THE RUPA POCKET DICTIONARY

ENGLISH – HINDI

अंग्रेज़ी – हिन्दी

THE RUPA POCKET DICTIONARY

ENGLISH – HINDI
अंग्रेज़ी – हिन्दी

V. P. SHARMA

RUPA
PUBLICATIONS INDIA

First Published 2009
Second Impression 2011

Published by
Rupa Publications India Pvt. Ltd.
7/16, Ansari Road, Daryaganj,
New Delhi 110 002

Sales Centres:

Allahabad Bengaluru Chennai
Hyderabad Jaipur Kathmandu
Kolkata Mumbai

Typeset in
Nikita Overseas Pvt. Ltd.
1410 Chiranjiv Tower,
43 Nehru Place
New Delhi 110 019

Printed in India by
Rekha Printers Pvt. Ltd.
A-102/1 Okhla Industrial Area, Phase-II
New Delhi-110 020

Some Important Abbreviations

(Many more are to be found in the main Dictionary)

AAI	Airport Authority of India
ACC	Auxiliary Cadet Corps
AICC	All India Congress Committee
AIDS	Acquired Immune Deficiency Syndrome
AIIMS	All India Institute of Medical Sciences
AITUC	All India Trade Union Congress
ANC	African National Congress
ASEAN	Association for South East Asian Nations
ASI	Archaeological Survey of India
ASLV	Augmented Satellite Launch Vehicle
ASSOCHAM	Associated Chamber of Commerce and Industry
BARC	Bhabha Atomic Research Centre
BBC	British Broadcasting Corporation
BCCI	Board of Control for Cricket in India
BHEL	Bharat Heavy Electricals Limited
BIFR	Board of Industrial and Financial Reconstruction
BJP	Bharatiya Janata Party
BOP	Balance of Payments
BOT	Build-Operate-Transfer
BPO	Business Process Outsourcing
BSE	Bombay Stock Exchange
BSF	Border Security Force

BSNL	Bharat Sanchar Nigam Limited
CBI	Central Bureau of Investigation
CBSE	Central Board of Secondary Education
CBDT	Central Board of Direct Taxes
CDMA	Code Division Multiple Access
CEO	Chief Executive Officer
CFL	Compact Fluorescent Lamp
CHOGM	Commonwealth Heads of Government Meeting
CII	Confederation of Indian Industries
CISF	Central Industrial Security Force
CID	Criminal Investigation Department
CITU	Congress of International Trade Union
CPCB	Central Pollution Control Board
CPI (M)	Communist Party of India (Marxist)
CRPF	Central Reserve Police Force
CRR	Cash Reserve Ratio
CSIR	Council of Scientific and Industrial Research
CVC	Central Vigilance Commission
DAVP	Directorate of Audio Visual Publicity
DGCA	Directorate General of Civil Aviation
DVD	Digital Video Disk
DOE	Department of Electronics
DRDO	Defence Research Development Organization
ECG	Electro Cardiogram
ECM	European Common Market
EEC	European Economic Commission
E&OE	Errors and Omissions Excepted
ESI	Employees' State Insurance
EU	European Union
FAO	Food and Agriculture Organization
FBI	Federal Bureau of Investigation (US)
FICCI	Federation of Indian Chambers of Commerce and Industry

GAIL	Gas Authority of India Limited
GDP	Gross Domestic Product
GMT	Greenwich Mean Time
GNP	Gross National Product
GPRS	General Packet Radio Service
GSM	Global System for Mobile
HAL	Hindustan Aeronautics Limited
HUDCO	Housing and Urban Development Corporation
IAA	International Airport Authority
IAEA	International Atomic Energy Agency
IAF	Indian Air Force
IARI	Indian Agricultural Research Institute
IAS	Indian Administrative Service
IATA	International Air Transport Association
IBM	International Business Machines
IBRD	International Bank for Reconstruction and Development
ICAR	Indian Council of Agricultural Research
ICC	International Cricket Council
IMF	International Monetary Fund
INTELSAT	International Telecommunication Satellite
INTERPOL	International Police Organization
IPL	Indian Premier League
IPR	Intellectual Property Rights
ISD	International Subscriber Dialling
ISRO	Indian Space Research Organization
IST	Indian Standard Time
KPO	Knowledge Process Outsourcing
LCD	Liquid Crystal Display
LED	Light Emitting Diode
LPG	Liquefied Petroleum Gas
MBA	Master of Business Administration
MLA	Member of Legislative Assembly

MoU	Memorandum of Understanding
NABARD	National Bank for Agriculture and Rural Development
NASA	National Aeronautics and Space Administration (USA)
NSE	National Stock Exchange
NATO	North Atlantic Treaty Organization
NCC	National Cadet Corp
NCERT	National Council of Educational Research and Training
NRI	Non-Resident Indian
NSG	Nuclear Suppliers Group/National Security Guards
OPEC	Organization of Oil Exporting Countries
PAN	Permanent Account Number
PIN	Personal Identification Number
PSLV	Polar Satellite Launch Vehicle
RAW	Research and Analysis Wing
RBI	Reserve Bank of India
RTI	Right To Information
SAARC	South Asian Association for Regional Cooperation
SEBI	Securities and Exchange Board of India
SEZ	Special Economic Zone
SIM	Subscriber Identification Module
SMS	Short Message Service
TRAI	Telecom Regulatory Authority of India
UK	United Kingdom
UNO	United Nations Organization
UNESCO	United Nations Educational Scientific and Cultural Organization
USA	United States of America
VAT	Value Added Tax

VDU	Visual Display Unit
VIP	Very Important Person
VOIP	Voice over Internet Protocol
VCD	Video Compact Disk
VRS	Voluntary Retirement Scheme
WPI	Wholesale Price Index
WWF	World Wild-Life Fund
WTO	World Trade Organization

Word That are Often Mispronounced

absentia (अब्ˊसेंन्टिअ)
acclimatize (अˊक्लाइमटाइज़)
aghast (अˊगास्ट)
annihilate (अˊनाइअलेट)
appall (अˊपॉल)
awry (ऑˊराइ)
bass (बिस)
blasé (ˊब्लाज़े)
blockade (ब्लॉˊकेड)
bomb (बॉम)
bowel (ˊबाउअल)
bowl (बोल)
bravado (ब्रˊवाडो)
bravo (ब्रावो)
breakfast (ˊब्रेंक्फस्ट)
bury (ˊबेंरि)
camaraderie (कैमˊराडरि)
celebrity (सिलेंब्रिटि)
cello (ˊचेंलो)
cemetery (ˊसेंमट्रि)
chagrin (ˊशैग्रिन)
charade (शˊराड)
chassis (ˊशैसि)
chauffeur (ˊशोफ़र)
chic (शिक)
chore (चॉर)
chortle (ˊचॉर्टल)
chutzpah (ˊहुट्स्पा)
climber (ˊक्लाइमर)
cognac (ˊकॉन्यैक)
comb (कोम)
conduct (n.) (ˊकॉनडक्ट)
conduct (v.) (कन्ˊडक्ट)
consortium (कन्ˊसॉटिअम)
culinary (ˊकलिनरि)
cupboard (ˊकबर्ड)
debris (ˊडेंबरि)
demolition (डेंमˊलिशन)
demonstrate (ˊडेंमन्स्ट्रेट)
demonstration (डेंमन्स्ˊट्रेशन)
demonstrative (डिˊमॉन्स्ट्रेटिव़)
dengue (ˊडेंङगि)
deter (डिˊटरा)
devotee (डेंव़ˊटी)
discrepancy (डिˊस्क्रेंपन्सि)
discretion (डिˊस्क्रेंशन)
donkey (ˊडॉङकि)
employee (इम्ˊप्लॉइ)

entourage (´आन्टुराझ़)
entrepreneur (आन्ट्र´प्रॅनर)
espionage (´ऍस्पिअनाझ़)
façade (फ़´साड)
feisty (´फ़ाइअस्टि)
fete (फेट)
fiery (´फाइअरि)
finale (फि´नालि)
flour (´फ्लाउर)
ghost (गोस्ट)
group (ग्रूप)
hauteur (ओ´टर)
healthy (´हॅल्थि)
hereditary (ह´रॅडिटरि)
housing (´हाउज़िंग)
husband (´हज़्बंड)
impetus (´इम्पिटस)
impious (´इम्पिअस)
indict (इन्´डाइट)
insatiable (इन्´सेशबल)
invalid (a.) (इन्´वैलिड)
invalid (b.) (इन्´व़लिड)
lettuce (´लॅटिस)
lion (´लाइअन)
loin (लॉइन)
locale (ल´काल)
loose (लूस)
machination (मैशि´नेशन्ज़)
macho (´मैचो)
maestro (´माइस्ट्रो)
malinger (म´लिंगर)
manger (´मेन्जर)
martyr (´मार्टर)
masochism (´मैसकिज़म)
mass (´मैस)
massage (´मैसाझ़)
meadow (´मॅडो)
measure (´मॅझ़र)
mechanism (´मॅकनिज़म)
menace (´मॅनिस)
menu (´मॅन्यु)
mien (मीन)
mirage (मि´राझ़)
moisten (´मॉइसन)
monk (मंक)
monkey (´मंकि)
morale (म´राल)
mortgage (मॉ´गिज)
nuptial (´नप्शल)
opera (´ऑपर्अ)
opposite (´ऑपज़िट)
pal (पैल)
par excellence (पार्ऍक्स´लांस)
penis (´पीनिस)
pint (पांइट)
plait (प्लैट)

plethora (´प्लेंथर्‌अ)

porpoise (´पॉर्पस)

prefer (प्रि´फर)

preference (´प्रेंफरंस)

prima facie (प्राइम्‌अ´फेशि)

rebel (n.) (´रेंबल)

rebel (v.) (रि´बेंल)

regime (रे´ज़ीम)

renege (रि´नेग)

row (रो, राउ)

sabotage (´सैबटाझ़)

salmon (´सैमन)

satiate (´सेशिएट)

satiety (स´टाइअटि)

sauté (´सोटे)

scenario (सि´नारिओ)

schizophrenia (स्किट्स´फ्रीनिअ)

sciatica (साइ´ऐटिक्‌अ)

scourge (स्क´र्जे)

sew (सो)

sieve (सिव़)

slough (स्लफ, स्लाउ)

sparse (स्पार्स)

steak (स्टेक)

strafe (स्ट्रेफ, स्ट्राफ़)

suite (स्वीट)

sycophant (´सकफंट)

thursday (´थज़डे)

tier (टिअर)

tomb (टूम)

tortoise (´टार्टस)

tribunal (ट्राइ´ब्यूनल)

tribune (ट्रि´ब्यून)

trilogy (´ट्रिलजि)

trio (´ट्रीओ)

vase (वाज़)

vignette (वि´न्‌यट)

vineyard (´विन्‌यार्ड)

wednesday (´वेंन्‌ज़डे)

whore (हॉर)

women (´विमिन)

wrath (राथ)

zoology (जू´आलजि)

A

a, an (ए, ऐन) संज्ञा से पहले एक के अर्थ में प्रयुक्त **indefinite article**; *an,* स्वर अथवा अनुच्चारित *h* से पहले प्रयुक्त

aback (अ'बैक) *adv.* – **taken aback** भौंचक, चकित, हैरान

abalone (ऐब'लोनि) *n.* घोंघे जैसी मछली जिस का मांस खाया जाता है और जिसमें मोती भी मिलते हैं

abandon (अ'बैंडन) *vt.* छोड़कर चल देना – *n.* असंयम; स्वच्छंदता – **abandoned** *a.* छोड़ा हुआ; परित्यक्त – **abandonment** *n.* परित्याग, छोड़े जाने की स्थिति

abase (अ'बेस) *vt.* नीचा दिखाना, अपमानित करना – **abasement** *n.* अपमान, अनादर

abash (अ'बैश) *vt.* (अधिकतर *passive* में प्रयुक्त) लज्जित या शर्मिंदा करना – **abashed** (अ'बैश्ट) *a.* लज्जित

abate (अ'बेट) *v.* (पीड़ा, तूफान आदि का) कम होना या करना

abattoir ('ऐबट्वा) *n.* कसाईघर

abbey ('ऐबि) *n.* ईसाई मठ जहाँ भिक्षु या भिक्षुणियाँ रहती हों; मठ का गिरजाघर

abbot ('ऐबट) *n.* ईसाई मठ का अध्यक्ष; महंत (**abbess** *fem.*)

abbr., abbrev. abbreviation का संक्षेप

abbreviate (अ'ब्रीविएट) *vt.* छोटा या संक्षिप्त करना – **abbreviation** (अब्रीवि'एशन) *n.* संकेताक्षर; संक्षिप्त रूप

abdicate ('ऐब्डिकेट) *v.* (विधिवत) त्यागना या छोड़ना (राज सिंहासन आदि) – **abdication** (ऐब्डि'केशन) *n.* राज्य त्याग; पदत्याग

abdomen ('ऐब्डमन) *n.* पेट – **abdominal** (ऐब्'डॉमिनल) *a.* पेट या उदर संबंधी

abduct (ऐब्'डक्ट) *vt.* अपहरण करना – **abduction** (ऐब्'डक्शन) *n.* अपहरण

aberration (ऐब'रेशन) *n.* सही या ठीक रास्ते से हटने की क्रिया; विपथन; पथभ्रष्ट होने की क्रिया; दोष, चूक – **aberrant** (ऐ'बेरंट) *a* पथभ्रष्ट

abet (अ'बेट) *vt.* सहायता या प्रोत्साहन देना विशे० किसी बुरे काम में, उकसाना, उभाड़ना – **abetter, abettor** *n.* अपराध-सहकारी

abeyance (अ'बेअंस) *n.* (निर्णय, कानून आदि की) लागू न होने की स्थिति

abhor (अब्'हॉर) *vt.* से अत्यधिक घ णा करना – **abhorrence** (अब्'हॉरन्स) *n.* घ णा – **abhorrent** *a.* घ णित, घिनौना

abide (अ'बाइड) *vt.* सहन या बर्दाश्त करना (**abode, abided, abiding**) – **abide by** आज्ञा मानना या पालन करना

ability (अ'बिलिटि) *n.* योग्यता; सामर्थ्य; शक्ति; (*skill*) गुण

ab initio (ऐबि'निशिओ) *Lat.* प्रारंभ से, शुरू से

abject ('ऐब्जेक्ट) *a.* नीच; घ णित; अधम, कमीना, दयनीय

abjure (अब्'ज्युअर) *vt.* शपथ या कसम खा कर छोड़ना; तौबा करना

ablaze (अ'ब्लेज़) *a.* जलता हुआ

able ('एब्ल) *a.* योग्य; समर्थ; कुशल, समक्ष – **ably** *adv.* कुशलता से – **able-bodied** *a.* हृष्ट-पुष्ट

ablution (अ'ब्लूशन) *n.* (प्राय: *pl.*) हाथ-मुँह धोना

abnegate ('ऐब्निगेट) *vt.* त्यागना – **abnegation** (ऐब्नि'गेशन) *n.* त्याग

abnormal (ऐब्'नॉर्मल) *a.* अनियमित, असामान्य; अस्वाभाविक; बेढंगा – **abnormality** (ऐब्नॉर्'मैलिटि) *n.* असामान्यता; अस्वाभाविकता – **abnormally** *adv.* अस्वाभाविक ढंग से

aboard (अ'बॉर्ड) *adv.* (जहाज, विमान या रेलगाड़ी) में सवार

abolish (अ'बॉलिश) *vt.* खत्म करना, उन्मूलन करना (प्रथा, कुरीति आदि) – **abolition** (एिब'लिशन) *n.* उन्मूलन, अंत

A-bomb *n.* परमाणु बम, **atomic bomb** का संक्षेप

abominate (अ'बॉमिनेट) *vt.* अत्यधिक घ णा करना – **abominable** (अ'बॉमिनबल) *a.* घ णित, बुरा – **abominably** *adv.* घ णित ढंग से – **abomination** (अबॉमि'नेशन) *n.* घ णित वस्तु या बात; घ णा; जुगुप्सा – **abominable snowman** बड़े आकार का बन्दर जैसा कल्पित प्राणी जिस के बारे में यह धारणा है कि वह हिमालय में रहता है

Aborigine (एब'रिजिनि) *n.* आस्ट्रेलिया का मूल निवासी – (**a** –) किसी देश का मूल निवासी; आदिवासी

abort (अ'बॉर्ट) *vt.* समय से पहले समाप्त करना; गर्भपात कराना – *vi.* गर्भपात होना – **abortion** (अ'बॉर्शन) *n.* गर्भपात – **abortive** *a.* असफल

abound (अ'बाउंड) *vi.* भरपूर, प्रचुर या अधिक संख्या, मात्रा में होना – **abounding in** *a.* से भरपूर

about (अ'बाउट) *adv.* चारों ओर; लगभग; आसपास; इधर-उधर; चलता-फिरता – *prep.* के चारों ओर; के पास या समीप; के बारे में; जाने आदि को तैयार – **about turn** बिल्कुल बदल जाने, पलट जाने की क्रिया; घूम जाना

above (अ'बव़) *adv.* अधिक ऊँचा; के ऊपर – *prep.* से ऊँचा; से अधिक; से अच्छा; से परे

abrasion (अ'ब्रेझ़न) *n. (skin)* खरोंच; घिसने, रगड़ने या छीलने की क्रिया – **abrasive** (अ'ब्रेसिव़) *n.* घिसने या चमकाने में प्रयुक्त पदार्थ (जैसे रेगमाल) – *a.* जिससे खरोंच या खराश लगे; रूखा (बर्ताव)

abreast (अ'ब्रेस्ट) *adv.* साथ-साथ, के बराबर-बराबर

abridge (अ'ब्रिज) *vt.* संक्षिप्त या छोटा करना – **abridg(e)ment** *n.*

abroad (अ'ब्रॉड) *adv.* विदेश में या बाहर; दूर-दूर तक

abrogate ('ऐब्रोगेट) *vt.* रद्द करना (करार, संधि आदि) – **abrogation** (एब्रो'गेशन) *n.* निरसन, रद्द करने की क्रिया

abrupt (अ'ब्रप्ट) *a.* आकस्मिक; रूखा; जल्दबाजी में; असम्बद्ध – **abruptly** *adv.* सहसा – **abruptness** *n.*

abscess ('ऐब्सेस) *n.* पीवदार फोड़ा

abscond (अब्'स्कॉण्ड) *vi.* फ़रार हो जाना विशे० चोरी करके

absent ('ऐब्सेंट) *a.* अनुपस्थित; अनमना; अन्यमनस्क – (एिब्'सेन्ट) *vt.* अनुपस्थित हो जाना – **absence** *n.* अनुपस्थिति – **absentee** (एब्सन्'टी) *n.* अनुपस्थित व्यक्ति – **absenteeism** *n.* (नौकरी, स्कूल आदि से) लगातार अनुपस्थित रहने की स्थिति – **absently** *adv.* – **absentminded** *a.* अन्यमनस्क, खोया हुआ

absinth(e) ('ऐब्सिन्थ) *n.* सौंफ से बनी शराब, अफसंतीन

absolute ('ऐब्सलूट) *a.* पूर्ण, सम्पूर्ण; असीम; बिना शर्त का; शुद्ध (**as absolute alcohol**) – *n.* सम्पूर्ण वस्तु – **absolutely** *adv.* पूर्णतया, बिल्कुल – *interj.* बेशक – **absoluteness** – *n.* पूर्णता – **absolute zero** (**–273.15°C**) न्यूनतम संभव तापमान

absolve (अब्'ज़ॉल्व़) *vt.* को बरी या दोष मुक्त करना

absorb (अब्'सॉर्ब,-ज़ार्ब) *vt.* सोख लेना, चूस लेना; तल्लीन कर देना; (धक्का आदि) सह लेना; समा लेना – **absorbent** *a.* नमी सोखने वाली (रूई आदि) – **absorption** *n.* सोख लेने की क्रिया; तल्लीनता

abstain (अब्'स्टेन) *vi.* (*from* के साथ) से अलग रहना; न करना, बचना या परहेज़ करना (शराब आदि से); (वोट आदि) न देना – **abstainer** *n.* परहेज़गार – **abstention** (अब्'स्टेन्शन) *n.* (मतदान में) तटस्थता – **abstinence** *n.* परहेज़

abstemious (अब्'स्टीमिअस) *a.* खाने और विशे० शराब पीने में मिताहारी; संयमी

abstract ('ऐब्स्ट्रैक्ट) *a.* जो केवल कल्पना में हो, यथार्थ में नहीं, काल्पनिक; अमूर्तः, निराकार – *n.* संक्षेप; सारांश – (ऐब्'स्ट्रैक्ट) *vt.* हटा लेना; घटाना – **abstracted** *a.* अन्यमनस्क

abstruse (अब्'स्ट्रूस) *a.* अस्पष्ट; दुर्बोध; गूढ़ – **abstrusely** *adv.*

absurd (अब्'सर्ड) *a.* तर्क के विपरीत; बेतुका – **absurdity** *n.* बेतुकापन; असंगति

abundance (अ'बन्डन्स) *n.* बाहुल्य; प्रचुरता – **abundant** *a.* प्रचुर, भरपूर – **abundantly** *adv.* पूरी तरह

abuse (अ'ब्यूज़) *vt.* गाली देना; दुरूपयोग करना – (अ'ब्यूस) *n.* गाली; दुरूपयोग – **abusive** *a.* गाली-गलौज भरा

abut (अ'बट) *vi.* से सटा या लगा होना; साथ लगना (-tt-)

abysmal (अ'बिज़्मल) *a.* अथाह, अगाध (अज्ञान आदि); *inf.* बहुत ही बुरा

abyss (अ'बिस) *n.* बहुत गहरा गड्ढा या खाई

AC alternating current (प्रत्यावर्ती विद्युत धारा) का संक्षेप

A/C account (लेखा) का संक्षेप

acacia (अ'केशअ) *n.* कीकर; बबूल

academy (अ'कैडमि) *n.* कला या विज्ञान के प्रसार का संगठन; विशेष प्रशिक्षण की संस्था; अकादमी – **academic** (ऐक'डेमिक) *a.* अकादमी का; शैक्षिक; विश्व विद्यालय आदि से संबंधित; सैद्धांतिक; पंडिताऊ – **academically** *adv.* – **academician** (अकैड'मिशन) *n.* कला, विज्ञान परिषद का सदस्य, विशेष प्रशिक्षण संस्था का सदस्य, परिषद-सदस्य

accede (ऐक्'सीड) *vi.* मान लेना; (पद या कार्यभार) संभालना

accelerate (ऐक्'सेलरेट) *vt.* की गति या चाल बढ़ाना – *vi.* गति बढ़ाना – **acceleration** *n.* गतिवर्धन – **accelerator** *n.* कार आदि में गति बढ़ाने का यंत्र, ऐक्सलरेटर

accent ('ऐक्संट) *n.* उच्चारण में किसी स्वर पर बल, स्वराघात, उच्चारण चिह्न; किसी स्थान या देश का उच्चारण, विशेष लहजा; विशेष बल या आघात – (ऐक्'सेन्ट) *vt.* बलाघात अथवा स्वराघात करना

accentuate (ऐक्'सेन्चुएट) *vt.* बल या जोर देना, बल देना

accept (अक्'सेप्ट) *vt.* लेना; ग्रहण करना; (*agree to*) स्वीकार करना; (*admit*) मानना; मिलाना; (सदस्य) बनाना; विश्वास करना – **acceptability** *n.* स्वीकार/ग्रहण किये जाने की क्षमता – **acceptable** *a.* स्वीकार्य, मंज़ूर – **acceptably** *adv.* – **acceptance** *n.* स्वीकृति, मंज़ूरी, अनुमोदन

access ('ऐक्सेस) *n.* प्रवेश, पहुंच; उसका अधिकार या साधन; पैठ – *vt.* *Computers* कम्प्यूटर पर जानकारी प्राप्त करना – **accessibility** *n.* सुलभता – **accessible** (अक्'सेसब्ल) *a.* सुलभ; जिस तक पहुँच आसान या संभव हो

accession (अक्'सेशन) *n.* अधिकार या पद की प्राप्ति, पद प्राप्ति; पदारोहण; वृद्धि; अधिक (संख्या, मात्रा) होने की क्रिया

accessory (अक्'सेसरि) *n.* कार आदि के अतिरिक्त पुर्ज़े; उपसाधन; महिलाओं की वेशभूषा; अपराध में सहायक व्यक्ति – *a.* अतिरिक्त, सहायक

accident ('ऐक्सिडंट) *n.* संयोगवश हुई घटना; दुर्घटना; अनावश्यक या असहज गुण – **accidental** (ऐक्सि'डेन्टल) *a.* आकस्मिक,

संयोग से हुई (घटना आदि) – **accidentally** *adv.* संयोग से; अनजाने – **accident prone** (व्यक्ति) जिसकी दुर्घटना की संभावना अधिक रहती हो; *India* दुर्घटना संभावित (क्षेत्र)

acclaim (अ'क्लेम) *vt.* की जयजयकार करना, अभिनंदन करना – *n.* जयजयकार – **acclamation** *n.* जयजयकार द्वारा अनुमोदन

acclimatize (अ'क्लाइमटाइज) *vt.* नये जलवायु या वातावरण के अनुकूल बनाना – **acclimatization** (अक्लाइमटाइ'ज़ेशन) *n.* वातावरण के अनुकूल बनने/बनाने की क्रिया

accolade ('ऐकलेड) *n.* प्रशंसा; सार्वजनिक अनुमोदन; पुरस्कार; प्रतिष्ठा

accommodate (अ'कॉमडेट) *vt.* किसी के रहने व भोजन की व्यवस्था करना; अनुग्रह करना, सहायता देना; जगह आदि देना; अनुकूल बनाना – **accommodating** *a.* सहायता देने को तैयार, उदार – **accommodation** (अकॉम'डेशन) *n.* आवास, ठहरने का स्थान; समझौता

accompany (अ'कम्पनि) *vt.* साथ जाना, संगीत में संगत करना; के साथ होना (**accompanied, accompanying**) – **accompaniment** *n.* सहायक स्वर, संगत-वाद्य आदि – **accompanist** *n.* संगत करने वाला कलाकार

accomplice (अ'कॉम्प्लिस) *n* सह अपराधी

accomplish (अ'कम्प्लिश) *vt.* पूरा करना – **accomplished** *a.* निपुण, कुशल; गुण-सम्पन्न – **accomplishment** *n.* पूरा होने की स्थिति; उपलब्धि – **accomplishments** *pl. n.* व्यक्तिगत प्रवीणता, दक्षता

accord (अ'कॉर्ड) *n.* (विशे० *in accord with*) मेल, संगति; समझौता – *v.* से मेल खाना, के अनुरूप होना – *vt.* प्रदान करना – **accordance** *n.* सहमति, संगति – **accordant** *a.* अनुकूल, संगत – **according** *adv.* के अनुसार – **accordingly** *adv.* अतः, इसलिए

accordion (अ'कॉर्डिअन) *n.* एक बाजा जिसमें धौंकनी और सुर होते हैं, अकॉर्डियन

accost (अ'कॉस्ट) *vt.* किसी (अपरिचित) को रोक कर उससे कुछ पूछना, अथवा अनुचित प्रस्ताव रखना

account (अ'काउंट) *n.* विवरण, ब्यौरा; महत्व; हिसाब-किताब; लेखा-खाता; (बैंक में) जमाधन; दुकान आदि में उधार-खाता – *vt.* अनुमान लगाना; समझना – *vi.* कारण बताना, जवाब देना – **accountability** *n.* जवाबदेही – **accountable** *a.* जिम्मेदार, उत्तरदायी – **accountancy** *n.* लेखा-शास्त्र – **accountant** *n.* लेखापाल, हिसाब-किताब रखने वाला – **accounting** *n.* लेखाकरण, लेखा, हिसाब-किताब – **accounts** *n.* लेखाकरण संबंधी बही खाते – **on account** उधार – **on any account** किसी भी कारण – **on account of** के कारण – **give a good/bad account of oneself** (परीक्षा, अभिनय आदि में) अच्छा/बुरा प्रदर्शन करके दिखाना

accredited (अ'क्रेडिटिड) *a.* अधिक त; स्वीकार या अधिकारियों द्वारा मान्य

accrue (अ'क्रू) *vi.* को प्राप्त होना; (ब्याज आदि) जुड़कर बढ़ना

acct. account (हिसाब-किताब) का संक्षेप

accumulate (अ'क्यूम्युलेट) *vt.* *(gather)* संचय या संग्रह करना; इकट्ठा करना – *vi.* अधिकाधिक मात्रा में संचित होना – **accumulation** *n.* संचयन, ढेर; अम्बार होने की क्रिया – **accumulator** (अ'क्यूम्युलेटर) *n.* कार आदि की बैटरी जो फिर से चार्ज हो सकती है; कम्प्यूटर का वह भाग जिसमें अंक संचित होते हैं

accurate ('ऐक्युरिट) *a.* शुद्ध, सही, जिसमें कोई गलती न हो – **accuracy** ('ऐक्युरिसि) *n.* शुद्धता, सही होने की स्थिति – **accurately** *adv.* सही-सही, ठीक-ठीक

accursed, accurst (अ'कर्सिड, अ'कर्स्ट) *a.* शापित, अभिशप्त; घिनौना; जघन्य

accuse (अ'क्यूज़) *vt.* दोष या आरोप लगाना, दोष देना – **accusation** *n.* – **accusatory** *a.* अभियोगात्मक – **accused** *n.* अभियुक्त

accustomed *a.* हमेशा वाली (वस्तु, आदत); (का) आदी

ace (एस) *n.* ताश का इक्का; पांसे का एक; (*Tennis*) टेनिस में फेंकी गयी गेंद जिसे विरोधी छू तक न सके; चोटी का विमान चालक (लड़ाकू विमान का); *inf.* किसी काम में प्रवीण या माहिर व्यक्ति – *a. inf.* श्रेष्ठतम

acetic (अ'सीटिक) *a.* सिरके से बना या उसके गुणों वाला

acetylene (अ'सेटिलीन) *n.* रंगहीन ज्वलनशील गैस जो धातुओं को टांका लगाने के काम आती है; असीटीलीन

ache (एक) *n.* लगातार होने वाली पीड़ा – *vi.* में पीड़ा होना – **aching** *a.* दर्द करता हुआ

achieve (अ'चीव़) *vt. (aim)* पूरा करना; सम्पन्न करना; (विजय, सफलता) प्राप्त करना; (काम) पूरा करना – **achievement** *n.* कार्यसिद्धि, उपलब्धि

Achilles' heel (अकिलीज़'हील) *n.* किसी व्यक्ति की चारित्रिक कमज़ोरी जो उसकी असफलता का कारण बन सकती है

acid ('ऐसिड) *a.* तीखा, खट्टा – *n.* अम्ल, तेज़ाब – **acidity** (अ'सिडिटि) *n.* अम्लता, खट्टापन – **acid rain** वर्षा जो वातावरण के प्रदूषण से तेज़ाबी बन जाये – **acid test** अग्नि परीक्षा

ack-ack ('ऐक-'ऐक) *n.* विमानभेदी तोप या उसके गोले-दगने की क्रिया

acknowledge (अक्'नॉलिज) *vt.* प्राप्ति-सूचना देना, स्वीकार करना, मानना – **acknowledg(e)ment** *n.* स्वीक ति; प्राप्ति-सूचना

acme ('ऐक्मि) *n.* सबसे ऊंचा बिन्दु; चरम बिंदु; पराकाष्ठा

acne ('ऐक्नि) *n.* मुहाँसा, चमड़ी का एक रोग

acoustics (अ'कूस्टिक्स) *pl. n.* ध्वनि शास्त्र; भवन में की गयी ध्वनि-व्यवस्था (लाउड स्पीकर, माइक्रोफोन आदि)

acquaint (अ'क्वेंट) *vt.* (*with* के साथ) (से) परिचित कराना, अवगत करना; जानकारी या सूचना देना – **acquaintance** *n.* परिचित व्यक्ति; परिचय, जानकारी

acquiesce (ऐक्वि'ऐस) *vi.* (*in* के साथ) स्वीकार कर लेना; बिना आपत्ति किये मान जाना – **acquiescence** *n.* मौन सम्मति

acquire (अ'क्वाइअर) *vt.* प्राप्त करना; अर्जित करना, पाना – **acquisition** (ऐक्वि'ज़िशन) *n.* लाभ, धन दौलत जमा करने या प्राप्त करने की क्रिया – **acquisitive** (अ'क्विज़िटिव़) *a.* धन दौलत आदि जमा करने की प्रव ति वाला; लोभी – **acquisitiveness** *n.* लोभी प्रव ति

acquit (अ'क्विट) *vt.* निर्दोष ठहराना; अपराध से मुक्त करना; (ऋण) चुकाना; अच्छी तरह पेश आना, अपना कार्य कुशलता से पूरा करना (- tt-) – **acquittal** *n.* अदालत द्वारा दोष मुक्ति, निरपराध ठहराया जाना – **acquittance** *n.* भुगतान

acre ('एकर) *n.* एकड़ – **acres** *pl. n.* जमीन, भूसम्पत्ति; *inf.* विशाल क्षेत्र या बहुत अधिक – **acreage** ('एकरिज) *n.* एकड़ों में भूमि का क्षेत्रफल

acrid ('ऐक्रिड) *a.* तीता, तीखा, चरपरा

acrimony ('ऐक्रिमनि) *n.* विचारों या भाषा की कटुता; कड़वाहट या तीखापन – **acrimonious** (ऐक्रि'मोनिअस) *a.* कटुता भरा (विवाद आदि)

acrobat ('ऐक्रबैट) *n.* कलाबाज़ विशे० सर्कस में – **acrobatic** (ऐक्रो'बैटिक) *a.* कलाबाज़ी संबंधी – **acrobatics** *pl. n.* कोई भी ऐसा काम जिसमें बहुत फुर्ती व कौशल की जरूरत हो

acronym (ऐक्रनिम) *n.* शब्दों के प्रथम अक्षरों को जोड़ कर बना शब्द; परिवर्णी शब्द जैसे ISRO, SAARC

across (अ'क्रॉस) *prep.* उस पार, दूसरी ओर; आर-पार – *adv.* पार, की ओर; चौड़ा – **get (or put) it across** (कोई बात) समझा देना

acrylic (अ'क्रिलिक) *n.* क त्रिम पदार्थ की किस्में विशे० क त्रिम कपड़े की

act (ऐक्ट) *n.* काम, कर्म, क्रिया; अधिनियम, कानून; (*drama*) अंक – *v.* अभिनय करना – *vi.* प्रभाव डालना; पेश आना; का स्वांग भरना, ढोंग करना – *vt.* का अभिनय करना, का रोल अदा करना – **acting** *n.* अभिनय – *a.* कार्य-वाहक, स्थानापन्न – **action** *n.* कार्यवाही; कार्य; व्यवहार; क्रिया; युद्ध, भिड़न्त; कानूनी कार्यवाही, काररवाई – **action replay** टेलीविज़न पर खेल के रोमांचक अंश (प्राय: सीधे प्रसारण में) तुरंत दोबारा दिखा देना – **activate** (ऐक्टिवेट) *vt.* क्रियाशील बनाना; रेडियोधर्मी बनाना – **active** *a.* सक्रिय; फुर्तीला, चुस्त; (ज्वालामुखी) जो चालू हो – **actively** *adv.* *n.* किसी राजनीतिक अथवा सामाजिक परिवर्तन के लिए कार्य करनेवाला व्यक्ति – **activity** *n.* सक्रियता; चहल-पहल, सरगर्मी – **actor** (ऐक्टर) *n.* (फिल्म, नाटक का) पात्र, अभिनेता (*fem.* **actress**)

actual (ऐक्चुअल) *a.* वास्तविक, यथार्थ; वर्तमान – **actuality** (ऐक्चु'ऐलिटि) *n.* वास्तविकता – **actually** *adv.* वास्तव में, सचमुच

actuate (ऐक्चुएट) *vt.* सक्रिय बनाना; प्रेरणा देना

acuity (अ'क्यूइटि) *n.* तीक्ष्णता, विशे० द ष्टि या विचारों की

acumen (ऐक्युमन) *n.* कुशाग्र बुद्धि; विदग्धता

acupuncture (ऐक्युपंक्चर) *n. orig.* चीन की चिकित्सा पद्धति जिसमें शरीर के विभिन्न अंगों में सूइयां चुभो कर इलाज किया जाता है – **acupuncturist** *n.* इस पद्धति का चिकित्सक

acute (अ'क्यूट) *a.* होशियार, कुशाग्र बुद्धि; नुकीला, पैना; 90° से कम का कोण; तीव्र; प्रखर; प्रचण्ड – *n.* किसी अक्षर पर दिया गया बलाघात (´) जिस से उसका उच्चारण स्पष्ट हो – **acutely** *adv.* तीव्रता से; तीक्षणता से – **acuteness** *n.* नुकीलापन, होशियारी; कुशाग्रता; तीव्रता

AD *Anno Domini* का संक्षेप, यीशु मसीह के बाद (वर्ष के साथ लिखा जाता है, जैसे AD 506)

ad (ऐड) *n. abbrev.* advertisement का संक्षेप

adage (ऐडिज) *n.* कहावत, लोकोक्ति

adamant (ऐडमन्ट) *a.* कठोर; बहुत कड़ा; अटल

Adam's apple (ऐडम्ज़ ऐप्ल) कंठमणि, टेंटुआ

adapt (अ'डैप्ट) *vt.* (किसी वस्तु को नए प्रयोग के) अनुकूल बनाना; रूपांतरण करना, बदलना – **adaptability** *n.* अनुकूल बनने की क्षमता – **adaptable** (अ'डैप्टब्ल) *a.* जो अनुकूल बन सके – **adaptation** *n.* रूपांतर, अनुकूलन – **adapter, adaptor** *n.* दो (विभिन्न आकार के) पुर्ज़ों को जोड़ने वाला पुर्ज़ा विशे० बिजली के उपकरणों का, उपायोजक

add (ऐड) *vt.* जोड़ना; मिलाना, बढ़ाना; आगे कहना – *vi.* जुड़ना – **addition** (अ'डिशन) *n.* जोड़, योग; जोड़ने की क्रिया; व द्धि – **additional** *a.* अतिरिक्त – **additive** (ऐडिटिव़) *n.* भोजन आदि में मिलाया जाने वाला तत्व (रंग आदि), संयोजी – **add-on** *n.* वस्तु आदि जो किसी योजना, करार आदि के साथ अतिरिक्त मिले, अतिरिक्त लाभ जैसे टेलीफोन के साथ इंटरनेट सेवा; उपकरण जो कम्प्यूटर की कार्य-प्रणाली अधिक अच्छी करने के लिए उससे जोड़ा जाय; संयोजक-उपकरण

addendum (अ'डेन्डम) *n.* जोड़ा गया अंश; परिशिष्ट (*pl.* **addenda**)

adder (ऐडर) *n.* गेहुअन (एक विषैला सांप)

addict *n.* (ऐडिक्ट) नशा करने वाला (जैसे *a drug addict*), व्यसनी – *vt.* (अ´डिक्ट) (प्रायः *passive*) की लत होना – **addicted** *a.* आदी – **addiction** (अ´डिक्शन) *n.* लत, किसी नशे के बिना रह न सकने की स्थिति – **addictive** *a.* (वस्तु) जिससे लत लगे

addle (ऐडल) *vt.* सड़ाना; बिगाड़ना; गड्डमड्ड कर देना – *vi.* सड़ना; बिगड़ना, गड्डमड्ड हो जाना

address (अ´ड्रैस) *n.* पता; सरनामा (चिट्ठी पर लिखा); स्थान जहां व्यक्ति रहता हो; भाषण – (~ **es**) *pl.* प्रणय निवेदन, प्यार का इज़हार – *vt.* पता लिखना; भाषण देना; सम्बोधित करना; (चिट्ठी आदि) भेजना – **addressee** (ऐड्रै´सी) *n.* (चिट्ठी आदि) पाने वाला

adept (अ´डेप्ट) *a.* निपुण या कुशल – *n.* विशेषज्ञ

adequate (ऐडिक्विट) *a.* पर्याप्त, समुचित, काफ़ी; यथेष्ट – **adequacy** *n.* यथेष्टता, पर्याप्त होने की स्थिति – **adequately** *adv.* यथेष्ट रूप से/मात्रा में

adhere (अड्´हिअर) *vi.* चिपकना; जुड़ जाना; (नियम, फैसले आदि पर) डटे या जमे रहना – **adherent** *n/a.* अनुनायी – **adhesion** (अड्´हीझ़न) *n.* चिपकाव; भक्ति – **adhesive** (अड्´हीसिव्) *a.* चिपकने वाला – *n.* ऐसा पदार्थ, आसंजक

ad hoc (ऐड्´हॉक) *a./adv.* किसी विशेष अवसर या काम के लिए; तदर्थ; काम चलाऊ (ढंग से)

adieu (अ´ड्यू) *interj.* अलविदा – *n.* विदाई *pl.* (**adieus, adieux** (अ´ड्यूज़))

adjacent (अ´जेसंट) *a.* साथ लगता, निकटवर्ती

adjective (ऐजिक्टिव) *n.* विशेषण

adjoin (अ´जॉइन) *vt.* से जोड़ देना; लगा देना – *vi.* से लगा होना; जुड़ा होना – **adjoining** *a.* साथ लगता, समीप, सन्निकट

adjourn (अ´जर्न) *vt.* (सभा आदि को) अस्थायी रूप से स्थगित करना – *vi.* कुछ समय के लिए स्थगित होना – **adjournment** *n.* (सभा) स्थगन

adjudicate (अ´जूडिकेट) *v.* निर्णय देना; फैसला सुनाना – **adjudication** (अजूडि´केशन) *n.* निर्णय – **adjudicator** *n.*

adjunct (ऐजंक्ट्) *a.* मिलाया या जोड़ा हुआ; अनुबद्ध – *n.* व्यक्ति या वस्तु जो जोड़ी जाय

adjust (अ´जस्ट) *vt.* अनुकूल बनाना; रूपान्तरण करना, विनियमित करना; समायोजन करना – *vi.* अनुकूल बन जाना – **adjustable** *a.* समायोज्य – **adjuster** *n.* समायोजक – **adjustment** *n.* समायोजन

adjutant (ऐजटंट) *n.* वरिष्ठ अधिकारियों की सहायता करने वाला सैनिक अधिकारी

adlib (ऐड्´लिब) *v.* बिना तैयारी या पूर्व योजना के भाषण/अभिनय/ संगीत आदि (में कोई अंश) तत्काल प्रस्तुत करना

adman (ऐड्मैन) *n.* विज्ञापन व्यवसाय से संबंधित व्यक्ति

administer (अड्´मिनिस्टर) *vt.* प्रबन्ध चलाना; देख-भाल करना; (न्याय आदि) करना; प्रशासन चलाना; लागू करना (नियम, कानून आदि); (दवाई) देना – **administrate** *vt.* प्रबन्ध चलाना (सरकारी विभाग, व्यापार, संस्था आदि का) – **administration** *n.* प्रशासन, प्रबन्ध – **administrative** *a.* प्रशासनिक, प्रबन्धकीय, सरकार सम्बन्धी – **administrator** *n.* प्रशासक, प्रबंधक – (*fem.* **adminstratrix**)

admiral (ऐड्मरल) *n.* नौसेनाध्क्ष, ऐडमिरल

admire (अड्´माइअर) *vt.* प्रशंसा करना; देखकर चकित होना; समादर करना – **admirable** (ऐड्मरबल) *a.* प्रशंसनीय; अति उत्तम – **admiration** (ऐड्म´रेशन) *n.* प्रशंसा, तारीफ; श्रद्धा – **admirer** *n.* प्रशंसक

admit (अड्´मिट) *vt.* स्वीकार करना, मान लेना; (*allow*) की गुंजाइश होना; प्रवेश करने देना –

(-tt-) – **admissible** (अड्'मिसबल) *a.* विचार योग्य; मंजूर – **admission** *n.* प्रवेश की अनुमति; प्रवेश-शुल्क; अपराध-स्वीकारोक्ति; कबूलने की क्रिया – **admittance** *n.* प्रवेश; प्रवेश अधिकार – **admittedly** *adv.* मान लिया, मानना होगा कि...

admixture (अड्'मिक्स्चर) *n.* मिश्रण; मिलाने की क्रिया; पदार्थ जो मिलाया जाय

admonish (अड्'मॉनिश) *vt.* डांटना, फटकारना; चेतावनी देना; समझाना – **admonition** (ऐड्म'निशन) *n.* डांट; चेतावनी

ad nauseam (ऐड्'नॉज़िऐम) *Lat.* ऊबा देने या घृणा उत्पन्न करने की सीमा तक

ado (अ'डू) *n.* झमेला; बतंगड़; हलचल

adolescence (ऐड'लेंसन्स) *n.* किशोरावस्था – **adolescent** (ऐड'लेंसंट) *n./a.* किशोर

adopt (अ'डॉप्ट) *vt.* अपनाना, अपना बनाना, विशे. किसी बच्चे को 'गोद' लेना; (कोई सिद्धान्त) अपनाना; (प्रस्ताव) पास करना – **adopted** *a.* गोद लिया (बच्चा), दत्तक – **adoption** (अ'डॉप्शन) *n.* गोद लेना

adore (अ'डॉर) *vt.* अत्यधिक प्यार करना, आराधना करना – **adorable** (अ'डॉरबल) *a.* श्रद्धा योग्य – **adoration** (ऐड'रेशन) *n.* श्रद्धा, आराधना

adorn (अ'डॉर्न) *vt.* संजाना, संवारना, सुन्दर बनाना – **adornment** *n.* सजावट, श्रृंगार

ADP automatic data processing (कम्प्यूटर आदि से आंकड़ों को सारणीबद्ध करना) का संक्षेप

adrenal (अ'ड्रीनल) *a.* गुरदे के समीप – **adrenalin(e)** (अ'ड्रेनलिन) *n.* इस ग्रंथि से निकलने वाला स्त्रव (जो दवा के रूप में प्रयुक्त होता है)

adrift (अ'ड्रिफ्ट) *a./adv.* बिना नियंत्रण बहता हुआ; (*fig.*) दिशाहीन; *inf.* डांवांडोल; *inf.* भटका हुआ

adroit (अ'ड्रॉइट) *a.* कुशल, दक्ष चतुर

adulation (ऐड्यु'लेशन) *n.* चाटुकारी, चापलूसी – **adulatory** *a.* अति प्रशंसात्मक

adult ('ऐडल्ट, अ'डल्ट) *a.* वयस्क, बालिग़; सयाना – *n.* वयस्क या सयाना व्यक्ति; भरापूरा पौधा या पशु जो जवान हो चुका हो

adulterate (अ'डल्टरेट) *vt.* मिलावट या अपमिश्रण करना – **adulterant** *n.* पदार्थ जिससे मिलावट की जाये – **adulterated** *a.* मिलावटी – **adulteration** *n.* मिलावट

adultery (अ'डल्टरि) *n.* किसी पति या पत्नी का दूसरी स्त्री या पुरूष से सम्बन्ध रखना, परगमन – **adulterous** *a.* व्यभिचारी

ad valorem (ऐड्व़'लॉरम) *a./adv. Lat.* मूल्य के अनुसार, यथामूल्य

advance (अड्'वांस) *vt.* आगे लाना, बढ़ाना; (सुझाव, दलील आदि) देना/पेश करना; पेशगी देना – *vi.* आगे जाना, बढ़ना; उन्नति, करना – *n.* प्रगति, सुधार; पेशगी, अग्रिमराशि – (~**s**) *pl.* मित्रता या प्रेम का निवेदन – **advanced** *a.* प्रगतिशील, समय से आगे; (कार्य) जो काफी पूरा हो चुका हो – **advancement** *n.* पदोन्नति, तरक्की

advantage (अड्'वांटिज) *n.* लाभ, श्रेष्ठता, अनुकूल परिस्थिति; (*TENNIS*) ऐडवांटिज, जीत के लिए अनुकूल अंक – **advantageous** (एड्वन्'टेजस) *a.* लाभदायक

advent ('ऐडवन्ट) *n.* आना, आगमन

adventure (अड्'वेन्चर) *n.* जोखिम, साहस का काम, अपूर्व या उल्लेखनीय अनुभव; सट्टेबाजी – *vt.* (जोखिम) उठाना – *vi.* जोखिम उठाना – **adventurer** *n.* जो साहसिक या जोखिम के काम करे; तिकड़मी (**adventuress** *fem.*) – **adventurous** *a.* साहसिक; तिकड़मी; जोखिम भरा

adverb ('ऐड्व़र्ब) *n.* क्रिया-विशेषण – **adverbial** (अड्'व़र्बिअल) *a.* क्रिया-विशेषण सम्बंधी

adverse (ऐड्वर्स) *a.* प्रतिकूल, विरुद्ध, हानिकारक – **adversary** (ऐड्वर्सरि) *n.* शत्रु; विरोधी – **adversely** *adv.* प्रतिकूल रूप से (प्रभाव पड़ना आदि) – **adversity** (ऐड् 'वर्सिटि) *n.* विपत्ति, दुर्भाग्य; तंगहाली

advert (ऐड्वर्ट) *n. inf.* **advertisement** का संक्षेप

advertise ('ऐड्वर्टाइज़) *vt.* समाचार पत्र आदि में) विज्ञापन देना; प्रचार करना – *vi.* सार्वजनिक सूचना देना – **advertisement** (अड् 'वर्टिस्मंट) *n.* विज्ञापन, इश्तहार – **advertiser** *n.* विज्ञापन देने वाला, विज्ञापनदाता – **advertising** *a./n.* विज्ञापन

advice (अड् 'वाइस) *n.* सलाह, परामर्श; सिफारिश, विधिवत सूचना या ज्ञापन

advise (अड् 'वाइज़) *vt.* सलाह या परामर्श देना; सुझाव देना; सूचना देना – **advisable** *a.* उपयुक्त; उचित, मुनासिब – **advised** *a.* सोच-समझकर किया या कहा हुआ जैसे **well-advised** में – **advisedly** (अड् 'वाइज़िड्लि) *adv.* सोच-समझकर किया(कार्य) – **advisor, adviser** *n.* सलाहकार, परामर्शदाता – **advisory** *a.* सलाहकार (समिति) – *n.* किसी विपत्ति की आशंका की सरकारी चेतावनी

advocate *n.* (ऐड्वकिट) वकील, ऐडवोकेट; समर्थक – *vt.* (ऐड्वकेट) किसी बात का समर्थन करना, सिफारिश करना

advt. advertisement का संक्षेप

adze (ऐड्ज़) *n.* बढ़ई का औज़ार, बसूला

aegis ('ईजिस) *n.* तत्वावधान; संरक्षण (मूल, यूनानी देवता ज़ूस की ढाल)

aerated ('ऍअरेटिड) *a.* गैस भरा (तरल पदार्थ सोडा, लैमन आदि)

aerial (ऍअरिअल) *a.* वायु का, हवाई; वायुयान सम्बन्धी – *n.* रेडियो, टी.वी. आदि का एरियल

aero (ऍअरो) (*comb. form*) वायु- या वायुयान जैसे, **aero engine** में

aerobatics (ऍअरो 'बैटिक्स) *pl. n.* विमानों की उड़ान के करतब, हवाई करतब

aerobics (ऍअ 'रोबिक्स) *pl. n.* एक व्यायाम की पद्धति जिस का उद्देश्य खून में आक्सीजन की मात्रा बढ़ाना है

aerodrome ('ऍअरड्रोम) *n.* हवाई अड्डा

aerodynamics (ऍअरोडाइ 'नैमिक्स) *n.* वायु के बहाव का अध्ययन, विशे. गतिमान ठोस वस्तुओं के आसपास

aeronautics (ऍअर 'नॉटिक्स) *n.* विमान विज्ञान – **aeronautical** *a.* विमान-विज्ञान सम्बन्धी

aeroplane ('ऍअरप्लेन) *n.* वायुयान, विमान

aerosol ('ऍअरसॉल) *n.* (हवा के दबाव से) छिड़का जाने वाला तरल पदार्थ

aerospace ('ऍअरस्पेस) *n.* वायुमण्डल व उसके आगे अंतरिक्ष

aesthetic (ईस् 'थेंटिक) *a.* सौंदर्य, रुचि और कला से सम्बंधित, सौंदर्य-बोध सम्बंधी – **aesthetics** *n.* सौंदर्य शास्त्र

afar (अ 'फ़ार) *adv.* दूर (तक, से)

affable ('एफ़बल) *a.* मिलनसार, हंसमुख

affair (अ 'फ़ेंअर) *n.* किया गया काम, कारोबार; घटना; मामला; प्रेम सम्बन्ध – **affairs** *pl. n.* व्यक्तिगत कामकाज के मामले, सार्वजनिक हित के मामले

affect (अ 'फ़ेंक्ट) *vt.* पर प्रभाव डालना, असर करना; भावनाओं को उद्धेलित करना; दिखावा करना, अभिनय करना, बनंना; पसंद करना – **affectation** (एफ़ेंक् 'टेशन) *n.* ढोंग, दिखावा – **affected** *a.* बनावटी (व्यवहार आदि), दिखावटी; ग्रस्त, (बाढ़ बीमारी आदि से) प्रभावित – **affection** (अ 'फ़ेंक्शन) *n.* स्नेह, प्यार – **affectionate** *a* स्नेहपूर्ण, स्नेही, कोमल – **affectionately** *adv.* स्नेहपूर्वक

affidavit (ऐफि डेविट) *n.* शपथ लेकर दिया लिखित बयान, शपथपत्र, हलफ़नामा
affiliate (अ फ़िलिएट) *vt.* मिलाना, किसी संगठन को किसी संघ से सम्बद्ध करना – **affiliation** (अफ़िलि एशन) *n.* सम्बन्ध, सम्बद्ध होना
affinity (अ फ़िनिटि) *n.* सहज पसंद; मिलते-जुलते होने की क्रिया, साद श्य; विवाह से उत्पन्न नाता
affirm (अ फ़र्म) *v.* द ढ़तापूर्वक या निश्चय से कहना, पुष्टि करना, प्रतिज्ञान करना – **affirmation** (ऐफ़र् मेशन) *n.* पुष्टि; प्रतिज्ञान; समर्थन; हां – **affirmative** *a.* स्वीकारात्मक – *n.* हां, स्वीकारोक्ति – **affirmative action** *US* भेदभाव के शिकार जाति, वर्ग आदि के लिए नौकरियों, कालिजों आदि में आरक्षण
affix (अ फ़िक्स) *vt.* जोड़ना, लगाना –(ऐफ़िक्स) *n.* जोड़ा गया अंश, विशे. शब्द के साथ, पहले (*prefix*) या बाद में (*suffix*) प्रत्यय, उपसर्ग
afflict (अ फ़्लिक्ट) *vt.* दुख देना या कष्ट पहुंचाना, सताना, तंग करना, परेशान करना – **affliction** (अ फ़्लिक्शन) *n.* कष्ट
affluent (ऐफ़्लुअन्ट) *a.* धनी; प्रचुर, बहुत – *n.* सहायक नदी – **affluence** *n.* धन-दौलत, सम द्धि, बहुलता
afford (अ फ़ॉर्ड) *vt.* खरीद सकना; (खर्च, समय आदि) दे सकना; समर्थ होना; देना, प्रदान करना
afforest (अ फ़ॉरिस्ट) *vt.* पेड़ लगाना, जंगल उगाना – **afforestation** (ऐफ़ॉरिस् टेशन) *n.* वनरोपण, पेड़ लगाना
affray (अ फ़्रे) *n.* हाथपाई, लड़ाई, दंगा, हंगामा
affront (अ फ़्रंट) *vt.* खुले आम या जानबूझ कर अपमान करना – *n.* अपमान, निरादर
afield (अ फ़ील्ड) *adv.* घर से परे; (कार्य) क्षेत्र में (होना)
afire (अ फ़ाइअर) *adv.* जलता हुआ
aflame (अ फ़्लेम) *adv.* जलता हुआ
afloat (अ फ़्लोट) *adv.* तैरता हुआ (समुद्र में); (अफ़वाहें) फैली हुई
afoot (अ फ़ुट) *adv.* पैदल; जारी, चालू; सक्रिय
afraid (अ फ़्रेड) *a.* डरा या सहमा हुआ
afresh (अ फ़्रेश) *adv.* दोबारा, नए सिरे से
African (ऐफ़्रिकन) *a.* अफ़्रीका का
Afrikaans (ऐफ़्रि कान्स) *n.* दक्षिण अफ़्रीका में प्रयुक्त भाषा – **Afrikaner** (ऐफ़्रि कानर) *n.* दक्षिण अफ़्रीका की गोरी जाति का व्यक्ति, जिस की मात भाषा अफ़्रीकांस हो
Afro (ऐफ़्रो) *a.* अफ़्रीकी
after (आफ़्टर) *adv.* बाद में; पीछे; के अनुसार; के जैसा – *prep.* पीछे, किसी के बाद, पीछे-पीछे – *conj.* किसी समय के बाद – *a.* पीछे का, बाद का, जहाज़ के पिछले भाग में – **after all** फिर भी
afterbirth (आफ़्टर्बर्थ) *n.* जन्म के बाद निकलने वाली झिल्ली (जिसमें शिशु लिपटा रहता है), आंवल, खेड़ी
aftercare (आफ़्टर्केअर) *n.* बीमारी के इलाज के बाद रोगी की देखभाल, विशे. प्रसूति के बाद की सेवा सुश्रुषा
aftereffect (आफ़्टरइफ़ेक्ट) *n.* किसी काम या घटना का बाद में होने वाला प्रभाव
aftermath (आफ़्टरमैथ) *n.* परिणाम, नतीजा
afternoon (आफ़्टर् नून) *n.* तीसरा पहर, अपरान्ह
aftershave (आफ़्टर्शेव) *n.* दाढ़ी बनाने के बाद लगाने का तरल पदार्थ (लोशन)
afterthought (आफ़्टर्थॉट) *n.* वह विचार जो बाद में आए, अनुबोध
afterward(s) (आफ़्टर्वड्(ज़)) *adv.* बाद में, पश्चात्
Ag *Chem* चांदी (के लिए प्रयुक्त चिह्न)
again (अ गेन) *adv.* फिर, दोबारा, अतिरिक्त, बदले में, के अलावा – **again and again** बार-बार

against (अ'गेंस्ट) *prep.* के विरुद्ध, के खिलाफ़, के विपरीत; पहले से; के लिए; के पास या सम्पर्क में; के सामने

agape (अ'गेप) *a./adv.* मुंहबाए, खुले मुंह (आश्चर्य से)

agate ('ऐगिट) *n.* रंगदार कीमती प्त्थर, गोमेद, अक़ीक़

age (एज) *n.* आयु, अवस्था; युग; व्यस्कता; लंबा समय – *v.* व द्ध होना या करना – **aged** *a.* ('एज़्ड) *a.* की उम्र का – *pl. n.* ('एजिड) बूढ़े लोग – **ag(e) ing** *n.* व द्ध होना – *a.* व द्ध होते हुए – **ageless** *a.* चिरयुवा, सदा ज़वान – **age-old** *a.* बहुत पुराना, पुरातन – **age of consent** जब कानून के अनुसार शादी की जा सकती है

agenda (अ'जेंन्डअ) *n.* विचारणीय कार्यों की सूची, कार्य सूची, (बैठक का) कार्यक्रम

agent ('एजंट) *n.* जिसे किसी ने अपनी ओर से कार्य करने का अधिकार दिया हो, अभिकर्ता, दलाल, एजेंट; प्रभाव दिखाने वाला व्यक्ति या पदार्थ; कारण, कारक; प्राक तिक शक्ति – **agency** *n.* शाखा; माध्यम, साधन; दलाल का व्यवसाय या उसका कार्यस्थान, एजेन्सी

agent provocateur (अ'झाँप्रवॉक 'तार) *Fr.* पुलिस या गुप्तचर विभाग का जासूस

agglomeration (अग्लॉम'रेशन) *n.* पिंड के रुप में संचित होने की क्रिया

aggrandize (अ'ग्रैन्डाइज़) *vt.* आकार, शक्ति, या दर्जे में बड़ा बनाना; बढ़ाना – **aggrandizement** *n.* वद्धि

aggravate ('ऐग्रवेट) *vt.* बिगाड़ देना; अधिक गंभीर बनाना; *inf.* चिढ़ाना, तंग करना – **aggravating** *a.* गंभीर बनाने वाला (कारण) – **aggravation** (ऐग्र'वेशन) *n.* बिगाड़ना, (समस्या) गंभीर बनना

aggregate ('ऐग्रिगिट) *a.* मिलाया या इकट्ठा किया हुआ, संकलित, सम्पूर्ण, कुल – ('ऐग्रिगिट) *n.* समूह, समुच्चय, कुल योग

aggression (अ'ग्रेशन) *n.* अकारण हमला, आक्रमण, लड़ाई के समान काररवाई; युद्ध की शुरूआत – **aggressive** *a.* आक्रमणशील, लड़ाका

aggrieve (अ'ग्रीव़) *vt.* दुःख या कष्ट देना, हानि पहुंचाना – **aggrieved** *a.* दुःखी, व्यथित; जिसे किसी से शिकायत हो, असंतुष्ट, अपक त

aghast (अ'गास्ट) *a.* भौंचक्का या मुंह बाए; डरा हुआ

agile ('ऐजाइल) *a.* फुर्तीला, तेज़, सक्रिय – **agility** (अ'जिलिटि) *n.* फुर्ती, तेज़ी

agitate ('ऐजिटेट) *vt.* परेशान कर देना; उत्तेजित करना; गतिशील रखना या चलता रखना, हिलाना – *vi.* आंदोलन करना – **agitated** *a.* उत्तेजित – **agitation** *n.* उत्तेजना, अशांति; आंदोलन – **agitator** *n.* आंदोलनकारी, उपद्रवी

aglow (अ'ग्लो) *a.* चमकता हुआ, प्रदीप्त

AGM Annual General Meeting का संक्षेप

agnostic (एेग्'नॉस्टिक) *n.* व्यक्ति जिस का विश्वास हो कि हम भौतिक संसार के बाहर की किसी वस्तु को नह जान सकते, अज्ञेयवादी – **agnosticism** *n.*

ago (अ'गो) *adv.* पहले – **long ago** बहुत समय पहले

agog (अ'गॉग) *a./adv.* उत्सुक; उत्तेजित

agony ('ऐगनि) *n.* घोर मानसिक या शारीरिक व्यथा या पीड़ा; कड़ा संघर्ष – **agonize** *vt.* व्यथा या क्लेश पहुंचाना, तड़पाना – *vi.* क्लेश पहुंचना; तड़पना, बहुत चिंतित होना – **agonizing** *a.* व्यथापूर्ण; चिंतापूर्ण

agoraphobia (एगर'फोबिअ) *n.* खुले स्थानों का डर

agrarian (अ'ग्रेंअरिअन) *a.* क षि भूमि या उस के प्रबन्ध से सम्बन्धित

agree (अ'ग्री) *v.* मान लेना; से सहमत होना; मेल खाना; के अनुकूल होना, माफिक आना; ठीक

करना (खाते) **(agreed, agreeing)** – **agreeability** *n.* – **agreeable** *a.* सहमत, राज़ी; रुचिकर, सुखद, बढ़िया – **agreement** *n.* सहमति, करार, अनुबंध; समझौता – **agree with** से सहमत होना, को मानना – **not agree with sb.** (खाद्य-पदार्थ/जलवायु) माफिक/रास न आना

agriculture (ऐग्रिकल्चर) *n.* कृषि – **agricultural** *a.* कृषि-सम्बन्धी – **agriculturist** *n.* किसान

aground (अ'ग्राउंड) *adv.* नदी आदि के तल में धंसी हुई (नाव आदि)

ahead (अ'हेंड) *adv.* आगे; आगे की ओर

AI artificial intelligence और artificial insemination का संक्षेप

aid (एड) *vt.* सहायता देना – *n.* सहायता

aide, aide-de-camp (एड, 'एड्ड 'कॉङ) *n.* सैनिक अधिकारी का सहायक अफसर, ए.डी.सी, परिसहायक (*pl.* **aides de-camp**)

AIDS (एड्ज़) *n.* घातक रोग जिसमें रोगों से लड़ने की शक्ति समाप्त हो जाती है, **acquired immune/immuno-deficiency syndrome** का संक्षेप, एड्ज़

ail (एल) *vt.* तकलीफ पहुंचाना – *vi.* बीमार होना – **ailing** *a.* बीमार – **ailment** *n.* बीमारी, रोग

aim (एम) *v.* निशाना बांधना, (बन्दूक आदि से) लक्ष्य करना, किसी (वस्तु आदि की प्राप्ति) के लिए प्रयत्न करना – *n.* निशाना; लक्ष्य; प्रयोजन; उद्देश्य – **aimless** *a.* निरुद्देश्य

ain't (एन्ट) **am not, is not, are not, has not, have not** के लिए बोलचाल की भाषा में प्रयुक्त शब्द

air (ऍअर) *n.* हवा, वायु; वायुमण्डल; लय, तान; हावभाव – **(~ s)** *pl.* नाज़-नखरा – *vt.* हवा लगाना; सुखाना – **airily** *adv.* नख़रे से, लापरवाही से – **airiness** *n.* खुला, हवादार होने की स्थिति; प्रफुल्लता – **airless** *a.* जहां हवा न हो, बंद – **airy** *a.* खुला, हवादार – **air base** सैनिक वायुयान अड्डा – **airborne** *a.* जो उड़ रहा हो – **air commodore** वायुसेना का एक पद – **air-condition** *vt.* किसी भवन में तापमान नियंत्रित करना, वातानुकूलित करना – **air conditioner** एयर कंडीशनर, वातानुकूलित करने का यंत्र – **air conditioning** वातानुकूलन – **aircraft** *n.* विमानों के लिए सामूहिक शब्द – **aircraft carrier** विमान-वाहक युद्धपोत – **airfield** *n.* हवाई अड्डा, वह स्थान जहां विमान उतरते हैं – **air force** वायु सेना – **air gun** छर्रेदार बन्दूक – **air hostess** विमान परिचारिका – **air letter** हवाई डाक से जाने वाली चिट्ठी – **airlift** *n.* आपात स्थिति में विमानों से सामान व लोगों को ढोने की क्रिया – *v.* – **airline** *n.* विमान कम्पनी – **airlock** *n.* पानी आदि की नली में हवा का बुलबुला जो पानी के जाने में रुकावट डालता है; कक्ष जिसमें वायु निकाल दी गयी हो – **air mail** हवाई डाक – **airman** *n.* वायु सैनिक – **airplay** *n.* ग्रामोफोन रिकार्ड का रेडियो पर बजना – **air pocket** वायुमंडल में हल्की वायु का वह क्षेत्र जिसमें पहुंच कर विमान अचानक नीचे की ओर गिरता हैं – **airport** *n.* हवाई अड्डा – **air pump** हवा निकालने या भरने का यंत्र – **air raid** हवाई हमला – **airsickness** *n.* विमान में बैठने पर उबकाई या उल्टी आना – **airstrip** *n.* छोटा हवाई अड्डा जहां विमानों के उतरने की एक ही पट्टी हो – **airtight** *a.* जिसमें वायु का प्रवेश न हो सके – **airworthy** *a.* (विमान) जो उड़ान भरने के योग्य हो – **airworthiness** *n.* – **be on the air** रेडियो/टि.वी. पर प्रसारित होना

aisle (आइल) *n.* गिरजाघर या थियेटर आदि में सीटों के बीच का रास्ता, गलियारा

ajar (अ'जार) *adv.* अधखुला (दरवाज़ा आदि)

a.k.a. also known as का संक्षेप
akimbo (अ´किंबो) *adv.* कमर पर हाथ रखे जिस से कुहनियां बाहर को निकली हों
akin (अ´किन) *a.* के जैसा; सद श (गुण या आकार में)
alabaster (´ऐलबास्टर) *n.* चिकना, सफेद और आधा पारदर्शक पत्थर, सेलखड़ी
a la carte (आला´कार्त) *Fr.* व्यंजन सूची; (मैन्यू) से अलग-अलग चुने गये (व्यंजन)
alacrity (अ´लैक्रिटि) *n.* चुस्ती, तत्परता
alarm (अ´लार्म) *n.* अचानक डर जाने की स्थिति, डर, अंदेशा; आशंका; खतरे की चेतावनी; खतरे की घंटी; युद्ध का आह्वान – *vt.* डरा देना; खतरे की चेतावनी देना – **alarming** *a.*आशंकापूर्ण, भयप्रद – **alarm clock** अलारम घड़ी
alas (अ´लैस) *interj.* हाय ! अफसोस !
albatross (´ऐल्बट्रॉस) *n.* एक बड़ा समुद्री पक्षी, कादूस
albeit (आल्´बीइट) *conj.* यद्यपि, हालांकि
albino (एेल्´बीनो) *n.* सफेद चमड़ी और बाल व गुलाबी आंखों वाला व्यक्ति या पशु, सूरज मुखी (व्यक्ति) (*pl.* **albinos**)
album (´ऐल्बम) *n.* पुस्तक जिसमें चित्र, हस्ताक्षर या डाक टिकट चिपकाए जाते हैं, अल्बम; एक से अधिक गानों का रिकार्ड आदि के रूप में संग्रह
albumen (´ऐलब्युमिन) *n.* अण्डे की सफ़ेदी
alchemy (´एल्कमि) *n.* मध्य युग का रसायन शास्त्र विशे. घटिया धातुओं से सोना बनाने का
alcohol (´ऐल्कहॉल) *n.* ऐल्कोहल, शराब; एक रसायनिक पदार्थ – **alcoholic** *a./n.* जिसे शराब की लत हो, शराबी, पियक्कड़ – **alcoholism** (´ऐल्कहॉलिज़्म) *n.* शराब की लत; उस से उत्पन्न रोग
alcove (´ऐल्कोव़) *n.* (दीवार में बना) आला, लता-कुंज
aldehyde (´ऐल्डिहाइड) *n.* कार्बनिक समिश्रणों के समूह में से कोई एक
alder (´ऑल्डर) *n.* भोजपत्र के व क्ष जैसा पेड़, भिदुर
alderman (´ऑल्डर्मन) *n.* नगर पालिका के प्रबन्ध मण्डल का सदस्य, पौर मुख्य
ale (एल) *n.* एक प्रकार की बीयर
alert (अ´लर्ट) *a.* चौकन्ना, चौकस; फुर्तीला, क्रियाशील – *n.* अचानक हमले की चेतावनी – *vt.* चेतावनी देना, विशे. खतरे की, सावधान करना, ध्यान दिलाना – **alertness** *n.* सतर्कता, सावधानी – **on the alert** चौकस, चौकन्ना, सावधान
algae (´ऐल्जी) *pl.n.* [*sing* **alga** ऐलग्अ] पानी में उगने वाला पौधा, विशे. शैवाल
algebra (´ऐल्जिब्रअ) *n.* बीज गणित
ALGOL *Computers* algorithmic oriented language का संक्षेप
algorithm (´ऐल्गरिदम) *n.* जटिल आंकलनों की विधि, कलन गणित
alias (´एलिअस) *adv.* अन्यथा, उर्फ – *n.* उपनाम (*pl.* **aliases**)
alibi (´ऐलिबाइ) *n.* अभियुक्त की यह दलील कि अपराध के समय वह मौके पर नह था; *inf.* बहाना
alien (´एलिअन) *a.* विदेशी, भिन्न स्वरूप वाला, अनमेल, असंगत, प्रतिकूल (*to* के साथ) – *n.* विदेशी – **alienate** *vt.* विमुख करना – **alienation** *n.* विमुखता, अलग होना, करना
alight[1] (अ´लाइट) *vi.* गाड़ी आदि से उतरना
alight[2] *a.* जलता हुआ; उज्जवल
align (अ´लाइन) *vt.* सीध मिलाना, इकट्ठे या सहमत करना – **alignment** *n.* सीध, पंक्तिबद्धता, सरेखण – **non-alignment** *n.* तटस्थता (की नीति)
alike (अ´लाइक) *a.* एक जैसा, समान – *adv.* एक ही प्रकार से, समान रूप से
alimentary (ऐलि´मेंन्टरि) *a.* – **alimentary canal** नली जिस से भोजन पेट में पहुंचता है

alimony (ऐलिमनि) *n.* (तलाक पाई पत्नी या पति का) निर्वाह व्यय

alive (अ´लाइव़) *a.* जीवित; सक्रिय; सजीव, फुर्तीला; जानकार; से भरा

alkali (´एल्कलाइ) *n.* पदार्थ जो तेज़ाब को बेअसर करे, क्षार (*pl.* **alkali(e)(s)** – **alkaline** *a.* क्षारीय, खारा

all (ऑल) *a.* सारा, समस्त, सब – *adv.* पूरी तरह; (*in games*) प्रत्येक का, दोनों ओर (जैसे **the score was two all**) – *n.* सम्पूर्ण, सब – **all fours** घुटनों और हाथों (के बल) – **all out** *a/adv.* पूरे जोर (से) – **all-rounder** *n.* हरफनमौला

allay (अ´ले) *vt.* तकलीफ, कष्ट, डर दूर या कम करना

allege (अ´लेंज) *vt.* आरोप लगाना, दलील पेश करना – **allegation** (एलि´गेशन) *n.* आरोप – **alleged** – *a.* आरोपित, तथाकथित – **allegedly** (अ´लेंजिड्लि) *adv.*

allegiance (अ´लीजंस) *n* राज्यभक्ति; स्वामिभक्ति

allegory (´ऐलिगरि) *n.* प्रतीक कथा; अन्योक्ति

allergy (´ऐलर्जि) *n.* किसी खाद्य या अन्य पदार्थ के प्रति असाधारण संवेदनशीलता, प्रत्यूर्जता, ऐलर्जी – **allergic** (अ´लर्जिक) *a.* एलर्जी से उत्पन्न; *inf.* जिसे किसी व्यक्ति या वस्तु विशेष से घ णा हो

alleviate (अ´लीविएट) *vt.* हल्का या कम करना, (कष्ट, क्रोध आदि) में कमी करना

alley (´ऐलि) *n.* संकरी गली, रास्ता या पगडंडी, स्किटल खेलने का बाड़ा; बड़ा कंचा (*pl.* **alleys**)

alliance (अ´लाइअन्स) *n.* मैत्री, साहचर्य; (परिवारों में) विवाह सम्बन्ध; (राष्ट्रों के बीच) संधि, राष्ट्र संघ

alligator (´ऐलिगेटर) *n.* मगरमच्छ जाति का जीव, जो अमरीकी महाद्वीप में पाया जाता है, घड़ियाल

alliteration (अलिट´रेशन) *n.* अनुप्रास अलंकार

allocate (´ऐलकेट) *vt.* हिस्से के रूप में बांटना या देना, निर्धारित करना, स्थित करना – **allocation** *n.* निर्धारण, आवंटन

allopathy (अ´लॉपथि) *n.* चिकित्सा की परम्परागत पद्धति डाक्टरी चिकित्सा

allot (अ´लॉट) *vt.* (हिस्से के रूप में) बांटना; (समय) निर्धारित कर देना, (कार्य) सिपुर्द कर देना (**allotted** *pt./pp*) – **allotment** *n.* बांटने की प्रक्रिया, आवंटन; खेती के लिए किराए पर दी गयी भूमि; बांटा गया हिस्सा

allow (अ´लाउ) *vt.* करने देना, मान लेना; किसी काम के लिए समय निर्धारित कर देना – *vi.* (प्राय: *for* के साथ) का ध्यान रखना; की गुंजाइश छोड़ना – **allowable** *a.* स्वीक ति योग्य – **allowance** (अ´लाउअन्स) *n.* भत्ता; (टैक्स में) छूट की राशि, गुंजाइश

alloy (´ऐलॉइ, अ´लॉइ) *n.* दो या अधिक धातुओं का मिश्रण, मिश्र धातु –*vt.* (अ´लॉइ) धातुओं का मिश्रण करना, खोट मिलाना

allude (अ´लूड) *vi.* हल्का सा संकेत या इशारा करना – **allusion** (अ´लूझ़न) *n.* संकेत

allure (अ´ल्युअर) *vt.* लुभाना, प्रलोभन देकर अपनी ओर करना – **alluring** *a.* लुभावना, मोहक

alluvial (अ´लूविअल) *a.* नदी के पानी से आई (मिट्टी, रेत आदि), कछारी

ally (अ´लाइ) *vt.* संधि, विवाह या मित्रता के नाते में बांधना, जोड़ना (**allied** *pt./pp.*, **allying** *pr.*) – **allied** (अ´लाइड, ´ऐलाइड) *a.* सहबद्ध, जुड़ा हुआ – **ally** (´ऐलाइ) *n.* राष्ट्र या शासक जो किसी संधि द्वारा दूसरे का मित्र बने, संधिबद्ध राष्ट्र (*pl.* **allies**)

alma mater (´ऐल्म´माटर, ´मेटर) *Lat.* अपना स्कूल, कालिज या विश्वविद्यालय

almanac (´ऑल्मनैक) *n.* पंचांग, तिथिपत्री, जन्तरी

almighty (ऑल्´माइटि) *a.* सर्वशक्तिमान – **The Almighty** ईश्वर
almond (´आमण्ड) *n.* बादाम (का पेड़)
almost (´ऑल्मोस्ट) *adv.* लगभग, करीब-करीब
alms (आम्ज़) *pl. n.* दान, भिक्षा
aloe (´ऐलो) *n.* घीकुंवार का पौधा, अगरू
aloft (अ´लॉफ्ट) *adv.* ऊपर, ऊंचाई पर जहाज़ के रस्सों आदि के ताने-बाने में
alone (अ´लोन) *a.* अकेला, एकाकी – *adv*. सिर्फ, केवल
along (अ´लॉङ) *adv.* लम्बाई में; साथ-साथ, आगे – *prep*. के समानान्तर, की बगल में – **alongside** *adv./prep*. की बगल में, पास-पास
aloof (अ´लूफ़) *adv.* अलग, दूर – *a.* जो किसी से मेल जोल न बढ़ाए – **aloofness** *n.* अलगाव, दूरी
aloud (अ´लाउड) *adv.* ऊंचे स्वर में, ज़ोर से
alp (ऐल्प) *n.* ऊंचा पर्वत – **Alps** *pl.* पर्वतमाला विशे. स्विट्ज़रलैंड में
alphabet (´ऐल्फ़बेंट) *n.* वर्णमाला, ककहरा – **alphabetical** *a.* वर्णक्रम में
already (ऑल्´रेंडि) *adv.* पहले से ही, इस से पहले, अपेक्षित समय से पहले
Alsatian (ऐल्´सेशन) *n.* बड़े आकार का शिकारी कुत्ता
also (´ऑल्सो) *adv.* भी; साथ ही; इसी तरह – **also-ran** *n.* असफल प्रतियोगी, उम्मीदवार आदि
altar (´ऑल्टर) *n.* वेदी (ऊंचा स्थान, जहां बलि आदि दी जाय; चर्च में पूजा का सामान रखने की मेज़
alter (´ऑल्टर) *vt.* बदलना; भिन्न कर देना – *vi.* बदलना; भिन्न हो जाना – **alterability** *n.* परिवर्तनशीलता – **alterable** *a.* परिवर्तनशील – **alteration** *n.* परिवर्तन, रद्दोबदल
altercation (ऑल्टर्´केशन) *n.* कहासुनी, विवाद
alter ego (´ऑल्टर्´ईगो) *Lat.* अन्तरंग मित्र; स्वयं का दूसरा रूप
alternate *v.* (´ऑल्टर्नेट) बारी- बारी से करना; बारी-बारी से आना या होना – *a.* (ऑल्´टर्निट) बारी-बारी से, एक के बाद एक, छोड़कर – **alternately** (ऑल्´टर्निट्लि) *adv.* बारी-बारी से – **alternative** (आल्´टर्नटिव़) *n.* विकल्प, दो में से एक – *a.* वैकल्पिक – **alternator** *n.* ए.सी. बिजली बनाने का यंत्र
although (ऑल्´दो) *conj.* (इसके बावजूद; यद्यपि, हालांकि
altimeter (ऐल्´टिमिटर) *n.* ऊंचाई मापने का यंत्र, तुंगतामापी
altitude (´ऐल्टिट्यूड) *n.* ऊंचाई, ऊंचा स्थान
altogether (ऑल्ट´गेंदर) *adv.* पूरी तरह, पूर्णतया; कुल मिलाकर, कुल
altruism (´ऐल्ट्रुइज़म) *n.* परोपकारिता
alum (´ऐलम) *n.* फिटकरी
aluminium, US **aluminum** (ऐल्यु´मिनियम, अ´लूमिनम) *n.* ऐल्युमिनियम धातु
always (´ऑल्वेज़) *adv.* सदा, हमेशा, सर्वदा
AM, a.m. amplitude modulation; ante meridiem का संक्षेप
am (ऐम) BE का *first person sing. present indefinite*
amalgam (अ´मैल्गम) *n.* पारे के साथ किसी अन्य धातु का मिश्रण; नरम मिश्रण जिसे कोई भी रूप दिया जा सके; कई तत्वों का मिश्रण
amalgamate (अ´मैल्गमेट) *vt.* मिलाना, सम्मलित करना – *vi.* मिलना – **amalgamation** (अमैल्ग´मेशन) *n.*
amass (अ´मैस) *v.* बड़ी संख्या में जमा या संचित करना; ढेर लगाना

amateur (ऐमटर, ऐमचर) *n.* व्यक्ति जो बिना धन की लालसा के केवल शौक के लिए किसी कला, खेल आदि में भाग ले, शौकीन, अव्यवसायी (खिलाड़ी, कलाकार आदि) – **amateurish** *a.* अनाड़ी

amaze (अ'मेज़) *vt.* (*surprise*) बहुत अधिक हैरान करना, अचम्भे में डालना – **amazement** *n.* विस्मय, अचम्भा – **amazing** *a.* आश्चर्यजनक; असाधारण

ambassador (एम्'बैसडर) *n.* राजदूत – (**ambassadress** *fem*)

amber (ऐम्बर) *n.* जीवाश्म (नीचे दबे हुए व क्षों से मिलने वाली पीले रंग की पारदर्शी राल), कहरुबा – *a.* इस से बना या इस जैसा; पीला

ambidextrous (ऐम्बि'डेक्स्ट्रस) *a.* जो दोनों हाथों से सभी काम कर सके, सव्यसाची, दुहथिया

ambience (ऐम्बिअंस) *n.* किसी स्थान का वातावरण

ambiguous (एम्'बिग्युअस) *a.* जिस का एक से अधिक अर्थ निकले, द्वयर्थक, अस्पष्ट – **ambiguity** (ऐम्बि'ग्यूइटि) *n.* अस्पष्टता

ambition (ऐम्'बिशन) *n.* आकांक्षा, महत्वाकांक्षा – **ambitious** *a.* (ऐम्'बिशस) महत्वाकांक्षी

ambivalence (ऐम्'बिव़लन्स), **ambivalency** (ऐम्'बिव़लन्सि) *n.* एक साथ परस्पर विरोधी इच्छाओं या विचारों का होना, उभयभाव – **ambivalent** *a.* उभयभावी, परस्पर विरोधी इच्छाओं वाला

ambulance (ऐम्ब्युलन्स) *n.* बीमार या घायल व्यक्तियों को ले जाने का वाहन, अस्पताल गाड़ी, एम्बुलेंस

ambush (ऐमुबुश) *n.* घात लगाने की क्रिया – *vt.* घात लगाकर हमला करना

ameliorate (अ'मील्यरेट) *vi.* सुधरना – *vt.* सुधारना – **amelioration** *n.* सुधार

amen (आ'मॆन) *interj.* तथास्तु, आमीन

amenable (अ'मीनबल) *a.* जिसे वश में करना अथवा प्रभावित करना आसान हो, आज्ञाकारी

amend (अ'मॆन्ड) *vi.* सुधर जाना – *vt.* सुधारना, संशोधन करना, परिवर्तन करना, जैसे संसद में विधयेक में – **amendment** *n.* संशोधन – **amends** *pl. n.* क्षतिपूर्ति, हरज़ाना

amenity (अ'मीनिटि) *n.* (प्राय: *pl.*) लाभकारी सुविधा या सेवा, सुख-साधन

American (अ'मॆरिकन) *a.* अमरीका महाद्वीप या संयुक्त राज्य अमरीका का, या उससे सम्बंधित, अमरीकी – *n.* अमरीकन, अमरीका वासी

amethyst (एमिथिस्ट) *n.* नीले बैंगनी रंग का रत्न, जम्बुमणि

amiable (एमिअबल) *a.* सौम्य, मिलनसार; उदार

amicable (ऐमिकब्ल) *a.* मैत्रीपूर्ण, सौहार्दपूर्ण

amid, amidst (अ'मिड, अ'मिड्स्ट) *prep.* में, बीच में

amiss (अ'मिस) *a.* गलत – **take amiss** किसी बात का बुरा मनना

amity (ऐमिटि) *n.* मित्रता, सौहार्द

ammeter (ऐमीटर) *n.* बिजली की धारा मापने का यंत्र, धारामापी

ammonia (अ'मोनिअ) *n.* अमोनिया गैस या द्रव, अमोनिया – **ammonium** *n.* अमोनिया

ammunition (एम्यु'निशन) *n.* गोला-बारूद; *fig* भी

amnesia (एम्'नीज़िअ) *n.* स्मरण शक्ति का लोप, स्म तिलोप

amnesty (ऐम्निस्टि) *n.* सर्वक्षमा, विशे. सरकार द्वारा अपराधियों को

amoeba (अ'मीबअ) *n.* एक सैल का जीवाणु जो तालाब आदि में मिलता है, अमीबा

among, amongst (अ'मंग, अ'मंग्स्ट) *prep.* में, बीच में, दरम्यान; मिलकर

amoral (ए'मॉरल) *a.* नैतिकता निरपेक्ष, नैतिक गुणों से खाली

amorous (ऐमरस) *a.* प्रेमातुर, प्रणयी; कामी

amorphous (अ'मॉर्फ़स) *a.* बिना किसी स्पष्ट

आकार या आक तियों के, अनाकार

amount (अˈमाउंट) *vi.* कुल जोड़ या योग होना, के बराबर होना – *n.* रकम, राशि, कुल योग; मात्रा

amp amperage; ampere(s) का संक्षेप

ampere (ˈऐम्पेंअर) *n.* बिजली के करंट का माप, ऐम्पियर

amphibious (ऐम्ˈफ़िबिअस) *a.* जो प थ्वी और जल दोनों मे जीवित रहे या काम कर सके, उभयचर – **amphibian** *n.* जीव जो पहले पानी में रहे और बाद में प थ्वी पर, उभयचर; गाड़ी जो पानी और प थ्वी दोनों पर चल सके; विमान जो पानी में भी उतर सके

amphitheatre (ˈऐम्फ़िथिअटर) *n.* रंगशाला जिसके चारों तरफ ऊपर से नीचे की ओर बैठने के स्थान बने हों

ample (ˈएम्पल) *a.* लम्बा-चौड़ा, विस्त त; पर्याप्त

amplify (ˈऐम्पलिफ़ाइ) *vt.* बढ़ाना (आकार, ध्वनि आदि); बड़ा या विस्त त करना (**amplified** *pt.*, **amplifying** *pr.p.*) – **amplification** (ऐम्प्लिफ़िˈकेशन) *n.* (ध्वनि आदि) बढ़ाने की क्रिया, प्रवर्धन; विस्तार – **amplifier** (ˈऐम्पलिफ़ाइअर) *n.* लाउडस्पीकर

amplitude (ˈऐम्प्लिट्यूड) *n.* विस्तार, आयाम

amputate (ˈऐम्प्युटेट) *v.* (शरीर का कोई अंग) काट देना – **amputation** (ऐम्प्युˈटेशन) *n.* शरीर का कोई अंग काटने की क्रिया

amuck, amok (अˈमक) *adv.* – **run amuck** गुस्से से पागल होना, सिर पर खून सवार होना

amulet (ˈएम्युलिट) *n.* ताबीज़, जन्तर

amuse (अˈम्यूज़) *vt.* जी, मन बहलाना, मनोरंजन करना, हंसाना – **amusement** *n.* मनोरंजन, दिल बहलाव – **amusing** *a.* मनोरंजक

an (एन) दे. A

anabolic steroid (एनˈबॉलिक-) खिलाड़ियों द्वारा शरीर को मांसल बनाने के लिए प्रयोग किए जाने वाले हारमोनों में से एक

anachronism (अˈनैक्रनिज़्म) *n.* इतिहास की घटना को किसी गलत काल में दिखाना, कालदोष; वस्तु जिसका प्रचलन न हो

anaconda (ऐनˈकॉन्ड्अ) *n.* बड़े आकार का सांप, अजगर

anaemia (अˈनीमिअ) *n.* रक्त में लाल कणों की कमी, रक्ताल्पता – **anaemic** *a.* जिसे रक्ताल्पता का रोग हो, जिस का रंग पीला हो या जो बीमार लगे।

anaesthetic (ऐनिस्ˈथैटिक) *n./a.* बेहोशी लाने की (दवा), निश्चेतक – **anaesthesia** (ऐनिस्ˈथीज़िअ) *n.* संज्ञाहीनता, बेहोशी लाने की दवा – **anaesthetist** (अˈनीस्थटिस्ट) *n.* इस दवा के प्रयोग का विशेषज्ञ डाक्टर

anal देखिए ANUS

analgesic (ऐनल्ˈजीज़िक) *a./n.* (दवाई) जो पीड़ा दूर करे

analog(ue) (ˈऐनलॉग) *a.* सूईयों वाली (घड़ी आदि)

analogy (अˈनैलजि) *n.* साद श्य, अनुरूपता; तुल्यता, समानता – **analogical** (ऐनˈलॉजिकल) *a.* साद श्यमूलक; समान, से मेल खाता – **analogous** (अˈनैलगस) *a.* सद श; अनुरूप, समान

analysis (अˈनैलिसिस) *n.* विश्लेषण [*pl.* **analyses**) (अˈनैलिसीज़)] – **analyse** (ˈऐनलाइज़) *vt.* विश्लेषण करना – **analyst** (ˈऐनलिस्ट) *n.* विश्लेषण करने वाला – **analytic (al)** (ऐनˈलिटिकल) *a.*

anarchy (ˈएनर्कि) *n.* किसी राष्ट्र या देश में सरकार का न होना, अराजकता, अव्यवस्था – **anarchist** *n.* अराजकतावादी, तोड़-फोड़ करने वाला

anathema (अˈनैथम्अ) *n.* वस्तु जिससे अत्याधिक घ णा हो

anatomy (अ'नैटमि) *n.* शरीर रचना-विज्ञान, शरीर का व्यापक विश्लेषण – **anatomical** (ऐन'टॉमिकल) *a.* शरीर रचना-विज्ञान सम्बंधी

ancestor ('ऐन्सेस्टर) *n.* पूर्वज, पुरखा; किसी वस्तु का पुराना रूप – **ancestral** *a.* पैतृक, पूर्वजों से मिली (सम्पत्ति आदि) – **ancestry** ('ऐनसेस्ट्रि) *n.* वंश, कुल, कुलपरंपरा

anchor ('ऐंकर) *n.* जहाज़ का लंगर – *vt.* लंगर डालना – **anchorage** *n.* लंगर डालने की क्रिया या स्थान – **anchor person** रेडियो या टी. वी. पर समाचार देने, रिपोर्ट आदि प्रस्तुत करने वाला व्यक्ति, प्रस्तुतकर्ता

ancient ('एन्शंट) *a.* पुराने समय का, पुरातन, प्राचीन; घिसापिटा, पुराना

ancillary (एन्'सिलरि) *a.* गौण; अनुषंगी, सहायक, पूरक

and (ऐन्ड) *conj.* और, तथा, एवं, व

androgynous ('एन्ड्रॉजिनस) *a.* जिसमें पुरुष व स्त्री दोनों के शारीरिक लक्षण हों, पुंजायांगी

anecdote ('ऐनिक्डोट) *n.* किस्सा (जिसमें एक ही घटना का वर्णन हो)

aneroid barometer ('ऐनरॉइड-) वायु का दबाव मापने का उपकरण जिसमें पारा या अन्य द्रव नहीं होता

anew (अ'न्यू) *adv.* फिर से, नए सिरे से

angel ('एंजल) *n.* देवदूत, फरिश्ता; देवदूत जैसे गुणों वाला व्यक्ति

anger ('ऐंगर) *n.* क्रोध, गुस्सा, नाराज़गी – *vt.* गुस्सा या ताव दिलाना – **angrily** *adv.* क्रोध से – **angry** *a.* क्रुद्ध, नाराज

angina (pectoris) (एन्'जाइन्अ-) ('पैक्टरिस) *n.* हृदय रोग में होने वाली छाती की तीव्र पीड़ा

angle[1] ('ऐंगल) *vi.* बंसी (कांटे) से मछली पकड़ना – **angler** *n.* कांटे से मछली पकड़ने वाला

angle[2] *n.* कोण, कोना; दृष्टिकोण; *inf.* गुप्त व बुरा उद्देश्य – *vt.* मोड़ देना

Anglicize ('ऐंग्लिसाइज़) *vt.* अंग्रेज़ी में व्यक्त करना, अंग्रेज़ी ढंग का बनाना

Anglo- ('ऐंग्लो) (*comb. form*) अंग्रेज़ जैसे **Anglo-American**

Anglophobia (ऐंग्लो'फ़ोबिअ) *n.* इंग्लैंड या अंग्रेजों के प्रति घृणा की भावना

angora (ऐंग्'गॉर्अ) *n.* सफेद, लम्बे और रेशमी बालों वाली बकरी जिसके बालों से ऊन या कपड़ा बनता है; इन बालों से बना कपड़ा या ऊन, अंगोरा

anguish ('ऐंग्विश) *n.* घोर शारीरिक या मानसिक व्यवस्था, पीड़ा

angular ('ऐंग्युलर) *a.* इकहरे बदन का या भद्दा (व्यक्ति); जिसमें कोण हों; कोण से माप किया गया – **angularity** *n.* भद्दापन

animal ('ऐनिमल) *n.* प्राणी, जीव, पशु – *a.* जीवों या पशुओं से सम्बंधित; शारीरिक या विषय भोग सम्बंधी – **animal husbandry** पशुपालन

animate ('ऐनिमेट) *vt.* प्राण या जीवन डालना, जीवित करना; प्रेरणा देना; सक्रिया बनाना; (की) कार्टून फिल्म बनाना – **animated** *a.* जोशभरा; ग़रमगरम (बहस); कार्टून (फिल्म) के रूप में – **animation** (ऐनि'मेशन) *n.* सजीवता, उत्साह; कार्टून फ़िल्म – **animator** *n.* कार्टून फिल्म बनाने वाला

animosity (ऐनि'मॉसिटि) *n.* वैर, शत्रुता; द्वेष

animus ('ऐनिमस) *n.* घृणा; शत्रुता; द्वेष

aniseed ('ऐनिसीड) *n.* सौंफ़ के दाने

ankle ('ऐंकल) *n.* टखना – **anklet** ('ऐंकलिट) *n.* पायल, नूपुर, पाजेब

annals ('ऐनल्ज़) *pl. n.* घटनाओं का ऐतिहासिक वृत्तांत, इतिहास

annex (ऐ'नेंक्स) *vt.* साथ जोड़ना, संलग्न करना; कब्जे में करना (क्षेत्र आदि) – **annexation** (ऐनेंक्'सेशन) *n.* किसी देश पर कब्जा करके अपने में मिला लेने की क्रिया

annexe, US **annex** ('ऐनेंक्स) *n.* साथ लगा भवन; किसी बड़े भवन का भाग; परिशिष्ट

annihilate (अ'नाइअलेट) *vt.* पूर्णतया नष्ट करना – **annihilation** (अनाइअ'लेशन) *n.* सर्वनाश, विध्वंस

anniversary (ऐनि'वर्सरि) *n.* वर्षगांठ, वार्षिकोत्सव

Anno Domini (ऐनो'डॉमिनाइ,-नी *Lat.* ईसवी, सन्

announce (अ'नाउंस) *vt.* सूचित करना; घोषणा करना – **announcement** *n.* घोषणा – **announcer** *n.* रेडियो स्टेशन पर कार्यक्रमों की सूचना देने वाला उद्घोषक, वाचक

annoy (अ'नॉइ) *vt.* चिढ़ाना व नाराज करना, खिजाना, परेशान करना – **annoyance** *n.* नाराज़गी

annual (ऐन्युअल) *a.* वार्षिक, सालाना – *n.* एक वर्षीय पौधा; प्रति वर्ष प्रकाशित होने वाली पुस्तक, वार्षिकी – **annually** *adv.* प्रतिवर्ष

annuity (अ'न्यूइटि) *n.* प्रत्येक वर्ष दी जाने वाली रकम या अनुदान, वार्षिक व ति

annul (अ'नल) *vt.* रद्द करना (करार आदि)

anode (ऐनोड) *n.* करेंट में प्रवेश का बिन्दु, धनाग्र – **anodize** *vt.* धातु पर बिजली के माध्यम से पानी चढ़ाना

anoint (अ'नॉइन्ट) *vt.* तेल या मरहम लगाना; तेल लगाकर पवित्र करना, अभिषेक करना – **anointment** *n.* तेल लगाने की क्रिया, विलेपन; अभिषेक

anomalous (अ'नॉमलस) *a.* अनियमित; असामान्य; असंगत – **anomaly** *n.* अनियमितता, असंगति

anonymous (अ'नॉनिमस) *a.* अनाम, (विशे. पुस्तक) जिसपर लेखक का नाम न हो – **anonymity** (एन'निमिटि) *n.* अनाम होना

anopheles (अ'नॉफ़िलीज़) *n.* मलेरिया फैलाने वाले मच्छर की जाति

anorexia (ऐनॉ'रेक्सिअ) *n.* भूख न लगने का रोग, क्षुधाभाव

another (अ'नदर) *a.* कोई दूसरा, एक और, दूसरा, भिन्न – *pron.* दूसरा

ans. answer का संक्षेप

answer ('आन्सर) *vt.* का उत्तर देना; हल कर देना; के लिए पर्याप्त होना; के अनुरूप होना; संतुष्ट करना; उपयुक्त होना – *vi.* उत्तर देना; ठीक उत्तर देना; (*for, to* के साथ) उत्तरदायी, जवाबदेह होना – *n.* उत्तर, हल – **answerable** *a.* उत्तरदायी – **answering machine** टेलीफोन से जुड़ा यंत्र जो घंटी बजने पर संदेश सुन लेता और रिकार्ड कर लेता है

ant (ऐन्ट) *n.* च टी – **anteater** *n.* च टी खाने वाला जंतु, च टीखोर – **ant hill** बांबी

antagonist (ऐन्'टैगनिस्ट) *n.* विरोधी, प्रतिद्वंद्वी – **antagonism** *n.* विरोध की भावना – **antagonistic** *a.* – **antagonize** *vt.* विरोधी बनाना, दुश्मनी मोल लेना

Antarctic (ऐन्ट्'आर्क्टिक) *a.* दक्षिण ध्रुवीय – *n.* दक्षिणी ध्रुव का क्षेत्र

ante- (ऐन्टि) (*comb. form*) पहले का; पहला

antecedent (ऐन्टि'सीडंन्ट) *a./n.* पहले आने वाली (घटना, वस्तु आदि)

antelope (ऐन्टिलोप) *n.* हिरण की एक जाति, कुरंग

ante meridiem (ऐन्टिम'रिडियम) *Lat.* दोपहर से पहले

antenatal (ऐन्टि'नेट्ल) *a.* गर्भ के दिनों में या जन्म से पूर्व (दिखभाल आदि)

antenna (ऐन्'टेन्अ) *n.* कीड़े-मकौड़ों के आगे को निकले धागे जैसे स ग जिन से वे टोह लेते हैं; रेडियो या टी.वी. का एरियल (*pl.* **antennae**)

anterior (एन्'टिअरिअर) *a.* जो आगे हो; पहले का

anthem (ऐन्थम) *n.* निष्ठा, विशे. देशभक्ति का गीत; राष्ट्रगीत– **national anthem** राष्ट्र-गीत या उस की धुन

anther (ऐन्थर) *n.* फूल का वह अंश जिसमें पराग होता है, पराग कोष

anthology (एन्'थॉलजि) *n.* कविताओं या साहित्यक क तियों का संग्रह, चयनिका

anthropoid (ऐंथ्रपॉइड) *a.* मानव जैसा – *a/n.* मानव जैसा (बन्दर)

anthropology (ऐंथ्र'पॉलजि) *n.* मानव जाति के उद्गम और विकास का विज्ञान, मानवशास्त्र

anti-ant- (ऐन्टि, ऐन्ट) *(comb. form)* विरोधी, रोधी, इस से **anti-aircraft, antispasmodic** *a./n.* जैसे शब्द बनते है

antibiotic (एन्टिबाई'ऑटिक) *n.* कई प्रकार के रसायन विशेष पेनिसलीन, जो जीवाणुओं से उत्पन्न रोगों के इलाज में काम आते हैं – *a.* ऐसे रसायन का

antibody (ऐन्टिबॉडि) *n.* रक्त में पाए जाने वाले या उसमें डाले गए पदार्थ जो रोग उत्पन्न करने वाले जीवाणुओं का असर दूर करते हैं

anticipate (एन्'टिसिपेट) *vt.* पहले से जान लेना या महसूस करना, प्रत्याशा करना, (के लिए) पहले से तैयार रहना, पूर्वानुमान करना – **anticipation** *n.* प्रत्याशा, पूर्वज्ञान – **anticipatory** *a.* पूर्वाभासी, पहले से

anticlimax (एन्टि'क्लाइमैक्स) *n.* अचानक उदात्त से निम्न पर आ जाना; अपकर्ष, रसापकर्ष

anticlockwise (ऐंन्टि'क्लॉक्वाइज़) *a./adv.* बाएं से दाएं (घूमने वाला)

antics (ऐन्टिक्स) *pl.n.* बेतुके, भोंडे या भद्दे काम या उछलकूद, मसखरापन, भंडौती

anticyclone (ऐंटि'साइक्लोन) *n.* अधिक दबाव वाले क्षेत्र में चलने वाली तेज़ हवाएं, प्रतिचक्रवात

antidote (ऐन्टिडोट) *n.* (किसी विष, रोग आदि का) प्रतिकार करने वाली औषधि, विषहर

antigen (ऐन्टिजन) *n.* शरीर में प्रवेशकर रोग उत्पन्न करने वाला पदार्थ जिसके कारण प्रतिरोधी-पदार्थ (antibody) पैदा होते हैं, प्रतिजन

antihistamine (ऐन्टि'हिस्टमीन) *n.* अलर्जी में दी जाने वाली औषधि

antioxidant (ऐन्टि'ऑक्सिडंट) *n.* कुछ भोज्य पदार्थों में पाया जाने वाला तत्व जो शरीर को कैंसर जैसे रोगों से बचाता है

antipathy (एन्'टिपथि) *n.* चिढ़, नफ़रत, घ णा

antipodes (एन्'टिपडीज़) *pl. n.* देश या राष्ट्र जो प थ्वी के दूसरी ओर हों

antipyretic (एन्टिपाइ'रैटिक) *a./n.* (औषधि) जिसमें बुख़ार उतर जाय, ज्वरहर

antique (एन्'टीक) *n.* पुराने समय की कोई वस्तु विशे. संग्रह की गई कुर्सी-मेज़ आदि; *inf.* पुराने ज़माने का – **antiquated** (ऐन्टिक्वेटिड) *a.* पुराना, अप्रचिलित – **antiquity** (एन्'टिक्विटि) *n.* प्राचीन काल, महान युग

antiseptic (एन्टि'सेप्टिक) *n./a.* (औषधि) जो रोगाणुओं को रोके, पूतिरोधक, रोगाणुरोधी – *a.*

antithesis (एन्'टिथिसिस) *n.* विरोध, विपरीतता, प्रतिपक्ष (विचारों की विपरीतता) [*pl.* **antitheses** (एन्'टिथिसीज़)]

anti-virus software *Computers* एक प्रकार का साफ्टवेयर जो कम्प्यूटर के कार्यक्रमों **(programs)** में आये दोष **(virus)** को दूर करता है

antler (ऐंट्लर) *n.* हिरण की कुछ जातियों के स ग

antonym (ऐन्टनिम) *n.* विपरीत अर्थ वाला शब्द, विलोम

anus ('एनस) *n.* मलद्वार – **anal** *a.* गुदा का

anvil (ऐन्विल) *n.* (लोहार की) निहाई, सन्दान, अहरन जिस पर रखकर लोहा कूटा जाता है

anxious (ऐङ्क्शस) *a.* चिंतित; उत्सुक – **anxiety** (ऐङ'ज़ाइटि) *n.* चिंता – **anxiously** *adv.* चिंता की स्थिति में

any (ऐनि) *a./pron.* कोई, कुछ; किसी; प्रत्येक – **anybody** *n.* कोई (भी) – **anyhow** *adv.*

जैसे-तैसे – **anyone** *n.* कोई भी व्यक्ति – **anything** *n.* कोई भी; कुछ भी (वस्तु) – **anyway** *adv.* जैसे भी; फिर भी – **anywhere** *adv.* कह भी

aorta (एˈऑर्टअ) *n.* रक्त की धमनी जो हृदय के बांए भाग में है, महाधमनी

apace (अˈपेस) *adv.* तीव्र गति से, तेज़ी से

apart (अˈपार्ट) *adv.* अलग; दूर; टुकड़ों में

apartheid (अˈपार्ट्हाइट) *n.* (विशे. दक्षिण अफ्रीका में) रंगभेद नीति

apartment (अˈपार्टमेंन्ट) *n.* कमरा, फ्लैट

apathy (ˈऐपथि) *n.* उदासीनता, भावशून्यता – **apathetic** (ऐपˈथेंटिक) *a.*

ape (एप) *n.* बिना पूंछ का बन्दर (जैसे चिम्पैंज़ी, गोरिल्ला); असभ्य फूहड़ व्यक्ति; नकल करने वाला – *vt.* नकल करना

aperture (ˈऐपर्चर) *n.* छेद, सूराख

apex (ˈएपेंक्स) *n.* शिखर, शीर्ष बिन्दु [*pl.* **apexes** (ˈऐपिसिज़), **apices** (ˈएपिसीज़)]

aphorism (ˈऐफ़रिज़म) *n.* सूक्ति, सूत्र, लोकोक्ति

aphrodisiac (ऐफ्रˈडिज़िऐक) *a.* (पदार्थ) जिससे कामेच्छा जागे, कामोद्दीपक – *n.*

apiary (ˈएपिअरि) *n.* स्थान जहां मधु मक्खियां पाली जायं, मधुवाटिका – **apiculture** *n.* मधुमक्खी पालन

apiece (अˈपीस) *adv.* प्रत्येक को/के लिए

aplomb (अˈप्लॉम) *n.* आत्मविश्वास

apocalypse (अˈपॉकलिप्स) *n.* विश्व-विध्वंस

apology (अˈपॉलजि) *n.* क्षमायाचना; घटिया विकल्प (*for* के साथ प्रयुक्त) – **apologetic** *a.* क्षमा मांगने की मुद्रा में – **apologize** *vi.* क्षमा मांगना; खेद प्रकट करना

apostle (अˈपॉसल) *n.* सुधार आन्दोलन का नेता

apostrophe (अˈपॉस्ट्रफ़ि) *n.* (') चिह्न जो वर्णलोप का परिचायक है; किसी म त या अनुपस्थित व्यक्ति से सम्बोधन

appal (अˈपॉल) *vt.* निराश करना, डराना, स्तब्ध कर देना – **appalling** *a. inf.* भयानक, डरावना, बहुत खराब

apparatus (ऐपˈरेटस) *n.* उपकरण, औजार आदि जो किसी परीक्षण अथवा प्रक्रिया में काम आएं

apparel (अˈपैरल) *n.* पहनने के कपड़े

apparent (अˈपैरंट) *a.* द ष्ट, प्रकट, ऊपरी; स्वीक त, जैसे **heir apparent** – **apparently** *adv.* प्रकट या द श्य रूप से

apparition (ऐपˈरिशन) *n.* किसी आक ति का प्रकट होना या दिखाई देना, विशे. किसी भूत प्रेत का

appeal (अˈपील) *vi.* (*to* के साथ) से अनुरोध करना, पसंद आना, लगना, के नाम पर सहायता या समर्थन मांगना; उच्च न्यायालय में अपील करना, याचना करना – *n.* अनुरोध, निवेदन, अपील

appear (अˈपिअर) *vi.* दिखाई देना या पड़ना, प्रकट होना; पेश होना, जनता के संमुख आना; लगना, प्रतीत होना – **appearance** (अˈपिअरन्स) *n.* दर्शन, प्रकटन; रूप-रंग, दिखावा

appease (अˈपीज़) *vt.* सन्तुष्ट करना; गुस्सा ठण्डा करना – **appeasement** *n.* तुष्टीकरण

append (अˈपेंन्ड) *vt.* साथ लगाना, जोड़ना, नत्थी करना

appendicitis (अपेंन्डिˈसाइटिस) *n.* बड़ी आंत के साथ लगती थैली (अपैन्डिक्स) की सूजन

appendix (अˈपेंन्डिक्स) *n.* पुस्तक के साथ जोड़ा अंश, परिशिष्ट; *Anatomy* बड़ी आंत के साथ लगती थैली, उण्डूक, अपैन्डिक्स [*pl.* **appendices** (अˈपेंण्डिसीज़), **appendixes**]

appertain (ऐपर्ˈटेन) *vi.* का होना, से सम्बन्धित या संगत होना; उचित होना

appetite (ˈऐपिटाइट) *n.* इच्छा, प्रव ति; भूख – **appetizer** (ˈऐपिटाइज़र) *n.* भोजन से पहले खाने या पीने का पदार्थ जो भूख बढ़ाता है, क्षुधावर्धक – **appetizing** *a.* क्षुधावर्धक; आकर्षक

applaud (अ'प्लॉड) *vt.* ताली बजाकर प्रशंसा व्यक्त करना, वाह-वाह करना – **applause** (अ'प्लॉज़) *n.* तालियां, अनुमोदन
apple ('ऐपल) *n.* सेब का पेड़
appliance (अ'प्लाइअंस) *n.* उपकरण, विशे. बिजली से चलने वाला
applique (ऐ'प्लीके) *n.* बेलबूटे आदि जो किसी वस्तु की सतह पर चिपकाए जाएं, चिपकव नक्काशी
apply (अ'प्लाइ) *vt.* लगाना, प्रयोग में लाना; (किसी काम में) लग जाना – *vi.* (पर) लागू होना, प्रार्थनापत्र देना, आवेदन करना (**applied** *pt./pp.*, **applying** *pr. p.*) – **applicability** *n.* उपयुक्तता – **applicable** *a.* संगत, जो लागू हो सके – **applicant** *n.* प्रार्थी – **application** (ऐप्लि'केशन) *n.* किसी विशेष प्रयोजन के लिए प्रयोग, संगति, प्रासंगिकता, (नौकरी के लिए) आवेदन-पत्र; एकाग्रता, परिश्रम; *Computers* कम्प्युटर सॉफ्टवेयर का भाग जो कार्य विशेष में काम आता है – **applied** *a.* व्यावहारिक, प्रयोगिक
appoint (अ'पॉइन्ट) *vt.* (किसी पद या नौकरी पर) नियुक्त करना, नियत या निर्धारित करना – **appointment** *n.* किसी से मिलने का समय, पूर्व नियोजित भेंट; नियुक्ति
apportion (अ'पॉर्शन) *vt.* बांटना
apposite ('ऐपज़िट) *a.* उपयुक्त, उचित
appraise (अ'प्रेज़) *vt.* कूतना, मूल्य निर्धारण करना
appreciate (अ'प्रीशिएट) *vt.* सही मूल्यांकन करना; आभार मानना; समझ लेना; रसास्वादन करना, आनंद लेना – *vi.* का मूल्य बढ़ना – **appreciable** *a.* अच्छा खासा, पर्याप्त – **appreciation** *n.* प्रशंसा; मूल्यव द्धि
apprehend (ऐप्रि'हेंण्ड) *vt.* गिरफ्तार करना; समझना; डरना – **apprehension** (ऐप्रि'हेन्शन) *n.* डर, आशंका – **apprehensive** *a.* आशंकित
apprentice (अ'प्रेन्टिस) *n.* प्रशिक्षार्थी, नौसिखिया – *vt.* किसी को प्रशिक्षार्थी बनाना – **apprenticeship** *n.*
apprise (अ'प्राइज़) *vt.* जानकारी देना
approach (अ'प्रोच) *v.* पास या निकट आना; शुरू करना; किसी से प्रार्थना करना; सद श होना – *n.* पास आने की क्रिया; पहुंचाने या करने का साधन; साद श्य – **approachable** *a.* सुगम्य; जहां आसानी से पहुंचा जा सके; मिलनसार
approbation (ऐप्र'बेशन) *n.* अनुमोदन, मंज़ूरी
appropriate *vt.* (अ'प्रोप्रिएट) हथिया लेना, किसी विशेष काम के लिए रखना – *a.* (अ'प्रोप्रिइट) उपयुक्त, उचित – **appropriately** *adv.*
approve (अ'प्रूव़) *vt.* (को) अच्छा समझना; पसंद करना; (खर्च करने का अधिकार देना; मान लेना या स्वीक ति देना – **approval** *n.* स्वीक ति; अच्छा समझने या पसंद करने की क्रिया – **approver** *n.* इकबाली गवाह, सरकारी गवाह
approx. approximate(ly) का संक्षेप
approximate *a.* (अ'प्रॉक्सिमिट) बहुत निकट; लगभग ठीक, मोटा (अनुमान) – *vt.* (अ'प्रॉक्सिमेट) समीप लाना – *vi.* समीप होना, सद श होना – **approximately** *adv.* लगभग, करीब-करीब – **approximation** (अप्रॉक्सि'मेशन) *n.* लगभग या करीब होना, मोटा अनुमान; साद श्य
apricot ('एप्रिकॉट) *n.* खूबानी, ज़रदालू – *a.* खूबानी के रंग का
April ('एप्रल) *n.* अप्रैल
apron ('एप्रन) *n.* कपड़ों को छ टों आदि से बचाने के लिए पहना कपड़ा, पेटबन्द; परदे के आगे का रंगमंच; हवाई अड्डे पर वह सड़क जहां विमान खड़े रहते हैं, जहां माल लादा जाता है आदि
apropos (ऐप्र'पो) *adv.* – **apropos of** के सम्बन्ध में

apt (ऐप्ट) *a.* उपयुक्त; संगत; तुरंत (जवाब) – **aptitude** (ऐप्टिट्यूड) *n.* प्रव त्ति, रुझान; योग्यता – **aptly** *adv.* – **aptness** *n.*

aqualung (ऐक्वलंग) *n.* पानी के नीचे (तैरते समय) सांस लेने का उपकरण

aquamarine (एक्वम'रीन) *n.* एक रत्न, बेरूज – *a.* हरा-नीला, समुद्र जैसे रंग का

aquarium (अ'क्वेंअरिअम) *n.* जलजीव शाला, मछली घर (*pl.* **aquariums, aquaria**)

Aquarius (अ'क्वेंअरिअस) *n.* राशिचक्र की ग्यारहव राशि कुम्भ, जिसका काल 21 जनवरी से 19 फरवरी तक होता है

aquatic (अ'क्वैटिक) *a.* पानी में रहने या उगने वाला, जलचर; पानी में किया जाने वाला खेल – **aquatics** *pl. n.* पानी पर खेले जाने वाले खेल, जैसे तैराकी, नौका-चालन आदि

aqueduct (ऐक्विडक्ट) *n.* पानी ले जाने की नाली विशे. वह जो पुल जैसी हो, क त्रिम जल प्रणाली; जलवाली सेतु

aqueous ('एक्विअस) *a.* पानी का या उस जैसा, जिसमें पानी हो

arable (ऐरबल) *a.* क षियोग्य, खेती लायक (ज़मीन)

arbiter ('आर्बिटर) *n.* विवाचक, मध्यस्थ निर्णायक, पंच – **arbitrarily** *adv.* – **arbitrary** ('आर्बिट्ररि) *a.* जो किसी नियम के अनुसार न हो; मनमाना; निरंकुश; स्वेच्छाचारिता पर आधारित – **arbitrate** *v.* झगड़े का फैसला करना, मध्यस्थ का काम करना – **arbitration** *n.* मध्यस्थता विशे. औद्योगिक व कानूनी झगड़ों में, विवाचन – **arbitrator** *n.* मध्यस्थ

arbour ('ऑर्बर) *n.* व क्षों से घिरा खुला स्थान, कुंज, लतामण्डप

arc (आर्क) *n.* गोले का एक भाग, चाप; दो संवाहकों के बीच बिजली का प्रकाश, आर्क

arcade (आर्'केड) *n.* खम्बों पर बनी महराबों की पांति; आच्छादित मार्ग, विशे. जिस के दोनों ओर दुकानें हों; छत्ता, तोरणपथ

arch[1]**-** (*comb. form*) मुख्य, जैसे **archenemy** *n.*

arch[2] (आर्च) *n.* महराब, चाप, डाट, मेहराब जैसी अन्य वस्तु, मेहराबदार आक ति; ऐड़ी और पंजे के बीच पैर का ऊपर उठा भाग – *v.* मेहराब बनाना – **arched** *a.* मेहराबी, चापदार – **archway** *n.* मेहराबदार रास्ता, तोरणद्वार

arch[3] *a.* मुख्य, प्रधान; नटखट; नखरेबाज़ – **archly** *adv.* नखरे से – **archness** *n.* नख़रा; ढिठाई; नटखटपन

archaeology (आर्कि'ऑलजि) *n.* पुरातत्व विज्ञान – **archaeological** (आर्किअ'लॉजिकल) *a.* **archaeologist** *n.* पुरातत्ववेत्ता

archaic (आर्'केइक) *a.* पुराना, पुरातन, आदिकालिक

archbishop ('आर्च्'बिशप) *n.* मुख्य बिशप

archery ('आर्चरि) *n.* धनुष-बाण की विद्या – **archer** *n.* धनुर्धर

archetype ('आर्किटाइप) *n.* आदिरूप; आदर्श, नमूना – **archetypal** ('आर्किटाइपल) *a.* आदिरूपी

archipelago (आर्कि'पेलगो) *n.* द्वीप पुंज

architect ('आर्किटेक्ट) *n.* जिसे भवनों के डिज़ाइन और निर्माण का कौशल प्राप्त हो, वास्तुविद – **architectural** *a.* वास्तुशिल्पीय – **architecture** ('आर्किटेक्चर) *n.* वास्तुकला, भवन-निर्माण कला

archives ('आर्काइव्ज़) *pl. n.* स्थान जहां अभिलेख रखे जाते हों, अभिलेखागार, पुरालेखागार; *Computers* अधिक समय तक उपयोग करने के इरादे से कम्प्यूटर या डिस्क में सहेज कर रखी गई फाइलों (जानकारी) की प्रतिलिपियां

Arctic ('आर्कटिक) *a.* उत्तरी ध्रुव के क्षेत्रों से

सम्बन्धित – *n.* उत्तरी ध्रुवक्षेत्र – **arctic** *a.* बहुत ठंडा

ardent (´आर्डन्ट) *a.* उत्साही – **ardour** *n.* उत्साह, जोश, गरमी

arduous (´आर्ड्यूअस) *a.* कठिन; परिश्रमी

are[1] (आर) BE का *present indefinte plural*, हैं, हो

are[2] *n.* एक माप, 100 वर्ग मीटर का क्षेत्र

area (´ऐंअरिअ) *n.* क्षेत्रफल; इलाका; विस्तार कार्य का क्षेत्र; छोटा सा निचला अहाता

areca (´ऐरिक्अ, अ´रीक्अ) *n.* सुपारी का पेड़

arena (अ´रीन्अ) *n.* अखाड़ा; कार्यक्षेत्र; रणभूमि, रंगभूमि

aren't (आर्न्ट) *are not* का संक्षेप

argue (´आर्ग्यू) *vi.* झगड़ा या विवाद करना; बहस करना; दलील पेश करना; तर्क करना – *vt.* वाद विवाद करना – **arguable** *a.* – **argument** *n.* झगड़ा; दलील, वाद-विवाद – **argumentative** *a.* विवाद प्रिय, झगड़ालू

arid (´ऐरिड) *a.* धूप से तपता हुआ; सूखा; नीरस – **aridity** *n.*

Aries (´ऐंअरीज़) *n.* राशिचक्र की पहली राशि, मेष, जिसकी समय 21 मार्च से 20 अप्रैल तक होता है

arise (अ´राइज़) *vi.* घटना; उठना; उत्पन्न होना; खड़े होना; ऊपर उठना (**arose, arisen, arising**) – **arise from** से उत्पन्न होना, का परिणाम होना

aristocracy (ऐरि´स्टॉक्रसि) *n.* कुलीन वर्ग द्वारा शासन; ऊंचे वर्ग के लोग, अभिजात वर्ग – **aristocrat** *n.* रईस, कुलीन – **aristocratic** (ऐरिस्ट´क्रैटिक) *a.* रईस; कुलीन; शानदार – **aristocratically** *adv.*

arithmetic (अ´रिथ्मटिक) *n.* अंक गणित

ark (आर्क) *n.* बाइबल के अनुसार नूह की नाव – **Ark** *n.* पेटी (बक्सा) जिसमें यहूदियों का नियम संग्रह था

arm[1] (आर्म) *n.* बांह, भुजा; शाखा, आगे को निकला भाग जैसे समुद्र का संकरा भाग; कुर्सी का हत्था; आस्तीन – **armchair** *n.*हत्थों वाली कुर्सी – **armful** *n.* बांहों में भरा/समाया हुआ सामान – **armhole** *n.* कमीज़ का मोढा (जहां से बांह आस्तीन में डाली जाये) – **armlet** *n.* बाजूबंद; (झील का) बाहर निकला भाग – **armpit** *n.* काँख, बगल

arm[2] (आर्म) *vt.* हथियारों से लैस करना – *vi.* हथियार उठाना – *n.* हथियार, अस्त्र-शस्त्र; सेना का भाग; (~ **s**) *pl.* हथियार, युद्ध; सेना के कारनामे; कुलचिन्ह – **armament** *n.* युद्ध-सामग्री (टैंक, तोप आदि), हथियार – **armed robbery** डाका जिसमें हथियारों का प्रयोग हो

armada (आर्´माड्अ) *n.* बहुत से समुद्री जहाजों या विमानों का समूह, बेड़ा

armadillo (आर्म´डिलो) *n.* अमरीकन महाद्वीप का चूहे की जाति का जीव जिसके शरीर पर कवच जैसी हड्डियां होती हैं

armature (´आर्मचर) *n.* बिजली की मशीन (मोटर) का घूमने वाला भाग, आर्मेचर

armistice (´आर्मिस्टिस) *n.* युद्ध विराम

armour (´आर्मर) *n.* कवच; टैंकों, जंगी जहाज़ों के बाहर का कवच, चद्दर; कवचित गड़ियों जैसे टैंकों का सामूहिक नाम – **armorial** (आर्´मॉरिअल) *a.* कुलचिन्ह संबंधी – **armourer** *n.* हथियार बनाने व उनकी मरम्मत करने वाला, शस्त्रसाज – **armoury** *n.*शस्त्रागार, हथियार घर – **armoured vehicle, car** बख्तरबंद गाड़ी

army (´आर्मि) *n.* सेना, लश्कर; बहुत अधिक संख्या; भीड़

aroma (अ´रोम्अ) *n.* सुगन्ध, सुवास; विशिष्ट आकर्षण – **aromatic** (ऐर´मैटिक) *a.* सुगंधित

arose (अ´रोज़) ARISE का *pt.*

around (अ'राउंड) *prep.* के चारों ओर, समीप या पास; लगभग (समय के बारे में) – *adv.* चारों ओर; वृत्त में; इधर-उधर किसी विशेष स्थान पर नहीं; *inf.* किसी स्थान में उपस्थित
arouse (अ'राउज़) *vt.* जगाना; सचेत करना; भड़काना, उत्तेजित करना
arraign (अ'रेन) *vt.* आरोप लगाना, अभियोग लगाना
arrange (अ'रेंज) *v.* क्रम या तरतीब में करना, इंतज़ाम करना; सजाना; समझौता करना; के अनुसार करना; आयोजित करना – **arrangement** *n.* प्रबंध; तरतीब, क्रम
array (अ'रे) *n.* व्यूह रचना, विशे. सेना की; सजधज, ठाट-बाट (विशभूषा की); प्रभावशाली या शानदार प्रदर्शन – *vt.* व्यूह रचना या व्यवस्था करना; किसी क्रम या तरतीब में रखना; कपड़े पहनाना, सजाना
arrears (अ'रिअर्ज़) *pl. n.* बकाया (रकम); बचा हुआ (काम)
arrest (अ'रेस्ट) *vt.* गिरफ्तार करना, बन्दी बनाना; रोकना; ध्यान आकृष्ट करना – *n.* गिरफ्तारी – **arresting** *a.* आकर्षक
arrive (अ'राइव़) *vi.* पहुंचना; आना; (*at* के साथ) पहुंचना; पाना; सफल होना या नाम पाना; पैदा होना – **arrival** *n.*
arrogance ('ऐरगन्स) *n.* घमण्ड; अक्खड़पन – **arrogant** *a.* घमण्डी, अक्खड़
arrow ('ऐरो) *n.* बाण, शर, तीर – **arrowhead** *n.* बाण का फल, कोई तिकोनी आकृति
arrowroot ('ऐरोरूट) *n.* वेस्ट इण्डीज़ के एक पौधे की मांड, अरारोट
arse (आर्स) *n. sl.* चूतड़
arsenal ('आर्सनल) *n.* युद्ध की सामग्री का भण्डार, शस्त्रागार
arsenic ('आर्सनिक) *n.* एक सफेद सलेटी रंग की धातु और उस से बना विष, संखिया
arson ('आर्सन) *n.* जानबूझकर सम्पत्ति को आग लगाने का अपराध, आगजनी
art (आर्ट) *n.* कौशल; निपुणता; कला; कलाकृति; व्यवसाय; शिल्प; चालाकी, धूर्तता – (~ **s**) *pl.* (विज्ञान की तुलना में) कुछ विधाएं, भाषाएं और इतिहास आदि – **artful** *a.* चालाक – **artist** *n.* कलाकार – **artiste** (आर्'टीस्ट) *n.* गायक या नर्तक – **artistic** (आर्'टिस्टिक) *a.* कलात्मक – **artistically** *adv.* – **artistry** – *n.* – **artless** *a.* स्वाभाविक; भोला-भाला, निष्कपट
artefact ('आर्टिफैक्ट) *n.* मनुष्य द्वारा बनाई गयी वस्तु, शिल्पकृति
artery ('आर्टिरि) *n.* हृदय से शरीर में रक्त लेने वाली धमनी; संचार का मुख्य साधन; मुख्य मार्ग – **arterial road** प्रमुख मार्ग
arthritis (आर्'थ्राइटिस) *n.* जोड़ों की सूजन, गठिया
article ('आर्टिकल) *n.* मद, वस्तु; निबन्ध, लेख; अनुच्छेद; भाग; *Grammar* the, a, an; करार का एक खण्ड या अनुच्छेद; नियम, शर्त – *vt.* प्रशिक्षार्थी से करार करना, अनुबन्ध करना **articled** *a.* प्रशिक्षार्थी
articulate *a.* (आर्'टिक्युलिट) जो अपनी बात साफ़-साफ़ ठीक तरह कह सके; जुड़ा हुआ; सुस्पष्ट, साफ़-साफ़ – *vt.* (आर्'टिक्युलेट) जोड़ना; साफ़ बोलना, – *vi* बोलना – **articulated** *a.* जुड़ा हुआ – **articulately** *adv.* स्पष्ट रूप से – **articulateness** *n.* स्पष्ट बोलने व कहने की क्षमता – **articulation** *n.* उच्चारण; संधियोजन
artifice ('आर्टिफ़िस) *n.* तिकड़म, चाल – **artificial** (आर्टि'फ़िशल) *a.* कृत्रिम, नकली; झूठा, बनावटी – **artificiality** (आर्टिफ़िश्'ऐलिटि) *n.* बनावटीपन – **artficially** *adv.* –**artificial intelligence** कम्प्यूटर की मनुष्य की तरह सोचने की क्षमता, यांत्रिक बुद्धि – **artificial**

respiration कृत्रिमश्वसन, जिस व्यक्ति की सांस बंद हो गई हो उसे सांस दिलाने की क्रिया
artillery (आर्'टिलरि) *n.* बड़ी तोपे; उन्हें चलाने वाला सैनिक दल; तोपखाना
artisan (आर्टि'ज़ैन) *n.* कारीगर
artiste देखिए ART
as (ऐज़) *adv/conj.* तुलना, सादृश्य; बराबरी, सहमति, तर्क के अर्थ में; जैसा, के समान; क्योंकि; जिस समय; ज्योंही; जैसे ही; जैसा कि
asap as soon as possible का संक्षेप
asbestos (ऐस्'बेस्टॉस) *n.* एस्बेस्टास धातु
ascend (अ'सेंण्ड) *vi.* चढ़ना; ऊपर उठना – *vt.* (पर) चढ़ना, ऊपर जाना – **ascendancy** *n.* प्रभुत्व, आधिपत्य – **ascendant** *a.* (व्यक्ति, पार्टी आदि) उदीयमान, चढ़ता हुआ – **ascension** (अ'सेंन्शन) *n.* आरोहण – **ascent** *n.* चढ़ाई, आरोहण; *fig.* उत्थान, उन्नति
ascertain (ऐसर्'टेन) *v.* जान लेना; निश्चित करना
ascetic (अ'सेंटिक) *n.* तपस्वी, संन्यासी – *a.*
ascorbic acid (अ'स्कॉर्बिक-) विटामिन सी
ascribe (अ'स्क्राइब) *vt.* (पर) के लिए उत्तरदायी ठहराना; श्रेय देना
aseptic (अ'सेंप्टिक) *a.* कीटाणु रहित, अपूतिक – **asepsis** *n.* कीटाणु रहित होना, अपूति
asexual (ए'सेंक्स्युल) *a.* अलिंगी अयौन, जिसका स्पष्ट लिंग न हो; (जनन) जिसमें नर व मादा युग्मक की आवश्यकता न हो
ash[1] (ऐश) *n.* राख, भस्म – (~ **es**) *pl.* दाह-संस्कार के अवशेष – **ashen** *a.* राख के समान, पीला
ash[2] *n.* इमारती लकड़ी वाला – **ashen** *a.*
ashamed (अ'शेम्ड) *a.* शर्मिंदा, लज्जित
ashore (अ'शॉर) *adv.* तटपर, किनारे पर (वि. समुद्र के)
Asian ('एशन, एझ़न) *a.* एशियाई – *n.* – **Asiatic** (एशि'ऐटिक) a. ऐशियाई
aside (अ'साइड) *adv.* एक ओर; एकांत में – *n.* स्वगत भाषण, दबी आवाज में बोले गए शब्द (वि. नाटक में) जो पास खड़े किसी व्यक्ति ने नह सुनने होते
asinine ('ऐसिनाइन) *a.* मूर्ख
ask (आस्क) *vt.* निवेदन करना; मांगना, पूछना; आमंत्रित करना; बुलाना – *vi.* पूछताछ करना अथवा निवेदन करना
askance (अ'स्कैन्स) *adv.* तिरछी नजर से, टेढ़ा – **look askance** संदेह से देखना
askew (अ'स्क्यू) *adv.* एक ओर, टेढ़ा
asleep (अ'स्लीप) *a./adv.* सोया हुआ; शांत
asp (ऐस्प) *n.* ज़हरीला सांप
asparagus (अ'स्पैरगस) *n.* पौधा जिस के डंठल सलाद की तरह खाये जाते हैं, शतावरी
aspect ('ऐस्पेंक्ट) *n.* रूप; आकार; पक्ष
aspersion (अ'स्पर्शन) *n.* (प्राय: *pl.*) लांछन; निंदात्मक आलोचना
asphalt ('ऐस्फ़ैल्ट) *n.* डामर, तारकोल
asphyxiate (ऐस्'फ़िक्सिएट) *v.* दम घोटना, बेहोश कर देना
aspire (अ'स्पाइअर) *vi.* आकांक्षा करना – **aspirant** ('ऐस्पिरंट) *n.* आकांक्षी, उम्मीदवार – **aspiration** (ऐस्पि'रेशन) *n.* अभिलाषा, आकांक्षा
aspirin ('ऐस्प्रिन) *n.* दर्द तथा ज्वर निवारक दवा (गोली), ऐस्प्रिन
ass (ऐस) *n.* गधा; *fig.* मूर्ख व्यक्ति
assail (अ'सेल) *vt.* आक्रमण करना; कटु आलोचना करना – **assailant** *n.* आक्रमणकारी
assassin (अ'सैसिन) *n.* हत्यारा (वि. विशिष्ट व्यक्ति की धोखे से हत्या करने वाला) – **assassinate** (अ'सैसिनेट) *vt.* – **assassination** (असैसि'नेशन) *n.* हत्या, कत्ल
assault (अ'सॉल्ट) *n.* आक्रमण – *vt.* हमला करना; बलात्कार का प्रयास करना

assay (अ'से) *vt.* परीक्षण करना, जांच करना (विशे मिश्रधातु या खनिज पदार्थ में धातुओं के अनुपात का)

assemble (अ'सेंम्बल) *vt.* एकत्र करना; (मशीन के कल पुर्ज़े) जोड़ना – *vi.* एकत्र होना – **assembly** *n.* सभा; जमाव; पुर्ज़े जोड़ने की व्यवस्था – **assembly line** मशीनों, कारीगरों की क्रमबद्ध व्यवस्था जिससे पुर्ज़े जोड़ कर कोई चीज़ बनाई जाय

assent (अ'सेंन्ट) *vi.* स्वीक ति देना – *n.* स्वीक ति

assert (अ'सर्ट) *vt.* निश्चयपूर्वक कहना, दावा करना – **assertion** (अ'सर्शन) *n.* **assertive** *a.*

assess (अ'सेंस) *vt.* मूल्य निर्धारित करना, मूल्यांकन करना – **assessable** *a* – **assessment** *n.* अंकित मूल्य; अनुमान – **assessor** *n.* मूल्यांकन अधिकारी

asset (ऐसेंट) *n.* मूल्यवान अथवा उपयोगी वस्तु/व्यक्ति – (~ **s**) *pl.* वह संपत्ति जो ऋण चुकाने के काम आ सके

assiduous (अ'सिड्युअस) *a.* अध्यावसायी; मेहनती

assign (अ'साइन) *vt.* नियुक्त करना; बांटना; सौंपना – **assignation** (ऐसिग्'नेशन) *n.* गुप्त मिलन – **assignment** *n.* नियुक्ति; नियत कार्य

assimilate (अ'सिमिलेट) *vt.* पढ़कर समझ लेना; सद श/के समान बनाना; पचाना; समो लेना – **assimilable** *a.* – **assimilation** *n.*

assist (अ'सिस्ट) *vt.* सहायता करना – **assistance** (अ'सिस्टन्स) *n.* – **assistant** *n.* सहायक

associate *vt.* (अ'सोशिएट) जोड़ना; मिलाना – *vi.* से मेल- जोल रखना, एक हो जाना – *n.* (अ'सोशिइट) संगी, साझीदार, सहयोगी, संस्था का अवर सदस्य – **association** (असोसि'एशन) *n.* संस्था, संघ; सम्बंध

assorted (अ'सॉर्टिड) *a.* मिले-जुले, फुटकर – **assortment** *n.*छंटाव, वर्गीकरण

assuage (अ'स्वेज) *vt.* (भावनाओं आदि की तीव्रता) कम करना

assume (अ'स्यूम) *vt.* मान लेना; (का) ढोंग करना; अपने ऊपर (उत्तरदायित्व, भार आदि) लेना – **assumption** (अ'सम्पशन) *n.* पूर्वधारणा; मान्यता; (कार्यभार) ग्रहण

assure (अ'शुअर) *vt.* विश्वास दिलाना, वायदा करना; निश्चित करना; बीमा करना (विशे. जीवन का) – **assurance** *n.* आश्वासन, विश्वास – **assured** *a.* निश्चित

asterisk (ऐस्टरिस्क) *n.* छपाई में प्रयुक्त तारा चिन्ह (*)

asteroid (ऐस्टरॉइड) *n.* छोटाग्रह – *a.* तारे जैसा, तारारूप

asthma (ऐस्म्अ) *n.* दमा – **asthmatic** (ऐस्'मैटिक) *a./n.* दमा का (रोगी)

astigmatism (अ'स्टिग्मटिज़म) *n.* द ष्टि वैषम्य, (आंख के) लेन्स का ठीक तरह से फोकस न कर पाने का दोष, अबिंदुकता – **astigmatic** *a.*

astir (अ'स्टर) *adv.* गतिमान; उत्तेजित

astonish (अ'स्टॉनिश) *vt.* चकित करना, अचंभे में डालना – **astonishing** *a.* आश्चर्यजनक – **astonishment** *n.*

astound (अ'स्टाउंड) *vt.* भौचक्का कर देना – **astounding** *a.* विस्मयकारी

astral (ऐस्ट्रल) *a.* नक्षत्र सम्बंधी

astray (अ'स्ट्रे) *adv.* पथभ्रष्ट, भटका हुआ

astride (अ'स्ट्राइड) *adv.* टांगें फैलाकर

astringent (अ'स्ट्रिन्जंट) *a.* तेज़, तीखा

astrology (अ'स्ट्रॉलजि) *n.* फलित ज्योतिष – **astrologer** (अस्'ट्रॉलजर) *n.* ज्योतिषी – **astrological** (ऐस्ट्र'लॉजिकल) *a.*

astronaut (ऐस्ट्रनॉट) *n.* अंतरिक्ष- यात्री

astronomy (अ'स्ट्रॉनमि) *n.* सितारों, ग्रह-नक्षत्रों आदि का वैज्ञानिक अध्ययन, खगोल-शास्त्र

– **astronomer** *n.* ज्योतिषविद् – **astronomical** (एस्ट्र 'नॉमिकल) *a.* बहुत बड़ा, खगोलीय

Astro turf घास जैसा लगने वाला कत्रिम तल (मैदान) जिस पर खेल खेल जाते हैं

astute (अ'स्ट्यूट) *a.* सूझ-बूझ वाला

asunder (अ'संडर) *adv.* अलग-अलग; टुकड़े-टुकड़े

asylum (अ'साइलम) *n.* शरण; शरण स्थल; सुरक्षित स्थान; (पुराना नाम) पागल खाना

asymmetry (ए'सिमिट्रि) *n.* विषमता – **asymmetrical** (ऐसि'मैट्रिकल) *a.* विषम

at (ऐट) *prep./adv.* में; पर; स्थान, समय, दर स्थिति, परिस्थिति, कीमत तथा कारण के साथ प्रयुक्त; की ओर

atheism ('एथिइज़म) *n.* नास्तिकता – **atheist** *n.* नास्तिक

athlete ('ऐथ्लीट) *n.* निपुण खिलाड़ी – **athletic** (ऐथ्'लेंटिक) *a.* (बलिष्ठ, कसरती) शरीर – **athletics** *pl. n.* दौड़ना, कूदना, फेंकना आदि जैसे खेल

athwart (अ'थ्वॉर्ट) *prep.* आड़ा – *adv.* तिरछा

atlas ('ऐट्लस) *n.* ऐटलस, मान-चित्रावली

ATM AUTOMATIC TELLER MACHINE का संक्षेप, बैंक के बाहर लगी मशीन जिससे ग्राहक खुद ही पैसे निकाल सकते हैं

atmosphere ('ऐट्मस्फ़िअर) *n.* वायुमण्डल; वातावरण; (किसी स्थान पर चल रही विचारों आदि की) हवा, लहर – **atmospheric** (ऐट्मस्'फ़ेरिक) *a.* वायुमण्डलीय

atom ('ऐटम) *n.* परमाणु; कण – **atomic** (अ'टॉमिक) *a.* परमाण्विक; परमाणु सम्बंधी – **atomizer** *n.* तरल पदार्थ को महीन फुहार में परिवर्तित करने का उपकरण – **atom(ic) bomb** परमाणु बम – **atomic energy** परमाणु ऊर्जा – **atomic reactor** दे. REACTOR

atone (अ'टोन) *vi.* क्षतिपूर्ति करना, प्रायश्चित करना – **atonement** *n.* प्रायश्चित

atop (अ'टॉप) *adv.* के शिखर पर; के ऊपर

atrocious (अ'ट्रोशस) *a.* अत्यधिक निर्दयी, क्रूर, दुष्ट; *inf.* बुरा, भद्दा – **atrociously** *adv.* – **atrocity** (अ'ट्रॉसिटि) *n.* अत्याचार

atrophy ('ऐट्रफि) *n.* क्षय; क्षीणता –*vi.* क्षीण होते जाना (**atrophied** *pt./pp.* **atrophying** *pr.p.*)

attach (अ'टैच) *v.* (मुख्य *tr.*) संलग्न करना; जोड़ना; लगाना; सम्बंधित होना, जुड़े होना; प्रदान करना; (विभाग आदि में) नियुक्त करना; कुर्क करना – **attachment** *n.*लगाव, प्रेम – **attached to** से बहुत ज्यादा लगाव रखे हुए

attaché (अ'टैशे) *n.* राजनयिक कार्यालय में नियुक्त विशेषज्ञ (*pl.* **attachés**) – **attaché case** अटैची केस

attack (अ'टैक) *vt.* आक्रमण करना; आलोचना करना; उत्साह से (कार्य) शुरू करना; (पीड़ा रोग आदि का किसी को) घेर लेना –*n.* आक्रमण; बीमारी का दौरा

attain (अ'टेन) *vt.* पहुंचना; पाने में सफल होना – **attainable** *a.* – **attainment** *n.* उप्लब्धि (विशे. निजी उप्लब्धि)

attar ('ऐटर) *n.* इत्र विशे. गुलाब का

attempt (अ'टेंम्ट) *vt.* प्रयत्न करना – *n.* प्रयत्न

attend (अ'टेंण्ड) *vt.* उपस्थित होना; साथ जाना – *vi* (**to** के साथ) का ध्यान रखना; पर ध्यान देना – **attendance** *n.* सेवा; उपस्थिति; उपस्थित लोगों की संख्या – **attendant** *n./a.* परिचारक; नौकर – **attention** *n.* ध्यान; देखभाल; सैनिकों की ड्रिल (कवायद) में सावधान की स्थिति – **attentive** *a.* सावधान, सतर्क

attenuated *a.* दुबला व लंबा

attest (अ'टेंस्ट) *vt.* सत्यापन करना; तस्दीक़ करना – **attestation** *n.*

attic (ऐटिक) *n.* अटारी

attire (अ´टाइअर) *vt.* कपड़े पहनाना – *n.* पोशाक, कपड़े

attitude (ऐटिट्यूड) *n.* मनोव ति, रुख; द ष्टिकोण; विचार; भाव; मुद्रा; व्यवहार

attorney (अ´टर्नि) *n.* अटार्नी, वह व्यक्ति (वि. वकील) जिसे दूसरे की ओर से कार्य करने का कानूनी अधिकार हो, मुख्तार (*pl.* **attorneys**) – **Attorney General** महान्यायवादी; न्यायमंत्री

attract (अ´ट्रैक्ट) *vt.* (ध्यान आदि) आकर्षित करना; की रुचि जाग त करना – *vi.* (चुम्बक आदि का) एक दूसरे को ख चना – **attraction** (अ´ट्रैक्शन) *n.* आर्कषण, खिंचाव – **attractive** *a.* आकर्षक

attribute *vt.* (अ´ट्रिब्यूट) (को) श्रेय देना – *n.*(ऐट्रिब्यूट) – *n.* वस्तु का गुण, विशेषता, लक्षण, खूबी – **attributable** *a.* (*to* के साथ) के कारण – **attribution** *n.*

attrition (अ´ट्रिशन) *n.* धीरे-धीरे शक्ति आदि क्षीण होना; घिसाई; रगड़ – **war of attrition** शत्रु को नष्ट करने के लिए लगातार हमले

attune (अ´ट्यून) *vt.* का सुर मिलाना; का मेल कराना

aubergine (´ओबर्ज़ीन) *n.* बैंगन (का पौधा)

auburn (´ऑबर्न) *a.* सुनहरा; ललाई लिए भूरा – *n.* सुनहरा रंग

auction (´ऑक्शन) *n.* नीलामी – *v.* नीलाम करना, की बोली लगाना – **auctioneer** (ऑक्श´निअर) *n.* नीलामकार

audacious (ऑ´डेशस) *a.* निर्भीक; साहसी; ढीठ – **audacity** *n.*

audible (ऑडिबल) *a.* श्रव्य; (ध्वनि) जो सुनी जा सके

audience (´ऑडिअन्स) *n.* श्रोतागण; (अदालती) सुनवाई; औपचारिक साक्षात्कार; किसी बड़े आदमी के साथ भेंट, मुलाकात

audio (´ऑडिओ) (*comb. form.*) ध्वनि अथवा श्रवण से संबंधित

audiovisual (ऑडिओ´विझ़ुअल) *a.* द श्य-श्रव्य, सुनने-देखने दोनों से ताल्लुक वाला

audit (´ऑडिट) *n.* लेखा-परीक्षण, हिसाब-किताब की जांच – *vt.* जांच करना – **auditor** *n.* लेखा-परीक्षक

audition (ऑ´डिशन) *n.* परीक्षण (रेडियो, टी.वी. आदि के कार्यक्रमों में भाग लेने के इच्छुक प्रत्याशियों के लिए), ध्वनि-परीक्षण – *vt.* ध्वनि-परीक्षा करना – **auditorium** (ऑडि´टॉरिअम) *n.* रंगशाला, सिनेमा आदि में दर्शकों के बैठने का हॉल, **US, C** हॉल (*pl.* **auditoriums, auditoria**) – **auditory** *n.* श्रवणशक्ति सम्बंधी

auger (´ऑगर) *n.* बरमा; बेधनी

augment (ऑग्´मेण्ट) *v.* अधिक करना, बढ़ाना

augur (´ऑगर) – *v.* भविष्यवाणी करना – **augury** *n.* भविष्य संकेत

august (ऑ´गस्ट) *a.* भव्य, आलीशान; सम्मान्य, रौबदार

August (´ऑगस्ट) *n.* अगस्त

aunt (आण्ट) *n.* चाची; ताई; मामी; मौसी; बुआ; **auntie, aunty** *n.* भी

aura (´ऑर्‌अ) *n.* गुण, विशेषता, वातावरण आदि जो व्यक्ति अथवा वस्तु के औरों से भिन्न होने, विशिष्ट होने का आभास कराये

auricle (´ऑरिकल) *n.* कान का बाहरी हिस्सा; हृदय का ऊपरी छेद

aurora (ऑ´रौर्‌अ) *n.* वायुमण्डल को आलोकित करने वाली रंग-बिरंगी ध्रुवीय-ज्योति

auspices (´आस्पिसिज़) *n.* – **under the auspices of** के तत्वाधान में

auspicious (ऑ´स्पिशस) *a.* मंगलमयी, शुभ, अनुकूल – **auspiciously** *adv.*

austere (ऑ´स्टिअर) *a.* कठोर; अतिसंयमी; आडम्बरहीन; गंभीर (मुद्रा) – **austerely** *adv.*

austerity (ऑ´स्टेरिटि) *n.* सादगी; संयम; आडम्बरहीनता

Australian (आ´स्ट्रेलिअन) *a./n.* (आस्ट्रेलिया का निवासी)

authentic (ऑ´थेन्टिक) *a.* असली, प्रामाणिक, विश्वसनीय – **authentically** *adv.* – **authenticate** *vt.* को प्रामाणिक ठहराना, का पुष्टीकरण करना – **authenticity** (आर्थेन्´टिसिटि) *n.* प्रामाणिकता, सच्चाई

author (´ऑथर) *n.* लेखक; जन्मदाता (**-ess** *fem.*) – **authorship** *n.*

authoritarian (अथॉरि´टेंअरिअन) *a.* निरंकुश

authoritative (ऑ´थॉरिटिव़) *a.* अधिकारपूर्ण – **authoritatively** *adv.*

authority (ऑ´थॉरिटि) *n.* कानूनी अधिकार, प्रदत्त अधिकार; प्रभाव; आज्ञा; विशेषज्ञ; प्राधिकरण – **the authorities** अधिकारी-वर्ग

authorize (´ऑथ्राइज़) *vt.* अधिकार देना

auto- (ऑटो-) (*comb. form*) स्वयं-/आत्म- जैसे **autograph**

autobiography (ऑटोबाइ´ऑग्रफ़ि) *n.* आत्मकथा – **autobiographical** *a.* (लेखक के) जीवन से संबंधित

autocrat (´ऑटक्रैट) *n.* निरंकुश शासक, तानाशाह – **autocracy** (ऑ´टॉक्रसि) *n.* – **autocratic** *a.*

autograph (´ऑटग्राफ़) *n.* हस्ताक्षर, स्वाक्षर – *vt.* हस्ताक्षर करना

automat (´ऑटमैट) *n.* विक्रय-यंत्र (मशीन जिसमें सिक्का डालने पर सिग्रेट, काफ़ी आदि बाहर आ जाती हैं)

automatic (ऑट´मैटिक) *a.* स्वचालित, बिना ध्यान से सोचे किया (कार्य) – *a./n.* (हथियार) जिसमें बारबार गोली नहीं भरनी पड़ती – **automatically** *adv.* अपने आप – **automation** *n.* औद्योगिक मशीनीकरण

automobile (´ऑटमबील) *n.* मोटर-कार

autonomy (ऑ´टॉनमि) *n.* स्वशासन, स्वायत्तता – **autonomous** (ऑ ´टॉनमस) *a.* स्वायत्त, आंतरिक मामलों में स्वतंत्र

autopsy (ऑ´टॉप्सि) *n.* शव-परीक्षा; विश्लेषण

autumn (´ऑटम्) *n.* शरत् ऋतु – *a.*– शरत्

auxiliary (ऑग्´ज़िलरि) *a.* – सहायक, पूरक

avail (अ´वे़ल) *v.* उपयोगी होना, हितकर होना, लाभदायक होना – *n.* लाभ – **avail oneself of** का लाभ उठाना – *n.* – **to no avail** बिना किसी परिणाम के, अकारथ

available (अ´वे़लबल) *a.* उपलब्ध, सुलभ – **availability** *adv.*

avalanche (´ऐव़लांच) *n.* हिमस्खलन, पहाड़ों पर हिमखंडों का फिसलकर नीचे आना; वस्तु की भारी मात्रा

avarice (´ऐव़रिस) *n.* धन का लोभ – **avaricious** (ऐव़´रिशस) *a.* लोभी

avenge (अ´वे़ंज) *vt.* बदला लेना या चुकाना – **avenger** *n.*

avenue (´ऐव़न्यू) *n.* चौड़ी सड़क; सड़क जिसके दोनों ओर व क्ष हों

aver (अ´व़र) *vt.* पुष्टि करना; निश्चयपूर्वक कहना (**-rr-**)

average (´ऐव़रिज) *n.* औसत – *a.* – *vt.* औसत निकालना अथवा निश्चित करना – *vi.* औसत होना; औसत पर पहुंचना – **on average** औसत से

averse (अ´व़र्स) *a.* अनिच्छुक; प्रतिकूल **aversion** (अ´व़र्शन) *n.* अनिच्छा; अरुचि; व्यक्ति अथवा वस्तु जो अच्छी न लगे

avert (अ´व़र्ट) *vt.* (मुंह, निगाहें) फेर लेना; (गंभीर स्थिति, दुर्घटना आदि) बचा लेना

aviary (´एव्यरि) *n.* पक्षी रखने का स्थान (बड़ा पिंजरा), दरबा

aviation (एवि´एशन) *n.* विमान चलाने की कला या विद्या, वायुवहन, उड्डयन – **aviator** *n.* विमानचालक

avid (ऐविड) *a.* उत्सुक, उत्कंठित; लालायित – **avidity** (अ'विडिटि) *n.*
avocado (एव'काडो) *n.* गरम प्रदेशों का एक पेड़, उसका फल
avocation (ऐव'केशन) *n.* पेशा
avoid (अ'वॉइड) *vt.* (से) दूर रहना, (से) बचना, (दुर्घटना आदि) न होने देना – **avoidable** *a.* – **avoidance** *n.*
avoirdupois (ऐवर्ड'पॉइज़) *n./a.* पाउंड तथा आउंस पर आधारित भार तोलने की प्रणाली
avowedly (अ'वाउइड्लि) *adv.* प्रकट रूप से
await (अ'वेट) *vt.* (की) प्रतीक्षा करना; नियत होना, जैसे *death awaited him.*
awake (अ'वेक), **awaken** (अ'वेकन) *v.* जगाना; सचेत होना अथवा करना (*pt.* **awoke,** *pp.* **awoken**) – **awakening** *n.* सजगता, जागरूकता
award (अ'वॉर्ड) *n.* इनाम, पुरस्कार; अदालती फैसला – *vt.* पुरस्कार, हर्जाना आदि देना
aware (अ'वेंअर) *a.* जानकार, अवगत – **awareness** *n.* जागति
away (अ'वे) *a./adv.* अनुपस्थित, बाहर; दूर (समय में) दूर; निरंतर – **away game** प्रतिद्वंदी के मैदान, देश आदि में खेला गया खेल
awe (ऑ) *n.* भय और श्रद्धायुक्त आदर – **awe-inspiring**, **awesome** *a.* जिस से भय उत्पन्न हो
awful ('ऑफुल) *a.* बहुत बुरा, अरुचिकर, भद्दा; *inf.* अत्यधिक – **awfully** *adv.* अप्रिय रूप में – *inf.* अत्यधिक
awhile (अ'वाइल) *adv.* कुछ देर के लिए
awkward ('ऑक्वर्ड) *a.* बेढंगा, भद्दा; भोंडा; कष्टकर; परेशान – **awkwardly** *adv.* – **awkwardness** *n.*
awl (ऑल) *n.* आल, लकड़ी, चमड़े आदि में सुराख करने का सुआ
awning ('ऑनिंग) *n.* सायबान; धूप, बारिश आदि से बचाने के लिये तिरपाल से बनी छत
awoke, awoken awake का *pt./pp.*
AWOL absent without leave का संक्षेप
awry (अ'राई) *adv./a.* – **go awry** कोई प्रयत्न, योजना असफल हो जाना
axe (ऐक्स) *n.* कुल्हाड़ी – *vt. inf* नौकरी से निकाला जाना; (योजना आदि को) छोड़ देना
axiom ('ऐक्सिअम) *n.* स्वयंसिद्धि; किसी तर्क अथवा प्रमाण के बिना ही माना जाने वाला कथन; अभिग हीत – **axiomatic** *a.*
axis ('ऐक्सिस) *n.* अक्ष; धुरी (*pl.* **axes** ('ऐक्सीज़)) – **axial** ('ऐक्सिअल) *a.* – **axially** *adv.*
aye (आइ) *adv.* हां – *n.* स्वीकारात्मक उत्तर अथवा समर्थन में वोट
azure ('ऐझ़र) *n.* आसमानी रंग; आसमान – *a.*

B

BA Bachelor of Arts का संक्षेप

babble (ˈबैबल) *v.* बकबक करना, बेतुकी बातें किये जाना या बच्चों की तरह बोले जाना; भेद खोलना – *n.*

babe (बिब) *n.* छोटा बच्चा; भोला-भाला व्यक्ति

babel (ˈबेबल) *n.* कोलाहल, शोर जिसमें कुछ समझ न आए

baboon (बˈबून) *n.* बैबून, अफ्रीका तथा एशिया में पाया जाने वाला बड़ा बंदर

baby (ˈबेबि) *n.* छोटा बच्चा, शिशु – **babyhood** *n.* शिशुकाल – **babyish** *a.* बच्चे जैसा – **baby-sit** *vi.* बच्चे को संभालना – **baby-sitter** *n.* व्यक्ति जो माता-पिता की अनुपस्थिति में कुछ समय के लिए बच्चे को संभाले

bachelor (ˈबैचलर) *n.* कुमार, अविवाहित; स्नातक (बी.ए., बी.एस.सी. आदि) – **bachelorhood, bachelorship** *n.* कुमारपन (पुरुष की) अविवाहित अवस्था

bacillus (बˈसिलस) *n.* अण्डाणु, सूक्ष्म जीवाणु जिनमें से कुछ बीमारियां फैलाते हैं; बैसिलस (*pl.* **bacilli** (बˈसिलाइ)

back (बैक) *n.* पीठ; पिछला हिस्सा; पिछवाड़ा; पीछे का खिलाड़ी – *a.* पीछे स्थित; पहला – *adv.* पीछे को; पहले का; वापिस – *vi.* पीछे हटना – *vt.* समर्थन करना; (घुडदौड़ आदि में) दांव लगाना; (कार को) पीछे ले जाना; पीछे कपड़ा आदि लगाना – **backer** *n.* समर्थक; दांव लगाने वाला – **backing** *n.* समर्थन; पीछे लगाने का कपड़ा आदि; पॉप-गायक के साथ संगत करने वाला वादक – **backwards** *adv.* पीछे को (चलना, मुड़ना); पीछे (समय में); अधिक बुरी हालत में (जाना), बदतर – **backward** *a.* पीछे को (चलने वाला); पिछड़ा हुआ; संकोचशील; शर्मीला – **backwardness** *n.* पिछड़ापन – **backbencher** *n. Brit, Aust, Canada* संसद-सदस्य जो सरकार अथवा विरोधीपक्ष में किसी पद पर न हो – **backbite** *vt.* चुगली करना, पीठ पीछे बुराई करना – **backbone** *n.* रीढ़ की हड्डी; *fig.* सबसे महत्वपूर्ण अंग – **backcloth, backdrop** *n.* रंगमंच पर पीछे का पर्दा – **backdate** *vt.* किसी पिछली तारीख से लागू करना – **back door** गुप्त, चुपचाप (*back door entry into Parliament/ politics*) – **backfire** *vi.* (किसी प्रयत्न, योजना का) विफल होना; उलटी आंतें गले पड़ना – **background** *n.* पृष्ठभूमि; भूमिका; (व्यक्ति का) पिछला इतिहास – **backhanded** *a.* (प्रशंसा) जिसमें आलोचना छिपी हो, कपट पूर्ण – **backlash** *n.* आकस्मिक प्रतिकूल प्रतिक्रिया – **backlog** *n.* पिछला इकट्ठा हुआ कार्य जो निपटाया जाना हो – **backpack** *n.* पीछे लटकाया जाने वाला एक प्रकार का थैला – **back seat** कम महत्व का स्थान – **backstroke** *n.* बैकस्ट्रोक तैराकी, पीठ के बल तैराकी – **backwater** *n.* अप्रवाही जल; पिछड़ा हुआ प्रदेश – **backwoods** *pl. n.* दूरस्थ वन्य प्रदेश

bacon (ˈबेकन) *n.* नमक लगा कर रखा सूअर का मांस

bacteria (बैक्ˈटिअरिअ) *pl. n.* (*sing.* **bacterium**) सूक्ष्म जीवाणु जो कुछ रोग पैदा करते हैं – **bacterial** *a.* जीवाणु संबंधी

bad (बैड) *a.* बुरा, खराब; घटिया; दुष्ट; भ्रष्ट; अत्याधिक (जुकाम); अप्रिय, अरुचिकर; सड़ा-गला – (**worse** *comp.*, **worst** *sup.*) – **badly** *adv.* बुरी तरह

bade (बैड, बेड) BID का *pt*

badge (बैज) *n.* बैज, बिल्ला; पहचान चिन्ह
badger (बैजर) *n.* लोमड़ी के आकार का बिल में रहने वाला जानवर, बिज्जू – *vt.* तंग करना, परेशान करना
badminton (बैड्मिंटन) *n.* बैडमिंटन का खेल
baffle (बैफ़ल) *vt.* रोकना, बाधा डालना; घबरा देना
bag (बैग) *n.* थैला, झोला, बोरा, भार-माप; महिलाओं का हैंडबैग – *vt.* थैले में भरना; शिकार मारना; पाना (**-gg-**) – **bagging** *n.* कपड़ा – **baggy** *a.* ढीला-ढाला
bagasse (ब'गैस) *n.* गन्ने का रस निकालने के बाद बचा कचरा; खोई
bagatelle (बैग'टेंल) *n.* तुच्छ वस्तु; बोर्ड पर नौ गोलियों और एक छोटे डन्डे से खेला जाने वाला खेल
baggage (बैगिज) *n.* सफर का सामान; *offens.* स्त्री; महिला
bagpipes (बैग्पाइप्स) *pl. n.* स्काटलैंड का एक वाद्य – **bagpiper** *n.* ऐसा वाद्य बजाने वाला
bail[1] (बिल) *n.* जमानत; जमानत देने वाला – *vt.* जमानत पर छोड़ना अथवा छुड़ाना – *inf.* (~ **out**) किसी व्यक्ति या फ़र्म को मुसीबत से निकालना
bail[2] *n. Cricket* बेल, विकिटों पर रखे जाने वाले लकड़ी के टुकड़े; अस्तबल में घोड़ों को अलग करने वाला लकड़ी का डण्डा
bail[3] *vt.* नाव में भरे पानी को बाहर निकाल कर फैंकना – **bail out** हवाई जहाज़ से पैराशूट (हवाई छतरी) द्वारा नीचे कूदना; (मुसीबत से) बचाना
bailiff (बेलिफ़) *n.* बेलिफ़; जमींदार या मकान मालिक का कारिन्दा; कुर्की कराने वाला कर्मचारी
bait (बिट) *n.* (मछली पकड़ने के लिये) चारा; प्रलोभन, लालच
baize (बिज़) *n.* चिकना ऊनी कपड़ा, बनात
bake (बिक) *vt.* (भट्टी में) पकाना – *vi.* डबल रोटी (ब्रैड), केक आदि बनाना; गर्मी में झुलस जाना अथवा तांबे जैसा लाल पड़ जाना –**baker** *n.* – **bakery** *n.* बेकरी – **baking powder** पकाने के काम आने वाला पदार्थ जिसमें मीठा सोडा (सोडियम बाइकार्बोनेट) आदि होते हैं
Bakelite (बेकलाइट) R एक प्रकार का प्लास्टिक
balance (बैलन्स) *n.* तराज़ू; संतुलन; बक़ाया, बकाया रोकड़; दो रकमों का अंतर – *vt.* तोलना; सन्तुलित करना, बराबर करना – **balanced** *a.* संतुलित – **balance of trade** व्यापारांतर – **balance sheet** तुलन-पत्र, पक्का चिट्ठा; देना-पावना विवरण
balcony (बैल्कनि) *n.* बालकनी, छज्जा; सिनेमा, थियेटर में ऊपर की सीटें
bald (बॉल्ड) *a.* गंजा; रूखा, साफ़ (शब्दों में) – **balding** *a.* जिसके बाल उड़ रहे हों – **baldness** *n.* गंजापन
bale[1] (बिल) *n.* गट्ठर, बोरियों का बंडल
bale[2] *vt.* देखिए – BAIL[3]
baleful (बेल्फुल) *a.* धमकी भरी (आखें आदि), अनिष्टकर
balk (बॉक, बॉल्क) *vi.* रास्ते से हट जाना; रुक जाना – *vt.* बाधा डालना, रोकना; जी चुराना – *n.* रुकावट; शहतीर – **balk at** पीछे हटना (कर्तव्य आदि से); रुक जाना
ball[1] (बॉल) *n.* गोलाकार वस्तु; गेंद; फेंकी गई गेंद; बन्दूक की गोली – **ball bearings** बाल बेयरिंग – **ballpoint (pen)** *n.* बाल-प्वाइंट पैन
ball[2] *n.* न त्य के विशे. समारोह पर एकत्रित समुदाय – **ballroom** *n.* नाचघर
ballad (बैलड) *n.* गाथागीत, कथात्मक कविता
ballast (बैलस्ट) *n.* जहाज़ को स्थिरता देने के लिये उसमें रखा गया भारी वज़न; स्थिरता देने वाला कोई भी पदार्थ, स्थिरक – *vt.* स्थिरक से भरना, स्थिर करना
ballet (बैले) *n.* न त्य नाटक; न त्य-नाट्य – **ballerina** (बैल'रीनअ) *n.* नर्तकी

ballistic (ब'लिस्टिक) *a.* प्राक्षेपिक, प्राक्षेप्य वस्तु; (गोली, गोले) के रूप में गतिमान, उसकी गति से संबंधित

balloon (ब'लून) *n.* गुब्बारा

ballot (बैलट) *n.* गुप्त मतदान – *vt.* वोट देना – *vi.* वोट मांगना – **ballot box** मतपेटी

balm (बाम) *n.* मरहम, मलहम

balsam (बाल्सम) *n.* गुलमेंहदी का पौधा

balustrade (बैलस्ट्रेड) *n.* जंगला

bamboo (बैम्'बू) *n.* बांस (*pl.* **bamboos**)

bamboozle (बैम्'बूज़ल) *vt.* चकराना, चकमा देना

ban (बैन) *vt.* प्रतिबंध लगाना; अवैध घोषित करना (**-nn-**) –*n.* प्रतिबंध, निषेध

banal (ब'नाल) *a.* मामूली, साधारण, तुच्छ या घिसीपिटी – **banality** (ब'नैलिटि) *n.* तुच्छता, घिसी-पिटी बात

banana (बना'न्अ) *n.* केले का पेड़; केला

band[1] (बैंड) *n.* पट्टी; दो सीमाओं के बीच मूल्यों का परास; रेडियों, आक ति आदि का परास – **bandage** (बैंडिज) *n.* घावों पर बांधने की पट्टी

band[2] *n.* दल, टोली, बाजा बजाने वालों की मण्डली, बैंड – *vt.* इकट्ठा करना, दल बनाना – *vi.* इकट्ठे होना

bandanna (बैन्'डैन्अ) *n.* रंगबिरंगा रेशमी या सूती रूमाल; बंधना

B & B bed and breakfast का संक्षेप

bandicoot (बैंडिकूट) *n.* आस्ट्रेलिया व भारत में पाया जाने वाला चूहे जैसा प्राणी, घूंस

bandit (बैंडिट) *n.* दस्यु, डाकू, पहाड़ों में छिपे लुटेरों के गिरोह का सदस्य

bandwagon (बैड्वैगन) *n.* **climb/jump or get on the bandwagon** उस संस्था, राजनीतिक पार्टी आदि में सम्मिलित हो जाना जिसकी सफलता निश्चित हो

band width जानकारी की मात्रा जो टेलीफोन की तार, इंटरनेट आदि पर एक ही समय में जा सकती है

bandy (बैंडि) *vt.* मार-पीट करना; किसी बात, नाम का बार-बार ज़िक्र करना (**bandied, bandying**) – **bandy, bandy-legged** *a.* (घुटनों से) बाहर की ओर झुकी टांगों वाला (व्यक्ति)

bane (बेन) *n.* (व्यक्ति अथवा वस्तु) दुख या मुसीबत का कारण, शाप – **baneful** *a.* हानिकारक, विनाशक

bang (बैंग) *n.* धमाका, गहरा वार – *vt.* धमाका करना; ज़ोरदार प्रहार करना, जोर से (दरवाज़ा) बन्द करना

bangle (बैंगल) *n.* चूड़ी, कड़ा

banish (बैनिश) *vt.* देश-निकाला देना, निकाल देना – **banishment** *n.*

banister(s) (बैनिस्टर्ज़) *pl. n.* जंगला; जीने के साथ लगी टेक

banjo (बैंजो) *n.* गिटार जैसा वाद्य; बैन्जो (*pl.* **jo(e)s**)

bank[1] (बैंक) *n.* नदी, झील आदि का किनारा, बांध; टीला; समुद्र में उठी हुई जमीन – *v.* बांध बनाना, ढेर लगाना; वायुयान का मुड़ते समय अंदर की ओर झुक जाना

bank[2] *n.* बैंक; जहां भविष्य में उपलब्ध कराने के लिए कोई वस्तु जमा की जाए जैसे **blood bank** – **banking** *n.* बैंक का व्यवसाय – **bank account** बैंक खाता – **banknote** *n.* बैंक नोट, भुगतान का लिखित वचन – **bankroll** *n.* पैसे से मदद, वित्तीय सहायता – **bank on** पर भरोसा करना

bankrupt (बैंक्रप्ट) *n.* दिवालिया – *a.* – **bankruptcy** *n.* दिवाला

banner (बैनर) *n.* ध्वजा, झण्डा; किसी सेना या राष्ट्र का झण्डा; लम्बी पट्टी के रूप में विज्ञापन – **banner headline** (अखबार में) एक सिरे से दूसरे तक समाचार सुरखी

banquet (ˈबैंक्विट) *n.* दावत, भोज

bantamweight *n.* बॉक्सिंग में बहुत हल्का भार

banter (ˈबैंटर) *vt.* हंसी-मज़ाक में छेड़ना – *n.* हंसी-मजाक, छेड़छाड़

banyan, banian (बैन्यन) *n.* बरगद, बड़

baptize (बैप्ˈटाइज़) *vt.* बपतिस्मा देना, ईसाई धर्म का विधिवत सदस्य बनाना; नामकरण करना – **baptism** (ˈबैप्टिज़्म) *n.* (ईसाई धर्म में) नामकरण संस्कार; बपतिस्मा

bar (बार) *n.* छड़, सलाख; रोक; नदी के मुहाने पर रेत का टीला; कचहरी में कठघरा; वकील समुदाय; होटल आदि में काउन्टर जहां पेय-पदार्थ (विशेषकर शराब) मिले; संगीत की इकाई – *vt.* दरवाज़े में अर्गल लगाना; रोक लगाना; वर्जित करना, निकाल देना (**-rr-**) – *prep.* के अतिरिक्त, सिवाय – **barring** *prep.* को छोड़कर – **bar code** वस्तुओं पर मोटी पतली रेखाओं का समूह जो मूल्य का सांकेतिक चिन्ह होता है व जिसे कम्प्यूटर पढ़ सकता है – **barmaid, barman, bartender** US,C *n.* बार में पेय (विशे. शराब) देने वाला (स्त्री या पुरुष) कर्मचारी

barb (बार्ब) *n.* भाले अथवा मछली पकड़ने के कांटे आदि में आगे लगी मुड़ी हुई तीखी नोक; तीखा व्यंग्य, चुभती टिप्पणी – **barbed wire** कांटेदार तार

barbarous (ˈबार्बरस) *a.* बर्बर, क्रूर, ज़ालिम – **barbarian** (बार्ˈबेंअरिअन) *n.* ज़ालिम, क्रूर व्यक्ति – **barbaric** (बार्ˈबैरिक) *a.* – **barbarism** *n.* – **barbarity** (बार्ˈबैरिटि) *n.* – **barbarously** *adv.*

barbecue (ˈबार्बिक्यू) *n.* बाहर खुले में आग पर पकाया मांस; इस कार्य में प्रयुक्त चूल्हा – *vt.* (सीख पर) भूनना

barber (ˈबार्बर) *n.* नाई, हज्जाम

barbiturate (बार्ˈबिट्यूरिट) *n.* नींद लाने की दवाई, शामक

bard (बार्ड) *n.* (CELTIC) कैल्टिक कवि; चारण; भाट – **the Bard** शेक्सपीयर

bare (बेंअर) *a.* नंगा, खुला; सादा, खाली; केवल, मात्र – *vt.* दिखाना; (आवरण, कपड़ा आदि) हटाना, उघाड़ना – **barely** *adv.* मुश्किल से, मात्रभर – **barefaced** (ˈबेंअर्फेस्ट) *a.* बेशर्म

bargain (ˈबार्गिन) *n.* सौदा; सस्ता सौदा; समझौता – *vi.* मोल-तोल करना

barge (बार्ज) *n.* बजरा, चपटी नौका – *vi. inf.* बीच में बोलना; *inf.* धक्का देना – **not touch sb/sth with a bargepole** *fig.* किसी व्यक्ति/वस्तु से कोई नाता न रखना

barium (ˈबेंअरिअम) *n.* सफेद धात्विक तत्व; बेरियम

bark[1] (बार्क) *n.* कुत्ते के भौंकने की क्रिया – *v.* भौंकना

bark[2] *n.* वक्ष की छाल

barley (ˈबार्लि) *n.* जौ

barmy (ˈबार्मि) *a. inf.* बेवकूफ़, पागल

barn (बार्न) *n.* बखार, खलिहान, खत्ता – **barnyard** *n.* बाड़ा

barnacle (ˈबार्नकल) *n.* छोटी मछली (शंख-मीन) जो चट्टानों तथा जहाज़ों के निचले भाग से चिपकी रहती है

barometer (बˈरॉमिटर) *n.* बैरोमीटर

baron (ˈबैरन) *n.* (ब्रिटेन में) सबसे नीची श्रेणी के सामंत (की उपाधि); शक्तिशाली व्यापारी या व्यवसायी (*fem*-**ess**)

baroque (बˈरोक) *a.* (शैली) अत्याधिक अलंकृत विशे. वास्तुकला व साहित्य, संगीत, चित्रकला आदि में

barrack (ˈबैरक) *n.* (प्राय: *pl.* में) बैरक; स्थान जहां सैनिक रहते हैं

barrage (ˈबैराझ़) *n.* तोपों से भारी गोलाबारी; (प्रश्नों आदि की) लगातार भारी बौछार; नदी पर बांध

barrel (ˈबैरल) *n.* बैरल, (लकड़ी का) पीपा; इसका आयतन; (बन्दूक व पिस्तौल आदि की) नली

barren ('बैरन) *a.* बांझ, बंध्या; बंजर; व्यर्थ, लाभहीन, निष्फल; मन्द – **barrenness** *n.* बांझपन; निष्फलता

barricade (बैरि'केड) *n.* मोर्चा, रुकावट – *vt.* मोर्चा बंदी करना, (सड़क आदि पर) रुकावट खड़ी करना

barrier ('बैरिअर) *n.* रोक, रुकावट, बाधा; (चुंगी आदि के लिए) सीमा – **barrier reef** समुद्र के किनारे समानान्तर प्रवालभित्ति

barrister ('बैरिस्टर) *n.* बैरिस्टर, हाईकोर्ट (तथा ऊपरी न्यायालयों) में वकील

barrow ('बैरो) *n.* (**wheel barrow** भी) हथठेला

barter ('बार्टर) *v.* वस्तु-विनिमय करना, सामान के बदले सामान लेना या देना – *n.* वस्तु-विनिमय

base[1] (बेस) *n.* पैंदा, तल, नींव; प्रारंभ रेखा बिन्दु; संचालन केन्द्र, अड्डा; आधार; पदार्थ जिसमें और चीजें मिलाई जाती हैं; *Chem.* क्षारक, बेस, यौगिक जो किसी ऐसिड से मिलकर लवण बनाता है – *vt.* (~ **on**) आधारित करना – **baseless** *a.* निराधार – **basement** *n.* तहखाना

base[2] *a.* नीच, कमीना, घृणा योग्य; खोटा, अशुद्ध – **basely** *adv.* – **baseness** *n.* नीचता – **baseborn** *a.* जारज, दोग़ला

baseball ('बेस्‌बॉल) *n.* खेल, मूल अमरीकन, बल्ले तथा गेंद से खेला जाने वाला खेल

bash (बैश) *inf. v.* ज़ोर से प्रहार करना – *n.* प्रहार; कोशिश; पार्टी, जश्न

bashful ('बैश्‌फुल) *a.* शर्मीला, संकोची

BASIC *Computers* Beginners' All-purpose Symbolic Instruction Code का संक्षेप

basic ('बेसिक) *a.* आधारभूत, बुनियादी, मूल; प्रधान; *Chem.* क्षारीय – **basically** *a.*

basil ('बैज़ल) *n.* तुलसी

basin ('बेसन) *n.* चिलमची, तसला; बन्दरगाह; नदी घाटी, तलहटी

basis ('बेसिस) *n.* आधार, तर्क का आधार (*pl.* - **ses** ('बेसीज़))

bask (बास्क) *vi.* धूप खाना, धूप का आनंद लेना (प्राय: *fig.*)

basket ('बास्किट) *n.* टोकरी, डलिया – **basketball** *n.* बास्केटबाल का खेल

bastard ('बास्टर्ड) *n.* अविवाहित माता-पिता का पुत्र, हरामज़ादा – *a.* नियमविरुद्ध, नकली

bastion ('बैस्टिअन) *n.* किलेबन्दी में आगे निकला हुआ भाग; बुर्ज, सुदृढ़ सुरक्षा व्यवस्था

bat[1] (बैट) *n. Cricket, Baseball* बैट, बल्ला – *v.* बल्लेबाज़ी करना – **batting** *n.* बल्लेबाज़ी – **batsman** ('बैट्‌स्मन) *n.* बल्लेबाज

bat[2] *n.* चमगादड़

bat[3] *vt.* (पलकें) झपकाना

batch (बैच) *n.* एक सी वस्तुओं का समूह, घान (एक ही बार में बनाई गई वस्तुओं का, जैसे केक, दवाईयों आदि का); दल, टोली

bated ('बेटिड) *a.*– **with bated breath** (चिंता, घबराहट, के कारण) सांस रोक कर

bath (बाथ) *n.* नहाने का टब अथवा स्थान; नहाने का पानी; स्नान – *vt.* धोना (टब आदि में)

bathe (बेद) *v.* तैरने के लिये जाना; नहाना; पानी में डुबाना (धोने, भिगोने आदि के लिये), नहलाना (**bathed, bathing**) – *n.* खुले पानी में तैराई – **bather** *n.* नहाने, तैरने वाला व्यक्ति

bathroom ('बाथ्‌रूम) *n.* स्नानगृह

batik ('बैटिक) *n.* बैटिक, कपड़ा-रंगाई की विधि जिसमें मोम का प्रयोग होता है

batsman *n.* दे० BAT[1]

baton ('बैटन) *n.* छड़ी, डण्डा विशे. पुलिसमैन, वृन्द-नायक (कन्डक्टर) व सर्वोच्च सैनिक अधिकारी मार्शल का

battalion (ब'टैल्यन) *n.* थल सेना की तीन या अधिक कम्पनियों का संगठन; बटालियन

batten (बैटन) *vi.* (प्राय: **batten on**) फलना-फूलना, मौज करना विशे. दूसरे के पैसे या माल पर; मुफ्तखोरी करना

batter (ˈबैटर) *vt.* लगातार टक्कर मारना – *n.* (खाद्य-पदार्थ बनाने के लिए) फेंटी हुई मैदा, अण्डे और दूध की लपसी

battery (ˈबैटरि) *n.* विद्युत बैटरी; एक स्थान पर एक ही प्रकार की इकट्ठी रखी गई वस्तुऐं

battle (ˈबैट्ल) *n.* लड़ाई; संघर्ष – *vi.* युद्ध करना, संघर्ष करना – **battle cry** लड़ाई या आंदोलन का नारा

battlement (ˈबैट्ल्मंट) *n.* किले का परकोटा तथा उसमें बने तोप व तीर चलाने के स्थान, फ़सील

battleship (ˈबैट्ल्शिप) *n.* जंगी जहाज़

baulk (बॉक) *v.* देखिए **BALK**

bauxite (ˈबॉक्साइट) *n.* बॉक्साइट, कच्ची धातु जिससे एल्यूमिन्यम बनता है

bawdy (ˈबॉडि) *a.* अश्लील; गंदा; कामोत्तेजक

bawl (बॉल) *vi.* चिल्लाना, चीखना; रोना

bay[1] (बे) *n.* खाड़ी; भवन का खंड या कक्ष; आला

bay[2] *vi.* कुत्ते का भौंकना विशे. शिकारी कुत्ते का

bayonet (ˈबेअनिट) *n.* संगीन, बेनट

BC before Christ ईसापूर्व, जो साल के बाद लिखते हैं जैसे **326** B.C.

BCG Bacillus Calmette Guerin (क्षयरोग का टीका) का संक्षेप

B.Com., B.Comm. Bachelor of Commerce का संक्षेप

B/D Bank Draft का संक्षेप

BDS Bachelor of Dental Surgery का संक्षेप

BE Bachelor of Engineering का संक्षेप

B/E bill of exchange का संक्षेप

be (बी) *vi.* रहना; होना; घटित होना; *pr. ind;* **I am** मैं...हूं; **he is** वह...है; **we are** हम...हैं; **you are** तुम...हो; **they are** वह...हैं – **was** *pt.,* **were** *pl.;* **been** *pp;* **being** *pr. p*

beach (बीच) *n.* समुद्र-तट – *vt.* नाव को किनारे चढ़ाना

beacon (ˈबीकन) *n.* संकेत-दीप, प्रकाश स्तंभ (ख़तरे का संकेत देने के लिये) समुद्र में उतराती स्थिर वस्तु, बोया; जहाज़रानी में प्रयुक्त (रेडियो) संकेत

bead (बीड) *n.* मनका, माला का दाना; बूंद; (भवन निर्माण में) मनका सज्जा पट्टी – **beaded** *a.* मनकेदार

beak (बीक) *n.* चोंच; (किसी वस्तु का) नुकीला या आगे बढ़ा हुआ भाग; *sl.* मैजिस्ट्रेट

beaker (ˈबीकर) *n.* बीकर, रसायनज्ञों द्वारा प्रयोग किया जाने वाला कांच का पात्र

beam (बीम) *n.* शहतीर; जहाज़ की कड़ी, चौड़ाई अथवा बग़ल; किरण; मुस्कान; तराजू की डंडी, तुलादण्ड – *vt.* प्रकाश किरण, रेडियो लहर आदि को फैलाना, प्रसारित करना – *vi.* मुस्कराना

bean (बीन) *n.* बीन, सेम (की फली)

bear[1] (बॅअर) *vt.* ले जाना, ढोना; जन्म देना, उपजाना, फल देना; भार डालना; प्रभावित करना (**bore** *pt.,* **born** *or* **borne** *pp.,* **bearing** *pr. p.*) – **bearer** *n.* वाहक, धारक; बैरा

bear[2] *n.* रीछ; रीछ जैसा दूसरा कोई प्राणी – **bear hug** *n.* बाहों में कस कर जकड़ना

beard (बिअर्ड) *n.* दाढ़ी – *vt.* साहसपूर्वक सामना करना

bearing (ˈबॅअरिङ) *n.* बेयरिंग, मशीन का वह भाग जिस पर मशीन की छड़ घूमती है; वह भाग जो घर्षण कम करता है; सम्बद्धता; आचरण; दिशाकोण, स्थिति

bearish *a.* (शेयर बाज़ार) जब शेयरों की कीमतें गिर रही हों

beast (बीस्ट) *n.* पशु, चौपाया; क्रूर मनुष्य, ज़ालिम आदमी – **beastly** *a.* पशु जैसा, पाशविक; क्रूर

beat (बीट) *vt.* मारना, पीटना; हराना; आगे निकल जाना; फेंटना; (पंख) फड़फड़ाना; (टक्करें

मारकर, कुचलकर) रास्ता बनाना – *vi.* धड़कना; हवा के विरुद्ध चलना (**beat** *pt.*, **beaten** *pp.*) – *n.* धड़कन; गश्त; (संगीत ताल) – *a. sl.* थककर चकनाचूर – **beater** *n.* कूटने, फेंटने आदि के काम आने वाली वस्तु; थापी, रई

beau (बो) *n.* प्रेमी (*pl.* **beaux** (बोज़)

beauty (ˈब्यूटि) *n.* सुंदरता, शोभा; सुंदर व्यक्ति या वस्तु – **beautician** (ब्यूˈटिशन) *n.* ब्यूटी पार्लर में काम करने वाला – **beauteous** *a.* सुंदर – **beautiful** *a.* सुंदर, आकर्षक – **beautifully** *adv.* – **beautify** *vt.* सुन्दर बनाना, सजाना (**-fied, -fying**) – **beauty parlour** ब्यूटी पार्लर

beaver (ˈबीव़र) *n.* ऊदबिलाव

became (बिˈकेम) BECOME का *pt.*

because (बिˈकॉज़) *adv./conj.* क्योंकि, इसलिए कि, के कारण

beck[1] (बॅक) *n.* इशारा – **at someone's beck and call** किसी के इशारों पर (रहना)

beckon (ˈबॅकन) *v.* संकेत से बुलाना

become (बिˈकम) *vi.* हो जाना, बन जाना – *vt.* उचित होना, जंचना, शोभा देना (**became** *pt.*, **become** *pp.*, **becoming** *pr. p.*) – **becoming** *a.* उचित, शोभनीय

bed (बॅड) *n.* पलंग, चारपाई; बिस्तर; क्यारी; *Architecture etc.* आधार, नींव; (नदी, समुद्र का) तल; तह, परत; (चट्टान) स्तर – **bedding** *n.* बिस्तरा – **bedpan** (ˈबॅड्पैन) *n.* बीमार व्यक्ति के लिए टट्टी-पेशाब का बर्तन, बेडपेन – **bedridden** *a.* (बीमार या वद्ध व्यक्ति) शय्याग्रस्त, बिस्तर से लगा हुआ – **bedrock** *n.* आधारशिला – **bedroom** *n.* शयनकक्ष – **bedsore** *n.* लंबे अरसे तक बिस्तर पर पड़े रहने से बने त्वचा पर छाले/घाव – **bedstead** *n.* पलंग

bedlam (ˈबॅड्लम) *n.* शोरशराबा

bee (बी) *n.* मधुमक्खी – **beehive** (ˈबीहाइव़) *n.* मधुमक्खी का छत्ता

beef (बीफ़) *n.* गोमांस

been (बीन, बिन) BE का *pp.*

beep (बीप) *n.* कार के हार्न की रुक-रुक कर होने वाली आवाज़, पीं-पीं की आवाज़ – *v.* ऐसी आवाज़ निकालना

beer (बिअर) *n.* बियर (एक मादक पेय)

beet (बीट) *n.* चुकंदर, *US* **beetroot**

beetle (ˈबीट्ल) *n.* एक प्रकार का भˈग, भंवरा

befall (बिˈफ़ॉल) *v.* घटित होना, आ पड़ना (**befell, befallen**)

befit (बिˈफ़िट) *vt.* (के लिए) उचित होना (**-tt-**)

before (बिˈफ़ॉर) *prep.* के सामने, के आगे, के पूर्व, के पहले – *adv.* पहले, सामने – *conj.* से पहले – **beforehand** *adv.* पहले से

beg (बॅग) *vt.* विनयपूर्वक मांगना, प्रार्थना करना – *vi.* भीख मांगना, भीख पर गुज़ारा करना (**-gg-**) – **beggar** *n.* भिखारी

began (बिˈगैन) BEGIN का *pt.*

begin (बिˈगिन) *v.* आरंभ करना, चलाना (**began** *pt.*, **begun** *pp.*, **beginning** *pr. p.*) – **beginner** *n.* नौसिखिया – **beginning** *n.* शुरुआत

beguile (बिगाइल) *vt.* बहकाना, फुसलाना

begun (बिˈगन) BEGIN का *pp.*

behalf (बिˈहाफ़) *n.* की ओर, के पक्ष में, के लिए विशे. **on behalf of** में

behave (बिˈहेव़) *vi.* व्यवहार करना, पेश आना – **behaviour** (बिˈहेव्यर) *n.* आचरण, व्यवहार

behead (बिˈहॅड) *vt.* सिर काट देना

beheld (बिˈहॅल्ड) BEHOLD का *pt./pp.*

behest (बिˈहॅस्ट) *n.* आदेश; अनुरोध

behind (बिˈहाइंड) *prep.* के पीछे; का समर्थक – *adv.* पीछे, पीछे की ओर – **behind hand** *a./adv.* काम में पीछे; सुस्त

behold (बि´होल्ड) *vt.* देखना, ध्यान से देखना (**beheld** *pt.*, **beheld**, **beholden** *pp.*) – **beholder** *n.* दर्शक

beholden (बि´होल्डन) *a.* आभारी

behove (बि´होव़) *vt.* (के लिए) उचित, आवश्यक होना (केवल भाववाच्य)

beige (बेझ़) *n.* बना, रंगा ऊनी कपड़ा; उस का रंग, हल्का भूरा

being (´बीइङ) *n.* अस्तित्व; प्राणी; जीव – BE का *pr. p.*

belated (बि´लेटिड) *a. (late)* विलम्बित, बहुत देर से (किया गया कार्य)

belch (बेल्च) *vi.* डकार लेना – *vt.* बाहर फेंकना

beleaguered (बि´लीगर) *a.* घेरे में फंसा

believe (बि´लीव़) *vt.* को सही मान लेना – *vi.* में विश्वास करना; विश्वास होना – **belief** *n.* विश्वास – **believer** *n.* (किसी धर्म में) विश्वास रखने वाला; आस्तिक

belittle (बि´लिट्ल) *vt.* महत्व घटाना, मज़ाक उड़ाना

bell (बेल) *n.* घंटा, घंटी

belle (बेल) *n.* सुंदरी, (अपने समय की) सर्व सुंदरी

bellicose (´बेलिकोस) *a.* युद्धप्रिय, लड़ाकू

belligerent (बि´लिजरंट) *a.* शत्रुतापूर्ण, आक्रामक, दुश्मनों जैसा (व्यवहार आदि) – **belligerence** *n.* आक्रामकता; युद्धस्थिति

bellows (´बेलोज़) *pl. n.* धौंकनी

belly (´बेलि) *n.* उदर, पेट – **belly button** *inf.* नाभि

belong (बि´लॉङ) *vi.* की सम्पत्ति होना, के अधिकार में होना; का सदस्य अथवा निवासी होना; (स्थान) का होना; से संबंध रखना – **belongings** *pl. n.* निजी सामान

beloved (बि´लविड) *a.* परमप्रिय, बहुत प्यारा – *n.* प्रिय व्यक्ति, प्रियतम, प्रेयसी

below (बि´लो) *adv.* नीचे – *prep.* से नीचे; से निचली सतह पर

belt (बेल्ट) *n.* पेटी; कमरबंद

bemoan (बि´मोन) *vt.* रोना, विलाप करना (किसी वस्तु के छिन जाने पर)

bemuse (बि´म्यूज़) *v.* हतप्रभ कर देना, चक्कर में डाल देना

bench (बेन्च) *n.* बैठने की बेंच; न्यायाधीशों के बैठने का स्थान या उन का समूह, न्यायपीठ; न्यायालय – **bench mark** कसौटी

bend (बेण्ड) *vt.* मोड़ना; झुकाना; टेढ़ा करना (**bent** *pt./pp.*) – *vi.* झुकना, मुड़ना – *n.* मोड़; झुकाव

beneath (बि´नीथ) *prep.* के नीचे; से नीचे

benediction (बेनि´डिक्शन) *n.* (ईश्वर से) मंगलकामना; आशीर्वाद

benefit (´बेनिफ़िट) *n.* लाभ, फायदा – *vt.* किसी का भला करना – *vi.* (**benefited, benefiting**) – **benefactor** *n.* उपकारी, (**benefactress** *fem.*) – **beneficent** *a.* उपकारी, दयालु – **beneficial** (बेनि´फ़िशल) *a.* लाभकारी – **beneficiary** *n.* लाभ पाने वाला; व त्तिभोगी

benevolent (बि´नेवलंट) *a.* हितैषी; परोपकारी – **benevolence** *n.*

benign (बि´नाइन) *a.* भद्र, सौम्य, हितकर; हितैषी; (रसौली आदि) जिसमें कैंसर न हो – **benignancy** (बि´निग्नन्सि) *n.*

bent (बेण्ट) BEND का *pt./pp.* – *a.* मुड़ा हुआ; टेढ़ा

benumb (बि´नम) *vt.* सुन्न या शिथिल कर देना

benzene, benzine, benzole, benzoline (´बेन्ज़ीन), (बेन्´ज़ीन) (´बेन्ज़ोल), (´बेन्ज़ोलिन) *n.* ज्वलनशील द्रवों का समूह जो रसायनों में, मिश्रणों में और सफ़ाई करने के रसायनों में प्रयुक्त होते हैं

bequeath (बि´क्वीद) *vt.* वसीयत कर के (किसी के लिए) सम्पत्ति छोड़ना – **bequest** (बि´क्वेस्ट) *n.* छोड़ी गयी सम्पत्ति

berate (बि´रेट) *vt.* डांटना, फटकारना

bereave (बि´रीव़) *vt.* (म त्यु द्वारा) छोड़ देना, वंचित कर देना (**bereaved, bereft** *pt./pp.*) – **bereaved** *a.* शोकसंतप्त (परिवार)

Bermuda shorts (बर्म्यूड्अ´शॉर्ट्स) *pl. n.* (**Bermudas** भी) घुटनों तक की निक्कर

berry (´बॅरि) *n.* बिना गुठली का बेर जैसा फल, बदरी, सरसफल

berserk (बर्´ज़र्क, बर्´सर्क) *a.* – **go berserk** पागल हो जाना व अनियंत्रित हो जाना

berth (बर्थ) *n.* जहाज़ के लंगर डालने का स्थान; घाट; गोदी; जहाज़ या रेलगाड़ी में सोने का स्थान; शायिका – *vt.* (जहाज को) घाट/डॉक पर लगाना

beset (बि´सॅट) *vt.* टूट पड़ना; खतरे या समस्याओं से घेर लेना (**beset, besetting**)

beside (बि´साइड) *prep.* पास या बगल में; की तुलना में – **besides** *adv./prep.* के अलावा, के अतिरिक्त

besiege (बि´सीज) *vt.* घेरा डालना (सैनिकों द्वारा)

best (बॅस्ट) *a./adv.* **good** या **well** का *sup.*

bestial (´बॅस्टिअल) *a.* पशु जैसा; बर्बर, क्रूर

bestow (बि´स्टो) *vt.* देना; प्रदान करना

bet (बॅट) *v.* बाज़ी या दांव (पर) लगाना; शर्त बदना या लगाना (**bet** *or* **betted** *pt./pp.* **betting** *pr. p.*) – *n.* दांव पर लगाई राशि

betel (´बीट्ल) *n.* पान; ताम्बूल – **betel nut** सुपारी

betray (बि´ट्रे) *vt.* विश्वासघात करना, विशे. शत्रु को सहायता करके – **betrayal** (बि´ट्रेअल) *n.* विश्वासघात

better (´बॅटर) *a./adv.* **good** या **well** का *comp.*, बेहतर, अधिक अच्छा – *v.* सुधारना, बेहतर बनाना – **betterment** *n.* सुधार

between (बि´ट्वीन) *prep./adv.* बीच या मध्य में (समय या स्थान के); परस्पर सम्बन्ध या तुलना का सूचक भी

beverage (´बेबरिज) n. पीने की वस्त, पेय

beware (बि´वेंअर) *vi.* सतर्क या चौकस रहना, सावधान रहना

bewilder (बि´विल्डर) *vt.* चक्कर में डालना, चकित करना, भ्रम में डालना

beyond (बि´यॉण्ड) *adv.* के परे; अतिरिक्त – *prep.* (के) दूसरी ओर; बाद में; पहुंच से बाहर; से अधिक

B/F brought forward का संक्षेप

bhp brake horsepower का संक्षेप

bias (´बाइअस) *n.* झुकाव; व्यक्तिगत झुकाव या पसंद; एकपक्षीय झुकाव, पूर्वग्रह (*pl.* **biases**) – *vt.* तरफ़दारी या पक्षपात करना (-**s**-या-**ss**-) – **bias(s)ed** *a.* एकतरफ़ा; पक्षपात भरा

bib (बिब) *n.* बच्चे की ठोड़ी के नीचे बंधा कपड़ा जिससे कि उसके कपड़ों पर दूध आदि न गिरे, गांती, गतिया

Bible (´बाइबल) *n.* ईसाई धर्म का पवित्र ग्रंथ, बाइबल – **biblical** (´बिब्लिकल) *a.*

bibliography (बिब्लि´ऑग्राफ़ि) *n.* किसी विषय संबंधी पुस्तकों की सूची

biceps (´बाइसॅप्स) *n.* दो सिर वाली मांसपेशी, विशे. (कन्धे और कुहनी के बीच) बाज़ू की, डौला

bicker (´बिकर) *vi./n.* छोटी छोटी बातों पर झगड़ा (करना)

bicycle (´बाइसिकल) *n.* बाइसिकल, साइकल – **bicyclist** (´बाइसिक्लिस्ट) *n.* साइकल-चालक

bid (बिड) *vt.* (नीलामी में) बोली देना; कहना; आदेश देना, आमंत्रित करना – *vi.* (~ **for**) के लिए बोली लगाना (**bade/bid, bidden**) – *n.* पेशकश (विशे. कीमत की), बोली; कोशिश; *Card Games* पत्ते दिखाने के लिए कहना – **bidder** *n.* बोली लगाने वाला – **bidding** *n.* आज्ञा, कहना

bide (बाइड) *vi.* रहना, निवास करना – *vt.* (उपयुक्त समय की) प्रतीक्षा करना – **biding** *n.* प्रतीक्षा

biennial (बाइ´ऐंनिअल) *a.* जो हर दो वर्ष बाद हो – *n.* पौधा जो दो वर्ष तक रहे, दो बरसी

bier (बिअर) *n.* अरथी (जिस पर मुर्दे को गाड़ने/जलाने के लिए ले जाते है)

bifocal (बाइ´फ़ोकल) *a.* (ऐनक) दो फोकस वाली, द्विफोकसी

bifurcate (´बाइफ़र्केट) *vt.* दो शाखाओं में बांटना

big (बिग) *a.* बड़े आकार, ऊंचाई, संख्या या शक्ति वाला; बड़ा; ऊंचा; विशाल; लम्बा चौड़ा; महत्वशाली; महान (**bigger** *comp.*, **biggest** *sup.*) – **bigness** *n.* विशालता – **big shot** *inf.* महत्त्वशाली या प्रभावशाली व्यक्ति

bigamy (´बिगमि) *n.* एक पति/पत्नि के होते दूसरे पुरुष/दूसरी स्त्री से विवाह करने का अपराध

bigotry (´बिगट्रि) *n.* कट्टरता, धर्मान्धता

bike (बाइक) *n.* BICYCLE या MOTOR BIKE का संक्षेप

bikini (बि´कीनि) *n.* स्त्रियों की तैरने की पोशाक जिसमें अंगिया और चड्डी मात्र होते हैं

bilateral (बाई´लैटरल) *a.* द्विपक्षीय, दो तरफ

bilingual (बाइ´लिंग्वल) *a.* द्विभाषी – **bilingualism** *n.* द्विभाषिकता

bill[1] (बिल) *n.* खरीदी गयी वस्तुओं की कीमत सहित सूची; बीजक; US करेंसी नोट; संसद के अधिनियम का मसौदा, विधेयक; इश्तहार; हुण्डी, विपत्र – *vt.* बीजक या बिल बनाना या देना; विज्ञापन के माध्यम से घोषणा करना

bill[2] *n.* पक्षी की चोंच

billion (´बिल्यन) *n.* दस खरब की संख्या; US, Fr, C एक अरब

bimonthly (बाइ´मन्थ्लि) *adv./a.* दो मास में एक बार, द्वैमासिक; मास में दो बार, पाक्षिक

bin (बिन) *n.* अनाज रखने की कोठड़ी; धानी; कचरा आदि डालने का डिब्बा आदि – **dustbin** *n.* कूड़ा डालने का कनस्तर

binary (´बाइनरि) *a.* दो का या दो को मिलाकर बना, दोहरा

bind (बाइण्ड) *vt.* कस कर बांधना; इर्दगिर्द लपेटना; इकट्ठे बांधना; उपकार या अहसान करना; वचन लेना, पक्का करना; रोकना; पट्टी बांधना; जमाना, जोड़ना या एक करना; (पुस्तक की) जिल्द बांधना (**bound** *pt./pp.*) – **binder** *n.* (जिल्द) बांधने वाला

binge (बिंज) *n. inf.* खाने पीने का दौर जिसमें संयम से काम न लिया जाय; रंगरलियां

bingo (´बिंगो) *n.* **housey-housey** खेल जिसमें संख्या पुकारी जाती है और उसमें भाग लेने वाले पुकारी गयी संख्या काट देते हैं, (भारत में) तम्बोला

binocular (बाइ´नॉक्युलर) *a.* जो दो आंखों से देखे या जो दो आंखों के लिए बना हो – **binoculars** *pl. n.* दूरबीन

binomial (बाइ´नोमिअल) *a./n.* बीज-गणित में दो पदों वाला, द्विपद

bio- (बाइओ) (*comb. form*) जीवन-जीवित

biochemistry (बाइओ´कैमिस्ट्रि) *n.* जीव रसायन

biodegradable (बाइओडि´ग्रेडबल) *a.* जो प्राक तिक साधनों से सड़गल जाय

biodiversity (बाइओडाइ´वर्सिटि) *n.* किसी स्थान पर पशु-पौधों की विविधता, जैव-विविधता

biog. biographical, biography का संक्षेप

biography (बाइ´ऑग्रफ़ि) *n.* जीवन चरित, जीवनी – **biographer** *n.* जीवनी लेखक – **biographical** (बाइअ´ग्रैफ़िकल) *a.* जीवन-संबंधी

biology (बाइ´ऑलजि) *n.* जीव विज्ञान, प्राणी-विज्ञान, जैविकी – **biological** (बाइअ´लॉजिकल) *a.* जीव-विज्ञान संबंधी

biophysics (बाइओ´फ़िजिक्स) *n.* जीव- भौतिकी (जैविक प्रक्रियाओं का भौतिकी अध्ययन)

biopsy (ˈबाइऑप्सि) *n.* शरीर का कोई ऊतक काट कर उसकी परीक्षा, जीवूति परीक्षा

bioscope (ˈबाइअस्कोप) *n.* (पुराना शब्द) सिनेमा

biosphere (ˈबाइअस्फ़िअर) *n.* जीव मण्डल

biotechnology (बाइओटॅक्ˈनॉलजि) *n.* कोशिका (cell), बेक्टीरिया आदि का कचरा नष्ट करने के लिए उपयोगी, जैव-प्रौद्योगिकी

bipartisan (बाइपार्टिˈज़ैन) *a.* दो राजनीतिक दलों को मिलाकर बना या उन से समर्थन पाने वाला

bipartite (बाइˈपार्टाइट) *a.* दो अंगों या दलों/पक्षों वाला

biped (ˈबाइपॅड) *n.* दो पैरों वाला जीव, दोपाया

birch (बर्च) *n.* पेड़ जिसकी छाल चांदी के समान चमकती है, भूर्ज, भोजपत्र

bird (बर्ड) *n.* पक्षी, पंछी; *sl.* युवती, जवान लड़की – **bird's-eye view** सरसरी निगाह

birth (बर्थ) *n.* जन्म, पैदाइश – **birth control** सन्तति निग्रह – **birthday** *n.* जन्मदिन – **birthmark** *n.* जन्म के समय शरीर पर कोई धब्बा या चिन्ह जो पहचान का कारण बने, जन्म-चिन्ह – **birth rate** जन्म दर

biscuit (ˈबिस्किट) *n.* बिस्कुट

bisect (बाइˈसॅक्ट) *vt.* दो बराबर-बराबर हिस्सों में बांटना

bisexual (बाइˈसॅक्सयुअल) *a.* जो स्त्री तथा पुरुष दोनों की ओर आकृष्ट हो, उभयलिंगी

bishop (ˈबिशप) *n.* पादरी जो एक अंचल का अधिकारी हो, बिशप; (शतरंज में) फ़ीला, हाथी

bismuth (ˈबिज़मथ) *n.* लाली लिए एक सफेद धातु, बिस्मथ

bison (ˈबाइसन) *n.* बड़े आकार का जंगली सांड, ग़वल; अमरीका की जंगली भैंस

bistro (ˈबीस्त्रो) *n.* छोटा सा रेस्तोरां या ढाबा

bit[1] (बिट) *n.* टुकड़ा, अंश; बरमे का अगला भाग; अनी; घोड़े की लगाम का दहाना (वह भाग जो उसके मुंह में डाला जाता है); कौर

bit[2] BITE का *pt./pp.*

bit[3] *n. Computers* जानकारी की सबसे छोटी इकाई

bitch (बिच) *n.* कुत्ते, लोमड़ी या भेड़िए की मादा; कुतिया; *offens., sl.* कुत्ती, असभ्य, दुर्भावपूर्ण स्त्री; *inf.* मुसीबत – *vi. inf.* शिकायत करना – **bitchy** *a.* कुतिया जैसा; दुर्भावपूर्ण

bite (बाइट) *vt.* काटना, विशे. दांत से पकड़ लेना; (मछली का) चारे की ओर आना; गला देना (**bit** *pt.* **bit, bitten** *pp.*, **biting** *pr. p.*)

bitter (ˈबिटर) *a.* कड़वा; तीखा; तीता; अप्रिय; नाराज़ या दुखी (व्यक्ति); व्यंग्यपूर्ण – **bitterly** *adv.* – **bitterness** *n.* कड़वाहट, वैमनस्य

bitumen (ˈबिट्युमिन) *n.* सड़कों पर बिछाने के तारकोल का एक तत्व, बिट्युमिन, डामर

bizarre (बिˈज़ार) *a.* अनोखा, असाधारण, बेतुका; भयानक

blab (ब्लैब) *v.* भेद खोल देना; बकबक करना (**-bb-**)

black (ब्लैक) *a.* काला, अंधकारमय; दुष्ट; अशुभ, मनहूस; निराशाभरा; कलंकित – *n.* काला रंग; काले कपड़े आदि; (**B-**) (काली जाति का) नीग्रो – **blacken** *vt.* काला करना – *vi.* काला होना – **black belt** *Judo, Karate* प्रशिक्षक या इसमें प्रवीण व्यक्ति द्वारा पहनी जाने वाली पेटी; ऐसी पेटी पहनने का हकदार – **blackbird** *n.* यूरोप की एक चिड़िया, कस्तूरा – **blackboard** *n.* ब्लैक बोर्ड, श्यामपट्ट – **black box** *inf.* विमान के फ्लाइट रिकार्डर का दूसरा नाम – **black coffee/tea** बगैर दूध की काफी, चाय – **black economy** काला धन; काले धन पर निर्भर अर्थ-व्यवस्था – **black eye** घूंसे की मार से आंखों के पास आयी सूजन – **blackhead** *n.* त्वचा (विशे. मुंह पर) कील – **black hole** बाहरी अंतरिक्ष

में वह क्षेत्र जो अपने आस-पास से सब कुछ अंदर खींच लेता है यहां तक कि प्रकाश भी – **blacklist** *n.* ऐसे लोगों की सूची जो संदिग्ध हों या जो विश्वासपात्र नहीं समझे जाते, काली सूची – *vt.* काली सूची में नाम लिखना – **black market** काला बाज़ार, चोर बाज़ार – **black sheep** व्यक्ति जो कुल या वर्ग के लिए कलंक समझा जाए – **black widow** अमरीका महाद्वीप की एक ज़हरीली मकड़ी – **be in the black** (कंपनी का) लाभ कमाते होना – **in black and white** लिखित में

blackguard (ˈब्लैगार्ड) *n.* गुंडा; बदमाश

blackmail (ˈब्लैक्मेल) *vt.* किसी से भंडाफोड़ का डर दिखाकर पैसे ऐंठना – *n.*

blackout (ˈब्लैक्आउट) *n.* बिजली का बंद हो जाना; चिराग गुल; क्षणिक अचेतना या बेहोशी; विमानों के आक्रमण से बचने के लिए सारी बत्तियों का बुझा देना या मद्धिम कर देना – **(black out)** *vt.* बत्तियां बुझा देना; समाचार न आने देना – *vi.* बेहोश होना

blacksmith (ˈब्लैक्स्मिथ) *n.* लोहार

bladder (ˈब्लैडर) *n.* द्रव पदार्थ डालने के लिए झिल्ली की थैली, विशे. मूत्राशय

blade (ब्लेड) *n.* चाकू या औज़ार का वह अंश जिससे काटते हैं; धार; तलवार; नाव के चप्पू का चपटा भाग – **blade of grass** घास का तिनका

blame (ब्लेम) *n.* निंदा करने की क्रिया; दोष – *vt.* दोष देना या निंदा करना – **blameworthy** *a.* निंदनीय, दोषी

bland (ब्लैंड) *a.* साधारण, फीका; भावहीन

blank (ब्लैंक) *a.* जिसपर कुछ लिखा न हो, खाली, रिक्त; भावशून्य; चकराया हुआ; (कविता) अतुकांत – *n.* शून्य; रिक्त स्थान; खाली कारतूस (जिसमें गोली नहीं होती) – **blank cheque** चेक जिस पर रकम न लिखी हो; पूरा अधिकार

blanket (ˈब्लैंकिट) *n.* कम्बल; आवरण – *vt.* पूरा ढँक देना; छिपाना

blare (ब्लेंअर) *v.* ऊंची आवाज़ निकालना – *n.*

blasphemous (ˈब्लैस्फिमस) *a.* ईशनिंदात्मक – **blasphemy** (ˈब्लैस्फ़िमि) *n.* ईशनिंदा

blast (ब्लास्ट) *n.* विस्फोट, धमाका; विस्फोट के कारण हवा का ज़ोर का झोंका; झोंका; जोर की आवाज – *vt.* उड़ा देना; विस्फोट द्वारा हटाना या खोलना – **blast furnace** इस्पात पिघलाने की भट्ठी जिसमें गर्म हवा का प्रयोग होता है – **blast-off** *n.* अंतरिक्षयान का प थ्वी से उड़ान का क्षण

blatant (ˈब्लेटंट) *a.* खुला, साफ, स्पष्ट, घोर

blaze[1] (ब्लेज़) *n.* धधकती हुई आग; चमक; प्रदीप्ति; उत्तेजित होकर भड़क उठने की क्रिया – *vi.* धू-धू कर जलना; भड़कना (गुस्से में)

blaze[2] *v.* (पेड़ों पर निशान लगा कर) रास्ता निश्चित करना – *n.* व क्ष पर बना ऐसा चिन्ह

blazer (ˈब्लेज़र) *n.* एक प्रकार का कोट जो विशे. खिलाड़ी पहनते हैं, ब्लेज़र

bleach (ब्लीच) *v.* सफ़ेद होना या करना – *n.* रंग काटने का पदार्थ, रंग काट

bleak (ब्लीक) *a.* ठंडा; रूखा; उजाड

bleary (-eyed) (ˈब्लिअरि) *a.* जिस की आंखें (आंसुओं या नींद से) धुंधला गयी हों

bleat (ब्लीट) *v.* भेड़ आदिका/मिमिआना; शिकायत भरे स्वर में बोलना – *n.* मिमियाहट

bleed (ब्लीड) *vi.* खून निकलना – *vt.* खून या कोई और तरल पदार्थ निकालना (**bled** *pt./pp.*)

blend (ब्लेंण्ड) *vt.* मिलाना; घोल मिलाना – *n.* मिश्रण – **blender** *n.* उपकरण जिसमें डाल कर खाद्य पदार्थ मिलाए जाते हैं, मिक्सी

bless (ब्लेंस) *vt.* (मंत्रादि से) पवित्र करना; आशीर्वाद देना; (प्राय: *passive*) वरदान देना; देना; धन्य कहना या मानना; की पूजा करना; प्रसन्न करना (**blessed, blest** (ब्लेंस्ट) – **blessed** (ˈब्लेंसिड, ब्लेंस्ट) *a.* धन्य; सौभाग्यशाली – **blessing** *n.* वरदान

blew (ब्लू) **BLOW** का *pt.*

blight (ब्लाइट) *n.* पौधों की एक बीमारी; अंगभारी; हानिकारक प्रभाव; अभिशाप – *vt.* मुरझा देना; सुखा देना; हानि पहुंचाना

blind (ब्लाइंड) *a.* अंधा; बेसमझ; विवेकहीन; अंधाधुंध; अंधेरा; मद्धिम; बन्द (जैसे गली) – *vt.* अंधा कर देना – *n.* खिड़की की झिलमिली; बहाना; धोखे की टट्टी – **blinding** *a.* बहुत तेज़ (प्रकाश, वर्षा आदि) – **blindly** *adv.* – **blindness** *n.* अंधापन – **blind alley** बंदगली – **blindfold** *vt.* आंखों पर पट्टी बांधना – **blind man's buff** आंख मिचौली या लुका छिपी का खेल

blink (ब्लिंक) *vi.* आंख से इशारा करना; आंख झपकाना या मिचकाना; टिमटिमाना – *n.* चमक – **blinkers** *pl. n.* घोड़े की आंख पर लगे चमड़े के टुकड़े जिससे कि वह इधर-उधर देख न सके, अंधेरी – **blink at** देख कर अनदेखी करना

bliss (ब्लिस) *n.* सम्पूर्ण सुख; परमानन्द – **blissful** a. – **blissfully** *adv.* – **blissfulness** *n.*

blister (ब्लिसटर) *n.* फफोला, छाला; सतह पर उभरा स्थान (जैसा लकड़ी पर रोगन सूखने पर पड़ जाता है) – *v.* छाले पड़ जाना – **blistering** *a.* अत्याधिक कटु, जैसे आलोचना – **blister pack** सामान लपेटने का सख्त खुरदरी सतह वाला पारदर्शी पदार्थ (प्लास्टिक) जिस पर बुलबुले बने हों

blithe (ब्लाइद) *a.* प्रसन्न; बहुत खुश, मस्त

B Litt Bachelor of Literature का संक्षेप

blitz (ब्लिट्स) *n.* अचानक ज़बरदस्त हवाई बमबारी

blitzkrieg (ब्लिट्स्क्रीग) *n.* दुश्मन को एकदम पस्त करने के लिए अचानक ज़बरदस्त फौजी हमला

blizzard (ब्लिज़र्ड) *n.* बर्फ़ का तूफान

bloat (ब्लोट) *v.* फूल या सूज जाना

blob (ब्लॉब) *n.* थक्का, विशे. तरल की बूंद; अस्पष्ट आक ति

bloc (ब्लॉक) *n.* व्यक्तियों या राष्ट्रों का (राजनीतिक) गुट

block (ब्लॉक) *n.* लकड़ी या पत्थर का ठोस, चौकोर टुकड़ा; कुन्दा; शिलाखण्ड; अवरोध; रुकावट; घिरनी; मकानों, भवनों आदि का समूह, खण्ड – *vt.* बाधा डालना; रोकना – **blockage** *n.* रुकावट – **blockbuster** *n.* अत्यंत सफल (फिल्म, पुस्तक) – **blockhead** *n.* मूर्ख; मन्द बुद्धि (व्यक्ति) – **block letters** अंग्रेजी वर्णमाला के capital अक्षर

blog (ब्लॉग) *n.* इंटरनेट पर विषय-विशेष का जानकारी-स्थल (वेबसाइट) जिसमें सबसे ताज़ा जानकारी सबसे ऊपर होती है – **blogger** *n.* ऐसी जानकारी वेबसाइट को देने वाला

blockade (ब्लॉ'केड) *n.* नाकेबन्दी; घेरा – *vt.* नाकेबन्दी करना, घेरा डालना

bloke (ब्लोक) *n. inf.* व्यक्ति; छोकरा

blond (ब्लॉण्ड) *a.* हल्के या भूरे रंग के (बाल) – *n.* भूरे बालों वाला व्यक्ति (*fem.* **blonde**)

blood (ब्लड) *n.* रक्त, खून; जाति; सगे-सम्बंधी; वंश, कुल; स्वभाव; गुस्सा – **bloodily** *adv.* – **bloodless** *a.* खून खराबे के बिना (क्रांति आदि) – **bloody** *a.* खून में सना; रक्तरंजित (क्रांति आदि) – *a./adv. sl.* भाववाचक शब्द जैसे **a bloody liar** (एकदम झूठा) में – *v.* खून से रंगना – **blood bank** रक्त (दान) बैंक – **blood donor** रक्तदानी – **blood group** रुधिरवर्ग, ब्लड-ग्रुप – **blood hound** भेदिया कुत्ता; जासूस – **blood pressure** रक्तचाप – **bloodshed** *n.* रक्तपात, खून-खराबा – **bloodshot** *a.* लाल-लाल (आंखे) – **blood-stained** *a.* रक्तरंजित – **bloodthirsty** *a.* रक्त-पिपासु, खून का प्यासा, खूंखार – **blood transfusion** एक व्यक्ति का खून दूसरे को देने की क्रिया, रक्त-आदन – **blood vessel** शिरा, रक्तवाहिका

bloom (ब्लूम) *n.* पौधे का फूल; फूल का खिलना; युवावस्था; पूर्णता; चमक; लाली *–vi.* पुष्प आना, पल्लवित होना – **blooming** *a.* खिला हुआ; प्रसन्न (मुख)

bloomer (ˈब्लूमर) *n. inf.* हास्यास्पद या मूर्खतापूर्ण भूल

blossom (ˈब्लॉसम) *n.* फूल; कली *–vi.* फूल आना; विकसित होना

blot (ब्लॉट) *n.* धब्बा, दाग; कलंक, लांछन – *vt.* धब्बा या दाग़ लगाना; मिटा देना (**-tt-**)

blouse (ब्लाउज़) *n.* (स्त्रियों की) कमर तक की ढीली-ढाली कुरती; कुरता

blow[1] (ब्लो) *vi.* फूंकना; हांफना; (हवा) चलना; बजना – *vt.* हवा फूंकना या हवा के ज़ोर से चलाना; बजाना, आवाज़ निकालना; (नाक) साफ करना; (बिजली का फ़्यूज़) उड़ा देना; *sl.* फिज़ूलखर्ची में उड़ा देना (**blew, blown**) – *n.* झोंका – **blower** *n.* धौंकनी – **blowlamp** *n.* बड़ी तेज़ आग वाला बर्नर जिससे लकड़ी/लोहे के रोगन को जलाते हैं (**blowtorch** भी) – **blow-out** *n.* गाड़ी के पहिए से अचानक हवा का निकल जाना (छेद के कारण); तेल कुंए से अनियंत्रित तेल या गैस का स्राव; *sl.* शानदार या डटकर भोजन – **blow out** बुझना; अचानक गाड़ी के टायर में छेद होना; बिजली का फ्यूज़ उड़ जाना – **blow up** विस्फोट या धमाका होना; हवा भरना; फोटो को बड़े आकार का बनाना; *inf.* अचनाक गुस्से में आ जाना – **blow-by-blow** *a.* विस्तार से (वर्णन)

blow[2] *n.* वार; धक्का; अचानक आई विपत्ति; हानि

blown BLOW का *pp.*

bludgeon (ˈब्लजन) *n.* छोटे आकार का मोटा सोटा, मोगरी – *vt.* सोंटे से मारना; (किसी को किसी काम के लिए विवश करना)

blue (ब्लू) *a.* नीला, आसमानी; गुस्से से लाल; निराशा में डूबा हुआ – *n.* नीला रंग; नील जो कपड़ों की धुलाई में काम आता है – *vt.* नीला करना; नीला रंग चढ़ाना (**blued** *pt./pp.*) – **blues** *pl. n. inf.* (बहुधा *sing v.* के साथ) उदासी; निराशा – **bluish** *a.* – **blue blood** राजघराने या कुलीन वंश के लिए प्रयुक्त – **blue chip** *a.* (कंपनी) अच्छी लाभ देने वाली – **blue-collar** *a.* औद्योगिक मज़दूरों के लिए प्रयुक्त – **blue film** अत्यंत अश्लील फिल्म – **blueprint** *n.* मानचित्र आदि की प्रति – **bluestocking** *n.* बुद्धिजीवी या विदुषी महिला

bluff *vt.* (शक्तिशाली होने का नाटक कर के) झांसा देना; रोब या धौंस से काम निकालना – *n.* झांसा

blunder (ˈब्लंडर) *n.* भद्दी भूल – *vi.* मूर्खतापूर्ण भूल करना

blunt (ब्लंट) *a.* जिसकी धार तेज़ न हो; कुन्द; कुंठित; भोथरा; स्पष्ट, रूखी (बात); मुंहफट (व्यक्ति) – *vt.* कुन्द या कुंठित करना – **bluntly** *adv.* – **bluntness** *n.* भोथरापन; रूखापन; स्पष्टवादिता

blur (ब्लर) *vt.* धुंधला या अस्पष्ट कर देना – *vi.* धुंधला हो जाना (**-rr-**) – *n.* – **blurred** *a.* धुंधला – **blurry** *a.*

blurb (ब्लर्ब) *n.* पुस्तक आदि का विज्ञापन या परिचय.

blurt (ब्लर्ट) *vt.* – **blurt out** अचानक या किसी के बिना कहे कुछ बता देना, कह डालना, फूट पड़ना

blush (ब्लश) *vi.* (लज्जा से) मुंह लाल हो जाना, शरमा या झेंप जाना – *n.*

bluster (ˈब्लस्टर) *vi.* घुड़कना, धमकाना; गरजना – *n.* – **blustering, blustery** *a.* प्रचण्ड, तेज़ (आंधी आदि)

boa (ˈबॉअ) *n.* बड़ा सांप जिसमें विष नहीं होता

boar (बॉअर) *n.* नर सूअर, बराह; जंगली सूअर

board (बॉर्ड) *n.* तख्ता; मेज; खानपान, भोजन; कम्पनी का प्रबंध-मण्डल; प्रबन्ध-परिषद; गत्ता

– *vt.* तख्ते लगाकर पाटना; प्रतिदिन खाद्य-पदार्थ या भोजन देना; चढ़ना, सवार होना – *vi.* प्रतिदिन भोजन करना – **boarder** *n.* छात्रावास आदि का निवासी – **board and lodging** खाने व रहने की व्यवस्था – **boarding card** जहाज़, विमान में बैठने का अनुमति पत्र – **boarding house** छात्रावास – **boarding school** छात्रावास सहित स्कूल – **boardroom** *n.* प्रबंध-मण्डल का सभा-भवन – **above board** जिस पर संदेह न हो सके, खरा – **on board** जहाज़ में, जहाज़ पर सवार – **go by the board** योजना आदि का कोई फल न निकलना

boast (बोस्ट) *v.* की डग या शेखी मारना – *n.* शेखी, डग, आत्मश्लाघा; गौरव; वस्तु जिस पर गौरव किया जाये – **boastful** *a.*

boat (बोट) *n.* नाव, कश्ती; जहाज़ – *vi.* नाव में सैर करना – **boating** *n.* नौका-विहार – **boathouse** *n.* शिकारा – **boatman** *n.* नाविक, मल्लाह

bob (बॉब) *vi.* ऊपर-नीचे होना; डूबना-उतराना – *vt.* झटके से चलना; (स्त्री के बाल) काट कर छोटे करना (**-bb-**) – *n.* झटक; छोटे बाल – **bobbed** *a.* छोटे कटे (बाल)

bobbin (ˈबॉबिन) *n.* फिरकी (जिस पर धागा चढ़ाते है); परेता; अटेरन

bobby (ˈबॉबि) *n. inf.* (इंग्लैंड में) पुलिस का सिपाही

bode (बोड) *vt.* का शकुन होना –**bode ill/well (for)** (के लिए) बुरा/अच्छा शकुन होना

bodice (ˈबॉडिस) *n.* स्त्रियों की पोशाक का ऊपरी भाग; चोली; कुरती

body (ˈबॉडि) *n.* शरीर, बदन, देह, काया; शरीर का मुख्य भाग; शव, लाश; किसी भी वस्तु का मुख्य भाग; सार; पिण्ड; व्यक्ति; व्यक्तियों का संगठित समूह; (आत्मा के विपरीत) पदार्थ – **bodily** *a.* शारीरिक – *adv.* सशरीर – **bodybuilding** *n.* व्यायाम द्वारा मांस-पेशिया सुद ढ़ करना – **bodyguard** *n.* अंग-रक्षक – **body warmer** बगैर आस्तीन की रूई आदि से भरी जाकिट – **bodywork** *n.* मोटरगाड़ी का ढांचा

bog (बॉग) *n.* दलदल – **boggy** *a.* दलदल वाला – **get bogged down** (वार्ता आदि) अड़चन के कारण रुक जाना

bogey (ˈबोगि) *n.* बुरी या शरारती प्रेतात्मा, हौआ – **bogeyman** *n.* (प्रायः काल्पनिक) व्यक्ति जिसके नाम से बच्चों को डराया जाए

bogie (ˈबोगि) *n.* रेलवे की यात्री गाड़ी का डिब्बा, बोगी

bogus (ˈबोगस) *a.* खोटा; बनावटी; जाली

boil[1] (बॉइल) *vi.* उबलना, *inf.* जोश या गुस्से में आना – *vt.* उबालना – *n.* उबलने की स्थिति – **boiler** *n.* उबालने का बर्तन, देग़, बायलर

boil[2] *n.* छाला

boisterous (ˈबॉइस्टरस) *a.* उच्छंखल, ऊधमी

bold (बोल्ड) *a.* निर्भीक, निडर; ध ष्ठ, ढीठ; मोटा (टाइप) – **boldly** *adv.* हिम्मत से, बेधड़क – **boldness** *n.*

boll (बोल) *n.* कपास आदि का डोडा; बीजकोष

bollard (ˈबॉलर्ड) *n.* सड़क या पगडंडी पर लगी सीमा दर्शानि की खूंटी या खूंटा

bolster (ˈबोल्स्टर) *vt.* सहारा देना, थामना – *n.* मसनद; सहारा (वि. इमारत को); हौसला

bolt (बोल्ट) *n.* काबला; छलांग; बिजली या गाज; कपड़े का थान – *vt.* काबले से कसना; जल्दी जल्दी खाना, भकोसना, सटकना – *vi.* एकदम भाग जाना; रस्से तुड़ाकर भागना

bomb (बॉम) *n.* बम, गोला *sl.* बहुत बड़ी राशि – **the bomb** परमाणु बम – *vt.* बमों से आक्रमण करना – **bombard** (बॉम्ˈबार्ड) *vt.* बम बरसाना, गोलाबारी करना; आपत्तियों की बौछार करना – **bombardier** *n.* आर्टिलरी (गोलंदाज) फौज का छोटा अफसर –

bombardment *n.* गोलाबारी – **bomber** *n.* बमवर्षक विमान – **bombshell** *n.* बम का ख़ोल; आश्चर्यजनक बात – *inf.* अत्यंत सुन्दर लड़की

bombast (ˈबॉम्बैस्ट) *n.* आडम्बरपूर्ण भाषा

bona fide (ˈबोनˈफ़ाइडि) *a./n. Lat.* सदाशयता (से), नेक नीयती (से) – **bona fides** (ˈफ़ाइडीज़) *a./n.* सदाशयता, नेक नीयती

bonanza (बˈनैन्ज़ूअ) *n.* अचानक मिलने वाली समृद्धि या सौभाग्य

bond (बॉण्ड) *n.* बेड़ी, बंधन; सम्बंध; पैसा लौटाने का लिखित वचन, बंधनपत्र; समझौता या अनुबन्ध पत्र, इकरारनामा –*vt.* बांधना; जोड़ना

bondage (ˈबॉण्डिज) *n.* दासता, गुलामी

bone (बोन) *n.* हड्डी – **bony** *a.* पतला-दुबला, मरियल

bonfire (ˈबॉन्फ़ाइअर) *n.* खुले में जलाई आग, अलाव

bonkers (बॉङ्कर्ज़) *a. sl.* पागल; ख़ब्ती

bonnet (ˈबॉनिट) *n.* स्त्रियों की टोपी जिसे रस्सी से ठोड़ी के नीचे बांधते हैं; टोपी; कार आदि के इंजन का ढक्कन

bonny (ˈबॉनि) *a.* सुन्दर, कमनीय

bonsai (ˈबॉन्साइ) *n.* गमलों में बौने पेड़ या झाड़ियां (उगाने की कला)

bonus (ˈबोनस) *n.* अतिरिक्त, (अप्रत्याशित) राशि या भेंट (*pl.* **bonuses**); लाभ का हिस्सा जो कर्मचारियों को दिया जाता है, लाभांश, बोनस

boo (बू) *interj.* तिरस्कार या नापसंद होने का चिन्ह; छी-छी – *v.* शोरगुल करना

booby (ˈबूबि) *n.* मूर्ख व्यक्ति – **booby trap** कोई वस्तु जिसमें विस्फोटक पदार्थ छिपाए गए हों जिसे हाथ लगाते ही विस्फोट हो जाता है

book (बुक) *n.* पुस्तक, किताब; साहित्यिक कृति; ग्रंथ का मुख्य खण्ड; हिसाब बही-खाता – *vt.* टिकट या कमरा आदि आरक्षित करना या कराना; अभियुक्त पर अभियोग लगाना; चालान करना – **booking** *n.* आरक्षण (टिकट आदि का) – **bookish** *a.* जिसे पढ़ने का शौक हो, पांडित्यपूर्ण – **bookbinder** *n.* जिल्दसाज़ – **bookcase** *n.* किताबें रखने की अलमारी – **book-keeping** *n.* व्यापार के बही खाते रखने का काम – **booklet** *n.* पुस्तिका – **bookworm** *n.* जो हर समय किताबों से चिपका रहे, किताबी कीड़ा

boom[1] (बूम) *n.* व्यापादिक कार्य कलाप में अचानक वृद्धि, तेजी, गरम बाज़ारी; समृद्धि – *vi.* समृद्ध हो जाना

boom[2] *vi./n.* गरज (की आवाज़ पैदा करना); धड़ाका या गूंज (पैदा होना)

boomerang (ˈबूमरैङ) *n.* आस्ट्रेलिया के आदिवासियों द्वारा फैंका जाने वाला लकड़ी का टेढ़ा हथियार जो फ़ैकने वाले के पास वापिस आ जाता है – *vi.* तदबीर उल्टी पड़ जाना; उल्टा असर होना, उल्टी आंतें गले पड़ना

boon (बून) *n.* सहायक या अनुकूल वस्तु; वरदान

boor (बुअर) *n.* असभ्य या गंवार व्यक्ति – **boorish** *a.* असभ्य, गंवारू

boost (बूस्ट) *n.* प्रोत्साहन; सहायता; बढ़ावा; बढ़त या वृद्धि – *vt.* प्रोत्साहन देना, वृद्धि करना – **booster** *n. Med.* पिछली खुराक का असर बढ़ाने के लिए दी गई दवा की खुराक

boot[1] (बूट) *n.* टख़ने तक का जूता, बूट; कार आदि में सामान रखने का स्थान, डिकी; *inf.* लात मारने की क्रिया – *vt. inf.* किसी को लात मारना

booth (बूथ) *n.* दूकान; छोटा कमरा या कोष्ठ – **polling/voting booth** मतदान स्थान

bootleg (ˈबूट्लेग) *v.* गैर कानूनी माल, विशे. शराब, बनाना, ले जाना या बेचना – **bootlegger** *n.* अवैध शराब बेचने वाला

booty (ˈबूटि) *n.* लूट का माल

booze (बूज़) *n./vi. inf.* ज्यादा शराब (पीना)

borax (ˈबॉरैक्स) *n.* बोरौन से बना पानी में घुल जाने वाला सफेद पदार्थ, सुहागा

border (ˈबॉर्डर) *n.* सीमांत प्रदेश; किनारा, हाशिया; सीमा; बाग की पट्टी – *vt.* हाशिया या किनारा लगाना – *vi.* साथ लगना – **borderline** *n.* सीमारेखा

bore[1] (ˈबॉर) *vt.* छेद करना – *n.* छेद; बन्दूक की नली का व्यास

bore[2] *vt.* ऊबा देना – *n.* कानखाऊ, ऊबा देने वाला व्यक्ति – **boredom** (ˈबॉर्डम) *n.* ऊब, बोरियत – **boring** *a.* ऊबा देने वाला (विषय)

bore[4] BEAR का *pt.*

born (बॉर्न) BEAR का *pp.*

borne (बॉर्न) BEAR का *pp.*

boron (ˈबॉरॉन) *n.* रासायनिक तत्व जो इस्पात को कड़ा बनाने के काम आता है

borough (ˈबर्अ) *n.* नगर

borrow (ˈबॉरो) *vt.* किसी से उधार या अमानत पर लेना; उधार लेना; (किसी के विचार आदि) अपना लेना

bosom (ˈबुज़म) *n.* (*arch., lit.*) वक्षःस्थल, छाती; भावनाओं का केन्द्र

boss[1] (बॉस) *n.* किसी संगठन का प्रभारी या स्वामी, मालिक – *v.* प्रभारी होना; दूसरों पर रोब गांठना – **bossy** *a.* दबंग, धांसू, धाकड़, रोब जमाने वाला

botany (ˈबॉटनि) *n.* वनस्पति विज्ञान – **botanical** (बˈटैनिकल) *a.* वनस्पति-विज्ञान संबंधी – **botanist** *n.* वनस्पति शास्त्री

botch (बॉच) *vt.* भोंडे तरीके से काम कर के काम खराब कर देना

both (बोथ) *a./pron.* दोनों – *adv./conj.* भी

bother (ˈबॉदर) *vt.* परेशान या तंग करना; घबरा देना – *vi.* कष्ट उठाना; चिंता करना – *n.* कष्ट, चिंता

bottle (ˈबॉट्ल) *n.* बोतल, शीशी; उसमें डाला द्रव – *vt.* बोतल में भरना; रोकना, दबाना (भावनाऐं आदि) – **bottlebrush** *n.* साफ करने का बुरुश – **bottle-gourd** *n.* लौकी – **bottleneck** *n.* संकरा रास्ता जो यातायात में अड़चन पैदा करे; जो उत्पादन में बाधा उत्पन्न करे; अड़चन, अवरोध

bottom (ˈबॉटम) *n.* निचला भाग, पैंदा; समुद्र या नदी का तला; चूतड़

bougainvill(a)ea (बूगन्ˈविलिअ) *n.* गरम प्रदेशों की एक बेल जिसमें लाल या बैंगनी गुच्छे लगते हैं, बोगन विलिया

bough (बाउ) *n.* व क्ष की टहनी

bought (बॉट) BUY का *pt./pp.*

boulder (ˈबोल्डर) *n.* बड़ी गोल चट्टान

boulevard (ˈबूल्वार, ˈबूल्वार्द) *n.* चौड़ी सड़क; मुख्य मार्ग

bounce (बाउन्स) *v.* उछालना (गेन्द आदि) – *n.* चैक का बैंक से लौटना (बिना अदायगी); उछलने की क्रिया; किस वस्तु में उछलने की क्षमता; *inf.* बल; तेज, ओज; उत्साह

bound[1] (बाउंड) *n.* सीमा – *vt.* सीमित करना – **boundary** (ˈबाउंड्रि) *n.* सीमा, हद – **boundless** *a.* असीम, अंतहीन

bound[2] *vi.* कूदना; छलांग लगाना – *n.*

bound[3] *a.* किसी स्थान की ओर गतिमान, जैसे **outward bound**

bound[4] BIND का *pt./pp.* – *a.* जिसने प्रण ले रखा हो, आबद्ध; निश्चित; सम्बद्ध या बंधा हुआ

bounty (ˈबाउन्टि) *n.* उदारता; भेंट या तोहफा, इनाम; उदार दान – **bounteous** (ˈबाउंटिअस), **bountiful** (ˈबाउंटिफुल) *a.* भरपूर; उदार, मुक्तहस्त

bouquet (बूˈके) *n.* फूलों का गुच्छा, गुलदस्ता; सुगन्धि (शराब की); प्रशंसा; बधाई

bourbon (ˈबर्बन) *n.* *US* मक्की से बनी व्हिस्की

bourgeois (ˈबुअर्ज़वा) *n./a.* (बहुधा तिरस्कार से) धनी मध्यवर्ग का सदस्य – **the bourgeoisie** (बुअर्ज़वा ˈज़ी) मध्यमवर्ग

bout (बाउट) *n.* अवधि, दौर; (बीमारी का) दौरा; बल परीक्षा; प्रतियोगिता या लड़ाई (जैसे मुक्केबाज़ी, कुश्ती)

boutique (बू´टीक) *n.* छोटी सी दुकान, विशे. फैशनवाले कपड़ों की
bovine (´बोवाइन) *a.* बैल या गाय का, गोजातीय
bow[1] (बो) *n.* धनुष; (सारंगी आदि का) गज़; रिबन आदि की गांठ़ – *vt.* झुकाना – *vi.* झुकना – **bowlegged** *a.* जिसकी टांगे मुड़ी हुई हों
bow[2] *vi.* (आदर से) झुक जाना; नमस्कार करना; मान लेना; (किसी के आगे) झुक जाना – *vt.* नीचे को झुकाना; कुचल देना – *n.* झुककर अभिवादन
bowel (´बाउअल) *n.* (बहुधा *pl.*) अंतड़ी का निचला भाग (विशे. मलत्याग के सन्दर्भ में); किसी वस्तु का आन्तरिक हिस्सा
bower (´बॉउअर) *n.* लतामण्डप; कुंज
bowl[1] (बोल) *n.* कटोरा, चौड़ा गहरा बरतन; इस रूप का भूमिक्षेत्र
bowl[2] *n.* लकड़ी की गेंद – *vt.* गेंद फेंकना – **bowler** *n.* (क्रिकेट आदि में) गेंदबाज़
box[1] (बॉक्स) *n.* (लकड़ी का) संदूक; गत्ते का डिब्बा, बकसा; कोठड़ी, खाना; बक्से जैसा प्रकोष्ठ; *inf.* टी. वी. – *vt.* बक्से में डालना; बंद कर देना – **box office** (सिनेमा, थियेटर में) टिकटघर; कलाकार या क ति (फिल्म आदि) के लिए जनता में आकर्षण, बॉक्स ऑफिस
box[2] *v.* मुक्केबाज़ी करना – *vt* मारना – *n.* मुक्का – **boxer** *n.* मुक्केबाज़; बुलडॉग जैसा कुत्ता
boy (बॉइ) *n.* लड़का; युवक – *interj.* आश्चर्यबोधक शब्द – **boyhood** *n.* लड़कपन – **boyish** *a.* – **boyfriend** *n.* प्रेमी
boycott (´बॉइकॉट) *vt.* बहिष्कार करना – *n.* बहिष्कार, बाइकाट
bra (ब्रा) *n.* brassiere का संक्षिप्त रूप
brace (ब्रेस) *n.* छेद करने का औज़ार, हथबर्मा, बंधनी; पट्टी; जोड़ा; दांत सीधे करने की तारें – (~ **s**) *pl.* गेलिस; धनुकोष्ठक { } – *vt.* (धक्का सहने के लिए) अपने आप को तैयार करना; सहारा देना, सुद ढ़ बनाना – **bracing** *a.* स्फूर्तिदायक – **bracelet** *n.* कंगन – *pl. sl.* हथकड़ी
bracket (´ब्रैकिट) *n.* दीवारगीर, ब्रैकट; टेक; बंधनी; वर्ग – *pl.* कोष्ठक {} () – *vt.* कोष्ठकों में रखना; जोड़ना; एक ही श्रेणी में रख देना
brackish (´ब्रैकिश) *a.* (पानी) खारा; अप्रिय
brag (ब्रैग) *vi.* शेख़ी मारना; डींग हांकना (**-gg-**) – *n.* शेख़ी, डींग – **braggart** (ब्रैगर्ट) *n.* शेखीबाज़, बड़बोला
braid (ब्रेड) *vt.* गूंथना; गोटा लगाना
braille (ब्रेल) *n.* उभरे हुए अक्षर छापने की प्रणाली (जिससे कि नेत्रहीन उन्हें छू कर पढ़ सकें), ब्रेल
brain (ब्रेन) *n.* मस्तिष्क, दिमाग – *vt.* सिर पर चोट मार कर जान ले लेना – **brainless** *a.* मूर्ख –**brainy** *a.* समझबूझ वाला – **brainchild** *n.* (मस्तिष्क की) उपज़, आविष्कार – **brain drain** अत्यंत कुशल व्यक्तियों (डाक्टर, इंजीनियर आदि) का स्वदेश छोड़कर दूसरे देश धन प्राप्ति के लिए जाना – **brainstorming** *n.* समस्या- समाधान के लिए गहन विचार-विमर्श – **brainwash** *vt.*किसी के विश्वासों या विचारों को बदल देना या बिगाड़ देना – **brainwave** *n.* अचानक आया विचार, सूझ
brake[1] (ब्रेक) *n.* पहिए या गाड़ी का ब्रेक – *vt.* ब्रेक लगाना, गाड़ी की गति धीमी करना
bran (ब्रैन) *n.* भूसी, चोकर
branch (ब्रांच) *n.* पेड़ की शाखा, डाल, डाली; किसी संगठन का अंग, शाखा – *vi.* डाल या शाखाएं निकलना या फूटना; अलग (रास्ता) हो जाना; फैल जाना
brand (ब्रैंड) *n.* छाप, छापा, ट्रेडमार्क; प्रकार, किस्म; गरम लोहे से दगने का निशान, दाग़; बदनामी का दाग़, कलंक – *vt.* गरम लोहे से दाग़ना; निशान या छाप लगाना; कलंक लगाना – **brand-new** *a.* बिल्कुल नया – **branded product** अच्छी कंपनी का उत्पादन

brandish (ब्रैंडिश) *vt.* घुमाना, लहराना (तलवार आदि)

brandy (ब्रैन्डि) *n.* ब्रांडी

brash (ब्रैश) *a.* निडर, ध ष्ठ, ढीठ

brass (ब्रास) *n.* पीतल; किसी वाद्य व ंद में पीतल के वाद्य; *inf.* रुपया-पैसा; *inf.* (सेना के) अधिकारी

brassiere (ब्रैसिअर, ब्रैज़िअर) *n.* अंगिया, चोली, स्त्री का नीचे पहनने का वस्त्र जो स्तनों को ढंकता है

brat (ब्रैट) *n.* बच्चे के लिए तिरस्कारपूर्ण शब्द, छोकरा

bravado (ब्र'वाडो) *n.* बहादुरी का दिखावा; डींग

brave (ब्रेव़) *a.* वीर, बहादुर; बढ़िया; शानदार – *n.* योद्धा – *vt.* सामना करना; ललकारना – **bravely** *adv.* – **bravery** *n.*

bravo (ब्रा'वो) *interj.* शाबाश! बहुत अच्छा!

brawl (ब्रॉल) *vi.* मारपीट व शोर शराबा करना – *n.* मारपीट

brawn (ब्रॉन) *n.* शारीरिक बल या शक्ति; सूअर के मांस का अचार – **brawny** *a.* हट्टा-कट्टा

bray (ब्रे) *n.* गधे की आवाज़, रेंकने का स्वर – *vi.* रेंकना

braze (ब्रेज़) *vt.* पीतल या जस्ते का टांका लगाना

brazen (ब्रेज़न) *a.* पीतल का या उस जैसा; ध ष्ठ, ढीठ, निर्लज्ज, बेशर्म – *vt.* ध ष्ठता या ढिठाई से कोई काम करना – **brazenness** *n.* ध ष्ठता, बेशर्मी

brazier[1] (ब्रेज़िअर) *n.* पीतल का काम करने वाला, ठठेरा

brazier[2] *n.* जलते कोयले रखने का पात्र, अंगीठी

breach (ब्रीच) *n.* दरार; नियम या कर्तव्य का उल्लंघन – *vt.* दरार डालना – **breach of contract** समझौते का उल्लघंन – **breach of peace** मार-पीट, दंगा

bread (ब्रेड) *n.* रोटी; डबल रोटी; भोजन; *sl.* रुपया-पैसा – **breadwinner** *n.* (परिवार का) कमाऊ व्यक्ति

breadth (ब्रेड्थ) *n.* चौड़ाई; उदारता

break (ब्रेक) *vt.* तोड़ना; टुकड़े करना; फोड़ना; चूर-चूर करना; नष्ट कर देना; पालन न करना या उल्लंघन करना; (~ **news**) बता देना; विद्युत-धारा में बाधा डालना; (रिकार्ड) तोड़ना; दिवालिया बना देना; (असर) कम करना; (घोड़े को) सधाना; (कूटभाषा) पढ़ लेना; का अचानक शुरू हो जाना (रोना, गाना, हंसी, आंसू); *Cricket* (गेंद का) टप्पा पड़ने पर रास्ता बदल देना – *vi.* टूटना; टुकड़े होना या चूर-चूर होना; अलग होना; खुल जाना; प्रकट होना; दरार पड़ जाना; (लहरों का) टकराना; (~ **with**) से झगड़ा हो जाना; भर्रा जाना; (~ **for**) भोजन के लिए काम रोकना (**broke, broken**) – *n.* भंग, दरार; रास्ता या छिद्र; संबन्ध-विच्छेद; क्रमभंग; अवकाश, विराम, अंतराल; *inf.* अवसर; प्रभात; *Cricket* गेंद का पिच पर गिर कर रास्ता बदलने की क्रिया; *Tennis* प्रतिद्वंदी की सर्विस तोड़ने की क्रिया – **breakable** *a.* – **breakage** *n.* टूट-फूट – **breaker** *n.* (विद्युत सर्कट को) तोड़ने वाला साधन; चट्टानों से टकराती लहर – **breakdown** *n.* एकदम बीमार पड़ जाना – **breakfast** (ब्रेक्फ़स्ट) *n.* नाश्ता – **break-in** *n.* चोरों द्वारा सेंध – **break-neck** *a.* अंधाधुंध, तेज़ (रफ्तार) – **breakthrough** *n.* सफलता; महत्वपूर्ण खोज या सुराग़ – **break-up** *n.* विवाह-संबध टूटना; कंपनी आदि का टुकड़ों में बंटना

breast (ब्रेस्ट) *n.* छाती, वक्षःस्थल, स्त्री के स्तन या कुच; भावनओं का केन्द्र; बाहर को निकली कोई उठान – *vt.* मुकाबला या सामना करना; दौड़ के अन्त में फीते से छाती भिड़ना – **breastfeed** *vt.* (मां का बच्चे को) अपना दूध पिलाना – **breaststroke** *n.* तैराकी की एक शैली

breath (ब्रेथ) *n.* सांस; दम; जीवन; हल्की हवा –

breathe (ब्रीद) – *vi.* सांस लेना; जीना; थोड़ा रुकना; सुस्ताना – *vt.* (हवा) सांस में छोड़ना या खींचना; धीमे बोलना, फुसफुसाना – **breather** (ब्रीदर) *n.* थोड़ी देर का विश्राम – **breathing** *n.* – **breathless** (ब्रेथ्लिस) *a.* जिसका सांस फूल रहा हो – **breathtaking** *a.* विस्मयकारी; बहुत सुंदर, अनुपम

Breathalyser (ब्रेथलाइज़र) **R** यंत्र जिससे श्सास का विश्लेषण कर के पी गयी शराब की मात्रा आंकी जा सकती है, श्वासपरीक्षक

bred BREED का *pt./pp*

breech (ब्रीच) *n.* नितम्ब, चूतड़; किसी भी वस्तु, विशे. बन्दूक का पिछला भाग – **breeches** (ब्रिचिज़) *pl. n.* तंग पतलून जो घुड़सवारी के लिए पहनते हैं

breed (ब्रीड) *vt.* उत्पन्न करना; जन्म देना, पालना – *vi.* पैदा होना; बच्चे पैदा करना (**bred** *pt./pp.*) – *n.* बच्चे; नस्ल, जाति या वंश; किस्म – **breeder** *n.* जानवर (मवेशी) पालने वाला व्यक्ति, प्रजनक – **breeding** *n.* अच्छा लालन-पालन, शिक्षा – **breeder reactor** परमाणु रिऐक्टर (संयंत्र)

breeze (ब्रीज़) *n.* मंद समीर – **breezily** *adv.* – **breezy** (ब्रीज़ि) *a.* जहां हवा बह रही हो; ज़िन्दादिल, हंसमुख, चुस्त

brevity (ब्रेविटि) *n.* संक्षिप्त अभिव्यक्ति, संक्षिप्तता; लघुता (समय की)

brew (ब्रू) *vt.* शराब बनाना जैसे माल्ट से बीअर; (गरम पानी डालकर) चाय आदि बनाना; रचना (षड्यंत्र आदि) – *vi.* तैयारी में होना – *n.* तैयार किया गया पेय (शराब, चाय आदि) – **brewer** *n.* – **brewery** *n.* शराब का कारख़ाना

bribe (ब्राइब) *n.* घूस, रिश्वत – *vt.* घूस या रिश्वत देना – **bribery** (ब्राइबरि) *n.* घूस, रिश्वत

brick (ब्रिक) *n.* ईंट – *vt.* ईंटों से चिनाई करना या (कोई रास्ता आदि) बंद कर देना – **bricklayer** *n.* राजगीर

bride (ब्राइड) *n.* दुल्हन, नववधु – **bridal** (ब्राइड्ल) *a.* नव-वधु का या विवाह-सम्बंधी – **bridegroom** (ब्राइड्ग्रूम) *n.* दूल्हा – **bridesmaid** (ब्राइड्ज़्मेड) *n.* वधू की सखी

bridge[1] (ब्रिज) *n.* पुल, दूसरे हिस्सों को मिलाने या सहारा देने वाली वस्तु, टेक; जहाज़ पर बना संकरा मंच; नाक का ऊपरी भाग, बांसा, नकली दांत जो प्राक तिक दांत से बंधा होता है – *vt.* पर पुल बनाना

bridge[2] *n.* ताश का एक खेल, ब्रिज

bridle (ब्राइड्ल) *n.* घोड़े के साज़ का वह भाग जो उसके सिर और मुंह पर बांधा जाता है, बाग, रोक – *vt.* को लगाम लगाना -- *vi.* – **bridle at** पर नाराज़गी प्रकट करना – **bridle path** रास्ता जहां घोड़े चल सकते हों

brief (ब्रीफ़) *a.* संक्षिप्त; थोड़े समय का, अल्प; अपर्याप्त – *n.* वकील के लिए तैयार किया गया मुकदमे का सारांश – (~ **s**) *pl.* चड्डी, जांघिया – *vt.* विवरण या आदेश देना – **briefing** (ब्रीफ़िङ) *n.* आदेश या जानकारी देने का काम – **briefly** *adv.* – **briefcase** (ब्रीफ़केस) *n.* काग़ज पत्र ले जाने का छोटा बक्सा, ब्रीफ़केस

brigade (ब्रि'गेड) *n.* सेना का एक अंग (जो डिवीज़न से छोटा होता है); किसी कार्य विशेष के लिए संगठित समूह – **brigadier** (ब्रिग'डिअर) *n.* ब्रिगेड का सेनापति, ब्रिगेडियर

bright (ब्राइट) *a.* चमकीला, प्रकाश भरा; प्रसन्नचित्त, चालाक, तेज – **brighten** *vt.* (**brighten up** भी) – **brightly** *adv.* – **brightness** *n.* चमक, प्रकाश

brilliant (ब्रिलयंट) *a.* चमकता हुआ; शानदार; प्रतिभाशाली; वैभवशाली या प्रतापी – **brilliance, brilliancy** *n.* चमक, प्रभा; प्रतिभा – **brilliantly** *adv.*

brim (ब्रिम) *n.* किनारा, विशे. नदी, प्याले या हैट का – **brimful** *a.* – **brimless** *a.* किनारे रहित (हैट) – **brimming** *a.* भरपूर

brimstone (´ब्रिम्स्टोन) *n.* गंधक
brine (ब्राइन) *n.* खारा पानी, नमकीन पानी; अचार
bring (ब्रिङ) *vt.* लाना; साथ ले जाना; पहुंचाना; बना देना (**brought** *pt/pp.*) – **bring about** का कारण बनना – **bring down** गिरा देना (सरकार, वायुयान आदि) – **bring off** (कार्य में) सफल होना – **bring out** स्पष्ट करना; प्रकाशित करना – **bring up** (सवाल) उठाना; (बच्चे को) पालना
brink (ब्रिंक) *n.* किसी ढालू स्थान का ऊपरी भाग, किनारा, कगार; बहुत नज़दीक
brisk (ब्रिस्क) *a.* फुर्तीला, तेज़; स्फूर्तिपूर्ण
bristle (´ब्रिसल) *n.* छोटा कड़ा बाल – *vi.* (बाल) खड़े होना; गुस्सा हो जाना
brittle (´ब्रिटल) *a.* जो आसानी से टूट जाय, भुरभुरा, कमज़ोर, भंगुर; रूखा
broad (ब्रॉड) *a.* चौड़ा, खुला; अश्लील, गंवारू (मज़ाक); सामान्य; उदार; बोली या क्षेत्र विशेष का (उच्चारण) – **broaden** *vt.* चौड़ा करना, फैलाना – **broadly** *adv.* मोटे तौर पर – **broadcast** (´ब्रॉड्कास्ट) – *vt.* रेडियो या टेलीविज़न पर प्रसारित करना; (बीज) फैलाना (**broadcast** *pt/pp.*) – *n.* रेडियो या टेलीविज़न पर प्रसारण, प्रोग्राम – **broadcaster** *n.* प्रसारक – **broadminded** *a.* सहिष्णु, विशाल हृदय – **broadside** *n.* एक ओर की सभी तोपें दागने की क्रिया; कड़ी आलोचना, घोर निंदा
broadband (बॉडबैंड) *n.* *Computers* इंटरनेट पर तीव्र गति से जानकारी, चित्र आदि के संचार का तरीका
brocade (ब्रो´केड) *n.* ज़री, कमख्वाब, कमखाब
broccoli (´ब्रॉकलि) *n.* एक प्रकार की फूलगोभी
brochure (´ब्रोश्युअर) *n.* पुस्तिका
broil[2] *vt.* भूनना
broke (ब्रोक) BREAK का *pt.*– *a. inf.* खाली जेब, तंग हाल – **broken** (´ब्रोकन) – BREAK का *pp.*
broker (´ब्रोकर) *n.* दलाल, आढ़तिया – **brokerage** (´ब्रोकरिज) *n.* दलाली
brolly (´ब्रॉलि) *n. inf.* छाता
bromide (´ब्रोमाइड) *n.* दवाओं और फोटोग्राफ़ी में काम आने वाला एक रसायन
bromine (´ब्रोमीन) *n.* एक तरल रसायन जो रासायनिक काम में आता है
bronchial (´ब्रॉङकिअल) *a.* श्वासनली सम्बन्धी – **bronchitis** (ब्रॉङ´काइटिस) *n.* श्वासनली की सूजन
brontosaurus (ब्रॉण्ट´सॉरस) *n.* इतिहास से पहले के युग का एक विशालकाय घासखोर डाइनोसॉर
bronze (ब्रॉन्ज़) *n.* तांबे और रांगे का मिश्रण, कांसा – *a.* कांसे का बना या उस जैसा – *vt.* कांसे जैसा बनाना – **Bronze Age** *n.* – **the Bronze Age** आज से लगभग 6000 से 4000 वर्ष पहले का समय जब मानव हथियारों आदि के लिए कांसे का प्रयोग करता था, कांस्य युग
brooch (ब्रोच) *n.* जड़ाऊ पिन
brood (ब्रूड) *n.* बच्चों विशे. पक्षियों के एक बार में पैदा हुए बच्चों का झुण्ड; समूह – *v.* (मुर्गी का) अंडे सेने के लिए बैठना; ध्यानमग्न होना; किसी बात को सोच कर परेशान होना
brook[1] (ब्रुक) *n.* छोटी नदी, सरिता – **brooklet** (´ब्रुक्लिट) *n.* छोटी सरिता
brook[2] *vt.* सहना, बर्दाश्त करना
broom (ब्रूम) *n.* झाड़ू, बुहारी; पीले रंग के फूलों वाली झाड़ी – **broomstick** *n.* झाड़ू का हत्था
broth (ब्रॉथ) *n.* गाढ़ा शोरबा
brothel (´ब्रॉथल) *n.* वेश्यालय, कोठा
brother (´ब्रदर) *n.* भाई; निकट सम्बन्धी – **brotherhood** *n.* भाई चारा; बिरादरी; भ्रातृसंघ – **brother-in-law** *n.* पति या पत्नी का भाई; देवर; जेठ; साला; बहनोई; बहिन का पति, नन्दोई; साढू

brought BRING का *pt./pp.*
brow (ब्राउ) *n.* (**eyebrow** भी) भौं, भृकुटी; माथा; (पहाड़ी का) किनारा – **browbeat** (ˈब्राउबीट) *vt.* धौंस देना, धमकाना (**browbeat** *pt.*, **brow-beaten** *pp.*)
brown (ब्राउन) *a.* भूरे रंग का – *n.* भूरा रंग – *v.* पका कर भूरा बनाना या करना – **brown sugar** शक्कर; एक नशीला पदार्थ
browse (ब्राउज़) *vi.* पुस्तक के पन्ने उलटना (खरीदने से पहले); (पशु का) कोपलें पत्ते आदि चरना; *Computers* इंटरनेट पर जानकारी-स्थल (**websites**) का अवलोकन करना – **browser** *n. Computers* इंटरनेट से संर्पक का माध्यम (प्रोग्राम)
bruise (ब्रूज़) *vt.* ऐसी चोट लगना कि त्वचा न कटे, गुमटा पड़ना – *n.*
brunch (ब्रंच) *n. inf.* सुबह के नाश्ते और दोपहर के खाने का सम्मिश्रण
brunette (ब्रूˈनेंट) *n.* श्वेत जाति की गहरे भूरे बालों वाली स्त्री, श्यामला – *a.* गहरा भूरा
brunt (ब्रंट) *n.* आक्रमण का आघात; जोर; मुख्य आघात (आक्रमण, तीव्र आलोचना का)
brush (ब्रश) *n.* कूंची; बुरुश; बुरुश से साफ़ करने की क्रिया; हल्का स्पर्श; भिड़ंत; घने बालों वाली पूंछ; झाड़ी; बिजली के जेनरेटर का एक पुर्जा – *vt.* बुरुश मारना या उससे साफ़ करना
brusque (ब्रुस्क, ब्रस्क) *a.* रूखा, अक्खड़
brute (ब्रूट) *n.* पशु, जीव (मानव को छोड़कर); अक्खड़, असभ्य और दुष्ट व्यक्ति – *a.* पाश्विक; बर्बर; विषयी; बुद्धिहीन – **brutal** (ˈब्रूटल) *a.* पशु जैसा, निर्मम या निर्दय – **brutality** (ब्रूˈटैलिटि) *n.* – **brutalize** (ˈब्रूटलाइज़) *vt.*
B.Sc. Bachelor of Science का संक्षेप
bubble (ˈबबल) *n.* बुलबुला; सारहीन या खोखली वस्तु – *vi.* बुलबुले उठना; बुदबुदाना; खदबदाना – **bubbly** *a.* – **bubble wrap, bubble pack** प्लास्टिक की शीट जो हवा के बुलबुलों से भरी होती है और सामान लपेटने के काम आती है
buck (बक) *n.* (हिरन आदि का) नर; कांधी मारने की क्रिया; *US, sl.* डालर – *v.* (घोड़े का) उछल कूद कर के सवार को गिराने की कोशिश करना; विरोध करना; (समस्या आदि) से बचना – **buckshot** *n.* (कारतूस में) छर्रा – **buckteeth** *pl. n.* बाहर निकले हुए ऊपर के दांत – **buck up** खुश करना, हौसला देना – **pass the buck** इलज़ाम या जिम्मेवारी दूसरे पर डालना
bucket (ˈबकिट) *n.* बालटी; डोल – *vt.* बाल्टी में रखना या ले जाना
buckle (ˈबकल) *n.* पेटी आदि बांधने का बकसुआ – *vt.* टूटना; झुकना
buckram (ˈबक्रम) *n.* गोंद आदि से कड़ा किया गया मोटा कपड़ा जो कोट आदि में अस्तर के काम आता है; बुकरम
bucolic (ब्यूˈकॉलिक) *a.* देहाती, ग्रामीण
bud (बड) *n.* कली; गुंचा – *vi.* खिलना, फूलना – *vt.* कलम लगाना (**budded** *pt./pp.*) – **budding** *a.* उभरता हुआ (कलाकार आदि); प्रारंभिक (प्यार आदि)
buddy (ˈबडि) *n. inf* मित्र; बन्धु
budge (बज) *vt.* सरकाना, हिलाना – *vi.* हटना, परे होना; सरकना
budget (ˈबजिट) *n.* वार्षिक वित्तीय विवरण, बजट – *vi.* बजट या खर्च की योजना तैयार करना
buff[1] (बफ़) *n.* भैंस या बैल की खाल से बना चमड़ा; हल्का पीला रंग; पालिश करने का पैड – *vt.* पालिश करना; चमकाना
buffalo (ˈबफ़लो) *n.* भैंस या भैंसा (*pl.* **-lo(e)s**)
buffer (ˈबफ़र) *n.* टक्कर रोकने का उपकरण; टक्कर, रोक
buffet[1] (ˈबफ़िट) *n.* प्रहार; थप्पड़; दुर्भाग्य – *vt.* थप्पड़ मारना; प्रहार करना

buffet² (´बुफ़े) *n.* काउंटर या मेज़ जहां पकवान रखे जाते हैं; भोज जहां अतिथि स्वयं अपने लिए व्यंजन परोसते हैं; खाने की मेज़ के पास रखी अलमारी

buffoon (ब´फून) *n.* भांड; विदूषक; मसख़रा – **buffoonery** *n.* भंडौती; मसख़रापन

bug (बग) *n.* कोई छोटा कीड़ा; खटमल; *inf.* रोगाणु; छिपाया गया माइक्रोफोन (जिस से वहां की बातें सुनी जा सकें) – *vt.* इस प्रकार का माइक्रोफोन लगाना

bugbear (´बगबेंअर) *n.* कोई चीज़ जिस से अकारण भय हो; हौआ; जूजू; परेशान करने वाली वस्तु

bugger (´बगर) *n.* लौंडिबाज़; *vulg. sl.* अप्रिय व्यक्ति या वस्तु

bugle (´ब्यूगल) *n.* एक बाजा; बिगुल

build (बिल्ड) *v.* बनाना, बनाना, निर्माण करना (**built** *pt./pp.*) – *n.* गठन, बनावट, रचना – **builder** *n.* भवन निर्माता – **building** (´बिल्डिंग) *n.* भवन, इमारत – **build-up** *n.* वद्धि

bulb (बल्ब) *n.* पौधे की गोलाकार जड़ जैसे प्याज़ की; बिजली का बल्ब – **bulbous** (´बल्बस) *a.*

bulge (बल्ज) *n.* उभार; अस्थायी व द्धि – *vi.* बाहर को निकलना; उभरना

bulk (बल्क) *n.* आकार; परिणाम; अधिकतर भाग माल (जो कह भेजा जाय) – **bulky** *a.* भारी, वज़नी

bull¹ (बुल) *n.* सांड, अन्य अनेक पशुओं का नर – **bulldog** *n.* बुलडॉग कुत्ता – **bulldoze** (´बुल्डोज़) *v.* बुलडोज़र से (भवन आदि) गिराना, ज़मीन समतल करना, (मिट्टी) हटाना आदि; ज़बरदस्ती कुछ करवाना; डराना – **bulldozer** *n.* बुलडोज़र, एक शक्तिशाली ट्रैक्टर जिसके आगे खुदाई का उपकरण लगा होता है – **bullock** (´बुलक) *n.* बैल – **bull's eye** (निशाने का) चांद

bullet (´बुलिट) *n.* बन्दूक आदि की गोली – **bulletproof** *a.* (कार, वस्त्र आदि) जिस पर गोली का असर न हो, अभेद्य, गोली-रोक

bulletin (´बुलिटिन) *n.* (सरकारी) विज्ञप्ति; पत्रिका, बुलेटिन

bullfight (´बुल्फ़ाइट) *n.* आदमी व सांड की लड़ाई का खेल

bullion (´बुल्यन) *n.* सोना-चांदी

bullish *n.* (शेयर बाजार) जब शेयर चढ़ रहे हों; (व्यक्ति, कंपनी आदि) जो भविष्य के बारे में आश्वस्त हो

bully (´बुलि) *n.* व्यक्ति जो कमज़ोर लोगों को धमकाए, तंग करे या हानि पहुंचाए, धौंसिया, दादा – *vt.* धमकाना; धौंस देना

bulrush (´बुल्रश) *n.* सरकंडे जैसा पौधा, नरकट

bulwark (´बुल्वर्क) *n.* (किले की) बाहरी दीवार, परकोटा; मोर्चा या सुरक्षा की व्यवस्था

bum (बम) *sl. n.* चूतड़; *US* आवारा; मुफ्तख़ोर

bumble (´बम्बल) *v.* भोंडे या फूहड़ ढंग से काम करना

bump (बम्प) *n.* धक्का; टक्कर; (चोट से उभरा) गुमटा – *vt.* धक्का या टक्कर मारना – **bumper** *n.* मोटर गाड़ी के आगे-पीछे लगी चौड़ी छड़े बम्पर – *a.* बहुत ज्यादा (फ़सल), बड़ा (पत्रिका अंक) – **bump off** *sl.* की हत्या करना, को खत्म कर देना

bun (बन) *n.* बंद, छोटा गोल केक; (बालों का) जूड़ा

bunch (बंच) *n.* (फूलों, चाबियों, केलों आदि का) गुच्छा; (लोगों का) छोटा सा झुंड – *vt.* गुच्छे में रखना, इकट्ठे बांधना – *vi.* इकट्ठे हो जाना

bundle (´बन्ड्ल) *n.* पोटली; गठड़ी; पुलिंदा; समूह – *vt.* (**bundle up** भी) पुलिंदे में बांधना

bung (बङ) *n.* (पीपे का) डाट

bungalow (´बंगलो) *n.* बंगला

bungee jumping (´बंजि जम्पिङ) *n.* खेल जिसमें व्यक्ति बहुत ऊंचे स्थान (पुल आदि) से

पैरों में रस्सी बांधकर कूदता है और नीचे तल को छुए बगैर रस्सी से ही ऊपर आ जाता है – **bungee jump** *vi.*

bungle (ˈबंगल) *vt.* (अनाड़ियों की तरह) काम बिगाड़ देना; घपला करना; गड़बड़ कर देना

bunk[1] (बंक) *n.* संकरा बिस्तर

bunk[2] (बंक) *n. sl.* जल्दी से निकल भागने की क्रिया

bunker (ˈबंकर) *n.* तेल, कोयला आदि रखने का पात्र; तहखाना; *Golf* मैदान में गड्ढा; (सेना में) भूमि के नीचे बनाया मोर्चा

bunkum (ˈबन्कम) *n.* बकवास, अनर्गल बात

bunny (ˈबनि) *n. inf.* खरगोश

bunting (ˈबन्टिंग) *n.* रंगबिरंगी झण्डिया बनाने की सामग्री; झंडियां

buoy (बॉइ) *n.* (रुकावटों आदि का सूचक) उपकरण जो समुद्र में लंगर से बंधा तैरता रहता है, बोया; डूबने से बचने के लिए बना बोया – *vt.* – **buoyancy** *n.* (शेयरों में) तेज़ी; उल्लास – **buoyant** (ˈबॉइअंट) *a.*

burden (ˈबर्डन) *n.* भार; बोझ; (लदा हुआ) माल; वस्तु या बात जिसे सहना कठिन हो, भार – *vt.* बोझ डालना; (ज़िम्मेवारी आदि) लादना; – **burdensome** *a.*

bureau (ˈब्यूअरो) *n.* लिखने की मेज़; कार्यालय, दफ्तर; सरकारी विभाग (*pl.* **-reaus, -reaux**); *US* दराज़ों वाली मेज़ – **bureaucracy** *n.* अधिकारी वर्ग, नौकरशाही; दफ्तरशाही – **bureaucrat** *n.* नौकरशाह; अफसर – **bureaucratic** *a.* दफ्तरशाही (कार्यविधि आदि)

burgeon (ˈबर्जन) *vi.* (कली का) खिलना; तेज़ी से विकसित होना

burglar (ˈबर्ग्लर) *n.* सेंधमार, चोर – **burglary** *n.* चोरी – **burglar alarm** चोर के अंदर घुसते ही आवाज करके सूचना देने का उपकरण, चोर-सूचक

burial दे० BURY

burlap (ˈबर्लैप) *n.* मोटा कैन्वास; टाट

burlesque (बर्ˈलेंस्क) *n.* (कलात्मक) नकल; स्वांग; प्रहसन

burly (ˈबर्लि) *a.* हट्टाकट्टा; स्थूलकाय

burn[1] (बर्न) *vt.* जलाना – *vi.* जलना, *lit or fig.;* जल जाना; राख हो जाना – *vt.* सी. डी. या डी. वी. डी. में संगीत भरना (**burned** *or* **burnt** *pp./pt.*) – *n.* जले का निशान या दाग़ – **burner** *n.* जलने वाला भाग (हीटर, स्टोव आदि का), बर्नर

burnish (ˈबर्निश) *vt.* रगड़कर चमकाना; पालिश करना

burp (बर्प) *vi. inf.* डकार लेना (विशे. दुधमुहे बच्चे का) – *n.* डकार

burrow (ˈबरो) *n.* (खरगोश आदि का बिल – *vt.* भूमि में छेद करना या उसे खोदना; में छिप जाना

bursar (ˈबर्सर) *n.* स्कूल, कालिज आदि का खज़ांची या कोषाध्यक्ष

burst (बर्स्ट) *vi.* फट जाना; फूटना; टुकड़े-टुकड़े हो जाना; (गुस्से आदि में) अचनाक फट पड़ना (**burst** *pt./pp.*) – *vt.* – *n.* फूटने की क्रिया; विस्फोट; दौर; (किसी क्रिया में) अचानक तेज़ी – **burst into** (कमरे में) एकदम घुस जाना

bury (ˈबेरि) *vt.* जमीन में गाड़ना; दफ़नाना; छिपाना (**buried, burying**) – **burial** *n./a.* दफ़नाने की क्रिया

bus (बस) (मूलत: omnibus) *n.* बस (*pl.* **buses**)

bush (बुश) *n.* झाड़ी; जंगल, झाड़-झंखाड़ – **bushy** *a.* घनी (दाढ़ी); गुच्छेदार; झाड़ीदार

bushel (ˈबुशल) *n.* सूखी वस्तुओं का माप जो आठ गैलन के बराबर होता है

business (ˈबिज़्निस) *n.* व्यवसाय; कारोबार; वाणिज्यिक या औद्योगिक संस्थान; व्यापार; लेनदेन; मामला; विषय; काम – **businesslike** *a.* व्यावहारिक; सुव्यवस्थित

bust[1] (बस्ट) *n.* सिर और कंधों की मूर्ति, अर्ध-प्रतिभा; स्त्री के स्तन

bust[2] *vt.* नष्ट करना, फोड़ना; छापा मारना; गिरफ्तार करना या होना; दिवालिया करना – *vi*. नष्ट होना, दिवालिया हो जाना – *a*. टूटा हुआ – *n*. पुलिस द्वारा छापा या गिरफ्तारी

bustard (ˈबस्टर्ड) *n.* तेज़ी से दौड़ने वाला बड़ा पक्षी, सोहन चिड़िया, हुकना

bustle (ˈबसल) *vi.* हड़बड़ाना; दौड़धूप करना – *n*. हलचल; हड़बड़ी

busy (ˈबिज़ि) *a.* व्यस्त; काम में लगा हुआ; क्रियाशील – *vt*. काम में लगाना; व्यस्त रखना (**busied, busying**) – **busily** *adv.* – **busybody** (ˈबिज़िबॉडि) *n.* दखलंदाज़

but (बट) *conj.* परंतु, लेकिन – *prep.* के बिना; के अतिरिक्त; केवल, सिर्फ

butcher (ˈबुचर) *n.* कसाई; क्रूर और रक्तपिपासु पुरुष – *vt*. हत्या करना, काम बिगाड़ देना – **butchery** *n.* बेरहमी से कत्ल

butler (ˈबट्लर) *n.* मुख्य नौकर, खानसामा

butt[1] (बट) *n.* मोटा सिरा; कुंदा; (उपहास का) पात्र; जिसका सब मज़ाक उड़ाएं; पैंदा – *v*. (सि) लगे होना

butt[2] *v.* (सिर से) टक्कर मारना; धक्का देना

butter (ˈबटर) *n.* मक्खन – *vt.* मक्खन चुपड़ना/लगाना; चापलूसी करना

buttercup (ˈबटर्कप) *n.* चमकदार, पीले फूलों वाला पौधा; बटरकप

butterfly (ˈबटर्फ्लाइ) *n.* तितली; अस्थिर बुद्धि वाला व्यक्ति; तैरने की एक शैली

buttermilk (ˈबटर्मिल्क) *n.* मथने के बाद बचा दूध, छाछ ·

butterscotch (ˈबटर्स्कॉच) *n.* एक कड़ी, भुरभुरी टाफ़ी (दूध और शक्कर से बनी मिठाई)

buttock (ˈबटक) *n.* चूतड़; पीछे को निकला भाग (प्राय: *pl.*)

button (ˈबट्न) *n.* बटन, घुण्डी; मशीन आदि चलाने के लिए लगी घुण्डी या बटन – *vt.* (**button up** भी) बटन लगाना – **buttonhole** *n.* काज; फूल जो कोट पर लगाया जाय – *vt*. किसी अनिच्छुक व्यक्ति को बातों में उलझाए रखना

buttress (ˈबट्रिस) *n.* दीवार की टेक या पुश्ता; सहारा, टेक – *vt.* सहारा देना

buxom (ˈबक्सम) *a.* स्वस्थ, मोटी ताज़ी, प्रसन्नचित, बड़े स्तनों वाली (स्त्री)

buy (बाइ) *v.* मोल लेना, खरीदना; रिश्वत या घूस देना; (बहाने आदि का) विश्वास करना (**bought** *pt./pp.*) – **buyer** *n.*

buzz (बज़) *vi.* भिनभिनाना, गुंजारना – *n.* मधुमक्खियों की गुंजार – *inf.* टेलीफोन पर बुलावा – **buzzer** *n.* (घंटी की तरह) भिनाभिनाहट की आवाज़ करने वाला उपकरण, बज़र – **buzz word** *inf.* किसी कार्य क्षेत्र का शब्द विशेष जो बहुत प्रचलित हो गया हो

buzzard (ˈबज़र्ड) *n.* बाज़ जाति का शिकारी पक्षी, टीसा

by (बाइ) *prep.* समीप, पास; साथ-साथ; पुराना या भूतकाल का; (इस) बीच; द्वारा, जारिये – *adv.* समीप; दूर; (सि) अलग; भूतकाल का – **by and by** शीघ्र ही; निकट भविष्य में – **by and large** कुल मिलाकर, सामान्यतया – **by-your-leave** *n.* आज्ञा

by- *(comb. form)* गौण; सहायक, आनुषंगिक; जो रास्ते से हट कर हो, जैसे **bypath, byproduct, bystander** *n.*

bye *n. Sport* ऐसी स्थिति जहां विरोधी टीम की चूक के कारण जीत हो जाए; *Cricket* ऐसा रन जो बल्लेबाज़ के गेंद छुए बिना मिल जाये

bye (-bye) (ˈबाइ (-ˈबाइ)) *excl.* विदा लेते समय 'नमस्ते!'

by(e)-election *n.* किसी सदस्य के इस्तीफ़े या म त्यु पर हुआ चुनाव, उपचुनाव

by(e)law (ˈबाइलॉ) *n.* कानून या विनियम जो स्थानीय अधीनस्थ प्रशासन ने बनाया हो, उप-विधि, उप-नियम

bygone (ˈबाइगॉन) *a.* जो बीत गया हो, पुराना, भूतकाल का, विगत –*n.* (प्राय: *pl.*) पुरानी घटनाएं; छोटी सी प्राचीन काल की पुरानी वस्तु

bypass(ˈबाइपास) *n.* भीड़ वाले रास्तों से बचने के लिए बनाई सड़कें;हृदय में रक्त-प्रवाह का रास्ता बदलने के लिए किया गया (आपरेशन) –*vt.* से बाहर-बाहर निकल जाना; किसी कार्य के लिए उपयुक्त अधिकारी की आज्ञा बिना कार्य कर लेना

bypath (ˈबाइपाथ) *n.* कम उपयोग में आने वाला मार्ग

by-product(ˈबाइप्रडक्ट) *n.* उपोत्पादन, गौण-उत्पादन, उपफल, मुख्य उत्पादन के साथ उत्पन्न पदार्थ

byte (बाइट) *n. Computers* जानकारी की एक इकाई के रूप में जोड़े गए टुकड़ों में से एक

byword (ˈबाइवर्ड) *n.* सुप्रसिद्ध नाम; कहावत

C

C (सी) *Chem.* Carbon, Celsius, Centigrade, Conservative का चिह्न
CA Chartered Accountant का संक्षेप
cab (कैब) *n.* टैक्सी; रेलवे इंजन या लारी में चालक का कक्ष; घोड़ागाड़ी – **cabby** *n.* टैक्सी चालक
cabal (क'बैल) *n.* षड़यंत्रकारियों का छोटा सा दल; गुप्त षड़यंत्र
cabaret ('कैबरे) *n.* क्लब या रेस्तोरां में न त्य का प्रदर्शन
cabbage ('कैबिज) *n.* बंद गोभी
cabin ('कैबिन) *n.* कोठड़ी; सायबान; कक्ष, छोटा कमरा, विशे. जहाज़ में दबूसा – *vt.* जकड़ना; कसना; बंद कर देना
cabinet ('कैबिनिट) *n.* दराज़ों वाली मेज़ या आलमारी; टी.वी. रेडियो आदि का बक्सा; मंत्रिमंडल
cable ('केबल) *n.* मजबूत रस्सा; लोहे आदि का तार या तारों का गुच्छा जो बिजली या तार-सन्देश भेजने के काम आता है; समुद्री तार; समुद्री माप (100/120 **fathom** के बराबर) – *v.* समुद्री तार भेजना – **cable-car** *n.* मोटे तारों पर लटकी गाड़ी जो मोटर से चलती है व प्राय: पहाड़ों में यात्रियों को एक चोटी से दूसरी तक ले जाने में काम आती है – **cable television** टी.वी. का प्रसारण जो तारों के माध्यम से हो
cacao (क'काओ) *n.* कोको नाम के पेड़ का बीज जिससे चॉकलेट बनता है
cache (कैश) *n.* (शस्त्रादि) छिपाने की गुप्त जगह; अनाज आदि का भंडार
cackle ('कैकल) *vi.* (मुर्गी का) कुड़कुड़ाना – *n.* कुड़कुड़ाने की आवाज़; हंसी की आवाज़
cacophony (क'कॉफ़नि) *n.* कर्णकटु ध्वनि/आवाज़
cactus ('कैक्टस) *n.* नागफ़नी, सेहुंड (*pl.* **cactuses, cacti** ('कैक्टाइ))
cad (कैड) *n.* नीच, पाजी, व्यक्ति जो शिष्टाचार से अनभिज्ञ हो
cadaver (क'डेवर) *n.* शव, लाश
caddie, caddy ('कैडि) *n.* गॉल्फ़ खिलाड़ी का नौकर जो उस का सामान लेकर चलता है
caddy ('कैडि) *n.* चाय रखने के लिए छोटा डिब्बा
cadence ('केडन्स) *n.* संगीत या कविता में स्वर का उतार-चढ़ाव, स्वर लहरी
cadet (क'डेंट) *n.* प्रशिक्षार्थी युवक, विशे. सैनिक अफसर पद के लिए प्रशिक्षण पाने वाला छात्र सैनिक
cadmium ('कैड्मियअम) *n.* कैडमियम धातु
cadre ('काडर) *n.* किसी संगठन का ढांचा; संवर्ग, विशे. रेजिमेंट के अधिकारी; राजनीतिक दलों के कार्यकर्ता
Caesarean section (सि'ज़ेंअरिअन) पेट चीर कर गर्भ से बच्चा निकालने की विधि
cafe ('कैफ़े) *n.* छोटा रेस्तोरां जहां खाने की छोटी मोटी चीज़े मिलती हैं – **cafeteria** (कैफ़ि'टिअरिअ) *n.* रेस्तोरां जहां ग्राहक स्वयं अपने लिए व्यंजन परोसते हैं
caffeine ('कैफ़ीन) *n.* चाय और काफ़ी के पौधे मे पाया जाने वाला उत्तेजक पदार्थ; कैफ़ीन
caftan *n.* देखिए KAFTAN
cage (केज) *n.* पिंजरा; कटघरा; बन्द करने का स्थान; लिफ्ट का पिंजरा जिसमें लोग बैठते हैं – *vt.* पिंजरे में डालना; बंद करना – **cagey** *a. inf.* सतर्क, चौकना
cajole (क'जोल) *vt.* खुशामद से राज़ी करना; फुसलाना – **cajolement** (क'जोल्मंट) *n.* खुशामद – **cajolery** (क'जोलरि) *n.* खुशामद; फुसलाने की क्रिया

cake (केक) *n.* केक; ठोस पिण्ड – *vi.* सूख कर कड़ा हो जाना (जैसे कीचड़) – **cake walk** आसान काम; आसान जीत

calamine (ˈकैलमाइन) *n.* गुलाबी रंग की मरहम

calamity (कˈलैमिटि) *n.* बहुत बड़ी विपित्ति

calcium (कैल्सिअम) *n.* चूना, कैलसियम

calculate (ˈकैल्क्युलेट) *vt.* हिसाब लगाना; कूतना; गिनना – *vi.* परिगणन करना – **calculable** *a.* – **calculating** *a.* चालाक; धूर्त – **calculation** *n.* गणना, हिसाब – **calculator** *n.* हिसाब लगाने, जोड़ आदि करने का इलेक्ट्रॉनिक यंत्र, परिकलक, कैलकुलेटर – **calculus** *n.* (ˈकैल्क्युलस) गणित की एक शाखा; परिकलन

caldron (ˈकॉल्ड्रन) देखिए CAULDRON

calendar (ˈकैलिंडर) *n.* पंचांग; तिथि पत्र; घटनाओं, दस्तावेज़ों की सूची; रजिस्टर – *vt.* सूची में लिखना; क्रमबद्ध करना

calendula (कैˈलॅन्डयुल्अ) *n.* गेंदा की जाति का एक पीले फूलों वाला पौधा

calf[1] (काफ़) *n.* बछड़ा; अन्य पशुओं का बच्चा; बछड़े की खाल का बना चमड़ा (*pl.* **calves** (काव्ज़)) – **calve** (काव) *vi.* गाय का ब्याना, बछड़े को जन्म देना

calf[2] *n.* पिंडली (*pl.* **calves**)

calibre (ˈकैलिबर) *n.* बंदूक, तोप आदि की नली का व्यास; चरित्रबल; सामर्थ्य, योग्यता – **calibrate** *vt.* नापने के उपकरण पर निशान लगाना, अंशाकन करना – **calibration** *n.*

calico (ˈकैलिको) *n.* सूती कपड़ा

call (कॉल) *vt.* बुलाना; बुला भेजना; नाम पुकारना; (प्रायः *up* के साथ) टेलीफ़ोन करना – *vi.* चिल्लाना; मिलने जाना – *n.* ज़ोर की आवाज़; पशुओं की आवाज़/बोली; भेंट; आंतरिक प्रेरणा; बुलावा; आह्वान; निमंत्रण; आवश्यकता; मांग – **caller** *n.* मिलने वाला – **calling** *n.* व्यवसाय, पेशा – **call box** सार्वजनिक टेलीफोन बूथ – **call centre** दफ़्तर जहां ग्राहकों से संपर्क, सौदा केवल टेलीफोन पर किया जाता है – **call girl** टेलीफोन पर सौदा तय करने वाली वेश्या– **call back** दुबारा फोन करना – **call for** की मांग करना – **call off** (हड़ताल आदि) समाप्त कर देना

calligraphy (कˈलिग्रफ़ि) *n.* सुलेख; सुलेख विद्या

calliper (ˈकैलिपर) *n.* टांग को सीधा रखने की धातु की खपची – (~ **s**) *pl.* व्यास नापने का उपकरण, परकार

callous (ˈकैलस) *a.* कठोर; निर्दय; अनदेखी करने वाला – **callousness** *n.* निर्दयता; कठोरता

calm (काम) *a.* शांत, चुपचाप; स्थिर – *n.* शांति; स्थिरता; बंद हवा – *vt.* शांत करना – *vi.* शांत हो जाना – **calmly** *adv.* शंतिपूर्वक

calorie, calory (ˈकैलरि) *n.* ऊष्मा या गरमी की इकाई; भोजन से प्राप्त ऊर्जा की इकाई; ऊष्मांक, कैलरी

calumny (ˈकैलम्नि) *n.* बदनामी; झूठा आरोप

calypso (कˈलिप्सो) *n.* वेस्ट इण्डीज का गाने के समय ही बनाया गया गीत

camaraderie (कैमˈराडरि) *n.* साथी या सखा होने की भावना; सौहार्द्र; परस्पर विश्वास

cambric (ˈकेम्ब्रिक) *n.* बढ़िया सन का या सूती सफ़ेद कपड़ा

camcorder (ˈकैम्कॉर्डर) *n.* संयुक्त वीडियो कैमरा व रिकार्डर जिसे हाथ में लेकर घूमा जा सके

came (केम) COME का *pt.*

camel (ˈकैमल) *n.* ऊंट

cameo (ˈकैमिओ) *n.* गोलाकार फलक या जड़ाऊ पिन जिसपर पच्चीकारी की गयी हो; (किसी प्रसिद्ध) अभिनेता का किसी फिल्म में एक लघु दृश्य

camera (ˈकैमर्अ) *n.* कैमरा – **cameraman** *n.* चित्र खचने वाला विशे. टी.वी. या सिनेमा

के लिए – **in camera** (कानूनी कार्यवाही आदि) जो बंद कमरे में हो

camisole (ˈकैमिसोल) *n.* कुरती जो ब्लाउज़ के नीचे पहनी जाय

camouflage (ˈकैमफ्लाझ़) *n.* छद्मवरण, शुत्र की द ष्टि से बचने के लिए तोपों को ढंकना व छिपाना (रंग, पत्तियों आदि से) – *vt.* (छद्मवरण से) छिपाना

camp (कैम्प) *n.* घुमक्कड़ों या सैनिकों के तम्बुओं का स्थान, शिविर; अस्थायी निवास के लिए कोठड़ियां आदि; पड़ाव; किसी राजनीतिक दल का समर्थक समूह – *vi.* शिविर बनाना या उस में ठहरना – **camper** (ˈकैम्पर) *n.* कैम्प में ठहरने वाला; US शिविर लगाने में काम आने वाली गाड़ी, कैम्प; रिहायशी-गाड़ी – **campfire** *n.* शिविर में बाहर जलाई गई आग, अलाव; शिविर-समारोह

campaign (कैम्ˈपेन) *n.* (राजनीतिक या सैन्य) किसी प्रयोजन के लिए किये गये कार्यों की श्रं खला, अभियान, आंदालेन – *vi.* (*fig* भी) किसी अभियान या आंदोलन में भाग लेना – **campaigner** *n.* आंदोलनकारी

camphor (ˈकैम्फ़र) *n.* कपूर, कर्पूर

campus (ˈकैम्पस) *n.* कालिज या विश्वविद्यालय का मैदान या अहाता, क्षेत्र, परिसर

can[1] (कैन) *vi.* समर्थ होना, सकना (**could** *pt.*)

can[2] *n.* तरल या ठोस पदार्थों के लिए टीन का डिब्बा – *vt.* डिब्बे में बंद करना (**canned** *pt./pp.*) – **canned** *a.* डिब्बा-बंद (पदार्थ); पहले से रिकार्ड किया हुआ (संगीत, कार्यक्रम आदि)

Canadian (कˈनेडिअन) *n.* कनाडावासी – *a.* कनाडा का

canal (कˈनैल) *n.* नहर; शरीर में कोई नालिका या नली

canary (कˈनेंअरि) *n.* पीले रंग की एक चिड़िया, पीत चटकी

cancel (ˈकैन्सल) *vt.* रद्द कर देना; (पार्टी, सभा, मुलाकात आदि) न करने की घोषणा करना; काट देना; हटा देना; (टिकट पर) मुहर लगा देना – **cancellation** *n.* रद्द किया जाना, मनसूखी; (आरक्षण) रद्द किया जाना

cancer[1] (ˈकैन्सर) *n.* कैन्सर रोग – **cancerous** (ˈकैन्सरस) *a.* कैन्सर सम्बन्धी

Cancer[2] *n.* राशि चक्र की चौथी राशि कर्क, जिस का समय 21 जून से 21जुलाई तक होता है – **tropic of Cancer** भूमध्य रेखा के उत्तर में 23 डिग्री से 27 डिग्री तक का क्षेत्र

candid (ˈकैंडिड) *a.* स्पष्टवादी; निष्कपट; तटस्थ; सरल – **candidly** *adv.* स्पष्ट रूप से – **candidness, candour** *n.* (ˈकैंडर) स्पष्टवादिता

candidate (ˈकैंडिडेट) *n.* उम्मीदवार, प्रत्याशी; प्रवेशार्थी; परीक्षार्थी – **candidature** (ˈकैंडिडचर) *n.* उम्मीदवारी

candle (ˈकैन्डल) *n.* मोमबत्ती; शमा; रोशनी – **candelabrum** *n.* झाड़ जिसमें बहुत सी बत्तियां लगती हैं; दीप व क्ष (*pl.* **candelabra**) – **candlestick** *n.* (**candleholder** भी) बत्तीदान, शमादान

candy (ˈकैंडि) *n.* मिसरी; US टॉफी आदि जैसी मिठाई, लैमनचूस – *vt.* चीनी में पगाना – *vi.* पगना (**candied** *pt./pp.*, **candying** *p.*) –**candied** *a.* – **candyfloss** *n.* पगाई चीनी से बनी हल्की रूई जैसी मिठाई, बुढ़िया के बाल

cane (केन) *n.* बेंत, छड़ी – *vt.* बेंत से मारना

canine (ˈकेनाइन) *a.* कुत्ते जैसा या उस से सम्बन्धित

canister (ˈकैनिस्टर) *n.* कनस्तर, टीन

canker (ˈकैंकर) *n.* फोड़ा, नासूर; वस्तु जो गला दे, नष्ट कर दे या विक त कर दे; विनाशकारी रोग

cannabis (ˈकैनबिस) *n.* (**cannabis plant** भी) भांग का पौधा; भांग

cannibal (ˈकैनिबल) *n.* नरभक्षी व्यक्ति – *a.* नरभक्षी – **cannibalism** *n.* नरभक्षण
cannon (ˈकैनन) *n.* तोप (*pl.* **cannon** *or* **cannons**)
cannot (ˈकैनॉट) = CAN का **negative** रूप
canny (ˈकैनि) *a.* समझदार; चौकस; होशियार
canoe (कˈनू) *n.* हल्की, चप्पू से चलने वाली नाव; डोंगी – **canoeist** *n.* डोंगी चालक
canon[1] (ˈकैनन) *n.* कानून या नियम, विशे. चर्च का; मापदण्ड; प्रामाणिक ग्रंथ-संग्रह; संतों की सूची – **canonization** (कैननाइˈज़ेशन) *n.* (चर्च द्वारा) संत घोषित करने की क्रिया – **canonize** (ˈकैननाइज़) *vt.* किसी मत व्यक्ति को संत घोषित करना
canopy (ˈकैनपि) *n.* (सिंहासन या शैया के ऊपर का) छत्र; सायबान
cantaloupe, -loup, -lope (ˈकैन्टलूप) *n.* एक प्रकार का खरबूज़ा
cantankerous (कैन्ˈटैंकरस) *a.* झगड़ालू
canteen (कैन्ˈटीन) *n.* कारखाने या स्कूल आदि का जलपान गह
canter (ˈकैन्टर) *n.* घोड़े की मद्धिम चाल, पोइया – *v.* ऐसी चाल चलना या चलाना
cantilever (ˈकैटिलीवर) *n.* शहतीर, कड़ी आदि जो केवल एक ओर टिकी हो, कैन्टीलीवर
canto (ˈकैंटो) *n.* लम्बी कविता का एक खण्ड; सर्ग (*pl.*-**tos**)
cantonment (कन्ˈटून्मन्ट) *n.* छावनी
canvas (ˈकैन्वस) *n.* मोटा कपड़ा जो नावों के पाल बनाने या चित्रकला में काम आता हैं, किरमिच, कैन्वस
canvass (ˈकैन्वस) *vt.* लोगों से वोट या चन्दा मांगना; पक्ष प्रचार करना; बहस करना; (विचार) जानना
canyon (ˈकैन्यन) *n.* गहरी घाटी (जिसमें से प्राय: नदी गुज़रती है)
cap (कैप) *n.* टोपी; ढक्कन; आवरण – *vt.* टोपी पहनाना
capable (ˈकेपबल) *a.* योग्य; प्रतिभाशाली; समर्थ – **capability** (केपˈबिलिटि) *n.*सामर्थ्य; योग्यता; क्षमता
capacity (कˈपैसिटि) *n.* सामर्थ्य, क्षमता; गुंजाइश; धारिता, समाई; हैसियत; योग्यता; मानसिक क्षमता या शक्ति – **capacious** (कˈपेशस) *a.* जिसमें बहुत स्थान हो
cape *n.* भूमि का संकरा/नुकीला भाग जो समुद्र में बढ़ा हुआ हो, अंतरीप
caper (ˈकेपर) *n.* उछलकूद; शरारत भरा या गैर कानूनी काम – *vi.* उछलना, नाचना
capillary (कˈपिलरि) *a.* बाल जैसा – *n.* सूक्ष्म छिद्र वाली नली, विशे. रक्तवाहिनी नली; कोशिका; कैपिलरी
capital (ˈकैपिटल) *n.* राजधानी; पूंजी, मूलधन; बड़े आकार का अक्षर जैसे (अंग्रेजी में) – *a.* मुख्य; महत्वपूर्ण; श्रेष्ठ – **capitalism** *n.* पूंजीवाद – **capitalist** *n.* पूंजीपति; पूंजीवाद समर्थक – *a.* पूंजीवादी – **capitalize** *v.* पूंजी में परिवर्तित करना – *vt.* (*on* के साथ) (का) लाभ उठाना – **capitally** *adv.* बहुत अच्छी तरह से – **capital punishment** मत्यु दण्ड
capitation (कैपिˈटेशन) *n.* प्रति व्यक्ति कर या अनुदान; गणना
capitulate (कˈपिट्युलेट) *vi.* आत्मसमर्पण करना (विशे. कुछ शर्तों के अनुसार), झुकना, हार मानना – **capitulation** (कपिट्यु ˈलेशन) *n.* आत्मसमर्पण
cappuccino (कैपुˈचीनो) *n.* काफ़ी जिसमें भाप से गरम किया दूध मिला हो
caprice (कˈप्रीस) *n.* मौज; सनक – **capricious** (कˈप्रीशस) *a.* सनकी – **capriciousness** *n.* सनकी प्रकति
Capricorn (ˈकैप्रिकार्न) *n.* मकर; राशिचक्र की दसव राशि जिस का समय 21 दिसम्बर से 19 जनवरी तक होता है; एक तारामंडल – **tropic**

of Capricorn भूमध्य रेखा के दक्षिण में 23 डिग्री से 27 डिग्री तक का क्षेत्र

capsicum (ˈकैप्सिकम) *n.* पहाड़ी/शिमला मिर्च

capsize (कैप्ˈसाइज़) *vt.* उलट देना – *vi.* उलट जाना

capsule (ˈकैपस्यूल) *n.* कैपसूल

Capt. Captain का संक्षेप

captain (ˈकैप्टिन) *n.* जहाज का मुख्य अधिकारी; कप्तान; सैनिक टुकड़ी का अधिकारी; (टीम का) कप्तान; प्रमुख, सरदार – *vt.* (का) कप्तान होना

caption (ˈकैप्शन) *n.* लेख या चित्र का शीर्षक

captive (ˈकैप्टिव़) *n.* बंदी – *a.* – **captivate** (ˈकैप्टिवेट) *vt.* मोहित करना, लुभाना – **captivating** *a.* मनोहर, लुभावना – **captivity** *n.* कैदी; बंदी-स्थिति – **captive market** ग्राहकों का समूह जिन्हें एक ही कंपनी का उत्पादन खरीदना पड़े

capture (ˈकैप्चर) *vt.* पकड़ लेना; बन्दी बना लेना; हासिल कर लेना; (द श्य) रिकार्ड कर लेना – *n.* – **captor** (ˈकैप्टर) *n.* पकड़ने/बंदी बनाने वाला

car (कार) *n.* मोटर गाड़ी, कार रेल का एक विशेष प्रकार का यात्री डिब्बा

carafe (कˈरैफ) *n.* मेज पर रखने की कांच की बनी पानी की बोतल या निथरनी

caramel (ˈकैरमल) *n.* जलाई गई चीनी जो खाद्य पदार्थों में काम आती हैं; एक प्रकार की मिठाई

carat (ˈकैरट) *n.* छोटा वज़न जो सोना या हीरे तोलने में प्रयुक्त होता है (0.20 ग्राम के बराबर); सोने की शुद्धता का माप (शुद्ध सोना 24 कैरट का होता है)

caravan (ˈकैरवैन) *n.* बड़ी गाड़ी जिसमें रहने की व्यवस्था होती है और जिसे कार आदि के पीछे लगा देते हैं; (पूर्व में) इकट्ठे यात्रा करते व्यापारियों की टोली, कारवां, काफ़िला

caraway (ˈकैरवे) *n.* जीरे का पौधा; जीरा

carbohydrate (कार्बोˈहाइड्रेट्) *n.* कार्बन, हाइड्रोजन और आक्सीजन का मिश्रण; विशे. भोजन के तत्व के रूप में; शक्कर और स्टार्च (जो चावल, आलू आदि में पाया जाता है)

carbolic (acid) (कार्ˈबॉलिक) कोलतार से बनी एक कीटनाशक दवा

carbon (ˈकार्बन) *n.* एक अधातुक तत्व जो सभी जीव परक पदार्थों में होता है – **carbonate** *n.* कार्बोलिक ऐसिड का लवण – **carbon dioxide** रंगहीन गैस जो जीवों के छोड़े गए सांस में होती है – **carbon paper** कार्बन पेपर – **carbon copy** कार्बन पेपर से तैयार प्रति

carbuncle (ˈकार्बन्कल) *n.* फोड़ा; सूजी हुई रसौली; लाल रंग का रत्न; माणिक्य, माणिक, लाल

carburettor (कार्ब्युˈरेंटर) *n.* कार आदि के इंजनों का पुर्जा जिसमें पेट्रोल और हवा का मिश्रण होता है, कार्बुरेटर

carcass, carcase (ˈकार्कस) *n.* पशु का शव; लोथ

carcinogen (कार्ˈसिनजन) *n.* पदार्थ जिससे कैंसर उत्पन्न हो; केन्सरजन – **carcinogenic** (कार्‌सिनˈजेनिक) *n.*

card[1] (कार्ड) *n.* मोटा, कड़ा कागज़, मोटे कागज़ पर छपा पहचान पत्र; शुभकामना का कार्ड; ताश के 52 पत्तों में से कोई एक – (~ **s**) *pl.* ताश का कोई खेल – **cardboard** *n.* गत्ता – **card game** ताश का खेल – **card index** कार्डों पर बनी अनुक्रमणिका – **lay your cards on the table** अपने इरादे स्पष्ट करना – **keep your cards close to your chest** अपने इरादे, भावनाएं छिपाए रखना – **trump card** *fig.* तुरूप का पत्ता

card[2] *n.* ऊन साफ करने का यंत्र, कंघा – *vt.* (ऊन) धुनना – **carder** *n.* धुनिया

cardiac (ˈकार्डिऐक) *a.* हृदय सम्बन्धी – **cardiograph** (ˈकार्डिओग्राफ) *n.* हृदय की

गति या धड़कन नापने का यंत्र – **cardiogram** ('कार्डिओग्रैम) *n.* हृदय की धड़कन का रेखाचित्र या ग्राफ – **cardiologist** *n.* हृदय-रोग विशेषज्ञ – **cardiology** *n.* हृदय-विज्ञान

cardigan ('कार्डिगन) *n.* बुनी हुई ऊनी खुली जाकेट

cardinal ('कार्डिनल) *a.* प्रधान; मुख्य; प्रमुख – *n.* रोमन कैथोलिक चर्च में पोप से दूसरे स्थान का पादरी; कार्डिनल – **cardinal numbers** गणन संख्या जैसे 1,2,3 – **cardinal points** दिश-बिन्दु उत्तर, दक्षिण (N,S,E,W) आदि

cardiologist दे० CARDIAC

care (कॅअर) *vi.* परवाह करना, (का) ध्यान रखना; पसंद करना – *n.* ध्यान; परवाह; देख-रेख; चिंता; सावधानी – **carefree** *a.* निश्चिंत – **careful** *a.* सतर्क, सावधान – **carefully** *adv.* – **caring** *a.* दूसरों का ख्याल रखने वाला; संवेदनशील – **carefulness** *n.* सावधानी – **careless** *a.* लापरवाह – **carelessness** *n.* – **caretaker** *n.* प्रभारी, रखवाला – *a.* अंतरिम; अस्थायी – **careworn** *a.* चिंतापूर्ण (भाव)

career (क'रिअर) *n.* जीवन का रास्ता; जीवन व त्ति, पेशा, व्यवसाय; तेज़ प्रगति – **career woman** स्त्री जो अपने व्यवसाय में प्रगति को विवाह या बच्चों की अपेक्षा प्राथमिकता दे

caress (क'रॅस) *vt.* पुचकारना; चूमना; (*embrace*) गले लगाना; प्यार करना – *n.* चुमकारने या प्यार करने की क्रिया

cargo ('कार्गो) *n.* माल जो जहाज़ आदि में लादा गया हो (*pl.* **cargoes**)

caribou ('कैरिबू) *n.* रेंडिअर (एक प्रकार का हिरन)

caricature ('कैरिकचुअर) *n.* व्यंग्य-चित्र – *vt.* (किसी का) व्यंग्य-चित्र बनाना

caries ('कॅअरिईज़) *n.* दांतों या हड्डियों का गल जाना, अस्थिक्षय

carnage ('कार्निज) *n.* हत्याकांड, बड़े पैमाने पर हत्याएं

carnal ('कार्नल) *a.* शारीरिक; विषयी; इन्द्रियासक्त, सांसारिक

carnation (कार्'नेशन) *n.* लाल रंग का फूल

carnival ('कार्निवल) *n.* आनन्दोत्सव, चलता फिरता मेला (जो स्थान स्थान पर लगे); मनोरंजन के लिए किया गया कार्यक्रम

carnivorous (कार्'निवरस) *a.* मांसभक्षी; मांसाहारी

carol ('कैरल) *n.* आनंद या ईश स्तुति का (विशे. क्रिस्मस के अवसर पर) गाया जाने वाला गाना

carouse (क'राउज़) *vi.* खूब शराब पीना, शराब के जाम पर जाम पीते जाना

carp *vi.* छोटी छोटी बातों की शिकायत करना; दोष निकालना; कुड़कुड़ाना

carpenter ('कार्पिन्टर) *n.* बढ़ई – **carpentry** ('कार्पिंट्रि) *n.* बढ़ई की कला/काम

carpet ('कार्पिट) *n.* कालीन; गलीचा; दरी – **carpetbagger** *n.* राजनीतिक कार्यकर्ता जो अपने स्वार्थ के लिए कह भी पैर जमाने की कोशिश करे – **carpet bombing** *n.* छोटे से क्षेत्र में भारी बम-वर्षा

carriage ('कैरिज) *n.* रेलगाड़ी का डिब्बा; ठवन; चाल; व्यवहार या चलन; घोड़ागाड़ी – **carriageway** *n.* सड़क का वह भाग जहां गड़ियों एक पंक्ति व एक दिशा में चलती हैं

carrion ('कैरिअन) *n.* सड़ती हुई लाश

carrot ('कैरट) *n.* गाजर

carry ('कैरि) *vt.* ले जाना; ढोना; पकड़ लेना; जीत लेना; कर दिखाना; व्यवहार करना; रोग-संवाहक होना; गर्भवती होना – *vi.* (फैंकी गयी वस्तु, आवाज आदि का) पहुंचना (**carried, carrying**) – *n.* भार (पहुंच); परास – **carrier** *n.* व्यक्ति जिस से दूसरों को रोग लगे

लेकिन वह स्वयं उस से पीड़ित न हो; विमान वाहक जाहज़; पत्रवाहक कबूतर

cart (कार्ट) *n.* घोड़ागाड़ी, बैलगाड़ी – *vt.* गाड़ी में ढो कर ले जाना – **cartage** *n.* गाड़ी-भाड़ा, ढुलाई – **cartwheel** *n.* तिरछी कलाबाज़ी

cartel (कार्'टॅल) *n.* उत्पादकों का संघ (जिससे कि उत्पादन, कीमतों आदि पर उन का अधिकार रहे)

cartilage ('कार्टिलिज) *n.* कुरकुरी (हड्डी), अस्थि

cartography (कार्'टॉग्रफ़ि) *n.* मानचित्र/नक्शा बनाने की क्रिया अथवा कला – **cartographer** *n.*

carton ('कार्टन) *n.* गत्ते या प्लास्टिक का डिब्बा

cartoon (कार्'टून) *n.* व्यंग्य चित्र – **cartoonist** *n.* व्यंग-चित्रकार

cartridge ('कार्ट्रिज) *n.* कारतूस, गोली (का आवरण); (पिन का) सिक्का; फ़िल्म, टेप, स्याही आदि रखने की डिबिया

carve (कार्व़) *vt.* काटना; तराशना; पत्थर तराश कर मूर्ति बनाना – **carving** *n.* नक्काशी

cascade (कैस्'केड) *n.* जलप्रपात; झरना

case[1] (केस) *n.* उदाहरण; घटना; परिस्थिति; वाद का विषय; वस्तु स्थिति; शर्त; किसी मामले के पक्ष में दलीलें; *Med.* रोगी जिसका उपचार हो रहा हो; मुकदमा; मुकदमे का आधार; विभक्ति कारक

case[2] *n.* डिब्बा, आवरण – *vt.* बकस या पेटी में डालना

casement ('केस्मंट) *n.* फरमेदार खिड़की (जिस का पट कब्जों पर खुलता हो

cash (कैश) *n.* नकदी; नकद – *vt.* (चैक) भुनाना, (चैक) का भुगतान करना – **cashier** *n.* खजांची, कोषाध्यक्ष – **cash-book** *n.* रोकड़ बही – **cash card** इलैक्ट्रानिक कार्ड जिसे मशीन में डालकर पैसा निकाला जाता है – **cash desk** स्थान जहां भुगतान किया जाय – **cash dispenser** यंत्र जिसमें कार्ड डाल कर पैसा निकाला जाय (ATM भी) – **cash register** रोकड़ का बक्स जिसमें रुपये-पैसे की गिनती यंत्र द्वारा होती है – **cash-strapped** जिसे धन का अभाव हो

cashew (कै'शू) *n.* काजू (**cashew nut** भी)

cashier (कै'शिअर) *vt.* नौकरी से निकालना (विशे. फौज से)

casino (क'सीनो) *n.* जुआघर, जुआखाना (*-pl* **casinos**)

cask (कास्क) *n.* काठ का पीपा

casket ('कास्किट) *n.* आभूषण रखने का डिब्बा; मंजूषा; US ताबूत

cassata (क'साट्अ) *n.* आइसक्रीम जिसमें बादाम आदि की गिरी और फल डाले जाते हैं

casserole ('कैसरोल) *n.* बरतन जो पकाने और परोसने दोनों काम आता हैं; ऐसे बरतन में पका खाद्य पदार्थ

cassette (कै'सेट) *n.* फिल्म या टेप आदि का प्लास्टिक का डिब्बा – **cassette player** कैसेट प्लेयर, कैसट चलाने का उपकरण – **cassette recorder** (संगीत आदि) कैसेट में भरने का उपकरण

cast (कास्ट) *v.* (प्रकाश, छाया/निगाह) फैंकना या डालना; नीचे फैंक देना; (पत्ते) गिराना; उतारना; मत या वोट डालना; देना (नाटक में भूमिका); (धातु को) सांचे में ढालना – *n.* फैंकने की क्रिया; दूरी जिस तक कोई वस्तु फैंकी जाय; सांचा; फैंकी गयी या उतारी गयी वस्तु; अभिनेताओं की टोली; प्रकार या गुण – **castaway** *n.* व्यक्ति जो डूबे हुए जहाज़ से बचकर अपरिचित भूमि पर आया हो – **casting vote** निर्णायक मत

caste (कास्ट) *n.* (भारत में) जाति, जात; सामाजिक दरजा

caster sugar ('कास्टर-) महीन पिसी चीनी (**castor sugar** भी)

castigate ('कैस्टिगेट) *vt.* दण्ड देना; फटकारना, लताड़ना; सुधारना

castle ('कासल) *n.* किला, दुर्ग; देहात में बनी हवेली; (शतरंज में) रुख़

castor oil (ˈकास्टर-) अरण्डी का तेल
castrate (कैˈस्ट्रेट) *vt.* बधिया करना, प्रजनन शक्ति से वंचित करना – **castration** *n.*
casual (ˈकैझुअल) *a.* प्रासंगिक या आकस्मिक; जिस का पहले से अनुमान न हो; यदा कदा होने वाला; लापरवाह; अनौपचारिक (विषभूषा) – **casually** *adv.* अकस्मात, संयोग से; यों ही – **casualty** (ˈकैझुअल्टि) *n.* व्यक्ति जो दुर्घटना में हताहत हुआ हो; दुर्घटना आदि में गुम या नष्ट हुई वस्तु -(*pl.* **-ties**)
cat (कैट) *n.* बिल्ली – **catcall** *n.* (सभा में श्रोता का मज़ाक उड़ाने के लिए) सीटी जैसी आवाज़ – **catnap** *n./vi.* झपकी – **cat's eye** R सड़क में लगाया चमकने वाला कांच जिससे यातायात के रास्ते निर्धारित होते हैं – **catwalk** *n.* उभरा हुआ संकरा (जिस पर मॉडल फैशन शो में प्रदर्शन करते हैं) मार्ग या तख्ता
cataclysm (ˈकैटक्लिज़म) *n.* विनाशकारी उथल-पुथल; महाप्रलय
catacomb (ˈकैटकोम) *n.* तहखाना जिसमें कब्रें बनी हों
catalogue (ˈकैटलॉग) *n.* सूची; सूची पत्र, ग्रंथ सूची – *vt.* ऐसी सूची बनाना
catalyst (ˈकैटलिस्ट) *n.* पदार्थ जो रसायन का रूप बदल दे लेकिन जिसमें स्वयं परिवर्तन न हो, उत्प्रेरक
catapult (ˈकैटपल्ट) *n.* गुलेल – *vi.* तेज़ी से ऊपर चढ़ना, प्रगति करना
cataract (ˈकैटरैक्ट) *n.* जलप्रपात; आंख की एक बीमारी, सफेद मोतियाबिन्द
catarrh (कˈटार) *n.* श्लेठमल झिल्ली की सूजन जिसके कारण जुकाम हो जाता है
catastrophe (कˈटैस्ट्रफ़ि) *n.* महाविपत्ति; अनर्थ; विध्वंस या विनाश; प्रलय; विपद् – **catastrophic** (कैटˈस्ट्रॉफ़िक) *a.* अनर्थकारी; विध्वंसक
catch (कैच) *vt.* हाथों में लेना; पकड़ना; समझना; सुनना; बीमारी हो जाना; (समय पर गाड़ी आदि) पकड़ना; अचानक या (चोरी आदि) करते देख लेना, लगना – *vi.* (छूत की बीमारी) होना; फंस जाना; जलने लगना (**caught** *pt./pp*) – *n.* पकड़ने की क्रिया; शिकार; *inf.* रोड़ा; रुकावट; असुविधा; प्रतिकूल स्थिति; वस्तु या व्यक्ति जो पाने योग्य हो – **catchy** *a.* मनमोहक, स्मरणीय – **catch** 22 ऐसी दुविधा जिस से बचना असंभव हो – **catchment area** क्षेत्र जहां वर्षा का पानी जमा होकर नदियों में जाता है
catechize (ˈकैटिकाइज़) *vt.* प्रश्नोत्तर के माध्यम से धर्म के विषय में सिखाना – **catechism** *n.*
category (ˈकैटिगरि) *n.* वर्ग; कोटि; श्रेणी – **categorical** (कैटिˈगॉरिकल) *a.* सुनिश्चित
cater (ˈकेटर) *vi.* आवश्यक वस्तुओं, विशे. खानपान, का प्रबंध करना – **caterer** *n.* पार्टी आदि के लिए खान-पान का प्रबंधकर्त्ता – **catering** *n.* खान-पान, भोजन-प्रबंध
caterpillar (ˈकैटर्पिलर) *n.* इल्ली; झांझा; सूंडी; एक प्रकार का ट्रैक्टर जिसमें चक्र पट्टी लगी हो
cathedral (कˈथीड्रल) *n.* किसी क्षेत्र का मुख्य गिरजाघर
cathode (ˈकैथोड) *n.* ऋणाग्र (नैगेटिव ऋणात्मक इलैक्टरोड); कैथोड – **cathode rays** इलैक्ट्रान्स की धारा; कैथोड किरण
catholic (ˈकैथलिक) *a.* सारे विश्व का या उसमें व्याप्त, सार्वभौम – **Catholic** – *n.* रोमन कैथलिक धर्म का अनुयायी – **Catholicism** *n.* **catholicity** (कैथˈलिसिटि) *n.* उदारता
cattle (ˈकैट्ल) *pl. n.* मवेशी विशे. गाय-बैल
caucus (ˈकॉकस) *n.* राजनीतिक दल के ऐसे सदस्य समूह की बैठक जिसे नीति निर्धारण का अधिकार हो
caught CATCH का *pt./pp.*
cauldron (ˈकॉल्ड्रन) *n.* कड़ाहा
cauliflower (ˈकॉलिफ़्लाउअर) *n.* फूल गोभी
cause (ˈकॉज़) *n.* कारण; हेतु;निमित्त; मूल; उद्देश्य;

प्रयोजन; (दान) धर्म का काम; आन्दोलन; मुकदमा; मामला – *vt.* उत्पन्न करना

causeway (ˈकॉज़्वे) *n.* दलदली भूमि आदि पर ऊंची सड़क; पक्की (ईंट, पत्थर लगी) गली या सड़क

caustic (ˈकॉस्टिक) *a.* जलता हुआ; कटु; तीखा; मर्मभेदी कास्टिक

cauterize (ˈकॉटराइज़) *vt.* कास्टिक या गरम लोहे से जलाना – **cauterization** *n.*

caution (ˈकॉशन) *n.* सावधानी; सतर्कता; चौकसी; चेतावनी – *vt.* चेतावनी देना – **cautionary** *a.* जिसमें चेतावनी या कोई शिक्षा हो – **cautious** (ˈकॉशस) *a.* सावधान, चौकस – **cautiously** *adv.*

cavalcade (कैवल्ˈकेड) *n.* घुड़सवारों का दस्ता या जुलूस

cavalier (कैवˈलिअर) *a.* लापरवाह; अवहेलना करने वाला

cavalry (ˈकैवल्रि) *n.* घुड़सवार सेना; रिसाला

cave (केव़) *n.* गुफ़ा – **cavern** (ˈकैवर्न) *n.* गहरी गुफ़ा – **cavernous** *a.* गहरी गुफ़ा समान – **cavity** (ˈकैविटि) *n.* कोटरिका, (दांत में) छोटा छिद्र; गड्ढा – **cave in** धंस जाना; हार जाना, आत्मसमर्पण करना

caviar(e) (ˈकैविआर) *n.* स्टर्जन नाम की मछली का अंडे सहित अंडाशय जिसे नमक लगाकर शराब के साथ खाया जाता है

cavil (ˈकैविल) *vi.* बेकार की मीन मेख या बाल की खाल निकालना (**cavilled** *pt./pp.*)

cavort (कˈवॉर्ट) *vi.* कूदफांद करना

caw (कॉ) *n.* कांय-कांय, कांव-कांव – *vi.* कांय-कांय या कांव कांव करना

cayenne (pepper) (केˈएॅन) *n.* लाल मिर्च

CBI *India* Central Bureau of Investigation का संक्षेप

cc carbon copy; cubic centimetres का संक्षेप

CCTV closed circuit television का संक्षेप

CBT computer based testing/training का संक्षेप

CD compact disc का संक्षेप

CD-ROM compact disc-read only memory का संक्षेप, सी. डी. जिसमें बड़ी मात्रा में जानकारी एकत्र होती है व जो कम्प्यूटर पर उपयोग की जा सकती है

cease (सीस) *v.* बंद होना या करना – **ceasefire** *n.* युद्ध-विराम, लड़ाई-बंदी – **ceaseless** *a.* लगातार

cedar (ˈसीडर) *n.* देवदार का पेड़ या उसकी लकड़ी

cede (सीड) *vt.* हार मानना; झुक जाना; सौंपना, छोड़ देना या दे देना विशे. क्षेत्र

ceiling (ˈसीलिंग) *n.* कमरे आदि की छत (छत के नीचे का भाग); उच्चतम कीमत, मज़दूरी आदि

celeb (सˈलेॅब) *n. inf.* celebrity का संक्षेप

celebrate (ˈसेॅलिब्रेट) *vi.* (किसी सुखद घटना या विशेष दिन पर) उत्सव मनाना – *vt.* जन्म दिन आदि मनाना; कोई धार्मिक अनुष्ठान करना, प्रशंसा करना – **celebrated** *a.* प्रसिद्ध; विख्यात – **celebration** (सेॅलिˈब्रेशन) *n.* उत्सव; समारोह – **celebrity** (सिˈलेॅब्रिटि) *n.* विख्यात या प्रसिद्ध व्यक्ति; प्रसिद्धि; ख्याति

celerity (सिˈलेॅरिटि) *n.* शीघ्रता; तेज़ी, फुर्ती

celery (ˈसेॅलरि) *n.* एक भाजी जिसके डंठल सलाद की तरह खाए जाते हैं, अजमोद

celestial (सिˈलेॅस्टिअल) *a.* स्वर्गीय; दिव्य; आकाश का

celibacy (ˈसेॅलिबसि) *n.* अविवाहित होने की स्थिति, ब्रह्मचर्य – **celibate** *n.* ब्रह्मचारी

cell (सेॅल) *n.* छोटा कमरा, कोठड़ी, विशे. जेल की; कोटर; (जीवों के शरीर में) कोशिका; बैटरी, सेल; किसी राजनीतिक या धार्मिक संगठन की स्थानीय शाखा; गुट्ट – **cellular** (ˈसैल्युलर) *a.* कोशिकीय – **cellular telephone** चलता-फिरता टेलिफोन, सैलफोन (**cellphone, mobile phone** भी)

cellar (सेलर) *n.* तहखाना
cello (चेलो) *n.* सारंगी या वायलिन जैसा वाद्य; चेलो
cellophane (सेलफ़ेन) *n.* कागज़ जैसा पतला, पारदर्शी पदार्थ जो चीज़ों को लपेटने के काम आता है
cell phone दे० **CELL**
celluloid (सेल्युलाइड) *n.* एक क त्रिम प्लास्टिक
cellulose (सेल्युलोस) *n.* पौधों से प्राप्त पदार्थ; कार्बोहाइड्रेट (चीनी, मांड आदि) का एक वर्ग
Celsius (सेल्सिअस) *n.* तापमान का क्रमांक, **0º** (जब बर्फ़ पिघलने लगती है) से **100º** (जब पानी उबलने लगता है) तक – *a.* भी
cement (सि मेन्ट) *n.* सीमेंट; जोड़ने वाला पदार्थ; सरेस – *vt.* सीमेंट से जोड़ना; जोड़ना; द ढ़ करना
cemetery (सेमिट्रि) *n.* कब्रिस्तान
cenotaph (सेनटाफ़) *n.* ऐसे व्यक्ति का स्मारक जो कह और दफ़नाया गया हो
censer (सेन्सर) *n.* धूपदान
censor (सेन्सर) *n.* व्यक्ति जिसे फिल्में, पुस्तकें आदि देखकर आपत्तिजनक अंश हटाने का अधिकार हो, खण्डवर्जक, सेन्सर – *vt.* सेन्सर करना – **censorship** *n.* सेन्सर व्यवस्था
censure (सेन्शर) *n.* निंदा; कटु आलोचना – *vt.* दोष देना; कटु आलोचना करना – **censure motion** (संसद आदि में) निंदा प्रस्ताव
census (सेन्सस) *n.* जनगणना; गणना
cent (सेण्ट) *n.* डालर आदि का सौवां भाग, सेंट
centaur (सेन्टॉर) *n.* काल्पनिक जीव जो आधा घोड़ा और आधा मानव होता है; किन्नर
centenary (सेन् टीनरि) *n.* सौ वर्ष; शताब्दी; शताब्दी समारोह – *a.* सौ का या उस से सम्बन्धित –**centenarian** (सेन्टि नेंअरिन) *n.* सौ साल का, शतायु
centigrade (सेन्टिग्रेड) *a.* **Celsius** का दूसरा नाम; जिसमें **100** डिग्री हों
centimetre (सेन्टिमीटर) *n.* मीटर का सौवां भाग
centipede (सेन्टिपीड) *n.* अनेक टांगों वाला कीड़ा, कनखजूरा, गोजर
centre (सेण्टर) *n.* केंद्र, मध्य बिन्दु; धुरी, अक्ष; किसी कार्यकलाप या संगठन का स्थान – *vt.*केंद्रित करना, एकाग्र करना – **central** *a.* केन्द्रीय – **centrality** *n.* केन्द्रीयता – **centralization** *n.* केन्द्रीकरण – **centralize** *vt.* केंद्रित करना – **centrally** *adv.* – **centrifugal** (सेन्ट्रिफ़्युगल) *a.* जो केन्द्र से परे को जाए; अपकेंद्रीय – **centripetal** (सेन्ट्रिपिटल) *a.* जो केन्द्र की ओर आए – **central processing unit** *Computers* कम्प्यूटर का वह भाग जहां गणितीय प्रक्रियाएं की जाती है; केन्द्रीय संसाधन एकक
century (सेन्चुरि) *n.* शताब्दी; सदी; शतक
CEO Chief Executive Officer का संक्षेप, कंपनी प्रमुख
ceramic (सि रैमिक) *n.* चीनी मिट्टी; उस से बनी वस्तु – *a.* चीनी मिट्टी से बना – **ceramics** *n.* चीनी मिट्टी के बरतन आदि बनाने की कला; ऐसे बरतन; कलावस्तु
cereal (सिअरिअल) *n.* अनाज (गेहूं, चावल आदि); नाश्ते में खाने का दलिया (जौ या गेहूं आदि का)
cerebral (सेरिब्रल) *a.* मस्तिष्क का या उस से सम्बन्धित
ceremony (सेरिमनि) *n.* समारोह; विधिवत अनुष्ठान, धार्मिक अनुष्ठान, शिष्टाचार – **ceremonial** (सेरि मोनिअल) *a.* औपचारिक, रीति अनुरूप – *n.* शिष्टाचार की औपचारिकता
certain (सर्टन) *a.* निश्चित; पक्का; तय, निर्णीत; अवश्यम्भावी; अनिवार्य; कोई; कोई एक; मध्यम (मात्रा आदि का), कुछ – **certainly** *adv.* निस्संदेह – **certainty** *n.* निश्चित रूप, बात आदि, निश्चय – **certitude** (सर्टिट्यूड) *n.* विश्वास, भरोसा

certify ('सर्टिफ़ाइ) *vt.* विधिवत घोषित करना, प्रमाण पत्र देना; सत्यापन करना, तसदीक करना, वस्तु के प्रामाणिक होने का आश्वासन देना (–**fied,-fying**) – **certificate** (सर्'टिफ़िकिट) *n.* प्रमाण पत्र, सार्टिफ़िकेट

cervix ('सर्विक्स) *n.* गरदन; गर्भाशय का निचला भाग – **cervical** (सर्'वाइकल) *a.* गर्भाशय-सम्बंधी; गर्दन-सम्बंधी

cessation (सें'सेशन) *n.* अन्त; अवसान; समाप्ति; विराम

CFC chlorofluorocarbon का संक्षेप

Cf. confer का संक्षेप (Lat. तुलना कीजिए), देखिए

c/f carried forward का संक्षेप

cg centigram का चिह्न

cgs units (सीजीएस यूनिट्स) दशमलव प्रणाली जिसका आधार सेंटीमीटर, ग्राम और सैकंड है

ch. chapter, church का संक्षेप

chafe (चेफ़) *vt.* रगड़ कर कड़ा कर देना या घिसा देना; (हाथ) रगड़ कर गरमाना; तंग या परेशान करना

chaff (चाफ़) *n.* अनाज की भूसी, चोकर; कुट्टी; कूड़ा-करकट

chaffinch ('चैफिंच) *n.* एक छोटी चिड़िया

chagrin ('शैग्रिन) *n.* झेंप; खीज़, निराशा – *vt.* परेशानी में डालना

chain (चेन) *n.* जंजीर; सिकड़ी; बांधने की वस्तु; वस्तुओं या घटनाओं का सिलसिला; क्षेत्र नापने की लम्बी जंजीर; जरीब; श्रंखला – *vt.* (**chain up** भी) जंजीर से बांधना; बंद करना; रोकना – **chain reaction** एक से दूसरी घटना या प्रक्रिया होने का सिलसिला

chair (चेंअर) *n.* कुर्सी; पद; पीठ; प्राध्यापक का पद – *vt.* अध्यक्षता करना; विजेता को (कुर्सी पर बिठाकर या कन्धों पर) ले जाना – **chairman** *n.* (बैठक, सभा का) (पुरुष) अध्यक्ष या सभापति – **chairmanship** *n.* अध्यक्षता – **chairperson** *n.* अध्यक्ष या सभापति

chalk ('चॉक) *n.* खड़िया; चाक – *v.* चाक से रगड़ना, कोई आकृति बनाना या निशान लगाना; रूप रेखा बनाना – **chalky** *a* खड़ियामय

challenge ('चैलिंज) *vt.* को चुनौती देना; ललकारना; (किसी के कथन आदि के) ग़लत होने का दवा करना; विरोध करना; आपत्ति करना – *n.* – **challenged** *a.* – **mentally/physically/visually challenged** – विकलांग व्यक्तियों के लिए प्रयुक्त शब्द (जो किसी मानसिक, शारीरिक या दृष्टि दोष के शिकार हों)

chamber ('चैम्बर) *n.* सभा भवन; सभा या सदन (विधानसभा आदि); व्यक्तियों का समूह; कोठड़ी; कोटर – (~**s**) *pl.* वकील का कार्यालय; निवास स्थान – **chamber of commerce** वाणिज्य मंडल

chameleon (क'मीलिअन) *n.* गिरगिट

champ[1] (चैम्प) *v.* (भोजन) चबाते समय घोड़े के समान आवाज़ करना; घबराया हुआ होना; अधीर होना

champ[2] *n.* *CHAMPION* का संक्षेप

champagne (शैम्'पेन) *n.* हल्की, फेनदार शराब, शैम्पेन

champion ('चैम्पिअन) *n.* जो (किसी खेल आदि में) सब से आगे हो, सर्वजेता, विजेता; समर्थक, हिमायती; जो दूसरों के लिए लड़े; नायक – *vt.* किसी लक्ष्य के लिए संघर्ष करना; समर्थन या हिमायत करना – **championship** *n.* समर्थन; सर्वविजय, खेल प्रतियोगिता में सर्वप्रथम स्थान

chance (चांस) *n.* घटनाक्रम जिसका पहले से अनुमान न हो सके; संयोग, भाग्य; अवसर; मौका; संभावना; जोखिम – *vt.* दांव पर रखना, जोखिम में डालना – *vi.* होना, घटना – *a.* संयोगवश, अप्रत्याशित

chancellor ('चान्सलर) *n.* राज्य का एक ऊंचा अधिकारी; मंत्री; विश्वविद्यालय का अध्यक्ष, कुलपति – **chancellorship** *n.*

chandelier (शैन्डि'लिअर) *n.* (टांगने का) झाड़ (जिसमें मोमबत्तियों या बल्बों के लिए स्थान हो); दीपाधार

change (चेंज) *v.* बदलना; भिन्न हो जाना या करना; कपड़े या आवरण बदलना – *vt.* किसी वस्तु के बदले कुछ और देना; विनिमय करना; बदलना; रुपये भुनाना या तुड़ाना – *n.* परिवर्तन; बदलाव; विभिन्नता; विविधता; रेज़गारी; छुट्टा; अदायगी के बाद बची रकम; शेष राशि – **changeable** *a.* परिवर्तनीय – **changing room** खेलने, तैरने आदि के लिए जाने से पहले कपड़े बदलने का कमरा, वस्त्र-कक्ष

channel ('चैनल) *n.* नदी तल; जलान्तराल; खाड़ी, बंदरगाह का गहरा भाग; खांचा; माध्यम; धारा; रेडियो फ्रीक्वेंसी; टी.वी. प्रसारण स्टेशन – *vt.* खांचा या नाली बनाना; ले जाना या पहुंचाना

chant (चांट) *n.* गीत; राग; नारा जो बार बार लगाया जाय – *v.* बराबर एक ही नारा लगाना; एक ही राग अलापना या रट लगाना

chaos ('केऑस) *n.* अव्यवस्था; गड़बड़झाला – **chaotic** *a.* अस्त व्यस्त; अव्यवस्थित

chap[1] (चैप) *v.* ठण्ड से त्वचा का सूख कर फट जाना या उसमें दरारें पड़ना (**-pp-**) – **chapped** *a.*

chap[2] *n. inf.* व्यक्ति; आदमी

chapel ('चैपल) *n.* किसी संस्था आदि का निजी गिरजाघर; ऐसे व्यक्तियों का पूजाघर जो मुख्य चर्च के अनुयायी नह हैं

chaperon(e) ('शैपरोन) *n.* व्यक्ति (बहुधा महिला) जो किसी अविवाहित युवती के साथ रहे, संरक्षिका – *vt.* संरक्षिका का काम करना

chapter ('चैप्टर) *n.* पुस्तक का भाग; अध्याय; अनुभाग; पादरियों की सभा या मण्डली किसी समाज या संस्था की संगठित शाखा; बिरादरी

char (चार) *vt.* झुलसाना (**-rr-**)

character ('कैरिक्टर) *n.* स्वभाव; व्यक्तित्व के सभी गुण; चरित्र, चालचलन; नैतिक गुण; चरित्र, सनकी व्यक्ति; (कहानी, उपन्यास का) पात्र; वर्ण; अक्षर; अंक; छाप; विशेष गुण – **characteristic** (-'रिस्टिक) *a.* विशिष्ट – *n.* – **characteristically** *adv.* – **characterization** *n.* चरित्र-चित्रण; लक्षण-वर्णन – **characterize** *vt.* चरित्र-चित्रण करना; की विशेषता या गुण बताना – **characterless** *a.* नीरस, फीका; व्यक्तित्वहीन

charade (श'राड) *n.* बेतुका या हास्यासपद काम; विक त रूप; नकल – *pl.* एक खेल जिसमें विरोधी टीम की भाव भंगिमा से किसी शब्द का अनुमान लगाया जाता है; शब्द-पहेली

charcoal ('चार्कोल) *n.* लकड़ी का कोयला

charge (चार्ज) *vt.* दाम या कीमत मांगना; आरोप लगाना; कार्य सौंपना; आदेश देना; आक्रमण करना; धावा बोलना या चढ़ाई करना; (न्यायाधीश का) आदेश देना; में बिजली उत्पन्न करना, भरना – *vi* धावा; बोलना, आक्रमण करना – *n.* मूल्य, अभियोग, जुर्म; धावा आदेश, (बिजली का) आवेश/चार्ज – *pl.* खर्च; प्रभार, शुल्क – **chargeable** *a.* जिस पर शुल्क लगे, जिसका मूल्य चुकाना पड़े; (खर्चा) जो दफ्तर आदि के नाम डाला जा सके; आदेय – **charger** *n.* युद्ध का घोड़ा; (बैटरी आदि में) बिजली भरने का उपकरण – **charge sheet** पुलिस स्टेशन में रखी सूची जिसमें अपराध-विशेष अपराधियों के नाम होते हैं; *India* अभियोग-पत्र

chariot ('चैरिअट) *n.* रथ; राजसी गाड़ी – **charioteer** *n.* सारथी

charisma (क'रिज़्मअ) *n.* व्यक्ति के विशेष गुण; आकर्षण – **charismatic** *a.*

charity ('चैरिटि) *n.* दया; दान, परोपकार; दान-राशि, दान की गई वस्तुएं आदि; हितैषिता, दयाभाव – **charitable** *a.* धमार्थ; दयालु

charlatan ('शार्लटन) *n.* ढोंगी; पाखंडी

charm (चार्म) *n.* आकर्षण; आकर्षक वस्तु; गंडा, तावीज़; जन्तर – *vt.* मुग्ध करना – **charmed** *a.* मोहित – **charmer** *n.* – **charming** *a.* आकर्षक, मोहक

chart (चार्ट) *n.* मानचित्र, रेखाचित्र; सारणी; विवरण – *vt.* मानचित्र या रेखाचित्र बनाना

charter ('चार्टर) *n.* अधिकार-पत्र; सनद; घोषणापत्र – *vt.* (सवारी) किराए पर देना या लेना – **chartered accountant** चार्टर्ड अकांउटैंट – **chartered bus** अनुबंधित बस

chary ('चेंअरि) *a.* चौकस; संकोची

chase (चेस) *vt.* शिकार करना; पीछे जाना; पीछे पड़ना; खदेड़ देना – *n.* पीछा; शिकार

chasm ('कैज़्म) *n.* गहरी खाई; (पहाड़ी आदि की) दरार

chassis ('शैसि) *n.* मोटर गाड़ी के नीचे का ढांचा; विमान के नीचे का ढांचा

chaste (चेस्ट) *a.* सती, साध्वी; पतिव्रता; शुद्ध; सुशील; सदाचारी – **chastity** *n.* सतीत्व; शुद्धता

chasten ('चेसन) *vt.* दण्ड देकर सुधारना; रोकना – **chastened** *a.* जो दण्ड पाकर सुधर जाये – **chastise** *vt.* दण्ड देना; बुरी तरह डांटना – **chastisement** *n.*

chat[1] (चैट) *vi.* इधर उधर की बातचीत करना; गप्प लड़ाना (**-tt-**) – *n.* बातचीत, गपशप – **chattily** *adv.* – **chatty** *a.* बातूनी; (बातचीत में) अनौपचारिक, मैत्रीपूर्ण – **chat room** इंटरनेट पर गपशप का स्थान – **chat show** रेडियो या टी.वी. कार्यक्रम जिसमें लोगों से बेतकल्लुफ़ बातचीत की जाती है

chatter ('चैटर) *vi.* बकबक करना; (सरदी या डर से) दांत बजना – *n.* बकबक – **chatterbox** *n.* बातूनी, बक्की

chauffeur ('शोफ़र) *n.* कार का वेतनभोगी चालक (**chauffeuse** *fem.*– फ़र्ज़)

chauvinism ('शोविनिज़्म) *n.* उग्रराष्ट्रीयता; अपने को ऊंचा समझने की प्रव ति – **chauvinist** *n.* उग्रराष्ट्रवादी

cheap (चीप) *a.* सस्ता; सुलभ; तुच्छ या निकम्मा, बेकार; घटिया – *adv.* सस्ते दामों में – **cheapen** *vt.* सस्ता या घटिया कर देना; (घटिया व्यवहार से किसी की नजरों में) गिर जाना – **cheaply** *adv.*

cheat (चीट) *v.* धोखा देना; ठगना– *n.* धोखेबाज

check (चेंक) *vt.* रोकना रुकावट डालना; जांच करना – *n.* रोक; रोध; रुकावट; जांच; कपड़े पर चारखाने; शतरंज में शह या किश्त – *a.* चारखाने वाला – **check-in (desk)** *n.* होटल, हवाई अड्डे पर पहुंचने की सूचना (देने का स्थान) – **checklist** *n.* करने वाले कार्यों की सूची – **checkmate** *n. Chess* शतरंज में शह मात; कोई भी हार – *vt. Chess* शहदेना; हराना – **checkout** *n.* सुपर बाज़ार आदि में सामान की कीमत चुकाने का स्थान; होटल छोड़ने का समय – **checkpoint** *n.* सामान, यातायात आदि की जांच की चौकी (प्राय: सीमा पर) – **checkup** *n.* रोगी की पूरी जांच, डाक्टरी जांच – **check in** होटल, हवाई अड्डे आदि पर पहुंचने की सूचना देना – **check out** बिल अदा करके होटल छोड़ना

checked (चेंक्ट) *a.* जिसपर छोटे छोट खाने बने हों

checker देखिए CHEQUER

Cheddar ('चेंडर) *n.* चिकना, कड़ा, पनीर

cheek (चीक) *n.* गाल – *vt. inf.* ध ष्टता, गुस्ताखी से पेश आना – **cheeky** *a.*

cheep (चीप) *vi.* पक्षियों का चींचीं करना – *n.*

cheer (चिअर) *vt.* दिलासा देना; धीरज बंधाना, की (तालियां बजा कर) जयजयकार करना – *vi.* – *n.* जयजयकार; आनंद, प्रसन्नता – **cheerful** *a.* प्रसन्नचित्त, प्रफुल्ल – **cheerfully** *adv.* प्रसन्नतापूर्वक, खुशी से

– **cheerfulness** *n.* प्रसन्नता – **cheerily** *adv* – **cheers**! शराब का पहला जाम उठाते समय उद्गार, 'शुभकामना!' – **cheerio** (चिअ'रिओ) *intej* (उद्गार) शुभकामना

cheese (चीज़) *n.* पनीर – **cheesecloth** *n.* झीना सूती कपड़ा – **cheeseparing** *a.* कंजूस – **cheesed off** *a.* नाराज; ऊबा हुआ

cheetah ('चीट्अ) *n.* चीता

chef (शेफ़) *n.* मुख्य रसोइया, विशे. रेस्तोरां में

chemistry ('कैमिस्ट्रि) *n.* रसायन-विज्ञान, रसायन शास्त्र – **chemical** ('कैमिकल) *a.* रासायनिक – *n.* रसायन – **chemically** *adv.* – **chemist** ('कैमिस्ट) *n.* कैमिस्ट, रसायनशास्त्री

chemotherapy (कैमो'थैरपि) *n.* रसायनों से रोगों (विशे. कैंसर) का उपचार

chenille (श'नील) *n.* शनील

cheque, *US* **check** (चैक) *n.* चैक – **chequebook** *n.* चैक बुक

chequer ('चैकर) *n.* चारखाना जैसा कि शतरंज की बिसात पर बना होता है; शतरंज जैसे खेलों में प्रयुक्त गोटियां – (~ **s**) *pl.* ऐसे चारखाने; ड्राफ्ट्स का खेल – *vt.* चारखाने बनाना – **chequered** ('चैकर्ड) *a.* चारखनेदार; रंग बिरंगा; उतार-चढ़ाव वाला

cherish ('चैरिश) *vt.* कद्र करना; दिल में संजोए रखना

cheroot (श'रूट) *n.* चुरुट

cherry ('चैरि) *n.* लाल रंग का बेर जैसा फल, चेरी – *a.* चमकीला लाल, बदरीरक्त

cherub ('चैरब) *n.* फरिश्ता; देवदूत (*pl.* **cherubim, cherubs**) – **cherubic** (च'रूबिक) *a.* देवदूत जैसा

chess (चैस) *n.* शतरंज

chest (चैस्ट) *n.* छाती; वक्षःस्थल; पेटी; सन्दूक – **chest of drawers** मेज़ जैसी अलमारी जिसमें दराज़ लगे होते हैं

chestnut ('चैस्नट) *n.* पांगर व क्ष और उस का फल (जो अखरोट जैसा होता है)

chew (चू) *v.* चबाना – *n.* – **chewy** *a.* कड़ा; जिसे चबाना पड़े – **chewing gum** *n.* चुइंग-गम

chic (शिक) *a.* बना-ठना, बांका – *n.* ऐसा व्यक्ति

chicanery (शि'केनरि) *n.* छल-फ़रेब; धोखा; झांसा-पट्टी

chick, chicken (चिक, 'चिकिन) *n.* चूजा, मुर्गी; *sl.* छोकरी, युवती –**chicken feed** मामूली रकम – **chicken-hearted** *a.* कायर, डरपोक – **chicken out** डर के मारे किसी काम से पीछे हट जाना – **chickenpox** *n.* छोटी माता – **chickpea** *n.* छोटे दाने का मटर

chicory ('चिकरि) *n.* कासनी (एक पौधा, जिस की जड़ का चूर्ण काफ़ी में मिलाया जाता है या उसके स्थान पर प्रयुक्त होता है)

chide (चाइड) *vt.* डांटना; (**chid** *pt.*, **chidden, chid** *pp.*, **chiding** *pr. p.*)

chief (चीफ) *n.* मुख्य अधिकारी; मुखिया – *a.* प्रमुख; सर्वोच्च – **chiefly** *adv.* मुख्यतया

chiffon (शि'फ़ॉन) *n.* झीना, महीन कपड़ा

child (चाइल्ड) *n.* बच्चा, बालक; संतान (*pl.* **children** ('चिल्ड्रन)) – **childish** *a.* बचकाना; मूर्खतापूर्ण – **childishly** *adv.* – **childless** *a.* निसंतान – **childlike** *a.* बालसुलभ; निष्कपट – **childbirth** *n.* प्रसव – **childhood** *n.* बचपन – **child abuse** बच्चे के साथ शारीरिक या भावनात्मक रूप से अनुचित व्यवहार – **child's play** बहुत आसान काम

chill (चिल) *n.* ठण्डक; कंपकंपी, उदासी या निराशा उत्पन्न करने वाली बात – *v.* (पेय, भोजन) ठण्डा करना – **chilly** *a.* ठण्डा (मौसम); रूखा

chilli ('चिलि) *n.* लाल मिर्च या उसका पौधा

chime (चाइम) *n.* घण्टी की आवाज़; लयपूर्ण घण्टानाद

chimney ('चिम्नि) *n.* चिमनी (*pl.* – **neys**)

chimpanzee (चिम्पैन्ˈज़ी) *n.* चिम्पैंज़ी
chin (चिन) *n.* ठोड़ी, ठुड्डी
china (ˈचाइन्अ) *n.* बढ़िया चीनी मिट्टी के बरतन; प्यालों, प्लेटों के लिए सामूहिक नाम
chink[1] (चिंक) *n.* दरार, दरक
chink[2] *n.* धातु गिरने आदि की हल्की आवाज़, खनक
chip (चिप) *n.* आलू का पतला, तला हुआ टुकड़ा (*US:* **potato chip** भी); (लकड़ी की) खपची; स्थान जहां से टुकड़ा टूट गया हो; टुकड़ा; (**microchip** भी) कम्प्यूटर आदि में लगने वाला सिलिकॉन का पतला टुकड़ा, चिप – *vt.* छोटा-सा टुकड़ा तोड़ना (**chipped** *pt./pp.*) – *vi.* **chip in** बात काटना
chirp, chirrup (चर्प, ˈचिरप) *n.* चहक; पक्षी की च ची – *vi.* चहकना; च च करना – **chirpy** *a. inf.* चहकता हुआ; प्रसन्नचित
chisel (ˈचिज़ल) *n.* (लकड़ी आदि काटने की) छैनी; रुखानी – *vt.* छैनी से काटना; *sl.* धोखाधड़ी करना (**chiselled** *pt./pp.*) – **chiselled** *a.* तीखे (नैन-नक्श)
chit[1] (चिट) *n.* पर्ची; रुक्का; चिट्ठी
chit[2] *n.* बालक; कम आयु की युवती, छोकरी
chitchat (ˈचिट्चैट) *n.* गपशप, बातचीत
chivalry (ˈशिवल्रि) *n.* वीरता और सज्जनता; मध्य युग की सामंत पद्धति – **chivalrous** *a.* उदारचेता; क्षात्रधर्मी – **chivalrously** *adv.*
chive (चाइव़) *n.* एक जड़ी जिस में प्याज़ जैसी गन्ध होती है
chloride (ˈक्लॉराइड) *n.* क्लोरिन का एक यौगिक; रंग काटने का पदार्थ – **chlorine** (ˈक्लॉरिन) *n.* क्लोरिन
chlorofluorocarbon (क्लॉरो ˈफ़्लुअरोकार्बन) *n.* (CFC), एक गैस जो वायुमंडल में ओज़ोन की सतह को हानि पहुंचाती है
chloroform (ˈक्लॉरफ़ॉर्म) *n.* हवा में उड़ जाने वाला द्रव जो पहले रोगियों को बेहोश करने के काम आता था, क्लोरोफ़ार्म – *vt.* क्लोरोफार्म सुंघा कर बेहोश करना
chlorophyll (ˈक्लॉरफ़िल) *n.* पौधों में हरे रंग का अंश, पर्णहरित, क्लोरोफ़िल
chock-a-block, chock-full *a.* ठसाठस (भरा हुआ)
chocolate (ˈचॉक्लिट) *n.* चॉकलेट – *a.* कत्थई रंग
choice (चॉइस) *n.* चुनने का कार्य या अधिकार; चुनाव; विकल्प; रुचि; चुना गया व्यक्ति या वस्तु – *a.* चुनिन्दा; बढ़िया
choir (क्वाइअर) *n.* गायक मण्डली, विशे. गिरजाघर की – **choir boy** गिराजाघर की गायक-मण्डली का सदस्य लड़का
choke (चोक) *vt.* सांस घोटना, गला दबाना; बाधा डालना – *vi.* दम घुटना – *n.* इंजन के कार्बुटर में पेट्रोल और हवा का मिश्रण सुधारने का पुर्जा – **choked** *a.* अवरुद्ध, दबा हुआ (स्वर)
cholera (ˈकॉलर्अ) *n.* हैज़ा
cholesterol (कˈलेस्टरॉल) *n.* जीवों के ऊतकों और चर्बी में मिलने वाला पदार्थ
chomp (चॉम्प) *v.* चबाते समय चप-चप की आवाज़ करना
choose (चूज़) *vt.* चुनना, पसंद करना; चुन कर लेना – *vi.* ठीक समझना; फ़ैसला करना (**chose, chosen, choosing**) – **choosy** *a.* जो आसानी से किसी चीज़ को पसंद न करे
chop[1] (चॉप) *vt.* (गंडासे आदि से) काटना या टुकड़े करना (**-pp-**) – *n.* वार जिससे कोई वस्तु काटी जा सके; काटने की क्रिया; काटा हुआ टुकड़ा; मांस का टुकड़ा जिसमें प्राय: सीने की हड्डी हो – **chopper** *n.* गंडासा; *inf.* हेलीकॉप्टर; *inf.* बड़ी मोटर साइकिल – **choppy** *a.* (समुद्र) जिसमें छोटी-छोटी ज़ोरदार लहरें उठ रही हों, अशांत (समुद्र)

chopsticks (ˈचॉप्स्टिक्स) *pl. n.* बांस आदि की लम्बी तीलियां या खपचियां जिन से चीन के लोग खाना खाते हैं

chord (कॉर्ड) *n.* स्वर संघात; **Math** जीवा

chore (चॉर) *n.* (अप्रिय) काम; इधर-उधर का काम – **household chores** घर का काम

choreography (कॉरिˈऑग्रफि) *n.* न त्यों, विशे. न त्य-नाटिका (बैले) को, नियोजित करने की कला; न त्य नाटिका की स्वर लिपि लिखने की कला – **choreographer** *n.* न त्यनियोजक/निर्देशक

chortle (ˈचाट्र्ल) *vi.* (खुशी से) घुरघुरा कर हंसना – *n.* ऐसी हंसी

chorus (ˈकॉरस) *n.* गायक-दल; व न्दगान; *fig.* सामूहिक रूप (से विरोध आदि)

chose (चोज़) CHOOSE का *pt* – **chosen** (चोज़न) *pp.*

Christ (क्राइस्ट) *n.* ईसा मसीह

Christian (ˈक्रिस्चन) *n.* ईसाई – *a.* ईसाई; ईसा या ईसाई धर्म सम्बंधी – **christen** (ˈक्रिसन) *vt.* बपतिस्मा देना; नाम रखना – **Christianity** (क्रिस्टिˈऐनिटि) *n.* ईसाई धर्म – **Christianize** (ˈक्रिस्यधनाइज़) *vt.* ईसाई धर्म का अनुयायी बनाना – **Christian name** व्यक्ति का नाम (कुलनाम, गोत्र आदि के विपरीत) जो ईसाईयों में बपतिस्मा के समय रखा जाता है

Christmas (ˈक्रिस्मस) *n.* यशु मसीह का जन्मोत्सव, क्रिसमस (25th **December**) बड़ा दिन

chromosome (ˈक्रोमसोम) *n.* कोशिका के ऊतक में सूक्ष्म तत्व जो आनुवंशिक गुणों के लिए जिम्मेदार है, गुणसूत्र, क्रोमोसोम

chronic (ˈक्रॉनिक) *a.* चिरकालिक; पुराना

chronicle (ˈक्रॉनिकल) *n.* समयक्रम में घटनाओं का वर्णन; इतिव त्त, इतिहास – *vt.* इतिव त लिखना – **chronicler** *n.* इतिहासकार

chronology (क्रˈनॉलजि) *n.* घटनाओं का सिलसिलेवार क्रम – **chronological** (क्रॉनˈलॉजिकल) *a.* सिलसिलेवार

chrysanthemum (क्रिˈसैंथमम) *n.* गुल दाउदी फूल

chubby (ˈचबि) *a.* गोल मटोल, मोटा

chuck (चक) *inf. vt.* फैंक देना; प्यार से थपथपाना (ठोड़ी के नीचे); छोड़ना या त्याग देना

chuckle (ˈचकल) *vi.* धीरे धीरे या मुंह बंद करके हंसना – *n.* दबी हुई हंसी

chum (चम) *n. inf.* घनिष्ट मित्र – **chummy** *a.*

chunk (चंक) *n.* टुकड़ा बड़ी मात्रा, भाग

church (चर्च) *n.* गिरजाघर – **Church** *n.* ईसाई मत; पादरी गण

churlish (ˈचर्लिश) *a.* असभ्य, उजड्ड

churn (चर्न) *n.* दूध का बड़ा बरतन, मटका – *vt.* बिलोना PARACHUTE का संक्षेप

chute (शूट) *n.* ढालू नाली

chutney (ˈचट्नि) *n.* चटनी

chutzpah (ˈहुट्स्पअ) *n.* हिम्मत, साहस (विशे० अपने अफसर आदि से स्पष्ट बात करने का)

CIA *US* Central Intelligence Agency केन्द्रीय गुप्तचर विभाग का संक्षेप

cicada (सिˈकाइअ) *n.* झ गुर जैसा कीड़ा, रइयां

CID Criminal Investigation Department का संक्षेप

cider (ˈसाइडर) *n.* सेब का आसव (एक हल्की शराब)

cigar (सिˈगार) *n.* सिगार, चुरुट – **cigarette** (सिगˈरैंट) *n.* सिगरेट

cilantro (सिˈलैन्ट्रो) *n. US* (*coriander*) हरा धनिया

C-in-C Commander-in-Chief का संक्षेप

cinch (सिंच) *n. inf.* आसान काम

cinder (ˈसिंडर) *n.* जले कोयले की राख

cinema (ˈसिनिम्अ) *n.* सिनेमाघर; चलचित्र (सामान्यतया या सामूहिक रूप से)

cineraria (सिन'रेंअरिअ) *n.* पौधा जिसमें डेज़ी जैसे फूल लगते हैं, सिनरेरिया

cinnamon ('सिनमन) *n.* दालचीनी; उसका पेड़ – *a.* हलके भूरे रंग का

cipher, cypher ('साइफ़र) *n.* गुप्त लिखाई, गूढ़लेख; शून्य; *fig.* नगण्य या महत्वहीन व्यक्ति; शब्द-चिन्ह; गुम्फाक्षर – *vt.* गूढ़ाक्षरों में लिखना

circa ('सर्‌कअ) *lat.* सन

circle ('सर्कल) *n.* वृत्त; घेरा; *Theatre* सभा भवन के तल के ऊपर के स्थान; समान उद्देश्यों वाला संगठन; मण्डली; समाज का वर्ग – *vt.* घेरा डालना – *vi* के इर्द गिर्द घूमना – **circular** ('सर्क्युलर) *a.* वृत्ताकार – *n.* चिट्ठी जो बहुत से व्यक्तियों को एक साथ भेजी जाये, सर्क्युलर, परिपत्र – **circulate** ('सर्‌क्युलेट) *vi.* घूमना; प्रचारित करना (व्यक्तियों और स्थानों में) – *vt.* परिचालित करना – **circulation** (सर्क्यु'लेशन) *n.* रक्त संचार; प्रसार; वितरण; संचार; समाचार पत्र की बिक्री की संख्या

circuit ('सर्किट) *n.* परिक्रमा, चक्कर; क्षेत्र; बिजली के करेंट का रास्ता, सर्किट; दौरा, विशे. न्यायाधीशों का; खेलों की श्रृंखला; मण्डल या जिला – **circuitous** (सर्‌'क्युइटस) *a.* चक्करदार

circumcise ('सर्कम्‌साइज़) *vt.* लिंग की ऊपरी त्वचा काटना, खतना या सुन्नत करना – **circumcision** (सर्कम्‌'सिझ़न) *n.* ख़तना

circumference (सर्‌'कम्फ़रन्स) *n.* सीमारेखा, विशे. वृत्त की परिधि; घेरा

circumlocution (सर्कम्‌ल'क्यूशन) *n.* घुमा फिरा कर कही गयी बात, वाग्जाल

circumscribe (सर्कम्‌'स्क्राइब) *vt.* सीमित या सीमाबद्ध करना; घेरना; बाधा डालना

circumspect ('सर्कम्‌स्पेक्ट) *a.* चौकस, सतर्क, सावधान; विवेकशील

circumstance ('सर्कम्सटन्स) *n.* ब्यौरा; घटना; तथ्य – (~ **s**) *pl.* परिस्थितियां – **circumstantial** (सर्कम्‌स्'टैन्शल) *a.* पारिस्थितिक

circumvent (सर्कम्‌वेन्ट) *vt.* बचना; से बच निकलना

circus ('सर्कस) *n.* सर्कस; सार्वजनिक प्रयोग के लिए रंगशाला; नगर का गोल चौक जहां कई सड़कें आ कर मिलती हैं (*pl.* **circuses**)

cirrhosis (सि'रोसिस) *n.* जिगर की बीमारी

cistern ('सिस्टर्न) *n.* पानी की टंकी

citadel ('सिटडल) *n.* गढ़, नगर-दुर्ग

cite (साइट) *vt.* उद्धरण या हवाला देना – **citation** *n.* उद्धरण; बहादुरी के लिए प्रशस्ति पत्र

citizen ('सिटिज़न) *n.* नागरिक; नगरवासी – **citizenship** *n.* नागरिकता

citron ('सिट्रन) *n.* निम्बू जैसा फल; गलगल – **citric acid** नींबू, संतरे आदि में मिलने वाला हलका तेज़ाब – **citrus fruit** ('सिट्रस-) नींबू; मुसम्मी; नारंगी जैसे फल

city ('सिटि) *n.* नगर, शहर

civic ('सिविक) *a.* नगर या नागरिकों से सम्बन्धित – **civics** *n.* नागरिक शास्त्र

civil ('सिविल) *a.* नागरिकों से सम्बन्धित; असैनिक; परिष्कृत, शिष्ट, सभ्य; *Law* दीवानी (फौजदारी के विपरीत) – **civilian** *n.* असैनिक व्यक्ति अथवा कर्मचारी – **civility** *n.* शिष्टता – **civil engineer** सड़क, पुल आदि के निर्माण से सम्बंधित इंजीनियर, सिविल इंजीनियर – **civil service** प्रशासनिक सेवा – **civil war** गृह युद्ध

civilize ('सिविलाइज़) *vt.* सभ्य बनाना; परिष्कृत करना – **civilization** (सिविलाइ'ज़ेशन) *n.* सभ्यता – **civilized** *a.* सभ्य

clack (क्लैक) *n./v.* खटखट (करना)

clad (क्लैड) CLOTHE का *pt./pp.*

claim (क्लेम) *vt.* अधिकार के रूप में मांगना, दावा

करना – *vi.* बीमे का दावा करना – *n.* (अधिकार का) दावा, अधिकार; दावे की वस्तु – **claimant** *n.* दावेदार

clairvoyance (क्लेअर् वॉइअन्स) *n.* भविष्य में होने वाली घटनाओं के बारे में बता सकने की शक्ति, अतीन्द्रिय द ष्टि – **clairvoyant** *n./a.* सूक्ष्मदर्शी

clamber (क्लैम्बर) *vi.* बड़ी कठिनाई से चढ़ना; हाथ-पैर के बल चढ़ना

clamour (क्लैमर) *n.* शोर; चीख-पुकार, दुहाई – *vi.* जोर-जोर से बोलना या कोई चीज मांगना

clamp (क्लैम्प) *n.* पकड़ने या दबाने का औज़ार, शिकंजा – *vt.* – **clampdown** *n.* (~ **on**) के विरूद्ध कार्यवाही; पकड़-धकड़

clan (क्लैन) *n.* कबीला; दल

clandestine (क्लैन् डैंस्टिन, – डैंस्टाइन) *a.* गुप्त; चोरी-छिपे

clang (क्लैङ) *v.* टनटनाना, टनटन की आवाज़ करना – *n.* टन-टन की आवाज़

clank (क्लैंक) *n.* धातु की वस्तुओं के परस्पर बजने की आवाज, टन-टन – *v.*

clap[1] (क्लैप) *vt.* थपकी देना, (ताली) बजाना; जल्दी से रख देना – *vi.* कड़कना; ताली बजाना; प्रशंसा करना (**-pp-**) – *n.* कड़कड़ाहट; गड़गड़ाहट (बादलों की); तालियां

clap[2] *n. sl.* सूज़ाक, उपदंश

claret (क्लैरट) *n.* फ्रांस की लाल रंग की शराब

clarify (क्लैरिफ़ाइ) *v.* स्पष्ट करना; शुद्ध हो जाना, समझ में आना (**clarified** *pt./pp.*, **clarifying** *pr.p.*) – **clarification** (क्लैरि फ़िकेशन) *n.* स्पष्टीकरण, सफ़ाई – **clarity** (क्लैरिटि) *n.* स्पष्टता

clarinet (क्लैरि नेंट) *n.* शहनाई जैसा एक बाजा, क्लैरिनेट

clash (क्लैश) *n.* (हथियारों के टकराने की) खटखटाहट; (*fig*) झगड़ा, टक्कर; संघर्ष – *vi.* टकराना; संघर्ष करना; (घटनाओं; कार्यक्रम आदि का) एक ही समय होना; (रंगों, विचारों का) मेल न खाना – *vt.* खटखटाना

clasp (क्लास्प) *n.* बकसुआ; आलिंगन – *vt.* बांधना, आलिंगन करना, गले लगाना; जकड़ना; जोर से पकड़ना

class (क्लास) *n.* वर्ग, श्रेणी कक्षा; योग्यता पर आधारित वर्ग; गुण; *inf.* श्रेष्ठता – *vt.* सही वर्ग में रखना – **classify** (क्लैसिफ़ाइ) *vt.* वर्गीकरण करना (**classified, classifying**) – **classification** *n.* वर्गीकरण – **classified** *a.* गुप्त(जानकारी); वर्गीक त (विज्ञापन) – **class-conscious** *a.* जिसे जाति या वर्ग विशेष का होने का अहसास हो – **class struggle** (**class war** भी) वर्ग-संघर्ष

classic (क्लैसिक) *a.* अति उत्तम; श्रेष्ठ (विशे. कलाक ति के लिए प्रयुक्त); आदर्श; चिरप्रतिष्ठित – *n.* सर्वमान्य, उच्च कोटि की साहित्यक रचना – *pl. n.* प्राचीन ग्रीक व लैटिन साहित्य – **classical** *a.* उच्च स्तर का (ग्रीक व रोमन साहित्य, कला, संस्क ति)

clatter (क्लैटर) *n.* खड़खड़ाहट

clause (क्लॉज़) *n. Grammar* उपवाक्य; संधि, अनुबंध-पत्र (इकरारनामा) आदि का खण्ड

claustrophobia (क्लॉस्ट्र फ़ोबिअ) *n.* बंद जगह (कमरा, लिफ्ट) से डर लगना

clavicle (क्लैविकल) *n.* हँसुली, कंधे को गर्दन से जोड़ने वाली हड्डी, कालरबोन

claw (क्लॉ) *n.* पशु, पक्षियों के नख, पंजा; पंजानुमा कोई वस्तु – *vt.* पंजों से दबोचना या पकड़ना

clay (क्ले) *n.* चिकनी मिट्टी; मिट्टी

clean (क्लीन) *a.* साफ़ शुद्ध; पवित्र; निर्मल; निर्दोष – *adv.* पूरी तरह से, साफ़-साफ़ – *vt.* सफ़ाई करना – **cleanliness** (क्लेंन्लिनिस) *n.* सफ़ाई, स्वच्छता – **cleanly** (क्लीन्लि) *adv.* सफ़ाई से – *a.* साफ – **cleanse** (क्लेंन्ज़) *vt.* शुद्ध करना, साफ़ करना; परिमार्जन करना

– **clean-shaven** *a.* जिसने दाढ़ी-मूंछ साफ कर रखी हो – **clean sweep** पूर्ण विजय

clear (क्लिअर) *a.* शुद्ध, साफ़; बाधा रहित –*adv.* चमकता हुआ, साफ़-साफ़, पूरी तरह से – *vt.* स्पष्ट करना; (दोष से) मुक्त करना; पार करना, लांघना; (मुनाफा) कमाना, (रास्ता) साफ़ करना, (मुश्किलें) दूर करना; (कर्ज़ा) चुकाना – *vi.* साफ़, स्वच्छ, निर्मल, पारदर्शक हो जाना – **clearance** *n.* – **clearing** *n.* भूमिखण्ड जहां से पेड़ साफ़ कर दिए गए हों

cleave[1] (क्लीव़) *vt.* टुकड़े करना, चीरना – *vi.* टुकड़े हो जाना, विभाजित होना (**clove, cleft** *pt.*, **cloven, cleft** *pp.*, **cleaving** *pr.p.*) – **cleavage** *n.* दरार; स्त्री के स्तनों के बीच का स्थान

cleave[2] *vi.* चिपकना, लगा रहना; वफादार रहना (**cleaved** *pt./pp.*) **cleaving** *pr. p.*,

cleft (क्लेफ़्ट) *n.* दरार, फटन; दरार के पड़ने से बना (चट्टान, पहाड़ी आदि में) खुला मुख अथवा छेद

clemency (ˈक्लेमंसि) *n.* दयाशीलता; राज्यक्षमा

clench (क्लेन्च) *vt.* (मुट्ठी) बांधना; (दांत) भ चना/पीसना; जकड़ना

clergy (ˈक्लर्जि) *n.* चर्च के पादरी वर्ग का सामूहिक नाम – **clergyman** *n.* पादरी

clerical (ˈक्लेरिकल) *a.* पादरियों से सम्बन्धित; सरकारी काम से सम्बन्धित या उस का; क्लर्क के काम से सम्बन्धित

clerk (क्लार्क, US क्लर्क) *n.* क्लर्क, लिपिक

clever (ˈक्लेव़र) *a.* बुद्धिमान; योग्य; दक्ष; कुशल, प्रवीण; चतुर; सूझ-बूझ या सोच-समझ वाला

cliché (ˈक्लीशे) *n.* घिसा-पिटा मुहावरा, अलंकार आदि (*pl.* **clichés**)

click[1] (क्लिक) *n.* 'खटाक' की आवाज़ –*vi.* 'खट' की आवाज़ करना; (जीभ) चटकाना

click[2] *vi.* *sl.* सफल होना; *inf.* समझ आ जाना; *inf.* दोस्त बन जाना

client (ˈक्लाइअंट) *n.* ग्राहक; मुवक्किल **clientele** (क्लीऑन्ˈटेल) *n.* ग्राहक-ग

cliff (क्लिफ़) *n.* सीधी खड़ी चट्टान **cliffhanger** *n.* तनावपूर्ण स्थिति

climate (ˈक्लाइमिट) *n.* जलवायु, आबोह वातावरण – **climatic** (क्लाइˈमैटिक)

climax (ˈक्लाइमैक्स) *n.* पराकाष्ठा; संभोग चरम बिन्दु – **climactic** (क्लाइˈमैक्टिक *a.* चरमोत्कर्ष वाला (द श्य)

climb (क्लाइम) *v.* (व क्ष, पर्वत आदि) पर चढ़ सीढ़ियां चढ़ना – *n.* चढ़ाई – **climb** (ˈक्लाइमर) *n.* (आरोही) बेल; चट्टानों आ पर चढ़ने वाला, आरोहक

clinch (क्लिंच) *vt.* समझौता या अनुबंध कर

cling (क्लिङ) *vi.* चिपकना; जुड़े रहना; लिपटन (पर) आश्रित होना (**clung** *pt./pp.*)

clinic (ˈक्लिनिक) *n.* दवाखाना, क्लीनिक **clinical** *a.* रोगियों की देखभाल आदि सम्बंधित; यथार्थ; भावशून्य; साधारण **clinical thermometer** थर्मामीटर

clink (क्लिंक) *n.* झनझनाहट (धातु की वस्तु के गिरने, टकराने की आवाज़) – *v.*

clip[1] (क्लिप) *vt.* कैंची से काटना; काट कर छो कर देना, कतरना (**-pp-**) – *n.* *inf.* तीव्र प्रहा

clip[2] (क्लिप) *n.* क्लिप, बालों को इकट्ठा रखने लिए) चुटकी; (**paper clip** भी) क्लिप **clipping** *n.* (अखबार आदि की) कतरन

clipper (ˈक्लिपर) *n.* तेज़ चलने वाला पानी जहाज़

clique (क्लीक) *n.* गुट – **cliquish** *a.*

clitoris (ˈक्लिटरिस) *n.* स्त्री की योनि में पुर के शिश्न के समानान्तर छोटा अंग; भगशिश् भगांकुर

cloak (क्लोक) *n.* लबादा; ओट; भेस; बहाना *vt.* लबादा पहनाना; ओट लेना; छिपाना **cloakroom** *n.* कोट, हैट आदि रखने कमरा; अमानती सामानघर

clobber (´क्लॉबर) *inf. vt.* बुरी तरह पीटना, करारी हार देना

clock (क्लॉक) *n.* घड़ी; मापकयंत्र (जैसे टैक्सी मीटर) – **clockwise** *adv./a.* बांये से दांये परिक्रमा (घड़ी की सुइयों की दिशा में) – **put the clock back** पुराने रूढ़िवादी तरीके/जीवन शैली अपनाना – **race against the clock** समय पर समाप्त करने के लिए तेज़ी से काम करना

clod (क्लॉड) *n.* मिट्टी का ढेला; गवांर

clog (क्लॉग) *vt.* रुकावट डालना, अड़ंगा लगाना; (पाइप में तेल आदि के बहाव को) रोक देना (*-gg-*) – *vi.* (**-gg-**) – *n.* रुकावट, बाधा; अर्गल; लकड़ी के तले वाले चमड़े के जूते

cloister (´क्लॉइस्टर) *n.* आच्छादित मार्ग; छत्ता; मठ – **cloistered** *a.* एकांत में

clone (क्लोन) *n.* बिना यौन सम्बंध के उत्पन्न एक ही जीव अथवा पौधों के वंशज जो मूल जीव/पौधे से हूबहू मिलते हैं, कंतक – *v.* कंतक बनाना

close[1] (क्लोस) *a.* निकट; घनिष्ठ; करीब-करीब बराबर; सतर्क; बंद; छिपाने वाला; गैर हवादार; (मौसम) घुटन वाला; चुप; कंजूस; तंग, संकीर्ण; सीमित – *adv.* करीब-करीब, निकट; ज़ोर से – *n.* बंद जगह, कैथीड्रल का अहाता – **closely** *adv.* – **closeness** *n.* – **close-fitting** *a.* तंग चुस्त (पोशाक) – **close-up** *n.* (फिल्म आदि में) निकट से लिया गया चित्र

close[2] (क्लोज़) *vt.* बंद करना; (सड़क) रोक देना; समाप्त करना – *vi.* जुड़ना, मिलना; बंद होना – *n.* समाप्ति; अंत

closed circuit television (CCTV) चोरी आदि रोकने के लिए व्यवसाय केंद्रों व सार्वजनिक भवनों में कैमरे व टेलीविज़न की व्यवस्था

closet (´क्लॉज़िट) *n.* **US, C** अलमारी; छोटा निजी कमरा; पाख़ाना, शौचगृह – *vt.* गुप्त परामर्श के लिए व्यक्तिगत कक्ष में बंद कर देना

clot (क्लॉट) *n.* थक्का, टुकड़ा; *inf.* मूर्ख; जमा हुआ खून – *vi.* खून जमना (**-tt-**) – **blood clot** खून का थक्का

cloth (क्लॉथ) *n.* कपड़ा – **clothes** (क्लोद्स) *pl. n.* कपड़े, पोशाक, बिछौना – **clothe** *vt.* वस्त्र पहनाना (**clothed** (क्लोद्ड) या **clad** *pt./pp.*) – **clothier** (´क्लोदिअर) *n.* – **clothing** *n.* वस्त्र, कपड़े

cloud (क्लाउड) *n.* बादल, घटा; *fig.* उदासी – *vt.* अंधेरा कर देना – *vi.* बादल घिर आना – **cloudburst** *n.* अचानक मूसलाधार वर्षा – **cloudy** *a.* घुटा हुआ (आकाश); मटमैला (द्रव), धुंधला – **under a cloud** शक के घेरे में

clout (क्लाउट) *n. inf.* प्रहार; प्रभाव, शक्ति – *vt.* प्रहार करना

clove[1] (क्लोव़) *n.* लौंग

clover (´क्लोव़र) *n.* पशुओं के चारे का पौधा, तिपतिया

clown (क्लाउन) *n.* मसख़रा, विदूषक

cloy (क्लॉइ) *vt.* मीठे के लगातार उपयोग का (व्यक्ति को) छका देना, परितृप्त कर देना, अघा देना

club (क्लब) *n.* मुगदर, मोटा डण्डा; एक प्रकार का बैट; क्लब, संघ; ताश में चिड़ी का पत्ता – *vt.* मुगदर से प्रहार करना – *vi.* सामूहिक हित के लिए इकट्ठे हो जाना (**-bb-**)

clue (क्लू) *n.* किसी रहस्य या पहेली का सुराग़

clump[1] (क्लंप) *n.* पेड़ों या पौधों का झुरमुट

clump[2] *vi.* बेढंगे तरीके से या भारी कदमों से चलना – *n.*

clumsy (´क्लम्ज़ि) *a.* बेढंगा, फूहड – **clumsily** *adv.*

clung (क्लङ) CLING का *pt./pp.*

cluster (´क्लस्टर) *n.* झुण्ड, समूह – *v.*

clutch[1] (क्लच) *v.* जकड़ना, पकड़ना – *n.* जकड़, पकड़; चंगुल; मशीन के दो घूमते भागों को जोड़ने

या अलग करने में सहायता करने वाला पुर्ज़ा, क्लच (कार आदि में)

clutter (´क्लटर) *v.* चीज़ें (कमरे आदि में) इधर-उधर फेंक देना, अव्यवस्थित कर देना – *n.*

cm centimetre (S) का संक्षेप

CNG Compressed Natural Gas का संक्षेप

CO Commanding Officer का संक्षेप

Co. Company का संक्षेप

c/o care of; carried over का संक्षेप

coach (कोच) *n.* लम्बी यात्रा वाली अथवा पर्यटक बस; बड़ी चार पहियों वाली (घोड़ा) गाड़ी; रेलगाड़ी का सवारी डिब्बा; शिक्षक; *Sport* कोच, प्रशिक्षक – *vt.* परीक्षा, खेल प्रतियोगिता आदि के लिए तैयार करना

coagulate (को´ऐग्युलेट) *v.* (खून का) जमना – **coagulation** (कोऐग्यु´लेशन) *n.* जमाव, स्कंदन

coal (कोल) *n.* पत्थर का कोयला; दहकता अंगारा – **coal tar** कोलतार

coalesce (कोअ´लेंस) *vi.* एक हो जाना – **coalescence** (कोअ´लेंसन्स) *n.*संलीन या एक होने की क्रिया

coalition (कोअ´लिशन) *n.* गठबंधन

coarse (कॉर्स) *a.* खुरदरा; रूखा; स्थूल; अश्लील, गवांरू – **coarsely** *adv.* – **coarseness** *n.*

coast (कोस्ट) *n.* समुद्र तट – *v.* गति संवेग के साथ (बिना इंजन चालू रखे) चलते चले जाना; बिना अधिक प्रयत्न के आगे बढ़ना; (जहाज़ आदि का) तट के किनारे-किनारे जाना – **coastal** *a.* समुद्रतटीय – **coastguard** *n.* तटरक्षक – **coastline** *n.* तट-रेखा

coat (कोट) *n.* कोट; जानवर की बालों वाली खाल, पक्षी के रोएं; आवरण – *vt.* तह चढ़ाना; पहनाना – **coating** *n.* लेप, तह

coax (कोक्स) *vt.* प्यार से बात मानने पर राजी करना

coaxial (को´ऐक्सिअल) *a.* समान अक्ष वाली (तारें आदि); समाक्षी

cob (कॉब) *n.* छोटी जाति का एक घोड़ा; नर राजहंस; भुट्टा; गोल डबलरोटी

cobalt (´कोबॉल्ट) *n.* कोबाल्ट धातु

cobble (´कॉबल) *vt.* पैबंद लगाना; जूतों की मरम्मत करना – *n.* गोल पत्थर – **cobbler** *n.* मोची

cobra (´कोब्रअ) *n.* नाग, काला सांप

cobweb (´कॉब्वेब) *n.* मकड़ी का जाला

cocaine (क´केन) *n.* एक नशीला पदार्थ कोकेन

cochineal (´कॉचि´नील) *n.* किरमिज़ी रंग

cock (कॉक) *n.* मुर्गा; नरपक्षी; नल की टोंटी; बन्दूक का घोड़ा – *vt.* घोड़ा चढ़ाना, बन्दूक चलाने की स्थिति में लाना); सिर ऊपर करना या घुमाना – **cockerel** (´कॉकरल) *n.* छोटा मुर्गा, पट्ठा – **cockeye(d)** *a.* भैंगा; टेढ़ा, तिरछा

cockpit (´कॉक्पिट) *n.* (वायुयान व रेसवाली कार में) चालक स्थान, छोटे जहाज़ में कक्ष

cockroach (´कॉक्रोच) *n.* काकरोच, तिलचट्टा

cocktail (´कॉक्टेल) *n.* शराब मिश्रित पेय; कॉकटेल

cocky (´कॉकि) *a.* घमंडी; ध ष्ट, ढीठ

cocoa (´कोको) *n.* ककेओ व क्ष के बीज से बना पाउडर; इस पाउडर से बना पेय, कोको

coconut (´कोकनट) *n.* नारियल (का व क्ष)

cocoon (क´कून) *n.* कोया, कोष जिसमें रेशम का कीड़ा पलता है, कोषा, क मिकोष

COD Cash on Delivery का संक्षेप

cod (कॉड) *n.* उत्तरी गोलार्ध की समुद्री मछली, स्नेहमीन, कॉड

coda (´कोडअ) *n. Mus.* संगीत रचना का अंतिम भाग

coddle (´कॉड्ल) *vt.* बहुत ज्यादा लाड़ प्यार करना

code (कोड) *n.* (गुप्त या संक्षिप्त संदेश भेजने के लिए) अक्षरों व संकेत-चिह्नों की पद्धति;

आचार-संहिता – **codify** *vt.* (संग्रह करके) संहिताबद्ध करना **(-fied-fying)** – **codification** *n.* वर्गीकरण, संहिताकरण
codeine (ˈकोडीन) *n.* पीड़ाहर दवा; क्षारीय दवा जिस से न द आए
codicil (ˈकॉडिसिल) *n.* वसीयत का परिशिष्ट
co-educational (कोएड्यु ˈकेशनल) *a.* सहशिक्षा सम्बंधित – **co-ed** *n.* स्कूल आदि जिसमें सहशिक्षा हो – *a.*
coefficient (कोइ ˈफ़िशंट) *n. Maths.* गुणांक
coerce (को ˈअर्स) *vt.* मजबूर करना – **coercion** (को ˈअर्शन) *n.* जबरदस्ती/बल प्रयोग द्वारा रोकने की क्रिया
co-exist (कोइग् ˈज़िस्ट) *vi.* सहअस्तित्व होना – **coexistence** *n.* सहअस्तित्व – **coexistent** *a.* सहवर्ती
coffee (ˈकॉफ़ि) *n.* काफ़ी, कहवा; काफ़ी का पेय – **coffee bar** *Brit* अल्पाहार ग ह – **coffee table** नीची लम्बी मेज, सेंटर टेबल
coffer (ˈकॉफ़र) *n.* तिजोरी
coffin (ˈकॉफ़िन) *n.* बाक्स जिसमें शव रखा जाता है, ताबूत, शवपेटी
cog (कॉग) *n.* मशीन के पहिये का दांता – **cog wheel** दांतेदार पहिया
cogent (ˈकोजन्ट) *a.* युक्तिसंगत
cogitate (ˈकॉजिटेट) *vi.* सोच-विचार करना
cognac (ˈकॉन्यैक) *n.* फ्रैंच ब्रांडी
cognition (कॉग् ˈनिशन) *n.* ज्ञान, बोध
cognizance (ˈकॉग्निज़न्स) *n.* ज्ञान; प्रत्यक्ष ज्ञान; संज्ञान, बोध; ध्यान देने की क्रिया – **cognizable** *a.* जो पहचाना जा सके, ज्ञेय; (अपराध) जिस पर अदालती कार्यवाही की जा सकती है
cohabit (को ˈहैबिट) *vi.* पति-पत्नी की तरह रहना, सहवास करना
cohere (को ˈहिअर) *vi.* चिपकना, संसक्त होना – **coherence** (को ˈहिअरन्स) *n.* सामंजस्य, सम्बद्धता – **coherent** *a.* सुसंगत (बात, विचार, तर्क) – **cohesion** (को ˈहीझ़न) *n.* सम्बद्धता – **cohesive** (को ˈहीसिव) *a.* जिसके विभिन्न अंग पूरी तरह सम्बद्ध हों
cohort (ˈकोहॉर्ट) *n.* एक सी उम्र या सामाजिक वर्ग के लोग; साथी
coiffeur (क्वा ˈफ़र) *n.* केशप्रसाधक, हेयर ड्रेसर
coiffure (क्वा ˈफ़्युअर) *n.* बाल संवारने का ढंग, केशविन्यास, हेयर-स्टाइल
coil (कॉइल) *vt.* लपेटना; की कुंडली बनाना – *vi.* लिपटना; कुंडली बन जाना – *n.* पिंडी; गर्भाशय में लगाया जाने वाला एक गर्भ निरोधक उपकरण
coin (कॉइन) *n.* सिक्का; मुद्रा – *vt.* सिक्के ढालना, अंकित करना; (शब्द) निर्माण करना – **coinage** *n.*
coincide (कोइन् ˈसाइड) *vi.* एक ही साथ होना; पूरी तरह मेल खाना, समान होना – **coincidence** (कोइन्सिडन्स) *n.* संयोग – **coincident** *a.* एक ही स्थान तथा समय में, समान, सम्पत्ति – **coincidental** *a.* संयोग से हुआ (कार्य आदि)
coir (ˈकॉइअर) *n.* नारियल जटा
coition (को ˈइशन) *n.* संभोग, मैथुन (**coitus** (ˈकोइटस) भी)
coke[1] (कोक) *n.* पत्थर के कोयले के आसवन के बाद बचा पदार्थ जो ईंधन के रूप में इस्तेमाल होता है
coke[2] (कोक) *sl. n.* कोका-कोला; कोकेन
Col. Colonel का संक्षेप
colander (ˈकॉलंडर), **cullender** *n.* छोटे छेदों वाली छलनी
cold (कोल्ड) *a.* ठण्डा, शीत; उदासीन; भावशून्य; तटस्थ; निरुत्साह; रूखा – *n.* ठंडक; सर्दी-जुकाम – **coldly** *adv.* रूखेपन से (पेश आना) – **coldness** *n.* रूखापन, बेरुखी – **cold-blooded** *a. fig* बेरहमी से, निष्ठुरता से;

(जीव) जिसका शारीरिक तापमान आसपास के तापमान के अनुकूल हो – **cold comfort** जिससे खास खुशी न हो – **cold feet** *sl*. डर – **cold war** आर्थिक, कूटनीतिक परंतु असैनिक संघर्ष, शीत-युद्ध – **throw cold water on** पर पानी फेर देना, निरुत्साहित करना

coleslaw (ˈकोल्स्लॉ) *n*. सलाद जिसमें मुख्यरूप से पत्ता गोभी के छोटे-छोटे टुकड़े होते हैं।

colic (ˈकॉलिक) *n*. आंतों का दर्द; अंत्रशूल – **colitis** बड़ी आंत की सूजन ब हदांत्र शोथ

collaborate (कˈलैबरेट) *vi*. किसी के साथ मिल कर कोई काम करना, सहयोग देना – **collaboration** (कलैबˈरेशन) *n*. सहयोग – **collaborator** *n*. सहयोगी

collage (कˈलाझ़) *n*. भांति-भांति की वस्तुओं के टुकड़ों को किसी भूमि पर चिपका कर बनाई गई कलाक ति

collapse (कˈलैप्स) *vi*. गिर जाना, बैठ जाना; असफल हो जाना – *n*. पतन; (का) गिरना या ढेर होना; बिल्कुल कार्य करना बंद कर देना

collar (ˈकॉलर) *n*. कालर, पट्टा – *vt*. कालर से पकड़ना – **collarbone** *n*. हंसुली, कंधों को गरदन से जोड़ने वाली हड्डी

collate (ˈकॉलेट) *vt*. मिलाना

collateral (कॉˈलैटरल) *n*. कर्ज़े की अदायगी के लिए गारंटी या प्रतिभूति, समर्थक ऋणाधार – *a*. समानांतर, समपार्श्विक (जैसे चचरे भाई); गौण

colleague (ˈकॉलीग) *n*. दफ्तर आदि में सहकर्मी

collect (कˈलेक्ट) *vt*. इकट्ठा करना, जमा करना; वसूल करना; (चंदा) उगाहना – *vi*. इकट्ठे होना; *inf*. उगाहना, वसूली करना – **collected** *a*. शांत; एकत्रित – **collection** (कˈलेक्शन) *n*. संग्रह – **collector** *n*. कलक्टर, जिलाधीश; (टैक्स) वसूल करने वाला कर्मचारी, संग्राहक – **collect call** टेलीफोन काल जिसका खर्च करने वाले के बजाय सुनने वाला दे

college (ˈकॉलिज) *n*. कालिज ; विद्वानों की संस्था; संघ – **collegiate** (कˈलीजिइट) *a*. कालिज या कालिज-छात्र सम्बन्धी

collide (कˈलाइड) *vi*. (से) टकराना; (से) टकराव होना – **collision** (कˈलिझ़न) *n*. टक्कर

collier (ˈकॉलिअर) *n*. कोयला खान मज़दूर – **colliery** (ˈकॉल्यरि) *n*. कोयले की खान

collision दे० COLLIDE

colloid (ˈकॉलॉइड) *n*. घोल में कणों का लटकना

colloquial (कˈलोक्विअल) *a*. बोल-चाल की भाषा में प्रयोग किया जाने वाला (शब्द, मुहावरा आदि), बोलचाल का – **colloquialism** *n*.

collusion (कˈलूझ़न) *n*. सांठ-गांठ, मिलीभगत

cologne (कˈलोन) *n*. कोलोन नाम की खुशबू या इत्र

colon[1] (ˈकोलन) *n*. (:) का चिन्ह, अपूर्ण विराम

colon[2] *n*. गुदा के ऊपर बड़ी आंत का भाग

colonel (ˈकर्नल) *n*. ब्रिगेडियर से नीचे का सैनिक अधिकारी

colonnade (कॉलˈनेड) *n*. खम्भों की कतार

colony (ˈकॉलनि) *n*. उपनिवेश; एक ही व्यवसाय के लोगों की बस्ती, कालोनी – **colonial** (कˈलोनिअल) *a*. औपनिवेशिक, कालोनी का – **colonialism** *n*. उपनिवेशवाद – **colonist** *n*. उपनिवेश निवासी, उपनिवेशक – **colonization** *n*. उपनिवेश बनाने की क्रिया – **colonize** *vt*. उपनिवेश या बस्ती बसाना

colossus (कˈलॉसस) *n*. विशालकाय मूर्ति; विशालकाय वस्तु या व्यक्ति (*pl*. **colossi** (कˈलॉसाइ), **colossuses**) – **colossal** (कˈलॉसल) *a*. विशालकाय, बहुत बड़ा

colour (ˈकलर) *n*. रंग, रंगत; आभा; (रंग) रोगन; वर्ण; *fig*. आभास; बहाना; ध्वनिरूप; विशेषता; मिज़ाज – (~ **s**) *pl*. झंडा; *Sport* विशिष्ट बिल्ला या चिन्ह – *vt*. रंगना, रंग (रोगन) करना, रंग भरना; छिपाना; बदल देना; (पर)

प्रभाव डालना या तोड़-मरोड़ देना – *vi.* शरमा जाना – **coloration** *n.* – **coloured** *a.* अश्वेत लोग – **colourful** *a.* रंग-बिरंगा

colt (कोल्ट) *n.* बछेड़ा, घोड़े का 4-5 साल तक का बच्चा

column (ˊकॉलम) *n.* खंभा; (लोगों की) लम्बी पंक्ति; पृष्ठ-कालम; (सैनिक) दस्ता – **columnist** (ˊकॉलम्निस्ट) *n.* समाचार पत्र के लिए नियमित रूप से लेख लिखने वाला पत्रकार

coma (ˊकोम्अ) *n.* बेहोशी की हालत

comb (कोम) *n.* कंघा, कंघी; मुर्गे की कलगी; मधुमक्खी का छत्ता – *vt.* (बालों में) कंघी करना; (क्षेत्र) छान डालना; तलाश करना

combat (ˊकॉम्बैट) *vt.* लड़ना, संघर्ष करना – *n.* लड़ाई – **combatant** (ˊकॉम्बटण्ट) *n.* संयोधी, लड़ाकू – **combative** *a.* युद्ध-प्रिय

combine *vt.* (कम्ˊबाइन्) जोड़ना, मिलाना – *vi.* मिलना, संघटित होना – *n.* (ˊकॉम्बाइन) व्यापार संघ, संघ – **combination** (कॉम्बिˊनेशन) *n.* संयोग; संयोजन; संगठन – **combine harvester** मशीन जो एक ही साथ अनाज काटती व गाहती (साफ करती) भी है

combustion (कम्ˊबस्चन) *n.* जलने की क्रिया, दहन – **combustibility** *n.* जलने का गुण, दाह्यता – **combustible** *a.* ज्वलनशील; *fig.* जल्द नाराज़ होने वाला

come (कम) *vi.* आना, पहुंचना; की ओर बढ़ना; होना, घटित होना; उप्लब्ध होना; हो जाना (**came, come, coming**) – **comeback** *n. inf.* अवकाश-ग्रहण के बाद फिर सक्रिय हो जाना; *inf.* मुंहतोड़ जवाब – **comedown** *n.* निराशाजनक अथवा घटिया वस्तु; सामजिक स्तर में गिरावट

comedy (ˊकॉमिडि) *n.* सुखान्त अथवा हास्य-नाटक, कामदी, प्रहसन – **comedian** (कˊमीडिअन) *n.* हास्य-अभिनेता, मसखरा

comely (ˊकम्लि) *a.* आकर्षक (स्त्री)

comet (ˊकॉमिट) *n.* धूमकेतु, पुच्छल तारा

comfort (ˊकम्फ़र्ट) *n.* आराम, चैन; दिलासा; सुख-साधन, सांत्वना देने वाली वस्तु, व्यक्ति आदि – *vt.* चैन या सुख पहुंचाना; दिलासा देना – (~ **s**) *pl.* सुख-साधन – **comfortable** *a.* आरामदेह; *inf.* आर्थिक रूप से सुखी या मज़े में – **comfortably** *adv.* आराम, चैन से

comic (ˊकॉमिक) *a.* (**comical** भी) कामदी से सम्बंधित, हास्यजनक, बेढंगा – *n.* हास्य अभिनेता, मसखरा; पत्रिका जिसमें कार्टून-कथाएं दी जाती हैं – **comical** *a.* – **comic strip** *n.* चित्रकथा

comma (ˊकॉम्अ) *n.* अल्प विराम (,)

command (कˊमांड) *vt.* आदेश देना; (पर) अधिकार रखना; प्रभुत्व रखना; नियंत्रित रखना; *MIL.* का अधिकारी होना; के योग्य होना; (आस पास के क्षेत्र से) ऊंचा होना – *vi.* (पर) शासन करना – *n.* आदेश, हुक्म, नियंत्रण; प्रभुता; शासन; ऊंची स्थिति; (किसी विषय का) ज्ञान, (पर) अधिकार; अधिकार (में); अधिकार क्षेत्र – *Computers* कम्प्यूटर निर्देश – **commandant** (ˊकॉमन्डैंट) *n.* सेना का एक अधिकारी – **commandeer** (ˊकॉमन्डिअर) *vt.* फ़ौजी इस्तेमाल के लिए कब्ज़े में ले लेना; हस्तगत कर लेना – **commander** *n.* सेनापति, कमांडर – **commanding** *a.* प्रधान; प्रभावशाली – **commandment** *n.* ईश्वरीय आदेश

commando (कˊमांडो) *n.* विशेष सैनिक टुकड़ी का सदस्य जिसे जल, थल व वायु से आक्रमण करने का प्रशिक्षण दिया गया हो, कमांडो (*pl.* **commandos**)

commemorate (कˊमेंमरेट) *vt.* स्मरणोत्सव मनाना; (की) यादगार होना

commence (कˊमेंन्स) *v.* शुरू करना या होना – **commencement** *n.*

commend (क'मेण्ड) *vt.* तारीफ़ करना, सौंपना – **commendable** *a.* तारीफ के लायक, प्रशंसनीय – **commendation** (कमेंन् 'डेशन) *n.* प्रशंसा; सिफारिश

commensurate (क'मेंन्सरिट) *a.* (आकार या अवधि में) के बराबर, अनुपातिक

comment ('कॉमेन्ट) *n.* टिप्पणी; आलोचना; चर्चा; नोट; व्याख्या – *vi.* टिप्पणी करना; की व्याख्या करना; की आलोचना करना; पर (संक्षिप्त) नोट लिखना – **commentary** ('कॉमंटरि) – *n.* विस्त त व्याख्या; टीका; फ़िल्म आदि के साथ जुड़ा हुआ वर्णन; *Sport* आंखों देखा हाल, कमेंट्री – **commentator** ('कॉमंटेटर) *n.* व्याख्याकार; आंखों देखा हाल सुनाने वाला

commerce ('कॉमर्स) *n.* वाणिज्य, व्यापार – **commercial** (क'मर्शल) *a.* व्यापारिक, वाणिज्य संबंधी; जिसका उद्देश्य लाभ हो – *n.* विज्ञापन विशे. रेडियो तथा टेलीविज़न पर – **commercialize** *vt.* व्यापारीकरण करना (वि० कला आदि का)

commiserate (क'मिज़रेट) *v.* (*with* के साथ प्रयुक्त) को दिलासा देना; से सहानुभूति प्रकट करना – **commiseration** (कमिज़ 'रेशन) *n.*

commission (क'मिशन) *n.* करने के लिए सिपुर्द किया गया कार्य; कार्याधिकार; आयोग, समिति, कमीशन; आढ़त, कमीशन; राजकीय अधिकार पत्र, नियुक्ति पत्र (सेना में अफ़सर के पद का); आचरण – *vt.* सौंपना, कार्याधिकार देना; *Mil* सेना में अफसर नियुक्त करना; (कलाक ति) बनवाना – **commissioner** *n.* आयुक्त; आयोग या सरकारी बोर्ड (समिति) का सदस्य, कमिश्नर

commit (क'मिट) *vt.* सिपुर्द करना, हवाले करना; (अपराध, भूल आदि) करना; वचनबद्ध हो जाना; बंध जाना; पर मुकदमा चलाने का आदेश देना (-tt-) – **commitment** *n.* विश्वास, प्रतिज्ञा; वचनबद्धता – **committal** *n.* गिरफ्तारी, जेल में जाना

committee (क'मिटि) *n.* समिति, कमेटी

commode (क'मोड) *n.* दराज़ों वाली मेज़; स्टूल जिसमें शौच के लिए पात्र लगा होता है, कमोड

commodious (क'मोडिअस) *a.* लंबा-चौड़ा, बड़ा

commodity (क'मॉडिटि) *n.* (व्यापार में) माल; उपयोगी वस्तु

common ('कॉमन) *a.* सार्वजनिक, लोक-; सामान्य, आम; साधारण; मामूली; प्रायः होने वाली (घटना आदि); घटिया; गंवारू – *n.* आम मैदान; पंचायती जमीन – **commonality** *n.* साधारण होने की स्थिति – **commoner** *n.* साधारण व्यक्ति – **commonly** *adv.* सामान्यतया – **commonplace** *a.* साधारण, घिसा-पिटा – *n.* घिसी-पिटी बात; सामान्य बात – **common sense** सामान्य बुद्धि, व्यावहारिक ज्ञान – **commonwealth** *n.* राष्ट्रमंडल

commotion (क'मोशन) *n.* गड़बड़ी, शोरगुल

commune[1] (क'म्यून) *vi.* (सि) बातचीत करना – **communion** (क'म्यून्यन) *n.* (विचारों, अनुभूतियों आदि में) सहभागी होने की स्थिति/क्रिया; भाईचारा

commune[2] ('कॉम्यून) *n.* व्यक्तियों, परिवारों का समुदाय जिसकी सांझे की सम्पत्ति व जिनका (काम में) समान उत्तरदायित्व हो – **communal** ('कॉम्युनल) *a.* सार्वजनिक उपयोग के लिए; *India* साम्प्रदायिक

communicate (क'म्यूनिकेट) *vt.* बताना, पहुंचाना (समाचार आदि) – *vi* जानकारी देना या उसका आदान प्रदान करना; सम्पर्क रखना; (कमरों आदि के बीच) गलियारा या दरवाज़ा होना; (रोग) संचारित करना – **communicable** *a.* संचारी (रोग), छूत का (रोग) – **communication** *n.* संचारण;

संदेश पहुंचाने की क्रिया; संदेश; सूचना, (प्राय: *pl.*) संचार-व्यवस्था या साधन (रेडियो, डाक आदि); यातायात साधन (सड़क, रेल आदि) – (~ s) *pl.* सैन्य आस्थान (अड्डा) व मोरचे के बीच संचार सम्बंध – **communicative** *a.* जानकारी देने के लिए तैयार या प्रस्तुत

communiqué (क´म्यूनिके) *n.* विज्ञप्ति, सरकारी सूचना

communism (´कॉम्युनिज़म) *n.* साम्यवाद – **communist** *n./a.* साम्यवादी

community (क´म्यूनिटि) *n.* समुदाय, समाज, समूह सम्प्रदाय; जनता; हिस्सेदारी; समानता – **community centre** सामुदायिक कार्यो के लिए भवन; सामुदायिक केंद्र, पंचायत घर

commute (क´म्यूट) *vi.* रोजाना घर से कार्य स्थान तक यात्रा करना – *vt.* विनियम करना; (दण्ड) में कमी करना; बदल देना, रूपांतरण कर देना – **commutation** (कम्यु´टेशन) *n.* विनिमय; रूपांतरण; (दण्ड में) कमी – **commutator** (´कॉम्यूटेटर) *n.* ए.सी. करंट को डी.सी. में बदलने का उपकरण – **commuter** *n.* दैनिक-यात्री

compact[1] (कम्´पैक्ट) *a.* अच्छी तरह से लगाया या बांधा हुआ; ठोस – *v.* – **compactness** *n.* ठोसपन, सघनता – **compact disc, CD,** छोटा रिकार्डनुमा तवा जिस पर आवाज़ तथा चित्र रिकार्ड किये जाते हैं और फिर लेज़र किरणों की मदद से सुने व देखे जा सकते हैं; *Computers* डिस्क जिसमें जानकारी संचित होती है, सी.डी.

compact[2] (´कॉम्पैक्ट) *n.* छोटी डिबिया जिसमें चेहरे का पाउडर, लगाने का पफ व आइना होता है

compact[3] (´कॉम्पैक्ट) *n.* समझौता, संधि

companion[1] (कम्´पैन्यन) *n.* साथी, सहचर – **companionable** *a.* मिलनसार – **companionship** *n.* साथ, साहचर्य

company (´कम्पनि) *n.* मण्डली, टोली; संगति; साथ; अतिथि; व्यापारिक कम्पनी; *Mil* कप्तान के आधीन रेजिमैंट की एक टुकड़ी; जहाज़ के कर्मचारी; नाटक कलाकार मंडली

compare (कम्´पेंअर) *vt.* तुलना करना; मिलाना; समानता बताना; विशेषण व क्रियाविशेषण के comparative तथा superlative रूप बताना – *vi.* समान होना; मिलना; तुलना योग्य होना – **comparability** *n.* तुलनात्मकता – **comparable** *a.* तुलनीय – **comparative** *a.* तुलनात्मक; सापेक्ष; *Grammar* विशेषण व क्रिया-विशेषण का रूप जो 'अधिक' होना बताए – *n.* – **comparison** *n.* तुलना

compartment (कम्´पार्ट्मंट) *n.* कक्ष, खाना; (रेल का) डिब्बा

compass (´कंपस) *n.* कुतुबनुमा; कम्पास; (प्राय: *pl.*) कोण आदि खचने की परकार; परिधि; घेरा; क्षेत्र, विस्तार; पहुंच – *vt.* घेर लेना; समझ लेना; पूरा करना

compassion (कम्´पैशन) *n.* दया, करुणा; सहानुभूति – **compassionate** *a.* दयालु; कपालु

compatible (कम्´पैटबल) *a.* संगत, अनुरूप; अनुकूल; मेल खाता हुआ

compatriot (कम्´पैट्रिअट) *n.* सहदेशवासी, हमवतन – *a.*

compeer (´कॉम्पिअर) *n.* बराबर का साथी, सहयोगी

compel (कम्´पेंल) *vt.* बलपूर्वक काम कराना; जरूरी कर देना (-ll-) – **compelling** *a.* जिसका जवाब न हो, अत्यावश्यक

compendium (कम्´पेंन्डिअम) *n.* संक्षेप, सार-संग्रह, सारांश (*pl.* **compendiums, compendia**)

compensate (´कॉम्पेंन्सेट) *vt.* क्षतिपूर्ति करना, हरजाना देना; बराबर कर देना –

compensation (कॉम्पेन् सेशन) *n.* हरजाना, क्षतिपूर्ति, मुआवज़ा

compere (ˈकॉम्पेंअर) *n.* टेलिविज़न कार्यक्रम आदि में कलाकारों को पेश करने वाला व्यक्ति – *vt.* कार्यक्रम पेश करना

compete (कम्ˈपीट) *vi.* (प्राय: *with* के साथ) मुकाबला करना; प्रतियोगिता में भाग लेना – **competition** *n.* प्रतियोगिता, प्रतिस्पर्द्धा – **competitive** (कम्ˈपेंटिटिव़) *a.* प्रतियोगी (खेल); मुकाबले की (कीमतें) – **competitor** (कम्ˈपेंटिटर) *n.* प्रतियोगी, प्रतिद्वंदी

competent (ˈकॉम्पिटंट) *a.* योग्य; कुशल; सक्षम; उचित; वैध; यथेष्ट; बहुत प्रशंसनीय (कार्य आदि) – **competence** *n.*

compile (कम्ˈपाइल) *vt.* (पुस्तक आदि) संकलित करना; इकट्ठा करना; तैयार करना; बनाना – **compilation** *n.* संकलन – **compiler** *n.*

complacent (कम्ˈप्लेसंट) *a.* आत्मसंतुष्ट; संतुष्ट – **complacence, complacency** *n.* आत्मसंतोष

complain (कम्ˈप्लेन) *vi.* शिकायत करना; इलज़ाम लगाना; (*of* के साथ) तकलीफ़ बताना – **complaint** *n.* शिकायत; इलज़ाम; बीमारी, तकलीफ़ – **complainant** *n.* फरियादी; शिकायत करने वाला

complement (ˈकॉम्प्लिमंट) *n.* पूरक; सम्पूरक; पूर्ण राशि, संख्या, पूरा साज-सामान – *vt.* जोड़ना; (को) पूरा करना – **complementary** *a.* पूरक

complete (कम्ˈप्लीट) *a.* सम्पूर्ण; सम्पन्न; समाप्त, सारा; सभी भांति से – *vt.* पूरा करना, समाप्त करना, सम्पूर्ण करना – **completely** *adv.* – **completeness** *n.* – **completion** (कम्ˈप्लीशन) *n.* पूरा होने की स्थिति

complex (ˈकॉम्प्लेंक्स) *a.* जटिल, पेचीदा; कठिन; गुथा हुआ; मिश्रित – *n.* बहुत से भागों से बनी वस्तु; सम्बंधित इमारतों का समूह; मनोवैज्ञानिक रोग; मनोग्रंथि; सनक – **complexity** *n.* जटिलता, पेचीदापन

complexion (कम्ˈप्लेंक्शन) *n.* (चेहरे का) रूप-रंग, स्वरूप; त्वचा विशे. मुंह का रंग; रंग-ढंग; रूप, प्रकार

compliant (कम्ˈप्लाइअंट) दे. COMPLY

complicate (ˈकॉम्पलिकेट) *vt.* जटिल या कठिन बनाना; उलझाना, मिलाकर गड़बड़ कर देना – **complicated** *a.* – **complication** *n.* उलझन, जटिलता, पेचीदगी

complicity (कम्ˈप्लिसिटि) *n.* (अपराध या ग़लत काम में) सहयोग

compliment (ˈकॉम्प्लिमंट) *n.* प्रशंसा अथवा सम्मान की अभिव्यक्ति – (~ **s**) *pl.* सम्मान, शुभकामनाएं – *vt.* प्रशंसा करना; बधाई देना – **complimentary** *a.* प्रशंसा भरा; मुफ्त (टिकट)

comply (कम्ˈप्लाइ) *vi.* पालन करना, पूरा करना (**complied, complying**) – **compliance** *n.* पालन – **compliant** *a.* आज्ञाकारी; के अनुरूप

component (कम्ˈपोनन्ट) *n.* एक संपूर्ण वस्तु का भाग, अवयव, अंग – *a.*

compose (कम्ˈपोज़) *vt.* व्यवस्थित करना, (टाइप-अक्षर) ठीक क्रम में लगाना; बनाना; लिखना; (संगीत) रचना करना; संयत या शांत करना – **composed** *a.* संयत, शांत – **composer** *n.* रचियता विशे. संगीतकार – **composite** (ˈकॉम्पज़िट) *a.* मिश्रित – **composition** (कॉम्प्ˈज़िशन) *n.* रचना – **composure** (कम्ˈपोझ़र) *n.* शांति, संयम, धैर्य

compost (ˈकॉम्पॉस्ट) *n.* पत्तों आदि के सड़ने से बनी खाद

compound[1] *n.* (ˈकॉम्पाउण्ड) *(Chem)* मिश्रण, यौगिक पदार्थ; शब्द जो दो या अधिक घटकों

को मिला कर बने – *a.* मिश्र, चक्रव द्धि (ब्याज); मिश्रित, संयुक्त – *vt.* (कम्ˈपाउण्ड) मिलाना, संयोजित करना; (चिंता) बढ़ाना; (समस्या) बिगाड़ना; समझौता करना

compound² (ˈकॉम्पाउण्ड) *n.* अहाता

comprehend (ˈकॉम्प्रिहेंन्ड) *vt.* समझना – **comprehensible** *a.* – **comprehension** (कॉम्प्रि ˈहेंन्शन) *n.* बोधशक्ति – **comprehensive** *a.* व्यापक; पूर्ण

compress (कम्ˈप्रेस) *vt.* दबाना; दबाकर आकार में छोटा कर देना – (ˈकॉम्प्रेस) *n.* चोट आदि पर लगाने की कपड़े की गद्दी – **compression** *n.* – **compressor** *n.* मशीन जो हवा या गैस को सम्पीड़ित करती है (दबाकर एकत्र करती है)

comprise (कम्ˈप्राइज़) *vt.* (*of* के साथ भी) समाविष्ट करना; के बराबर होना; (को) समोए होना

compromise (ˈकॉम्प्रमाइज़) *n.* समझौता; बीच का रास्ता – *vi.* समझौते द्वारा झगड़ा निपटाना – *vt.* खतरे में डालना; (किसी को) संदेह या बदनामी की स्थिति में डालना – *a.* **compromising situation** बदनामी की स्थिति

comptroller (कन्ˈट्रोलर) *n.* लेखा-नियन्ता (कुछ पदनामों में प्रयुक्त)

compulsion (कम्ˈपल्शन) *n.* मजबूरी, दबाव; नियंत्रित मनोवेग – **compulsive** *a.* (आदत से) मजबूर – **compulsory** *a.* अनिवार्य, अत्यावश्यक

compunction (कम्ˈपंक्शन) *n.* गलत काम पर पश्चाताप का अनुभव; खेद

compute (कम्ˈप्यूट) *vt.* हिसाब लगाना; परिकलन करना विशे. कम्प्यूटर पर – **computation** (कॉम्प्युˈटेशन) *n.* हिसाब, गणना; अनुमान (खर्च आदि का) – **computer** (कम्ˈप्यूटर) *n.* कम्प्यूटर – **computerize** *v.* कम्प्यूटर लगाना, इससे (कोई) कार्य करना – **computer literate** *a.* कम्प्यूटर-कुशल – **computer programmer** व्यक्ति जो कम्प्यूटर द्वारा किये जाने वाले कार्य की योजना तैयार करता है, प्रोग्रामर

comrade (ˈकॉम्रेड) *n.* सहचर, साथी, दोस्त – **comradeship** *n.* साथ; मित्रता; साहचर्य

con¹ (कॉन) *v. inf.* (*confidence trick* का संक्षेप) धोखा देना, ठगना

con² *n.* **contra** (विरोधी) का संक्षेप – **pros and cons** पक्ष में व विरोध में (तर्क)

concave (ˈकॉन्केव़) *a.* अवतल, नतोदर (कांच या लैन्स), अंदर की ओर गोलाईवाला – **concavity** *n.*

conceal (कन्ˈसील) *vt.* छिपाना – **concealment** *n.*

concede (कन्ˈसीड) *vt.* मान लेना; स्वीकार कर लेना

conceit (कन्ˈसीट) *n.* घमंड, अपने बारे में बहुत अच्छी राय; दूरारूढ़ कल्पना – **conceited** *a.* अहंकारी

conceive (कन्ˈसीव़) *v.* सोचना; कल्पना करना, समझना; बनाना (योजना आदि); गर्भवती होना – **conceivable** *a.* कल्पनीय

concentrate (ˈकॉन्सन्ट्रेट) *vt.* (कोशिशें आदि) केन्द्रित करना; गाढ़ा करना – *vi.* (पर) ध्यान लगाना; इकट्ठा होना – *n.* गाढ़ा पदार्थ – **concentrated** *a.* – **concentration** (कॉन्सन्ˈट्रेशन) *n.* एकाग्रता, केन्द्रीकरण

concentric (कन्ˈसेंन्ट्रिक) *a.* एक ही केन्द्र वाले (व त); सकेंद्र

concept (ˈकॉन्सेप्ट) *n.* धारणा; संकल्पना

conception (कन्ˈसेप्शन) *n.* विचार; धारणा; गर्भधारण

concern (कन्ˈसर्न) *vt.* से संबंध रखना; के लिए महत्त्वपूर्ण होना; पर लागू होना; में दिलचस्पी रखना; चिंतित करना – *n.* मामला; महत्त्व; चिंता; व्यापारिक संस्था – **concerned** *a.* से

संबंधित चिंतित – **concerning** *prep.* के बारे में

concert *n.* (´कॉन्सर्ट) संगीत समारोह; मेल; सहमति

concertina (कॉन्सर्´टीना) *n.* अकार्डियन जैसा एक बाजा

concession (कन्´सेंशन) *n.* अनुदान; रियायत; छूट; विशेष सुविधा – **concessionary** *a.* (*India:* **concessional**) रियायती

conch (कॉङ्क, कॉन्च) *n.* शंख

conciliation (कन्सिलि´एशन) *n.* सुलह, समझौता – **conciliatory** *a.* मैत्रीपूर्ण, समझौते के रुख वाला

concise (कन्´साइस) *a.* संक्षिप्त, थोड़े शब्दों में (लेखन-शैली आदि) – **concisely** *adv.* संक्षेप में – **conciseness** *n.*

conclave (´कॉन्क्लेव़) *n.* गुप्त सभा

conclude (कन्´क्लूड) *vt.* समाप्त करना, निष्कर्ष निकालना; निर्णय करना या कर लेना – *vi.* समाप्त होना; सम्पन्न होना; निर्णय कर लेना – **conclusion** (कन्´क्लूझ़न) *n.* समाप्ति; निष्कर्ष – **conclusive** (कन्´क्लूसिव) *a.* निर्णायक; पक्का (सबूत आदि) – **conclusively** *adv.*

concoct (कन्´कॉक्ट) *vt.* कई चीज़ें मिलाकर (पकवान) तैयार करना; गढ़ना; कल्पना करना; कोरा बहाना बनाना – **concoction** *n.*

concord *n.* (´कॉङ्कॉर्ड) समझौता; मेल; सामंजस्य

concourse (´कॉन्कॉर्स) *n.* जमघट, भीड़; सार्वजनिक क्षेत्र में खुला मैदान

concrete (´कॉन्क्रीट) *n.* रेत, सीमेन्ट आदि का मिश्रण जो मकान आदि बनाने में इस्तेमाल होता है, कंक्रीट – *a.* कंक्रीट से बना; निश्चित; प्रत्यक्ष; ठोस

concubine (´कॉङ्क्युबाइन) *n.* उपपत्नी, रखैल

concur (कन्´कर) *vi.* सहमत होना; सहमति प्रकट करना या देना; एक साथ होना; एक ही समय पड़ना (-rr-) – **concurrence** (कन्´करन्स) *n.* सहमति – **concurrent** *a.* समवर्ती, एक साथ घटित/विद्यमान होने वाले

concussion (कन्´कशन) *n.* मस्तिष्क की चोट; आघात

condemn (कन्´डेम) *vt.* तीव्र निंदा करना; दोषी या अपराधी ठहराना; बुरी स्थिति में पहुंचा देना; किसी वस्तु को बेकार ठहराना – **condemnation** (कन्डेम्´नेशन) *n.* तीव्र निंदा; दंडादेश

condense (कन्´डेन्स) *vt.* गाढ़ा करना; अधिक ठोस बनाना; गैस से द्रव्य में परिवर्तित करना; थोड़े से शब्दों में वर्णन कर देना – *vi.* गैस से द्रव्य बन जाना – **condensation** (कॉण्डेन्´सेशन) *n.* संघनन, गाढ़ा होना

condescend (कॉन्डि´सेन्ड) *vi.* अपने से नीचे के स्तर के व्यक्ति से भद्रता का व्यवहार करना, झुक जाना – **condescending** *a.* कपालु – **condescension** (कॉण्डि ´सेन्शन) *n.*

condiment (´कॉन्डिमंट) *n.* मसाला

condition (कन्´डिशन) *n.* स्थिति, हालत; दशा; अवस्था; शर्त; स्वास्थ्य – *vt.* अनुकूलित करना; प्रशिक्षित करना; ठीक करना – **conditional** *a.* परिस्थितियों अथवा घटनाओं पर निर्भर

condole (कन्´डोल) *vi.* प्रियजन की म त्यु पर उसके प्रति संवेदना अथवा सहानुभूति प्रकट करना – **condolence** (कन्´डोलन्स) *n.* संवेदना

condom (´कॉन्डम) *n.* पुरुषों द्वारा प्रयोग किया जाने वाला रबड़ से बना गर्भनिरोधक

condone (कन्´डोन) *vt.* माफ़ करना, क्षमा करना, जाने देना

conducive (कन्´ड्यूसिव) *a.* उपयोगी; सहायक

conduct *n.* (´कॉन्डक्ट) व्यवहार, आचरण, प्रबंध – *vt.* (कन्´डक्ट) मार्ग दिखाना; आगे चलना; (आर्केस्ट्रा) संचालन करना; (कार्यक्रम) संचालन करना; प्रबंध करना; चालन करना (ताप, विद्युत का) – **conduction** *n.* चालन –

conductivity *n.* (धातु की) विद्युत, ताप आदि चालन करने की क्षमता, चालकता – **conductor** *n.* बस-कन्डक्टर; आरकेस्ट्रा संचालक; मार्गदर्शक; चालक पदार्थ जिनमें से ताप व विद्युत आदि गुज़र सकें

conduit (ˈकॉन्डिट, ˈकॉन्ड्युइट) *n.* पानी, बिजली के तार आदि ले जाने के लिए नाली या पाइप

cone (कोन) *n.* ठोस तिकोनी आकृति जिसका आधार वृत्ताकार होता है; कोन; शंकु; चीड़, देवदार आदि का फल – **conic(al)** *a.* शंकुरूपी

confectionery (कन्ˈफ़ेक्शनरी) *n.* मिष्ठान्न, केक, पेस्ट्री आदि

confederate *n.* (कन्ˈफ़ेडरिट) साथी, षड़यंत्र में सहभागी – *v.* (कनˈफ़ेडरेट) संगठित होना – **confederation** (कन्फ़ेडˈरेशन) *n.* राजनीतिक इकाइयों का संगठन, राजमंडल

confer (कन्ˈफ़र) *vt.* पदवी आदि प्रदान करना, देना, पुरस्कार के रूप में देना – *vi.* परामर्श करना; सलाह लेना (-rr-) – **conference** (ˈकॉन्फ़रन्स) *n.* सम्मेलन; परामर्श

confess (कनˈफ़ेस) *vt.* मानना, स्वीकार करना – *vi.* मान लेना; पादरी के सामने अपने पाप स्वीकार करना – **confession** (कन्ˈफ़ेशन) *n.* अपराध/पाप स्वीकरण

confetti (कन्ˈफ़ेटि) *pl. n.* रंगीन कागज़ के टुकड़े जो प्रायः ईसाई विवाह में नव दम्पत्ति पर फैंके जाते हैं

confide (कन्ˈफ़ाइड) *vi.* (*in* के साथ) (को) रहस्य बतलाना; (पर) भरोसा रखना; (पर) दृढ़ विश्वास करना – *vt.* बताना – **confidant** (कॉन्फ़िˈडैन्ट) *n.* विश्वासपात्र, अंतरंग मित्र (**confidante** *fem.*) – **confidence** (ˈकॉन्फ़िडन्स) *n.* विश्वास, भरोसा; आत्मविश्वास; भेद; गोपनीय बात – **confident** *a.* विश्वस्त, आत्मविश्वासपूर्ण – **confidential** *a.* निजी; गोपनीय – **confidently** *adv.* – **confidence trick** (**con** भी) किसी का विश्वास प्राप्त कर के धोखा करने की क्रिया, ठगी

configuration (कन्फ़िग्युˈरेशन) *n.* आकृति; स्वरूप

confine (कन्ˈफ़ाइन) *vt.* सीमित रखना; घर के अन्दर या बिस्तर आदि पर ही रखना; (अंदर) बन्द कर देना; कैद रखना – **confines** *pl. n.* सीमा; सीमांत – **confinement** *n.* बच्चे के जन्म के समय अंदर रहना, प्रसव; कैद

confirm (कन्ˈफ़र्म) *vt.* पक्का करना; पता करना; पुष्टि करना; अनुमोदन करना; (नियुक्ति) स्थायी करना – **confirmation** (कॉन्फ़र्ˈमेशन) *n.* दृढ़ करने या पक्का करने की क्रिया, पुष्टि; नौकरी स्थायी करने की क्रिया – **confirmative, confirmatory** *a.* – **confirmed** *a.* (आदत आदि के बारे में) बहुत पुराना, न बदल सकने वाला; पुष्ट; स्थायी

confiscate (ˈकॉन्फ़िस्केट) *vt.* जब्त कर लेना – **confiscation** (कॉन्फ़िस्ˈकेशन) *n.* जब्ती

conflagration (कॉन्फ़्लˈग्रेशन) *n.* भीषण अग्निकांड

conflict *n.* (ˈकॉन्फ़्लिक्ट) संघर्ष; द्वन्द, झगड़ा; विरोध – *vi.* (कन्ˈफ़्लिक्ट) प्रतिकूल होना; मेल न खाना – **conflicting** *a.* परस्पर-विरोधी (रिपोर्ट आदि)

confluence (ˈकॉन्फ़्लुअंस), **conflux** (ˈकॉन्फ़्लक्स) *n.* नदियों का संगम; मिलन-स्थल

conform (कन्ˈफ़ॉर्म) *v.* मान्य परम्परा आदि का पालन करना; नियम, रिवाज, आदर्श आदि के अनुरूप होना – **conformist** *n.* जो परम्पराओं आदि का पालन करे विशे. आवश्यकता से अधिक – **conformity** *n.* पालन, अनुरूपता

confound (कन्ˈफ़ाउन्ड) *vt.* चकरा देना; हैरान कर देना; उलझन में डालना; गड़बड़ कर देना;

हरा देना – **confounded** *a.* विशे. *inf.* चकराया हुआ, हैरान; *inf.* घणित

confront (कन् 'फ्रन्ट) *vt.* का सामना करना, सामने रखना – **confrontation** (कॉनफ्रन् 'टेशन) *n.* सामना; मुकाबला, टक्कर

confuse (कन् 'फ़्यूज़) *vt.* चकरा देना, मिला कर गड़बड़ कर देना; उलझा देना; भ्रम में डालना; एक वस्तु को दूसरी समझना; घबरा देना – **confused** *a.* चकराया हुआ – **confusing** *a.* चकराने वाला – **confusion** (कन् 'फ़्यूझन) *n.* गड़बड़, अस्त व्यस्तता; भ्रम

confute (कन् 'फ्यूट) *vt.* गलत साबित करना; खंडन करना – **confutation** (कॉन्फ्यु 'टेशन) *n.* खण्डन

congeal (कन् 'जील) *v.* ठंडा होकर या जमकर ठोस हो जाना

congenial (कन् 'जीन्यल) *a.* प्रिय; रुचि के अनुकूल; समान प्रक ति व रुचि वाले (व्यक्ति) – **congeniality** (कनजीनि 'ऐलिटि) *n.* समान प्रक ति व रुचि – **congenially** *adv.*

congenital (कन् 'जेंनिट्ल) *a.* जन्मजात, जन्म से

congest (कन् 'जेस्ट) *v.* भीड़ करना; प्रवाह रोकना – **congestion** (कन् 'जेस्चन) *n.* संकुलन; बहुत ज्यादा इकट्ठा होना (फेफड़ों आदि में कफ, रक्त आदि का); भीड़-भाड़ – **congested** *a.* भीड़भाड़ वाला (क्षेत्र आदि)

conglomeration (कन्लॉम 'रेशन) समूह, ढेर; राशि

congratulate (कन् 'ग्रैट्युलेट) *vt.* बधाई देना – **congratulation** (कंग्रैट्यु 'लेशन) *n.* बधाई – **congratulatory** *a.* बधाई का (तार, संदेश)

congregate ('कॉङग्रिग्रेट) *v.* एकत्र होना या करना; इकट्ठे होना/करना– **congregation** (कॉङग्रि 'गेशन) *n.* सभा, मंडली विशे. पूजा पाठ के लिए

congress ('कॉंग्रेस) *n.* सम्मेलन; विचार-विमर्श के लिए विधिवत बुलाई गई सभा; विधान सभा – **Congressman** *n.* US संयुक्त राष्ट्र अमेरिका की संसद का सदस्य; *India* राजनीतिक दल कांग्रेस (*Indian National Congress*) का सदस्य

congruent ('कॉङ्ग्रुअंट) *a.* संगत, समरूप गणित में एक ही आकार और आक ति वाले (त्रिकोण), सर्वांगसम (त्रिकोण)

conifer ('कोनिफ़र, 'कॉनिफ़र) *n.* पतली नुकीली पत्तियों वाले ठण्डे इलाके के सदाबहार पेड़ जैसे चीड़, देवदार आदि, शंकुव क्ष

conjecture (कन् 'जेंक्चर) *n.* अटकल लगाना, अनुमान लगाना

conjugal ('कॉन्जुगल) *a.* वैवाहिक; पति-पत्नी के संबंध का

conjugate ('कॉन्जुगेट) *v.* क्रिया के रूप बनाना (जैसे **to be** से **is, am, are, was, were** बनते हैं)

conjunction (कन् 'जंक्शन) *n.* संयुक्त होने की स्थिति: संयोग; समुच्चय-बोधक शब्द

conjunctivitis (कन्जङटि 'वाइटिस) *n.* इस झिल्ली की सूजन अथवा शोथ

conjure ('कंजर) *v.* जादू का खेल करना, जादुई करतब दिखाना; भूत-प्रेत बुलाना

conk (कॉङक) *inf. vt.* प्रहार करना (विशे. सिर पर) – **conk out** खराब हो जाना, बिगड़ जाना (कार आदि)

conman ('कॉन्मैन) *n.* ठग

connect (क 'नेंक्ट) *v.* जोड़ना; मिलाना; (मन में) सम्बद्ध करना – **connection, connexion** (क 'नेंक्शन) *n.* सम्बंध, संयोजन; रेलगाड़ी आदि जिसका पहुंचने का समय ऐसा हो कि यात्री दूसरी गाड़ी पकड़ सकें; रिश्तेदार

connive (क 'नाइव़) *vi.* (~ **at**) गुप्त रूप से षड़यंत्र में सहयोग देना; (~ **with**) (कुकर्म की) मौन सहमति देना – **connivance** *n.* कुकर्म की मौन सहमति/अनदेखी/उसमें सहयोग

connoisseur (कॉनि´सर) *n.* गुण ग्राहक, पारखी, विशे. कलाक तियों का

connotation (कॉन´टेशन) *n.* लक्षणा, शब्दों के मूल अर्थ के अतिरिक्त (छिपा हुआ) अर्थ

connubial (क´न्यूबिअल) *a.* वैवाहिक, विवाह सम्बन्धी

conquer (´कॉङकर) *vt.* विजय पाना, (पर) काबू पाना – *vi.* विजयी होना – **conqueror** *n.* विजेता – **conquest** (´कॉन्वेंस्ट) *n.* विजय

conscience (कॉन्शन्स) *n.* अन्तःकरण, अन्तर आत्मा– **conscientious** (कॉन्शि´ऍन्शस) *a.* ईमानदार, अन्तःकरण की बात मानने वाला

conscious (´कॉन्शस) *a.* सतर्क; अपनी स्थिति तथा अपने व्यक्तित्व से परिचित; चेतन; जानकर (किया गया कार्य आदि) – **consciously** *adv.* जानकर (कुछ करना) – **consciousness** *n.* होश में होने की स्थिति; चेतनावस्था

conscript *n.* (´कॉन्स्क्रिप्ट) सेना में अनिवार्य भरती के कानून के अंतर्गत भरती किया गया व्यक्ति – *vt.*(कन्´स्क्रिप्ट) अनिवार्य भरती करना – **conscription** (कन्´स्क्रिप्शन) *n.*

consecrate (´कॉन्सिक्रेट) *vt.* पवित्र करना; पवित्र कार्य आदि के लिए अर्पित करना – **consecration** (कॉन्सि´क्रेशन) *n.*

consecutive (कन्´सेंक्युटिव़) *a.* जो एक के बाद एक आए; लगातार; निरंतर

consensus (कन्´सेंन्सस) *n.* आम राय, सर्वसम्मति

consent (कन´सेंन्ट) *vi.* राज़ी होना, मान जाना; स्वीक ति देना – *n.* सहमति, अनुमति

consequence (´कॉन्सिक्वंस) *n.* फल, नतीजा, परिणाम; प्रभाव; महत्व – **consequent** *a.* परिणाम-स्वरूप – **consequential** (कान्सि´क्वेंन्शल) *a.* महत्वपूर्ण – **consequently** *adv.* अतः, इसलिए, फलस्वरूप

conserve (कन्´सर्व़) *vt.* सुरक्षित रखना, बनाए रखना; सड़ने या खराब होने से बचाए रखना – *n.* जैम, मुरब्बा आदि – **conservation** (कॉन्सर्´वेशन) *n.* सरंक्षण – **conservationist** *n./a.* प्राक तिक संसाधनों के सरंक्षण का पक्षधर – **conservative** *a.*संतुलित, रूढ़िवादी, दकियानूसी – *n. Politics* परिवर्तन- विरोधी – **conservatism** *n.* रूढ़िवाद –**conservatory** *n.*कांच का बना पौधा-घर

consider (कन्´सिडर) *vt.* (के बारे में) सोचना, विचार करना; का ध्यान करना, को ध्यान में रखना; मानना; विचार-विनिमय करना – **considerable** *a.* महत्वपूर्ण, बहुत बड़ा – **considerably** *adv.* – **considerate** *a.* दूसरों की भावनाओं का ध्यान रखने वाला; विचारशील – **consideration** *n.* सोच-विचार; लिहाज़; महत्व; रिश्वत; क्षतिपूर्ति

consign (कन्´साइन) *vt.* में डालना या रख देना; के हवाले कर देना, संवाहक को सौंप देना; भेजना – **consignee** (कन्साई´नी) *n.* जिसे माल भेजा गया हो, प्राप्तकर्ता – **consignment** *n.* भेजने के लिए सौंपा गया सामान – **consignor** *n.* प्रेषक, भेजने वाला

consist (कन्´सिस्ट) *vi.* (सि, का) बना होना – **consistency** (कन्´सिस्टन्सि) *n.* संगति, सामंजस्य; सदैव एक-सा होना; गाढ़ेपन का माप – **consistent** (कन्´सिस्टंट) *a.* संगत, सदैव एक-सा (व्यवहार) आदि – **consistently** *adv.*

console[1] (कन्´सोल) *vt.* सान्त्वना या दिलासा देना – **consolation** *n.* सांत्वना – **consolatory** *a.* सांत्वनापूर्ण

console[2] (´कॉन्सोल) *n.* बोर्ड (सतह) जिस पर इलैक्ट्रानिकी यंत्र चलाने के स्विच आदि लगे हों

consolidate (कन्´सॉलिडेट) *vt.* मिलाकर एक करना; द ढ़ या मज़बूत करना; पक्का करना –

consolidation *n.* संघटित या मजबूत होने की क्रिया; (भूमि की) चकबन्दी

consonant (´कॉन्सनंट) *n.* (व्याकरण में) व्यंजन – *a.* अनुरूप, से मेल खाता हुआ, संगत – **consonance** *n.* अनुरूपता; *Grammar* सन्नाद

consort *vi.* (कन्´सॉर्ट) से मेल-जोल रखना; की संगति में रहना – *n.* (´कॉन्सॉर्ट) शासक की पत्नी/पति – **consortium** (कन्´सॉर्टियम) *n.* बैंकों, कम्पनियों आदि का संघ; सहायता-संघ

conspicuous (कन्´स्पिक्युअस) *a.* ध्यान आकर्षित करने वाला

conspire (कन्´स्पाइअर) *vi.* षड़यंत्र रचना, षड़यंत्र की योजना बनाना – **conspiracy** (कन्´स्पिरसि) *n.* षड़यंत्र, साज़िश – **conspirator** *n.* षड़यंत्रकारी

constable (´कन्स्टबल) *n.* पुलिस का सिपाही, कान्सटेबल

constant (´कॉन्सटंट) *a.* स्थिर; अपरिवर्तनीय, न बदलने वाला– *n.* स्थिरांक, (विज्ञान, गणित आदि में) – **constancy** *n.* स्थिरता; एकनिष्ठा; वफ़ादारी – **constantly** *adv.* लगातार

constellation (कॉन्स्टि´लेशन) *n.* तारामण्डल

consternation (कॉन्स्टर्´नेशन) *n.* डर, भय; घबराहट

constipation (कॉन्स्टि´पेशन) *n.* कब्ज़

constituent (कन्´स्टिट्यूअंट) *a.* घटक, अवयव, अंश– *n.* अवयव, अंग, घटक; निर्वाचक **constituency** (कन्´स्टिट्युअन्सि) *n.* मतदाता-गण; चुनाव-क्षेत्र – **constituent assembly** संविधान सभा

constitute (´कॉन्स्टिट्´यूट) *vt.* बनाना, स्थापित करना; संघटित करना; के बराबर होना; का भाग होना – **constitution** (कॉन्स्टि´ट्यूशन) *n.* सरंचना, बनावट; गठन; स्वास्थ्य; स्वभाव; नियम-संग्रह; (देश का) संविधान – **constitutional** *a.* संवैधानिक; मूलभूत – *n.* स्वास्थ्य लाभ के लिए की जाने वाली सैर – **constitutionally** *adv.*

constrain (कन्´स्ट्रेन) *vt.* बाध्य करना – **constraint** (कन्´स्ट्रेंट) *n.* मजबूरी; दबाव; प्रतिबंध; नियंत्रण

constriction (कन्´स्ट्रिक्शन) *n.* संकुचन, कसा होना – **constrict** *vt.* कसना

construct *vt.* (कन्´स्ट्रक्ट) बनाना, निर्माण करना, रचना – *n.* (´कॉन्स्ट्रक्ट) सामान्य विचारों/सिद्धांतों के संयोजन से प्राप्त एक संश्लिष्ट विचार/सिद्धांत – **construction** (कन्´स्ट्रक्शन) *n.* निर्माण, रचना; निर्मित वस्तु – **constructive** *a.* रचनात्मक

construe (कन्´स्ट्रू) *vt.* अर्थ लगाना; निष्कर्ष निकालना

consul (´कॉन्सल) *n.* एक देश का दूसरे देश में प्रतिनिधि; दूत – **consular** (´कॉन्स्युलर) *a.* दूत अथवा उसके कार्य सम्बंधी – **consulate** (´कान्सलिट) *n.* दूतावास

consult (कन्´सल्ट) *v.* परामर्श लेना, सलाह करना; (पुस्तक आदि को) किसी बारे में जानकारी के लिए देखना – **consultancy** (´कन्सल्टन्सि) *n.* व्यक्तियों, कम्पनियों व संगठनों को परामर्श देने वाली कंपनी – **consultant** *n.* विशेषज्ञ, व्यावसायिक परामर्शदाता; अस्पताल में वरिष्ठ डाक्टर अथवा सर्जन – **consultation** (कॉन्सल्´टेशन) *n.* परामर्श; सलाह लेने के लिए पूर्व निश्चित भेंट, विशे. डाक्टर या वकील से – **consultative** *a.* सलाहकार

consume (कन´स्यूम) *vt.* उपभोग करना; खा लेना; पी लेना; दिल-दिमाग पर छा जाना; खर्च कर देना, उड़ा देना; नष्ट कर देना – **consumer** *n.* उपभोक्ता – **consumption** (कन्´सम्प्शन) *n.* उपभोग, खपत; यक्ष्मा, तपेदिक – **consumptive** *a./n.* तपेदिक से पीड़ित –

consumer goods उपभोक्ता वस्तुएँ – **consumer society** उपभोक्ता समाज
consumerism *n.* उपभोक्तावाद
consummate *vt.* (ˈकॉन्समेट) पूरा करना; पूर्णता तक पहुंचाना (विशे. विवाह को संभोग द्वारा) – *a.* (कन्ˈसमिट) पूरा, पक्का; अतिकुशल
consumption दे० CONSUME
contact (ˈकॉन्टैक्ट) *n.* स्पर्श, संपर्क; दो या अधिक विद्युत संवाहकों (कंडक्टर) का संधिस्थल या जोड़; उपयोगी परिचित व्यक्ति – *vt.* संपर्क करना; मिलना – **contact lenses** चश्मे की बजाय आँखों में लगाए जाने वाले लेन्स
contagious (कन्ˈटेजस) *a.* (रोग) संचारी संक्रामक, छूत से फैलने वाला
contain (कन्ˈटेन) *vt.* (अपने में) रखना; के लिए स्थान होना; समाए होना; अपने आपको रोकना, नियंत्रण करना – **container** *n.* (रखने के लिए) डिब्बा आदि जैसे पात्र
contaminate (कन्ˈटैमिनेट) *vt.* गंदा या दूषित करना – **contamination** (कन्टैमिˈनेशन) *n.* प्रदूषण, संदूषण
contemplate (ˈकॉन्टेम्प्लेट) *vt.* विचार करना, चिन्तन करना; (करने का) विचार होना – **contemplation** (कॉन्टेम्ˈप्लेशन) *n.*
contemporary (कन्ˈटेम्परिर) *a.* समकालीन – **contemporaneous** *a.* समकालीन
contempt (कन्ˈटेम्प्ट) *n.* किसी के प्रति तिरस्कार, घृणा, निकम्मा समझने आदि की भावना – **contemptible** *a.* घृणा योग्य; घटिया – **contemptuous** *a.* तिरस्कारपूर्ण
contend (कन्ˈटेन्ड) *vi.* मुकाबला करना; तर्क करना – *vt.* जोर देकर कहना – **contention** (कन्ˈटेन्शन) *n.* संघर्ष, विवाद; झगड़े का विषय – **contentious** (कन्ˈटेन्शस) *a.* झगड़ालू; विवादास्पद
content[1] (ˈकॉन्टेन्ट) *n.* विषय-वस्तु, वस्तु जो किसी पात्र में रखी हो; वस्तु की मात्रा जो समा सकती है, धारिता – *pl.* विषय, विषय-वस्तु, विषय-सूची
content[2] (कन्ˈटेन्ट) *a.* सन्तुष्ट; सहमत – *vt.* संतुष्ट करना – *n.* संतोष – **contented** *a.* संतुष्ट – **contentment** *n.* संतोष
contest (ˈकॉन्टेस्ट) *n.* प्रतियोगिता – *vt.* (कन्ˈटेस्ट) विरोध करना; (चुनाव आदि) लड़ना; प्रतियोगिता में भाग लेना – **contestant** *n.*
context (ˈकॉन्टेक्स्ट) *n.* संदर्भ, प्रसंग – **contextual** *a.* प्रासंगिक
contiguous (कन्ˈटिग्युअस) *a.* संसक्त, सटा हुआ, लगा हुआ – **contiguity** *n.* सटे होने की स्थिति
continent[1] (ˈकॉन्टिनन्ट) *n.* महाद्वीप – **continental** *a.* महाद्वीप का (विशे. युरोप के लिए प्रयुक्त), महाद्वीपीय
continent[2] (ˈकॉन्टिनन्ट) *a.* संयमी
contingent (कन्ˈटिन्जन्ट) *a.* संभावित; आकस्मिक; सांयोगिक – *n.* सैनिकों, खिलाड़ियों आदि का दल जो एक बड़े दल का भाग हो अथवा प्रतिनिधित्व करता हो – **contingency** *n.* संभावित घटना/स्थिति
continue (कन्ˈटिन्यू) *v.* जारी रखना – *vi.* चलता रहना या चलाते रहना; रुक कर/रोक कर फिर से शुरू करना, होना; आगे बढ़ाना – **continual** *a.* लगातार चलने वाली (क्रिया) – **continually** *adv.* – **continuation** (कन्टिन्युˈएशन) *n.* विस्तार; पुनरारंभ, जारी रहना –**continuity** (कॉन्टिˈन्यूइटि) *n.* निरंतरता, जारी रहने की स्थिति – **continuous** *a.* – **continuously** *adv.*
contort (कन्ˈटॉर्ट) *vt.* मरोड़ कर आकृति या शक्ल बिगाड़ देना – **contortion** *n.* ऐंठन, मरोड़
contour (ˈकॉन्टुअर) *n.* रूपरेखा, परिरेखा; आकृति विशे. पर्वत, समुद्र तट आदि की
contra-(*comb form*) विरुद्ध

contraband (´कॉन्ट्रबैंड) *n.* तस्करी का सामान
contraception (कॉन्ट्र´सेप्शन) *n.* (प्राय:) क त्रिम उपायों से गर्भ निरोध; संतति-निग्रह – **contraceptive** *a./n.* गर्भ-निरोधक
contract *vi.* (कन्´ट्रैक्ट) सिकोड़ना या सिकुड़ना, छोटा करना या होना – *vt.* (´कॉन्ट्रैक्ट) ठेका लेना, अनुबंध करना; (बीमारी) लगा लेना – *n.* (´कॉन्ट्रैक्ट) सौदा; ठेका; इकरारनामा, अनुबंध-पत्र – **contraction** *n.* सिकुड़न – **contractor** *n.* ठेकेदार – **contractual** *a.* ठेके सम्बन्धी, अनुबंधित – **breach of contract** अनुबंध तोड़ना
contradict (कॉन्ट्र´डिक्ट) *vt.* खण्डन करना – **contradiction** *n.* खण्डन, परस्पर विरोध – **contradictory** *a.* परस्पर विरोधी, विरोधात्मक
contraption (कन्´ट्रैप्शन) *n.* यंत्र, जुगत
contrary (´कॉन्ट्ररि) *a.* विरुद्ध, विरोधी; विपरीत, दूसरा; (कन्´ट्रेअरि) अड़ियल – *n.* वस्तु जो किसी अन्य वस्तु के एकदम विपरीत हो; विपर्याय – *adv.* विरोध में, के प्रतिकूल – **on the contrary** इसके विपरीत
contrast *vt.* (कन्´ट्रास्ट) तुलना करना – *vi.* बहुत अधिक अंतर अथवा वैषम्य होना – *n.* (´कॉन्ट्रास्ट) विषमता; अंतर; टेलिविज़न पर चित्र की स्पष्टता
contravene (कॉन्ट्र´वीन) *vt.* उल्लंघन करना; – **contravention** (कॉन्ट्र´वेन्शन) *n.* उल्लंघन; विरोध
contribute (कन्´ट्रिब्यूट) *v.* चंदा देना; योगदान देना; समाचारपत्रों में लेख लिखना – **contribution** (कॉन्ट्रि´ब्यूशन) *n.* चंदा; योगदान; लेख – **contributor** *n.* समाचारपत्रों में लेख लिखने वाला; चंदा देने वाला, अंशदाता
contrite (कन्´ट्राइट, ´कॉन्ट्राइट) *a.* जिसे अपने कुकर्म पर पश्चाताप हो; अनुतापी – **contrition** (कन्´ट्रिशन) *n.* पश्चाताप, पछतावा
contrive (कन्´ट्राइव़) *vt.* चालाकी से काम निकालना या बनाना; आविष्कार करना – **contrivance** *n.* युक्ति, जुगत, यंत्र – **contrived** *a.* पहले से सोचा व तैयार किया हुआ; बनावटी
control (कन्´ट्रोल) *vt.* संचालन करना; नियंत्रण करना, नियंत्रित करना; निरीक्षण करना (**-ll-**) – *n.* शासन; संचालन; निरीक्षण – (~ **s**) *pl. n.* कार, वायुयान आदि को नियंत्रित रखने वाले पुर्ज़ों की व्यवस्था – **controller** *n.* नियंत्रक; व्यय नियंत्रक
controversy (´कॉन्ट्रव़र्सि, कन्´ट्रॉव़र्सि) *n.* विवाद, वाद विवाद विशे. सार्वजनिक विषयों पर – **controversial** (कॉन्ट्र´व़र्शल) *a.* विवादास्पद
contusion (कन्´ट्यूझ़न) *n.* चोट, नील, गुमटा
conundrum (क´नन्ड्रम) *n.* पहेली
convalesce (कान्व़´लेस) *vi.* स्वास्थ्य-लाभ करना (बीमारी, आपरेशन आदि के बाद) – **convalescence** *n.* स्वास्थ्य लाभ – **convalescent** *a./n.* स्वास्थ्य- लाभ कर रहा रोगी
convection (कन्´व़ेक्शन) *n.* प्रसारण विशे. द्रव्य व गैस में ताप का; संवहन – **convector** *n.* संवहनकारक (पदार्थ)
convene (कन्´व़ीन) *vt.* (समिति आदि की बैठक) बुलाना; एक संयोजन करना, (सभा आदि) आयोजित करना – **convener, -or** *n.* संयोजक – **convention** (कन्´वेन्शन) *n.* सम्मेलन, सभा; समझौता; प्रथा – **conventional** *a.* परम्परागत (हथियार, युद्ध आदि) जिसमें परमाणु हथियार न हों
convenient (कन्´व़ीनिअंट) *a.* उपयुक्त, सुविधाजनक, आरामदेह – **convenience** (कन्´व़ीनिअन्स) *n.* सुविधा, आराम;

(सार्वजनिक) शौचालय – *a.* (खाद्य पदार्थ) जो जल्दी बनाया जा सके – **conveniently** *adv.* आसानी से, सुविधापूर्वक

convent (ˈकॉन्वंट) *n.* धार्मिक-समुदाय विशे. ईसाई साध्वियों का; उनका मठ, आश्रम

converge (कन्ˈवर्ज) *vi.* की ओर अभिमुख होना; एक स्थान, बिंदु आदि पर मिलने या इकट्ठे होने के लिए आगे बढ़ना – **convergence, -gency** *n.* अभिबिंदुता, अभिसरण

conversant (कन्ˈवर्सन्ट) *a.* परिचित, भिज्ञ, जानकार; निपुण, कुशल

conversation (कॉनवर्ˈसेशन) *n.* दे. CONVERSE

converse[1] (कन्ˈवर्स) *vi.* से बातचीत करना – **conversation** *n.* (कॉन्वर्ˈसेशन) *n.* बातचीत, वार्तालाप – **conversational** *a.*

converse[2] (ˈकॉन्वर्स) *a.* विपरीत, दूसरी (ओर) – *n.* विपर्याय; उलटा – **conversely** (कॉन्ˈवर्सलि) *adv.* इसके विपरीत

convert (कन्ˈवर्ट) *vt.* अन्य उपयोग कर लेना; बदलना, परिवर्तित करना, रूपांतरित करना; धर्म, विचार, मत परिवर्तन करा देना – *n.* (ˈकॉन्वर्ट) व्यक्ति जिसने धर्म परिवर्तन किया हो -- **conversion** (कन्ˈवर्शन) *n.* रूपांतरण; परिवर्तन; धर्म परिवर्तन – **convertible** *n.* कार जिसे छत पीछे हटा कर खुली कार में परिवर्तित किया जा सकता है

convex (ˈकॉन्वेक्स, कन्ˈवेक्स) *a.* बाहर की ओर गोलाई लिए हुए, उत्तल, उन्नतोदर, कनवेक्स (लेंस, दर्पण) – **convexity** *n.*

convey (कन्ˈवे) *vt.* ले जाना; ढोना; (सूचना आदि) पहुंचाना, देना; *Law* हस्तान्तरित करना, दे देना – **conveyance** *n.* ले जाना; वाहन, सवारी; सम्पत्ति का अधिकार सौंपने की क्रिया, हस्तान्तरण – **conveyor belt** सामान ढोने का (विशे. कारखानों में) लगातार चलने वाला पट्टा; वाहक-पट्टा

convict *vt.* (कन्ˈविक्ट) अपराधी या दोषी ठहराना अथवा घोषित करना – *n.* (ˈकॉन्विक्ट) अपराधी, कैदी – **conviction** *n.* दोषी ठहराने का न्यायिक फैसला; विश्वास; द ढ़ विश्वास; पूरा यकीन

convince (कन्ˈविन्स) *vt.* मनवाना – **convincing** *a.* (प्रमाण, तथ्य आदि) जिससे यकीन आ जाए

convivial (कन्ˈविविअल) *a.* मिलनसार

convocation (कॉन्वˈकेशन) *n.* सभा; दीक्षान्त समारोह

convoluted (ˈकॉन्वलूटिड) *a.* कुण्डलित, मरोड़ा हुआ; जटिल, घुमा-फिरा कर (दलील आदि)

convoy (ˈकॉन्वॉइ) *n.* जहाजों, सैनिकों, बसों आदि का काफ़िला, कानवाई – *vt.* संरक्षण में साथ ले जाना

convulse (कन्ˈवल्स) *vt.* बुरी तरह हिला देना; (शरीर को) मरोड़ना – **convulsion** (कन्ˈवल्शन) *n.* जबरदस्त खलबली – *pl.* ऐंठन, मरोड़; लगातार ठहाके; हिस्टीरिया का दौरा

cook (कुक) *vt.* खाना पकाना; *inf.* नकली (लेखा, हिसाब-किताब आदि) बनाना – *vi.* पकना; रसोइये, बावर्ची का काम करना – *n.* रसोइया, बावर्ची – **cookbook** *n.* पाक-विद्या पुस्तक – **cooker** *n.* पकाने का बर्तन, कुकर – **cookery** *n.* पाक विद्या (कला) – **cookie** *n.* (विशे. *US*) बिस्कुट; *Computers* जानकारी जो वेबसाइट किसी के कम्प्यूटर पर छोड़ देती है ताकि दुबारा इस्तेमाल किये जाने पर उपभोक्ता को पहचाना जा सकें – **cook up** *inf.* (कहानी) गढ़ना; खाना बनाना

cool (कूल) *a.* शीतल; हल्का ठंडा; शांत, धैर्यवान; रूखा, उदासीन; *inf.* ध ष्ट, ढीठ – *v.* ठण्डा करना; शांत करना या होना – **coolant** *n.* औज़ार, मशीन आदि को ठंडा रखने का तरल पदार्थ

coolie (´कूलि) *n.* (बहुधा तिरस्कारपूर्ण) कुली; मज़दूर

coop[1] (कूप) *n.* (मुर्गियों का) दरबा – *vt.* दरबे में बंद करना, छोटी सी जगह में बंद रखना

coop[2], **co-op** (´कोऑप) *n.* सहकारी संस्था

cooperate (को´ऑपरेट) *vi.* मिलकर काम करना – **cooperation** (कोऑप´रेशन) *n.* सहयोग – **cooperative** *a.* (को´ऑपरटिव) सहयोग देने को तैयार – *n.* सहकारी संस्था

coordinate (को´ऑर्डिनेट) *vt.* अनेक व्यक्तियों द्वारा किए जा रहे कार्य को समन्वित करना – *a.* समान, तुल्य – **coordination** (कोऑर्डि´नेशन) *n.* समन्वय, तालमेल

coot (कूट) *n.* टिकरी, छोटा काले रंग का जल-पक्षी; *sl.* बेवकूफ (बूढ़ा) व्यक्ति

cop (कॉप) *sl. vt.* पकड़ना – *n.* पुलिस का सिपाही

copal (´कोपल) *n.* वार्निश (रोगन) में इस्तेमाल की जाने वाली, राल

cope (कोप) *vi.* (~ **with**) (से) निपटना; संभालना

Copernican (क´पर्निकन) *a.* कापरनिकस, पोलेंडवासी खगोलशास्त्री (1473-1543), से अथवा उसके सिद्धांत से सम्बंधित

copier (´कॉपिअर) *n.*फोटोकापी-मशीन

coping (´कोपिङ) *n.* प्रायः गोलाई में दीवार की ऊपरी सतह ताकि वर्षा का पानी न रुक सके

copious (´कोपिअस) *a.* काफी मात्रा में, भरपूर

copper[1] (´कॉपर) *n.* तांबा; तांबे या काँसे का सिक्का – **coppersmith** *n.* तांबे का कारीगर, ताम्रकार

copper[2] (´कॉपर) *n. sl.* पुलिस का सिपाही

coppice (´कॉपिस), **copse** (कॉप्स) *n.* छोटे व क्षों व झाड़ियों का जंगल

copra (´कॉप्रअ) *n.* खोपरा, सूखे नारियल की गरी

copulate (´कॉप्युलेट) *vi.* (~ **with**) से मैथुन करना, संभोग करना – **copulation** (कॉप्यु´लेशन) *n.* मैथुन, संभोग

copy (´कॉपि) *n.* नकल, प्रतिलिपि; छपाई के लिए सामग्री, (पुस्तक की) प्रति – *vt.* प्रतिलिपि बनाना; नकल करना; अनुकरण करना (**copied** *pt./pp.*, **copying** *pr. p.*) - **copyist** *n.* – **copycat** *a.* पहले जैसा (अपराध) – **copyright** *n.* कापीराइट, पुस्तक, लेख आदि छापने व प्रकाशित करने का एकमात्र वैध अधिकार – *vt.* **copywriter** *n.* विज्ञापन लेखक

coquette (को´केंट, कॉ´केंट) *n.* नख़रेबाज़ स्त्री, स्त्री जिसे इश्कबाज़ी या प्रेम का खिलवाड़ करने की आदत हो – **coquettish** *a.* नख़रेवाली

coral (´कॉरल) *n.* मूंगा, प्रवाल

cord (कॉर्ड) *n.* रस्सी; कपड़े पर उठी हुई धारियां; ऐसा कपड़ा (जैसे कार्डराइ)

cordial (´कॉर्डिअल) *a.* हार्दिक, मैत्रीपूर्ण, स्नेहपूर्ण – *n.* मीठा, फलों के रस से बना पेय – **cordiality** *n.* मित्रभाव

cordon (´कॉर्डन) *n.* सेना अथवा पुलिस द्वारा घेरा – *vt.* घेरा डालना

corduroy (´कॉर्डरॉइ, कॉर्ड´रॉइ) *n.* सूती कपड़ा जिस पर मखमली (उठी हुई) धारियां होती हैं, कार्डराई

core (कॉर) *n.* सेब तथा अन्य फलों का कड़ा भाग, बीजकोष; मुख्यतम भाग – *vt.* गूदा निकालना

coriander (कॉरि´ऐन्डर) *n.* धनिया

cork (कॉर्क) *n.* कार्क; उसका टुकड़ा जो बोतलों आदि के डाट – *vt* कार्क से बंद करना – **corkscrew** *n.* कार्क ख चकर निकालने का औज़ार

cormorant (´कॉमरन्ट) *n.* एक बड़ा समुद्री पक्षी, जलकाग

corn[1] (कॉर्न) *n.* अनाज, गल्ला; *US* मक्का – *vt.* मांस को नमक लगाकर सुखाना – **corny** *a.* *inf.* घिसा-पिटा – **corncob** *n.* मक्का का भुट्टा – **cornflakes** *pl. n.* कॉर्नफ्लेक – **cornflour** *n.* मक्का का आटा

corn[2] (कॉर्न) *n.* पैर या पैर के अंगूठे पर कड़ी खाल का घट्ठा जिसमें पीड़ा होती है

cornea (´कॉर्निअ) *n.* आंख की पतली सफेद झिल्ली, स्वच्छमण्डल

cornelian (कार्'नीलिअन) *n.* गोमद जैसा एक कीमती पत्थर

corner ('कार्नर) *n.* कोना; दूर छोटी सी जगह, कार्नर, मैदान के कोने से सीधी किक रक्षक टीम के गोल की ओर (रेफ़री के आदेश पर) – *vt.* मुसीबत में फंसाना या बचने का रास्ता न छोड़ना; *Business* किसी वस्तु का सारा स्टाक खरीद कर एकाधिकार जमाना – *vi.* मोड़ काटना – **cornered** *a.* जो फंस गया हो – **cornerstone** *n.* सबसे महत्वपूर्ण भाग, आधार – **round the corner** बहुत नज़दीक

corollary (क'रॉलरि) *n.* उपप्रमेय, किसी पूर्व कथन से निकला निष्कर्ष; अनुमिति; परिणाम

coronary ('कॉरनरि) *a.* हृदय की रक्त- शिराओं सम्बंधित – **coronary thromobosis** दिल की बीमारी जिसमें हृदय की नाड़ी में लहू का थक्का बन जाता है

coronation (कॉर'नेशन) *n.* राज्याभिषेक

coronet ('कॉरनिट) *n.* छोटा मुकुट

corporal ('कॉर्परल) *a.* शारीरिक; दैहिक; भौतिक – **corporal punishment** पीटना, बेंत लगाना

corporal[2] ('कॉर्परल) *n.* सेना में सार्जेंट से छोटा पद, नायक; नौसेना में एक छोटा अफ़सर

corporation (कॉर्प'रेशन) *n.* संघ, निगम – **corporate** ('कॉर्परिट) *a.* निगम- विषयक; सामूहिक

corporeal (कॉर्'पॉरिअल) *a.* शारीरिक; भौतिक; मूर्त

corps (कॉर) *n.* सैनिक दल, कोर; निकाय; संगठित समूह – *pl.* **corps** कॉर्ज़

corpse (कॉर्प्स) *n.* लाश, शव

corpulent ('कॉर्प्युलंट) *a.* मोटा; स्थूल

corpus ('कॉर्पस) *n.* रचनाओं का संग्रह (विशे. एक ही लेखक की); किसी वस्तु का मुख्य भाग

corpuscle ('कॉर्पसल) *n.* सूक्ष्म जीव अथवा कण, कणिक; रक्त में श्वेताणु व लोहिताणु

correct (क'रेक्ट) *vt.* सुधारना, (में) गलतियां बताना; डांटना; दण्ड देना; सही करना –*a.* सही, बिल्कुल ठीक; उचित – **correction** *n.* सुधार; शुद्धि; डांट-डपट – **corrective** *a./n.* दोष दूर करने वाले (उपाय) – **correctly** *adv.* – **correctness** *n.*

correlate ('कॉरिलेट) *vt.* परस्पर सम्बंध स्थापित करना – **correlation** *n.* पारस्परिक सम्बंध

correspond (कॉरि'स्पॉन्ड) *vi.* अनुकूल होना, से मेल खाना, के जैसा होना; पत्र व्यवहार करना – **correspondence** *n.* मेल, सादृश्य; पत्र व्यवहार; प्राप्त चिट्ठियां – **correspondent** *n.* पत्र-लेखक, संवाददाता – **corresponding** *a.* से मेलखाता, जैसा ही

corridor ('कॉरिडर) *n.* गलियारा

corrigendum (कॉरि'जेंन्डम) *n.* शुद्धि-पत्र (*pl.* **corrigenda**)

corroborate (क'रॉबरेट) *vt.* पुष्टि करना, समर्थन करना (कथन आदि का)

corrode (क'रोड) *vt.* धीरे-धीरे खा जाना, काट देना, नष्ट कर देना – *vi.* कट जाना या नष्ट हो जाना – **corrosion** (क'रोझ़न) *n.*

corrugated ('कॉरूगेटिड) *a.* लहरदार (जैसे लोहे की चादर)

corrupt (क'रप्ट) *a.* बेइमान, भ्रष्ट, रिश्वतख़ोर; दुश्चरित्र; दूषित; परिवर्तन कर के बिगड़ा (शब्द साहित्यिक लेख आदि) – *vt.* चरित्र बिगाड़ना, भ्रष्ट करना; विकृत करना – **corruption** (क'रप्शन) *n.* भ्रष्टाचार; दूषण; विकार

cortege (कॉर'टेझ़) *n.* शव-यात्रा

cortisone ('कॉर्टिज़ोन) *n.* विभिन्न प्रकार की बीमारियों में प्रयुक्त कृत्रिम हारमोन

cosmetic (कॉज़्'मेंटिक) *n.* सौंदर्य-प्रसाधन सामग्री, कॉस्मटिक – *a.*

cosmic ('कॉज़्मिक) *a.* बह्माण्ड अथवा अंतरिक्ष से सम्बंधित

cosmic rays अंतरिक्ष से आने वाली विद्युत चुम्बकीय किरणें, अंतरिक्ष-किरण

cosmonaut (´कॉज़्मनॉट) *n.* सोवियत अंतरिक्ष-यात्री

cosmopolitan (कॉज़्म´पॉलिटन) *n.* व्यक्ति जो अनेक देशों में रहा हो व यात्रा की हो

cosmos (´कॉज़्मॉस) *n.* सुव्यवस्थित विश्व अथवा ब्रह्माण्ड

cost (कॉस्ट) *n.* लागत, मूल्य, कीमत; (समय, मेहनत आदि का) व्यय; खर्च – (~**s**) *pl.* मुकदमे का खर्च – *vt.* का दाम होना, की हानि होना या (को) गंवा देना (**cost** *pt./pp*) – **costing** *n* लागत-निर्धारण (उत्पादन का) – **costliness** *n.* महंगापन – **costly** *a.* महंगा – **cost-cutting** *n.* खर्चे में कटौती – **cost-effective** *a.* लागत-सार्थक, काम जिस पर खर्च की तुलना में अधिक लागत न हो – **cost of living** निर्वाह-खर्च

costume (´कॉस्ट्यूम) *n.* वेषभूषा या पोशाक, समय या स्थान विशेष की

cosy (´कोज़ि) *a.* सुखद, आरामदेह; सुरक्षा की अनुभूति कराने वाला (स्थान) – *n.* चायदानी आदि को गरम रखने के लिए उस पर डालने का आवरण

cot (कॉट) *n.* बच्चे का पालना

coterie (´कोटरि) *n.* समान हितों वाले व्यक्तियों का गुट

cottage (´कॉटिज) *n.* झोंपड़ी, कुटीर, छोटा मकान – **cottage cheese** हल्का, मुलायम पनीर – **cottage industry** कुटीर उद्योग

cotton (´कॉटन) *n.* कपास; रूई

couch (काउच) *n.* कोच, सोफा, गद्देदार पलंग

couch potato *n.* बहुत अधिक टेलीविज़न देखने वाला व्यक्ति

cougar (´कूगर) *n.* प्यूमा, उत्तरी अमरीका का (बिल्ली की जाति का) एक हिंस्र जीव

cough (कॉफ़) *vi.* खांसना – *n.* खांसी

could CAN[1] का *pt.*

council (´काउन्सल) *n.* परिषद; इसकी बैठक; नगर प्राधिकरण – **councillor** *n.* पार्षद

counsel (´काउन्सल) *n.* परामर्श, सलाह; वकील – *vt.* सुझाव देना (-**ll**-) – **counsellor** *n.* परामर्शदाता; (अमरीका में) वकील

count[1] (काउंट) *vt.* गिनना; जोड़ना; शामिल करना; समझना – *vi.* गिना जाना; (~ **on**) (पर) भरोसा करना; महत्व रखना – *n.* गणना; संख्या; गिनती – **countable** *a.* – **countless** *a.* असंख्य, अनगिनत – **countdown** *n.* उलटी गिनती (जैसे अंतरिक्ष-यान छोड़ने से पहले)

count[2] *n.* (कुछ देशों में) सामन्त की पदवी – **countess** *n. fem.*

countenance (´काउंटिनन्स) *n.* मुखाक ति; मुख पर भावों की अभिव्यक्ति – *vt.* अनुमोदन करना, समर्थन करना

counter[1] (´काउंटर) *n.* बैंक, दुकान आदि में पट्टा, काउंटर, कैरम-बोर्ड जैसे खेलों में डिस्क या टोकन – **over the counter** खुली बिकने वाली (दवाइयां) – **under the counter** अवैध रूप से बिकने वाली (वस्तुएं)

counter[2] (´काउंटर) *adv.* विपरीत दिशा में; के प्रतिकूल – *vi.* विरोध करना

counter-(*comb. form*) प्रतिकूल, उलटा; विपरीत; बदले में, जैसे कि **counterattack** *n.*

counteract (काउंटर्´ऐक्ट) *vt.* प्रभावहीन या बेअसर कर देना

counterattack (´काउंटर्अटैक) *n./v.* जवाबी हमला (करना)

counterfeit (´काउंटर्फ़िट) *a.* नकली, जाली, खोटा – *n.* नकल, जालसाज़ी – *vt.* नकली, जाली वस्तुएं बनाना

counterfoil (´काउंटर्फ़ॉइल) *n.* चैक, रसीद, पोस्टल आर्डर का वह भाग जो भेजने वाला रिकार्ड के लिए रखता है

countermand (काउंटर्'मांड) *vt.* रद्द करना (पिछले आदेश को)

counter-productive (काउंटरप्र'डक्टिव़) *a.* विपरीत-प्रभावी

counterpart ('काउंटरपार्ट) *n.* एक वस्तु या व्यक्ति जैसी दूसरी वस्तु, प्रतिमूर्ति

countersign ('काउंटर्साइन) *vt.* किसी अन्य (अफसर आदि) द्वारा हस्ताक्षरित दस्तावेज़ पर हस्ताक्षर करना, अनुमोदन करना

countess ('काउंटिस) *n.* दे. COUNT[2]

country ('कन्ट्रि) *n.* देश; ग्रामीण क्षेत्र – **countryman** *n.* देशवासी; चिन्हदेहाती, ग्रामीण – **countryside** *n.* ग्रामीण क्षेत्र

county ('काउंटि) *n.* प्रांत, ज़िला

coup (कू) *n.* सफल चाल – **coup d'état** ('कू'देता) हिंसा द्वारा सरकार का तख्ता पलटने की क्रिया

coupé ('कूपे) *n.* दो दरवाज़ों तथा चार सीटों वाली छोटी कार, रेल का छोटा डिब्बा

couple ('कप्ल) *n.* दो; जोड़ा; पति-पत्नी – *vt.* जोड़ना, बांधना, मिलाना – *vi.* जुड़ना, सम्बंधित होना – **coupler** *n.* जोड़ने वाला, योजक – **couplet** ('कप्लिट) *n.* दोहा, द्विपदी – **coupling** *n.* जोड़ विशे. रेल के डब्बों को जोड़ने वाला भाग; संभोग

coupon ('कूपॉन) *n.* कूपन

courage ('करिज) *n.* साहस, हिम्मत, वीरता – **courageous** (क'रेजस) *a.* साहसी – **courageously** *adv.*

courier ('कुअरिअर) *n.* संदेशवाहक

course (कॉर्स) *n.* गति; अवधि; दिशा, पथ, मार्ग; प्रगति; क्रम; कार्य-संचालन के स्वरूप की दिशा; व्याख्यान माला; पाठ्यक्रम; विषय; (भोजन में) दौर; गोल्फ का मैदान; घुड़दौड़ का मैदान – *vt.* पीछा करना, पीछे दौड़ाना – *v.* तेज़ बहना; (रक्त) संचार होना – **in the course of time** समय बीतने के साथ – **of course** बेशक

court (कॉर्ट) *n.* चौक, आंगन; खेल का मैदान, कोर्ट; दरबार; न्यायालय, कचहरी; खुशामद; प्रेम (जताना) – *vt.* से प्रेम जताना; (मुसीबत आदि) बुलाना – **courtier** ('कॉर्टिअर) *n.* दरबारी – **court card** ताश में बादशाह, बेगम, गुलाम – **court martial** फौजी अदालत – *vt.* फौजी अद्दालत में मुकदमा चलाना – **courtyard** *n.* आंगन

courtesy ('कर्टिसि) *n.* भद्रता; शिष्टाचार – **courteous** ('कर्टिअस) *a.* शिष्ट – **courteously** *adv.*

courtship ('कॉर्ट्शिप) *n.* प्रणय निवेदन काल (जब युवक युवती मिलते जुलते हैं)

cousin ('कज़न) *n.* चचेरा, फुफेरा, मौसेरा, ममेरा भाई या बहिन

covenant ('कव़नन्ट) *n./v.* प्रसंविदा; समझौता (करना); प्रतिज्ञापत्र (भरना)

cover ('कव़र) *vt.* ढकना, ढक्कन बंद करना; (~ **with**) फैला देना, बिछा देना; ओढ़ लेना, आड़ा या पर्दा करना, रक्षा करना, बचाना; क्षेत्र (दूरी, इलाका आदि) तय करना, पार करना; शामिल करना; पर्याप्त होना; *Journalism etc.* विवरण देना; (पर) बंदूक तान कर रखना – *n.* ढक्कन; आवरण; लिफ़ाफ़ा; कोई भी ढकने वाली चीज़ – **coverage** *n.* (बीमा) राशि; क्षेत्र; विस्तार, विवरण-मात्रा – **covering** *n.* आवरण, जिसमें वस्तु ढंकी/लिपटी हो – **coverlet** *n.* पलंगपोश – **cover girl** लड़की जिसका फोटो किसी पत्रिका के मुख-प ष्ठ पर हो

covert ('कव़र्ट) *a.* गुप्त; छिपी हुई (धमकी)

covet ('कव़िट) *vt.* ललचाना विशे. दूसरे की वस्तु आदि के लिए – **covetous** *a.* लालची, लोभी

cow (काउ) *n.* गाय; मादा हथिनी, ह्वेल आदि

coward ('काउअर्ड) *n.* कायर, डरपोक – **cowardice** *n.* कायरता – **cowardly** *a.* कायरतापूर्ण

cower (ˈकाउअर) *vi.* दुबक जाना

cowrie (ˈकाउरि) *n.* कौड़ी

cowslip (ˈकाउस्लिप) *n.* एक जंगली फूल

coy (कॉइ) *a.* संकोची; नखरेबाज

coyote (ˈकॉइओट) *n.* उत्तरी अमेरिका के मैदानों का भेड़िया

CPU *Computers* central processing unit का संक्षेप

crab (क्रैब) *n.* केकड़ा

crack (क्रैक) *vt.* तोड़ना; फोड़ना; चटकाना *inf.* चुटकुले सुनाना/हल करना – *vi.* कड़कना, चटकना, फूटना; दरार पड़ना; वयस्क होने पर लड़के की आवाज का भारी होना; मानसिक संतुलन खो बैठना – *n.* चटक की आवाज; दरार, दरक; कमी; मज़ाक विशे. व्यंग भरा; गपशप; *sl.* कोकेन से बना नशीला पदार्थ – *a. inf.* दक्ष, कुशल – **cracker** *n.* पटाखा; पतला नमकीन बिस्कुट – **crackers** *a. sl.* सनकी, पागल – **crackle** *n.* चट-पट की लगातार आवाज़ – *vi.* चट-चट की आवाज़ करना – **crack down on** ज़ोर-शोर से धर-पकड़ शुरू करना

cradle (ˈक्रेडल) *n.* पालना – *vt.* पालना झुलाना; (शुरू से) लालन-पालन करना

craft[1] (क्राफ्ट) *n.* कौशल, शिल्प विशे. हस्तकला या दस्तकारी में; चालाकी; दस्तकारी; शिल्पी-संघ – **craftily** *adv.* – **crafty** *a.* चालाक, धूर्त – **craftsman** *n.* दस्तकार, शिल्पी, कारीगर – **craftsmanship** *n.*

craft[2] (क्राफ्ट) *n.* बड़ी नाव, समुद्री जहाज़

crag (क्रैग) *n.* ऊंची खड़ी चट्टान – **craggy** *a.* पथरीला

cram (क्रैम) *vt.* ठूंसना, पूरी तरह भरना; खिलाना; परीक्षा के लिए रटना (**-mm-**) – *n.*, रट्टा

cramp (क्रैम्प) *n.* ऐंठन, मरोड़ – *vt.* नियंत्रण लगाना; जकड़ना – **cramped** *a.* तंग (जगह)

crane (क्रेन) *n.* सारस, क्रौंच; क्रेन – *vi.* गरदन आगे बढ़ाकर देखना

cranium (ˈक्रेनिअम) *n.* कपाल, खोपड़ी (*pl.* **craniums, crania**)

crank (क्रैंक) *n.* मशीन का हैंडल जो मशीन के शाफ्ट को गोलाकार गति देता है; झक्की, सनकी व्यक्ति – *v.* क्रैंक घुमाकर इंजन चालू करना/होना – **cranky** *a.* सनकी, US, C गर्म मिज़ाज

crash (क्रैश) *v.* धमाका करना/कराना, धमाके के साथ ढहना/ढहाना – *vi.* टूटना, टुकड़े होना; ढह जाना; नष्ट होना (विशे. व्यापार आदि में); (शेयर बाजार) एकदम गिरना; जहाज़ का गिरना; (एक कार आदि का दूसरी से) टकराना; *Computers* कम्प्यूटर व्यवस्था/मशीन का अचानक काम करना बंद कर देना – *n.* ज़ोर का धमाका, टकरा कर गिरना; टक्कर विशे. वाहनों की; जहाज़ का गिरना; ढहना या विध्वंस होना, अचानक पतन, दिवाला; (शेयर बाजारों) में अचानक गिरावट, लुढ़कना – *a.* शीघ्र परिणाम हेतु – **crash helmet** सिर की सुरक्षा के लिए मोटर-साइकिल सवार द्वारा पहनी जाने वाली हेलमेट – **crash-land** *v.* (वायुयान) संकट की स्थिति में नीचे उतरना या उतारना

crass (क्रैस) *a.* अत्यधिक मूर्खतापूर्ण – **crassness** *n.* मूर्खता – **crassly** *adv.*

crate (क्रेट) *n.* सामान रखने के लिए (प्राय: लकड़ी का) बड़ा कण्डा (खुला बाक्स), क्रेट

crater (ˈक्रेटर) *n.* ज्वालामुखी का मुहाना; गोल गहरा गड्ढा

crave (क्रेव़) *v.* (किसी वस्तु आदि की) तीव्र लालसा रखना, तरसना – *vt.* मांगना

craven (ˈक्रेव़न) *a./n* कायर

crawl (क्रॉल) *vi.* रेंगना, हाथ व घुटनों के बल चलना; घिघियाना – *n.* ; बहुत धीमी चाल; एक प्रकार की तैराकी – **be crawling with sth** (लोगों, कीड़ों आदि से) भरा होना, ढका होना

crayfish (ˈक्रेफ़िश), **crawfish** *n.* नदियों में मिलने वाला झींगा जैसा जीव; चिंगर
crayon (ˈक्रेअन) *n.* रंगीन खड़िया, मोम से बनी पेंसिल या बत्ती
craze (क्रेज़) *n.* थोड़ी देर तक अत्यधिक लोकप्रिय रहने वाली कोई वस्तु आदि; तीव्र इच्छा, धुन, सनक, पागलपन – **crazed** *a.* पागल; (चीनी मिट्टी की वस्तु पर) महीन दरारें – **crazy** (ˈक्रेज़ि) *a.* पागल, ख़ब्ती, सनकी, किसी वस्तु के लिए अत्यंत व्यग्र
creak (क्रीक) *n.* चरमराहट – *vi.* चरमराना
cream (क्रीम) *n.* क्रीम, मलाई; सौंदर्य प्रसाधन हल्का पीला रंग; सर्वोत्तम अंश या व्यक्ति – *vt.* से क्रीम निकाल लेना; सर्वोत्तम अंश ले लेना – **creamy** *a.*
crease (क्रीस) *n.* चुन्नट, सिलवट, गेंदबाज़ और बल्लेबाज़ के नियत स्थान को बताने वाली रेखा; – *v.* चुन्नट डालना, सिलवट पड़ना
create (क्रीˈएट) *vt.* रचना, उत्पन्न करना, सृष्टि करना, बनाना – *vi. inf.* निरर्थक तमाशा करना – **creation** *n.* – **creative** *a.* रचनात्मक, मौलिक – **creator** *n.* बनाने वाला, परमात्मा
creature (ˈक्रीचर) *n.* जीव, प्राणी – **creature comforts** सांसारिक सुख-साधन
crêche (क्रॅश, क्रेश) *n.* शिशुसदन, क्रैच
credence (ˈक्रीडन्स) *n.* विश्वास
credentials (क्रिˈडॅन्शल्ज़) *pl. n.* प्रत्यय पत्र; राजदूत आदि को दिया जाने वाला नियुक्ति व पहचान पत्र; योग्यता का प्रमाण
credible (ˈक्रॅडिबल) *a.* विश्वास-योग्य, विश्वसनीय – **credibility** *n.*
credit (ˈक्रॅडिट) *n.* श्रेय, प्रतिष्ठा का कारण व स्रोत; विश्वास; आस्था; गौरव; उधार; बैंक खते में जमा राशि; साख; *(study) US* स्कूल, कालिज में पाठ्यक्रम की इकाई; इकाई सफलता पूर्वक समाप्त करने का प्रतीक अंक – (~**s**) *pl.* फिल्म के निर्माण में भाग लेने व सहयोग देने वालों की सूची – *vt.* श्रेय देना; व्यक्ति के पास गुण आदि होने का विश्वास करना; (रकम) खाते में जमा करना – **creditable** *a.* प्रशंसनीय, श्रेयस्कर – **creditably** *adv.* – **creditor** *n.* लेनदार
credit card एक प्लास्टिक का कार्ड जो सामान उधार खरीदने के लिए इस्तेमाल होता है
credulous (ˈक्रॅड्युलस) *a.* सहज में विश्वास करने वाला – **credulity** *n.* सहज विश्वास करने का स्वभाव – **credulousness** *n.*
creed (क्रीड) *n.* धर्ममत सिद्धांत; पन्थ
creek (क्रीक) *n.* तट के समीप
creep (क्रीप) *vi.* रेंगना, सरकना; *fig.* आहिस्ता-आहिस्ता आगे बढ़ना; खिसकना; डर आदि से रोंगटे खड़े हो जाना (**crept** *pt./pp.*) – *n.* रेंगने आदि की क्रिया; *sl.* घृणित व्यक्ति – *pl.* डर व नफ़रत का अनुभव – **creeper** *n.* बेल, लता – **creepy** *inf. a.* डरावनी, भयावह
cremation (क्रिˈमेशन) *n.* दाह-संस्कार – **cremate** (क्रिˈमेट) *vt.* दाह-संस्कार करना – **crematorium** (क्रॅम ˈटॉरिअम) *n.* शमशान घाट
crepe (क्रेप) *n.* एक प्रकार का लहरदार कपड़ा – **crepe rubber** जूते के तले पर लगाया जाने वाला खुरदरा रबड़ – **crepe bandage** जोड़ों के दर्द में बांधने की लचीली पट्टी
crept CREEP का *pt./pp.*
crescendo (क्रिˈशॅन्डो) *n.* संगीत में आरोह, धीरे-धीरे स्वर ऊंचा होते जाना – *a./adv.*
crescent (ˈक्रॅसंट, ˈक्रॅज़ंट) *n.* बालचन्द्र, अर्धचन्द्र, इस प्रकार की कोई भी आकृति; घुमाव लिए हुए मकानों की पंक्ति
crest (क्रॅस्ट) *n.* कलगी, तुर्रा, पर्वत शिखर; चोटी; कगार; लहर का ऊपरी भाग – **crestfallen** *a.* निराश, हतोत्साह
cretin (ˈक्रॅटिन) *n.* थायराइड ग्रंथि के दोष के कारण बौना रह गया व्यक्ति; *inf.* मूर्ख

crevice (´क्रेविस) *n.* दरार; फटन; तरेड़
crew (क्रू) *n.* विमान, जहाज़ आदि के कर्मचारी; कर्मीदल; *inf.* जत्था या गिरोह
crib (क्रिब) *n.* पालना; खटोला; नांद; खोल; किसी की क ति का अपने नाम से प्रकाशन
cribbage (´क्रिबिज) *n.* ताश का खेल
crick (क्रिक) *n.* ऐंठन या मरोड़, विशे. गर्दन में
cricket[1] (´क्रिकिट) *n.* झ गुर, झिल्ली
cricket[2] *n.* क्रिकेट का खेल – **cricketer** *n.*
crime (क्राइम) *n.* कानून का उल्लंघन; अपराध; बुरा या निषिद्ध काम; *inf.* ऐसा काम जिसपर पछतावा हो – **criminal** *a.* अपराध सम्बन्धी – *n.* अपराधी
crimp (क्रिम्प) *vt.* चुन्नट डालना; शिकन डालना
crimson (´क्रिम्ज़न) *a./n.* गहरे लाल रंग का
cringe (क्रिंज) *vi.* दुबक जाना; *fig.* किसी के आगे नाक रगड़ना/दांत निपोरना
crinkle (´क्रिङ्कल) *v./n.* (सिलवट) डालना
cripple (´क्रिपल) *n.* अपंग, विकलांग – *vt.* अपंग बना देना; कमज़ोर कर देना; बिगाड़ना; कार्यकुशलता घटाना
crisis (´क्राइसिस) *n.* बीमारी आदि में विकट स्थिति; संकट (*pl.* **crises** ´क्राइसीज़)
crisp (क्रिस्प) *a.* भुरभुरा, खस्ता; स्पष्ट; ताजा; स्फूर्तिदायक; फुर्तीला; घुंघराले (बाल) – *n.* – (~ **s**) *pl.* आलू का तला हुआ पतला टुकड़ा – **crispy** *a.* कुरकुरा; लहरदार
crisscross (´क्रिस्क्रॉस) *a.* आड़ा-तिरछा
criterion (क्राइ´टिअरिअन) *n.* कसौटी; मापदण्ड (*pl.* **criteria**)
critical (´क्रिटिकल) *a.* छिद्रान्वेषी; आलोचना करने वाला; अत्यधिक महत्वपूर्ण; (*serious*) गंभीर, नाज़ुक (*critical situation/illness*) – **critic** (´क्रिटिक) *n.* आलोचक – **criticism** *n.* आलोचना; समीक्षा – **criticize** *vt.* आलोचना करना
croak (क्रोक) *v.* टर्राना; कांव-कांव करना; निराशापूर्ण बातें करना; रुंधे गले से बोलना
crochet (´क्रोशे) *n.* कांटेदार (आगे से मुड़ी) सलाई से बुनने की कला – *v.* ऐसी बुनाई करना
crockery (´क्रॉकरि) *n.* चीनी मिट्टी के प्याले, प्लेट आदि
crocodile (´क्रॉकडाइल) *n.* मगर, मगरमच्छ
crocus (´क्रवैसाँ) *n.* छोटा गोल जड़ वाला पौधा, कुंकुम
croissant (´क्रवैसाँ) *n.* अर्द्ध-चंद्राकार छोटी रोटी
crony (´क्रोनि) *n.* अंतरंग मित्र
crook (क्रुक) *n.* कंटिया लगी लाठी; हुक; *inf.* धोखेबाज़; अपराधी – **crooked** (´क्रुकिड) *a.* मुड़ा हुआ; टेढ़ा; बेइमान
croon (क्रून) *v.* गुनगुनाना, धीमी आवाज़ में गाना
crop (क्रॉप) *n.* फसल, उपज पक्षी की गलथैली; चाबुक की मूठ; चाबुक; छोटे कटे बाल – *v.* छोटे (बाल) काटना; फसल उगाना; (पशुओं द्वारा) चर जाना; कतरना (**-pp-**) – **cropper** *inf. n.* भीषण असफलता
cross (क्रॉस) *n.* *90* डिग्री कोण पर परस्पर काटती हुई रेखाएं; लकड़ी की सलीब, ईसाई मत का चिन्ह; सलीब की शक्ल की कोई वस्तु या चिन्ह; दुर्भाग्य; मुसीबत; खीज उत्पन्न करने वाली बात या वस्तु; नस्लों का सम्मिश्रण; संकर; दोग़ला – *v.* पार करना; काटना; रास्ते में मिलना और आगे निकल जाना – *vt.* (*out* के साथ प्रयुक्त) रेखा डाल कर काट देना; (किसी पर) सलीब का निशान बनाना; पशुओं की नस्लों या पौधों को संकरा या कलम लगा कर सुधारना – *a.* नाराज़; खीजा हुआ; उल्टा; आड़ा; तिरछा; आर-पार; विरोधी; प्रतिकूल – **crossing** *n.* चौराहा, चौक; पैदल पारपथ – **crosswise** *adv./a.* आड़े-तिरछे – **crossbreed** *n.* संकर नस्ल (पशु जिसके माता पिता अलग अलग नस्ल के हों) – **cross-country** *a./n.* खुले मैदानों में (लम्बी दौड़) – **cross-examine** *vt.* गवाह से जिरह करना –

cross-eyed *a.* भैंगा – **cross-legged** *a.* पालथी मारे हुए – **cross-ply** *a.* (टायर) जिस की रबड़ में आड़े धागे डाले गए हों – **cross-reference** *n.* पुस्तक आदि के एक अंश में किसी दूसरे अंश का संदर्भ – **crossroads** *n.* चौराहा – **cross section** आड़ा/तिरछा भाग; किसी समुदाय या देश का प्रतिनिधि समूह – **crossword puzzle** वर्ग पहेली – **cross your fingers** अपनी सफलता की आशा करते रहना – **cross your mind** ख्याल आना

crotch (क्रॉच) *n.* टांगों के बीच का भाग जहां जननेन्द्रियाँ स्थित हैं; कांटा

crouch (क्राउच) *vi.* नीचे झुकना; दुबकना; भूमि के साथ लग जाना; नाक रगड़ना – *n.* झुकाव; दुबकने की क्रिया

crow[1] (क्रो) *n.* कौआ

crow[2] (क्रो) *vi.* मुर्गे का बांग देना; ड ग हांकना – *n.* मुर्गे की बांग

crowbar (ˈक्रोबार) *n.* सब्बल

crowd (क्राउड) *n.* भीड़, जनसमूह – *vi.* इकट्ठे होना – *vt.* ठसाठस भर देना; मस्तिष्क (विचारों से) भर देना जिससे कुछ और न सूझे – **crowded** *a.* भीड़-भाड़ वाला (स्थान)

crown (क्राउन) *n.* मुकुट; सम्राट; सम्राट तंत्र; सम्राट की शक्ति; कई विदेशी सिक्के; शिखर, सिर का ऊपरी भाग; चोटी; किसी वस्तु की पूर्णता या सम्पूर्णता; *(Sports)* खिताब; दांत पर नकली आवरण – *vt.* मुकुट पहनाना; उपाधि देना; किसी घटनाक्रम का चरमबिन्दु पर पहुंचाना; दांत को क त्रिम पदार्थ से ढंकना – **crown prince** युवराज

crucial (ˈक्रूशल) *a.* निर्णायक; संगीन; संकटकाल का; *inf.* अत्यधिक महत्वपूर्ण

crucible (ˈक्रूसिबल) *n.* धातु गलाने का छोटा पात्र; कुठाली

crucify (ˈक्रूसिफ़ाइ) *vt.* सलीब पर लटकाना; सूली चढ़ाना – **crucifix** *n.* सलीब (*pl.* **crucifixes**) – **crucifixion** (क्रूसि फ़िक्शन) *n.* सलीब पर लटकाने की क्रिया

crude (क्रूड) *a.* असभ्य; कच्चा; अशोधित; खुरदरा; जो अधूरा रह गया हो – **crudity** *n.* असभ्यता

cruel (क्रूअल) *a.* निर्दय; जिस से पीड़ा या कष्ट उत्पन्न हो – **cruelly** *adv.* – **cruelty** *n.* निर्दयता

cruet (ˈक्रूइट) *n.* नमक मिर्च आदि रखने की शीशी

cruise (ˈक्रूज़) *vi.* समुद्री जहाज़ में यात्रा करना; (विमान, कार आदि का) सुरक्षित, औसत रफ्तार से चलना – *n.* समुद्री यात्रा – **cruiser** *n.* यात्री जहाज़; तेज़-रफ्तार जंगी जहाज़

crumb (क्रम) *n.* टुकड़ा, विशे. रोटी का – *vt.* टुकड़े करना

crumble (ˈक्रम्बल) *v.* चूर चूर कर देना – *vi.* छोटे-छोटे टुकड़े हो जाना – **crumbly** *a.* भुरभुरा

crumple (ˈक्रम्पल) *v.* चूर-चूर या टुकड़े टुकड़े कर देना या हो जाना; सिलवट डालना या पड़ना – **crumpled** *a.*

crunch (क्रंच) *n.* कुरकरे पदार्थ के चबाने की आवाज़; कंकड़ पर चलने की आवाज़; *inf.* संकट या निर्णय की घड़ी – *v.* चबाने/चरमराहट की आवाज़ करना; *Computers* आंकड़ों की बड़ी मात्रा से निपटना – *a.* महत्वपूर्ण (मैंच, मीटिंग आदि)

crusade (क्रू ˈसेड) *n.* किसी बुराई के विरुद्ध आन्दोलन; धर्मयुद्ध; जिहाद – *vi.* जिहाद करना/छेड़ना – **crusader** *n.*

crush[1] (क्रश) *vt.* कुचल देना; टुकड़े टुकड़े कर देना; करारी मात देना – *n.* पेराई, कुचलने की क्रिया; अत्यधिक भीड़-भाड़

crush[2] (क्रश) *n. inf.* – **crush on sb** किसी से अत्यधिक प्रेम जो कुछ ही देर चले

crust (क्रस्ट) *n.* पपड़ी; ऊपरी (कड़ी) परत – **crusty** *a.* गुस्सैल; चिड़चिड़ा

crustacean (क्र ˈस्टेशन) *n.* सीपी, शंख आदि में रहने वाला जीव जैसे केकड़ा

crutch (ˈक्रच) *n.* बैसाखी; सहारा; संबल
crux (क्रक्स) *n.* निर्णय का आधार; मूल प्रश्न (*pl.* **cruxes, cruces** (ˈक्रूसीज़))
cry (क्राइ) *vi.* रोना, चिल्लाना; मांगना (**out** भी); याचना करना (*for* के साथ) – *vt.* जोर से चिल्लाना; घोषणा करना (**cried, crying**) – *n.* घोषणा; चीख़; चिल्लाहट; (जानवर की) बोली; विलाप; नारा – **in full cry** पूरे ज़ोर-शोर/उत्साह सहित
cryogenics (क्राइअˈजेनिक्स) *n.* निम्नताप विज्ञान (भौतिकी की एक शाखा) – **cryogenic** *a.* निम्नताप विज्ञान संबंधी
crypt (क्रिप्ट) *n.* तहखाना, विशे. गिरजाघर के नीचे – **cryptic** *a.* रहस्यमय; गूढ़, गुप्त
crystal (ˈक्रिस्टल) *n.* एक पारदर्शी खनिज स्फटिक, बिल्लौर, क्रिस्टल; बहुत साफ कांच; तराशे हुए कांच के बरतन; रवा – **crystalline** (ˈक्रिस्टलाइन) *a.* क्रिस्टल जैसा – **crystallize** *v.* क्रिस्टल बनाना या बनना
crystal ball कांच का गोला जिसमें देख कर कुछ ज्योतिषी भविष्यवाणी करते हैं
CBSE Central Board of Secondary Education का संक्षेप
CST US, C Central Standard Time का संक्षेप
cu. Cubic का संक्षेप
cub (कब) *n.* लोमड़ी या अन्य हिंसक पशुओं का बच्चा; शावक; बाल स्काऊट – *v.* (पशु का) बच्चे देना, ब्याना (**-bb-**)
cube (क्यूब) *n.* घन (छः वर्गाकार पक्षों वाला ठोस ढांचा); घन जैसा कुन्दा; किसी राशि को उसी से दो बार गुणा कर के प्राप्त राशि, त्रिघात; घन – *vt.* इस प्रकार गुणा करना – **cubic(al)** *a.*
cubicle (ˈक्यूबिकल) *n.* बड़े कमरे में (चारों ओर से घिरा) कक्ष
cuckold (ˈककल्ड) *n.* पुरुष जिसकी पत्नी पर-पुरुषों से सम्बन्ध रखे, कुलटा-पति – *vt.* ऐसा पति बन जाना
cuckoo (ˈकुकू) *n.* कोयल जैसा पक्षी
cucumber (ˈक्यूकम्बर) *n.* खीरा
cud (कड) *n.* जुगाली
cuddle (ˈकडल) *vt.* गले लगाना
cudgel (ˈकजल) *n.* छोटी, मोटी लाठी या डंडा
cue[1] (क्यू) *n.* अभिनेता के भाषण के अंतिम शब्द जो अगले अभिनेता के लिए बोलने का संकेत हैं; संकेत; इशारा; कार्यवाही के लिए उदाहरण
cue[2] (क्यू) *n.* बिलियर्ड के खेल में प्रयुक्त लम्बा पतला डंडा
cuff (कफ़) *n.* आस्तीन की मोहरी; कलाई बन्द
cuisine (क्विˈज़ीन) *n.* पाक प्रणाली या शैली; व्यंजनों की सूची
culinary (ˈकलिनरि) *a.* भोजन पकाने या रसोई घर से सम्बन्धित या उसका
cull (कल) *vt.* चुनना; इकट्ठे करना; कुछ पशुओं को चुनकर औरों से अलग करना व मार देना
culminate (ˈकल्मिनेट) *vi.* चरमबिन्दु या पराकाष्ठा तक पहुंचना – **culmination** (कल्मिˈनेशन) *n.* चरमोत्कर्ष; समाप्ति
culpable (ˈकल्पबल) *a.* जिसे दोष दिया जा सके; निन्दनीय
culprit (ˈकल्प्रिट) *n.* दोषी
cult (कल्ट) *n.* पूजा या उपासना की पद्धति; किसी वस्तु, व्यक्ति या कार्य के प्रति निष्ठा का भाव
cultivate (ˈकल्टिवेट) *vt.* खेती करना, जमीन जोतना; विकास, सुधार या परिष्करण करना; किसी से परिचय बढ़ाना, दोस्ती करना; पोषण करना; आचरण करना – **cultivation** (कल्टिˈवेशन) *n.* खेतीबाड़ी – **cultivator** *n.* किसान, खेतिहर
culture (ˈकल्चर) *n.* संस्कृति; खेती; संवर्धन (कृत्रिम ढंग से); इस प्रकार संवर्द्धित जीवाणु – **cultural** (कल्चरल) *a.* सांस्कृतिक – **cultured** *a.* सुसंकृत; सभ्य – **cultured pearl** कृत्रिम मोती

culvert (´कल्वर्ट) *n.* पुलिया
cum (कम) *Lat* (के) साथ
cumbersome (´कम्बर्सम) *a.* बोझिल
cum(m) in (´कमिन) *n.* सफेद जीरा
cumulative (´क्यूम्युलटिव़) *a.* जो बार बार जोड़ने से बढ़ता जाय, संचयी
cunning (´कनिङ) *a.* चालाक; धूर्त – *n.* चालाकी; धूर्तता
cup (कप) *n.* प्याला; छोटा कटोरा; प्याले जैसी आक तियां या गड्ढे; पुरस्कार में दिया जाने वाला प्याले जैसा पात्र – *vt.* हाथों को जोड़ कर प्याले जैसा बनाना – **cupful** *n.* प्याला भर – **cupboard** (´कबर्ड) *n.* अल्मारी
Cupid (´क्यूपिड) *n.* कामदेव
cupidity (क्यू´पिडिटि) *n.* लोभ, अर्थलिप्सा
cur (कर) *n.* बाजारू कुत्ता; पाजी, नीच
curative (´क्युअरटिव़) *a.* रोगहर – *n.* रोगहर
curator (क्युअ´रेटर) *n.* अभिभावक या अध्यक्ष विशे. संग्रहालय आदि का
curb (कर्ब) *n.* रोक; पाबन्दी
curd (कर्ड) *n.* (**curds** *pl. n.* भी) *n.* दही – **curdle** (´कर्डल) *v.* दही जमाना; थक्केदार बनाना – **bloodcurdling** *a.* अत्यधिक भयावह
cure (क्युअर) *vt.* इलाज करना ठीक करना; (नमक आदि लगाकर) मांस, मछली सुखाना; चमड़ा/खाल कमाना – *n.* औषधि; उपचार; रोगमुक्ति– **curable** *a.* साध्य
curfew (´कर्फ्यू) *n.* घरबन्दी, कर्फ्यू
curie (´क्युअरि) *n.* रेडियम किरणों की मानक इकाई
curio (´क्युअरिओ) *n.* विरली या विलक्षण संग्रह योग्य कलाक ति या वस्तु (*pl.* **curios**)
curious (´क्युअरिअस) *a.* जिज्ञासु; कुतूहली; विलक्षण, असाधारण; अजीब – **curiosity** *n.* जिज्ञासा – **curiously** *adv.*
curl (कर्ल) *vi.* कुण्डलाकार होना – *vt.* कुण्डलाकार बनाना – *n.* बालों का कुण्डल, छल्ला; छल्लेदार आक ति – **curly** *a.* घुंघराले, छल्लेदार
curlew (´कर्ल्यू) *n.* लम्बी चोंच वाला जलपक्षी, गुलिंदा
currant (´करन्ट) *n.* किश्मिश
current (´करंट) *a.* चालू; प्रचलित; वर्तमान; सामयिक; ताज़ा; नया – *n.* (पानी की) धारा; (हवा का) वेग; प्रव ति; बहाव; बिजली का करन्ट – **currency** *n.* मुद्रा; प्रचलन; लोकप्रियता – **currently** *adv.* – **current account** बैंक में चालू खाता
curriculum (क´रिक्युलम) *n.* पाठ्यक्रम (*pl.* **curriculums, curricula**) – **curriculum vitae** (–´व़ाइटी) (CV) किसी व्यक्ति की शिक्षा, क तत्व आदि का व तांत
curry[1] (´करि) *n.* कढ़ी
curry[2] (´करि) *vt.* – **curry favour with** खुशामद या चिकनी चुपड़ी बातों से किसी का क पापात्र बनना
curse (कर्स) *n.* (**cuss** भी) गाली; शाप; अभिशाप; लानत; दुर्भाग्य – *v.* गाली देना; कोसना – **cursed** (´करसिड, कर्स्ट) *a.* घ णित; अभिशप्त
cursory (´कर्सरि) *a.* सरसरी; ऊपरी – **cursorily** *adv.*
curt (कर्ट) *a.* रूखा; टका सा – **curtly** *adv.* – **curtness** *n.* रुखाई; बेलिहाज़ी
curtail (कर्´टेल) *vt.* घटाना या संक्षिप्त करना; काटना – **curtailment** *n.*
curtain (´कर्टन) *n.* परदा; परदे के लिए लटकाया कपड़ा; रंगमंच का परदा, यवनिका – *vt.* लगाना – **curtain-raiser** *n.* मुख्य नाटक से पहले की छोटी नाटिका; कोई प्रारंभिक घटना (जो मुख्य घटना की सूचक हो)
curts(e)y (´कर्ट्सि) *n.* स्त्री द्वारा घुटने झुका कर किसी (बड़े) आदमी का अभिवादन – *vi.* इस प्रकार अभिवादन करना

curve (कर्व्) *n.* वक्ररेखा; वक्र – *vt.* वक्र बनाना – *vi.* सड़क आदि का मुड़ना

cushion (ˈकुशन) *n.* गद्दी; गद्दा – *vt.* गद्दी लगाना; किसी कुप्रभाव को कम करना/से बचाना – **cushion against** के विरुद्ध सुरक्षा/सहारा

cushy (ˈकुशि) *a. inf.* आरामदेह; नरम

custard (ˈकस्टर्ड) *n.* दूध और अंडों से बना व्यंजन; दूध में मक्की का महीन आटा और चीनी मिला कर बना हलुआ

custody (ˈकस्टडि) *n.* सुरक्षित रखने की क्रिया; अभिभावकता; हिरासत; हवालात – **custodian** (कˈस्टोडिअन) *n.* अभिभावक; अभिरक्षक – **custodial** *a.*हिरासत में

custom (ˈकस्टम) *n.* स्वभाव, आदत; व्यवहार; प्रथा; रीति-रिवाज; प्रचलन; ग्राहक-गण; सीमा-शुल्क, सीमाकर – *pl.* आयात-शुल्क; सीमा-शुल्क विभाग; हवाई अड्डे का वह क्षेत्र जहां सीमा शुल्क अधिकारी सामान की जांच करते हैं – **customarily** *adv.* – **customary** *a.* सदा की तरह; साधारण; प्रथानुसार – **customer** *n.* ग्राहक – **custom-made** *a.* नाप देकर सिलवाए गए (कपड़े); विशेष आर्डर पर बनी (वस्तु) – **customs duties** सीमा शुल्क; आयात तथा निर्यात कर

cut (कट) *vt.* काटना; कतरना; अन्दर तक जाना; हिस्से करना; किसी औज़ार से टुकड़े करना; काट कर संवारना; कम करना; घटाना; कटौती करना; छोटा या संक्षिप्त करना; *inf.* (किसी को) अनदेखा करना या पहचानने से इनकार करना; क्रिकेट में गेंद पाइंट के बाईं ओर मारना **(cut, cutting)** – *n.* काटने की क्रिया; चोट; प्रहार; (चाकू या चाबुक का) घाव; कटौती; कमी; (*fashion*) शैली; (*shape*) शक्ल; बनावट; काट; तराश, पच्चीकारी; कटा हुआ टुकड़ा; भाग; *inf.* हिस्सा, विशे. मुनाफे का – **cutter** *n.* काटने वाला (व्यक्ति या वस्तु); जंगी जहाज़ की नाव; छोटा मस्तूलों वाला जहाज़ – **cutting** *n.* काटने की क्रिया; काटी गयी वस्तु; पौधे की टहनी, कलम; (अखबार की) कतरन – *a.* व्यंग्य भरा – **cutthroat** *a.* निर्मम – *n.* हत्यारा

cute (क्यूट) *a.* आकर्षक; मनोहर; मनमोहक; सुन्दर

cuticle (ˈक्यूटिकल) *n.* मोटी त्वचा विशे. नाखूनों के नीचे की; उपत्वचा; उपचर्म

cutlery (ˈकट्लरि) *n.* छुरी, कांटा, चम्मच आदि

cutlet (ˈकट्लिट) *n.* भुना या तला मांस का टुकड़ा; तिक्का; कतला; (भारत में) तले हुए आलू से बना कतला, कटलेट

cut-off *n./a.* रुक जाने की सीमा (**cut-off point**)

cut-out *n.* गत्ते/लकड़ी से बनी आक ति; विद्युत धारा रोकने के लिए पुरज़ा

CV curriculum vitae (व्यक्ति का शिक्षा और उस के काम का व तांत)

Cwt. hundredweight का संक्षेप

cyanide (ˈसाइनाइड) *n.* अत्यधिक विषैला रासायनिक संमिश्रण

cyber (ˈसाइबर) *a.* इंटरनेट संबंधी – **cyber cafe** दुकान जहां इंटरनेट सेवा उपलब्ध हो – **cyber crime** इंटरनेट संबंधी अपराध

cybernetics (साइबर्ˈनेटिक्स) *n.* इलैक्ट्रानिकी और जीवों के शरीर की नियंत्रण व्यवस्था का तुलनात्मक अध्ययन

cyberspace *n.* काल्पनिक स्थान जहां कम्प्यूटरों द्वारा एक दूसरे को भेजे जा रहे संदेश आदि होते हैं, साइबर-स्थान

cycle (ˈसाइकल) *n.* आवर्ती श्र ंखला या काल; चक्र; घटना चक्र; पूरी श्र ंखला या काल; माला; घटनाएं जो क्रमबद्ध हों; बाइसिकल – *vi.* चक्रों में चलना; बाइसिकल चलाना – **cyclic(al)** (ˈसाइक्लिकल, ˈसिक्लिकल) *a.* चक्रबद्ध – **cyclist** (ˈसाइक्लिस्ट) *n.* बाइसिकल चलाने वाला, साइकल-सवार

cyclone (ˈसाइक्लोन) *n.* चक्रवात, समुद्री तूफान, साइक्लोन – **cyclonic** *a.* चक्रवाती

cyclopedia (साइक्लोˈपीडिअ) देखिए ENCYCLOPEDIA

cyclostyle (ˈसाइक्लस्टाइल) *vt.* (बांटने के लिए पर्चे आदि की) बड़ी संख्या में प्रतिलिपियां विशेष मशीन से तैयार करना – *a./n.* ऐसा करने का (तरीका, मशीन)

cylinder (ˈसिलिन्डर) *n.* बेलन जैसी चीज़; सिलंडर – **cylindrical** (सिˈलिंड्रिकल) *a.* बेलनाकार

cymbals (ˈसिम्बल्ज़) *pl. n.* झांझर; करताल

cynic (ˈसिनिक) *n.* जो सभी की नीयत बुरी समझे या सोचे कि कुछ अच्छा नह होगा, दोष-दर्शक – **cynical** *a.* जो नैतिक मापदण्डों को तिरस्कार की द ष्टि से देखे – **cynicism** (ˈसिनिसिज़म) *n.* दोष-दर्शिता

cynosure (ˈसिनज़्युअर, ˈसिनशुअर) *n.* आकर्षण का केन्द्र

cypher (ˈसाइफ़र) *n.* देखिए CIPHER

cypress (ˈसाइप्रस) *n.* सरू का पेड़

cyst (सिस्ट) *n.* द्रव या पीव से भरी थैली

D

dab (डैब) *vt.* हल्के दबाव से कोई गीली और नरम चीज़ लगाना; थपकी देना – *n.* पुचारा; थपकी; लगाई गयी मात्रा

dabble ('डैबल) *vi.* पानी में खेलना; किसी काम में सरसरी तौर से लगना या ऊपरी तौर से दिलचस्पी लेना

dad, daddy (डैड, 'डैडि) *n. inf.* पिता

daffodil ('डैफ़डिल) *n.* वसन्त ऋतु का फूल, पीला नरगिस, डैफ़ोडिल

dagger ('डैगर) *n.* छुरा, कटार

dahlia ('डेल्यअ) *n.* मैक्सिको से आया एक रंग-बिरंगे फूलों वाला पौधा, डालिया

daily ('डेलि) *a.* दैनिक; जो प्रतिदिन हो या प्रकाशित हो – *adv.* प्रतिदिन – *n.* दैनिक अखबार; घर का काम काज करने वाली नौकरानी

dainty ('डेन्टि) *n.* स्वादिष्ट व्यंजन – *a.* नाजुक; नाजुक मिज़ाज; बढ़िया; नकचढ़ा; जिसे कोई चीज़ आसानी से पसन्द न आए – **daintily** *adv.* – **daintiness** *n.* नाजुक मिज़ाजी

dairy ('डेंअरि) *n.* दुग्धशाला, डेरी – **dairying** *n.* – **dairyman** *n.*

dais ('डेइस, डेस) *n.* मंच

daisy ('डेज़ि) *n.* पीले केन्द्र और सफ़ेद पत्तियों वाला फूल, डेज़ी

dale (डेल) *n.* घाटी

dally ('डैलि) *vi.* खिलवाड़ करना; बेकार समय गंवाना; इधर उधर घूमना या खड़े रहना; मन बहलाना (**dallied, dallying**)

dam[1] (डैम) *n.* बांध; बांध में रुका हुआ पानी – *vt.* बांध बनाना (**-mm-**)

dam[2] (डैम) *n.* मां (पशु के लिए प्रयुक्त)

damage ('डैमिज) *n.* क्षति, हानि; टूटफूट; नुकसान – *pl.* हरजाना; क्षतिपूर्ति – *vt.* हानि या क्षति पहुंचाना

dame (डेम) *n. obs.* महिला

damn (डैम) *vt.* लानत भेजना; नरक में डालना; तबाह करना; निंदा या कटु आलोचना करना – *vi.* कोसना, धिक्कारना (**damned** डैम्ड, **damning**) – *interj.* लानत है ! धिक्कार है ! – **damnation** *n.*

damp (डैम्प) *a.* नम; आद्र, गीला, तर – *n.* नमी, सील; कोयला खान में खतरनाक गैस – *vt.* गीला या तर करना; (बहुधा *down* के साथ) दबाना, निरुत्साहित करना – **dampen** *v.* गीला करना या होना – *vt.* कम करना – **damper** *n.* जो निरुत्साहित करे – **damp squib** *coll.* आयोजन, कार्यक्रम जो आशा के विपरीत फीका निकले

damsel ('डैम्ज़ल) *n. obs.* लड़की

dance (डाँ'साज़) *vi.* नृत्य करना; नाचना, उछलना – *vt.* नृत्य करना या कराना – *n.* नृत्य, नाच; उस का संगीत; नाचने के लिए लोगों का जमा होना – **dancer** *n.* नर्तक

dandruff ('डैंड्रफ) *n.* सिर पर जमा होने वाली रूसी

dandy ('डैन्डि) *n.* ऐसा पुरुष जिसे अपने पहनावे का बहुत अधिक ध्यान हो, छैला, बांका – *a. inf.* बढ़िया; बहुत अच्छा

danger ('डेन्जर) *n.* खतरा; जोखिम; भ्रम – **dangerous** *a.* खतरनाक; जोखिम भरा – **dangerously** *adv.*

dangle ('डैंगल) *vt.* झुलाना; प्रलोभन देना – *vi.* झूलना, अस्थिर होना

dank (डैंक) *a.* सीला और ठण्डा – **dankness** *n.*

dapper ('डैपर) *a.* साफ़-सुथरा; बना ठना

dare (डेंअर) *vt.* हिम्मत या साहस दिखाना; सामना करना; चुनौती देना – *n.* चुनौती – **daring**

a. साहसी – *n.*साहस – **daredevil** *a./n.* निधड़क, दुस्साहसी; जांबाज (व्यक्ति) – **I dare say** मेरा ख्याल है/मुझे लगता है...

dark (डार्क) *a.* अंधेरा; अंधकारपूर्ण; काला; गहरा; धुंधला; गुप्त; अज्ञानी; बुरा – *n.* अंधकार; कालापन; अज्ञान – **darken** *v.* काला करना; अंधेरा करना या होना - **darkly** *adv.* - **darkness** *n.* -**dark horse** छुपा रुस्तम – **darkroom** *n.* फोटोग्राफ़र का अंधेरा कमरा जहां फ़िल्म धोई जाती है

darling (ˊडार्लिंग) *a./n.* प्रेमपात्र या बहुत प्रिय (व्यक्ति)

darn (डार्न) *vt.* रफू करना – *n.* रफू किया स्थान

dart (डार्ट) *n.* तीर के फल जैसा तीखा अस्त्र; सांग; लपकने की क्रिया; कपड़े की सीवन या तुरपन – *pl.* सांग को निशाने पर फैंकने का खेल – *vt.* फैंकना – *vi.* झपटना; लपकना; अचानक चल देना

dash (डैश) *vt.* पटक देना; टुकड़े-टुकड़े कर देना; टक्कर देना या मारना; छ टे डालना या पुट देना – *vi.* झपटना; लपकना – *n.* आघात; टक्कर; झपटने की क्रिया; थोड़ा सा, पुट; तेज़ दौड़; शब्दों के बीच पड़ी रेखा (-) – **dashing** *a.* निर्भीक; बना ठना – **dashboard** *n.* कार आदि में चालक के आगे लगा चौखटा जिसमें गतिमापक और अन्य यंत्र होते है

data (ˊडेट्अ, ˊडाट्अ) *pl. n.* (बहुधा *sing v.*के साथ) आंकड़े; जानकारी; ब्यौरा – **data bank** किसी विषय विशेष पर कम्प्यूटर में संग्रहीत जानकारी – **data base** आंकड़ों का व्यवस्थाबद्ध संग्रह जो किसी प्रयोजन विशेष के लिए सारणीबद्ध किया जा सके – **data processing** कम्प्यूटर के माध्यम से आँकड़ों को व्यवस्थाबद्ध करना

date[1] (डेट) *n.* तिथि, तारीख, दिनांक; घटना का काल; कलाक ति का काल (कि वह कब बनी); मिलने का निर्धारित समय या वादा – *vt.* पर तारीख लगाना; तारीख का संकेत देना/बताना; की आयु बताना; *inf* के साथ घूमने-फिरने जाना

date[2] *n.* खजूर; खजूर का पेड़

datum (ˊडेटम) *n.* आंकड़ा; जानकारी (*pl.* **data**)

daughter (ˊडॉटर) *n.* पुत्री, बेटी – **daughterly** *adv.* – **daughter-in-law** *n.* बेटे की पत्नी, बहू

daunt (डॉन्ट) *vt.* डराना, भयभीत करना (विशे. किसी को काम से रोकने के लिए) – **dauntless** *a.* निडर, निर्भीक – **daunting** (ˊडान्टिङ) *a.* निरुत्साहित करने वाला

dawdle (ˊडॉड्ल) *vi.* समय गंवाना; आवारागर्दी करना, व्यर्थ ही इधर-उधर चक्कर लगाना

dawn (डॉन) *n.* ऊषाकाल, भोर, सवेरा; पहली किरण या किसी चीज़/बात का प्रारंभ – *vi.* भोर होना; प्रारंभ होना; समझ आने लगना

day (डे) *n.* दिन, दिवस; चौबीस घण्टे का समय; युग, अवधि, काल; विशेष (महत्व का) दिन – **daybook** *n.*बही, दैनिक पत्री – **daybreak** *n.* भोर, ऊषाकाल – **day care** छोटे बच्चों, बूढ़ों की देखभाल का इंतज़ाम – **daydream** *n.* दिवास्वप्न – *vi.*दिन में सपने लेना – **daylight** *n.* दिन का प्रकाश – **daystar** *n.* शुक्र ग्रह (जो भोर से पहले दिखाई पड़ता है – **daytime** *n.* सूर्योदय और सूर्यास्त के बीच का समय, दिन का समय – **day by day** हर समय; धीरे-धीरे – **make sb's day** (ऐसी खबर जो) सारा दिन खुश रखे

daze (डेज़) *vt.* हक्का-बक्का, चकित या भौंचक्का कर देना

dazzle (ˊडैज़ल) *vt.* अत्यधिक प्रकाश से चका चौंध कर देना या चौंधिया देना – *n.* चकाचौंध

D.D.T. (डी.डी.टी.) *n.* एक कीटनाशक दवाई

de- (*comb. form*) से हटाना या अलग करना, जैसे **delouse** (शरीर से जुएं साफ करना)

dead (डेड) *a.* म तक, मरा हुआ; पुराना; जो काम न कर रहा हो; बुझा हुआ; जिसमें चमक, गति

या शक्ति न रही हो, निर्जीव, निश्चेष्ट – *n.* मुरदा व्यक्ति (प्राय: *pl.* में, **the dead**) – *adv.* पूरी तरह – **deaden** *vt.* – **deadly** *a.* मृत्यु समान – *adv.* मुरदे या मृतक के समान – **dead-and-alive** *a.* निस्तेज; नीरस – **deadbeat** *n. inf.* आलसी, नाकारा व्यक्ति – **dead heat** दौड़ जिसमें दो या अधिक प्रतियोगी बराबर रहें – **dead letter** कानून जिसे कोई मानता न हो; चिट्ठी जिसे व्यक्ति तक पहुंचाया न जा सके – **deadline** *n.* अंतिम तिथि – **deadlock** *n.* गतिरोध – **dead set** पूर्णतया; दृढ़तापूर्वक कार्यवाही – **dead of night** रात का सन्नाटा – **deadweight** *n.* बहुत भारी वस्तु; परिवर्तन या सफलता के रास्ते में रुकावट – **deadwood** *n.* संगठन में बेकार वस्तु/व्यक्ति

deaf (डॅफ़) *a.* बहरा, बधिर; उदासीन; जो (किसी की बात) सुनना न चाहे – **deafen** *vt.* बहरा कर देना – **deafness** *n.*

deal (डील) *vt.* बांटना; देना; से सम्बन्ध रखना – *vi.* व्यापार करना (*with, in* के साथ); व्यवहार करना; कार्यवाही करना (**dealt** *pt./pp.*) – *n.* सौदा; करार, व्यवहार; हिस्सा – **dealer** *n.* (ताश में पत्ते) बांटने वाला; व्यापारी – **dealings** *pl. n.* दूसरों के साथ व्यवहार; लेन-देन, व्यापार – **deal with** कार्यवाही करना; निपटना

dean (डीन) *n.* विश्वविद्यालय या कालिज का अधिकारी; गिरजे का अधिकारी

dear (डिअर) *a.* प्रिय; प्यारा; बहुमूल्य, कीमती; महंगा – *n.* प्रिय व्यक्ति; प्रियतम – *adv.* ऊंची कीमत पर – **dearly** *adv.* – **dearness** *n.* महंगाई

dearth (डर्थ) *n.* अभाव, कमी; दुर्लभता

death (डॅथ) *n.* मृत्यु, मौत; समाप्ति; विनाश – **deathless** *a.* अमर

debacle (डि'बाकल, डि'बाकल) *n.* पूर्ण पराजय; करारी हार; विनाश

debar (डि'बार) *vt.* वंचित करना; निकाल देना; रोकना या प्रतिबन्ध लगाना; मना करना (**-rr-**)

debase (डि'बेस) *vt.* मूल्य, गुणवत्ता या स्वरूप में घटाना – **debasement** *n.*

debate (डि'बेट) *v.* बहस या वाद विवाद करना, विशे. किसी सभा में; विचार करना – *n.* वाद विवाद, बहस, विवाद – **debatable** *a.* विवादास्पद

debauch (डि'बॉच) *vt.* व्यभिचार करना, भ्रष्ट करना – *n.* व्यभिचार; विषयासक्ति, लम्पटता – **debauchee** (डॅबा'ची) *n.* विलासी; लम्पट – **debauchery** *n.* विलासिता; लम्पटता

debenture (डि'बॅन्चर) *n.* (कम्पनी आदि का) ऋणपत्र

debility (डि'बिलिटि) *n.* शारीरिक दुर्बलता, कमज़ोरी, आलस्य

debit ('डॅबिट) *Accounting n.* किसी द्वारा देय राशि जो उस के नाम लिखी जाय; खाते का पन्ना जहां ऐसी राशियां लिखी जाती है – *vt.* के नाम लिखना; देय खाते में डालना – **debit card** प्लास्टिक कार्ड जिससे वस्तुऐं खरीदने पर सीधा बैंक में खाते से भुगतान हो जाता है, डेबिट-कार्ड

debonair (डॅब'नेंअर) *a.* फैशनेबल; मिलनसार; खुशमिज़ाज; सौम्य; भद्र

debris ('डेब्रि) *n. sing & pl.* मलबा, कचरा

debt (डॅट) *n.* कर्ज़, ऋण; ऋण की राशि – **debtor** (डॅटर) *n.* ऋणी; देनदार

debug (डी'बग) *vt. Computers* कम्प्यूटर प्रोग्राम में आयी खराबियों को निकालना, दोष रहित करना

debunk (डी'बंक) *vt.* (किसी के झूठ या दंभ का) पर्दाफ़ाश करना, विशे. खिल्ली उड़ा कर

debut ('डेब्यू, 'डॅब्यू) *n.* पहली बार जनता के सामने आना; अभिनेता/अभिनेत्री का प्रथम अभिनय

– **debutante** (डॅब्युटांट) *n.* युवती जो पहली बार समाज में प्रवेश कर रही है

)ec. December का संक्षेप

leca- (डॅक्अ) (*comb. form*) दस, जैसे **decalitre** दस लीटर

lecade (डॅकेड) *n.* दस वर्ष की अवधि, दशक; दशाब्द

lecadent (डॅकडंट) *a.* हासोन्मुख; जिस का नैतिक पतन हो रहा हो – **decadence** (डॅकडंस) *n.*

lecamp (डि'कैम्प) *vi.* भाग जाना; रफूचक्कर हो जाना; फरार हो जाना

lecanter (डि'कैन्टर) *n.* ढक्कन वाली कांच की बोतल जिसमें शराब रखी जाती है

lecapitate (डि'कैपिटेट) *vt.* सिर काट लेना – **decapitation** (डिकैपि'टेशन) *n.*

lecathlon (डि'कैथ्लॉन) *n.* एक प्रतियोगिता जिसमें दस प्रकार के खेल होते हैं

lecay (डि'के) *v.* सड़ जाना, गल जाना; बिगड़ना; हस होना – *n.* सड़न, गलन; क्षय; हस

lecease (डि'सीस) *n.* म त्यु; मौत – *vi.* मर जाना – **deceased** (डि'सीस्डट) *a.* मतक – *n.* व्यक्ति जो कुछ ही समय पहले भरा हो

deceive (डि'सीव़) *vt.* गलत रास्ते पर डालना; धोखा या छल करना; ठगना – **deceit** *n.* धोखा; छल; धूर्तता – **deceitful** *a.*

decelerate (डी'सॅलरेट) *vi.* गति या रफ्तार मद्धिम करना; धीमे हो जाना

December (डि'सॅम्बर) *n.* दिसम्बर

decent ('डीसन्ट) *a.* सम्मानजनक; उचित; मर्यादा वाला; शालीन; समुचित; *inf.* दयालु; दयामय – **decency** *n.* शालीनता; सज्जनता – **decently** *adv.*

decentralize (डी'सॅन्ट्रलाइज़) *vt.* विकेन्द्रीकरण करना

deception (डि'सॅप्शन) *n.* छल, धोखा; कपट; चाल, दांव; इंद्रजाल – **deceptive** (डि'सॅप्टिव) *a.* भ्रमजनक, भ्रांति पैदा करने वाला

decibel (डॅसिबल) *n.* ध्वनि/आवाज़ (की गहनता मापने की) इकाई

decide (डि'साइड) *vt.* तय करना; निर्णय/फैसला करना; निर्णय देना (न्यायाधीश आदि का) – *vi.* किसी निष्कर्ष या निर्णय पर पहुंचना – **decided** *a.* निश्चित – **decidedly** *adv.* निश्चय ही, निस्संदेह – **decision** (डि'सिझ़न) *n.* निर्णय; फैसला; निश्चय; संकल्प – **decisive** (डि'साइसिव़) *a.* निश्चयात्मक; निर्णायक – **decisively** *adv.*

deciduous (डि'सिड्युअस) *a.* (व क्ष) जिसके पत्ते हर साल झड़ें; (स ग, दांत) जो एक अवधि तक बढ़ कर गिर जाय

decimal (डॅसिमल) *a.* दस से सम्बन्धित, दशमिक – *n.* दशमलव – **decimal point** दशमलव बिन्दु – **decimal system** भार या सिक्कों की दशमलव प्रणाली (जिसमें हर भार या सिक्के से छोटा उसका दसवां भाग हो) – **decigram** *n.* ग्राम का दसवां भाग – **decilitre** *n.* लीटर का दसवां भाग – **decimetre** *n.* मीटर का दसवां भाग, डेसीमीटर

decimate (डॅसिमेट) *vt.* दसवां भाग या बड़ा अंश मार देना/का विनाश कर देना

decipher (डि'साइफ़र) *vt.* अर्थ निकालना; गूढ़लिपि पढ़ना

deck (डॅक) *n.* मंच या तख्तों का बना फर्श, विशे. जहाज़ की छत; रिकार्ड बजाने के बाजे का वह भाग जहां रिकार्ड लगाया जाता है; टेप रिकार्डर का वह अंश जहां टेप रखे जाते हैं – *vt.* सजाना; संवारना

declaim (डि'क्लेम) *v.* नाटकीय ढंग से या भावावेश में भाषण देना; आपत्ति या विरोध प्रदर्शन करना – **declamation** (डॅक्ल'मेशन) *n.* भाषण, वक्त ता – **declamatory** (डि'क्लैमटरि) *a.*

declare (डि´क्लेंअर) *vt.* (विधिवत) घोषणा करना; जोर दे कर कहना; बताना (कि किन वस्तुओं पर सीमा शुल्क लग सकता है) – *vi.*किसी का पक्ष लेना (*for* के साथ); *Cricket* पूरी टीम के खेले बिना पारी समाप्ति की घोषणा करना – **declaration** (डेंक्ल´रेशन) *n.* घोषणा, एलान – **declarative, declaratory** *a.* – **declarer** *n. Bridge* ताश के खेल में जो खिलाड़ी रंग बताए या कहे कि उस के पास रंग का पत्ता नह है

decline (डि´क्लाइन) *vt.* इनकार करना, मना करना – *vi.* नीचे की ओर झुकना या ढालू होना; धीरे धीरे बिगड़ना या क्षय होना; छोटा होते या घटते जाना; संज्ञा में विभक्ति लगाना – *n.* अवनति; धीरे धीरे बिगड़ने की क्रिया; ह्रास, क्षय; घटाव; ढलान

decoction (डि´कॉक्शन) *n.* (जड़ी बूटी आदि) उबालकर काढ़ा बनाने की क्रिया; काढ़ा

decode (डी´कोड) *vt.* गूढ़ भाषा का अर्थ निकालना; गुप्त लेख पढ़ना

decompose (डीकम्´पोज़) *vt.* किसी वस्तु को उसके घटकों में विभाजित करना – *vi.* सड़ या गल जाना – **decomposition** *n.* सड़ने या गलने की क्रिया

decongestant (डीकन्´जेंस्टंट) *a./n.* (दवा) जो विशे. नाक की बलगम को दूर करे

decontaminate (डीकन्´टैमिनेट) *vt.* विषाक्तता या परमाणु पदार्थों के प्रभाव को दूर करना, प्रदूषण हटाना – **decontamination** (डीकन्टैमि´नेशन) *n.* विषाक्तता या प्रदूषण हटाने की क्रिया

decontrol (डीकन्´ट्रोल) *vt.* राज्य के नियंत्रण से मुक्त करना; विनियंत्रित करना (**-ll-**)

decor (´डेकॉर) *n.* कमरे आदि की सजावट, सज्जा; रंग सज्जा, मंच सज्जा

decorate (´डेंकरेट) *vt.* सजाना, अलंक त करना; कमरे में रोगन करना या उसकी दीवारों पर छपा कागज़ चिपकाना; पदक या सम्मान प्रदान करना – **decoration** (डेंक´रेशन) *n.* सजावट; तमग़ा, सम्मान – **decorative** *a.* – **decorator** *n.* सजाने वाला

decorum (डि´कॉरम) *n.* शिष्ट व्यवहार, शिष्टाचार; मर्यादा; शालीनता – **decorous** *a.* शिष्ट; शालीन; मर्यादित

decoy (डि´कॉइ) *n.* दूसरों को फंसाने या उनका ध्यान बंटाने के लिए प्रयुक्त वस्तु

decrease *v.* (डि´क्रीस) घटना या घटाना; कम होना या करना – *n.* (´डीक्रीस) कमी, घटाव

decree (डि´क्री) *n.* कानूनी आदेश; डिगरी – *v.* कानूनी फैसला करना; आदेश देना

decrepit (डि´क्रेंपिट) *a.* पुराना और कमज़ोर; जर्जर; जीर्ण

decry (डि´क्राइ) *vt.* तुच्छ समझना; निंदा करना (**decried, decrying**)

dedicate (´डेंडिकेट) *vt.* किसी प्रयोजन विशेष के लिए समर्पित करना; (पुस्तक आदि किसी को) समर्पित करना; ईश्वर की सेवा में लगाना – **dedication** *n.*

deduce (डि´ड्यूस) *vt.* (तथ्यों से निष्कर्ष निकालना – **deduct** (डि´डक्ट) *vt.* घटाना; काटना; निकाल देना – **deduction** *n.* घटाने की क्रिया; कटौती; निष्कर्ष; सामान्य को ध्यान में रखकर विशेष निष्कर्ष

deed (डीड) *n.* काम; कारनामा; कानूनी दस्तावेज़

deem (डीम) *vt.* समझना; मानना

deep (डीप) *a.* गहरा; गहराई में; गंभीर; किसी गहराई विशेष तक; मार्मिक; गहन; जिसे समझना कठिन हो; गूढ़; दुर्बोध; चालाक; डूबा हुआ; निमग्न; गहरा (रंग); गंभीर (आवाज़) – *n.* गहरा स्थान या तल; समुद्र – *adv.* बहुत नीचे या गहराई पर – **deepen** *v.* – **deeply** *adv.* – **in deep waters** मुसीबत में, संकट में

deer (डिअर) *n.* हिरन (*pl.* **deer**)

deface (डि´फ़ेस) *vt.* (शक्ल) बिगाड़ना; विक त करना; (चैक आदि पर) लिखकर खराब/बेकार

करना – **defacement** *n.* शक्ल बिगाड़ने की क्रिया; खराब करना

de facto (डि´फ़ैक्टो) *Lat.* जो वास्तव में हो (चाहे कानून उसे स्वीकार न करे), वस्तुतः

defame (डि´फ़ेम) *vt.* की बदनामी करना; (बदनामी या अफवाहों से) मानहानि करना – **defamation** (डॅफ़´मेशन) *n.* मानहानि – **defamatory** *a.*

default (डि´फ़ॉल्ट) *n.* चूक; कार्यवाही न करने की स्थिति; अनुपस्थिति; बाकीदारी (ऋण चुकाने या अदायगी में चूक); *Computers* कोई और विकल्प या परिवर्तन न चुनने की स्थिति में जो हो – *v.* अदायगी न करना – **defaulter** *n.* चूक करने वाला विशे. सैनिक जिसने आदेश का पालन न किया हो – **in default of** की अनुपस्थिति में

defeat (डि´फ़ीट) *vt.* हराना; व्यर्थ या विफल कर देना – *n.* पराजय; हार; विफलता – **defeatism** *n.* पराजयवाद (हार मानने की प्रवृति) – **defeatist** *a./n.*

defecate (´डॅफ़िकेट) *vt.* मल त्याग (पाख़ाना) करना – **defecation** (डॅफ़ि´केशन) *n.*

defect *n.* (डि´फ़ॅक्ट, ´डीफ़ॅक्ट) दोष, खराबी; त्रुटि; कमी; कमज़ोरी – *vi.* (´डी´फ़ॅक्ट) अपने देश या साथियों को छोड़ कर विरोधियों से मिल जाना; दल बदल करना – **defection** (डि´फ़ॅक्शन) *n.* दल-बदल – **defective** *a.* दोषपूर्ण; अपूर्ण; त्रुटिपूर्ण – **defector** *n.* *India* दल-बदलू

defend (डि´फ़ॅन्ड) *vt.* बचाव या रक्षा करना; आक्रमण रोकना; (तर्क या साक्ष्य से) पक्ष लेना; सफाई पेश करना; (खेलों में) विजेता का चुनौती देने वाले को हराने की कोशिश करना – **defence** *n.* प्रतिरक्षा; रक्षा; सफाई; मोर्चा बन्दी – **defenceless** *a.* – **defendant** *n.* प्रतिवादी; अभियुक्त – **defender** *n.* समर्थक – **defensible** *a.* जिस का बचाव संभव हो – **defensive** *a.* रक्षात्मक – *n.*

defer[1] (डि´फ़र) *vt.* टालना, स्थगित करना (**-rr-**) – **deferment** *n.* टालने या स्थगित करने की क्रिया

defer[2] *vi.* **defer to** किसी और की राय या फैसला मान लेना (**-rr-**) – **deference** *n.* सम्मान; श्रद्धा

defiance (डि´फ़ाइअंस) *n.*, **defiant** *a.* देखिए DEFY

deficient (डि´फ़िशंट) *a.* अपूर्ण; अपर्याप्त – **deficiency** (डि´फ़िशंसि) *n.* अपूर्णता, कमी; अपर्याप्तता – **deficit** (´डॅफ़िसिट) *n.* घाटा; कमी; अभाव

defile (डि´फ़ाइल) *vt.* गंदा, अपवित्र या दूषित करना; कलुषित करना – **defilement** *n.*

define (डि´फ़ाइन) *vt.* निरूपण करना; परिभाषा देना; निश्चित करना; निर्धारित करना; सीमांकन करना; निशानदेही करना – **definable** *a.* – **definition** *n.* (डॅफ़ि´निशन) परिभाषा; निरूपण; स्पष्टता – **definite** (´डॅफ़िनिट) *a.* निश्चित; सुस्पष्ट; निश्चयात्मक; अवश्यंभावी – **definitely** *adv.* निश्चय ही

deflate (डी´फ़्लेट) *v.* हवा निकालना; (व्यक्ति का) मानमर्दन करना; *Economics* अपस्फीति करना (मुद्रा की राशि कम कर के उसका मूल्य बढ़ाना) – **deflation** *n.* आर्थिक और औद्योगिक क्रियाकलाप में कमी, अपस्फीति

deflect (डि´फ़्लॅक्ट) *v.* मोड़ना; दिशा बदल देना – **deflection** *n.*

deflower (डी´फ़्लाउअर) *vt.* कौमार्य भंग करना

deforest (डी´फ़ॉरिस्ट) *vt.* वृक्षों की कटाई कर के जंगल साफ़ करना – **deforestation** (डीफ़ॉरि´स्टेशन) *n.* जंगलों की कटाई

deform (डि´फ़ार्म) *vt.* रूप या शक्ल बिगाड़ना; कुरूप बनाना; टेढ़ा मेढ़ा कर देना –

deformation (डिफ़ॉर्'मेशन) *n.* विकृति – **deformed** *a.* विकृत; कुरूप – **deformity** *n.*
defraud (डि'फ़्रॉड) *vt.* ठगना
defray (डि'फ़्रे) *vt.* (खर्च हुआ पैसा) अदा करना
defrost (डी'फ़्रॉस्ट) *v.* (ठंड से जमी वस्तु को) पिघलाना
deft (डॅफ्ट) *a.* दक्ष, निपुण; कुशल
defunct (डि'फ़ंक्ट) *a.* मृत; पुराना; अप्रचलित
defuse (डी'फ़्यूज़) *vt.* बम आदि का पलीता निकालना (जिससे वह फटे नहीं); किसी स्थिति में तनाव दूर करना
defy (डि'फ़ाइ) *vt.* चुनौती देना; सफलतापूर्वक विरोध करना; न मानना (**defied, defying**) – **defiance** *n.* अवज्ञा; विरोध – **defiant** *a.* जो खुले आम विरोध करे
degenerate *vi.* (डि'जॅनरेट) अवनति होना; नैतिक, मानसिक और शारीरिक स्तर का गिरना; बिगड़ना या भ्रष्ट हो जाना – *a.* (डि'जॅनरिट) विकृत; भ्रष्ट; पतित – *n.* चरित्रहीन या भ्रष्ट व्यक्ति – **degeneration** (डीजॅन'रेशन) *n.* चरित्र-पतन
degrade (डि'ग्रेड) *vt.* अपमानित करना; भ्रष्ट करना; दरजा घटाना – *vi.* रासायनिक रूप से सड़ जाना – **degradable** *a.* जो रासायनिक या जैविक दृष्टि से गल या सड़ जाने वाला हो – **degraded** *a.* अपमानित; बदनाम – **degradation** (डॅग्र'डेशन) *n.*
degree (डि'ग्री) *n.* किसी प्रक्रिया, माप, दर्जे, व्यवस्था, स्थिति आदि की अवस्था; सोपान; कोटि; दर्जा; कोण या तापमान का माप; अंश; अशांक; *Gr.* धातु; उपाधि – **third degree** लम्बी, कड़ी पूछताछ (प्राय: यातना देकर)
dehydrate (डी'हाइड्रेट) *vt.* निर्जल करना; नमी दूर करना – **dehydration** (डीहाइ'ड्रेशन) *n.* (शरीर में) पानी की कमी
deign (डेन) *vt.* किसी पर कृपा करना
deity ('डीइटि) *n.* ईश्वरीय सत्ता या गुण; देवता
dejected (डि'जॅक्टिड) *a.* उदास; हतोत्साह, निराश
dekko (डॅको) *n. sl.* निगाह मारने की क्रिया
delay (डि'ले) *vt.* स्थगित करना; देर करना या लगाना – *vi.* देर लगाना; अटकाना (**delayed, delaying**) – *n.* देर
delectable (डि'लॅक्टबल) *a.* रूचिकर; स्वादिष्ट
delegate *n.* ('डॅलिगेट, 'डॅलिगिट) प्रतिनिधि – *vt.* ('डॅलिगेट) प्रतिनिधि के रूप में भेजना; किसी को अधिकार आदि देना – **delegation** (डॅलि'गेशन) *n.* प्रतिनिधि मण्डल; प्रत्यायोजन
delete (डि'लीट) *vt.* हटाना; काटना; मिटाना – **deletion** (डि'लीशन) *n.*
deleterious (डॅलि'टिअरिअस) *a.* हानिकर
deliberate *a.* (डि'लिबिरिट) जानबूझ कर (किया गया); सोच समझ कर (किया गया) – *v.* (डि'लिबरेट) सोच विचार, विचार-विमर्श या वाद-विवाद करना – **deliberation** (डिलिब'रेशन) *n.* सोच विचार; वाद-विवाद
delicate ('डॅलिकिट) *a.* कोमल; नाज़ुक; जिसमें सावधानी या कौशल की आवश्यकता हो – **delicacy** ('डॅलिकसि) *n.* स्वादिष्ट व्यंजन – **delicately** *adv.*
delicious (डि'लिशस) *a.* सुखद; रुचिकर, स्वादिष्ट
delight (डि'लाइट) *vt.* बहुत आनंद देना – *vi.* (*in* के साथ) किसी काम/बात में बहुत सुख मिलना – *n.* आनंद, हर्ष – **delightful** *a.* आनंदप्रद; रुचिकर; सुन्दर
delimitation (डिलिमि'टेशन) *n.* सीमाएं निर्धारित करने की क्रिया
delineate (डि'लिनिएट) *vt.* रूपरेखा प्रस्तुत करना – **delineation** *n.*
delinquent (डि'लिंक्वंट) *n.* व्यक्ति विशे. अवयस्क जो छोटा मोटा अपराध करे – *a.* – **delinquency** *n.* छोटा मोटा अपराध या दुष्कर्म

delirium (डि´लिरिअम) *n.* मानसिक विकार, (विशे. बुखार में), प्रलाप – **delirious** (डि´लिरिअस) *a.*

deliver (डि´लिव़र) *vt.* (सामान आदि) निश्चित स्थान तक ले जाना; देना; सौंपना; छोड़ना; मुक्ति दिलाना; बांटना; बच्चे को जन्म देना; (भाषण आदि) देना – **deliverance** (डि´लिव़रन्स) *n.* मुक्ति, रिहाई – **deliverer** *n* – **delivery** *n.* सुपुर्दगी; माल छुड़ाई; वितरण; प्रसव; शैली (भाषण आदि की)

delta (´डेल्ट्अ) *n.* त्रिकोणभूमि जो नदी के कई भागों में बंट गयी हो; यूनानी वर्णमाला का चौथा अक्षर (Δ)

delude (डि´लूड) *vt.* धोखा देना; बहकाना – **delusion** (डि´लूझ़न) *n.* भ्रांति; भ्रम

deluge (´डेल्यूज) *n.* बाढ़; भारी वर्षा – *vt.* जलमग्न कर देना

de luxe (ड´लक्स, ड´लुक्स) *a.* बढ़िया; सर्वोत्तम

delve (डेल्व) *v.* (*into* के साथ) खोजबीन करना

demand (डि´मांड) *vt.* मांगना (आदेश देकर, अधिकार के रूप में); अपनी देय राशि, अधिकार या आवश्यकता समझ कर मांगना – *n.* मांग; दावा; आवश्यकता – **demanding** *a.* (काम) श्रमसाध्य; जिसके लिए कौशल या धैर्य आवश्यक हो

demarcate (´डीमार्केट) *vt.* सीमा निर्धारित करना अथवा अंकित करना – **demarcation** *n.*

demean (डि´मीन) *vt.* दर्जा कम करना, नीचा करना

demat (डि´मैट) *a.* **demateralized** का संक्षेप; *India* कम्पनियों के शेयर जो निजी कागज़ी दस्तावेज़ के बजाये एक बड़ी कम्प्यूटर व्यवस्थ पर हों

demeanour, US demeanor (डि´मीनर) *n.* आचरण; व्यवहार

demented (डि´मेंन्टिड) *a.* पागल, विक्षिप्त

demerit (डी´मेरिट) *n.* अवगुण

demi- (*comb. form*) आधा, जैसे – **demigod** (आधा देवता)

demilitarize (डी´मिलिटराइज़) *vt.* (किसी क्षेत्र से) सेनाएं हटाना, विसैन्यीकरण करना

demise (डि´माइज़) *n.* (विचार, संस्था आदि का) अंत; *formal* मृत्यु, देहांत; वसीयत या पट्टे द्वारा सम्पत्ति का हस्तांतरण

demo (डेमो) *n. inf.* DEMONSTRATION का संक्षेप

demobilize (डी´मोबिलाइज़) *vt.* सेना का विघटन करना; सैनिक को सेवा मुक्त करना

democracy (डि´मॉक्रसि) *n.* लोकतंत्र, प्रजातंत्र – **democrat** (´डेमक्रैट) *n.* लोकतंत्रवादी – **democratic** (डेम´क्रैटिक) *a.*

demolish (डि´मॉलिश) *vt.* ढा देना; पूरी तरह नष्ट कर देना – **demolition** (डेम´लिशन) *n.*

demon (´डीमन) *n.* शैतान; दानव; पिशाच; असुर; नर-पिशाच; राक्षस; किसी काम में माहिर या अत्यधिक लगन वाला व्यक्ति

demonstrate (´डेम्न्स्ट्रेट) *vt.* तर्क द्वारा सिद्ध करना; दिखाना; प्रयोग द्वारा सिद्ध करना, प्रदर्शित करना – *vi.* (~ **in support of**) जलूस या सभा द्वारा किसी पक्ष का समर्थन करना; प्रदर्शन करना – **demonstration** (डेमन्´स्ट्रेशन) *n.* स्पष्ट करने की क्रिया, साक्ष्य द्वारा प्रमाणित करने की क्रिया, प्रदर्शन (जनता के विचारों का संगठित रूप से) – **demonstrative** (´डिमॉन्सट्रटिव़) *a.* जो अपनी भावनाओं का प्रदर्शन करे; जिससे कोई बात स्पष्ट होती हो; निर्णायक – **demonstrator** (´डेमन्सट्रेटर) *n.* जो उपकरणों आदि और उनका प्रयोग दिखाए; सार्वजनिक प्रदर्शनों में भाग लेने वाला प्रदर्शनकारी; प्रयोगशाला में अध्यापक का सहायक

demoralize (डि'मॉरलाइज़) *vt.* नैतिक बल तोड़ना –**demoralization** (डिमॉरलाइ'ज़ेशन) *n.*
demote (डि'मोट) *vt.* दर्जा या पद घटाना – **demotion** *n.* पदावनति
demur (डि'मर) *vi.* आनाकानी करना (**-rr-**)
demure (डि'म्युअर) *a.* संकोची
demurrage (डि'मरिज) *n.* विलम्ब शुल्क
den (डॅन) *n.* (जंगली पशु की) मांद; **US** छोटा कमरा, (अपराधियों का) अड्डा
denationalize (डी'नैश्नलाइज़) *vt.* (privatize) (उद्योग आदि को) राज्य के स्वामित्व से निजी हाथों में सौंपना – **denationalization** (डीनैश्नलाइ'ज़ेशन) *n.* विराष्ट्रीयकरण
dengue ('डॅङगि) *n.* उष्ण प्रदेशों का एक ज्वर; दण्डक ज्वर
denial (डि'नाइअल) देखिए DENY
denigrate ('डॅनिग्रेट) *vt.* तुच्छ बताना
denim ('डॅनिम) *n.* मोटा सूती कपड़ा – **denims** *pl. n.* नीले रंग की जीन
denizen ('डॅनिज़न) *n.* वासी, निवासी
denomination (डिनामि'नेशन) *n.* विशिष्ट नाम वाला गिरजा या सम्प्रदाय; नाम, विशे. किसी वर्ग या समूह का – **denominator** *n.*संख्या जिस से भाग दिया जाय; हर
denote (डि'नोट) *vt.* द्योतक या नाम होना – **denotation** *n.* अभिधा, शाब्दिक अर्थ
denounce (डि'नाउन्स) *vt.* भर्त्सना या निन्दा करना – **denunciation** (डिनन्सि 'एशन) *n.*
dense(डॅन्स) *a.* घना, सघन; मन्द बुद्धि, मूर्ख – **density** *n.* घनत्व
dent (डॅन्ट) *n.* (दबाव या चोट से बना) गड्ढा, पिचक – *vt.* चोट या दबाव से गड्ढा बनाना
dental ('डॅन्टल) *a.* दांतों का; दंत्य- (स्वर) – **dentist** *n.* – दांतों का डाक्टर – **dentistry** *n.* दंत-चिकित्सा – **denture** ('डॅन्चर) *n.* (बहुधा *pl.*) नकली दांत

denude (डि'न्यूड) *vt.* नंगा करना; मिट्टी, व क्षों आदि के साफ़ हो जाने से चट्टान का निकल आना – **denudation** (डॅन्यु'डेशन) *n.*
denunciation (डिनन्सि'एशन) देखिए DENOUNCE
deny (डि'नाइ) *vt.* नकारना, खण्डन करना; अस्वीकार करना; रद्द करना; त्यागना; देने से इनकार करना
deodorize (डी'ओडराइज़) *vt.* (किसी पदार्थ को) गंध रहित करना – **deodorant** (डी'ओडरंट) *n.* गंध रहित करने वाला पदार्थ – **deodorizer** *n.* गंधहर पदार्थ
dep. depart(s), departure का संक्षेप
depart (डि'पार्ट) *vi.* चले जाना; चल पड़ना, प्रस्थान करना; से हट जाना; बदल जाना; *formal* मर जाना – **departure** (डि' पार्चर) *n.*
department (डि'पार्ट्मन्ट) *n.* विभाग; महकमा; क्षेत्र – **departmental** *a.* विभागीय – **departmentally** *adv.* – **department store** बड़ी दुकान जिसमें सभी प्रकार की वस्तुएं बिकती हों
depend (डि'पॅण्ड) *vi.* (~ **on**) निर्भर करना; पर भरोसा या विश्वास होना; जीना; पर आधारित होना; (निर्णय या फैसले पर) निर्भर होना – **dependable** *a.* विश्वास के योग्य – **dependant** *n.* (के परिवार का) सदस्य, आश्रित व्यक्ति – **dependent** *a.* आश्रित – **dependence** *n.* निर्भरता
depict (डि'पिक्ट) *vt.* चित्रण करना; वर्णन करना – **depiction** *n.* चित्रण; वर्णन
deplete (डि'प्लीट) *vt.* खाली, कम, या समाप्त करना – **depletion** (डि'प्लीशन) *n.* समाप्ति, खाली हो जाने की क्रिया/स्थिति
deplore (डि'प्लॉर) *vt.* (पर) खेद प्रकट करना; बुरा कहना; शिकायत करना; (के कारण) दुखी होना – **deplorable** *a.* खेदजनक, निन्दनीय; शोचनीय

deploy (डि'प्लॉइ) *v.* सैनिक या जहाज़ आदि (युद्ध के लिए) तैनात करना – **deployment** *n.* सैन्य विन्यास

depopulate (डि'पॉप्युलेट) *v.* जनसंख्या घटा देना

deport (डि'पॉर्ट) *vt.* देश से निकालना (किसी विदेशी को); देश निकाला देना – **deportation** (डीपॉर्'टेशन) *n.* निर्वासन

depose (डि'पोज़) *vt.* अपदस्थ करना, सम्राट को गद्दी से उतारना – *vi.* शपथ लेकर बयान देना

deposit (डि'पॉज़िट) *vt.* नीचे रखना, विशे. सावधानी से; पैसा जमा करना, विशे. बैंक में; नीचे गिराना (तलछट के रूप में) – *n.* जमा की गयी या रखी गयी वस्तु; कीमत के अंश के रूप में या जमानत के रूप में दी गयी राशि; तलछट – **depositor** *n.* जमा करने वाला

depot ('डेंपो) *n.* गोदाम; भण्डार

depraved (डि'प्रेव्ड) *a.* चरित्रहीन – **depravity** (डि'प्रैविटि) *n.*

deprecate ('डेंप्रिकेट) *vt.* (की) निंदा करना

depreciate (डि'प्रीशिएट) *vt.* कीमत, मूल्य या क्रय क्षमता घटाना; तुच्छ समझना; मुद्रा का अवमूल्यन करना – *vi* का मूल्य या महत्व कम हो जाना; मुद्रा अवमूल्यन होना – **depreciation** (डिप्रीशि'एशन) *n.* मुद्रा अवमूल्यन; अवज्ञा; निंदा

depredation (डेंप्रि'डेशन) *n.* लूटमार, लूटपाट

depress (डि'प्रेंस) *vt.* निराश करना, उदास करना; घटाना, दबाना – **depressed** *a.* निराश, खिन्न, उदास; दलित (वर्ग); दबा हुआ (क्षेत्र) – **depression** (डि'प्रेंशन) *n.* निराशा, विषाद, उदासी; गड्ढा, गर्त; आर्थिक मंदी जो गरीबी व बेरोज़गारी का कारण बने

deprive (डि'प्राइव़) *vt.* छीन लेना; ले लेना – **deprivation** (डेंप्रि'वेशन) *n.* अभाव, तंगी, तंगहाली – **deprived** *a.* वंचित; गरीब, भूखा-नंगा

dept. department का संक्षेप

depth (डेंप्थ) *n.* गहराई; गहरा स्थान; खाई; गंभीरता, (ज्ञान की) गहनता

depute *vt.* (डि'प्यूट) सौंपना, देना; किसी व्यक्ति को प्रतिनिधि नियुक्त करना, के स्थान पर नियुक्त करना – *a./n.* (डेंप्यूट) स्कॉटलैंड में, सहायक – **deputation** (डेंप्यु'टेशन) *n.* किसी वर्ग की ओर से बातचीत करने के लिए भेजे गए व्यक्तियों का समूह, प्रतिनिधि-मंडल, शिष्ट मंडल – **deputize** ('डेंप्युटाइज़) *vi.* के स्थान पर कार्य करना – *vt.* के स्थान पर नियुक्त करना – **deputy** ('डेंप्युटि) *n.* सहायक; प्रति-, उप-; प्रतिनिधि

derail (डि'रेल) *v.* - **be derailed** (गाड़ी का) पटरी से उतरना; *fig* रास्ते से हट जाना – **derailment** *n.*

derange (डि'रेंज) *vt.* अस्त व्यस्त कर देना, अव्यवस्थित कर देना; उलट-पलट देना; पागल कर देना – **derangement** *n.*

deregulate (डी'रेंग्युलेट) *vt.* (व्यापार आदि पर) से नियंत्रण हटाना

derelict ('डेंरिलिक्ट) *a.* परित्यक्त, छोड़ा हुआ; टूटा-फूटा, खंडहर जैसा – *n.* आवारा – **dereliction** *n.* कर्तवय-विमुखता

deride (डि'राइड) *vt.* से तिरस्कारपूर्ण व्यवहार या बात करना; की हंसी उड़ाना – **derision** (डि'रिझ़न) *n.* उपहास – **derisive** (डि'राइसिव़) *a.* – **derisory** (डि'राइसरि) *a.*

derive (डि'राइव़) *vt.* प्राप्त करना; परिणाम निकालना – **derivation** (डेंरि'वेशन) *n.* व्युत्पत्ति, निसक्ति; मूल, उद्‌भव – **derivative** (डि'रिव़टिव़) *a.* व्युत्पन्न – *n.* व्युत्पत्ति

dermatitis (डर्म'टाइटिस) *n.* त्वचा की सूजन व जलन

dermatology (डर्म'टॉलजि) *n.* त्वचा विज्ञान – **dermatologist** *n.* त्वचा-विशेषज्ञ

derogatory (डि'रॉगटरि) *a.* अपमानजनक

descend (डि'सेंन्ड) *vi.* नीचे आना या जाना; का ढलान होना; मान जाना; (~ **from**) (का) वंशज होना; उत्तराधिकार में मिलना; (~**on**) टूट पड़ना –*vt.* (सीढ़ियाँ आदि) से नीचे उतरना – **descendant** *n.* वंशज

describe (डि'स्क्राइब) *vt.* का वर्णन करना; कहना या नाम देना; ज्यामिति की आकृति बनाना – **description** (डिस्'क्रिप्शन) *n.* विवरण; चित्रण; अंकन; हुलिया – **descriptive** *a.* वर्णनात्मक; विवरणात्मक

desecrate ('डेंसिक्रेट) *vt.* की पवित्रता भंग करना – **desecration** (डेंसि'क्रेशन) *n.*

desert[1] ('डेंज़र्ट) *n.* रेगिस्तान, मरुस्थल – *a.* उजाड़, निर्जन, वीरान

desert[2] (डि'ज़र्ट) *vt.* का साथ छोड़ देना; को छोड़ कर चले जाना – *vi.* (विशे. सैनिक का) काम छोड़ कर भाग जाना – **deserter** *n.* भगोड़ा

desert[3] *n.* (बहुधा *pl.*) अपने किये का पुरस्कार या दुष्फल, फल, दण्ड या पुरस्कार

deserve (डि'ज़र्व) *vt.* के योग्य या का पात्र होना; का अधिकारी होना

design (डि'ज़ाइन) *vt.* का खाका खींचना, प्रारूप तैयार करना; योजना बनाना; (के इस्तेमाल का) इरादा बनाना –*n.* खाका; सजावटी नमूने बनाने की कला; परिकल्पना, योजना; षड़यंत्र; बनावट; इरादा – **designer** *n.* प्रारूप, नमूने आदि तैयार करने वाला, रूपकार, अभिकल्पक – **designing** *a.* धूर्त; जोड़ तोड़ करने वाला, षड़यंत्रकारी

designate ('डेंज़िग्नेट) *vt.* नामोद्दिष्ट करना, नाम देना, चुनना; किसी पद पर नियुक्ति करना – *a.* ('डेंज़िग्निट) नामोद्दिष्ट (जिसे पद विशे. के लिए चुना गया हो परंतु जिसने पद ग्रहण न किया हो) – **designation** (डेंज़िग्'नेशन) *n.* पदनाम, ओहदा

desire (डि'ज़ाइअर) *vt.* इच्छा करना, चाहना; मांगना –*n.* इच्छा, आकांक्षा; प्रार्थना; कामेच्छा *n.* – **desirable** *a.* वांछनीय, अभीष्ट – **desirous** *a.* इच्छुक

desist (डि'ज़िस्ट) *vi.* (~**from**) बंद करना, छोड़ देना; (से) बाज़ आना

desk (डेंस्क) *n.* लिखने पढ़ने के लिए मेज़, डेस्क; (आफिस आदि का) काउंटर

desolate *a.* ('डेंसलिट) निर्जन, सुनसान, उजाड़; अकेला; नीरस; उदास, निराश –*vt.* ('डेंसलेट) उजाड़ देना

despair (डिस्'पेंअर) *vi.* निराश हो जाना – *n.* पूर्ण निराशा; विषाद

despatch (डिस्'पैच) देखिए **DISPATCH**

desperate ('डेंस्परिट) *a.* निराशा के कारण कुछ भी करने को तैयार, दुस्साहसी; ख़तरनाक; अति निराशाजनक, घोर, भयंकर – **desperado** (डेंस्प'राडो) *n.* दुस्साहसी, बदमाश (**pl. -do(e)s**) – **desperately** *adv.* – **desperation** (डेंस्प'रेशन) *n.* घोर निराशा

despise (डिस्'पाइज़) *vt.* नीचा समझना; तिरस्कार करना – **despicable** ('डेस्पिकबल, डिस्'-) *a.* कमीना, तुच्छ; नीच; घिनावना

despite (डि'स्पाइट) *prep.* के बावजूद, के होते हुए भी

despoil (डि'स्पॉइल) *vt.* लूटना, छीनना

despondent (डि'स्पॉन्डंट) *a.* निराश; उदास – **despondency** *n.*

despot ('डेंस्पॉट) *n.* तानाशाह; निरंकुश शासक – **despotic** (डेंस्'पॉटिक) *a.*

dessert (डि'ज़र्ट) *n.* भोजनोपरांत खाया जाने वाला मीठा पकवान या फल

destabilize (डी'स्टेबलाइज़) *vt.* (व्यवस्था, सरकार आदि को) अस्थिर करना

destination (डेंस्टि'नेशन) *n.* गंतव्य स्थान

destined (´डॅस्टिन्ड) *vt.* नियत
destiny (´डॅस्टिनि) *n.* नियति; भाग्य, किस्मत
destitute (´डॅस्टिट्यूट) *a.* जिसके पास कुछ न हो, अकिंचन; दीन-हीन; निराश्रय
destroy (डिस्´ट्रॉइ) *vt.* नष्ट, तबाह या बर्बाद करना; टुकड़े-टुकड़े कर देना; समाप्त कर देना; ढा देना, गिरा देना; विनाश कर देना – **destroyer** *n.* तबाह करने वाला; तेज़ चलने वाला छोटा जंगी जहाज़ – **destructible** *a.* जो नष्ट किया जा सके – **destruction** (डि´स्ट्रक्शन) *n.* विनाश, तबाही – **destructive** *a.* विनाशकारी, विध्वंसक; नकरात्मक (रचनात्मक के विपरीत)
desultory (´डॅसल्टरि) *a.* बेतरतीब, असम्बद्ध, बे सिलसिला
detach (डि´टैच) *vt.* खोल देना; अलग करना – **detachable** *a.* – **detached** *a.* जो अलग-अलग रहे; तटस्थ – **detachment** *n.* अनासक्तता; अलग कर देना किसी विशेष काम के लिए भेजी सैन्य टुकड़ी
detail (´डीटेल) *n.* विवरण; तफ़सील, प्रत्येक वस्तु की चर्चा; सेना में किसी काम के लिए तैनात व्यक्ति या दल, टुकड़ी – *vt.* ब्यौरा देना; काम पर तैनात करना
detain (डि´टेन) *vt.* रोकना हवालात में रखना; रोक रखना – **detention** (डि´टॅन्शन) *n.* नज़रबंदी, हिरासत; रोके रखना
detect (डि´टॅक्ट) *vt.* पता लगाना, ढूंढ निकालना; सुराग निकालना – **detection** *n.* खोज; पहचान, अभिज्ञान – **detective** *n.* जासूस – *a.* – **detector** *n.* यंत्र जिससे रेडियो संकेतों का पता चलाया जा सके
detente (डि´टांट) *n.* राजनीतिक अथवा अतर्राष्ट्रीय मामलों में तनाव की कमी
detention (डि´टॅन्शन) *n.* देखिए **DETAIN**
deter (डि´टर) *vt.* निरुत्साहित करना; रोकना, न करने देना (**-rr-**) – **deterrent** *a./n.* रोकने का (साधन), निवारण
detergent (डि´टर्जन्ट) *n.* (कपड़े) साफ करने वाला पदार्थ, प्रक्षालक – *a.* जिसमें साफ़ करने की क्षमता हो
deteriorate (डि´टिअरिअरेट) *v.* (स्थिति) बिगड़ना या बिगाड़ना
determine (डि´टर्मिन) *vt.* फैसला करना; निर्धारित करना; नियत करना, निर्णायक तत्व होना; *Law* अवधारणा करना, समाप्त करना – *vi.* फैसले पर पहुचंना; समाप्त हो जाना – **determination** (डिटर्मि´नेशन) *n.* दृढ़ निश्चय; संकल्प – **determined** *a.* पक्का इरादा किए हुए
detest (डि´टॅस्ट) *vt.* घृणा करना
dethrone (डि´थ्रोन) *vt.* (राजा को) गद्दी से उतारना
detonate (´डॅटनेट) *v.* बम, सुरंग, विस्फोटक पदार्थ आदि का विस्फोट करना, दागना – **detonation** (डॅट´नेशन) *n.* विस्फोट – **detonator** *n.* विस्फोटक
detour (´डीटुअर) *n.* लम्बा चक्करदार रास्ता
detract (डि´ट्रैक्ट) *v.* घटना, कम करना – **detractor** *n.* निंदक
detrain (डी´ट्रेन) *v.* गाड़ी से उतरना या उतार देना
detriment (´डॅट्रिमंट) *n.* हानि – **detrimental** (डॅट्रि´मंटल) *a.* हानिकारक
deuce (ड्यूस) *n.* दो; ताश की दुक्की; *Tennis* दोनों खिलाड़ियों के 40 अंक होने की स्थिति; विस्मयादिबोधक 'शैतान!'
Deutsche Mark (´डॉइच -) जर्मन मुद्रा
devalue (डी´वैल्यू), **devaluate** (डी´वैल्युट) *v.* मुद्रा का मूल्य घटना या घटाना – **devaluation** (डीवैल्यु´एशन) *n.* अवमूल्यन
devastate (´डॅवस्टेट) *vt.* उजाड़ना करना, विध्वंस करना; *inf.* अभिभूत करना

develop (डि´वेंलप) *vt.* विकसित करना; बनाना; (कहानी आदि) बढ़ाना; ब्यौरा देना; उत्पन्न करना; विकास करना; (नैगेटिव से) फोटो (चित्र) उभारना; निर्माण कार्य द्वारा भूमि का विकास करना – *vi.* विकसित होना (**developed, developing**) – **developer** *n.* भूमि विकासकर्त्ता; नैगेटिव से फोटो उभारने का रसायन – **development** *n.* विकास; घटना; नया निर्माण (इमारतों का)

deviate (´डीविएट) *vi.* रास्ते से हटना; पथभ्रष्ट होना – **devious** *a.* धोखेबाज़, धूर्त, कपटी; टेढ़ा-मेढ़ा, चक्करदार, असम्बद्ध, असंगत

device (डि´वाइस) *n.* युक्ति, तरकीब, उपाय; साधन; उपकरण

devil (´डेंवल) *n.* शैतान; नरक दूत; राक्षस; पापी, दुष्ट या क्रूर व्यक्ति; मुश्किल या परेशानी वाली चीज़/बात; *inf.* बदमाश – **devilish** *a.* शैतान जैसा, पैशाचिक; बुरा, दुष्टतापूर्ण – **devil-may-care** *a.* बेफ़िक्र, मस्त

devious (´डीविअस) *a.* देखिए **DEVIATE**

devise (डि´वाइज़) *vt.* (तरकीब, युक्ति, जुगत) सोच निकालना; आविष्कार करना

devoid (डि´वॉइड) *a.* – **devoid of** खाली, रहित, विहीन

devolve (डि´वॉल्व) *vi.* (पर) जिम्मेदारी आना; (को) मिलना, मिल जाना – *vt.* (कार्य) के जिम्मे करना – **devolution** (डिव´लूशन) *n.* जिम्मेदारी सौंपने की क्रिया

devote (डि´वोट) *vt.* अर्पित करना; दे देना; किसी व्यक्ति विशेष या प्रयोजन के लिए समर्पित करना – **devoted** *a.* निष्ठावान – **devotee** (डेंव´टी) *n.* भक्त, उपासक; शौकीन – **devotion** (डि´वोशन) *n.* भक्ति; श्रद्धा

devour (डि´वाउअर) *vt.* निगलना; खा जाना

devout (डि´वाउट) *a.* धर्मपरायण; श्रद्धालु

dew (ड्यू) *n.* ओस

dexterity (डेंक्´स्टेंरिटि) *n.* दक्षता, निपुणता, कौशल – **dexterous** *n.*दक्ष, निपुण

di- *comb. form* दो-, द्वय

dia -(डाइअ-) *comb. form* के द्वारा

diabetes (डाइअ´बीटीज़) *n.* मधुमेह रोग – **diabetic** (डाइअ´बेंटिक) *n./a.* मधुमेह का (रोगी)

diabolic(al) (डाइअ´बॉलिक्(ल)) *a.* शैतानी, राक्षसी; *inf.* बहुत खराब (मौसम)

diagnosis (डाइअग्´नोसिस) *n.* रोग-निदान, रोग की पहचान (*pl.* **diagnoses** (डाइग्´नोसीज़)) – **diagnose** (´डाइअग्नोज़) *vt.* रोग-निदान करना – **diagnostic** (डाइअग्´नॉस्टिक) *a.*

diagonal (डाइ´ऐगनल) *a.* कोने से कोने तक, तिरछा – *n.* कोने से कोने तक रेखा, विकर्ण – **diagonally** *adv.*

diagram (´डाइअग्रैम) *n.* रेखाचित्र

dial (´डाइअल) *n.* घड़ी का डायल; मीटर, वज़न तौलने की मशीन आदि का अंकपट्ट; टेलीफ़ोन का डायल; *sl.* चेहरा, थोबड़ा – *vt.* टेलीफ़ोन का नंबर घुमाना (**-ll-**)

dialect (´डाइअलेंक्ट) *n.* बोली, उपभाषा

dialectic (डाइअ´लेंक्टिक) *n.* तर्क विद्या

dialogue (´डाइअलॉग) *n.* बातचीत (दो व्यक्तियों के बीच); (नाटक, उपन्यास आदि में) संवाद

dialysis (डाइ´एलिसिस) *n. Med.* गुर्दे की बीमारी से पीड़ित रोगी का रक्त साफ करने की क्रिया, व क्क-शोधन

diameter (डाइ´ऐमिटर) *n.* व्यास; मोटाई – **diametrical** (डाइअ´मेंट्रिकल) *a.* विरोधी, उलटा

diamond (´डाइअमंड) *n.* हीरा; समचतुर्भुज; ताश में ईंट का पत्ता – **diamond jubilee, wedding** 60 व (कभी-कभी 75 व) वर्षगांठ, हीरक-जयंती

diaper (´डाइअपर) *n.* (**nappy**) **US** बच्चे का पोतड़ा

diaphanous (डाइ´ऐफ़नस) *a.* पारदर्शी

diaphragm (´डाइअफ़्रैम) *n.* शरीर के दो गहवरों के बीच मांसपेशियों की दीवार, मध्यपट; झिल्ली जो शरीर की किसी नली का मुंह थोड़ा सा बंद करे या खोले, तंतुपट, तनुपट

diarrhoea (डाइअ´रिअ) *n.* दस्तों की बीमारी, अतिसार

diary (´डाइअरि) *n.* दैनिकी, डायरी

diaspora (डाइ´ऐस्पर्अ) *n.* स्वदेश छोड़कर दूसरे देश में जाने व बसने की क्रिया; प्रवासी

diatribe (´डाइअट्राइब) *n.* कटु निंदा

dice (डाइस) *pl. n.* (*sing* भी) पासा – *vi.* पासा खेलना – *vt.* सब्ज़ी के छोटे-छोटे टुकड़े करना – **dicer** *n.* टुकड़े करने का उपकरण – **dicey** *a. inf.* खतरनाक, जोखिम भरा

dichotomy (डाइ´कॉटमि) *n.* दो भागों में विभाजन

dictate *v.* (डिक्´टेट) लिखाना, लिखवाना; तय, निर्धारित करना; (शर्त आदि) थोप देना; हुक्म देना – *n.* (´डिक्टेट) हुक्म, आदेश; मांग – **dictation** (डिक्´टेशन) *n.* – **dictator** *n.* तानाशाह, अधिनायक – **dictatorial** (डिक्ट´टॉरिअल) – **dictatorship** *n.*

diction (´डिक्शन) *n.* बोलने व लिखने में शब्दों का चुनाव और प्रयोग

dictionary (´डिक्शनरि) *n.* शब्दकोश; कोश

did (डिड) DO का *pt.*

didactic (डि´डैक्टिक) *a.* उपदेशात्मक

die[1] (डाइ) *vi.* मर जाना; समाप्त हो जाना; *inf.* (के लिए/करने के लिए, अत्यधिक उत्सुक होना **(died, dying)** – **diehard** *n.* कट्टरपंथी

die[2] (डाइ) *n.* ठप्पा, रूपदा; चूड़ी डालने का औज़ार

diesel (´डीज़ल) *a.* डीजल इंजन से सम्बधित – *n.* इस प्रकार का इंजन; यह तेल, डीज़ल

diet (´डाइअट) *n.* पथ्य; आहार – *vi.*वज़न घटाने के लिए नियमित आहार, खाना – **dietary** *a.* आहार-सम्बंधी – *n.* नियमित आहार; आहार पद्धति – **dietician** *n.* आहार-विशेषज्ञ

differ (´डिफ़र) *vi.* भिन्न या अलग होना; असहमति या मतभेद रखना – **difference** (´डिफ़रंस) *n.* भिन्नता; विशिष्टता; मतभेद, असहमति; बाकी, शेष – **different** *a.* भिन्न, अलग – **differently** *adv.*

differential (डिफ़´रैन्शल) *a.* जो परिस्थिति के साथ बदले; विशेष कार का पुर्ज़ा जो पिछले पहियों की (मोड़ते समय) गति नियंत्रित करता है; भिन्नक; भिन्न प्रकार के काम की मज़दूरी की दरों का अन्तर – **differentiate** *vt.* भिन्न करना; भेद या विशिष्टता दिखाना – *vi.* अन्तर या भेदभाव करना – **differentiation** *n.*

difficult (´डिफ़िकल्ट) *a.* श्रमसाध्य, मुश्किल, कठिन, दुर्बोध; अस्पष्ट – **difficulty** *n.* कठिनाई; दुर्बोधता; मुश्किल; समस्या; अड़चन, परेशानी; रुकावट; अस्पष्टता; मुसीबत

diffident (´डिफ़िडंट) *a.* जिसमें आत्मविश्वास न हो; संकोची; झेंपू

diffraction (डिफ़्´रैक्शन) *n.* प्रकाश किरणों का विवर्तित होना

diffuse *vt.* (डि´फ्यूज़) फैलाना या बिखेरना – *a.* (डि´फ्यूस) विकीर्ण, फैला हुआ; ढीला; शब्दाडम्बरी, वाचाल – **diffusion** (डि´फ्यूझन) *n.* फैलने की क्रिया

dig (डिग) *vi.* खोदना, खुदाई करना; खोजना, खोज निकालना – *vt.* खोदना; गढ़ा बनाना; छेद करना; खोदकर निकालना; जा घुसना; तलाश कर के खोज निकालना **(dug, digging)** – *n.* खुदाई का काम; (पुरातत्त्व विज्ञानी द्वारा) खुदाई; ताना; बोली-ढोली; छेड़छाड़ – **(~ s)** *pl. inf.* मकान या आवास **(diggings** भी) – **digger** *n.*

digest *vt.* (डि´जेस्ट, ´डाइजेस्ट) पचाना, हज़म करना, क्रमबद्ध संक्षेप या सार तैयार करना; आत्मसात् करना; खा पी जाना – *vi.* भोजन का पचना, हज़म होना – *n.* (´डाइजेस्ट) सार-संग्रह, विशे. कानूनों का; पत्रिका जिसमें पहले से

प्रकाशित लेखों का सार या संक्षिप्त रूप प्रकाशित होता है – **digestible** *a.* – **digestion** (डि'जेंस्चन) *n.* पाचन शक्ति; हाज़मा – **digestive** *a.*

digit ('डिजिट) *n.* (हाथ या पैर की) उंगली; 0 से 9 तक की कोई संख्या, अंक – **digital** *a.* उंगली का या उस जैसा; उंगली से किया जाने वाला; (घड़ी आदि) जिसमें समय सुइयों से नह बल्कि अंकों में दिखाई देता है

dignity ('डिग्नटि) *n.* गौरव, प्रतिष्ठा; वैभव; ऊंचा पद – **dignify** *vt.* गौरव या गरिमा प्रदान करना (**-fied, -fying**) – **dignified** *a.* वैभवशाली – **dignitary** *n.* प्रतिष्ठित व्यक्ति

digress (डाइ'ग्रेस) *vi.* बात बदलना; भटक जाना (मुख्य विषय से) – **digression** *n.* विषयान्तर

dilapidated (डि'लैपिडेटिड) *a.* टूटा-फूटा

dilate (डाइ'लेट) *vt.* फैलाना – *vi.* विस्तार से कहना या लिखना – **dilation** (डाइ'लेशन)

dilatory ('डिलटरि) *a.* धीमा, सुस्त; विलम्ब या देरी करने वाला

dilemma (डाइ'लेंम्अ, डि'लेंम्अ) *n.* उभयसंकट, द्विविधा, असमंजस

dilettante (डिलि'टांटि) *n.* व्यक्ति, जिसे कला का थोड़ा सा ज्ञान हो, शौकीन (*pl.* **dilettanti**) – *a.* नौसिखिया; शौकीन

diligent ('डिलिजंट) *a.* कर्मठ, परिश्रमी – **diligence** *n.*

dilly-dally ('डिलिडैलि) *vi. inf.* इधर-उधर (अकारण) घूमना; आगा पीछा करना, हिचकना

dilute (डाइ'ल्यूट) *vt.* पतला करना; हल्का, कम या मन्द करना – *a.* इस प्रकार पतला हुआ – **dilution** *n.* हल्का, कम, पतला या मंद करने की क्रिया

dim (डिम) *a.* धुंधला; मंदबुद्धि (**dimmer** *comp.*, **dimmest** *sup.*) – *vi.* धुंधला हो जाना – *vt.* रोशनी मंदी/कम कर देना (**-mm-**) - **dimly** *adv.* अस्पष्ट रूप से

dime (डाइम) *n.* **US** 10 सेंट का सिक्का

dimension (डाइ'मेंन्शन, डि'मेंन्शन) *n.* माप; आकार; लम्बाई-चौड़ाई; पहलू – **dimensional** *a.* – **fourth dimension** *Physics* समय

diminish (डि'मिनिश) *v.* कम करना – **diminution** (डिमि'न्यूशन) *n.* कमी, ह्रास – **diminutive** (डि'मिन्युटिव़) *a.* बहुत छोटा, लघु

dimple ('डिम्पल) *n.* त्वचा में, विशे.गाल पर पड़ा गड्ढा; कोई छोटा गड्ढा

din (डिन) *n.* शोरगुल – *vt.* कोई बात दोहराते रहना, कान खाना (**-nn-**)

dine (डाइन) *vi.* भोजन करना (विशे. दिन का मुख्य भोजन) – *vt.* किसी को भोजन खिलाना – **diner** *n.* जो किसी रेस्तरां में खाना खा रहा हो; छोटा, सस्ता रेस्तरां

dingy ('डिंजि) *a.* गंदा, मैल भरा; नीरस; धुंधला – **dinginess** *n.*

dinner ('डिनर) *n.* दिन का मुख्य भोजन; रात्रि भोज; सरकारी दावत

dinosaur ('डाइनसॉर) *n.* इतिहासपूर्व युग का विशालकाय जीव जो अब लुप्त हो चुका है, डाइनासौर

dint (डिंट) *n.* – **by dint of** से, के द्वारा, के माध्यम से

dioxide (डाइ'ऑक्साइड) *n.* आक्साइड जिसमें दो हिस्से आक्सीजन और एक हिस्सा अन्य पदार्थ हो

dip (डिप) *vt.* (कुछ समय के लिए तरल पदार्थ में) डुबाना; झुकाना; में डालना; डुबा कर निकाल लेना; कार की रोशनी नीचे कर देना – *vi.* कुछ समय के लिए या थोड़ा सा डूब जाना; नीचे की ओर जाना या ढलान होना (**-pp-**) – *n.* झुकाने या डुबाने की क्रिया; डुबकी; नीचे को जाता रास्ता

या ढलान; गड्ढा; लाटरी – **dip into** उड़ती नज़र डालना

diphtheria (डिप् थिअरिअ) *n.* गले का रोग, रोहिणी

diploma (डि'प्लोम्अ) *n.* उपाधिपत्र; सनद; डिप्लोमा

diplomacy (डि'प्लोमसि) *n.* अन्तराष्ट्रीय सम्बन्धों की कला, कूटनीति; बातचीत और व्यवहार में कौशल – **diplomat** ('डिप्लमैट) *n.* कूटनीतिज्ञ – **diplomatic** (डिप्ल'मैटिक) *a.* – **diplomatically** *adv.*

dipsomania (डिप्सो'मेनिअ) *n.* मद्यपान की तीव्र इच्छा

dipstick ('डिप्स्टिक) *n.* कार में तेल (मोबिल आयल) मापने की लोहे की छड़

dire (डाइअर) *a.* भीषण, भयानक, घोर

direct (डि'रैक्ट, डाइ'रैक्ट) *vt.* रास्ता बताना; नियंत्रण करना, प्रबंध देखना, आदेश देना; निशाना साधना, चलाना; (चिट्ठी आदि) प्रेषित, सम्बोधित करना; नाटक या चलचित्र में निर्देशन देना – *a.* सीधा (सम्बंध, परिणाम, गाड़ी आदि); स्पष्टवादी, ईमानदार, कुछ न छिपाने वाला; सीधी बात कहने वाला; तुरंत; वंशानुगत – **direction** (डि'रैक्शन) *n.* निर्देशन; लक्ष्य; दिशा, रास्ता या गति – **directive** *a./n.* निर्देश – **directly** *adv.* सीधे – **director** *n.* (फिल्म का) निर्देशक; कम्पनी के प्रबन्ध मण्डल का सदस्य – **directorate** *n.* निदेशालय – **directory** *n.* नामों, पतों आदि की पुस्तक, डायरेक्टरी

dirt (डर्ट) *n.* मैल, गन्दगी, कीचड़, मिट्टी; अश्लील सामग्री; दूषण – **dirtiness** *n.* – **dirty** *a.* गंदा, मैला; अश्लील; अनुचित; बेईमानी का – **dirt track** कच्ची सड़क या रास्ता

dis - (*comb. form*) विलोम, नकार, विरोध के अर्थ में प्रयुक्त

disable (डिस्'एब्ल) *vt.* अयोग्य या बेकार कर देना; अपंग बना देना – **disabled** *a.* अपंग, विकलांग – **disability** (डिसअ'बिलिटि) *n.* अयोग्यता, असमर्थता, विकलांगता; कमी

disabuse (डिसअ'ब्यूज़) *vt.* भ्रम या ग़लतफ़हमी दूर करना

disadvantage (डिसअड्'वॉन्टिज) *n.* कमी; असुविधा; प्रतिकूल परिस्थिति – *vt.* बाधा डालना – **disadvantaged** *a.* समाज के कमजोर वर्ग के (लोग) – **disadvantageous** *a.*

disaffected (डिसअ'फ़ेक्टिड) *a.* असंतुष्ट; विद्रोही – **disaffection** *n.* अनिष्ठा; असंतोष; राजद्रोह

disagree (डिसअ'ग्री) *vi.* असहमत होना; मेल न खाना; (भोजन आदि का किसी पर) बुरा प्रभाव होना, हानिकर होना – **disagreement** *n.* मतभेद, असहमति; झगड़ा, विवाद; अंतर – **disagreeable** *a.* अप्रिय, झगड़ालू

disallow (डिसअ'लाउ) *vt.* ग़लत या अमान्य होने के आधार पर अस्वीकार करना, रद्द करना

disappear (डिसअ'पिअर) *vi.* अदृश्य या ग़ायब हो जाना लुप्त हो जाना – **disappearance** *n.*

disappoint (डिसअ'पॉइंट) *vt.* निराश करना – **disappointment** *n.* निराशा

disapprove (डिस'प्रूव) *v.* पर नाराज़गी दिखाना – **disapproval** *n.*

disarm (डिस्'आर्म) *v.* हथियार डलवाना; देश का अस्त्र भंडार कम करना; मुग्ध कर लेना – **disarmament** *n.* निरस्त्रीकरण

disarray (डिसअ'रे) *vt.* अस्तव्यस्त करना – *n.* अस्तव्यस्तता

disassociate (डिस'सोशिएट) दे० DISSOCIATE

disaster (डि'ज़ास्टर) *n.* घोर संकट, विनाश, विपदा – **disastrous** *a.* विनाशकारी

disavow (डिस'वाउ) *vt.* सार्वजनिक रूप से किसी वस्तु, विषय विशेष की जानकारी न होने का एलान करना – **disavowal** *n.*

disband (डिस्´बैंड) *vt.* (सेना, संगठन) भंग करना
disbelief (डिस्´बिलीफ़) *n.* अविश्वास – **disbelieve** *vt.* विश्वास न करना
disburse (डिस्´बर्स) *vt.* रुपये-पैसे का भुगतान करना, वितरण करना – **disbursement** *n.* भुगतान
disc (डिस्क) *n.* कोई भी तश्तरीनुमा पतली, चपटी, गोल वस्तु; ग्रामोफ़ोन रिकार्ड; *Computers* जानकारी संग्रह करने की डिस्क – **disc jockey** रेडियो पर संगीत के रिकार्ड बजाने वाला व्यक्ति
discard (डिस्´कार्ड) *v.* अस्वीकार करना; छोड़ देना, निकाल देना, अलग करना
discern (डि´सर्न) *vt.* पहचानना; देखना, समझ लेना – **discernible** *a.* – **discerning** *a.* पारखी; विवेकी; कुशाग्र बुद्धि – **discernment** *n.* अंतर्दृष्टि, पहचान, परख
discharge (डिस्´चार्ज) *vt.* रिहा करना; बर्खास्त करना; (पानी आदि) छोड़ना; (कर्तव्य) निभाना; (बंदूक) दागना; (जहाज़ का) माल उतारना; (कर्ज़ा) चुकाना; (हस्पताल से) छुट्टी देना –*n.* बर्खास्तगी; (पानी आदि) छोड़ा जाना; रिहाई; छोड़ी गई वस्तु (द्रव्य, गैस आदि); (हस्पताल से) छुट्टी; रिहाई-पत्र; भुगतान-पत्र आदि
disciple (डि´साइपल) *n.* अनुयायी, शिष्य
discipline (´डिसिप्लिन) *n.* अनुशासन, आज्ञाकारिता; आत्मसंयम – *vt.* शिक्षण देना, दण्ड देना – **disciplinary** *a.* अनुशासनात्मक
disclaim (डिस्´क्लेम) *vt.* दावा छोड़ देना; न मानना
disclose (डिस्´क्लोज़) *vt.* प्रकट करना, बताना – **disclosure** (डिस्´क्लोझ़र) *n.* प्रकट की गई बात
disco (´डिस्को) DISCOTHEQUE का संक्षेप
discolour (डिस्´कलर) *vt.* रंग बिगाड़ना
discomfiture (डिस्´कम्फ़िचर) *n.* परेशानी, क्षुब्धता
discomfort (डिस्´कम्फ़र्ट) *n.* तकलीफ; असुविधा; परेशानी
discomposure (डिस्कम्´पोझ़र) *n.* परेशानी
disconcert (डिस्कन्´सर्ट) *vt.* घबरा देना; व्याकुल करना
disconnect (डिस्क´नैक्ट) *vt.* अलग करना; (बिजली, पानी आदि) काटना
disconsolate (डिस्´कॉन्सलिट) *a.* निराश, मायूस
discontent (डिस्कन्´टैन्ट) *n.* असंतोष
discontinue (डिस्कन्´टीन्यू) *vt.* रोकना (कार्य आदि), बंद कर देना
discord (´डिस्कॉर्ड) *n.* कलह; फूट; अनबन; बेसुरी ध्वनि – **discordant** *a.*
discotheque (´डिस्कटेक) *n.* क्लब आदि जहां रिकार्ड किए हुए संगीत की धुन पर युवक, युवती नाचते हैं; नृत्य के साथ संगीत के लिए साज-सामान जो एक स्थान से दूसर स्थान पर ले जाया जा सकता है
discount *vt.* (डिस्´काउंट) संभव परंतु अनुपयुक्त, अनुचित आदि समझना; विश्वास न करना; (कीमत में) छूट देना – *n.* (´डिस्काउंट) छूट, कटौती; मिती-काटा (ब्याज में)
discourage (डिस्´करिज) *vt.* का उत्साह या आत्मविश्वास कम करना; रोकना; नापसंदगी ज़ाहिर करना
discourse *n.* (´डिस्कॉर्स) वार्तालाप; भाषण; प्रवचन – *vi.* (डिस्´कॉर्स)
discourteous (डिस्´कर्टिअस) *a.* अशिष्ट – **discourtesy** *n.*
discover (डि´स्कवर) *vt.* खोज निकालना; (का) पता चलाना या लगाना, सामने लाना – **discovery** *n.* खोज
discredit (डिस्´क्रैडिट) *vt.* बदनाम करना; विश्वास न करना –*n.* बदनामी; साख उठ जाना – **discreditable** *a.*

discreet (डि'स्क्रीट) *a.* सावधान व सतर्क; समझदार
discrepancy (डि'स्क्रेंपन्सि) *n.* असंगति, मेल न खाना
discrete (डिस्'क्रीट) *a.* अलग
discretion (डि'स्क्रेशन) *n.* समझ बूझ, सावधानी, मरजी, कार्य करने की स्वतंत्रता – **discretionary** *a.* विवेकात्मक
discriminate (डि'स्क्रिमिनेट) *vi.* भेदभाव करना; में अंतर जानना; विवेकशील होना – **discrimination** (डिस्क्रिमि'नेशन) *n.* भेदभाव; तमीज़
discursive (डि'स्कर्सिव़) *a.* (चर्चा, लेख) लक्ष्यहीन
discus ('डिस्कस) *n.* चक्का जिसे फेंकने की खेल प्रतियोगिता होती है, डिस्कस
discuss (डि'स्कस) *vt.* (के विषय में) विचार-विनिमय या परामर्श करना; बहस करना – **discussion** *n.*
disdain (डिस्'डेन) *n./v.* तिरस्कार या घणा (करना)
disease (डि'ज़ीज़) *n.* बीमारी, रोग
disembark (डिसिम्'बार्क) *v.* जहाज़ आदि से उतरना
disembodied (डिसिम्'बॉडिड) *a.* देहमुक्त (आत्मा)
disenchanted (डिसिन्'चांटिड) *a.* मोह या भ्रम से मुक्त
disfavour (डिस्'फ़ेवर) *n.* नापसंदगी, नाराज़ी
disfigure (डिस्'फ़िगर) *vt.* आकति या शक्ल बिगाड़ना
disgorge (डिस्'गॉर्ज) *vt.* उगलना
disgrace (डिस्'ग्रेस) *n.* कलंक बदनामी – *vt.* (को) बदनामी दिलाना – **disgraceful** *a.* शर्मनाक
disgruntled (डिस्'ग्रंटल्ड) *a.* असंतुष्ट; चिड़चिड़ा
disguise (डिस्'गाइज़) *vt.* भेष बदलना, छिपा लेना; ढंकना, असलियत छिपाना – *n.* छद्मवेश; धोखा, पहचान छिपाने का तरीका
disgust (डिस्'गस्ट) *n.* घिन; घणा, तीव्र अरुचि; विरक्ति – *vt.* जुगुप्सा, घणा आदि उत्पन्न करना
dish (डिश) *n.* तश्तरी, रकाबी; परोसा हुआ भोजन
disharmony (डिस्'हार्मनि) *n.* अंसगति; झगड़ा
dishevelled (डि'शेंवल्ड) *a.* बिखरे बालों वाला
dishonest (डिस्'ऑनिस्ट) *a.* बेइमान
dishonour (डिस्'ऑनर) *n.* बेइज्ज़ती, बदनामी, कलंक
disillusion (डिसि'लूझन) *vt.* मोह या भ्रम दूर करना
disincentive (डिसिन्'सेंन्टिव़) *n.* वस्तु, आदि जो कुछ कार्य विशेष से विमुख करे
disinclination (डिसिन्क्लि'नेशन) *n.* अनिच्छा
disinfectant (डिसिन्'फ़ेक्टंट) *n.* रोगाणु नाशक – **disinfect** *vt.* रोगाणुओं को समाप्त करना
disinformation (डिसिन्फ़र्'मेशन) *n.* धोखा देने या भ्रम में डालने के इरादे से दी गई गलत सूचना या जानकारी
disingenuous (डिसिन्'जेंन्युअस) *a.* कपटी
disinherit (डिसिन्'हेंरिट) *vt.* उत्तराधिकार से वंचित करना
disintegrate (डिस्'इंटिग्रेट) *v.* टुकड़े-टुकड़े हो जाना, विघटित होना – **disintegration** (डिसिंटि'ग्रेशन) *n.*
disinterest (डिस्'इन्ट्रिस्ट) *n.* निष्पक्षता; निर्लिप्तता
disinvest (डिस्'इन्वेंस्ट) *vi.* (कंपनी आदि से) अपनी पूंजी निकालना अथवा कम करना
disjoint (डिस्'जॉइंट) *vt.* जोड़ अलग कर देना; अव्यवस्थित कर देना, अलग कर देना – **disjointed** *a.* असम्बद्ध, असंगत (वार्ता); न जुड़ा हुआ
disk (डिस्क) *n. Computers* डिस्क – **disk drive** रिकार्ड प्लेयर का पुर्ज़ा जो उसे चलाता है; कम्प्यूटर में ऐसा पुर्ज़ा – **diskette** *n. US* डिस्क

dislike (डिस´लाइक) *v.* नापसंद करना; से चिढ़ना – *n.*
dislocate (´डिस्लकेट) *vt.* जोड़ अलग कर देना; अस्तव्यस्त करना, इधर-उधर कर देना – **dislocation** (डिस्ल´केशन) *n.* बिखराव; अस्त-व्यस्तता
dislodge (डिस्´लॉज) *vt.* छिपने के स्थान से निकाल देना; पद आदि से हटा देना
disloyal (डिस´लॉइअल) *a.* देशद्रोही, विश्वासघाती – **disloyalty** *n.*
dismal (´डिज़्मल) *a.* निराशाजनक
dismantle (डिस्´मैन्टल) *vt.* ढाना; (पुरज़े) अलग-अलग कर देना
dismay (डिस्´मे) *vt.* निराशा अथवा भय से भर देना – *n.* भय; निराशा; घबराहट
dismember (डिस्´मेंम्बर) *vt.* (शरीर के) टुकड़े कर देना, हाथ-पैर अलग कर देना; विभाजन कर देना – **dismemberment** *n.*
dismiss (डिस्´मिस) *vt.* नौकरी से बरख़ास्त करना, पदच्युत करना; (कमरे आदि से) बाहर भेज देना; (किसी बात को) सच न मानना – **dismissal** *n.* बर्खास्तगी
disobey (डिसअ´बे) *v.* आज्ञा न मानना या मानने से इन्कार कर देना – **disobedience** (डिस´बीडिअंस) *n.* अवज्ञा – **disobedient** *a.*
disorder (डिस्´ऑर्डर) *n.* अव्यवस्था, गड़बड़; दंगा; रोग, बीमारी – *vt.* क्रम तोड़ना; अस्त-व्यस्त कर देना; बीमार कर देना – **disorderly** *a.* हंगामे वाली (सभा आदि); अस्त-व्यस्त (कमरा आदि)
disown (डिस्´ओन) *vt.* अपना मानने से इन्कार करना
disparage (डिस्´पैरिज) *vt.* को तुच्छ समझना
disparity (डि´स्पैरिटि) *n.* असमानता; विषमता
dispassionate (डिस्´पैशनिट) *a.* शांत; निष्पक्ष
dispatch, despatch (डि´स्पैच) *vt.* (विशेष कार्य के लिए) भेजना, रवाना करना; निपटाना – *n.* प्रेषण, रवानगी; संवाददाता की रिपोर्ट (विदेश से)
dispel (डि´स्पेंल) *vt.* मिटाना; भगा देना (-ll-)
dispense (डि´स्पेंन्स) *vt.* देना; (दवाई) तैयार करना; (न्याय) करना – **dispensable** *a.* अनावश्यक, गौण – **dispensary** *n.* औषधालय – **dispensation** (डिस्पेंन्´सेशन) *n.* (से) छूट या मुक्ति दिया जाना; प्रक ति अथवा ईश्वर का विधान – **dispense with** छोड़ देना, के बिना काम चला लेना
disperse (डि´स्पर्स) *vt.* तितर-बितर करना; बिखेरना
dispirited (डि´स्पिरिटिड) *a.* हतोत्साह, खिन्न
displace (डिस्´प्लेस) *vt.* का स्थान बदलना; का स्थान छीन लेना – **displacement** *n.* – **displaced person** विस्थापित व्यक्ति
display (डि´स्प्ले) *vt.* प्रदर्शन करना, दिखाना
displease (डिस्´प्लीज़) *v.* नाराज़ करना, अप्रसन्न करना – **displeasure** (डिस्´प्लेंझ़र) *n.*
dispose (डि´स्पोज़) *vt.* क्रम से रखना; निपटना; (की ओर) झुकाव करना; झुका लेना; ठिकाने लगाना; निपटाना – *vi.* (कार्य) पूरा करना – **disposable** *a.* प्रयोग के तुरंत बाद फैंकी जा सकने वाली (वस्तु), प्रयोज्य – **disposal** *n.* व्यवस्था; निपटान; वस्तु या व्यक्ति से काम लेने का अधिकार या अवसर – **disposition** (डिस्प´ज़िशन) *n.* झुकाव; प्रव ति; व्यवस्था – **dispose of** बेचना; रास्ते से हटाना; निपटाना
dispossess (डिस्प´ज़ेंस) *vt.* बेदखल करना
disproportionate (डिस्प्र´पॉर्शनट) *a.* अनुपात में बहुत बड़ा या बहुत छोटा
disprove (डिस्´प्रूव़) *vt.* को गलत या झूठा सिद्ध करना
dispute (डि´स्प्यूट) *vi.* विवाद करना, झगड़ा करना – *vt.* चुनौती देना; खण्डन करना – *n.*

विवाद; झगड़े का विषय **disputable** *a.* विवाद्य, जो विवाद का विषय हो या बन सके

disqualify (डिस्'क्वॉलिफाइ) *vt.* (परीक्षा, चुनाव आदि के लिए) अयोग्य ठहराना – **disqualification** *n.*

disquiet (डिस्'क्वाइट) *n.* चिंता, परेशानी

disrupt (डिस्'रप्ट) *vt.* गड़बड़ कर देना/करा देना – **disruption** *n.*

dissatisfied (डिस्'सैटिस्फ़ाइड) *a.* असंतुष्ट – **dissatisfaction** *n.* असंतोष

dissect (डि'सेक्ट) *vt.* सूक्ष्म परीक्षण के लिए चीर-फाड़ करना या काटना – **dissection** *n.* विच्छेदन, चीरफाड़

disseminate (डि'सेमिनेट) *vt.* प्रसार करना

dissent (डि'सेन्ट) *vi.* असहमति प्रकट करना; राजधर्म अस्वीकार करना – *n.* विमति, विसम्मति – **dissension** (डि'सेन्शन) *n.* मतभेद, फूट – **dissenter** *n.*

dissertation (डिसर्'टेशन) *n.* शोध-प्रबंध

disservice (डिस्'सर्विस) *n.* हानि, अपकार

dissident ('डिसिडंट) *n./a.* असहमत व्यक्ति विशे. सरकार विरोधी – **dissidence** *n.* असहमति

dissimilar (डि'सिमिलर) *a.* असमान, विषम

dissipate ('डिसिपेट) *vt.* बरबाद करना; (भय आदि को) दूर करना, मिटाना – **dissipated** *a.* दुराचारी

dissociate (डि'सोशिएट) *v.* (से) सम्बंध तोड़ना

dissolute ('डिसलूट) *a.* दुराचारी, बदचलन

dissolution (डिस'लूशन) *n.* टूटना; संसद, साझेदारी, विवाह आदि का भंग होना/विसर्जन

dissolve (डि'ज़ॉल्व) *vt.* घोलना, पिघलाना; विसर्जन करना, समाप्त करना – *vi.* घुलना, पिघलना; विलीन होना, गायब होना; भंग होना, रद्द होना – **dissoluble** *a.* जो घुल जाए, विलयनीय

dissonant ('डिसनंट) *a.* कर्कश, बेसुरा

dissuade (डि'स्वेड) *vt.* (कुछ) न करने की सलाह देना, करने से रोकना, मना करना – **dissuasion** (डि'स्वेझ़न) *n.*

distance ('डिस्टन्स) *n.* फासला, दूरी; सम्बंधों में दूरी, रूखापन – *vt.* दूरी पर रखना, दूरी बनाए रखना – **distant** *a.* बहुत दूर (स्थान व समय में); रूखा; उदासीन

distaste (डिस्'टेस्ट) *n.* खाने-पीने की वस्तु के लिए अरुचि; नफ़रत

distemper (डिस्'टेम्पर) *n.* कुत्तों में एक रोग; दीवारों के पलस्तर पर बगैर तेल का रोगन करने का एक ढंग; इस प्रकार का रोगन, डिस्टैम्पर

distend (डिस्'टेण्ड) *v.* फुलाना या फूलना – **distension** (डिस्'टेन्शन) *n.*

distil (डिस्'टिल) *vt.* द्रव को भाप बनाकर (ठंडा कर के) दुबारा से द्रव बनाना, आसवन करना; इस प्रणाली से द्रवों को शुद्ध करना – **distillate** *n.* आसव – **distillation** (डिस्टि'लेशन) *n.* आसवन – **distillery** *n.* स्थान जहां शराब बनाई जाती है

distinct (डि'स्टिंक्ट) *a.* स्पष्ट; साफ दिखाई देने या सुनाई पड़ने वाला; निश्चित; अलग, भिन्न – **distinction** *n.* भिन्नता, भेद; विशिष्टता; श्रेष्ठता का गुण, उत्कर्ष; सम्मान-सूचक अंक – **distinctive** *a.* विशिष्ट भिन्नता का संकेतक

distinguish (डि'स्टिंग्विश) *vt.* भेद दिखलाना; पहचानना; (~ **oneself**) सम्मान व ख्याति प्राप्त करना; वर्गीकरण करना – *vi.* अंतर पहचान व समझ सकना – **distinguished** *a.* सम्मानित; प्रख्यात, प्रतिष्ठित

distort (डि'स्टॉर्ट) *vt.* तोड़ मरोड़ देना, किसी बात को गलत ढंग से बयान करना – **distortion** (डि'स्टॉर्शन) *n.* विकृति; मिथ्या वर्णन

distract (डि'स्ट्रैक्ट) *vt.* (काम आदि से) ध्यान हटाना, घबरा देना पागल बना देना – **distracted** *a.* खोया हुआ – **distraction** *n.*

distraught (डि´स्ट्रॉट) *a.* परेशान, शोक से व्याकुल, विक्षुब्ध

distress (डि´स्ट्रेस) *n.* अत्यधिक संकट; मानसिक वेदना – *vt.* दु:ख देना, व्यथित करना

distribute (डि´स्ट्रिब्यूट) *vt.* बांटना, वितरण करना; फैलाना; वर्गीकरण करना – **distribution** (डिस्ट्रि´ब्यूशन) *n.* वितरण, फैलाव, विस्तार – **distributor** *n.* माल-वितरक

district (´डिस्ट्रिक्ट) *n.* जिला; क्षेत्र

distrust (डिस्´ट्रस्ट) *n.* अविश्वास – *v.* का विश्वास न करना

disturb (डि´स्टर्ब) *vt.* परेशान करना; बेचैन करना; अस्त-व्यस्त करना – **disturbance** *n.* अशांति – **disturbing** *a.* चिंताजनक

disuse (डिस्´यूस) *n.* वस्तु की प्रचिलित अथवा प्रयोग में न होने की स्थिति – **disused** (डिस्´यूज़्ड) *a.*

ditch (डिच) *n.* खाई – *vt. inf.* साथ छोड़ जाना, अलग कर देना

dither (´डिदर) *vi.* असमंजस में होना, फैसला न कर पाना – *n.* ऐसी स्थिति

ditto (´डिटो) *n. It.* वैसा ही जैसा ऊपर दिया गया है – **do.** DITTO का संक्षेप

ditty (´डिटि) *n.* गाना

diva (´डीव्अ) *n.* प्रसिद्ध गायिका

divan (डि´वैन) *n.* दिवान, बिना पीठ का लम्बा, नीचा गद्देदार सोफा

dive (डाइव्) *vi.* गोता मारना, पानी में ऊपर से छलांग लगाना; **(of plane)** अचानक नीचे आना – *n.* गोता; *sl.* बदनाम बार या क्लब – **diver** *n.* गोताखोर

diverge (डाइ´वर्ज) *vi.* एक दूसरे से दूर होना – **divergence** *n.* भिन्नता – **divergent** *a.* भिन्न

diverse (डाइ´वर्स) *a.* भिन्न, विविध – **diversify** *vt.* विविधता उत्पन्न करना **(-fied, -fying)** – **diversely** *adv.* – **diversification** (डाइवर्सिफि´केशन) *n.* विविधता (की क्रिया) – **diversity** *n.* विविधता

divert (डाइ´वर्ट) *vt.* दूसरी दिशा में मोड़ देना; मनोरंजन करना – **diversion** (डाइ´वर्शन) *n.* दिशा- परिवर्तन; मुख्य मार्ग बंद होने की दशा में यातायात के लिए दूसरा मार्ग; मनोरंजन – **diverting** *a.* मनोरंजक

divest (डाइ´वेस्ट) *vt.* आवरण या अलंकार उतारना – **divestment** *n.* (कंपनी के शेयर आदि) छोड़ने की क्रिया

divide (डि´वाइड) *vt.* दो या अधिक भागों में बांटना, अलग करना; भाग देना; वितरण करना – *vi.* अलग हो जाना – *n.* किसी क्षेत्र को विभाजित करने वाली नदी आदि; दो वर्गों में अंतर – **dividend** (´डिविडेंड) *n.* लाभांश; विभाज्य संख्या – **dividers** *pl. n.* कम्पास, परकार

divine (डि´वाइन) *a.* दैवी, पवित्र – *n.* पुरोहित (पादरी) – *v.* अनुमान लगाना, भविष्यवाणी करना – **divinity** (डि´विनिटि) *n.* देवत्व; धर्म-विज्ञान

division (डि´विझ़न) *n.* विभाजन, बंटवारा; मंडल, खण्ड; सीमा; विभाग; राजनीतिक क्षेत्र, मतभेद; *Math.* भाग; सैन्य दल, डिवीज़न; अलग होने की क्रिया, फूट – **divisible** (डि´विज़बल) *a.*विभाज्य, भाज्य – **divisional** *a.* विभागीय, मंडलीय – **divisive** (डि´वाइसिव) *a.* फूट डालने वाला – **divisor** (डि´वाइज़र) *n. Math.* भाजक, गुणक

divorce (डि´वॉर्स) *n.* तलाक – *vt.* – तलाक देना **divorced** *a.* – **divorcee** (डिवॉर्´सी) *n.* तलाकशुदा (व्यक्ति)

divulge (डाइ´वल्ज) *vt.* बताना, भेद खोलना

DIY do -it -yourself का संक्षेप

dizzy (ˈडिज़ि) *a.* चकराया हुआ, अस्थिर – **dizziness** *n.* चक्कर, सिर घूमना

DJ disc jockey का संक्षेप

DNA *n.* deoxyribonucleic acid का संक्षेप जो सभी जीवों में क्रोमोसोम का मुख्य तत्त्व होता है

do[1] (डू) *vt.* करना; काम पूरा करना; (प्रश्न) हल करना; उपयुक्त या पर्याप्त होना; (फासला) तय करना; तैयार करना, *sl.* ठगना; लूटना; ध्यान रखना – *vi.* (व्यवहार) करना; (सि) काम चलाना, काफ़ी होना; होना (जैसे *doing well*) – *v. aux.* से नकारात्मक और प्रश्नसूचक वाक्य बनते हैं और किसी बात पर बल दिया जा सकता है (**did, done, doing**) – *n. inf.* उत्सव, रागरंग – **do away with** नष्ट करना – **do up** बांधना; मरम्मत करना – **do's and don'ts** नियम जिनका किसी कार्य-विशेष के समय ध्यान रखना जरूरी हो

do. ditto का संक्षेप

docile (ˈडोसाइल) *a.* आज्ञा परायण, सीधा (व्यक्ति); दब्बू – **docility** (डोˈसिलिटि) *n.*

dock[1] (डॉक) *n.* बंदरगाह में गोदी – *v.* जहाज़ बंदरगाह पर लगना या लगाना; अंतरिक्ष-यानों का अंतरिक्ष में जुड़ना – **docker** *n.* गोदी-मजदूर – **dockyard** *n.* डॉकयार्ड, गोदी सहित वह स्थान जहां जहाज़ बनाए अथवा मरम्मत किए जाते है

dock[2] *n.* पूंछ का हड्डी वाला भाग; कटी हुई दुम, ठूंठ – *vt.* (पूंछ आदि) काट कर छोटा कर देना; कम कर देना; (मज़दूरी में) कटौती करना

dock[3] *n.* अदालत में कटघरा

docket (ˈडॉकिट) *n.* वस्तुओं के पैकेट के साथ भेजा गया विवरण-पत्र

doctor (ˈडॉक्टर) *n.* डाक्टर, चिकित्सक; विश्वविद्यालय से किसी भी विषय में डॉक्टर की उपाधि प्राप्त व्यक्ति (पी.एच.डी आदि) – *vt.* चिकित्सा करना; ठीक करना, मरम्मत करना; रद्दोबदल करके जाली हिसाब-किताब आदि तैयार कर देना –– **doctorate** (ˈडॉक्टरिट) *n.* डॉक्टर की उपाधि – **Doctor of Philosophy** *n.* संक्षेप Ph.D.

doctrine (ˈडॉक्ट्रिन) *n.* शिक्षा; धर्म सिद्धांत; मत

document (ˈडॉक्युमन्ट) *n.* प्रलेख; लिखित प्रमाण, कागज़ात; दस्तावेज़ – *vt.* प्रलेख, प्रमाण-पत्र, सर्टिफिकेट प्रस्तुत करना – **documentary** (डॉक्युˈमेंन्टरि) *a./n.* प्रमाण-रूपी; व त-चित्र – **documentation** (डाक्युमेंन्ˈटेशन) *n.*

dodder (ˈडॉडर) *vi.* लड़खड़ाना या कांपना (वि. बुढ़ापे के कारण)

dodge (डॉज) *v.* इधर-उधर होकर बचना या बचने की कोशिश करना, चकमा देना – *n.* चाल; युक्ति; बचने की क्रिया – **dodger** *n.* चालबाज़ – **dodgy** *inf. a.* खतरनाक

doe (डो) *n.* हिरनी; मादा खरगोश

does (डज़) *do* का *third person sing, pres, ind. active;* देखिए **do** – **doesn't** = **does not**

doff (डॉफ) *vt.* (हैट, कपड़े) उतारना; अलग करना, परे रख देना

dog (डॉग) *n.* कुत्ता; नर भेड़िया, लोमड़ी तथा अन्य पशु; व्यक्ति (घ णा, गाली अथवा मज़ाक में प्रयुक्त शब्द) – **dogged** (ˈडॉगिड) *a.* जिद्दी, हठी, धुन का पक्का – **dog collar** कुत्ते का पट्टा – **dog-ear** *n.* पुस्तक के पन्ने का मुड़ा हुआ कोना – *vt.* – **dogfight** *n.*लड़ाकू वायुयानों का आपसी युद्ध – **doggy bag** थैला जिसमें भोजन के बाद बचे हुए खाने को ले जा सकते है – **go to the dogs** बरबाद होना

dogma (ˈडॉग्मअ) *n.* धर्म सिद्धांत, सिद्धांत, मत (*pl.* **-s. -ata**) – **dogmatic** (डॉग्ˈमैटिक) *a.* हठधर्मी (व्यक्ति), मताग्रही – **dogmatically** *adv.* – **dogmatism** (ˈडॉग्मटिज़म) *n.* मताग्रह, हठधर्मिता – **dogmatist** *n.* – **dogmatize** (ˈडॉग्मटाइज़) *vi*

doldrums (´डॉल्ड्रम्ज़) *pl. n.* उदासी, विषाद; विषुवत-रेखा के समीप शांत क्षेत्र जहां धीमी हवाएं चलती हैं, विषुवत प्रशांत मण्डल

dole (डोल) *n.* दान; *inf.* बेरोज़गारी बीमा के अंतर्गत भत्ता; थोड़ा-थोड़ा करके बांटना – *vt.* – **dole out**

doleful (´डोल्फुल) *a.* दुःखी, उदास, शोकग्रस्त

doll (डॉल) *n.* गुड्डा, गुड़िया; *sl.* आकर्षक लड़की अथवा स्त्री

dollar (´डॉलर) *n.* संयुक्त राज्य अमेरिका, आस्ट्रेलिया, कनाडा आदि अनेक देशों का प्रचलित सिक्का, डालर ($)

dollop (´डॉलप) *n. inf.* (चम्मच भर) नरम भोज्य पदार्थ की मात्रा; थोड़ी सी मात्रा

dolly (´डॉलि) *n.* गुड़िया; फिल्म व टी.वी. कैमरा रखने की पहिये वाली धातु की टेक

dolour (´डॉलर) *n.* शोक, व्यथा, वेदना – **dolorous** *a.* शोकपूर्ण

dolphin (´डाल्फ़िन) *n.* डाल्फ़िन मछली

dolt (डोल्ट) *n.* मूर्ख, बुद्धू

domain (ड´मेन) *n.* रियासत; क्षेत्र; अधिकार-क्षेत्र, प्रांत

dome (डोम) *n.* गुम्बद, गुम्बज; ऐसा उभार लिये कोई वस्तु

domestic (ड´मेस्टिक) *a.* घरेलू, पारिवारिक; पालतू (जानवर); आंतरिक, देशीय – *n.* घरेलू नौकर – **domesticate** *vt.* पालतू बनाना; घरेलू जिंदगी का अभ्यस्त बनाना

domicile (´डॉमिसाइल) *n.* निवास- स्थान – **domiciled** *a.*अधिवासी

dominate (´डॉमिनेट) *vt.* शासन करना, अधिकार में रखना; (पर) छाये होना; (स्थान) से ऊंचा होना – *vi.* सबसे अधिक प्रभावशाली या महत्वपूर्ण भाग या सदस्य होना – **dominant** *a.* – **domination** (डॉमि´नेशन) *n.* – **domineer** (डॉमि´निअर) *vi.* रोब जमाना

dominion (ड´मिनियन) *n.* प्रभुत्व, शासन, राज्य; अधिकार-क्षेत्र

don[1] (डॉन) *vt.* (कपड़े) पहनना (**-nn-**)

don[2] *n.*विश्वविद्यालय का अध्यापक; स्पेन में उपाधि; सर (**Sir**); *inf.* माफिया नेता

donate (डो´नेट) *vt.* दान करना – **donation** *n.* दान, चन्दा – **donor** *n.* दाता

done (डन) DO का *pp.*

donkey (´डॉङकि) *n.* गधा (*pl.* **-eys**)

doodle (´डूडल) *vi.* टेढ़ी-मेढ़ी रेखाएं खींचना – *n.*

doom (डूम) *n.* भाग्य, प्रारब्ध; सर्वनाश, दुर्भाग्य; दण्डाज्ञा; (मानव का अंतिम) न्याय – *vt.* दण्डाज्ञा देना; म त्यु अथवा कष्ट भाग्य में लिख देना – **doomsday** (´डूम्ज़्डे) *n.*कयामत अथवा प्रलय का दिन

door (डॉर) *n.* द्वार, दरवाज़ा – **doorbell** *n.* दरवाज़े की घंटी – **doormat** *n.* पायदान – **doorstep** *n.* देहरी – **doorway** *n.* अंदर आने का रास्ता, प्रवेश-द्वार – **behind closed doors** चुपचाप, गुप्तरूप से (सलाह आदि करना)

dope (डोप) *n.* एक प्रकार की वारनिश; दवा, वि. गैरकानूनी नशीली दवा; *inf.* मूर्ख – *vt.* नशीली दवा खिलाना

dormant (´डारमंट) *a.* निष्क्रिय; सोया हुआ

dormitory (´डॉर्मिट्रि) *n.* कई बिस्तरों वाला शयनागार

dormouse (´डॉर्माउस) *n.* चूहे जैसा एक छोटा जीव, स्वपमूष

dose (डोस) *n.* दवा की एक खुराक – *vt.* खुराक देना – **dosage** *n.* दवा की निर्धारित खुराक

dossier (´डॉसिए) *n.* विषय अथवा घटना-विशेष पर बनी हुई फ़ाइल

dot[1] (डॉट) *n.* बिंदी, चिन्ह – *vt.* बिन्दु लगाना; बिखराना – **dotty** *a. sl.* सनकी

dote (डोट) *vi.* (– **dote on/upon**) बेहद पसंद करना या प्यार करना – **dotage** *n.* सठियाना – **doting** *a.* अति स्नेही

double (ˊडबल) *a.* दोहरा; दुगना; दो प्रकार का, दो तरफा, दो के लिए (*double bed*) – *adv.* दो बार, दुगनी (राशि देना, लेना); जोड़े में – *n.* प्रतिरूप, एक जैसा दूसरा; दुगनी मात्रा; तेज़ मोड़; डबल मार्च; तेज दौड़ – *v.* दुगना करना या होना; दो गुना बढ़ाना या बढ़ना; दोहरा करना; एकदम मुड़ जाना – **double agent** दो विरोधी पक्षों का जासूस – **double-cross** *v.* दो विरोधी पक्षों के लिए कार्य करने वाले व्यक्ति का दोनों को दूसरे का भेद बताकर धोखा देना – *n.* – **double-dealing** *n.*कपट, धोखा – **double standard** दोहरे मानदण्ड, धूर्तता – **double take** किसी टिप्पणी या घटना आदि पर देर से हुई प्रतिक्रिया

doubt (डाउट) *vt.* सन्देह करना; विश्वास न करना – *vi.* विश्वास अथवा मत में पक्का न होना – *n.* सन्देह; अनिश्चय – **doubtful** *a.* सन्देहास्पद – **doubtless** *adv.* निस्सन्देह

dough (डो) *n.* गुंधा हुआ आटा; लोई; *inf.* रूपये-पैसे – **doughnut** *n.* आटे से बना एक मीठा खाद्य पदार्थ

doughty (ˊडाउटि) *a.* बहादुर, साहसी

dour (डुअर) *a.* ज़िद्दी, कठोर

douse (डाउस) *vt.* पानी में डुबाना, तर कर देना; (रोशनी) बुझाना

dove (डव) *n.* फ़ाख्ता; युद्ध-विरोधी व्यक्ति – **dovetail** (ˊडव्टेल) *v. fig.* समन्वय करना, मेल मिलाना

dowager (ˊडाउअजर) *n.* विधवा जिसे अपने पति की उपाधि व संपत्ति मिली हुई हो

dowdy (ˊडाउडि) *a.* फूहड़, भद्दा

down[1] (डाउन) *adv.* नीचे, नीचे की ओर ढलान या उतार पर, क्षितिज से नीचे, उसी समय (भुगतान), तुरंत – *prep.* ऊपर से नीचे, निचले भाग पर – *a.* दुखी, उदास – *vt.* गिरा देना, (नीचे) खच च लेना, उतार देना; *inf.* पी जाना (वि. तेज़ी से) – **downward** *a./adv.* – **downwards** *adv.* – **downcast** *a.* उदास, खिन्न – **downfall** *n.* पतन – **download** *vt.* वेबसाइट आदि से जानकारी निजी कम्प्यूटर पर उतारना – **downplay** *vt.* किसी घटना, वस्तु को कम महत्व देना – **downpour** *n.* मूसलाधार वर्षा – **downright** *a.* पूर्ण, पक्का – **downstream** *a.* नदी के बहाव की दिशा में – **down-and-out** बेरोज़गार व बगैर पैसे – **down-to-earth** *a.* समझदार व व्यवहारवादी

down[2] *n.* पक्षी के नरम पर; रोम, रोंआ, रोयेंदार वस्तु – **downy** *a.*

downtown (ˊडाउन्टाउन) *n.* शहर का केंद्रीय भाग/मुख्य व्यावसायिक केन्द्र

downtrodden (ˊडाउन्ट्रॉडन) *a.* पिछड़े, गरीबी, शोषण का शिकार (लोग)

dowry (ˊडाउअरि) *n.* दहेज

doz. dozen का संक्षेप

doze (डोज़) *vi.* ऊंघना, झपकी लेना – *n.*

dozen (ˊडज़न) *n.* दर्जन

Dr. doctor; *US* **drive** का संक्षेप

drab (ड्रैब) *a.* नीरस; एकरस; हलका भूरा – *n.* मटमैला रंग

drachm (ड्रैम) *n.* माप की इकाई, द्रव आउंस का 1/4 भाग; ठोस वज़न के आउंस का सोलहवां भाग

Draconian (ड्रिˊकोनिअन) *a.* कठोर, क्रूर, बेरहम

draft[1] (ड्राफ्ट) *n.* खाका, रूपरेखा; (बैंक) ड्राफ्ट; टुकड़ी, दस्ता – *vt.* खाका आदि तैयार करना; पाण्डुलिपि बनाना; (सैनिकों आदि को) अलग करके दूसरी इकाई (यूनिट) में भेज देना

draft[2] **US** *vt.* अनिवार्य सैन्य सेवा के लिए (सैनिकों आदि का) चयन करना – *vi.* दे. DRAUGHT – *n.*

drag (ड्रैग) *vt.* घसीटना, जाल या कांटा-लंगर डालकर आगे ख चना; (बहस, मामला आदि) लम्बा ख चना – *vi.* पिछड़ना, (मामला आदि) लम्बा खिंचना (**-gg-**) – *n.* प्रगति में रोक या बाधा; हेंगा, पटेला; स्लेज; जाल; कांटा; *inf.* नीरस व्यक्ति अथवा वस्तु – *sl.* नाच-गान करने वाले पुरुषों द्वारा पहने जाने वाले स्त्रियों के वस्त्र – **dragnet** *n.* ज़बरदस्त तलाश वि. पुलिस द्वारा अपराधी की

dragon (ड्रैगन) *n.* काल्पनिक मगरमच्छ जैसा पंखों वाला अजगर जो आग उगलता है; छिपकली, गिरगिट आदि की जाति का एक बड़ा जीव

drain (ड्रेन) *vt.* पाइप आदि से द्रव्य ख चना; सुखा देना; (पानी की टंकी) खाली कर देना; समाप्त कर देना – *vi.* बह जाना; सूख जाना – *n.* नाली, नाला; अपव्यय; धीरे-धीरे बरबादी (धन, शक्ति आदि की) – **drainage** *n.* निकास-व्यवस्था – **go down the drain** (पैसा आदि) बर्बाद हो जाना (विशे. किसी योजना पर)

drake (ड्रेक) *n.* नर बतख़

drama (ड्राम्अ) *n.* नाटक; नाट्य-साहित्य व कला; घटनाओं का नाटक जैसा सिलसिला – **dramatic** (ड्र'मैटिक) *a.* नाटक-संबंधी; प्रभावशाली, उत्तेजनापूर्ण – **dramatist** (ड्रैमटिस्ट) *n.* नाटककार – **dramatization** (ड्रैमटाइ'ज़ेशन) *n.* – **dramatize** (ड्रैमटाइज़) *vt.* टी.वी., सिनेमा के लिए (उपन्यास को) नाटक का रूप देना; किसी बात को नाटकीय ढंग से प्रस्तुत करना

drank (ड्रैंक) DRINK का *pt.*

drape (ड्रेप) *vt.* ढंकना, वस्त्र पहनाकर सजाना – **draper** *n.* बज़ाज़, कपड़े बेचने वाला – **drapery** *n.* वस्त्र विशे. सजाए हुए; (बहुधा *pl.*) परदे – **drapes** *pl. n.* परदे

drastic (ड्रैस्टिक) *a.* उग्र, कठोर, कड़ा

draught, US draft (ड्राफ्ट) *n.* कमरे में दरवाज़े आदि की दरारों में से हवा का झोंका; खिंचाव; दवा की खुराक, घूंट; पीना; सांस ख चना; पानी में जहाज़ की गहराई, डुबाव – (**~s**) *pl.* ड्राफ्टस का खेल जो चपटे गोल मोहरों से शतरंज के बोर्ड पर खेला जाता है – *a.* लद्दू, भारवाही (पशु) – *vt.* देखिए DRAFT – **draughtsman** *n.* नक्शानवीस, ड्राफ्ट्समैन– **draughtsmanship** *n.* नक्शानवीसी

draw (ड्रॉ) *vt.* ख चना, घसीटना; सांस लेना; फँसाना; रेखाचित्र, खाका आदि बनाना; (नतीजा आदि) निकालना; (मसौदा, वसीयत आदि) तैयार करना; (चैक) लिखना; (ध्यान) आक ष्ट करना; (*out* के साथ) भावनाओं आदि को प्रकट कराना; (हथियार बाहर) निकालना; लाटरी द्वारा पाना; (जहाज़ का तैरने योग्य पानी की) आवश्यकता रखना; (कुंए, पीपे आदि से पानी आदि) ख चना निकालना; (बैंक से पैसा) प्राप्त करना – *vi* ख चना; आक ष्ट होना; (हवा अंदर) आने देना; पेंसिल आदि से रेखाचित्र बनाना; *Sports* (टीम द्वारा) मैच बराबरी पर समाप्त करना; (नजदीक) आना (**drew** *pt.*, **drawn** *pp.*) – *n.* ख चने, रेखांकित करने आदि की क्रिया; लाटरी निकालने की क्रिया; अपूर्ण खेल; बराबर का परिणाम – **drawer** *n.* (पैसा आदि) निकालने वाला, प्राप्त करता; मेज़ में दराज़ – **drawing** *n.* रेखांकन कला; रेखा चित्र; क्रिया (DRAW) का कार्य – **drawback** *n.* कमी, त्रुटि – **drawing room** बैठक – **draw near** पास आना – **draw up** तैयार करना; रुकना

drawl (ड्रॉल) *v.* धीरे-धीरे बोलना – *n.* ऐसे बोलने की क्रिया

drawn (ड्रॉन) DRAW का *pp.*

dread (ड्रेड) *vt.* डरना, भयभीत होना – *n.* भय, आशंका, त्रास – *a.* जिससे डर लगे, भयानक – **dreadful** *a.* अरुचिकर; भयानक; बुरा

dream (ड्रीम) *n.* स्वप्न, कपोल-कल्पना; दिवास्वप्न, ख्याली-पुलाव, महत्वाकांक्षा – *vi.*

स्वप्न देखना कल्पना करना – *vt.* स्वप्न में देखना, कल्पना करना; असंभव कल्पना करना ((**dreamt**) (ड्रॅम्ट) *or* **dreamed** (ड्रीम्ड) *pt./pp.*) – **dreamer** *n.* – **dreamy** *a.* विचारों में खोया रहने वाला, अव्यवहारिक, अस्पष्ट; *inf.* अद्भुत – **dreamland** *n.* सपनों का संसार

dreary (ड्रिअरि) *a.* नीरस, उदासी भरा

dredge[1] (ड्रॅज) *v.* समुद्र तल से मिट्टी कीचड़ आदि निकालना – *n.* कीचड़ आदि निकालने का औजार – **dredger** *n.* मिट्टी, कीचड़ निकालने का जहाज़

dregs (ड्रॅग्ज़) *pl. n.* कूड़ा करकट, तलछट, तल; बेकार भाग

drench (ड्रॅन्च) *vt.* बुरी तरह भिगो देना – *n.* बुरी तरह भीग जाना

dress (ड्रॅस) *vt.* (*clothing*) पहनाना, सजाना; संवारना; तैयार करना; मरहम-पट्टी करना – *vi.* कपड़े पहनना – *n.* स्त्रियों की चोली तथा स्कर्ट मिलाकर बनी एक ही पोशाक; वर्दी; सांयकाल पहने का औपचारिक परिवेश – **dresser** *n.* विशेष वस्त्र पहनाने वाला (वि. अभिनेता व अभिनेत्री को); रसोई की अलमारी – **dressing** *n.* ऊपर लगाने की वस्तु जैसे चटनी; मरहम; *inf.* डांट – **dress circle** रंगशाला में पहली गैलरी – **dress rehearsal** नाटक आदि के खेले जाने से पहले अंतिम अभ्यास

drew (ड्रू) DRAW का *pt.*

dribble (ड्रिबल) *v.* टपकाना; चुआना; लार टपकाना; *Football* फुटबाल को पैर से ठेलते हुए आगे जाना – *n.* टपकना; बूंद

drift (ड्रिफ्ट) *vi.* हवा, पानी के बहाव के साथ-साथ जाना – *n.* बहाव; अपने रास्ते से दूर चले जाना; आशय, वक्ता का वास्तविक अर्थ; हवा द्वारा एकत्रित बर्फ, रेत आदि का ढेर – **drifter** *n.* घुमक्कड़, जो कभी किसी एक स्थान या नौकरी में न रहे – **driftwood** *n.* समुद्र द्वारा बहाकर तट पर लाई गई लकड़ी

drill[1] (ड्रिल) *n.* सूराख़ करने का औजार या मशीन; बरमा; सैनिकों की कवायद, ड्रिल; (शिक्षा में) बार-बार अभ्यास – *vt.* सुराख़ करना; कवायद करना; अभ्यास करना – *vi.* तेल की खोज में खुदाई करना; अभ्यास करना

drill[2] *n.* एक मोटा कपड़ा, ज़ीन

drink (ड्रिंक) *v.* (**drank** *pt.*, **drunk** *pp*) पीना; सोखना; शराब पीना विशे. बहुत अधिक – *n.* पीने की वस्तु, शराब – **drinker** *n.* पियक्कड़ – **drink to, drink the health of** शराब का घूंट पीकर किसी की शुभकामना करना

drip (ड्रिप) *v.* बूंद-बूंद टपकना या टपकाना (**-pp-**) – *n.* बूंद बूंद टपकने की क्रिया; बूंद; नाड़ी में (ग्लुकोज़ आदि) द्रव्य पहुंचाने की क्रिया; नीरस, मूर्ख व्यक्ति – **dripping** *n.* भुनते हुए मांस से टपकती चर्बी – *a.* बहुत गीला – **drip-dry** *a.* (कपड़ा) जिसे यदि गीला ही टांग दिया जाए तो सूखने पर उसकी सलबटे दूर हो जाएं

drive (ड्राइव़) *vt.* हांकना, (गाड़ी आदि) चलाना; प्रेरित करना; (कील) ठोंक देना; पीछा करना; गाड़ी में ले जाना; (गोल्फ, टैनिस आदि में) गेंद जोर से फेंकना – *vi.* मशीन, पशु चलना; (~ **to**) गाड़ी से (कह) पहुंचना; दौड़ पड़ना; (~ **into/against**) टकरा जाना; (तेज हवा से बादलों का) उड़ जाना (**drove, driven, driving**) – *n.* चालन, संचालन; गाड़ी में सैर; काम कराने की शक्ति; आंदोलन; क्रिकेट, गोल्फ, टैनिस में गेंद पर तेज़ प्रहार – **driver** *n.* ड्राइवर, चालक; गोल्फ़ का बल्ला – **drive-in** *a.* (सिनेमा, होटल) जहां फिल्म देखने/भोज्य-पदार्थ खरीदने के लिए कार से उतरने की जरूरत न हो

drivel (ड्रिव़ल) *vi.* लार टपकना; बकवाद करना – *n.* बकवाद, बकबक

drizzle (ड्रिज़ल) *n.* बूंदाबांदी *n.* (होना)
dromedary (ड्रमडरि) *n.* एक कूबड़ वाला ऊंट
drone (ड्रोन) *n.* नर-मुधमक्खी; आलसी, निकम्मा व्यक्ति; भिनभिनाहट – *v.* भिनभिनाना; अस्पष्ट बोलना
drongo (ड्रॉङ्गो) *n.* उष्ण प्रदेश का काले रंग का पक्षी
drool (ड्रूल) *vi.* लार टपकना; नाक बहना
droop (ड्रूप) *vi.* कुम्हला जाना; निरुत्साह होना; झुक जाना – *vt.* झुका देना – *n.* झुके होने की स्थिति – **droopy** *a.*
drop (ड्रॉप) *n.* बूंद; बहुत कम मात्रा; गिरावट; गिरने की दूरी; गिरने की क्रिया – *vt.* गिराना; टपकाना; यूं ही कुछ कह देना; (यात्री व माल) उतारना; (किसी विषय पर बातचीत) बन्द कर देना; (टीम से) निकाल देना; (~ **a line**) संक्षिप्त पत्र लिखना; को गाड़ी से कहीं छोड़ना – *vi.* गिरना; टपकना; समाप्त हो जाना; कम होना; अनौपचारिक रूप से आना और जाना (**-pp-**) – **droplet** *n.* छोटी सी बूंद – **droppings** *pl. n.* लीद, मेंगनी आदि; पक्षी की बीट – **drop-out** *n.* जो शिक्षा अधूरी छोड़ दे; जो अपने (रूढ़िवादी) समाज से अलग हो जाए
dropsy (ड्रॉप्सि) *n.* जलोदर रोग जिसमें शरीर में पानी इकट्ठा हो जाता है
dross (ड्रॉस) *n.* मैल; कूड़ा करकट; बेकार पदार्थ
drought (ड्राउट) *n.* सूखा, अनाव ष्टि
drove[1] (ड्रोव़) DRIVE का *pt.*
drove[2] *n.* झुंड, भीड़ (वि. चलती हुई)
drown (ड्राउन) *vt.* डुबाकर मारना; ऊंची आवाज का किसी आवाज़ को दबा देना – *vi.* डूब जाना
drowsy (ड्राउज़ि) *a.* उन दा, निद्रालु; सुस्त; न द लाने वाली (वस्तु) – **drowsiness** *n.*
drubbing (ड्रबिङ) *n.* करारी हार
drudge (ड्रज) *vi.* कोल्हू के बैल की तरह काम करना – *n.* कोल्हू का बैल, गुलाम – **drudgery** (ड्रजरि) *n.* कड़ी मेहनत का नीरस काम
drug (ड्रग) *n.* औषधि, दवा; नशीली दवा –*vt.* दवा खिलाना या पिलाना वि. बेहोशी लाने वाली दवा (**-gg-**) – **drug addict** लतिया, नशेबाज़ – **druggist** *n.* **US** दवा बेचने वाला
drugget (ड्रगिट) *n.* मोटी ऊनी दरी
drum (ड्रम) *n.* ढोल; (पीपा आदि) ढोलनुमा वस्तुएं; ड्रम; कान का परदा – *v.* ढोल बजना; लगातार ठपठपाना (**-mm-**) – **drummer** *n.* ढोलकिया – **drumstick** *n.* ढोल बजाने की छड़ी; पकाये हुए पक्षी की टांग का निचला जोड़; सहिजन फली
drunk (ड्रंक) *a.* मदहोश, नशे में धुत्त; *fig.* मस्त – DRINK का *pp.* – **drunkard** *n.* नशे में धुत्त – **drunken** *a.* नशे में; नशे के कारण – **drunkenness** *n.* पियक्कड़ होने की स्थिति
dry (ड्राइ) *a.* सूखा; दूध न देने वाली (गाय आदि); भावनाहीन; मद्य-निषेद सम्बन्धी; नीरस (विषय आदि); जिसमें मिठास न हो – *vt.* सुखाना (**dried, drying**) – *vi.* सूखना – **drily** *adv.* – **dryness** *n.* – **dryer, drier** *n.* सुखाने वाला; सुखाने का यंत्र – **dry battery** बिना द्रव्य की बिजली की बैटरी – **dry-clean** *v.* कपड़े बिना पानी किसी अन्य द्रव्य (पिट्रोल आदि) से साफ करना – **dry-cleaner** *n* – **dry ice** ठोस कार्बन डाइआक्साइड
DTP Desktop Publishing का संक्षेप
dual (ड्यूअल) *a.* दोहरा, दो का, दुगना – **dualism** *n.* द्वैतवाद, दो विशिष्ट शक्तियों अथवा सिद्धांतों के होने में विश्वास
dub (डब) *vt.* उपाधि प्रदान करना, फिल्म में मूल भाषा से भिन्न भाषा, ध्वनि-पट्टी (साउंड-ट्रैक) लगाना, डब करना; (चमड़े पर) चर्बी लगाना (**-bb-**)

dubious (´ड्यूबिअस) *a.* संदिग्ध
duchess (´डचिस) *n.* ड्यूक की पत्नी अथवा विधवा
duck[1] (डक) *n.* बत्तख़ (**drake** *masc.*); *Cricket* बल्लेबाज के शून्य रन – *vi.* डुबाना; एकदम नीचे झुक जाना या सिर नीचा कर लेना – **duckling** *n.* बत्तख़ का बच्चा
duct (डक्ट) *n.* नाली, नलिका – **ductile** *a.* तार बनाने योग्य, तन्य, प्रत्यस्थ, लचीला व कड़ा; विनीत, वश्य – **ductility** (डक्´टिलिटि) *n.* – **ductless** *a.* नाली रहित, निस्रोत (ग्रंथियां) जो स्वास्थ्य के लिए आवश्यक पदार्थ बनाती हैं
dud (डड) *n.* असफल योजना; निकम्मा व्यक्ति या वस्तु – *a.* बेकार
dude (´ड्यूड) *n.* **US** पर्यटक वि. पशु-फ़ार्म पर; *US* छैला, बांका
duds (डड्ज़) *pl. n. inf.* वस्त्र, कपड़े
due (ड्यू) *a.* जो देना हो; प्राप्य, पावना; समुचित; उचित, आनेवाला, अपेक्षित, निश्चित (तिथि) – *adv.* बिल्कुल ठीक दिशा में – *n.* व्यक्ति का अधिकार; (बहुधा **dues** *pl.*) फीस, शुल्क आदि – **duly** *adv.* बाकायदा; उचित रूप से; यथा समय – **due to** के कारण
duel (´ड्यूअल) *n.* घातक हथियारों (तलवार, पिस्तौल) से द्वंद-युद्ध; दो पक्षों का कड़ा संघर्ष – *vi.* द्वन्द-युद्ध करना (**-ll-**)
duet (´ड्यूऍट) *n.* युगलगान, युगलवादन
duffer (´डफर) *n.* मूर्ख, अनाड़ी व्यक्ति
dug (डग) DIG का *pt.pp.*
duke (ड्यूक) *n.* यूरोप में, युवराज से नीचे सामंत; छोटी रियासत (डची) का शासक (**duchess** *fem.*)
dull (डल) *a.* (व्यक्ति) मन्द बुद्धि, सुस्त; (वस्तु, कार्य आदि) नीरस, उबाने वाला; उदास; धुंधला; बादलों से ढंका – *v.* दर्द, दुःख, संवेदना आदि मंद या कुण्ठित करना या होना – **dullard** *n.* मंदबुद्धि
duly (´ड्यूलि) दे. DUE
dumb (डम) *a.* मूक, गूंगा; *inf.* मंदबुद्धि – **dumbness** *n.* – **dumbbell** *n.* (व्यायाम के लिए) डम्बल – **dumbfounded** *a.* हक्का-बक्का
dummy (´डमि) *n.* डमी, पुतला (कपड़ों को प्रदर्शित करने के लिए); *Cards* डमी, ब्रिज के खेल में मेज़ पर खोला गया हाथ (ताश)
dump (डम्प) *vt.* ढेर लगा देना, फेंक देना, पटक देना; (सस्ती वस्तुएं) विदेशों में बड़ी मात्रा में बिकने भेज देना; *Computers* जानकारी उतार कर संग्रह के लिए कहीं और भेज देना – *n.* कूड़े का ढेर; *inf.* गंदी जगह; गोला-बारूद आदि का अस्थायी गोदाम; कम्प्यूटर में संग्रहीत जानकारी उतारने की क्रिया; ऐसी जानकारी की विषय-सूची; (**dumps** *pl.*) उदासी, मायूसी
dunce (डन्स) *n.* देर में समझने वाला; मूर्ख
dune (ड्यून) *n.* समुद्र तट अथवा रेगिस्तान में रेत का टीला, टिब्बा
dung (डंग) *n.* गोबर, लीद, खाद
dungaree (डंग´री) *n.* मोटा सूती कपड़ा
dungeon (´डंजन) *n.* तहखाने में कारागार, काल कोठरी
dunk (डंक) *vt.* डबलरोटी आदि खाने के लिए (चाय, दूध आदि में) डुबोना; डुबाना
duo (´ड्यूओ) *n.* कलाकारों का जोड़ा
duodenum (ड्यूओ´डीनम) *n.* छोटी आँत का ऊपर का भाग
dupe (ड्यूप) *n.* धोखाधड़ी का शिकार, भोला-भाला व्यक्ति – *vt.* उल्लू बनाना, धोखा देना
duplex (´ड्यूप्लेक्स) *a.* दोहरा, द्वैध; दो भागों में (ऊपर-नीचे) बना फ्लैट
duplicate *vt.* (´ड्यूप्लिकेट) किसी वस्तु की ठीक नकल बनाना – *a.* (´ड्यूप्लिकिट) दोहरा, दुगुना; ठीक एक वस्तु जैसी दूसरी (वस्तु) – *n.* (´ड्यूप्लिकिट) प्रतिकृति, नकल – **duplication** (ड्यूप्लि´केशन) *n.* –

duplicator *n.* प्रतिलिपियां बनाने की मशीन – **duplicity** (ड्यू'प्लिसिटि) *n.* कपट, छल; दोगलापन; धोखा

durable ('ड्युअरबल) *a.* टिकाऊ (वस्तु) – **durability** (ड्युअर'बिलिटि) *n.*

duration (ड्यु'रेशन) *n.* अवधि, मियाद

duress (डयुअ'रेंस) *n.* – **under duress** दबाव/बल प्रयोग के कारण (कोई अनिच्छित बयान देना)

during ('ड्युअरिंग) *prep.* की अवधि में, के दौरान

dusk (डस्क) *n.* (शाम का) झुटपुटा; संध्या – **dusky** *a.* सांवला; मटमैला, धुंधला

dust (डस्ट) *n.* धूल, गर्द, किसी भी पदार्थ का चूरा, राख – *vt.* पाउडर, (चूर्ण) बुरकना; धूल झाड़ना – **duster** *n.* झाड़न – **dusty** *a.* धूल भरा – **dustbin** *n.* कूड़ेदान

Dutch (डच) *a.* नीदरलैंड संबंधित, वहां का निवासी, वहां की भाषा – **Dutch courage** शराबी का साहस या शेख़ी; झूठा साहस; जोशे-जाम – **go Dutch** (दावत आदि में) प्रत्येक व्यक्ति का अपना खर्चा आप देना

duty ('ड्यूटि) *n.* कर्त्तव्य, फ़र्ज; ड्यूटी, शुल्क, सैन्य-सेवा; नौकरी; कार्य – **dutiable** *a.* जिस पर सीमा शुल्क लगे – **dutiful** *a.* कर्त्तव्य-परायण – **duty-free** *a.* नि:शुल्क

dwarf (ड्वॉर्फ) *n.* बौना (मनुष्य, पशु, पौधा); पौराणिक बहुत छोटा मनुष्य जैसा जीव; (*pl.* **dwarf, dwarves**) – *a.* बहुत ज्यादा छोटा – *vt.* तुलना में बहुत छोटा दिखलाना; सामान्य आकार तक बढ़ने से रोकना

dwell (ड्वेंल) *vi.* रहना; बसना; पर विचार करना; (पर) विस्तार से लिखना या बोलना (**dwelt** *pt./pp.*) – **dweller** *n.* – **dwelling** *n.* घर

dwindle ('ड्विंड्ल) *vi.* क्षीण होना, कम होना

dye (डाइ) *vt.* कपड़ा रंगना (घुले रंग में डुबो कर) (**dyed , dyeing**) – *n.* द्रव में घुला या घुल सकने वाला रंग; रंग; वर्ण – **dyer** *n.*

dyke (डाइक) *n.* समुद्र का पानी रोकने के लिए बना बाँध

dynamics (डाइ'नैमिक्स) *n.* गति-विज्ञान; भौतिक बल – **dynamic** (डाइ'नैमिक) *a.* गतिशील, सक्रिय; ओजस्वी

dynamism ('डाइन्अमिज़म) *n.* कुछ करने का जोश, उत्साह व ऊर्जा, ओज

dynamite ('डाइनमाइट) *n.* डाइनामाइट – *vt.* डाइनामाइट से उड़ा देना

dynamo ('डाइनमो) *n.* डाइनमो, बिजली उत्पन्न करने वाला यंत्र (*pl.* **-mos**)

dynasty ('डिनस्टि) *n.* वंश, राजवंश – **dynastic** (डि'नैस्टिक) *a.* राजवंशीय

dysentery ('डिसंट्रि) *n.* पेचिश, संग्रहणी

dysfunction (डिस्'फंक्शन) *n.* सामान्य रूप से कार्य न करना (वि. शरीर के अंगों का), दुष्क्रिया

dyslexia (डिस्'लेंक्सिअ) *n.* मानसिक विकार से उत्पन्न पठन-अक्षमता; ठीक तरह से लिखने व पढ़ने में कठिनाई

dyspepsia (डिस्'पेंप्सिअ) *n.* अजीर्ण, बदहज़मी

E

E Earl, East, Eastern, English का संक्षेप

each (ईच) *a./pron.* प्रत्येक, हर एक (अलग, अलग) – **each other** एक दूसरे (को, की ओर आदि)

eager (ˈईगर) *a.* उत्सुक, बेसब्र – **eagerly** *adv.* उत्सुकता से – **eagerness** *n.* उत्सुकता

eagle (ˈईगल) *n.* गरुड़, उकाब

ear[1] (इअर) *n.* कान; सुनने की शक्ति; स्वर की पहचान; ध्यान – **earmark** *vt.* किसी विशेष प्रयोजन के लिए अलग रख देना – **earphone** *n.* कान पर लगाकर रेडियो सुनने का रिसीवर – **earring** *n.* कान की बाली, कर्ण फूल – **earshot** *n.* सुनने की सीमा का फासला – **be all ears** सुनने के लिए उत्सुक

ear[2] ***n.*** अनाज की बाली

earl (अर्ल) *n.* इंगलैंड में मारकीस से नीचे सामंत

early (ˈअर्लि) *a./adv.* प्रारंभिक, शीघ्र; प्राचीन; पहले भाग में; पूर्व; सवेर-सवेरे; प्राचीन काल में

earn (अर्न) *vt.* कमाना; प्राप्त करना; के योग्य होना – **earnings** *pl. n.* कमाई, उपार्जन

earnest[1] (ˈअर्निस्ट) *a.* गंभीर; उत्साही; निष्ठावान – **earnestly** *adv.* निष्ठा से – **in earnest** गंभीर, गंभीरता से पक्के निश्चय से, मन लगाकर

earnest[2] *n.* अग्रिम राशि, बयाना

earth (अर्थ) *n.* पृथ्वी, स्थल; मिट्टी; खनिज; विद्युत-सयंत्र को पृथ्वी से जोड़ने वाली तार, भूसंपर्क, अर्थ – *vt.* विद्युत-संयत्र को तार द्वारा पृथ्वी से जोड़ना – **earthen** *a.* मिट्टी का बना – **earthly** *a.* संभव – **earthy** *a.* पृथ्वी का; स्वभाविक – **earthenware** *n.* मिट्टी के बरतन – **earthquake** *n.* भूचाल, भूकम्प – **earthworm** *n.* केंचुआ

ease (ईज़) *n.* आराम; परेशानी, दर्द, मुसीबत से छुटकारा; आलस्य; आसानी –*v.* (भार, चिंता आदि) कम करना; शारीरिक व मानसिक सुख, आराम पहुंचाना; ढीला करना; (पीड़ा) कम करना – **easily** *adv.* आसानी से – **easy** *a.* आसान, चिंता, परेशानी, दर्द आदि से मुक्त; सहज ही बात मानने वाला – **easy-going** *a.* आरामतलब – **at ease** आराम से – **take it easy** ज़्यादा चिंता न करना

east (ईस्ट) *n.* पूर्व दिशा – *a.* पूर्व (क्षितिज) पर, पूर्व में, के समीप; पूर्वी, पूर्वीय – *adv.*पूर्व से, की ओर – **easterly** *a./adv.* पूर्वी – **eastern** *a.* – **eastward** *a/n.* – **eastward(s)** *adv.*

Easter (ˈईस्टर) *n.* ईसा के पुनर्जीवित होने की खुशी में पर्व

easy (ˈईज़ि) दे. EASE

eat (ईट) *v.* खाना; भोजन करना; नष्ट करना; कुतरना; खा जाना (**ate** *pt.*, **eaten** *pp.*) – **eatable** *a.* खाने योग्य – **eatery** *n. inf.* रेस्तंरा, ढाबा – **eat out** घर के बजाय रेस्तरां जाकर खाना खाना

eau de Cologne (ओ ड कˈलोन) *n. Fr.* एक हल्की सुगंधित इत्र

eaves (ˈईव्ज़) *pl. n.* छत का वह भाग जो दीवार के आगे की ओर निकला हो, ओरी – **eavesdrop** *v.* छिपकर बातें सुनना

ebb (ऍब) *vi.* (समुद्र में भाटे का) उतरना, हटना; अवनति – *n.* भाटा; अवनति, घटना – **ebb tide** भाटा – *fig.* **ebb away** धीरे-धीरे घटकर समाप्त हो जाना

ebony (ˈऍबनि) *n.* आबनूस की लकड़ी (एक सख्त काली लकड़ी) – *a.* आबनूस का बना, के जैस काला

ebullient (इ'बल्यंट, इ'बुल-) *a.* उल्लास भरा, खुशी से भरा हुआ – **ebullience** *n.* उल्लास

e-business ('ईबिज़्निस) *n.* **electronic business** का संक्षेप, इंटरनेट के माध्यम से व्यापार, इंटरनेट-व्यापार

eccentric (इक'सेंन्ट्रिक) *a.* सनकी; विचित्र; अनियमित; जिसकी धुरी केंद्र में स्थित न हो – *n.* सनकी, विचित्र व्यक्ति – **eccentricity** *n.*

ecclesiastic (इक्लीज़ि'एस्टिक) *n.* पुरोहित, पादरी – *a.* गिरजे-सम्बन्धी

ECG electrocardiogram, electrocardiograph का संक्षेप

echelon ('ऐशलॉन) *n.* उत्तरदायित्व अथवा प्रशासनिक महत्व का सोपान या दरजा, सोपानक; सैनिकों, वायुयानों आदि की ऐसी विरचना (व्यवस्था)

echo ('ऐको) *n.* प्रतिध्वनि, गूंज; अनुकरण (*pl.* **echoes**) – *vt.* प्रतिध्वनित करना – *vi.* गूंजना, दुहराना, दुहराये जाना (**echoed, echoing**)

éclair (ए'क्लेअर) *n.* उंगली नुमा जमाया हुआ केक जिसमें क्रीम भरी होती है

eclectic (इ'क्लेक्टिक, ऐ'क्लेक्टिक) *a.* विचाराधारा में ग्रहणशील, उदार (विचार, पसंद आदि में) – *n.* – **eclecticism** *n.*

eclipse (इ'क्लिप्स) *n.* (सूर्य या चंद्र) ग्रहण; वस्तु, व्यक्ति आदि की प्रसिद्धि का बहुत कम होना – *vt.* (को) ग्रहण लगाना; एक वस्तु, व्यक्ति द्वारा दूसरे को श्रीहीन या फीका कर देना; छिपाना; (से) आगे बढ़ जाना

ecology (इ'कॉलजि) *n.* वनस्पति तथा जीवों के अपने पर्यावरण से सम्बंध का अध्ययन **ecological** *a.* पर्यावरण-सम्बंधी – **ecologist** *n.* पर्यावरण-विज्ञानी

e-commerce ('ईकॉमर्स) *n.* **electronic commerce** का संक्षेप, इंटरनेट के माध्यम से क्रय-विक्रय व्यवस्था, इंटरनेट- व्यापार

economy (इ'कॉनमि) *n.* धन का किफायत से व उचित उपयोग, मितव्ययता; अर्थ-व्यवस्था – **economic** (ईक'नॉमिक) *a.* अर्थशास्त्र-सम्बंधी, किफायती – **economical** *a.* मितव्ययी, किफायती – **economically** *adv.* – **economics** *n.* (*as sing.*) अर्थशास्त्र; (*as pl.*) आर्थिक पहलू – **economist** (इ'कॉनमिस्ट) *n.* अर्थशास्त्री – **economize** *v.* व्यय, अपव्यय आदि सीमित अथवा कम करना

ecstasy ('ऐक्स्टसि) *n.* उल्लास, हर्षोन्माद; भाव-समाधि; तन्मयता – **ecstatic** (ऐक्'स्टैटिक) *a.* अत्यंत हर्षित, समाधि-मग्न

eczema ('ऐक्सिमअ) *n.* ऐक्ज़ीमा, दाद

eddy ('ऐडि) *n.* भंवर, बवण्डर – *vi.* भंवर या बवण्डर में चक्कर खाना (**eddied, eddying**)

Eden ('ईडन) *n.* (बाइबल में) वह उद्यान जिसमें स ष्टि के आरंभ में आदम व ईव (हौवा) रहे थे; कोई सुख व आनन्ददायक स्थान व स्थिति

edge (ऐज) *n.* किनारा, कोर; सीमा; (उस्तरे, तलवार आदि की) धार, पैनापन; कडुवाहट – *vt.* (चाकू आदि) तेज़ करना; किनारा बनाना; आहिस्ता-आहिस्ता खिसकाना – *vi.* तिरछा चलना, सावधानी से चले जाना या आ जाना

edible ('ऐडिबल) *a.* भोज्य, खाने योग्य – **edibility** *n.*

edict ('ईडिक्ट) *n.* राजाज्ञा, आदेश, पत्र, फ़रमान

edifice ('ऐडिफ़िस) *n.* भवन, इमारत

edify ('ऐडिफ़ाइ) *vt.* नैतिक रूप से सुधारना; उपदेश देना (**-fied, -fying**) – **edification** (ऐडिफ़ि'केशन) *n.* नैतिक सुधार या उन्नति, सुशिक्षा

edit ('ऐडिट) *vt.* सम्पादन करना; फिल्म, टेप आदि को प्रसारण के लिए ठीक करना या तैयार करना – **edition** *n.* संस्करण; किसी छापी गई पुस्तक आदि की संख्या – **editor** *n.* सम्पादक – **editorial** *a.* सम्पादक का – *n.* सम्पादकीय

educate (ऍजुकेट) *vt.* शिक्षित करना, पढ़ाना, प्रशिक्षित करना – **education** *n.* शिक्षा – **educational** *a.* – **education(al)ist** *n.* शिक्षा-शास्त्री – **educative** *a.* शिक्षाप्रद – **educator** *n.* शिक्षक

EEC European Economic Community का संक्षेप

eel (ईल) *n.* सांपनुमा मछली, ईल, बाम

eerie (ˈइअरि) *a.* भयानक, अजीबोगरीब

EEG Electroencephalogram का संक्षेप

efface (इˈफ़ेस) *vt.* मिटा देना, (रगड़ कर) गायब कर देना

effect (इˈफ़ेक्ट) *n.* परिणाम, प्रभाव, लागू रहने की स्थिति; (~ **s**) *pl.* फिल्म, रेडियो प्रसारण, नाटक आदि से जुड़ी वस्तुऐं (प्रकाश, ध्वनि आदि सम्बंधी) – *vt.* उत्पन्न करना, सम्पन्न करना – **effective** *a.* प्रभोवात्पादक, कारगर – **effectively** *adv.* – **effectual** *a.* – **with immediate effect** तुरंत (लागू)

effeminate (इˈफ़ेमिनिट) *a.* हाव-भाव में स्त्री जैसा (पुरुष), जनाना

effervesce (ऍफ़रˈवेंस) *vi.* (द्रव का) बुदबुदाना; अत्यंत्र प्रसन्न होना – **effervescent** *a.*

effete (इˈफ़ीट) *a.* जीर्ण, क्षीण, दुर्बल

efficacious (ऍफ़िˈकेशस) *a.* प्रभावोत्पादक, असरदार – **efficacy** *n.* असर

efficient (इˈफ़िशंट) *a.* कार्य कुशल – **efficiency** *n.*

effigy (ˈऍफ़िजि) *n.* मूर्ति; पुतला

effluent (ˈऍफ़्लुअंट) *n.* (कारख़ाने आदि से) छोड़ा गया पानी अथवा अन्य द्रव, निस्सारी

effort (ˈऍफ़र्ट) *n.* परिश्रम; प्रयत्न; उप्लब्धि

effrontery (इˈफ़्रंटरि) *n.* गुस्ताख़ी

effusive (इˈफ़्यूसिव) *a.* भावपूर्ण उद्गारों को भावात्मक रूप से प्रकट करने वाला; जोश भरा

e.g. *exempli gratia (Lat. for example)* उदाहरण के लिए

egalitarian (इगैलिˈटैंअरिअन) *a.* यह विश्वास करने वाला कि सभी मनुष्य समान होने चाहिए, समतावादी – *n.*

egg[1] (ऍग) *n.* अण्डा

egg[2] *vt.* – **egg on** उकसाना

ego (ˈईगो, ˈऍगो) *n.* अहम्, अहंभाव – **egoism** *n.* स्वार्थ, अहंभाव – **egoist** *n.* अहंकारी, स्वार्थी – **egoistic(al)** *a.* – **egotism** *n.* स्वार्थ, अहंकार – **egotist** *n.* अपनी ही प्रशंसा आप करने वाला – **egocentric** *a.* आत्म-केन्द्रित, अहंकारी, अहंकेन्द्रिक

e-governance (इˈ-गवर्नन्स) *n.* सरकारी दफ्तरों व जनता के बीच सम्पर्क के लिए इंटरनेट का उपयोग

egregious (इˈग्रीजस) *a.* स्पष्ट, भयंकर (भूल)

egret (ˈईग्रिट) *n.* सफेद रंग का लम्बी गर्दन वाला पक्षी

eight (एट) *n.* आठ (की संख्या) – *a.* – **eighteen** (एˈटीन) *a./n.* अठारह – **eighteenth** *a./n.* अठारवाँ – **eighth** *a./n.* (एट्थ) आठवाँ – **eightieth** (ˈएटिइथ) *a./n.* अस्सीवां – **eighty** *a./n.* अस्सी

either (ˈआइदर, ईदर) *a./pron.* दोनों में से एक, दोनों में से प्रत्येक, प्रत्येक – *adv./conj.* दो संभावनाओं को जोड़ने के लिए **"or"** (या) से पहले प्रयुक्त *e.g.* **either he or you will go** नकारात्मक उक्ति को बल देने के लिए

ejaculate (इˈजैक्युलेट) *v.* (वीर्य) निकलना या निकालना; सहसा बोल उठना – **ejaculation** (इजैक्युˈलेशन) *n.* – **ejaculatory** *a.*

eject (इˈजेंक्ट) *vt.* निकाल बाहर करना, फेंक देना – **ejection** (इˈजेंक्शन) *n.*

eke out (ईक-) मुश्किल से गुज़ारा करना

elaborate *a.* (इˈलैबरिट) विस्त त (वर्णन आदि); लम्बा-चौड़ा (आयोजन); जटिल – *vi.* (इˈलैबरेट) (वर्णन आदि का) खुलासा करना

– *vt.* (इ'लैबरेट) विस्तार से वर्णन करना; उत्पन्न करना – **elaboration** (इलैब'रेशन) *n.*

elapse (इ'लैप्स) *vi.* (समय) गुज़रना

elastic (इ'लैस्टिक) *a.* लचीला – *n.* लचीला फ़ीता – **elasticity** *n.* लचीलापन

elation (इ'लेशन) *n.* उल्लास; गर्व, घमण्ड

elbow ('ऍल्बो) *n.* कोहनी, इसे ढकने वाला (कमीज की) आस्तीन का हिस्सा; मोड़ – *vt.* कोहनी मारना – **elbowroom** *n. fig.* पर्याप्त स्थान

elder ('ऍल्डर) *a.* बड़ा, ज्येष्ठ – (~ **s**) *pl.* सम्मानीय – OLD का *comp.* – *n.* (दो व्यक्तियों में आयु में) बड़ा; वद्ध व्यक्ति; कुछ गिरजाघरों में एक अधिकारी – **elderly** *a.* वयोवद्ध, अधेड़ – **eldest** *a.* सबसे बड़ा – OLD का *sup.* – **the elderly** बड़े-बूढ़े

elect (इ'लेंक्ट) *vt.* वोट द्वारा चुनना, (वस्तु कार्य आदि) चुनना – *a.* चुना हुआ; मनोनीत, निर्वाचित; चुनिन्दा – **election** *n.* चुनाव, निर्वाचन – **electioneer** *vi.* राजनीतिक चुनाव में दौड़-धूप – **elective** *a.* निर्वाचित, वैकल्पिक (विषय आदि); चयनात्मक – **elector** *n.* निर्वाचक, मतदाता – **electoral** *a.* – **electorate** *n.* निर्वाचक समूह

electricity (इलेंक्'ट्रिसिटि) *n.* विद्युत, बिजली – **electric** (इ'लेंक्ट्रिक) *a.* बिजली का संचार करने वाला, अथवा उससे चलने वाला (यंत्र या उपकरण); उत्तेजित – **electrical** *a.* – **electrician** (इ'लेंक्ट्रिशन) *n.* बिजली-मिस्त्री – **electrification** *n.* विद्युतीकरण – **electrify** *vt.* विद्युतीकरण करना (**-fied, -fying**) – **electrifying** *a.* जोशीला (भाषण, अभिनय)

electro- (*comb. form*) विद्युत- (द्वारा) जैसे **electrotherapy** (इलेंक्ट्रो'थेरपि) *n.*

electrocardiograph (इलेंक्ट्रो-'कार्डिओग्राफ़), **ECG** *n.* हृदय की विद्युतीय क्रिया को अंकित (रिकार्ड) करने का यंत्र – **electrocardiogram** *n.* इस यंत्र से बनाया गया रेखांकन, ई.सी.जी.

electrocute (इ'लेंक्ट्रक्यूट) *vt.* बिजली द्वारा प्राण दण्ड देना; (*passive* में) बिजली के झटके से मर जाना – **electrocution** (इलेंक्ट्र'क्यूशन) *n.* बिजली के झटके से मत्यु

electrode (इ'लेंक्ट्रोड) *n.* बैटरी आदि में संचालक जिसके जरिये विद्युत-करंट अंदर आती अथवा बाहर जाती है, इलैक्ट्रोड

electroencephalograph (इलेक्ट्रोऍन्-'सॅफलग्राफ़), **EEG** *n.* मस्तिष्क की विद्युत क्रिया को रेखांकित करने का यंत्र – **electroencephalogram** *n.* इससे बनाया गया रेखांकन

electrolyse (इ'लेंक्ट्रोलाइज़) *vt.* (रासायनिक यौगिक के) तत्वों को विद्युत द्वारा अलग-अलग करना – **electrolysis** *n.* ऐसा करने की क्रिया, विद्युत-अपघटन

electrolyte (इ'लेंक्ट्रोलाइट) *n.* घोल या पिघला हुआ पदार्थ जिसमें बिजली प्रवाहित होती है

electromagnet (इलेंक्ट्रो'मैग्निट) *n.* चुम्बक जिस पर तार लिपटी होती है जिसमें से विद्युत-धारा प्रवाहित होती है, विद्युत-चुम्बक – **electromagnetic** (इलेक्ट्रोमैग्'नैटिक) *a.*

electron (इ'लेंक्ट्रॉन) *n.* परमाणु का एक मूल घटक – **electronic** (इलेंक्'ट्रॉनिक) *a.* इलेक्ट्रॉन अथवा इलेक्ट्रॉनिक्स सम्बन्धी; इलेक्ट्रॉन की क्रिया पर निर्भर साधन – **electronics** *n.* इलेक्ट्रॉनिक साधनों, उपकरणों व परिपथ (सरकिट) के विकास सम्बंधी प्रौद्योगिकी (टैक्नॉलजी)

electroplate (इ'लेंक्ट्रोप्लेट) *vt.* विद्युत-अपघटन (इलेक्ट्रोलिसिस) द्वारा चांदी आदि की परत चढ़ाना

elegant (ऍलिगंट) *a.* सुरुचिपूर्ण, शिष्ट; आचार-व्यवहार में बहुत अच्छा – **elegance** *n.* बहुत सुरूचिपूर्ण आचार-व्यवहार

elegy (ऍलिजि) *n.* शोकगीत, शोक कविता

element (ऍलिमंट) *n.* तत्व, मूलतत्व; अवयव, हिस्सा, (राशि का) अंश; बिजली की केतली व स्टोव में गरम करने की तार; स्वाभाविक या अनुकूल वातावरण – (~ s) *pl.* मौसम, आंधी-तूफान; प्रारंभिक ज्ञान – **elemental** *a.* मूल प्राक तिक शक्तियों से सम्बंधित – **elementary** *a.* प्राथमिक, प्रारंभिक, सरल

elephant (ऍलिफ़ंट) *n.* हाथी

elevate (ऍलिवेट) *vt.* ऊपर उठाना, ऊंचा करना; (मन) गर्व व उल्लास से भर देना, उन्नत करना – **elevation** (ऍलि वेशन) *n.* उठाना; ऊंचाई वि. समुद्र तल से भवन आदि के एक पक्ष का रेखाचित्र – **elevator** *n. US* लिफ्ट

eleven (इ लेंव्न) *n.* ग्यारह; ग्यारह की टीम – *a.* – **eleven fold** *a./adv.* ग्यारहगुना – **eleventh** *a.* ग्यारहवाँ – **eleventh hour** बिल्कुल अंतिम क्षण (पर पहुंचना आदि)

elf (ऍल्फ) *n.* छोटी परी, वन की परी (*pl.* **elves**)

elicit (इ लिसिट) *vt.* (बात को) प्रकाश में लाना

eligible (ऍलिजबल) *a.* योग्य, उपयुक्त, उचित (पात्र) – **eligibility** (ऍलिजि बिलिटि) *n.* योग्यता; निर्वाच्यता

eliminate (इ लिमिनेट) *vt.* हटाना, अलग कर देना, (से) मुक्ति पा लेना – **elimination** (इलिमि नेशन) *n.* – **eliminator** *n.* जो हटाये या निकाले आदि

elite (इ लीट, ए लीट) *n.* विशिष्ट वर्ग, समाज के सर्वोत्क ष्ट, सबसे उत्तम लोग – **elitism** *n.*

elixir (इ लिक्सर) *n.* पारसमणि; अम त

elk (ऍल्क) *n.* एक बड़ा हिरण

ellipse (इ लिप्स) *n.* अण्डाकार आक ति

ellipsis (इ लिप्सिस) *n. Grammar* वाक्य अथवा शब्द के किसी भाग का लोप, पदलोप

elm (ऍल्म) *n.* (एक व क्ष) चिराबेल, हिमरोई, उपकर; इसकी लकड़ी

elocution (ऍल क्यूशन) *n.* सार्वजनिक भाषण देने की कला; वक्त त्व कला

elongate (ईलॉङगेट) *vt.* लंबा करना, बढ़ाना – **elongation** (ईलॉङ गेशन) *n.*

elope (इ लोप) *vi.* प्रेमी के साथ घर से भाग जाना – **elopement** *n.*

eloquence (ऍलक्वन्स) *n.* भाषा का धारा-प्रवाह प्रयोग, वाक्पटुता – **eloquent** *a.*

else (ऍल्स) *adv.* अतिरिक्त, (कोई) और; वरना – **elsewhere** *adv.* कहीं और

ELT English Language Teaching उन लोगों को अंग्रेज़ी पढ़ाना जिनकी यह प्रथम/मात भाषा न हो

elucidate (इ लूसिडेट) *vt.* व्याख्या करना; स्पष्ट करना – **elucidation** (इलूसि डेशन) *n.*

elude (इ लूड) *vt.* बच निकलना; टाल मटोल करना; (अर्थ, भाव) समझ में न आना – **elusive** (इ लूसिव) *a.* आसानी से पकड़ में न आने वाला; धोखेभरा

e-mail (ईमेल) *n.* electronic mail का संक्षेप, इंटरनेट के माध्यम से पत्र-व्यवहार, ईमेल – *vt.* इस प्रकार पत्र व्यवहार करना

emaciate (इ मेशिएट) *v.* क्षीण काय, दुबला पतला हो जाना या करना – **emaciation** (इमेसि एशन) *n.*

emanate (ऍमनेट) *vi.* (से) निकलना, उत्पन्न होना – **emanation** *n.* निर्गम, प्रसर्जन

emancipate (इ मैन्सिपेट) *vt.* स्वाधीन करना, उद्धार करना – **emancipation** *n.* उद्धार

emasculate (इ मैस्क्युलेट) *vt.* बधिया करना; प्रभावहीन करना – **emasculation** *n.*

embankment (इम् बैंक्मंट) *n.* बांध, तटबंध; सड़क या रेलमार्ग के लिए बना मिट्टी का भराव

embargo (ऍम् बार्गो) *n.* निषेध-आज्ञा (*pl.* -**goes**) – *vt.* निषेध-आज्ञा लागू करना

embark (ऍम्'बार्क) *v.* जहाज, वायुयान आदि पर चढ़ना; या चढ़ाना (*on* या *upon* के साथ) – **embarkation** *n.* – **embark on** नया/कठिन/ महत्वपूर्ण कार्य शुरु करना·

embarrass (इम्'बैरस) *vt.* परेशान करना; उलझन में डालना – **embarrassment** *n.* लज्जा; परेशानी, घबराहट; उलझन

embattled (इम'बैट्ल्ड) *a.* मुसीबतों, समस्याओं से घिरा हुआ

embassy ('ऍम्बसि) *n.* राजदूतावास, दूतावास, राजदूत का कार्य

embellish (इम्'बेंलिश) *vt.* सजाना, सुदंर बनाना – **embellishment** *n.*

ember ('ऍम्बर) *n.* अंगारा – *pl.* लाल-तपते कोयले

embezzle (इम्'बेंज़ल) *vt.* ग़बन करना – **embezzlement** *n.*

embitter (इम्'बिटर) *vt.* कटुता, कड़वाहट बढ़ाना

emblem ('ऍम्ब्लम) *n.* सूचक चिन्ह; बैज

embody (इम्'बॉडि) *vt.* साकार रूप देना, मूर्त रूप देना; अभिव्यक्त करना, सम्मिलित करना (**embodied, embodying**) – **embodiment** *n.* मूर्त रूप

embolden (इम्'बोल्डन) *vt.* (की हिम्मत बढ़ाना

emboss (इम्'बॉस) *vt.* नक्काशी किया हुआ; उभरा (शब्द, मुहर आदि)

embrace (इम्'ब्रेस) *vt.* को आलिंगन करना, बाहों में लेना, गले लगाना; को ग्रहण करना – *n.* आलिंगन

embroider (इम्'ब्रॉइडर) *vt.* बेलबूटा काढ़ना; (कहानी आदि में) नमक मिर्च लगाना, बढ़ा-चढ़ा देना – **embroidery** *n.* कशीदाकारी, कढ़ाई

embryo ('ऍम्ब्रिओ) *n.* गर्भ में (अविकसित) बच्चा, भ्रूण

emerald ('ऍमरल्ड) *n.* एक कीमती हरे रंग का पत्थर, पन्ना – *a.* इसके रंग का

emerge (इ'मर्ज) *vi.* ऊपर या बाहर आना; प्रकट होना; (तहकीकात करने पर) सामने आना – **emergence** (इ'मर्जन्स) *n.* आविर्भाव, सामने आने की क्रिया – **emergent** *a.* उभरता हुआ

emergency (इ'मर्जन्सि) *n.* आपात-स्थिति – **emergency exit** संकट-द्वार

emetic (इ'मेंटिक) *n./a.* उल्टी कराने वाली दवा

emigrate ('ऍमिग्रेट) *vt.* अपना देश छोड़कर दूसरे देश में जाकर बस जाना – **emigrant** *n.* प्रवासी – **emigration** *n.* प्रवास

eminent ('ऍमिनंट) *a.* विशिष्ट, विख्यात (व्यक्ति); श्रेष्ठ, प्रतिष्ठित – **eminence** *n.* प्रतिष्ठा, ऊंचाई, श्रेष्ठता, ख्याति – **eminently** *adv.* बहुत ही (अच्छा, उचित, उपयुक्त आदि)

emissary ('ऍमिसरि) *n.* दूत; प्रतिनिधि आदि (वि. सरकारी)

emit (इ'मिट) *vt.* (किरणें, ध्वनि आदि) छोड़ना, प्रसारित करना – **emission** *n.* छोड़े जाना

emolument (इ'मॉल्युमंट) *n.* वेतन, आय, पारिश्रमिक, परिलाभ

emotion (इ'मोशन) *n.* मन की उत्तेजना; भावावेश, (हर्ष, भय आदि के कारण) मनोभाव – **emotional** *a.* भावुक, भावात्मक

emperor ('ऍम्परर) *n.* सम्राट (**empress** *fem.*)

emphasis ('ऍम्फ़सिस) *n.* बल, जोर; शब्दों पर बलाघात; महत्व (*pl.* **-ses** (सीज़)) – **emphasize** ('ऍम्फ़साइज़) *vt.* जोर देना – **emphatic** (इम्'फ़ैटिक) *a.* जोरदार, स्पष्ट, प्रभावशाली

empire ('ऍम्पाइअर) *n.* साम्राज्य

empirical (ऍम्'पिरिकल) *a.* सिद्धांत के विपरीत अनुभव अथवा प्रयोग से प्राप्त (ज्ञान)

employ (इम्'प्लॉइ) *vt.* (व्यक्ति को) नौकरी देना, काम पर लगाना; उपयोग करना (**employed, employing**) –

employee (ऍम्पलॉइ'ई) *n.* कर्मचारी – **employer** *n.* मालिक – **employment** *n.*नौकरी, कार्य, व्यवसाय

emporium (ऍम्'पॉरिअम) *n.* एम्पोरियम; वाणिज्य-केन्द्र (**pl. -riums, -ria**)

empower (इम्'पाउअर) *vt.* (कार्य विशेष करने का) अधिकार देना

empress ('ऍम्प्रिस) *n.* साम्राज्ञी; सम्राट की पत्नी

empty ('ऍम्पटि) *a.* खाली, निरर्थक; खोखला; निरुद्देश्य –*v.* खाली करना या होना; (किसी अन्य बरतन आदि में) उंडेलना, डालना (**emptied, emptying**) – **empties** *pl. n.* खाली बक्से, बोंतलें आदि – **emptiness** *n.*

emu ('ईम्यू) *n.* आस्ट्रेलिया का शुतुरमुर्ग जैसा विशाल पक्षी जो उड़ नह सकता

emulate ('ऍम्युलेट) *vt.* अनुकरण करना – **emulation** *n.* प्रतिस्पर्धा, मुकाबला

emulsion (इ'मल्शन) *n.* फोटो फ़िल्म पर एक पतली तरल परत जो प्रकाश से प्रभावित होती है; दूधिया द्रव जिसमें तेल अथवा अन्य चिकनाई वाले पदार्थो के कण मिले होते हैं; इस प्रकार का रंग-रोगन, पायस; मिश्रण – **emulsifier** *n.*

enable (इ'नेबल) *vt.* समर्थ करना; अधिकार देना; (कुछ करने के लिए) साधन उप्लब्ध कराना

enact (इ'नैक्ट) *vt.* कानून बनाना; अभिनय करना – **enactment** *n.* अधिनियमन

enamel (इ'नैमल) *n.* धातु आदि पर लेप किया जाने वाला चमकीला पदार्थ जो उसे जंग आदि से बचाता है, एनैमल, तामचीनी; दांत की चमकीली तह; कोई भी सख्त बाहरी तह – *vt.* (**-ll-**)

enamour (इ'नैमर) *vt.* – **enamoured of** पर आसक्त या मोहित होना

en bloc (ऑं'ब्लॉक) *Fr. adv.* सामूहिक रूप से, इकट्ठे

encamp (इन्'कैम्प) *v.* पड़ाव या डेरा डालना – **encampment** *n.* डेरा

encapsulate (इन'कैप्सयुलेट) *vt.* कैप्सूल में बंद करना; *fig.* (विषय आदि को) संक्षिप्त रूप देना

encash (इन्'कैश) *vt.* (चैक) भुनाना

enchant (इन्'चांट) *vt.* मंत्रमुग्ध करना (**-tress** *fem.*) – **enchanting** *a.* मोहक; मनोहर – **enchantment** *n.* जादू, वशीकरण

encircle (इन्'सर्कल) *vt.* चारों ओर से घेर लेना

enclave ('ऍन्क्लेव़) *n.* क्षेत्र जो चारों ओर से विदेशी भूमि से घिरा हो, विदेशी अंत: क्षेत्र

enclose (इन्'क्लोज़) *vt.* चारों ओर से बंद कर देना; घेरना; संलग्न करना, साथ जोड़ना या रखना (पत्र आदि में) – **enclosure** (इन्'क्लोझ़र) *n.* संलग्न वस्तु, घेरा, बाड़ा

encomium (ऍन्'कोमिअम) *n.* गुणगान

encompass (इन्'कम्पस) *vt.* घेरना, समाना या सम्मिलित करना

encore ('ऑङकॉर) *interj.* दुबारा, फिर से, मुकर्रर

encounter (इन्'काउंटर) *vt.* से अचानक मिलना; (मुश्किल) का सामना करना; से मुठभेड़ होना – *n.*

encourage (इन्'करिज) *vt.* हिम्मत बढ़ाना, प्रोत्साहित करना; समर्थन देना, प्रेरित करना – **encouragement** *n.* प्रोत्साहन

encroach (इन्'क्रोच) *vi.* (**up/on** के साथ) में अनाधिकार हस्तक्षेप या प्रवेश करना; पर गैर कानूनी कब्ज़ा करना; अधिकाधिक क्षेत्र में फैलते जाना – **encroachment** *n.* अनाधिकार कब्ज़ा

encrust, incrust (इन्'क्रस्ट) *v.* पपड़ी जमना या जमाना, जड़ना

encumber (इन्'कम्बर) *vt.* बाधा डालना; बोझ लाद देना – **encumbrance** (इन'कम्ब्रन्स) *n.*

encyclop(a)edia (ऍन्साइक्लो'पीडिअ) *n.* विश्वकोश – **encyclop(a)edic** *a.*

end (ऍण्ड) *n.* सीमा, छोर; समाप्ति, अंत; फल, परिणाम; टुकड़ा; दूसरा भाग; म त्यु; उद्देश्य, लक्ष्य, ध्येय; *Sport* खेल के मैदान में दो में से कोई भाग – *v.* समाप्त करना या होना – **ending** *n.* – **endless** *a.* अंतहीन; – **endways** *adv.* खड़ा; लम्बाई में; सिरे से सिरा मिलाकर – **make both ends meet** मुश्किल से गुज़ारा करना

endear (इन् डिअर) *vt.* प्रिय बनाना – **endearing** *a.* मोहित करने वाला – **endearment** *n.* प्यार भरे शब्द, लाड़-प्यार

endeavour (इन डॅव़र) *vi.* प्रयत्न करना – *n.* प्रयत्न, कोशिश

endemic (ऍन् डॅमिक) *a.* किसी क्षेत्र अथवा देश में बार-बार होने वाला (बाढ़, बीमारी आदि) – *n.* ऐसा रोग

endorse (इन् डॉर्स) *vt.* प ष्ठांकन द्वारा पुष्टीकरण करना, समर्थन करना; विज्ञापन के रूप में किसी उत्पाद का) अनुमोदन करना; (चैक आदि के पीछे) हस्ताक्षर करना; मोटर चालक का लाइसेंस (उसमें उसका अपराध दर्ज करके) प ष्ठांकित करना – **endorsement** *n.*

endow (इन् डाउ) *vt.* (के लिए) स्थायी आय का स्रोत प्रदान करना; देना – **endowment** *n.* दान; स्थायी-निधि

endue (इन् ड्यू) *vt.* प्रदान करना, (गुण आदि से) सम्पन्न करना

endure (इन् ड्युअर) *vt.* झेलना – *vi.* बने रहना, टिकना – **endurable** *a.* सहनीय – **endurance** *n.* सहनशक्ति – **enduring** *a.* चिरकालीन

enema (ऍनिम्अ) *n.* औषधि अथवा द्रव जो गुदा से पेट में चढ़ाया जाय

enemy (ऍनमि) *n.* शत्रु

energy (ऍनर्जि) *n.* बल, शक्ति, कार्य करने की शक्ति, ऊर्जा; मशीन, बैटरी आदि का कार्य-सामर्थ्य अथवा शक्ति उत्पन्न करने की क्षमता – **energetic** (ऍनर् जॅटिक) *a.* चुस्ती से कार्य करने वाला – **energize** *vt.* बल देना; ऊर्जा संचार आरंभ करना

enervate (ऍनर्व़ेट) *vt.* कमज़ोर बनाना – **enervation** *n.* शिथिलता, दुर्बलता

enfeeble (इन् फ़ीबल) *vt.* कमज़ोर या शक्तिहीन करना

enfold (इन् फ़ोल्ड) *vt.* बाहों में भरना, आलिंगन करना; लपेटना

enforce (इन् फ़ॉर्स) *vt. (Law)* लागू करना – **enforced** *a.* जबरदस्ती लागू किया गया

enfranchise (इन् फ़्रैन्चाइज़) *vt.* मताधिकार देना

Eng. England, English का संक्षेप

engage (इङ गेज) *vt.* आकर्षित करना; काम पर रखना, अपने लिए रखना, लेना; *(Military)* से संघर्ष करना; (टैक्सी आदि) किराये पर लेना; सगाई करना; काम में लगाना; उलझाना; लगाना – *vi.* व्यस्त होना, वचनबद्ध होना; से लड़ना; मशीन के दो पुर्ज़ों का जुड़ना – **engaged** *a.* जिसकी सगाई हो चुकी हो, वाग्दत्त, वाग्दत्ता; व्यस्त; उपयोग किया जा रहा (टेलीफोन) – **engagement** *n.* सगाई; पूर्व निश्चित समय पर किसी से मिलने या कह जाने आदि का कार्यक्रम; मुठभेड़ – **engaging** *a.* आकर्षक

engender (इन् जॅण्डर) *vt.* उत्पन्न करना

engine (ऍन्जिन) *n.* इंजन, यंत्र – **engineer** (ऍन्जि निअर) *n.* अभियन्ता, इंजीनियर – *vt.* इंजीनियर के रूप में निर्माण करना; चालाकी से कोई कार्य कराना – **engineering** *n.* इंजीनियरी, अभियंत्रिकी

English (इंग्लिश) *n.* अंग्रेज़ी; इंगलैंड के लोग, अंग्रेज़ – *a.* इंगलैंड से सम्बंधित, अंग्रेज़ी

engrave (इन् ग्रेव़) *vt.* धातु पर छापने के लिए अक्षर, चित्र आदि खोदना; नक्श करना, (मन में) जमाना – **engraver** *n.* – **engraving** *n.* नक्काशी

engross (इन् ग्रोस) *vt.* तल्लीन करना – **engrossed** *a.* तल्लीन, (में) खोया हुआ
engulf (इन् गल्फ़) *vt.* निगलना, पूरी तरह ढंक लेना
enhance (इन् हान्स) *vt.* अधिक करना
enigma (इ निग्मअ) *n.* रहस्यमय व्यक्ति अथवा वस्तु; पहेली; बुझौवल – **enigmatic(al)** (ऍनिग् मैटिक्(ल)) *a.* रहस्यमय
enjoin (इन् जॉइन) *vt.* आदेश देना; लागू करना
enjoy (इन् जॉइ) *vt.* आनंद लेना; भोगना; उपभोग करना – *v. refl.* प्रसन्नचित होना – **enjoyable** *a.* – **enjoyment** *n.*
enlarge (इन् लार्ज) *vt.* बढ़ाना; बड़े आकार में परिवर्तित करना – *vi.* बढ़ना, विस्तारपूर्वक लिखना; बड़े आकार में परिवर्तित हो सकना – **enlargement** *n.* बड़े आकार में परिवर्तित करने की क्रिया – **enlarger** *n.* ऐसा करने वाला प्रकाशिक (आप्टिकल) यंत्र
enlighten (इन् लाइट्न) *vt.* जानकारी देना; सूचित करना; प्रकाश डालना, प्रबुद्ध करना, अज्ञान दूर करना – **enlightenment** *n.* ज्ञानोदय – **the enlightened** प्रबुद्ध, ज्ञान सम्पन्न
enlist (इन् लिस्ट) *vt.* सिपाही भर्ती करना; (सहयोग) प्राप्त करना – *vi.* भरती होना – **enlistment** *n.* भरती
enliven (इन् लाइव़न) *vt.* सजीव बना देना, जान डाल देना
en masse (आँ मास) *adv.* सामूहिक रूप से
enmesh (इन् मेंश) *vt.* फँसाना
enmity (ऍन्मिटि) *n.* शुत्रता
ennui (आन्वी) *n.* ऊब, बोरियत
enormous (इ नॉर्मस) *a.* विशाल – **enormity** (इ नॉरमिटि) *n.* घोर अपराध, दोष, स्थिति आदि; *inf.* दीर्घ आकार
enough (इ नफ़) *a.* पर्याप्त, काफ़ी – *n.* समुचित मात्रा – *adv.* पर्याप्त (ही)
enquire (इन् क्वाइअर) दे. INQUIRE
enrage (इन् रेज) *vt.* बेहद गुस्सा दिलाना
enrapture (इन् रैप्चर) *vt.* आनंद-विभोर करना; मोहित करना
enrich (इन् रिच) *vt.* धनी बनाना, (में) व द्धि करना
enrol (इन् रोल) *vt.* सूची में नाम लिखना; भरती करना, सदस्य बनाना (-ll-) – *vi.* सदस्य बनना – **enrolment** *n.*
en route (आन् रूट) *Fr.* रास्ते में
ensconce (इन् स्कॉन्स) *vt.* छिपाना; सुरक्षित व आराम से रहते होना
ensemble (आन् साम्बल) *n.* संपूर्ण, समष्टि; स्त्री के सारे वस्त्र, सज्जा; अभिनेता, नर्तक आदि कलाकारों का दल अथवा समूह
enshrine (इन् श्राइन) *vt.* पूजा-स्थल में स्थापित करना; श्रद्धा व प्रेम से सुरक्षित रखना
enslave (इन् स्लेव़) *vt.* गुलाम बनाना; वशीभूत करना
ensnare (इन् स्नेंअर) *vt.* जाल आदि में फंसाना, बहकाना
ensue (इन् स्यू) *vi.* के परिणाम स्वरूप घटित होना
ensure (ऍन् शुअर) *vt.* सुरक्षित या सुनिश्चित करना
entail (इन् टेल) *vt.* के लिए आवश्यक होना
entangle (इन् टैंगल) *vt.* फंसाना, उलझाना
enter (ऍण्टर) *vt.* में प्रवेश कराना, घुसाना; (व्यवसाय आदि) में जाना; की शुरुआत करना; सम्मिलित होना; (नाम, आँकड़े आदि) दर्ज करना; सदस्य बनाना, भाग लेने के लिए नाम लिखाना – *vi.* अंदर आना – **entrance** (ऍन्ट्रन्स) *n.* प्रवेश; प्रवेश-द्वार; प्रवेश-मार्ग; प्रवेश-अधिकार; प्रवेश-शुल्क – **entrant** *n.* प्रवेशक (वि. प्रतियोगिता में) – **entry** *n.* प्रवेश; प्रवेश करना; दर्ज की गई संख्या, वस्तु आदि, जैसे लेखा सूची में – **enter into** पर बहस करना; में सक्रिय रूप से भाग लेना;

समझौता/अनुबन्ध करना; (बातचीत) शुरू करना

enterprise (ऍंण्टर्‌प्राइज़) *n.* साहसिक अथवा कठिनाइयों भरा कार्य; साहस; उत्साह (नया उद्यम प्रारंभ करने का); व्यापार; व्यापार-संगठन (कम्पनी) – **enterprising** *a.* उद्यमी; उत्साही

entertain (ऍण्टर्‌ˊटेन) *vt.* का मन बहलाना; अतिथि-सत्कार करना; विचार करना – **entertainer** *n.* नर्तक/नर्तकी; गायक/गायिका – **entertaining** *a.* मनोरंजक – **entertainment** *n.* मनोरंजन

enthral (इन्‌ˊथ्रॉल) *vt.* मोहित करना (-ll-)

enthusiasm (इन्‌ˊथ्यूज़िऐज़म) *n.* उत्साह, उमंग – **enthusiast** (इन्‌ˊथ्यूज़िऐस्ट) *n.* का ज़ोरदार समर्थक, उत्साही – **enthusiastic** (इन्थ्यूज़िˊऐस्टिक) *a.*

entice (इन्‌ˊटाइस) *vt.* फुसलाना, लालच देना

entire (इन्‌ˊटाइअर) *a.* सम्पूर्ण, सारा – **entirely** *adv.*पूर्ण रूप से – **entirety** (इन्‌ˊटाइअर्टि) *n.* सम्पूर्णता, अखण्डता

entitle (इन्‌ˊटाइटल) *vt.* अधिकार देना; (करने की) अनुमति देना; शीर्षक या नाम देना

entity (ˊऍण्टिटि) *n.* अस्तित्व; वास्तविक वस्तु

entomology (ऍण्टˊमॉलजि) *n.* कीट-विज्ञान

entomb (इन्‌ˊटूम) *vt.* मकबरे में म तशरीर को दफना देना

entourage (ऑन्टुˊराझ़) *n.* संगी-साथी; अनुचर

entrance[1] (ˊऍण्ट्रन्स) *n.* दे. ENTER

entrance[2] (इन्‌ˊट्रान्स) *vt.* मंत्रमुग्ध करना; सम्मोहित करना

entrap (इन्‌ˊट्रैप) *vt.* जाल में फांसना

entreat (इन्‌ˊट्रीट) *vt.* अनुनय-विनय करना – **entreaty** *n.* विनती

entrench (इनˊट्रैन्च) *vt.* खाइयों से घेरा बनाना, जमना – **entrenchment** *n.* – **entrenched** (इन्‌ˊट्रैन्चट) *a.* डटा हुआ

entrepreneur (ऑन्ट्रप्रˊनर) *n.* उद्यमकर्ता, उद्यमी

entropy (ˊऍण्ट्रपि) *n.* किसी तंत्र (सिस्टम) में व्यवस्था की कमी तथा समय के साथ इस कमी का बढ़ते जाना

entrust (इन्‌ˊट्रस्ट) *vt.* सौंपना, सुपुर्द करना

entwine (इन्‌ˊट्वाइन) *vt.* गूंथना; लिपटना

enumerate (इˊन्यूमरेट) *vt.* एक-एक का बारी-बारी नाम बताना; गिनना – **enumeration** (इन्यूमˊरेशन) *n.* गणना

enunciate (इˊनन्सिएट) *vt.* स्पष्ट रूप से व्यक्त करना; उच्चारण करना – **enunciation** (इनन्सिˊएशन) *n.* घोषणा, कथन, उच्चारण

envelop (इन्‌ˊवैलप) *vt.* लपेटना; ढंकना; घेरना

envelope (ˊऍन्वलोप, ऑन्व-) *n.* लिफ़ाफ़ा; आवरण

environment (इन्‌ˊवाइरन्‌मंट) *n.* वातावरण, पर्यावरण; अड़ोस-पड़ोस का – **environmental** *a.* – **environmentalist** *n.* पर्यावरण-विज्ञानी – **environs** *pl. n.* नगर के बाहर का शहरी क्षेत्र, उपनगरीय क्षेत्र

envisage (इन्‌ˊविज़िज) *vt.* की संभावना देखना; परिकल्पना करना

envoy (ˊऍन्वॉइ) *n.* विशेष राजदूत, राजदूत से पद में दूसरे स्थान पर राजनयिक

envy (ˊऍन्वि) *vt.* ईर्ष्या करना (**envied, envying**) – *n.* ईर्ष्या – **enviable** *a.* जो ईर्ष्या उत्पन्न करे – **envious** *a.* ईर्ष्यालु

enzyme (ˊऍन्ज़ाइम) *n.* कोशिकाओं द्वारा उत्पन्न प्रोटीनों का समूह जो अनेक जीव-रासायनिक प्रक्रियाओं में उत्प्रेरक का काम करता है, ऐन्ज़ाइम, किण्वक

ephemeral (इˊफ़ेमरल) *a.* क्षणिक, क्षण भंगुर

epic (ˊऍपिक) *n.* महाकाव्य, वीरगाथा – *a.* प्रभावशाली, भव्य (साहित्य रचना)

epicentre (ˊऍपिसेंण्टर) *n.* भूकम्प का अधिकेन्द्र, उत्केन्द्र

epicure (ऍंपिक्युअर) *n.* स्वादलोलुप, भोगवादी – **epicurean** (एपिक्युअ'रीअन) *a.*
epidemic (ऍपि'डेंमिक) *a.* (रोग) जो चारों ओर फैला हुआ हो – *n.* महामारी
epigram ('ऍपिग्रैम) *n.* सूक्ति, कहावत
epigraph ('ऍपिग्राफ़) *n.* शिलालेख; पुस्तक आदि के शुरू में उद्ध तवाक्य
epilepsy ('ऍपिलेंप्सि) *n.* मिरगी, अपस्मार – **epileptic** *n.* मिरगी का रोगी – *a.*
epilogue ('ऍपिलॉग) *n.* नाटक की अंतिम कविता या संवाद, भरत वाक्य
episcopal (इ'पिस्कपल) *a.* बिशप का या उसके अधिकार में
episode ('ऍपिसोड) *n.* घटना; प्रसंग; पुस्तक या दूरदर्शन के धारावाहिक कार्यक्रम का अंश
epistemology (इपिस्टि'मॉलजि) *n.* ज्ञान के स्रोत, स्वरूप और सीमाओं का अध्ययन, ज्ञान मीमांसा
epistle (इ'पिस्ल) *n.* चिट्ठी; पत्र; कविता लंबा पत्र
epitaph ('ऍपिटाफ़) *n.* समाधि लेख
epithet ('ऍपिथेंट) *n.* अतिरिक्त, या गुणसूचक शब्द या नाम, उपनाम; उपाधि – **epithetical** *a.*
epitome (इ'पिटमि) *n.* विशिष्ट उदाहरण; सार, सारांश
epoch ('ईपॉक) *n.* महत्वपूर्ण अवधि या काल का प्रारंभ, युग – **epoch-making** *a.* अत्यंत महत्वपूर्ण घटना जो अपना प्रभाव इतिहास पर छोड़ जाय
equal ('ईक्वल) *a.* (संख्या, आकार या गुण में) बराबर, समान; तुल्य; एक जैसा, सद श; सन्तुलित –*n.* जो किसी और के समान हो –*vt.* के बराबर होना – **equality** (इ'क्वॉलिटि) *n.* समानता, बराबरी, समता; सद श्यता – **equalization** (ईक्वलाइ'ज़ेशन) *n.* – **equalize** *v.* बराबर या समान बनाना या बनना
equanimity (इक्व'निमिटि) *n.* धीरज, धैर्य
equate (इ'क्वेट) *vt.* – **equate with** किसी को बराबर मानना या बनाना; एक समान स्तर पर लाना – **equation** (इ'क्वेशन) *n.* समीकरण; बराबर करने की क्रिया
equator (इ'क्वेटर) *n.* भूमध्य रेखा – **equatorial** (ऍक्व'टॉरिअल) *a.*
equestrian (इ'क्वेंस्ट्रिअन) *a.* घुड़सवारी का या उसमें दक्ष; घुड़सवार
equi-(*comb. form*) बराबर, जैसे **equilibrium** में
equidistant (ईक्वि'डिस्टंट) *a.* दो स्थानों से समान दूरी पर
equilateral (ईक्वि'लैटरल) *a.* समभुज, समबाहु
equilibrium (ईक्वि'लिब्रिअम) *n.* संतुलन, साम्य (*pl.* – **riums, -ria**)
equinox ('ईक्विनॉक्स) *n.* समय, जब सूर्य भूमध्य रेखा पार करता है और दिन और रात बराबर होते हैं (20 मार्च, 22 सितम्बर)
equip (इ'क्विप) *vt.* सजाना, सज्जित या लैस करना; तैयार करना (**-pp-**) – **equipment** (इ'क्विपमंट) *n.* उपकरण; (बिजली आदि का) सामान
equipoise ('ऍक्वपॉइज़) *n.* साम्यावस्था – *vt.* सन्तुलन स्थापित करना
equity ('ऍक्विटि) *n.* कंपनी के शेयरों का मूल्य; (**equities**) *pl.* कंपनी के शेयर – **equitable** *a.* न्यायसंगत; उचित
equivalent (इ'क्विवलंट) *a.* **equivalent(to)** के बराबर, समान, तुल्य; पर्यायवाची, समानार्थी; अनुरूप – **equivalence** *or* **equivalency** *n.* समानता, बराबरी
equivocal (इ'क्विव़कल) *a.* जिस के दो अर्थ या संदिग्ध अर्थ हो; जिस पर सन्देह हो सके – **equivocate** (इ'क्विव़केट) *vi.* किसी को गुमराह करने के लिए गोलमोल बात कहना –

equivocation (इक्विव´केशन) *n.* वाक्छल

era (´इअर्अ) *n.* युग; संवत्; काल

eradicate (इ´रैडिकेट) *vt.* मिटाना; नष्ट कर देना – **eradicable** *a.* **eradication** *n.* उन्मूलन

erase (इ´रेज़) *vt.* मिटाना (रबर के टुकड़े से लिखावट आदि); टेप पर रिकार्ड की गयी आवाज़ मिटाना – **eraser** *n.* लिखावट मिटाने का रबर – **erasure** *n.*

erect (इ´रेक्ट) *a.* सीधा खड़ा; खड़ा (पुरुष-लिंग) – *vt.* खड़ा करना; निर्माण करना, बनाना – **erection** (इ´रेक्शन) *n.* (पुरुष-लिंग, भवन) खड़े होने/करने की क्रिया

ermine (´अर्मिन) *n.* उत्तरी क्षेत्रों का नेवले जैसा जीव जिसकी खाल सफेद और रोएंदार होती है; उसकी सफेद खाल

erode (इ´रोड) *vt.* काटना; खा जाना; धीरे-धीरे समाप्त कर देना – **erosion** (इ´रोझ़न) *n.* कटाव

erotic (इ´रॉटिक) *a.* काम विषयक, काम सुख से सम्बन्धित – **eroticism** *n.* श्रृंगारिकता; कामुकता

err (अर) *vi.* भूल करना – **erratic** (इ´रैटिक) *a.* अनियमित (गति या व्यवहार में); सनकी, मनमौजी – **erratically** *adv.* – **erroneous** (इ´रोनियस) *a.* भ्रांतिपूर्ण, गलत – **error** (´ऐरर) *n.* भूल, गलती

errand (´ऐरंड) *n.* किसी काम के लिए संक्षिप्त यात्रा; काम (जो किसी को सौंपा जाय); सन्देशवाहक का काम; उद्देश्य

errant (´ऐरंट) *a.* जो साहसिक कामों के लिए इधर उधर घूमता फिरे; पथभ्रष्ट, गुमराह

erst, erstwhile (अर्स्ट, ´अर्स्ट्वाइल) *adv.* कुछ समय पहले तक का, भूतपूर्व

erudite (´ऐरुडाइट) *a.* विद्वान – **erudition** (ऐरु´डिशन) *n.* पण्डित्य

erupt (इ´रप्ट) *vi.* फूटना; अचानक व तेजी से (लड़ाई आदि) होने लगना – **eruption** (इ´रप्शन) *n.* फूटना

escalate (´ऐस्कलेट) *v.* (व्यापकता या प्रचंडता) बढ़ना

escalator (´ऐस्कलेटर) *n.* चलती सीढ़ी, चल-सोपान

escape (इ´स्केप) *vi.* मुक्त हो जाना; बच निकलना; दण्ड से बच जाना; भाग निकलना, (गैस आदि) निकल जाना – *vt.* से बच जाना; भुला दिया जाना – *n.* पलायन; बचाव; (गैस) निकलने की क्रिया – **escapade** (´ऐस्क पेड) *n.* शरारत भरा साहसिक काम – **escapism** *n.* कड़वे यथार्थ से बचने के लिए कल्पना का सहारा लेने की प्रव ति; पलायनवाद

eschew (इस्´चू) *vt.* परे रहना, से बचना, परहेज़ करना

escort *n.* (´ऐस्कॉर्ट) यात्री आदि का रक्षा गारद; व्यक्ति जो किसी को लिवा ले जा रहा हो – *vt.* (इस्´कार्ट) रक्षा गारद का किसी को लिवा कर ले जाना

Eskimo (´ऐस्किमो) *n.* एस्कीमो, उत्तर अमरीका महाद्वीप, ग्रीनलैंड आदि शीत प्रधान देशों की आदिम जाति; उस की भाषा (*pl.*-**mos**)

esoteric (ऐसो´टेरिक) *a.* गूढ़; अस्पष्ट; गुप्त

esp. especially का संक्षेप

especial (इ´स्पेशल) *a.* विशिष्ट, विशेष – **especially** *adv.* विशेष रूप से, खास तौर पर

espionage (´ऐस्पिअनाझ़) *n.* जासूसी; गुप्तचरों का प्रयोग

esplanade (´ऐस्प्ल´नेड) *n.* मैदान, विशे. जहां लोग सैर के लिए जाते हों

espouse (इ´स्पाउज़) *vt.* समर्थन करना

espresso (ऐ´स्प्रेसो) *n.* काफ़ी में से भाप गुज़ार कर बनायी काफ़ी

esprit de corps (एस्प्री ड ´कॉर) अपने समाज/संगठन के प्रति प्यार/निष्ठा की भावना

espy (इ'स्पाइ) *vt.* देखना; ताड़ना

essay *n.* (ऍसे) निबन्ध, लेख; प्रयत्न – *vt.* (ऍसे) प्रयत्न या कोशिश करना; परिश्रम या जांच करना (**essayed, essaying**) – **essayist** *n.* निबन्ध-लेखक

essence (ऍसंस) *n.* सार, तत्व, सारांश; अस्तित्व; जीवन; सत्ता; यथार्थ; आसव, अरक, सुगन्धि – **essential** (इ'सेंन्शल) *a.* आवश्यक या अनिवार्य (तत्व) – *n.* मुख्य बातें – **essentiality** – **essentially** *adv.* आवश्यक रूप से

establish (इ'स्टैब्लिश) *vt.* द ढ़ या स्थिर करना; स्थापित करना; प्रतिष्ठित करना; प्रमाणित करना – **establishment** *n.* संगठित संगठन आदि, संस्थान; प्रतिष्ठान; घर-ग हस्थी; उद्यम या व्यापार; सार्वजनिक संस्था – **the Establishment** *n.* किसी समाज का सत्ता सम्पन्न वर्ग या समूह

estate (इ'स्टेट) *n.* जमीन-जायदाद, जागीर; सम्पत्ति, सम्पदा; सम्पत्ति के विकास का क्षेत्र, विशे. जहां कारखाने और मकान हों; राष्ट्र के अंग के रूप में वर्ग; जीवन में दर्जा, स्थिति या परिस्थिति – **estate agent** मकानों के खरीदने बेचने वाला दलाल

esteem (इ'स्टीम) *vt.* सम्मान या आदर करना; समझना, मानना – *n.* सम्मान, आदर, श्रद्धा

estimate (ऍस्टिमेट) *vt.* (राशि, नाप आदि का) अनुमान लगाना; कूतना, आंकना; के बारे में राय बनाना; संभावित मूल्य बताना – *n.* (ऍस्टमिट) अनुमान, अंदाजा; राय; अनुमानित या आंकलित राशि; ठेकेदार द्वारा बताई गयी कीमत – **estimable** *a.* आदरणीय – **estimation** *n.* राय, विचार; आदर, सम्मान

estrange (इ'स्ट्रेंज) *vt.* (किसी का) प्यार खो बैठना; से अलग कर देना – **estrangement** *n.* अलगाव, मनमुटाव

estuary (ऍस्ट्युअरि) *n.* नदी का मुहाना (जहां ज्वार आते हों)

etc. & c. et cetera का संक्षेप

et cetera (इट् 'सेंट्रा) *Lat.* आदि, वगैरा, इत्यादि (संक्षेप etc. & c.)

etch (ऍच) *vt.* धातु की पट्टी पर तेज़ाब से लिखना या आक ति बनाना, उकेरना; स्पष्ट छाप छोड़ना

eternal (इ'टर्नल) *a.* जिस का आदि अंत न हो, शाश्वत, नित्य – **eternally** *adv.* – **eternity** (इ'टर्निटि) *n.* अनन्तकाल, शाश्वत्व – **eternal triangle** स्थिति जिसमें दो पुरुष एक स्त्री से या दो स्त्रियां एक पुरुष से प्रेम करें या सम्बंध रखें

ethereal (इ'थिअरिअल) *a.* हल्का, वायु जैसा; पारलौकिक; प्रेतात्मा जैसा

ethic(al) (ऍथिक, 'ऍथिकल) *a.* नैतिकता सम्बन्धी – **ethically** *adv.* – **ethics** (ऍथिक्स) *n.* नीति शास्त्र, आचरण शास्त्र; नैतिक सिद्धांत; आचरण-नियम

ethnic ('ऍथ्निक) *a.* एक ही सांस्क तिक परम्परा में बंधे राष्ट्र, जाति अथवा कबीले से संबन्धित

ethos ('ईथॉस) *n.* किसी समाज विशेष या उस की संस्क ति के विशिष्ट गुण या उन का सार, जातिगत स्वभाव या आचार

etiquette (ऍटिकेंट) *n.* शिष्टाचार

etymology (ऍटि'मॉलजि) *n.* शब्दों की व्युत्पति का विज्ञान, निरुक्त

EU European Union का संक्षेप

eucalyptus (यूक'लिप्टस) *n.* गन्ध सफ़ेदा, सफ़ेदा

eugenic (यू'जेंनिक) *a.* अच्छी संतान की उत्पत्ति से सम्बन्धित या उसमें सहायक, सुजननिक – **eugenics** *n.* सुजनन विज्ञान

eulogy ('यूलजि) *n.* गुणगान – **eulogize** *vt.* प्रशंसा करना, का गुणगान करना

eunuch ('यूनक) *n.* हिजड़ा; नपुंसक; शक्तिहीन, प्रभावहीन व्यक्ति

euphemism (´यूफ़िमिज़म) *n.* कठोर या अप्रिय शब्द के स्थान पर हल्के शब्द का प्रयोग; प्रियोक्ति – **euphemistic** *a.* मंगलभाषी
euphoria (यू´फ़ॉरिअ) *n.* सुखबोध, सुखाभास
euphuism (´यूफ़्यूइज़म) *n.* शब्दाडम्बर, लच्छेदार भाषा
eureka (यु´रीकअ) *interj.* पा लिया-मिल गया!
euro (´युअरो) *n.* (*symbol* €) युरोपियन यूनियन के अनेक देशों में मुद्रा की इकाई
Euro- (´युअरो) *comb. form* युरोप/युरोपियन यूनियन संबन्धी/का
European (युअर´पिअन) *n./a.* युरोप का (निवासी या नागरिक); **European Economic Community** (EEC) युरोप के देशों का व्यापार संघ
euthanasia (यूथ´नेज़िअ) *n.* बिना पीड़ा के म त्यु, सुखम त्यु; किसी को प्राणान्तक पीड़ा से बचाने के लिए इस प्रकार मार डालना
evacuate (इ´वैक्युएट) *vt.* खाली करना; मलोत्सर्ग करना – **evacuation** (इवैक्यु´एशन) *n.* – **evacuee** (इवैक्यु´ई) *n.* शरणार्थी; व्यक्ति जिसे खतरे के स्थान से हटा लिया गया हो
evade (इ´वेड) *vt.* टालमटोल करना; बच निकलना – **evasion** (इ´वेझ़न) *n.* टाल मटोल, बहाने बाजी; संदिग्ध या द्व्यर्थक बात – **evasive** (इ´वेसिव़) *a.*
evaluate (इ´वैल्युएट) *vt.* मूल्यांकन करना – **evaluation** (इवैल्यु´एशन) *n.* मूल्यांकन
evangelical (ईवैन्´जेलिकल) *a.* ईसाई मत का प्रबल प्रचारक जो प्रयत्न करें कि लोग उसके विचारों को अपना लें – *n.* इस मत का अनुयायी
evaporate (इ´वैपरेट) *vi.* भाप बन कर सूख जाना – *vt.* भाप बना कर सुखा देना – **evaporation** (इवैप´रेशन) *n.* वाष्पीकरण – **evaporator** *n.*
evasion (इ´वेझ़न) दे. EVADE

eve (ईव़) *n.* पूर्व संध्या (उत्सव आदि की), किसी घटना से तुरंत पहले का समय
even (´ईव़न) *a.* समतल, बराबर, संतुलित; (संख्या) जिसे दो से भाग दिया जा सके, निष्पक्ष – *vt.* बराबर या समतल बनाना; सन्तुलित करना – *adv.* भी; से भी; जैसा कि; जिस समय; के बावजूद (किसी बात पर बल देने के लिए प्रयुक्त)
evening (´ईव़्निंग) *n.* संध्या, शाम; *Fig* ह्रास; अंत
event (इ´वेंण्ट) *n.* घटना; उल्लेखनीय घटना; परिस्थिति, खेलों में कोई कार्यक्रम – **eventful** *a.* महत्वपूर्ण; जिसमें सनसनीखेज़ घटनाएं हों – **eventual** (इ´वेन्चुअल) *a.* अंतिम; संभावित – **eventuality** *n.* संभावित घटना – **eventually** *adv.* अंत में
ever (´एव़र) *adv.* सदा, हमेशा; लगातार, किसी भी समय – **evergreen** *n./a.* सदाबहार (पौधा, झाड़ी आदि) – **evermore** *adv.* सदा, हमेशा
every (´एव़्रि) *a.* प्रत्येक, हर कोई; हर संभव – **everybody** *n.* प्रत्येक व्यक्ति – **everyday** *a.* सामान्य; साधारण – **everyone** *n.* हर एक – **everything** *n.* सब कुछ – **everywhere** *adv.* सर्वत्र, सब जगह
evict (इ´विक्ट) *vt.* निकाल देना; (कानूनी प्रक्रिया से) बेदख़ल करना – **eviction** *n.* बेदखली
evident (´एविड़ंट) *a.* प्रत्यक्ष; सुस्पष्ट – **evidence** (´एविड़ंस) *n.* प्रमाण, सबूत; लक्षण, संकेत; गवाही, साक्ष्य – *vt.* बताना या संकेत करना; प्रमाणित करना – **evidently** *adv.*
evil (´ईव़ल) *a.* बुरा; हानिकर – *n.* बुराई; दुष्टता; पाप – **evildoer** *n.* पापी
evince (इ´विन्स) *vt.* दिखाना, प्रदर्शित करना
evocative (इ´वॉकटिव़) *a.* जो कोई पुरानी अच्छी याद जगाये (गंध, भाव, स्थान आदि की), प्रबोधक

evoke (इ'वोक) *vt.* आह्वान करना; याद करना – **evocation** (ऍव'केशन) *n.*

evolve (इ'वॉल्व) *v.* धीरे धीरे विकसित करना या होना – *vi.* वृद्धि की प्रक्रिया में धीरे धीरे बदल जाना – **evolution** (ईव'लूशन) *n.* विकास; विकास क्रम

ewe (यू) *n.* मादा भेड़

ex. example, excepted, extra का संक्षेप

ex-, (*comb. form*) से बाहर, से पहले, जैसे **ex-president**

exacerbate (इग्'ज़ैसर्बेट, इक्'सैसर्बेट) *vt.* तीव्र या प्रचण्ड करना; कटु बनाना; और खराब करना

exact (इग्'ज़ैक्ट) *a.* सही, यर्थाथ, यथा तथ्य – *vt.* मांगना; बलपूर्वक ले लेना; कर लेना – **exacting** *a.* कड़ा, सख्त – **exaction** (इग्'ज़ैक्शन) *n.* बलपूर्वक लेने की क्रिया – **exactitude** (इग्'ज़ैक्टिट्यूड) *n.* – **exactly** *adv.* ठीक यही – **exactness** *n.* यथा तथ्य, यथार्थता

exaggerate (इग्'ज़ैजरेट) *vt.* बढ़ा चढ़ा कर कहना – **exaggeration** *n.* अतिश्योक्ति

exalt (इग्'ज़ॉल्ट) *vt.* उन्नत करना, ऊंचा उठाना; प्रशंसा करना; उदात्त बनाना; प्रतिष्ठा देना

exam. *n.* **examination** का संक्षेप

examine (इग्'ज़ैमिन) *vt.* जांच पड़ताल करना; पता लगाना; परीक्षा लेना – **examination** *n.* – **examinee** (इग्ज़ैमि'नी) *n.* परीक्षार्थी – **examiner** *n.* परीक्षक

example (इग्'ज़ाम्पल) *n.* उदाहरण, दृष्टांत; नमूना, बानगी; चेतावनी

exasperate (इग्'ज़ास्परेट) *vt.* चिढ़ाना; गुस्सा दिलाना – **exasperation** (इग्ज़ास्प'रेशन) *n.*

excavate ('ऍक्सकवेट) *vt.* खुदाई करना, खोखला करना – **excavation** (ऍक्सक'वेशन) *n.* खुदाई – **excavator** *n*

exceed (इक्'सीड) *vt.* से अधिक होना, से आगे बढ़ जाना

excel (इक्'सेंल) *vt.* से बढ़ कर होना, से बेहतर होना – *vi.* (किसी क्षेत्र में) बहुत अच्छा होना, विशिष्ट होना (-ll-) – **excellence** ('ऍक्सलन्स) *n.* – **excellency** *n.* राजदूत आदि का सम्बोधन, महामहिम – **excellent** *a.* श्रेष्ठ, उत्तम

except (इक्'सेंप्ट) *prep.* को छोड़ कर, के सिवाय; परन्तु; *conj.* यदि – *vt.* छोड़ देना, निकाल देना-**excepting** *prep.* को छोड़ कर – **exception** (इक्'सेंप्शन) *n.* अपवाद; आपत्ति – **exceptionable** *a.*आपत्ति योग्य – **exceptional** *a.* असाधारण – **take exception to sth** पर कड़ा एतराज़ करना

excerpt *n.* ('ऍक्सर्प्ट) पुस्तक आदि से उद्धरण – *vt.* (ऍक्'सर्प्ट) उद्धरण या हवाला देना

excess (इक्'सेंस) *n.* मात्रा जो फालतू हो, अधिशेष; बाहुल्य, प्राचुर्य; अति, असंयम, मर्यादा रहित आचरण – **excessive** *a.* बहुत अधिक

exchange (इक्स्'चेंज) *vt.* आदान प्रदान, अदला बदली या विनिमय करना – *n.* विनिमय; आदान प्रदान; मुद्रा विनिमय; किसी वस्तु के बदले दी गयी वस्तु; बातचीत; टेलिफोन केन्द्र

exchequer (इक्स्'चेंकर) *n.* राजस्व विभाग, राजकोष – **the Exchequer** ब्रिटेन का राजस्व विभाग

excise[1] (ऍक्'साइज़) *n.* उत्पादन शुल्क, आबकारी

excise[2] (इक्'साइज़) *vt.* काट निकालना – **excision** (ऍक्'सिझन) *n.* काट देने की क्रिया

excite (इक्'साइट) *vt.* उत्तेजित करना, भड़काना, उकसाना, उभाड़ना; उत्पन्न करना – **excitable** *a.* शीघ्र उत्तेजित हो जाने वाला – **excitement** (इक्'साइट्मंट) *n.* उत्तेजना

exclaim (इक्स्'क्लेम) *v.* अचानक बोल उठना; चिल्ला उठना – **exclamation** (ऍक्स्क्ल'मेशन) *n.* सहसा बोल उठने की क्रिया, विस्मयादिबोधक चिन्ह (!) – **exclamatory** *a.*

exclude (इक्स्'क्लूड) *vt.* सम्मिलित न करना, निकाल देना, अलग रखना करना –**exclusion** (इक्स्'क्लूझ़न) *n.* बहिष्करण; बहिष्कार – **exclusive** (इक्स्'क्लूसिव़) *a.* एकमात्र; विशिष्ट – *n.* एकमात्र, वि. कोई समाचार या लेख जो एक ही समाचार पत्र में प्रकाशित हो

excommunicate (ऍक्स्क'म्यूनिकेट) *vt.* बहिष्क त करना, निकाल देना (चर्च आदि से) – **excommunication** *n.*

excrement ('ऍक्स्क्रिमंट) *n.* मल, विष्ठा

excruciating (इक्'स्क्रूशिएटिंग) *a.* भीषण (पीड़ा आदि)

excursion (इक्'स्कर्शन) *n.* सैर-सपाटा, भ्रमण; विषयान्तर

excuse *vt.* (इक्'स्क्यूज़) क्षमा करना, माफ़ करना; (दोष, भूल की) अनदेखी करना; छोड़ देना; माफ़ करना (जुर्माना आदि) – *n.* (इक्'स्क्यूस) बहाना; क्षमा याचना – **excusable** *a.* – **excuse me!** प्रयोग किये जाने वाले शब्द जब ध्यान आकर्षित करना हो; निकलने के लिए रास्ता मांगना हो; थोड़े से अनुचित व्यवहार के लिए माफी मांगनी हो

execrable ('ऍक्सिक्रबल) *a.* घिनौना

execute ('ऍक्सिक्यूट) *vt.* प्राण दण्ड या फांसी देना; पूरा करना, पालन करना; बनाना; कानूनी दस्तावेज़ पर हस्ताक्षर करना – **executant** *n.* निष्पादक; वादक या गायक – **execution** (ऍक्सि'क्यूशन) *n.* फांसी, प्राणदण्ड – **executioner** *n.* जल्लाद – **executive** (इग्'जेंक्यटिव़) *n.* प्रशासन में अधिकारी; कार्यकारी या प्रशासनिक संगठन; किसी समाज/संगठन की कार्यकारिणी – *a.* कार्यकारी, विशे. सरकारी कानून लागू करने वाली शाखा – **executor** *n.* वसीयत लागू करने के लिए नियुक्त व्यक्ति, निष्पादक (**executrix** *fem.*)

exemplar (इग्'ज़ेम्प्लर) *n.* आदर्श – **exemplary** (इग्ज़ेम्'प्लरि) *a.* अनुकरणीय

exemplify (इग्'जेंम्प्लिफ़ाइ) *vt.* का उदाहरण या द ष्टांत होना (**-fied, -fying**)

exempt (इग्'ज़ेम्प्ट, इग्'ज़ेम्ट) *vt.* से मुक्त करना, से छूट या माफ़ी देना – *a.* जिसे छूट या विमुक्ति मिली हो, विमुक्त – **exemption** (इग्'ज़ेम्पशन इग्'जैम्शन) *n.* छूट, विमुक्ति

exercise ('ऍक्सर्साइज़) *vt.* का प्रयोग करना, प्रयोग में लाना; अभ्यास या व्यायाम कराना; (आदेश या जिम्मेदारी का) पालन करना; परेशान करना – *vi.* व्यायाम करना – *n.* व्यायाम; अभ्यास; कसरत; पाठ; पालन; प्रयोग (किसी अंग या इन्द्रिय का); (अधिकार) प्रयोग – **exercise book** अभ्यास पुस्तिका, कापी, नोटबुक

exert (इग्'ज़र्ट) *vt.* प्रयास या परिश्रम करना; दबाव, प्रभाव आदि डालना – **exertion** (इग्'ज़र्शन) *n.* प्रयास; परिश्रम

ex gratia (ऍक्स 'ग्रेश्अ) *a.* अनुग हपूर्वक दी गयी (राशि आदि)

exhale (ऍक्स्'हेल, इग्'ज़ेल) *v.* सांस या धुंआ छोड़ना

exhaust (इग'ज़ॉस्ट) *vt.* थका देना; इस्तेमाल कर लेना; (जिस से कुछ न बचे) समाप्त करना; (किसी विषय) पर सभी पहलुओं से विचार करना – *n.* कार आदि के इंजन से निकली गैस; ऐसी गैस के निकलने का रास्ता – **exhausted** *a.* थका हुआ – **exhaustion** (इग्'ज़ॉस्चन) *n.* अत्यधिक थकान, क्लांति – **exhaustive** *a.* सर्वांगीन, ब्यौरेवार

exhibit (इग्'ज़िबिट) *vt.* प्रदर्शन करना – *n.* प्रदर्शित वस्तु – **exhibition** (ऍक्सि'बिशन) *n.* प्रदर्शनी, नुमाइश – **exhibitionist** *n.* व्यक्ति जिसे आत्मप्रदर्शन की ललक हो – **exhibitor** (इग्'ज़िबिटर) *n.* प्रदर्शक, विशे. किसी नाटक, फिल्म आदि का

exhilarate (इग्'ज़िलरेट) *vt.* सजीव बना देना; प्रसन्न या आल्हादित कर देना –

exhilarating (इग् ज़िलरेटिंग) *a.* – **exhilaration** (इग्ज़िल 'रेशन) *n.* उल्लास
exhort (इग् 'जॉर्ट) *vt.* प्रेरित या उत्साहित करना; आग्रह करना (किसी काम के लिए) – **exhortation** (इग्जॉर् 'टेशन) *n.*
exhume (ऍक्स 'हयूम) *vt.* गड़ी हुई वस्तु (शव आदि) खोद कर निकालना – **exhumation** (ऍक्सहयू 'मेशन) *n.*
exigent ('ऍक्सिजंट) *a.* अत्यावश्यक, लाज़मी; बहुत जल्दी का – **exigence, exigency** *n.* अत्यावश्यकता; आपातकाल, संकट
exile ('ऍग्ज़ाइल, 'ऍक्साइल) *n.* देश निकाला, निर्वासन; व्यक्ति जिसे देश निकाला मिला हो – *vt.* देश निकाला देना
exist (इग् 'ज़िस्ट) *vi.* होना, अस्तित्व होना, जीवित होना; विद्यमान होना, बने रहना – **existence** (इग् 'ज़िस्टन्स) *n.* अस्तित्व – **existent** *a.* – **existing** *a.* वर्तमान
exit ('एग्ज़िट, 'एक्सिट) *n.* निकास, बाहर का रास्ता; बाहर जाने की क्रिया; मत्यु; रंगमंच से अभिनेता का जाना – *vi.* बाहर जाना – **exit poll** चुनाव परिणाम का अनुमान लगाने के लिए मतदान के तुरंत बाद लोगों से पूछना कि उन्होंने किसे वोट दिया है
exodus ('ऍक्सडस) *n.* जाना, विशे. भीड़ का; (E-) बाइबल के पुराने खण्ड (**Old Testament**) का दूसरा भाग
ex officio ('ऍक्स् अ 'फ़िशिओ) *Lat.* पद के अधिकार से, पदेन
exonerate (इग् 'ज़ॉनरेट) *vt.* बरी करना, निर्दोष ठहराना
exorbitant (इग् 'ज़ॉर्बिटंट) *a.* बहुत अधिक, हद से ज्यादा
exorcise ('ऍक्सॉर्साइज़) *vt.* भूत-प्रेत को भगाना – **exorcism** ('ऍक्सॉर्सिज़म) *n.* भूत-प्रेत भगाने की क्रिया, झाड़-फूंक; बुरे अनुभव या कटु स्मतियों को भुलाने की क्रिया – **exorcist** *n.* ओझा
exotic (इग् 'ज़ाटिक) *a.* जो विदेश से लाया जाय, विदेशी, विरला; अनोखा; आकर्षक; मनोहारी – **exotica** विदेशी या अन्य स्थानिक वस्तुओं का संग्रह
expand (इक् 'स्पैंड) *v.* फैलाना, प्रसारित करना; फुलाना; बढ़ाना, विस्तार करना, विकसित करना – **expandable,** – **ible** *a.* – **expanse** (इक् 'स्पैंस) *n.* विस्तत स्थान; खुला मैदान – **expansion** (इक् 'स्पैंशन) *n.* विस्तार; विकास – **expansionism** *n.* विस्तार/प्रभाव बढ़ाने की प्रवत्ति – **expansive** *a.* लम्बा चौड़ा, विस्तत; मिलनसार; बातूनी
expatiate (इक् 'स्पेशिएट) *vi.* (*on* के साथ) सविस्तार बोलना या लिखना; विस्तार में जाना
expatriate (एक्स् 'पैट्रिएट) – *a./n.* जो अपना देश छोड़ कर दूसरे देश में बस गया हो, प्रवासी
expect (इक् 'स्पेक्ट) *vt.* प्रतीक्षा करना या राह देखना; आशा करना – **expectancy** (इक् 'स्पेक्टंसि) *n.* प्रत्याशा; आशा – **expectant** (इक् 'स्पेक्टंट) *a.* प्रत्याशी; मां बनने वाली (स्त्री) – **expectation** (ऍक्स्पेक् 'टेशन) *n.* भविष्य के उज्जवल होने की आशा; अपेक्षा; संभावना – (~ **s**) *pl.* किसी की वसीयत से लाभ होने की आशा – **be expecting a child** मां बनने वाली होना
expectorate (ऍक् 'स्पेक्टरेट) *v.* (*formal*) थूकना
expedient (इक् 'स्पीडिअंट) *a.* उचित, सुविधाजनक; कार्यसाधक – *n.* कार्य साधक उपाय (जो संकट में काम आए) – **expediency** *n.* कार्य साधकता
expedite ('ऍक्स्पिडाइट) *vt.* काम में तेज़ी लाना; शीघ्र पूरा करना – **expedition** (ऍक्सपि 'डिशन) *n.* अभियान; खोज यात्रा; अभियान के सदस्य व उपकरण – **expeditionary** *a.*
expel (इक् 'स्पेल) *vt.* बाहर निकालना, निष्कासित करना; बहिष्कार करना (**-ll-**) –

expulsion *n.* निष्कासन; खदेड़ने की क्रिया – **expulsive** *a.*

expend (इक्'स्पेंण्ड) *vt.* खर्च करना; लगा देना – **expendable** *a.* इस्तेमाल हो जाने या नष्ट होने वाला या होने के लिए रखा गया – **expenditure** (इक्'स्पेंन्डिचर) *n.* खर्च; व्यय – **expense** (इक्'स्पेंन्स) *n.* लागत; खर्च (का कारण) – *pl.* खर्च; व्यय की गयी राशि – **expensive** *a.* महंगा, बहुमूल्य, कीमती

experience (इक्'स्पिअरिअंस) *n.* अनुभव; तजुर्बा; अनुभूति (किसी घटना की); घटना – *vt.* (का) अनुभव करना; भोगना; मिलना या साक्षात्कार होना – **experienced** *a.* अनुभवी; कार्यकुशल या दक्ष

experiment (इक्'स्पेरिमन्ट) *n.* प्रयोग; परीक्षण – *vi.* प्रयोग या परीक्षण करना – **experimental** (एक्स्पेरि'मेंन्टल) *a.*

expert ('ऐक्स्पर्ट) *n.* विशेषज्ञ, माहिर – *a.* कुशल, प्रवीण – **expertise** (एक्स्पर्'टीज़) *n.* विशेषज्ञ ज्ञान

expiate ('ऐक्सपिएट) *vt.* दण्ड भोगना; प्रायश्चित करना

expire (इक्'स्पाइअर) *vi.* की अवधि समाप्त होना; मर जाना – *vt.* (सांस) छोड़ना – **expiry** (इक्'स्पाइअरि) *n.* अन्त; समाप्ति (अवधि आदि की)

explain (इक्'स्प्लेन) *vt.* स्पष्ट करना; समझाना; व्याख्या करना, अर्थ बताना; कारण बताना, सफाई देना – **explanation** *n.* स्पष्टीकरण व्याख्या – **explanatory** *a.* व्याख्यात्मक

expletive (इक्'स्प्लीटिव़) *n.* सहसा निकला उद्गार; गाली

explicable ('ऐक्स्प्लिकबल) *a.* जिस की व्याख्या की जा सके

explicit (इक्'स्प्लिसिट) *a.* ब्यौरेवार; स्पष्ट

explode (इक्'स्लोड) *vi.* धमाके से फटना; विस्फोट होना; (जनसंख्या का) तेज़ी से बढ़ना – *vt.* विस्फोट करना; खण्डन करना – **explosion** (इक्'स्लोझ़न) *n.* विस्फोट – **explosive** (इक्'स्लोसिव़) *a./n.* विस्फोटक (पदार्थ)

exploit *n.* ('ऐक्स्प्लॉइट) कारनामा, करतब – *vt.* (इक्स्'प्लॉइट) से लाभ उठाना; शोषण करना – **exploitation** *n.* शोषण

explore (इक्'स्लॉर) *vt.* छानबीन करना; खोज करना; पता लगाना; परीक्षण या जांच पड़ताल करना; किसी देश की यात्रा करके उसके बारे मे पता लगाना – **exploration** (ऐक्स्प्लॉ'रेशन) *n.* खोज; खोजबीन – **exploratory** *a.* – **explorer** *n.* खोजी; अन्वेषक

explosion (इक्'स्लोझ़न) देखिए EXPLODE

expo ('ऐक्स्पो) *n. inf.* **exposition** का संक्षेप

exponent (इक्'स्पोनंट) *n.* व्यक्ति जो किसी विचाराधारा का प्रतिपादन करे; *Math* घातांक – **exponential** (ऐक्स्पो'नेंन्शल) *a.*

export *vt.* (इक'स्पॉर्ट) निर्यात करना – *n./a.* ('एक्सपॉर्ट) निर्यात (का) – **exporter** *n.* निर्यातक

expose (इक्'स्पोज़) *vt.* प्रदर्शन करना, दिखाना; खोल देना, उघाड़ना; पोल खोलना, बताना (रहस्य आदि); बिना सहारे के छोड़ देना; खतरे आदि में डालना; फोटो ख चना – **exposure** (इक्'स्पोझ़र) *n.* अनावरण; प्रदर्शन; तजुर्बा; फोटो ख चने की क्रिया – **exposed** *a.* अनाव त; बिना किसी ओट के

exposé (ऐक्स्'पोज़े) *n.* समाचारपत्र आदि में किसी घोटाले या अपराध का भण्डाफोड़

exposition (ऐक्स्प'ज़िशन) देखिए EXPOUND

expostulate (इक्'स्पॉस्ट्युलेट) *vi.* विरोध प्रकट करना; बहस करना या आपत्ति करना – **expostulation** (इक्स्पॉस्ट्यु'लेशन) *n.*

expound (इक्'स्पाउंट) *vt.* प्रतिपादन करना; व्याख्या करना – **exposition** (ऍक्स्प'ज़िशन) *n.* व्याख्या; विवरण; प्रदर्शनी **expositor** (इक्'स्पॉज़िटर) *n.* प्रतिपादक, व्याख्याकार; टीकाकार – **expository** *a.* व्याख्यात्मक

express (इक्'स्प्रेस) *vt.* प्रकट करना; अभिव्यक्त करना – *a.* स्पष्ट साफ़, सुनिश्चित; सोचा समझा; विशेष रूप से तैयार; तेज़गामी; विशेष रूप से भेजा गया; तेज़ (गाड़ी) – *adv.* विशेष रूप से; विशेष उद्देश्य से; तेज़ी से – *n.* तेज़ चलने वाली गाड़ी या द्रुत; जल्दी पार्सल पहुंचाने की सेवा – **expression** (इक्'स्प्रेशन) *n.* अभिव्यक्ति; शब्द या शब्दावली, मुहावरा; (चेहरे का) भाव, भंगिमा, मुद्रा; भावना; कही गयी बात – **expressive** *a.* अर्थपूर्ण, सार्थक – **expressionless** *a.* भावहीन

expulsion (इक्'स्पल्शन) *n.* देखिए EXPEL

expunge (इक्'स्पंज) *vt.* (नाम, टिप्पणी) काट देना; (स्म ति) मिटा देना, (कार्यवाही से) निकाल देना – **expunction** (इक्'स्पंक्शन) *n.* कार्यवाही से निकाल देने की क्रिया

expurgate (ऍक्स्पर्गेट) *vt.* (पुस्तक आदि से) आपत्तिजनक शब्द निकाल देना; परिशोधन करना

exquisite (ऍक्स्क्विज़िट) *a.* उत्क ष्ट उत्तम – **exquisitely** *adv.*

extant (ऍक्'स्टेंन्ट) *a.* वर्तमान, विद्यमान

extempore (इक्'स्टेंम्परि) *a./adv.* बिना पहले से तैयारी किए; तत्काल प्रस्तुत – **extemporize** (इक्'स्टेंम्पराइज़) *vt.* बिना तैयारी के बोलना या प्रस्तुत करना

extend (इक्'स्टेंण्ड) *vt.* तानना, फैलाना; लम्बा करना; (अवधि) बढ़ाना; विस्त त करना (क्षेत्र); देना – *vi.* बढ़ना; क्षेत्र में फैलना – **extendable, extendible, extensible** *a.* जिसे बढ़ाया जा सके – **extension** (इक्'स्टेंन्शन) *n.* विस्तार, प्रसार, फैलाव; समय या अवधि बढ़ाने की क्रिया; अतिरिक्त उपकरण (लाइन) जैसे टेलिफोन का – **extensive** *a.* व्यापक – **extent** *n.* विस्तार; प्रसार; फैलाव; परिमाण; सीमा; आयाम – **extension cord/lead** विद्युत उपकरण के साथ लगी अतिरिक्त तार

extenuate (इक्'स्टेंन्युएट) *vt.* प्रकोप कम करना (दोष, अपराध का); घटाना, हल्का करना – **extenuation** (इकस्टेंन्यु'एशन) *n.*

exterior (इक्'स्टिअरिअर) *n.* बाहरी भाग; बाहरी रूप – *a.* बाहरी

exterminate (इक्'स्टर्मिनेट) *vt.* पूरी तरह नष्ट कर देना – **extermination** *n.* विध्वंस, उन्मूलन – **exterminator** *n.*

external (इक्'स्टर्नल) *a.* बाहर का, बाहरी – **externally** *adv.*

extinct (इक्'स्टिंक्ट) *a.* जो समाप्त या लुप्त हो गया हो; बुझा हुआ – **extinction** (इक्'स्टिंक्शन) *n.* समाप्ति, विनाश, लोप

extinguish (इक्'स्टिङ्विश) *vt.* बुझाना; मिटाना; समाप्त करना – **extinguishable** *a.* – **extinguisher** *n.* आग बुझाने का उपकरण, अग्नि-शमक

extol (इक्'स्टोल) *vt.* गुणगान करना, अत्यधिक प्रशंसा करना (**-ll-**)

extort (इक्'स्टॉर्ट) *vt.* किसी से ऐंठना; बलपूर्वक या धमकी से लेना – **extortion** (इक्'स्टॉर्शन) *n.* लूटने-खसोटने की क्रिया – **extortionate** *a.* (कीमत) जो लूट खसोट की हद तक हो

extra (ऍक्स्ट्रअ) *a.* अतिरिक्त; अधिक; अधिक अच्छा, सामान्य से बेहतर – *adv.* अतिरिक्त; सामान्य से अधिक – *n.* अतिरिक्त वस्तु; अतिरिक्त राशि (जो कीमत से अलग ली जाय), *Cricket* अतिरिक्त रन जो गेंद द्वारा बैट छू कर न बनी हो; *Films* अभिनेता जो भीड़ के द श्य के लिए रखा जाय

extra- (*comb. form*) इतर-, परे-, जैसे **extramarital** में
extract *vt.* (इक्'स्ट्रैक्ट) निकालना, विशे. बलपूर्वक; दबाव डाल कर लेना; सार या निचोड़ निकालना; प्राप्त करना; उद्धरण या हवाला देना – *n.* ('एक्सट्रैक्ट) उद्धरण; सार तत्व, निचोड़, अरक, सत्व – **extraction** (ऍक्स्'ट्रैक्शन) *n.* निकालना या उखाड़ना, विशे. दांत का
extra-curricular *a.* जो पाठ्यक्रम का भाग न हो, पढ़ाई के अतिरिक्त (गति- विधियां)
extradition (ऍक्सट्र'डिशन) *n.* सन्धि के अनुसार किसी अपराधी को उस के देश की सरकार को सौंपना, प्रत्यार्पण करना – **extradite** *vt.* ऐसे अपराधी को सौंपना या लाना
extramarital *a.* विवाह से बाहर (सम्बंध आदि), विवाहेतर
extramural (ऍक्स्ट्र'म्युअरल) *a.* विश्वविद्यालय, कालिज आदि के पाठ्यक्रम, विभाग आदि जो बाह्य क्षात्रों (नियमित क्षात्रों के विपरीत) के लिए हों; जो किसी स्थान की सीमाओं से बाहर स्थित हो
extraneous (इक्'स्ट्रेनिअस) *a.* बाहरी विषयेतर; असंगत; जो बाहर से जोड़ा गया हो
extraordinary (इक्'स्ट्रॉर्डिनरि) *a.* असाधारण, असामान्य; आश्चर्यजनक; अपूर्व – **extraordinarily** *adv.*
extrasensory (एक्स्ट्र'सॅन्सरि) *a.* इन्द्रियेतर ज्ञान सम्बन्धी; ऐसे ज्ञान का जो ज्ञानेन्द्रियों से प्राप्त न हुआ हो
extraterrestrial (ऍक्स्ट्र'टॅरॅस्ट्रियल) *a.* पृथ्वी के वायुमण्डल से बाहर का या उस से सम्बन्धित
extravagant (इक्'स्ट्रैविगंट) *a.* अपव्ययी; अत्यधिक – **extravagance** *n.* फिज़ूलखर्ची – **extravagantly** *adv.* – **extravaganza** (इक्सट्रैव'गैन्ज़अ) *n.* अत्यधिक भड़कीला प्रदर्शन, नाटक आदि, अतिरंजिका
extravert (ऍक्सट्र'वर्ट) देखिए EXTROVERT
extreme (इक्'स्ट्रीम) *a.* अत्यधिक; उग्र, छोर का, सिरे का, सीमा का; संयम की सीमा से परे का – *n.* सिरा, छोर, सीमा, किसी श्रृंखला का पहला और अंतिम सिरा/भाग – **extremely** *adv.* – **extremist** *n.* उग्रवादी – **extremism** *n.* – **extremity** (इक्'स्ट्रॅमिटि) *n.* सीमा, अंत – (~ **ties**) *pl.* हाथ, पैर; अत्यधिक कठिनाई या मुसीबत
extricate ('ऍक्सट्रिकेट) *vt.* निकालना; छुड़ाना
extrinsic (ऍक्'स्ट्रिन्सिक) *a.* सहायक; बाहरी – **extrinsically** *adv.*
extrovert ('ऍक्सट्रवर्ट) *n.* व्यक्ति जो बाहर की वस्तुओं और लोगों में अधिक रुचि ले, बहिर्मुखी
exuberant (इग्'ज़्यूबरंट) *a.* अत्यधिक ज़िन्दादिल, चुलबुला – **exuberance** *n.* – **exuberantly** *adv.*
exude (इग्'ज़्यूड) *vi.* (आत्मा-विश्वास) दिखाना; टपकाना – *vt.* चुआना, टपकाना
exult (इग्'ज़ल्ट) *vi.* उल्लसित होना; फूले न समाना – **exultancy** *n.* – **exultant** *a.* विजयोल्लास से भरा – **exultation** (ऍग्ज़ल्'टेशन) *n.* विजयोल्लास
eye (आइ) *n.* आंख; दृष्टि, नज़र; ध्यान; नाका (सूई का) छेद; दृष्टिकोण; विवेक; निगरानी; तूफान आदि का केंन्द्र; आंख जैसी वस्तु – *vt.* देखना – **eyeball** *n.* कोया, नेत्रगोलक – **eyebrow** *n.* भौंह, भृकुटि – **eyelash** *n.* बरौनी – **eyelid** *n.* पलक – **eye-opener** *n.* आंखें खोलने वाला (समाचार/बात) – **eyesore** *n.* घृणित वस्तु – **eyewash** *inf. n.* बहाना; धोखा – **eyewitness** *n.* प्रत्यक्षदर्शी, चश्मदीद गवाह – **not see eye to eye with sb** से किसी बात पर सहमत न होना
eyrie (इ'अरि, 'आइअरि) *n.* शिकारी पक्षी विशे. चील या बाज़ का घोंसला

F

F Fahrenheit का संक्षेप

fab (फ़ैब) *a.* बहुत बढ़िया

fable (ˊफ़ेबल) *n.* नीति कथा; जिस के पात्र जीव जन्तु हों; किस्सा; पौराणिक कथा; झूठ, गप्प – **fabled** *a.* चर्चित परंतु विरल – **fabulous** (ˊफ़ैब्युलस) *a.* आश्चर्यजनक; *inf.* सर्वश्रेष्ठ

fabric (ˊफ़ैब्रिक) *n.* कपड़ा; बनावट; ढांचा, गढ़त – **fabricate** (ˊफ़ैब्रिकेट) *vt.* बनाना, ढांचा तैयार करना; गढ़ना (झूठ आदि); जाली दस्तावेज़ तैयार करना – **fabrication** (फ़ैब्रिˊकेशन) *n.* निर्माण; सांचना; गढ़ना; जालसाज़ी – **fabricator** *n.*

facade (फ़ˊसाड) *n.* इमारत का अगला भाग, माथा; *fig* दिखावा; मुखौटा

face (फ़ेस) *n.* चेहरा; विक त भाव भंगिमा; बाहरी आकार; अगला भाग, माथा; ऊपरी सतह या मुख्य भाग; घड़ी का डायल; प्रतिष्ठा, इज्जत – *vt.* की ओर अगला भाग होना, सामने होना; हिम्मत से सामना करना – *vi.* मुड़ना – **facet** (ˊफ़ैसिट) *n.* पहलू – **facial** (ˊफ़ेशल) *a.* चेहरे का – *n.* चेहरा सुन्दर बनाने की प्रक्रिया – **faceless** *a.* गुमनाम, अनाम – **face-lifting** *n.* भवन आदि को आकर्षक बनाने के लिए उसकी मरम्मत, उद्धार – **on the face of it** ऊपर से, पहली नज़र में

facetious (फ़ˊसीशस) *a.* जो असमय हंसी ठिठोली करे

facile (ˊफ़ैसाइल) *a.* आसान, सरल; ऊपरी; मूर्खतापूर्ण – **facilitate** (फ़ˊसिलिटेट) *vt.* आसान बना देना, सहायता करना – **facilitation** (फ़सिलिˊटेशन) *n.* – **facilitator** *n.* आसान बनाने वाला; शिक्षक – **facility** (फ़ˊसिलिटि) *n.* सुविधा; आसानी; दक्षता, कौशल – (~ **ties**) *pl.* अवसर; अच्छी परिस्थितियां; कोई काम करने के साधन या उपकरण

facsimile (फ़ैक्ˊसिमिलि) *n.* हू-ब-हू नकल; प्रतिक ति (दे० **fax** भी)

fact (फ़ैक्ट) *n.* तथ्य, सत्य, सच्चाई; असलियत; वास्तविकता – **factual** (ˊफ़ैक्चुअल) *a.* वास्तविक, तथ्यों पर आधारित

faction (ˊफ़ैक्शन) *n.* गुट – **factionalism** *n.* गुटबन्दी

factor (ˊफ़ैक्टर) *n.* कारक, घटक; संख्या जो किसी अन्य संख्या से गुणा करने पर निश्चित संख्या बन जाय, गुणक; दलाल

factory (ˊफ़ैक्टरि) *n.* कारखाना

faculty (ˊफ़ैकल्टि) *n.* क्षमता; मानसिक शक्ति; सामर्थ्य; रुझान; संकाय, विश्वविद्यालय का विभाग; किसी पेशे के लोग; अधिकार

fad (ˊफ़ैड) *n.* रिवाज या फैशन जो कुछ समय तक रहे; सनक, झक

fade (ˊफ़ेड) *vi.* रंग फीका या हल्का पड़ जाना; क्षीण या कमज़ोर हो जाना; मद्धिम हो जाना; धीरे धीरे लुप्त हो जाना – *vt.* हल्का, फीका या क्षीण कर देना

faeces (ˊफ़ीसीज़) *pl. n.* मल, विष्ठा

fag (फ़ैग) *n. inf.* ऊबाने वाला या नीरस काम; *sl.* सिगरेट – *v. inf.* (विशेष **fag out** में) थक जाना (**-gg-**) – **fag end** अंतिम हिस्सा; घटिया किस्म की बची खुची चीज़ें

faggot (ˊफ़ैगट) *n.* लकड़ी का गट्ठर

Fahrenheit (ˊफ़ैरन्हाइट) (*abbr.* F) *a.* गरमी के माप से सम्बन्धित (इस माप के अनुसार पानी 32°पर जम जाता है और 212°पर उबल जाता है)

fail (ˊफ़ेल) *vi.* असफल होना; (यंत्र आदि का) बंद हो जाना; अनुत्तीर्ण होना; अपर्याप्त होना; जरूरत

पड़ने पर काम न आना; शक्ति क्षीण हो जाना; समाप्त हो जाना; दिवाला निकल जाना – *vt.* निराश करना; सहायता न देना; उपेक्षा करना; भूल जाना; अनुत्तीर्ण करना – **failed** *a.* असफल (विद्यार्थी, लेखक) – **failing** *n.* कमी; कमज़ोरी – *prep.* न होने पर, के अभाव में – **failure** *n.* असफलता; चूक; ख़राबी; क्षय – **without fail** निश्चय ही

faint (फ़ेंट) *a.* कमज़ोर हल्का, धुंधला; फीका शिथिल; जिसे चक्कर आ रहे हों; जो बेहोश होने को हो – *vi.* बेहोश हो कर गिर पड़ना

fair[1] (फ़ेंअर) *a.* न्यायी; निष्पक्ष; नियमानुसार; कानूनी; गोरा, सुन्दर; पर्याप्त; अच्छी किस्म का; उपयुक्त मात्रा वाला; निष्कलंक; युक्ति युक्त; मध्यम; सुहाना (मौसम) – *adv.* ईमानदारी से – **fairness** *n.* निष्पक्षता – **the fair sex** नारी

fair[2] (फ़ेअर) *n.* मेला; प्रदर्शनी

fairy (फ़ेंअरि) *n.* परी – *a.* परियों का; परी जैसा – **fairy-tale** *a.* परियों की कहानी का या उस जैसा – **fairy tale** परियों की कहानी

fait accompli (फ़ेट्अ कम्प्लि) *Fr.* जो पहले ही हो चुका हो, सम्पन्न कार्य

faith (फ़ेथ) *n.* भरोसा, विश्वास; निष्ठा, वफादारी – **faithful** *a.* एकनिष्ठ, वफ़ादार – **faithfully** *adv.* – **faithless** *a.*

fake (फ़ेक) *vt.* नकली माल बनाना; बनावटी भाव व्यक्त करना – *n.* नकली या जाली वस्तु, व्यक्ति या काम – *a.*

fakir (फ़ किअर) *n.* फ़कीर

falcon (फ़ॉल्कन, फ़ॉकन) *n.* बाज़, विशे. वह जिसे पक्षियों का शिकार करने के लिए सधाया गया हो

fall (फ़ॉल) *vi.* गिरना, नीचे आना; नीचे हो जाना; घट जाना; नीचे लटक जाना; भूमि पर आ गिरना; ढह जाना; किसी के कब्ज़े मे आ जाना; फिर पीछे पहुंच जाना; समाप्त हो जाना; मुंह से निकलना या कहा जाना; घटना हो जाना (**fell** *pt.* **fallen** *pp.*) – *n.* गिरावट, पतन; गिरावट की मात्रा या राशि; कमी; घटाव; पतन, विनाश; तबाही; (प्राय: *pl.*) जल प्रपात; आरोह-अवरोह; प्रलोभन में आ जाना, नैतिक पतन; US पतझड़ का मौसम – **fallout** *n.* परमाणु बम के विस्फोट के बाद वातावरण में फैला विषैला बादल; प्रभाव

fallacy (फ़ैलसि) *n.* गलत, भ्रामक विचार या तर्क – **fallacious** *a.* भ्रामक, भ्रमपूर्ण – **fallibility** (फ़ैलि बिलिटि) *n.* भूल कर बैठने का दोष – **fallible** (फ़ैलबल) *a.* जो भूल कर सकता है

fallen (फ़ॉलन) FALL का *pp.*

fallow (फ़ैलो) *a.* परती (भूमि); जिस पर खेती न हो; उपेक्षित

false (फ़ॉल्स) *a.* गलत, भूल भरा; झूठा; दिखावटी, भ्रामक, भ्रांतिजनक; कपट पूर्ण, नकली – **falsely** *adv.* – **falsify** (फ़ॉल्सिफ़ाइ) *vt.* झूठे दस्तावेज़ बनाना; (उम्मीदों पर) पानी फेरना (**falsified, falsifying**) – **falsehood** *n.* झूठ, असत्य; कपट, बेइमानी, धोखा

falter (फ़ॉल्टर) *vi.* झिझकना; हकलाना; लड़खड़ाना, डगमगाना

fame (फ़ेम) *n.* कीर्ति, ख्याति, प्रसिद्धि – **famous** *a.* प्रसिद्ध, विख्यात

familiar (फ़ मिलिअर) *a.* प्रसिद्ध; सुपरिचित; प्राय: होने वाला; घनिष्ठ; ज़रूरत से ज़्यादा बेतल्लुफ़; मुंहलगा – *n.* अंतरंग या घनिष्ठ मित्र; सुपरिचित भूत – **familiarity** *n.* घनिष्ठता; बेतकल्लुफ़ी – **familiarize** *vt.* (किसी को) परिचित कराना (किसी विषय या काम से)

family (फ़ैमिलि) *n.* परिवार, वंश; कुल, जाति; वर्ग

famine (फ़ैमिन) *n.* अकाल – **famished** *a.* बहुत अधिक भूखा

famous (फ़ेमस) देखिए FAME

fan[1] (फ़ैन) *n.* पंखा (बिजली या हाथ का) पक्षी की पूंछ के फैले हुए पंख – *vt.* पंखा करना – *vi.* पंखे की तरह फैल जाना (**-nn-**) – **fanlight** *n.* दरवाज़े पर पंखे के आकार का झरोखा

fan[2] (फ़ैन) *inf. n.* भक्त, प्रेमी; शौकीन, विशे. किसी खेल आदि का

fanatic (फ़ नैटिक) *a.* मतांध, कट्टरपंथी; धर्मान्ध – *n.* कट्टरपंथी व्यक्ति – **fanatical** *a.* कट्टरपंथी – **fanatically** *adv.* – **fanaticism** *n.* धर्मांधता, कट्टरपंथी

fancy (ˈफ़ैन्सि) *a.* रंग बिरंगा, भड़कीला – *n.* मौज, सनक; पसंद, झुकाव; कल्पना शक्ति; कल्पना – *vt.* कल्पना करना; विश्वास करना या रुझान होना – **take a fancy to** *inf.* किसी को पसंद करना या चाहने लगना (**fancied, fancying**) – **fanciful** *a.* कल्पना पर आधरित; अवास्तविक

fanfare (ˈफ़ैन्फ़ेंअर) *n.* तुरही नाद, धूमधाम; तड़क भड़क

fang (फ़ैन्ग) *n.* सांप का विष दंत

fanlight (ˈफ़न्लाइट) *n.* दरवाज़े के ऊपर खिड़की

fantasy (ˈफ़ैन्टसि) *n.* अत्यधिक उपजाऊ कल्पना; स्वप्न चित्र; भड़कीला आविष्कार या डिज़ाइन – **fantasia** (फ़ैन् ˈटेज़िअ) *n.* अत्यधिक कल्पनाशील संगीत/रचना – **fantasize** *v.* स्वप्न देखना (किसी प्रिय व्यक्ति या वस्तु के) – **fantastic** (फ़ैन् ˈटैस्टिक) *a.* अदभुत, अजीब; विलक्षण; *inf.* बहुत अच्छा; *inf.* बहुत बड़ा; बहुत ज़्यादा – **fantastically** *adv.*

FAQ frequently asked questions का संक्षेप

far (फ़ार) *adv.* दूर, परे; पहले समय का; अधिक (अच्छा, बड़ा आदि) (**farther, further** *comp*, **farthest, furthest** *sup.*) – *a.* दूर का; अधिक दूर – **far-fetched** *a.* कहानी आदि जिस पर विश्वास न किया जा सके – **far-flung** *a.* काफी दूर; दूर तक फैला हुआ, व्यापक – **far-off** *a.* बहुत दूर; बहुत पहले

farce (फ़ार्स) *n.* प्रहसन; तमाशा, ढोंग – **farcical** (ˈफ़ार्सिकल) *a.* नाटकीय

fare (फ़ेंअर) *n.* भाड़ा, किराया; यात्री; भोजन – *vi.* आगे बढ़ना; होना; यात्रा करना; उन्नति करना – **farewell** *interj.* अलविदा – *n.* विदा लेने की क्रिया

farm (फ़ार्म) *n.* फ़ारम; खेत, खेती – *v.* खेती करना; पशु पालना – **farmer** *n.* किसान – **farmhand** *n.* खेत मज़दूर – **farmhouse** *n.*

farrow (ˈफ़ैरो) *n.* सूअर के बच्चों का झुंड – *v.* सूअर (की मादा) का ब्याना

fart (फ़ार्ट) *vulg. n.* पाद; अधोवायु का निकलना – *vi.* पादना

farther (ˈफ़ार्दर) *adv./a.* आगे, और आगे; FAR का *comp.* – **farthest** *adv./a* सब से दूर; FAR का *sup.*

farthing (ˈफ़ार्दिङ) *n.* एक पुराना ब्रिटिश सिक्का

fascia, facia (ˈफ़ेशिअ) *n.* दुकान की खिड़की के ऊपर की चपटी सतह

fascinate (ˈफ़ैसिनेट) *vt.* मोहित करना, मोह लेना – **fascination** *n.* सम्मोहन; आकर्षण

fascism (ˈफ़ैशिज़्म) *n.* निरंकुश शासन व्यवस्था का सिद्धान्त – **fascist** *a./n.* इस सिद्धान्त में विश्वास रखने वाला (व्यक्ति)

fashion (ˈफ़ैशन) *n.* फ़ैशन; रिवाज, रीति, लोकाचार; ढंग – *vt.* बनाना, रूप देना, गढ़ना – **fashionable** *a.* प्रचलित, लोकप्रिय; शौकीन (व्यक्ति)

fast[1] (फ़ास्ट) *a.* तेज़, जिस के कारण तेज़ प्रगति हो सके; (घड़ी) जो अधिक समय दिखाती हो; स्थिर (दोस्त); मजबूत, पक्का (रंग); – *adv.* तेज़ी से, मज़बूती से – **fastness** *n.* द ढ़ता; दुर्ग; किला – **fast food** भोजन, विशे. ऐसे व्यंजन जो पहले से तैयार रहते हैं – **fast track** तेज़ी से कुछ पाने का तरीका

fast[2] *vi.* उपवास करना – *n.* उपवास, रोज़ा – **fasting** *n.* उपवास या रोज़ा

fasten (ˈफासन) *vt.* बांधना; कसना – *vi.* बंध जाना; जकड़ा जाना – **fastener** (ˈफासनर), **fastening** *n.* बांधने/जोड़ने का उपकरण

fastidious (फ़ैस्टि ˈडिअस) *a.* जिसे खुश करना कठिन हो; नाज़ुक मिज़ाज

fat (फ़ैट) *n.* चर्बी, वसा – *a.* मोटा जिसमें बहुत लाभ हो; उपजाऊ (**fatter** *comp,* **fattest** *sup.*) – *vt.* पशु को खिला खिलाकर मोटा/मांसल बनाना (**-tt-**) – **fatness** *n.* – **fatten** *v.* – **fatty** *a.* जिसमें बहुत चर्बी हो – **fathead** *n. inf.* मूर्ख

fate (फ़ेट) *n.* भाग्य, किस्मत, विनाश – *vt.* किस्मत में लिखा होना – **fatal** *a.* घातक – **fatalism** *n.* भाग्यवाद; भाग्य के आगे सिर झुकाने की प्रव ति – **fatalist** *n.* भाग्यवादी – **fatalistic** (फ़ेट ˈलिस्टिक) *a.* – **fatality** (फ़ ˈटैलिटि) *n.* दुर्घटना जिसमें म त्यु हो जाय; युद्ध या दुर्घटना में मरने वाला व्यक्ति – **fatally** *adv.* – **fateful** *a.* महत्वपूर्ण

father (ˈफ़ादर) *n.* पिता, बाप; पूर्वज, पुरखा; (F-) परमात्मा, पादरी; समाज के वयोव द्ध सदस्य के लिए सम्बोधन – *vt.* पैदा करना; प्रारंभ करना; पिता या लेखक होना स्वीकार करना; पिता के रूप में काम करना – **fatherhood** *n.* पित त्व – **fatherly** *a.* पिता समान – **father-in-law** *n.* ससुर – **father figure** पिता समान व्यक्ति – **Father's Day** जून का तीसरा रविवार जब बच्चे पिता को उपहार देते हैं

fathom (ˈफ़ैदम) *n.* पानी की गहराई का माप (6 फुट) – **fathomable** *a.* – **fathomless** *a.* अथाह

fatigue (फ़ ˈटीग) *n.* थकान, थकावट कठोर परिश्रम; दबाव पड़ने पर धातु की कमज़ोरी; सैनिक का (गैर-सैनिक) काम – *vt.* थकाना, चूर-चूर करना

fatuous (ˈफ़ैट्युअस) *a.* बहुत मूर्खतापूर्ण

faucet (ˈफ़ॉसिट) *n.* (**tap**) US नल की टोंटी

fault (फ़ॉल्ट) *n.* दोष; त्रुटि; कुकर्म; कसूर; गलती, चूक; *Tennis* गलत ढंग से फैंकी गेंद; *Geology* किसी स्तर (चट्टानों आदि) में दरार या फटन – *v.* दोष निकालना – **faulty** *a.* दोष भरा; गलत

fauna (ˈफ़ॉन्अ) *n.* किसी क्षेत्र या युग के जीवों का सामूहिक नाम (*pl.* **-s, - ae**)

faux pas (फ़ो ˈपा) *n.* विवेक रहित काम; असावधानी; बेवकूफी

favour (ˈफ़ेवर) *n.* क पा द ष्टि; अहसान; समर्थन; पक्षपात; फीता, बैज – *vt.* पक्षपात या तरफ़दारी करना; क पा करना; समर्थन देना; *US* सद श होना – **favourable** *a.* – **favourably** *adv.* – **favourite** *n.* क पापात्र, प्रेमभाजन; जिस के जीतने की आशा हो – **favouritism** *n.* पक्षपात

fawn[1] (फ़ॉन) *n.* हिरन का बच्चा, हिरनौटा – *a.* हल्का भूरा

fawn[2] (फ़ॉन) – *vi.* चापलूसी करना

fax (फ़ैक्स) *n.* इलेक्ट्रिक प्रतिलिपि भेजने की इलेक्ट्रानिकी व्यवस्था, फैक्स; इस प्रकार भेजे गए कागज़ात – *v.*

fear (फ़िअर) *n.* डर; भय; आशंका – *vt.* डरना, भयभीत होना; झिझकना; डर कर पीछे हट जाना – **fearful** *a.* – **fearless** *a.* निडर – **fearlessly** *adv.* – **fearsome** *a.* भयानक, भयंकर

feasible (ˈफ़ीज़बल) *a.* जो किया जा सके, व्यवहार्य; संभाव्य – **feasibility** (फ़ीज़ि ˈबिलिटि) *n.*

feast (फ़ीस्ट) *n.* दावत; धार्मिक वर्षगांठ – *vi.* दावत उड़ाना; जी भर कर खाना – *vt.* प्रीतिभोज देना

feat (फ़ीट) *n.* करतब, कमाल

feather (ˈफ़ेदर) *n.* पक्षी के पर, पंख; पंख से मिलती जुलती वस्तु – **feathery** *a.* हल्का व मुलायम

– **feather-weight** *n.* वज़न में हल्का व्यक्ति या वस्तु – **the white feather** कायरता

feature (ˈफ़ीचर) *n.* (प्राय: *pl.*) चेहरा-मोहरा, नयन-नक्श; विशेषता, विशेष लक्षण – *vt.* रूपरेखा प्रस्तुत करना, चित्रित करना; *Cinema* फिल्म में मुख्य भूमिका में प्रस्तुत करना – *vi.* प्रमुख होना – **featureless** *a.* जिसमें कोई विशेष बात न हो

Feb. February का संक्षेप

febrile (ˈफ़ीब्राइल) *a.* ज्वर का या उस से सम्बन्धित; उत्तेजित व बहुत सक्रिय

February (ˈफ़ेब्रुअरि) *n.* फरवरी का माह

feckless (ˈफ़ेक्लिस) *a.* निर्जीव; निस्तेज

fecund (ˈफ़ीकंड) *a.* उपजाऊ, उर्वर उत्पादकता

fed FEED का *pt./pp.* – **fed up** तंग आया; परेशान

federal (ˈफ़ेडरल) *a.* संघीय – **federalism** *n.* संघवाद – **federation** *n.* संघ; राज्यसंघ

fee (फ़ी) *n.* पारिश्रमिक, फीस

feeble (ˈफ़ीबल) *a.* दुर्बल प्रभावहीन

feed (फ़ीड) *vt.* खिलाना; देना; पहुंचाना – *vi.* भोजन करना (**fed** *pt./pp.*) – *n.* भोजन करने की क्रिया; चारा; चारागाह; चारे की मात्रा; यंत्र में डाली गयी सामग्री; यंत्र का वह भाग जिस में से हो कर सामग्री जाती है; टी. वी. कार्यक्रम जो केंद्रीय स्टेशन से नेटवर्क के अन्य स्टेशनों को भेजे जांय – **feed-back** *n.* पूछने पर भेजी गयी जानकारी

feel (फ़ील) *v.* छूना, स्पर्श करना; अनुभव करना; टटोलना; अनुभूति होना; भावनाओं का प्रदर्शन करना (*for* के साथ); विश्वास करना; समझना (**felt** *pt./pp.*) – *n.* महसूस करने की क्रिया या घटना; अनुभूति; स्पर्श की सामर्थ्य या गुण – **feeler** *n.* कुछ जीवों की स्पर्शेन्द्रिय; दूसरों के विचार जानने के लिए रखा गया प्रस्ताव; वह जो महसूस करे – **feeling** *n.* बोध; अनुभव; मनोभाव, भावना; संवेदनशीलता; सहानुभूति; कोमल हृदयता (~**s**) – *pl.* भावनाएं – *a.* संवेदनशील – **feel-good** *a.* सुख व प्रसन्नता की अनुभूति वाला (अनुभव)

feet FOOT का *pl.*

feign (फ़ेन) *v.* बहाना करना; का स्वांग भरना या नाटक करना

felicity (फ़िˈलिसिटि) *n.* आनंद; सुख-शांति; उचित शब्द प्रयोग करने की योग्यता – **felicitate** (फ़िˈलिसिटेट) *vt.* बधाई देना – **felicitation** (फ़िलिसिˈटेशन) (प्राय: *pl.* में) *n.* बधाई

feline (ˈफ़ीलाइन) *a.* बिल्ली का; बिल्ली जैसा

fell[1] (फ़ेल) FALL का *pt.*

fell[2] (फ़ेल) *vt.* गिराना; (पेड़) काट कर गिरा देना – **feller** *n.*

fellow (ˈफ़ेलो) *n. inf.* पुरुष; लड़का; व्यक्ति; साथी; सहकर्मी; जोड़ा; वैसी ही वस्तु; समाज या कालिज का सदस्य – *a.* एक ही वर्ग या कक्षा का; सम्बद्ध; साथी – **fellowship** *n.* बिरादरी; समाज; मैत्री; (विश्वविद्यालय में) शोधकर्ता का पद या विशेष छात्रव ति – **fellow feeling** संवेदना, सहानुभूति

felon (ˈफ़ेलन) *n.* गंभीर अपराध का दोषी – **felony** (ˈफ़ेलनि) *n.* गंभीर अपराध

felt[1] (फ़ेल्ट) FEEL का *pt./pp.*

felt[2] (फ़ेल्ट) *n.* नमदा; नमदे की बनी वस्तु

fem. feminine का संक्षेप

female (ˈफ़ीमेल) *a.* स्त्री या मादा का या उस से सम्बन्धित – *n.* स्त्री; मादा – **female plug** छेदवाला प्लग

feminine (ˈफ़ेमिनिन) *a.* स्त्रियों का, स्त्री सुलभ; स्त्रियोचित; (व्याकरण में) स्त्रीलिंग – **feminism** *n.* स्त्रियों के लिए बराबर के अधिकारों की मांग, स्त्री अधिकारवाद – **feminist** *a./n.* – **femininity** *n.* नारीत्व; नारीवर्ग

femoral (´फ़ेमरल) *a.* जांघ का
femur (´फ़ीमर) *n.* जांघ की हड्डी
fence (फ़ॅन्स) *n.* बाड़ा, बाड़, घेरा, अहाता – *v.* (**fence in** भी) बाड़ लगाना; पटे बाज़ी करना (तलवारों से खेलना); प्रश्न का उत्तर देने में आनाकानी करना; *sl.* चोरी का माल खरीदना, बेचना – **fencing** *n.* पटेबाज़ी की कला
fend (फ़ॅण्ड) *vt.* (वार) रोकना – *vi.* अपना प्रबन्ध स्वयं करना – **fender** (´फ़ॅन्डर) *n.* आतिशदान का जंगला; US; कार के मडगार्ड
feng shui (फ़ॅङ´शूइ) *n.* चीनी पद्धति जिसके अनुसार किसी भवन की दिशा व उसमें वस्तुएं सजाने का स्थान निर्धारित किया जाता है ताकि उसके निवासी सुखी रहें
fennel (´फ़ॅनल) *n.* सौंफ़
ferment (´फ़र्मेंण्ट) *n.* खमीर उत्तेजना – *v.* खमीर उठाना या उठना; उत्तेजित होना या करना – **fermentation** *n.* खमीर उठने की क्रिया
fern (फ़र्न) *n.* रोएंदार पत्तों वाला एक पौधा; पर्णांग
ferocious (फ़´रोशस) *a.* उग्र, क्रूर; निर्दयी – **ferocity** (फ़´रॉसिटि) *n.*
ferret (´फ़ॅरिट) *n.* नेवले जैसा जीव – *vt.* निकालना या ढूंढना – *vi.* ढूंढना, खोज निकालना
ferric, ferr(e)ous (´फ़ॅरिक, ´फ़ॅरिअस) *a.* लोहे का या उस से बना
Ferris wheel (´फ़ॅरिस-) मेलों में लगा गोल झूला जिसमें बैठने के लिए सीटें लगी होती है
ferry (´फ़ेरि) *n.* (**ferry boat** भी) नौका जो यात्रियों को नदी पार कराती है; नौका-सेवा – *v.* ऐसी नौका में यात्री ले जाना; नौका में यात्रा करना (**ferried, ferrying**)
fertile (´फ़र्टाइल) *a.* उपजाऊ; जनन क्षम – **fertility** (फ़र्´टिलिटि) *n.* उर्वरता; जनन-क्षमता – **fertilization** (फ़र्टिलाइ´ज़ेशन) *n.* – **fertilize** *vt.* खाद देना/लगाना – **fertilizer** *n.* उर्वरक, खाद
fervent, fervid (फ़र्वेन्ट ´फ़र्विड) *a.* उत्साही, जोशीला; उग्र – **fervently** *adv.* – **fervour** (´फ़र्वर) *n.* जोश, उत्साह
fester (´फ़ॅस्टर) *v.* (घाव में) पीब पैदा कर देना/हो जाना – *vi.* किसी बात का खटकना या कांटे के समान चुभना; कड़वाहट उत्पन्न हो जाना
festival (´फ़ॅस्टिवल) *n.* उत्सव या पर्व, विशे. धार्मिक; त्यौहार; समारोहों की श्रंखला – **festive** *a.* उत्सव सम्बन्धी; आनन्दमय – **festivity** *n.* आनन्दोत्सव; आमोद-प्रमोद – *pl.* उत्सव या खुशी मनाने की प्रक्रिया
festoon (फ़ॅस्´टून) *n.* (स्वागत में टंगी) फूलों, झंडियों आदि की लड़ी – *vt.* लड़ी लगाना, लड़ियों से सजावट करना
fetch (फ़ॅच) *vt.* जाकर लाना, लाना, ले आना; आकर्षित करना; (कीमत) पर बिकना – *n.* चाल – **fetching** *a.* आकर्षक
fete, fête (फ़ेट) *n.* मेला, उत्सव – *vt.* भोज आदि से सम्मानित करना
fetid, foetid (´फ़ॅटिड, ´फ़ीटिड) *a.* बदबूदार; दुर्गन्धयुक्त
fetish (´फ़ॅटिश, ´फ़ीटिश) *n.* काम भावना जो कोई वस्तु विशेष देखकर जाग्रत हो; ऐसी बात या वस्तु जिस पर अत्यधिक ध्यान दिया जाय
fetter (´फ़ॅटर) *n.* बेड़ी; बाधा, बंधन, नियंत्रण – *pl.* बन्दी होने की स्थिति – *vt.* बेड़ियां पहनाना; रोकना; नियंत्रित करना; बाधा डालना
fettle (´फ़ॅट्ल) *n. inf.* स्वास्थ्य (**in fine fettle**)
fetus (´फ़ीटस) देखिए FOETUS
feud (फ्यूड) *n.* पुश्तैनी बैर, विशे. कबीलों या कुटुम्बों में – *vi.* पुश्तैनी दुश्मनी रखना
feudal (´फ्यूड्ल) *a.* मध्य युग की सामाजिक और आर्थिक व्यवस्था जैसा, सामन्ती; *inf.* बहुत पुराने तर्ज़ का – **feudalism** *n.* सामन्तवाद

fever (फ़ीव़र) *n.* ज्वर, बुखार; व्यग्रता, उत्तेजना – **feverish** *a.* जिसे बुखार हो; व्यग्र, विह्वल – **fever pitch** बहुत तेज़ गति; अत्यधिक उत्तेजना

few (फ़्यू) *a.* थोड़े से, कुछ, इने गिने; – *n.* थोड़ी सी संख्या – **good few, quite a few** कई, बहुत से – **few and far between** कभी-कभी, बहुत कम (किसी का आना)

fez (फ़ेज़) *n.* नमदे की बनी लाल रंग की तुर्की टोपी

ff folios, following का संक्षेप

fiancé (फ़ि'आन्से) *n.* पुरुष मंगेतर (**fiancée** (फ़ि'आन्से) *fem.*)

fiasco (फ़ि'ऐस्को) *n.* पूर्ण असफलता; विफलता (*pl.* **-co(e)s**)

fiat ('फ़ाइअट) *n.* आदेश; आज्ञा; सरकारी या अधिकारी अनुमति

fib (फ़िब) *n.* छोटा-मोटा झूठ – *vt.* झूठ बोलना, गप्प हांकना (**-bb-**) – **fibber** *n.* गप्पी, झूठा

fibre ('फ़ाइबर) *n.* रेशा; तन्तु; धागा जो बटा जा सके (जैसे रूई, ऊन का) – **fibreglass** *n.* कांच के महीन तन्तुओं से बना पदार्थ – **fibre optics** लम्बे पारदर्शी कांच तन्तुओं के जरिये जानकारी प्रकाश किरणों के रूप में भेजने की प्रक्रिया

fickle ('फ़िकल) *a.* अस्थिर; चंचल – **fickleness** *n.*

fiction ('फ़िक्शन) *n.* गल्प साहित्य, कल्पना पर आधारित साहित्य – **fictional** *a.* कल्पित – **fictitious** (फ़िक्'टिशस) *a.* काल्पनिक, मनगढ़ंत; नकली; झूठा; बनावटी

fiddle ('फ़िड्ल) *n.* वायलिन या बेला जैसा वाद्य; तुच्छ वस्तु; गैर कानूनी और धोखा धड़ी पर आधारित काम – *vt.* अशांत होना – *v. sl.* ध गोखा देना; छल करना – **fiddling** *a.* तुच्छ – **fiddly** *a.* छोटा; जिसे पकड़ना कठिन हो – **fiddlestick** *interj.* बकवास – **play the second fiddle to sb** किसी की अपेक्षा कम महत्व दिया जाना; अपेक्षतया कम महत्व पूर्ण पद पर होना

fidelity (फ़ि'डॅलिटि) *n.* ईमानदारी; आवाज़ की तद्रूपता

fidget ('फ़िजिट) *vi.* बेचैन होना; अशांत होना

fiduciary (फ़ि'डूशिअरि) *a.* न्यास (ट्रस्ट) में रखी या दी गयी – *n.* न्यासधारी या ट्रस्टी

field (फ़ील्ड) *n.* क षि भूमि, खेत; क्षेत्र जिसमें कोई खनिज आदि प्रचुर मात्रा में हो; किसी खेल के सभी खिलाड़ियों का सामूहिक नाम; संभावित विजेता को छोड़ कर सभी प्रतियोगी; युद्ध-भूमि; क्षेत्र जिस पर बिजली, गुरूत्वाकर्षण या चुम्बकत्व का प्रभाव डाला जा सकता है; ज्ञान का क्षेत्र; कार्यक्षेत्र या उस की व्यापकता – *v. Cricket* आदि में गेन्द को रोकना; खिलाड़ी या टीम को मैदान में भेजना – **fielder** *n.* – **field day** अभ्यास, युद्धाभ्यास या क्षेत्र में काम का दिन; महत्वपूर्ण अवसर – **field glasses** दूरबीन – **field marshal** सेना का सब से बड़ा अधिकारी – **fieldwork** *n.* अनुसंधान या काम जो कक्षा या प्रयोगशाला की बजाय बाहर किया जाता है

fiend (फ़ ड) *n.* नरक दूत, राक्षस; बदमाश या दुराचारी व्यक्ति – **fiendish** *a.* बदमाश, दुष्ट क्रूर, निष्ठुर

fierce (फ़िअर्स) *a.* हिंस्र, खूंखार; भीषण, उग्र – **fiercely** *adv.* – **fierceness** *n.*

fiery ('फ़ाइअरि) *a.* जलता हुआ; उग्र; उत्तेजित, (**fierier** *comp*, **fieriest** *sup.*)

fiesta (फ़ि'ऍस्ट्अ) *n.* (धार्मिक) उत्सव या त्यौहार

fife (फ़ाइफ़) *n.* तेज़ आवाज़ वाला बांसुरी जैसा वाद्य

fifteen ('फ़िफ़्टीन) *n.* पंद्रह की संख्या

fifth दे० FIVE

fig (फ़िग) *n.* अंजीर, गूलर; उसका पेड़

fight (फ़ाइट) *v.* लड़ना; (अधिकारों आदि के लिए) संघर्ष करना; विरोध करना; लड़ाई के माध्यम

से तय या निश्चित करना; वाद-विवाद करना (**fought** (फ़ॉट) *pt./pp.*) – *n.* लड़ाई, संघर्ष – **fighter** *n./a.* लड़ाकू, योद्धा; *Mil.* विमान जो अन्य विमानों को मार गिराए – **fighting** *n.* लड़ाई – **fighting fit** एकदम स्वस्थ – **fighting spirit** लड़ने और पाने की हिम्मत

figment (ˈफ़िग्मंट) *n.* – **a figment of imagination** कल्पित वस्तु; कल्पना की उड़ान

figure (ˈफ़िगर) *n.* संख्या; अंक; राशि; रूप; आकार; शरीर की बनावट; शक्ल विशे. विशिष्ट रंगरूप और आकार; चित्र, रेखाचित्र; आकृति; मूर्ति, प्रतिमा; प्रारूप; नृत्य या स्केटिंग में गति; अलंकार या लाक्षणिक प्रयोग – *vt.* अनुमान लगाना, आंकलन करना; रेखाचित्र या चित्र बनाना – *vi.* (प्रायः **figure in**) दीखना, दिखाई पड़ना; दृष्टिगोचर होना; में शमिल होना – **figurative** (ˈफ़िगरटिव़) *a.* लाक्षणिक, अलंकारमय – **figuratively** *adv.* लाक्षणिक रूप से – **figurine** (फ़िगˈरीन) *n.* छोटी मूर्ति – **figurehead** *n.* नाम मात्र का नेता या शासक – **figure of speech** अलंकार

filament (ˈफ़िलमंट) *n.* बिजली के बल्ब आदि में महीन तार जो गरम हो कर प्रकाश देती है; तन्तु:केशर

filch (फ़िल्च) *vt.* चुराना; उड़ा ले जाना

file[1] (फ़ाइल) *n.* फ़ाइल, मिसिल; किसी व्यक्ति या विषय सम्बन्धी जानकारी; सुव्यवस्थित पंक्ति, कतार (सैनिकों आदि की) – *vt.* कागज़ मिसिल मे लगाना या नत्थी करना; मुकदमा दायर करना – *vi.* कतार में चलना – **filing** *n.*

file[2] (फ़ाइल) *n.* घिसाई करने का औज़ार, रेती – *vt.* रेती लगा कर घिसना – **filing** *n.* रेती लगाने का काम; रेती से उखड़ा धातु का कण

filial (ˈफ़िल्यल) *a.* पुत्र या पुत्री के समान; पुत्रोचित

filigree (ˈफिलिग्री) *n.* सोने चांदी के तार का काम; ज़रदोज़ी

fill (फ़िल) *vt.* भरना, भर देना; पूरी तरह भर देना या छा जाना; (पद) ग्रहण करना और उसका काम करना; (छेद आदि) रोक देना; सन्तुष्ट करना; पूरा करना – *vi.* भर जाना – *n.* पूरा सामान; जितना जी चाहे उतनी मात्रा – **filling** *n.* – **filling station** पैट्रोल पम्प – **fill the bill** *inf.* आवश्यक पूर्ति करना

fillip (ˈफ़िलिप) *n.* प्रोत्साहन, बढ़ावा

filly (ˈफ़िलि) *n.* चार वर्ष से कम की घोड़ी, बछेड़ी

film (फ़िल्म) *n.* चलचित्र, फ़िल्म; फोटोग्राफ़ी की फ़िल्म; झिल्ली या परत; आंखों का धुंधलापना; हल्की धुंध – *a.* सिनेमा से संबन्धित – *vt.* चलचित्र बनाना – *v.* झिल्ली या परत चढ़ाना या चढ़ जाना – **filmy** *a.* झीना; जाली जैसा – **film star** चलचित्रों का लोकप्रिय अभिनेता या अभिनेत्री

filter (ˈफ़िल्टर) *n.* तरल पदार्थ छानने का कपड़ा या उपकरण; छन्ना; साफ़ी; फ़िल्टर – *v.* छन्ने या फिल्टर का काम करना – *vi.* धीरे धीरे किसी स्थान, वस्तु में से गुज़रना – **filtrate** *n.* छनी गैस या तरल पदार्थ

filth (फ़िल्थ) *n.* गन्दगी, मैल; प्रदूषण; अश्लीलता – **filthily** *adv.* – **filthiness** *n.* – **filthy** *a.* मैला, घिनावना, गन्दा; अश्लील

fin (फ़िन) *n.* मछली का पंख; उससे मिलती जुलती वस्तु जैसे विमान का पंख

final (ˈफ़ाइनल) *a.* अंतिम, आखिरी; निर्णायक; अपरिवर्तनीय – *n.* प्रतियोगिता, निर्णायक खेल या परीक्षा जो अन्त में हो, अंतिम प्रतियोगिता आदि – (~ **s**) *pl.* अंतिम परीक्षा, प्रतियोगिता – **finale** (फ़िˈनालि) *n.* संगीत रचना या नृत्य नाटिका का अंतिम भाग – **finality** (फ़ाइˈनैलिटि) *n.* अंतिम रूप या अवस्था – **finalize** (ˈफ़ाइनलाइज) *v.* अंतिम रूप देना – **finally** *adv.* अंतिम रूप से

finance (फ़ˈनैन्स; फ़ाइनैन्स) *n.* धन का प्रबन्ध या व्यवस्था, वित्त-व्यवस्था; वित्त, धन (*pl.* भी)

– *vt.* पूंजी या धन जुटाना या लगाना (किसी काम के लिए) – **financial** (फि'नैन्शल, 'फ़ाइ-) *a.* वित्तीय – **financially** *adv.* – **financier** (फि'नैंसिअर, फ़ाइ-) *n.* पैसा लगाने वाला

finch (फिंच) *n.* एक पक्षी, तूती

find (फ़ाइण्ड) *vt.* पाना; मिलना; पता लगाना; पहचानना; अनुभव करना; खोज निकालना; जान लेना; निर्णय करना, (दोषी) ठहराना; *Law* निर्णय पर पहुंचना करना (**found** *pt./pp.*) – *n.* प्राप्ति; उप्लब्धि; कोई मूल्यवान वस्तु मिलने की क्रिया – **finder** *n.* – **finding** *n.* अदालती निर्णय

fine[1] (फ़ाइन) *a.* बढ़िया, उत्तम, श्रेष्ठ; कोमल, नाजुक; शुब्द्ध, बारीक या महीन; पतला; सूक्ष्म; मनोहर; सुन्दर; भड़कीला; *inf.* स्वस्थ; मज़े में; सुहाना – *vt.* साफ़ या शुब्द्ध करना; मैल निकालना; पतला करना – **finely** *adv.* – **fineness** *n.* शुब्द्धता – **finery** *n.* भड़कीली पोशाक – **finesse** (फ़ि'नेंस) *n.* चातुर्य, कौशल (स्थिति संभालने का) – **fine art** ललित कला – **fine print** दे० **small print**

fine[2] (फ़ाइन) *n.* जुर्माना – *vt.* जुर्माना करना – **in fine** अन्त में; संक्षेप में

finger ('फिंगर) *n.* उंगली, उसकी आक ति की वस्तु – *vt.* उंगली से छूना या टटोलना – **fingerprint** *n.* उंगली की छाप विशे. वह जिससे अपराधी की पहचान की जा सके – **fingerstall** *n.* उंगली का कवच; अंगुलि घानी – **little finger** छोटी उंगली – **index finger** तर्जनी

finicking ('फ़िनिकिंग), **finicky** ('फ़िनिकि) *a.* जिसे खुश करना कठिन हो; नाजुक मिज़ाज

finis ('फ़िनिस) *Lat.* अन्त, इति, विशे. पुस्तक की

finish ('फ़िनिश) *v.* समाप्त करना या होना, अंत करना; पूरा करना (काम आदि) – *n.* अंत; परिष्करण, पालिश आदि; अंतिम रूप

finite ('फ़ाइनाइट) *a.* सीमित; सीमाबद्ध – *n.* समापिका क्रिया

fir (फ़र) *n.* देवदारू; उस पेड़ की लकड़ी

fire (फाइअर) *n.* आग; जलने की क्रिया, दहन; लपट, ज्वाला; दीप्ति; जलते ईंधन का पुंज; विनाशक आग; कमरा गरम रखने का उपकरण आदि; उत्साह, जोश, उमंग; गोलीबारी – *vt.* गोली दागना; *inf.* नौकरी से निकाल देना; पकाना (ईंट आदि); जलाना; ईंधन डालना; प्रेरणा देना; फट जाना – *vi.* बन्दूक आदि चलना; जलने लगना; उत्तेजित हो जाना – **firearm** *n.* बन्दूक, पिस्तौल आदि – **firebrand** *n.* जलती लकड़ी का टुकड़ा; उत्साही व्यक्ति जो दूसरों को प्रेरित करे या भड़काए – **firebreak** *n.* (जंगल में) साफ़ की गयी भूमि की पट्टी जिससे कि आग फैलने न पाए – **fire brigade** दमकल; आग बुझाने वाले व्यक्ति और उन के उपकरण – **firebug** *n. inf.* व्यक्ति जो जान बूझकर इमारत आदि को आग लगाए – **fire drill** आग लगने पर बचाव विधि का अभ्यास – **fire engine** दमकल, आग बुझाने का इंजन – **fire escape** जीना या सीढ़ियां जिससे इमारत में आग लगने पर बचकर निकला जा सके – **fire extinguisher** छोटी आग बुझाने का पानी व रासायनिक पदार्थ भरा सिलेंडर – **firefly** *n.* जुगनू – **fireman** *n.* दमकल दल का सदस्य – **fireplace** *n.* कमरे का आतिशदान या अंगीठी – **firepower** *n.* सेना/जहाज़ के पास उपलब्ध तोपें: *fig.* शक्ति, क्षमता – **fireside** *n.* अंगीठी या चूल्हा; घर; पारिवारिक जीवन – **fire station** दमकल केंद्र – **firewall** *Computers* कम्प्यूटर व्यवस्था जो जानकारी विशेष को अनधिक त लोगों के पास नहीं जाने देती – **firewood** *n.* ईंधन की लकड़ी – **firework** *n.* (बहुधा (~ s) *pl.*) आतिशबाज़ी – (~s) *pl.* गुस्से, आवेश का प्रदर्शन – **firing squad** सैनिकों का दल या दस्ता

जो किसी अपराधी को गोली मारने के लिए भेजा जाय

firm ('फ़र्म) *a.* ठोस, पक्का; स्थिर; स्थायी; सुदृढ़; दृढ़प्रतिज्ञ; निश्चित – *v.* पक्का, स्थिर करना या होना – *n.* वाणिज्यिक उद्यम, फ़र्म या कम्पनी; साझेदारी – **firmly** *adv.* मज़बूती से

firmament ('फ़र्ममंट) *n.* आकाश

first (फ़र्स्ट) *a.* पहला; प्रथम, समय या क्रम में पहला; पहला (दर्जे या वर्ग में); श्रेष्ठ; मुख्य – *n.* प्रारंभ; किसी चीज़ का पहली बार घटना; विश्व विद्यालय में प्रथम श्रेणी की आनर्स की उपाधि – *adv.* पहले; पहली बार – **firstly** *adv.* – **first aid** डाक्टर के आने से पहले रोगी/घायल का उपचार; प्रथम उपचार – **first-hand** *a.* प्रत्यक्ष या आंखों देखा; मुख्य स्रोत से प्राप्त (जानकारी आदि) – **first-rate** *a.* सर्वोत्तम, पहले दर्जे का; सर्वोत्कृष्ट

fiscal ('फ़िस्कल) *a.* राजकोष सम्बन्धी

fish (फ़िश) *n.* मछली (*pl.* **fish, fishes**) – *v.* मछली पकड़ना; परोक्ष रूप से जानकारी प्राप्त करना – **fisher** *n.* – **fishery** *n.* मछली पकड़ने का काम; क्षेत्र जहां मछली मिलती हो – **fishy** *a.* मछली जैसा या मछली भरा; संदिग्ध – **fisherman** *n.* मछुआरा

fishplate ('फ़िश्प्लेट) *n.* रेल की पटरी के नीचे लगी पट्टी; जकड़ पट्टी

fissure ('फ़िशर) *n.* दरार, फटन – **fissile** ('फ़िसाइल) *a.* जो फट सके या जिसमें दरार पड़े – **fission** ('फ़िशन) *n.* विखंडन; परमाणु ऊर्जा से परमाणु का विस्फोट – **fissiparous** (फ़ि'सिपरस) *a.* जो फटन या विस्फोट से उत्पन्न हो या टुकड़े टुकड़े हो जाय

fist (फ़िस्ट) *n.* मुट्ठी, मुक्का – **fisticuffs** *pl. n.* हाथापाई

fit (फ़िट) *vt.* उपयुक्त होना; ठीक होना या ठीक बैठ जाना; पूरा उतरना; ठीक करना या बैठाना; अन्दर डालना या लगाना; देना – *vi.* ठीक बैठ जाना या जम जाना; उपयुक्त होना; उपयुक्त आकार का होना (**-tt-**) – *a.* उपयुक्त, ठीक, अनुरूप; अच्छी हालत में; स्वस्थ (**fitter** *comp.*, **fittest** *sup.*) – *n.* (वस्त्र की) काट; शैली या रिवाज; फ़ैशन; वेशभूषा य कपड़ों के ठीक बैठने की स्थिति – **fitment** *n.* मेज कुर्सी आदि में से कोई एक – **fitness** *n.* उपयुक्तता; अच्छा स्वास्थ्य – **fitter** *n.* व्यक्ति या वस्तु जो किसी वस्तु को उपयुक्त बना दे; दर्जी आदि जो कपड़े की कटाई व सिलाई करता है; मिस्त्री – **fitting** *a.* उपयुक्त, पर्याप्त – *n.* उपकरण; उसे लगाने या बैठाने की क्रिया

fit[2] (फ़िट) *n.* (बीमारी, बेहोशी आदि का) दौरा; बीमारी का अचानक आना; तरंग; आवेश – **fitful** *a.* अनियमित – **fitfully** *adv.* बीच बीच में, रुक-रुक कर (जैसे *sleep fitfully*)

five (फ़ाइव़) *a./n.* पांच का अंक – **fifth** (फ़िफ़्थ) *a./n.* पांचवां – **fifthly** *adv.* – **fives** *n.* एक खेल जो गेंद बल्ले से खेलते हैं – **fifteen** ('फ़िफ़्टीन) *a./n.* पंद्रह – **fifteenth** *a./n.* पंद्रहवां – **fiftieth** *a./n.* ('फ़िफ़्टिअथ) पचासवां – **fifty** ('फ़िफ़्टि) *a./n.* पचास – **fifth column** युद्धकाल में किसी देश में शुत्र की जासूसी करने वाला संगठन

fix (फ़िक्स) *vt.* जमाना, जड़ना, बैठाना; स्थापित करना; नियुक्त करना; देना (किसी के जिम्मे काम डालना); नियत या निर्धारित करना; पक्का करना; मरम्मत करना; *inf.* गलत ढंग या धोखे से किसी घटना के परिणाम पर प्रभाव डालना; घूस देना; *sl.* किसी के होश ठिकाने लगाना, उसे ठीक करना – *vi.* पक्का या ठोस हो जाना; निर्णय करना – *n.* उलझन, कठिनाई – **fixation** (फ़िक्'सेशन) *n.* किसी बात की सनक या तीव्र इच्छा – **fixture** ('फ़िक्स्चर) *n.* वस्तु जो कहीं जड़ी हो; मकान के साथ लगी वस्तु; खेल प्रतियोगिता की तिथि – **fix up** प्रबन्ध या व्यवस्था करना

fizz (फ़िज़) *vi.* सी-सी की आवाज़ करना – *n.* सी-सी की आवाज़; सोडे जैसा पेय जिस पर झाग आ जाए – **fizzle** (ˈफ़िज़ल) *vi.* झाग निकलने जैसी हल्की आवाज़ करना – *n.* सी-सी की आवाज़; पूरी असफलता – **fizzle out** *inf.* किसी प्रयत्न का असफल होना, टांय टांय फिस होना

fjord, fiord (फ्यॉर्ड) *n.* (विशे. नार्वे में) उपखाड़ी (समुद्र का संकरा भाग जो तट के अन्दर तक आ गया हो)

flabbergasted (ˈफ्लैबर्गास्टिड) *a.* हक्का-बक्का

flabby (ˈफ़्लैबि) *a.* लटका हुआ, ढीला; मोटा – **flab** *n. inf.* शरीर पर चर्बी, थुलथुलापन

flaccid (ˈफ़्लैक्सिड) *a.* ढीला, शिथिल

flag[1] (फ़्लैग) *n.* झण्डा; झण्डी – *vt.* झण्डे से संकेत द्वारा सूचित करना (**-gg-**) – **flagstone** *n.* पत्थर की चपटी सिल

flag[2] *vi.* मुरझाना, मंद पड़ जाना

flagellate (ˈफ्लैजिलेट) *vt.* कोड़े लगाना

flagrant (ˈफ्लेग्रंट) *a.* घोर, जघन्य, लज्जाजनक

flail (फ़्लेल) *n.* (अनाज गाहने का) मूसल – *v.* मूसल से मारना, मूसल की तरह चलाना

flair (फ्लेंअर) *n.* जन्मजात योग्यता

flak (फ़्लैक) *n.* विमानभेदी तोपों की गोलाबारी; *inf.* प्रतिकूल आलोचना

flake (फ़्लेक) *n.* छोटा, पतला टुकड़ा, विशे. बर्फ़ का, हिमकण; पपड़ी या परत का टुकड़ा – *v.* पपड़ी उतारना, उतरना

flamboyant (फ़्लैम्ˈबॉइअंट) *a.* भड़कीला

flame (फ़्लेम) *n.* लपट; आवेश, विशे. प्रेम का; *inf.* प्रेमी या प्रेमिका – *vi.* लपटें उठना; जलना; चमकना

flamingo (फ़्लˈमिंगो) *n.* लम्बी गर्दन वाला जलपक्षी, हंसावर

flammable (ˈफ़्लैमबल) *a.* जो शीघ्र आग पकड़ ले

flank (फ्लैंक) *n.* नितम्ब और पसलियों के बीच का भाग; पार्श्व भाग; बाज़ू, बगल – *vt.* सेना के बाज़ू की मोर्चे बन्दी करना; बाज़ू से आक्रमण करना; दोनों में से किसी ओर से आगे बढ़ना

flannel (ˈफ़्लैनल) *n.* नरम, सूती कपड़ा, फ़लालैन

flap (फ़्लैप) *v.* फड़फड़ाना (पंखों का); बाहों को ऊपर नीचे हिलाना; डगमगाना; *inf.* (**in a flap**) उत्तेजित या घबराए हुए होना (**-pp-**) – *n.* कड़कड़ाहट; थपथपाहट, किसी चौड़ी वस्तु का इधर उधर हिलना; विमान के पंख का वह भाग जो ऊपर नीचे हिलता है; *inf.* उत्तेजना, चिंता या घबराहट की स्थिति

flare (फ़्लेंअर) *vi.* लपटों का धधकना; *inf.* (**up** के साथ) अचानक गुस्से से भड़क उठना; बाहर को फैलना जैसे घाघरे के घेरे का – *n.* धधक; संकेत के लिए छोड़ा गया प्रकाश का गोला, फ्लेअर

flash (फ़्लैश) *n.* प्रकाश या लपटों की कौंध या चमक; (छोटा) पल; संक्षिप्त समाचार; प्रदर्शन; तड़क-भड़क – *vt.* स्विच दबाना; सन्देश भेजना; चमका देना; कौंधा देना; अचानक प्रकाश दिखाना – *vi.* अचानक कौंधना या चमकना; अचानक दिखाई पड़ना; लपकना या तेजी से जाना – **flashback** *n.* पुस्तक, नाटक या चलचित्र में किसी पिछली घटना का वर्णन या प्रदर्शन – **flash flood** तेज़ बारिश के कारण अचानक आयी बाढ़

flask (फ़्लास्क) *n.* लम्बी गर्दन वाली बोतल (वैज्ञानिक काम के लिए); (**vacuum flask** भी) थर्मस

flat[1] (फ्लैट) *a.* समतल; सपाट; कोरा (जवाब आदि); नीरस, स्वादहीन; निर्जीव, पहिए का टायर जिसमें हवा न हो या छेद हो गया हो (**flatter** *comp.*, **flattest** *sup.*) – *n.* जो चपटा हो – **flatly** *adv.* – **flat rate** समान दर – **flat out** अधिकतम गति या परिश्रम से

flat[2] (फ़्लैट) *n.* बड़ी इमारत में कुछ कमरों का मकान, फ्लैट

flatter (´फ़्लैटर) *vt.* चापलूसी करना; झूठी प्रशंसा करना; बढ़ा चढ़ा कर तारीफ़ करना – **flatterer** *n.* खुशामदी, चाटुकार – **flattery** *n.* खुशामद, चाटुकारी

flatulent (´फ़्लेंट्युलंट) *a.* जिससे पेट मे वायु उत्पन्न हो, बादी; जिसके पेट में अत्याधिक वायु हो – **flatulence** *n.* बादी, उदरवायु

flaunt (फ़्लॉण्ट) *v.* शान से दिखाना, इतरा कर दिखाना

flautist (´फ़्लॉटिस्ट) *n.* बांसुरी वादक

flavour (´फ़्लेवर) *n.* सुगन्धि और स्वाद की मिश्रित अनुभूति – *vt.* सुगन्धि डालना; (व्यंजन में) मिर्च मसाले डालना – **flavouring** *n.* व्यंजनों में डालने की सुगंधि

flaw (फ़्लॉ) *n.* दोष; त्रुटि – *vt.* दोष या त्रुटि बनाना, बिगाड़ना – **flawless** *a.* परिपूर्ण; बेऐब

flax (फ़्लैक्स) *n.* अलसी का पौधा जिसके रेशे से कपड़ा बनता है, फ्लैक्स – **flaxen** *a.* फ्लैक्स का; भूसे जैसे रंग का

flay (फ़्ले) *vt.* चमड़ी उधेड़ना; कटु आलोचना करना

flea (फ़्ली) *n.* पिस्सू – **fleabag** *n.* व्यक्ति या घोड़ा जो गंदा रहता हो

fleck (फ़्लेंक) *n.* धब्बा, चकत्ती

fled (फ़्लेंड) FLEE का *pt./pp.*

fledg(e)ling *n.* चिड़िया का बच्चा; अनुभवहीन व्यक्ति

flee (फ़्ली) *v.* (कह से) भाग जाना (**fled, fleeing**)

fleece (फ़्लीस) *n.* भेड़ की ऊन – *vt. inf.* ऐंठना; लूटना

fleet[1] (फ़्लीट) *n.* जंगी जहाज़ों का बेड़ा; जहाज़, कारें आदि जो एक साथ चलती हों

fleet[2] (फ़्लीट) *a.* तेज़ – **fleeting** *a.* क्षणिक; क्षणभंगुर

flesh (फ़्लेंश) *n.* मांस; पौधों या फलों का गूदा – **fleshy** *a.* मोटा, गूदाभरा

flew (फ़्लू) FLY का *pt.*

flex (फ़्लेंक्स) *n.(cord)* बिजली का लचीला तार – *v.* झुकना या मुड़ना; झुकाना या मोड़ना – **flexibility** (फ्लेक्स´बिलिटि) *n.* लचीलापन, लचक – **flexible** *a.* लचीला; जिसे मोड़ा या बदला जा सके; जिसे परिस्थिति के अनुकूल बनाया जा सके

flick (फ़्लिक) *vt.* हल्का प्रहार करना या झटका – *n.* – *pl. sl.* सिनेमा – **flick through** पन्ने पलटना (पुस्तक, पत्रिका के)

flicker (´फ़्लिकर) *vi.* टिमटिमाना, झिलमिलाना; फड़फड़ाना; कांपना – *n.* टिमटिमाता प्रकाश या अस्थिर गति

flight (फ़्लाइट) *n.* उड़ान; विमान द्वारा यात्रा; उड़ने की शक्ति; सीढ़ी, ज़ीना (**flight of steps** भी); पलायन, भाग जाने की क्रिया – **flight recorder** विमान में इलैक्ट्रॉनिक उपकरण जिसमें उसकी उड़ान की जानकारी होती है

flimsy (´फ़्लिम्ज़ि) *a.* कमज़ोर; झीना, महीन

flinch (फ़्लिंच) *vi.* पीछे हट; जाना हिचकना

fling (फ़्लिंग) *v.* (मुख्यतया) फैंकना, पटकना, दे मारना; (बिस्तर पर) गिर पड़ना (गाली) देना (**flung** *pt./pp.*) – *n.* पटकने की क्रिया; जल्दबाज़ी में किया प्रयास; रंगरलियां

flint (फ़्लिंट) *n.* चकमक (पत्थर) – *a.* चकमक का या उस जैसा; कठोर; निर्दय

flip (फ़्लिप) *v.* उछालना; उलटा कर देना (**-pp-**) – *n.* उछालने या उलटा करने की क्रिया – **flippancy** (´फ़्लिपन्सि) *n.* चंचलता, छिछोरापन – **flippant** *a.* जो गंभीर बात को भी हंसी मज़ाक समझे, चंचल – **flippantly** *adv.* – **flipper** *n.* मछली का पंख जिससे वह तैरती है – (~ **s**) *pl.* रबड़ के पंख जैसे उपकरण जो पैरों में पहन कर तैरने में सहायक होते हैं – **flip side** किसी विचार का अप्रिय पहलू

flirt (फ़्लर्ट) *vi.* प्रेम का ढोंग करना; खिलवाड़ करना – *n.* इश्कबाज़ी या चोंचले करने वाली/वाला – **flirtation** (फ़्लर्´टेशन) *n.*

flit (फ़्लिट) *vi.* फुदकना

float (फ़्लोट) *vi.* तैरना, तिरना – *vt.* तरल पदार्थ में बहाना; कोई कम्पनी या व्यापार संगठन शुरू करना; शेयर, बांड आदि बेचने का प्रस्ताव करना – *n.* तैरने वाला उपकरण, तिरौंदा; छोटी नाव विशे. जो बैटरी से चलती है; मोटर गाड़ी जिस पर झांकिया सजाई जाती हैं (किसी जलूस आदि के लिए)

flock (फ़्लॉक) *n.* रेवड़, झुंड; *fig.* लोगों का समूह या झुंड; धार्मिक लोगों का समूह; शिष्य वंद – *vi.* भीड़ या झुंड के रूप में इकट्ठे होना

floe (फ़्लो) *n.* बर्फ़ की तैरती चादर

flog (फ़्लॉग) *vt.* चाबुक या सोटे से पीटना; *sl.* बेचना **(-gg-)**

flood (फ़्लड) *n.* बाढ़, सैलाब; ज्वार; जल प्रवाह; बहता पानी; (शब्दों की) झड़ी – *vt.* बाढ़ ला देना; भर देना; पानी से भर देना; बहुत बड़ी संख्या में आना या चलना – **floodlight** *n.* मंच आदि पर प्रयुक्त तेज़ प्रकाश

floor (फ़्लॉर) *n.* फ़र्श; मंज़िल; चपटी, समतल भूमि; (सभा आदि में) बोलने का अधिकार – *vt.* फ़र्श बनाना; ढा देना; चकरा देना – **flooring** *n.* फ़र्श बनाने की सामग्री – **floor show** क्लब में नाच गाने का कार्यक्रम

flop (फ़्लाप) *vi.* नीचे को झुकना या गिर जाना; फ़र्श पर गिर कर चित्त हो जाना; *inf.* सो जाना; *inf.* असफल होना **(-pp-)** – *n.* गिरने की क्रिया या उस की आवाज़; *inf.* असफलता – **floppy** *a.* ढीला – **floppy disk** *Computer* लचीला चक्र या डिस्क जिस पर जानकारी अंकित की जाती है

flora (ˈफ़्लॉर्अ) *n.* किसी क्षेत्र के पेड़ पौधे; उन की सूची (*pl.* **-ras, -rae**) – **floral** *a.* फूलों का – **florist** *n.* फूल बेचने वाला

florid (ˈफ़्लॉरिड) *a.* लाल दमकते मुंह वाला; तड़क भड़क वाली (भाषा)

flotation, floatation (फ़लोˈटेशन) देखिए FLOAT

flotilla (फ़लोˈटिल्अ) *n.* छोटे जहाज़ों का बेड़ा; जंगी जहाज़ों का बेड़ा

flotsam (ˈफ़्लॉट्सम) *n.* (जहाज या नाव के डूबने या नष्ट होने के बाद) समुद्र में तैरता सामान; फैंका हुआ रद्दी माल

flounce (फ़्लाउन्स) *vi.* अचानक, अधीर हो कर चल देना

flounder[1] (ˈफ़्लाउंडर) *vi.* पानी या कीचड़ में गिर पड़ना और निकलने के लिए हाथ पैर मारना; बोलते समय अटकना; (कंपनी आदि) डावां-डोल होना

flour (ˈफ़्लाउअर) *n.* आटा; मैदा; चूर्ण

flourish (ˈफ़्लरिश) *vi.* फलना-फूलना – *vt.* घुमाना, हिलाना, हवा में लहरा कर दिखाना – *n.* सजावटी घुमाव या गोलाई; अलंक त या लच्छेदार भाषा; ज़ोर से हाथ हिलाने की क्रिया

flout (फ्लाउट) *vt.* अनादर या तिरस्कार करना

flow (फ़्लो) *vi.* बहना; का संचार होना; प्रवाहित होना; लहराना; लटकना; प्रचुर मात्रा में होना – *n.* बहाव, संचार; बहाव की मात्रा प्रचुरता – **flow chart** औद्योगिक प्रक्रिया के क्रम का रेखाचित्र

flower (ˈफ़्लाउअर) *n.* फूल; सब से उत्क ष्ट भाग; चुनी हुई वस्तु – *vi.* फूल आना या खिलना; यौवन पर आना; विकसित होना व सफल होना – **flowery** *a.* फूलों भरा; लच्छेदार या अलंक त (भाषा आदि) – **flower girl** फूल बेचने वाली लड़की

flown (फ़्लोन) FLY का *pp.*

fl. oz. fluid ounce(S) का संक्षेप

flu (फ़्लू) *n.* INFLUENZA का संक्षेप

fluctuate (ˈफ़्लक्टयुएट) *v.* बदलते रहना; घटना-बढ़ना – **fluctuation** *n.* उतार - चढ़ाव

flue (फ़्लू) *n.* चिमनी, धुआंकश

fluent (ˈफ़्लूअंट) *a.* जिसमें कोई भाषा धारा प्रवाह बोलने की क्षमता हो – **fluency** (ˈफ़्लूअन्सि)

fluff (फ़्लफ) *n.* पक्षी के पतले पर; *inf.* गलती, भूल – *v.* हलका व नरम हो जाना या करना; *inf.* गलती करना – **fluffy** *a.* रोएंदार

fluid ('फ़्लूइड) *a.* तरल; परिवर्तनशील (स्थिति) – *n.* गैस या तरल पदार्थ – **fluidity** (फ़्लू'इडिटि) *n.* – **fluid ounce** एक माप, पाइंट के बीसवें भाग के बराबर

fluke *n.* संयोग, तुक्का

flume (फ़्लूम) *n.* पानी की संकरी नाली

flummox ('फ़्लमक्स) *vt.* हैरान करना; चकरा देना

flung (फ़्लंग) FLING का *pt./pp.*

flunk (फ़्लंक) *v.* परीक्षा में फ़ेल होना/करना

flunkey ('फ़्लंकि) *n.* नौकर, चपरासी; पिछलग्गू

fluoride ('फ़्लुअराइड) *n.* फ़्लोरीनयुक्त लवण

fluorescence (फ़्लुअ'रेंसन्स) *n.* किसी पदार्थ पर इलैक्ट्रॉन आदि डालने से उत्पन्न प्रकाश या अन्य किरणें जैसा कि बिजली की ट्यूबों में होता है – **fluorescent** *a.* प्रकाशमान, प्रतिदीप्त

flurry ('फ़्लरि) *n.* हलचल; सरगर्मी (**flurried, flurrying**)

flush[1] (फ़्लश) *vi.* (लज्जा से) मुंह लाल हो जाना; चमड़ी का रंग लाल हो जाना; अचानक या जोर से बह जाना; उत्तेजित होना – *vt.* पाखाने में जंजीर खच कर पानी चलाना; उत्तेजित करना – *n.* – **flush out** ढूंढ निकालना

flush[2] (फ़्लश) *v.* (जंगली पशु आदि को) छिपने के स्थान से खदेड़ना

flush[3] (फ़्लश) *n.* ताश में एक ही रंग के पत्ते

fluster ('फ़्लस्टर) *v.* घबरा देना – *n.* घबराहट

flute(फ़्लूट) *n.* बांसुरी, खड़ी गोल झिरी – *vi.* बांसुरी बजाना – *vt.* झिरी डालना – **fluted** *a.* जिसमें झिरी पड़ी हो

flutter ('फ़्लटर) *v.* (पर) फड़फड़ाना; कांपना; उत्तेजित या आशंकित करना; घबरा देना – *n.*

flux (फ़्लक्स) *n.* प्रवाह; निरन्तर परिवर्तन; स्राव; धातुओं का टांका लगाने में सहायक पदार्थ – **in a state of flux** जहां निरंतर परिवर्तन हो रहा हो

fly[1] (फ़्लाइ) *v.* उड़ना; हवा में तेज़ी से गुज़रना; हवा में तैरना; कूदना; तेज़ी से जाना; भाग जाना; कह से तुरंत और अचानक चल देना – *vt.* विमान चलाना; उड़ाना; उड़ा देना – *vi.* (झंडा) लहराना; (से) भाग जाना; (**flew** *pt.*, **flown** *pp.*) – *n.* पतलून के बटन या ज़िप; कपड़े में शिगाफ़; तम्बू में घुसने का रास्ता; उड़ने की क्रिया – **flying** *a.* जल्दबाज़ी से की गयी (यात्रा); संक्षिप्त (प्रवास) – **fly-by-night** *a.* बेइमान व्यक्ति या कंपनी जो जल्दी से पैसा बनाने को तत्पर हो – **flying colours** सफलता; जीत – **flying saucer** उड़न तश्तरी (उड़ते हुए यान जो समझा जाता है कि अन्तरिक्ष से आते हैं) – **flying squad** पुलिस, सेना आदि की विशेष टुकड़ी जो जल्दी कार्य करती है, तूफानी दल – **flying start** अच्छी तेज़ शुरूआत – **flyleaf** *n.* पुस्तक के शुरू और अन्त का खाली पन्ना (*pl.* **fly leaves**) – **flyover** *n.* सड़क के ऊपर पुल – **fly-past** *n.* विशेष अवसर पर हवाई दस्ते की उड़ान – **flywheel** *n.* भारी पहिया जो मशीन की गति को नियंत्रित करता है

fly[2] (फ़्लाइ) *n.* मक्खी

FM Field Marshal, Frequency Modulation का संक्षेप

foal (फ़ोल) *n.* (घोड़े या गधे का) बछेड़ा – *v.* घोड़ी या गधी का बच्चे देना, ब्याना

foam (फ़ोम) *n.* झाग, हल्के वज़न का फेन जैसा पदार्थ जो गरमी सर्दी से बचने और वस्तुएं लपेटने के काम आता है (**plastic foam** भी) – *v.* झाग या फेन उठाना; बहुत गुस्से में होना – **foamy** *a.* झाग भरा – **foam rubber** रबड़ जिस में बहुत से छेद होते हैं

fob off किसी की तिरस्कार से उपेक्षा करना या टाल देना; भगा देना (**-bb-**)

focus (फ़ोकस) *n.* बिन्दु जहां किरणें केन्द्रित होती है; किरण बिन्दु; स्थिति जहां चित्र या बिम्ब बिल्कुल स्पष्ट होता है; (आकर्षण, दिलचस्पी का) केंद्र, मिलन बिन्दु या केन्द्र बिंदु (*pl.* **focuses, foci** (फ़ो'साइ)) – *vt.* केन्द्रित करना; चित्र स्पष्ट करना – *vi.* केन्द्रित होना; स्पष्ट होना (**focused, focusing**) – **focal** *a.* केन्द्र बिन्दु का या केन्द्र बिन्दु

fodder ('फ़ॉडर) *n.* चारा

foe (फ़ो) *n.* शत्रु, दुश्मन

foetus, fetus ('फ़ीटस) *n.* गर्भ में विकसित बच्चा, भ्रूण – **foetal** *a.*

fog (फ़ॉग्) *n.* धुन्ध, कोहरा – *vt.* कुहरे से ढक देना; धूमिल कर देना; घबरा देना; चकरा देना (**-gg-**) – **foggy** *a.* जब धुन्ध या कोहरा छाया हो – **not have the foggiest idea** कुछ न पता होना

fog(e)y ('फ़ोगि) *n.* दकियानूसी (आदमी)

foible ('फ़ॉइबल) *n.* छोटा अवगुण या कमज़ोरी

foil[1] (फ़ॉइल) *vt.* विफल कर देना; हरा देना

foil[2] (फ़ॉइल) *n.* पन्नी; कोई वस्तु जिसकी तुलना में किसी अन्य वस्तु के गुण अधिक स्पष्ट हो जाय

foist (फ़ॉइस्ट) *vt.* – **foist off/on** घटिया या अनचाही वस्तु को मूल्यवान कह कर बेच देना; किसी के गले मढ़ना

fold[1] (फ़ोल्ड) *vt.* दोहरा करना; तह करना; मोड़ना; जोड़ना (बाहें, हाथ आदि); लपेटना; गले लगाना; *Cooking* लपेटना – *vi.* – **fold up** तह होना; लिपट जाना; गिर पड़ना; (कंपनी आदि) बंद हो जाना – *n.* तह; मोड़; लपेट; तह या शिकन (जो कपड़ा मोड़ने से पड़ी हो); भूमि के गर्भ में लिपटी हुई तह – **folder** *n.* मिसिल या फाइल

fold[2] (फ़ोल्ड) *n.* भेड़ों का बाड़ा; श्रद्धालुओं की मण्डली; शिष्य मण्डली

foliage ('फ़ोलिइज) *n.* पत्तों के लिए सामूहिक शब्द, पर्णावली

folk (फ़ोक) *n.* जनसाधारण; जनता, लोक; परिवार, सम्बन्धी; जाति – (**~ s**) *pl.* लोग; माता पिता – **folk dance** लोक नत्य – **folklore** *n.* लोगों की परम्पराएं, रीति रिवाज और विश्वास; लोक साहित्य – **folk song** लोक गीत

follow ('फ़ॉलो) *v.* पीछे जाना या आना, पीछे-पीछे चलना; बाद में आना – *vt.* साथ होना; चाकरी करना; किसी रास्ते आदि पर चलना; अनुयायी होना; ग्रहण करना (उपदेश आदि); बहुत अधिक रुचि या दिलचस्पी होना; परिणाम होना; अर्थ समझना – *vi.* आगे आना; परिणाम होना – **follower** *n.* अनुयायी, शिष्य, समर्थक – **following** *a.* निम्नलिखित – *n.* समर्थकों का समूह – **follow-up** *n.* किसी योजना आदि के लागू करने के बाद का काम

folly ('फ़ॉलि) *n.* मूर्खता; मूर्खतापूर्ण विचार या काम

foment (फ़'मेन्ट) *vt.* भड़काना, उकसाना, प्रोत्साहन देना; (गर्म पानी आदि से) सिकाई या टकोर करना – **fomentation** (फ़मेन्'टेशन) *n.* टकोर; सिकाई

fond (फ़ॉण्ड) *a.* स्नेही; प्रिय – **fondly** *adv.* – **fondness** *n.* चाव, स्नेह

fondle ('फ़ॉन्डल) *vt.* पुचकारना; दुलारना, प्यार से हाथ फेरना

font (फ़ॉन्ट) *n.* छपाई के अक्षर का आकार व शैली

food (फ़ूड) *n.* आहार, खाद्य, भोजन – **food mixer, food processor** मिक्सी – **food-stuff** *n.* खाद्य पदार्थ

fool (फ़ूल) *n.* मूर्ख या मन्दबुद्धि व्यक्ति – *vt.* मूर्ख या बुद्धू बनाना; धोखा देना – *vi.* मूर्खतापूर्ण व्यवहार करना; समय व्यर्थ के कामों में नष्ट करना (**fool around** भी) – **foolery** *n.* स्वभावगत मूर्खता; मूर्खों जैसा व्यवहार; हंसी-दिल्लगी; बेतुकी बात – **foolhardy** *a.* बेकार में जोखिम उठाने वाला – **foolish** *a.* मूर्खतापूर्ण; मूर्ख (व्यक्ति) – **fool-proof** *a.* जिसके खराब या असफल होने की आशंका न हो

foot (फुट) *n.* पैर; निचला भाग (किसी भी वस्तु का); पाया; पायता, पैताना; पैदल दूरी का माप (12 इंच); (कविता का) चरण, पाद (*pl.* **feet**) – *v.* (प्राय: *tr.*) नाचना, चलना (विशे. **foot it** में); कीमत चुकाना (विशे. **foot the bill** में) – **footage** *n.* फुटों में लम्बाई; इस्तेमाल की गयी फिल्म – **footing** *n.* आध ार, न व – **football** *n.* फुटबाल; उस की गेंद –**foothill** *n.* पर्वत के नीचे की ओर पहाड़ियां – **foothold** *n.* ऊपर चढ़ते समय पैर रखने की जगह; (*fig.* भी) स्थान जहां से आगे बढ़ा जा सकता है – **footlights** *pl. n.* रंगमंच के आगे प्रकाश की व्यवस्था – **footloose** *a.* जो हर प्रकार के बन्धनों से मुक्त हो, स्वच्छंद – **footnote** *n.* प ष्ठ के अंत में छपी टिप्पणी, पाद-टिप्पणी – **footprint** *n.* पदचिन्ह – **footwear** *n.* जूते, चप्पल आदि

fop (फ़ॉप) *n.* बांका, छैला, बना-ठना

for (फ़ॉर) *prep.* के लिए; के कारण, की वजह से; के हेतु, के निमित; के बजाय; की ओर; के पक्ष/नाम में; के बारे में; के दौरान; की तलाश में; की अदायगी के लिए; के स्वरूप में; के होते हुए भी – *conj.* क्योंकि

forage (ˊफ़ॉरिज) *n.* चारा; रातिब – *vi.* (जानवर द्वारा) चारे की तलाश करना, – *n.* चारों ओर तलाश (किसी वस्तु की)

forasmuch (फ़रज़्ˊमच) *conj.* (*as* के साथ) क्योंकि, चूंकि

foray (ˊफ़ॉरे) *n.* छापा, आक्रमण; किसी क्षेत्र में घुसने की क्रिया – *vi.*

for(e)bear (फ़ॉर्ˊबेंअर) *n.* पूर्वज, पुरखा

forbear (ˊफॉर्बेंअर) *v.* (विशे. *from* के साथ) न करना, परहेज़ करना; बाज़ आना; धीरज रखना (**forbore** *pt.*, **forborne** *pp.*) – **forbearance** (ˊफ़ॉर्बेंअरन्स) *n.* आत्मसंयम; धीरज; सहिष्णुता

forbid (फ़र्ˊबिड) *vt.* मना करना, निषेध करना (**forbade** *pt.*, **forbidden** (फ़र्ˊबिडन) *pp.*, **forbidding** *pr. p.*) –**forbidding** *a.* भीषण, डरावना

force (फ़ॉर्स) *n.* बल; शक्ति; ज़ोर; ताकत; मानसिक या नैतिक बल; सैनिकों की टुकड़ी या दस्ता; किसी विशेष उद्देश्य के लिए संगठित समूह; प्रभावोत्पादकता; (**in** ~) लागू होने की स्थिति; प्रचण्डता – *vt.* विवश करना; तोड़ डालना; धकेलना, खदेड़ना; समय से पहले परिपक्व करना; बलर्पूवक करवाना – **forced** *a.* जो बल प्रयोग या जबर्दस्ती से कराया जाय; अनिवार्य; अस्वाभाविक; अत्यधिक – **forceful** *a.* शक्तिशाली; ओजस्वी; जो दूसरे से अपनी बात मनवा सके – **forcible** *a.* बल प्रयोग से या जबर्दस्ती किया, विवशकारी – **forcibly** *adv.* ज़बरदस्ती – **force the pace** कार्य तेज़ी से करने के लिए मजबूर कर देना

forceps (ˊफ़ॉर्सिप्स) *pl. n.* चिमटी

ford (फ़ॉर्ड) *n.* नदी का छिछला भाग जिसे पैदल लांघा जा सके – *vt.* पैदल नदी पार करना

fore (फ़ॉर) *a.* आगे (**former, further** *comp.*, **foremost, first, furthest,** *sup.*) – *n.* अगला भाग

fore- (*comb. form*) पहले; पीछे; आगे

forearm (फ़ॉर्ˊआर्म) *n.* हाथ और कुहनी के बीच का भाग – *vt.* पहले से तैयारी करना या हथियार ले रखना

forebode (फ़ॉर्ˊबोड) *vt.* पहले से सूचना देना – **foreboding** (फ़ॉर्ˊबोडिंग) *n.* अनिष्ट की आशंका या पूर्वाभास

forecast (ˊफ़ॉर्कास्ट) *vt.* पहले से अनुमान लगाना (विशे. मौसम का) – *n.* भविष्यवाणी; पूर्वानुमान

forecastle (ˊफ़ोकसल) *n.* जहाज़ का आगे का ऊपर उठा भाग; नाविकों के रहने का स्थान

foreclose (फ़ॉर्ˊक्लोज़) *vt.* (बैंक द्वारा) कर्ज़ा न दिये जाने पर बंधक संपति को कब्ज़े में ले लेना; निषेध करना – **foreclosure** (फ़ॉर्ˊक्लोझ़र) *n.* रोक, मोचन; निषेध

forecourt (ˈफ़ॉर्कॉर्ट) *n.* भवन के आगे की खुली जगह, अहाता
forefathers (ˈफ़ॉर्फ़ादर्ज़) *pl. n.* पूर्वज
forefinger (ˈफ़ॉर्फ़िंगर) *n.* अंगूठे के साथ की उंगली, तर्जनी (**index finger** भी)
foregather (फ़ॉर्ˈगैदर) देखिए FORGATHER
forego[1] (फ़ॉर्ˈगो) *vt.* (समय, स्थान में) पहले होना या घटना (– **went** *pt.*, – **gone** *pp.*, – **going** *pr. p.*) – **foregoing** *a.* पूर्वलिखित; पहले का – **foregone** *a.* जिस का निर्णय हो चुका हो; पहले का
forego[2] (फ़ॉर्ˈगो) देखिए FORGO
foreground (ˈफ़ॉर्ग्राउंड) *n.* चित्र में अनुभाग या अग्रभूमि
forehead (ˈफ़ॉरिड) *n.* माथा, पेशानी
foreign (ˈफ़ॉरिन) *a.* विदेशी; असंगत; बाहरी – **foreigner** *n.* विदेशी नागरिक
forelock (ˈफ़ॉर्लाक) *n.* बालों की लट जो माथे पर लटकती हो, अलक
foreman (ˈफ़ॉर्मन) *n.* मज़दूरों से काम लेने वाला; फोरमैन; ज्यूरी का प्रमुख
foremost (ˈफ़ॉर्मोस्ट) *a./adv.* समय, स्थान या महत्व में पहला; प्रमुख; श्रेष्ठ – **first and foremost** पहला और सबसे महत्वपूर्ण
forenoon (ˈफ़ॉर्नून) *n.* दोपहर से पहले का समय,पूर्वान्ह
forensic (फ़ˈरेंन्सिक) *a.* अपराध/अपराधी की पहचान के लिए किये जाने वाले वैज्ञानिक परीक्षण से सम्बंधित; न्यायालय व अपराधियों को पकड़ने से सम्बन्धित – **forensic medicine** कानूनी मामलों में चिकित्सा ज्ञान का प्रयोग
foreplay (ˈफ़ॉर्प्ले) *n.* संभोग से पहले की चूमाचाटी
forerunner (ˈफ़ॉर्रनर) *n.* पहले आने वाला; अग्रदूत
foresee (फ़ॉर्ˈसी) *vt.* पहले से जान लेना, पूर्व ज्ञान रखना, पूर्वानुमान लगा लेना (**foresaw** *pt.*, **foreseen** *pp*) – **foreseeable** *a.* जिसे पहले से जाना जा सके
foreshadow (फ़ॉर्ˈशैडो) *vt.* पूर्वाभास या पूर्व लक्षण होना
foresight (ˈफ़ॉर्साइट) *n.* दूरदर्शिता; भविष्य की चिंता
foreskin (ˈफ़ॉर्स्किन) *n.* लिंग के अग्र भाग की चमड़ी, खलड़ी
forest (ˈफ़ॉरिस्ट) *n.* वन, जंगल – *vt.* वनारोपण करना – **forestry** *n.*वन विद्या
forestall (फ़ॉर्ˈस्टाल) *vt.* पहले से किसी बात को रोकने की तैयारी करना; रोकथाम करना, पेशबन्दी करना
foretaste (ˈफ़ॉर्टेस्ट) *n.* पूर्वास्वादन
foretell (फ़ॉर्ˈटैल) *vt.* भविष्यवाणी करना (**foretold** *pt./pp.*)
forethought (ˈफ़ॉर्थॉट) *n.* दूरदर्शिता; आने वाली घटनाओं का पूर्वानुमान
forever (फ़ॉˈरेंवर) *adv.* सदा के लिए, अनन्तकाल तक
forewarn (फ़ॉरˈवॉर्न) *vt.* पहले से चेतावनी दे देना
forewent (फ़ॉरˈवेंन्ट) देखिए FOREGO[1]
foreword (ˈफ़ॉर्वर्ड) *n.* भूमिका, प्राक्कथन
forfeit (ˈफ़ॉर्फ़िट) *n.* अपराध अथवा चूक के कारण जब्त हुई वस्तु: जुर्माना; दण्ड – *a.* जब्ती – *vt.* खो बैठना; जब्त हो जाना – **forfeiture** *n.*
for(e)gather (फ़ॉर्ˈगैदर) *vi.* मिलना, इकट्ठे या जमा होना; साथ मिलाना
forgave (फ़र्ˈगेव) FORGIVE का *pt.*
forge[1] (फ़ॉर्ज) *n.* लोहार की दुकान; भट्टी; धातु शोधन या धातु गलाने का कारखाना – *vt.* धातु को तपा कर गढ़ना; बनाना, आक ति देना; आविष्कार करना; जालसाज़ी करना, नकली वस्तु बनाना – **forger** *n.* जालसाज़ –

forgery *n.* जाली दस्तावेज़; जाली चीज़ें बनाने का धंधा; जालसाज़ी
forge[2] (फ़ॉर्जे) *vi.* (धीरे धीरे लेकिन लगातार) आगे बढ़ना
forget (फ़र्'गेंट) *vt.* भूल जाना; भुला देना; अपेक्षा या अनदेखी करना (**forgot** *pt.*, **forgotten** या US *obs.* **forgot** *pp.*, **forgetting** *pr.p.*) – **forgetful** *a.* भुलक्कड़
forgive (फ़र्'गिव) *v.* क्षमा या माफ़ करना – **forgiveness** *n.* क्षमा, माफ़ी
forgo (फ़ॉर्'गो) *vt.* के बिना काम चलाना
forgot (फ़र्'गॉट), **forgotten** (फ़र्'गॉटन) दे. FORGET
fork (फ़ॉर्क) *n.* कांटा (जिससे खाना खाते हैं); पुआल आदि उठाने का यंत्र, पांचा; जंदरा; शाखाओं में विभाजन; उस विभाजन का बिन्दु; मोड़ – *vi.* शाखाओं में बंटना – *vt.* पांचे या कांटे से उठाना या फैंकना; पांचे जैसा बनाना – **fork out** *inf.* (अनिच्छा से) देना या अदा करना
forlorn (फ़र्'लॉर्न) *a.* परिव्यक्त; असहाय; निरावलम्ब; निराश (व्यक्ति); निर्जन (प्रदेश) – **forlorn hope** (प्रयत्न) जिसकी सफलता की आशा न हो
form (फ़ॉर्म) *n.* रूप, आकार; आक ति; ढांचा; स्वभाव; जाति; श्रेणी; प्रपत्र; हालत; अच्छी हालत; स्कूल की कक्षा; काम करने का स्वाभाविक तरीका; शब्दों की निश्चित व्यवस्था, वर्ण विन्यास; बैंच – *vt.* बनाना, गढ़ना, रचना-रूप देना; प्रबन्ध करना; संगठित करना; प्रशिक्षण देना; सोचना; से मिलकर बनना, अंग बनाना – *vi.* अस्तित्व या शक्ल होना – **formation** (फ़ॉर्'मेशन) *n.* निर्माण, निर्मित वस्तु; ढांचा; आक ति; व्यवस्था; सैनिक व्यूह रचना – **formative** *a.* विकास सम्बन्धी; जो विकसित हो रहा हो; जिसका प्रयोग बनाने में हो – **formless** *a.* निराकार
formal ('फ़ॉर्मल) *a.* रस्मी, औपचारिक; नियमानुसार; ऊपरी, बाहरी, दिखावटी; बाहरी रूप या दिनचर्या के अनुरूप; औपचारिक अवसर के लिए, नियम के अनुकूल, जिसका कोई महत्व नह ; सुस्पष्ट और नियमानुकुल; रूखा – **formality** (फ़ॉर्'मैलिटि) *n.* औपचारिकता, तकल्लुफ, औपचारिकता बरतने का स्वभाव; रीति रिवाज का पालन; रूढ़िवाद; केवल रूप या आक ति की चिंता (मौलिकता के विपरीत) – **formally** *adv.* औपचारिक ढंग से
format ('फ़ॉर्मैट) *n.* पुस्तक का आकार और रूप; टेलीविज़न आदि के रूपक की व्यवस्था
former ('फ़ॉर्मर) *a.* पुराना, पुराने समय का; भूतपूर्व; पूर्वोल्लिखित – *pron.* पूर्वोल्लिखित वस्तु, व्यक्ति या तथ्य – **formerly** *adv.* पहले
formidable ('फ़ॉर्मिडबल) *a.* भयानक; विकट; दुर्जेय; भीषण, भयंकर; कठिन (काम आदि) – **formidably** *adv.*
formula ('फ़ॉर्म्युलअ) *n.* सूत्र (*pl.* **-ulae, -s**) – **formulate** *vt.* नुस्खे या फार्मूले के रूप में व्यक्त करना; बनाना – **formulation** *n.*
fornication (फ़ॉर्नि'केशन) *n.* पति या पत्नी के अतिरिक्त किसी से संभोग
forsake (फ़र्'सेक) *vt.* छोड़ देना; त्याग देना; छोड़ कर चल देना (**forsook, forsaken, forsaking**)
forswear (फ़ॉर्'स्वेंअर) *vt.* त्यागना; अस्वीकार करना; छोड़ देना – *refl.* झूठी कसम खाना ~ **swore** *pt.*, ~ **sworn** *pp.*)
fort (फ़ॉर्ट) *n.* किला; दुर्ग
forte (फ़ॉर्ट, 'फ़ार्टे) *n.* विशेष योग्यता या क्षमता; काम जिसमें महारत हो
forth (फ़ॉर्थ) *adv.* सामने, आगे – **forthcoming** *a.* आगामी; निकट, उपलब्ध; जो बात करने को तैयार हो – **forthwith** *adv.* तुरंत, एकदम

forthright (ˊफ़ॉर्थ्राइट) *a.* निष्कपट, खरा; स्पष्टवादी

fortieth (ˊफ़ॉर्‌टिअथ) देखिए FOUR

fortify (ˊफ़ॉर्टिफ़ाइ) *vt.* मजबूत या सुद ढ़ करना; किलेबन्दी करना; (इरादा) पक्का करना (**fortified**, **fortifying**) – **fortification** (फ़ॉर्टिफ़िˊकेशन) *n.* किलेबन्दी; मोर्चाबन्दी

fortitude (ˊफ़ॉर्टिट्यूड) *n.* साहस; धीरज; सहनशक्ति

fortnight (ˊफ़ॉर्ट्नाइट) *n.* दो सप्ताह का समय; पखवाड़ा, पक्ष – **fortnightly** *a.* पाक्षिक (पत्रिका आदि) – *adv.* जो पखवाड़े में एक बार हो

fortress (ˊफ़ॉर्ट्रिस) *n.* गढ़, गढ़ी, किला

fortuitous (फॉर्ˊट्यूइटस) *a.* आकस्मिक; संयोगवश

fortune (ˊफ़ॉर्चन) *n.* सौभाग्य; सम द्धि; धन दौलत – **fortunate** (ˊफ़ॉर्चनिट) *a.* भाग्यशाली – **fortunately** *adv.* सौभाग्य से – **fortune-teller** *n.* ज्योतिषी

forty (ˊफ़ॉर्टि) देखिए FOUR

forum (ˊफ़ॉरम) *n.* मंच; सभा

forward (ˊफ़ॉर्वर्ड) *a.* जो आगे हो, प्रगतिशील; भविष्य का; वादे का (सौदा आदि) – *n.* खिलाड़ी जो आगे हट कर खेलता हो (फुटबाल, हाकी आदि में) – *adv.* आगे (को); भावी; जो दिखाई दे; जहाज़ के अगले भाग में; आगे बढ़ा हुआ – *vt.* आगे बढ़ाना; भेजना – **forwardness** *n.* –**forwards** *adv.*

forewent देखिए FORGO

fossil (ˊफ़ॉसल) *n.* भूमि के नीचे दबे विशे. प्रागैतिहासिक जीव या पौधे के अवशेष, जीवाश्म – *a.* दकियानूसी, पुराना प्राचीन – **fossilize** (ˊफ़ॉसिलाइज़) *v.* जीवश्म बन जाना; पत्थर का हो जाना – **fossil fuel** कोयला, तेल आदि, खनिज ईंधन

foster (ˊफ़ॉस्टर) *vt.* व द्धि या विकास को प्रोत्साहन देना; पालन करना (विशे. किसी दूसरे के बच्चे का) – **foster father/mother** गैर के बच्चे को पालने वाला, पालक पिता/माता – **foster parent** पालक माता-पिता – **foster child** पोष्य-बालक

fought (फ़ॉट) FIGHT का *pt./pp.*

foul (फ़ाउल) *a.* खराब, घ णित; दुर्गन्ध भरा, बदबूदार (भोजन); गन्दा; अन्यायपूर्ण या अनुचित; गाली गलौज भरी (भाषा); गंदगी भरा, अवरुद्ध या रुका हुआ – *n.* जानबूझ कर किया नियम विरूद्ध काम; नियमों का उल्लंघन – *adv.* अनुचित ढंग से – *v.* (मुख्यतया *tr.*) गंदा करना या होना; रोक देना या अवरुद्ध करना; (खेल में) टकरा जाना

found[1] (फ़ाउंड) FIND का *pt./pp.*

found[2] *vt.* स्थापित करना; न व डालना; आधार बनाना – **foundation** *n.* आधार, न व – **founder** *n.* संस्थापक – **foundation stone** न व का पत्थर विशे. जिसे समारोह में लगाया जाय – **founding father** विचारधारा, संस्था, आंदोलन का प्रवर्ता, संस्थापक

found[3] *vt.* गला कर सांचे में डालना; ढालना – **foundry** *n.* ढलाई का कारखाना; ढलाई की कला

founder (ˊफ़ाउंडर) *vi.* ढह जाना, ढेर हो जाना, गिर जाना; जहाज़ आदि का डूब जाना या कीचड़ में धंस जाना

foundling (ˊफ़ाउंड्लिंग) *n.* बच्चा जिसे उसके माता पिता ने फैंक दिया हो, बटबहाऊ

fount (फाउंट) *n.* स्रोत; छपाई के एक प्रकार के अक्षर या टाइप

fountain (ˊफ़ाउन्टिन) *n.* फ़व्वारा, फौआरा (विशे. सजावटी); स्रोत, झरना – **fountainhead** *n.* स्रोत; मूल स्रोत – **fountain pen** फाउंटेन पैन

four (फ़ॉर) *n./a.* चार, चार की संख्या – **fourth** (फ़ॉर्थ) *a.* चौथा – **fourthly** *adv.* – **fortieth** (ˈफ़ॉर्टिइथ) *a.* चालीसवां – **forty** *a./n.* चालीस – **fourteen** (ˈफॉर्टीन) *n./a.*चौदह – **fourteenth** *a.* चौदहवां – **four-poster** *n.* चारपाई जिसमें मच्छरदानी आदि के लिए चार डंडे लगे होते है – **forty winks** हल्की, थोड़ी सी नींद – **on all fours** घुटनों और हाथों के बल

fowl (फ़ाउल) *n.* मुरगा या मुरगी; पक्षी; उस का मांस – *vi.* पक्षियों का शिकार करना

fox (फ़ॉक्स) *n.* लोमड़ी; उसकी खाल; धूर्त या चालाक व्यक्ति – *vt.* चक्कर में डाल देना, चकरा देना – *vi.* मक्कारी दिखाना – **foxy** *a.* मक्कार

foyer (ˈफ़ॉइअर) *n.* रंगशाला, होटल आदि की ड्योढ़ी

fps फुट प्रति सैकेंड; फुट-पाउंड-सैकेंड

fracas (ˈफ्रैका) *n.* उपद्रव; मारपीट

fraction (ˈफ्रैक्शन) *n.* संख्या जो पूरी न हो; भिन्न; टुकड़ा, अंश, खंड – **fractional** *a.* अपूर्ण

fracture (ˈफ्रैक्चर) *n.* टूटने की क्रिया; हड्डी का टूटना; फटन, दरार – *v.* टूटना

fragile (ˈफ्रैजाइल) *a.* भुरभुरा; नाजुक, – **fragility** (फ्रˈजिलिटि) *n.*

fragment (ˈफ्रैग्मंट) *n.* टूटा हुआ या छोटा टुकड़ा – *v.* – **fragmentary** *a.* आंशिक, अपूर्ण – **fragmentation** *n.*

fragrant (ˈफ्रैग्रंट) *a.* सुगन्धित – **fragrance** *n.* सुगन्धि – **fragrantly** *adv*

frail (फ्रेल) *a.* भंगुर, कमज़ोर, जिसका स्वास्थ्य खराब हो; नैतिक द ष्टि से कमज़ोर – **frailty** (ˈफ्रेल्टि) *n.* दुर्बलता, कमज़ोरी

frame (फ्रेम) *n.* चौखटा (तस्वीर का); चौखट (दरवाज़े की); ढांचा; बनावट, गठन (शरीर का); मनोदशा; फिल्म पर ख चा गया एक चित्र – *vt.* बनाना, गठन करना; संरचना करना; (किसी के) अनुरूप बनाना; शब्दों में व्यक्त करना; किसी पर झूठा आरोप लगाना – **frame of mind** मनोदशा – **frame-up** *n. sl.*षड़यंत्र; झूठी गवाही से फंसा देने की क्रिया – **framework** *n.* ढांचा जिसमें पूरक टुकड़े जोड़े जा सकें; सहारा देने के लिए बना ढांचा

franc (फ्रैंक) *n.* फ्रांस, स्विटजरलैंड और अन्य देशों की मुद्रा, फ्रांक

franchise (ˈफ्रैन्चाइज़) *n.* मताधिकार; विशेषाधिकार, विशे. कुछ सामान बेचने का – **franchisee** (फ्रैन्चाइˈज़ी) *n.* विशेष विक्रय अधिकारी

frank (फ्रैंक) *a.* स्पष्टवादी; सच्चा, सरल, निष्कपट – *n.* चिट्ठी पर लगी सरकारी मुहर – *vt.* चिट्ठी पर मुहर लगाना – **frankly** *adv.* साफ़-साफ़ – **frankness** *n.* स्पष्टवादिता

Frankenstein's monster (ˈफ्रैंकिन्सटाइन्ज़) राक्षस जो विपत्ति लाए और अपने निर्माता के काबू में न रहे, भस्मासुर

frantic (ˈफ्रैंटिक) *a.* गुस्से, शोक, चिंता आदि से उद्दिन या उत्तेजित; व्यग्र; उग्र; प्रचण्ड – **frantically** *adv.* व्यग्रता से

fraternal (फ्रˈटर्नल) *a.* भाई का या भाई जैसा – **fraternity** (फ्रˈटर्निटि) *n.* बन्धुता; भाईचारा, US कालिज का समाज – **fratricide** (ˈफ्रैट्रिसाइड) *n.* भाई या बहिन की हत्या

fraud (फ्रॉड) *n.* अपराधपूर्ण छल या धोखा; धोखे से कुछ छीन लेने की प्रक्रिया; ढोंग या पाखंड – **fraudulent** *a.*

fraught (फ्रॉट) *a.* – **fraught with** (खतरों आदि) से भरा हुआ

fray[1] (फ्रे) *n.* लड़ाई; झगड़ा; दंगा

fray[2] (फ्रे) *v.* घिस जाना, कोनों का घिस जाना

freak (फ्रीक) *n.* अपसामान्य व्यक्ति, पशु या वस्तु; अजूबा; अनूठा – *a.* **freak out** *inf.* रहन-सहन का अपना ही तरीका अपनाना

freckled (ˈफ्रेकल्ड) *a.* भूरे चकत्तों वाली (चमड़ी)

free (फ़्री) *a.* आज़ाद, मुक्त; जिस पर कोई बन्धन न हो; निर्बाध; निःशुल्क, मुक्त; करमुक्त; (*of translation*) मुक्त (जो शब्दिक न हो); उदार; खाली (जो इस्तेमाल न हो रहा हो जैसे सीट); व्यक्ति जिसे कोई काम न हो; जो नियत न हो, अनियत – *vt.* आज़ाद कर देना; रिहा करना; हटाना (बाधा, पीड़ा आदि); छुटकारा दिलाना (**freed, freeing**) – **freedom** *n.* स्वतंत्रता, स्वाधीनता, आज़ादी – **freely** *adv.* अबाध रूप से – **freebie** *n.* मुफ़्त दी जाने वाली वस्तु – **freebooter** *a.* लुटेरा सैनिक – **free enterprise** मुक्त अर्थ-व्यवस्था (बिना सरकारी नियंत्रण के) – **free-for-all** *n.* हाथापाई – **free hand** कार्य करने की स्वतंत्रता –**freehold** *n.* जमीन का पट्टा जिसमें किराया न देना पड़े; ऐसी ज़मीन – **freelance** *a./n.*जो किसी संगठन में न हो बल्कि अपना स्वतंत्र काम करता हो – **free trade** मुक्त व्यापार, जिसमें सीमाशुल्क आदि के बन्धन न हों – **freeware** मुफ्त मिलने वाला कम्प्यूटर सॉफ्टवेयर – **freeway** *n.* US मुख्य सड़क – **free will** परमात्मा या भाग्य के विपरीत अपने निर्णय स्वयं करने का मानव का अधिकार, स्वतंत्र इच्छा

freeze (फ्रीज़) *v.* ठंड से जमा देना, बर्फ़ जमाना – *vt.* ठंडे स्थान में रख कर खाद्य पदार्थों को ताज़ा रखना; (फिल्म) बीच में रोक देना, कीमतें, वेतन एक स्तर पर बनाये रखना; बैंक खाते से पैसे न निकालने देना – *vi.* बहुत ठंड लगना; डर से जड़ हो जाना; रुक जाना (**froze, frozen, freezing**) – **freezer** *n.* ठंडी अल्मारी जिसमें रखी चीज़ें बासी नहीं होती – **freezing point** तापमान जिस पर तरल पदार्थ जम जाय

freight (फ़्रेट) *n.* रेल, जहाज़ आदि द्वारा माल भेजने की क्रिया; भाड़ा – **freighter** *n.* माल वाहक जहाज़ आदि

French (फ़्रैंच) *n.* फ्रांस के लोगों की भाषा, फ़्रैंच – *a.* फ्रांस का, फ्रांसीसी – **French fries/ potatoes** तले हुए आलू – **French leave** बिना पूछे ली गयी छुट्टी

frenetic (फ्रि'नैंटिक) *a.* (गुस्से से) उन्मत्त

frenzy ('फ्रेंन्ज़ि) *n.* उन्माद, पागलपन, अत्यधिक उत्तेजना – **frenzied** *a.* उन्मत्त

frequent ('फ़्रीक्वंट) *a.* बारम्बार होने या घटने वाला; सामान्य; बहुल – *vt.* (फ़्रि'क्वेंट) बार बार जाना, प्रायः जाना – **frequency** ('फ़्रीक्वंसि) *n.* बारम्बारता – **frequently** *adv.* बहुधा

fresco ('फ्रेंस्को) *n.* दीवार पर प्लस्तर सूखने से पहले बनाया रंगीन चित्र, भित्ति चित्र (*pl.* - **co(e)s**)

fresh (फ्रेंश) *a.* ताज़ा; नया; अतिरिक्त; भिन्न; हाल का; अनुभवहीन; शुद्ध; ताज़ा (फल आदि) जो धुंधला या पुराना न हो गया हो; जो थका न हो, तरोताज़ा; तेज़ (हवा) – **freshen** *v.* तरोताज़ा होना/करना – **freshman, fresher** *n.* पहले वर्ष का छात्र (विश्वविद्यालय में) – **freshness** *n.* ताज़गी

fret (फ्रेंट) *v.* चिढ़ना; कुढ़ना; खीजना; खिजाना, चिंता करना (**-tt-**) – *n.* खीज, कुढ़न; चिढ़ – **fretful** *a.* खीजा या चिढ़ा हुआ; गुस्सैल

Freudian ('फ्रॉइडिअन) *a.* आस्ट्रिया के मनोवैज्ञानिक सिग्मंड फ़्रायड का या उन के सिद्धांतों से सम्बन्धित

friable ('फ़्राइअबल) *a.* भुरभुरा

friar ('फ़्राइअर) *n.* एक भिक्षु सम्प्रदाय का सदस्य; भिक्षु

friction ('फ़्रिक्शन) *n.* रगड़, घर्षण; मनमुटाव

Friday ('फ़्राइडे) *n.* शुक्रवार – **Good Friday** ईस्टर से पहले का शुक्रवार

fridge (फ़्रिज) *n. inf.* **refrigerator** (रेफ़्रिजरेटर) का संक्षेप

fried (फ़्राइड) FRY का *pt./pp.*

friend (फ्रेण्ड) *n.* मित्र, निकट सहकर्मी; समर्थक – **friendless** *a.* – **friendliness** *n.* – **friendly** *a.* मैत्रीपूर्ण; स्नेही; अनुकूल – **friendship** *n.* मित्रता – **friendly fire** सैनिकों पर अपनी ही सेना, विमान आदि द्वारा गलती से गोलाबारी

frieze[1] (फ्रीज़) *n.* (दीवार पर बनी) सजावटी पट्टी, चित्रवल्लरी

frieze[2] (फ्रीज़) *n.* एक प्रकार का मोटा ऊनी कपड़ा

frigate (फ्रिगिट) *n.* तेज़ जंगी जहाज़ जो दूसरे जहाज़ों की रक्षा करता है या पनडुब्बियों को नष्ट करता है

fright (फ्राइट) *n.* अचानक डर; धक्का, झटका; त्रास; बेढंगा या हास्यास्पद व्यक्ति या वस्तु – **frighten** *vt.* डराना – **frightful** *a.* डरावना, भयंकर; *inf.* बहुत अधिक या बड़ा – **frightfully** *adv. inf.* बहुत अधिक

frigid (फ्रिजिड) *a.* औपचारिक, रस्मी, रूखा; मन्दकाम (स्त्री जिसकी कामेच्छा अधिक न हो); ठण्डा – **frigidity** (फ्रि'जिडिटि) *n.* उदासीनता, रूखापन; निर्ममता

frill (फ्रिल) *n.* झालर; बालों की कंठी – *vt.* झालर बनाना या उससे सजाना

fringe (फ्रिंज) *n.* झब्बा, फुंदना; बाल जो माथे पर डाल कर काटे गए हों; किनारा; हाशिया; सीमा – *vt.* झब्बा लगाना या उस का काम देना – *a.* (रंगमंच आदि) गैर सरकारी; परम्परा या लीक से हट कर; अतिरिक्त – **fringe benefits** सुविधाएं; वेतन के अलावा मिलने वाले लाभ

frisk (फ्रिस्क) *vi.* उछल कूद करना – *vt.* हिलाना; *inf.* जामा तलाशी लेना – *n.* तलाशी – **frisky** *a.* चंचल

fritter[1] (फ्रिटर) *vt.* गंवाना; नष्ट करना

frivolous (फ्रिवलस) *a.* जो गंभीर न हो, छिछोरा – **frivolity** (फ्रि'वॉलिटि) *n.* छिछोरपन

fro (फ्रो) *adv.* उधर (परे) (केवल **to and fro** में)

frock (फ्रॉक) *n.* फ्रॉक या वैसा वस्त्र – *vt.* पादरी का पद देना

frog (फ्रॉग) *n.* मेंढक – **frogman** *n.* साज सामान से लैस तैराक जो गोताखोर का काम करता है, गोताखोर – **frogmarch** *n.* किसी व्यक्ति को उस की इच्छा के विरुद्ध ले जाने का तरीका वि. हाथ कसकर पकड़ कर

frolic ('फ्रॉलिक) *n.* आमोद-प्रमोद; कल्लोल – *vi.* कल्लोल करना (**frolicked, frolicking**) – **frolicsome** *a.* कल्लोल करने वाला; विनोदशील

from (फ्रॉम) *prep.* प्रस्थान, स्रोत, दूरी, कारण या परिवर्तन के बिन्दु का सूचक, से

frond (फ्रॉण्ड) *n.* पौधे का डंठल (पत्तों समेत); पर्णांग पत्र

front (फ्रंट) *n.* अगला या सामने का भाग, भाग; अगवाड़ा; माथा; आगे की स्थिति; (**sea front** भी) समुद्र के पास सैर की जगह; मोर्चा; युद्ध स्थल; रुख, व्यवहार; *inf.* शरीफों जैसा आगा जिसकी आड़ में कोई अपराध किया जा रहा हो; कार्यक्षेत्र; समान लक्ष्य वाले व्यक्तियों का समूह, मोर्चा – *v.* देखना, सामने होना; *inf.* आड़ होना – *a.* आगे का – **frontage** *n.* भवन का अगवाड़ा, माथा – **frontal** *a.* आगे का – **frontier** ('फ्रंटिअर) *n.* सीमा प्रदेश – **frontispiece** ('फ्रंटिस्पीस) *n.* पुस्तक के मुखपृष्ठ के सामने छपा चित्र, मुखचित्र

frost (फ्रॉस्ट) *n.* पाला, तुषार; जमने की क्रिया या स्थिति; मौसम जब तापमान हिमांक से कम हो जाय – *v.* पाले से या वैसी अपारदर्शी वस्तु से ढकना – **frosted** *a.* अपारदर्शी (कांच) – **frostbite** *n.* शीतदंश (जब अत्यधिक ठंड से शरीर का कोई अंग, बहुधा हाथ पैर या कान, जम कर बेकार हो जाये)

froth (फ्रॉथ) *n.* झाग, फेन – *v.* झाग या फेन उठाना, उठना – **frothy** *a.*

frown (फ्राउन) *vi.* त्योरी चढ़ाना, नाराज़गी प्रकट करना – *n.* तेवर; नाराज़गी

froze (फ्रोज़) FREEZE का *pt.* – **frozen** (फ्रोज़न) FREEZE का *pp.*
FRS Fellow of Royal Society का संक्षेप
fructify (फ़्रक्टिफ़ाइ) *v.* फलदार बनाना; सफल बनाना/होना (**fructified**, **fructifying**)
frugal (फ़्रूगल) *a.* मिताहारी; किफायती – **frugality** (फ़्रू गैलिटि) *n.* मिताहार; मितव्ययिता
fruit (फ़्रूट) *n.* फल; (*usu. pl.* में) परिणाम, नतीजा; लाभ, फायदा – *vi.* फलना, फल आना – **fruitful** *a.* लाभदायक – **fruition** (फ़्रू इशन) *n.* उपयोग, आशाएं पूरी होना – **fruitless** *a.* लाभरहित, बेकार
frustrate (फ़्र स्ट्रेट) *vt.* निष्फल करना (प्रयत्न आदि), होने न देना; निराश कर देना – **frustrated** *a.* कुंठित; जिसकी आशाओं पर पानी फिर गया हो – **frustration** *n.* कुंठा
fry[1] (फ़्राइ) *vt.* तलना – *vi.* तला जाना (**fried, frying**) – *n.* कोई तला हुआ व्यंजन – **frying pan** तलने का चपटा बरतन
fry[2] (फ़्राइ) *n.* मछली का बच्चा; पोना – **small fry** छोटी तुच्छ या महत्वहीन वस्तु या व्यक्ति, छुटभैया
ft. **feet,** foot, fort का संक्षेप
fuck (फ़क) *vt. sl./taboo* से संभोग करना; गुस्सा आदि व्यक्त करने के लिए गाली
fuddled (फ़ड्ल्ड) *v.* (बुढ़ापे या अधिक पी लेंने के कारण) चकराया हुआ; भ्रमित
fuel (फ्युअल) *n.* ईंधन; पोषक तत्व – *vt.* ईंधन देना
fugitive (फ़्यूजिटिव) *n.* भगोड़ा – *a.* फ़रार
fulfil (फुल फ़िल) *vt.* पूरा करना (शर्तें आदि); पालन करना; आज्ञा मानना; (इच्छा) पूरी करना (**-ll-**) – **fulfilment** *n.* (इच्छा की) पूर्ति
full (फुल) *a.* पूरा, परिपूर्ण; भरा हुआ, प्रचुर; काफ़ी – *adv.* पूर्णतया; भरा पूरा; ठीक ठीक; अत्यधिक – **fully** *adv.* – **fullness**, **fulness** *n.* पूर्णता –**fulsome** *a.* बहुत अधिक – **full-blown** *a.* जो पूर्णतया विकसित हो – **full-fledged** *a.* पूर्णरूप से विकसित
fulminate (फ़ल्मिनेट) *vi.* (विशे. *against* के साथ) घोर निन्दा करना – *n.* – **fulmination** *n.* निंदा, दोषारोपण
fulsome (फुल्सम) देखिए FULL
fumble (फ़म्बल) *v.* टटोलना; भौंडे ढंग से काम करना – *n.* भौंडा तरीका
fume (फ़्यूम) *vi.* लाल पीला होना; धुआं या भाप छोड़ना – *n.* धुआं, भाप – **fumigate** (फ़्यूमिगेट) *vt.* धुआं छोड़ना, विशे. कीटाणु मारने के लिए – **fumigation** *n.* धूमन – **fumigator** *n.* धूमक
fun (फ़न) *n.* आमोद प्रमोद; मज़ाक; तमाशा – **funny** *a.* जिसे देख कर हंसी आए; अजीब या अद्भुत
function (फ़ंक्शन) *n.* क्रिया, क त्य; समारोह, उत्सव; कर्तव्य; पेशा – *vi.* काम करना; चलना (मशीन आदि का) – **functional** *a.* व्यावहारिक; आवश्यक; चालू या क्रियाशील – **functionary** *n.* अधिकारी या कर्मचारी
fund (फ़ंड) *n.* निधि, कोष; भंडार; मात्रा – *pl.* धनराशि – *vt.* विभिन्न तरीकों से वित्त की व्यवस्था करना, धन जुटाना
fundamental (फ़ंड मेंण्टल) *a.* आधारभूत, मूलभूत; परमावश्यक; प्रारंभिक – *n.* आधार – **fundamentalism** *n.* धार्मिक कट्टरता, रूढ़िवाद – **fundamentalist** *n.* (धार्मिक मामलों में) कट्टरपंथी
funeral (फ़्यूनरल) *n.* म तक के दफ़नाने या जलाने की क्रिया; अन्त्येष्टि – **funereal** (फ़्यू निअरिअल) *a.* शोकमय, निराशा या अंधकार में डूबा
fungus (फ़ंगस) *n.* फफूंद, भुकड़ी; बिना फूल पत्तियों या जड़ वाला पौधा जैसे कुकरमुत्ता (*pl.*

fungi (´फ़न्जि, ´फ़न्जाइ) **-guses**) – **fungal, fungous** (´फ़ंगस) *a.* फफूंद जैसा या उस से सम्बन्धित – **fungicide** (´फ़ंजिसाइड) *n.* फफूंद नाशक पदार्थ

funky (´फ़ेंकि) *inf.* तेज़ लय वाले पॉप-संगीत सम्बंधी; फेशनेबल (कपड़े आदि)

funnel (´फ़नल) *n.* कीप, कुप्पी; (जहाज़ या रेलवे इंजन की) चिमनी या धुआंकश; (सुरंग आदि में) हवा आने का रास्ता – *v.* चिमनी आदि के माध्यम से पहुंचाना/पहुंचना; चुपचाप देना

funny (´फ़नि) देखिए FUN

fur (फ़र) *n.* पशु की खाल के नरम बाल, रोएं; ऐसी रोयेंदार खाल (जो कमाई गयी हो); रोएंदार ऊपरी सतह – *vt.* रोयों से भर देना (**-rr-**) – **furry** *a.* रोयों का या उन जैसा

furbish (´फ़र्बिश) *vt.* चमकाना; मांजना

furious (´फ़्युअरिअस) *a.* जिसे बहुत क्रोध आया हो, आगबबूला; हिंसा पर उतारू – **furiously** *adv.*

furl (फ़र्ल) *vt.* लपेटना, बांधना

furlong (´फ़रलॉङ्ग) *n.* दूरी का एक माप, मील का आठवां भाग, 201.17 मीटर

furlough (´फ़र्लो) *n.* US छुट्टी, विशे. सैनिक की

furnace (´फ़र्निस) *n.* (धातु गलाने की) भट्ठी; बॉयलर गरम करने की बंद अंगीठी; बहुत गरम स्थान

furnish (´फ़र्निश) *vt.* घर में मेज़ कुर्सी आदि लाना; साज़ सामान से लैस करना; देना; जुटाना – **furnishings** *pl. n.* घर सजाने का सामान, परदे आदि – **furniture** (´फ़र्निचर) *n.* मेज़, कुर्सी आदि

furore (फ़्यु´रॉरि, ´फ़्युअरॉर) *n.* शोर-शराबा, विशे. विरोध प्रदर्शन

furrow (´फ़रो) *n.* हलरेखा, सीता कूंड – (**furrows**) *pl. fig.* (माथे पर) शिकन – *vt.* हल से कूंड या लीक बनाना – **furrowed** *a.* शिकन भरी (भवें आदि)

further (´फ़र्दर) *adv.* और; के अतिरिक्त; आगे, और आगे – *a.* और, अधिक, अतिरिक्त – FAR, FORE[1] का *comp.* – *vt.* आगे बढ़ाना; सहायता या प्रोत्साहन देना – **furtherance** (´फ़र्दरन्स) *n.* आगे बढ़ाने की क्रिया – **furtherer** *n.* – **furthermore** *adv.* इसके अतिरिक्त/अलावा – **furthest** *a.* FAR, FORE [1] का *sup.* – *adv.* – **furthermost** *a.* दूरतम; सब से आगे

furtive (´फ़र्टिव़) *a.* चोर के समान; नज़र छिपा कर काम करने वाला – **furtively** *adv.*

fury (´फ़्युअरि) *n.* आक्रोश; आवेश; (तूफान आदि की) प्रचण्डता

fuse, US fuze (फ़्यूज़) *v.* गलाकर मिलाना; गरमी से पिघल जाना; संमिश्रण; (बिजली का) फ़्यूज उड़ा देना; विफल बना देना – *n.* बिजली का फ़्यूज़ (पतली तार जो गल जाय); बम आदि का पलीता – **fusion** (´फ़्यूझ़न) *n.* गलने या पिघलने की क्रिया; वस्तु का परस्पर गल कर मिलना जैसे परमाणुओं का

fuselage (´फ़्यूज़िलाझ़) *n.* विमान का ढांचा

fuss (फ़स) *n.* अनावश्यक परेशानी; (बात का) बतंगड़ (बनाने की क्रिया); शिकायत; आपत्ति (बिकार की) – *vi.* बात का बतंगड़ बनाना; छोटी छोटी बातों पर ध्यान न देना या उनकी चिंता करना – **fussy** *a.* नकचढ़ा; जिसे आसानी से कुछ पसंद न आए – **make a fuss of** तिल का ताड़ बनाना

futile (´फ़्यूटाइल) *a.* व्यर्थ; बेकार; निष्प्रभाव – **futility** (फ़्यू´टिलिटि) *n.* असारता, व्यर्थता

future (´फ़्यूचर) *n.* भविष्य, भावी जीवन; भाग्य – *a.* भावी; आने वाले समय का

fuzz (फ़ज़) *n.* रूआं; रूएंदार बाल (या उन के गुच्छे); *sl.* पुलिस का सिपाही

G

gram(s); gravity (गुरुत्वाकर्षण) (के कारण गति में तेज़ी) का संक्षेप

abble (गैबल) *v.* बड़बड़ाना – **gift of the gab** वाक्पटुता, वाग्मिता

aberdine, gabardine (गैबर्डीन) *n.* बढ़िया ऊनी कपड़ा जिससे बरसाती कोट बनते हैं

ad (गैड) *vi.* (विशे. **gad about** में) मौज-मस्ती करते घूमना **(-dd-)**

adget (गैजिट) *n.* छोटी मशीन आदि जो किसी काम आए; मशीनी जुगत; वस्तु जो अपनी नवीनता या अद्‌भुत होने के कारण प्रिय हो – **gadgetry** *n.* छोटी मशीनें सामूहिक रूप से; इनका उपयोग

affe (गैफ़) *n.* भयंकर भूल; असामयिक बात; बिना सोचे समझे कही बात

ag[1] (गैग) – *vt.* मुंह में कपड़ा ठूसना; बोलने न देना – *n.* मुंह में ठूंसा कपड़ा या उस पर बन्धी पट्टी; सार्वजनिक रूप से किसी बारे में कुछ न कहने का (सरकारी) आदेश

ag[2] (गैग) *n.* मज़ाक; लतीफ़ा

aggle(गैगल) *n.* बतखों का समूह; *inf.* अनियंत्रित भीड़

aiety (गेइअटि) *n.* देखिए GAY

ain (गेन) *vt.* पाना; कमाना (लाभ आदि); जीतना; पहुंचना; कमाई करना – *vi.* बढ़ना; सुधरना; समीप पहुंचना; (मशीन, घड़ी आदि का) तेज़ चलना – *n.* लाभ; व द्धि; सुधार – **gainfully** *adv.* लाभ सहित; मज़दूरी या वेतन के साथ

ainsay (गेन्‌ से) *vt.* खण्डन करना

ait (गेट) *n.* चाल, ठवन

aiter (गेटर) *n.* टांग के निचले हिस्से को ढकने का कपड़ा या चमड़ा

ala (गाल्अ) *n.* उत्सव, समारोह; नाटक आदि का प्रदर्शन; खेल प्रतियोगिता आदि

galaxy (गैलक्सि) *n.* आकाशगंगा (तारों का समूह); विशिष्ट या प्रसिद्ध व्यक्तियों का समूह

gale (गेल) *n.* तेज़ हवा, झंझा

gall[1] (गॉल) *n. inf.* ध ष्टता, गुस्ताखी; कटुता; चिढ़ – **gall bladder** जिगर के साथ लगी पित्त की थैली; पित्ताशय – **gallstone** *n.* पित्ताशय की पथरी

gallant (गैलंट) *a.* बढ़िया; भव्य; प्रतापी; वीर, बहादुर; (गैलांट भी) नारीभक्त; नारीसेवा-परायण – *n.* – **gallantly** *adv.* प्रेमी, आशिक; बना ठना, बांका युवक बहादुरी से – **gallantry** *n.* वीरता, बहादुरी

gallery (गैलरि) *n.* दीर्घा, गलियारा, गैलरी; गिरजा या रंगशाला में आगे की बढ़ी हुई दूसरी मंजिल; दर्शक समूह; भवन के बाहर लम्बा संकरा प्लेटफ़ार्म; कमरा या कमरे जो विशेष प्रयोजनों के लिए इस्तेमाल हों जैसे कला प्रदर्शनी के लिए; दीवार में हो कर मकान के अन्दर जाने का रास्ता

galley (गैलि) *n.* पाल और पतवार वाली बड़ी नाव जिसे दास या अपराधी खेते थे; विमान या जहाज़ का रसोईघर; पतवार वाली बड़ी नाव

gallon (गैलन) *n.* तरल पदार्थों का नाप, *Brit* 4.55 लीटर; *US* 3.79 लीटर

gallop (गैलप) *v.* सरपट दौड़ना; तेज़ चलना

gallows (गैलोज़) *n.* टिकठी, फांसी का तख्ता

Gallup poll (गैलप-) *n.* किसी विषय पर जनसाध ारण के विचार जानने की विधि, जनमत संग्रह

galore (ग'लॉर) *adv.* ढेर सा, बहुत सा

galoshes (ग'लॉशिज़) *pl. n.* ऊपरी जूता

galvanize (गैल्वनाइज़) *vt.* क्रियाशील बनाना; लोहे आदि पर जस्ता चढ़ाना

gambit (गैम्बिट) *n. Chess* पहली चाल; *fig.* कोई पहली कार्यवाही; टिप्पणी, चाल आदि जिस का उद्देश्य अपना पलड़ा भारी करना हो

gamble (गैम्बल) *vi.* जुआ खेलना – *n.* जोखिम खतरा; दांव; शर्त; जूएबाज़ी – **gambler** *n.* जुआरी

gambol (गैम्बल) *vi.* उछल कूद या कल्लोल करना *(-ll-)* - *n.*

game (गेम) *n.* खेल; शौक; कार्य या व्यवसाय; मज़ाक; योजना; चाल, तिकड़म; तरकीब; शिकार – *a.* साहसी; इच्छुक – *vi.* जुआ खेलना – **gamester** *n.* जुआरी – **gamekeeper** *n.* शिकारी रक्षक; चौकीदार जो जंगल में अनधिक त शिकार रोकने के लिए रखा जाता है – **game plan** (राजनीति, व्यापार आदि में) सफल होने की योजना

gamma (गैम्अ) *n.* ग्रीक भाषा का तीसरा अक्षर – **gamma ray** एक पैनी विद्युत चुम्बकीय किरण

gamut (गैमट) *n.* सप्तक, स्वरग्राम; पूरा विस्तार

gander (गैंडर) *n.* नर बतख

gang (गैङ) *n.* (अपराधियों की) टोली, गिरोह; मज़दूरों का दस्ता – *vi.* (विशे. *together* के साथ) गिरोह बनाना – **gang up (on)** *inf.* किसी के विरुद्ध संगठित होना – **gang rape** सामूहिक बलात्कार

gangrene (गैंग्रीन) *n.* घाव या बीमारी से मांस का गल जाना, कोथ – **gangrenous** *a.*

gangster (गैंग्स्टर) *n.* अपराधी गिरोह का सदस्य

gangway (गैंग्वे) *n.* जहाज़ से तट तक का पुल या वैसा ढांचा; सीटों की पत्तियों के बीच का रास्ता – *interj.* रास्ता दीजिए!

gap (गैप) *n.* छेद, दरार; खाली जगह; अंतराल; अंतर; फटन *fig.* त्रुटि

gape (गेप) *vi.* (आश्चर्य से) मुंह खुले का खुला रहना; जम्हाई लेते समय मुंह खोलना; पूरा खुलना या खोलना – *n.* टकटकी; दरार; जंभाई

garage (गैराझ़, गैरिज) *n.* कार खड़ी करने या उसकी मरम्मत का स्थान – *vt.* कार गैराज में रखना

garb (गार्ब) *n.* पहनावा, पोशाक; पहनावे का फ़ैशन – *vt.* कपड़े पहनाना

garbage (गार्बिज) *n.* कूड़ा, कचरा; बकवास – **garbage can** *US* कूड़ा डालने का कनस्तर

garbled (गार्बल्ड) *vt.* (कहानी, विवरण आदि) जो तोड़-मरोड़ कर या गलत रूप में पेश की जाय

garden (गार्डन) *n.* उद्यान, बाग़ – *vi.* बाग़ीचा उगाना – **gardener** *n.* माली, बागबान – **gardening** *n.* बागवानी

gargantuan (गार्गैण्ट्युअन) *a.* विशालकाय

gargle (गार्गल) *vi.* ग़रारे करना

garish (गेंअरिश) *a.* भड़कीला, चटकीला

garland (गार्लण्ड) *n.* माला (फूलों की) – *vt.* माला पहनाना

garlic (गार्लिक) *n.* लहसुन

garment (गार्मंट) *n.* पहनने का कपड़ा या वस्त्र – **garments** *pl. n.* कपड़े

garner (गार्नर) *vt.* इकट्ठे या एकत्र करना

garnet (गार्निट) *n.* एक कीमती पत्थर, तामड़ा

garnish (गार्निश) *vt.* सजाना (विशे. किसी व्यंजन को) – *n.* उसमें प्रयुक्त पदार्थ

garret (गैरिट) *n.* दुछत्ती, अटारी

garrison (गैरीसन) *n.* किसी नगरी या किले में तैनात सैनिक; स्थान जिस की किलेबंदी की गयी हो – *vt.* किले में सैनिक ठहराना

garrulous (गैरुलस) *a.* (*talkative*) बातूनी, वाचाल

garter (गार्टर) *n.* गेटिस, मोज़ाबंद

gas (गैस) *n.* गैस; *inf.* (विशे. *US*) पेट्रोल; *inf.* बेकार की शेखी भरी बातें *(pl.* **gases**) – *vt.* गैस छोड़ना; गैस से विषाक्त कर देना – *vi.* शेखी बघारना (**-ss-**) – **gaseous** (गैसिअस, गैशस) *a.* गैस का या उस जैसा – **gas station** *US* पेट्रोल पंप

gash (गैश) *n.* खुला या गहरा घाव – *vt.* गहरी काट मारना

gasket (ʹगैस्किट) *n.* धातु के पुर्जों (विशे. इंजनों) को बंद करते समय उन में रबड़ या अस्बस्टस का प्रयोग (जिससे कि तेल आदि बाहर न निकले)

gasoline, -ene (ʹगैसलीन) *n.* **US** पेट्रोल

gasp (गास्प) *vi.* हांफना; भौंचक रह जाना – *n.* हांफने की क्रिया

gastric (ʹगैस्ट्रिक) *a.* आमाशय या मेदे का – **gastronomy** (गैस्ʹट्रॉनमि) *n.* अच्छे व्यंजन खाने का शौक, चटोरापन

gastroenteritis (गैस्ट्रोएॅण्टʹराइटिस) *n.* आमाशय और अन्तड़ियों की सूजन

gate (गेट) *n.* (दीवार में) फाटक, दूरी या बाड़ा अथवा जंगला; पानी का द्वार, जल-कपाट; आने जाने का रास्ता; – (**gate money** भी) प्रवेश शुल्क – **gatecrash** *v.* किसी सभा या समारोह में बिना निमंत्रण के जाना – **gateway** *n.* रास्ता, प्रवेश द्वार

gather (ʹगैदर) *vt.* इकट्ठे करना; धीरे-धीरे जमा करना या बढ़ाना; समेटना, बटोरना – *vi.* बढ़ना; जमा होना; समझना; जानना – **gathering** *n.* सभा, जनसमूह

gauche (गोश) *a.* फूहड़; भद्दा

gaudy (ʹगॉडि) *n.* भड़कीला

gauge (गेज) *n.* मानक माप, जैसे तार की गोलाई का; धातु की चादर की मोटाई; रेल के बीच की पटरियों की दूरी; सामर्थ्य; धारिता; विस्तार; तारों की मोटाई, वर्षा आदि मापने का यंत्र – *vt.* मापना या अनुमान लगाना

gaunt (गॉण्ट) *a.* दुबला पतला

gauntlet (ʹगॉण्ट्लिट) *n.* – **run the gauntlet** (पुराने समय में) दो पंक्तियों में लाठियां आदि लिए लोगों में से गुज़रना; आलोचना या अप्रिय व्यवहार का सामना करना; विपत्ति सहना

gauze (गॉज़) *n.* जालीदार कपड़ा; जाली

gave (गेव़) **GIVE** का *pt.*

gavel (ʹगैवल) *n.* अध्यक्ष या नीलाम करने वाले की छोटी मुंगरी

gawky (ʹगॉकि) *a.* फूहड़; बेढंगा

gay (गे) *a.* समलिंगकामी (लौंडा, लौंडेबाज़); प्रसन्नचित्त, खुशमिज़ाज; भड़कीला – **gaiety** (ʹगेइअटि) *n.* प्रसन्नता – **gaily** *adv.*

gaze (गेज़) *vi.* टकटकी बांध कर देखना – *n.* टकटकी

gazelle (गʹज़ेल) *n.* छोटे आकार का हिरन, चिंकारा

gazette (गʹज़ेट) *n.* राजपत्र; कुछ समाचार पत्रों का नाम – *vt.* राजपत्र में प्रकाशित करना – **gazetteer** (गैज़िʹटिअर) *n.* भूगोल कोष (किसी क्षेत्र के नगरों का विवरण)

GDP Gross Domestic Product का संक्षेप

gear (गिअर) *n.* गरारी, गियर (कार आदि के इंजन में); साज़ सामान; कपड़ा लत्ता; माल; बरतन; उपकरण; औज़ार; साज़ – *vt.* गियर में डालना या लगाना; साज़ लगाना या कसना – **gearbox** *n.* बक्सा जिसमें गरारियां लगी होती हैं – **gear up for** के लिए तैयार होना

geek (गीक) *n.* अनाकर्षक वस्त्र पहने वाला व बोर करने वाला व्यक्ति

geese (गीस) GOOSE का *pl.*

Geiger counter (ʹगाइगर-) *n.* रेड़ियो धर्मिता (*radio activity*) का पता लगाने का उपकरण

geisha (ʹगेशअ) *n.* (जापान में) पुरुषों की पेशेवर संगिनी

gel (जेॅल) *n.* अवलेह जैस गाढ़ा पदार्थ जो विशे॰ बाल संवारते समय लगाया जाता है – *vi.* ऐसा पदार्थ बनाना (**-ll-**), **jell** भी

gelatin(e) (ʹजेॅलटीन) *n.* सरेस, जिलेटिन; उससे मिलती जुलती वस्तु – **gelatinous** (जिʹलैटिनस) *a.* जिलेटिन युक्त; जिलेटिन जैसा

geld (गेॅल्ड) *vt.* बधिया करना

gem (जेॅम) *n.* मणि या रत्न, विशे. जब वह तराशा गया हो

Gemini (जॅमिनाइ, जॅमि´नी) *n.* राशि चक्र का तीसरा चिन्ह मिथुन (युग्म) जिस का समय 22 मई से 21 जून तक होता है
gender (´जॅण्डर) *n.* लिंग (पुल्लिग या स्त्रीलिंग)
gene (जीन) *n.* एक जीविका तत्व जो माता पिता के गुणों का समावेश उनके बच्चों में करने के लिए जिम्मेदार है
genealogy (जीनि´ऐलजि) *n.* वंशावली
general (´जॅनरल) *a.* साधारण, आम, सामान्य; व्यापक; सार्वजनिक, आम; जो सभी पर लागू हो, कुछ विभागों तक सीमित न हो; सामान्य, व्याप्त; फुटकर; जिसका सम्बन्ध केवल मुख्य तत्व से हो; अस्पष्ट; अनिश्चित – *n.* कर्नल से ऊंचा सैनिक अधिकारी, जनरल – **generalization** *n.* (सामान्य निष्कर्ष) – **generalize** *vt.* सामान्य नियम का रूप देना – *vi.* सामान्य निष्कर्ष निकालना – **generally** *adv.* सामान्यतया – **general knowledge** सामान्य ज्ञान
generate (´जॅनरेट) *vt.* उत्पन्न करना – **generation** (जॅन´रेशन) *n.* उत्पादन; पीढ़ी, पुश्त – **generative** *a.* उत्पादक – **generator** *n.* बिजली, भाप आदि बनाने का उपकरण; पैदा करने वाला, जनक
generic (जि´नॅरिक) *a.* जातीय, जातिगत; (उत्पादन विशे० दवाई) जिसका नाम कम्पनी विशेष से संम्बधित न होकर उसके मुख्य अवयव पर आधारित हो (जैसे *aspirin*) – **generically** *adv.*
generous (´जॅनरस) *a.* उदार; दानी, दानशील; प्रचुर, भरपूर – **generosity** (जॅन´रॉसिटी) *n.* उदारता, दानशीलता
genesis (´जॅनिसिस) *n.* उत्पत्ति, उद्‌गम
genetics (जि´नॅटिक्स) *n.* आनुवंशिकता और जीवों में परिवर्तन का अध्ययन, आनुवंशिकी – **genetic** *a.*
genial (´जीन्यल) *a.* हंसमुख; मिलनसार; अनुकूल
genie (´जीनि) *n.* परियों की कहानियों में प्रकट होने वाला दास, दासी; जिन्न (*pl.* **genii**)
genital (´जॅनिट्ल) *a.* जननेन्द्रियों से सम्बन्धित – **genitals** (´जॅनिटल्ज़) *pl. n.* जननेन्द्रियां
genius (´जीनिअस) *n.* प्रतिभा; प्रतिभाशाली व्यक्ति
genocide (´जॅनोसाइड) *n.* जाति संहार
genome (´जिनोम) *n.* किसी भी जीव (*organism*) में समाविष्ट जीविका तत्वीय (*genetic*) सामग्री
genre (झ़ांर्अ) *n.* किस्म, प्रकार; शैली
gent (जॅन्ट) *n.* सभ्य व्यक्ति – *pl.* पुरुषों का शौचालय
genteel (जॅन्´टील) *a.* (*disapproving*) सुसंस्क त, भद्र; फ़ैशन के अनुसार; जो सभ्य होने का आडम्बर करे
gentle (´जॅण्ट्ल) *a.* म दु स्वभाव का; चुप रहने वाला; कोमल; (मौसम आदि) सौम्य; हल्का; सभ्य, नरम, धीमा; कुलीन – **gentility** (जॅन्टिलिटि) *n.* अच्छा व्यवहार; कुलीनता – **gentleness** *n.* सौम्यता का गुण; म दुता – **gently** *adv.* – **gentry** *n.* भद्र या कुलीन लोग (अभिजात वर्ग से नीचे के) – **gentleman** *n.* सज्जन पुरुष; संभ्रांत पुरुष; पुरुष (विनयपूर्वक मर्द के लिए प्रयुक्त) – **gentlemanly, gentlemanlike** *a.* – **gentlewoman** *n.* संभ्रांत महिला
genuine (´जॅन्युइन) *a.* असली, सच्चा, शुद्ध हृदय
genus (´जीनस) *n.* वर्ग; गण; प्रकार (*pl.* **genera** (´जॅनर्अ))
geography (जि´ऑग्रफ़ि) *n.* भूगोल (शास्त्र) – **geographer** *n.* भूगोल शास्त्री – **geographic(al)** (जिअ´ग्रैफिकल) *a.* भौगोलीय – **geographically** *adv.*
geology (जि´ऑलजि) *n.* भू-विज्ञान – **geological** (जिअ´लॉजिकल) *a.* भू-विज्ञान संबंधी – **geologist** (जि´ऑलजिस्ट) *n.* भू-विज्ञान विशेषज्ञ

geometry (जि´ऑमिट्रि) *n.* रेखागणित, ज्यामिति – **geometrical** (जिअ´मैट्रिकल) *a.*

geophysics (जीओ´फ़िज़िक्स) *n.* भू-भौतिकी

georgette (जॉर्´जेंट) *n.* महीन, रेशमी और झीना कपड़ा जॉर्जेट

geostationary (जीओ´स्टेशनरि) *a.* (कत्रिम उपग्रह) जो प थ्वी का 24 घंटे में चक्कर लगाये अतः अपने स्थान पर स्थिर होने का आभास दे, स्थिर-स्थित

geranium (जि´रेनिअम) *n.* लाल, गुलाबी या सफेद फूलों वाला एक सामान्य पौधा; तेज़ गुलाबी रंग

geriatrics, gerontology (जेंरि´ऐट्रिक्स, जेंरॉन्´टॉलजि) *n.* व द्धों और उन के रोगों की चिकित्सा का विज्ञान; जरा चिकित्सा – **geriatric** *a./n.* व द्ध (व्यक्ति)

germ (जर्म) *n.* रोगाणु; प्रारंभिक वस्तु या रूप – **germicidal** (जर्मि´साइडल) *a.* – **germicide** (´जर्मिसाइड) *n.* रोगाणु नाशक औषधि या तत्व

German (´जर्मन) *n./a* जर्मनी का (नागरिक या भाषा)

germinate (´जर्मिनेट) *v.* अंकुरित होना या फूटना – **germination** *n.* अंकुरण

gerund (´जेंरड) *n.* क्रियावाची संज्ञा जैसे living

gestation (जेंस्´टेशन) *n.* गर्भ में रहने की स्थिति; गर्भ की अवधि; विकसित होने की अवधि

gesticulate (जेंस्´टिक्युलेट) *vi.* बोलते समय (भाव व्यक्त करने के लिए) हाथ हिलाना, इंगित करना – **gesticulation** *n.*

gesture (´जेंस्चर) *n.* चेष्टा, इंगित, इशारा; मनोदशा का इशारा – *vi.*

get (गेंट) *vt.* पाना, प्राप्त करना, लेना; पकड़ना; कमाना; भेजना या मंगाना; किसी स्थिति में लाना; तैयार करना; उत्पन्न करना; किसी वस्तु का कब्ज़े में होना; कराना (काम आदि); *inf.* समझना – *vi.* जाने या आने में सफल होना; पहुंचना; प्राप्त करना; बन जाना (**got, getting**) – **getaway** *n.* भाग निकलना (बच कर)

geyser (´गीज़र) *n.* गरम पानी का चश्मा; पानी गरम करने का गीज़र

ghastly (´गास्ट्लि) *a. inf.* भयंकर, डरावना *inf.* अस्वस्थ, अप्रिय – *adv.* देखने में घिनौना

ghetto (´गेंटो) *n.* घनी आबादी वाली गन्दी बस्ती जिसमें एक ही जाति के लोग रहते हों (*pl.*-**tos**)

ghost (गोस्ट) *n.* भूत; प्रेतात्मा; छाया, आभास; (~ **writer**) व्यक्ति जो दूसरों के नाम से लिखे – **ghostly** *a.* भूत जैसा

giant (´जाइअंट) *n.* दैत्य, दानव; असाधारण गुणों से सम्पन्न या बड़े कद का व्यक्ति; विशाल पौधा आदि – *a.* भीमकाय – **gigantic** (जाइ´गैन्टिक) *a.* विशाल, भीमकाय

gibber (´जिबर) *vi.* मुंह से निरर्थक आवाज़ें निकालना – **gibberish** (´जिबरिश) *n.* अर्थहीन भाषण या शब्द

gibbon (´गिबन) *n.* एक प्रकार का बन्दर, ऊलक

gibe, jibe (´जाइब) – *v.* ताना मारना – *n.* ताना

giddy (´गिडि) *a.* जिसे चक्कर आ रहे हों, जो गिरने को हो; (ऊंचाई) जिससे सिर चकराए – **giddiness** *n.* सिर चक्कर

gift (गिफ्ट) *n.* भेंट, उपहार; प्रतिभा; सामर्थ्य – *vt.* उपहार या दान देना – **gifted** *a.* प्रतिभाशाली

gigantic देखिए GIANT

giggle (´गिगल) *vi.* मूर्खों की तरह हंसना – *n.* इस प्रकार की हंसी

gigolo (´झ़िगलो, ´जिगलो) *n.* भाड़े का आशिक (जिसे उससे उम्र में बड़ी स्त्री ने पाल रखा हो)

gild (गिल्ड) *vt.* सोने का पानी चढ़ाना; मुलम्मा करना (**gilded** *pt.*, **gilt** *or* **gilded** *pp.*) – **gilt** *a.* जिस पर मुलम्मा चढ़ा हो – *n.* सोने का पानी, मुलम्मा; ऊपरी तड़क भड़क

gill (गिल) *n.* मछली का गलफड़ा (बहुधा *pl.*)

gimmick (´गिमिक) *n.* चाल या तिकड़म जो ध्यान आक ष्ट करने या प्रचार के लिए चली जाय

gin (जिन) *n.* एक प्रकार की शराब

ginger (´जिंजर) *n.* अदरक – *vt.* जोश दिलाना – **gingerbread** *n.* अदरक से बना केक – **ginger group** किसी दल या संगठन में उत्साही लोगों का समूह जो उसे क्रांतिकारी रूप देना चाहता है

gingerly (´जिंजर्लि) *adv.* सावधानी से, संकोच पूर्वक – *a.*

Gipsy (´जिप्सि) *n.* देखिए GYPSY

giraffe (जि´राफ़) *n.* लम्बी गर्दन वाला अफ्रीकी जीव, जिराफ़

gird (गर्ड) *vt.* कमरबन्द या पेटी बांधना; तलवार कमर में बांधना; तैयारी करना, कमर कसना; घेरा डाल लेना (**girt, girded** *pt./pp.*) – **girder** (´गर्डर) *n.* बड़ा शहतीर, विशे. इस्पात का बना

girdle (´गड्र्ल) *n.* स्त्रियों का कमर से जांघ तक ढकने वाला तंग वस्त्र; कमरबंद; मेखला; पेटी; घेरा; (*griddle*) तवा – *vt.* घेरा डालना

girl (गर्ल) *n.* लड़की – **girlfriend** *n.* प्रेमिका; सहेली – **girlhood** *n*

girth (गर्थ) *n.* घेरे का माप; घोड़े की कसन या तंग (जिस पर काठी रहती है) – *vt.* घेरा डालना; कमरबंद कसना या तंग बांधना

gist (जिस्ट) *n.* सार, सारांश

give (गिव़) – *vt.* देना; प्रदान करना; भेंट देना; स्वामित्व प्रदान करना; पहुंचाना; जिम्मे लगाना (काम आदि); प्रसारित करना; (दावत आदि) देना; दिलाना – *vi.* झुक जाना; रास्ता छोड़ना; चलना (**gave, given, giving**) – *n.* लचक; दाब – **give up** हार मान लेना; की आशा छोड़ देना; त्याग देना

glacier (´ग्लैसिअर, ´ग्लेसिअर) *n.* हिमनदी, पहाड़ों की घाटियों में जमी बर्फ़ का दरिया – **glacial** (´ग्लेसिअल, ´ग्लेशल) *a.* बर्फ़ या हिम नदी का, बहुत ठंडा

glad (ग्लैड) *a.* खुश, प्रसन्न, आनंद मग्न; सुहावना, मनोहर; प्रसन्न करने वाला – **gladden** *vt.* खुश करना – **gladly** *adv.* – **gladness** *n.* – **glad rags** *pl. n. sl.* बढ़िया कपड़े जो विशेष अवसरों पर पहने जाते हैं

glade (ग्लेड) *n.* जंगल में खाली स्थान जहां घास उगी हो

gladiator (´ग्लैडिएटर) *n.* प्राचीन रोम का प्रशिक्षित योद्धा जो मालिक के मन बहलावे के लिए दूसरे योद्धाओं से तलवार आदि से लड़ता था

gladiolus (ग्लैडि´ओलस) *n.* आइरिस जाति का पौधा जिसकी पत्तियां तलवार जैसी होती हैं

glamour (´ग्लैमर) *n.* मनोहरता; आकर्षण – **glamorize** *vt.* मनमोहक बनाना – **glamorous** *a.* मोहक, आकर्षक

glance (ग्लांस) *vi.* सरसरी नज़र या उचटती निगाह डालना; सरसरी निगाह से पढ़ना; (गेंद का) हल्का सा छूना – *n.* उचटती निगाह; झांकी; चमक; *Cricket* गेंद जो बल्ले से हलका सा टकरा कर रास्ता बदल ले – **glancing** (´ग्लांसिंग) *a.* तिरछी

gland (ग्लैंड) *n.* शरीर के अंग जिन का स्राव अन्य अंगों को नियंत्रित करता है; ग्रन्थि

glare (ग्लेंअर) – *vi.* गुस्से से देखना, आंखें तरेरना; तेज़ चमकना; चमचमाना – *n.* चौंध, चमचमाहट – **glaring** *a.* भद्दी या बड़ी (भूल)

glass (ग्लास) *n.* कांच, शीशा; कांच की बनी वस्तु; ग्लास; उसमें भरा पेय आदि; कैमरे का लेंस; (**looking glass** भी) आइना; दूरबीन; बैरोमीटर; खुर्दबीन या सूक्ष्मदर्शी यंत्र – (~ **es**) *pl.* ऐनक, चश्मा – **glassy** *a.* कांच जैसा; भाव शून्य (आंखें) – **glass-house** *n.* कांच घर जहां क त्रिम गर्मी में पौधे उगाए जाते हैं

glaucoma (ग्लॉ´कोमअ) *n.* काला मोतिया (आंखों का एक रोग)

glaze (ग्लेज़) *vt.* कांच लगाना; कांच जैसे पदार्थ से ढंकना या लपेटना – *vi* कांच जैसा हो जाना – *n.* कांच जैसा पारदर्शी पदार्थ; चमकीली सतह

gleam (ग्लीम) *n.* प्रकाश की झलक; हल्की या क्षणिक चमक – *vi.* झलकना या चमकना – **gleaming** *a.* चमकता, चमचमाता हुआ

glean (ग्लीन) *v.* जानकारी इकट्ठी करना; बटोरना; सिल्ला बीनना – **gleaner** *n.*

glee (ग्ली) *n.* उल्लास; आनन्द – **gleeful** *a.* आनंदित, उल्लसित

glib (ग्लिब) *a.* धारा प्रवाह परन्तु ऊपरी और झूठी (बातें)

glide (ग्लाइड) *vi.* सरकना; बहना; विमान का बिना इंजन के उड़ना – *n.* सरकने की क्रिया – **glider** *n.* विमान जो बिना इंजन के, हवा के बहाव पर उड़ता है, ग्लाइडर – **gliding** *n.* ग्लाइडर उड़ाने का खेल

glimmer (ˈग्लिमर) *vi.* टिमटिमाना; झलकना – *n.* टिमटिमाहट – **glimmering** *n.* हल्का प्रकाश; टिमटिमाहट; आभास; अस्पष्ट धारणा या विचार

glimpse (ग्लिम्प्स) *n.* झलक; आभास; झांकी – *vt.* झलक देखना

glint (ग्लिंट) *v.* चमकना; झिलमिलाना; झांकना; चमकना – *n.* चमक, झिलमिलाहट

glisten (ˈग्लिसन) *vi.* झिलमिलाना; टिमटिमाना (प्रकाश पड़ने पर)

glitch (ग्लिच) *n. inf.* अड़चन

glitter (ˈग्लिटर) *vi.*तेज, झिलमिलाते प्रकाश में जगमगाना; चमचमाना; भड़कीला होना – *n.*

globe (ग्लोब) *n.* गोला जिस पर प थ्वी या तारों का मानचित्र बना होता है; प थ्वी; गोला – **global** *a.* गोले का; सारी प थ्वी का – **globular** (ˈग्लॉब्युलर) *a.* गोले जैसा – **globalize** *vt.* सारे विश्व से नाता जोड़ना, अंतर्राष्ट्रीय बनाना – **globalization** *n.* भूमण्डलीकरण, विश्वीकरण – **globule** (ˈग्लॉब्यूल) *n.* गोली, गोलिका – **globulin** (ˈग्लॉब्युलिन) *n.* एक प्रकार की प्रोटीन – **globetrotter** *n.* व्यक्ति जो दुनियाभर में भ्रमण करता फिरे, विश्वभ्रमणकर्ता – **global warming** पथ्वी पर बढ़ती कार्बन डाईऑक्साइड के कारण वातावरण के तापमान में व द्धि

gloom (ग्लूम) *n.* अंधेरा; निराशा, उदासी; विषाद – **gloomily** *adv.* – **gloomy** *a.* अंधकारमय; विषादपूर्ण, उदासीभरा

glory (ˈग्लॉरि) *n.* प्रसिद्धि; महिमा; वैभव; शान शौकत – *vi.* गर्व करना (**gloried, glorying**) – **glorification** *n.* – **glorify** *vt.* महिमा प्रदान करना (**-ified, -ifying**) – **glorified** *a.* थोथी शानवाला – **glorious** *a.* महिमामय; वैभवशाली, शानदार; मनोहर

gloss[1] (ग्लॉस) *n.* चमक-दमक; मुलम्मा – *vt.* मुलम्मा चढ़ाना; (विशे. *over* के साथ) (भूल आदि) अनदेखी करना; उपेक्षा करना – **glossiness** *n.* – **glossy** *a.* चमकदार – *n.* चमकीले कागज़ पर छपी पत्रिका

gloss[2] *n.* टिप्पणी, व्याख्या – *vt.* व्याख्या, टीका या भाष्य करना – **glossary** (ˈग्लॉसरि) *n.* विशेष प्रकार के शब्दों का संग्रह या कोश

glove (ग्लव) *n.* दस्ताना – *vt.* दस्ताने से ढकना, दस्ताना पहनाना – **glove box, compartment** कार में आगे की ओर एक छोटा सा खाना जिसमें छोटी मोटी चीज़े रखी जा सकती हैं

glow (ग्लो) *vi.* चमकना; दीप्ति देना; उल्लास या उत्साह से भरे होना; गरम होना या दीखना; भावावेश में होना – *n.* चमक; लाली; उत्साह – **glow-worm** *n.* जुगनू

glower (ˈग्लॉउअर) *vi.* क्रोध भरी द ष्टि से देखना, आंखें तरेरना

glucose (ˈग्लूकोस) *n.* फलों में पायी जाने वाली शक्कर, ग्लूकोज़

glue (ग्लू) *n.* गोंद, सरेस; कोई भी चिपचिपा पदार्थ – *vt.* गोंद से चिपकाना

glum (ग्लम) *a.* रूठा हुआ; उदास

glut (ग्लट) *n.* बाहुल्य, भरमार – *vt.* छक कर खाना; अत्यधिक माल भर लेना **(-tt-)**

glutton[1] (ˈग्लट्न) *n.* पेटू, खाऊ; लालची व्यक्ति; व्यक्ति जो किसी चीज़ को बहुत पसंद करता हो या जिसकी सामर्थ्य उसमें बहुत हो – **gluttony** (ˈग्लटनि) *n.* पेटूपन

glycerin(e) (ˈग्लिसरिन) *n.* (ग्लिसरीन)

gm gram का संक्षेप

GMT Greenwich Mean Time (ग्रीनिच मानक समय) का संक्षेप

gnarled (नार्ल्ड) *a.* गांठदार (व क्ष)

gnash (नैश) *v.* दांत पीसना या किटकिटाना (क्रोध से)

gnat (नैट) *n.* छोटी डांस (मक्खी)

gnaw (नॉ) *v.* कुतरना या चबाना; (विशे. *at* के साथ) सताना, तंग या परेशान करना, खाये जाना

GNP Gross National Product (सकल राष्ट्रीय उत्पाद) का संक्षेप

gnu (नू) *n.* दक्षिणी अफ्रीका का भैंस जैसा हिरन या बारहसिंगा

go (गो) *vi.* जाना, चलना; रास्ता देना; चलते रहना; चले जाना या प्रस्थान करना; काम करना (यंत्र आदि का); टूट जाना या रुक जाना; समाप्त हो जाना (अवधि आदि); रखा जाना; रखना; रखने योग्य होना; प्रव ति होना; परिणाम में सहायक होना; स्वीकार किया जाना; प्रचलित होना; हो जाना (**went** *pt.*, **gone** *pp.*) – *n.* जाने की क्रिया; ऊर्जा; तेज; प्रयत्न; बारी – **go-slow** *n.* मज़दूरों का विरोध प्रदर्शन के लिए काम की गति जान बूझकर धीमी कर देना

goad (गोड) *n.* अंकुश (जिससे पशु हांके जाते है); प्रेरणा – *vt.* किसी को परेशान करना जब तक कि वह प्रतिक्रिया न करे; प्रोत्साहित करना

goal (गोल) *n.* (दौड़ आदि का) गंतव्य स्थान; लक्ष्य; (खेलों में) गोल – **goal-keeper** *n.* गोल कीपर – **goal post** *n.* चौखटा जिसमें गेंद जाने पर गोल होता है

goat (गोट) *n.* बकरा, बकरी – **goatee** (गोटी) *n.* बकरे जैसी दाढ़ी – **goatherd** *n.* गड़रिया – **get (someone's) goat** *sl.* किसी को तंग या परेशान करना; खिजाना

gobble (ˈगॉबल) – *vt.* (**gobble down/up** भी) जल्दी-जल्दी, मरभुक्खों की तरह खाना, भकोसना; (पैसे आदि) चट कर जाना

gobbledegook, gobbledygook (ˈगॉबल्डिगूक) *n.* आडम्बरपूर्ण भाषा

goblet (ˈगॉब्लिट) *n.* शराब पीने का पात्र

goblin (ˈगॉब्लिन) *n. Folklore* छोटे कद का पिशाच या बेताल

god (गॉड) *n.* देवता; पूज्य व्यक्ति या वस्तु (मूर्ति आदि); मूर्ति; (**God**) ईश्वर (**goddess** *fem.*) – **godlike** *a.* – **godliness** *n.* पवित्रता, धार्मिकता –**godly** *a.* धर्मपरायण; पवित्र – **godfather** *n.* धर्मपिता; अपराधी-गिरोह का मुखिया – **god-fearing** *a.* धर्म परायण – **god-forsaken** *a.* निराशा या अंधकार में डूबा हुआ – **godhead** *n.* दैवी स्वभाव वाला या देवता – **godsend** *n.* ईश्वरीय वरदान, सौभाग्य

goggles (ˈगॉगल्ज़) *n.* धूप का चश्मा

goitre (ˈगॉइटर) *n.* थायराइड ग्रंथि की सूजन, गलगण्ड

gold (गोल्ड) *n.* सोना; धन-दौलत; सुन्दर या कीमती वस्तु; सुनहरा रंग – *a.* सोने का या उस जैसा – **golden** *a.* स्वर्णिम, सुनहरी – **golden handshake** कंपनी नीति के अंतर्गत स्वेच्छा से समयपूर्ण अवकाश लेने/नौकरी छोड़ने वाले कर्मचारी को मिलने वाली एक मुश्त रकम – **golden mean** बीच का रास्ता – **golden rule** महत्वपूर्ण सिद्धान्त – **goldfish** *n.* सुनहरी या रंग बिरंगी छोटी मछली जो सजावट के लिए पाली जाती है – **gold-plated** *a.* जिस पर सोने का पतरा चढ़ा हो – **gold rush** सोने/सम द्धि

की खोज में लोगों की किसी स्थान विशेष के लिए दौड़ – **goldsmith** *n.* सुनार

golf (गॉल्फ़) *n.* गॉल्फ का खेल – *vi.* यह खेल खेलना – **golf course** गॉल्फ़ खेलने का मैदान

gondola (ˈगॉण्डलअ) *n.* वीनस नगर की नहरों में चलने वाली नाव; गौन्डोला

gone (गॉन) Go का *pp.*

gong (गॉङ) *n.* घड़ियाल, घण्टा

gonorrhoea (गॉनˈरिअ) *n.* सूज़ाक

good (गुड) *a.* प्रशंसनीय, अच्छा, ठीक, उपयुक्त, सर्वोत्क ष्ट; लाभकारी; भलामानस; साधु; दयालु; सुरक्षित; समुचित; बढ़िया; शुध्द, खरा (**better** *comp.*, **best**, *sup.*) – *n.* लाभ; कल्याण; मुनाफा – *pl.* माल-अस्बाब, सम्पत्ति – **goodly** *a.* बड़ा, प्रचुर – **goodness** *n.* – **good will** सद्भाव साख – **for good** सदा के लिए – **up to no good** निकम्मा, बेइमान

goodbye (गुड्ˈबाइ) *interj./n.* विदा लेते समय कहा जाने वाला शब्द, अलविदा

goof (गूफ़) *inf. n.* भूल; मूर्ख व्यक्ति – *vi.* भूल करना

googly (ˈगूग्लि) *n. Cricket* गेंद जो उछलने के बाद अचानक रास्ता बदल लेती है

goon (गून) *n. inf.* मूर्ख व्यक्ति; *us* बदमाश, गुंडा

goose (गूस) *n.* बतख (*pl.* **geese** (गीस)

gooseberry (ˈगूज़बरि) *n.* काक बदरी की झाड़ी और उसका फल

gory (ˈगॉरि) *a.* भयानक (कहानी); मारकाट भरी (लड़ाई आदि)

gore *vt.* पशु का सींग भौंक देना

gorge (गॉर्ज) *n.* खड्ड; जुगुप्सा; घ णा; नाराज़गी – *vi.* भकोसना; डट कर खाना

gorgeous (ˈगॉर्जस) *a.* शानदार, बढ़िया; भड़कीला; चमचमाता हुआ – *inf.* बहुत सुन्दर

gorilla (गˈरिलअ) *n* अफ्रीका का विशाल काय जीव, गोरिल्ला

gory (ˈगॉरि) देखिए GORE

go-slow *n.* दे० Go

gospel (ˈगॉस्पल) *n.* ब्रह्म वाक्य; ऐसा सत्य जिस पर आपत्ति न की जा सके – **Gospel** *n.* बाइबल के न्यू टेस्टामेंट के पहले चार खण्डों में से कोई एक

gossamer (ˈगॉसमर) *n.* मकड़ी के जाले जैसा पारदर्शी पदार्थ; रेशमी जालीदार महीन कपड़ा

gossip (ˈगॉसिप) *n.* गप्प; ऐसी बातें करने वाला – *vi.* गप्पें हांकना; बेकार की बातें करना

got (गॉट) देखिए GET

gouge (ˈगाउज) *vt.* खुरच कर या औज़ार से निकालना

gourd (गुअर्ड) *n.* कद्दू या उस जैसे फल; तूंबा (सुखाए कद्दू का खोल)

gourmand (ˈगुअर्मंड) *n.* खाऊ, पेटू, भकोसने वाला व्यक्ति

gourmet (ˈगुअर्मे) *n.* व्यक्ति जिसे अच्छे व्यंजनों, शराब आदि की पहचान हो; जो अच्छे व्यंजनों आदि का शौकीन हो

gout (गाउट) *n.* गठिया

Gov. Government, Governor का संक्षेप

govern (ˈगर्वन) *vt* शासन करना; निर्देश देना; पथ प्रदर्शन करना; नियंत्रण रखना; निर्णय या फैसले करना; अन्वय होना (व्याकरण) – **governance** *n.* शासन चलाने का काम – **governess** *n.* अध्यापिका जो किसी के घर में रह कर बच्चों को पढ़ाती हो – **government** (ˈगवर्न्मेंट) *n.* सरकार, शासन; शासन पद्धति; सरकार के अधिकारी वर्ग; मंत्रिमण्डल; नियंत्रण; अधिकारों का प्रयोग – **governmental** *a.* – **governor** (ˈगवर्नर) *n.* शासक; राज्यपाल; किसी संस्था का सर्वोच्च अधिकारी; किसी संगठन की संचालन समिति का सदस्य; इंजन की गति नियंत्रित करने वाला उपकरण

gown (गाउन) *n.* चोग़ा, लबादा; स्त्री की टखनों तक की पोशाक, गाउन

grab (ग्रैब) *vt.* अचानक पकड़ लेना, झपट लेना; हड़प लेना **(-bb-)**; जल्दी से हथिया लेना; ध्यान आकर्षित करना – *n.* झपट; झटके से पकड़ने की कोशिश; पकड़ने का उपकरण आदि

grace (ग्रेस) *n.* लालित्य, मनोहरता; लावण्य; क पा द ष्टि, उपकार; सदभावना; औचित्य; भोजन से पहले या बाद ईश्वर को धन्यवाद देने की क्रिया – *vt.* शोभा बढ़ाना, सम्मानित करना – **graceful** *a.* ललित, मनोहर, लावण्यपूर्ण – **gracefully** *adv.* – **graceless** *a.* बेशर्म; भ्रष्ट – **gracious** (ग्रेशस) *a.* दयामय, क पालु; रमणीय; लाभकारी; दीनबन्धु (अपने से छोटों पर क पा द ष्टि रखने वाला) – **graciously** *adv.* – **with bad/good grace** अशोभनीय/ शोभनीय ढंग से

grade (ग्रेड) *n.* सोपान; श्रेणी; कोटि; वर्ग; दरजा; ढलान – *vi.* क्रमबद्ध करना; श्रेणियों में बांटना या रखना – **make the grade** सफल होना

gradient (ग्रेडिअंट) *n.* ढाल का ढालूपन या प्रवणता

gradual (ग्रैड्युअल) *a.* जो धीरे-धीरे हो, क्रमिक; जो ढालू न हो – **gradually** *adv.* क्रमशः, धीरे-धीरे

graduate *vi.* (ग्रैड्युएट) स्नातक बनना – *vt.* क्रमबद्ध करना, श्रेणीबद्ध करना; माप के निशान लगाना (जैसे थर्मामीटर पर); अधिक मुश्किल व महत्वपूर्ण काम शुरू कर देना – *n.* (ग्रैड्युइट) स्नातक – **graduation** (ग्रैड्यु एशन) *n.* स्नातक बनने की क्रिया

graffiti (ग्रै फ़ीती) *pl. n.* (*sing.* **graffito**) दीवारों पर लिखे (प्रायः अश्लील) शब्द या वैसे चित्र

graft[1] (ग्राफ्ट) *n.* पौधे में लगाई क़लम; कलम लगाने की प्रक्रिया; एक स्थान की चमड़ी दूसरे स्थान पर लगाने की क्रिया – *vt.* कलम लगाना; चमड़ी एक स्थान से दूसरे पर लगाना; एक विचार को दूसरे का भाग बनाना

graft[2] (ग्राफ्ट) *inf. n.* कठोर परिश्रम; अनुचित उपायों विशे. सरकारी या राजनीतिक विशेषाधिकारों से उन्नति करना; घूस

grain (ग्रेन) *n.* अनाज; उसका दाना; गेहूँ और उस जैसे अन्य अनाज; कण; कणिका; वजन का माप; बुनत या बुनाई; बहुत छोटी मात्रा – **grainy** *a.* दानेदार

gram(me) (ग्रैम) *n* किलोग्राम का हज़ारवां भाग, ग्राम

grammar (ग्रैमर) *n.* व्याकरण – **grammarian** (ग्र मैंअरिअन) *n.* व्याकरण- शास्त्री – **grammatical** (ग्र मैटिकल) *a.* जो व्याकरण के अनुरूप – **grammatically** *adv.*

gramophone (ग्रैमफ़ोन) *n.* ग्रामोफोन (बाजा जिस पर रिकाई बजाते है)

gran, granny (ग्रैन, ग्रैनि) *n. inf.* दादी; नानी

granary (ग्रैनरि) *n.* धान्यागार, अन्न का भंडार, कोठार

grand (ग्रैंड) *a.* भव्य, विशाल, शानदार; महत्वपूर्ण; ऊंचा; उदात्त; प्रमुख; कुल (जोड़) – **grandeur** (ग्रैंजर) *n.* शान; वैभव; प्रताप; महानता; महत्व – **grandiloquence** (ग्रैन् डिलक्वंस) *n.* शब्दाडम्बर – **grandiose** *a.* भव्य; आडम्बरपूर्ण – **grandchild** (ग्रैन्चाइल्ड) *n.* पोता-पोती; नाती, नातिन – **granddaughter** *n.* पोती; नातिन – **grandfather** *n.* दादा; नाना – **grand master** शतरंज का श्रेष्ठतम खिलाड़ी – **grandmother** *n.* दादी; नानी – **grandparent** *n.* नाना/नानी; दादा/दादी – **grandson** *n.* पोता, नाती – **grandstand** (ग्रैन्स्टैंड, ग्रैंड् स्टैंड) *n.* दर्शकों के बैठने का स्थान जिसमें ऊपर नीचे कुर्सियों की कतारें लगी हों

Grand Prix (ग्राँ प्री) *n.* (*pl.* **Grands Prix** (ग्राँ प्री) कारों/मोटरसाइकिलों की प्रतिष्ठित दौड़ों में से कोई भी

grand slam कोई प्रतिष्ठित खेल प्रतियोगिता
granite (ˈग्रैनिट) *n.* कड़ी दानेदार चट्टान
grant (ग्रान्ट) *vt.* (प्रार्थना) स्वीकार करना; अनुदान देना; मान लेना – *n.* अनुदान; भेंट; भत्ता
granule (ˈग्रैन्यूल) *n.* कण, कनी – **granular** (ˈग्रैन्युलर) *a.* दानेदार
grape (ग्रेप) *n.* अंगूर – **grapevine** (ˈग्रेप्वाइन) *n.* अंगूर की बेल; *inf.* अफ़वाह
grapefruit *n.* चकोतरा (नारंगी की जाति का, बड़े आकार का फल)
graph (ग्राफ़) *n.* लेखाचित्र; आलेख
graphic (ˈग्रैफ़िक) *a.* सजीव (चित्रण); जीती जागती (तस्वीर); लिखने, चित्रकला आदि से सम्बंधित – **graphics** *pl. n.* कम्प्यूटर की सहायता से बनाये गए चित्र, लेखाचित्र आदि
graphite (ˈग्रैफाइट) *n.* पेंसिल बनाने का सीसा या सिक्का
grapple (ˈग्रैपल) *vi.* हाथापाई करना; सामना करना – *n.* हाथापाई; अंकोड़ा या कांटेदार लंगर – **grappling iron** कांटेदार लंगर
grasp (ग्रास्प) *v.* कस कर पकड़ना; समझना – *n.* – **grasping** *a.* लालची, लोभी
grass (ग्रास) *n.* घास चरागाह; *sl.* चरस – **grasshopper** *n.* टिड्डा – **grass roots** आधारभूत तत्व – **grassroots** *a.* जो जन साधारण में से आए
grate[1] (ग्रेट) *n.* लोहे का ढांचा जो आतिशदान के बाहर लगा होता है; झांझरी, जाली – **grating** *n.* छड़ों का बना ढांचा
grate[2] (ग्रेट) *vt.* पीसना – *vi* रगड़ने की आवाज़ करना; किसी को खिजाना – **grater** *n.* पीसने या छोटे टुकड़े करने का उपकरण, कद्दूकस आदि – **grating** *a.* कर्कश; खीज उत्पन्न करने वाला
grateful (ˈग्रेट्फुल) *a.* कृतज्ञ, एहसानमंद – **gratefulness** *n.* कृतज्ञता – **gratitude** (ˈग्रैटिट्यूड) – *n.* कृतज्ञता
gratify (ˈग्रैटिफ़ाइ) *vt.* संतुष्ट करना – **gratification** *n.* संतुष्टि, संतोष; इनाम
gratis (ˈग्रैटिस) *adv./a.* मुफ्त
gratuitous (ग्रˈट्यूइटस) *a.* मुफ्त; अकारण; बिन-मांगे – **gratuity** (ग्रˈट्यूइटि); सेवा के लिए दी गयी अनुग्रह राशि
grave[1] (ग्रेव़) *n.* कब्र; मृत्यु – **gravestone** *n.* मकबरा; कब्र का पत्थर – **graveyard** *n.* कब्रिस्तान
grave[2] (ग्रेव़) *a.* गंभीर; महत्वपूर्ण; गौरवपूर्ण; सीधा सादा; गहरे रंग का; भारी (स्वर); घोर, विकट, संगीन (अपराध आदि) – **gravely** *adv.*
gravel (ˈग्रैव़ल) *n.* कंकड़, बजरी – *vt.* कंकड़, बजरी बिछाना
gravitate (ˈग्रैविटेट) *vi.* गुरूत्वाकर्षण से चलना या हिलना; *Physics* आकर्षण केन्द्र की ओर प्रवृत होना; तह में बैठ जाना – **gravitation** (ग्रैविˈटेशन) – *n.* गुरूत्वाकर्षण – **gravitational** *a.*
gravity (ˈग्रैविटि) *n.* पिण्डों, विशे. पृथ्वी और अन्य पिण्डों का परस्पर आकर्षण, गुरूत्वाकर्षण; गुरूत्व; महत्व; गंभीरता
gravy (ˈग्रेवि) *n.* पकते समय मांस से निकला रस, यख़नी
gray (ग्रे) *a.* *GREY* की *US* स्पैलिंग
graze[1] (ग्रेज़) *v.* पशु का घास चरना या चराना
graze[2] (ग्रेज़) *vt.* छू जाना; खुरच जाना; रगड़ खा जाना – *n.* खरौंच
grease (ग्रीस) *n.* पिघली हुई चर्बी; गाढ़ा तेल जो मशीनी पुर्ज़ों में डाला जाता है – *vt.* (ग्रीज़) ग्रीस देना – **grease sb's palm** को रिश्वत देना
great (ग्रेट) *a.* बड़ा, विशाल, महान, महत्वपूर्ण, प्रतिष्ठित; *inf.* उत्कृष्ट, बहुत (*great help*)– *prefix* दूर का संबंध जैसे **great-grandfather** *n.* पड़दादा, पड़नाना – *n.*

महान व्यक्ति – greatly adv. – greatness n. महानता

greed (ग्रीड) n. लालसा; लोभ, लालच – greedy a. पेटू; लालची; लोभी; धन लोलुप – greedily adv. – greediness n.

Greek (ग्रीक) n. यूनान की भाषा – a यूनान का या यूनानवासी

green (ग्रीन) a. हरे रंग का; कच्चा (फल आदि); अनाड़ी; अनुभवहीन व्यक्ति; भोला-भाला; ईर्ष्यालु; पर्यावरण-रक्षा सम्बंधी (green issues) – n. हरा रंग; घास भरा क्षेत्र – (~ s) pl. हरी शाक भाजी – greenery n. हरियाली – green back US नोट (डालर) – green belt किसी नगर के पास हरा भरा क्षेत्र, हरित पट्टी – green card विदेशियों को अमरीका में रहने व काम करने का अनुमति-पत्र – greengrocer n. फल और सब्ज़ी बेचने वाला, कुंजड़ा – greengrocery n. फल और सब्ज़ी – greenhorn n. अनाड़ी, नौसिखिया – greenhouse n. कांच लगा पौधा घर – greenhouse effect प्रदूषण के कारण बढ़ती गरमी से प थ्वी के वातावरण की बढ़ती गरमी – green light चौराहे की हरी बत्ती; कार्य शुरू करने की अनुमति – greenroom n. अभिनेताओं का विश्राम कक्ष, नेपथ्यशाला

greet (ग्रीट) vt. स्वागत, अभिवादन या नमस्कार करना; अगवानी करना – greeting n. अभिवादन; स्वागत – greeting card छपे बधाई पत्र

gregarious (ग्रि ग्रेंअरिअस) a. मिलनसार; यूथचर (पशु जो झुंडों में रहें) – gregariousness n.

grenade (ग्रि नेड) n. हथगोला

grew (ग्रू) GROW का pt.

grey (ग्रे) a. धूसर; धुंधला; अंधकारमय; जो सफेद हो रहा हो (बाल); बूढ़ा; बीच का; अनिर्णीत; नीरस – n. धूसर रंग – v. मटमैला बनाना या होना – greyness n. मटमैलापन, धुंधलापन; सफेदी (बालों की) – grey market वैध बाज़ार जहां सस्ती आयातित वस्तुएं मिल जाती हैं – grey matter inf. बुद्धि

greyhound (ग्रेहाउंड) n. तेज़ रफ्तार शिकारी कुत्ता

grid (ग्रिड) n. झांझरी, जाली; एक दूसरे से जुड़ी हुई प्रणालियाँ; राष्ट्र भर के लिए बिजली की व्यवस्था

griddle, girdle (ग्रिड्ल, गर्डल) n. तवा

gridlock (ग्रिड्लॉक) n. जबरदस्त यातायात अवरोध (ट्रैफिक जैम)

grief (ग्रीफ़) n. शोक – grievance (ग्रीव़न्स) n. शिकायत – grieve (ग्रीव़) vi. शोक मनाना, दुखी होना – vt. किसी को दुख देना – grievous (ग्रीव़स) a. दुखद; गहरा (घाव आदि); घोर

grill (ग्रिल) n. खाना पकाने के उपकरण में पुर्ज़ा जो गरमी नीचे को करता है (जिससे मांस भूना जा सके); इस प्रकार भूना मांस आदि – v. भूनना; कड़ी जिरह करना (पुलिस द्वारा अपराधी से) – grilling a. बहुत गरम – n. कड़ी जिरह

grim (ग्रिम) a. कड़ा; कठोर; निर्दय, निष्ठुर; विकराल; जो पीछा न छोड़े; अशुभ, निरानंद – grimly adv.

grimace (ग्रि मेस) n. टेढ़ा मुंह या मुख विक ति – vi मुंह बनाना

grime (ग्राइम) n. जमी हुई मैल, कालिख – vt. मैला कर देना; काला कर देना – grimy a. जिस पर मैल जमी हो

grin (ग्रिन) vi. खीसें निकालना (हंसते समय) (-nn-) – n. मुस्काराहट, खीस

grind (ग्राइंड) vt. पीसना; दमन करना; तेज करना; सान पर धरना; रगड़ना – vi पीसना inf. डटकर मेहनत करना (विशे. अध्ययन में); कद्दूकस आदि से छोटे-छोटे टुकड़े करना (ground *pt./pp.*) – *n. inf.* कड़ी मेहनत; पीसने की क्रिया – **grinder** *n.* चक्की, पीसने की मशीन – **grindstone** *n.* चक्की का पाट; सान – **grind to a halt** (गाड़ी) एकदम रुक जाना; (काम आदि) एकदम बन्द हो जाना

grip (ग्रिप) *n.* पकड़; मूठ; समझ; अधिकार या जानकारी – *vt.* पकड़ना (कस कर); ध्यान आक ष्ट करना या रुचि बनाए रखना – **gripping** *a.* बहुत दिलचस्प

grisly (ˈग्रिज़ूलि) *a.* डरावना घिनौना

grist (ग्रिस्ट) *n.* पिसने के लिए गया अनाज – **grist for one's mill** वस्तु/स्थिति जिससे लाभ उठाया जा सकता हो

grit (ग्रिट) *n.* रेत के कण; बजरी; कंकड़; गिट्टी; हिम्मत, साहस, जीवट – *pl.* गेहूं का दलिया – *vt.* दांत पीसना (**-tt-**) – **gritty** *a.* रेत मिला; साहसी; इरादे का पक्का

grizzle[1] (ˈग्रिज़ल) *v.* भूरा या खाकी हो जाना या बना देना – **grizzly (bear)** उत्तरी अमरीका का विशालकाय रीछ

groan (ग्रोन) *vi.* कराहना; कष्ट सहना – *n.*

grocer (ˈग्रोसर) *n.* पनसारी – **groceries** *pl. n.* पनसारी का सामान – **grocery** *n.* पनसारी का व्यवसाय, उसकी दुकान

groggy (ˈग्रॉगि) *a. inf.* डगमग

groin (ग्रॉइन) *n.* स्थान जहां टांगे मिलती हैं, चड्डा

groom (ग्रूम) *n.* साईस; (**bridegroom** भी) दूल्हा – *vt.* देखभाल करना; किसी चीज़ का प्रशिक्षण देना; साज सिंगार करना; (किसी को) किसी काम/पद के योग्य बनाना; घोड़े को संवारना – **well-groomed** *a.* सजा- संवरा

groove (ग्रूव़) *n.* खांचा; नाली; दिनचर्या – *vt.* खांचा बनाना – **groovy** *a. sl.* फैशनेबल

grope (ग्रोप) *vi.* टटोलना – **groping** *n.* तलाश, टटोलना

gross (ग्रोस) *a.* बहुत मोटा; कुल (जमा आदि); असभ्य; अश्लील; भीषण – *n.* बारह दर्जन – **grossness** *n.* असभ्यता

grotesque (ग्रो'टॆस्क) *a.* बुरी तरह विक त, भोंडा, भद्दा – **grotesquely** *adv.*

grouch (ˈग्राउच) *inf. n.* सदा बड़बड़ाने या कुड़कुड़ाने की क्रिया – *vi.* बड़बड़ाना

ground[1] (ग्राउंड) *n.* जमीन, भूमि; मिट्टी; कारण; प्रेरणा; विशेष क्षेत्र; खेल का मैदान – (~ **s**) *pl.* मकान के आसपास अहाता; कारण – *vt.* स्थापित करना; प्रारंभिक ज्ञान देना, हवाई जहाज़ या चालक के उड़ान भरने पर रोक लगा देना; (जहाज़ को) भूग्रस्त कर देना – *vi.* (नाव का) तट पर जा चढ़ना – **groundless** *a.* निराध ार, अकारण – **ground breaking** नई दिशा देने वाला (कार्य, आविष्कार) – **ground floor** भूतल – **groundnut** *n.* मूंगफली – **groundwork** *n.* प्रारंभिक काम, तैयारी – **ground zero** स्थान जहां बम फटता है

ground[2] GRIND का *pt./pt.*

group (ग्रूप) *n.* दल, समूह, वादकों या गायकों का व ंद या टोली – *vt.* समूह में रखना – *vi.* समूह में आना, इकट्ठे होना

grouse (ग्राउस) *vi.* बड़बड़ाना, शिकायत करना

grout (ग्राउट) *n.* पतला मसाला (ईंटों के बीच डालने का) – *vt.* ऐसा मसाला लगाना

grove (ग्रोव़) *n.* व क्षों का झुंड

grovel (ग्रॉव़ल) *vi.* किसी के सामने नाक रगड़ना (**-ll-**)

grow (ग्रो) *vi.* बढ़ना, विकसित होना; उत्पन्न होना – *vt.* उगाना (**grew** *pt.*, **grown** *pp.*) – **growth** *n.* बढ़त, विकास; व द्धि; जो उगा या उग रहा हो – **grown-up** *a./n.* वयस्क व्यक्ति

growl (ग्राउल) *vi.* गुर्राना; बड़बड़ाना – *n* गुर्राहट

grub (ग्रब) *vt.* जड़ से निकाल लेना – *vi.* खोदना; ढूँढना (**-bb-**) – *n.* लाखा (सूंडी); *sl.* खाना – **grubby** *a.* गंदा, मैला

grudge (ग्रज) *vt.* (किसी को कुछ) देने की इच्छा न होना – *n.* दुर्भाव, नाराज़गी

gruel (ग्रूअल) *n.* दूध या पानी में उबाल कर बनाया दलिया – **gruelling** *a./n.* बुरी तरह थका देने वाला (अनुभव)

gruesome (ग्रूसम) *a.* वीभत्स, डरावना, घ णाजनक

gruff (ग्रफ़) *a.* रूखा (स्वर अथवा व्यवहार), बदमिज़ाज (व्यक्ति) – **gruffly** *adv.*

grumble (ग्रम्बल) *vi.* (शिकायत के रूप मे) बड़बड़ाना – *n.* बड़बड़ाना – **grumbler** *n.* हमेशा बड़बड़ाने, शिकायत करने वाला

grumpy (ग्रम्पि) *a.* चिड़ाचिड़ा, बदमिज़ाज

grunt (ग्रंट) *vi.* (सूअर का) घुरघुराना – *n.* सूअर की आवाज़; कानों को चुभने वाली भारी आवाज़

guarantee (गैरन्‌टी) *n.* गारंटी, आश्वासन; जमानत – *vt.* गारंटी देना; जिम्मा लेना (**guaranteed, guaranteeing**) – **guarantor** *n.* गारंटी देने वाला, जमानती

guard (गार्ड) *vt.* रक्षा करना, चौकसी करना – *vi* सतर्क रहना, सावधानी बरतना – *n.* रक्षक-दल; संतरी; सुरक्षा सैनिक, रेल का गार्ड; पहरा, रखवाली, खतरनाक चीज़ के चारों ओर लगाया गया आवरण (जाल आदि), सतर्कता, चौकसी – *pl.* (**Guards**) कुछ ब्रिटिश रेजिमेंटों के लिए प्रयुक्त शब्द, गार्डज़ – **guardian** (गार्डिअन) *n.* अभिभावक – **guardianship** *n.* संरक्षण, अभिभावकता – **guard rail** पुल के साथ लगा जंगला जो लोगों को नीचे गिरने से बचाता है

guava (ग्वावूअ) *n.* अमरूद

guer(r)illa (ग रिलूअ) *n.* गुरिल्ला, छापामार सैनिक – *a.*

guess (गेंस) *vt.* अनुमान लगाना; ताड़ना; *US* विश्वास करना; विचार रखना – *vi.* अनुमान करना, अटकल लगाना – *n.* अनुमान – **guesswork** *n.* अटकलबाज़ी

guest (गेंस्ट) *n.* अतिथि – **guesthouse** *n.* आवास-ग ह

guffaw (ग फॉ) *n.* हंसी का ठहाका लगाना

guide (गाइड) *n.* मार्ग-दर्शक, पथ-प्रदर्शक; गाइड; संदर्शिका (पुस्तक); गति निर्देशन का उपकरण – *vt.* पथ-प्रदर्शन करना, मार्ग दिखाना, निर्देशन करना, संचालन करना – **guidance** (गाइडन्स) *n.* मार्ग दर्शन – **guided missile** नियंत्रित प्रक्षेपास्त्र – **guideline** *n.* किसी कार्य आदि को सम्पन्न करने के लिए बनाए गए सामान्य निर्देश

guild (गिल्ड) *n.* संघ, क्लब

guile (गाइल) *n.* छल-कपट, धोखा

guillotine (गिल टीन) *n.* सिर काटने का यंत्र, गिलोटिन; कागज़ काटने की मशीन; संसद आदि में किसी विषय पर मतदान का समय निश्चित कर के बहस सीमित करने का उपाय – *vt.* सिर काटना; पर गिलोटिन का इस्तेमाल करना; मतदान का समय निशचित करके बहस को सीमित करना

guilt (गिल्ट) *n.* दोष, अपराध, पाप – **guilty** *a.* दोषी

guinea (गिनि) *n.* गिन्नी, 21शिलिंग का एक सोने का सिक्का – **guinea pig** (गिनि पिग) मूलत: दक्षिण अमेरिका का बड़े चूहे जैसा जानवर, गिनी-पिग; *inf.* शोध में प्रयुक्त व्यक्ति अथवा जानवर

guise (गाइज़) *n.* (छद्म) रूप, वेष; बहाना

guitar (गि टार) *n.* गिटार – **guitarist** *n*

gulf (गल्फ़) *n.* खाड़ी

gull (गल) *n.* एक समुद्री पक्षी, गल

gullible (गलिबल) *a.* भोला भाला; किसी की बात का आसानी से विश्वास कर लेने वाला

gullet (गलिट) *n.* (गले से पेट तक) आहार नली

gully (गलि) *n.* तेज बहते पानी द्वारा बनाई गई संकरी नाली

gulp (गल्प) *vt* तेज़ी से निगलना, गटकना – *n.*

gum¹ (गम) *n.* मसूड़ा

gum² (गम) *n.* गोंद; चुइंग गम (चबाने का एक लचीला मीठा पदार्थ); गोंद वाला व क्ष; सफेदे

का व क्ष – *vt.* गोंद से चिपकाना (**-mm-**) – **gummy** *a.* चिपचिपा – **gumboots** *pl. n.* रबड़ के टखनों से ऊपर के जूते

gumption (ˈगम्पशन) *n.* सूझबूझ, समझदारी व साहस

gun (गन) *n.* बंदूक, तोप, पिस्तौल आदि; पिचकारी नुमा कोई भी उपकरण जिससे दबाव द्वारा वस्तु फैंकी जाए – **gunner** *n.* तोपची – **gunboat** *n.* छोटा जंगी जहाज़ – **gunfire** *n.* गोलियां चलने की आवाज़ – **gunman** *n.* सशस्त्र लुटेरा – **gunmetal** *n.* तांबे, टिन और जस्ता (ज़िंक) से बनी मिश्रधातु – **gunpowder** *n.* बारूद – **gun running** हथियारों की तस्कारी – **gunshot** *n.* तोप या बंदूक की मार की सीमा; चलाई गई गोली – *a.* गोली से (घाव आदि) – **gun down** को गोली से उड़ा देना

gung-ho (गङˈहो) *a.* कुछ करने को अत्यंत उत्सुक व उत्साहित

gunny (ˈगनि) *n.* टाट

gurgle (ˈगर्गल) *n.* (पानी की) गड़गड़ की आवाज़ – *vi.* गड़गड़ करना, गड़गड़ करते पानी निकलना

gush (गश) *vi.* तेज धारा के रूप में बाहर निकलना, फूट पड़ना – *n.* अचानक तेज़ धार; *fig.* भावावेग

gust (गस्ट) *n.* हवा या वर्षा का तेज़ झोंका – **gusty** *a.* तेज़ हवा (का मौसम)

gusto (ˈगस्टो) *n.* उत्साह, जोश

gut (गट) *n.* (प्रायः *pl.*) आंत, अंतड़ी; जानवर की आंतों से बने सारंगी आदि की तार – (~ **s**) *pl. inf.* साहस और धैर्य – *vt.* आंतें निकालना (मछली आदि से); सामान नष्ट कर देना (विशेष आग लगाकर) या ले जाना – **gutless** *a.* डरपोक – **gutsy** *a. inf.* साहसी

gutta-percha (ˈगट्अ ˈपर्च्अ) *n.* सफेद रबड़ जैसा पदार्थ (उत्पन्न करने वाला व क्ष)

gutter (ˈगटर) *n.* परनाला, गंदे पानी की नाली – *vt.* (में) नाली बनाना – *vi.* धाराओं में बहना; मोम का पिघल कर धाराओं में नीचे बह जाना व मोमबत्ती का समाप्त हो जाना

guy (गाइ) *n. inf.* आदमी, लड़का – **wise guy** *inf.* (प्रायः व्यंग्य) चालाक, चतुर व्यक्ति

guzzle (ˈगज़ल) *v.* (खाने-पीने की वस्तु) ठूंसना, गटकना – *n.* ठूंसने, गटकने की क्रिया

gym (जिम) *n.* GYMNASIUM या GYMNASTICS का संक्षिप्त रूप

gymkhana (जिम्ˈकान्अ) *n.* घुड़सवारी की प्रतियोगिता या प्रदर्शन

gymnasium (जिम्ˈनेज़िअम) *n.* व्यायामशाला (*pl.* **-s, -nasia** (–ˈनेज़िअ)) – **gymnast** (जिम्नैस्ट) *n.* व्यायाम में निपुण खिलाड़ी – **gymnastics** (जिम्ˈनैस्टिक्स) *pl. n.* मांस-पेशियों को सुद ढ़ बनाने वाले व्यायाम, जिमनास्टिक – *n.* व्यायाम विद्या

gynaecology (गाइनिˈकॉलजि) *n.* स्त्री-रोग-विज्ञान – **gynaecological** (गाइनिकˈलॉजिकल) *a.* स्त्री-रोग सम्बंधी – **gynaecologist** (गाइनिˈकॉलजिस्ट) *n.* स्त्री-रोग विशेषज्ञ

gypsum (ˈजिप्सम) *n.* खड़िया मिट्टी, सेलखड़ी

Gypsy, Gipsy (ˈजिप्सि) *n.* एक खानाबदोश जाति का सदस्य; खानाबदोश

gyrate (जाइˈरेट) *vi.* चक्राकार घूमना, चक्कर काटना – **gyration** (जाइˈरेशन) *n.*

H

habeas corpus (हेबिअस ˈकॉर्पस) *n.* बंदी को न्यायालय में उपस्थित करने का आदेश, बंदी-प्रत्यक्षीकरण

habit (हैबिट) *n.* आदत; स्वभाव – **habitual** (ह ˈबिट्युअल) *a.* अभ्यस्त, आदी; नियमित – **habituate** *vt.* की आदत डाल देना

habitable (हैबिटबल) *a.* रहने योग्य – **habitat** (हैबिटैट) *n.* प्राक तिक आवास स्थान – **habitation** (हैबि ˈटेशन) *n.* रहने का स्थान

hack[1] (हैक) *vt.* टुकड़े-टुकड़े कर देना, काटना; *inf.* खौं-खौं (सूखी खांसी) करना – *n.* काटने से बना जख्म; *inf.* सूखी खांसी – **hacker** *n. sl.* व्यक्ति जो कंप्यूटर के जरिये किसी कंपनी अथवा सरकारी कंप्यूटर के गोपनीय आंकड़ों तक पहुंच जाये – **hacking** *n.*

hack[2] (हैक) *n.* – **hack work** (रोज़ी कमाने के लिए) नीरस काम

hackneyed (ˈहैक्निड) *a.* सामान्य, घिसा-पिटा

hacksaw (ˈहैक्सॉ) *n.* धातुओं को काटने की आरी

had HAVE का *pt./pp.*

haemoglobin (हीमो ˈग्लोबिन) *n.* रक्तकणों को लाल रंग प्रदान करने व ऑक्सीजन ले जाने वाला पदार्थ, रुधिर वर्णिका

haemophilia (हीमो ˈफ़िलिअ) *n.* खून न जम सकने के कारण अत्यधिक खून बहने की वंशानुगत प्रव ति, रक्त स्कंदन हीनता, हीमोफ़ीलिया – **haemophiliac** *n.* व्यक्ति जिसमें यह कमी हो

haemorrhoids (ˈहैमराइड्ज़) *n.* बवासीर, अर्श

hag (हैग) *n.* खूसट बुढ़िया

haemorrhage (ˈहैमरिज) *n.* बहुत अधिक खून बहना, रक्त स्राव

haggard (ˈहैगर्ड) *a.* अजीब जंगली सा; चिंतित; मरियल

haggle (ˈहैगल) *vi.* सौदेबाज़ी करना – *n.*

hail[1] (हेल) *n.* ओला; बौछार (शब्दों आदि की) – *v.* ओले गिरना – **hailstone** *n.* ओला

hail[2] (हेल) *vt.* का अभिवादन करना; स्वागत करना; पुकारना, बुलाना – **hail from** का रहने वाला होना

hair (हेअर) *n.* बाल; रोएं – **hairy** *a.* अधिक बालों वाला – **hairdo** *n.* बाल संवारने का ढंग, केश-विन्यास – **hairdresser** *n.* केश-प्रसाधक, हेअर ड्रैसर – **hairsplitting** *n.* बाल की खाल निकालना – **let your hair down** मस्ती करना – **make someone's hair stand on end** (डर से) रोएं खड़े कर देना

hale (हेल) *a.* तगड़ा, स्वस्थ विशे. **hale and hearty** में

half (हाफ़) *n.* आधा भाग (*pl.* **halves** (हाव्ज़)) – *a.* आधा – *adv.* आधे तक, आधा – **halfback** *n. Football* खिलाड़ी का फारवर्ड (अग्रिमपंक्ति) के पीछे स्थान – **half-baked** *a.* अधपका (विचार आदि); *inf.* नासमझ, अधपका; मूर्ख – **half-brother, half-sister** *n.* सौतेला भाई, सौतेली बहिन – **half-cocked** *a.* अपूर्ण तैयार (होने के कारण विफल होना) – **half-hearted** *a.* बेमन से किया (कार्य) – **half-life** *n.* रेडियोधर्मी पदार्थों के आधे परमाणु नष्ट होने में लगने वाला समय – **half-mast** *n.* झुका हुआ (झंडा) (किसी की म त्यु पर शोक का प्रतीत – **half-time** *n. Sport* अर्ध-समय, विश्राम-काल – **half-wit** *n.* अल्पबुद्धि, मूर्ख

halibut (ˈहैलिबट) *n.* एक बड़ी खाने-योग्य मछली

hall (हॉल) *n.* सभा-भवन, हाल

hallelujah (हैलि´लूय्अ) *n. interj.* ईश स्तुति, परमात्मा के नाम का उदार, "हैलिलूया"

hallmark (´हॉल्मार्क) *n.* सोने व चांदी की शुद्धता-स्तर का प्रमाण-चिन्ह

hallo (ह´लो) *interj.* HELLO दे.

Halloween (हैला´ईन) *n.* 31 अक्तुबर सांय, ईसाई धर्म में एक पवित्र दिन

hallucination (हलूसि´नेशन) *n.* दष्टि भ्रम (वस्तु सामने न होने पर भी दिखाई देने का भ्रम) – **hallucinatory** *a.* दष्टि भ्रम सम्बन्धी

halo (´हेलो) *n.* चन्द्रमा, सूर्य आदि व चित्रों में संतों के सिर के चारों ओर दिखाया गया प्रभामण्डल (प्रकाश); व्यक्ति से जुड़ी महत्ता (*pl.* **-lo(e)s**) – *vt. inf.* प्रभामण्डल बनाना

halt[1] (हॉल्ट) *n.* रोक, विराम (विशे. सैनिकों आदि को मार्चिंग में रुकने का आदेश); बिना स्टेशन की इमारत वाला छोटा रेलवे स्टेशन, पड़ाव– *vt.* रोकना, रुकना

halt[2] (हॉल्ट) *vi.* हिचकना, आगा-पीछा करना

halve (हाव़) *vt.* दो भाग करना; आधा कर देना, बांट लेना

ham (हैम) *n.* सूअर की रान के ऊपरी भाग का मांस; *inf.* अभिनेता जो बढ़ा चढ़ा कर अस्वभाविक अभिनय करे; *inf.* जो शौकिया बेतार-संचार में रुचि ले – **ham-fisted, ham-handed** *a.* अनाड़ी, बेढंगा

hamburger (हैम्बर्गर) *n.* पावरोटी के टुकड़ों के बीच मांस आदि का टुकड़ा रख कर बनाया व्यंजन, हैम्बर्गर

hamlet (हैम्लिट) *n.* छोटा गांव

hammer (´हैमर) *n.* हथौड़ा – *vt.* हथौड़ा मारना; ठोकना; *inf.* बुरी तरह पछाड़ देना – **hammer and tongs** पूरे जोर-शोर से – **hammer out** (समस्या का हल) निकाल लेना

hammock (´हैमक) *n.* रस्सियों पर झूलता कपड़े, कैनवस आदि का बिस्तर, झूला, दलारा

hamper[1] (हैम्पर) *n.* ढक्कन सहित टोकरा (डला); बॉक्स आदि विशे. जो क्रिसमस के उपहार के रूप में भेजा जाय, डाली

hamper[2] (हैम्पर) *vi.* बाधा डालना, उलझाना

hamstrung (हैम्स्ट्रंग) *a.* पंगु; (ऐसा कार्य, व्यक्ति आदि) जिसके रास्ते में रुकावट, बाधा डाली गयी हो अवरोधित

hand (हैंड) *n.* हाथ; (दायें, बायें) ओर, दिशा, तरफ; लिखावट; मज़दूर; (घड़ी की) सूई; बांटे गए ताश (का हाथ) – *vt.* देना या आगे बढ़ाना, पकड़ाना – **handful** *n.* मुट्ठी भर – **handy** *a.* सुविधाजनक – **handbag** *n.* हैंडबैग – **handbill** *n.* इश्तहार – **handbook** *n.* निर्देश-पुस्तिका – **handcuff** *n.* हथकड़ी – *vt.* हथकड़ी लगाना – **handicraft** *n.* हस्त-शिल्प – **handiwork** *n.* कारनामा, करतूत – **handkerchief** (´हैंकर्चिफ़) *n.* रूमाल – **handout** *n.* विज्ञप्ति-पत्रक, सूचना सामग्री – **handwriting** *n.* लिखाई, लिखावट; लिपि; हस्तलिपि – **hand over** (कार्य भार) सुपुर्द करना

handicap (´हैंडिकैप) *n.* अड़चन; बाधा-दौड़, बाधा-प्रतियोगिता; विकलांगता – *vt.* बाधा डालना, रोक लगाना, प्रतिबंध लगाना (**-pp-**) –**mentally handicapped** मंद बुद्धि – **physically handicapped** विकलांग

handle (´हैंडल) *n.* मूठ, दस्ता, हत्था – *vt.* छूना, पकड़ना; संभालना; निपटाना, (से) निपटना, का व्यापार करना; कार्य संचालन करना

handsome (´हैंड्सम) *a.* सुन्दर (पुरुष); प्रचुर

hang (हैंग) *vt.* लटकाना टांगना; फांसी देना (**hanged** *pt./pp.*) – *vi* टंगे होना, टंगना; (बादल) छाये होना; पकड़े रहना (**hung** *pt./ pp.*) –**hanger** *n.* खूंटी, कपड़े टांगने का हैंगर – **hangman** *n.* जल्लाद – **hangover** *n.* ज्यादा शराब पीने के बाद होने वाला असर, खुमार

hangar (´हैंगर) *n.* हवाई जहाज़ रखने का स्थान, विमान शाला

hanker (हैंकर) *vi.* – **hanker after** को पाने के लिए बहुत उत्सुक होना
hankie, hanky (हैंकि) *n.* HANDKERCHIEF का संक्षेप
hanky-panky (हैंकि पैंकि) *inf. n.* चालाकी, चालबाज़ी; अवैध यौन-संबंध
haphazard (हैप् हैज़र्ड) *a.* अव्यवस्थित, बेतरतीब – **haphazardly** *adv.*
hapless (हैप्लिस) *a.* अभागा, बेचारा
happen (हैपन) *vi.* होना, घटित होना; संयोग होना – **happening** *n.* घटना – **as it happens** ऐसा है कि...
happy (हैपि) *a.* प्रसन्न, भाग्यवान, उपयुक्त – **happily** *adv.* – **happiness** *n.* प्रसन्नता – **happy-go-lucky** *a.* मौजी, मस्त
harass (हैरस) *vt.* तंग करना, परेशान करना, सताना – **harassment** *n.*
harbinger (ˈहार्बिंजर) *n.* अग्रदूत, आने वाली (घटना आदि) की (शुभ) सूचना देने वाला
harbour (ˈहार्बर) *n.* बंदरगाह; आश्रय – *vt.* शरण, आश्रय देना; छिपाना; (दुर्भाव आदि) मन में रखना
hard (हार्ड) *a.* सख्त; ठोस; समझने में कठिन; कठोर; असहनीय; व्यावहारिक, घोर (परिश्रम); (ऐसी नशीली दवा) जिसकी जल्दी लत पड़ जाए – *adv.* ज़ोर से, परिश्रम से; कठिनाई से; (के) पीछे ही – **harden** *v.* कड़ा बनाना; कठोर बनाना – **hardly** *adv.* मुश्किल से, ना के बराबर – **hardness** *n.* कड़ाई, सख्ती; कठोरता – **hardship** *n.* दुर्भाग्य, कष्ट – **hardboard** *n.* प्लाई का तख्ता, हार्ड बोर्ड – **hard-boiled** *a.* खूब उबालने पर सख्त हो गया (अण्डा); *inf.* अनुभवी, अभावुक – **hard copy** कम्प्यूटर फ्लॉपी/सी.डी. के विपरीत लिखित रूप में दस्तावेज़ – **hardcore** *a.* कट्ट – **hard cover** पक्की जिल्द में पुस्तक – **hard disk** *Computers* कम्प्यूटर में अंदर लगी डिस्क जिसमें आंकड़े व प्रोग्राम संचित होते हैं – **hard-headed** *a.* चतुर, व्यावहारिक – **hard-hearted** कठोर, निर्मम – **hard luck** दुर्भाग्य – **hardware** *n.* लोहे का सामान; मशीन के पुर्ज़े; *Computers* मशीनी व इलेक्ट्रॉनिकी पुर्ज़े – **hard of hearing** ऊंचा सुनने वाला – **hard-up** *inf.* तंगहाल
hardy (ˈहार्डि) *a.* तगड़ा; साहसी; कष्ट सहने में समर्थ; खुले में सारा साल उगे रह सकने वाले पौधे – **hardihood** *n.* निर्भीकता
hare (हेंअर) *n.* ख़रगोश
harem (हेंअरम, हाˈरीम) *n.* हरम, जनानख़ाना, अंतपुर
hark (हार्क) *vi.* सुनना – **hark back** बहस की पिछले बातों पर लौट कर आ जाना
harm (हार्म) *n.* हानि, नुकसान; चोट – *vt.* हानि या चोट पहुंचाना – **harmful** *a.* हानिकारक – **harmfully** *adv.* – **harmless** *a.* हानिरहित
harmony (ˈहार्मनि) *n.* मेल, सहमति, संगति; शांति; स्वर-संगति, स्वरों का तालमेल – **harmonious** *a.* संगत, मेल में; मैत्रीपूर्ण – **harmoniously** *adv.* – **harmonium** *n.* हार्मोनियम – **harmonize** *v.* तालमेल स्थापित करना; या होना; मेल कराना या होना; सहमति कराना या होना
harness (ˈहार्निस) *n.* घोड़े का साज़, बैलों का जूआ आदि – *vt.* साज चढ़ाना, जोतना; (जल प्रपात आदि की) ऊर्जा को काम में लाना
harp (हार्प) *n.* एक वीणा जैसा संगीत वाद्य, हार्प – *vi.* **harp on** का राग अलापना
harpoon (हार्ˈपून) *n.* व्हेल मछली पकड़ने के लिए कांटेदार बर्छी, हार्पून
harrow (हैरो) *n.* हैरो, पटरा, सुहागा, हल चलाने के बाद भूमि समतल करने का औज़ार – *vt.* पर सुहागा फेरना – **harrowing** *a.* हृदय-विदारक

harry (ˈहैरि) *vt.* तंग करना

harsh (हार्श) *a.* रूखा, कठोर, कटु, निर्मम – **harshly** *adv.* कठोरता या कटुता से – **harshness** *n.*

harvest (ˈहार्विस्ट) *n.* फसल (काटने का मौसम), पैदावार, उपज; कार्य का परिणाम – *vt.* फसल काटना व जमा करना – **harvester** *n.* फसल काटने वाला, फसल काटने की मशीन

has (हैज़) HAVE का **third person** *singular* – **has-been** *n. inf.* व्यक्ति जो कभी बहुत लोकप्रिय और सफल था परंतु अब नहीं है

hash (हैश) *n.* कीमा; *inf.* HASHISH का संक्षेप – *vt.* छोटे-छोटे टुकड़े करना – **make a hash of** गड़बड़ कर देना, बरबाद कर देना

hash browns *US* आलू व प्याज़ के छोटे टुकड़ों को तलकर बनाया व्यंजन

hashish (ˈहैशीश) *n.* भांग (**hashesh** भी)

hasp (हास्प) *n.* कुण्डा

hassle (ˈहैसल) *inf. n.* झगड़ा; परेशानी

hast (हैस्ट) *obs.* HAVE का *second person sing. pres. indicative*

haste (हिस्ट) *n.* जल्दी, जल्दबाज़ी, हड़बड़ी – *vi.* जल्दी करना – **hasten** (ˈहेसन) *v.* जल्दी करना या कराना – **hastily** *adv.* जल्दबाज़ी में – **hasty** *a.* उतावला – **make haste!** जल्दी करो!

hat (हैट) *n.* हैट, टोप – **hat trick** लगातार तीन सफलनाएं विशे. खेल में – **hats off to sb** किसी की प्रशंसा में उद्गार

hatch[1] (हैच) *v.* (अण्डे) सेना; (षड्यंत्र) रचना, (योजना) बनाना – **hatchery** *n.* कमरा, मशीन जिसमें अंडे सेए जाते हैं

hatch[2] (हैच) *n.* (प्राय: जहाज़ की) दीवार, फ़र्श या छत में कब्ज़े वाला दरवाज़ा वायुयान या अंतरिक्ष यान का दरवाज़ा – **hatchback** *n.* कार जिसमें पीछे की ओर उठाने वाला दरवाज़ा होता है – **hatchway** *n.* जहाज़ के डैक का दरवाज़ा, फलका-मुख

hatchet (ˈहैचिट) *n.* छोटी कुल्हाड़ी – **bury the hatchet** दुश्मनी भूलकर समझौता करना

hate (हिट) *vt.* घृणा करना – *n.* घृणा, वस्तु जिससे घृणा हो – **hateful** *a.* घृणित – **hatefully** *adv.* – **hatred** (ˈहेट्रिड) *n.* बहुत ज्यादा नफ़रत, द्वेष

haughty (ˈहॉटि) *a.* घमण्डी, अकड़ वाला – **haughtily** *adv.*

haul (हॉल) *vt.* घसीटना, खींचना – *n.* खींची गयी वस्तु, पकड़ी गयी मछलियां, पकड़ा गया माल; तै करने वाला रास्ता – **haulage** (ˈहॉलिज) *n.* वहन; ढुलाई (कीमत) – **long haul** जिसमें सफल होने में बहुत समय व मेहनत लगे

haunch (हांच) *n.* चूतड़, पट्ठा, कूल्हा; हिरन की टांग और पुट्ठे का मांस

haunt (हॉण्ट) *vt.* किसी स्थान पर आते रहना; भूतों का (स्थान विशेष पर) आना-जाना या अड्डा होना; (का) किसी को बार-बार ध्यान आना – *n.* अड्डा – **haunted** *a.* भुतहा (मकान आदि); चिंतित – **haunting** *a.* अत्यंत मनमोहक या दुखद

haute couture (ओट् कुˈट्यर) *n. French* आधुनिकतम फ़ैशन, ऊंचे दर्ज़े का फ़ैशन

hauteur (ओˈटर) *n.* अभिमान, दर्प

have (हैव़) *vt.* होना, पास रखना या होना; (रोग) होना; (करने के लिए) बाध्य होना; धोखा देना; (में) शामिल होना; पाना; में होना (CONTAIN के अर्थ में); अनुमति देना; कराना; जन्म देना; (auxiliary के रूप में इससे *perfect* तथा अन्य *tenses* बनते है) (**had, having**) – **have-nots/haves** दे० **the** के नीचे

haven (ˈहेव़न) *n.* बन्दरगाह; *fig.* आश्रय, सुरक्षित स्थान

haversack (हैव़र्सैक) *n.* *(backpack)* पैदल यात्रा आदि में पीठ पर सामान भर कर ले जाने का कैन्वस का झोला

havoc (हैव़क) *n.* बरबादी, विध्वंस; *inf.* अस्तव्यस्तता, अव्यवस्था

hawk (हॉक) *n.* बाज़; युद्ध की ओर ले जाने वाली नीतियों का समर्थक – **hawk-eyed** *a.*पैनी निगाह वाला

hawker (हॉकर) *n.* फेरी वाला

hawthorn (हॉथॉर्न) *n.* कांटेदार झाड़ियाँ

hay (हे) *n.* सूखी कटी हुई घास – **haystack** *n.* सूखी घास का ढेर – **haywire** (हेवाइअर) *a.* गड़बड़, अस्त-व्यस्त

hazard (हैज़र्ड) *n.* खतरा, जोखिम, संभावित संकट – *vt.* जोखिम में पड़ना, खतरा उठाना – **hazardous** *a.* जोखिम भरा, ख़तरनाक

haze (हेज़) *n.* धुंध (प्राय: गर्मी के कारण); धुंधलापन – **hazy** *a.* अस्पष्ट

hazel (हेज़ल) *n.* बादाम जैसे फलों वाली झाड़ी; बादामी रंग – *a.* भूरा (रंग)

H bomb HYDROGEN BOMB का संक्षेप

he (ही) *pron.* *(third person masculine pronoun)* वह, उसी ने (व्यक्ति, जानवर); *(comb. form)* नर, जैसे he-goat बकरा

head (हेंड) *n.* सिर; किसी भी वस्तु का सबसे ऊपर का भाग; (संस्था, स्कूल आदि का) अध्यक्ष, प्रधान; मुख्य भाग; योग्यता; संकट का चरम बिंदु; नेता; अध्याय का भाग; शीर्षक; अंतरीप; एक व्यक्ति; जीव; चित या पट; (जानवरों की) संख्या *(20 heads of cattle)*; टेप रिकार्डर आदि का टेप को छूने वाला भाग – *a.* मुख्य, प्रधान; प्रतिकूल (पवन), उल्टी – *vt.* सबसे ऊपर होना, प्रधान होना; नेत त्व करना; निर्देशन करना; शीर्षक देना; फुटबाल को सिर से मारना – *vi.* की ओर जाना – **heading** *n.* शीर्षक – **heads** *adv. inf.* सिक्के का चेहरे/चित्र वाला पक्ष – **heady** *a.* मादक, उत्तेजक – **headache** (हेंड्एक) *n.* सिर दर्द – **headboard** *n.* पलंग का सिरहाना – **headcount** (कर्मचारियों, दर्शकों आदि की) संख्या – **headlight** *n.* कार आदि की आगे की रोशनी, हैडलाइट – **headline** *n.* शीर्षक, सुर्खी – **headlong** *adv.* सिर के बल; बिना सोचे विचारे – **head office** मुख्य कार्यालय – **headquarters** *pl. n.* सेना के प्रधान का कार्यालय; मुख्यालय – **headstrong** *a.* अड़ियल, हठी, ज़िद्दी – **headway** *n.*, प्रगति

heal (हील) *vi.* स्वस्थ करना या होना – **health** (हैल्थ) *n.* स्वांस्थ्य; व्यक्ति के सम्मान में पिया जाने वाला जाम – **healthily** *adv.* – **healthiness** *n.* – **healthy** (हैल्थि) *a.* स्वस्थ, नीरोग – **health food** भूमि से प्राप्त पौष्टिकता के लिए खाया जाने वाला शाकाहारी भोजन

heap (हीप) *n.* ढेर – *vt.* ढेर लगाना; लादना

hear (हिअर) *vt.* सुनना; *Law* मुकदमे की सुनवाई करना; पर ध्यान देना – *vi.* सुन सकना; पता चलना (**heard** (हर्ड) *pt./pp.*) – **hearer** *n.* सुनने वाला – **hearing** *n.* श्रवण-शक्ति, सुनने की सीमा; अदालत में सुनवाई – **hear! hear**! *interj.* वाह! वाह! – **hearsay** *n.* सुनी-सुनाई बात, अफ़वाह – *a*

hearse (हर्स) *n.* शववाहन

heart (हार्ट) *n.* हृदय, दिल; मन, आत्मा, साहस; केंद्र; (ताश में) पान का पत्ता – **hearten** *v.* प्रोत्साहित करना या होना – **heartily** *adv.* खुले दिल से – **heartless** *a.* कठोर, निर्दय – **hearty** *a.* हार्दिक, सच्चा; स्वस्थ; पर्याप्त व जी भर कर (खाना) – **heart attack** दिल का दौरा – **heartbroken** *a.* जिसका दिल टूट गया हो – **heartburn** *n.*ऊपर की आंत में पीड़ा, अम्लशूल; ईर्ष्या – **heart failure** दिल का दौरा – **heart-rending** *a.* हृदय-विदारक – **by heart** याद, रटा हुआ

hearth (हार्थ) *n.* चूल्हा, भट्टी; घर

heat (हीट) *n.* गर्मी, ताप, गरमी का मौसम; उत्तेजना; मादा जीवों में काम भावना की उत्तेजना, मस्ती; अंतिम दौड़ में भाग लेने वालों के चुनाव हेतु प्रारंभिक दौड़ या प्रतियोगिता – *v.* गरम करना या होना – **heated** *a.* गरम; *fig* उत्तेजनापूर्ण – **heatedly** *adv.* – **heater** *n.* हीटर

heathen (ˈहीदन) *a.* विधर्मी; काफ़िर; असभ्य – *n.* ऐसा व्यक्ति

heave (हीव़) *vt.* ज़ोर लगाकर उठाना; (भारी चीज़) फेंकना; (लम्बी सांस) भरना – *vi.* फूलना; उभरना; मतली आना – *n.* ज़ोर, धक्का

heaven (हॅव़न) *n.* स्वर्ग; आकाश (*pl.* भी) – **heavenly** *a.* स्वर्ग जैसा

heavy (हॅवि) *a.* भारी; सघन; बहुत अधिक व धीमा (यातायात); कठिन; तीव्र; दुःखी, नीरस – **heavily** *adv.* – **heaviness** *n.*

Hebrew (ˈहीब्रू) *n.* यहूदी, हीब्रू (इब्रानी) भाषा

heckle (हॅकल) *vt.* वक्ता को प्रश्न पूछ-पूछ कर व उपहास आदि द्वारा तंग करना; बार-बार टोकना

hectare (हॅक्टार) *n.* सौ आर अथवा 10,000 वर्ग मीटर

hectic (ˈहेक्टिक) *a.* बहुत व्यस्त (जीवन आदि)

hedge (हॅज) *n.* कटी झाड़ियों से बना घेरा, बाड़ा, हैज – *vt.* ऐसा घेरा बनाना, रुकावट डालना; (समस्या आदि) बीच में आना; दोनों ओर दाव लगाना – *vi.* बाड़ा लगाना या उसकी छंटाई करना; हिचकिचाना; भविष्य की हानि से बचाव का प्रबंध करना

hedonist (ˈहीड्निस्ट) *n.* सुखवादी

heed (हीड) *vt.* ध्यान देना – **heedless** *a.* असावधान

heel (हील) *n.* एड़ी; जूते की एड़ी, अवांछनीय व्यक्ति; *sl.* घटिया या कमीना आदमी – *vt.* एड़ी लगाना

hefty (हॅफ़्टि) *a.* भारी-भरकम, तगड़ा (व्यक्ति); बहुत अधिक (कीमत)

hegemony (हिˈजॅमनि) *n.* राजनीतिक व सैनिक प्रभुत्व

heifer (हॅफ़र) *n.* छोटी उम्र की गाय

height (हाइट) *n.* कद; ऊंचाई; शिखर; ऊंची भूमि; चरम सीमा, पराकाष्ठा; (प्रायः (~ s) *pl.*) पहाड़ की चोटी – **heighten** *vt.* अधिक ऊंचा करना

heinous (ˈहेनस, ˈहीनस) *a.* बर्बर, जघन्य

heir (ऍअर) *n.* उत्तराधिकारी, वारिस (*few.* **heiress** *n.*) – **heirloom** *n.* पुश्तों से चली आ रही वस्तु, कलाक ति

held (हॅल्ड) HOLD का *pt./pp.*

helicopter (हॅलिकॉप्टर) *n.* हेलीकॉप्टर

helium (ˈहीलिअम) *n.* हीलियम गैस

hell (हॅल) *n.* नरक; प्रेतलोक; दुष्टता, दुःख या यातना का स्थान अथवा स्थिति – **hellish** *a.* नारकीय – **to hell with you!** भाड़ में जाओ!

hello (हॅˈलो) (**hallo, hullo** भी) *interj.* हलो; आश्चर्यसूचक शब्द, अरे!

helm (हॅल्म) *n.* पतवार; मुख्य सहारा

helmet (हॅल्मिट) *n.* (लोहे आदि का) टोप, हेल्मेट

help (हॅल्प) *vt.* सहायता करना, सहारा देना; आराम पहुंचाना – *n.* सहायता – **helper** *n.* सहायक – **helpful** *a.* सहायक, उपयोगी – **helping** *n.* भोजन का एक बार में खाया भाग, कौर, ग्रास – **helpless** *a.* बेकार, लाचार

helter-skelter (हॅल्टर-ˈस्कॅल्टर) *adv./a./n.* जल्दबाज़ी, हड़बड़ी (में)

hem (हॅम) *n.* कपड़े का किनारा, गोट – *vt.* गोट लगाना; रोक लगाना, घेरना (**-mm-**)

hemi- (हॅमि) (*comb. form*) आधा

hemisphere (हॅमिस्फ़िअर) *n.* गोलार्द्ध; प थ्वी का (उत्तरी व दक्षिणी) गोलार्द्ध

hemp (हॅम्प) *n.* सन्, जिससे रस्सी बनाई जाती है; गांजा

hen (हॅंन) *n.* मुर्गी – **henpecked** (हॅंन्पेंक्ट) *n.* जोरू का गुलाम

hence (हॅंन्स) *adv.* यहां से; इसलिए – **henceforward, henceforth** *adv.* अब से

henchman (हॅंन्च्मन) *n.* अनुचर, पिछलगू

henna (हॅंन्अ) *n.* मेहंदी की झाड़ी; मेहंदी

hepatitis (हॅप'टाइटिस) *n.* जिगर की सूजन

hepta- (हॅप्ट्अ) (*comb. form*) सात

heptagon (हॅंप्टगन) *n.* सप्तभुज

her (हर) *a/pron.* उस (स्त्री का); उसे – **hers** *pron.* उसका (स्त्री का) – **herself** pro*n.* स्वयं

herald (हॅंरल्ड) *n.* अग्रदूत, शासक की ओर से सार्वजनिक घोषणा करने वाला उद्घोषक – *vt.* घोषणा करना

herb (हर्ब) *n.* जड़ी-बूटी – **herbaceous** (हर्'बेशस) *a.* जड़ी-बूटी का या जैसा; सदा फूल देने वाला – **herbal** *a.* जड़ी-बूटी का, की (बनी दवा आदि) – **herbicide** *n.* वनस्पति-नाशक रसायन, शाकनाशी – **herbivorous** (हर्'बिव्रस) *a.* शाकभक्षी

herculean (हरक्यु'लीअन) *a.* अत्यधिक शक्ति व साहस की आवश्यकता वाला (कार्य आदि)

herd (हर्ड) *n.* पशुओं (विशे. एकसे) का झुण्ड – *v.* भीड़ बना लेना, एकत्र हो जाना – *v.* चराना – **herdsman** *n.* चरवाहा

here (हिअर) *adv.* यहां – **hereafter** *adv.* इसके बाद, भविष्य में – *n.* भविष्य, परलोक – **hereby** *adv.* इस बयान के द्वारा – **herewith** पत्र के साथ

heredity (हि'रॅडिटि) *n.* जीव की अपने लक्षण बच्चों में पहुंचा देने की प्रव ति, आनुवंशिकता – **hereditary** (हि'रॅडिटरि) *a.* वंशानुगत, पैत क, पुश्तैनी

heresy (हॅंरसि) *n.* रूढ़िवादी मत या सिद्धांत के विपरीत मत – **heretic** (हॅंरटिक) *n.* विधर्मी

heritage (हॅंरिटिज) *n.* पैत क सम्पत्ति, विरासत

hermetic (हर्'मॅटिक) *a.* वायुरुद्ध, इस प्रकार सील-बंद कि हवा अंदर न जा सके

hermit ('हर्मिट) *n.* एकांतवासी (साधु, सन्यासी आदि)

hernia ('हर्निअ) *n.* शरीर के किसी अंग (या उसके भाग) का अपनी त्वचा की परत से बाहर आ जाना, अन्त्र व द्धि, हर्निया

hero ('हिअरो) *n.* अपनी सफलताओं व गुणों के लिए सम्मानित व्यक्ति; साहित्यक क ति का नायक; शूरवीर (*pl.* **heroes, heroine** *fem.*) – **heroic** (हि'रोइक) *a.* वीरोचित, साहसिक – **heroically** *adv.* – **heroics** *pl. n.* बेतुका, असंयत व्यवहार – **heroism** ('हॅंरोइज़म) *n.* वीरता – **hero worship** वीर पूजा, महान व्यक्तियों की प्रशंसा, भक्ति

heroin (हॅंरोइन) *n.* मॉरफीन से बना एक नशीला पदार्थ

heron (हॅंरन) *n.* बगुला

herpes ('हर्पीज़) *n.* चर्म रोग

hertz (हर्ट्स) *n.* (रेडियो) आव ति (फ्रीक्वेन्सी) की एस.आई. इकाई (*pl.* **hertz**)

hesitate (हॅंज़िटेट) *vi.* हिचकिचाना, झिझकना – **hesitancy, hesitation** *n.* हिचकिचाहट – **hesitant** *a.* हिचकिचाने वाला

hessian (हॅंसिअन) *n.* पटसन का कपड़ा, टाट

hetero- (*comb. form*) विभिन्न, विषम

heterodox (हॅंटरोडॉक्स) *a.* प्रचलित मत, सिद्धांत आदि के विपरीत, असनातनी, विपंथी – **heterodoxy** *n.* विपंथिता

heterogeneous (हॅंटरो'जीनिअस) *a.* विभिन्न तत्वों से बना जातीय – **heterogeneity** (हॅंटरोजि'नीटि) *n.* विजातीयता

heterosexual (हॅंटर्अ'सॅक्शुअल) *a.* जो विपरीत लिंग व्यक्ति की ओर आकर्षित हो, विषम लिंगकामी

hew(ह्यू) *v.* (कुल्हाड़ी से) काटना, चीरना (**hewn, hewed** *pp.*)

hex-, hexa- (*comb. form*) छः

hexagon(´हेक्सगन) *n.* षटकोण

heydey(´हेडे) *n.* बहार, यौवन

HF high frequency का संक्षेप

HGV heavy goods vehicle (भारी माल वाहन) का संक्षेप

hiatus(हाइ´एटस) *n.* क्रमभंग (वार्ता या अभिलेखन में), अंतर, रिक्ति

hibernate(´हाइबर्नेट) *vi.* (जीवों का) शीतकाल निष्क्रय या सुप्त अवस्था में बिताना – **hibernation** (हाइबर्´नेशन) *n.*

hibiscus (हि´बिस्कस) *n.* जवाकुसुम, गुड़हर की झाड़ी

hiccup (´हिकप) *n.* हिचकी – *vi.* हिचकी लेना

hide[1] (हाइड) *vt.* छिपाना, गुप्त रखना – *vi.* छिपना (**hid** *pt.*, **hidden** *or* **hid** *pp.*, **hiding** *pr.p.*) – *n.* छिपने का स्थान (जैसे शिकारियों का) – **hide-and-seek** *n.* लुका-छिपी का खेल

hide[2] (हाइड) *n.* जानवर की खाल – **hiding** *n. sl.* पिटाई; करारी हार – **hide-bound** *a.* संकीर्ण, दकियानूसी

hideous (´हिडिअस) *a.* घ णित, घिनौना, वीभत्स

hierarchy (´हाइअरार्कि) *n.* श्रेणी बद्ध संगठन, समाज या समूह, सोपानतंत्र – **hierarchical** (हाइअ´रार्किकल) *a.* अधिक्रमिक, सोपानिक

hi-fi (´हाइ´फ़ाइ) *a.* HIGH FIDELITY का संक्षिप्त रूप – *n.* इस प्रकार के उपकरण

higgledy-piggledy (´हिगल्डि ´पिगल्डि) *adv./a.* अस्त-व्यस्त, गड़बड़

high (हाइ) *a.* ऊंचा, उच्च; मुख्य (मार्ग); पूरे ज़ोर पर (शीत, ग्रीष्म आदि); तेज़, ऊंची (ध्वनि), महंगा, अधिक (मूल्य); उत्तम (गुण); उच्च, बड़ा (पद), कुलीन; महत्वपूर्ण, श्रेष्ठ, उत्क ष्ट; *inf.* मस्ती में विशे. नशीली दवाइयों के प्रभाव में – *adv.* ऊंचा; अत्यधिक – **highly** *adv.* – **highness** *n.* ऊंचा होने की स्थिति, का गुण – **highbrow** *n. sl.* उच्चवर्गीय – *a.* बौद्धिक, दुर्बोध, कठिन – **high fidelity** *a.* प्राय: रिकार्ड किये हुए संगीत ध्वनि आदि के उच्चकोटि के पुनरुत्पादन का (उपकरण), उच्चतद्रूप – **high-flown** *a.* ऊंचे-ऊंचे (विचार आदि) – **high-handed** *a.* हठधर्मी, मनमाना – **highlight** *n.* चित्र, फोटो आदि में सबसे अधिक चमकता भाग; विशिष्टता – (~ **s**) *pl.* (खेल के) मुख्य अंश जो टी. वी. पर मैच के बाद दिखाये जांय – *vt.* पर ज़ोर देना, (का) महत्व बताना – **high-powered** *a.* उच्च-स्तरीय – **high-rise** *a.* बहुतल, बहुमंज़िला (भवन) – **high-sounding** *a.* आडम्बरपूर्ण – **high tech** आधुनिक औद्योगिक उपकरणों के उपयोग पर आधारित आंतरिक सजावट की शैली, **high technology** का संक्षेप, आधुनिकतम तकनीक जैसे इलैक्ट्रानिकी – **high-tech** *a.* आधुनिकतम तकनीक व यंत्रों से बना **high-tension** *a.* शक्तिशाली विद्युतधारा वाला (तार) – **high tide** (समुद्र में) ज्वार – **high time** अंतिम संभावित समय या अवसर – **high-up** *n.* महत्वपूर्ण व्यक्ति जो ऊंचे पद पर आसीन हो – **highway** *n.* राजमार्ग

hijack (´हाइजैक) *vt.* किसी वाहन (विशे. विमान) आदि का अपहरण करना – **hijacker** *n.* अपहरणकर्ता

hike (हाइक) *vi.* लम्बी पदयात्रा करना – *vt.* बढ़ाना (जैसे कीमतें) – *n.* व द्धि, बढ़ौती (कीमतों, भत्ते आदि में) – **hiker** *n.* लम्बी पदयात्रा करने वाला

hilarity (हि´लैरिटि) *n.* उल्लास – **hilarious** (हि´लेंअरिअस) *a.* अत्यंत आनंददायक, बहुत हंसाने वाला (कार्यक्रम, बात आदि), उल्लसित

hill (हिल) *n.* पहाड़ी, टीला – **hillock** *n.* छोटी पहाड़ी – **hilly** *a.* पहाड़ी (इलाका)

hilt (हिल्ट) *n.* – **to the hilt** पूरी तरह
him (हिम) *pron.* he सर्वनाम का object रूप, संप्रदान कारक – **himself** *pron.* उसने स्वयं
hind[1] (हाइंड) *n.* हिरनी
hind[2] (हाइंड) *a.* पीछे का, पिछला
hinder (ˈहिंडर) *vt.* रुकावट डालना, बाधा डालना – **hindrance** (ˈहिंड्रन्स) *n.*
Hindi (ˈहिन्दी) *n.* हिन्दी भाषा – **Hindu** *n.* हिन्दू – **Hinduism** *n.* हिंदू धर्म
hinge (हिंज) *n.* (दरवाज़े आदि का) कब्ज़ा, चूल – *vt.* कब्ज़ा लगाना – *vi.* घूमना; (पर) निर्भर करना
hint (हिंट) *n.* संकेत, इशारा – *v.* संकेत देना
hinterland (ˈहिटर्लैंड) *n.* समुद्रतट के पीछे, अथवा महानगर, बंदरगाह आदि के पास का क्षेत्र, पश्च भूमि, प ष्ठ प्रदेश
hip[1] (हिप) *n.* कूल्हा, पुट्ठा, नितम्ब
hip[2] (हिप) *a.* फैशन वाला (वस्त्र, संगीत) **hipper** *comp.*, **hippest** *sup.*
hippie, hippy (ˈहिपि) *n.* व्यक्ति जिसके वस्त्र, व्यवहार आदि उसके द्वारा परंपरागत मान्यताओं को अस्वीकार करने के सूचक हैं, हिप्पी
hippopotamus (हिपˈपॉटमस) *n.* दरयाई घोड़ा
hire (ˈहाइअर) *vt.* किराये या भाड़े पर लेना; नौकर रखना – *n.* भाड़े पर लेना या लिया जाना; किराया, भाड़ा – **hireling** (ˈहाइअर्लिङ) *n.* भाड़े का टट्टू – **hire-purchase** *n.* किश्तों में भुगतान योज़ना; किराया-खरीद
his (हिज़) *pron./a.* उस (पुरूष) का, की
hiss (हिस) *vi.* (सांप का) फुफकारना; सी-सी की आवाज़ करना विशे. गुस्से में – *vt.* नाराज़गी ज़ाहिर करना – *n.* फुफकार; सी-सी की आवाज़
history (ˈहिस्टरि) *n.* इतिहास – **historian** (हिस्ˈटॉरिअन) *n.* इतिहासकार – **historic** (हिस्ˈटॉरिक) *a.* ऐतिहासिक, महत्त्वपूर्ण – **historical** *a.* ऐतिहासिक, अतीत में घटित
histrionic (हिस्ट्रिˈऑनिक) *a.* (हावभाव में) नाटकीय, पाखण्डी, बनावटी – **histrionics** *pl. n.* इस प्रकार का व्यवहार; अभिनय कला
hit (हिट) *vt.* (पत्थर आदि से) मारना, वार करना, ठोकर मारना; चोट पहुंचना, अचानक पा लेना; पर बुरा प्रभाव डालना – *vi.* वार करना, अचानक (योजना आदि) सोच पाना (**hit, hitting**) – *n.* वार; सफलता; लोकप्रिय गाना आदि – **hit the jackpot** अचानक पैसा पा लेना
hit-and-run *a.* (दुर्घटना) जिसमें चालक मारकर भाग जाय
hitch (हिच) *vt.* (रस्सी आदि से) बांधना, झटके से खींचना – *vi.* अटक जाना; बंध जाना – *n.* अड़चन; गाँठ; बांधना; झटका – **hitch (hike)** *vi.* मुफ्त सवारी मांग कर यात्रा करना
hither (ˈहिदर) *adv.* इधर – **hitherto** *adv.* अब तक
HIV human immunodeficiency virus का संक्षेप, वायरस जो बाद में एड्स् की बीमारी का कारण बन सकता है
hive (हाइव़) *n.* मधुमक्खी-पेटी – **hive off** अलग कर देना
hoard (हॉर्ड) *n.* ज़खीरा, भंडार – *vt.* जमा करना
hoarding (ˈहॉर्डिङ) *n.* विज्ञापन के लिए बड़ा बोर्ड, होर्डिंग
hoarse (हॉर्स) *a.* फटा-फटा (स्वर), कर्कश (ध्वनि)
hoary (ˈहॉरि) *a.* पके बालों वाला, धूसर; पुराना; आदरणीय – **hoarfrost** *n.* जमी हुई ओस
hoax (होक्स) *n.* मज़ाक
hobble (ˈहॉबल) *vi.* लंगड़ाना
hobby (ˈहॉबि) *n.* शौक, हॉबी
hobgoblin (हॉब्ˈगाब्लिन) *n.* शरारती परी
hobnob (ˈहॉब्नॉब) *vi.* साथ शराब पीना; (से) मेलजोल रखना (**-bb-**)
hobo (ˈहोबो) *n.* **US, C** आवारा; घुमक्कड़
hockey (ˈहॉकि) *n.* हॉकी का खेल; **US,C** बर्फ पर हाकी का खेल

hocus-pocus (ˊहोकस्ˊपोकस) *n.* हेराफेरी
hod (हॉड) *n.* गारा, ईंट आदि ढोने का तसला
hoe (हो) *n.* फावड़ा, कुदाली – *vt.* फ़ावड़े से खोदना **(hoed, hoeing)**
hog (हॉग) *n.* खस्सी नर सूअर; लोभी नीच व्यक्ति – *vt. inf.* खाना; (किसी वस्तु का) केवल अपने लिए उपयोग करना – **hogwash** *n.* बकवास – **go the whole hog** किसी कार्य को (विशे. नये कार्य को) पूरी तरह कर डालना
hoist (हॉइस्ट) *vt.* (काँटे से) ऊपर उठाना
hold[1] (होल्ड) *vt.* पकड़ना, पकड़े रखना, स्थिर रखना, थामना; धारण करना, का अधिकारी होना; (प्रदर्शन सभा आदि) करना; हिरासत में लेना; (समारोह आदि) मनाना; रोके रखना; विश्वास रखना – *vi.* दृढ़ रहना, बना रहना, डटे रहना, लागू रहना, पर्याप्त होना **(held** *pt./pp.*) –*n.* पकड़; प्रभाव – **holder** *n.* धारी, स्वामी – **holding** *n.* (प्राय: *pl.*) सम्पत्ति जैसे ज़मीन, शेयर आदि – **holdall** *n.* बिस्तर बंद– **holdup** *n.* सशस्त्र डाका; देरी; सड़क पर भीड़ में रुके रहना – **hold back** हिचकिचाना – **hold out** डटे रहना; (रसद) चलना
hole (होल) *n.* छेद, छिद्र, सुराख; गड्ढा; बिल; *inf.* गन्दा (रहने का) स्थान; *inf.* कठिन स्थिति, परेशानी – *v.* सुराख करना, खोदना; छेद में डालना
holiday (ˊहॉलिडे) *n.* छुट्टी का दिन
hollow (ˊहॉलो) *a.* खोखला; बनावटी, झूठा – *n.* गड्ढा; छेद; घाटी – *vt.* खोखला बनाना; छेद करना; खोदना
holocaust (ˊहॉलकास्ट) *n.* सर्वनाश, विध्वंस
holy (ˊहोलि) *a.* धार्मिक, पवित्र, दैवी – **holiness** *n.* पवित्रता – **holy day** धार्मिक त्यौहार
homage (ˊहॉमिज) *n.* श्रद्धांजलि, सम्मान
home (होम) *n.* घर; मातृभूमि; वृद्ध, असहाय आदि व्यक्तियों के लिए संस्था – *a.* घर से सम्बंधित; स्वदेश – *adv.* घर को, घर पर; लक्ष्य तक – *v.* लक्ष्य तक पहुंचना, पहुंचना – **homeless** *a.* बेघर – **homely** a. सीधा-सादा, घरेलू – USC (दिखने में) साधारण – **homeward** *a./adv.* घर की ओर – **homewards** *adv.* घर की ओर – **homemaker** *n.* गृहिणी – **homesick** *a.* जो घर-परिवार या स्वदेश की याद से दु:खित हो, गृह-वियोगी – **homework** *n.* स्कूल का काम, होमवर्क – **bring home to** अपनी बात समझा देना, (अपने विचार से) प्रभावित करना
homicide (ˊहॉमिसाइड) *n.* नर हत्या; मानव घाती, हत्यारा
homily (ˊहॉमिलि) *n.* प्रवचन, धर्म- उपदेश; उपदेश
homo-*(comb. form)* सम-, समान, जैसे **homogeneous, homosexual**
hom(o)eopathy (होमिˊऑपथि) *n.* होम्यौपैथी चिकित्सा प्रणाली – **homoeopath** (ˊहोमिओपैथ) *n.* होम्योपैथी चिकित्सक
homogeneous (होमˊजीनियस) *a.* समरूप, समांगी, सदृश – **homogeneity** (होमोजिˊनीटि) *n.* समरूपता, एकरूपता – **homogenize** *vt.* (दूध व क्रीम में वसा-कणों को तोड़ कर दूध को) समांगीकृत करना
homonym (ˊहॉमनिम) *n.* समनाम शब्द, समउच्चारण परंतु भिन्नार्थक शब्द – **homonymous** *a.* समध्वनिक
Homo sapiens (होमोˊसेपिअन्ज़) *n.* आज का मानव/मानव जाति
homosexual (होमोˊसैक्स्युअल) *n./a.* समलिंगकामी – **homosexuality** (होमोसैक्स्युˊऐलिटि) *n.* समलिंग कामुकता
Hon. Honourable **(also h-) honorary** का संक्षिप्त रूप
hone (होन) *n.* धार तेज करने का सान – *vt.* सान पर धार चढ़ाना

honest (´ऑनिस्ट) *a.* सच्चा, ईमानदार; खरा, असली; निष्कपट –**honestly** *adv.* सच्चाई से, सचमुच – **honesty** *n.* ईमानदारी, सच्चाई

honey (´हनि) *n.* शहद – **honeycomb** (´हनिकोम) *n.* मधुमक्खियों का छाता – **honeycombed** *a.* गढ्ढे, सुरंगों से भरा हुआ (क्षेत्र) –**honeymoon** *n.* मधुमास

honk (हॉङ्क) *n.* कार की पों-पों –*vi.*

honour (´ऑनर) *n.* आदर, सम्मान; प्रतिष्ठा, ईमानदारी; मर्यादा; सतीत्व; सम्मान-सूचक (गुण, उपाधि); (पत्र में प्रयुक्त) प्रसन्नता; सौभाग्य – (~ **s**) *pl.* सम्मान; परीक्षा में विशिष्ट श्रेष्ठता – *vt.* आदर करना, (वायदा) पूरा करना; सम्मान प्रदान करना; चेक, हुंडी आदि सकारना, का भुगतान करना – **honourable** (´ऑनरबल) *a.* आदरणीय; प्रतिष्ठित; ईमानदार – **honourably** *adv.* – **honorarium** (ऑन´रैंअरिअम) *n.* मानदेय, फीस (*pl.* **-ria**) – **honorary** (´आनररि) *a.* सम्मान सूचक (उपाधि); अवैतनिक (पद व कार्य) – **your Honour** जज के लिए सम्बोधन

hood[1] (हुड) *n.* टोप, सिर व गरदन को ढंकने वाला टोप, हुड; कार, बच्चा गाड़ी की खुल सकने वाली छत; बरसाती; *US* कार के इंजन का ढक्कन –**hoodwink** *vt.* धोखा देना

hooch (हूच) *n.* देसी अवैध शराब

hood (हुड) *n.* टोप; *US* कार के इंजन का ढक्कन – **hoodwink** *vt.* धोखा देना

hoodlum (´हूड्लम) *n.* गुण्डा, दादा

hoodoo (´हूडू) *n.* दुर्भाग्य का कारण (वस्तु, व्यक्ति आदि)

hoof (हूफ़) *n.* (*pl.* **hoofs** या **hooves**) खुर

hook (हुक) *n.* आंकड़ा, काँटा, हुक; खूंटी; हँसिया; *Boxing* कुहनी मोड़ कर मारा गया मुक्का – *vt.* पकड़ना, हुक से बांधना, फंसाना; *Golf* (गेंद) काफी बांयें मारना; *Cricket* लेग की ओर गेंद को घुमा देना – **hooked** हुक जैसी आक ति वाला; पकड़ा हुआ, फंसा हुआ; *sl.* (की) लत पड़ी हुई – **hook-up** *n.* रेडियो, टेलिविज़न स्टेशनों का (कार्यक्रम विशेष के लिए) जुड़ना; (में) सम्पर्क स्थापित होना – **hookworm** (´हुक्वर्म) *n.* आँतों का एक कीड़ा, हुकवर्म – **by hook or by crook** किसी भी तरह – **off the hook** टेलीफोन रिसीवर अपने स्थान से हटा होना – **let sb off the hook** (अपराधी, दोषी आदि को) आसानी से छोड़ देना

hookah (´हुक्अ) *n.* हुक्का

hooligan (´हूलिगन) *n.* गुण्डा, बदमाश, तोड़-फोड़ करने वाला (युवा) व्यक्ति – **hooliganism** *n.*

hoop (हूप) *n.* पीपे आदि के चारों ओर चक्करदार पट्टी; खिलौने या खेलों में कूदने का छल्ला – *vt.* इससे बांधना, घेर लेना

hoot (हूट) *n.* उल्लू की आवाज; नाराज़गी दिखाने व मज़ाक उड़ाने के लिए हू-हू की आवाज़ें; *inf.* हास्यास्पद व्यक्ति या वस्तु – *vi.* सीटी बजाना, हूट करना; कार आदि के हॉर्न का पों-पों करना – **hooter** *n.* (कारखाने आदि का) भोंपू; *sl.* नाक

hop (हॉप) *vi.* एक पैर से कूदना; *inf.* उछल कर आगे बढ़ना; फुदकना (**-pp-**) – *n.* उछाल, कूद; यात्रा का एक भाग – **hopscotch** (´हॉप्स्कॉच) *n.* बच्चों का लंगड़ी टांग या टापू का खेल, चिबिड्डी

hope (होप) *n.* आशा, अभिलाषा अभिलाषित वस्तु – *v.* आशा करना – **hopeful** *a.* आशावान, आशापूर्ण (स्थिति) – **hopefully** *adv. inf.* (विशे. आजकल) आशा की जाती है – **hopeless** *a.* निराशाजनक (स्थिति आदि)

hopper (´हॉपर) *n.* उछलने वाला व्यक्ति या वस्तु; चक्की या मशीन में (अनाज आदि) पदार्थ डालने का उपकरण

horde (हॉर्ड) *n.* भीड़, झुण्ड

horizon (ह´राइज़न) *n.* क्षितिज; क्षितिज-रेखा – **horizontal** (हॉरि´जॉण्टल) *a.* समतल

hormone (´हॉर्मोन) *n.* कुछ ग्रंथियों से निकलने वाला एक पदार्थ जो शरीर के अवयवों का कार्य करने में सहायक है – **hormonal** *a.*

horn (हॉर्न) *n.* सींग; इससे बनी अथवा मिलती-जुलती अनेक वस्तुएं; इससे बने सुषिर-वाद्य (तुरही जैसे); कार आदि का हार्न, भोंपू

horoscope (´हॉरस्कोप) *n.* जन्मपत्री, जन्म कुण्डली

horrendous (हॉ´रेंण्डस) *a.* भयंकर, रोमांचकारी

horror (´हॉरर) *n.* आतंक; घ णा – **horrible** (´हॉरबल) *a.* भयंकर; वीभत्स, जिससे घ णा उत्पन्न हो – **horribly** *adv.* – **horrid** *a.* अप्रिय, घ णित, डरावना; *inf.* रूखा – **horrify** *vt.* भयभीत करना (– **ified,** – **ifying**)

horse (हॉर्स) *n.* घोड़ा; घुड़सवार सेना; रिसाला; (जिमनास्टिक्स में) कूदने का घोड़ा; कपड़े सुखाने का ढांचा, घोड़ी – **horseman** *n.* (**horsewoman** *fem.*) घुड़सवार – **horsepower** *n.* इंजन-शक्ति की इकाई, अश्व शक्ति, हार्स पावर – **horseracing** *n.* घुड़दौड़ – **horseradish** मूली *n.* – **horseshoe** *n.* नाल; नालाकार वस्तु – **horse-trading** *n.* राजनीतिज्ञों, व्यापारियों में सौदे बाज़ी

horticulture (´हॉर्टिकल्चर) *n.* बाग़बानी, उद्यानक षि – **horticultural** (हॉर्टि´कल्चरल) *a.* बाग़बानी-, उद्यान- – **horticulturist** (हॉर्टि´कल्चरिस्ट) *n.* उद्यानक षि विशेषज्ञ

hose (होज़) *n.* (**hose pipe** भी) द्रव या गैस ले जाने के लिए रबर आदि का लचीला पाइप; जुराबें – **hosiery** (´होज़िअरि) *n. obs.* होज़री, जुराब, बनियान आदि

hospice (´हॉस्पिस) *n.* म त्यु के निकट व्यक्तियों के लिए अस्पताल

hospital (´हॉस्पिटल) *n.* अस्पताल– **hospitalization** *n* अस्पताल में भरती कराना – **hospitalize** *vt.*

hospitality (हॉस्पि´टैलिटि) *n.* अतिथि-सत्कार, आवभगत – **hospitable** (हॉ´स्पिटबल) *a.* अतिथि-सत्कारशील, मेहमाननवाज़

host (होस्ट) *n.* (**hostess** *fem.* (होस्टिस)) मेज़बान, अतिथियों का सत्कार करने वाला; सराय या होटल का मालिक; किसी (टी.वी. /रेडियो, कार्यक्रम का) संचालक; ऐसा जानवर, पौधा जिसमें परजीवी (कीटाणु आदि) रहते हैं – *vt.* मेज़बानी करना

hostage (´हॉस्टिज) *n.* बन्धक व्यक्ति

hostel (´हॉस्ट्ल) *n.* होस्टल

hostile (´हॉस्टाइल) *a.* विरोधी, प्रतिकूल; बैरपूर्ण – **hostility** (हॉ´स्टिलिटि) *n.* शत्रुता – **hostilities** *pl. n.* युद्ध, युद्ध-स्थिति

hot (हॉट) *a.* गरम; तपता हुआ; क्रोधित, तीव्र, नवीन; अतिप्रिय (*hot favourite*); चरपरा, तीता (स्वाद), *sl.* उत्तम, तेज़, चुस्त; कामोत्तेजक (व्यक्ति); *sl.* चोरी का (माल) (**hotter** *comp.*, **hottest** *sup.*) – **hotly** *adv.* गुस्से से, पूरे ज़ोर से – **hotness** *n.* गरमी – **hotbed** *n.* अड्डा (षड्यंत्र का) – **hot dog** हॉट डॉग, गोल डबलरोटी के टुकड़ों में रखा गर्म सॉसेज (कीमे से बना पदार्थ) – **vegetable hotdog** *India* सब्ज़ी भरकर बनाया हॉटडॉग – **hothead** *n.* क्रोधी, उतावला – **hothouse** *n.* शीत प्रदेशों में उष्ण प्रदेशों के पौधे उगाने के लिए क त्रिम रूप से गरम रखा हुआ भवन, काँच घर – **hot pants** स्त्रियों की तंग निकर – **hotplate** *n.* बिजली के कुकर पर लगी प्लेट जो गरम की जा सकती है, तप्त प्लेट – **hot-tempered** *a.* गर्म मिज़ाज – **get into hot water** मुसीबत में फंसना – **blow/go hot and cold** किसी काम के बारे में कभी 'हां' कभी 'ना' कहना

hotchpotch (´हॉच्पॉच) *n.* खिचड़ी; गड़बड़झाला
hotel (हो´टैल) *n.* होटल; **hotel keeper, hotelier** (हॉ´टैल्यर) *n.* होटल मालिक या प्रबंधक
hound (हाउंड) *n.* शिकारी कुत्ता – *vt.* पीछा करना
hour (आउअर) *n.* घंटा; दिन का समय, निश्चित समय – *pl.* कार्य, प्रार्थना आदि की निश्चित अवधि; प्रार्थना संग्रह – **hourly** *adv.* हर घंटे होने वाला – *a.*
house *n.* (हाउस) मकान, गृह, भवन; सभा भवन, सदन आदि; परिवार; व्यापारिक फर्म (प्रतिष्ठान); (हाल में बैठे) श्रोतागण (*pl.* **houses** ´हाउज़िज) – *vt.* (हाउज़) आश्रय, रहने का स्थान, माल रखने का स्थान आदि देना या लेना; ढंकना या रखना – **housing** (´हाउज़िङ) *n.* मकान (देना); ढकने, सुरक्षित रखने या रखने के लिए विशेषकर बना ढांचा अथवा भाग – **house arrest** *n.* नज़रबंदी – **house-boat** (´हाउस्बोट) *n.* नौकाघर – **housebreaker** *n.* घर में सेंध लगाने वाला चोर – **household** *n.* गृहस्थी – **householder** *n.* गृहस्वामी – **housekeeper** *n.* घर का प्रबंधक – **housekeeping** *n.* घर चलाना, उसका खर्चा – **housemaid** *n.* नौकरानी – **house-to-house** घर-घर जाकर करने का (काम) – **house-warming** *n.* गृह प्रवेश – **housewife** (´हाउस्वाइफ़) *n.* गृहस्वामिनी – **house work** घर-गृहस्थी का काम – **on the house** भोजन/पेय पदार्थ जो होटल में ग्राहकों को मुफ्त मिलें
hovel (´हॉवल) *n.* झोंपड़ी, घरोन्दा
hover (´हॉव़र) *vi.* पक्षियों का मंडराना – **hovercraft** (´हॉव़र्क्राफ्ट) *n.* एक प्रकार का यान जो पृथ्वी व पानी दोनों पर सतह से ऊपर वायु के दबाव से चलता है
how (हाउ) *adv.* कैसे, किस दिशा में, किस सीमा तक – **however** *conj.* परंतु, लेकिन, फिर भी, तथापि – *adv.* किसी भी तरह, कितना भी
howdah (´हाउड्अ) *n.* हाथी पर बैठने का हौदा
howl (हाउल) *vi.* हू-हू करना, (विशे. भेड़िये व शिकारी कुत्तों का) चिल्लाना – *n.* ऐसी आवाज़ – **howler** *n.* ऐसी आवाज़ निकालने वाला; *inf.* भारी, मूर्खतापूर्ण भूल
hub (हब) *n.* पहिये का केंद्र; नाभि; *fig.* गतिविधियों का केंद्र
hubby (´हबि) *n. inf.* पति
huddle (´हड्ल) *n.* घनी भीड़; *inf.* तात्कालिक (और गुप्त) विचार-विमर्श – *v.* सटकर इकट्ठा होना, सिमट कर बैठ जाना
hue (´ह्यू) *n.* रंग, वर्ण
hue and cry (सार्वजनिक) विरोध
huff (हफ़) *n.* खीज या झुंझलाहट – *vi.* हांफना – **in a huff** गुस्से में (चले जाना)
hug (हग) *vt.* चिपटाना, गले लगाना – *n.* स्नेहपूर्ण आलिंगन
huge (ह्यूज) *a.* बहुत बड़ा, विशाल
hulk (हल्क) *n.* जहाज का (बिकार) ढांचा; *offens.* विशालकाय भद्दा व्यक्ति या वस्तु – **hulking** *a.* भद्दा; बड़ा, मोटा
hull (हल) *n.* जहाज़ का ढांचा, मुख्य भाग; स्ट्रॉबेरी, रसभरी आदि फलों का पुटक या छिलका – *vt.* ऊपर का खोल व छिलका हटाना, छीलना
hullabaloo (हलब´लू) *n.* शोरगुल
hum (हम) *vi.* (मधुमक्खी का) भिनभिनाना; *sl.* बहुत सक्रिय होना – *vt.* गुनगुनाना (**-mm-**) – *n.* गुंजन; *sl.* गंध; *sl.* चहल पहल, गतिविधि; रेडियो में आवाज़ में खराबी
human (´ह्यूमन) *a.* मानवीय, मानव- सम्बन्धी – **humane** (ह्यू´मेन) *a.* उदार, दयामय; सहृदय – **humanism** (´ह्यूमनिज़्म) *n.* मानववाद, मानवतावाद, धर्म के विपरीत कर्म में विश्वास – **humanist** *n.* –

humanitarian (ह्यूमैनि'टेंअरिअन) *n.* लोकोपकारी व्यक्ति – *a.* – **humanity** (ह्यू'मैनिटि) *n.* मानव स्वभाव; मानव जाति; दयालुता – **humanities** *pl. n.* साहित्य, दर्शन, कला का अध्ययन – **humanize** *vt.* मानवीय या सभ्य बनाना – **humanly** *adv.* – **humankind** *n.* सम्पूर्ण मानव जाति – **human being** मनुष्य, इन्सान

humble ('हंबल) *a.* विनम्र, दीन – *vt.* नीचा दिखाना, अपमानित करना – **humbly** *adv.*

humbug ('हंबग) *n.* धोखेबाज; कपटी

humdrum ('हमड्रम) *a.* साधारण; फीका, रूखा

humid ('ह्यूमिड) *a.* सीलन भरा, आर्द्र – **humidity** ऽ(ह्यू'मिडिटि) *n.* आर्द्रता

humiliate (ह्यू'मिलिएट) *vt.* अपमानित करना; नीचा दिखाना – **humiliation** (ह्यूमिलि'एशन) *n.* अपमान

humility (ह्यू'मिलिटि) *n.* विनम्रता; दीनता

humour (ह्यूमर) *n.* हास्य, परिहास, मज़ाक; मनोदशा; मिज़ाज; स्वभाव – *vt.* (को) प्रसन्न करना – **humorist** *n.* विनोदी; हास्य लेखक – **humorous** ('ह्यूमरस) *a.* हास्यकर, मज़ाकिया – **humorously** *adv.*

hump (हम्प) *n.* (ऊंट आदि का) कूबर; छोटी पहाड़ी; *inf.* उदासी – *vt.* कूबर के आकार का बनाना – **humpback** *n.*कुबड़ा

humus ('ह्यूमस) *n.* सड़ी हुई वनस्पति व गोबर आदि से बनी खाद, खाद-मिट्टी

hunch (हंच) *n. inf.* पूर्वाभास; कूबर – *vt.* (कूबर के आकार में शरीर का भाग) झुकाना – **hunchback** *n.*कुबड़ा

hundred ('हंड्रड, 'हंड्रिड) *n./a.* सौ – **hundredth** *a.* सौवां – **hundredfold** *a./adv.* सौ गुना – **hundredweight** *n.* 112 पौंड, 50.4 किलोग्राम का भार, टन का बीसवां भाग – **hundreds of** सैंकड़ों

hung (हङ) HANG का *pt./pp.* – *a.* निर्णय न देने की स्थिति में (ज्यूरी); जिसमें किसी का बहुमत न हो

hunger ('हंगर) *n.* भूख; प्रबल इच्छा या कामना – *vi.* भूख लगना; प्रबल कामना रखना – **hungrily** *adv.* भूखे की तरह – **hungry** *a.* भूखा – **hunger strike** भूख हड़ताल

hunk (हंक) *n.* मोटा टुकड़ा

hunt (हंट) *v.* शिकार करना; को तलाश करना – *n.* शिकारी; पीछा; खोज; आखेट-मार्ग; शिकारी कुत्तों का समूह; शिकारी दल; शिकार-क्षेत्र – **hunter** *n.* शिकारी (**huntress** *fem.*)

hurdle ('हड्र्ल) *n.* बाधा, रुकावट – *pl.* बाधा-दौड़ – *vi.* बाधा दौड़ में बाधा पार करना – **hurdler** *n.* बाधा-दौड़ धावक

hurl (हर्ल) *vt.* ज़ोर से फेंकना – **hurly-burly** *n.* हुल्लड़, गड़बड़ी

hurrah (हु'रा), **hurray** (हू'रे) *interj.* प्रसन्नता या प्रशंसा का विस्मयादिबोधक शब्द

hurricane ('हरिकन) *n.* तूफान विशे. समुद्री तूफान – **hurricane lamp** लालटेन

hurry ('हरि) *v.* जल्दी करना या कराना (**hurried, hurrying**) – *n.* जल्दबाज़ी, उत्सुकता, उतावलापन, बेचैनी

hurt (हर्ट) *vt.* चोट पहुंचाना, नुकसान पहुंचाना; दर्द करना; दुःख देना – *vi. inf.* दर्द अनुभव कराना (**hurt** *pt./pp.*) – *n.* घाव, चोट, हानि – **hurtful** *a.* दुःखदायी, कष्टप्रद

hurtle ('हट्र्ल) *vi.* (वस्तु आदि का) तेज़ी से चलना, घूमना

husband ('हज़्बंड) *n.* पति – *vt.* संभल कर खर्च करना, बचत से (पैसों आदि का) पूरा उपयोग करना – **husbandry** *n.* क षि कार्य; अर्थव्यवस्था – **animal husbandry** पशु-पालन

hush (हश) *v.* एकदम चुप होना या करना – *n.* सन्नाटा, चुप्पी, पूरी शांति – **hush-hush** *a. inf.* गुपचुप, गुप्त – **hush up** मामला आदि दबा देना

husk (हस्क) *n.* भूसा, छिलका; वस्तु का व्यर्थ का भाग – *vt.* भूसा निकालना – **husky** (´हस्कि) *a.* भारी (आवाज़); भूसे जैसा सूखा; सूखा (गला); भूसे या छिलके का, से भरा; *inf.* लम्बा, तगड़ा

hustings (´हस्‌टिंङ्ज़) *pl. n.* चुनाव सम्बंधी राजनीतिक अभियान; संसदीय चुनाव क्रिया

hustle (´हसल) *v.* धकेलना, आगे बढ़ना, किसी से जल्दी कराना – *vi.US C sl.* (विश्या का ग्राहकों को) ललचाना – *n.* – **hustler** *n.* धोखे से पैसा ऐंठने वाला, ठग; वेश्या – **hustle and bustle** चहल-पहल

hut (हट) *n.* झोंपड़ी, कुटिया

hy(a)ena (हाइ´ईना) *n.* लकड़बग्घा

hybrid (´हाइब्रिड) *n./a.* संकर, दोग़ला पौधा अथवा जानवर

hydrant (´हाइड्रंट) *n.* सड़क के किनारे आग बुझाने में प्रयोग के लिए लगा नल

hydraulic (हाइ´ड्रॉलिक) *a.* पाइप में द्रव-दाब से सम्बंधित अथवा उससे चलने वाला (यंत्र) – **hydraulics** *n.* द्रव- इंजीनियरी

hydro- (*comb. form*) जल

hydrocarbon (हाइड्रो´कार्‌बन) *n.* कार्बन व हाइड्रोजन का यौगिक

hydrochloric acid (हाइड्र´क्लॉरिक-) गंधक का तेजाब

hydroelectric (हाइड्रोइ´लेॅक्ट्रिक) *a.* जल-विद्युत सम्बंधी

hydrogen (´हाइड्रिजन) *n.* हाइड्रोजन गैस – **hydrogen bomb** हाइड्रोजन बम, उदजन बम

hydrophobia (हाइड्र´फ़ोबिअ) *n.* पानी से डरना, जलभीति, पागल कुत्ते के काटने से हुए रोग का लक्षण

hydrotherapy (हाइड्रो´थेॅरपि) *n. Med.* जल-चिकित्सा

hydrous (´हाइड्रस) *a.* सजल, जलीय

hygiene (´हाइजीन) *n.* स्वास्थ्य-विज्ञान – **hygienic** (हाइ´जीनिक) *a.* स्वास्थ्यकर – **hygienically** *adv.* – **hygienist** *n.* दंत-चिकित्सक का सहायक

hymen (´हाइमेॅन) *n.* कौमार्य-झिल्ली; योनिच्छद; (H-) ग्रीक विवाह-देवता

hymn (हिम) *n.* स्तुति, ईश-भजन, स्त्रोत – *vt.* स्तुति करना – **hymnal** (´हिम्‌नल) *a.* भजन, स्तुति सम्बंधित – *n.* भजन-संग्रह (**hymn book** भी)

hype (हाइप) *sl. n.* धोखा; जालसाज़ी; टी. वी., रेडियो पर ज़ोरदार प्रचार – *v.* (किसी उत्पादन का) ज़ोरदार प्रचार करना – **hyped up** बहुत उत्सुक व बेचैन

hyper- (*comb. form*) से अधिक, बहुत अधिक

hyperbole (हाइ´पर्‌बलि) *n.* अतिशयोक्ति

hypersensitive (हाइपर्´सेॅन्सिटिव़) *a.* अतिसंवेदनशील, बहुत नाज़ुक

hypertension (हाइपर्´टेॅन्शन) *n.* उच्चरक्तचाप

hypnosis (हिप्´नोसिस) *n.* सम्मोह, सम्मोहन विद्या – **hypnotic** *a.* सम्मोहन सम्बंधी – **hypnotism** (´हिप्‌नटिज़्म) *n.* सम्मोहन – **hypnotize** *vt.* सम्मोहन करना

hypochondriac (हाइप´कॉन्ड्रिऐक) *n./a.* अकारण रोग का भ्रम करने वाला व्यक्ति, रोगभ्रमी

hypocrisy (हि´पॉक्रसि) *n.* धूर्तता, पाखण्ड, ढोंग – **hypocrite** (´हिपक्रिट) *n.* धूर्त, पाखण्डी

hypothesis (हाइ´पॉथिसिस) *n.* परिकल्पना, अनुमान; प्राक्कल्पना पर आधारित (*pl.* **-eses** सीज़) – **hypothetical** (हाइप´थेॅटिकल) *a.* परिकल्पित, अनुमानित

hysteria (हि´स्टअरिअ) *n.* हिस्टीरिया, मानसिक रोग; उन्माद – **hysterical** (हिस्´टेॅरिकल) *a.* उन्मत्त, हिस्टीरिया-पीड़ित – **hysterically** *adv.* – **hysterics** *n.* हिस्टीरिया के दौरे

Hz hertz का संक्षिप्त रूप

I

I (आइ) *pron.* मैं

ibex (´आइबेंक्स) *n.* बड़े सींगों वाली जंगली बकरी, साकिन (*pl.* **ibex**)

ibid (इ´बिड) *Lat.* **ibidem** का संक्षेप, (पुस्तक में) पूर्वोक्त, वहीं, वही

ibis (´आइबिस) *n.* सारस जैसा जलपक्षी, बुज्जा

I/C in charge (प्रभारी, कार्यभारी) का संक्षेप

ICBM Intercontinental Ballistic Missile (अंतरमहाद्वीपीय प्रक्षेपास्त्र) का संक्षेप

ice (आइस) *n.* (जमी हुई) बर्फ; आइसक्रीम – *vt.* से ढंकना या ढंके जाना; बर्फ से ठंडा करना; (केक पर) चाशनी चढ़ाना – *vi.* – **icicle** (´आइसिकल) *n.* छतों आदि से लटकती बर्फ, हिमलंब, हिमवर्तिका – **icily** *adv.* बहुत शांत परंतु रुखे पन से (बात) – **iciness** *n.* – **icing** *n.* केक पर लगी चाशनी – **icy** *a.* बर्फीला – **ice age** हज़ारों वर्ष पहले लम्बा समय जब प थ्वी बर्फ से ढंकी थी, हिमयुग – **iceberg** *n.* समुद्र में तैरता हिमशैल – **icebound** *a.* बर्फ से ढका – **ice cream** आइसक्रीम, कुल्फी – **ice floe** समुद्र पर तैरती बर्फ की मोटी परत – **ice rink** बर्फ जमाकर बनाया गया स्केटिंग का क्षेत्र/रिंक – **ice skating** बर्फ पर स्केटिंग का खेल

icon (´आइकॉन) *n.* प्रतिमा, मूर्ति (विशे. देवी, देवताओं की) – **iconoclasm** (आइ´कॉनोक्लैज़्म) *n.* मूर्तिभंजन; रूढ़ि-भंजन – **iconoclast** *n.* मूर्तिभंजक, मूर्तियां तोड़ने वाला; रूढ़िभंजक – **iconoclastic** (आइकॉनो´क्लैस्टिक) *a.*

ICU (हस्पताल में) intensive care unit का संक्षेप

ID (आइ´डी) *n.* पहचान-पत्र (identification का संक्षेप)

id (इड) *n.* मूल व त्यात्मक मानसिक शक्तियां, इद, इदम्

I'd (आइड) I had/I would का संक्षेप

idea (आइ´डिअ) *n.* विचार, भाव, धारणा; अंदाज़ा; योजना, मत, उद्देश्य

ideal (आइ´डिअल) *n.* आदर्श; आदर्श-स्वरूप – *a.* सर्वांगपूर्ण; आदर्श – **idealism** *n.* आदर्शवाद – **idealist** *n.* आदर्शवादी; अव्यावहारिक व्यक्ति – **ideally** *adv.*

identity (आइ´डेंण्टिटि) *n.* व्यक्तित्व, पहचान – **identical** *a.* समान, एक से – **identically** *adv.* – **identifiable** *a.* सरलता से पहचाना जा सकने वाला – **identification** *n.* पहचान, परिचय, एकीकरण – **identify** *vt.* पहचानना; तादात्म्य स्थापित करना, (स्वयं को) वर्ग, वाद आदि से जोड़ना, अभिन्न समझना (**identified, identifying**)

ideology (आइडि´ऑलजि) *n.* विचारधारा, (आर्थिक, राजनीतिक आदि) सिद्धांत, वाद – **ideological** (आइडिअ´लॉजिकल) *a.* सैद्धांतिक

idiocy (´इडिअसि) *n.* दे. IDIOT

idiolect (´इडिअलेंक्ट) *n.* व्यक्ति विशेष के बोलने की शैली, व्यक्ति बोली

idiom (´इडिअम) *n.* मुहावरा; बोली; अभिव्यक्ति की विशिष्ट शैली – **idiomatic** *a.* मुहावरेदार, चलित भाषा में

idiosyncrasy (इडिओ´सिंक्रिसि) *n.* व्यक्ति की मानसिक, स्वाभाविक, चारित्रिक विशेषता, सनकीपन

idiot (´इडिअट) *n.* जड़ बुद्धि, मूर्ख – **idiocy** *n.* जड़-बुद्धिता, निपट मूर्खता – **idiotic** (इडि´ऑटिक) *a.* महामूर्ख

idle (´आइड्ल) *a.* बेकार; सुस्त; बंद (मशीन); बेरोज़गार; खाली (समय) – *vi.* (इंजन का)

बिना गीयर लगे धीरे-धीरे चलना– **idle away** समय व्यर्थ गंवाना – **idleness** *n.* सुस्ती – **idler** *n.* निठल्ला – **idly** *adv.*

idol (´आइड्ल) *n.* पूजा हेतु देवी-देवता की मूर्ति; भक्ति या श्रद्धा योग्य वस्तु – **idolater** (आइ´डॉलटर) *n.*, (**idolatress** *fem.*) मूर्तिपूजक – **idolatry** (आइ´डॉलट्रि) *a.* मूर्ति पूजा; अत्यधिक लगाव व श्रद्धा – **idolize** *vt.* (व्यक्ति आदि) की पूजा करना

idyll (इडिल) *n.* जीवन के सरल, सुंदर (विशे. गांव में) समय का वर्णन, ग्राम-गीत – **idyllic** (आइ´डिलिक) *a.* ऐसे जीवन का, से संबंधित, रमणीय

i.e. *Lat. id est* (का संक्षेप), अर्थात

if (इफ़) *conj.* यदि, अगर– *n.* अनिश्चितता या संदेह (विशे. **ifs and buts** में, अगर-मगर) – **iffy** *a. inf.* संदिग्ध – **if so** यदि ऐसा है – **if not** यदि नहीं – **if only** यदि बस

igloo (´इग्लू) *n.* एस्कीमो का गुम्बदनुमा बर्फ का घर

ignite (इग्´नाइट) *vt.* सुलगाना, आग लगाना – *vi.* सुलगना, आग पकड़ना – **ignition** (इग्´निशन) *n.* सुलगने, सुलगाने की क्रिया; इंजन चालू होने की क्रिया

ignoble (इग्´नोबल) *a.* नीच, अधम; घटिया (विचार, भावना)

ignominy (´इग्नमिनि) *n.* बदनामी, कलंक – **ignominious** (इग्नो´मिनिअस) *a.* बदनाम, घ णित

ignore (इग्´नॉर) *vt.* पर ध्यान न देना, उपेक्षा करना – **ignoramus** (इग्न´रेमस) *n.* अज्ञानी, ज्ञान-शून्य (*pl.* – **muses**) – **ignorance** (´इग्नरन्स) *n.* अज्ञान, मालूम न होना – **ignorant** *a.* अज्ञानी; अनपढ़; अनजान, अनभिज्ञ – **ignorantly** *adv.*

iguana (इ´ग्वान्अ) *n.* अमरीका का एक बहुत बड़ा गिरगिट जैसा जीव, गोह, इगवाना

ill (इल) *a.* अस्वस्थ; बुरा; दोषपूर्ण; अशुभ – *n.* बुराई; हानि; बीमारी – *adv.* बुरी तरह से; मुश्किल से (जैसे *ill afford* में) – **illness** *n.* बीमारी – **ill-advised** *a.* असावधान, अविवेकी, नासमझी का (कार्य) – **ill-fated** *a.* दुर्भाग्यपूर्ण – **ill-gotten** *a.* बेइमानी की/हराम की (कमाई) – **ill-mannered** *a.* अशिष्ट, बदतमीज़ – **ill-treat** *vt.* दुर्व्यवहार करना – **ill will** द्वेष, दुर्भावना, मन में मैल

ill. illustrated, illustration का संक्षिप्त रूप

illegal (इ´लीगल) *n.* अवैध, गैर कानूनी – **illegality** *n.* अवैधता

illegible (इ´लेंजिबल) *a.* अपाठ्य, जो पढ़ा न जा सके, अस्पष्ट

illegitimate (इलि´जिटिमिट) *a.* अविवाहित माता-पिता से उत्पन्न, जारज – *n.* जारज – **illegitimacy** *n.* अवैधता

illicit (इ´लिसिट) *a.* गैर कानूनी, अवैध

illiterate (इ´लिटरिट) *a.* निरक्षर, अनपढ़, अशिक्षित – *n.* – **illiteracy** *n.* निरक्षरता

illogical (इ´लॉजिकल) *a.* असंगत, तर्क विरुद्ध; (*behaviour*) नासमझी भरा

ill-tempered (इल्´टेंम्पर्ड) *a.* गुस्सैल, रूखा

illuminate (इ´लूमिनेट) *vt.* आलोकित करना; स्पष्ट करना, पर प्रकाश डालना – **illuminant** *n.* प्रकाशमान करने वाली (वस्तु); प्रदीपक – **illumination** (इलूमि´नेशन) *n.* आलोकित करने की क्रिया, रोशनी, दीपमाला; चित्रावली; ज्ञान होना

illusion (इ´लूझ़न) *n.* भ्रांति, भ्रम, वहम – **illusionist** *n.* जादूगर – **illusory** (इ´लूसरि) *a.* भ्रामक

illustrate (´इलस्ट्रेट) *vt.* चित्र, उदाहरण आदि (समझाने के लिए) साथ देना, उदाहरण देना – **illustration** (इल´स्ट्रेशन) *n.* चित्र; आरेख; उदाहरण – **illustrative** *a.* व्याख्यापूर्ण – **illustrator** *n.*

illustrious (इ´लस्ट्रिअस) *a.* प्रसिद्ध, सुविख्यात
image (´इमिज) *n.* प्रतिमा, चित्र; छाया; प्रतिबिम्ब; प्रतिरूप; धारणा, मन में बना चित्र, शब्द-चित्र, विशे. साहित्य में – *vt.* (की) प्रतिमा, चित्र आदि बनाना – **imagery** (´इमिजरि) *n.* (साहित्य में) बिम्ब - विधान
imagine (इ´मैजिन) *vt.* कल्पना करना, सोचना, अनुमान लगाना – **imaginable** *a.* जिसकी कल्पना की जा सके – **imaginary** (इ´मैजिनरि) *a.* काल्पनिक – **imagination** (इमैजि´नेशन) *n.* कल्पना-शक्ति – **imaginative** *a.* कल्पनाशील
imam (इ´माम) *n.* मुस्लिम धार्मिक नेता, इमाम
imbalance (इम्´बैलन्स) *n.* असंतुलन
imbecile (´इम्बिसील) *n.* मूर्ख, जड़ बुद्धि
imbibe (इम्´बाइब) *vt.* (मदिरा) पीना; (मन में) पूर्ण रूप से ग्रहण कर लेना – *vi.* पीना
imbue (इम्´ब्यू) *vt.* (भावनाओं आदि से ओत-प्रोत करना
imitate (´इमिटेट) *vt.* अनुकरण करना, नकल उतारना, के जैसा बनाना – **imitable** *a.* – **imitation** (इमि´टेशन) *n.* नकल, सदश्यता, के जैसी वस्तु; नकली वस्तु
immaculate (इ´मैक्युलिट) *a.* निष्कलंक, बेदाग़, निर्मल, साफ; त्रुटिहीन
immaterial (इम´टिअरिअल) *a.* महत्वहीन
immature (इम´ट्युअर, इम´चुअर) *a.* अपरिपक्व, नासमझ – **immaturity** *n.*
immediate (इ´मीडिअट) *a.* तुरंत होने वाला, तात्कालिक, निकटतम – **immediacy** *n.* तात्कालिकता – **immediately** *adv.* तुरंत
immemorial (इमि´मॉरिअल) *a.* अति प्राचीन, बहुत पुराना
immense (इ´मेंन्स) *a.* विशाल, बहुत बड़ा – **immensely** *adv.* – **immensity** *n.*
immerse (इ´मर्स) *vt.* डुबोना; में लीन करना – **immersion** (इ´मर्शन) *n.* निमज्जन, डुबाने की क्रिया
immigrate (´इमिग्रेट) *vi.* किसी देश में आकर बस जाना – **immigrant** (´इमिग्रंट) *n./a.* अप्रवासी – **immigration** (इमि´ग्रेशन) *n.* आप्रवास
imminent (´इमिनंट) *a.* निकट भविष्य में घटित होने वाला, सन्निकट – **imminence** *n.* सन्निकटता – **imminently** *adv.*
immobile (इ´मोबाइल) *a.* जड़वत्, एक स्थान पर स्थिर – **immobilize** (इ´मोबलाइज़) *vt.* को चलने या काम करने से रोक देना
immolate (´इमोलेट) *vt.* मारना, बलि देना – **immolation** *n.* बलि
immoral (इ´मॉरल) *a.* अनैतिक, भ्रष्ट
immortal (इ´मॉरट्ल) *a.* अमर, अविस्मरणीय – *n.* देवता; अविनाशी वस्तु या व्यक्ति – **immortality** (इमॉर्´टैलिटि) *n.* – **immortalize** *vt.* अमर कर देना
immune (इ´म्यून) *a.* (रोग आदि से) प्रतिरक्षित, निरापद; मुक्त – **immunity** *n.* प्रतिरक्षा, निरापदता, मुक्त (मुकदमे, कर आदि से) – **immunization** (इम्युनाइ´ज़ेशन) *n.* – **immunize** (´इम्युनाइज़) *vt.* प्रतिरक्षित करना
impact (´इम्पैक्ट) *n.* टक्कर, संघात; (*fig.*) गंभीर प्रभाव – *vt.* (इम्´पैक्ट) ठूंसना; जमाना, बैठाना
impair (इम्´पेंअर) *vt.* कमजोर करना; हानि पहुंचाना – **impairment** *n.* हानि, क्षति
impart (इम्´पार्ट) *vt.* (सूचना आदि) देना, बताना; देना
impartial (इम्´पार्शल) *a.* निष्पक्ष
impassable (इम्´पासबल) *a.* (दर्रा आदि) जिसे पार न किया जा सके, दुर्गम
impasse (´इम्पैस, ऐम्पास) *n.* गतिरोध
impassioned (इम्´पैशण्ड) *a.* जोशीला, आवेगपूर्ण (भाषण आदि)
impassive (इम्´पैसिव़) *a.* भावशून्य; शांत

impatient (इम्´पेशंट) *a.* अधीर, बेसब्र
impeach (इम्´पीच) *vt.* अभियोग लगाना, गंभीर आरोप लगाना – **impeachment** *n.* (राज्य के विरुद्ध अपराध का) महाभियोग
impeccable (इम्´पेॅकबल) *a.* त्रुटिहीन
impecunious (इम्पि´क्यूनिअस) *a.* गरीब – **impecuniosity** (इम्पिक्यूनि´ऑसिटि) *n.* गरीबी
impede (इम्´पीड) *vt.* रोकना, बाधा डालना – **impediment** (इम्´पेॅडिमंट) *n.* अड़चन, बाधा; हकलाहट
impel (इम्´पेॅल) *vt.* प्रेरित करना, उकसाना
impending (इम्´पेॅन्डिङ) *a.* शीघ्र ही घटित होने वाला
impenetrable (इम्´पेॅनिट्रबल) *a.* जिसको भेदा न जा सके, अभेध, दुरूह
imperative (इम्´पेॅरटिव़) *a.* अत्यावश्यक, अनिवार्य; आज्ञात्मक – *n. Grammar* आज्ञार्थक व ति
imperceptible (इमपर्´सेॅप्टबल) *a.* अति सूक्ष्म, अगोचर
imperfect (इम्´पर्फ़िक्ट) *a.* अपूर्ण, अधूरा; त्रुटिपूर्ण
imperial (इम्´पिअरिअल) *a.* शाही, साम्राज्य का, शानदार, भव्य – **imperialism** *n.* साम्राज्यवाद – **imperialist** *n.*
imperil (इम्´पेॅरिल) *vt.* खतरे में डालना (-ll-)
imperious (इम्´पिअरिअस) *a.* घमण्डी, अकड़वाला
impersonal (इम्´पर्सनल) *a.* भावनाओं से अप्रभावित
impersonate (इम्´पर्सनेट) *vt.* दूसरे व्यक्ति का रूप धारण करना; का अभिनय करना – **impersonation** (इम्पर्स´नेशन) *n.* – **impersonator** *n.*
impertinent (इम्´पर्टिनंट) *a.* ढीठ, गुस्ताख – **impertinence** *n.*
imperturbable (इमपर्´टर्बबल) *a.* शांत, अविचलित – **imperturbably** *adv.*
impervious (इम्´पर्विअस) *a.* जिसमें से (पानी आदि) न निकल सके; (भावनाओं, तर्क आदि से) अप्रभावित; अभेद्य – **imperviously** *adv.* – **imperviousness** *n.* अभेद्यता, अप्रभावित रहने की प्रक ति
impetuous (इम्´पेॅट्युअस) *a.* उतावला – **impetuosity** (इम्पेॅटयु´ऑसिटि) *n.* उतावलापन
impetus (´इम्पिटस) *n.* संवेग; प्रेरणा
impinge (इम्´पिंज) *vi.* (*on* के साथ) के क्षेत्र में जाना; पर प्रभाव डालना; टकराना
impious (इम्´पिअस) *a.* अधर्मी
implacable (इम्´लैकबल) *a.* कठोर; अपरिवर्तनीय (घ णा आदि)
implant (इम्´प्लांट) *vt.* रोपना, (विचार मन में) बैठाना
implausible (इम्´प्लॉज़बल) *a.* तर्क विरुद्ध, अविश्वसनीय
implement (´इम्प्लिमंट) *n.* औज़ार, उपकरण – *vt.* लागू करना, अमल में लाना
implicate (´इम्प्लिकेट) *vt.* फंसाना; का संकेत देना – **implication** (इम्प्लि´केशन) *n.* अभिप्राय – **implicit** (इम्´प्लिसिट) *a.* अव्यक्त; पूर्ण (विश्वास आदि)
implore (इम्´प्लॉर) *vt.* याचना; प्रार्थना करना
imply (इम्´प्लाइ) *vt.* का संकेत देना; का अर्थ होना **(implied, implying)**
import (इम्´पॉर्ट) *vt.* लाना, आयात करना – *n.* (´इम्पॉर्ट) आयात; आयातित वस्तु; अर्थ; महत्व – **importer** *n.* आयातकर्ता
important (इम्´पॉर्टंट) *a.* महत्वपूर्ण, आवश्यक; प्रभावशाली – **importance** (इम्´पॉर्टन्स) *n.* महत्व; प्रभाव
importune (इम्´पॉट्यून) *vt.* आग्रह करना – **importunate** (इम्´पॉट्युनिट) *a.* दुराग्रही, बार-बार मांगने वाला – **importunity** *n.*

impose (इम्ˈपोज़) *vt.* (कर) लगाना; (विचार आदि) थोपना – *vi.* का लाभ उठाना; दुरुपयोग करना – **imposing** *a.* शानदार, भव्य – **imposition** (इम्पˈज़िशन) *n.* आरोपण, थोपा जाना; कर; भार – **impost** *n.* आयात कर, महसूल

impossible (इम्ˈपॉसिबल) *a.* असंभव; बिलकुल अनुचित – **impossibility** *n.* असंभवता – **impossibly** *adv.*

impostor (इम्ˈपॉस्टर) *n.* ढोंगी – **imposture** (इम्ˈपॉस्चर) *n.* ढोंग

impotent (ˈइम्पटण्ट) *a.* बेबस; नपुंसक – **impotence** (ˈइम्पटन्स) *n.* लाचारी; नपुंसकता

impound (इम्ˈपाउण्ड) *vt.* (वाहन, मवेशी आदि) कानूनन जब्त करना

impoverish (इम्ˈपॉवरिश) *vt.* दरिद्र कर देना; कमज़ोर कर देना – **impoverishment** *n.* दरिद्रता

impracticable (इम्ˈप्रैक्टिकबल) *a.* जिसको कार्यान्वित करना असंभव या कठिन हो

impractical (इम्ˈप्रैक्टिकल) *a.* अव्यावहारिक

impregnable (इम्ˈप्रेग्नबल) *a.* अजेय, अटल

impregnate (ˈइम्प्रेग्नेट) *vt.* भर देना, संसेचित करना; गर्भित करना – **impregnation** *n.*

impress (इम्ˈप्रेस) *vt.* प्रभावित करना; मोहर लगाना; (के दिमाग में) बैठाना – *n.* (ˈइम्प्रेस) छाप, छाप लगाने की क्रिया – **impression** (इम्ˈप्रेशन) *n.* अंकित प्रभाव (विशे. मन पर); धारणा, विश्वास; छाप; छपाई; (मुद्रित) संस्करण; मुद्रित कापी (पुस्तक की) – **impressionable** (इम्ˈप्रेशनबल) *a.* सहज में प्रभावित होने वाला – **impressive** *a.* प्रभावशाली

imprest (इम्ˈप्रेस्ट) *vt.* पेशगी – *n.*

imprint (ˈइम्प्रिंट) *n.* छाप – *vt.* छाप लगाना

imprison (इम्ˈप्रिज़न) *vt.* बन्दी बनाना – **imprisonment** *n.* कारावास

impromptu (इम्ˈप्रॉम्प्ट्यू) *adv./a.* तुरंत, बिना अभ्यास के (भाषण आदि)

improve (इम्ˈप्रूव़) *v.* सुधरना या सुधारना – **improvement** *n.* सुधार

improvident (इम्ˈप्रॉविडंट) *a.* फिज़ूलखर्च; लापरवाह, नासमझ – **improvidence** *n.* असावधानी, लापरवाही

improvise (ˈइम्प्रवाइज़) *v.* उपलब्ध वस्तुओं से काम चलाना; बिना तैयारी के बोलना (कविता आदि) – **improvisation** *n.*

impudent (ˈइम्प्यूडंट) *a.* बदतमीज़, गुस्ताख़ – **impudence** *n.* गुस्ताखी

impulse (ˈइम्पल्स) *n.* आवेश, कुछ करने की अचानक इच्छा – **impulsive** (इम्ˈपल्सिव़) *a.* बिना सोचे-विचारे कार्य करने वाला

impunity (इम्ˈप्यूनिटि) *n.* दंड के डर से मुक्ति

impute (इम्ˈप्यूट) *vt.* आरोप लगाना

in (इन) *prep.* (स्थान, सकाल, स्थिति, क्षेत्र आदि) में, अंदर – *adv.* अवस्था, स्थान आदि में; *inf.* प्रचिलित – *a. inf.* लोकप्रिय, फैशन में

in. inch(es) का संक्षिप्त रूप

inability (इन्अˈबिलिटि) *n.* असमर्थता

in absentia (इन्ऐबˈसेंन्टिअ) *adv.* अनुपस्थिति में

inaccessible (इनऐकˈसेंसबल) *a.* जहां/ जिस तक पहुंचा न जा सके, अगम्य

inaccurate (इन्ˈऐक्युरिट) *a.* गलत, यथार्थ से परे

inaction (इनˈऐक्शन) *n.* निष्क्रियता, आलस्य – **inactive** *a.* निष्क्रिय

inadequate (इन्ˈऐडिक्विट) *a.* अपर्याप्त – **inadequacy** (इन्ˈऐडिक्वसि) *n.*

inadvertent (इन्अड्ˈवर्टंट) *a.* असावधान; भूल से हुई (त्रुटि आदि)

inadvisable (इनड्ˈवाइज़बल) *a.* अनुचित

inalienable (इन´एलिअनबल) *a.* (अधिकार) अहस्तान्तरणीय
inane (इ´नेन) *a.* मूर्ख, अर्थहीन
inanimate (इन्´ऐनिमिट) *a.* जड़, अचेतन
inappropriate (इन्अ´प्रोप्रिअट) *a.* अनुपयुक्त, असंगत
inarticulate (इनार्´टिक्यलट) *a.* जो अपने विचार आदि स्पष्ट न कर सके
inasmuch (इनज़्´मच) *adv.* इस कारण, क्योंकि (केवल **inasmuch as** में)
inaudible (इन´ऑडिबल) *a.* जो सुनाई न दे
inaugurate (इ´नॉग्युरेट) *vt.* आरंभ करना, उद्‌घाटन करना – **inaugural** *a.* उद्‌घाटन – **inauguration** (इनॉग्यु´रेशन) *n.* उद्‌घाटन (समारोह)
inauspicious (इनॉस्´पिशस) *a.* अशुभ
inborn (´इन्´बॉर्न) *a.* जन्मसिद्ध
inbuilt (´इन्बिल्ट) *a.* गुण जो किसी वस्तु का आवश्यक अंग हो, निहित
incalculable (इन्´कैल्क्युलबल) *a.* बहुत अधिक; अनिश्चित
in camera गुप्त (सभा, अधिवेशन आदि)
incandescent (इन्कैन्´डेंसंट) *a.* तापदीप्त, तपती, चमकती (वस्तु)
incantation (इन्कैन्´टेशन) *n.* जादू-टोना, झाड़-फूंक, जादू-मन्तर
incapable (इन्´केपबल) *a.* असमर्थ, अशक्त
incarnation (इनकार्´नेशन) *n.* अवतार
incendiary (इन्´सेंन्डिअरि) *a.* वैर के कारण संपत्ति को आग लगाने का (कार्य)
incense[1] (इन्´सेंन्स) *vt.* बेहद गुस्सा दिलांना
incense[2] (´इन्सेंन्स) *n.* धूप या अगरबत्ती; इसका सुगंधित धुआं
incentive (इन्´सेंन्टिव़) *n.* प्रोत्साहन, प्रेरणा
inception (इन्´सेप्शन) *n.* प्रारंभ, शुरूआत
incessant (इन्´सेसंट) *a.* निरंतर, लगातार
incest (´इन्सेस्ट) *n.* सगे संबंधियों (जिनका विवाह नहीं हो सकता) में संभोग – **incestuous** (इन्´सेस्ट्युअस) *a.* अगम्यागमन विषयक
inch (इंच) *n.* इंच, फुट का बारहवां भाग, **0.0254** मीटर – *v.* बहुत धीरे-धीरे आगे बढ़ना
incident (´इन्सिडंट) *n.* घटना – *a.* प्रासंगिक, संबद्ध – **incidence** (´इन्सिडंस) *n.* घटित होने की सीमा या आव ति (बारम्बारता) – **incidental** *a.* छोटा व अपेक्षाक त कम महत्व का, आकस्मिक, प्रासंगिक – **incidentally** *adv.* संयोग से, अकस्मात; इसी प्रसंग में – **incidentals** *pl. n.* छोटे-मोटे खर्च
incinerate (इन्´सिनरेट) *vt.* भस्म कर देना
incipient (इन्´सिपिअंट) *a.* आरंभिक
incision (इन्´सिझ़न) *n.* चीरा – **incisive** (इन्´साइसिव़) *a.* पैना, तीखा (व्यंग आदि)
incite (इन्´साइट) *vt.* भड़काना
inclement (इन्´क्लेमंट) *a.* (मौसम के लिए प्रयुक्त) बहुत खराब
incline (इन्´क्लाइन) *v.* झुका होना, झुकाना; ढालू होना या बनाना, की ओर झुकाव होना या करना – (´इन्क्लाइन) *n.* ढलान – **inclination** (इन्क्लि´नेशन) *n.* झुकाव; ढाल
include (इन्´क्लूड) *vt.* सम्मिलित करना, में लगा देना – **inclusion** (इन्´क्लूझ़न) *n.* समावेश – **inclusive** *a.* (सब) मिलाकर
incognito (इन्कॉग्´नीटो) *adv./a.* अज्ञात रूप से, छद्‌म वेष में (*pl.* **-tos**)
incoherent (इन्को´हिअरंट) *a.* अस्पष्ट; असम्बद्ध – **incoherence** *n.* असम्बद्धता – **incoherently** *adv.*
income (´इन्कम) *n.* आय (विशे. वार्षिक) – **income tax** आयकर
incoming (´इन्कमिङ) *a.* आता हुआ, आगमिक
incomparable (इन्´कॉम्प्रबल) *a.* अतुलनीय
incompatible (इन्कम्´पैटबल) *a.* असंगत, अनमेल – **incompatibility** असंगति
incompetence (इन्´कॉम्पिटन्स) *n.* असमर्थता, अयोग्यता – **incompetent** *a.*

incomprehensible (इन्काम्प्रि'हॅन्सबल) *a.* जो समझ न आये
inconceivable (इन्कन्'सीवबल) *a.* कल्पना के बाहर, कल्पनातीत
incongruous (इन्'कॉङ्ग्रुअस) *a.* असंगत
inconsequent (इन्'कॉन्सिक्वंट), **inconsequential** (इन्कॉन्सि'क्वेन्शल) *a.* महत्वहीन
inconsistent (इन्कन्'सिस्टंट) *a.* असंगत; परस्पर विरोधी
inconsolable (इन्कन्'सोलबल) *a.* जिसे दुख में धीरज न बंधाया जा सके, शोकातुर
inconspicuous (इन्कन्'स्पिक्युअस) *a.* जिसपर ध्यान न जाय, अप्रकट
incontrovertible (इन्कॉण्ट्र'व़ र्टिबल) *a.* (तर्क आदि) जोकाटा न जासके, अकाट्य
inconvenience (इन्कन्'वीनिअन्स) *n.* असुविधा – *vt.* परेशान करना – **inconvenient** *a.* असुविधाजनक
incorporate (इन्'कॉर्परेट) *vt.* सम्मिलित करना, निगम बना लेना – **incorporation** *n.* सम्मिलित करने, निगम बनाने की क्रिया
incorrigible (इन्'कॉरिजबल) *a.* जो सुधर न सके
increase *v.* (इन्'क्रीस) आकार, संख्या आदि में वृद्धि करना या होना – *n.* ('इन्क्रीस) वृद्धि, बढ़ती; लाभ
incredible (इन्'क्रेंडबल) *a.* अविश्वासनीय
incredulous (इन्'क्रेंडुलस) *a.* जो विश्वास न करे
increment ('इन्क्रिमंट) *n.* वृद्धि विशे. क्रमिक (वेतन-वृद्धि)
incubator ('इन्क्युबेटर) *n.* अण्डे सेने व अकाल प्रसव में जन्मे बच्चों को पालने की मशीन
inculcate ('इन्कल्केट) *vt.* मन में बैठाना
incumbent (इन्'कम्बंट) *a.* (*on* के साथ) के लिए आवश्यक – *n.* पदधारी, विशे. चर्च में
incur (इन्'कर) *vt.* अपने ऊपर (ऋण आदि) लेना; (किसी की नाराज़गी) मोल लेना **(-rr-)**
incurable (इन्'क्युअरबल) *a.* लाइलाज, असाध्य
indebted (इन्'डेंटिड) *a.* आभारी ऋणी – **indebtedness** *n.* आभार; कर्ज़ में डूबे होना
indecent (इन्'डीसंट) *a.* अशोभनीय
indecipherable (इन्डि'साइफ़बल) *a.* जो पढ़ा न जा सके, अपाठ्य
indecisive (इन्डि'साइसिव़) *a.* (व्यक्ति) जो निर्णय न कर सके, ढुलमुल, डावांडोल – **indecision** *n.* अनिश्चय दुविधा, हिचकिचाहट
indeed (इन्'डीड) *adv.* निस्संदेह, वास्तव में
indefatigable (इन्डि'फ़ैटिगबल) *a.* ना थकने वाला, अथक – **indefatigably** *adv.*
indefensible (इन्डि'फ़ेंन्सबल) *a.* असमर्थनीय
indefinite (इन्'डेंफ़िनिट) *a.* अनिश्चित; अनिश्चित कालीन – **indefinitely** *adv.* अनिश्चित काल तक; अनिश्चित रूप से
indelible (इन्'डेंलिबल) *a.* अमिट
indelicate (इन्'डेंलिकिट) *a.* अशिष्ट; भद्दा, रूखा
indemnity (इन्'डेम्निटि) *n.* हरजाना, क्षतिपूर्ति; बीमा; आश्वासन
indent (इन्'डेंन्ट) *vt.* हाशिये से हटकर अन्दर की ओर लिखना या छापना; (किसी से) माल मंगाना; मांग-पत्र से माल मंगाना – *n.* ('इंडेंण्ट) मांग; मांग-पत्र, इंडेंट
independent (इंडि'पेंडंट) *a.* स्वतंत्र; निर्दलीय – **independence** (इंडि'पेंन्डन्स) *n.* स्वतंत्रता, स्वाधीनता
in-depth (इन्'डेंप्थ) *a.* विस्तृत
indescribable (इंडिस्'क्राइबबल) *a.* अकथनीय – **indescribably** *adv.*
indestructible (इन्डि'स्ट्रक्टबल) *a.* अविनाशी

indeterminate (इंडि´टर्मिनिट) *a.* अनिश्चित, अनिर्धारित, अनिर्धार्य

index (´इंडेक्स) *n.* पुस्तक के अंत में विषय-सूची, अनुक्रमणिका; *Math.* घातांक (*pl.* **indexes,** *Math.* **indices** (-सीज़)) – *vt.* विषय-सूची बनाना – **index finger** तर्जनी उंगली

Indian (´इंडिअन) *n.* भारतीय – *a.* भारतीय – **Indian hemp** गांजा; भांग का पौधा – **Indian ink** गहरा काला रंग – **Red Indian** अमरीका का मूल निवासी, रेड इंडियन

India rubber रबड़, मिटाने का रबड़

Indian summer शरद ऋतु में सूखा गर्म मौसम; जीवन में लगातार सफलता का समय

indicate (´इंडिकेट) *vt.* संकेत करना; बताना – **indication** (इंडि´केशन) *n.* संकेत, लक्षण, चिन्ह, निर्देश – **indicative** (इन्´डिकटिव़) *a.* निर्देशक – **indicator** *n.* सूचक

indict (इन्´डाइट) *vt.* अभियोग लगाना – **indictment** *n.* इलज़ाम लगाया जाना

indifferent (इन्´डिफ़रंट) *a.* उदासीन; न अच्छा न बुरा; घटिया – **indifference** *n.* उदासीनता; तटस्थता

indigenous (इन्´डिजिनस) *a.* देशी, देशज

indigestion (इंडि´जेंस्चन) *n.* बदहज़मी

indignant (इन्´डिग्नंट) *a.* (से/पर), क्रुद्ध, नाराज़ – **indignation** (इंडिग्´नेशन) *n.* नाराज़गी, रोष – **indignity** *n.* अपमान

indigo (´इंडिगो) *n.* (कपड़ों में लगाने का) नील; नील का पौधा (*pl.* **-go(e)s**) – *a.* गहरा नीला

indirect (इन्ड´रेक्ट) *a.* अप्रत्यक्ष

indiscipline (इन्´डिसिप्लिन) *n.* अनुशासनहीनता

indiscreet (इन्डि´स्क्रीट) *a.* बिना सोचे-समझे किया गया (कार्य)/कहा गया (शब्द आदि), अविवेकी – **indiscretion** (इन्डि´स्क्रेशन) *n.* अविवेक

indiscriminate (इंडिस्´क्रिमिनिट) *a.* अविवेकी, अंधाधुंध (गोली आदि दागने की क्रिया); अव्यवस्थित

indispensable (इंडि´स्पेंन्सबल) *a.* अनिवार्य, आवश्यक

indisposition (इंडिस्प´ज़िशन) *n.* अस्वस्थता – **indisposed** *a.* अस्वस्थ, अनिच्छुक

indisputable (इन्डि´स्प्यूटबल) *a.* निर्विवाद

indissoluble (इंडि´सॉल्युबल) *a.* चिर स्थायी, अटूट

indistinct (इन्डि´स्टिंग्ट) *a.* अस्पष्ट – **indistinctly** *adv.*

indistinguishable (इन्डि´स्टिङ्विशबल) *a.* जब दो वस्तुओं में अंतर न किया जा सके; अस्पष्ट

individual (इंडि´विड्युअल) *a.* एक, पथक, व्यक्तिगत, विशिष्ट – *n.* एक व्यक्ति या वस्तु – **individualism** *n.* व्यक्तिवाद – **individuality** *n.* वैयक्तिकता

indivisible (इन्डि´विज़बल) *a.* जिसके टुकड़े/भाग न किए जा सकें; अभाज्य (संख्या) – **indivisibility** *n.* अविभाज्यता

indoctrinate (इन्´डॉक्ट्रिनेट) *vt.* दिमाग में कूट-कूट कर (विचार, विश्वास) भर देना

indolent (´इंडलंट) *a.* आलसी, निष्क्रिय – **indolence** (इंडलंस) *n.*

indomitable (इन्´डॉमिटबल) *a.* जो न झुके, अदम्य

indoor (´इन्डॉर) *a.* अंदर, घर में; ढंका हुआ – **indoors** *adv.* अंदर – **indoor patient** अंतरंग रोगी

indubitable (इन्´ड्यूबिटबल) *a.* असंदिग्ध

induce (इन्´ड्यूस) *vt.* राजी करना; (रिश्वत देकर) फुसलाना – **inducement** *n.* प्रलोभन; लालच, घूस

induct (इन्´डक्ट) *vt.* पद पर प्रतिष्ठित करना; भरती करना

indulge (इन्´डल्ज) *vt.* संतुष्ट करना; आनंद लूटना – **indulgence** *n.* आनंद लूटना;

(अति) भोग, (अति) सेवन; अनुग्रह, क पा – **indulgent** *a.* आसक्त; क पालु, मेहरबान उदार – **indulgently** *adv.*

industry (´इंडस्ट्रि) *n.* उद्योग; अध्यवसाय, कठिन परिश्रम करने की शक्ति; कठिन परिश्रम – **industrial** (इन्´डस्ट्रिअल) *a.* औद्योगिक – **industrialize** *vt.* औद्योगीकरण करना – **industrious** *a.* परिश्रमी

inebriate (इन्´ईब्रिएट) *vt.* नशे में धुत्त करना

inedible (इन्´ऐडिबल) *a.* अखाद्य, अभोज्य

ineffective (इनि´फ़ैक्टिव़) *a.* प्रभावहीन, बेअसर

inefficient (इनि´फ़िशंट) *a.* अयोग्य, अकुशल – **inefficiency** *n.*

inelegant (इन´ऐलिगंट) *a.* भद्दा, बेढंगा

ineligible (इन´ऐलिजबल) *a.* अयोग्य

inept (इन्´ऐप्ट) *a.* भद्दा; अनाड़ी – **ineptitude** (इन्´ऐप्टिट्यूड) *n.* अनाड़ीपन

inequality (इनि´क्वालिटि) *n.* असमानता

inequitable (इन्´ऐक्विटबल) *n.* जो सबको बराबर न मिले, अनुचित – **inequity** *n.* पक्षपात, अन्याय

inert (इन्´अर्ट) *a.* जड़, निष्क्रिय, सुस्त; *Chem.* अक्रिय (गैस) – **inertia** (इन्´र्शअ) *n.* जड़ता, निष्क्रियता – **inertness** *n.*

inescapable (इनि´स्केपबल) *a.* स्थिति, तथ्य जिससे बचा न जा सके

inevitable (इन्´ऐविटबल) *a.* जिससे बचा न जा सके, अवश्यंभावी – **inevitability** *n.* अवश्यंभाविता – **inevitably** *adv.* हर हालत में, अनिवार्य रूप से

inexcusable (इनिक्´स्क्यूज़बल) *a.* (व्यवहार, त्रुटि) जिसे क्षमा न किया जा सके

inexorable (इन्´ऐक्सरबल) *a.* अटल व कठोर

inexplicable (इन्´ऐक्स्प्लिकबल) *a.* जिसे स्पष्ट न किया जा सके

infallible (इन्´फैलबल) *a.* अचूक, अमोघ

infamous (´इन्फ़मस) *a.* कुख्यात, बदनाम – **infamy** *n.* बदनामी

infant (´इन्फ़ंट) *n.* बहुत छोटा बच्चा, शिशु – **infancy** (´इन्फ़ंसि) *n.* बचपन, प्रारंभिक अवस्था – **infanticide** *n.* शिशु हत्या

infantry (´इन्फ़ंट्रि) *n.* पैदल सेना

infatuated (इन्´फ़ैट्युटटिड) *a.* दीवाना – **infatuation** (इन्फ़ैट्यु´एशन) *n.* दीवानापन

infect (इन्´फ़ैक्ट) *vt.* छूत लगाना – **infection** (इन्´फ़ैक्शन) *n.* संक्रामक रोग, छूत – **infectious** (इन्´फ़ैक्शस) *a.* संक्रामक, छूत का

infer (इन्´फ़र) *vt.* निष्कर्ष निकालना (-rr-) – **inference** *n.* निष्कर्ष – **inferential** (इन्फ़´रंशल) *a.* अनुमान-सिद्ध, अनुमित

inferior (इन्´फ़िअरिअर) *a.* गुण में घटिया, निम्न – *n.* (पद, महत्व आदि में) नीचे – **inferiority** (इन्फ़िअरि´ऑरिटि) *n.* घटियापन, हीनता

infernal (इन्´फ़र्नल) *a.* नारकीय

inferno (इन्´फ़र्नो) *n.* नरक; भयानक आग

infertile (इन्´फ़र्टाइल) *a.* बंजर (भूमि); बांझ स्त्री, पौधा

infest (इन्´फ़ैस्ट) *vt.* (कीड़ों आदि का) बड़ी संख्या में रहते होना, या सब तरफ फैले होना – **infestation** (इन्फ़ैस्´टेशन) *n.*

infidelity (इन्फ़ि´डैलटि) *n.* (पति/पत्नी से) विश्वासघात; धर्म-विशेष में अविश्वास – **infidel** (´इन्फ़िडल) *n.* काफ़िर – *a.*

in-fighting (´इन्फाइटिङ) *n.* अन्दरूनी झगड़े

infiltrate (´इन्फ़िल्ट्रेट) *v.* घुसपैठ करना – **infiltration** (इन्फ़िल्´ट्रेशन) *n.*

infinite (´इन्फ़िनिट) *a.* असीमित, अनंत – **infinitely** *adv.* बहुत अधिक – **infinitesimal** (इन्फ़िनि´टैसिमल) *a.* बहुत ही छोटा, सूक्ष्म – **infinity** *n.* अनन्तता, असीमता

infinitive (इन् 'फ़िनिटिव़) *a. Grammar* काल, लिंग – *n.* क्रियार्थक संज्ञा; अकाल क्रिया
infirm (इन् 'फ़र्म) *a.* दुर्बल डांवांडोल – **infirmity** (इन् 'फ़र्मिटि) *n.* दुर्बलता
inflammable (इन् 'फ़्लैमबल) *a.* ज्वलनशील उत्तेजनशील – **inflammation** *n.* सूजन व जलन – **inflammatory** *a.* उत्तेजक, भड़काने वाला
inflate (इन् 'फ़्लेट) *v.* हवा, गैस से फुलाना; हवा भरना (गुब्बारे, ट्यूब आदि में); मुद्रा स्फीति करना, कीमत बढ़ाना या बढ़ना – **inflation** *n.* मुद्रास्फीति – **inflationary** *a.* स्फीतिकारी, कीमतें बढ़ाने वाला
inflection, inflexion (इन् 'फ़्लेक्शन) *n.* विभक्ति; आवाज़ में उतार-चढ़ाव
inflexible (इन् 'फ़्लेक्सबल) *a.* अनम्य, न मुड़ सकने वाला, हठीला – **inflexibility** *n.*
inflict (इन् 'फ़्लिक्ट) *vt.* (प्राय: **inflict on**) (कष्ट, पीड़ा आदि) पहुंचाना, लगाना, देना
influence ('इनफ़्लुअन्स) *n.* प्रभाव, असर; प्रभावशाली व्यक्ति, वस्तु – *vt.* प्रभावित करना, (कार्य) करा लेना – **influential** (इनफ़्लु 'एन्शल) *a.* प्रभावशाली – **influentially** *adv.*
influenza (इनफ़्लु 'एन्ज़ा) *n.* इन्फ़्लूऐंज़ा, फ़्लू
influx ('इनफ़्लक्स) *n.* (लोगों, वस्तुओं आदि की) बाढ़
info *n. inf.* **information** का संक्षिप्त रूप
inform (इन् 'फ़ार्म) *vt.* बताना, सूचना देना – *vi.* (के बारे में) जानकारी देना – **informant** *n.* सूचना देने वाला – **information** (इनफ़र् 'मेशन) *n.* सूचना; जानकारी – **informative** *a.* सूचनात्मक; ज्ञानप्रद – **informer** *n.* मुखबिर – **information retrieval** कम्प्यूटर पर संचित जानकारी प्राप्त करने की प्रक्रिया – **information superhighway** इंटरनेट – **information technology** (संक्षेप में **IT**) कम्प्यूटर के माध्यम से जानकारी संचित करने व भेजने की क्रिया व तकनीक; उसका विज्ञान; *inf.* **Info Tech** भी
infra dig *inf.* शान के खिलाफ़ – **infrared** *a.* अवरक्त (किरणें), स्पेक्ट्रम के लाल छोर से नीचे (की किरणें)
infrastructure ('इन्फ़्रस्ट्रक्चर) *n.* किसी आर्थिक-व्यवस्था या संगठन की आधारिक संरचना
infringe (इन् 'फ़्रिंज) *vt.* (नियम आदि का) उल्लंघन करना – **infringement** *n.* उल्लंघन
infuriate (इन् 'फ़्युअरिएट) *vt.* बहुत अधिक क्रोधित करना
ingenious (इन् 'जीन्यस) *a.* (नई वस्तु, योजना आदि बनाने में) चतुर, कुशल; चतुरता से बनाई – **ingenuity** (इन्जि 'न्यूइटि) *n.* कुशलता, प्रवीणता
ingenuous (इन् 'जेन्युअस) *a.* सरल, भोला
ingrained (इन् 'ग्रेंड), **engrained** *a.* पक्की, बहुत पुरानी (लत या आदत)
ingratiate (इन् 'ग्रेशिएट) *v. refl.* स्वयं को किसी का क पापात्र बनाना
ingratitude (इन् 'ग्रैटिटयूड) *n.* अक तज्ञता, ग़ैर-अहसानमंदी
ingredient (इन् 'ग्रीडिअंट) *n.* मिश्रण का एक अवयव, तत्व या उपादान
inhabit (इन् 'हैबिट) *vt.* में रहना, निवास करना – **inhabitable** *a.* रहने योग्य – **inhabitant** *n.* निवासी – **inhabitation** (इनहैबि 'टेशन) *n.* निवास
inhale (इन् 'हेल) *v.* साँस लेना, कश लेना – **inhalation** *n.* कश वि. सांस के साथ खींचने की औषधि – **inhaler** *n.* रोग-हर औषधि की वाष्प लेने का साधन, श्वासयंत्र

inherent (इन् हिंअरंट) *a.* निहित, अंतर्निष्ठ; जन्मजात, स्वाभाविक रूप में

inherit (इन् हैरिट) *vt.* उत्तराधिकार में पाना, दाय पाना; माता-पिता से विरासत में पाना – *vi.* उत्तराधिकारी बनना – **inheritance** *n.* उत्तराधिकार, विरासत – **inheritor** *n.*

inhibit (इन् हिबिट) *vt.* रोकना (आवेग, इच्छा आदि); (कार्य में) विघ्न डालना – **inhibited** *a.* स्वभाविक रूप से व्यवहार करने या भावनाएं व्यक्त करने में असमर्थ – **inhibition** *n.* निषेध, निरोध; मनोभावों का दमन

inhospitable (इन्हॉस्पिटबल) *a.* जहां रहा न जा सके, बंजर; खराब (वातावरण); असत्कारशील/रूखे (लोग)

in-house *a.* आंतरिक (कंपनी, सस्था आदि के अंदर)

inhuman (इन् ह्यूमन) *a.* निर्दय, अमानुषिक – **inhumanity** *n.*

inimical (इ निमिकल) *a.* प्रतिकूल, विरोधी, अमैत्रीपूर्ण, वैरपूर्ण

inimitable (इ निमिटबल) *a.* जिसकी नकल न की जा सके, अद्वितीय

iniquity (इ निक्विटि) *n.* घोर अन्याय; पक्षपात – **iniquitous** *a.* अन्यायपूर्ण

initial (इ निशल) *a.* आरंभिक – *n.* आद्यक्षर, (व्यक्ति के नाम का) प्रथम अक्षर – *vt.* नाम के प्रथम अक्षरों में हस्ताक्षर करना (-ll-) – **initially** *adv.* प्रारंभ में

initiate (इ निशिएट) *vt.* प्रारंभ करना, चलाना – **initiative** *n.* पहला कदम, अगुआई; स्वतंत्र रूप से कार्य करने की योग्यता

inject (इन् जेंक्ट) *vt.* अन्दर पहुंचाना, टीका लगाना – **injection** *n.* इंजेक्शन

injunction (इन् जंक्शन) *n.* न्यायालय का निषेधादेश, निषेधाज्ञा

injury (इंजरि) *n.* चोट, हानि, अन्याय – **injure** (इंजर) *vt.* को चोट, हानि या क्षति पहुंचाना – **injured** *a.* घायल – **injurious** (इन् जुअरिअस) *a.* हानिकारक

injustice (इन् जस्टिस) *n.* अन्याय

ink (इंक) *n.* स्याही – *vt.* स्याही से चिन्ह लगाना, ढकना; स्याही से गन्दा करना – **inkjet printer** कम्प्यूटर से जुड़ा छपाई यंत्र

inkling (इंक्लिङ) *n.* संकेत, आभास

inland (इन्लंड) *n.* देश का भीतरी भाग – *a.* अंतर्देशीय – (इन् लैंड) *adv.* अंदर

in-laws (इन्लॉज़) *n.* सास, ससुर, साले आदि, ससुराल के लोग

inlay (इन् ले) *vt.* जड़ना, सजावटी डिज़ाइन जड़ना – (इन्ले) *n.* जड़ाऊ काम

inmate (इन्मेट) *n.* निवासी विशे. कारावास, हस्पताल आदि का

inmost (इन्मोस्ट) *a.* बिल्कुल अंदर की ओर, अधिकतम गहरा; **IN** का *sup.*

inn (इन) *n.* सराय, होटल – **innkeeper** *n.* सराय का मालिक

innate (इ नेट) *a.* जन्मजात, स्वाभाविक

inner (इनर) *a.* आन्तरिक, भीतरी – **innermost** *a.* अंतरतम

innings (इनिंग्ज़) *n. Cricket* बल्लेबाज़ी की पारी; अवधि; पारी – **good innings** लंबा जीवन

innocent (इनसंट) *a.* भोला, मासूम; निर्दोष – *n.* निर्दोष, निष्कपट; अबोध व्यक्ति विशे. बालक – **innocence** *n.*

innocuous (इ नॉक्युअस) *a.* हानिरहित

innovate (इनवेट) *vt.* नए विचार, प्रणाली आदि सम्मुख लाना – **innovation** (इन् वेशन) *n.* नवीनता; नूतन परिवर्तन – **innovator** *n.* प्रवर्तक

innumerable (इ न्यूमरबल) *a.* असंख्य, बहुत

inoculate (इ नॉक्युलेट) *vt.* बीमारी से बचाने वाला टीका लगाना – **inoculation** *n.* टीका

inoperable (इन् ऑपरबल) *a.* जो कार्यान्वित न हो सके – **inoperative** *a.* अमान्य, जो लागू न हो

inopportune (इन ऑपर्ट्यून) *a.* असामयिक, बेवक्त
inordinate (इन ऑर्डिनिट) *a.* बहुत अधिक
inorganic (इनॉर् गैनिक) *a.* जिसकी संरचना या गुण जीव जैसे न हों, अजैव; *Chem.* अकार्बनिक पदार्थ
inpatient (इन्पेशंट) *n.* अस्पताल में भरती बीमार, अंतरंग रोगी
input (इनपुट) *n.* जो औद्योगिक उत्पादन के संसाधन रूप में उपयोग किया जाए, आगत, निवेश; कम्प्यूटर में भरे गए आंकड़े आदि
inquest (इन्क्वेस्ट) *n.* म त्यु संबंधी तथ्य पता लगाने के लिए सरकारी जांच; विस्त त जांच
inquire, enquire (इन् क्वाइअर) *vi.* पूछताछ करना – **inquiry, enquiry** *n.* पूछताछ; जांच
inquisition (इन्क्वि ज़िशन) *n.* कड़ी जांच, सख्त सरकारी जांच या तहकीकात
inquistive (इन् क्विज़िटिव) *a.* जिज्ञासु
insane (इन् सेन) *a.* पागल, खब्ती, मूर्ख – **insanely** *adv.* पागल की तरह, बहुत अधिक – **insanity** (इन् सैनिटि) *n.* पागलपन
insanitary (इन् सैनटरि) *a.* गंदा, अस्वास्थ्यकर
insatiable (इन् सेशबल) *a.* संतुष्ट न की जा सकने वाली (भूख, लोभ आदि)
inscription (इन् स्क्रिप्शन) *n.* अभिलेख, शिलालेख
inscrutable (इन स्क्रूटबल) *a.* रहस्यमय
insect (इन्सेक्ट) *n.* कीड़ा – **insecticide** *n.* कीटनाशक दवा – **insectivorous** *a.* कीटभक्षी
insecure (इन्सि क्युअर) *a.* असुरक्षित; चिंतित – **insecurity** *a.*
inseminate (इन् सेमिनेट) *vt.* मादा में वीर्यारोपण करना
insensible (इन् सेन्सबल) *a.* वेदनाशून्य; अनभिज्ञ; अनुभूतिहीन
inseparable (इन् सेप्रबल) *a.* जो अलग न किया जा सके, अवियोज्य
insert (इन् सर्ट) *vt.* अंदर डालना, (में, बीच में) रखना – *n.* (इन्सर्ट) (वि. पुस्तक, पत्रिका आदि में) अलग से रखा गया अंश – **insertion** (इन् सर्शन) *n.* अंदर रखने/डालने की क्रिया
in-service *a.* कार्यकाल में किया गया
inset *n.* (इन्सेट) बीच में लगाई अतिरिक्त वस्तु विशे. सजावट हेतु – *vt.* (इन् सेट) इस प्रकार वस्तु, आंतरिक चित्र, नक्शा आदि लगाना
inside (इन् साइड) *n.* भीतरी भाग – *a.* आंतरिक, भीतरी – *adv.* भीतर – *prep.* अंदर, में
insidious (इन् सिडिअस) *a.* अप्रत्यक्ष परन्तु घातक
insight (इन्साइट) *n.* अंतर्द ष्टि, गहरी पहुंच, सूक्ष्म द ष्टि – **insightful** *a.*
insignia (इन् सिग्निअ) *pl. n.* बैज, आदर, पद सूचक चिन्ह
insignificant (इन्सिग् निफ़िकंट) *a.* महत्वहीन – **insignificance** *n.*
insincere (इन्सिन् सिअर) *a.* कपटी, पाखण्डी – **insincerity** *n.*
insinuate (इन् सिन्युएट) *vt.* संकेत देना; धीरे-धीरे व चुपचाप स्थान बना लेना – **insinuation** (इन्सिन्यु एशन) *n.* छिपा अर्थ
insipid (इन् सिपिड) *a.* नीरस, फीका
insist (इन् सिस्ट) *vi.* (पर) ज़ोर देना; (बात पर) अड़े रहना; (का) आग्रह करना – **insistence** *n.* आग्रह – **insistent** *a.* आग्रही
insolent (इन्सलंट) *a.* गुस्ताख – **insolence** *n.*
insolvent (इन् सॉल्वंट) *a.* दिवालिया – **insolvency** *n.* दिवालियापन
insomnia (इन् सॉम्निअ) *n.* अनिद्रा रोग – **insomniac** *a./n.* अनिद्रा रोगी
insomuch (इन्सो मच) *adv.* यहां तक (कि)

inspect (इन्'स्पेक्ट) *vt.* निरीक्षण करना – **inspection** *n.* – **inspector** *n.* निरीक्षक; थानेदार

inspire (इन्'स्पाइअर) *vt.* प्रेरणा देना, प्रेरित करना; भावनाओं, विचारों को जन्म देना – **inspiration** (इन्सपि'रेशन) *n.* उत्तम विचार; सृजनात्मक प्रभाव या प्रेरणा

instability (इन्स्ट'बिलिटि) *n.* अस्थिरता; (मानसिक आदि) असंतुलन

install (इन्'स्टॉल) *vt.* (उपकरण, यंत्र आदि) लगाना; (व्यक्ति को) विधिपूर्वक पदासीन करना – **installation** (इन्स्ट'लेशन) *n.* संस्थापन; अधिष्ठापन; स्थापित संयंत्र आदि

instalment (इन्'स्टॉल्मंट) *n.* किश्त, अंशिका; (टी.वी. सीरियल आदि का) भाग, कड़ी

instance ('इन्स्टन्स) *n.* उदाहरण, दृष्टांत, अनुरोध; (कार्यवाही का) चरण – *vt.* दिखलाना; उदाहरण देना; उल्लेख करना

instant ('इन्स्टंट) *n.* क्षण – *a.* तात्कालिक; (*of foods*) जिनके बनाने में बहुत कम समय लगे – **instantaneous** (इन्स्टन्'टेनिअस) *a.* तात्कालिक – **instantaneously** *adv.* तुरंत– **instantly** *adv.* तुरंत

instead (इन्'स्टेंड) *adv.* के बजाय

instigate ('इन्स्टिगेट) *vt.* भड़काना, उकसाना, (विद्रोह आदि) कराना – **instigation** *n.* – **instigator** *n.* भड़काने वाला

instil (इन्'स्टिल) *vt.* मन में बैठाना; की शिक्षा देना, साहस देना (-ll-) – **instilation** *n.*

instinct ('इन्स्टिक्ट) *n.* जन्मजात, मूल प्रवृत्ति, स्वाभाविक प्रवृति; सहज-बोध, सहज-बुद्धि – **instinctive** *a.* सहज, स्वाभाविक

institute ('इन्स्टिट्यूट) *vt.* स्थापित करना, बनाना, आरंभ करना – *n.* संस्थान – **institution** (इन्स्टि'ट्यूशन) *n.* संस्थापन; संस्था; प्रथा अथवा कानून आदि

instruct (इन्'स्ट्रक्ट) *vt.* शिक्षा देना, सिखाना; आदेश देना; समझाना – **instruction** (इन्'स्ट्रक्शन) *n.* शिक्षा; आदेश – **instructive** *a.* शिक्षाप्रद; लाभदायक – **instructively** *adv.* – **instructor** *n.* प्रशिक्षक (**instructress** *fem.*)

instrument ('इन्स्ट्रमंट) *n.* औज़ार; उपकरण; यंत्र; साधन; संगीत-वाद्य, बाजा; दस्तावेज़ – **instrumental** (इन्स्ट्र'मेन्टल) *a.* का कारण, सहायक; वाद्य से उत्पन्न (संगीत)

insubordinate (इन्स'बार्डिनिट) *a.* आज्ञा न मानने वाला – **insubordination** (इन् सबार्डि'नेशन) *n.* अवज्ञा, आज्ञा भंग

insufferable (इन्'सफ्रबल) *a.* असह्य

insular ('इन्स्युलर) *a.* द्वीपीय; संकीर्ण विचारों वाला – **insularity** *n.* संकीर्णता

insulate ('इन्सुलेट) *vt.* विद्युत, ताप अथवा ध्वनि आदि रोधी बनाना; अलग करना – **insulation** (इन्सु'लेशन) *n.* रोधन – **insulator** *n.* (विद्युत अथवा ताप) रोधक

insulin ('इन्स्युलिन) *n.* शरीर द्वारा उत्पन्न पदार्थ जो शक्कर को ऊर्जा में परिवर्तित होने में साहायक होता है

insult (इन्'सल्ट) *vt.* अपमान करना – *n.* ('इनसल्ट) अपमानजनक बात, अपमान – **insulting** *a.* अपमानजनक

insuperable (इन्'सूपरबल) *a.* जिस पर काबू न पाया जा सके, दुस्तर, अत्यंत कठिन

insure (इन्'श्युअर) *v.* बीमा करना या कराना; सुरक्षित करना – **insurance** (इन्'श्युअरन्स) *n.* बीमा – **insurer** *n.* बीमाकर्ता

insurgent (इन्'सर्जंट) *a./n.* विद्रोही, बाग़ी – **insurgence** *n.* विद्रोह

insurmountable (इन्सा'माउंटबल) *a.* अत्यंत कठिन, दुष्कर

insurrection (इन्सा'रेंक्शन) *n.* विद्रोह, बगावत

intact (इन्'टेंक्ट) *a.* समूचा, अक्षत

intake ('इंटेक) *n.* ग्रहण किया जाने वाला पदार्थ; ग्रहण-मात्रा; मुंह, रास्ता

integer (ˈइंटिजर) *n.* पूर्णांक, पूर्ण संख्या
integral (ˈइंटिग्रल) *a.* सम्पूर्ण; कुल का एक जरूरी (हिस्सा) – **integrate** (ˈइंटिग्रेट) *vt.* मिलाकर एक करना, संगठित करना – **integration** (इंटिˈग्रेशन) *n.* एकीकरण
integrity (इन्ˈटेंग्रिटि) *n.* सच्चाई, ईमानदारी, अखंडता
intellect (ˈइंटिलेंक्ट) *n.* बुद्धि, सोच-विचार की शक्ति – **intellectual** (इंटिˈलेंक्चुअल) *a.* बौद्धिक, बुद्धिमान – *n.* बुद्धिजीवी – **intellectualism** *n.* बुद्धिवाद
intelligent (इन्ˈटेलिजंट) *a.* बुद्धिमान; समझदार – **intelligence** *n.* समझ; बुद्धि; ज्ञान-शक्ति; गुप्त सूचना विशे. सामरिक महत्व की – **intelligentsia** (इंटेलिˈजेंण्ट्सिअ) *n.* बुद्धिजीवी वर्ग – **intelligibility** *adv.* – **intelligible** *a.* समझ आने वाला
intemperate (इन्ˈटेम्परिट) *a.* असभ्य (भाषा); बहुत अधिक शराब पीने वाला – **intemperance** *n.*
intend (इन्ˈटेण्ड) *vt.* (करने का) विचार रखना; (करने, कहने आदि का) इरादा करना या होना, ठान लेना; अभिप्राय होना – **intended** *a.* अभीष्ट
intense (इन्ˈटेन्स) *a.* तीव्र; उत्तेजित, जोशीला, भावपूर्ण – **intensification** *n.* – **intensify** *v.* तीव्र करना या हो जाना; बढ़ जाना – **intensity** *n.* तीव्रता – **intensive** *a.* तीव्र, घना, ज़ोरदार – **intensively** *adv.*
intent (इन्ˈटेण्ट) *n.* उद्देश्य – *a.* एकाग्र; दढ़ संकल्प; (कार्य में) लगा हुआ – **intention** (इन्ˈटेन्शन) *n.* अभिप्राय – **intentional** *a.* जानकर (किया गया/कहा गया) – **intently** *adv.* एकाग्रता से, बहुत ध्यान से
inter (इन्ˈटर) *vt.* दफ़न करना (-rr-) – **internment** *n.*
inter -(*comb. form*) अंतर, अन्तः जैसे **inter-caste** में
interact (इंटर्ˈऐक्ट) *vi.* एक दूसरे को प्रभावित करना – **interaction** (इंटर्ˈऐक्शन) *n.* पारस्परिक क्रिया या प्रभाव; पारस्परिक बातचीत – **interactive** *a.*
intercede (इंटर्ˈसीड) *vi.* की ओर से बोलना; मध्यस्थता करना – **intercession** (इंटर्ˈसैशन) *n.* मध्यस्थता
intercept (इंटर्ˈसेप्ट) *vt.* पकड़ लेना, रास्ते में रोक लेना – **interception** *n.* रोकने की क्रिया, अवरोधन
intercity (ˈइंटर्सिटि) *n./a.* दो मुख्य नगरों के बीच तीव्रगति रेल-सेवा
intercom (ˈइंटर्कॉम) *n.* आंतरिक टेलीफोन व्यवस्था
intercontinental (इंटर्कॉण्टि-ˈनैण्ट्ल) *a.* अंतरमहाद्वीपीय
intercourse (ˈइंटर्कॉर्स) *n.* संभोग
interest (ˈइंट्रिस्ट, ˈइंटरिस्ट) *n.* रुचि, दिलचस्पी, ब्याज, (*fig.* भी); हित; स्वार्थ; अधिकार; हिस्सा, अंश – *vt.* दिलचस्पी पैदा करना – **interested** *a.* संबद्ध; दिलचस्पी लेने वाला – **interesting** *a.* रोचक, दिलचस्प
interface (ˈइंटर्फ़ेस) *n.* *Technical* दो व्यवस्थाओं को जोड़ने वाला क्षेत्र, तल, सीमा; पारस्परिक प्रभाव क्रिया
interfere (इंटर्ˈफ़िअर) *vi.* हस्तक्षेप करना, दखल देना; (उपकरणों आदि से) छेड़छाड़ करना – **interference** *n.* हस्तक्षेप
interim (ˈइंटरिम) *n.* अंतरिमकाल, मध्य की अवधि – *a.* अंतरिम, अस्थायी
interior (इन्ˈटिअरिअर) *a.* भीतरी, आंतरिक; देशीय, अंतरस्थलीय – *n.* भीतरी भाग
interject (इंटर्ˈजेंक्ट) *vt.* बीच में बोलना – **interjection** *n.* उद्गार
interlock (इंटर्ˈलॉक) *v.* गुथना, गूंथ देना
interlude (ˈइंटर्लूड) *n.* मध्यांतर; मध्यांतर में दिखाया जाने वाला कार्यक्रम
intermediary (इंटर्ˈमीडिअरि) *n.* मध्यस्थ

intermediate (इंटर् 'मीडिइट) *a.* मध्यम; मध्यवर्ती

interminable (इन् 'टर्मिनबल) *a.* अंतहीन, बहुत लम्बा – **interminably** *adv.*

intermingle (इंटर्मि 'गल) *v.* लोगों, विचारों, रंगों आदि को मिलाना या उनका मिलना

intermission (इंटर् 'मिशन) *n.* अवरोध; मध्यांतर

intermittent *a.* रुक-रुक कर होने वाला

intern[1] (इन् 'टर्न) *vt.* नज़रबंद करना – **internment** *n.* नज़रबंदी

intern[2] *n.* प्रशिक्षार्थी डॉक्टर

internal (इन् 'टर्नल) *a.* आंतरिक, भीतरी; (देश, संस्था आदि के) आंतरिक विषयों से संबंधित – **internally** *adv.* अंदर से – **internal combustion engine** अंतर्दहन इंजन (जैसे कार में)

international (इंटर् 'नैश्नल) *a.* अंतर्राष्ट्रीय – *n.* विभिन्न देशों के बीच खेल प्रतियोगिता या मैच

Internet ('इंटर्नेट) *n.* अंतर्राष्ट्रीय स्तर पर एक दूसरे से जुड़े कम्प्यूटरों की व्यवस्था जिसका उपयोग (टेलीफोन के समान) कम्प्यूटर पटल पर जानकारी के आदान-प्रदान के लिए किया जाता है, इंटरनेट

interpersonal ('इंटर्पर्सनल) *a.* पारस्परिक सम्बंध विषयक

interpolate (इन् 'टर्पलेट) *vt.* (पुस्तक में) नई सामग्री (परिच्छेद आदि) जोड़ देना, विशे. भ्रामक सामग्री

interpret (इन् 'ट्रप्रिट) *vt.* की व्याख्या करना, अर्थ लगाना, स्पष्ट करना; अनुवाद करना (विशे. मौखिक) – **interpretation** *n.* अर्थ निर्णय – **interpreter** *n.* दुभाषिया

interracial (इंट 'रेशल) *a.* अंतरजातीय

interrogate (इन् 'टॆरगेट) *vt.* (सरकारी तौर पर, कड़ी) पूछताछ करना – **interrogation** (इंटर 'गेशन) *n.* पूछताछ – **interrogative** *a.* प्रश्नात्मक – *n.* प्रश्न-शब्द – **interrogator** *n.* – **interrogatory** *a.* प्रश्नात्मक – *n.* प्रश्न, प्रश्न-माला

interrupt (इंट 'रप्ट) *v.* टोकना, बीच में बोलना या रोकना; बाधा डालना – **interruption** (इंट 'रप्शन) *n.* टोक, हस्तक्षेप; बाधा; रोक

intersect (इंटर् 'सॆक्ट) *vt.* (रेखाओं को) काटना – *vi.* (*roads*) एक दूसरे को काटना; प्रतिच्छेद करना – **intersection** *n.* रेखाओं, मार्गों का संगम, चौराहा

intersperse (इंटर् 'स्पर्स) *vt.* छितराना, फैलाना, बिखराना; बीच में कुछ और प्रस्तुत करना

interstate ('इंटर्स्टेट) *a.* अंतर्राज्यीय

interstellar ('इंटर् 'स्टॆलर) *a.* तारों के बीच का रिक्त स्थान, अन्तर-तारकीय

intertwine (इंटर् 'ट्वाइन) *v.* गूंथना, लिपटना

interval ('इंटर्वल) *n.* अंतर, अंतराल; मध्यांतर; मध्यावकाश

intervene (इंटर् 'वीन) *vi.* बीच में पड़ना; हस्तक्षेप करना; बीच में घटित होना – **intervention** (इंटर् 'वॆन्शन) *n.* हस्तक्षेप, दखल; मध्यस्थता

interview ('इंटर्व्यू) *n.* भेंटवार्ता; साक्षात्कार, इंटरव्यू – *vt.* का साक्षात्कार करना, इंटरव्यू लेना – **interviewee** (इंटरव्यू 'ई) *n.* जिसका इंटरव्यू लिया गया हो – **interviewer** *n.* भेंटकर्ता

intestate (इन् 'टॆस्टेट) *a.* (म त व्यक्ति) जिसने वसीयत न की हो – *n.* ऐसा व्यक्ति

intestine (इन् 'टॆस्टिन) *n.* आन्त्र, आँत – **intestinal** *a.*

intimate[1] ('इंटिमिट) *a.* घनिष्ठ, गहरा (मित्र), आत्मीय; परिचित; निजी; खुलकर (बातचीत); अनैतिक (स्त्री-पुरुष संबंध) – *n.* अंतरंग मित्र – **intimacy** ('इंटिमसि) *n.*

intimate[2] *vt.* सूचना देना, संकेत देना – **intimation** (इंटि 'मेशन) *n.* सूचना

intimidate (इन्'टिमिडेट) *vt.* डराना, धमकाना – **intimidation** (इंटिमि'डेशन) *n.*
into ('इंटू, 'इंटु) *prep.* के भीतर (बाहर से भीतर की ओर गति के लिए); *Maths.* गुणा; में
intolerant (इन्'टॉलरंट) *a.* (के प्रति) असहिष्णु, को सहन करने में असमर्थ – **intolerable** *a.* असहनीय – **intolerance** *n.* असहिष्णुता
in toto (इन्'टोटो) *adv. Lat.* सम्पूर्णतया
intoxicate (इन्'टॉक्सिकेट) *vt.* नशे में धुत्त कर देना – **intoxicated** *a.* नशे में; बहुत उत्तेजित – **intoxicant** *a./n.* मादक (पदार्थ) – **intoxication** (इंटॉक्सि'केशन) *n.* नशा
intra – (*comb. form*) में, अंदर
intractable (इन्'ट्रैक्टबल) *a.* हठीला; (समस्या) जिसका निदान कठिन हो
intransigent (इन्'ट्रैन्सिजंट) *a.* हठी
intransitive (इन्'ट्रैन्सिटिव) *a.* अकर्मक (क्रिया)
intravenous (इंट्र'वीनस) *a.* अन्त:शिरा, शिरा में (इंजेक्शन आदि)
intrepid (इन्'ट्रेपिड) *a.*निडर, साहसी
intricate ('इंट्रिकिट) *a.* उलझा हुआ (बनावट); जटिल, पेचीदा – **intricacy** *n.* जटिलता
intrigue (इन्'ट्रीग) *n.* षड्यंत्र – *vi.* षडयंत्र रचना – *vt.* कुतूहल उत्पन्न करना – **intriguing** *a.* कुतूहल उत्पन्न करने वाला, आकर्षक
intrinsic (इन्'ट्रिन्सिक) *a.* आन्तरिक, मूलभूत
intro- (*comb. form*) में, के अन्दर, जैसे **introduce** में
introduce (इंट्र'ड्यूस) *vt.* परिचय कराना; प्रस्तुत करना; लाना; प्रयोग में लाना; घुसेड़ना – **introduction** *n.* परिचय; भूमिका, प्रस्तावना – **introductory** *a.* प्रारंभिक, परिचायक
introspection (इंट्र'स्पेक्शन) *n.* आत्मविश्लेषण
introvert ('इंट्रवर्ट) *n. Psychoanalysis* अन्तर्मुखी
intrude (इन्'ट्रूड) *vi.* अनुचित रूप से घुस जाना – **intruder** *n.* घुसपैठिया – **intrusion** (इन्'ट्रूझन) *n.* अनाधिकार प्रवेश, घुसपैठ; (बातचीत में) हस्तक्षेप
intuition (इन्ट्यु'इशन) *n* अंतर्ज्ञान, तत्थ्य के विपरीत केवल अनुभूति द्वारा कुछ जान लेने की क्रिया, मन की आंखे; अंतर्दृष्टि
inundate ('इनन्डेट) *vt.* जलमग्न कर देना; की भरमार कर देना
invade (इन्'वेड) *vt.* (पर) आक्रमण या हमला करना, चढ़ाई करना; सब तरफ फैल जाना – **invader** *n.* आक्रमणकारी – **invasion** (इन्'वेझन) *n.* चढ़ाई, हमला; दखलंदाजी
invalid[1] ('इन्वलीड) *n.* रोगी – *a.* रोग अथवा चोट से लाचार, असमर्थ – *v.* असमर्थ या अपंग हो जाना
invalid[2] (इन्'वैलिड) *a.* अमान्य, रद्द (नियम आदि) – **invalidate** *vt.*
invaluable (इन्'वैल्युअबल) *a.* अमूल्य
invariable (इन्'वेंअरिअबल) *a.* अपरिवर्ती, जो बदले ना – *n. Math.* निश्चय – **invariably** *adv.* निरंतर, सदा ही
invasion (इन्'वेझन) *n.* दे. INVADE
invective (इन्'वेंक्टिव) *n.* गाली भरा, कटु कथन अथवा लेखन
inveigle (इन्'वीगल) *vt.* बहकाना
invent (इन्'वेण्ट) *vt.* आविष्कार करना, (कहानी आदि) गढ़ना – **invention** *n.* आविष्कार, ईजाद; आविष्कार प्रतिभा; मनगढ़न्त कहानी; झूठ – **inventive** *a.* उपाय-कुशल; आविष्कारशील – **inventor** *n.* आविष्कारक
inventory ('इन्वंटरि) *n.* सामान आदि की विस्त त सूची
invert (इन्'वर्ट) *vt.* उलटाना, (वस्तुओं आदि की) स्थिति, संबंध विपरीत करना
inverse (इन्'वर्स) *a.* उलटा, विपरीत *n.* – **inversely** *adv.* उल्टा, विपरीत – **inversion** (इन्'वर्शन) *n.* उलटाव, उत्क्रमण

invertebrate (इन्ˈवर्टिब्रिट, -ब्रेट) *n.* मेरूदंडहीन प्राणी – *a.* बिना रीढ़ का; कमज़ोर

invest (इन्ˈवेस्ट) *vt.* लाभ के लिए (पूंजी, समय, शक्ति आदि) लगाना; प्रतिष्ठापित/ पदासीन करना; प्रदान करना – **investment** *n.* पूंजी लगाना; लगी हुई पूंजी, निवेश; खरीदे हुए शेयर आदि – **investor** *n.*

investigate (इन्ˈवेस्टिगेट) *vt.* जाँच-पड़ताल करना – **investigation** (इन्वेस्टिˈगेशन) *n.*

inveterate (इन्ˈवेटरिट) *a.* गहरा, पुराना

invidious (इन्ˈविडिअस) *a.* (कार्य, टिप्पणी आदि) जो लोगो को नाराज़ कर दे, अप्रिय; द्वेषजनक

invigilate (इन्ˈविजिलेट) *vi.* (परीक्षार्थियों की) निगरानी करना – **invigilator** *n.*

invigorate (इन्ˈविगरेट) *vt.* शक्ति देना

invincible (इन्ˈविन्सिबल) *a.* अजेय – **invincibility** *n.*

inviolable (इन्ˈवाइअलबल) *a.* जो अपवित्र या दूषित न किया जा सके; अपरिवर्तनीय – **inviolate** *a.* अक्षत; अदूषित

invisible (इन्ˈविज़बल) *a.* अदृश्य; अप्रकट **invisibility** *n.*

invite (इन्ˈवाइट) *vt.* निमंत्रण देना; मांगना, आकर्षित करना, बुलाना – *n.* (ˈइन्वाइट) *inf.* निमंत्रण – **inviting** *a.* चित्ताकर्षक, ललचाने वाला – **invitation** *n.*

in vitro (इन्ˈविट्रो) – **in vitro fertilization** (IVF) प्रक्रिया जिसमें स्त्री के डिम्ब (egg) को शरीर के बाहर निषेचित (fertilize) करने के बाद गर्भाशय में स्थापित किया जाता है ताकि वह बच्चे के रूप में विकसित हो सके

invoice (ˈइन्वॉइस) *n.* बीजक, कीमतों सहित सामान सूची – *vt.* बीजक बनाना, देना

invoke (इन्ˈवोक) *vt.* से प्रार्थना करना, को (सहायतार्थ) पुकारना, बुलाना – **invocation** *n.*

involuntary (इन्ˈवॉलंटरि) *a.* अनजाने में किया गया; सहज स्वभाव से

involve (इन्ˈवाल्व) *vt.* सम्मिलित करना; आवश्यक होना; (व्यक्ति को) फंसाना, से संबंधित होना; उलझाना – **involved** *a.* जटिल; में फंसा या से संबंद्ध

inward (ˈइन्वर्ड) *a.* आंतरिक; भीतरी; मानसिक – *adv.* (**inwards** भी) मन में, अंदर की ओर – **inwardly** *adv.* मन ही मन में

iodine (ˈआइअडीन) *n.* आयोडीन

ion (ˈआइअन) *n.* विद्युत-चार्ज सहित परमाणु अथवा परमाणु समूह, आयन – **ionosphere** (आइˈऑनस्फ़िअर) *n.* पृथ्वी की सतह से **60** से **100** कि.मी. ऊपर का वायुमंडल क्षेत्र, आयनमण्डल

iota (आइˈओट्अ) *n.* (प्राय: *not* के साथ) बहुत कम

I.O.U. I OWE YOU का संक्षेप, 'मैंने तुमसे ऋण लिया है'

IQ intelligence quotient का संक्षेप, बुद्धि-मापक अंक, बुद्धिलब्धि

irate (आइˈरेट) *a.* क्रुद्ध, उत्तेजित

ire (आइअर) *n.* क्रोध, रोष – **irascible** (इˈरैसिबल) *a.* चिड़चिड़ा

iridescent (इरिˈडेंसंट) *a.* इन्द्रधनुष की तरह रंग बदलता हुआ

iris (ˈआइरिस) *n.* (आंख का) तारामण्डल जिसमें पुतली होती है; आइरिस फूल

irk (अर्क) *vt.* तंग करना, (किसी में) झुंझलाहट पैदा करना – **irksome** *a.* थकाने वाला

iron (ˈआइअन, ˈआइरन) *n.* लोहा, लोहे का औज़ार, इस्तरी – *pl.* (कैदी की) बेड़ियाँ – *a.* लोहे का, लोहे जैसा; अटल, लौह, सशक्त – *vt.* इस्तरी करना – **iron out** (मतभेद आदि) दूर करना

irony (ˈआइरनि) *n.* व्यंग्य, व्यंग्योक्ति – **ironic** (आइˈरॉनिक), **ironical** (आइˈरॉनिकल, *a.* व्यंग्योक्तिपूर्ण, व्यंग्यपूर्ण

irradiate (इˈरेडिएट) *vt.* एक्स-रे, प्रकाश किरणों से किरणित (व्याप्त) करना; को प्रदीप्त, प्रकाशमान करना – **irradiation** *n.*

irrational (इ'रैशनल) *a.* असंगत; अकारण; निर्मूल; विवेकहीन – **irrationality** *n.*
irregular (इ'रॅग्युलर) *a.* अनियमित, गैरकानूनी; विषम
irrelevant (इ'रॅलवंट) *a.* असंगत, अप्रासंगिक – **irrelevance** *n.*
irreparable (इ'रॅपरबल) *a.* जिसकी मरम्मत या पूर्ति न की जा सके
irresistible (इरि'ज़िस्टबल) *a.* जिससे बचना कठिन हो; अत्यंत आकर्षक
irrespective (इरि'स्पॅक्टिव) *a.* का ध्यान किए या विचार किए बिना
irresponsible (इरि'स्पॉन्सबल) *a.* गैरज़िम्मेदार
irrevocable (इ'रॅवकबल) *a.* अपरिवर्तनीय
irrigate ('इरिगेट) *vt.* सिंचाई करना – **irrigation** *n.* सिंचाई – **irrigator** *n.*
irritate ('इरिटेट) *vt.* गुस्सा दिलाना; उत्तेजित करना – **irritable** *a.* चिड़चिड़ा – **irritant** *a./n.* व्यक्ति, वस्तु जो गुस्सा दिलाये – **irritating** *a.* गुस्सा या खीज दिलाने वाला (व्यवहार आदि) – **irritation** *n.*
is है, BE का third person singular, present indicative
Islam ('इस्लाम, 'इज़्लाम) *n.* इस्लाम – **Islamic** *a.* इस्लामी
island ('आइलंड) *n.* द्वीप; (*traffic island* भी) सड़क के बीच पैदल चलने वालों की सुविधा के लिए (गोलाई में बना) हुआ स्थान – **islander** *n.* द्वीप-निवासी
isle (आइल) *n. Poet.* द्वीप – **islet** ('आइलिट) *n.* छोटा द्वीप
isn't ('इजंट) is not का संक्षेप
isobar ('आइसोबार) *n.* समदाब रेखा
isolate ('आइसलेट) *vt.* अलग करना, (औरों से) दूर रखना – **isolated** *a.* इक्का-दुक्का – **isolation** *n.* एकाकीपन; वियोजन
isometric (आइसो'मॅट्रिक) *a.* सममितीय; बिना पूरे शरीर के हिले मांस-पेशियों के व्यायाम संबंधी – **isometrics** *pl. n.* सममितीय व्यायाम
isosceles (आइ'सॉसिलीज़) *a.* समद्विबाहु (त्रिभुज)
isotherm ('आइसोथर्म) *n.* समताप रेखा (मानचित्र पर)
isotope ('आइसटोप) *n.* किसी तत्व का परमाणु जिसकी नाभिक मात्रा व परमाणु भार उसी तत्व के अन्य परमाणु से भिन्न हो, आइसोटोप
issue ('इश्यू) *n.* प्रकाशन, अंक; निर्गमन, जारी की गई मात्रा की क्रिया; (*discharge*) निकास; संतान; विवाद का विषय या प्रश्न; परिणाम – *vi.* निकलना; (का) परिणाम होना; (से) उत्पन्न होना – *vt.* निकालना; देना, बांटना; प्रकाशित करना
isthmus ('इस्मस) *n.* दो समुद्रों के बीच भू-संधि, स्थल-संयोजक
it (इट) *pron.* (*neuter pronoun*) यह, ये – **its** *a.* इसका – **it's** *it is* 'इस' का संक्षेप – **itself** *pron.* अपने आप को, स्वयं
IT Information Technology का संक्षेप
ital. **italic** (type) का संक्षिप्त रूप
Italian (इ'टैल्यन) *n.* इटली की भाषा या वहां का निवासी, इटालियन – *a.* इटली का
italic (इ'टैलिक) *a.* तिरछे (अक्षर) – **italics** *pl. n.* तिरछा टाइप, छपाई में (शब्दों पर) बल देने के लिए प्रयुक्त – **italicize** *vt.* तिरछे टाइप में छापना
itch (इच) *n./vi.* खुजली (होना), खुजलाना – **itchy** *a.* खुजली करने को बेचैन
item ('आइटम) *n.* (*on agenda*) विषय; संग्रह आदि की एक मद, वस्तु; समाचार (**news item** भी); खाते आदि में प्रविष्टि या इंदराज – **itemize** *vt.*
itinerant (इ'टिनरंट) *n.* सैलानी; विभिन्न स्थानों पर थोड़े-थोड़े समय नौकरी करना

itinerary (आइ'टिनररि) *n.* यात्रा वृत्तांत; यात्राक्रम; मार्ग विवरण

IUD Intrauterine device का संक्षेप, गर्भ निरोध का एक साधन

IVF दे० in vitro

ivory ('आइव़रि) *n.* हाथी दांत – **ivory tower** आम ज़िंदगी की परेशानियों से परे स्थान या स्थिति

I've (आइव़) I have का संक्षेप

ivy ('आइवि़) *n.* एक सदाबहार बेल, मारवल्ली

J

jab (जैब) *vt.* चुभाना, गड़ाना, भोंकना (**-bb-**) – *n.* चुभोना, धक्का; *inf.* इंजेक्शन

jacaranda (जैक'रैण्ड्अ) *n.* दक्षिणी अमरीका का एक बैंगनी फूलों वाला व क्ष, जैकरण्डा

jack (जैक) *n.* व्यक्ति; *inf.* कुछ जानवरों में नर; कार आदि उठाने की मशीन, जैक; अनेक यांत्रिक उपकरण; (ताश में) गुलाम का पत्ता; बोल्ज़ (*bowls*) के खेल में गेंद; इलेक्ट्रॉनिकी उपकरणों में सॉकेट व प्लग लगाने का स्थान –*vt.* – **jack up** जैक से किसी वस्तु को उठाना; (कीमतें आदि) बढ़ाना

jackal ('जैकल) *n.* गीदड़

jackass ('जैकैस) *n.* नर गधा; मूर्ख

jacket ('जैकिट) *n.* जैकेट; बाहरी आवरण (जैसे किताब का)

jackknife ('जैक्नाइफ़) *n.* खटकेदार चाकू – *v.* तेज मोड़ काटना जैसे ट्रेलर वाले ट्रक द्वारा

jackpot ('जैक्पॉट) *n.* बड़ा इनाम, इकट्ठी हुई दांव-राशि

jack rabbit US खरगोश

Jacuzzi (ज'कूज़ी) *n.* स्नान के टब (हमाम) में पानी को भंवरदार बनाने का उपकरण; इस उपकरण सहित हमाम

jade[1] (जेड) *n.* एक रत्न (प्राय: हरे रंग का), हरिताश्म

jaded ('जेडिड) *a.* थकामाँदा; उदास

jagged ('जैगिड) *a.* नुकीला, दांतेदार

jaguar ('जेग्युअर) *n.* दक्षिणी अमरीका का एक हिंसक (बाघ जैसा) वन-प्राणी, जगुआर

jail (जेल) *n.* जेल – *vt.* कैद करना – **jailer** *n.* जेलर – **jailbird** *n.* पक्का अपराधी

jam (जैम) *vt.* ठूंसना; ठसाठस भरना; जकड़ना; (ब्रेक) ज़ोर से लगाना; *Radio* रेडियो स्टेशन का प्रसारण जाम कर देना या गड़बड़ कर देना (**-mm-**) – *n.* मुरब्बा, जैम; रुका हुआ यातायात, ट्रैफिक जैम; उलझन, परेशानी – **jam-packed** *a.* ठसाठस भरा हुआ

jamboree (जैम्ब'री) *n.* बालक स्काउटों का जमघट; मौज-मस्ती, जश्न, जम्बूरी

Jan. January का संक्षिप्त रूप

jangle ('जैंगल) *v.* (वस्तुओं का) खड़खड़ाना; नसें खिंचना (परेशानी से) – *n.* खड़खड़ाहट

janitor ('जैनिटर) *n.* (इमारत का) रखवाला; सफाई करने वाला

January ('जैन्युअरि) *n.* जनवरी मास

jar[1] (जार) *n.* मर्तबान, जार; *inf.* ग्लास (विशे. बीयर का)

jar[2] (जार) *v.* जोर-जोर से कंपा देना या कांपना (हिलना); प्रभाव डालना (**-rr-**) – *n.* अप्रिय खड़खड़ाहट की ध्वनि; (*shock*) धक्का

jargon ('जार्गन) *n.* किसी विषय या व्यवसाय की विशिष्ट शब्दावली, वर्ग-बोली; शब्दजाल; अनाप-शनाप

jasmin(e), 'जैज़्मिन) *n.* चमेली, जूही

jasper ('जैस्पर) *n.* एक रत्न, कपिश्मणि

jaundice ('जॉण्डिस) *n.* पीलिया रोग – **jaundiced** ('जॉन्डिस्ट) *a.* पीलिया पीड़ित; निराशावादी

jaunt (जॉन्ट) *n.* सैर, छोटी यात्रा

jaunty ('जॉन्टि) *a.* जिंदादिल, चुस्त

javelin ('जैवलिन) *n.* भाला, बरछा, विशे. खेल प्रतियोगिता में फेंकने में प्रयुक्त

jaw (जॉ) *n.* जबड़ा – *pl.* मुंह (अंदर की सारी हड्डियों समेत)

jay (जे) *n.* नीलकण्ठ – **jaywalker** *n.* (सड़क पर) लापरवाह पैदल यात्री

jazz (जैज़) *n.* द्रुतगति वाला एक प्रकार का पश्चिमी संगीत व न त्य – **jazzy** *a.* भड़कीला, दिखावटी

jealous ('जेलस) *a.* ईर्ष्यालु, सशंकित – **jealousy** *n.* ईर्ष्या

jeans (जीन्ज़) *pl. n.* जीन

jeep (जीप) **R** जीप

jeer (जिअर) *v.* ताना मारना, खिल्ली उड़ाना – *n.* उपहास

jelly (ˈजेंलि) *n.* जेली; फलों से बना अवलेह; जेली जैसा पदार्थ – **jellyfish** *n.* जेली फिश, एक बहुत छोटा समुद्री जीव

jeopardy (ˈजेंपर्डि) *n.* संकट, खतरा – **jeopardize** *vt.* संकट में डालना

jerk (जर्क) *n.* झटका; ऐंठन; *sl.* मूर्ख व्यक्ति – *v.* झटकना, झटका देना – **jerky** *a.* झटके से रुक-रुक कर चलने वाली (वस्तु)

jerkin (ˈजर्किन) *n.* बिना आस्तीन की जैकेट विशे. चमड़े की

jersey (ˈजर्ज़ि) *n.* जर्सी, ऊनी बण्डी

jest (जेंस्ट) *n./vi.* मज़ाक या हंसी-दिल्लगी (करना) – **jester** *n.* मसखरा

jet[1] (जेंट) *n.* द्रव, गैस आदि की तेज धार विशे. पतले छिद्र से निकलती हुई; पतला छिद्र, टोंटी; जेट विमान – *v.* धार फेंकना, फूट निकलना (**-tt-**) – **jet-black** *a.* काला स्याह – **jet engine** जेट विमान का इंजन – **jet lag** जेट-विमान यात्रा में समय-क्षेत्र पार करने के कारण हुई थकावट – **the jet set** अमीर, फ़ैशनेबल समाज के लोग जो दुनियां भर में घूमते रहते हैं

jet[2] (जेंट) *n.* चमकाया जा सकने वाला काला कड़ा पत्थर, क ष्णाश्म

jettison (ˈजेंटिसन) *vt.* जहाज से फेंक देना; छोड़ देना

jetty (ˈजेंटि) *n.* जेटी, घाट

Jew (जू) *n.* यहूदी; – **Jewess** *n. fem.* यहूदी लड़की/स्त्री – **Jewish** *a.* यहूदी

jewel (ˈजूअल) *n.* रत्न, रत्न-जड़ित आभूषण; बहुमूल्य वस्तु – **jeweller** *n.* जौहरी – **jewellery** *n.* ज़ेवरात, जवाहरात

jibe (जाइब) *n.* उपहास, ताना (**gybe**) भी

jiffy (ˈजिफ़ि) *n. inf.* कुछ क्षण, थोड़ा सा समय

jig (जिग) *n.* एक सजीव न त्य, इसके लिए संगीत; एक छोटा सा यांत्रिक उपकरण; काटने आदि में उपयुक्त एक उपकरण – **jigsaw** (ˈजिग्सॉ) *n.* छोटा चौखटी आरा – **jigsaw puzzle** चित्र के बेतरतीब लगाए हुए टुकड़े जिन्हें जोड़कर पूरी तस्वीर बन सकती है; जटिल समस्या

jihad (जिˈहाद) *n.* इस्लाम विरोधियों के खिलाफ़ मुसलमानों का धर्म-युद्ध

jilt (जिल्ट) *vt.* (प्रेमी को) छोड़ देना, अस्वीकार करना

jingle (ˈजिंगल) *n. inf.* छनकने की आवाज़, सरल तुकांत कविता, गाना आदि – *vi.* छनकना

jingoism (ˈजिंगोइज़म) *n.* उद्धत राष्ट्रवादिता – **jingoistic** *a.* उग्रराष्ट्रवादी

jinx (जिंक्स) *n.* अशुभ शक्ति, व्यक्ति, वस्तु (जो किसी के लिए दुर्भाग्य सूचक हो) – *v.* दुर्भाग्य सूचक बनना

jitters (ˈजिटर्ज़) *pl. n.* छटपटी, घबराहट, परेशानी – **jittery** *a.* घबराया हुआ

jiujitsu (जूˈजित्सू) *n.* दे JUJITSU

job (जॉब) *n.* काम, नौकरी; *inf.* मुश्किल कार्य; *inf.* अपराध विशे. डाका – **jobless** *a./pl. n.* बेकार (लोग) – **job work** फुटकर काम; ठेके पर काम

jockey (ˈजॉकि) *n.* (घुड़दौड़ में) पेशेवर घुड़सवार (*pl.* **-eys**) – *vi.* – **jockey for** के लिए तिकड़म लड़ाना

jocular (ˈजॉक्युलर) *a.* विनोदी, विनोदपूर्ण, मज़ाकिया – **jocularity** (जॉक्युˈलैरिटि) *n.* मज़ाकिया तबियत

jog (जॉग) *vi.* धीरे-धीरे दौड़ना (व्यायाम के लिए) – *vt.* झटका, धक्का देना; याद कराना, प्रेरित करना (**-gg-**) – *n.* धीमी दौड़ – **jogger** *n.* धीमे दौड़कर व्यायाम करने वाला

join (जॉइन) *vt.* जोड़ना, जोड़ मिलाना; (का) सदस्य बनना – *vi.* जुड़ना, मिल जाना (विशे. **join**

in में), भाग लेना – *n.* जोड़, संधि – **join hands with sb** से मिलकर काम करना – **join in** हाथ बंटाना

joint (जॉइंट) *n.* जोड़, संधि; भूनने के लिए मांस का टुकड़ा (प्राय: हड्डी सहित); *inf.* घर, स्थान आदि; *sl.* बदनाम बार (शराबघर) या नाइट क्लब; *sl.* नशीली सुलफे वाली सिगरेट – *a.* संयुक्त, अनेक व्यक्तियों द्वारा मिलाकर – *vt.* जोड़ना – **jointly** *adv.* इकट्ठे

joke (जोक) *n.* मज़ाक, दिल्लगी, परिहास – *vi.* मज़ाक करना – **joker** *n.* मज़ाकिया व्यक्ति, मसखरा, जोकर; *sl.* व्यक्ति; ताश में अतिरिक्त पत्ता, जोकर

jolly (ˊजॉलि) *a.* खुश, मस्ती में – *vt.* (विशे, *along* के साथ) व्यक्ति, अवसर आदि को प्रफुल्लित बनाना

jolt (जोल्ट) *n.* झटका, धक्का; हिचकोला – *vi.* झटके से चलना, घूमना – *vt.* झटका देना

joss stick धूप-बत्ती

jostle (ˊजॉसल) *v.* धक्का देना, ढकेलना

jot (जॉट) *n.* ज़रा सा – *vt.* – **jot down** संक्षेप में जल्दी से लिख लेना (**-tt-**) – **jotter** *n.* नोटबुक – **jotting** *n.*संक्षेप में लिखी हुई बातें

joule (जूल) *n. Electricity* काम या विद्युत की इकाई, जूल

journal (ˊजर्नल) *n.* समाचार पत्र; पत्रिका; रोज़नामचा, घटनाओं आदि का दैनिक लेखा – **journalism** *n.* पत्रकारिता – **journalist** *n.*

journey (ˊजर्नि) *n.* यात्रा, सैर, यात्रा-दूरी – *vi.* यात्रा करना

jovial (ˊजोविअल) *a.* मिलनसार, खुश मिज़ाज – **joviality** *n.* खुश मिज़ाजी

joy (जॉइ) *n.* हर्ष, खुशी; हर्ष आदि का कारण – **joyful, joyous** *a.* हर्षित, खुश – **joyless** *a.* उदास, नीरस – **joy ride** (चोरी की कार में) सैर – **joystick** *n. inf.* वायुयान का गति नियंत्रक यंत्र

Jr., Junior का संक्षिप्त रूप

jubilant (ˊजूबिलंट) *a.* उल्लासित, बेहद खुश – **jubilation** *n.* उल्लास

jubilee (ˊजूबिली) *n.* खुशी मनाने का मौका, जयंती विशे. 25 अथवा 50 वर्षीय

Judaism (ˊजूडेइज़म) *n.* यहूदी धर्म

Judas (ˊजूडस) *n.* विश्वासघाती मित्र

judge (जज) *n.* न्यायाधीश; निर्णायक (प्रतियोगिता, विवाद आदि में); सूझ-बूझ वाला व्यक्ति, पारखी; (विवाद, झगड़े आदि में) विवाचक – *vi.* न्याय करना; न्यायधीश के रूप में कार्य करना – *vt.* की सुनवाई करना; आंकना; फैसला देना – **judg(e)ment** *n.* निर्णय शक्ति, न्यायलय का निर्णय; विचार

judicial (जूˊडिशल) *a.* न्यायिक – **judicially** *adv.* – **judiciary** (जूˊडिशिअरि) *n.* न्यायतंत्र, न्यायपालिका, न्यायालयों की व्यवस्था – **judicious** (जूˊडिशस) *a.* विवेकपूर्ण, समझदारी का (निर्णय आदि)

judo (ˊजूडो) *n.* जुजुत्सु पर आधारित आधुनिक खेल

jug (जग) *n.* सुराही, जग; इसमें रखी वस्तु (**-gg-**)

juggernaut (ˊजगर्नॉट) *n.* भारी भरकम ट्रक; कोई भी विनाशकारी शक्ति

juggle (ˊजगल) *v.* बाज़ीगरी करना; (हिसाब-किताब में) हेरा फेरी करना – *n.* – **juggler** *n.* बाज़ीगर – **jugglery** *n.* बाज़ीगरी, धोखाधड़ी

jugular vein (ˊजग्युलर-) कण्ठ-शिरा – **go for the jugular** *inf.* बहस के दौरान किसी की सबसे कमज़ोर बात को पकड़ना

juice (जूस) *n.* रस; *fig.* बल, उत्साह, जीवन शक्ति – **juicy** (ˊजूसि) *a.* रसभरा

jujitsu, jujutsu, jiujitsu (जूˊजित्सू) *n.* जापानी कुश्ती व आत्मरक्षा का ढंग

July (जूˊलाइ) *n.* जुलाई मास

jumble (ˈजम्बल) *vt.* (वस्तुओं को) मिलाकर गड़बड़ कर देना – *n.* बेतरतीब, फुटकर वस्तुओं का ढेर

jumbo (ˈजंबो) *inf. n.* हाथी; कोई भी विशालकाय वस्तु – **jumbo jet** जम्बो जेट विमान

jump (जम्प) *v.* कूदना, उछलना, उछालना; (पन्ने आदि) छोड़ कर आगे पढ़ना, कूद कर परे होना – *vi.* जल्दी से दूर होना; ऊंचा उठना, पैराशूट से नीचे कूदना, चौंक जाना – *vt.* (पटरी आदि से) उतर जाना; *inf.* अचानक हमला करना – *n.* कूद, छलांग; छलांग द्वारा तै की गयी दूरी, ऊंचाई – **jumper** *n.* कूदने, छलांग लगाने वाला (व्यक्ति, वस्तु आदि); स्वेटर, पुलोवर – **jumpy** *a.* घबराया हुआ – **jump the queue/ the lights** पंक्ति तोड़कर आगे बढ़ जाना लालबत्ती पर न रूकना

junction (ˈजंक्शन) *n.* रेलवे जंक्शन; कोई भी संगम, संधि स्थान, जोड़

juncture (ˈजंक्चर) *n.* परिस्थिति

June (जून) *n.* जून मास

jungle (ˈजंगल) *n.* गर्म प्रदेश के घने जंगल; जीने के लिए संघर्ष, होड़, प्रतिस्पर्धा

junior (ˈजून्यर) *a.* अवर; छोटा; पद आदि में छोटा – *n.* अवर व्यक्ति

juniper (ˈजूनिपर) *n.* सदाबहार झाड़ी, हपुषा

junk (जंक) *n.* कबाड़, कूड़ा-करकट – **junk food** भोजन, प्रायः कम पोषक तत्वों वाला जो नियमित भोजन के अतिरिक्त या उसके स्थान पर खाया जाता है – **junk mail** पत्र, विशे० विज्ञापन, जो व्यापारिक संस्थान अनेक लोगों को भेजते हैं – **junk shop** कबाड़ी की दुकान

junket (ˈजंकिट) *n.* सरकारी खर्चे पर सैर-सपाटा

junta (ˈजंट्अ) *n.* सैनिक शासक दल

Jupiter (ˈजूपिटर) *n.* बृहस्पति ग्रह

jurisdiction (जुअरिस्ˈडिक्शन) *n.* न्याय-अधिकार, अधिकारक्षेत्र

jury (ˈजुअरि) *n.* (न्यायालय में) जूरी, पंच – **juror** (ˈजुअरर), **juryman** *n.* जूरी का सदस्य

just (जस्ट) *a.* उचित, ईमानदार, न्यायोचित – *adv.* ठीक-ठीक, यही, मुश्किल से; अभी-अभी, इसी समय, केवल – **justice** *n.* न्यायपरायणता, इंसाफ; न्यायमूर्ति – **justify** *vt.* उचित ठहराना या सिद्ध करना – **justifiable** *a.* – **justifiably** *adv.* – **justification** *n.* औचित्य, सफाई – **justified** *a.* उचित; ठीक – **justly** *adv.* उचित ही

jut (जट) *vi* आगे या बाहर निकला हुआ होना – *n.* आगे निकला भाग (**-tt-**)

jute (जूट) *n.* जूट, पटसन

juvenile (ˈजुविनाइल) *a.* तरुण, किशोर; तरुणों के लिए – *n.* किशोर व्यक्ति – **juvenile delinquent** बाल- अपराधी, किशोर-अपराधी

juxtapose (जक्स्टˈपोज) *vt.* पास-पास रखना – **juxtaposition** *n.* सन्निधि, पास-पास रखा जाना

K

K Kelvin; *one thousand* का संक्षेप

kaftan (ˈकैफ़्टैन) *n.* स्त्रियों का बाजू वाला ढीला लम्बा कुरता

kaleidoscope (कˈलाइडस्कोप) *n.* एक खिलौना जिसमें कांच के रंगीन टुकड़ों पर विभिन्न कोणों से प्रकाश के प्रभाव से विविध सुंदर डिज़ाइन बनते हैं, बहुमूर्तिदर्शी, कलाइडोस्कोप; स्थिति आदि जिसके विविध आयाम लगातार बदलते रहें – **kaleidoscopic** *a.* तीव्रता से बदलने वाला

kangaroo (कैंगˈरू) *n.* कंगारू – *v. inf.* कार का झटके से आगे बढ़ना या बढ़ाना

karate (कˈराटि) *n.* बिना शस्त्रों के जापानी ढंग का द्वंद-युद्ध जिसमें हाथ, पैर, कुहनी आदि का शस्त्रों के रूप में प्रयोग होता है; कराटे

Kb kilobyte का संक्षेप

keel (कील) *n.* जहाज़ के ढांचे का आधार, नौतल – **keel** *vi.* उलट जाना – **keel over** उलट जाना; *inf.* अचानक बेहोश हो जाना

keen (कीन) *a.* तीक्ष्ण; प्रखर; पैना; उत्सुक; कुशाग्र बुद्धि – **keenly** *adv.* – **keenness** *n.* उत्सुकता

keep (कीप) *vt.* रखना, पास रखना; जारी रखना; देख-रेख करना; बनाये रखना, भरण पोषण करना; रोक रखना – *vi.* ठीक रहना, बना रहना, नहीं बिगड़ना; चालू रहना (**kept** *pt./pp.*) – *n.* भरण-पोषण; देख-रेख; किले की मुख्य मीनार, गढ़ी – **keeper** *n.* – **keeping** *n.* अनुरूपता, संगति, देख-रेख, अधिकार – **keep going** किसी तरह जीना – **keep off sth** (नशा, सिगरेट आदि से) दूर रहना – **keep it up!** शाबाश, ऐसे ही अच्छा कार्य करते रहो! – **keepsake** *n.* निशानी, यादगार, स्म ति चिन्ह

keg (कॅग) *n.* छोटा पीपा; बीयर रखने का धातु का पात्र

Kelvin (कॅल्विन) *a.* थर्मामीटर के परम शून्य (-273.15 सेल्सियस) से शुरू होने वाले मापक्रम सम्बंधी – *n.* ताप की एस.आई. इकाई

kennel (ˈकॅनल) *n.* कुत्ता घर

kept KEEP का *pt./pp.*

kerb (कर्ब) *n.* फुटपाथ का पत्थर से बना किनारा

kerchief (ˈकर्चिफ़) *n.* सिर ढंकने का कपड़ा; रूमाल

kernel (ˈकर्नल) *n.* बादाम, अखरोट आदि की गिरी, (*fig.*) समस्या का केन्द्र; तत्व

kerosene (ˈकॅरसीन) *n.* मिट्टी का तेल

ketchup (ˈकॅचप) *n.* सिरका व टमाटर आदि से बनाया सॉस (चटनी)

kettle (ˈकॅट्रल) *n.* केतली, देगची

key (की) *n.* ताले की चाबी, घड़ी आदि की चाबी; कुंजी, किसी पुस्तक आदि की व्याख्या, समाधान, नियंत्रण-स्रोत; *Mus.* सम्बंधित स्वर-समूह; टाइपराइटर, प्यानो, अन्य अनेक बाजों आदि को संचालित करने का लीवर, टाइपराइटर की कुंजी (अक्षर) – *vt.* मानचित्र आदि स्थान, क्षेत्र की पहचान के लिए संकेत चिह्न लगाना; (**key in** भी) सुर ठीक करना – *a.* महत्वपूर्ण – **keyboard** *n.* प्यानो, टाइपराइटर आदि का कुंजी-फलक – **keynote** *n.* (**keynote address**) मुख्य व्याख्यान; मूल सिद्धांत – **keypad** *n.* केलकुलेटर, टेलीटेक्सट उपकरण आदि का कुंजी फलक – **keystone** *n.* चाप के केंद्र का पत्थर, संघान-प्रस्तर, डाट; *fig.* आधार – **keyed up** किसी साक्षात्कार आदि से पहले घबराया हुआ, उत्तेजित

kg. kilogram(s) का संक्षिप्त रूप

khaki (ˈकाकि) *a.* खाकी रंग – *n.* खाकी कपड़ा; फौजी वरदी

kHz. kilohertz का संक्षिप्त रूप

kick (किक) *vi.* पैर से ठोकर मारना, पैर से मारकर (रगबी आदि में) गोल करना; (*of rifle*) झटके से पीछे आना; (बुरी आदत से) पीछा छुड़ाना – *n.* ठोकर; पीछे झटका; उत्तेजना, रोमांच – **kickback** *n.* रिश्वत – **kick off** *v.* फुटबाल आदि का खेल आरंभ करना – **pick-start** *vt.* (योजना आदि) तेज़ी से शुरू करना

kid (किड) *n.* बकरी, भेड़ का बच्चा, मेमना; मेमने की खाल; *inf.* बच्चा – *vt. inf.* परेशान करना, धोखा देना – *vi. inf.* मज़ाक करना (**-dd-**) – **kids' stuff** आसान काम

kidnap ('किड्नैप) *vt.* अपहरण करना (*-pp*) – **kidnapper** *n.* अपहरणकर्ता

kidney ('किड्नि) *n.* गुर्दा, वृक्क; भोजन के रूप में प्रयुक्त जानवर का गुर्दा; स्वभाव, प्रकार (*pl.* **-neys**) – **kidney bean** मोठ; राजमा (दाल)

kill (किल) *vt.* मारना, हत्या करना; नष्ट करना; समाप्त करना; विफल कर देना; (समय) काटना; फीका कर देना; *inf.* थका देना; *inf.* पीड़ा देना – *n.* मारने का कार्य; शिकार में मारा गया जंतु – **killing** *a. inf.* थकाने वाला; बहुत हास्यकर – *n.* आकस्मिक सफलता विशे. शेयर बाज़ार में – **killjoy** *n.* रंग में भंग करने वाला – **kill time** इंतज़ार में समय काटना

kiln (किल्न) *n.* भट्ठा, भट्टा

kilo kilogram(me) का संक्षिप्त रूप

kilo- (*comb. form*) एक हज़ार जैसे **kilolitre** और **kilometre** में

kilogram(me) ('किलोग्रैम) *n.* किलोग्राम, **1000** ग्राम के बराबर

kilohertz ('किलोहर्ट्स) *n.* **1000** चक्र (साइकल) प्रति सैकिंड

kilowatt ('किलोवॉट) *n. Electricity* **1000** वाट

kin (किन) *n.* सम्बंधी, रिश्तेदार – *a.* सगा – **kindred** (किन्ड्रिड) *n.* सम्बंध; सम्बंधी, परिवार के सदस्य – a. सदृश, संबद्ध

kind (काइंड) *n.* प्रकार, जाति, वर्ग – *a.* दयालु, सहृदय; भला उदार; भद्र – **kindliness** *n.* दयालुता, उदारता – **kindly** *a.* दयालु, भला; सुहावना – *adv.* कृपया, कृपापूर्वक – **kindness** *n.* कृपा, मेहरबानी – **kindhearted** *a.* दयालु, सहृदय – **in kind** पैसे के स्थान पर वस्तुओं से भुगतान

kindergarten ('किंडर्गार्टन) *n.* चार से छः वर्ष तक की आयु के बच्चों की क्लास या स्कूल

kindle ('किंड्ल) *vt.* आग जलाना, सुलगाना; प्रेरित करना, उकसाना – *vi.* जलना – **kindling** *n.* आग शुरू करने के लिए छोटी-छोटी सूखी लकड़ियां, छिपटी

kinetic (कि'नेटिक) *a.* गति सम्बंधी, गतिज – **kinetics** *pl. n.* बलगति-विज्ञान

king (किंग) *n.* राजा; शतरंज में एक मोहरा, बादशाह; ताश में बादशाह; *Draughts* एक के ऊपर दूसरी गोटी जो दोनों चली जा सकती हैं – **kingship** *n.* – **kingdom** *n.* राज्य-क्षेत्र – **kingfisher** *n.* मछली पकड़ने वाला एक छोटा पक्षी, कौड़िल्ला – **kingpin** *n. inf.* मुखिया, संस्था, गुट आदि का सबसे महत्वपूर्ण व्यक्ति – **kingsize (d)** *a. inf.* बड़ा, सामान्य आकार से बड़ा

kink (किंक) *n.* रस्सी, तार, बाल आदि में बल; ऐंठन जैसे गर्दन में; *inf.* सनक – *v.* बल डालना या पड़ना, मरोड़ना – **kinky** *a.* बलदार; *inf.* सनकी विशे. जो असामान्य यौन क्रियाएं करे

kiosk ('कीऑस्क) *n.* छतरी, बूथ (छोटी दुकान); सार्वजनिक टेलिफोन बूथ

kismet ('किस्मेंट) *n.* भाग्य, किस्मत

kiss (किस) *n.* चुम्बन; हलका सा छूना – *v.* चूमना – **kiss of life** सीधे मुंह से मुंह में हवा भरकर पुनर्जीवित करना

kit (किट) *n.* सामान, निजी प्रयोग की सभी वस्तुएं विशे. यात्रा की; किसी उपकरण आदि के इकट्ठे बिकने वाले सभी भाग जो तुरंत जोड़े जा सकते हैं, किट – **kitbag** *n.* यात्रा या फौजी के सामान का थैला, किट थैला

kitchen (ˈकिचिन) *n.* रसोईघर – **kitchenette** (किचिˈनेंट) *n.* छोटा रसोईघर – **kitchen garden**

kite (काइट) *n.* पतंग; *sl.* वायुयान; चील

kith (किथ) *n.* मित्र, सम्बंधी (केवल – **kith and kin** में)

kitsch (किच) *n.* घटिया दर्जे का साहित्य, कला आदि जो भावुकता से ओत-प्रोत हो

kitten (ˈकिट्न) *n.* बिल्ली का बच्चा

kitty (ˈकिटि) *n.* KITTEN का संक्षिप्त रूप; सामुदायिक या पंचायती कोष

kiwi (ˈकीवि) *n.* न्यूजीलेंड का न उड़ने वाला पक्षी, कीवी; *sl.* न्यूजीलेंड निवासी – **kiwi fruit** एक एशियाई बेल का खाने योग्य फल, चीनी गूज़बरी (झरबेरी)

kleptomania (क्लेंप्टोˈमेनिअ) *n.* चोरी करने का मानसिक रोग, चौर्योन्माद – **kleptomaniac** *n.* ऐसे रोग से पीड़ित व्यक्ति

km **kilometre(s)** का संक्षिप्त रूप

knack (नैक) *n.* अनुभवों से प्राप्त कौशल, दक्षता

knapsack (ˈनैप्सैक) *n.* पीठ पर बांधने का फौजी या यात्री झोला, रकसैक

knave (निव़) *n.* ताश में गुलाम का पत्ता; *obs.* बदमाश – **knavery** *n.* दुष्टता, कुटिलता – **knavish** *a.* दुष्टतापूर्ण

knead (नीड) *vt.* (आटा) गूंधना, सानना; मालिश करना

knee (नी) *n.* घुटना – *vt.* घुटने से धक्का देना, धकेलना – **kneecap** *n.* घुटने की हड्डी, चपनी, – **knee-jerk** *a.* बिना सोचे विचारे अचानक (प्रतिक्रिया)

kneel (नील) *vi.* घुटने टेकना, घुटनों के बल बैठना (**knelt** *pt./pp.*)

knell (नेंल) *n.* घंटे बजाने की ध्वनि विशे. म त्यु या दफ़न के समय; विनाश-संकेत

knew (न्यू) **KNOW** का *pt.*

knickers (ˈनिकर्ज़) *pl. n.* स्त्रियों की नीचे पहनने की एक प्रकार की निकर

knickknack (ˈनिक्नैक) *n.* छोटी-मोटी नुमाइशी वस्तु, सस्ता जेवर

knife (नाइफ़) *n.* चाकू, छुरा, छुरी (*pl.* **knives**) – *vt.* छुरा मारना, घोंपना – **knife edge** संकटपूर्ण स्थिति

knight (नाइट) *n.* नाइट, मध्यकालीन समय में सामंत;शूरवीर; शतरंज में घोड़ा – *vt.* 'सर' की उपाधि प्रदान करना – **knighthood** *n.* 'सर' की उपाधि

knit (निट) *v.* बुनना; खींच कर पास-पास करना; एकत्र करना, जोड़ना; जुड़ना (**knitted, knit** *pt./pp.*, **knitting** *pr. p.*) – **knitting** *n.* बुना हुआ वस्त्र, बुनाई कला – **knit your brow** (गुस्से/ सोचने की मुद्रा में) भवें सिकोड़ना

knob (नॉब) *n.* लाठी आदि की मूठ, दस्ता; गुमटा – **knobb(l)y** *a.* गुमटेदार

knock (नॉक) *vt.* वार करना, मारना; *inf.* तीव्र आलोचना करना; खटखटाना; (इंजन का) खड़खड़ाना – *n.* वार, खटखट, दस्तक – **knocker** *n.* खटखटाने के लिए दरवाज़े पर लगी धातु की वस्तु, खटखटाने वाला व्यक्ति, वस्तु – **knock-kneed** *a.* अंदर की ओर मुड़ी हुई टांगों वाला – **knock out** *inf.* बेहोश कर देना; (विशे. बॉक्सिंग में) पछाड़ देना, चकरा देना – **knockout** *n.* बेहोश कर देने वाला वार; अत्यंत आकर्षक व्यक्ति या वस्तु

knoll (नोल) *n.* टीला

knot (नॉट) *n.* गांठ; समूह, पुंज; छोटा संगठित दल; बंधन; (व क्ष के शाखा व तने के जोड़ पर) गांठ;

जहाज़ी मील; कठिनाई, उलझन – *vt.* गांठ बांधना, लगाना (**-tt-**) – **knotty** *a.* गांठदार; पेचीदा, जटिल

know (नो) *vt.* जानना; जानकारी होना; से परिचित होना, पहचानना; अनुभव करना, समझना – *vi.* के बारे में जानकारी या समझ होना (**knew** *pt.*, **known** *pp.*) – **knowing** *a.* चालाक – **knowingly** *adv.* चतुरता से, जान बूझ कर – **knowledge** (ˈनॉलिज) *n.* जानकारी; ज्ञान – **knowledg(e)able** *a.* जानकार – **know-how** *n. inf.* व्यावहारिक ज्ञान, अनुभव

knuckle (ˈनकल) *n.* उंगली की गांठ, पोर – *vt.* पोरों से दबाना – **knuckle down** काम में लगना – **knuckle under** झुकना, हार जाना

KO knockout का संक्षेप

koala (कोˈआल्अ) *n.* रीछ से मिलता जुलता एक आस्ट्रेलियाई वन-प्राणी, कोआला

kohl (कोल) *n.* सुरमा

Koran (कुˈरान, कॉˈरान) *n.* कुरान

kosher (ˈकोशर) *a.* अच्छा, जैसे भोजन आदि; जो यहूदी भोजन-नियमों के अनुसार हो; *inf.* वैध, प्रामाणिक

kowtow (ˈकाउटाउ) *n.* झुकना – *vi.* – **kowtow to** की जी हजूरी करना; चापलूसी करना

krypton (ˈक्रिप्टॉन) *n.* वायुमंडल में बहुत कम मात्रा में विद्यमान गैस रूपी तत्व, क्रिप्टान

kudos (ˈक्यूडॉस) *n.* ख्याति; गौरव

kukri (ˈकुकरि) *n.* गोरखा चाकू, खुखरी

kung fu (ˈकंग ˈफू) *n.* चीनी कुश्ती जिसमें जूडो व कराटे के दाव-पेचों का समावेश है

KWh kilomatt-hours का संक्षेप

L

L Latin; Learner (driver) का संक्षेप
l litre का संक्षेप
l. lake; left; line का संक्षेप
lab *n. inf.* LABORATORY का संक्षेप
label (लेबल) *n.* लेबिल, नामपत्र– *vt.* लेबिल लगाना (**-ll-**)
labial (´लेबिअल) *a.* ओठों से उच्चारित (ध्वनि), ओष्ठ्य
laboratory (ल´बॉरटरि) *n.* प्रयोगशाला
labour (´लेबर) *n.* मेहनत; कार्य; श्रमिक वर्ग; मज़दूर; प्रयत्न; प्रसव-पीड़ा, प्रसव – *vi.* कठोर परिश्रम करना, प्रयत्न करना; कठिनाई से आगे बढ़ना – *vt.* पर जरूरत से ज्यादा बल देना – **laboured** *a.* कठिनाई से कहा/किया गया – **labourer** *n.* श्रमिक, मज़दूर – **laborious** (ल´बॉरिअस) *a.* कड़ी मेहनत वाला – **laboriously** *adv.* मेहनत से – **labour-intensive** *a.* श्रमिक-प्रधान (उद्योग)
Labrador (´लैब्रडॉर) *n.* एक बड़े आकार के कुत्ते की जाति
laburnum (ल´बर्नम) *n.* अमलतास
labyrinth (´लैबरिंथ) *n.* भूलभूलैया; जटिल स्थिति आदि
lac (लैक) *n.* लाख (मुहर लगाने में प्रयुक्त)
lace (लेस) *n.* (कपड़े में) लेस, जाली; डोरी; फीता (जैसे जूते का) – *vt.* फीता बांधना; (किसी खाद्य- पदार्थ/पेय को शराब आदि का) पुट देना – **lacy** *a.* जाली जैसा महीन
lacerate (´लैसरेट) *vt.* चीरना, फाड़ना, दुखाना – **laceration** *n.* चीरा
lack (लैक) *n.* अभाव, कमी, आवश्यकता – *vt.* कमी होना, की आवश्यकता होना – **lacklustre** *a.* भावशून्य, निस्तेज, नीरस
lackadaisical (लैक´डेज़िकल) *a.* सुस्त, निरुत्साह
lackey (´लैकि) *n.* नौकर, पिछलग्गा (*pl.* **-eys**)
laconic (ल´कॉनिक) *a.* संक्षिप्त (उत्तर); अल्पाक्षरिक; बिना ज़्यादा सोचे (उत्तर आदि)
lacquer (´लैकर) *n.* चमकीला रोग़न, मोटी वार्निश – *vt.* इससे पालिश (रंग) करना
lacuna (ल´क्यूनअ) *n.* रिक्त-स्थान, अंतराल; कमी विशे. कागज़ात में या श्रृंखला में (*pl.* **-nae**) (–नी), **-nas**)
lad (लैड) *n.* लड़का, किशोर
ladder (´लैडर) *n.* सीढ़ी
laden (´लेडन) *v.* (जहाज़) लदा होना
ladle (´लेड्ल) *n.* कढ़छी, कलछी – *vt.* कढ़छी से द्रव पदार्थ परोसना
lady (´लेडि) *n.* महिला; संभ्रांत महिला; कुछ कुलीन महिलाओं की उपाधि – **ladybird** *n.* सोनपंखी (कीट) – **ladylike** *a.* महिला-सुलभ, शालीन – **ladies' room** *US* (*toilet*) स्त्रियों का प्रसाधन-कक्ष – **lady-killer** *n.* बांका, छैला – **lady's finger** भिण्डी – **Our Lady** माता मरियम
lag (लैग) *vi.* बहुत धीरे चलना, पिछड़ जाना (**-gg-**) – *n.* पिछड़ना, दो घटनाओं के मध्य कालांतर – **laggard** *n.* फिसड्डी, मंद बुद्धि
lager (´लागर) *n.* एक प्रकार की बीयर
lagoon (ल´गून) *n.* लेगून, समुद्रताल
laid (लेड) LAY का *pt./pp.* – **laid-back** *a. inf.* शांत व स्थिर
lain (लेन) LIE का *pp.*
lair (लेंअर) *n.* (शेर आदि की) माँद
laissez-faire (लेसे´फ़ेंअर) *n.* अहस्तक्षेप नीति विशे. सरकार द्वारा देश के वाणिज्य क्षेत्र में
lake (लेक) *n.* झील, ताल
lama (´लामअ) *n.* बौद्ध पुरोहित, लामा
lamb (लैम) *n.* मेमना; (*fig.*) सीधा-सादा, असहाय प्राणी

lambast(e) (लैम्'बेस्ट) *vt.* तीव्र आलोचना करना; लताड़ना

lame (लेम) *a.* लंगड़ा, पंगु; (*fig.*) असंतोषजनक (बहाना) – *vt.* पंगु या लंगड़ा कर देना – **lame duck** पंगु; प्रभावहीन व्यक्ति, सरकार या वस्तु

lament (ल'मेंन्ट) *v.* शोक या विलाप करना, शोक व्यक्त करना – *n.* विलाप, शोक गीत – **lamentable** *a.* शोचनीय, दयनीय – **lamentation** (लमें'टेशन) *n.* विलाप

laminate ('लैमिनेट) *v.* दो या अधिक शीट (परत) जोड़कर एक शीट बनाना, कूटकर पतली शीट बनाना; पदार्थ (जैसे प्लास्टिक) की पतली परत चढ़ाना – *n.* इस प्रकार बनाई गई शीट – **lamination** *n.* पतली परत चढ़ाने की क्रिया

lamp (लैम्प) *n.* बत्ती, लैम्प, दिया– **lamppost** *n.* बत्ती का खम्बा – **lampshade** *n.* लैम्पशेड

lampoon (लैम्'पून) *n.* किसी व्यक्ति या साहित्यिक रचना पर व्यंग्य रचना (गद्य या पद्य में), निन्दा-लेख – *vt.* निंदालेख लिखना

LAN *Computers* Local Area Network का संक्षेप, किसी भवन में एक दूसरे से जुड़े कम्प्यूटरों के माध्यम से संचार व्यवस्था

lance (लान्स) *n.* घुड़सवार की बरछी, बल्लम – *vt.* नश्तर से चीरना – **lancer** *n.* पुराने युग का बल्लमधारी घुड़सवार सैनिक – **lancet** *n.* डाक्टरों का दुधारा चाकू, नश्तर

land (लैंड) *n.* भूमि, जमीन; मिट्टी; देश; जायदाद – (~ **s**) *pl.* जागीर – *vi.* भूमि पर उतरना (जहाज़ आदि से); *fig.* गिरना – *vt.* भूमि पर लाना; किसी बिन्दु या स्थिति तक पहुंचना; *inf.* पाना, प्राप्त करना; पकड़ना; *inf.* प्रहार करना – **landed** *a.* जिस के पास भूमि हो, भूमि वाली (सम्पत्ति आदि) – **landing** *n.* भूमि पर उतरने की क्रिया; सीढ़ियों में चौकी; उतरने का स्थान – **landless** *a.* भूमिहीन (किसान आदि) – **landfill** *n.* नगर का कूड़ा भरने/दबाने का स्थान – **landlocked** *a.* (देश) जिसके आसपास समुद्र न हो, स्थल-रुद्ध – **landlord** *n.*, **landlady** *fem.* जमींदार, व्यक्ति जिसने ज़मीन या मकान किराए पर उठा रखा हो; सराय आदि का मालिक या मालकिन – **landmark** *n.* सीमा चिन्ह; महत्वपूर्ण घटना या निर्णय (जिसे विकास की प्रक्रिया में विशिष्ट स्थान प्राप्त हो) – **landmine** *n.*ज़मीनी बम (सुरंग) – **landscape** *n.* (भूमि का) प्राक तिक द श्य – *v.* उद्यान, पार्क आदि बनाना – **landslide, landslip** *n.* पहाड़ की ढलान से मिट्टी, चट्टानों का गिरना; चुनाव में भारी बहुमत से विजय – **landing stage** घाट जहां से यात्री जहाज़ में चढ़ते उतरते हैं – **land sb/yourself in trouble** *etc.* मुसीबत में फँसाना/फँसना

lane (लेन) *n.* गली, वीथि; विमान या जहाज़ का निर्धारित रास्ता; सड़क का भाग जहां एक ओर ही जा सकते हैं

language ('लैंग्विज) *n.* भाषा

languish ('लैंग्विश) *vi.* कमज़ोर हो जाना; दुख में दिन काटना; तरसना – **languid** ('लैंग्विड) *a.* निस्तेज; उत्साहरहित – **languidly** *adv.* – **languor** ('लैंगर) *n.* निस्तेज होने की स्थिति, उत्साहहीनता – **languorous** *a.*

lank (लैंक) *a.* दुबला-पतला और लम्बा – **lanky** *a.* छरहरा, लम्बू

lantern ('लैंटर्न) *n.* लालटैन

lap[1] (लैप) *n.* गोद, गोदी; बैठे हुए व्यक्ति के घुटने; *fig.* स्थान जहां कोई वस्तु सुरक्षित पड़ी हो; घुड़दौड़ या खेल के मैदान का एक चक्कर; यात्रा का पड़ाव या अंश – *vt.* लपेट लेना; (प्रतिद्वंदी से) एक चक्कर या अधिक से आगे हो जाना (**-pp-**) – **lapdog** *n.* छोटा, पालतू कुत्ता; व्यक्ति जो अन्य व्यक्ति या संगठन के इशारों पर नाचे – **laptop** *n.* बैटरी से चलने वाला छोटा, हल्का कम्प्यूटर जो कहीं भी आसानी से ले जाया जा सकता है

lap[2] *vt.* (कुत्ते, बिल्ली के समान) जीभ से पीना; (लहरों का) किनारे से छपछपाना **(-pp-)**
lapel (ल'पॅल) *n.* कोट (के गरेबान) की लौट या मोड़ी
lapse (लैप्स) *n.* (मापदण्ड स्थिति या चरित्र की) गिरावट; चूक; भूल; गलती; दोष; समय का बीतना – *vi.* समाप्त हो जाना, विशे. प्रयुक्त न होने पर, रद्द या कालातीत हो जाना
lapwing ('लैप्विङ) *n.* एक पक्षी, टिटहरी
larceny ('लार्सिनि) *n.* चोरी
lard (लार्ड) *n.* सूअर की चर्बी
larder ('लार्डर) *n.* खाद्य भण्डार/अल्मारी
large (लार्ज) *a.* बड़ा, आकार या संख्या में अधिक; लम्बा-चौड़ा, विशाल; प्रचुर – *adv.* बड़े पैमाने पर – **largely** *adv.* – **largess(e)** (लार्'जॅस) *n.* दान; भेंट; चन्दा – **large scale** बड़े पैमाने पर – **at large** स्वतंत्र, अबाध; सामान्यतया
lark (लार्क) *n.* चंडूल (पक्षी); भरत
larva ('लार्व्अ) *n.* अपरिपक्व अवस्था में कीड़ा, इल्ली (*pl.* **-ae**) – **larval** *a.*
larynx ('लैरिंक्स) *n.* स्वरतंत्री; कंठ (*pl.* **larynges** (ल'रिन्जीज़)) – **laryngitis** (लैरिन्'जाइटिस) *n.* (गले में) स्वरतंत्री की सूजन
lasagne (ल'ज़ैन्यअ) *n.* पैस्टा (एक पकवान)
lascivious (ल'सिविअस) *a.* कामुक
laser ('लेज़र) *n.* विद्युत-चुम्बकीय किरणों या प्रकाश किरणों को संकेंद्रित करने की विधि; इस प्रकार उत्पन्न किरणें, लेज़र – **laser printer** (कम्प्यूटर से जुड़ा) लेज़र के प्रयोग द्वारा छपाई करने का यंत्र, लेज़र प्रिंटर
lash[1] (लैश) *n.* कोड़ा, चाबुक; कोड़े की मार; बरौनी, पलक – *vt.* चाबुक या कोड़े से मारना; टकराना (लहरों का); कटु आलोचना करना; लताड़ना; घुमाना – *vi.* – **lash out** मारना, प्रहार करना; तीव्र आलोचना करना
lash[2] *vt.* रस्सी आदि से कसकर बांधना
lass, lassie (लैस, 'लैसि) *n.* लड़की, छोकरी
lassitude ('लैसिट्यूड) *n.* थकावट, क्लांति
lasso (लै'सू, 'लैसो) *n.* रस्से के आगे बना फंदा जो पशुओं को पकड़ने के लिए फैंका जाता है, फांदा (*pl.* **lasso(e)s**) – *vt.* (**lassoed** (ल'सूड) **lassoing**)
last[1] (लास्ट) *a./adv.* अंतिम; पिछला – *a.* अंतिम – LATE का *sup.* – *n.* अंतिम व्यक्ति या वस्तु – **lastly** *adv.* अन्त में, अन्ततः – **last name** नाम का अंतिम भाग, कुटुम्ब नाम
last[2] *vi.* जारी रहना, बने रहना; जीवित रहना, बिना थके चलते/काम करते रहना
last[3] *n.* कल बूत (ढांचा जिस पर जूता बनता है या ठीक किया जाता है), कालिब
latch (लैच) *n.* अर्गला; सिटकिनी; खटकेदार ताला – *vt.* सिटकिनी, अर्गला लगाना
late (लेट) *a.* नियत समय के बाद का, देर से आने या होने वाला; पिछला; स्वर्गीय, दिवंगत; हाल का; पछेती (फसल) (**later** *comp.* **latest, last** *sup.*) – *adv.* देर से, देर तक, हाल में – **lately** *adv.* हाल में
latent ('लेटंट) *a.* जो विकसित न हुआ हो; छिपा हुआ
lateral ('लैटरल) *a.* बाज़ू का, पार्श्विक
latex ('लेटॅक्स) *n.* पौधों का दूध, विशे. रबड़ का
lath (लाथ) *n.* लकड़ी की पतली खपची (*pl.* **-s**)
lathe (लेद) *n.* खराद (मशीन), चाक
lather ('लादर) *n.* साबुन की झाग; फेन जैसा पसीना – *v.* मुंह पर साबुन की झाग लगाना, झाग उठाना; *inf.* पीटना
Latin ('लैटिन) *n.* प्राचीन रोम की भाषा, लातीनी, लैटिन – **Latin America** दक्षिण व मध्य अमरीका के भाग जहां स्पेनिश या पोर्चगीज़ (पुर्तगाली भाषा) बोली जाती है
latitude ('लैटिट्यूड) *n.* अक्षांश (भूमध्य रेखा से) उत्तर या दक्षिण की दूरी; किसी कसौटी से परे

हटने की क्रिया; स्वच्छंदता; गुंजाइश – **latitudes** *pl. n.* क्षेत्र

latrine (ल`ट्रीन) *n.* शौचालय

latter (`लैटर) *a.* दो में से बाद का, पिछला; हाल का – **latterly** *adv.* अभी हाल में

lattice (`लैटिस) *n.* जाली, झंझरी

laudable (`लॉडनल) *a.* प्रशंसनीय

laugh (लाफ़) *vi.* हंसना – *n.* हंसी – **laughable** *a.* हास्यास्पद – **laughably** *adv.* – **laughter** (`लाफ़्टर) *n.* हंसी – **laughing stock** हंसी या उपहास का पात्र, व्यक्ति जिस पर सभी हंसें – **laugh up your sleeve** मन-ही-मन हंसना – **laugh your head off** हंसते-हंसते दुहरा हो जाना

launch[1] (लॉन्च) *vt.* जल में उतारना (नौका आदि); शुरू करना; राकेट या उपग्रह को अन्तरिक्ष में छोड़ना; फैंकना, भेजना – **launch pad** अंतरिक्षयान आदि छोड़ने का स्थान (प्लेटफार्म)

launch[2] *n.* इंजन से चलने वाली नाव, मोटरबोट

laundry (`लॉन्ड्रि) *n.* धुलाइघर, धोबीखाना; धुलने के लिए रखे कपड़े – **launder** *vt.* कपड़े धोना और उन पर इस्तरी करना – **Laundrette** (`लांडरिट) **R** दुकान जहां ग्राहक मशीन में स्वयं कपड़े धोते हैं

laureate (`लॉरिइट) *a.* सम्मानित या प्रतिष्ठित – **poet laureate** राजकवि

laurel (`लॉरल) *n.* चमकीले पत्तों वाली झाड़ी, जयपत्र – **laurels** *pl. n.* इस झाड़ी के पत्ते जो विजेताओं या गुणी लोगों को पहनाए जाते थे; (*fig.*) शाबासी

lava (`लाव्अ) *n.* ज्वामुखी फटने से निकला लावा

lavatory (`लैव्टरि) *n.* शौच घर

lavender (`लैव्ंडर) *n.* सुगंधित फूलों की एक झाड़ी; उसके फूलों का रंग, चमेलिया

lavish (`लैविश) *a.* दिल खोल कर देने या खर्च करने वाला; उदार; विपुल, प्रचुर, खूब – *vt.* दिल खोल कर देना या खर्च करना

law (लॉ) *n.* कानून; नियम; विधि संहिता; कानून का ज्ञान; विधि का प्रशासन – *inf.* पुलिस (का सिपाही या अधिकारी); तथ्यों पर आधारित सिद्धांत – **lawful** *a.* कानूनी, वैध – **lawfully** *adv.* नियम से, वैधानिक रूप से – **lawless** *a.* जो कानून की अवहेलना करे; उपद्रवी, हिंसक – **lawyer** (`लॉयर) *n.* वकील – **law-abiding** *a.* जो कानूनों का पालन करे; शरीफ़ – **law-giver** *n.* विधि निर्माता, विधायक – *lawsuit n.* मुकदमा

lawn[1] (लॉन) *n.* बाग या घर के आंगन में उगाई घास का मैदान – **lawn mower** घास काटने की मशीन – **lawn tennis** टेनिस का खेल जो घास पर खेला जाय

lax (लैक्स) *a.* जो कठोर न हो; ढीला, लचीला – **laxative** (`लैक्सटिव्) *a.* विरेचक, दस्तावर – *n.* जुलाब – **laxity** (`लैक्सिटि) *n.* ढिलाई, शिथिलता (नैतिक कसौटियों की)

lay[1] (ले) **LIE**[1] का *pt.* – **layabout** *n.* आलसी आदमी; आवारा

lay[2] *vt.* रखना, (*table*) लगाना; (बजट आदि) प्रस्तुत करना; जिम्मेवारी डालना; (पर) ज़ोर देना; (जाल) बिछाना; (शर्त) लगाना (*lay a bet*) **(laid, laying)** – **layer** *n.* तह, परत; पौधे की नई टहनी जिसे मिट्टी में दबा देते हैं जिससे नई जड़ें बन जाए; दाब-डाली – *vt.* इस प्रकार टहनी को जमीन में गाड़ना, दाब कलम लगाना – **layout** *n.* विन्यास, निमार्ण-खाका – **lay off** काम कम होने पर मज़दूरों की छंटनी – **lay-off** *n.* काम-बंदी – **lay sth by** (भविष्य के लिए) बचाकर रखना – **be laid up with** (रोग, चोट आदि के कारण) पड़े होना/काम न कर सकना

layman *n.* साधारण व्यक्ति (जिसे किसी विषय का विशेष ज्ञान न हो)

lay figure छुटभैया, नगण्य व्यक्ति

lazy (लेज़ि) *a.* आलसी – **laze** (लेज़) *vi.* निठल्ले बैठे रहना – **laziness** *n.* आलस्य

lb. Pound का संक्षेप, पौंड का वज़न

l.b.w. (एल.बी.डबल्यू.) *Cricket* **leg before wicket** का संक्षेप

lead[1] (लीड) *vt.* पथ प्रदर्शन करना, आगे आगे चलना; नेत त्व करना; राज़ी करना; निर्देश करना; ले चलना – *vi.* सब से पहले होना, जाना या खेलना; परिणाम होना, का कारण बनना; तक पहुंचाना (**led, leading**) – *n.* नेत त्व, आगे होने की क्रिया; जो आगे हो या आगे जाने का काम करे; उदाहरण; अगला भाग; मुख्य स्थान या भूमिका (अभिनेता आदि की); तार जिस से किसी यंत्र में बिजली आए – **leader** *n.* नेता, अगुआ; समाचार पत्र में सम्पादकीय लेख, अग्रलेख (**leading article** भी) – **leadership** *n.* नेत त्व; नेतागण

lead[2] (लॅड) *n.* सीसा; पानी की गहराई नापने का उपकरण, साहुल; एक प्रकार का कार्बन जिससे पेंसिल बनती है, सिक्का (~ **s**) – *pl.* छत का भाग जिस पर सीसे की परत चढ़ी हो – *vt.* सीसे की परत चढ़ाना (**leaded, leading**) – **leaden** *a.* सीसे जैसा या उसका; भारी; धूसर – **lead-free** *a.* सीसारहित (पिट्रोल)

leaf (लीफ़) *n.* पत्ता, पत्ती; पन्ना; वरक; पत्तल, किवाड़; मेज़ के ऊपर का भाग जो अलग किया जा सकता है (*pl.* **leaves** (लीव्ज़)) – *vt.* (पुस्तक) के पन्ने उलटना – **leafless** *a.* पत्ते रहित (पेड़, शाखा आदि) – **leaflet** *n.* छोटा पत्ता, पत्रक; इश्तहार (जो तह किया हो), पुस्तिका – **leafy** *a.* पत्तेदार (सब्ज़ी)

league[1] (लीग) *n.* परस्पर सहायता का करार; संघ; क्लबों का संघ; *inf.* वर्ग, श्रेणी; स्तर; माप – *vi.* संघ बनाना; संघटन बनाने के लिए मिल जाना

league[2] *n. obs.* दूरी का माप = लगभग तीन मील

leak (लीक) *n.* छेद, रिसाव; (*fig.*) रहस्योद्‌घाटन – *vi.* (*liquid etc.*) रिसना; (*pipe*) चूना – *vt.* (*liquid*) निकलने देना – *v.* भेद, गुप्त जानकारी आदि का धीरे-धीरे पता दे देना, का पता चल जाना – **leakage** *n.* रिसाव, टपकन; (गैस) का निकलना – **leaky** *a.* जिससे रिसाव हो रहा हो, सूराखदार

lean[1] (लीन) *a.* दुबला-पतला; क्षीण – *n.* बिना चर्बी का मांस

lean[2] *v.* झुकना; का सहारा या टेक लेना; की ओर झुकाव या प्रव ति होना; निर्भर करना; आश्रित होना; (*on* के साथ) सहारा लेना (**leaned** या **leant** *pt./pp.*) – **leaning** *n.* झुकाव, प्रव ति – **lean-to** *n.* किसी दीवार के सहारे बना कमरा या सायबान

leap (लीप) *vt.* कूदना, छलांग लगाना – *vt.* के ऊपर से फांद जाना; (शेयर आदि) तेज़ी से बढ़ने (**leaped** या **leapt** (लॅप्ट) *pt./pp.*) *n.* छलांग; अचानक तेज़ी से व द्धि

learn (लर्न) *vt.* सीखना, ज्ञान या शिक्षा प्राप्त करना – *vi.* ज्ञान प्राप्त करना; अध्ययन करना; जान लेना; का तरीका सीखना (**learnt, learned** *pt./pp.*) – **learned** (लर्निड) *a.* विद्वान; पाण्डित्य पूर्ण – **learnedly** *adv.* – **learner** *n.* शिक्षार्थी

lease (लीस) *n.* पट्टा, इजारा – *vt.* पट्टे पर देना या लेना; किराए पर देना या लेना – **lease-hold** *a.* पट्टे पर (दी गयी भूमि) – **new lease of life** नया जीवन

leash (लीश) *n.* कुत्ते को बांधने की चमड़े की पट्टी

least (लीस्ट) *a.* सब से कम – LITTLE का *sup.* – *n.* सब से छोटा – *a./adv.* (मात्रा या परिणाम में) सब से कम

leather (लॅदर) *n.* चमड़ा – **leathery** *n.* चमड़े जैसा

leave[1] (लीव) *vt.* छोड़ना; छोड़कर चले जाना; रखना; रहने देना; सौंपना; वसीयत में देना –

vi. चले जाना; यात्रा पर रवाना होना (**left, leaving**)

leave² *n.* अनुमति; छुट्टी; छुट्टी की अवधि; विदा – **leave of absence** छुट्टी – **leave-taking** *n.* विदा लेने की क्रिया

leaves (लीवूज) LEAF का *pl.*

lecher (ˈलेंचर) *n.* कामुक पुरुष; लम्पट – **lecherous** (ˈलेंचरस) *a.* लम्पट; कामुक – **lechery** *n.* लम्पटता

lectern (ˈलेंक्टर्न) *n.* मंच पर रखा डेस्क (विशे. गिरजाघर में)

lecture (ˈलेंक्चर) *n.* व्याख्यान; सीख या डांट – *vi.* व्याख्यान देना – *vt.* सीख या डांट देना – **lecturer** *n.* प्राध्यापक – **lectureship** *n.* प्राध्यापक का पद

LED light emitting diode का संक्षेप

led (लेंड) LEAD का pt./pp.

ledge (लेंज) *n.* कगार; मेढ़; समुद्र तल के नीचे की कगार

ledger (ˈलेंजर) *n.* बही; बही खाता

lee (ली) *n.* शरण, ओट; जहाज़ का वह बाजू जो हवा से परे हो – **leeway** *n.* जहाज़ का ओट की ओर जाना; गुंजाइश; कमी, कसर

leech (लीच) *n.* जोंक; पैसे के लिए दूसरों पर आश्रित व्यक्ति, जोंक

leek (लीक) *n.* प्याज़ जैसा पौधा, गन्दना

leer (लिअर) *vi.* बुरी नीयत, शरारत या कामुकता से देखना, बुरी नज़र डालना – *n.* बुरी नज़र – **leery** *a.*

lees (लीज़) *pl. n.* (शराब की) तलछट

left¹ (लेंफ्ट) *a.* बांया – *n.* बांया हाथ या अंग; *Politics* वामपक्ष (**left wing** भी) – *adv.* बायें या बाएं ओर – **leftist** *n./a.* वामपक्ष (का सदस्य)

left² LEAVE का *pt./pp.* – **left-over** बचा-खुचा भोजन

leg (लेंग) *n.* टांग, लात; (पतलून आदि का) पांयचा; (मेज़ आदि का) पाया; (यात्रा का) पड़ाव, चरण, भाग – **leggings** *pl. n.* टांगों पर चमड़े का (लम्बी जुराबनुमा) वस्त्र – **leggy** *a.* जिसकी टांगें लम्बी हों, लमढींग

legacy (ˈलेंगसि) *n.* वसीयत द्वारा छोड़ी सम्पत्ति, बपौती, थाती; उत्तराधिकारी को दी गयी वस्तु

legal (ˈलीगल) *a.* कानून का, उस द्वारा नियुक्त या उस पर आधारित, वैध, कानूनी – **legality** (लिˈगैलिटि) *n.* वैधता – **legalization** (लीगलाइ- ˈज़ेशन) *n.* वैधीकरण – **legalize** *vt.* वैध बनाना – **legally** *adv.* वैध तरीके से, कानूनी तौर पर – **legal tender** वैध मुद्रा

legation (लिˈगेशन) *n.* कूटनीतिक प्रतिनिधि और उसके कर्मचारी; उस का निवास स्थान

legend (ˈलेंजंड) *n.* दंतकथा, किंवदंती, परम्परागत साहित्य; प्रसिद्ध व्यक्ति या घटना; लेख या शीर्षक – **legendary** *a.* पौराणिक; परम्परागत; प्रसिद्ध

legible (ˈलेंजिबल) *a.* जिसे आसानी से पढ़ा जा सके – **legibility** *n.* आसानी से पढ़े जा सकने का गुण

legion (ˈलीजन) *n.* प्राचीन रोम में एक बड़ा सैनिक दल; पुराने सैनिकों का संघ; बहुत बड़ी संख्या – **legionary** *a./n.*

legislator (ˈलेंजिस्लेटर) *n.* विधायक – **legislate** *vi.* कानून बनाना – **legislation** (लेंजिस्ˈलेशन) *n.* कानून बनाने की क्रिया; कानून – **legislative** *a.* कानून-संबंधी – **legislature** (ˈलेंजिस्लेचर) *n.* विधानसभा, विधायिका

legitimate (लिˈजिटिमिट) *a.* विवाहित स्त्री-पुरुष की (औलाद), औरस; वैध; नियमानुकूल तर्कसंगत – **legitimacy** *n.* वैधता – **legitimize** *vt.* वैध बनाना

leguminous (लिˈग्यूमिनस) *a.* (पौधे) जिनमें फलियां लगती हों (जैसे दालों के)

leisure (ˊलेंझ़र) *n.* फुरसत, अवकाश; खाली समय – **leisurely** *a.* धीमी – *adv.* धीरे धीरे फुरसत से, धीमी गति से – **leisured** *a.* जिसे फुर्सत ही फुर्सत हो

lemon (ˊलेंमन) *n.* नींबू; उस का पेड़; उस का रंग; *sl.* बेकार की वस्तु या गुणहीन व्यक्ति – **lemonade** *n.* नींबू के रस से बना पेय

lemur (ˊलीमर) *n.* पेड पर रहने वाले, बंदर जैसे जीव

lend (ˊलेंण्ड) *vt.* उधार या किराए पर देना; देना, प्रदान करना **(lent, lending)** – **lender** *n.* साहूकार – **lend an ear to** की बात ध्यान से सुनना – **lend a helping hand** मदद करना

length (लेंङ्थ) *n.* लंबाई; एक सिरे से दूसरे सिरे तक का माप; दूरी; समयावधि; टुकड़ा – **lengthen** *v.* लम्बा करना या होना, बढ़ाना या बढ़ना – **lengthily** *adv.* – **lengthwise** *a./adv.* लम्बाई में – **lengthy** *a.* अधिक लम्बा – **at length** पूरे ब्यौरे सहित; अंततः, आखिरकार

lenient (ˊलीनिअंट) *a.* म दु, नरम; सहिष्णु; सदय, दयालु; ढील देने वाला – **lenience, leniency** *n.* नरमी; सदयता

lens (ˊलेंन्ज़) *n.* कैमरा; एनक और दूरबीन में लगा पारदर्शी कांच का टुकड़ा जो प्रकाश किरणों को केन्द्रित या विकेन्द्रित करता है, लेन्स (*pl.* **lenses**)

lent LEND का *pt./pp.*

Lent (ˊलेंण्ट) *n.* ईस्टर से पहले व्रत रखने की अवधि

lentil (ˊलेंण्टिल) *n.* दाल

Leo (ˊलीओ) *n.* सिंह; पांचवीं राशि जिस की अवधि 23 जुलाई से 22 अगस्त तक होती है

leopard (ˊलेंपर्ड) *n.* तेंदुआ

leper (ˊलेंपर) *n.* कोढ़ी, कुष्ठरोगी; व्यक्ति जिस की उपेक्षा हो या जिस से लोग घ णा करें – **leprosy** (ˊलेप्रसि) *n.* कोढ़, कुष्ठ रोग

lesbian (ˊलेंज़ूबिअन) *n.* स्त्री जो स्त्रियों से काम संबंध रखे, समलिंगकामी स्त्री – **lesbianism** *n.*

lesion (ˊलीझ़न) *n.* घाव; शरीर के किसी अंग की बनावट या कार्य में हानिकारक परिवर्तन

less (लेंस) *a.* LITTLE का *comp.*, कम – *n.* छोटा अंश या मात्रा; छोटा परिमाण – *adv.* कम, थोड़ा – *prep.* घटाने के बाद – **lessen** *vt.* घटाना, कम करना – **lesser** *a.* कम, छोटा; कम महत्व वाला

lessee (लेंˊसी) *n.* जिसे पट्टा दिया गया हो, पट्टेदार

lesson (ˊलेंसन) *n.* पाठ, शिक्षा; सीख

lessor (ˊलेंसर) *n.* पट्टा देने वाला; किराए पर देने वाला

lest (लेंस्ट) *conj.* ऐसा न हो कि

let[1] (लेंट) *vt.* अनुमति देना; होने देना; निकलने देना; पट्टे पर या किराए पर देना – *vi.* किराए पर उठना – *v. aux.* प्रस्ताव, आदेश, धमकी आदि की अभिव्यक्तियों में प्रयुक्त **(let, letting)** – **let-down** *n.* आशा के विपरीत बहुत अधिक निराशा

let[2] *n.* बाधा, रोक टोक; कुछ खेलों (जैसे *tennis*) में गेंद के रोकने या नियमों का उल्लंघन जिस के लिए फिर खेलना पड़ता है

lethal (ˊलीथल) *a.* घातक, जान-लेवा

lethargy (ˊलेंथर्जि) *n.* उपेक्षा भाव; निर्जीवता – **lethargic** (लिˊथार्जिक) *a.* अकर्मण्य, सुस्त

let's Let us का संक्षेप

letter (ˊलेंटर) *n.* अक्षर, वर्ण; पत्र, चिट्ठी; शुद्ध अर्थ, व्याख्या – (~ **s**) *pl.* साहित्य, विद्या – *vt.* अक्षरों में लिखना – **lettered** *a.* विद्धान

lettuce (ˊलेटिस) *n.* सलाद के लिए उगाया पौधा, काहू

let-up *n.* (तीव्रता में) कमी, ढील

leucoma (ल्यूˊकोम्अ) *n.* एक प्रकार का मोतियाबिन्द

leukaemia (ल्यू´कीमिअ) *n.* रोग जिसमें श्वेताणु बढ़ जाते हैं, रक्त-कैंसर

level (´लेंवल) *a.* क्षैतिज; समतल, सपाट – *n.* क्षैतिज रेखा या तल; (**spirit level** भी) तलमापी यंत्र, साधनी; संतुलन; मानक स्तर – *vt.* समतल करना; एक ही तल या स्तर पर लाना; गिराना, ढाना, निशाना साधना (बन्दूक आदि का); *fig.* (आरोप) लगाना – *vi.* (विशे. **be level with** में) *inf.* बराबर के स्तर पर होना – **level crossing** रेलवे का फाटक

lever (´लीवर) *n.* टेक के पास की कड़ी छड़, उत्तोलक; कमानी (जिसे खींच कर यंत्र चलाया जाय) – *vt.* उत्तोलक या कमानी से चलाना या उठाना – **leverage** (´लीवरिज़) *n.* उत्तोलक की शक्ति या क्रिया, उत्तोलन; प्रभाव

leveret (´लेंवरिट) *n.* खरगोश का बच्चा

leviathan (लि´वाइअथन) *n.* विकराल समुद्री जीव; कोई विशालकाय या विकराल वस्तु

levitation (लेंवि´टेशन) *n.* अलौकिक शक्ति से किसी शरीर या पिण्ड को हवा में उठाने की क्षमता – **levitate** (´लेंविटेट) *v.* हवा में उठाना या उठना

levity (´लेंविटि) *n.* गंभीर बातों की हंसी उड़ाने की प्रव त्ति; छिछोरपन, हल्कापन

levy (´लेंवि) *vt.* (कर) लगाना (**levied, levying**) – *n.* कर की राशि

lewd (लूड) *a.* कामुक; अश्लील

lexicon (´लेंक्सिकन) *n.* शब्द कोष – **lexical** *a.* – **lexicographer** (लेंक्सि´कॉग्रफर) *n.* शब्दकोष-रचयिता

liable (´लाइअबल) *a.* जवाबदेह, उत्तरदायी; जिसे खतरा, संभावना आदि हो – **liability** (लाइअ´बि-लिटि) *n.* जवाबदेही, उत्तरदायित्व; बाधा; देयता; असुविधा – **liabilities** *pl. n.* ऋण

liaison (लि´एज़न) *n.* सम्पर्क; संबंध; घनिष्ठता; विवाहित पुरूष व विवाहित स्त्री (जो पति-पत्नी नहीं हैं) के गुप्त संबंध – **liaison officer** सम्पर्क अधिकारी

liar (´लाइअर) *n.* झूठा

lib (लिब) *n. inf.* LIBERATION का संक्षेप

libel (´लाइबल) *n.* लिखित बयान जिस से किसी की मानहानि हो, अपमान लेख

liberal (´लिबरल) *a.* (**L-**भी) राजनीतिक दल का जिसका लोकतांत्रिक सुधारों या व्यक्तिगत स्वतंत्रता में विश्वास हो; उदार, सहिष्णु; प्रचुर; संस्क ति से लगाव उत्पन्न करने वाली (शिक्षा) – *n.* उदार नेता – **liberalization** *n.* उदारीकरण विशे. व्यापार में – **liberalize** *vt.* उदार बनाना – **liberally** *adv.* उदारता से

liberate (´लिबरेट) *vt.* आज़ाद कराना, बंधन से मुक्त कराना – **liberation** *n.* मुक्ति – **liberator** *n.*

liberty (´लिबर्टि) *n.* स्वतंत्रता – (**liberties**) *pl.* अधिकार – **at liberty** स्वतंत्र, (कुछ करने) के लिए स्वतंत्र – **take liberties (with)** से ध ष्टता, गुस्ताखी करना

libido (लि´बीडो) *n.* जीवन शक्ति; काम वासना

Libra (´लाइब्रअ) *n.* तुला; राशिचक्र का सातवां चिन्ह जिस का समय 23 सितम्बर से 22 अक्तूबर है

library (´लाइब्ररि) *n.* पुस्तकालय; पुस्तकों, ग्रामोफोन रिकार्डों का संग्रह; घर में पढ़ने लिखने का कमरा – **librarian** (लाइ´ब्रेंअरिअन) *n.* पुस्तकाध्यक्ष

lice (लाइस) *pl. n.* दे. LOUSE

licence, US license (´लाइसन्स) *n.* लाइसेन्स, अनुज्ञापत्र; स्वेच्छाचारिता, मनमानी; व्याभिचार, लंपटता – **license** *vt.* को लाइसेंस देना – **licensed** *a.* लाइसेंस द्वारा अनुमत, वैध – **licensee** (लाइसन्´सी) *n.* लाइसेंसधारी

licentious (लाइ´सेंन्शस) *a.* व्यभिचारी

lichen (´लाइकन, ´लिचिन) *n.* चट्टानों या पेड़ों के तनों पर (काई के समान) उगने वाले फूलों के छोटे पौधे

lick (लिक) *vt.* चाटना; हल्के से छूना; *sl.* हराना; *sl.* पिटाई करना – *n.* चाटने की क्रिया; रोगन आदि की थोड़ी सी मात्रा; *inf.* गति, रफ्तार – **licking** *n. sl.* पिटाई

licorice (ˈलिकरिस) *n.* देखिए LIQUORICE

lid (लिड) *n.* ढक्कन, पलक; *sl.* हैट या टोपी

lie[1] (लाइ) *vi.* पड़े होना, लेटना; किसी स्थिति में होना; (अस्तित्व) होना; **(lay, lain, lying)**

lie[2] *vi.* झूठ बोलना **(lied, lying)** – *n.* झूठ – **white lie** अहानिकारक झूठ (जिससे किसी का दिल न दुखे)

lien (लिअन, ˈलीअन) *n.* किसी की जमीन जायदाद, ऋण आदि चुकाए जाने तक रखने का अधिकार

lieu (ल्यू) *n.* स्थान – **in lieu of** के बदले में

lieutenant (लेॅफ़् ˈटेॅनंट) *n.* सहायक; *Army* कप्तान से नीचे का अधिकारी; *Navy* (ल ˈटेॅनंट) कमांडर से नीचे का अधिकारी; **US** (ˈलूटेॅनन्ट) पुलिस अधिकारी – **lieutenancy** *n.*

life (लाइफ़) *n.* जीवन, ज़िन्दगी; जीवनकाल; जीवन चर्चा, जीवन चरित, जीवन शैली; प्राण, जान; स्फूर्ति, बल (*pl.* **lives**) – **lifeless** *a.* निर्जीव, मुरदा – **lifelong** *a.* जो जीवन भर रहे – **lifeblood** *n.* प्राण-शक्ति – **life boat** जहाज़ के डूबते लोगों को बचाने के लिए विशेष नाव – **life cycle** जीवन चक्र – **life expectancy** संभावित आयु – **life sentence** आजीवन कारावास का दण्ड – **life style** जीवन शैली

lift (लिफ़्ट) *vt.* उठाना; उठाकर रख देना; उन्नत बनाना; मनःस्थिति सुधारना; *inf.* चुराना, उठा लेना – *vi.* मन: स्थिति सुधरना; (बादल) छटना; उठना – *n.* (भवन में लगी) लिफ़्ट; (सामान आदि) उठाकर ले जाने की क्रिया; कार आदि में सवारी ले जाने की क्रिया, सवारी (देना) – **lift-off** *n.* राकेट, अंतरिक्षयान की उड़ान आरंभ

ligament (ˈलिगमंट) *n.* ऊतकों **(tissues)** का पुंज जो हड्डियों को जोड़ता है, अस्थिबंध – **ligature** (ˈलिगचर) *n.* बंधन, पट्टी; रक्त वाहिनी जोड़ने का धागा

light[1] (लाइट) *a.* हल्का; मदु, सौम्य; आसान, मामूली; (उद्योग) जिस में खपत की वस्तुएं छोटी मशीनों से बनती हो – *adv.* हल्के ढंग से – *vi.* गाड़ी आदि से उतरना; संयोगवश पा लेना **(upon** के साथ प्रयुक्त) **(lighted, lit** *pt./pp.*) – **lighten** *vt.* कम करना, हल्का करना – **lightly** *adv.* – **lightness** *n.* – **light-headed** *a.* जिसे चक्कर आ रहे हों; जो बेहोश होने को हो; प्रलापी – **light-hearted** *a.* जिसे कोई चिन्ता न हो – **light-weight** *n./a.*

light[2] *n.* प्रकाश, रोशनी; दीपक, बत्ती; खिड़की; दष्टिकोण; किसी वस्तु का हल्का या प्रकाशित अंश; जलाने की क्रिया या उस का उपकरण; समझने की क्रिया – (**~ s**) *pl.* सड़कों पर यातायात की बत्तियां – *a.* चमकीला; हल्के रंग का – *vt.* आग लगाना या जलाना; प्रकाशित करना – *vi.* जलने लगना; चमकने लगना **(lighted** *or* **lit** *pt./pp.*) – **lighten** *vt.* प्रकाश देना – **lighting** *n.* प्रकाश या रोशनी देने का उपकरण, रोशनियां – **lightning** *n.* आकाश से गिरने वाली बिजली – **lighthouse** *n.* (जहाज़ों को रास्ता दिखाने का) प्रकाश-स्तंभ

lighter (ˈलाइटर) *n.* सिग्रेट आदि जलाने का उपकरण, लाइटर

like[1] (लाइक) *a.* समान, सदश; अनुसार, अनुरूप; विशिष्ट – *adv.* के समान – *pron.* समान या सदश वस्तु; संभाव्यता – **likelihood** *n.* संभावना – **likely** *a.* शायद – **liken** *vt.* तुलना करना – **likeness** *n.* सदश्यता; प्रतिकति – **likewise** *adv.* उसी प्रकार

like[2] *vt.* पसंद करना, अच्छा समझना; चाहना; में रुचि होना – **likeable** *a.* – **liking** *n.* पसन्द, रुचि; अनुराग, प्रेम

lilac (ˈलाइलक) *n.* हल्के बैंगनी रंग के फूलों वाली झाड़ी, नीलक, बकायन; हल्का बैंगनी रंग – *a.* हल्का बैंगनी

Lilliputian (लिलिˈप्यूशिअन) *a.* छोटे कद का, बौना – *n.* बौना

lilt (लिल्ट) *v.* झूम कर गाना, झूमना – *n.* संगीत की लय पर झूमने की क्रिया – **lilting** *a.*

lily (ˈलिलि) *n.* कुमुदिनी – **lily-white** *a.* शुभ्र

limb (लिम) *n.* बांह या टांग; पक्ष; पेड़ की शाखा

limber *vi.* (ˈलिम्बर) – **limber up** व्यायाम द्वारा सभी मांसपेशियों में लचक लाना

lime[1] (लाइम) *n.* चूना – *vt.* जमीन पर चूना लगाना – **limelight** *n.* तेज़ प्रकाश; प्रचार, प्रसिद्धि – **limestone** *n.* चूने का पत्थर

lime[2] *n.* नींबू जैसा एक खट्टा फल, खट्टा – **lime-juice** *n.* खट्टे नींबू से बना एक पेय

lime[3] *n.* लाइम, खुशबूदार फूलों वाला एक पेड़

limerick (ˈलिमरिक) *n.* पांच पंक्तियों की हास्यपूर्ण कविता; तुक्तक

limit (ˈलिमिट) *n.* सीमा; अंतिम सीमा (समय या क्षेत्र की) – *vt.* सीमित करना; रोकना; सीमाबद्ध करना – **limitation** (लिमिˈटेशन) *n.* परिसीमन, सीमाबंधन – **limitable** (ˈलिमिटबल) *a.* – **limitless** *a.* असीम – **limited company** कंपनी जिसकी देनदारी सीमित हो, लिमिटेड कंपनी

limp[1] (लिम्प) *a.* ढीला, लचलचा; शिथिल – **limply** *adv.* ढीला

limp[2] *vi.* लंगड़ा कर चलना, लंगड़ाना – *n.* लंगड़ाहट

limpid (ˈलिम्पिड) *a.* निर्मल, पारदर्शी

linchpin (ˈलिंच्पिन) *n.* धुरे की कील; व्यक्ति या वस्तु जो अनिवार्य हो

line (लाइन) *n.* रेखा, लकीर, लीक; पंक्ति; कतार; श्रंखला; रास्ता; टेलीफोन का कनेक्शन; क्षेत्र या कार्य; पेशा, व्यवसाय; रेलवे की पटरी; रस्सी; तार; तर्क (*line of argument*); क्षेत्र (*enemy lines*) – *vt.* अस्तर लगाना; रेखांकित करना; पंक्ति में लाना – **lineage** (ˈलिनिइज) *n.* वंश; वंशज – **linear** (ˈलिनिअर) *a.* रेखाकार – **liner** (ˈलाइनर) *n.* जहाज़ या विमान जो यात्री ले जाता हो – **line printer** तेज़ छपाई की मशीन – **in line with sth** के अनुरूप

linen (ˈलिनिन) *a.* सन का बना हुआ – *n.* सन का बना महीन कपड़ा; इस कपड़े की बनी वस्तुएं

linger (ˈलिंगर) *vi.* देर लगाना; इधर उधर डोलना; अधिक समय तक ठहरना

lingerie (ˈलैन्झरि) *n.* स्त्रियों के नीचे या रात को पहनने के वस्त्र

lingua franca (ˈलिंग्वफ्रैंक्अ) *It.* विभिन्न भाषा भाषियों की सांझी भाषा, सम्पर्क भाषा

linguist (ˈलिंग्विस्ट) *n.* भाषाविद्; भाषा विज्ञानी – **linguistic** (लिंग्ˈग्विस्टिक) *a.* – **linguistics** *n.* भाषा-विज्ञान

liniment (ˈलिनिमंट) *n.* लेप करने की औषधि

lining (ˈलाइनिंङ) *n.* अस्तर

link (लिंक) *n.* कड़ी; जोड़, संबंध; दूरी का माप = लगभग **7.92** इंच – *vt.* जोड़ना; संबंध स्थापित करना – *vi.* जुड़ जाना – **linkage** *n.* जोड़

links (लिंक्स) *pl. n.* गोल्फ़ का मैदान

linnet (ˈलिनिट) *n.* तूती की जाति की एक चिड़िया

lino, linoleum (लिˈनोलिअम) *n.* फर्श पर बिछाने का जाजम जो टाट, अल्सी के तेल और काग आदि से बनता है

linseed (ˈलिन्सीड) *n.* अलसी

lint (लिंट) *n.* घावों पर रखने का नरम कपड़ा, सूफ़

lintel (ˈलिंट्ल) *n.* खिड़की या दरवाज़े के ऊपर समस्तरी शहतीर

lion (ˈलाइअन) *n.* शेर, सिंह (**lioness** *fem.*)

lip (लिप) *n.* होंठ, अधर; किनारा; *sl.* गुस्ताखी – **lip service** दिखावटी प्रशंसा या सम्मान – **lipstick** *n.* लिपस्टिक

liqueur (लि'क्युअर) *n.* मीठी शराब

liquid ('लिक्विड) *a.* तरल (पदार्थ); द्रव; प्रवाही; (सम्पत्ति) जो रुपये के रूप में हो, नकदी – *n.* तरल पदार्थ – **liquefaction** (लिक्वि'फ़ैक्शन) *n.* द्रवीकरण – **liquefy** ('लिक्विफ़ाइ), **liquidize** ('लिक्विडाइज़) *v.* तरल बनाना या हो जाना (**liquefied, liquefying**) – **liquidity** *n.* वित्तीय देनदारी पूरी करने की क्षमता

liquidate ('लिक्विडेट) *vt.* ऋण आदि चुका कर (कम्पनी को) समाप्त करना; समाप्त करना; मार डालना – **liquidation** *n.* (कम्पनी आदि) समाप्त करने की प्रक्रिया; दिवालिया होने की स्थिति – **liquidator** *n.* कम्पनी आदि को समाप्त करने के लिए नियुक्त अधि ाकारी

liquor ('लिकर) *n.* शराब

liquorice ('लिकरिस), *US,* **licorice** *n.* मुलैठी; उस का पौधा, गुंजा

lira (लिअर्अ, 'लीर्अ) *n.* इटली और तुर्की का सिक्का (*pl.* **-re, -ras**)

lisp (लिस्प) *v.* तुतलाना ('ज़' और 'स' का गलत उच्चारण करना) – *n.* तुतलाहट

lissom ('लिसम) *a.* लचीला; फुर्तीला

list¹ (लिस्ट) *n.* सूची, तालिका – *vt.* सूची में लिखना

list² *vi.* (जहाज़ का) एक ओर झुकना – *n.* जहाज़ का झुकाव

listen ('लिसन) *vi.* कान लगा कर सुनना, (की बात) ध्यान से सुनना – **listener** *n.* श्रोता

listless ('लिस्ट्लिस) *a.* उदासीन; निर्जीव, निरुत्साह – **listlessly** *adv.*

lit LIGHT का *pt./pp.*

literal ('लिटरल) *a.* शाब्दिक; यथातथ्य; अक्षरों से संबंधित – **literally** *adv.* अक्षरशः

literate ('लिटरिट) *a.* पढ़ा-लिखा, साक्षर – *n.* साक्षर व्यक्ति – **literacy** ('लिटरसि) *n.* साक्षरता

literature ('लिटरिचर) *n.*) साहित्य; किसी भी विषय/वस्तु पर विस्त त लिखित (या छपी हुई) जानकारी – **literary** *a.* साहित्यिक

lithe (लाइद) *a.* लचीला; लचकीला – **lithesome** *a.* लचीला, फुरतीला

lithography (लि'थॉग्रफ़ि) *n.* धातु की प्लेट या पत्थर की सिल से छपाई की विधि – **lithograph** ('लिथग्राफ़) *n.* इस प्रकार छपा कागज़, चित्र आदि – *vt.* इस प्रकार छपाई करना

litigant ('लिटिगंट) *a./n.* मुकदमा करने वाला, वादी – **litigation** *n.* मुकदमा; मुकदमेबाज़ी

litmus ('लिट्मस) *n.* नीला रंग जो तेज़ाब पड़ने पर लाल हो जाता है और क्षार से फिर नीला, लिटमस – **litmus paper** इस रंग से बना कागज़ जो प्रयोगशाला में प्रयुक्त होता है

litotes ('लाइटोटीज़) *n.* (*understatement*) पर्यायोक्ति

litre ('लीटर) *n.* लिटर

litter ('लिटर) *n.* कूड़ा-कचरा; बेकार की टूटी-फूटी वस्तुएं; पशुओं का झोल (एक ही बार में जन्मे बच्चे); घायलों को ले जाने की डांडी – *vt.* (जगह) पर कूड़ा करकट बिखेरना; (पशु का) बच्चे देना – **litter bin** कूड़ेदान

little ('लिट्ल) *a.* छोटा; थोड़ा (*comp.* **less,** *sup.* **least**) – *n.* थोड़ा सा – *adv.* मामूली तौर पर

littoral ('लिटरल) *a.* समुद्र तट का – *n.* तटीय प्रदेश

live¹ (लिव़) *v.* जीना, जीवित रहना; जीवन बिताना; बने रहना; चलते या जारी रहना; निवास करना; (खा कर) जीना – **liveable, livable** *a.* जीने योग्य – **living** *n.* जीवित रहने की क्रिया; जीवित लोग; जीवन शैली; जीवन का उपाय, रोज़गार या काम

live² (लाइव़) *a.* जीवित; सक्रिय; ओजस्वी; जलता हुआ; लाइन आदि जिसमें बिजली हो; (*bomb*) जो फट सके; (प्रसारण) जो घटना के साथ-साथ

प्रसारित किया जाय; चर्चित (विषय) – **lively** *a.* सजीव, फुर्तीला; सक्रिय; चमकीला – **liveliness** *n.* ज़िन्दादिली, फुरती – **liven** *vt.* (विशे. **up** के साथ) जान डाल देना, सजीव बना देना – **live-in** (ʹलाव-इन) *a.* सहवासी (बिना विवाह के : *live-in lover*) – **livestock** (ʹलाइव्स्टॉक) *n.* मवेशी – **live wire** (ʹलाइव् वाइअर) तार जिसमें बिजली हो; उत्साही, व्यक्ति – **living death** मौत से बदतर ज़िन्दगी – **living hell** पृथ्वी पर नरक – **living wage** निर्वाह वेतन/मज़दूरी

livelihood (ʹलाइव्लिहुड) *n.* रोज़ी, आजीविका; सहारा

liver (ʹलिव़र) *n.* जिगर

livery (ʹलिव़रि) *n.* वरदी, विशे. नौकरों की

livid (ʹलिव़िड) *a.* सुरमई रंग का; नीले धब्बे जैसा जो गुमटे से पड़ता है; *inf.* बहुत नाराज़, लाल पीला

lizard (ʹलिज़र्ड) *n.* छिपकली

llama (ʹलाम्अ) *n.* दक्षिण अमरीका का छोटे आकार के ऊट जैसा एक लद्दू ढोर

LL.B. Bachelor of Laws का संक्षेप

load (लोड) *n.* बोझ, भार, बोझा; खेप, (माल की) लदान; (प्रयोग में ली जाने वाली बिजली का) भार – *vt.* डालना, (बंदूक आदि में) गोली भरना; (कैमरे में) रील भरना; *Computers* कम्प्युटर में आंकड़े/प्रोग्राम डालना, लोड करना – **loaded** *a.* जिस पर माल लदा हो, भरा; पक्षपात पूर्ण; (प्रश्न) जिसमें प्रश्नकर्ता का पूर्वाग्रह झलकता हो या जिससे जवाब देने वाला फंस सके

loadstar, -stone *n.* देखिए LODE

loaf[1] (लोफ़) *n.* डबलरोटी, पावरोटी (*pl.* **loaves** (लोव्ज़))

loaf[2] *vi.* इधर उधर घूमना, आवारागर्दी करना – **loafer** *n.* आवारागर्द

loam (लोम) *n.* उर्वरा भूमि, दुमट

loan (लोन) *n.* कर्ज़ा, उधार; उधार दी गयी वस्तु – *vt.* उधार देना – **loan word** दूसरी भाषा से लिया गया शब्द

lo(a)th (लोथ) *a.* अनिच्छुक – **loathe** (लोद) *vt.* घृणा करना, नफरत करना – **loathing** (ʹलोदिङ) *n.* घृणा – **loathsome** (ʹलोद्सम) *a.* घृणित

lob (लॉब) *n.* (टेनिस आदि खेलों में) गेन्द को बहुत ऊंचे उछालने की क्रिया; (पत्थर आदि) फेंकना – *vt.* गेंद को ऊंचे उछालना (**-bb-**)

lobby (ʹलॉबि) *n.* कमरों के आगे का बरामदा; (विधानसभा में) सभा भवन तक का रास्ता, व्यक्तियों का समूह जो संसद सदस्यों को प्रभावित करने की चेष्टा करे

lobe (लोब) *n.* गोलाई में बाहर को निकला भाग; शरीर के अंग का भाग; कान के नीचे लटकता मांस, लोलकी, ललरी

lobster (लॉब्स्टर) *n.* समुद्री झींगा मछली

local (ʹलोकल) *a.* स्थानीय; किसी क्षेत्र, शरीर के अंग तक सीमित; किसी स्थान का – *n.* किसी स्थान विशेष का निवासी – **locale** (लोʹकाल) *n.* घटनास्थल – **locality** (लोʹकैलिटि) *n.* स्थान; बस्ती, इलाका – **localize** (ʹलोकलाइज) *vt.* किसी स्थान तक सीमित करना – **locally** *adv.* – **local call** स्थानीय टेलीफोन

locate (लोʹकेट) *vt.* पता लगाना; स्थान निर्धारित करना; रखना, स्थापित करना – **location** (लोʹकेशन) *n.* स्थान निर्धारण; स्टुडिओ से परे स्थान जहां चलचित्र बनाया जाता है

lock[1] (लॉक) *n.* ताला; (बन्दूक का) घोड़ा; (नहर आदि में) जलपाश, बांध; पहिया घूमने से रोकने का उपकरण, कांटा, दो उपकरणों का बंधन; अवरोध, रोक – *vt.* ताला लगाना; ताले वाले बॉक्स आदि में रखना; जोड़ या बांध देना; स्थिर कर देना; बाहों में जकड़ लेना – *vi.* (दरवाज़े आदि का) ताला बंद हो जाना; जुड़ या बंध जाना – **locker** *n.* (बैंक में) बहुमूल्य वस्तुएं रखने का छोटा खाना जिसमें ताला लगा हो – **lockjaw** *n.* एक रोग जिसमें मांस पेशियां जकड़ जाती हैं, धुनक-बाई – **lockout** *n.* मालिकों द्वारा

तालाबंदी – **locksmith** *n.* तालों का मिस्तरी – **lockup (garage)** हवालात; गराज; गोदाम जो मुख्य भवन से परे हो

lock[2] *n.* बालों की लट, गुच्छा

locket (´लॉकिट) *n.* लॉकेट

locomotive (लोक´मोटिव़) *n.* रेलवे इंजन – *a.* संचलनशील – **locomotion** *n.* गति क्रिया

locus (´लोकस) *n.* स्थान या बस्ती; बिन्दुओं या रेखाओं की स्थिति; बिन्दुपथ (*pl.* **loci** (´लोसाइ))

locust (´लोकस्ट) *n.* टिड्डी

lode (´लोड) *n.* खान में धातु-रेखा – **lodestar** *n.* ध्रुव तारा – **lodestone** *n.* चुम्बक पत्थर

lodge (लॉज) *n.* मकान या कोठड़ी जो कभी कभी प्रयुक्त हो; वन के रक्षक की कोठड़ी – *vt.* मकान में रहने की व्यवस्था करना; जमा करना, (किसी के विरुद्ध शिकायत या आरोप) दर्ज कराना – *vi.* किसी के घर में किराया देकर रहना; आ टिकना (**in, on** -के साथ) – **lodger** *n.* किराएदार – **lodgings** *pl. n.* किराए के कमरे (किसी दूसरे के मकान में)

loft (लॉफ्ट) *n.* अटारी; गिरजाघर की दीर्घा या गैलरी – *vt.* (गेंद) ऊंची उछाल देना – **loftily** *adv.* घमंड से – **loftiness** *n.* – **lofty** *a.* बहुत ऊंचा; घमण्डी, अहंकारी

log[1] (लॉग) *n.* लकड़ी का लट्ठा या कुन्दा; रोज़नामचा (विमान, जहाज़ आदि की यात्रा का) – *vt.* रिकार्ड या अभिलेख रखना; (निश्चित दूरी) तय करना; समय लगाना (यात्रा में) (**-gg-**) – **logger** *n.* लकड़हारा – **logbook** *n.* यात्रा का रोज़नामचा

log[2] *n.* **logarithm** का संक्षेप

logarithm (´लॉगरिदम) *n.* लघुगणक – **logarithmic** (लॉग´रिद्‌मिक) *a.*

loggerhead (´लॉगरहेड) *n.* – **at loggerheads** (से) अनबन या झगड़ा

logic (´लॉजिक) *n.* तर्क; तर्क शास्त्र; तर्क संगत दलील या विचार – **logical** *a.* तर्क का; तर्क संगत; ठीक तर्क देने वाला

logistics (लॉ´जिस्‌टिक्स) *pl. n.* (*sing.* या *pl. v.* के साथ) सैनिक ले जाने, ठहरने और भोजन आदि की व्यवस्था; संभारतंत्र; किसी भी परियोजना का संगठन या संचालन – **logistical** *a.* संभारतंत्र-संबंधी

logo (´लोगो) *n.* कम्पनी आदि का चिह्न; प्रतीक-चिह्न

loin (लॉइन) *n.* कमर, कटि; इस अंग का मांस – *pl.* कमर और नितम्ब – **loin cloth** धोती, लुंगी; लंगोटी

loiter (´लॉइटर) *vi.* बेमतलब इधर-उधर घूमना, आवारा फिरना – **loiterer** *n.* आवारागर्द

loll (लॉल) *vi.* आराम से बैठे या लेटे रहना; (जीभ का) बाहर को लटकना

lollipop (´लॉलिपॉप) *n.* लकड़ी की तीली से चिपकाई मीठी गोली

lolly (´लॉलि) *n. inf.* लॉलीपॉप या कुल्फी; *sl.* रुपया-पैसा

lone (लोन) *a.* अकेला – **lonely** *a.* एकाकी होने के कारण उदास; सुनसान (स्थान); अकेला – **loneliness** *n.* एकाकीपन – **loner** *n. inf.* व्यक्ति जो अकेले रहना या काम करना पसंद करे – **lonesome** *a.*

long[1] (´लॉङ) *a.* लम्बा (दूरी या समय में); दीर्घ; व्यापक; जो देर तक चले – *adv.* लम्बे समय तक – **long-awaited** *a.* जिसकी देर से प्रतीक्षा हो – **long-distance** *a.* दूर की (टेलीफोन काल, गाड़ी) – **longhand** *n.* शब्द, पत्र आदि हाथ से लिखने की क्रिया – **long-range** *a.* भविष्य का; (विमान आदि) जो एक बार ईंधन लेकर लम्बी दूरी तय कर सके; हथियार जो दूर तक मार करे – **long-winded** *a.* लम्बी चौड़ी और ऊबाऊ बातें करने वाला

long² *vi.* लालायित होना, तरसना – **longing** *n.* लालसा

longevity (लॉन्'जेंविटि) *n.* लम्बी आयु

longitude ('लॉन्जिट्यूड) *n.* शून्य रेखांश से पूर्व या पश्चिम की दूरी, देशान्तर रेखांश – **longitudinal** *a.* देशान्तरीय; लम्बाई का

loo (लू) *n. inf.* शौचालय

look (लुक) *vi.* देखना; नज़र डालना; सामना करना; दीखना या लगना; टटोलना या ढूंढना (*for* के साथ); आशा करना (*for* के साथ); देखभाल करना (*after* के साथ) – *n.* दृष्टि, नज़र; दृश्य; तलाश; (बहुधा *pl.*) रूपरंग – **good looks** सौन्दर्य – **lookalike** *n.* व्यक्ति, जिसकी शक्ल किसी दूसरे से बिल्कुल मिलती हो – **lookout** *n.* चौकसी; पहरेदार; पहरे या निगरानी का स्थान; आशा या संभावना – **look after** देखभाल करना – **look forward to** की उत्सुकता से प्रतीक्षा करना – **look into** जांच करना

loom¹ (लूम) *n.* करघा (कपड़े बुनने का)

loom² *vi.* धुंधला दिखाई देना; छाया सी दीखना

loop ('लूप) *n.* फंदा, फांद, पाश; छल्ला; गर्भ-निरोधक उपकरण; विमान की गोलाई में उड़ान – *v.* फंदा या छल्ला बनाना

loophole ('लूप्होल) *n.* बच निकलने का साधन; नियम से बचने की क्रिया बिना उस का उल्लंघन किए; दीवार में छेद जहां से बन्दूक, तोप आदि दागी जा सके

loose ('लूस) *a.* ढीला; अस्पष्ट; लम्पट – *vt.* ढीला करना; खोलना – **loosely** *adv.* बिना विचारे – **loosen** *vt.* ढीला करना – **looseness** *n.* ढीलापन – **loose change** रेज़गारी, छुट्टा

loot ('लूट) *n.* लूट का माल – *vt.* लूटना

lop ('लॉप) *vt.* (पेड़ की टहनियां) काटना; छांटना; काट देना **(-pp-)**

loquacious (लॉ'क्वेशस) *a.* बातूनी

loquat ('लोक्वाट) *n.* लोकाट (फल)

lord (लॉर्ड) *n.* ब्रिटेन का सामन्त; की उपाधि, लार्ड; जागीरदार; मालिक; **(L-)** ईश्वर – *vi.* हुक्म चलाना, रोब छांटना – **lordly** *a.* गर्वीला, घमण्डी; भव्य; लार्ड के अनुकूल

lore (लॉर) *n.* जानकारी; दंतकथा; जनश्रुति

lorry ('लॉरि) *n.* **UK** माल ढोने का ट्रक

lose (लूज़) *vt.* हार जाना, से वंचित हो जाना, खो बैठना; इस्तेमाल न कर सकना या अपने पास न रख सकना; गंवा देना; पा न सकना; (घड़ी आदि का कुछ समय) पीछे रहना – *vi.* हानि उठाना (**lost** *pt./pp.*, **losing** *pr. p.*) – **loser** *n.* हारने वाला – **loss** *n.* हानि, घाटा; खोने की क्रिया; खोई वस्तु; क्षति – **lost** *a.* जो गुम हो गया हो, खोया हुआ; भटका हुआ; हारा हुआ; अप्रयुक्त – **loss-making** *a.* घाटे वाली (कम्पनी) – **get lost!** दफा हो जाओ!

lot ('लॉट) *pron.* बड़ी संख्या – *n.* समूह, ढेर; बहुत बड़ी मात्रा; हिस्सा; भाग्य; नीलामी की वस्तु; पर्ची (जिसे डाल कर किसी बात का निर्णय हो); भूमि का टुकड़ा – *pl. inf.* बहुत अधिक संख्या या मात्रा – *adv. inf.* बहुत अधिक

lotion ('लोशन) *n.* लोशन

lottery ('लॉटरि) *n.* लाटरी; जुआ

lotus ('लोटस) *n.* एक काल्पनिक पौधा जिसका फल खा कर व्यक्ति सब कुछ भूल जाता है; कमल (का फूल)

loud (लाउड) *a.* ऊंचा (स्वर); कोलाहल पूर्ण; चटकीला (रंग आदि) – **loudly** *adv.* ऊंचे स्वर में, जोर से – **loud mouth** *n. inf.* ज़्यादा बोलने वाला व्यक्ति

lounge ('लाउंज) *vi.* आराम से बैठना, लेटना, चलना – *n.* हवाई अड्डे, होटल आदि में लोगों के आराम से बैठने का स्थान

louse (लाउस) *n.* जूं (*pl.* **lice** (लाइस)) – **lousy** ('लाउज़ि) *a.* घिनौना; *sl.* बहुत अमीर, रईस; *sl.* घटिया; जूं भरा

lout (लाउट) *n.* असभ्य, गंवारू व्यक्ति

louvre *n.* (`लूव़र) *n.* (दरवाज़े, खिड़की पर) झिलमिली

love (लव़) *n.* प्रेम, स्नेह; दानशीलता; (*passion*) काम; प्रेमी या प्रेमिका; *Tennis etc.* शून्य का स्कोर – *v.* प्यार करना; पसंद करना – **lov(e)able** *a.* प्यारा – **loveliness** *n.* सौन्दर्य – **lovely** *a.* सुन्दर, चारु – **lover** *n.* प्रेमी/प्रेमिका – **make love (to)** के साथ संभोग करना

low[1] (लो) *a.* नीचा; निचले स्तर का; साधारण; दीन; गंवारू, निराश; बीमार; मद्धिम (**lower** *comp.* **lowest** *sup.*) – **lower** *vt.* नीचे कर देना, नीचे आने देना, उतारना; दर्जा घटाना, मात्रा मे कम कर देना – *a.* दर्जे में निचला; विकास के प्रारंभिक काल का – **lowliness** *n.* – **lowly** *a.* नीचा, निम्न; दीन – **lowbrow** *n./a.* जिसे पढ़ने लिखने या संस्क ति के मामलों में कोई रुचि न हो – **low-cut** *a.* (स्त्रियों का ब्लाउज़ आदि) जिसका गला बहुत बड़ा हो – **low-key** *a.* मद्धिम स्वर में; संयत तरीके से – **low-tension** *a.* बिजली का तार या उपकरण जिसमें वोल्टेज कम हो

low[2] (लो) *vi.* (गाय आदि का) रंभाना – *n.*

loyal (`लॉइअल) *a.* निष्ठावान, वफ़ादार; स्वामिभक्त – **loyalist** *n.* राजभक्त – **loyally** *adv.* – **loyalty** *n.* निष्ठा; वफादारी

lozenge (`लॉज़िंज) *n.* चूसने की मीठी गोली; दवा की चूसने की गोली

LSD lysergic acid diethylamide (एक नशीली दवा) का संक्षेप

Lt. Lieutenant का संक्षेप

Ltd. Limited (Liability) का संक्षेप

lubricate (`लूब्रिकेट) *vt.* तेल या ग्रीस डालना, चिकना करना – **lubricant** (`लूब्रिकंट) *n.* चिकना बनाने के लिए प्रयुक्त पदार्थ, स्नेहक – **lubrication** (लूब्रि`केशन) *n.*

lucid (`लूसिड) *a.* स्पष्ट; सुबोध, जो आसानी से समझ में आ जाय; स्वस्थचित्त (जो पागल न हो) – **lucidity** *n.* स्पष्टता

luck (लक) *n.* भाग्य, नियति; संयोग – **luckily** *adv.* सौभाग्यवश – **luckless** *a.* बदकिस्मत – **lucky** *a.* सौभाग्यशाली व्यक्ति

lucrative (`लूक्रटिव़) *a.* आर्थिक द ष्टि से बहुत लाभदायक

ludicrous (`लूडिक्रस) *a.* बेतुका; हास्यास्पद

ludo (`लूडो) *n.* एक खेल

lug[1] (लग) *vt.* जोर लगा कर घसीटना – *vi.* घसीट कर ले जाना (**-gg-**)

lug[2] *n.* मूठ या पकड़; *inf.* कान

luggage (`लगिज) *n.* यात्री का सामान

lugubrious (लु`गूब्रिअस) *a.* निराशामय

lukewarm (`लूक्वॉर्म) *a.* गुनगुना; उपेक्षाशील; शिथिल

lull (`लल) *vt.* शांत करना; चुप कराना – *vi.* चुप या शांत हो जाना – *n.* तूफान के दौरान थोड़े समय के लिए शांति या सन्नाटा – **lullaby** (`ललबाई) *n.* लोरी

lumber (`लम्बर) *n.* काठ-कबाड़; कचरा; कटी हुई इमारती लकड़ी *vi.* बेढंगे तरीके से चलना

luminous (`लूमिनस) *a.* चमकीला, प्रकाशमान – **luminary** *n.* प्रकाण्ड विद्वान – **luminosity** (लूमि`नॉसिटि) *n.* दीप्ति, ज्योति

lump (लम्प) *n.* ढेला, पिंड; गुमटा, सूजन – *vt.* (**lump together** भी) ढेर लगा देना, गड्डमड्ड कर देना – *vi.* घिसट कर आगे बढ़ना – **lumpish** *a.* ऊबड़-खाबड़; जिसमें ढेले हों – **lump sum** इकट्ठी/एकमुश्त रकम

lumpen (लम्पन) *a.* अनपढ़, गरीब (मज़दूर)

lunar (`लूनर) *a.* चांद का या उससे संबंधित

lunatic (`लूनटिक) *a.* पागल – *n.* पागल आदमी – **lunacy** (`लूनसि) *n.* पागलपन

lunch (लंच) *n.* दोपहर का खाना – *v.* दोपहर का खाना खाना या किसी को

खिलाना – **luncheon** (ˈलंचन) *n.* दोपहर का भोजन

lung (लंग) *n.* फेफड़ा

lunge (लंज) *vi.* (**lunge forward** भी) तलवार आदि से झपटना – *n.* झपटने की क्रिया, झपट्टा

lupin (ˈलूपिन) *n.* फलीदार पौधा जिस की लम्बी नालों पर फूल लगते हैं

lurch (लर्च) *n.* अचानक एक ओर झुक जाने की क्रिया – *vi.* लड़खड़ाना – **leave in the lurch** कठिनाई, मुसीबत में छोड़ देना

lure (ल्युअर) *n.* प्रलोभन; चारा (मछली पकड़ने का) – *vt.* लुभाना, आक ष्ट करना

lurid (ˈलुअरिड) *a.* भयंकर, डरावने (ब्यौरे वाला) – **luridly** *adv.*

lurk (लर्क) *vi.* घात में बैठना; छिपे रहना – **lurking** *a.* (सन्देह) जो स्पष्ट न हो

luscious (ˈलशस) *a.* मीठा, रसीला; अत्यधिक आकर्षक

lush[1] (लश) *a.* हरी भरी (घास, पौधे); सुंदर, आरामदेह व महंगा (मकान आदि)

lust (लस्ट) *n.* अत्यधिक तीव्र कामेच्छा; लालसा; उत्कण्ठा – *vi.* अत्यधिक लालसा होना – **lustful** *a.* कामुक, कामातुर – **lustily** *adv.* उत्साह से, ज़ोर-ज़ोर से (ताली बजाना आदि) – **lusty** *a.* स्वस्थ, ओजस्वी

lustre (ˈलस्टर) *n.* चमक, कांति; ख्याति; चमकदार सामग्री – **lustrous** *a.* चमकदार, मुलायम

lute[1] (लूट, ल्यूट) *n.* वीणा जैसा वाद्य

luxury (ˈलक्शरि) *n.* भोग विलास की वस्तुएं और उन का प्रयोग; ऐश्वर्य की वस्तु (जो जीवन के लिए अनिवार्य न हो), सुख साधन; विषय सुख – **luxuriance** (लग्ˈज़्युअरिअंस) *n.* प्रचुरता – **luxuriant** *a.* – **luxuriantly** *adv.* – **luxuriate** (लग्ˈज़्युअरिएट) *vi.* भोग विलास करना; किसी बात का आनंद लेना – **luxurious** (लग्ˈज़्युअरिअस) *a.* विलास प्रिय; ठाठदार, राजसी – **luxuriously** *adv.*

Lycra (ˈलाइक्र) *n.* R एक क त्रिम कपड़ा जो खिंच सकता है व चुस्तु वस्त्र बनाने में प्रयुक्त होता है

lying (ˈलाइंग) **LIE** का *pr. p.*

lymph (लिम्फ़) *n.* शरीर का श्वेत रक्त कण युक्त रंगहीन द्रव, लसीका – **lymphatic** (लिम्ˈफ़ैटिक) *a.*

lynch (लिंच) *vt.* बिना मुकदमा चलाए मार डालना; भीड़ का कथित अपराधी को मार डालना

lyre (लाइअर) *n.* वीणा जैसा एक वाद्य – **lyric(al)** (ˈलिरिकल) *a.* गीत काव्य; गाए जाने योग्य – **lyric** (ˈलिरिक) *n.* गीत – **lyrics** *pl.* लोकप्रिय गीत के शब्द

M

m metre(s) का संक्षेप
MA Master of Arts का संक्षेप
macabre (म´काबर) *a.* घिनौना, वीभत्स
macaroni (मैक´रोनि) *n.* मैदे का नलियों के आकार का खाद्य पदार्थ (*pl.* **-ni(es)**)
macaw (म´कॉ) *n.* तोते की एक जाति
mace[1] (मेस) *n.* चोब (पद का चिह्न); गदा
mace[2] (मेस) *n.* जावित्री (एक मसाला)
Mach (number) (मैक) *n.* ध्वनि की गति का विमान की गति से अनुपात
machination (मैकि´नेशन) *n.* (बहुधा ~ s *pl.*) षड़यंत्र, साज़िश
machine (म´शीन) *n.* यंत्र, मशीन; नियंत्रक संगठन; उपकरण – *vt.* यंत्र से सीना, छापना या बनाना – **machinery** *n.* मशीन के कल पुर्जे; मशीनें – **machinist** *n.* मिस्तरी, कारीगर – **machine gun** मशीन गन
machismo (मै´किज़्मो) *n.* अत्यधिक पुरुषोचित गर्व; – **macho** (´मैचो) *a.* पुरुष होने में गर्व का सूचक या उस का प्रदर्शन, मर्द – *n.* (*pl.* **-os.**)
mackerel (´मैकरल) *n.* एक समुद्री मछली, बांगड़ा
mackintosh (´मैकिंटॉश) *n.* (रबड़ मिले कपड़े का) बरसाती कोट
mad (मैड) *a.* पागल; उत्तेजित; किसी बात के बारे में अत्याधिक उत्साही; आगबबूला – **madden** *vt.* पागल सा कर देना
madam (´मैडम) *n.* स्त्री के लिए सम्मानसूचक सम्बोधन
madcap (´मैड्कैप) *n.* दुस्साहसी या सिरफिरा व्यक्ति – *a.*
made MAKE का *pt./pp.*
Madonna (म´डॉन्अ) *n.* कुमारी मरियम
maestro (´माइस्ट्रो) *n.* सर्वश्रेष्ठ संगीतज्ञ; किसी भी कला का श्रेष्ठ कलाकार; आचार्य
Mafia (´मैफ़िअ´*US* माफ़िअ) *n.* गुप्त अन्तर्राष्ट्रीय अपराधी संगठन जो इटली में प्रारंभ हुआ था
magazine (मैग´ज़ीन) *n.* पत्रिका; रिसाला; बन्दूक की गोलियों का पुंज, मैगज़ीन; गोला बारूद रखने का भण्डार, बारूदखाना
magenta (म´जेंण्ट्अ) *n./a.* ललाई लिए गहरा बैंगनी रंग (या उस का)
maggot (´मैगट) *n.* कई प्रकार के कीड़ों का प्रारंभिक रूप
magic (´मैजिक) *n.* जादू, जादूगरी; मायाजाल; जादू-टोना – *a.* जादुई – **magical** *a.* जादुई, मायिक – **magically** *adv.* – **magician** *n.* जादूगर; ऐन्द्रजालिक; बाज़ीगर – **magic wand** जादू की छड़ी
magistrate (´मैजिस्ट्रेट) *n.* मैजिस्ट्रेट – **magisterial** (मैजि´स्टिअरिअल) *a.* दण्डाधिकारी से सम्बन्धित या उस का; अधिनायकों जैसा
magnanimous (मैग्´नैनिमस) *a.* उदार, दानशील, विशाल हृदय – **magnanimity** (मैग्न´निमिटि) *n.* उदारता
magnate (´मैग्नेट) *n.* प्रभावशाली या धनी व्यक्ति
magnesium (मैग्´नीज़िअम) *n.* एक धातु का तत्व, मैग्नीज़ियम – **magnesia** (मैग्´नीश्अ) *n.* इससे बना चूर्ण जो दवाओं में पड़ता है
magnet (´मैग्निट) *n.* चुम्बक; चुम्बक पत्थर – **magnetic** (मैग्´नैटिक) *a.* चुम्बकीय – **magnetically** *adv.* – **magnetism** (´मैग्निटिज़्म) *n.* चुम्बकत्व; आकर्षण – **magnetization** (मैग्निटाइ´ज़ेशन) *n.* –

magnetize (ˈमैग्निटाइज़) *vt.* चुम्बकत्व प्रदान करना (किसी धातु आदि को) – **magnetic tape** प्लास्टिक का फीता जिस पर ध्वनि या दृश्य रिकार्ड किए जा सकते हैं

magnificent (मैग्ˈनिफ़िसंट) *a.* भव्य; शानदार; उत्कृष्ट – **magnificence** (मैग्ˈनिफ़िसन्स) *n.* वैभव, शान

magnify (ˈमैग्निफ़ाइ) *vt.* बढ़ाना (आकार आदि का); बढ़ा-चढ़ा कर कहना – **magnification** *n.* आवर्धन; प्रशंसा – **magnifier** *n.* आवर्धक – **magnifying glass** आवर्धक लेन्स

magnitude (ˈमैग्निट्यूड) *n.* महत्व; विस्तार

magnolia (मैग्ˈनोलिअ) *n.* चम्पा की झाड़ी या पेड़; इसके फूल

magpie (ˈमैग्पाइ) *n.* एक पक्षी, मुटरी

mahogany (मˈहॉगनि) *n.* आबनूस (का पेड़)

maiden (ˈमेड्न) *n.* कुंवारी युवती – *a.* कुंवारी; पहली बार; जिसमें कुछ काम न हुआ हो – **maid** *n. Literary* कुंवारी, युवा नौकरानी – **maidenly** *a.* कुमारी सुलभ – **maiden name** विवाह से पहले स्त्री का कुल नाम – **maiden over** *Cricket* ओवर जिसमें कोई रन न बना हो

mail¹ (मेल) *n.* डाक; एक बार ले जाई चिट्ठियां; डाक-व्यवस्था; तेज़ रेलगाड़ी – *vt.* डाक से भेजना – **mailbox** *n.* **US** घर के बाहर लगा डाकिये द्वारा पत्र डालने का डिब्बा

mail² (मेल) *n.* कवच, ज़रहबख्तर – **mailed** *a.* जिस पर कवच चढ़ा हो

maim (मेम) *vt.* अपंग कर देना; बिगाड़ना

main (मेन) *a.* मुख्य; प्रमुख–*n.* (**mains** भी) पानी का मुख्य पाइप; बिजली की तार जिससे घरों आदि में बिजली पहुंचती है; मुख्य अंग – **mainly** *adv.* मुख्यतया – **mainland** *n.* भूमि जो देश के क्षेत्र का मुख्य भाग हो – **main line** *n.* मुख्य रेल रास्ता – **mainspring** *n.* घड़ी की बड़ी कमानी; मुख्य कारण या प्रेरणा – **mainstay** *n.* मुख्य आधार – **mainstream** *n.* मुख्य

maintain (मेन्ˈटेन) *vt.* जारी रखना; सहारा देना; चालू रखना; भरण पोषण करना; दावा करना या निश्चयपूर्वक कहना – **maintenance** (ˈमेंटिनन्स) *n.* भरण पोषण; मकानों आदि का रख-रखाव; तलाक के बाद पत्नी को मिलने वाला गुज़ारा भत्ता

maize (मेज़) *n.* मकई, मक्का

majesty (ˈमैजिस्टि) *n.* वैभव, तेज; प्रभुत्व, राज-सत्ता; शान-शौकत – **majestic** (मˈजेस्टिक) *a.* राजसी; वैभवशाली – **majestically** *adv.*

major (ˈमेजर) *n.* सेना के कप्तान से बड़ा पद; संगीत में सरगम; **US** विश्व विद्यालय में अध्ययन का मुख्य विषय; वयस्क व्यक्ति – *vi.* **US** (अध्ययन के लिए मुख्य विषय में) अध्ययन समाप्त करना – *a.* मुख्य, प्रधान – **majority** (मˈजॉरिटि) *n.* अधिकांश, प्रमुख दल बहुमत; वयस्कता

make (मेक) *vt.* बनाना, निर्माण करना; उत्पन्न करना; स्थापित करना; नियुक्त करना; के बराबर होना; करवाना; पहुंचना; कमाना; तैयार करना, सजाना – *vi.* रुझान होना; सहायक होना (**made, making**) – *n.* किस्म, प्रकार या शैली – **make-believe** *n.* कल्पना – **make-over** *n.* कायापलट – **makeshift** *n.* अस्थायी, कार्यसाधक – **make-up** *n.* बनाव सिंगार की वस्तुएं; विशेषताएं; बनावट

mal-, male- (*comb. form*) बुरा, बुरी तरह, जैसे – **malfunction** (मैल्ˈफ़ंक्शन) *n./vi.*

maladjusted (मैलˈजस्टिड) *a.* जो सभ्य समाज की आवश्यकताएं पूरी न कर सके; जो परिवेश के अनुकूल न बन पाया हो – **maladjustment** *n.*

maladministration (मैलड्मिनिस् 'ट्रेशन) *n.* कुशासन

maladroit (मैल'ड्रॉइट) *a.* फूहड़; भोंडा

malady ('मैलडि) *n.* बीमारी, रोग

mala fide ('मेल'फ़ाइडि) *a.* बदनीयत, दुर्भावपूर्ण – *adv.*

malaise (मै'लेज़) *n.* एक अस्पष्ट बेचैनी/ रोग

malapropism ('मैलप्रॉपिज़्म) *n.* शब्दों का दुष्प्रयोग जिस से हंसी आए

malaria (म'लैंअरिअ) *n.* मलेरिया

malcontent ('मैल्कंटेन्ट) *a.* असन्तुष्ट

male (मिल) *a.* नर पुरुष से सम्बन्धित; पुरुषों या नर पशुओं का – *n.* पुरुष; पशु का नर

malediction (मैलि'डिक्शन) *n.* अभिशाप

malefactor ('मैलिफ़ैक्टर) *n.* अपराधी

malevolent (म'लेवलंट) *a.* द्वेषपूर्ण

malice ('मैलिस) *n.* दुर्भावना; विद्वेष – **malicious** (म'लिशस) *a.* बुराई करने या चाहने वाला; विद्वेषपूर्ण

malign (म'लाइन) *a.* अहितकर, अशुभ – *vt.* बदनाम करना – **malignancy** (म'लिग्नन्सि) – *n.* दुर्भाव; कैंसर की गांठ – **malignant** (मंलिग्नंट) *a.* अहितकर, अशुभ; द्वेषपूर्ण; असाध्य (कैंसर की गांठ) – **malignantly** *adv.* – **malignity** (म'लिग्निटि) *n.* द्वेष, दुश्मनी, बैर; (रोग की) असाध्यता

malinger (म'लिंगर) *vi.* काम से बचने के लिए (सख्त) बीमारी का बहाना करना

mall (मॉल) *n.* समतल छायादार रास्ता; छत्ता; **(shopping mall)** एक छत के नीचे बहुत सी दुकानों वाला बाज़ार

mallard ('मैलर्ड) *n.* जंगली बतख

malleable ('मैलिअबल) *a.* (धातु) जिसे कूट पीट कर नया आकार दिया जा सके; जिसे अनुकूल बनाया जा सके

mallet ('मैलिट) *n.* लकड़ी की हथौड़ी, मूंगरी

malnourished (मैल्'नरिश्ट) *a.* कुपोषित

malnutrition (मैल्न्यु'ट्रिशन) *n.* अपर्याप्त आहार, कुपोषण

malpractice (मैल्'प्रैक्टिस) *n.* गैर कानूनी आचारण; अनाचार

malt (मॉल्ट) *n.* जौ आदि के सूखाये हुए दाने जिस से शराब बनती है, माल्ट

maltreat (मैल्'ट्रीट) *vt.* बुरा व्यवहार करना

mammal ('मैमल) *n.* कोई भी स्तनपायी जीव

mammary ('मैमरि) *a.* स्तनों या दूध बनाने वाली ग्रन्थियों का

mammon ('मैमन) *n.* सभी बुराइयों की जड़ के रूप में धन सम्पत्ति

mammoth ('मैमथ) – *a.* विशालकाय

man (मैन) *n.* मानव, इंसान; मानव जाति; पुरुष; नौकर; शतरंज का मोहरा, पैदल या प्यादा; पति (*my man*) (*pl.* **men** (मॅन)) – *vt.* कर्मचारियों को जहाज़ आदि पर तैनात करना (**-nn-**) – **manful** *a.* वीर, बलशाली – **manfully** *adv.* – **manlike** *a.* पुरुषोचित – **manliness** *n.* पुरुषों जैसे गुण; पौरुष – **manly** *a.* पुरुषोचित – **manhandle** *vt.* पीटना – **manhole** *n.* भूमि के नीचे की नाली का ऊपर से रास्ता व उस का ढक्कन – **manhood** *n.* पौरुष – **mankind** *n.* मानव जाति, मानवता – **manpower** *n.* मानव शक्ति; उपलब्ध मज़दूरों की संख्या – **manslaughter** *n.* हत्या जो जानबूझ कर न की गयी हो; नरहत्या

manacle ('मैनकल) *n.* बेड़ी; हथकड़ी – *vt.* बेड़ियां डालना

manage ('मैनिज) *vt.* प्रबंध करना; करने में सफल होना; पर नियंत्रण करना, संभालना; चलाना – **manageable** *a.* नियंत्रणीय – **management** ('मैनिज़्मंट) *n.* प्रबंध, प्रबंधकर्त्ता जैसे प्रबंध बोर्ड के सदस्य; प्रशासन – **manager** ('मैनिजर) *n.* प्रबंधक, मैनेजर –

managerial (मैनि'जिअरिल) *a.* प्रबंधकीय, प्रबंध – **managing** *a.* प्रबंध

mandarin ('मैंडरिन) *n.* (भूतकाल में) चीन का बड़ा अधिकारी; *fig.* कोई बड़ा सरकारी अधिकारी

mandate ('मैन्डेट) *n.* अध्यादेश, जनादेश, किसी की ओर से कार्य करने का आदेश – **mandatory** *a.* अनिवार्य

mandolin(e) (मैंड'लिन) *n.* सारंगी जैसा एक साज़

mane (मेन) *n.* घोड़े, शेर की गरदन के लम्बे बाल, अयाल

manganese (मैंग'नीज़) *n.* एक धातु, उस का काला ऑक्साइड

manger ('मेन्जर) *n.* (जानवर के चारे की) नांद, चरनी

mangle[1] ('मैंगल) *n.* कपड़े निचोड़ने की मशीन – *vt.* मशीन में कपड़े निचोड़ना

mangle[2] (मैंगल) *vt.* बुरी तरह काटपीट देना; क्षत विक्षत करना

mango ('मैंगो) *n.* आम (*pl.* **-go(e)s** (–गोज़))

mangrove ('मैंग्रोव) *n.* समुद्र के पास नदी मुहाने कीचड़ में उगने वाला एक पेड़; चमरंग

manhole दे० MAN

mania ('मेनिअ) *n.* पागलपन; सनक, झक, शौक – **maniac** ('मेनिऐक) *n.* पागल; सनकी

manicure ('मैनिक्युअर) *n.* नाखूनों का तराशना और हाथों की सफाई

manifest ('मैनिफेंस्ट) *a.* स्पष्ट; निस्सन्देहात्मक – *a.* सीमा-शुल्क के लिए सामान की सूची – *vt.* व्यक्त करना, स्पष्ट करना – **manifestation** *n.* प्रकटीकरण – **manifestly** *adv.* स्पष्ट रूप से – **manifesto** *n.* राजनीतिक दल का घोषणा-पत्र (*pl.* **-to(e)s**)

manifold ('मैनिफ़ोल्ड) *a.* बहुसंख्यक और विविध – *n.*

manipulate (म'निप्युलेट) *vt.* चलाना, चालाकी से काम लेना; झूठे (खाते आदि) तैयार करना – **manipulation** (मनिप्यु'लेशन) *n.* चलाने की क्रिया; हाथ से काम करने या हाथों का कुशलता से प्रयोग करने की क्रिया; जोड़-तोड़ की क्रिया

mankind दे० MAN

mannequin ('मैनिकिन) *n.* पुतला जिसे कपड़े पहना दिये जाते हैं (दुकान में)

manner ('मैनर) *n.* ढंग, तौर तरीका; किस्म; रीति – *pl.* सामाजिक व्यवहार; आचरण – **mannerism** *n.* व्यक्ति का विशेष स्वभाव या व्यवहार की विशिष्टता, स्वभाव-विशिष्टता

manoeuvre (म'नूवर) *n.* चाल; तिकड़म; युक्ति – *v.* तिकड़म लड़ाना, चाल; या दांव पेच चलना; से काम कराना – **manoeuvrable** *a.* जिससे काम कराया जा सके

mansion ('मैन्शन) *n.* हवेली, कोठी, बड़ा मकान

mantelpiece *n.* आतिशदान के ऊपर बनी कार्निस

mantis ('मैंटिस) *n.* टिड्डा (*pl.* **mantes** ('मैंटीज़))

mantle ('मैंटल) *n.* ढीला-ढाला लबादा; आवरण; गैसकी लालटेन का मैन्टल –*vt.* ढक लेना

manual ('मैन्युअल) *a.* हाथ का या उस से किया जाने वाला; जो यंत्रचालित न हो – *n.* नियमावली

manufacture (मैन्यु'फ़ैक्चर) *vt.* निर्माण करना, बनाना, उत्पादन करना; गढ़ना – *n.* निर्माण; उत्पादन – **manufacturer** *n.* निर्माता

manure (म'न्युअर) – *n.* खाद

manuscript ('मैन्युस्क्रिप्ट) *n.* हाथ से लिखी पुस्तक या दस्तावेज

many ('मैनि) *a.* बहुत से, अनेक (**more** *comp.*; **most** *sup.*) – *n.* बहुत बड़ी संख्या

Maoism (´माओइज़्म) *n.* चीन में माओत्से तुंग द्वारा प्रचलित साम्यवाद – **Maoist** *n./a.*
Maori (´माउरि) *n.* न्यूज़ीलैंड की आदिमजाति; उसकी भाषा
map (मैप) *n.* मानचित्र, नक्शा – *vt.* मानचित्र या नक्शा बनाना (*-pp-*); (**out** के साथ) की योजना बनाना
maple (´मेपल) *n.* एक पेड़, द्विफल
mar (मार) *vt.* खराब कर देना, बिगाड़ देना (**-rr-**)
Mar. March का संक्षेप
marathon (´मैरथन) *n.* लगभग 42 कि.मी. लम्बी दूरी की दौड़
marble (´मार्बल) *n.* संगमरमर; बच्चों के खेलने की गोली, कंचा
March (मार्च) *n.* वर्ष का तीसरा महीना, मार्च
march[1] (मार्च) *vi.* (सैनिक के समान) चलना, कवायद करना; जाना; आगे बढ़ना; प्रदर्शन करना – *vt.* चलाना, कवायद कराना – *n.* कवायद; एक दिन में तय की गयी दूरी; मार्च करने की धुन; प्रदर्शन
mare (मेअर) *n.* घोड़ी
margarine (मार्जे´रीन) *n.* वनस्पति चिकनाई से बना मक्खन
margin (´मार्जिन) *n.* हाशिया; किनारा; अतिरिक्त मात्रा/संख्या; लाभ; गुंजाइश – **marginal** *a.* हाशिये का; किनारे का; सीमावर्ती – **marginalize** *vt.* का महत्व/प्रभाव घटा देना
marigold (´मैरीगोल्ड) *n.* गेन्दा
marijuana (मैरिजु´आन्अ), **marihuana** (मैरि´हान्अ) *n.* भांग के सूखे फूल व पत्ते; सुल्फ़ा (एक नशीला पदार्थ)
marina (म´रीन्अ) *n.* नावों के खड़े करने का घाट
marine (म´रीन) *a.* समुद्र या जहाज़ों का या समुद्र में मिलने वाला – *n.* जहाज़ी बेड़ा; समुद्र या भूमि पर युद्ध के लिए प्रशिक्षित सैनिक – **mariner** *n.* नाविक
marionette (मैरीअ´नेंट) *n.* कठपुतली
marital (´मैरिट्ल) *a.* वैवाहिक
maritime (´मैरिटाइम) *a.* समुद्री या नौवहन से सम्बन्धित
mark[1] (मार्क) *n.* निशान; संकेत, निर्देश; अक्षर; अंक या नम्बर; निशाना – *vt.* निशान या छाप लगाना; चिह्न विशेष होना; बताना, लक्षण होना; ध्यान/ नजर रखना; मूल्यांकन कर के नम्बर देना – *vi.* ध्यान देना – **marker** *n.* खेलों में अंको का हिसाब रखने वाला; ताश आदि खेलों के अंकों की गिनती का उपकरण; (**marker pen** भी) मोटी नोंक वाला पेन – **marksman** *n.* कुशल निशानेबाज़
mark[2] (मार्क) *n.* जर्मन सिक्का, मार्क
market (´मार्किट) *n.* बाज़ार; (माल की) मांग; व्यापार केन्द्र – *vt.* बेचना – **marketable** *a.* विक्रय योग्य – **marketing** *n.* बेचने की व्यवस्था
marmalade (´मार्मलेड) *n.* नारंगी, नींबू आदि का मुरब्बे जैसा पदार्थ
maroon[1] (म´रून) *n.* भूरापन लिए लाल रंग
maroon[2] (म´रून) *vt.* (व्यक्ति को) निर्जन द्वीप या तट पर छोड़ देना
marquee (मार्´की) *n.* बड़ा तम्बू
marrow (´मैरो) *n.* हड्डियों का गूदा, मज्जा; महत्वपूर्ण अंश; वनस्पतियों का गूदा; कुम्हड़ा
marry (´मैरि) *v.* विवाह करना या कराना (**married, marrying**) – **marriage** (´मैरिज) *n.* विवाह, शादी – **marriageable** *a.* विवाह योग्य
Mars (मार्ज़) *n.* प्राचीन रोम में युद्ध का देवता; मंगल ग्रह
marsh (मार्श) *n.* दलदल – **marshy** *a.*
marshal (´मार्शल) *n.* बड़ा सरकारी अधिकारी; US पुलिस अधिकारी – **field marshal** सेना का सब से बड़ा अधिकारी (वायु सेना में **air marshal**) – *vt.* क्रमबद्ध करना;

विधिपूर्वक ले चलना – **marshalling yard** मालगाड़ियों का केन्द्र या डिपो

marsupial (मार्ˊस्यूपिअल) *n.* जानवर जो अपने बच्चे को पेट की थैली में लेकर चलता है जैसे कंगारू, धानी प्राणी

mart (मार्ट) *n.* व्यापार केन्द्र; बाज़ार

martial (ˊमार्शल) *a.* युद्ध सम्बन्धी या उस जैसा; लड़ाकू – **martial art** युद्ध-समान खेल जैसे जूडो व कराटे – **martial law** सैनिक शासन

martini (मार्ˊटीनि) *n.* शराब का एक पेय

martyr (ˊमार्टर) *n.* शहीद; हुतात्मा; जो सदा कष्ट सहता रहे – *vt.* शहीद बना देना – **martyrdom** *n.* शहादत, बलिदान

marvel (ˊमार्वल) *vi.* आश्चर्यचकित होना **(-ll-)** – *n.* अदभुत वस्तु; चमत्कार – **marvellous** *a.*

Marxism (ˊमार्क्सिज़्म) *n.* कार्लमार्क्स का दर्शन, मार्क्सवाद – **Marxist** *n./a.* मार्क्सवादी

mascara (मैस्ˊकार्अ) *n.* पलकों को गहरा करने का अंजन

mascot (ˊमैस्कट) *n.* सौभाग्य चिह्न

masculine (ˊमैस्क्युलिन) *a.* पुरुष या नर जाति से सम्बन्धित, पुल्लिंग – **masculinity** (मैस्क्युˊलिनिटि) – *n.* पौरुष, मर्दानगी

mash (मैश) – *vt.* पीस कर घोल आदि बनाना

mask (मास्क) *n.* नकाब; *Surgery* कपड़ा जिससे नाक और मुंह ढक जाये; भेस; बहाना

masochism (ˊमैसकिज़्म) *n.* मानसिक विकार जिसमें पीड़ा या अपमान सहने में आनंद, विशे. लैंगिक सुख, मिलता है, पर पीड़ित-कामुकता – **masochist** *n.*

mason (ˊमेसन) *n.* राज(गीर), राज मिस्त्री – **masonry** *n.* चिनाई

Mass (मैस, मास) *n.* यशु मसीह के अंतिम भोज से सम्बन्धित प्रार्थना

mass (मैस) *n.* ढेर; अंबार, समूह; बहुत बड़ी मात्रा या संख्या – *v.* इकट्ठे करना एकत्र करना – **massive** *a.* विशाल और भारी – **mass media** जन संचार माध्यम (समाचारपत्र, रेडियो, टी.वी. आदि) – **the masses** जनसाधारण, जनता-जनार्दन

massacre (ˊमैसकर) *n.* कत्लेआम– *vt.*

massage (ˊमैसाज) *n.* मालिश – *vt.* मालिश करना – **masseur** (मैˊसर) *n.* मालिशिया (**masseuse** (मैˊसज़) *fem.*)

mast (मास्ट) *n.* जहाज़ का मस्तूल; एरियल, झण्डे आदि का सीधा खड़ा डंडा

master (ˊमास्टर) *n.* कप्तान; नियंत्रक; मालिक; ग हस्वामी; स्वामी; मूल (दस्तावेज़ जिसकी प्रतियां बनायी जाये); विशेषज्ञ; महान कलाकार; गुरु; छोटे लड़कों के नाम से पहले प्रयुक्त शब्द – *vt.* वश में कर लेना; ज्ञान या कौशल प्राप्त कर लेना – **masterful** *a.* दबंग, रोबीला – **masterly** *a.* जिसमें बहुत कौशल या उत्क ष्टता हो – **mastery** *n.* पूर्णज्ञान; विशेषज्ञता; अधिकार; विजय – **mastermind** *vt.* योजना बनाना; निर्देश करना – *n.* नियंता – **masterpiece** *n.* सर्वोत्क ष्ट क ति – **master plan** किसी परियोजना का विस्त त खाका, मास्टर प्लान – **master stroke** चाल; अद्वितीय युक्ति

masticate (ˊमैस्टिकेट) *vt.* चबाना – **mastication** (मैस्टिˊकेशन) *n.*

masturbate (ˊमैस्टर्बेट) *v.* हस्तमैथुन करना – **masturbation** (मैस्टर्ˊबेशन) *n.*

mat[1] (मैट) *n.* चटाई; पायदान; (उलझे हुए बाल आदि का) गुच्छा – *v.* ऐसा गुच्छा बनाना **(-tt-)**

mat[2] (मैट) *a.* मद्धिम; चमकहीन, धूसर

matador (ˊमैटडॉर) *n.* आदमी जो सांड से लड़ाई में उसका वध करता है

match[1] (मैच) *n.* प्रतियोगिता, खेल; बराबर का; व्यक्ति, वस्तु जो दूसरे जैसी हो, जोड़ा; विवाह – *vt.* रंग से रंग मिलाना; विरोध करना;

प्रतियोगिता में सामने लाना – **matching** *a.* मेल खाता – *vi.* जोड़ होना – **matchless** *a.* बेजोड़ – **find/meet your match** बराबर का/सेर को सवा सेर मिलना

match² (मैच) *n.* माचिस – **matchbox** *n.* माचिस की डिबिया – **matchwood** *n.* छोटे-छोटे लकड़ी के टुकड़े

mate¹ (मेट) *n.* साथी; सखा; पति या पत्नी; जोड़े में से कोई एक; व्यापारिक जहाज़ का एक अधिकारी – *v.* विवाह करना; (नर-मादा का) जोड़ा बनाना; संभोग करना

mate² (मेट) *n./vt.* (शतरंज में) शह मात (देना)

material (म´टिअरिअल) *n.* सामान (जिस से कोई चीज बने); कपड़ा – *a.* भौतिक; जिस का शारीरिक कल्याण पर प्रभाव हो, सांसारिक; महत्वपूर्ण – **materialism** (म´टिअरिअलिज़म) – *n.* धन दौलत में अत्यधिक रुचि; सांसारिकता; भौतिकवाद – **materialist** *a./n.* – **materialistic** ***a.*** – **materialize**. (म´टिअरिअलाइज़) *vi.* – **materially** *adv.* पर्याप्त मात्रा में

maternal (म´टर्नल) *a.* माता का या उस से सम्बद्ध – **maternity** (म´टर्निट) *n.* मातृत्व – *a.* गर्भवती स्त्री/स्त्री जो बच्चे को जन्म देकर चुकी हो, संबंधित

mathematics (मैथ´मैटिक्स) *n.* गणित शास्त्र – **mathematical** (मैथ´मैटिकल) *a.* गणित – **mathematician** *n.* गणितज्ञ

maths (मैथ्स) *n. inf.* गणितशास्त्र

matinee (´मैटिने) *n.* दोपहर बाद दिखाया गया चलचित्र, नाटक आदि

matriarch (´मेट्रिआर्क) *n.* कुल-माता – **matriarchal** *a.* व्यवस्था जिसमें माता का शासन हो – **matriarchy** *n.* मातृतंत्र

matriculate (म´ट्रिक्युलेट) *v.* मैट्रिक (दसवीं कक्षा) की परीक्षा पास करना – **matriculation** *n.* मैट्रिक की परीक्षा

matrimony (´मैट्रिमनि) *n.* विवाह – **matrimonial** (मैट्रि´मॉन्यल) *a.* विवाह सम्बन्धी

matrix (´मैट्रिक्स) *n.* पदार्थ या (सामाजिक, राजनीति आदि) स्थिति जिसमें कुछ जन्म ले (जैसे संस्कृति); उत्पत्ति स्थान (*pl.* **matrices** (मैट्रिसीज़))

matron (´मेट्रन) *n. old use* विवाहित स्त्री; प्रबन्धिका – **matronly** *a.* भारी, पुष्ट शरीर की

matter (´मैटर) *n. Physics* द्रव्य, पदार्थ; जड़ वस्तु; विषय, वस्तु; मामला; झगड़े की जड़; पुस्तक आदि की विषय वस्तु; बात – *vi.* महत्व होना – **matter-of-fact way** भावहीन तरीके (से)

mattock (´मैटक) *n.* गैन्ती (बागबानी का औज़ार)

mattress (´मैट्रिस) *n.* गद्दा

mature (मॅ´ट्युअर, म´चुअर) *a.* पका हुआ, विकसित; वयस्क – *v.* परिपक्व होना या करना – *vi.* (हुंडी का) देय हो जाना – **maturity** (म´ट्युअरिटि, म´चुअरिटि) *n.* परिपक्वता; *Business* पालिसी आदि के भुगतान का समय

maul (मॉल) *vt.* मारना-पीटना

mausoleum (मॉस´लीअम) *n.* मकबरा (*pl.* **-leums, -lea**)

mauve (मोव़) *a./n.* हल्के बैंगनी रंग (का)

maverick (´मैव़रिक) *n.* स्वतंत्र विचारों का रूढ़ि विरोधी व्यक्ति

maw (मॉ) *n.* पेट; (पक्षी का) पोटा

mawkish (´मॉकिश) *a.* भावुक; फीका; स्वादहीन; कमज़ोर, बीमार

max MAXIMUM का संक्षेप

maxim (´मैक्सिम) *n.* सूक्ति; आचरण नियम; सिद्धांत

maximum (´मैक्सिमम) *n.* अधिकतम – **maximize** *vt.* अधिकतम करना

May (मे) *n.* वर्ष का पांचवां महीना; **(m-)** एक पौधा, बनसंजली या उसके फूल

may (मे) *v. aux.* संभावना, अनुमति, अवसर आदि का द्योतक (**might** *pt.*) – **maybe** *adv.* शायद; संभवत:

mayhem (ˈमेहॅम) *n.* मारकाट, उत्पात

mayonnaise (मेअˈनेज़) *n.* अंडे, मलाई आदि फैंट कर बनाया घोल जो सलाद में मिलाया जाता है

mayor (मॅअर) *n.* महापौर, मेयर – **mayoress** *n.* मेयर की पत्नी या महिला मेयर

maze (मेज़) *n.* भूलभूलैंया; पगडंडियों आदि का बाहुल्य

MCP male chauvinist pig (घमंडी मरदों के लिए, अपने अधिकारों के लिए लड़ने वाली स्त्रियों द्वारा प्रयुक्त शब्द-समूह) का संक्षेप

MD Doctor of Medicine का संक्षेप

me (मी) *pron.* मुझे, मुझसे

mead (मीड) *n.* शहद से बनी शराब

meadow (ˈमॅडो) *n.* घास का मैदान

meagre (ˈमीगर) *a.* दुबला, पतला; अपर्याप्त

meal[1] (मील) *n.* भोजन

meal[2] (मील) *n.* आटा

mean[1] (मीन) *vt.* आशय या अर्थ होना; लक्षण या प्रतीक होना – *vi.* अर्थ होना; इरादा होना (**meant** (मॅन्ट) *pt./pp.*, **meaning** *pr. p.*) – **meaning** *n.* अर्थ, मतलब; महत्व – **meaningful** *a.* बड़े महत्व का; अभिव्यक्तिपूर्ण

mean[2] (मीन) *a.* नीच, कमीना; निक ष्ट, घटिया; कंजूस; बहुत साधारण

mean[3] (मीन) *n.* औसत या मध्यम दर्जे की वस्तु; मध्य बिन्दु – (**means**) *pl.* उपाय; धन-दौलत; साधन – *a.* औसत या मध्यम – **meantime, meanwhile** *adv./n.* इसी बीच – **by all means** निश्चय ही, अवश्य – **by no means** कदापि नहीं

meander (मिˈऐन्डर) *vi.* टेढ़ मेढ़े बहना; निरुद्देश्य घूमना

measles (ˈमीज़ल्ज़) *n.* खसरा

measure (ˈमॅझ़र) *n.* आकार; मात्रा, आकार या मात्रा नापने का बरतन या डंडा, माप; आकार या मात्रा की इकाई; उपाय – *vt.* नापना, माप लेना; प्रतिस्पर्धा करना – **measurable** *a.* – **measured** *a.* नपा-तुला; सुविचारित – **measurement** *n.* नापने की क्रिया; आकार

meat (मीट) *n.* मांस; भोजन

mechanic (मिˈकैनिक) *n.* मिस्त्री, मकैनिक, मशीनें आदि ठीक करने वाला – **mechanical** *a.* यंत्रों का या उनके संचालन से सम्बन्धित, बिना सोचे समझे किया गया, यंत्रवत

mechanism (ˈमॅकनिज़म) *n.* मशीन का ढांचा; मशीन – **mechanization** (मॅकनाइˈज़ेशन) *n.* यंत्रीकरण – **mechanize** *vt.* मशीनों का उपयोग करना; यंत्रवत या स्वचालित बनाना

medal (ˈमॅड्ल) *n.* पदक, तमगा, मैडल – **medallion** (मिˈडैल्यन) *n.* बड़ा पदक; फलक आदि जो सजावट में काम आए – **medallist** (ˈमेडॅलिस्ट) *n.* जिसे पदक मिला हो

meddle (ˈमॅड्ल) *vi.* हस्तक्षेप करना – **meddlesome** *a.* टांग अड़ाने वाला

media (ˈमीडिअ) *n.* MEDIUM का *pl.* विशेष रूप से रेडियो, टेलिविज़न जैसे संचार साधनों के लिए प्रयुक्त

medial (ˈमीडिअल) *a.* औसत से सम्बन्धित – **median** *a./n.* माध्य

mediate *vi.* (ˈमीडिएट) (बीच बचाव करने के लिए) मध्यस्थता करना – **mediation** (मीडिˈएशन) *n.* मध्यस्थता – **mediator** *n.*

medicine (ˈमॅडिसिन) *n.* दवा, औषधि; चिकित्सा शास्त्र – **medical** *a.* – **medically** *adv.* – **medicate** (ˈमॅडिकेट) *vt.* इलाज करना, दवा देना – **medication** *n.*

medico ('मेंडिको) *n. inf.* डाक्टर
medieval, mediaeval (मेंडि'ईवल) *a.* मध्य युग का
mediocre (मीडि'ओकर) *a.* साधारण, मामूली – **mediocrity** (मीडि'ऑक्रिटि) *n.* सामान्य या साधारण योग्यता
meditate ('मेंडिटेट) *vi.* मनन या चिन्तन करना; ध्यानमग्न होना – *vt.* सोचना, योजना बनाना – **meditation** (मेंडि'टेशन) *n.* ध्यान योग – **meditative** *a.* चिन्तनशील
medium ('मीड्यम) *a.* मध्यम, मंझला, बीच का; औसत – *n.* मध्यम श्रेणी; माध्यम, साधन; संचार साधन जैसे समाचार पत्र, रेडियो आदि; वातावरण; पर्यावरण (*pl.* **mediums, media**)
meek (मीक) *a.* विनीत, विनम्र; दब्बू – **meekly** *adv.* – **meekness** *n.* विनम्रता, दब्बूपन
meet (मीट) *vt.* मिलना सामने, होना, टकराना; पूरा करना (शर्त आदि); चुकाना, देना – *v.* सामने आना; किसी बिन्दु पर मिलना; इकट्ठे होना; सम्पर्क में आना (सभा आदि के लिए); (खेल में) का मुकाबला होना (**met** *pt./pp.*) – *n.* जमाव, इकट्ठे होने की क्रिया – **meeting** *n.* सभा, गोष्ठी
mega- ('मेंग्अ) (*comb. form*) विशाल (*mega store*); 10 लाख (*megawatt*)
megabucks ('मेंग्अबक्स) *n. inf.* बहुत बड़ी रकम
megabyte ('मेंगबाइट) *n. Computers* जानकारी की 10 लाख इकाइयां, 2^{20} इकाइयां
megalomania (मेंगलो'मेनिअ) *n.* महत्व या बड़प्पन का उन्माद
megaphone ('मेंगफ़ोन) *n.* भोंपू
megaton ('मेंगटन) *n.* दस लाख टन टी.एन.टी की विस्फोटक शक्ति
melamine ('मेंल्अमीन) *n.* सख़्त प्लास्टिक पदार्थ जो और पदार्थों पर चढ़ाया जाता है
melancholy ('मेंलन्कलि) *n.* उदासी; निराशा; विषाद – *a.* उदास; निराश
melee ('मेंले) *n.* भीड़ या उसमें परस्पर हाथापाई करते लोग
mellifluous, -luent (में'लिफ़्लुअस, में'लिफ़्लुअंट) *a.* मधुर, सुरीली (आवाज़)
mellow ('मेंलो) *a.* पका हुआ (फल आदि); मृदुस्वभाव; नरम; मिलनसार – *v.* नरम या मृदु (स्वभाव वाला) हो जाना या कर देना
melodrama ('मेंलड्राम्अ) *n.* नाटक जिसमें अत्यधिक भावुकतापूर्ण घटनाएं हों – **melodramatic** (मेंलोड्र'मैटिक) *a.* भावुकतापूर्ण, अतिनाटकीय
melody ('मेंलडि) *n.* सुरीली लय या तान – **melodious** (मि'लोडिअस) *a.* सुरीला
melon ('मेंलन) *n.* खरबूज़ा; तरबूज़
melt ('मेंल्ट) *v.* पिघलना या पिघलाना, गलना या गलाना; घुलना; नरम हो जाना; घुल जाना; मिल जाना; विलीन हो जाना, गायब हो जाना (**melted** *pt./pp.* **molten** *pp.*) – **melting** *a.* नरम; मृदु; स्नेही
member ('मेंम्बर) *n.* (किसी सभा या संगठन का) सदस्य; (शरीर का) अंग (वि० पुरुषलिंग); घटक – **membership** *n.* सदस्यता
membrane ('मेंम्ब्रेन) *n.* झिल्ली
memento (मि'मेंन्टो) *n.* निशानी, यादगार; स्मृति चिह्न (*pl.* **-to(e)s**)
memo ('मेंमो, 'मीमो) *n.* MEMORANDUM का संक्षेप
memoirs ('मेंम्वार्ज़) *pl. n.* आत्मकथा; व्यक्ति का इतिहास
memory ('मेंमरि) *n.* स्मृति, याद; स्मरण शक्ति, याद आई बात/घटना; स्मरणार्थ उत्सव आदि; कम्प्यूटर में स्थान जहां जानकारी सुरक्षित रखी जाती है – **memorable** *a.* स्मरणीय – **memorandum** (मेंम'रैण्डम) *n.* स्मरण पत्र; ज्ञापन; औपचारिक चिट्ठी (*pl.* **-dums,**

-da) – **memorial** (मि´मॉरिअल) *a.* स्म ति का या उसे बनाए रखने से सम्बन्धित – *n.* स्मारक – **memorize** (´मेंमराइज़) *vt.* याद कर लेना

men (´मेंन) *n.* MAN का *pl.*

menace (´मेंनिस) *n.* खतरा – *vt.* खतरे में डालना

mend (मेंण्ड) *vt.* मरम्मत करना; सुधारना; ठीक करना – *vi.* सुधरना विशे. स्वास्थ्य का – *n.* मरम्मत किया टुकड़ा

mendicant (´मेंन्डिकंट) *a.* – *n.* भिखारी

menial (´मीनिअल) *a.* मामूली काम से सम्बन्धित – *n.* नौकर

meningitis (मेंनिन्´जाइटिस) *n.* गरदन तोड़ बुखार

menopause (´मेनोपॉज़) *n.* बढ़ती उम्र के साथ मासिक धर्म का बंद होना, रजोनिव ति

men's room (*toilet*) पुरुष शौचालय

menstruation (मेंन्सट्रु´एशन) *n.* मासिक धर्म।

mensuration (मेंन्श´रेशन) *n.* मापने की क्रिया, विशे. क्षेत्रों की

mental (´मेंन्टल) *a.* मानसिक, मनोगत; *inf.* क्षीण बुद्धि; पागल – **mentality** *n.* मनोव ति – **mentally** *adv.*

menthol (´मेंन्थॉल) *n.* पोदीने का सत (एक दवा)

mention (´मेंन्शन) *vt.* चर्चा, उल्लेख या ज़िक्र करना – *n.* चर्चा उल्लेख, ज़िक्र – **mentionable** *a.* उल्लेखनीय

mentor (´मेंन्टर) *n.* विश्वस्त मार्गदर्शक

menu (´मेंन्यू) *n.* व्यंजन सूची

mercantile (´मर्कन्टाइल) *a.* व्यापारिक

mercenary (´मर्सिनरि) *a.* धन लोलुप; जो केवल पैसे की खातिर काम करे – *n.* भाड़े का सैनिक

merchant (´मर्चंट) *n.* व्यापारी; थोक का व्यापारी – **merchandise** (´मर्चन्डाइस, -डाइज़) *n.* व्यापारी का माल, सौदा – **merchant navy** व्यापारिक जहाज़ों का बेड़ा

mercury (´मर्क्युरि) *n.* पारा; (M –) बुध ग्रह – **mercurial** (मर्´क्युअरिअल) *a.* ज़िन्दादिल; जो जल्दी जल्दी बदले, चंचल

mercy (´मर्सि) *n.* दया, करुणा – **merciful** *a.* – **merciless** *a.*

mere (मिअर) *a.* केवल, मात्र; निरा, शुद्ध – **merely** *adv.* केवल

merge (मर्ज) *v.* विलीन हो जाना या कर देना – **merger** *n.* कम्पनियों का मिल कर एक हो जाना; विलीन हो जाना

meridian (म´रिडिअन) *n.* याम्योतर रेखा; आकाश में काल्पनिक व त्त जो ध्रुवों से गुज़रता है; तारे, ग्रह आदि का सब से ऊंचा बिन्दु; वैभव आदि की पराकाष्ठा – *a.*

merit (´मेंरिट) *n.* उत्कर्ष, अच्छाई, गुण; योग्यता – *pl.* उत्क ष्टता – *vt.* के योग्य होना – **meritorious** (मेंरि´टॉरिअस) – *a.* प्रशंसा योग्य, सराहनीय; योग्य

mermaid (´मर्मेड) *n.* जलपरी, मत्स्य कन्या

merry (´मेंरि) *a.* प्रफुल्लित; हंसमुख विनोदी – **merrily** *adv.* – **merriment** *n.* मौजमस्ती – **merry-go-round** *n.* चक्रदोला, गोल झूला

mesh (मेंश) *n.* जाली – *v.* फंसाना या फंस जाना; इंजन की गरारियों का परस्पर लगना

mesmerize (´मेंज़मराइज़) *vt.* सम्मोहित करना; आक ष्ट करना; जादू करना

mess (मेंस) *n.* गड़बड़झाला, बखेड़ा; सैनिकों का समूह जो इकट्ठे भोजन करते हों; स्थान जहां भोजन करते हों, मेस – *v.* गड़बड़ करना – **messy** *a.* अव्यवस्थित

message (´मेंसिज) *n.* सन्देश; शिक्षा, सीख; सौंपा गया काम – **messenger** (´मेंसिंजर) *n.* सन्देशवाहक

Messrs (´मेंसर्ज़) Mr. का *pl.*

Met. (मेंट) *a./n. inf.* **Meteorological** का संक्षेप

met (मेंट) MEET का *pt./pp.*

meta-(*comb. form*) परिवर्तन जैसे *metamorphose, metathesis* आदि में

metabolism (मिं टैबलिज़्म) *n.* शरीर में रासायनिक प्रक्रिया

metal (मैंट्ल) *n.* धातु; **(road metal)** सड़क पर बिछाने की मिट्टी, रोड़ी – **metallic** (मि टैलिक) *a.* धातु का – **metallurgy** *n.* धातुकर्म

metamorphosis (मेंट मॉर्फ़सिस) *n.* रूपांतरण, कायापलट (*pl.* – **phoses**)

metaphor (मेंटफ़र) *n.* रूपक, रूपकालंकार – **metaphorical** (मेंट फ़ॉरिकल) *a.* लाक्षणिक – **metaphorically** *adv.*

metaphysics (मेंट फ़िज़िक्स) *n.* तत्वमीमांसा – **metaphysical** *a.* तत्वमीमांसा सम्बन्धी

meteor (मीटिअर) *n.* उल्का – **meteoric** (मीटि ऑरिक) *a.* उल्का समान (उन्नति आदि) – **meteorite** (मीटिअराइट) *n.* भूमि पर गिरा उल्का खण्ड

meteorology (मीटिअ रॉलजि) *n.* मौसम विज्ञान – **meteorological** (मीटिअर लॉजिकल) *a.* मौसम-विज्ञान संबंधी – **meteorologist** *n.*

meter (मीटर) *n.* मापक यंत्र, मापी; बिजली आदि का मीटर

methane (मीथेन) *n.* कार्बन और हाइड्रोजन से मिल कर बनी ज्वलनशील गैस, मीथेन

method (मेंथड) *n.* ढंग, तरीका, प्रणाली, पद्धति – **methodical** *a.* सुव्यवस्थित – **methodology** *n.* प्रणाली विशेष; प्रक्रिया

methylated spirits मीथनोल मिली अलकोहल

meticulous (मि टिक्युलस) *a.* बारीकी में जाने वाला

metre (मीटर) *n.* लम्बाई का माप **39.37** इंच; (कविता का) छंद – **metric** (मेंट्रिक) *a.* मीटर प्रणाली का – **metrical** *a.* कविता के छंद का; छंदोबद्ध

metropolis (मि ट्रॉपलिस) *n.* महानगर (*pl.* - **lises**) – **metropolitan** (मैट्र पॉलिटन) *a.* महानगर का

mettle (मेंट्ल) *n.* साहस, हिम्मत; उत्साह

mew (म्यू) *n.* बिल्ली की आवाज़, म्याऊं – *vi.* (बिल्ली का) म्याऊं-म्याऊं करना

mezzanine (मेंज़नीन) *n.* दो तल्लों के बीच का तल्ला; म्यानी

mg मिलिग्राम का चिह्न

MHz (मेगाहर्ट्ज़) रेडियो तरंगों का माप

miasma (मि ऐज़्मअ) *n.* हानिकर या डरावना वातावरण

mica (माइक्अ) *n.* अभ्रक

microbe (माइक्रोब) *n.* जीवाणु; रोगाणु

microbiology (माइक्रोबाइ ऑलजि) *n.* अति सूक्ष्य जीवाणुओं का वैज्ञानिक अध्ययन

microcosm (माइक्रोकॉज़्म) *n.* किसी बड़ी चीज़ की लघु, प्रतिक ति

micron (माइक्रॉन) *n.* दूरी की इकाई; मीटर का दस लाखवां भाग

microorganism (माइक्रो ऑर्गनिज़्म) *n.* बहुत सूक्ष्म जीव

microphone (माइक्रफ़ोन) *n.* माइक, माइक्रोफ़ोन

microscope (माइक्रस्कोप) *n.* सूक्ष्मदर्शी यंत्र – **microscopic** *a.* इस यंत्र का; अति क्षुद्र (मात्रा आदि)

microwave (माइक्रोवेव़) *n.* कुछ सेंटीमीटर लम्बी विद्युत चुम्बकीय तरंग जिसका प्रयोग रेडार और खाना पकाने में होता है – **microwave oven** खाना पकाने का उपकरण जिसमें ऐसी किरणों का प्रयोग होता है

mid (मिड) *a.* बीच का – **mid- day** *n.* दोपहर

middle (मिडल) *a.* बीच का; मध्यवर्ती – *n.* मध्यवर्ती भाग – **middle-aged** *a.* अधेड़

उम्र का – **middle class** मध्यम वर्ग – **middle-class** *a.* मध्यम-वर्गीय – **middle finger** बीच की उंगली – **middleman** *n.* बिचौलिया

midge (मिज) *n.* मच्छर जैसा कीड़ा

midget (ˈमिजिट) *n.* बौना (व्यक्ति); छोटे आकार की वस्तु

midnight (ˈमिड्नाइट) *n.* अर्धरात्रि, मध्यरात्रि

midriff (ˈमिड्रिफ़) *n.* शरीर का बीच का भाग

mid-sized *a.* औसत आकार का

midst (मिड्स्ट) *prep.* के बीच में

midway (मिड ˈवे) *a.* आधे रास्ते

midwife (ˈमिड्वाइफ़) *n.* दाई; धाय

mien (मीन) *n.* व्यक्ति का रंग ढंग, तेवर या मुखाक ति

might[1] (माइट) देखिए MAY

might[2] (माइट) *n.* शक्ति, बल, सामर्थ्य – **mightily** *adv.* शक्तिशाली ढंग से – **mighty** *a.* शक्तिशाली, बलवान – *adv. inf.* बहुत अधिक

migraine (ˈमीग्रेन, ˈमाइग्रेन) *n.* आधे सिर का दर्द

migrate (माइ ˈग्रेट) *vi.* एक स्थान, देश छोड़ कर दूसरी जगह जाना, प्रवास करना – **migrant** *a./n.* प्रवासी (व्यक्ति) – **migration** *n.* प्रवास – **migratory** *a.* मौसम के अनुसार प्रवास करने वाले (जीव जन्तु)

mike (माइक) *n. inf.* **microphone** का संक्षेप

milch (मिल्च) *a.* दुधारू (पशु)

mild (माइल्ड) *a.* मंद, नरम, कोमल, शांत

mildew (ˈमिल्ड्यू) *n.* फफूंद, भुकड़ी

mile (माइल) *n.* लम्बाई का नाप, मील – **mileage** *n.* मीलों में दूरी; प्रति मील खर्च; पेट्रोल से प्रति गैलन तय की गयी दूरी – **milestone** *n. fig.* महत्वपूर्ण घटना या सफलता

milieu (ˈमील्यअ) *n.* वातावरण; जीवन की परिस्थितियां

militant (ˈमिलिटंट) *a. n.* उग्रवादी; किसी पक्ष का उग्र समर्थक – **militancy** *n.* उग्रवाद

military (ˈमिलिटरि) *a.* सैनिकों, सेनाओं या युद्ध से सम्बन्धित, सैन्य – *n.* सशस्त्र सेनाएं – **militia** (मि ˈलिश्अ) *n.* नागरिकों की सेना, मिलिशया

militate (ˈमिलिटेट) *vi.* (विशे. *against* के साथ) बहुत अधिक (प्रतिकूल) प्रभाव होना

milk (मिल्क) *n.* दूध; पौधों से रिसता रस – *vt.* दूध निकालना या दोहना; *fig.* धोखे से उमेठना – **milky** *a.* दूध मिला या उस जैसा, दूधिया – **Milky Way** आकाश गंगा, मन्दाकिनी

mill (मिल) *n.* कारखाना; चक्की (आटा आदि पीसने की) – *vt.* पीसना; सिक्के पर दांते बनाना – **millstone** *n.* चक्की का पाट

millennium (मि ˈलेंनिअम) *n.* **1000** वर्ष की अवधि, सहस्त्राब्दि; शांति और सुख का युग (*pl.* **-iums, -ia**)

millepede, millipede (ˈमिलिपीड) *n.* कनखजूरा, गोजर

millet (ˈमिलिट) *n.* बाजरा, मण्डुआ आदि मोटा अनाज

milli-(*comb. form*) हज़ारवां जैसे, **milligram** (ˈमिलिग्रैम) *n.* मिलीग्राम, ग्राम का हज़ारवां भाग

million (ˈमिल्यन) *n.* दस लाख – **millionaire** (मिल्य ˈनेंअर) *n.* करोड़पति; अमीर आदमी

mime (माइम) *n.* मूक अभिनय – *v.*

mimic (ˈमिमिक) *vt.* किसी की नकल उतारना, विशे. व्यंग्य के लिए (**mimicked, mimicking**) – *n./a.* नकलची, स्वांगिया – **mimicry** (ˈमिमिक्रि) *n.* नकल, स्वांग

mimosa (मि ˈमोसअ, –ज़अ) *n.* छुईमुई का पौधा, लाजवन्ती

min. minimum, minute का संक्षेप

minaret (मिन'रेंट) *n.* मस्जिद की मीनार

mince (मिन्स) *vt.* छोटे छोटे टुकड़े करना, कीमा बनाना – *vi.* ठुमक ठुमक कर चलना; चबा चबा कर बातें करना – *n.* मांस का कीमा – **mincer** *n.* कीमा करने की मशीन – **mincemeat** *n.* कीमा और मसालों का मिश्रण **not mince (your) words** दो टूक बात करना

mind (माइंड) *n.* मन बुद्धि, मस्तिष्क; स्मृति; इरादा; मनोवृत्ति – *vt.* (किसी बात का) बुरा मानना; परवाह करना, ध्यान रखना; सावधान रहना – *vi.* सावधानी बरतना; ध्यान देना – **mind-boggling** *a.* कल्पना से परे – **mindset** *n.* दृष्टिकोण, विचार धारा

mine[1] (माइन) *pron.* मेरा

mine[2] (माइन) *n.* खान; बारूदी सुरंग – *vt.* खान से निकालना या खोदना; बारूदी सुरंगें लगाना – **miner** *n.* खान मज़दूर – **minefield** *n.* भूमि या समुद्र क्षेत्र जहां बारूदी सुरंगें बिछी हों

mineral ('मिनरल) *n.* खनिज पदार्थ – *a.* खनिज

mingle ('मिंगल) *v.* मिलना; मिलाना; से मिलकर एक हो जाना

mini ('मिनि) *n.* कोई भी छोटी वस्तु; मिनि स्कर्ट, स्त्रियों की ऊंची स्कर्ट – *a.* छोटी

miniature ('मिनिचर) – *n.* छोटा चित्र; छोटे आकार की कोई वस्तु – *a.*

minimize ('मिनिमाइज़) *vt.* यथासंभव छोटा, या न्यूनतम करना – **minimal** *a.* अल्पतम – **minimum** *n.* न्यूनतम मात्रा या आकार – *a.* न्यूनतम (*pl.* **-mums, -ma**)

minion ('मिन्यन) *n.* कृपापात्र व्यक्ति

miniskirt ('मिनिस्कर्ट) *n.* स्त्रियों की बहुत छोटी स्कर्ट

minister ('मिनिस्टर) *n.* मंत्री; राजनयिक प्रतिनिधि; पादरी – *vi.* सेवा-सुश्रूषा करना – **ministerial** (मिनि'स्टिअरिअल) *a.* पादरी अथवा उसके पद से संबंधित; मंत्री मंडल संबंधी; मंत्री मंडल का समर्थक; (*of clerks*) लिपिकवर्गीय – **ministerialist** *n.* सरकार समर्थक – **ministry** *n.* पादरी का पद; मंत्री मंडल; सेवा-कार्य

mink (मिंक) *n.* नेवले की जाति का जीव; उस की भूरी खाल

minnow ('मिनो) *n.* छोटी दरियाई मछली

minor ('माइनर) *a.* छोटा; नाबालिग़ – *n.* अवयस्क व्यक्ति; संगीत का एक सुर – **minority** (माइ'नॉरिटि) *n.* अल्पसंख्या; अल्पसंख्यक दल; किसी राज्य के अल्पसंख्यक व्यक्ति; अवयस्कता

mint[1] (मिंट) *n.* टकसाल, टंकशाला – *vt.* सिक्के बनाना; आविष्कार करना

mint[2] (मिंट) *n.* पोदीना

minus ('माइनस) *prep./a.* कम; घटा कर ऋणात्मक – *n.* ऋण चिह्न (–)

minute[1] (माइ'न्यूट) *a.* क्षुद्र, सूक्ष्म; ठीक-ठीक, शुद्ध *adv.* –**minutiae** (मि'न्यूशिई) *pl. n.* छोटी छोटी बातों का ब्यौरा

minute[2] ('मिनिट) *n.* घण्टे या डिग्री का साठवां भाग, मिनट, पल; क्षण; ज्ञापन – *pl.* बैठक आदि की कार्यवाही का वृत्तांत – *vt.* कार्यवाही का वृत्तांत तैयार करना

miracle ('मिरकल) *n.* चमत्कार – **miraculous** (मि'रैक्युलस) *a.* चमत्कारपूर्ण

mirage ('मिराझ़) *n.* मृग मरीचिका, मृग-तृष्णा

mired (माइअर्ड) मुसीबत में फंसा हुआ

mirror ('मिरर) *n.* दर्पण, आइना – *vt.* प्रतिबिम्बित करना

mirth (मर्थ) *n.* आमोद प्रमोद; उल्लास – **mirthful** *a.* प्रसन्नचित

mis – (*comb. form*) गलत या बुरी तरह जैसे: **misdeed**

misadventure (मिसड्'वेंन्चर) *n.* अनिष्ट; दुर्घटना; दुर्भाग्य

misanthrope ('मिज़न्थ्रोप), **misanthropist** (मि'ज़ैन्थ्रपिस्ट) – *n.* मानवद्वेषी

misapprehension (मिसैप्रि'हॅन्शन) *n.* गलतफहमी
misappropriate (मिस्अ'प्रोप्रिएट्) *vt.* बेइमानी से काम में लाना; गबन करना
misbehave (मिस्बि'हेव्) *vi.* बदतमीज़ी करना – **misbehaviour** *n.*
miscalculate (मिस्'कैल्क्यूलेट) *vt.* गलत अनुमान लगाना
miscarry (मिस्'कैरि) *vi.* गर्भपात होना; असफल होना – **miscarriage** – *n.* गर्भपात
miscellaneous (मिस'लेनिअस) *a.* फुटकर, प्रकीर्ण, विविध – **miscellany** (मि'सॅलनि) *n.* पुस्तक में विविध प्रकार के लेखों का संग्रह; घालमेल
mischief ('मिस्चिफ़) *n.* नटखटपन, शरारत; हानि– **mischievous** ('मिस्चिव़स) *a.* शरारती; अनिष्टकारी
misconception ('मिस्कन्'सॅप्शन) *n.* गलत विचार, भ्रांत धारणा
misconduct (मिस्'कॉन्डक्ट) *n.* दुराचरण, अनुचित व्यवहार
miscreant ('मिस्क्रिअंट) *n.* दुष्ट, बदमाश
misdeed (मिस्'डीड) *n.* दुष्कर्म, अपराध
misdemeanour (मिस्डि'मीनर) *n.* मामूली अपराध
miser ('माइज़र) *n.* कंजूस, सूम, क पण व्यक्ति
miserable ('मिज़रबल) *a.* अत्यंत दुखी; दुखदायक; बेकार का; घिनावना – **misery** *n.* दुख भरा जीवन; गरीबी
misfire (मिस्'फ़ाइअर) *vi.* गोली, इंजन आदि का न चलना; किसी काम का न होना
misfit ('मिस्फ़िट) *n.* बेमेल वस्तु या व्यक्ति
misfortune (मिस्'फॉर्चून) *n.* दुर्भाग्य
misgiving (मिस्'गिविङ) *n.* (बहुधा *pl.*) आशंका, संदेह, भय
misguided (मिस्'गाइडिड) *a.* जिसे बहकाया गया हो
mishap ('मिस्हैप) *n.* मामूली दुर्घटना
misinform (मिसिन्'फॉर्म) *vt.* गलत सूचना देना
misinterpret (मिसिन्'टर्प्रिट) *vt.* गलत अर्थ निकालना – **misinterpretation** *n.*
mislead (मिस्'लीड) *vt.* गलत सूचना देना; बहकाना (**misled** *pp.*)
misnomer (मिस्'नोमर) *n.* गलत नाम या शब्द
misogyny (मि'सॉजिनि) *n.* स्त्रियों के प्रति घ णा, नारी द्वेष – **misogynist** *n.*
Miss (मिस) *n.* अविवाहित स्त्री का सम्बोधन, सुश्री; (**m-**) लड़की
misplace (मिस्'प्लेस) *vt.* (वस्तु) गलत स्थान पर रख देना
misprint (मिस्'प्रिन्ट) *n.* छपाई में भूल
misrepresent (मिस्रॅप्रि'जंट) *vt.* को गलत रूप में प्रस्तुत करना
miss (मिस) *vt.* निशाना चूकना; देख, सुन, पहुंच, आदि न पाना; किसी की अनुपस्थिति खलना; बचना – *n.* चूक, भूल, अभाव
missile ('मिसाइल) *n.* जो वस्तु निशाने पर फैंकी जा सके; प्रक्षेपास्त्र
mission ('मिशन) *n.* विशिष्ट काम या कर्तव्य; शिष्ट मण्डल – **missionary** *n.* धर्म प्रचारक, मिशनरी – *a.*
mist (मिस्ट) *n.* कुहासा, कुहरा – **misty** *a.* कुहरे भरा; धुंधला
mistake (मिस्'टेक) *n.* भूल, गलती; अशुद्धि – *vt.* गलत धारणा बना लेना; (व्यक्ति, वस्तु को) दूसरा समझ बैठना (**mistook** *pt.*, **mistaken** *pp*) – *vi.* भूल करना – **mistaken identity** गलत पहचान
mister ('मिस्टर) *n.* पुरुष का सम्बोधन (संक्षिप्त रूप **Mr.**)
mistress ('मिस्ट्रिस) *n.* रखैल, उपपत्नी; स्वामिनी
misunderstand (मिसंडर्'स्टैंड) *vt.* गलत समझना, गलत अर्थ निकालना

misuse (मिस्यूस) *n.* दुरुपयोग – *vt.*
mitigate (ˈमिटिगेट) *vt.* उग्रता, प्रचण्डता कम करना – **mitigation** *n.*
mix (मिक्स) *vt.* इकट्ठे करना; मिलाना; मिश्रण करना – *vi.* इकट्ठे होना; मिलना जुलना – **mixed** *a.* मिला जुला; जिसमें विभिन्न घटक जातियां, स्त्री पुरुष हों – **mixture** (ˈमिक्स्चर) *n.* सम्मिश्रण, घोल – **mix–up** *n.* गड़बड़ वाली स्थिति
ml millilitre (s) का संक्षेप
mm millimetre (s) का संक्षेप
moan (मोन) *n.* कराह – *v.* कराहना
moat (मोट) *n.* खाई, विशे. जो किले के आसपास हो, परिखा
mob (मॉब) *n.* अव्यवस्थित या उत्तेजित भीड़ – *vt.* भीड़ का आक्रमण करना, घेर लेना या दुर्व्यवहार करना (**-bb-**)
mobile (ˈमोबाइल) *a.* जो चल सके – *n.* मोबाइल फोन – **mobility** (मोˈबिलिटि) – *n.* गतिशीलता
mobilize (ˈमोबिलाइज़) *v.* लामबन्दी करना – *vt.* किसी प्रयोजन के लिए संगठित करना – **mobilization** *n.*
mock (मॉक) *vt.* हंसी या खिल्ली उड़ाना, उपहास करना; नकल उतारना – *a.* नकली, बनावटी – **mockery** *n.* उपहास, विडम्बना; स्वांग
mod (मॉड) modern का संक्षेप
mode (मोड) *n.* विधि, फ़ैशन – **modish** *a.* फ़ैशन के अनुसार
model (ˈमॉडल) *n.* नमूना, प्रतिमान; ढांचा; अनुकरणीय व्यक्ति या वस्तु; मॉडल – *vt.* नमूना या प्रतिमान बनाना; सांचा बनाना – *vi.* कपड़े पहन कर दिखाना (**-ll-**) – *a.* नमूने का; आदर्श – **modelling** *n.* मॉडल बनने का व्यवसाय
modem (ˈमोर्डेम) *n. Computers* दो कम्प्यूटरों को (टेलीफोन) लाइन द्वारा जोड़ने का उपकरण
moderate *a.* (ˈमॉडरिट) सन्तुलित, संयमी; मिताचारी; मध्यम – *n.* (ˈमॉडरिट) मध्य मार्गी या नरमपंथी व्यक्ति – *v.* (ˈमॉडरेट) हल्का या मंद करना; सभा आदि का संचालन करना – **moderation** *n.* संयम; नरमी – **moderator** *n.* मध्यस्थ
modern (ˈमॉडर्न) *a.* आधुनिक; नया, प्रचलित – *n.* आधुनिक युग का व्यक्ति – **modernity** (मॉˈडर्निटि) – **modernize** *vt.* आधुनिक बनाना
modest (ˈमॉडिस्ट) *a.* विनम्र, मर्यादित, सन्तुलित; जो अधिक न हो; भला, शिष्ट – **modesty** *n.* विनम्रता; संकोच; शालीनता
modicum (ˈमॉडिकम) *n.* थोड़ी सी मात्रा
modify (ˈमॉडिफ़ाइ) *vt.* थोड़ा परिवर्तन या फेरबदल करना (**-fied, -fying**) – **modification** *n.* परिवर्तन; रूपांतरण
modulate (ˈमॉड्युलेट) *vt.* नियमित करना; स्वर ऊंचा या नीचा करना – **modulation** *n.*
module (ˈमॉड्यूल) *n.* किसी ढांचे या यंत्र का भाग जो अलग हो जाता हो – **modular** *a.* अनेक ईकाइयों का (पाठ्यक्रम) जिसमें से कुछ को विद्यार्थी चुन सके
modus operandi (ˈमोडस ऑपˈरैन्डी) *Lat.* काम करने का तरीका, कार्य विधि
mogul (ˈमोगल) *n.* (किसी क्षेत्र में) महत्वपूर्ण व्यक्ति
moist (मॉइस्ट) *a.* नम, आर्द्र – **moisten** (मॉइसन) *v.* गीला या तर करना – **moisture** (ˈमॉइस्चर) *n.* नमी, आर्द्रता
molar (ˈमोलर) *a.* चबाने का (दांत) – *n.* दाढ़
molasses (मˈलैसिज़) *n.* शीरा (जो शक्कर बनाने के बाद बच रहता है)
mole[1] (मोल) *n.* तिल (शरीर पर)
mole[2] (मोल) *n.* छछूंदर; जासूस
molecule (ˈमॉलिक्यूल) *n.* अणु कण – **molecular** *a.* अणु, आण्विक
molest (मˈलेंस्ट) *vt.* छेड़खानी करना; सताना, तंग करना – **molestation** (मलेंस्ˈटेशन) – *n.*

moll (मॉल) *n. sl.* गुण्डे की सहायक स्त्री; वेश्या

mollify (ˊमॉलिफ़ाइ) *vt.* शांत करना; उग्रता कम करना; मनाना (**-fied, -fying**)

mollusc (ˊमॉलस्क) *n.* घोंघे जैसा कोई भी पानी का जीव

mollycoddle (ˊमॉलिकॉड्ल) *v.* लाड़ प्यार करना

Molotov cocktail (ˊमॉलटॉफ-) पेट्रोल भरा आग लगाने का बम

molten (ˊमॉल्टन) देखिए MELT

moment (ˊमोमंट) *n.* पल, क्षण – **momentarily** *adv.* क्षणभर के लिए – **momentary** *a.* क्षणिक

momentous (मोˊमेंण्टस) *a.* महत्वपूर्ण

momentum (मोˊमेंन्टम) *n.* संवेग; गति से उत्पन्न वेग (*pl.* **-ta, -tums**)

monarch (ˊमॉनर्क) *n.* सम्राट – **monarchy** *n.* सम्राट तंत्र; सम्राट का शासन

monastery (ˊमॉनस्टरि) *n.* मठ, विहार

Monday (ˊमण्डे) *n.* सोमवार

money (ˊमनि) *n.* रुपया-पैसा (*pl.* **-eys, -ies**) – **monetary** (ˊमनिट्रि) *a.* मुद्रा-सम्बन्धी – **moneyed, monied** *a.* धनी, अमीर – **money lender** साहूकार

mongoose (ˊमॉङ्गूस) *n.* नेवला (*pl.* **-gooses**)

mongrel (ˊमॉङ्ग्रल) *n.* दोग़ला पशु, विशे. कुत्ता; संकर जाति – *a.* दोग़ला, संकर

monitor (ˊमॉनिटर) *n.* व्यक्ति या यंत्र जो किसी प्रक्रिया पर द ष्टि रखे या उस का रिकार्ड रखे; अध्यापक का सहायक छात्र; कम्प्यूटर का टी. वी. समान उपकरण, मॉनीटर; एक प्रकार की बड़ी छिपकली, गोह – *vt.* द ष्टि या नज़र रखना

monk (मन्क) *n.* मठवासी (भिक्षु)

monkey (ˊमंकि) *n.* बन्दर – *vi.* छेड़छाड़ करना

mono- (*comb. form*) एक, जैसे **monosyllabic** *a.* एकाक्षरीय

monochrome (ˊमॉनक्रोम) *n.* एक रंग में बना चित्र आदि – *a.* एक रंग का – **monochromatic** *a.* एकरंगा

monogamy (मॉˊनॉगमि) *n.* एक समय एक ही पत्नी या पति होने की प्रथा

monograph (ˊमॉनग्राफ) *n.* एक विषय पर संक्षिप्त पुस्तक

monolith (ˊमॉनलिथ) *n.* एक सीधी खड़ी चट्टान का स्मारक, एकाश्म; संगठन जो जल्दी से परिवर्तन के लिए तैयार न हो

monologue (ˊमॉनलॉग) *n.* एक व्यक्ति द्वारा लम्बा भाषण, एकालाप

monopoly (मˊनॉपलि) *n.* एकाधिकार – **monopolize** *vt.* एकाधिकार प्राप्त करना, किसी वस्तु का कब्ज़ा लेना

monotone (ˊमॉनटोन) *n.* एक स्वर – **monotonous** (मˊनॉटनस) *a.* एकरस; फीका; उबाने वाला – **monotony** (मˊनॉटनि) *n.* एकरसता; नीरसता; ऊबाहट

monsoon (मॉन्ˊसून) *n.* मानसून

monster (ˊमॉन्सटर) *n.* काल्पनिक दैत्य; क्रूर व्यक्ति; भीमकाय जीव या वस्तु – *a.* विशाल, भीमकाय – **monstrosity** (मॉन्ˊस्ट्रॉसिटि) *n.* दैत्याकार जीव; विक ति – **monstrous** (ˊमॉन्स्ट्रस) *a.* भीमकाय, विकराल, डरावना

month (मंथ) *n.* मास, महीना – **monthly** *a.* मासिक – *adv.* महीने में एक बार – *n.* मासिक पत्रिका

monument (ˊमॉन्युमंट) *n.* स्मारक, विशे. भवन या मूर्ति – **monumental** *a.* व्यापक, विशाल; चिरस्थायी; स्मारक का या उस जैसा

moo (मू) *n.* गाय के रंभाने की आवाज – *vi.* रंभाना

mood[1] (मूड) *n.* मनोदशा, मनःस्थिति – **moody** *a.* उदास; तुनक मिज़ाज

moon (मून) *n.* चंद्रमा; उपग्रह – *vi.* खोये-खोये से इधर-उधर घूमते रहना – **moonlight** *n.* चांदनी

moor[1] (मुअर) *n.* बंजर भूमि; बीहड़
moor[2] (मुअर) *vt.* जहाज़ को रस्सों से तट से बांधना – **moorings** *pl. n.* जहाज़ बांधने के रस्से; स्थायित्व, सुरक्षा देने वाली बात या वस्तु
moose (मूस) *n.* उत्तरी अमरीका का एक हिरण
moot (मूट) *a.* जिस पर बहस हो सके; विवादास्पद – *vt.* बहस के लिए पेश करना
mop (मॉप) *n.* पुचारा; बालों आदि का गुच्छा – *vt.* पुचारे या झाड़न से साफ़ करना **(-pp-)**
moped (ˊमोपेंड) *n.* साइकल जो हल्के इंजन से चलती है
moral (ˊमॉरल) *a.* नैतिक; सदाचार सम्बन्धी – *n.* सीख, शिक्षा – **(~s)** *pl.* आचरण या स्वभाव विशे. लैंगिक सम्बन्धों में – **moralist** *n.* जो सदाचार की शिक्षा दे; नीतिज्ञ – **morality** (मˊरैलिटि) *n.* नैतिकता; नैतिक आचरण – **moralize** – *vi.* नैतिकता के बारे में कहना या लिखना; उपदेश देना – **morally** *adv.*
morale (मˊराल) *n.* मनोबल; हौसला
morass (मˊरैस) *n.* दलदल; बखेड़ा
moratorium (मॉरˊटॉरिअम) *n.* अधिकृत रूप से भुगतान, किसी कार्य आदि का स्थगित होना (*pl.* **-ria**)
morbid (ˊमॉर्बिड) *a.* जिसे मृत्यु में बहुत अधिक दिलचस्पी हो; वीभत्स; रोगग्रस्त
more (मॉर) *a.* (मात्रा या संख्या में) अधिक, ज्यादा; MANY और MUCH का *comp.* – *adv.* के अतिरिक्त; अधिक हद तक – *pron.* अतिरिक्त मात्रा या संख्या – **moreover** (मॉˊरोवर) *adv.* इसके अतिरिक्त, और फिर
morgue (ˊमॉर्ग) *n.* मुरदाघर
moribund (ˊमॉरिबन्ड) *a.* मृतप्राय, मरणासन्न
morning (ˊमॉर्निंग) *n.* प्रातः – **morn** *n. Poet* प्रभात, ऊषाकाल
moron (ˊमॉरॉन) *n.* मन्दबुद्धि व्यक्ति; *inf.* मूर्ख
morose (मˊरोस) *a.* उदास; चिड़चिड़ा
morphia, morphine (ˊमॉर्फ़िअ, ˊमॉर्फ़ीन) *n.* अफ़ीम से बना नशीला पदार्थ
Morse (मॉर्स) *n.* (**Morse code** भी) तार भेजने की मोर्स पद्धति
morsel (ˊमॉर्सल) *n.* ग्रास, छोटा टुकड़ा
mortal (ˊमॉट्र्ल) *a.* नश्वर, मरणशील; घातक; जानी (दुश्मन) – *n.* नश्वर जीव – **mortality** (मॉर्ˊटैलिटि) *n.* नश्वरता मृत्यु-दर – **mortally** *adv.* घातक रूप से अत्यधिक
mortar (ˊमॉर्टर) *n.* चूने, रेत आदि का मसाला; थोड़ी दूर मार करने वाली तोप; खरल (औषधि आदि पीसने की); ऊखल
mortgage (ˊमॉर्गिज) *n.* बंधक, रहन, गिरवी – *vt.* ज़मानत के रूप में देना
mortify (ˊमॉर्टिफ़ाइ) *vt.* नीचा दिखाना; त्याग, आत्मसंयम द्वारा दमन करना – *vi.* मांस का गल जाना **(-fied–fying)** – **mortification** *n.* इंद्रियदमन; मानमर्दन
mortuary (ˊमॉर्च्युअरि) *n.* मुरदाघर
mosaic (मˊज़ेइक) *n.* रंगीन कांच, पत्थर के टुकड़ों का जोड़ कर बना चित्र या नमूना; पच्चीकारी की यह विधि
mosque (मॉस्क) *n.* मस्जिद
mosquito (मस्ˊकीटो) *n.* मच्छर (*pl.* **-toes**)
moss (मॉस) *n.* काई – **mossy** (ˊमॉसि) *a.* जिस पर काई जमी हो
most (मोस्ट) *a.* आकार, संख्या या मात्रा में सब से अधिक; अधिकतम, अधिकांश; MUCH और MANY का *sup.* – *n.* अधिकतम संख्या, मात्रा आदि – *adv.* सब से अधिक – *US* ALMOST का संक्षेप – **mostly** *adv.*
motel (मोˊटेंल) *n.* होटल जिसमें ठहरने व मोटर गाड़ियों के रखने की व्यवस्था हो
moth (मॉथ) *n.* पतंगा; कपड़े में लगने वाला कीड़ा – **mothball** *n.* (कपड़ों में रखने की) फिनाइल, काफूर आदि की गोली – *vt.* फिनाइल की गोली रखना (कपड़ों में); उठाकर रख देना, उपयोग स्थगित कर देना

mother (ˈमदर) *n.* मां; भिक्षुणियों के मठ की अध्यक्षा – *a.* प्राकृतिक; देशज; जन्मजात – *vt.* माता के समान देख रेख, पालन पोषण करना – **motherhood** *n.* मातृत्व – **motherly** *a.* मातृ सुलभ – **motherboard** *n.* कम्प्यूटर का मुख्य भाग (पटल) जिस पर तमाम सर्किट बने होते हैं – **mother-in-law** *n.* सास – **mother of pearl** मुक्ता, सीप – **mother-to-be** *n.* जो मां बनने वाली हो, गर्भिणी – **mother tongue** मातृ भाषा

motif (मोˈटीफ़) *n.* मूलभाव

motion (ˈमोशन) *n.* गति, गतिशीलता; प्रस्ताव; मल त्याग – *vt.* इशारा करना – **motionless** *a.* स्थिर

motive (ˈमोटिव़) *n.* प्रेरणा; अभिप्राय – *a.* प्रेरक – **motivate** *vt.* प्रेरणा देना – **motivation** (मोटिˈव़ेशन) *n.*

motley (ˈमॉट्लि) *a.* फुटकर; रंग बिरंगा

motor (ˈमोटर) *a.* चालक; प्रेरक – *n.* चलाने वाली मशीन; मोटर कार – *vi.* मोटर कार द्वारा यात्रा करना – **motorist** *n.* कार का मालिक या सवार – **motorbike, motorcycle, motorboat**, *etc. n.* मोटर से चलने वाली गाड़ियाँ

mottled (ˈमॉटल्ट) *a.* चितकबरा, चित्तीदार

motto (ˈमॉटो) *n.* आदर्श वाक्य; आचरण नियम के रूप में अपनाई सूक्ति (*pl.* **-es**)

mould[1] (मोल्ड) *n.* सांचा; ढांचा; चरित्र; आकार – *vt.* ढालना, गढ़ना – **moulding** *n.* सजावटी किनारा

mould[2] (मोल्ड) *n.* फफूंद, भूकड़ी – **mouldy** *a.* फफूंद या भूकड़ी लगा

moult (मोल्ट) *v.* (पक्षियों का) पर, (पशुओं का) रोएं आदि गिराना – *n.*

mound (माउंड) *n.* (मिट्टी या पत्थरों का) टीला

mount (माउंट) *vi.* उठना; बढ़ना; (**mount up** भी) घोड़े पर चढ़ना – *vt.* चढ़ाना; चित्र को चौखटे में लगाना; बैठाना; (अंˈदोलन आदि) शुरू करना – *n.* जिस पर कोई वस्तु टिकी हो; घोड़ा; पहाड़ी

mountain (ˈमाउंटिन) *n.* ऊंची पहाड़ी; पर्वत – **mountaineer** *n.* पर्वतारोही पर्वतवासी; – **mountaineering** *n.* पर्वतारोहण – **mountainous** (ˈमाउंटिनस) *a.* पर्वतीय; बहुत ऊंचा

mourn (मॉर्न) *v. inf.* शोक मनाना, दुख प्रकट करना – **mourner** *n.* मातम करने वाला – **mournful** *a.* शोकग्रस्त; उदास – **mourning** *n.* शोक, मातमी पोशाक

mouse[1] (माउस) *n.* चूहा (*pl.* **mice**) – **mousy** *a.* चूहे जैसा (विशे. रंग में); दब्बू;शर्मीला – **mousetrap** *n.* चूहे पकड़ने का पिंजरा

mouse[2] (माउस) *n.* कम्प्यूटर से जोड़कर उसके कार्य संचालन में प्रयुक्त एक छोटा सा उपकरण

moustache (मस्ˈटाश) *n.* मूंछ

mouth *n.* (माउथ, *pl.* माउद्ज़) मुंह, मुख; मुहाना, दहाना; किसी खोखली वस्तु, स्थान का छिद्र – *vt.* (माउद) सुनाना, विशे. खुले में, चबा-चबा कर बात करना – **mouthpiece** *n.* होठों से पकड़ी हुई या होठों के पास किसी वस्तु का सिरा जैसे टेलिफोन का; प्रवक्ता, प्रतिनिधि

move (मूव़) *vt.* हटाना; उकसाना; प्रस्ताव रखना – *vi.* स्थान बदलना; मकान बदलना; कार्यवाही करना – *n.* हटाने, खिसकाने आदि की क्रिया; चाल; किसी लक्ष्य की प्राप्ति के लिए कार्यवाही – **mov(e)able** *a./n.* – **movement** *n.* चलने, हटाने की प्रक्रिया; गति, मशीन के चलने वाले पुर्ज़े; संगीत का अंश; आन्दोलन

movie (ˈमूवि़) **US** *inf. n.* फ़िल्म *pl.* सिनेमा

mow (मो) *v.* काटना (घास आदि) (**mown** *pp.*) – **mower** *n* (**lawn mower** भी) घास काटने वाला व्यक्ति या मशीन

MP Member of Parliament, Military Police का संक्षेप

MP-3 इंटरनेट से रिकार्ड किया संगीत – **MP-3 player** ऐसा संगीत सुनने का यंत्र
mph miles per hour का संक्षेप
Mr. mister का संक्षेप
Mrs. (ˈमिसिज़) विवाहित स्त्री का सम्बोधन
Ms. (मिज़) Miss या Mrs. के स्थान पर प्रयुक्त सम्बोधन
Ms(s) manuscripts(s) का संक्षेप
MSc Master of Science का संक्षेप
Mt. Mount का संक्षेप
much (मच) *a.* बहुत (**more** *comp.*, **most** *sup.*) – *n.* बहुत बड़ी मात्रा; बहुत सा; महत्वपूर्ण विषय – *adv*. बहुत; प्रायः, लगभग
muck (मक) *n.* मवेशियों का गोबर; कूड़ा-करकट
mucus (ˈम्यूकस) *n.* बलगम, श्लेष्मा
mud (मड) *n.* कीचड़ – **muddy** *a.* – **mudguard** *n.* कार आदि के पहिए का आवरण, मडगार्ड
muddle (ˈमड्ल) *vt.* (**muddle up** भी) गड़बड़ी कर देना; घबरा देना; काम बिगाड़ना – *n.* गड़बड़ी, अव्यवस्था
muezzin (मूˈएज़िन) *n.* मस्जिद में नमाज़ के लिए पुकारने वाला, मुअज़िन
muff (मफ़) *n.* हाथ गरम रखने का बड़ा दस्ताने जैसा आवरण
muffin (ˈमफ़िन) *n.* गोल, मोटी मीठी रोटी
muffle (ˈमफ़ल) *vt.* लपेटना, विशे. आवाज़ दबाने के लिए – **muffler** (ˈमफ़लर) *n.* गुलूबन्द
mufti (ˈमफ़्टि) *n.* साधारण कपड़े (वरदी के विपरीत)
mug[1] (मग) *n.* प्याला
mug[2] (मग) *n. sl.* चेहरा; *sl.* मूर्ख – *vt.* मारपीट कर लूट लेना – **mugger** *n.* लुटेरा – **mugging** *n.* लूटने की क्रिया
mug[3] (मग) *vi.* – **mug up** *inf.* रट्टा लगाना
mulberry (ˈमॅल्बरि) *n.* शहतूत
mule (म्यूल) *n.* खच्चर – **mulish** (ˈम्यूलिश) *a.* ज़िद्दी
mull (मल) *vt.* (शराब को) चीनी और मसाले डाल कर गरम करना – **mull over** के बारे में सोचना, पर विचार करना
multi- (*comb. form*) बहु-, जैसे **multiparty** *a.*
multifarious (मल्टिˈफ़ॅअरिअस) *a.* विभिन्न प्रकारों या हिस्सों वाला
multimedia (मल्टिˈमीडिअ) *n.* कम्प्यूटर तथा मनोरंजन में चल व अचल चित्रों, ध्वनि संगीत, रेखाचित्रों आदि का मिलाकर उपयोग
multiple (ˈमल्टिपल) *a.* बहुविध; बहुखंड – *n.* गुणज (दो संख्याओं के गुणा करने से प्राप्त संख्या) – **multiplication** *n.* गुणा; प्रजनन – **multiplicity** (मल्टिˈप्लिसिटि) *n.* विविधता; बहुलता – **multiply** (ˈमल्टिप्लाइ) *v.* संख्या, मात्रा आदि में बढ़ाना – *vt.* गुणा करना (**-plied–plying**)
multiplex (ˈमल्टिप्लेॅक्स) *n.* सिनेमाघर जिसमें एक साथ कई चलचित्र अलग-अलग पर्दों पर दिखाए जांय
multitude (ˈमल्टिट्यूड) *n.* बहुलता; बहुत बड़ी संख्या; बड़ी भीड़; जनताजनार्दन – **multitudinous** (मल्टिˈट्यूडिनस) *a.* बहुसंख्यक
mum[1], **mummy** (मम, ˈममि) *n. inf.* मां
mum[2] (मम) *a.* चुप, खामोश – **keep mum** चुप रहना
mumble (ˈमम्बल) *v.* बुदबुदाना; अस्पष्ट बोलना
mumbo-jumbo (मम्बोˈजम्बो) *n. inf.* निरर्थक भाषा या अनुष्ठान
mummy[1] (ˈममि) *n.* पुराना शव (जिसे लेप लगा कर रखा हो जिससे वह गले नही); परिरक्षित शव
mummy[2] (ˈममि) *n.* मम्मी, मां
mumps (ˈमम्प्स) *pl. n.* कनफेड़
munch (मंच) *v.* चबाना; चबाते हुए आवाज़ करना

mundane (ˈमन्डेन) *a.* साधारण; सांसारिक, इहलौकिक

municipal (म्यूˈनिसिपल) *a.* नगर से सम्बन्धित – **municipality** (म्यूनिसिˈपैलिटि) *n.* नगर पालिका

munificent (म्यूˈनिफ़िसंट) *a.* बहुत उदार – **munificence** (म्यूˈनिफ़िसन्स) *n.*

mural (ˈम्युअरल) *n.* भित्तिचित्र

murder (ˈमर्डर) *n.* हत्या – *vt.* हत्या करना – **murderous** *a.* खूनी या हत्यारे जैसा

murk (मर्क) *n.* गहरा अंधेरा – **murky** (ˈमर्कि) *a.* विषादमय; अंधकारपूर्ण

murmur (ˈमर्मर) *n.* मद्धिम, अस्पष्ट आवाज; फुसफुसाहट – *vi.* फुसफुसाना; शिकायत करना – *vt.* धीमी आवाज़ में कहना

muscle (ˈमसल) *n.* मांसपेशी; मांसपेशी व्यवस्था – **muscular** (ˈमस्क्युलर) *a.* हृष्ट पुष्ट; मांसपेशी का या उस जैसा – **muscleman** अपराधी का हट्टा-कट्टा अंगरक्षक, पहलवान, बाहुबली

muse (म्यूज़) *vi.* चिन्तन करना; विचारमग्न होना – *n.* चिन्तन; अन्यमनस्कता; दिवास्वप्न

museum (म्यूˈज़िअम) *n.* (प्राक तिक, कलात्मक ऐतिहासिक या वैज्ञानिक वस्तुओं का) संग्रहालय, अजायबघर

mush (मश) *n.* गूदा, लुगदी – **mushy** *a.* बहुत अधिक भावुकतापूर्ण

mushroom (ˈमश्रूम) *n.* खुम्बी, कुकुरमुत्ता – *vi.* तेज़ी से बढ़ना या फैलना

music (ˈम्यूज़िक) *n.* संगीत; संगीत रचना – **musical** *a.* संगीत का या उस जैसा; मधुर – *n.* संगीत प्रधान नाटक, फिल्म आदि – **musician** (म्यूˈज़िशन) *n.* संगीतज्ञ; संगीतकार – **musical instrument** संगीतवाद्य, बाजा

musk (मस्क) *n.* कस्तूरी; कस्तूरी जैसी सुगंध वाले पौधे – **musk deer** कस्तूरी म ग

Muslim (ˈमुस्लिम) *n.* मुसलमान – *a.*

muslin (ˈमज़लिन) *n.* मलमल

mussel (ˈमसल) *n.* शंखमीन; कोई भी सीपी में बंद मछली

must[1] (मस्ट) *v. aux.* आवश्यक, अनिवार्य या निश्चित होना, अवश्य (करना) चाहिए – *n.* अनिवार्य काम

mustache US दे० **moustache**

mustang (ˈमस्टैङ) *n.* जंगली घोड़ा

mustard (ˈमस्टर्ड) *n.* राई; सरसों, उसका पौधा – **mustard gas** विषैली गैस

muster (ˈमस्टर) *v.* इकट्ठे या जमा करना या होना (लोगों का) – *n.* जमा होने वाला समूह विशे. व्यायाम या प्रदर्शन के लिए

musty (ˈमस्टि) *a.* फफूंद या भुकड़ी लगा

mutate (म्यूˈटेट) *v.* परिवर्तन करना – **mutable** *a.* परिवर्तनशील – **mutant** *n.* परिवर्तित जीव, पौधा आदि – **mutation** (म्यूˈटेशन) *n.* परिवर्तन, विशे. जिस से जातिगत या पुश्तैनी गुण बदले जायें

mute (म्यूट) *a.* गूंगा, मूक; मौन – *n.* गूंगा व्यक्ति; *Mus.* वाद्य के स्वर को हलका करने की युगत – **muted** (ˈम्यूटिड) *a.* दबा हुआ (स्वर); मद्धिम (प्रकाश)

mutilate (ˈम्यूटिलेट) *vt.* अंग-भंग करना; बिगाड़ना – **mutilation** (म्यूटिˈलेशन) *n.* विक ति

mutiny (ˈम्यूटिनि) *n.* विद्रोह, ग़दर – *vi.* विद्रोह करना (**mutinied, mutinying**) – **mutineer** (म्यूटिˈनिअर) *n.* विद्रोही – **mutinous** *a.* विद्रोही, बाग़ी

mutter (ˈमटर) *vi.* बुदबुदाना, बड़बड़ाना – *vt.* कुछ बड़बड़ाना – *n.*

mutton (ˈमट्न) *n.* भेड़ का मांस

mutual (ˈम्यूचुअल) *a.* पारस्परिक, आपसी –*inf.* सब का – **mutually** *adv.* – **mutual fund** व्यवस्था जिसके अंतर्गत कंपनी निवेशकों का पैसा शेयर बाज़ार में लगाकर उससे हुए लाभ का अंश उन्हें देती है

muzzle (ˈमज़ल) *n.* जानवर की थूथनी; इसे बांधने का छींका, बन्दूक का मुंह, नालमुख – *vt.* पर छींका बांधना; मुंह बंद करना; (आवाज़) दबाना

MV motor vessel का संक्षेप

MW megawatt(s) का संक्षेप

my (माइ) *a.* मेरा, अपना; मेरे, अपने – **myself** *pron.* मेरा ही, मेरा स्वयं का; मैंने अपने आप (को)

myna(h) (ˈमाइन्अ) *n.* मैना

myopia (माइˈओपिअ) *n.* निकट दृष्टिता, दूर की चीज़ें ठीक न देख पाना

myriad (ˈमिरिअड) *a.* असंख्य – *n.* एक बहुत बड़ी संख्या

myrtle (ˈमट्‌र्ल) *n.* एक सदाबहार फूलों वाली झाड़ी

myself (माइˈसेल्फ़) दे. MY

mystery (ˈमिस्टरि) *n.* रहस्य, भेद; मर्म – **mysterious** (मिस्ˈटिअरिअस) *a.* रहस्यमय

mystic (ˈमिस्टिक) *n.* रहस्यवादी, व्यक्ति जो प्रार्थना, ध्यान आदि द्वारा ईश्वरीय व आत्मिक ज्ञान खोजता है – *a.* गूढ़ अर्थ सम्बंधी विशे. धार्मिक अर्थ में – **mystical** *a.* – **mysticism** (ˈमिस्टिसिज़म) *n.* रहस्यवाद

mystify (ˈमिस्टिफ़ाइ) *vt.* रहस्यमय बना देना (**-fied, -fying**) – **mystification** (मिस्टिफ़िˈकेशन) *n.* चकराने या उलझाने की क्रिया, बहकावट

mystique (मिस्ˈटीक) *n.* रहस्यपूर्ण वातावरण, रहस्यात्मकता

myth (मिथ) *n.* पौराणिक कथा; काल्पनिक व्यक्ति या वस्तु – **mythical** (ˈमिथिकल) *a.* काल्पनिक – **mythological** (मिथˈलॉजिकल) *a.* पौराणिक – **mythology** (मिˈथॉलजि) *n.* पौराणिक कथा समूह, पुराण शास्त्र, पुराण शास्त्र अध्ययन

N

nab (नैब) *inf. vt.* अपराधी को गिरफ्तार करना; अचानक धर लेना **(-bb-)**

nachos (नैचोज़) *sing. n.* मैक्सिको का व्यंजन

nadir (नेडिअर) *n.* अधो बिन्दु; *fig.* सबसे नीची स्थिति

nag (नैग) *v.* लगातार परेशान करना, सिर खाना **(-gg-)** – **nagging** *a.* परेशान करने वाला (संदेह, दर्द)

nail (नेल) *n.* नख, नाखून; कील – *vt.* कील ठोकना या लगाना, जकड़ देना; *inf.* पकड़ लेना

naive (ना'ईव़) *a.* सीधा, निष्कपट, भोला – **naivetè, naivety** (नाईव़'टे, नाइ'ईवटि) *n.*

naked ('नेकिड) *a.* नंगा; बिना ढंका, उघड़ा हुआ – **nakedly** *adv*. **nakedness** *n.* नग्नता

name (नेम) *n.* नाम; ख्याति; गौरव; वंश; प्रसिद्ध व्यक्ति – *vt.* नाम रखना; नाम लेना; उपाधि देना; नियुक्त करना; जिकर करना, निश्चत या निर्धारित करना – **nameless** *a.* अनाम; अकथनीय, अत्यंत भयावना या घ णित; अज्ञात – **namely** *adv*. अर्थात्, यानि – **name-calling** *n.* गाली/ अपशब्द का प्रयोग **namesake** *n.* हमनाम, समनाम

nanny ('नैनि) *n.* आया – **nanny goat** बकरी

nano- नैनो) *comb. form* दस अरब का एक भाग (जैसे *nanosecond*)

nap (नैप) *vi.* झपकी लेना, (दिन में) थोड़ा सो लेना **(-pp-)** – *n.* झपकी

nape (नेप) *n.* – **nape of the neck** गर्दन का पिछला भाग, गुद्दी

napkin ('नैपकिन) *n.* कागज या कपड़े का बड़ा रूमाल, नैपकिन, छोटा तौलिया

nappy ('नैपि) *n.* तौलिये के कपड़े अथवा मुलायम कागज का पोतड़ा, लंगोट

narcissus (नार्'सिसस) *n.* नरगिस (का फूल) (*pl.* **narcissi** (नार्'सिसाइ)

narcotic (नार्'कॉटिक) *n.* नशीली दवा; न द की दवा, स्वापी – *a.*

narrate (न'रेट) *vt.* वर्णन करना, बताना, (कहानी) सुनाना – **narration** (न'रेशन) *n.* वर्णन – **narrative** ('नैरटिव़) *n.* वर्णन, कथा – *a.* कथात्मक – **narrator** (न'रेटर) *n.* कथाकार

narrow ('नैरो) *a.* संकीर्ण, तंग; *fig.* सीमित; (बचने में) मुश्किल से कामयाब – *v.* संकीर्ण होना या करना; सीमित करना – **narrowness** *n.* – **narrow-minded** *a.* संकीर्ण विचारों वाला, असहिष्णु

nasal ('नेज़ल) *a.* नाक का – *n.* (आंशिक रूप से) नाक से उत्पन्न स्वर, अनुनासिक – **nasalize** *vt.* अनुनासिक

nasty ('नास्टि) *a.* गंदा; खीज पैदा करने या गुस्सा दिलाने वाला

nat. national; native; natural का संक्षेप

natal ('नेटल) *a.* जन्म सम्बन्धी

nation ('नेशन) *n.* राष्ट्र; कौम, जाति – **national** ('नैशनल) *a.* राष्ट्रीय – *n.* राष्ट्र का नागरिक – **nationalism** *n.* राष्ट्रवाद – **nationalist** *n./a.* राष्ट्रवादी – **nationality** (नैश'नैलिटि) *n.* राष्ट्रीयता – **nationalization** *n.* (नैश्नलाइ'ज़ेशन) *n.* (उद्योग आदि का) राष्ट्रीयकरण – **nationalize** *vt.* राष्ट्रीयकरण करना – **nationally** *adv.* – **nationwide** *a.* राष्ट्रीय पैमाने पर – **national park** क्षेत्र जहां शिकार, व क्ष काटने आदि की मनाही हो

native ('नेटिव़) *a.* मूल निवासी; मूलतः किसी स्थान पर पाये जाने वाले (पौधे, पक्षी, प्राणी),

जन्मजात – *n.* देशी, आदिवासी; किसी स्थान पर मूलतः पाये जाने वाले पौधे या प्राणी – **native language** देशीय भाषा

nativity (न'टिविटि) *n.* जन्म, इसका समय, **(N-)** ईसा का जन्म

natty ('नैटि) *a. inf.* बना-ठना – **nattily** *adv.*

nature ('नेचर) *n.* स्वभाव, प्रकृति; स्वरूप; **(N-)** सृष्टि, प्रकृति; भौतिक संसार; प्राकृतिक दृश्य, स्थान – **natural** ('नैचरल) *a.* प्राकृतिक; स्वाभाविक, नैसर्गिक; सामान्य – *n.* किसी कार्य/ स्थान के योग्य वस्तु, व्यक्ति – **naturalist** *n.* प्रकृति-विज्ञान का अध्येता – **naturalize** ('नैचरलाइज़) *vt.* नागरिकता प्रदान करना – **naturally** *adv.* स्वाभाविक ढंग से, सहज ही, निस्सन्देह – **naturism** ('नेचरिज़म) *n.* प्रकृति-पूजा; नग्नावस्था में रहने का सिद्धांत – **natural gas** ईंधन के रूप में प्रयुक्त ज़मीन/समुद्र के नीचे मिलने वाली गैस, प्राकृतिक गैस – **natural history** पशु, पक्षी व पौधों का अध्ययन, प्रकृति-विज्ञान

naughty ('नॉटि) *a.* नटखट, शरारती; *inf.* हल्की-सी अश्लील

nausea ('नॉज़िअ, 'नॉसिअ) *n.* मितली, मितलाई, उबकाई

nautical ('नॉटिकल) *a.* समुद्री, नौ- (जहाज़, नाविक, सामुद्रिक विषय-वस्तुओं के लिए प्रयुक्त) – **nautical mile** समुद्री मील, 1852 मीटर के बराबर

naval ('नेव़ल) *a.* दे. NAVY

navel ('नेव़ल) *n.* नाभि, तुन्दी

navigate ('नैविगेट) *v.* जहाज़ आदि का मार्ग निर्देशन करना या चलाना; यात्रा करना – **navigable** ('नैविगबल) *a.*– **navigation** (नैवि'गेशन) *n.* जहाज़, नौका, वायुयान, आदि का संचालन – **navigator** ('नैविगेटर) *n.* नौचालक

navy ('नेवि) *n.* नौसेना – *a.* गहरा नीला – **naval** ('नेव़ल) *a.* नौसेना सम्बंधी – **navy-blue** *a.* गहरा नीला

nay (नि) *adv. obs.* नहीं

NB *nota bene* (कृप्या नोट कीजिए) का संक्षेप

NCO Non-Commissioned Officer का संक्षेप

neap (नीप) *a.* नीचा – **neap tide** लघु ज्वार-भाटा

near (निअर) *prep.* निकट, पास, नज़दीक – *adv.* निकट, पास, करीब-करीब – *a.* लगभग; निकट का, नज़दीकी (रिश्तेदार), मुश्किल से (बचाव) – *v.* नज़दीक पहुंचना – **nearby** *a.* निकट के – **nearly** *adv.* लगभग, तकरीबन

neat (नीट) *a.* सुव्यवस्थित; साफ-सुथरा; दक्ष; विशुद्ध (शराब आदि)

nebulous ('नेंब्युलस) *a.* अस्पष्ट

necessary ('नेंसिसरि) *a.* आवश्यक, अनिवार्य – **necessarily** *adv.* – **necessitate** (निसें'सिटेट) *vt.* अनिवार्य कर देना – **necessity** (नि'सेंसिटि) *n.* आवश्यकता, आवश्यक वस्तु; अनिवार्यता; निर्धनता

neck ('नेंक) *n.* गर्दन; (बोतल का) तंग भाग; दो चौड़े भागों के बीच कोई भी तंग भाग – **necklace** ('नेंक्लिस) *n.* कण्ठी, नैकलेस – **necktie** *n.* टाई – **neck and neck (with sb)** दौड़, आदि में, साथ-साथ

nectar ('नेंक्टर) *n.* अमृत, सुधा; फूलों का रस, मकरंद – **nectary** *n.* मकरंद कोष

née, nee (ने) *a.* विवाहित स्त्री का विवाह पूर्व के नाम का संकेत

need (नीड) *vt.* की आवश्यकता होना, का अभाव होना; चाहना – *n.* अभाव, आवश्यकता – **needful** *a.* आवश्यक – **needless** *a.* अनावश्यक, निरर्थक – **needy** *a.* निर्धन, अभावग्रस्त

needle ('नीड्ल) *n.* सुई, बुनने की सलाई; सूचक-यंत्र, रिकार्ड-प्लेयर की सुई; देवदार आदि

की नुकीली पत्ती; *inf.* इंजेक्शन लगाने की सिरिंज – *vt. inf.* उकसाना, चिढ़ाना

nefarious (नि'फ़ेंअरिअस) *a.* दुष्ट, अपराधिक

negate (नि'गेट) *vt.* खण्डन करना, व्यर्थ कर देना – **negation** (नि'गेशन) *n.* खण्डन

negative ('नैंगटिव़) *a.* नकरात्मक, नकारी (शब्द या वाक्य); उत्साहहीन; रुचिविहीन;ऋणात्मक; किसी विद्युत-चार्ज की ऋणास्तक ध्रुवता –*n.*नह अर्थ वाले शब्द या वाक्य; *Photography* नैगेटिव प्लेट; प्रतिचित्र – *vt.* खण्डन करना, अस्वीकार करना

neglect (नि'ग्लेंक्ट) *vt.* अवहेलना करना, का ध्यान न रखना; की देखभाल न करना, (कर्तव्य आदि) न करना; उपेक्षा करना; छोड़ देना –*n.* अवहेलना, उपेक्षा, अनादर – **neglected** *a.* उपेक्षित – **neglectful** *a.* लापरवाह

negligee ('नैंग्लिझ़े) *n.* स्त्रियों का रात्रि वस्त्र, ड्रेसिंग गाउन

negligence ('नैंग्लिजन्स) *n.* लापरवाही; असावधानी; उपेक्षा – **negligent** ('नैंग्लिजंट) *a.* असावधान – **negligible** ('नैंग्लिजबल) *a.* नाममात्र को, महत्वहीन

negotiate (नि'गोशिएट) *vi.* समझौते के लिए बातचीत करना – *vt.* बातचीत द्वारा समझौता करना; (चैक, हुण्डी आदि) हस्तांतरित करना; (बाधा) पार करना – **negotiable** (नि'गोशबल) *a.* विक्रेय, विनिमेय – **negotiation** (निगोशि'एशन) *n.* समझौता वार्ता; मोल-तोल; चैक आदि का हस्तांतरण – **negotiator** *n.* मध्यस्थ

Negro ('नीग्रो) *n. offens.* नीग्रो, हब्शी

neigh (ने) *n.* घोड़े की हिनहिनाहट – *vi.* (घोड़े का) हिनहिनाना

neighbour ('नेबर) *n.* पड़ौसी – **neighbourhood** *n.* पड़ौस; पड़ौस का क्षेत्र व वहां के निवासी – **neighbouring** *a.* निकटवर्ती – **neighbourly** *a.* पड़ौसी जैसे (सम्बंध आदि); मिलनसार

neither ('नाइदर, 'नीदर) *a./pron.* (दोनों में से) कोई भी नह –*adv.* न तो … और नाहीं … *(She can neither read nor write)* - *conj.* अभी तक नह

neo- (*comb. form*) नव-, परिवर्तित रूप में;

neon ('नीऑन) *n.* वायुमण्डल में एक अक्रिय गैस, जो विज्ञापन बोर्ड आदि को प्रकाशमान करने के काम आती है

nephew ('नैंफ़्यू 'नैंव्यू,) *n.* भतीजा, भानजा

nepotism ('नैंपटिज़्म) *n.* भाई-भतीजावाद

Neptune ('नैंप्ट्यून, 'नैंप्चून) *n.* वरुण देवता; नेपचून नक्षत्र

nerve (नर्व़) *n.* स्नायु, नस; आत्माविश्वास, संकट में शांत रहना, धैर्य, साहस – (~ **s**) *pl.* चिड़चिड़ापन, शीघ्र आशंकित या उत्तेजित होना – *vt.* को साहस व शक्ति देना – **nerveless** ('नर्व़लिस) *a.* दुर्बल; डरपोक – **nervous** ('नर्व़स) *a.* उत्तेजित; आशंकित – **nervous breakdown** मानसिक व भावात्मक संतुलन भंग हो जाना

nest ('नैंस) *n.* घोंसला; बसेरा – *vi.* घोंसला बनाना

nestle ('नैंसल) *vi.* सुख से बस जाना या बसा होना; (प्राय: किसी स्थान आदि के निकट) से लगा होना

nestling ('नैंस्ट्लिंग, नैंस्लिंग) *n.* चिड़िया का बच्चा (जो घोंसला नह छोड़ सकता)

net[1] ('नैंट) *n.* जाल; **(N-)** देखिये INTERNET – *vt.* जाल बिछाना या जाल में पकड़ना, फंसाना **(-tt-)** – **netting** *n.* (रस्सी या तार का) जाल

net(t) (निट) *a.* सभी कटौतियों के बाद बचा (लाभ, अमादनी)

nether ('नैंदर) *a.* निचला

nettle ('नैंट्ल) *n.* बिच्छू-बूटी – *vt.* तंग करना

network ('नैंट्वर्क) *n.* रेलों, नहरों आदि का जालतंत्र, सुसम्बद्ध लोगों या वस्तुओं का संगठन या व्यवस्था; रेडियो स्टेशनों का वर्ग जो एक ही समय पर कोई एक कार्यक्रम प्रसारित करने

के लिए जुड़े हों; *Computers* किसी दफ्तर या संगठन में कम्प्यूटरों का जालतंत्र

neural (ˈन्युअरल) *a.* स्नायु-सम्बंधी

neurologist (ˈन्युरॉलजिस्ट) *n.* तंत्रिका-विज्ञानी

neurosis (न्युˈरोसिस) *n.* मानसिक असंतुलन, न्युरोसिस – **neurotic** (न्युˈरॉटिक) *a.* मानसिक असंतुलन से पीड़ित – *n.* ऐसा व्यक्ति

neuter (ˈन्यूटर) *a.* नपुंसक (लिंग)

neutral (ˈन्यूट्रल) *a.* तटस्थ, निरपेक्ष, अनिश्चित – *n.* तटस्थ देश; तटस्थ देशवासी; इंजन से असम्बद्ध गीयर – **neutrality** (न्यू ˈट्रैलिटि) *n.* तटस्थता – **neutralize** (ˈन्यूट्रलाइज़) – *vt.* प्रभावहीन करना

neutron (ˈन्यूट्रॉन) *n.* न्यूट्रॉन, परमाणु का एक कण – **neutron bomb** आणविक बम जो केवल मनुष्यों को नष्ट करेगा, इमारतों को नह

never (ˈनेंव़र) *adv.* कभी नह ; कदापि नह – **nevertheless** (नेंव़रदलेंस) *adv.* फिर भी, तदापि

new (न्यू) *a.* नवीन, नया; ताज़ा, अपरिचित – *adv.* (प्राय: **newly**) अभी, हाल में, फिर से – **newly** *adv.* – **newness** *n.* नवीनता – **newcomer** (ˈन्यूकमर) *n.* नवागन्तुक – **newfangled** *a.* नये ढंग के (विचार आदि)

news (न्यूज़) *n.* समाचार, खबर, खबरें; नयी जानकारी – **newsagent** *n.* समाचारपत्र वितरणकर्ता व विक्रेता – **newscaster** *n.* (**newsreader** भी) समाचार प्रसारणकर्ता – **newspaper** *n.* समाचार पत्र – **newsprint** *n.* अखबारी कागज – **newsreader** *n.* दे० **newscaster** – **newsreel** *n.* समाचार-दर्शन, समाचार-चित्र (फिल्म) – **newsworthy** *a.* समाचार के रूप में देने योग्य (घटना आदि)

newt (न्यूट) *n.* एक छोटा पूंछ वाला जल-स्थल चर जीव, सरटिका

next (नेंक्स्ट) *a.* अगला; निकटतम – *adv.* इसके बाद – **next-of-kin** *n.* निकटतम सम्बन्धी

nexus (नेंक्सस) *n.* सम्बंध, जोड़ (*pl.* **nexus**)

nibble (ˈनिबल) *v.* कुतरना – *n.* छोटा सा (खाने का) कौर

nice (नाइस) *a.* रुचिकर, सुखद; अच्छा, सहृदय; बारीक (फर्क, बात) – **nicely** *adv.* अच्छी तरह से, ठीक से – **nicety** (ˈनाइसिटि) *n.* बारीकी, सूक्ष्मता

niche (निच, नीश) *n.* दीवार में आला; जीवन में, जनता की नज़रों में उपयुक्त स्थान

nick (निक) *vt.* खांचा काटना या बनाना; *inf.* चुराना; गिरफ्तार कर लेना, पकड़ लेना – *n.* खांचा; अंतिम क्षण, बिल्कुल ठीक समय; *sl.* जेल – **in good nick** अच्छी हालत में, ठीक-ठाक

nickel (ˈनिकल) *n.* निकल धातु; **US**, पांच सैंट का सिक्का

nickname (ˈनिक्नेम) *n.* उपनाम; प्यार का नाम

nicotine (ˈनिकटीन) *n.* तम्बाकू का विषैला तरल पदार्थ, निकोटीन

niece (नीस) *n.* भतीजी, भानजी

nifty (ˈनिफ़्टि) *inf. a.* आकर्षक; चुस्त

niggard (ˈनिगर्ड) *n.* कंजूस, घटिया व्यक्ति – **niggardly** *a./adv.*

nigger (ˈनिगर) *n. offens.* नीग्रो

niggle (ˈनिगल) *vi.* आलोचना करते रहना; कमी निकालते रहना; गुस्सा दिलाना

nigh (नाइ) *a./adv./prep. obs.* or *Poet.* निकट

night (नाइट) *n.* रात, रात्रि – **nightie, nighty** (ˈनाइटि) *n.* स्त्रियों की रात की पोशाक – **nightcap** *n.* सोते समय पहनने की टोपी; सोने से पहले पी गयी शराब आदि – **nightclub** *n.* रात को नाच-गान आदि के लिए स्थान, नाइट क्लब – **nightdress** *n.*

स्त्रियों की रात को पहनने की ढीली-ढाली पोशाक – **nightingale** (´नाइटिंगेल) *n.* बुलबुल – **nightmare** *n.* दुःस्वप्न, डरावना सपना; भयानक अनुभव – **night-time** *n.* रात्रि समय/काल – **night life** किसी नगर की रात्रि की चहल-पहल (मनोरंजन के साधन आदि) – **nightspot** रात्रि-मनोरंजन स्थल

nil (निल) *n.* शून्य, कुछ नह

nimble (´निम्बल) *a.* फुरतीला, चुस्त; तेज, कुशल – **nimbly** *adv.* चुस्ती से; दक्षता से

nimbus (´निंबस) *n.* वर्षा-मेघ; प्रभा मण्डल (*pl.* **-bi** (-बाइ), **-buses**)

nine (नाइन) *a./n.* नौ – **ninth** *a.* नौंवा **nineteen** *a./n.* उन्नीस – **nineteenth** *a.* उन्नीसवां – **ninety** *a./n.* नब्बे – **ninetieth** *a.* नब्बेवां

nip (निप) *vt.* जोर से दबाना, चुटकी काटना, दबा कर काट लेना (अलग कर लेना); काटना, पौधों की छंटाई करके उनका विकास रोकना; रोकना; *sl.* चुराना – *vi. inf.* जल्दी करना (**-pp-**) – *n.* चुटकी; छंटाई; ठण्ड का तीखापन; चुस्की – **nippy** *inf. a.* सर्द; तेज़

nipple (´निपल) *n.* स्तन का अगला भाग, चूची; इसके आकार-प्रकार की वस्तु

nit (निट) *n.* जूं का अण्डा, लीख; अन्य छोटे कीड़ों के अण्डे; *inf.* **nitwit** का संक्षिप्त रूप – **nitpicking** *a. inf.* छोटी-छोटी कमियां निकालने वाला, छिद्रान्वेषी – **nitwit** *n. inf.* बुद्धू – **nitty-gritty** *n. inf.* आधारभूत तत्व, मुख्य बातें

nitrogen (´नाइट्रजन) *n.* नाइट्रोजन गैस – **nitrate** *n.* नाइट्रिक ऐसिड (शोरे का तेजाब) व अल्कली (क्षार) का यौगिक, नाइट्रेट – **nitric,** *a.* – **nitroglycerin(e)** (नाइट्रो´ग्लिसरिन) *n.* एक विस्फोटक द्रव

nix (निक्स) *n. sl.* कुछ नह

no (नो) *a.* कोई नह , बिल्कुल नह , एक भी नह – *adv.* नह , ना; असहमति प्रकट करने या खण्डन करने का शब्द – *n.* अस्वीक ति, खण्डन; प्रतिकूल मत या मतदाता (*pl.* **noes**) – **no-one, no one** कोई भी नह **no man's land** दो देशों की सीमाओं के बीच खाली क्षेत्र

no. number (संख्या) का संक्षिप्त रूप

noble (´नोबल) *a.* कुलीन वर्ग का; उच्च गुणों, योग्यताओं वाला, प्रभावशाली – *n.* सामन्त वर्ग का सदस्य, कुलीनता – **nobility** (नो´बिलिटि) *n.* सामन्त वर्ग; कुलीनता; उच्चता, श्रेष्ठता – **nobleman** (´नोबल्मन) *n.* कुलीन पुरुष – **nobly** *adv.*

nobody (´नोबडि) *n.* कोई नह , नगण्य व्यक्ति

nocturnal (नॉक्´टर्नल) *a.* रात में सक्रिय निशाचर (जीव)

nod (नॉड) *v.* सिर हिलाकर स्वीक ति देना, सहमति या आदेश देने के लिए सिर हिलाना; झपकी लेना, ऊंघना (**-dd-**) – *n.* सिर हिलाकर सहमति; आदेश

node (नोड) *n.* गांठ, संधिस्थान – **nodal** *a.*

nodule (´नॉड्यूल) *n.* छोटी सी गांठ, ग्रंथिका, खनिज-पिण्ड

noise (नॉइज़) *n.* आवाज़, ध्वनि, शोरगुल– *vt.* फैलाना, प्रचारित करना – **noisy** *a.* शोरभरा

nomad (´नोमैड) *n.* खानाबदोश, बंजारा – **nomadic** (नो´मैडिक) *a.*

nominal (´नॉमिनल) *a.* नाममात्र (का); (फीस आदि) बहुत कम, नगण्य; – **nominally** *adv.* नाम मात्र के लिए

nominate (´नॉमिनेट) *vt.* मनोनीत करना, नियुक्त करना – **nomination** (नॉमि´नेशन) *n.* – **nominee** (नॉमि´नी) *n.* उम्मीदवार, नामज़द, नामांकित

non- (*prefix*) *non-* लगाने से शब्द का विलोम बनता है: जैसे **nonaligned**

nonaligned (नॉन्अ´लाइंड) *a.* गुट-निरपेक्ष

nonbeliever (नॉन्बि´लीव़र) *n.* नास्तिक

nonchalant (ˈनॉन्शलंट) *a.* अनासक्त, उदासीन, भावहीन – **nonchalance** *n.* भावहीनता, उदासीनता

noncommittal (नॉन्कˈमिट्ल) *a.* जो निश्चित पसन्द या राय जाहिर न करे, निश्चित वादा न करे, हाँ-न-ना का (उत्तर), अनिबद्ध

non-compliance (नॉन् ˈकम्प्लाइअंस) *n.* आज्ञा पालन न करना, अपालन

nonconformist (नॉन्कन्- ˈफ़ॉर्मिस्ट) *n.* परंपरा-विरोधी

non-cooperation (नॉन्कोऑपˈरेशन) *n.* असहयोग

nondescript (ˈनॉन्डिस्क्रिप्ट) *a.* अवर्गीकृत; जिसकी (वर्णन योग्य) कोई विशिष्टता न हो

none (नन) *pron.* कोई नह , कोई भी नह – *a.* कोई सा भी नह – *adv*. बिल्कुल नह – **nonetheless** *adv*. फिर भी

nonentity (नॉन्ˈऐंण्टिटि) *n.* नगण्य व्यक्ति

nonflammable (नॉन्ˈफ्लैमबल) *a.* अज्वलनशील

non-negotiable (नॉन्ˈनियोशिअबल) *n.* (मांगे आदि) जो बदली न जा सकें, अपरिवर्तनीय

nonplus (नॉन्ˈप्लस) *vt.* परेशानी में डाल देना

nonsense (ˈनॉन्सन्स) *n.* अर्थहीन बातें, बकवास

nonstick (नान्ˈस्टिक) *n.* बर्तन जिसपर पकते समय पकवान चिपके नहीं

nonverbal (नॉन्ˈवर्बल) *n.* शब्दों के बिना (इशारों आदि से)

noodles (ˈनूडल्ज़) *pl. n.* नूडल (खाद्य पदार्थ)

nook (नुक) *n.* कोना; एकांत स्थान

noon (नून) *n.* दोपहर

noose (नूस) *n.* फंदा, पाश

nor (नॉर) *conj.* ना ही, और न

norm (नॉर्म) *n.* मानक, मान दण्ड, प्रतिमान – **normal** (नॉर्मल) *a.* सामान्य, साधारण, नियमित – *n.* – **normalcy** (ˈनॉर्मल्सि) *n.* सामान्य स्थिति, शांति – **normality** (नॉर्ˈमैलिटि) *n.* सामान्य स्थिति – **normally** *adv.* सामान्यतया

north (नार्थ) *n.* उत्तर दिशा –*adv.* उत्तर में – **northern** *a.* (ˈनॉर्दर्न) – **northwards** (नॉर्थ्वर्ड्ज़) *adv.* उत्तर की ओर

nos. numbers का संक्षिप्त रूप

nose (नोज़) *n.* नाक ; (जहाज या वायुयान आदि का) आगे निकला हुआ भाग– *v.* धीरे-धीरे आगे बढ़ना या बढ़ाना – *vt*. को नाक से छूना; सूंघना – *vi.* सूंघना; ताकझांक करना – **nosey** *a. inf.* जानने को उत्सुक – **nose dive** वायुयान का सीधा गिरना/ नीचे आना

nostalgia (नॉˈस्टैल्ज़्अ) *n.* भूतकाल का (सुखद) समय, घटनाएं याद आना – **nostalgic** *a.*

nostril (ˈनॉस्ट्रिल) *n.* नथुना, नासाछिद्र

not (नॉट) *adv.* नह , न, मत

nota bene (ˈनोट्अ ˈबीनि) *Lat.* ध्यान दीजिए

notable (ˈनोटबल) *a.* उल्लेखनीय – *n.*विशिष्ट, प्रख्यात व्यक्ति – **notably** (ˈनोटब्लि) *adv.* विशेष रूप से, विशेषकर; काफी अधिक

notary (ˈनोटरि) *n.* (**notary public** भी) अदालत के लिए अनुबंध, विलेख आदि को तैयार करने वाला, लेख्य प्रमाणक, नोटरी

notation (नोˈटेशन) *n.* अंकन पद्धति, संकेत चिह्न

notch (नॉच) *n.* **V-** आकृति का खांचा; श्रेणी – *vt.* खांचा बनाना

note (नोट) *n.* संक्षिप्त टिप्पणी या विवरण; छोटा पत्र, नोट; (बैंक) नोट (जैसे 10 रु का नोट); स्वर चिह्न; एकल स्वर; चिह्न, संकेत; सूचना; ख्याति; ध्यान; (दफ्तर में) नोट – (~ **s**) *pl.* नोट की हुई सामग्री जो भविष्य में काम आ सकती हैं, नोट्स – *vt.* ध्यान देना, देखना; नोट करना – **noted** *a.* विख्यात, नामी – **notebook** *n.* – नोटबुक – **noteworthy** *a.* ध्यान देने योग्य; असाधारण

nothing (ˈनथिङ) *n.* कुछ नह , शून्य – *adv.* कुछ भी नह – **nothingness** *n.* शून्यता; असारता

notice (ˈनोटिस) *n.* ध्यान; अधिसूचना, चेतावनी; घोषणा; अनुबंध समाप्त करने, नौकरी से निकालने आदि की पूर्व सूचना – *vt.* देख लेना, उल्लेख करना; पर ध्यान देना; पहचानना – **noticeable** (ˈनोटिसबल) *a.*

notify (ˈनोटिफ़ाइ) *vt.* सूचित करना – (**-fied, -fying**) – **notifiable** *a.* सूचनीय – **notification** (नोटिफ़िˈकेशन) *n.* अधिसूचना, विज्ञप्ति

notion (ˈनोशन) *n.* धारणा; विचार; मत, सनक – **notional** *a.* मीमांसात्मक; काल्पनिक, वैचारिक; अनुमानित (मूल्य)

notorious (नोˈटॉरिअस) *a.* कुख्यात, बदनाम – **notoriety** (नोटˈराइटि) *n.*

notwithstanding (नॉट्‌विथ्ˈस्टैंडिङ) *prep.* के होते हुए भी, के बावजूद – *adv.* फिर भी, – *conj.* यद्यपि

nought (नॉट) *n.* कुछ नह ; शून्य

noun (नाउन) *n.* संज्ञा

nourish (ˈनरिश) *vt.* खिलाना; पोषण करना, (विचार, भावना) पनपने देना – **nourishing** *a.* पुष्टिकर (आहार) – **nourishment** *n.* पोषण, आहार

Nov. November का संक्षेप

novel[1] (ˈनॉवल) *n.* उपन्यास – **novelist** *n.* उपन्यासकार

novel[2] (ˈनॉवल) *a.* नूतन, अनूठा – **novelty** (ˈनॉवल्टि) *n.* नवीनता, अनूठी वस्तु; मामूली आभूषण

November (नोˈवेम्बर) *n.* नवम्बर मास

novice (ˈनॉविस) *n.* नौसिखिया, अनाड़ी

now (नाउ) *adv.* अब, अभी, इसी समय; (प्रायः **just now**) अभी-अभी – *conj.* क्योंकि – **nowadays** (ˈनाउअडेज़) *adv.* आजकल – **now and again/then** कभी-कभी

nowhere (ˈनोवेअर) *adv.* (कह (भी)

noxious (ˈनॉक्शस) *a.* विषाक्त, हानिकर

nozzle (ˈनॉज़ल) *n.* टोंटी, चुंच विशे. रबड़ के पाइप (होज़) के सिरे पर

nuance (न्यूˈआन्स) *n.* सूक्ष्मभेद (रंग, स्वर आदि में); अभिप्राय

nub (नब) *n.* गाँठ; (कहानी का) सार

nucleus (ˈन्यूक्लिअस) *n.* केंद्र; (*of atom*) केंद्रक, परमाणु का नाभिक (*pl.* **-lei** (-लिआइ)) – **nuclear** (ˈन्यूक्लिअर) *a.* (परमाणु का) नाभिकीय – **nuclear energy** नाभिकीय विखण्डन से उत्पन्न ऊर्जा, आणुविक ऊर्जा – **nuclear family** नाभिकीय परिवार, परिवार जिसमें केवल माता, पिता व बच्चे हों – **nuclear fission** परमाणु नाभिक के टूटने की क्रिया, नाभिकीय विखण्डन – **nuclear reaction** नाभिकीय प्रतिक्रिया; दो परमाणु नाभिकों की पारस्परिक क्रिया के कारण परमाणु-नाभिक की सरंचना व ऊर्जा-मात्रा में परिवर्तन की क्रिया – **nuclear reactor** दे. REACTOR

nude (न्यूड) *n.* नग्नता; नग्न व्यक्ति (चित्र, प्रतिमा आदि में) – **nudism** (ˈन्यूडिज़्म) *n.* नंगा रहने की प्रथा – **nudist** *n.* – **nudity** *n.* नग्नता

nudge (नज) *vt.* कुहनी मारकर कोई संकेत देना, टहोका देना – *n.* टहोका

nugget (ˈनगिट) *n.* सोने का ढेला

nuisance (ˈन्यूसन्स) *n.* परेशान करने या तंग करने वाला व्यक्ति या वस्तु, उपद्रवी

nuke (न्यूक) *vt. sl.* आणुविक शस्त्रों से आक्रमण करना या नष्ट करना

null (नल) *a.* रद्द, अमान्य – **nullify** *vt.* रद्द करना, प्रभावहीन कर देना (**-fied, -fying**)

numb (नम) *a.* सुन्न – *vt.* सुन्न कर देना – **numbing** *a.* – **numbness** *n.*

number (ˈनंबर) *n.* संख्या; अंक, नंबर, (समाचार पत्र आदि का) अंक; (एक–, बहु–) वचन; गाना, संगीत का स्वर समूह; प्रदर्शन; समूह; (घर, टेलिफोन आदि का) नंबर– *vt.* अंक लगाना; (*include*) में सम्मिलित करना; की संख्या तक पहुंचना – **numberless** *a.* असंख्य

numeral (ˈन्यूमरल) *n.* अंक, संख्याक – **numerate** (ˈन्यूमरिट) *a.* जो गणन, हिसाब-किताब में अंकों का प्रयोग कर सके – *vt.* गिनना – **numeration** (न्यूमˈरेशन) *n.* – **numerator** *n. Maths* भिन्न का अंश – **numerical** (न्यूˈमेरिकल) *a.* संख्यात्मक – **numerous** (ˈन्यूमरस) *a.* बहुसंख्यक

numskull (ˈनम्स्कल) *n.* मूर्ख

nun (नन) *n.* मठवासिनी, (ईसाई धर्म में) साधुनी, भिक्षुणी – **nunnery** *n.* भिक्षुणी-विहार, भिक्षुणी-मठ

nuptial (ˈनप्शल) *a.* वैवाहिक – **nuptials** *pl. n.* विवाह-संस्कार

nurse (नर्स) *n.* नर्स,उपचारिका– *vt.* की सेवा-सुश्रूषा करना; को दूध पिलाना, (क्षेत्र आदि पर) विशेष ध्यान देना; (दुर्भाव) मन में रखना – **nursery** (ˈनर्सरि) *n.* शिशु सदन; पौधों की नर्सरी – **nursery rhyme** बच्चों की कविता – **nursing home** उपचार व सेवा-सुश्रुष्मा के लिए छोटा (प्राइवेट) अस्पताल – **nursing officer** उपचर्या अधिकारी

nurture (ˈनर्चर) *n.* पोषण; शिक्षा; लालन-पालन, पोषाहार – *vt.* लालन-पालन करना, शिक्षा लेना

nut (नट) *n.* गिरीदार फल, मेवा (अखरोट, बादाम आदि); नट, ढिबरी; *sl.* सिर; (**nutcase** भी) *inf.* सिरफिरा व्यक्ति– **nutty** (ˈनटि) *a.* गिरीदार फल का/जैसा; स्वादिष्ट; *sl.* सिरफिरा (**nuts** भी) – **nutcrackers** *pl. n.* सरौता – **nutmeg** *n.* जायफल

nutrient (ˈन्यूट्रिअंट) *a.* पोषक, पुष्टिकर – *n.* पोषक पदार्थ

nutriment (ˈन्यूट्रिमंट) *n.* पोषक आहार – **nutrition** (न्यूˈट्रिशन) *n.* आहार, पोषण **nutritionist** *n.* आहार-विशेषज्ञ – **nutritious** (न्यूˈट्रिशस), **nutritive** (न्यूˈट्रिटिव़) *a.* पौष्टिक

nuzzle (ˈनज़ल) *vi.* थूथनी से खोदना; नाक से छूना, चिपटना

nylon (ˈनाइलन) *n.* नाइलोन (कपड़ा) – *pl.* नाइलोन की जुराबें

nymph (निम्फ़) *n.* , परी (समुद्र, वन, पर्वतों आदि में)

O

oak (ओक) *n.* बांज, शाहबलूत, बलूत का व क्ष
oar (ओर) *n.* चप्पू, डांड – *v.* (नाव) खेना – **oarsman** (´ओरर्ज़ूमन) *n.* खेवैया – **oarsmanship** *n.* नाव खेने में दक्षता
oasis (ओ´एसिस) *n.* नख़लिस्तान (*pl.* **oases** (ओ´एसीज़))
oat (ओट) *n.* (बहुधा ~ **s** *pl.*) जई का दाना, जई का पौधा – **oaten** (´ओटन) *a.* जई का – **oatmeal** *n.* जई का दलिया
oath (ओथ) *n.* शपथ
obdurate (´ऑब्ड्युरिट) *a.* हठी, दुराग्रही – **obduracy** *n.*
obedience (अ´बीडिअन्स) *n.* आज्ञाकारिता – **obedient** *a.*
obeisance (ओ´बेसन्स) *n.* झुककर प्रणाम
obese (ओ´बीस) *a.* मोटा, स्थूल – **obesity** (ओ´बीसिटि) *n.* मोटापा
obey (अ´बे) *vt.* की आज्ञा मानना, के अनुसार काम करना – *vi.* आज्ञा पालन करना
obituary (अ´बिट्युअरि) *n.*, निधनसचूना (*inf.* **obit** भी) – **obituarist** *n.* निधन-सूचना लेखक
object[1] (´ऑब्जिक्ट) *n.* पदार्थ, वस्तु, चीज़; विषय, पात्र (भावनाओं व क्रिया का केंद्र); उद्देश्य, लक्ष्य; *Grammar* कर्म
object[2] (अब्´जेंक्ट) *v.* विरोध करना, आपत्ति उठाना (कि...) – **objection** (अब्´जेंक्शन) *n.* आपत्ति, ऐतराज़ – **objectionable** *a.* आपत्तिजनक
objective (अब्´जेंक्टिव) *a.* वस्तुनिष्ठ, वास्तविक, निष्पक्ष – *n.* उद्देश्य, लक्ष्य – **objectivity** *n.* निष्पक्षता
oblige (अ´ब्लाइज) *vt.* कुछ करने के लिए प्रतिबद्ध करना, विवश करना – **obligate** (ऑब्लि´गेट) *vt.* कानूनी करारनामे से वचनबद्ध करना –**obligation** (ऑब्लि´गेशन) *n.* कर्तव्य, वचन; आभार – **obligatory** (अ´ब्लिगटरि) *a.* अनिवार्य – **obliging** *a.* उपकारी; सहयता करने के लिए तत्पर
oblique (अ´ब्लीक) *a.* तिरछा; अप्रत्यक्ष
obliterate (अ´ब्लिटरेट) *vt.* बिलकुल नष्ट कर देना
oblivion (अ´ब्लिविअन) *n.* पूरी तरह भूल जाना, विस्मरण – **oblivious** (अ´ब्लिविअस) *a.* (से) अनजान या बेख़बर
oblong (´ऑब्लॉङ) *a.* आयाताकार – *n.* ऐसे आकार का चित्र
obnoxious (अब्´नॉक्शस) *a.* घ णित, घिनौना
obscene (अब्´सीन) *a.* अश्लील, गंदा – **obscenity** (अब्´सेंनिटि) *n.* अश्लीलता
obscure (अब्´स्क्युअर) *a.* अस्पष्ट, धुंधला; गूढ़ – *vt.* न समझने योग्य, दुर्बोध, अस्पष्ट या धुंधला बना देना; छिपा लेना – **obscurantism** (अब्सक्युअ´रंटिज़म) *n.* रूढ़िवादिता, दकियानूसी – **obscurity** (अब्´स्क्युअरिटि) *n.* अंधकार; धुंधलापन; अस्पष्टता; दुर्बोधता; स्थान विशेष पर बहुत कम आने जाने की स्थिति, गुमनामी
obsequious (अब्´सीक्विअस) *a.* चापलूस, जी हजूरी करने वाला
observe (अब्´ज़र्व) *vt.* ध्यानपूर्वक देखना; टिप्पणी करना, अवलोकन करना, निरीक्षण करना; पालन करना, मानना – *vi.* टिप्पणी देना, करना – **observance** *n.* ध्यान; अनुपालन – **observant** (अब्´ज़र्वंट) *a.* सतर्क, शीघ्र ध्यान देने वाला – **observation** (ऑब्ज़र्´वेशन) *n.* अवलोकन, प्रेक्षण,

सावधानी से देखना; टिप्पणी, कथन – **observatory** (अब्ˈज़र्वट्रि) *n.* नक्षत्र आदि का दूरबीन से अध्ययन करने का स्थान, वेधशाला – **observer** (अब्ˈज़र्वर) *n.* प्रेक्षक, पर्यवेक्षक

obsess (अब्ˈसेंस) *vt.* दिमाग पर छाये रहना, (विचार आदि का) सताते रहना – **obsession** (अब्ˈसेंशन) *n.* सनक, धुन, दिमाग पर छाया हुआ विचार आदि – **obsessive** *a.* दिमाग पर छाया हुआ

obsolete (ˈऑब्सलीट) *a.* अप्रचिलित, लुप्त – **obsolescent** (ˈऑब्सˈलेंसंट) *a.* अप्रचिलित होता हुआ

obstacle (ˈऑब्स्टकल) *n.* रुकावट, अड़चन

obstetrics (ऑब्ˈस्टेंट्रिक्स) *n.* प्रसूति-विज्ञान – **obstetrician** (ऑब्सटेंˈट्रिशन) *n.* प्रसूति-विशेषज्ञ

obstinate (ˈऑब्सटिनिट) *a.* जिद्दी, अड़ियल – **obstinacy** (ˈऑब्सटिनसि) *n.*

obstreperous (अब्ˈस्ट्रेंपरस) *a.* ऊधमी

obstruct (अब्ˈस्ट्रक्ट) *vt.* बाधा डालना – **obstruction** *n.* बाधा, रुकावट – **obstructive** *a.* बाधक

obtain (अब्ˈटेन) *vt.* प्राप्त करना, पाना – **obtainable** *a.* प्राप्य

obtrude (अब्ˈट्रूड) *vt.* थोपना – **obtrusion** (अब्ˈट्रूझन) *n.* दख़लंदाजी – **obtrusive** (अब्ˈट्रूसिव़) *a.*

obtuse (अब्ˈट्यूस) *a.* मंदबुद्धि, 90° से अधिक (कोण); कुण्ठाग्र (जो पैना न हो)

obverse (ˈऑब्व़र्स) *n.* सिक्के, मैडल आदि का मुख्य (चित्रांकित) पासा – *a.* पूरक; सामने का

obviate (ˈऑब्व़िएट) *vt.* दूर करना, अनावश्यक कर देना

obvious (ˈऑब्व़िअस) *a.* स्पष्ट, प्रकट, सीधा – **obviously** *adv.* स्पष्टतया

occasion (अˈकेझ़न) *n.* अवसर; कारण; आवश्यकता; मौका, विशेष अवसर (समारोह आदि) – *vt.* का कारण बनना – **occasional** *a.* अवसरिक, यदाकदा होने वाला – **occasionally** *adv.* कभी-कभी, यदा-कदा

Occident (ˈऑक्सिडंट) *n.* पश्चिम (यूरोप, अमरीका)

occult (ऑˈकल्ट) *a.* गुप्त, रहस्यमय, गूढ़, अलौकिक

occupy (ˈऑक्युपाइ) *vt.* में रहना; घेरना; जगह भरना; (काम में) व्यस्त रखना; पर कब्ज़ा करना (**-pied, -pying**) – **occupancy** *n.* अधिकार में होना; में रहते होना – **occupation** (ऑक्युˈपेशन) *n.* जीविका, व्यवसाय, पेशा; अधिकार, कब्ज़ा – **occupational** *a.* व्यवसायजनित; जिसका पुनर्वास हेतु उपयोग हो – **occupier** (ˈऑक्युपाइअर) *n.* किरायेदार, रहने वाला

occur (अˈकर) *vi.* पाया जाना; सूझना; (**-rr-**) – **occurrence** (अˈकरंस) *n.* घटना

ocean (ˈओशन) *n.* महासागर – **oceanic** (ओशिˈऐनिक) *a.* महासागरीय, समुद्री

ochre (ˈओकर) *n.* गेरू

o'clock (अˈक्लॉक) *adv.* घड़ी में, घड़ी में बजे; **it is 5 o'clock** पांच बजे हैं

oct-, octa-, octo- (*comb. form*) आठ-

OCR Optical Character Recognition/ Reader का संक्षेप

octagon (ˈऑक्टगन) *n.* अष्टभुज (आक ति)

octane (ˈऑक्टेन) *n.* मोटर-इंधन का एक अवयव, ऑक्टेन

October (ऑक्ˈटोबर) *n.* अक्तूबर का मास

octogenarian (ऑक्टोजिˈनेंअरिअन) *n.* 80 व 89 वर्ष की आयु के बीच का व्यक्ति

octopus (ˈआक्टपस) *n.* आठ भुजाओं वाला समुद्री जीव, ऑक्टोपस

ocular (ˈऑक्युलर) *a.* नेत्र, नेत्र द ष्टि सम्बंधी

odd (ऑड) *a.* विचित्र, अजीब; आकस्मिक; विषम (संख्या); समुच्चय (सेट) में से अलग निकला हुआ; बराबर समूह बना देने के बाद बचा एक – **odds** *pl. n.* शर्त या दाव में एक ओर दिया गया अधिक लाभ; संभावना (घटना होने की) – **oddity** *n.* विचित्र वस्तु, व्यक्ति या आचरण – **odd jobs** *pl. n.* छोटे-मोटे काम – **odds and ends** बचा खुचा फुटकर सामान – **odd man/one out** एक व्यक्ति/वस्तु जो वर्ग में बाकियों से अलग हो

ode (ओड) *n.* सम्बोधगीत, भावगीत, ओड

odium (´ओडिअम) *n.* घ णा, बड़े पैमाने पर नापसन्दगी, अलोकप्रियता – **odious** (ओडिअस) *a.* घिनौना

odour (´ओडर) *n.* गन्ध – **odorous** (´ओडरस) *a.* सुगन्धित – **odourless** *a.* गंधहीन

of (ऑफ़) *prep.* का, की, के; से; के बारे में

off (ऑफ) *adv.* दूर – *prep.* दूर; से लगा हुआ – *a.* रद्द, स्थगित, बंद, खराब, खट्टा आदि; दूर; *Cricket* गेंदबाज़ के बांयी ओर – **offbeat** *a.* सामान्य से हटकर – **off colour** मामूली सा अस्वस्थ – **off-day** *n.* छुट्टी का दिन (व्यक्तिगत) – **off hand** *a./adv.* तुरंत, बिना विचारे, रूखा – **offset** (´ऑफ़्सेंट) *n.* जो बराबर कर दे; छपाई की एक प्रणाली – **offset** (ऑफ़्´सेंट) *vt.* – **offshoot** (´ऑफ़्शूट) *n.* उपशाखा – **offshore** (ऑफ़्शोर) *a.* किनारे से दूर समुद्र में; दूसरे देश में (व्यवसाय, निष्पत्ति आदि) – **off-white** *a.* पीलापन लिए सफेद – **offspring** *n.* बच्चे, संतान

offal (´ऑफ़ल) *n.* खाने में प्रयुक्त पशु की अंतड़ियां; कूड़ा-करकट

offend (अ´फ़ेंण्ड) *vt.* को नाराज़ करना – **offence** (अ´फ़ेंन्स) *n.* दोष, अपराध; अपमान – **offender** *n.* अपराधी, दोषी – **offensive** *a.* घ णाजनक; आक्रामक, हमलावर – *n.* आक्रमण

offer (´ऑफ़र) *vt.* भेंट करना, देना, प्रस्तुत करना; चेष्टा करना – *vi.* प्रस्तुत होना – *n.* भेंट; अर्पण; प्रस्ताव – **offering** *n.* क ति (लेखक आदि की); भेंट, प्रसाद

office (´ऑफ़िस) *n* कार्यालय, दफ्तर; (व्यापारिक या व्यावसायिक संगठन), पद; सेवा; कार्य; उपासना, अनुष्ठान – *pl.* कार्य; चर्च में प्रार्थना का कार्य – **officer** *n.* पदाधिकारी, अफसर

official (अ´फ़िशल) *a.* सरकारी, शासकीय – *n.* कर्मचारी, अधिकारी

officiate (अ´फ़िशिएट) *vi.* (के) स्थान पर कार्य करना, स्थानापन्न होना

officious (अ´फ़िशस) *a.* दखलंदाज

offing (ऑ´फ़िङ) *n.* – **in the offing** जल्द होने वाला

off-line *a.* जो कम्प्यूटर या इंटरनेट से सीधा जुड़ा हुआ न हो

offside (ऑफ़्´साइड) *a./adv. Sport* नियम विरूद्ध आगे (हो जाना), आफ़ साइड

often (´ऑफ़न) *adv.* प्राय: बहुत बार (*Poet.* **oft**)

ogle (´ओगल) *v.* घूरना – *n.* इस प्रकार देखना

ogre (´ओगर) *n. Folklore* नरभक्षी राक्षस, दानव (**ogress** *fem.*)

oh (ओ) *interj.* आश्चर्य, पीड़ा आदि बोधक शब्द

oil (ऑइल) *n.* तेल, पेट्रोलियम पदार्थ – *vt.* ग्रीस डालना, तेल देना – **oily** *a.* चिकना, तेल युक्त; चिकनाई वाला (भोजन) – **oilfield** *n.* तेल-क्षेत्र – **oil painting** तैल चित्र – **oilseeds** *pl. n.* तिलहन – **oilskin** *n.* मोम जामा – **oil tanker** तेल वाहक जहाज़ – **well oiled** *sl.* नशे में

ointment (´ऑइंटमंट) *n.* मरहम

O.K., okay (ओ´के) *a./adv. inf. excl.* ठीक है! अच्छा! ओके! – *vt.* का अनुमोदन करना, मंजूरी देना

okra (ओक्रअ) *n. US* भिंडी

old (ओल्ड) *a.* वृद्ध; प्राचीन; आयु में बड़ा (**older, elder** *comp.*, **oldest, eldest** *sup.*) – **olden** *a.* पुराना – **old-fashioned** *a.* पुराने ढंग का; दकियानूसी – **the old guard** संगठन के पुराने सदस्य जो परिवर्तन नहीं चाहते

oligarchy (´ऑलिगार्कि) *n.* अल्पतंत्र, कुलीन-तंत्र, केवल कुछ लोगों का शासन

olive (´ऑलिव़) *n.* जैतून; – *a.* (**olive green** भी) भूरापन लिए हरा – **olive oil** जैतून का तेल

ombudsman (´ऑम्बुड्ज़्मन) *n.* लोकपाल

omega (´ओमिग्अ) *n.* ग्रीक वर्णमाला का अंतिम अक्षर; अंत

omelette (´ऑम्लिट) *n.* आमलेट

omen (´आमन) *n.* शकुन, लक्षण – **ominous** (´ऑमिनस) *a.* धमकी भरा; अनिष्ट-सूचक

omit (ओ´मिट) *vt.* छोड़ देना; जाने देना, नहीं करना (-tt-) – **omission** (ओ´मिशन) *n.* चूक, त्रुटि

omni- (*comb. form*) सब, सर्व-

omnibus (´ऑम्निबस) *n.* निश्चित मार्ग पर चलने वाली यात्री बस (दे. **bus**); जिसमें विभिन्न प्रकार की रचनाएं संकलित हो – *a.* विविध वस्तुओं आदि से सम्बंधित

omnipotent (ऑम्´निपटंट) *a.* सर्वशक्तिमान

omnipresent (ऑम्नि´प्रेंज़ंट) *a.* सर्वव्यापी

omniscient (ऑम्´निसिअंट) *a.* सर्वज्ञ, सब कुछ जानने वाला

on (ऑन) *prep.* पर, के ऊपर; पास; पास (*no money on me*); के समय ; के दिन ; पर कार्यक्रम ; नित्य प्रयोग करते होना *on the pill* ; के विषय में ; (वाहन) से – *a.* चालू; *Cricket* बल्लेबाज के बायीं ओर का क्षेत्र – *adv.* निरंतर (*Go on*); आगे (*move on*) आदि – **on and on** लगातार

on- (*comb. form*) on के अर्थ में जैसे onlooker में

once (वन्स) *adv.* एक बार, किसी समय; कभी – **at once** तुरंत; साथ ही

one (वन) *a.* एक, एक ही; संयुक्त, केवल, अकेला, एक सा – *n.* 1 की संख्या या अंक, वह एक; एक इकाई – *pron.* सामान्य रूप में कोई, कोई व्यक्ति – **oneness** *n.* ऐक्य, एकत्व; अभिन्नता – **oneself** *pron.* स्वयं – **onesided** *a.* एक पक्षीय– **one-way** *a.* एक ओर चलने वाला (यातायात) – **one and only** प्रसिद्ध – **one by one** बारी-बारी से – **one up** किसी की अपेक्षा लाभ की स्थिति में

onerous (´ऑनरस) *a.* भारी, दूभर

onion (´अन्यन) *n.* प्याज़

only *a.* एक मात्र, अकेला – *adv.* केवल सिर्फ – *conj.* परंतु

onomatopoeia (ऑनोमैटपीअ) *n.* ध्वनि-अनुकरण (शब्द)

onset (´ऑन्सेंट) *n.* आरंभ, शुरूआत

onslaught (´ऑन्स्लॉट) *n.* आक्रमण

onto (´ऑन्टू) *prep.* पर, का जानकार

one-upmanship *n.* अपने आपको दूसरे से अच्छा सिद्ध करने की कला

onus (´ओनस) *n.* जुम्मेवारी, दायित्व

onward (´ऑन्वर्ड) *a.* आगे बढ़ता हुआ या बढ़ने वाला – *adv.* आगे – **onwards** *adv.* आगे

onyx (´ऑनिक्स) *n.* एक प्रकार की मणि, सुलेमानी

ooze (ऊज़) *vi.* रिसना, टपकना – *n.* कीचड़, पंक; बहती हुई गंदगी

op. opera; operation; opus का संक्षिप्त रूप

opal (´ओपल) *n.* विविध रंगों का चमकदार रत्न; दूधिया पत्थर

opaque (ओ´पेक) *a.* अपारदर्शी – **opacity** (ओ´पैसटि) *n.* अपारदर्शिता

op. cit. (´ऑप´सिट) *Lat.* **opere citato** in the work cited पहले उद्धृत रचना (पुस्तक आदि) से

open (´ओपन) *a.* खुला; प्रकट; फैला हुआ; साफ़ (दिल), सच्चा; सबके लिए; उदारमति; अनिश्चित (*open question*); खाली – *vt.*

खोलना; चालू करना, आरंभ करना (बहस आदि)– *vi.* खुलना, आरंभ होना – *n.* खुला स्थान, खुला ग्राम्यक्षेत्र– **opening** *n.* छिद्र; उद्घाटन, सुअवसर – *a.* आरंभिक, प्रथम – **openly** *adv.* खुले आम – **open-handed** *a.* उदार – **open-hearted** *a.* साफ़, उदार

opera (´ऑपरअ) *n.* ऑपिरा, गीति-नाट्य – **opera house** रंगशाला (जहां गीति-नाट्यों का मंचन होता हो)

operation (ऑप´रेशन) *n.* संचालन; क्रिया, काम, प्रचलन; चीरफाड़, शल्यक्रिया, सैनिक कार्रवाई – **operate** (´ऑपरेट) *vt.* (यंत्र, व्यापार आदि) चलाना – *vi.* कार्य करना; पर इच्छित प्रभाव डालना; आपरेशन (शल्य-क्रिया) करना – **operational** (ऑप´रेशनल) *a.* संचालन सम्बंधी; चालू, जारी – **operator** *n.* मशीन चलाने वाला; (टेलीफोन) ऑपरेटर

ophthalmic (ऑफ़्´थैल्मिक) *a.* नेत्र सम्बंधी, नेत्र – **ophthalmologist** (आफ़्थैल्´मॉलजिस्ट) *n.* नेत्र रोग-चिकित्सक – **ophthalmology** (ऑफ़्´थैल्´मॉलजि) *n.* , नेत्र विज्ञान, नेत्र-रोग विज्ञान

opiate (´ओपिइट) दे. OPIUM

opinion (अ´पिन्यन) *n.* विचार, राय – **opinionated** *a.* हठीला, अपने विचारों पर अड़ा रहने वाला – **opinion poll** जनमत संग्रह

opium (´ओपिअम) *n.* अफीम – **opiate** (´ओपिइट) *n.* अफीम युक्त औषधि – *a.* स्वापक, नींद लाने वाली

opossum (अ´पॉसम) *n.* छोटे आकार का जीव, अमरीकन व आस्ट्रेलियाई कंगारू जैसा जीव, ओपोसम

opponent (अ´पोनंट) *n.* विरोधी, प्रतिद्वंदी

opportune (´ऑपर्ट्यून) *a.* उपयुक्त, समयानुकूल – **opportunism** (ऑपर्´ट्यूनिज़्म) *n.* अवसरवाद – **opportunist** *n./a.* अवसरवादी – **opportunity** (ऑपर्´ट्यूनिटि) *n.* उपयुक्त, सुअवसर मौका

oppose (अ´पोज़) *vt.* का विरोध करना, का सामना करना – **opposite** (´ऑपज़िट) *a.* विरुद्ध, सम्मुख, विपरीत, उल्टा – *n.* विपरीत – *prep./adv.* सम्मुख, के सामने, दूसरी ओर – **opposition** (आप´ज़िशन) *n.* विरोध; सामना; विरोधी दल

oppress (अ´प्रेस) *vt.* अत्याचार करना, दबाना– **oppression** (अ´प्रेशन) *n.* दमन; अत्याचार, जुल्म – **oppressive** *a.* अत्याचारी, दमनकारी; असहनीय; भारी; (मौसम) गर्म व थका देने वाला – **oppressor** *n.* अत्याचारी

opprobrium (अ´प्रोब्रिअम) *n.* अपयश, बदनामी

opt (ऑप्ट) *vi.* चुनना

optic (´ऑप्टिक) *a.* द ष्टि या नेत्र सम्बंधी – *n.* आंख – **optics** *n.* प्रकाश विज्ञान – **optical** *a.* – **optician** *n.* चश्मे बनाने व बेचने वाला, ऑप्टिशियन – **optical character recognition** इलैक्ट्रॉनिकी प्रक्रिया जिसके द्वारा कम्प्यूटर लिखे हुए शब्द व अंक पहचान सकता है

optimism (´आप्टिमिज़म) *n.* आशावादिता – **optimist** (´आप्टिमिस्ट) *n.* आशावादी व्यक्ति – **optimistic** *a.* आशावान, आशावादी – **optimistically** *adv.*

optimum (´ऑप्टिमम) *a./n.* अनुकूलतम; श्रेष्ठ, सबसे अच्छा

option (´ऑप्शन) *n.* विकल्प, चुनाव; पसंद; चुनी गई वस्तु; छात्र का विषय चुनने का अधिकार; *Computers* प्रोग्राम में दिये गये विकल्पों में से कोई एक – **optional** *a.* वैकल्पिक, ऐच्छिक

opulent (´ऑप्युलंट) *a.* अत्यधिक धनी; भरपूर – **opulence** *n.*

opus (ओपस) *n.* रचना; संगीत रचना (*pl.* **opera** ('ऑपर्अ)

or (ऑर) *conj.* अथवा, या (*negative* में) – **or else** नह तो; वरना

oracle (´ऑरकल) *n.* देववाणी, देवस्थान पर की गई (प्रायः अनेकार्थी) भविष्यवाणी, देवस्थान; आप्त पुरुष; बुद्धिमान अथवा रहस्यमय परामर्शदाता – **oracular** (ऑ´रैक्युलर) *a.*

oral (´ऑरल) *a.* मौखिक, जबानी – *n.* मौखिक परीक्षा – **orally** *adv.*

orange (´ऑरिंज) *n.* नारंगी, संतरा, या मुसम्मी आदि; इसका पेड़; नारंगी रंग

orangutang (´ऑरैंग् ´ऊटैंग); **orang-utan** (´ऑरैंग´ऊटैन) *n.* बड़े लंगूर के सद श जानवर, औरंग-उटान

orator (´ऑरटर) *n.* कुशल वक्ता – **oration** (ऑ´रेशन) *n.* औपचारिक भाषण – **oratorical** (ऑर´टॉरिकल) *a.* वक्ता या भाषण सम्बंधी – **oratory** (´ऑरटरि) *n.* व्याख्यान, वाक्पटुता

orbit (´ऑर्बिट) *n.* नक्षत्र, ग्रह आदि का परिक्रमा-पथ, कक्षा; प्रभाव क्षेत्र, दायरा – *v.* कक्षा में घूमना या छोड़ना

orchard (´ऑर्चर्ड) *n.* फल-उद्यान; फल-व क्षों का समूह

orchestra (´ऑर्किस्ट्रअ) *n.* वाद्य-वंद, वाद्य-मण्डल; थियेटर में वादक-स्थान – **orchestral** *a.*

orchid (´ऑर्किड), **orchis** (´ऑर्किस) *n.* आर्किड जाति के अनेक फूलों वाले पौधे

ordain (ऑर्´डेन) *vt.* नये पुरोहित (पादरी) का अभिषेक करना, को नियुक्त करना; विधान करना, (ईश्वर, शासक द्वारा) निश्चय करना

ordeal (ऑर्´डील, आर्´डीअल) *n.* कठोर, कष्टकर अनुभव

order (´आर्डर) *n.* व्यवस्था; क्रम, (समाज में) शांति-व्यवस्था; श्रेणी; वर्ग; आदेश, आज्ञा; मंगवाने का आर्डर; पद्धति; धार्मिक वर्ग (सन्यासियों का वर्ग विशेष आदि), सम्प्रदाय – *vt.* आदेश देना; (माल) मंगवाना या बनवाना; व्यवस्थित करना, प्रबंध करना – **orderliness** *n.* – **orderly** *a.* शांत, व्यवस्थित – *n.* अस्पताल में परिचारक (नौकर); सैनिक अर्दली – **in order to** (करने, जाने आदि) के लिए – **out of order** (मशीन आदि) खराब, बंद

ordinance (´ऑर्डिनन्स) *n.* अध्यादेश

ordinary (´ऑर्ड्न्रि) *a.* साधारण; सामान्य; मामूली – **ordinarily** (´आर्ड्न्रिलि) *adv.* आमतौर पर

ordnance (´आर्ड्नन्स) *n.* तोपखाना; सैन्य सामग्री

ore (ऑर) *n.* कच्ची धातु, धातुक

organ (´ऑर्गन) *n.* आर्गन वाद्य; शरीर का अंग, इन्द्रिय; साधन; सूचना, समाचार प्रसारण माध्यम– **organic** (´ऑर्´गैनिक) *a.* जैव, जीव से सम्बंधित; शारीरिक-अवयव सम्बंधी, आंगिक, जैविक; *Chem.* कार्बन से बने यौगिक सम्बंधी; प्राक तिक खाद से उगाया गया; सुव्यवस्थित – **organically** *adv.* – **organist** (´ऑर्गनिस्ट) *n.* आर्गन-वादक

organdie (´ऑर्गंडि) *n.* पारदर्शक, महीन मलमल

organize (´ऑर्गनाइज़) *vt.* संगठित करना; संघटित करना; निश्चित रूप देना; आयोजित करना – **organism** *n.* संघटित व्यवस्था; पौधे व जीव – **organization** (आर्गनाइ´ज़ेशन) *n.* संगठन, संस्था, संघ – **organizer** *n.* संगठन करने वाला व्यक्ति

orgasm (´ऑर्गैज़म) *n.* कामोत्कर्ष

orgy (´ऑर्जि) *n.* अनियंत्रित रंगरलियां (विशे. मदिरापान व व्यभिचार सहित)

orient (´ऑरिअंट) *n.* (**O**) पूर्व (के देश), एशिया; मोतियों की चमक – *a.* (सूर्य आदि) निकला हुआ; (**O-**) पूर्वी (एशियाई) – *vt.* पूर्व की ओर अभिमुख करना; स्थान निश्चित करना, अपनी स्थिति जानना; (से स्वयं को) परिचित करना – **oriental** (ऑरि´ऍन्टल) *a./n.* पूर्व का वि०

चीन, जापान का – **orientation** *n.* दिशा-निर्धारण
orifice (´ऑरिफ़िस) *n.* छिद्र, सुराख
origin (´ऑरिजिन) *n.* आरंभ, उत्पत्ति, मूल, स्रोत; कुल, वंश
original (ऑ´रिजिनल) *a.* आदि-, मूल, प्रारंभिक; नवीन; मौलिक; सनकी – *n.* मूल (प्रति, बनावट, वस्तु जिसकी नकल की गई हो) – **originality** (अरिजि´नैलिटि) *n.* मौलिकता – **originally** *adv*. आरंभ में; मूलतः
originate (अ´रिजिनेट) *v.* आरंभ होना या करना, उत्पन्न होना या करना – **originator** *n.* प्रवर्तक
ornament (´ऑर्नमंट) *n.* आभूषण, जेवर; सजावट का सामान – *vt.* सजाना – **ornamental** (´ऑर्न´मैन्टल) *a.* सजावटी
ornate (ऑर्´नेट) *a.* सजाया हुआ
ornithology (ऑर्नि´थॉलजि) *n.* पक्षी-विज्ञान – **ornithologist** *n.* पक्षी-विज्ञानी
orphan (´ऑर्फ़न) *n.* अनाथ, यतीम – **orphanage** *n.* यतीमखाना, अनाथाश्रम
orthodox (´ऑर्थडॉक्स) *a.* परम्परा निष्ठ, रूढ़िवादी, कट्टरपंथी – **orthodoxy** *n.* रूढ़िवादिता, कट्टरपंथिता
orthopaedic (ऑर्थ´पीडिक) *a.* विकलांग उपचार सम्बंधी, टूटी या मुड़ी हड्डियों का (इलाज)
oscillate (´ऑसिलेट) *vi.* डोलना, झूलना; नियमित रूप से घटना बढ़ना
osprey (´ऑस्प्रे) *n.* मत्स्य-भक्षी उकाब; कलग़ी
ostensible (ऑस्´टैन्सिबल) *a* प्रकट; प्रत्यक्ष, कहने को – **ostensibly** *adv.*
ostentation (ऑसटॅन्´टेशन) *a.* दिखावा, आडम्बर – **ostentatious** *a.* आडम्बरपूर्ण, दिखावटी
osteopathy (आस्टि´ऑपथि) *n.* अस्थि-चिकित्सा
ostracize (´ऑस्ट्रसाइज़) *vt.* बहिष्कार करना, जात-बिरादरी से निकालना – **ostracism** *n.*
ostrich (´ऑस्ट्रिच) *n.* शुतुरमुर्ग
other (´अदर) *a.* दूसरा, अन्य, भिन्न, कोई और – *pron.* अन्य (व्यक्ति या वस्तु) – **otherwise** *adv.* अन्य प्रकार से, भिन्न रूप में – *conj.* वरना, नह तो, अन्यथा
otter (´ऑटर) *n.* ऊदबिलाव (एक जल जीव)
ouch (आउच) *interj.* अचानक दर्द का उद्गार, विस्मयादि बोधक शब्द हाय!
ought to (´ऑट् टु) *v. aux.* कर्तव्य, अनिवार्यता व परामर्श बोधक, अवश्य (करना) चाहिए (*I ought to go* मुझे अवश्य जाना चाहिए); संभावना सूचक (*It ought to rain* बारिश की पूरी संभावना है)
ounce (आउन्स) *n.* औंस (28.4 ग्राम के बराबर)
our (आउअर) *a.* हमारा – **ours** *pron.* हमारा – **ourselves** *pl. pron.* हम स्वयं
oust (आउस्ट) *vt.* बाहर निकाल देना, बेदखल करना
out (आउट) *adv.* बाहर; दूर, परे; हड़ताल पर – *a.* विचार के अयोग्य; अप्रचिलित; बेहोश; बुझी हुई; वर्जित; *Cricket* आउट हुआ (बल्लेबाज़); समाप्त – **outer** *a.* बाहरी – **outermost, outmost** *a.* बिल्कुल बाहरी – **outing** *n.* सैर – **outward** *a./adv.* बाहर का/बाहरी – **outwardly** *adv.* – **outwards** *adv.* – **out-and-out** पूरी तरह
out- (*comb. form*) से परे; से अधिक जैसे **outclass** *vt.*
outbid (´आउट्बिड) *vt.* (से) बड़ी बोली लगाना, ज्यादा कीमत देने को तैयार होना
outbreak (´आउट्ब्रेक) *n.* (बीमारी या झगड़े आदि का) अचानक फैल जाना, प्रकोप
outburst (´आउट्बर्स्ट) *n.* फूट पड़ना, विशे. तीव्र भावनाओं का जैसे क्रोध
outcast (´आउट्कास्ट) *n.* बहिष्कृत व्यक्ति या निर्वासित व्यक्ति
outclass (´आउट्क्लास) *vt.* से बढ़कर होना
outcome (´आउट्कम) *n.* परिणाम, फल
outcry (´आउट्क्राइ) *n.* सार्वजनिक विरोध
outdated (आउट्´डेटिड) *a.* पुराना, अप्रचिलित

outdo (आउट´डू) *vt.* से बढ़कर रहना

outdoors (आउट्´डोर्ज़) *adv.* खुले स्थान में – **outdoor** *a.*बाहर का, खुल का

outfit (´आउट्फ़िट) *n.* उपकरण, सज्जा (वस्त्र आदि); *inf.* इकाई के रूप में लोगों का दल

outflank (आउट्´फ्लैंक) *vt.* शत्रु के बाजू से जाकर पीछे पहुंच जाना

outgoing (´आउट्गोइङ) *a.* मिलनसार; मित्र जैसा

outgrow (आउट्´ग्रो) *vt.* से अधिक बढ़ जाना, ज्यादा बड़ा हो जाना; के कपड़ों का तंग या छोटा हो जाना – **outgrowth** *n.* परिणाम

outhouse (´आउट्हाउस) *n.* मुख्य भवन के पास बना शैड या छोटा मकान आदि, उपभवन

outing (´आउटिङ) *n.* सैर, पिकनिक

outlandish (आउट्´लैंडिश) *a.* अजीबोगरीब (सूरत, बरताव आदि में)

outlast (आउट्´लास्ट) *vt.* किसी की अपेक्षा अधिक देर तक चलना

outlaw (´आउट्लॉ) *n.* विधि-बहिष्क त (बदमाश, डाकू आदि), भगोड़ा, फरार – *vt.* भगोड़ा घोषित करना; वर्जित करना

outlay (´आउट्ले) *n.* लागत

outlet (´आउट्लेट) *n.* निकास

outline (´आउट्लाइन) *n.* रूपरेखा, खाका, सामान्य योजना; रेखाचित्र – *vt.* रेखाचित्र, रूपरेखा तैयार करना

outlook (´आउट्लुक) *n.* द ष्टिकोण, नज़रिया; संभावित परिणाम, द श्य

outlying (´आउट्लाइङ) *a.* दूरस्थ, सुदूर

outmoded (आउट्´मोडिड) *a.* पुराना

outnumber (आउट्´नम्बर) *vt.* से अधिक संख्या में होना

out-of-date (आउटऑफ़´डेट) *a.* जिसकी अवधि समाप्त हो गयी हो (विचार, सिद्धान्त या प्रथा); अप्रचिलित

outpatient (´आउट्पेशंट) *n.* रोगी जो अस्पताल में इलाज कराए लेकिन वहां रहे नह

outpouring (´आउट्पॉरिङ) *n.* भावों का उद्गार

output (´आउट्पुट) *n.* उत्पादन, पैदावर; *Computers* प्राप्त जानकारी

outrage (´आउट्रेज) *n.* दूसरे के अधिकारों का हनन, घोर अपमान, अन्याय; इससे उत्पन्न आक्रोश – *vt.* अपमान करना, गुस्सा दिलाना – **outrageous** *a.* घ णित, निन्दनीय

outright (´आउट्राइट) *a.* निर्विवाद; स्पष्ट – *adv.* पूर्णतया, एकदम

outset (´आउट्सैट) *n.* आरंभ

outside *n.* (´आउट्´साइड) बाहर, बाहरी भाग – (´आउट्´साइड) *adv.* बाहर, खुले में – (´आउट्´साइड) *a.* बाहरी; कम संभावित; अधिकतम – **outsider** *n.* बाहरी व्यक्ति; प्रतियोगी जिसकी जीतने की बहुत कम संभावना हो

outskirts (´आउट्स्कर्ट्स) *pl. n.* नगर का बाहरी क्षेत्र

outsource (´आउट्सॉर्स) *vt.* कम्पनी का काम बाहर से करवाना/या माल बाहर से मंगवाना

outspoken (आउट्´स्पोकन) *a.* स्पष्टवादी, खरा

outstanding (आउट्´स्टैंडिङ) *a.* श्रेष्ठ, उत्क ष्ट; बकाया

outstrip (आउट्´स्ट्रिप) *vt.* (मांग का आपूर्ति) से आगे बढ़ जाना

outward (´आउट्वर्ड) *a.* बाहरी – **outwardly** *adv.* बाहर से – **outward bound** बाहर जाने वाली (गाड़ी) आदि

outweigh (आउट्´वे) *vt.* अधिक भारी या महत्वपूर्ण होना

oval (´ओवल) *a.* अण्डाकार – *n.* अण्डाकार वस्तु

ovary (´ओवरि) *n.* स्त्रियों में डिम्बग्रंथि, अण्डाशय

ovation (ओ´वेशन) *n.* जय-जयकार, करतल-ध्वनि

oven (´अवन) *n.* ओवन, तन्दूर

over (´ओव़र) *adv.* ऊपर; पार; से अधिक; अत्यधिक; के बाद; पूर्णतया; फिर से, दुबारा, दूसरी ओर, नीच की ओर आदि – *prep.* के ऊपर; पर; से अधिक; के साथ आदि – *a.* ऊपरी, बाहरी – *n. Cricket* बॉलर का गेंद फेंकने का ओवर

over- (*comb. form*) अधिक, अत्यधिक, से अधिक, ऊपर, जैसे **overcoat** में

overall *n.* (´ओवर्‌ऑल) कपड़ों को धूल-मिट्टी से बचाने के लिए उनके ऊपर पहना जाने वाला ढीला-ढाला लबादा (*pl.* भी) – *a.* कुल मिलाकर (**overall cost**)

overbearing (ओवर्´बेंअरिङ) *a.* धौंसिया, रोब जमाने वाला

overcast (´ओव़र्‌कास्ट) *a.* घिरा हुआ विशे. बादलों से

overcome (ओवर्´कम) *vt.* पर काबू पाना, पराजित करना

overdraft (´ओव़र्‌ड्राफ्ट) *n.* बैंक में जमा राशि से अधिक निकाली गई धनराशि, ओवरड्राफ्ट

overdue (ओव़र्´ड्यू) *a.* जिसे आने में देर हो गयी हो, बहुत देर से मिला (सामान)

overdrive (´ओव़र्‌ड्राइव़) *n.* कुछ मोटर वाहनों में बहुत अधिक रफ़्तार पर प्रयोग के लिए अतिरिक्त विशेष गीयर

overflow *vi.* (ओवर्´फ़्लो) बहने लगना – *n.*

overfly (ओवर्´फ्लाइ) *vt.* के ऊपर उड़ना

overgrown (ओव़र्´ग्रोन) *a.* (बागीचा) जिसमें झाड़-झंखाड़ उग आया हो

overhaul *vt.* (ओव़र्´हॉल) जांच के बाद ठीक-ठाक कर देना, मरम्मत करना; से आगे निकल जाना – *n.* (´ओव़र्‌हाल) पूरी जांच, जीर्णोद्धार

overhead *a.* (´ओव़र्‌हेंड) सिर पर, ऊपर – (ओव़र´हेंड) *adv.* ऊपर, ऊपर से; ऊपर की (बत्ती) – **overheads** (´ओव़रहेंड्ज़) *pl. n.* व्यापार में उत्पादन व कच्चे माल की लागत के अतिरिक्त व्यय, उपरिव्यय

overhear (ओव़र्´हिअर) *vt.* किसी की बातें/बातचीत सुन लेना

overjoyed (ओव़र्´जॉयड) *a.* बहुत अधिक खुश

overland (´ओव़र्‌लैंड) *a./adv.* थल मार्ग (से)

overlook (ओव़र्´लुक) *vt.* अनेदखी करना, नज़रअंदाज करना, उपेक्षा करना; ऊपर से (द श्य) देखना

overnight (ओव़र्´नाइट) *adv.* (रात में) होना; *fig.* अचानक होना – *a.* रात का, रात में; अचानक

overpower (ओव़र्´पावर) *vt.* काबू पा लेना, वश में कर लेना

overrate (ओव़´रेट) *vt.* (किसी के महत्व को) बहुत अधिक आंकना

override (ओव़र्´राइड) *vt.* रद्द कर देना (आदेश, आपत्ति)

overrule (ओव़´रूल) *vt.* (फैसले को) रद्द करना; (दावा) स्वीकार न करना

overrun (ओव़´रन) *vt.* कब्ज़ा कर लेना; (समय, सीमा) पार कर जाना; उजाड़ देना, लूट लेना

overseas (´ओव़र्‌सीज़) *a.* विदेशी (व्यापार) – *a./adv.* समुद्र पार का

overseer (´ओव़र्‌सिअर) *n.* ओवरसिअर – *vt.* निरीक्षण करना

overshadow (ओवर्´शैडो) *vt.* पर छा जाना

oversight (´ओव़र्‌साइट) *n.* चूक, भूल; गलती

overt (´ओव़र्ट) *a.* प्रत्यक्ष, खुला

overtake (ओव़र्´टेक) *vt.* (वाहन, व्यक्ति) से आगे निकल जाना, बराबर आ पहुंचना

overthrow *vt.* (ओव़र्´थ्रो) (तख्ता) पलट देना; हरा देना – *n.* (´ओवर्‌थ्रो) विनाश, पतन

overtime (´ओव़र्‌टाइम) *n.* कार्य के घंटों के अतिरिक्त समय (में किया गया कार्य); अतिरिक्त समय भत्ता, ओवरटाइम

overtone (´ओव़र्टोन) *n.* (**overtones** भी) अतिरिक्त अर्थ, व्यंजना

overture (´ओव़र्ट्युअर) *n. Mus.* पूर्वरंग, बातचीत का आरंभ; प्रस्तावना

overweening (ओव़र्´वीनिङ) *a.* अहंकारपूर्ण, अक्खड़

overweight (ओव़र्´वेट) *a.* (व्यक्ति) जिस का वज़न अधिक हो

overwhelm (ओव़र्´वेल्म) *vt.* दबा देना, को पूरा ढंक लेना; बुरी तरह हराना – **overwhelming** *a.* भारी, ज़बरदस्त

overwork (ओवर्´वर्क) *vi/vt.* बहुत अधिक काम करना, अधिक काम करवाना – *n.*

overwrought (ओव´रॉट) *a.* अति उत्तेजित

owe (ओ) *vt.* ऋणी होना; आभारी होना – **owing** *a.* बाकी, देय – **owing to** के कारण

owl (आउल) *n.* उल्लू – **owlet** *n.* उल्लू का बच्चा

own (ओन) *a.* अपना, निजी – *vt.* का स्वामी होना, स्वीकार करना – *vi.* मान लेना – **owner** *n.* स्वामी, मालिक – **ownership** *n.* स्वामित्व

ox (ऑक्स) *n.* बैल, गाय या बैल (*pl.* **oxen**)

oxide (´ऑक्साइड) *n.* आक्सीजन और एक अन्य तत्व का सम्मिश्रण

oxygen (´ऑक्सिजन) *n.* आक्सीजन गैस

oxymoron (ऑक्सि´मॉरॉन) *n.* विरोधाभास अलंकार जैसे *cruel kindness*

oyster (´ऑइस्टर) *n.* खाने योग्य शुक्ति, घोंघा, कस्तूरा मछली

Oz (´ऑज़) *n. inf.* आस्ट्रेलिया

Oz. ounce (s) का संक्षेप

ozone (´ओज़ोन) *n.* ओज़ोन गैस

P

PA Personal Assistant, Public Address System का संक्षेप

p.a. per annum का संक्षेप

pace (पेस) *n.* कदम; गति; चाल – *vi* कदम-कदम चलना, टहलना – *vt.* गति निर्धारित करना; पार करना; कदम से मापना – **pacemaker** *n.* हृदय रोग वालों के लगाया जाने वाला उपकरण, पेस मेकर

pacify (ˈपैसिफ़ाइ) *vt.* शांत करना (**-fied, -fying**) – **pacific** *a.* शंतिपूर्ण; शांत, प्रशांत, स्थिर – **pacifism** (ˈपैसिफ़िज़्म) *n.* – **pacifist** *n.* युद्ध-विरोधी, व्यक्ति जो युद्ध में सहायता देने से इनकार करे

pack (पैक) *n.* गठरी, जानवरों का झुंड; दल, गिरोह, समूह, पैकेट; ताश की गड्डी – *vt.* सूटकेस आदि में रखना, बंडल बनाना; ठूंसना; में भरना, ठसाठस भरना; (**off** के साथ) चलता कर देना – **package** (ˈपैकिज) *n.* पार्सल; इकट्ठी प्रस्तावित रियायतें आदि – *vt.* पैकेज बनाना – **packet** *n.* छोटा पार्सल, पैकट; *sl.* बड़ी रकम – **pack up** काम बंद कर देना

pact (पैक्ट) *n.* समझौता, संविदा

pad[1] (पैड) *n.* गद्दी; कागज़ों का पैड, जानवर के पैर का तला; मुहर लगाने का पैड; रॉकेट छोड़ने का स्थान; *sl.*निवास – *vt.* मुलायम पदार्थ भरकर, गद्दीदार बनाना; (**-dd-**) – **padding** *n.* भरने का पदार्थ; साहित्यिक कृति में अनावश्यक विस्तार

pad[2] (पैड) *vi.* हल्के कदमों से चलना; धीरे-धीरे (पैदल) यात्रा करना (**-dd-**) – *n.* पैरों की आहट

paddle[1] (ˈपैड्ल) *n.* पैडल, छोटा चप्पू; **US** टेबल टैनिस का रैकट – *v* पैडल से नाव खेना, धीरे-धीरे खेना – **paddle wheel** जहाज़ का चप्पूदार चक्कर

paddle[2] (ˈपैड्ल) *vi.* नंगे पाँव उथले पानी में चलना

paddock (ˈपैडक) *n.* छोटा घास का मैदान या बाड़ा (घोड़ों के लिए)

paddy (ˈपैडि) *n.* धान

padlock (ˈपैड्लॉक) *n.* कुण्डे में लगाने वाला ताला – *vt.* ताला लगाना

padre (ˈपाड्रि) *n.* पादरी (विशे. सेना में)

paean (ˈपीअन) *n.* विजय-गीत

paediatrics (पीडिˈऐट्रिक्स) *n.* बाल-चिकित्सा (US **pediatrics** भी) – **paediatrician** (पीडिअˈट्रिशन) *n.* बाल-चिकित्सक

pagan (ˈपेगन) *a./n.* मूर्ति पूजक; काफ़िर – **paganism** *n.* मूर्ति पूजा; विधर्म

page[1] (पेज) *n.* पृष्ठ

page[2] (पेज) *n.* लड़का-नौकर, परिचर (**page boy** भी); दूल्हे का अनुचर – *v.* लाउडस्पीकर पर नाम पुकार कर बुलाना; पेजर द्वारा बुलाना – **pager** *n.* इलैक्ट्रानिकी उपकरण जिसमें संक्षिप्त लिखा हुआ संदेश प्राप्त किया जा सकता है, पेजर

pageant (ˈपैजंट) *n.* जलूस, शोभा यात्रा; विशेष वस्त्रों में शानदार प्रदर्शन विशे. नाटक में ऐतिहासिक दृश्यों आदि का – **pageantry** *n.* आकर्षक प्रदर्शन

pagoda (पˈगोड्अ) *n.* पिरामिड के आकार का (बौद्ध) मंदिर, पगोडा

paid (पेड) PAY का *pt.*

pail (पेल) *n.* बाल्टी

pain (पेन) *n.* पीड़ा, दर्द, तकलीफ़ – *pl.* कष्ट; परिश्रम – *vt.* कष्ट पहुंचाना, दुख देना – **painful** *a.* – **painfully** *adv.* – **painless** *a.* – **painlessly** *adv.* – **painkiller** *n.* दर्द निवारक दवा – **painstaking** *a.* परिश्रमी; श्रमसाध्य – **take (great) pains** ध्यान व मेहनत से कुछ करना

paint (पेंट) *n.* रंग, रोगन – *vt.* रंग करना, रंग भरना, चित्र बनाना, मेकअप करना – **painter** (पेंटर) *n.* चित्रकार – **painting** (पेंटिंग) *n.* चित्र

pair (पेंअर) *n.* जोड़ी – *v.* जोड़ा बनाना या बनना – **pair of scissors** कैंची – **pair of trousers** पतलून

pajamas (प'जामज़) *pl. n.* **US** दे. PYJAMAS

pal (पैल) *n. inf.* मित्र

palace (पैलिस) *n.* राजप्रासाद, महल, भवन – **palatial** (प'लेशल) *a.* महल जैसा, भव्य

palate (पैलिट) *n.* तालू, स्वाद-शक्ति – **palatable** (पैलटबल) *a.* स्वादिष्ट

palatial दे. PALACE

pale (पेल) *a.* पीला, फीका, धुंधला – *vi.* फीका पड़ जाना; महत्वहीन हो जाना – **beyond the pale of** (समाज की) मर्यादा से बाहर

palette (पैलिट) *n.* चित्रकार की रंगपट्टिका

pall[1] (पॉल) *n.* धुंए का बादल, ताबूत ढकने का कपड़ा– **pallbearer** *n.* ताबूत उठाने वाला

pall[2] (पॉल) *vi.* अरुचिकर, स्वादहीन हो जाना

pallet (पैलिट) *n.* माल रखने व स्थानांतरित करने का (पोर्टेबल) प्लेटफार्म

palliate (पैलिएट) *vt.* (व्याधि, पीड़ा) कम करना; सफ़ाई देना – **palliative** *a.* (औषधि आदि) जिससे रोग की प्रचण्डता कम हो

pallid (पैलिड) *a.* पीला – **pallor** (पैलर) *n.* पीलापन

palm (पाम) *n.* हथेली; (**palmtree** भी) ताड़, खजूर; ताड़ पत्र विजय-चिन्ह के रूप में – **palmist** (पामिस्ट) *n.* हस्तरेखा-शास्त्री – **palmistry** *n.* हस्तरेखाशास्त्र – **palmtop** *n.* हथेली में समा जाने वाला छोटा कम्प्यूटर

palpable (पैल्पबल) *a.* सुस्पष्ट

palpitate (पैल्पिटेट) *vi.* धड़कना, धक-धक करना – **palpitation** (पैल्पि'टेशन) *n.* (हृदय की) धड़कन; अनियमित ढंग से ज़ोर-ज़ोर से धड़कने की स्थिति

palsy (पॉल्ज़ि) *n.* पक्षाघात, फालिज

paltry (पॉल्ट्रि) *a.* तुच्छ, बेकार

pamper (पैम्पर) *vt.* ज्यादा लाड़ प्यार करना, लाड़-प्यार से बिगाड़ देना

pamphlet (पैम्फ़्लिट) *n.* पैम्फ्लेट, पुस्तिका

pan[1] (पैन) *n.* (**sauce pan** भी) कड़ाह, कड़ाही, तसला, तवा; तलने का पात्र (**frying pan** भी); शौचघर का पात्र; नमक बनाने का गड्ढा – *vt. inf.* कटु आलोचना करना (**-nn-**) – **pan out** *vi.* परिणाम होना

pan[2] (पैन) *v.* पूरे सीन की फिल्म बनाते हुए फिल्म कैमरा धीरे-धीरे घूमना या घुमाना

pan-, pant-, panto- *(comb. form)* – अखिल-सर्व- जैसे- panacea, में

panacea (पैन'सिअ) *n.* सर्वरोगहर, रामबाण औषधि

panache (प'नैश) *n.* अनोखा तौर-तरीका, बांकापन

pancake (पैन्केक) *n.* माल-पुए के प्रकार का पकवान, पुआ

panchromatic (पैन्क्रो'मैटिक) *a.* *Photography* सभी रंगों से प्रभावित होने वाली (फिल्म), सर्ववर्णिक

pancreas (पैंक्रिअस) *n.* अग्न्याशय, पाचक ग्रंथि

panda (पैंड्अ) *n.* एक चीनी वन्य प्राणी जो रींछ से मिलता जुलता है, पैंडा

pandemic (पैन्'डेमिक) *a.* देशांतरगामी (महामारी)

pandemonium (पैंडि'मोनिअम) *n.* ज़बरदस्त हंगामा, हो हल्ला

pander (पैण्डर) *v.* – **pander to** (बुरी हच्छाओं आदि) की संतुष्टि करना

pane (पेन) *n.* (खिड़की या शीशे का) कांच, कांच पट्ट

panel (पैनल) *n.* (दरवाज़े का) दिल्ला; कार आदि का वह भाग जिस पर गतिमापक आदि लगे होते हैं; फलक; विशेष कार्य के लिए जूरी, डाक्टरों आदि की तालिका, नामिका; चित्र-फलक – *vt.* दिल्ला लगाना

pang (पैङ) *n.* टीस, कसक, पीड़ा

panic (पैनिक) *n.* आतंक, भय – *a.* आतंक सम्बंधी – *v.* आतंकित, भयभीत आदि होना (**-icked, icking**) – **panicky** *a.* शीघ्र संत्रस्त होने या घबराने वाला

panoply (पैनप्लि) *n.* शानदार, ठाटबाट की वेशभूषा या तामझाम

panorama (पैन'रामअ) *n.* सर्वद श्य चित्र; दर्शक के चारों ओर लगे या चलते चित्र – **panoramic** (पैन'रैमिक) *a.* विशालदर्शी

pansy (पैंजि) *n.* पैंज़ी फूल

pant (पैंट) *vi.* हांफना

pantaloon (पैंटलून) *n.* मूक-अभिनय में बेवकूफ बुड्ढा – *pl. inf.* ढीली पतलून

panther (पैंथर) *n.* तेंदुआ

panties (पैंटिज़) *pl. n.* स्त्रियों का जांघिया

pantomime (पैंटमाइम) *n.* परी-कथा पर आधारित क्रिसमस-नाटक; मूक अभिनय, मूक नाटक

pantry (पैंट्रि) *n.* रसोई-भण्डार

pants (पैंट्स) *pl. n.* जांघिया; **US** पैंट

pap[1] (पैप) *n.* दलिया; गूदा

pap[2] (पैप) *n.* स्तन

papacy (पेपसि) *n.* पोप का पद – **papal** (पेपल) *a.* पोप से सम्बद्ध

paper (पेपर) *n.* कागज़; (**newspaper** भी) समाचार-पत्र; लेख; परीक्षा का प्रश्नपत्र – *pl* कागज़ात – *a.* कागज़ का बना – *vt.* कागज़ लगाना या चिपकाना – **paperback** *n.* पतली जिल्द वाली पुस्तक

papier-mâché (पैप्ये'मैशे) *n.* रद्दी कागज़, चीथड़ों आदि की लुगदी से बना सख्त पदार्थ, कुट्टी

papyrus (प'पाइरस) *n.* पपाइरस, एक पानी का पौधा, श्रीपत्र; इससे बने कागज़ पर पाण्डुलिपि (*pl.* **papyri**)

par (पार) *n.* मूल्यों व साख में समता; (शेयरों का) अंकित मूल्य; *Golf* अनुमानित औसत स्कोर – **parity** (पैरिटि) *n.* समता, बराबरी

para-, par-, pa- (*comb. form*) अतिरिक्त; से अधिक, से परे, जैसे **parallel, parody** में

parable (पैरबल) *n.* द ष्टांत, नीति-कथा

parachute (पैरशूट) *n.* पैराशूट, (हवाई) छतरी – *v.* पैराशूट से उतरना या उतारना – **parachutist** *n.* छतरी-सैनिक

parade (प'रेड) *n.* परेड, सैन्य प्रदर्शन – *vi.* कवायद करना, प्रदर्शन करना

paradise (पैरडाइस) *n.* वैकुण्ठ, स्वर्ग; पूर्ण आनंद की स्थिति

paradox (पैरडॉक्स) *n.* विरोधाभास

paraffin (पैरफ़िन) *n.* मोमबत्ती आदि में प्रयुक्त नरम पैट्रोलियम पदार्थ, पैराफ़िन – **paraffin oil** मिट्टी का तेल

paragon (पैरगन) *n.* श्रेष्ठता का आदर्श

paragraph (पैरग्राफ़) *n.* पैराग्राफ़, अनुच्छेद – *vt.* (लेख आदि) पैराग्राफ़ों में बांटना

parakeet (पैरकीट) *n.* एक तोते की जाति

parallel (पैरलेंल) *a.* समानांतर – *n.* समांतर, प्रतिरूप, अक्षांश – *vt.* साद श्य दिखाना; तुलना करना – **parallelism** *n.* समानांतरता, साद श्य – **parallelogram** (पैर'लेंलग्रैम) *n.* समानान्तर चतुर्भुज

paralysis (प'रैलिसि) *n.* पक्षाघात, लकवा (*pl.* **-yses** (-सीज़) – **paralyse** (पैरलाइज़) *vt.* लकवा मारना; ठप्प करना – **paralytic** (पैर'लिटिक) *a./n.* लकवाग्रस्त (रोगी)

paramilitary (पैर मिलिटरि) *a.* सैन्य व्यवस्था के अनुरूप अथवा सेना के सहायक अंग के रूप में संगठित असैनिक दल, परा सैनिक दल

paramount (पैरमाउंट) *a.* सर्वोपर, सर्वोच्च, मुख्यतम

paramour (पैरमुअर) *n.* प्रेमी या प्रेमिका (वि. विवाहित स्त्री का, विवाहित पुरुष की)

paranormal (पैर्अ नॉर्मल) *a.* सामान्य से परे

parapet (पैरपिट) *n.* मुंडेर; पुल के दोनों ओर की नीची दीवार, प्राकार

paraphernalia (पैरफ़र् नेलिअ) *n.* निजी सामान या छुट-पुट सामग्री, तामझाम

paraphrase (पैरफ्रेज़) *n.* भावनुवाद; मुक्त अनुवाद – *vt.* भावानुवाद करना

parasite (पैरसाइट) *n.* परजीवी (प्राणी या पौधा), पराश्रयी (व्यक्ति) – **parasitic** (पैर सिटक) *a.*

parasol (पैरसॉल) *n.* छाता (विशे. महिलाओं का)

paratroops (पैरट्रूप्स), **-troopers** (-ट्रूपर्ज़) *pl. n.* छतरी-सैनिक

paratyphoid (पैर टाइफ़ॉइड) *n.* मोतीझरा से मिलता-जुलता परंतु उससे भिन्न संक्रामक रोग

parcel (पार्सल) *n.* पार्सल – *vt.* (**parcel up** भी) लपेटना; (टुकड़ों में) बांटना (*-ll-*)

parch (पार्च) *v.* सुखाना; झुलसाना – **parched** *a.* (व्यक्ति) जिसे बहुत प्यास लगी हो; सूखे (होठ); सूखी (ज़मीन)

parchment (पार्च्मंट) *n.* चर्म पत्र, पार्च मंट; (इस पर लिखी) पाण्डुलिपि

pardon (पार्डन) *n.* क्षमा, माफी – *vt.* क्षमा करना, माफ करना – **pardonable** *a.* क्षमा योग्य

pare (पेंअर) *vt.* तराशना, छीलना; कतरना

parent (पेंरंट) *n.* माता या पिता – **parentage** *n.* पित त्व, वंश, वंशावली – **parental** (प रेंन्टल) *a.* पैत क – **parenthood** *n.* – **parenting** *n.* बच्चों का लालन-पालन

parenthesis (प रेंन्थिसिस) *n.* वाक्य के भीतर कोष्ठक, कॉमा या डैश में शब्द या वाक्यांश, निक्षेप – **parentheses** (-सीज़) *pl. n.* ऐसे वाक्यांश या शब्द के लिए प्रयुक्त लघु कोष्ठक ( )

par excellence (पार् ऐक्सलांस) *a. Fr* लाजवाब

pariah (पै रिअ) *n.* जाति-बहिष्क त

parish (पैरिश) *n.* पैरिश, यजमानी (क्षेत्र); एक पादरी का क्षेत्र – **parishioner** *n.* पैरिशवासी

parity (पैरिटि) दे. PAR

park (पार्क) *n.* सार्वजनिक उद्यान, पार्क; कार आदि खड़ी करने का सार्वजनिक स्थान – *vt.* (कार) पार्क करना, खड़ी करना

parlance (पार्लन्स) *n.* भाषा-शैली, बोली, बोलचाल का तरीका, शब्दावली, मुहावरा

parley (पार्लि) *n.* दो विरोधी गुटों, देशों आदि के नेताओं या प्रतिनिधियों के मध्य संधिवार्ता अथवा विचार-विमर्श (*pl.* **- leys**) – *vi*

parliament (पार्लमंट) *n.* संसद, पार्लियामेंट – **parliamentarian** (पार्लमेंन् टेंअरिन) *n.* संसद-सदस्य–**parliamentary** (पार्ल मेंन्टरि) *a.* संसदीय

parlour (पार्लर) *n.* बैठक, वार्ता-कक्ष; US व्यवसाय-कक्ष, दुकान

parochial (प रोकिअल) *n.* संकीर्ण सीमित

parody (पैरडि) *n.* क ति जिसमें किसी लेखक की शैली की नकल हो (प्राय: व्यंगात्मक), पैरोडी, विडंबन काव्य – *v.* की पैरोडी बनाना (**-odied, -odying**)

parole (प रोल) *n.* अच्छे आचरण के वचन पर अवधि से पूर्व कारावास से मुक्ति, परोल – *vt.* इस शर्त पर जेल से अस्थायी रिहाई कि बन्दी का आचरण ठीक रहेगा

paroxysm (पैरक्सिज़्म) *n.* पीड़ा आदि का अचानक ज़ोर, दौरा; क्रोध का आवेश; हंसी का दौरा

parricide (पैरिसाइड) *n.* पित अथवा मात हत्या, पित घातक, पित हंता

parrot (पैरट) *n.* तोता

parry (पैरि) *vt.* वार बचाना, दूर हटना **(parried, parrying)**

parse (पार्ज़) *vt. Grammar* पद व्याख्या करना, शब्दों, वाक्यों का व्याकरणिक पद परिचय देना

parsimony (ˈपार्सिमनि) *n.* कंजूसी – **parsimonious** *a.* मितव्ययी

parsley (ˈपार्स्लि) *n.* अजमोद, अजवायन की तरह सुगंधित पत्तियों वाला एक पौधा

parsnip (ˈपार्स्निप) *n.* चुकंदर जैसी एक तरकारी

parson (ˈपार्सन) *n.* चर्च का पादरी, पुरोहित

part (पार्ट) *n.* भाग, खण्ड; सदस्य; अभिनेता का पार्ट, भूमिका; कर्तव्य; (प्राय: *pl.*) क्षेत्र; मामला, काम – *v.* विभाजित करना, (से) अलग होना या करना – **parting** *n.* बालों में मांग; जुदाई; विदाई लेना – **partly** *adv.* अंशतः, कुछ अंश तक – **part and parcel** अभिन्न अंग – **part-time** *a.* अंशकालिक

partake (पार्ˈटेक) *v.* भाग लेना, सम्मिलित होना, भागी होना; खाना या पीना **(partook, -taken, -taking)**

partial (ˈपार्शल) *a.* आंशिक, अपूर्ण; पक्षपाती; का शौकीन – **partiality** *n.* (पारशिˈऐलिटि) *n.* पक्षपात; पसंद – **partially** *adv.* आंशिक रूप से, अंशतः

participate (पार्ˈटिसिपेट) *v.* भाग लेना; भागी या साझेदार होना – **participant** *n.* भागी, हिस्सेदार – **participation** *n.* भाग, सहयोग

participle (ˈपार्टिसिपल) *n.* क दन्त रूप जैसे *lose* का **present participle** रूप *losing*

particle (ˈपार्टिक्ल) *n.* कण, ज़र्रा

particular (पर्ˈटिक्युलर) *a.* विशेष, सूक्ष्म; नाज़ुक मिज़ाज, सख्त; सावधान – *n.* विशेष बात, स्थिति आदि – *pl.* विवरण, ब्यौरा – **particularity** *n.* विशिष्टता – **particularly** *adv.* विशेष रूप से

partisan (पार्टिˈज़ैन) *n./a.* अंधभक्त, तरफदार, समर्थक – **partisanship** *n.* पक्षपात, तरफदारी

partition (पार्ˈटिशन) *n.* विभाजन, बंटवारा; (कमरे, हॉल आदि की) विभाजक दीवार – *vt.* विभक्त करना, बांट देना

partner (ˈपार्ट्नर) *n.* साथी; साझेदार – **partnership** *n.* व्यवसाय आदि में साझेदारी

partridge (ˈपार्ट्रिज) *n.* तीतर

party (ˈपार्टि) *n.* दल, टोली (यात्रियों की), मण्डली; पार्टी (राजनीतिक); गोष्ठी; व्यक्ति; प्रीतिभोज – *a.* सहायक, समर्थक; भाग लेने वाला

pass (पास) *vt.* आगे बढ़ना, गुजरना, पार करना; से बढ़कर होना; स्वीक त होना; उत्तीर्ण करना; (समय) व्यतीत करना; को दे देना; उपेक्षा करना, ध्यान न देना; (सम्पत्ति आदि का म त्यु के बाद किसी को) मिलना; (तूफान आदि) चले जाना; पारित करना – *v.* चले जाना; एक हाथ से दूसरे हाथ में जाना, (समय) गुज़रना; (संसदीय बिल) पारित करना – *n.* दर्रा, घाटी; पास, पारपत्र; सफलता (परीक्षा में) – **passable** *a.* कामचलाऊ – **passing** *a.* क्षणिक; प्रासंगिक – **passer-by** *n.* राहगीर, राही – **pass away** का देहान्त होना – **pass for** समझा जाना – **pass out** बेहोश हो जाना

passage (पैसिज) *n.* (**passageway** भी) रास्ता, मार्ग; पुस्तक का परिच्छेद; गुज़रना; (समुद्र) यात्रा; यात्रा-भाड़ा; संसद आदि का कानून बनाने की क्रिया; (समय का) बीत जाना,

passenger (पैसिंजर) *n.* यात्री

passion (ˈपैशन) *n.* मनोभाव, तीव्र इच्छा विशे. कामेच्छा – **passionate** (ˈपैशनिट) *a.* भाव प्रवाह; क्रोधी; कामुक

passive (ˈपैसिव़) *a.* निष्क्रिय, निश्चेष्ट अकर्मण्य; *Grammar* कर्म वाच्य – **passivity** *n.*

passport (ˈपास्पॉर्ट) *n.* पासपोर्ट, पारपत्र

password (ˈपास्वर्ड) *n.* गुप्त शब्द या वाक्यांश जो मित्र व शुत्र में अंतर स्पष्ट करे, पहचान-शब्द; कम्प्यूटर, ई-मेल आदि को प्रयोग करने के लिए आवश्यक पासवर्ड

past (पास्ट) *a.* समाप्त, विगत, भूत – *n.* भूतकाल, अतीत – *adv.* से होकर (रास्ता), सीधा, के पार – *prep.* के बाद (तक); से अधिक; के परे

pasta (ˈपैस्ट्अ) *n.* गुंधे आटे से बने विविध प्रकार के खाद्य-पदार्थ जैसे स्पागैटी (सेवईं)

paste (पेस्ट) *n.* लेई, लेई जैसी मुलायम वस्तु जैसे टुथपेस्ट; पतला लेई जैसा चिपकाने वाले मिश्रण – *vt.* लेई से चिपकाना

pastel (ˈपैस्टल) *n.* रंग भरने की रंगीन चाक, पैस्टल-चित्र कला; हलका पीला रंग – *a.*

pasteurize (ˈपैस्टराइज़) *vt.* ताप से कीटाणु रहित करना – **pasteurization** *n.* पास्चुरीकरण

pastime (ˈपास्टाइम) *n.* मनोरंजन, मन बहलाव

pastor (ˈपास्टर) *a.* ईसाई पुरोहित – **pastoral** *a.* ग्रामीण-जीवन व चरवाहों से सम्बंधित; पास्तर के पद से सम्बद्ध

pastry (ˈपेस्ट्रि) *n.* पेस्ट्री (एक मिठाई)

pasture (ˈपास्चर) *n.* चरागाह – *v.* चरना, चराना

pat[1] (पैट) *vt.* थपथपाना (**-tt-**) – *n.* हल्की सी चपत, छोटा टुकड़ा (जैसे मक्खन का)

pat[2] (पैट) *adv.* तुरंत, ठीक मौके पर

patch (पैच) *n.* पैबंद, धब्बा; जमीन का टुकड़ा, एक छोटी अवधि – *vt.* थिकली लगाना, मरम्मत करना, उलटा-सीधा जोड़ लगाना – **patchy** *a.* असमान गुण वाला (कार्य)

pate (पेट) *n.* सिर, खोपड़ी

patent (ˈपेटंट) *n.* किसी आविष्कार पर एकाधिकार का दस्तावेज़, पेटेंट – *a.* प्रत्यक्ष; स्पष्ट – **patently** *adv.* स्पष्टतया, बिलकुल

paternal (पˈटर्नल) *a.* पैतृक – **paternalism** *n.* पिता के समान अधिकार का प्रयोग – **paternity** (पˈटर्निटि) *n.* पितृत्व

path (पाथ) *n.* पथ, रास्ता; कार्यवाही का तरीका

pathetic (पˈथैटिक) *a.* करुणाजनक, दयनीय

pathology (पˈथॉलजि) *n.* रोग-विज्ञान – **pathological** (पैथˈलॉजिकल) *a.* रोग-विज्ञान संबंधी; *inf.* जो स्वभाव से विवश हो (जैसे *pathological liar*) – **pathologist** *n.*

pathos (ˈपेथॉस) *n.* करुणा, करुणारस

patient (ˈपेशंट) *a.* धैर्यवान, सहनशील – *n.* रोगी, मरीज़ – **patience** (ˈपेशंस) *n.* धीरज, धैर्य

patriarch (ˈपेट्रिआर्क) *n.* परिवार का (पिता) मुखिया

patricide (ˈपैट्रिसाइड) *n.* पित्रघातक; पित्रहत्या

patrimony (ˈपैट्रिमनि) *n.* पैतृक सम्पत्ति, पुश्तैनी सम्पत्ति

patriot (ˈपैट्रिअट) *n.* देश-भक्त – **patriotic** (पैट्रिˈऑटिक) *a.* देश भक्ति से प्रेरित – **patriotism** (ˈपैट्रिअटिज़म) *n.* देश-भक्ति

patrol (पˈट्रोल) *n.* नियमित गश्त; गश्त लगाने वाला व्यक्ति या दल – *v.* गश्त लगाना

patron (ˈपेट्रन) *n.* संरक्षक (कलाकारों, दान संस्थाओं आदि का); समर्थक; नियमित ग्राहक; संरक्षक संत – **patronage** (ˈपैट्रनिज) *n.* (संरक्षक द्वारा दिया गया) समर्थन – **patronize** *vt. fig.* किसी की ओर अपनी श्रेष्ठता का भाव अपनाना; का नियमित ग्राहक होना

patter (ˈपैटर) *vi.* पट-पट या तड़-तड़ (जैसे बारिश की) आवाज़ करना; प्रार्थना आदि

बार-बार बोलना; अनाप-शनाप बोलना – *n.* ऐसी आवाज़; *inf.* तेज़ धारा प्रवाह में बोलना (सेल्समैन का)

pattern (पैटर्न) *n.* बनावट, डिज़ाइन, (काटने के लिए) कपड़ों आदि पर आक ति; आदर्श, नमूना, ढांचा; प्रतिमान, प्रतिरूप – *vt.*

patty (पैटि) *n.* एक समोसे जैसा पकवान, पैट्टी

paucity (ˈपॉसिटि) *n.* अभाव, कमी

paunch (पॉन्च) *n.* पेट, तोंद

pauper (ˈपॉपर) *n.* कंगाल, दरिद्र

pause (पॉज़) *vi.* कुछ समय के लिए रुकना, ठहरना – *n.* विश्राम

pave (पेव्) *vt.* खड़ंजा डालना, ईट-पत्थर से (गली आदि को) पक्का करना – **pavement** *n.* पटरी की पटड़ी – **pave the way for** के लिए मार्ग प्रशस्त करना

pavilion (पˈविल्यन) *n.* पैविलियन; (प्रदर्शनी) मंडप

paw (पॉ) *n.* जानवर का पंजा – *v.* पंजे से कुरेदना, पंजा मारना

pawn[1] (ˈपॉन) *vt.* गिरवी रखना, बन्धक या रेहन रखना – *n.* गिरवी रखी वस्तु – **pawnbroker** *n.* वस्तुएं गिरवी रखकर पैसा उधार देनेवाला, साहूकार – **pawnshop** *n.* गिरवीघर

pawn[2] (पॉन) *n.* शतरंज में प्यादा (पैदल); *fig.* व्यक्ति जो दूसरे के हाथों में कठपुतली हो

pay (पे) *vt.* पैसे देना, अदा करना; क्षतिपूर्ति करना; (शुभकामनाएँ) देना; (प्रशंसा के शब्द) कहना; के लिए लाभकर होना– *vi.* लाभकर होना; (*out* के साथ) खर्च करना (**paid, paying**) – *n.* वेतन – **payable** *a.* देय – **payee** *n.* पाने वाला – **payment** *n.* (ऋण) भुगतान, अदायगी – **payload** *n.* प्रक्षेपास्त्र (मिसाइल) आदि की विस्फोटक शक्ति – **paying guest** व्यक्तिगत घर में रहने व खाने-पीने आदि का खर्चा देकर रहने वाला अतिथि, पेइंग-गैस्ट – **payphone** *n.* सिक्के या कार्ड से चलने वाला सार्वजनिक टेलीफोन

PC Personal Computer का संक्षेप

p.c. per cent; postcard का संक्षेप

pea (पी) *n.* मटर

peace (पीस) *n.* शांति; मेलजोल; मानसिक शांति; नीरवता; आराम – **peaceful** *a.* शांतिपूर्ण, शांत, नीरव – **peacefully** *adv.*

peach (पीच) *n.* आड़ू

peacock (ˈपीकॉक) *n.* मोर (**peahen** *fem.* मोरनी)

peak (पीक) *n.* चोटी, नुकीला सिरा; चरम सीमा, एकदम व द्धि; टोपी की नोक – *v.* व द्धि की चरम सीमा पहुंचना या पहुंचाना – **peaked, peaky** *a.* नुकीला – **peak hours** दिन का वह समय जब काम का बहुत ज़ोर हो या लोग/गाड़ियां अधिक संख्या में आ जा रही हों, व्यस्त समय

peal (पील) *n.* गरज, गड़गड़ाहट; घण्टानाद – *vi.* गड़गड़ाना, झनझनाना – **peals of laughter** हंसी का ठहाका

peanut (ˈपीनट) *n.* मूंगफली – *pl. inf.* बहुत छोटी रकम

pear (ˈपैंअर) *n.* नाशपाती

pearl (पर्ल) *n.* मोती, मुक्ता

peasant (ˈपैंज़ंट) *n.* किसान, देहाती – **peasantry** *n.* किसान-वर्ग

peat (पीट) *n.* दलदल में पाये जाने वाले सड़े-गले पौधे; सूखने के बाद बना इसका ईंधन

pebble (ˈपैंबल) *n.* रोड़ा, कंकड़– *vt.* रोड़े बिछाना

peccadillo (पैंकˈडिलो) *n.* छोटा-मोटा अपराध या दोष, लघुपाप (*pl.* **-es, -s**)

peck (पैंक) *v.* (**peck at** भी) चोंच मारना; चुगना; *inf.* जल्दी से चुम्बन लेना

peculiar (पि´क्यूलिअर) *a.* अनोखा, निराला, अजीब – **peculiarity** (पिक्यूलि´ऐरिटि) *n.* विशिष्टता, अनोखापन, विलक्षणता, विशेषता
pecuniary (पि´क्यूनिअरि) *a.* धनसम्बंधी
pedagogue (´पेंडगॉग) *n.* स्कूल मास्टर, शिक्षक; पांडित्य प्रदर्शन करने वाला व्यक्ति – **pedagogic** (पेंड´गॉजिक) *a.* शैक्षिक
pedal (´पेंडल) *n.* पैडल – *a.* पैर का – *v.* पैडल मारकर साइकिल चलाना, पैडल मारना (*-ll-*)
pedant (´पेंडंट) *n.* पंडिताऊ – **pedantic** (पि´डैंटिक) *a.* – **pedantry** (´पेंडंट्रि) *n.* पांडित्य-प्रदर्शन
peddle (´पेंडल) *vt.* फेरी लगाना – **peddler** (´पेंड्लर) *n.* नशीली दवाएं बेचने वाला
pedestal (´पेंडिस्टल) *n.* स्तंभ-आधार; (मूर्ति की) मंचिका
pedestrian (पि´डेंस्ट्रिअन) *n.* पैदल चलने वाला – *a.* पैदल; साधारण; नीरस
pediatrics *n.* दे. PAEDIATRICS
pedicure (´पेंडिक्युअर) *n.* पैरों की चिकित्सा अथवा प्रसाधन, पाद चिकित्सा, नख-श्रं गार
pedigree (´पेंडिग्री) *n.* वंशावली, वंश व क्ष; (कुत्तों आदि की) नसल
pedlar (´पेंड्लर) *n.* फेरी लगाने वाला
pee (पी) *vi. inf.* पेशाब करना (**peed** *pt./pp*)
peek (पीक) *vi.* निगाह मारना, झांकना – *n.* झांकी
peel (पील) *vt.* छीलना – *vi.* (खाल) उतरना, छिलना; रोगन की परतें उतरना – *n.* छिलका, खाल – **peeled** *a. inf.* सर्तक, खुली (आंखे) – **peelings** *pl. n.* छिलके आदि
peep[1] (पीप) *vi.* झांकना; ताक झांक करना – *n.* ताक-झांक – **peep-hole** *n.* झरोखा, गवाक्ष
peep[2] (पीप) *vt.* च -च करना (मुर्गी के चूज़े की तरह) – *n.* च -च
peer[1] (पिअर) *n.* सामन्त, अभिजात (**peeress** *fem.*); समकक्ष व्यक्ति, बराबर का व्यक्ति – **peerless** *a.* बेजोड़, अद्वितीय
peer[2] (पिअर) *vi.* घूर कर देखना
peeved (पीव्ड) *a.* चिड़चिड़ा, रूठा हुआ
peevish (´पीविश) *a.* चिड़चिड़ा
peg (पेंग) *n.* खूंटी, मेख, कपड़ों की चिमटी (**clothes peg** भी); स्तर या मानक चिन्ह – *vt.* खूंटियों से बांधना, जकड़ना; (मूल्य) स्थिर करना; *inf.* फेंकना – *vi.* – **peg away** परिश्रम करते रहना
pejorative (पि´जॉरटिव) *a.* अप्रत्यक्ष निंदात्मक शब्द
Pekin(g)ese (पीक´नीज़, पिकिङ´ईज़) *n.* छोटा चीनी कुत्ता
pelican (´पेंलिकन) *n.* एक जलपक्षी, पेलिकन
pellet (´पेंलिट) *n.* गोली, छर्रा
pell-mell (´पेंल्मेंल) *adv.* गड्डमड्ड, अस्त व्यस्त
pelmet (´पेंल्मिट) *n.* परदे लटकाने का लकड़ी का ढांचा
pelt[1] (पेंल्ट) *vt.* (पत्थर आदि) मारना – *vi.* पत्थर आदि फेंकना; लगातार (वर्षा आदि का) गिरना
pelt[2] पेल्ट) *n.* जानवरों की रोंयेंदार खाल
pelvis (´पेंल्विस) *n.* कूल्हा, पेड़ू, (*pl.* **pelvises, -ves** (वीज़)) – **pelvic** *a.* श्रोणि-प्रदेश से सम्बद्ध, कूल्हे का
pen[1] (पेंन) *n.* पेन, कलम – *vt.* रचना लिखना (**-nn-**) – **pen name** लेखक का उपनाम, तख़ल्लुस
pen[2] (पेंन) *n.* (भेड़ों आदि का) छोटा बाड़ा
penal (´पीनल) *a.* दण्ड-, दण्ड देने, दण्ड भागी बनने से सम्बंधित – **penalize** (´पीनलाइज़) *vt.* दण्ड देना – **penalty** (´पेंनल्टि) *n.* दण्ड, सज़ा, जुर्माना; *Sport* नियम भंग करने का दण्ड
penance (´पेंनन्स) *n.* तपस्या, तप, प्रायश्चित
pence (´पेंन्स) *n.* PENNY का *pl.*
penchant (´पेंन्चंट, पाँ´शाँ) *n.* झुकाव
pencil (´पेंन्सल) *n.* पेन्सिल – *vt.* चित्र बनाना; पेन्सिल से निशान लगाना (**-ll-**)

pendant (पेंन्डंट) *n.* लटकन, लटकने वाला आभूषण – **pendent** (पेंन्डंट) *a.* लटका हुआ, आगे निकला हुआ

pending (पेंन्डिङ) *prep.* तक, के समय – *a.* विचाराधीन, अनिर्णीत

pendulum (पेंण्ड्युलम) *n.* लोलक, पेंडुलम (विशे. दीवार घड़ी का)

penetrate (पेंनिट्रेट) *vt.* प्रवेश करना; घुसना, घुसाना, छेदना; (गूढ़) अर्थ समझ लेना – **penetrable** *a.*– **penetrating** *a.* तीखा, भेदने वाला (स्वर); सूक्ष्म; तीक्ष्ण बुद्धि, मर्मज्ञ – **penetration** (पेंनि ट्रेशन) *n.* विवेक, भेद या अर्थ समझ सकने वाला; प्रवेश

penguin (पेंङविन) *n.* अंटार्कटिका का एक उड़ न सकने वाला जल पक्षी

penicillin (पेंनि सिलिन) *n.* अनेक प्रकार के रोगों में प्रभावशाली ऐंटीबायटिक औषधि, पेन्सलीन

peninsula (पि निन्स्युलअ) *n.* प्रायःद्वीप – **peninsular** *a.* प्रायःद्वीपीय

penis (पीनिस) *n.* पुरुष (व अन्य नर प्राणियों का) लिंग, शिश्न (*pl.* **penises, penes** (ईज़))

penitent (पेंनिटंट) *a.* पश्चातापी –**penitence** *n.* पश्चाताप

penny (पेंनि) *n.* ब्रिटेन का सिक्का, पाउंड का 100 वां भाग, पैनी (*pl.* **pence, pennies**) – **penniless** *a.* दरिद्र, निर्धन – **penny-pinching** *a.* कंजूस

pension (पेंन्शन) *n.* पेंशन – *vt.* पेंशन देना – **pensioner** *n.* पेंशन भोगी

pensive (पेंन्सिव़) *a.* विचार मग्न, उदास

pent (पेंण्ट) *a.* बंद – **pent-up** *a.* घुटी हुई (भावनाएं आदि)

pentagon (पेंण्टगॉन) *n.* पंचभुज

penthouse (पेंन्ट्हाउस) *n.* भवन की सबसे ऊपर की मंज़िल पर महंगा, आरामदेह फ्लैट आदि

penultimate (पि नल्टमिट) *a.* अंतिम से पहला, उपांतिम

penury (पेंन्युरि) *n.* घोर दरिद्रता, गरीबी – **penurious** (पि न्युअरिअस) *a.* कंजूस, गरीब, अंकिचन

peon (पीअन) *n.* चपरासी

people (पीपल) *pl. n.* लोग; जाति; जनता; राष्ट्र; परिवार – *vt.* आबाद करना, बसाना

pep (पेंप) *n. inf.* शक्ति, उत्साह– *vt.* जोश दिलाना, स्फूर्ति देना (**-pp-**)

pepper (पेंपर) *n.* (गोल या काली) मिर्च; शिमला मिर्च जैसी सब्ज़ियां – *vt.* मिर्च डालना; बुरकना, लगाना, छिड़कना; पत्थर आदि की बौछार करना – **peppermint** *n.* पोदीना, पिपरमिंट, इसके स्वाद वाली मिठाई

peptic (पेंप्टिक) *a.* पाचक, पाचकरस संबंधी – **peptic ulcer** आमाशय में फोड़ा

per (पर) *prep.* प्रति, द्वारा, के अनुसार

per-, par, pel-, pil (*comb. form*) में से, पूर्णतय जैसे *perfect* में

perambulator (प रैम्ब्युलेटर) *n.* बच्चागाड़ी, प्रैम

per annum *Lat.* (पर् ऐनम) *adv.* प्रति वर्ष

per capita (पर् कैपिट्अ) *adv.* प्रति व्यक्ति

perceive (पर् सीव़) *vt.* महसूस करना; ध्यान से देख लेना; समझ लेना – **perceivable** *a.* – **perceptibility** *n.* – **perceptible** *a.* इंद्रियगोचर – **perception** *n.* ज्ञान, बोध, समझ – **perceptive** *a.* अनुभावशील; शीघ्र समझ सकने वाला

percentage (पर् सेंन्टिज) *n.* प्रतिशतता – **per cent** (पर् सेंन्ट) प्रतिशत, प्रति सैंकड़ा

perception (पर् सेंप्शन) *n.* दे. PERCEIVE

perch (पर्च) *n.* बैठने का स्थान (विशे. चिड़ियों का), ठिकाना – *vt.* (ठिकाने पर) बैठना – *vi.* उतरना, टिकना, पर संतुलन करना

percolate (पर्कलेट) *v.* रिसना, चूना, छनना – **percolation** (पर्क लेशन) *n.* रिसाव, छनाई

– **percolator** ('पर्‌कलेटर) *n.* फिलटर सहित काफी बनाने का बरतन

percussion (पर्'कशन) *n.* आघात, टक्कर; थपक – **percussion instrument** ताल-वाद्य जैसे ढोल, तबला आदि

perdition (पर्'डिशन) *n.* सर्वनाश (विशे. आत्मिक)

peremptory (प'रैम्प्टरि) *a.* अधिकारपूर्ण, दबंग

perennial (प'रैनिअल) *a.* बारहमासी, चिरस्थायी – *n.* दो वर्ष से अधिक उगते रहने वाला पौधा

perfect *a.* ('पर्‌फ़िक्ट) सम्पूर्ण, पक्का, दोष रहित, उत्कष्ट – *n.* पूर्णकाल (**perfect tense** भी) – *vt.* (पर्'फ़ैक्ट) सुधारना, दक्ष बनाना – **perfection** (पर्'फ़ैक्शन) *n.* पूर्णता, आदर्श – **perfectly** *adv.* पूर्णतया

perfidy ('पर्फ़िडि) *n.* विश्वासघात

perforate ('पर्‌फ़रेट) *vt.* छेद करना, पार करना – **perforation** (पर्‌फ़'रेशन) *n.* वस्तु में बनाए गए छेद

perform (पर्'फ़ॉर्म) *vt.* पूरा करना, सम्पन्न करना; मंच पर अभिनय करना – *vi.* कार्य करना (कुशलता से, गलत ढंग से, आदि); निष्पादित करना; अभिनय करना; संगीत-वाद्य बजाना – **performance** *n.* पालन; निष्पादन; क्रिया, प्रदर्शन आदि – **performer** *n.* कलाकार – **performing arts** मंच कलाएं

perfume ('पर्‌फ़्यूम) *n.* सुगंधि, महक – *vt.* (पर्'फ़्यूम) सुगंधित करना

perfunctory (पर्'फ़ंकटरि) *a.* लापरवाही, बेमन से किया गया

perhaps (पर'हैप्स) *adv.* शायद, कदाचित

peri- *(comb. form)* गोल, नज़दीक जैसे - **perimeter, period,** में

peril ('पैरिल) *n.* खतरा, जोखिम – **perilous** *a.* संकट पूर्ण, जोखिम भरा

perimeter (प'रिमिटर) *n.* परिधि, किसी क्षेत्र की बाहरी सीमा

period ('पिअरिअड) *n.* अवधि, युग, काल; स्त्रियों का मासिक-स्राव, रजोधर्म; पूर्ण विराम (.) – *a.* काल-विशेष का – **periodic** (पिअरि'ऑडिक) *a.* आवर्ती, मियादी – **periodical** *a./n.* काल विशेष का, आवर्ती; निश्चित समयान्तर पर निकलने वाली पत्रिका

peripatetic (पैरिप'टैटिक) *a.* भ्रमणशील, घुमक्कड़

periphery (प'रिफ़रि) *n.* परिधि; बाहरी सतह – **peripheral** (प'रिफ़रल) *a.* छोटा-मोटा, कम महत्व वाला; *n. Computers* जानकारी अंकित करने के मानिटर, प्रिंटर आदि

periscope ('पैरिस्कोप) *n.* पेरिस्कोप, जिसके द्वारा समुद्र की सतह के ऊपर देखा जा सकता है

perish ('पैरिश) *vi.* मर जाना, नष्ट हो जाना, सड़ या गल जाना – *n.* – **perishable** *a.* ज्यादा समय न टिकने वाला (पदार्थ), बिगड़ने वाला – (~ **s**) *pl. n.* जल्दी खराब होने वाले खाद्य पदार्थ

perjury ('पर्जरि) *n.* झूठी गवाही देने या झूठी कसम खाने का अपराध, शपथ-भंग

perk (पर्क) *n.* लाभ, सुविधा या रियायत (किसी नौकरी की); *inf.* PERQUISITE का संक्षिप्त रूप

perky ('पर्कि) *a.* चुस्त; प्रसन्न

permanent ('पर्मनंट) *a.* स्थायी, चिरस्थायी; पक्का – **permanence** *n.* स्थायित्व

permeate ('पर्मिएट) *vt.* (गंध आदि) समा जाना, द्रव का फैल जाना; *fig.* (विचार, प्रभाव आदि) व्याप्त हो जाना – **permeable** *a.*

permit *vt.* (पर्'मिट) अनुमति देना, करने देना; संभव करना – *n.* ('पर्‌मिट) परमिट, कुछ करने की अनुमति, अनुज्ञापत्र – **permissible** (पर्'मिसबल) *a.* अनुमति योग्य – **permission** (पर्'मिशन) *n.* अनुमति –

permissive *a.* अत्यधिक उदार विशे. यौन सम्बंधों के मामले में

permutation (पर्म्यु´टेशन) *n.* *Maths*. अंकों आदि को सभी संभव क्रमों में रखना, क्रम परिवर्तन

pernicious (पर्´निशस) *a.* हानिकर; दुष्टतापूर्ण

perpendicular (परपन्´डिक्युलर) *a.* किसी रेखा पर 90° का कोण बनाती सीधी खड़ी (रेखा), अभिलम्ब; सीधा खड़ा – *n.* लम्ब

perpetrate (´पर्पिट्रेट) *vt.* (बुरा काम) करना, का जिम्मेवार होना – **perpetration** (पर्पि´ट्रेशन) *n.* अपराधकर्म – **perpetrator** *n.*

perpetual (पर्´पेंचुअल) *a.* निरंतर – **perpetually** *adv.* – **perpetuate** (पर्´पेंचुएट) *vt.* स्थायी बनाना – **perpetuity** *n.* स्थायित्व, निरंतरता

perplex (पर्´प्लेक्स) *vt.* चक्कर में डालना, हैरान कर देना – **perplexity** ***n.***; हैरानी की हालत

perquisite (´पर्क्विज़िट) *n.* (बहुधा ~ s *pl.*) नौकरी में वेतन के अतिरिक्त मिलने वाली सुविधा या लाभ

per se (पर्´ से) *Lat.* स्वतः, अपने आप

persecute (´पर्सिक्यूट) *vt.* धर्म, जाति आदि के कारण किसी को सताना – **persecution** (पर्सि´क्यूशन) *n.* अत्याचार, उत्पीड़न – **persecutor** *n.* अत्याचारी

persevere (पर्सि´विअर) *vi.* डटे रहना; प्रयत्न करते रहना – **perseverance** *n.* द ढ़ता, अध्यवसाय

persist (´पर्सिस्ट) *vi.* रुकावटों, आपत्तियों आदि के सामने भी डटे रहना – **persistence** *n.* – **persistent** *a.* द ढ़, जिद्दी; स्थायी; निरंतर

person (´पर्सन) *n.* व्यक्ति; *Grammar* पुरुष **first** (उत्तम), **second** (मध्यम), **third** (अन्य) **person**) – **persona** (पर्´सोन्अ) *n.* (नाटक, उपन्यास आदि का) चरित्र – **personable** *a.* रूपवान, रूपवती – **personage** (´पर्सनिज) *n.* मान्य व्यक्ति – **personal** (´पर्सनल) *a.* व्यक्तिगत, निजी, *Grammar* पुरुष वाचक – **personality** (पर्स´नैलिटि) *n.* व्यक्तित्व; विख्यात व्यक्ति – **personally** *adv.* स्वयं, खुद – **personal computer** *n.* (संक्षेप में **PC**) एक व्यक्ति के प्रयोग के लिए बना छोटा कम्प्यूटर

persona non grata (पर्सोन्अ नॉन ग्राट्अ) *n.* अवांछित व्यक्ति

personalize (´पर्सनलाइज़) *vt.* (प्राय: *passive*) व्यक्ति-विशेष की आवश्यकताओं के अनुरूप बनाना

personify (पर्´सॉनिफ़ाइ) *vt.* मानवीकरण करना; (कोई गुण) चरित्र में उतारना (**-ified, -ifying**) – **personification** *n.* मानवीकरण

personnel (पर्स´नैल) *n.* कर्मचारीगण

perspective (पर्स्´पेक्टिव़) *n.* परिप्रेक्ष्य, मन में बना द श्य या विचार; सपाट तल पर रेखाचित्र जिसमें ठोसपन, चित्रित वस्तुओं की अपेक्षाक त दूरी व आकार का आभास हो

perspicacious (पर्स्पि´केशस) *a.* कुशाग्र बुद्धि, तेज सूझबूझ वाला – **perspicacity** *n.*

perspicuous (पर्´स्पिक्युअस) *a.* सुस्पष्ट – **perspicuity** (पर्स्पि´क्यूइटि) *n.* सुस्पष्टता

perspire (पर्स्प´पाइअर) *v.* पसीना आना – **perspiration** *n.* पसीना

persuade (पर्´स्वेड) *vt.* राज़ी कर लेना, समझा लेना – **persuasion** (पर्´स्वेझ़न) *n.* राज़ी करने की क्रिया; धारणा, विश्वास – **persuasive** (पर्´स्वेसिव़) *a.* राजी करने में समर्थ (व्यक्ति, तरीका)

pert (पर्ट) *a.* ढीठ, चंट (विशे. लड़की या युवती)

pertain (पर्´टेन) *vi.* से संबंधित होना, के बारे में होना; का होना; के लिए उपयुक्त होना

pertinacious (पर्टि´नेशस) *a.* हठी – **pertinacity** (पर्टि´नैसिटि) *n.* दृढ़ता, हठ

pertinent (´पर्टिनंट) *a.* बिलकुल उपयुक्त, संगत – **pertinence** *n.* प्रासंगिकता

perturb (पर्´टर्ब) *vt.* व्याकुल करना

peruse (प´रूज़) *vt.* धीरे-धीरे व गौर से या आराम से पढ़ना – **perusal** *n.* ध्यानपूर्वक अध्ययन

pervade (पर्´वेड) *vt.* में फैल जाना या समा जाना, व्याप्त होना – **pervasion** (पर्´वेझ़न) *n.* व्याप्ति – **pervasive** (पर्´वेसिव़) *a.* व्यापक

pervert (पर्´वर्ट) *vt.* बिगाड़ना, भ्रष्ट करना – *n.* (´पर्वर्ट) पथभ्रष्ट या बिगड़ा हुआ, दुराचारी (विशे. यौन आचार में) – **perverse** (पर्´वर्स) *a.* (गलत बात के लिए) जिद्दी; दुष्ट; बिगड़ा हुआ, भृष्ट – **perversely** *adv.* – **perversity** *n.* दुष्टता, दुराग्रह – **perversion** (पर्´वर्शन) *n.* विकार, काम विकृति

pessimism (´पेंसिमिज़्म) *n.* निराशावाद – **pessimist** *n.* निराशवादी व्यक्ति – **pessimistic** *a.* निराशावादी

pest (पेंस्ट) *n.* कष्टकारी या हानिकारक वस्तु, व्यक्ति या कीड़ा – **pesticide** (´पेंस्टिसाइड) *n.* कीटनाशक रसायन

pester (´पेंस्टर) *vt.* परेशान करना

pestilence (´पेंस्टिलन्स) *n.* महामारी

pestle (´पेंसल) *n.* मूसली, मूसल

pet (पेंट) *n.* दुलारा (पशु या व्यक्ति); पालतू जानवर – *vt.* दुलारना; *inf.* चिपटाना, पुचकारना (-tt-) – **pet name** घर का नाम

petal (´पेंटल) *n.* फूल की पंखुड़ी, दल – **petalled** *a.* पंखुड़ीदार

peter (´पीटर) *vi.* – **peter out** *inf.* (मात्रा, उत्तेजना आदि) कम होते जाना

petit bourgeois (पेंटि´बुर्ज़ुवा) *a.* (**petty bourgeois** भी) निम्न मध्यम वर्ग का सदस्य

petite (प´टीट) *a.* छोटे कद की, नाज़ुक, कमनीय (युवती)

petition (पि´टिशन) *n.* अर्जी, याचिका, आवेदन (विशे. जो राष्ट्र के प्रमुख अथवा संसद के सम्मुख प्रस्तुत की जाए) – *vt.* आवेदन या याचिका प्रस्तुत करना – **petitioner** *n.* आवेदक

petrel (´पेंट्रल) *n.* एक समुद्री पक्षी

petrify (´पेंट्रिफ़ाइ) *vt.* पत्थर में परिवर्तित कर देना; *fig.* (व्यक्ति को) (भय से) स्तंभित कर देना

petroleum (प´ट्रोलिअम) *n.* खनिज तेल – **petroleum jelly** वैसलीन – **petrol** (´पेंट्रल) *n.* पैट्रोल

petticoat (´पेंटिकोट) *n.* पेटीकोट

petty (´पेंटि) *a.* तुच्छ, बहुत मामूली; संकीर्ण विचारों वाला

petulant (´पेंट्युलंट) *a.* बदमिज़ाज; चिड़चिड़ा – **petulance** *n.* चिड़चिड़ापन

phalanx (´फ़ैलैंक्स) *n.* दीवार की तरह खड़ा हुआ व्यक्तियों (विशे. पुलिस आदि) का दल (*pl.* **phalanxes, phalanges** (-जीज़))

phallus (´फ़ैलस) *n.* पुरूष का लिंग; आदिकालीन धार्मिक कृत्यों में इसका प्रतिरूप – **phallic** *a.* लिंग-लैंगिक

phantom (´फ़ैंटम) *n.* भूत, प्रेत; अवास्तविक छाया; माया

Pharaoh (´फ़ेअरो) *n.* प्राचीन काल में मिस्त्र के राजाओं की उपाधि, फ़रऊन

pharisee (´फ़ैरिसी) *n.* पाखण्डी, ढोंगी

pharmaceutical (फ़ार्म´स्यूटिकल) *a.* औषधि/औषधि निर्माण संबंधी – **pharmacist** (´फ़ार्मसिस्ट) *n.* औषधि निर्माण करने वाला, भेषजज्ञ – **pharmacology** (फ़ार्म´कॉलजि) *n.* औषधि अध्ययन – **pharmacy** (´फ़ार्मसि) *n.* औषधि निर्माण; औषधालय

pharynx (´फ़ैरिंक्स) *n.* मुंह के पिछले भाग से ग्रसिका तक की नली, ग्रसनी (*pl.* **pharynges** (फ़ै´रिन्जीज़)) – **pharyngitis** (-´जाइटिस) *n.* ग्रसनी की सूजन, ग्रसनी शोथ

phase (फ़ेज़) *n.* विकास या घटना-क्रम की विशेष अवस्था, स्थिति या दशा

Ph D Doctor of Philosophy (विद्या वाचस्पति) का संक्षेप

pheasant (ˈफ़ेजंट) *n.* तीतर की जाति का पक्षी, फ़ेजंट, चेड़

phenol (ˈफ़ीनॉल) *n.* कार्बॉलिक ऐसिड

phenomenon (फ़िˈनॉमिनन) *n.* कोई भी द श्य, घटना, तथ्य; उल्लेखनीय व्यक्ति या वस्तु (*pl.* **phenomena**) – **phenomenal** *a.* असाधारण, चमत्कारिक

phial (ˈफ़ाइअल) *n.* शीशी

philanthropy (फ़िˈलैंथ्रपि) *n.* परोपकार, मानव-प्रेम – **philanthropic** (फ़िलन्ˈथ्रॉपिक) *a.* लोकोपकारी – **philanthropist** (फ़िˈलैंथ्रपिस्ट) *n.* लोकोपकारी व्यक्ति

philately (फ़िˈलैटलि) *n.* डाक-टिकट इकट्ठे करना, डाक-टिकट संग्रहिकी – **philatelist** *n.* डाक टिकट संग्रही

philharmonic (फ़िल्हार्ˈमॉनिक) *a.* संगीत-

philistine (ˈफ़िलिस्टाइन) *a./n.* अज्ञानी, असभ्य व दम्भी व्यक्ति; संस्क ति व कला का विरोधी

philosophy (फ़िˈलॉसफ़ि) *n.* दर्शन शास्त्र; द ष्टिकोण – **philosopher** *n.* दार्शनिक – **philosophic(al)** (फ़िलˈसॉफ़िकल) *a.* दार्शनिक; बुद्धिमान, विद्धान; शांत चित्त

phlegm (फ़्लेंम) *n.* बलग़म, कफ, श्लेष्मा – **phlegmatic** (फ़्लेग्ˈमैटिक) *a.* भावशून्य, शांत, स्थिर

phobia (ˈफ़ोबिअ) *n.* भय या घ णा; अकारण नापसंदगी या नफ़रत

phoenix (ˈफ़ीनिक्स) *n.* एक पौराणिक पक्षी, अमर पक्षी; अद्वितीय वस्तु

phone (फ़ोन) *n. inf.* टेलीफोन – *a.* टेलीफोन संबंधी –*vi.* टेलीफ़ोन करना

phonetic (फ़ˈनैंटिक) *a.* ध्वनि सम्बंधी, स्वनिक – **phonetics** (फ़ˈनैंटिक्स) *n.* स्वन-विज्ञान

phoney (ˈफ़ोनि) *a. inf.* जाली, नकली

phosphorus (ˈफ़ॉस्फ़रस) *n.* फ़ासफ़ोरस – **phosphate** *n.* – **phosphite** *n.* फ़ासफ़ोरस से बने यौगिक – **phosphorescence** (फ़ॉस्फ़ˈरैंसन्स) *n.* अंधेरे में हलकी सी चमक, स्फुरदीप्ति

photo (ˈफ़ोटो) *n. inf.* फोटोग्राफ़

photocopy (ˈफ़ोटोकॉपि) *n.* फोटो प्रतिलिपि – *vt.* फोटो प्रतिलिपि बनाना

photoelectricity *n.* प्रकाश की क्रिया से उत्पन्न अथवा प्रभावित विद्युत, प्रकाश-विद्युत

photogenic (फ़ोटˈजैंनिक) *a.* (व्यक्ति) जिसका चेहरा चित्र में आकर्षक लगता हो, फोटो-योग्य

photograph (ˈफ़ोटग्राफ़) *n.* फोटो चित्र – *vt.* का फोटो ख चना – **photographer** (फ़ˈटॉग्रफ़र) *n.* – **photographic** (फ़ोटˈग्रैफ़िक) *a.* फोटो- **photography** (फ़ˈटॉग्रफ़ि) *n.*फ़ोटोग्राफी – **photo finish** ध ावकों के जीतने का क्रम दिखाने के लिए दौड़ के अंत में लिया गया फोटो

Photostat R (ˈफ़ोटोस्टैट) *n.* फोटोस्टैट – *vt.* फोटोस्टैट क्रिया द्वारा प्रतिलिपि बनाना

photosynthesis (फोटोˈसिंथिसिस) *n.* प्रक्रिया जिसके द्वारा हरे पौधे सूर्य की ऊर्जा से कार्बोहाइड्रेट का भंडार बनाते हैं

phrase (फ्रेज़) *n.* शब्द-समूह, वाक्यांश; मुहावरा; शैली – *vt.* शब्दों में व्यक्त करना – **phraseology** (फ्रेज़िˈऑलजि) *n.* शब्द-चयन

physics (ˈफ़िज़िक्स) *n.* भौतिकी, भौतिक-विज्ञान – **physical** *a.* शारीरिक (मानसिक व नैतिक के विपरीत); भौतिक; शरीर सम्बंधी – **physically** *adv.* – **physician** (फ़िˈज़िशन) *n.* चिकित्सक, डाक्टर – **physicist** (ˈफ़िज़िसिस्ट) *n.* भौतिक-विज्ञानी

physiognomy (फ़िज़ि ऑनमि) *n.* चेहरा देखकर चरित्र-चित्रण; चेहरा; रूप

physiology (फ़िज़ि ऑलजि) *n.* चेतन वस्तुओं के सामान्य प्रकार्यों का विज्ञान, शरीर विज्ञान – **physiologist** *n.* शरीर-विज्ञानी

physiotherapy (फ़िज़िओ थेरपि) *n.* मालिश, शारीरिक अंगों के विशेष व्यायाम आदि का चिकित्सा के लिए उपयोग, भौतिक-चिकित्सा – **physiotherapist** *n.* भौतिक-चिकित्सक

physique (फ़ि ज़ीक) *n.* शरीर का गठन, डील-डौल व विकास

pi (पाइ) *n. Maths.* वृत्त की परिधि व उसके व्यास का अनुपात जिसका मूल्य लगभग 3.14 होता है

piano (पि ऐनो) *n.* (मूल **pianoforte**) पियानो (एक वाद्य) (*pl.* **pianos**) – *a./adv. Mus.* धीमा; धीमे – **pianist** (पिऐनिस्ट) *n.* पियानो-वादक

piazza (पि ऐट्सअ, प्यात्सा) *n.* चौक, बाज़ार

pic (पिक) *n. inf.* चित्र (*pl.* **pics, pix**)

pick[1] (पिक) *vt.* छांटना, ध्यान से चयन करना; (फूल आदि) तोड़ना, इकट्ठे करना, चोंच मारना; चुगना; नोकदार वस्तु से छेद करना या कुरेदना; मौका ढूंढ लेना – *n.* इकट्ठा करने या चुनने की क्रिया; चुनिन्दा, (प्रस्तुत वस्तुओं आदि में) सबसे बढ़िया वस्तु आदि – **pick-me-up** *inf. n.* टॉनिक, स्फूर्तिदायक पेय – **pickpocket** *n.* जेबकतरा – **pick-up** *n.* बल्कृत (*mechanical*) ऊर्जा को विद्युतीय संकेतों में परिवर्तित करने का साधन जैसे रिकार्ड प्लेयर में, ध्वनि-ग्रह; छोटा ट्रक – **pick on** सताने या दोष देने के लिए किसी को चुनना – **pick up** उठाना, (सामान, यात्री आदि) लेना; सुधरना, अच्छा होना; (गति) तेज़ होना

pick[2] (पिक) *n.* सख्त जमीन खोदने की कुदाली, गैन्ती, खोदनी – **pickaxe** *n.* कुदाली

picket (पिकिट) *n.* खूंटा; हड़ताल के दौरान काम के इच्छुक कामगारों को रोकने के लिए हड़ताली कामगारों का धरना देने वाला दल – *vt.* धरना देना

pickle (पिकल) *n.* अचार; परेशानी की स्थिति – *vt.* अचार बनाना

picnic (पिक्निक) *n.* सैर-सपाटा, पिकनिक – *vi.* पिकनिक में भाग लेना (**picnicked, picnicking**)

picture (पिक्चर) *n.* चित्र, तसवीर; मन में छवि – *pl.* सिनेमा – *vt.* चित्रित करना – **pictorial** (पिक् टॉरिअल) *a.* चित्रात्मक, सचित्र, चित्र में – *n.* सचित्र पत्रिका या समाचार पत्र – **pictorially** *adv.* – **picturesque** (पिक्च रैस्क) *a.* चित्र जैसा मनोहर, सजीव

pidgin (पिजिन) *n.* दो या अधिक भाषाओं से मिलकर बनी मिश्रित भाषा

pie (पाइ) *n.* मांस, फल आदि से बना केक पकवान

piebald (पाइबॉल्ड) *a* चितकबरा – **pied** *a.* चितकबरा, विविध रंगों में

piece (पीस) *n.* टुकड़ा, खण्ड; अंश, हिस्सा, एक वस्तु (जिन्स), साहित्य, संगीत आदि की रचना, रचनांश – *vt.* ठीक करना, जोड़ना – **piecemeal** *adv.* थोड़ा-थोड़ा करके (कार्य जिसका मेहनताना दिया जाय) – **give sb a piece of your mind** खरी-खरी सुनाना

pier (पिअर) *n.* समुद्रतट पर बना घाट; खंभा विशे. पुल का

pierce (पिअर्स) *vt.* छेद करना, बेधना, भेदना, पार करना; प्रभावित करना – **piercing** *a.* तीखा (स्वर)

piety (पाइइटि) *n.* धार्मिकता, धर्म निष्ठा, भक्ति भाव

pig (पिग) *n.* सूअर; उसका मांस; *inf.* लोभी, गंदा व्यक्ति – **pig-headed** *a.* जिद्दी, अड़ियल – **piggyback** (पिगिबैक) *n.* पीठ पर सवारी, वि बच्चे को – **piggybank** *n.* गुल्लक

pigeon (ˈपिजिन) *n.* कबूतर – **pigeonhole** *n.*डेस्क आदि में कागज रखने के लिए खाना, कोष्ठ – *vt.* वर्गीकरण करना

pigment (ˈपिग्मंट) *n.* रंजक (रंग देने वाला) पदार्थ; वर्णक; रंग, रोगन

pigmy (ˈपिग्मि) दे. PYGMY

pike[1] (पाइक) *n.* नदी, झील आदि में पाई जाने वाली बड़ी मछली, पाइक

pilau (पिˈलाउ), **pilaf(f)** (पिˈलैफ़) *n.* पुलाव

pile[1] (पाइल) *n.* ढेर, अम्बार; राशि; भव्य भवन; भवन समूह – *vt.* ढेर लगाना – *vi.* (*in, out, off* आदि के साथ) अव्यवस्थित झुंड में चलना

pile[2] (पाइल) *n.* न व के रूप में गाड़ी गयी शहतीर

pile[3] (पाइल) *n.* कालीन, मखमल आदि की रोंएंदार सतह

piles (पाइल्ज़) *pl. n.* बवासीर (के मस्से)

pilfer (ˈपिल्फ़र) *v.* छोटी या कम मात्रा में वस्तुओं की चोरी करना – **pilferage** *n.* चोरी

pilgrim (ˈपिल्ग्रिम) *n.* तीर्थयात्री – **pilgrimage** *n.* तीर्थयात्रा

pill (पिल) *n.* दवाई की गोली – **a bitter pill** कड़वा घूंट – **the pill** खाने की गर्भनिरोधक गोली

pillage (ˈपिलिज) *v.* लूटपाट करना – *n.* लड़ाई में लूटपाट

pillar (ˈपिलर) *n.* खम्भा, स्तंभ

pillion (ˈपिल्यन) *n.* मोटर साइकिल, स्कूटर आदि पर पिछली सीट

pillory (ˈपिलरि) *vt.* भर्त्सना व तिरस्कार करना (**pilloried, pillorying**)

pillow (ˈपिलो) *n.* तकिया – **pillow case** तकिए का गिलाफ़

pilot (ˈपाइलट) *n.* वायुयान या अंतरिक्षयान चालक, पायलट; बंदरगाह पर जहाज़ का मार्ग दर्शक; मार्ग दर्शक – *a.* प्रायोगिक व आरंभिक (योजना आदि) – *vt.* पथ प्रदर्शन करना; चलाना; (संसद आदि में विधेयक) प्रस्तुत करना

pimp (पिम्प) *n.* वेश्या का दलाल, भड़ुवा – *vi.* वेश्या की दलाली करना

pimple (ˈपिंपल) *n.* फुंसी

pin (पिन) *n.* पिन; लकड़ी या धातु की खूंटी; बिजली के प्लग का पिन; बोलिंग के खेल में गोल डंडा; हथगोले के ऊपर लगा पिन – *vt.* पिन लगाना, पिन से नत्थी करना; जकड़ देना (**-nn-**) – **pin code** दे. **POST**– **pinpoint** *vt.* का ठीक-ठीक पता लगाना या पता देना

pinafore (ˈपिनफॉर) *n.* ऐप्रन, बच्चों के कपड़ों के ऊपर पहनाया जाने वाला कपड़ा

pincers (ˈपिन्सर्ज़) *pl. n.* चिमटी, चिमटा; झ गा आदि के पंजे

pinch (पिंच) *vt.* चुटकी से पकड़ना; चुटकी भरना या काटना; ऐंठना; *inf.* चोरी करना; *inf.* गिरफ्तार करना – *vi.* (जूते का) काटना – *n.* चुटकी; चुटकी भर; तकलीफदेह; दबाव; विपत्ति

pine[1] (पाइन) *n.* (**pine tree** भी) चीड़ का व क्ष, इसकी लकड़ी

pine[2] (पाइन) *vi.* (के लिए) लालायित होना, पाने की तीव्र इच्छा करना, दुःख आदि से घुलना

pineapple (ˈपाइन्ऐपल) *n.* अनानास

Ping-Pong (ˈपिङ-पॉङ) *n.* **R** टेबल-टैनिस

pinion[1] (ˈपिन्यन) *n.* पंख – *vt.* पक्षी को पंख या व्यक्ति के बाज़ू बांध कर जकड़ देना, मुश्कें बांधना

pink (पिंक) *n.* गुलाबी रंग; अत्युत्तम स्थिति – *a.* गुलाबी; थोड़ा वामपंथी – *vt.* चुभाना; संवारना, (किनारे का डिज़ाइन बनाना – *vi.* इंजन का आवाज़ करना – **pink slip** बर्खास्तगी की चिट्ठी

pinnacle (ˈपिनकल) *n.* शिखर, चोटी; नुकीली बुर्ज, कलश; *fig.* पराकाष्ठा

pint (पाइंट) *n.* द्रव माप, 1/8 गैलन (.568 लिटर)

pin-up (ˈपिन-अप) *n.* कामोत्तेजक व्यक्तित्व वाले व्यक्ति विशे. (अर्ध-) नग्न स्त्री का चित्र

pioneer (पाइअˈनिअर) *n.* अन्वेषक, खोजी; (किसी

स्थान पर) सबसे पहले बसने वाला; प्रवर्तक; अगुआ – *vi.* अगुआ बनना, रास्ता तैयार करना

pious (ˈपाइअस) *a.* भक्त, धर्म परायण

pip[1] (पिप) *n.* फल का बीज

pip[2] (पिप) *n.* रेडियो में समय की संकेतध्वनि; ताश आदि पर बुंदकी, बिन्दु; *inf.* छोटे सैनिक अफसर के पद का संकेत देने वाला उसके कंधे पर लगा पद-चिन्हक सितारा

pipe (पाइप) *n.* पाइप, नली; तम्बाकू भरकर पीने का पाइप; बांसुरी; (~ **s**) *pl.* मशकबीन – *v.* मुरली बजाना; चीख कर बोलना; पाइप से (पानी आदि) पहुंचाना; वस्त्र पर गोट लगाना – **piper** *n.* मुरली या मशकबीन बजाने वाला – **piping** *n.* पाइप व्यवस्था, नल-तंत्र; केक पर सजी चाशनी; कपड़ों पर लगी गोट – **pipe dream** अवास्तविक, असंभव योजना – **pipeline** *n.* तेल, पानी दूर ले जाने के लिए नल तंत्र – **piping hot** बहुत गर्म, उबालता हुआ – **in the pipeline** आने वाला

piquant (ˈपीकंट) *a.* तीखा, चरपरा

pique (पीक) *n.* अपमान की भावना, खीज; उत्सुकता; चिढ़

pirate (ˈपाइरिट) *n.* समुद्री डाकू; कापीराइट (प्रकाशनाधिकार) का उल्लंघन करने वाला प्रकाशक; वीडियो टेप/कैसेट, कम्प्यूटर प्रोग्राम चोरी से नकल करके बेचने वाला व्यक्ति – *n./a.* अनधिक त रेडियो प्रसारण करने वाला – *vt.* बिना अधिकार मूल पुस्तक, कम्प्यूटर सामग्री आदि की प्रतिलिपि बनाकर बेचना – **piracy** (ˈपाइरसि) *n.* – **pirated** *a.* जो मूल क ति की अनधिक त प्रतिलिपि हो

Pisces (ˈपाइसीज़) *n.* मीन, राशि-चक्र की 12 व राशि (जिसका काल 20 फरवरी से 20 मार्च तक होता है)

piss (पिस) *vi. sl.* पेशाब करना

pistachio (पिस्ˈटाशिओ) *n.* पिस्ता

pistol (ˈपिस्ट्ल) *n.* पिस्तौल, तमंचा – *vt.* पिस्तौल से मारना (**-ll-**)

piston (ˈपिस्टन) *n.* इंजन की पश्चाग्र (आगे-पीछे) गति को घूर्णी (घूमने वाली) गति में परिवर्तन करने वाला एक भाग, पिस्टन

pit (पिट) *n.* गड्ढा; खान, खदान; रंगशाला में संगीत-मंडली (आरकेस्ट्रा) का स्थान;श्मोटर-रेस मार्ग पर कारों की मरम्मत व उनमें तेल भरने का स्थान – *vt.* से लड़ाना; (बीमारी आदि का) गड्ढे, दाग बनाना (**-tt-**) – **pitfall** *n.* छिपा हुआ खतरा

pitch[1] (पिच) *vt.* फेंकना; (तंबू) लगाना; (सुर) मिलाना – *vi.* धड़ाम से गिरना; (जहाज़ का) डूबना-उतरना – *n.* फेंक; ऊंचाई; अवस्था; पराकाष्ठा; ढाल; डूबना-उतराना; पेच की चूड़ियों के बीच की दूरी; स्वर तारत्व; खेल का मैदान– **pitcher** *n.* US बेसबॉल में गेंदबाज़ – **pitchfork** *n.* घास आदि उठाने की जेली, पांजा – *vt.* जेली से या उस के समान किसी चीज़ से तेज़ी से उठाकर फेंकना – **pitched battle** (दो समूहो के बीच) जमकर लड़ाई

pitch[2] (पिच) *n.* डामर, तारकोल – *vt.* डामर डालना या लगाना – **pitch-black, -dark** *a.* गहरा काला

pitcher (ˈपिचर) *n.* घड़ा, बड़ी सुराही

pith (पिथ) *n.* (कुछ पौधों की डाली में) गूदा, मज्जा; *fig.* सार, महत्वपूर्ण अंश – **pithy** *a.* संक्षिप्त एवं ज़ोरदार; सारगर्भित

pittance (ˈपिटंस) *n.* बहुत कम मेहनताना

pituitary (पिˈट्यूइटरि) *a.* मस्तिष्क के निचले भाग में स्थित पीयूष ग्रंथि संबंधी

pity (ˈपिटि) *n.* दया, तरस, सहानुभूति, खेद का विषय – *vt.* पर तरस खाना, पर दया आना, सहानुभूति रखना; (**pitied, pitying**) – **piteous** (ˈपिटिअस) *a.* सहानुभूति के योग्य; करुणाजनक – **pitiable** (ˈपिटिअबल) *a.* दयनीय, शोचनीय – **pitiably** *adv.* – **pitiful**

a. दयनीय; अवहेलना योग्य – **pitiless** *a.* निर्मम, बेरहम– **what a pity** ! कितने दु:ख की बात है

pivot (ˈपिवट) *n.* चूल, कीली, धुरी; *fig.* केंद्र बिंदु – *vt.* धुरी लगाना, धुरी पर रखना – *vi.* धुरी पर घूमना – **pivotal** *a.*

pizza (ˈपीत्सअ) *n.* (मूलत:) इटली का एक पकवान, पीत्सा

placard (ˈप्लैकार्ड) *n.* कागज़ या गत्ते पर एक ओर लिखा विज्ञापन, सूचना आदि, पोस्टर, प्लेकार्ड, सूचना पत्रक

placate (प्लˈकेट) *vt.* शांत करना, संतुष्ट करना

place (प्लेस) *n.* स्थान, दरजा, स्थिति; नगर; गाँव; रहने का स्थान; इमारत, दफ्तर; नौकरी, सीट, खाली जगह – *vt.* विशेष स्थान पर रख देना, लगाना; पहचानना; स्थान निश्चित करना; (शर्त) लगाना; (माल) मंगाना – **placement** *n.* नौकरी दिलवाने की क्रिया

placebo (प्लˈसीबो) *n.* रोगी को बिना बताए औषधि के स्थान पर दी गयी मीठी या अन्य औषधि-रहित गोली

placid (ˈप्लैसिड) *a.* शान्त, स्थिर (पानी)

plagiarism (ˈप्लेजरिज़्म) *n.* साहित्यिक चोरी – **plagiarize** *v.*

plague (प्लेग) *n.* प्लेग, ताऊन; *inf.* आफ़त, मुसीबत – *vt. fig.* परेशान करना, सताना

plain (प्लेन) *a.* सपाट; सरल; स्पष्ट; साधारण, निष्कपट, साफ़-साफ़ (बोलने वाला); असुंदर – *n.* सपाट मैदान – *adv.* साफ़-साफ़ – **plainly** *adv.* – **plainness** *n.*

plaintiff (ˈप्लेंटिफ़) *n. Law* मुकदमा दायर करने वाला, वादी, मुद्दई – **plaintive** *a.* दु:खपूर्ण, शोकपूर्ण, उदासी भरा

plait (प्लैट) *n.* बालों की चोटी, बट दिया हुआ फूस – *vt.* बंटना, गूंथना

plan (प्लैन) *n.* इरादा; योजना; रूपरेखा, ख़ाका; नक्शा– *vt.* की योजना बनाना; व्यवस्था करना; इरादा होना (**-nn-**)

plane[1] (प्लेन) *n.* समतल, तल – *vt.* रंदा फेरना – *a.* स्तर, बढ़ई का रंदा

plane[2] (प्लेन) – *n.* वायुयान

plane[3] (प्लेन) *n.* चिनार का व क्ष

planet (ˈप्लैनिट) *n.* ग्रह – **planetary** *a.* ग्रह-संबंधी

planetarium (प्लैनिˈटेंअरिअम) *n.* , तारा घर, नक्षत्रकक्ष

plank (ˈप्लैंक) *n.* फर्श आदि बनाने के लिए लकड़ी का तख्ता, पटरा

plant (प्लांट) *n.* पौधा; संयंत्र, प्लांट – *vt.* पौधा लगाना, बीज डालना; (दिल, दिमाग में) जमाना; बसाना; (बम आदि) रखना– **planter** *n.* बागान-मालिक

plantain[2] (ˈप्लैंटिन) *n.* केला

plantation (प्लैन्ˈटेशन) *n.* चाय, तंबाकू आदि के बाग़ान

plaque (प्लैक, प्लाक) *n.* सजावटी पटिया, तख्ती; बैज (बिल्ला); जड़ाउ पिन; दांतों पर जमी सफेदी

plasma (ˈप्लैज़्मअ) *n.* रक्त का द्रव भाग, जीव द्रव्य

plaster (ˈप्लास्टर) *n.* दीवारों आदि पर लगाने का पलस्तर (**plaster of Paris** भी); चोट आदि पर चिपकाने का औषधि युक्त प्लास्टर (**sticking plaster** भी) – *vt.* पलस्तर लगाना, पोतना, पलस्तर जैसा पोतना

plastic (ˈप्लैस्टिक, ˈप्लास्टिक) *n.* प्लास्टिक – *a.* प्लास्टिक का बना; लचीला – **plasticity** (प्लैसˈटिसिटि) *n.* ढलनशीलता; म दुता – **plastic surgery** शरीर के विक्षत अंग को सुधारने के लिए आपरेशन

plate (प्लेट) *n.* तश्तरी, थाली, प्लेट; धातु की चद्दर; सोने या चांदी के बरतन; छपाई का एक साधन, मुद्रा पट्ट; पुस्तक में छपा चित्र, चित्र प ष्ठ; बच्चों के दांतों पर चढ़ी प्लेट; *inf.* नकली दांत – *vt.*

सोना-चांदी आदि की पत्तर चढ़ाना, मुलम्मा चढ़ाना

plateau (ˈप्लैटो) *n.* पठार; (व्यापार आदि में) ठहराव

platform (ˈप्लैट्फार्म) *n.* चबूतरा; मंच; (रेलवे) प्लेटफार्म; राजनीतिक दल का कार्यक्रम या मंच, मोरचा आदि; *Computers* उपयोग किया जा रहा सॉफ्टवेयर अथवा कम्प्यूटर व्यवस्था (सिस्टम)

platinum (ˈप्लैटिनम) *n.* प्लैटिनम धातु

platitude (ˈप्लैटिट्यूड) *n.* सामान्य घिसी-पिटी बात

platonic (प्लˈटॉनिक) *a.* आध्यात्मिक, निष्काम (प्रेम), मैत्रीपूर्ण (स्वभाव का)

platoon (प्लˈटून) *n.* सैनिक प्लाटून, पलटन

platter (ˈप्लैटर) *n.* चपटा कम गहरा बरतन; कठौती

plaudit (ˈप्लॉडिट) *n.* शाबाशी, प्रशंसा

plausible (ˈप्लॉज़बल) *a.* तर्कसंगत, ठीक लगने वाली (बात)

play (प्ले) *vi.* खेलना, खेलों में भाग लेना; (व्यक्ति या व्यक्ति की भावनाओं आदि) से खिलवाड़ करना; अभिनय करना; (वाद्य) बजाना– *n.* नाटक; अभिनय; खेल; मज़ाक; व्यवहार; गतिविधि, जूआ, जुएबाजी – **playback** *n.* पहले से रिकार्ड किया संगीत, फिल्म, टेलीफोन संदेश सुनाना/दिखाना – **playback singer** *India* पार्श्व-गायक – **player** *n.* – **playful** *a.* ज़िंदादिल – **playhouse** *n.* नाट्यशाला, रंगशाला – **playing cards** ताश के पत्ते – **playing fields** खेल का मैदान – **playing** *n.* खिलौना – **playwright** (ˈप्लेराइट) *n.* नाटककार

plaza (ˈप्लाज़अ) *n.* नगर-चौक

plea (प्ली) *n.* निवेदन, अनुनय; कैदी या प्रतिवादी का (सफ़ाई) बयान; बहाना, सफ़ाई – **plead** (प्लीड) *vi.* याचना करना; वकालत करना, बहस करना – *vt.* सफ़ाई मे कुछ कहना (**pleaded** *or US*, **pled, pleading**)

please (प्लीज़) *vt.* को प्रसन्न या संतुष्ट करना, अच्छा लगना, सुहाना – *vi.* चाहना – *adv.* कृपया – **pleasant** (ˈप्लेज़ंट) *a.* सुखकर, मनोहर; नम्र – **pleasantly** *adv.* – **pleasantry** (ˈप्लेज़ंट) *n.* हंसी-मज़ाक, दिल्लगी – **pleasurable** (ˈप्लेझ़रबल) *a.* आनंद, सुख देने वाला – **pleasure** (ˈप्लेझ़र) *n.* आनंद, इच्छा

pleat (प्लीट) *n.* चुन्नट; वेणी – *vi.* चुनट डालना

plebeian (प्लˈबीअन) *a.* साधारण (व्यक्ति) – *n.* जनता, *offens. sl.* **pleb**, गंवार

plebiscite (ˈप्लेबिसाइट, -सिट) *n.* जनमत-संग्रह

pledge (प्लेज) *n.* वचन, प्रतिज्ञा; बंधक; रेहन; गिरवी; समर्थन या शुभेच्छा का जाम – *vt.* वचन देना, प्रतिज्ञा करना, बन्धक रखना, गिरवी रखना

plenty (ˈप्लेण्टि) *n.* प्रचुरता, यथेष्ट, काफ़ी – **plentiful** *a.* बहुत मात्रा में

plethora (ˈप्लेथर्अ) *n.* बहुत ज्यादा मात्रा

pleurisy (ˈप्लुअरिसि) *n.* फेफड़ों व छाती के बीच झिल्ली की सूजन, फुप्फुसावरण-शोथ, उरोग्रह

pliable (ˈप्लाइअबल) *a.* जो आसानी से मुड़ सके; आसानी से प्रभावित होने वाला, अनम्य – **pliant** *a.* **pliable** के अर्थ में प्रयुक्त

pliers (ˈप्लाइअर्ज़) *pl. n.* प्लायर, प्लास

plight (प्लाइट) *n.* दुर्दशा; परेशानी

plimsolls (ˈप्लिम्सल्ज़) *pl. n.* रबड़ के तले वाले कपड़े (कैन्वस) के जूते

plinth (प्लिथ) *n.* पत्थर जिस पर खंभा या मूर्ति खड़ी हो, स्तम्भ मूल

plod (प्लॉड) *vi.* लगातार धीरे-धीरे चलते या काम करते जाना (**-dd-**)

plop (प्लॉप) *n.* छपाक से पानी में गिरने की आवाज़ – *v.*

plot[1] (प्लॉट) *n.* गुप्त योजना, षड़यंत्र; कथानक, कथा

वस्तु – *vt.* षड़यंत्र रचना; स्थिति अंकित करना; नक्शा बनाना – *vi.* षड़यंत्र करना (**-tt-**)

plot² (प्लॉट) *n.* छोटा भूखण्ड, प्लाट

plough (प्लाउ), **US plow** *n.* हल; बर्फ हटाने का हल – *vt.* हल चलाना, जोतना – *vi.* धीरे-धीरे काम करना – **ploughman** *n.* हलवाहा – **ploughshare** *n.* (हल का) फाल

ploy (प्लॉइ) *n.* तिकड़म, युक्ति

pluck (प्लक) *vt.* ख चना, तोड़ना; नोंचना; गिटार आदि के उंगली से ख चकर तार बजाना – *n.* साहस; झटका – **plucky** *a.* साहसी

plug (प्लग) *n.* छेद बंद करने की डाट; *Electricity* प्लग – *vt.* डाट लगाना (**-gg-**) – *vi.*

plum (प्लम) *n.* आलूचा, आलू बुखारा; सबसे बढ़िया या चुनिंदा भाग, टुकड़ा, नौकरी, कार्य आदि – *a.* बढ़िया, चुनिंदा

plumage (´प्लूमिज) दे. PLUME

plumb (प्लम) *n.* पानी की गहराई नापने, दीवार की सिंचाई देखने आदि के लिए डोरी से बंधा सीसे का टुकड़ा, साहुल – *a.* सीधा, लम्ब – *adv.* सीधे – **US** *inf.* ठीक-ठीक – *vt.* सीधा करना; थाह लेना; तक पहुंचना; समझ लेना (नल व्यवस्था आदि से) जोड़ना – **plumber** (´प्लमर) *n.* नल व पाइप लगाने व ठीक करने वाला कारीगर – **plumbing** (´प्लमिंग) *n.* नलसाज़ी, नल व पाइप आदि की व्यवस्था – **plumb line** (´प्लम्लाइन) *n.* साहुल लगी डोरी (रस्सी)

plume (प्लूम) *n.* पंख; पंख या घोड़े के बालों से हैट आदि पर सजावट – *vt.* पंखों से सजाना; अभिमान करना – **plumage** (´प्लूमिज) *n.* पक्षी के पंख

plummet (´प्लमिट) *vi.* सीधे गिर जाना – *n.* डोरी सहित साहुल

plump¹ (प्लम्प) *a.* गोल-मटोल – *v.* मोटा करना, मोटा होना

plump² (प्लम्प) *vi.* धड़ाम से बैठना या गिरना; (**plump for** में) चुन लेना – *adv.* अचानक, धड़ाम से, सीधे

plunder (´प्लंडर) *vt.* लूटना, योजना बनाकर लूटना – *vi.* लूटपाट करना – *n.* लूट; लूट का माल

plunge (प्लंज) *vt.* डुबाना – *vi.* गोता लगाना, (में) छलांग लगाना, झपटना, तेज़ी से लपकना – *n.* गोता, डुबकी – **plunger** *n.* रुकी नाली खोलने का रबड़ का उपकरण; पम्प का पिस्टन – **take the plunge** *inf.* कुछ महत्वपूर्ण कार्य करने का निर्णय लेना

plural (´प्लुअरल) *a.* बहुवचन – *n.* शब्द का बहुवचन रूप – **plurality** (प्लुअ´रैलिटि) *n.* बहुमत; अनेकत्व; बाहुल्य

plus (प्लस) *prep.* मिलाकर; धन (जिसका चिन्ह + होता है) – *a.* घनात्मक; अतिरिक्त; अच्छा (*plus point*)

plush (प्लश) *n.* मखमल – *a.* आलीशान व महंगी वस्तुओं से सजाया हुआ

Pluto (´प्लूटो) *n.* पाताल लोक का ग्रीक देवता; प्लूटो ग्रह

plutonium (प्लू´टोनिअम) *n.* रेडियोधर्मी प्लूटोनियम धातु

ply¹ (प्लाइ) *vt.* चलाना; काम में लेना – *vi.* (जहाज़ आदि) आना जाना (**plied, plying**) – **ply with** (किसी को भोजन, शराब आदि) दिये जाना; (सवालों की) झड़ी लगा देना

ply² (प्लाइ) *n.* लकड़ी की परत, प्लाई; (सूत आदि की) लड़ – **plywood** (´प्लाइवुड) *n.* परतदार लकड़ी, प्लाईवुड

PM paymaster; postmaster; Prime Minister का संक्षेप

pm, PM; post meridiem (*Lat.* after noon); post mortem का संक्षेप

pneumatic (न्यु´मैटिक) *a.* हवा से भरा हुआ या दबी हुई हवा से चलने वाला (बरमा)

pneumonia (न्यू´मोनिअ) *n.* निमोनिया रोग

poach[1] (पोच) *vt.* अनधिक त शिकार करना – *vi.* अनाधिकार प्रवेश करना – **poacher** *n.* अनधिक त शिकारी

poach[2] (पोच) *vt.* (अण्डा,मछली आदि) पानी में हलका उबालना

pock (पॉक) *n.* – **pockmarked** *a.* जिस पर चेचक जैसे दाग़ हों

pocket (ˈपॉकिट) *n.* जेब; गड्ढा जहां धातु के भण्डार हों; थैली, गड्ढा; अलग-थलग वर्ग या स्थान– *vt.* जेब में रखना; हथिया लेना, चुरा लेना – *a.* लघु, छोटा – **pocket money** जेब खर्च

pod (पॉड) *n.* मटर आदि की फली

podium (ˈपोडिअम) *n.* मंच, चबूतरा

poem (ˈपोइम) *n.* कविता – **poet** *n.* कवि (**poetess** *fem.*) – **poetry** (ˈपोइट्रि) *n.* काव्य, काव्य कला – **poetic(al)** (ˈपोएँटिक(ल)) *a.* – **poetics** *n.* काव्यशास्त्र

poignant (ˈपॉइन्यंट) *a.* हृदय विदारक, मार्मिक – **poignancy** (ˈपॉइन्यन्सि) *n.* मार्मिकता

point (पॉइंट) *n.* बिन्दु; विराम चिन्ह; विषय, बात; गुण, विशेषता (*good points*); स्थिति; समय; बहस, तर्क आदि का सार, सारांश; लक्ष्य, उद्देश्य; अंतरीप; नोक; (पर्दाथ के गलने, जमने आदि का) अंक; अंक (खेल आदि में); स्थल, जगह; कम्पास पर दिशा-सूचक चिन्ह, रेल की लाइन बदलने का कांटा; वस्त्रों पर लगाने की एक प्रकार की लेस; संकेत, निर्देश; स्थान जहां तार जोड़ कर बिजली की करंट बल्ब, पंखे आदि में चालू की जाय – *vi.* दिशा संकेत करना, ध्यान दिलाना – *vt.* निशाना लगाना, लक्ष्य करना; संकेत करना, बतलाना; पैना या तेज़ करना; सीमेंट आदि से दरारें भरना, टीप करना – **pointed** *a.* नुकीला, सीधा – **pointer** *n.* निर्देशक, सूचक, संकेतक – **pointless** *a.* भोथरा, कुंद; निरर्थक – **pointblank** *a.* सीधा, साफ़-साफ़, रूखा – *adv.* अत्यंत निकट से – **point of view** द ष्टिकोण, नज़रिया

poise (पॉइज़) *n.* संतुलन; आत्मविश्वास, प्रभावशाली हाव भाव व चलने का ढंग, ठवन – *v.* संतुलन रहना या रखना, लटकना, झूलना – *vt.* तैयार करना – **poised** *a.* शांत, आत्मविश्वासपूर्ण; तैयार

poison (ˈपॉइज़न) *n.* विष, ज़हर – *vt.* विष देना; विष मिलाना-**poisonous** *a.* ज़हरीला

poke (पोक) *vt.* ढकेलना; कुरेदना; (हाथ आदि) बाहर निकालना– *vi.* धक्का मारना; टोह लेना – *n.* – **poker** *n.* कुरेदनी, पोकर – **poke fun at** का मज़ाक उड़ाना

poker (ˈपोकर) *n.* ताश का एक खेल

polar (ˈपोलर) *a.* दे. POLE

pole[1] (पोल) *n.* स्तंभ, खंभा; लट्ठा – *vt.* लट्ठे से धकेलना

pole[2] (पोल) *n.* (उत्तरी व दक्षिणी) ध्रुव; चुम्बक, विद्युत-बैटरी आदि के ध्रुव (दोनों छोर) – **polar** *a.* ध्रुवीय – **polarity** (पोˈलैरिटि) *n.* – **pole vault** लम्बे बांस से ऊंचे कूदने का खेल, पोल वाल्ट

police (पˈलीस) *n.* पुलिस – *vt.* कानून व्यवस्था बनाए रखना – **policeman** *n.* पुलिसमैन (**policewoman** *fem.*) – **police station** पुलिस थाना

policy[1] (ˈपॉलिसि) *n.* नीति, कूटनीति; समझदारी, चालाकी

policy[2] (ˈपॉलिसि) *n.* (**insurance policy** भी) बीमा-पालिसी, बीमा पत्र

polish (ˈपॉलिश) *vt.* चमकाना, पालिश करना; परिष्क त करना, सुधारना – *n.* चमक; चिकनी सतह; चमकाने का पदार्थ, पालिश; सुसंस्क ति, सभ्यता – **polished** *a.* *fig.* सुसंस्क त, सभ्य

polite (पˈलाइट) *a.* विनम्र, सभ्य

politic (ˈपॉलिटिक) *a.* विवेकपूर्ण – **politics** *n.* राजनीति, राजनीति-शास्त्र – **political** (पˈलिटिकल) *a.* राजनीतिक – **politically**

adv. – **politician** (पॉलि'टिशन) *n.* राजनीतिज्ञ – **polity** *n.* राज्यतंत्र, राज्य-व्यवस्था

poll (पोल) *n.* मतदान; मतगणना; मत संख्या; आम राय जानने के लिए आंशिक जनमत-संग्रह (**opinion poll** भी) – *vt.* (वोट) पाना; मतदान करना – *vi.* मत देना, वोट डालना – **polling booth** मतदान-कक्ष

pollen ('पॉलिन) *n.* (फूलों का) पराग – **pollinate** ('पॉलिनेट) *vt.* पराग स चना – **pollination** *n.*

pollute (प'लूट) *vt.* दूषित करना; अपवित्र करना – **pollutant** (प'लूटंट) *n.* प्रदूषक (पदार्थ) – **pollution** (प'लूशन) *n.* प्रदूषण

polo ('पोलो) *n.* पोलो (चौगान) का खेल – **polo neck** गोल गले का – **polo shirt** एक प्रकार की टी-शर्ट

polyester ('पॉलिएँस्टर) *n.* प्लास्टिक, कपड़ा आदि बनाने में प्रयुक्त एक क त्रिम पदार्थ

polygamy (पॉ'लिगमि) *n.* , बहुपत्नी प्रथा

polyglot ('पॉलिग्लॉट) *a./n.*, बहुभाषी

polygon ('पॉलिगन) *n.* बहुभुज (आक ति) – **polygonal** (पॉ'लिगनल) *a.*

polygraph ('पॉलिग्रैफ़) *n.* दे० LIE DETECTOR

polyp ('पॉलिप) *n.* एक अत्यंत सूक्ष्म समुद्री जीव (**polypus** भी); (शरीर में) एक प्रकार की गांठ, अर्बुद

polystyrene (पॉलि'स्टाइरीन) *n.* सामान पैक करने में प्रयुक्त एक क त्रिम पदार्थ विशे. एक सफेद कड़ा परंतु हल्का पदार्थ *a.*

polytechnic (पॉलि'टैक्निक) *n.* कालिज जहां मुख्यता विभिन्न शिल्प (दस्तकारी) सिखाये जाते हैं

polythene ('पॉलिथीन) *n.* एक कड़ा थर्मोप्लास्टिक पदार्थ – **polythene bag** पोलिथीन की थैली

polyunsaturated (पॉलिअन्'सैचुरेटिड) *a.* (ऐसी वसा) जो रक्त में कलैस्टराल नह बनाता

pomegranate ('पॉमिग्रैनिट) *n.* अनार

Pomeranian (पॉम'रेनिअन) *n.* एक छोटे कद के कुत्ते की नस्ल

pomp (पॉम्प) *n.* धूमधाम; आडम्बर; तड़क-भड़क

pompous ('पॉम्पस) *a.* आडम्बरपूर्ण – **pomposity** (पॉम्'पॉसिटि) *n.* आडम्बर

pond (पॉण्ड) *n.* पोखर, जोहड़

ponder ('पॉण्डर) *v.* विचारना, गंभीर चिंतन करना

ponderous ('पॉण्डरस) *a.* भारी, आसानी से न संभलने वाला; नीरस

pontiff ('पॉन्टिफ़) *n.* पोप, धर्माध्यक्ष; बिशप – **pontificate** (पॉन्'टिफ़िकेट) *vi.* लंबे-चौड़े शब्दों में शिक्षा देना

pontoon (पॉन्'टून) *n.* अस्थायी पुल बनाने में काम आने वाली चपटे तले की नाव या बड़ा पीपा, पंटून

pony ('पॉनि) *n.* टट्टू – **ponytail** *n.* सिर के पीछे लंबे बालों का बनाया गुच्छा

poodle ('पूड्ल) *n.* बहुत छोटे कुत्ते की नस्ल, पूडल

Pooh-Bah ('पू-बा) *n.* आडम्बरपूर्ण अधिकारी, ज्यादा शान दिखाने वाला अफसर

pool[1] (पूल) *n.* पोखर; तैरने का तालाब

pool[2] (पूल) *n.* धनराशि; संघ (जैसे इंजीनियरों का जिनमें से कोई भी किसी भी मलिक के लिए कार्य कर सके), निकाय; बिलियर्ड्स का एक खेल – *vt.* इकट्ठा करना

poor (पुअर) *a.* निर्धन; घटिया; थोड़ा; बेचारा; कम उपजाऊ (ज़मीन) – **poorly** *adv.* खराब – *a.* अस्वस्थ, बीमार

pop[1] (पॉप) *v.* 'तड़ाक' या 'फक्' की आवाज़ करना; *inf.* अचानक आ जाना या चले जाना; घुस पड़ना (**-pp-**) – *n.* 'तड़ाक' या 'फक्' की ध्वनि – **popcorn** *n.* भुने हुए मक्का के दाने

pop[2] (पॉप) *inf. n.* पिता; बूढ़ा व्यक्ति

pop[3] (पॉप) *n.* सार्वजनिक रूप से (विशे. युवाओं को) पसंद संगीत

pop. popular, population का संक्षिप्त रूप

Pope (पोप) *n.* रोमन-कैथलिक चर्च का परम धर्माध्यक्ष, पोप

poplar (ˈपॉप्लर) *n.* पहाड़ी पीपल, बन पीपल

poplin (ˈपॉप्लिन) *n.* सूती, कमीज़ का कपड़ा, पापलीन

poppy (ˈपॉपि) *n.* पोस्त का पौधा

populace (ˈपॉप्युलस) *n.* जन-साधारण

popular (ˈपॉप्युलर) *a.* लोकप्रिय – **popularity** (पॉप्यु ˈलैरिटि) *n.* लोकप्रियता – **popularize** *vt.* लोकप्रिय बनाना

populate (ˈपॉप्युलेट) *vt.* आबाद करना, बसाना – **population** (पॉप्यु ˈलेशन) *n.* जनसंख्या – **populous** (ˈपॉप्युलस) *a.* घनी आबादी वाला

populist (ˈपॉप्युलिस्ट) *n.* जनहित में कार्य करने का दावा करने वाला राजनीतिज्ञ – *a* – **populism** *n.* ऐसी राजनीति

porcelain (ˈपॉर्सलिन) *n.* चीनी-मिट्टी के बर्तन

porch (पॉर्च) *n.* पोर्च, प्रवेश द्वार के आगे ढका हुआ भाग

porcupine (ˈपॉर्क्युपाइन) *n.* साही

pore[1] (पॉर) *vi.* **pore over** ध्यान से अध्ययन करना

pore[2] (पॉर) *n.* रोमकूप, रोएँ का छिद्र – **porous** (ˈपॉरस) *a.* जिसमें से पानी आदि रिस सके; छिद्रपूर्ण

pork (पॉर्क) *n.* सूअर का गोश्त

porn (पॉर्न), **porno** (ˈपॉर्नो) *n. inf.* pornography का संक्षिप्त रूप

pornography (पॉर् ˈनॉग्रफ़ि) *n.* अश्लील साहित्य, फ़िल्म आदि – **pornographer** *n.* – **pornographic** (पॉर्न ˈग्रैफ़िक) *a.* अश्लील

porpoise (ˈपार्पस) *n.* डॉल्फ़िन जैसा एक समुद्री स्तनपायी जीव, सूँस, शिंशुक

porridge (ˈपॉरिज) *n.* दलिया

port[1] (पॉर्ट) *n.* बंदरगाह; बंदरगाह से लगा शहर

port[2] (पॉर्ट) *n.* जहाज़ का बायां भाग

port[3] (पॉर्ट) *n.* एक लाल मीठी शराब

port[4] (पॉर्ट) *n.* जहाज़ के पार्श्व में खुला भाग – **porthole** *n.* जहाज़ के पार्श्व में बनी खिड़की या मूका, मोखा

portable (ˈपॉर्टबल) *n./a.* (वस्तु) जिसे आसानी से उठाकर ले जा सकें, सुबाह्य

portage (ˈपॉर्टिज) *n.* माल ले जाने का भाड़ा

portal (ˈपॉर्ट्ल) *n.* फाटक, प्रवेश द्वार

portend (पॉर् ˈटेण्ड) *vt.* पूर्व सूचना देना, का शकुन होना – **portent** (ˈपॉर् ˈटेन्ट) *n.* शकुन; अपशकुन

porter (ˈपॉर्टर) *n.* कुली; दरबान, द्वारपाल

portfolio (पॉर्ट् ˈफ़ोलिओ) *n.* कागज़ात रखने का बस्ता (प्राय: चमड़े का); सरकार में मंत्री का विभाग; शेयर, बांण्ड आदि के रूप में किसी की सम्पत्ति की लिस्ट (*pl.* **-s**)

portico (ˈपॉर्टिको) *n.* द्वार मण्डप, ड्योढ़ी (*pl.* -os)

portion (ˈपॉर्शन) *n.* भाग, अंश; भाग्य, किस्मत – *vt.* हिस्सों में बाँटना

portly (ˈपॉर्ट्लि) *a.* मोटा-तगड़ा

portmanteau (पॉर्ट् ˈमैंटो) *n.* चमड़े का सूटकेस (*pl.* **-s, -x** (–टोज़) – *a.* कई विशेषताओं/कार्यक्रमों आदि से बना एक कार्यक्रम आदि

portray (पॉर् ˈट्रे) *vt.* का (मुख) चित्र बनाना; सजीव वर्णन करना – **portrait** (ˈपॉर्ट्रिट) *n.* चित्र; प्रतिक ति – **portraiture** (ˈपॉर्ट्रिचर) *n.* (मुख) चित्रण – **portrayal** (पॉर् ˈट्रेअल) *n.* चित्रण; अभिनय

pose (पोज़) *vt.* रुख अपनाना; पेश करना – *vi.* (चित्र के लिए) खड़ा होना या बैठना; का ढोंग रचना, दिखावा करना – *n.* मुद्रा, ढोंग, आडम्बर – **poseur** (पोज़र) दिखावा करने वाला, आडम्बरी

poser (ˈपोज़र) *n.* पहेली, चकराने वाला प्रश्न
posh (पॉश) *a. inf.* सुंदर, शानदार (भवन आदि)
position (पˈज़िशन) *n.* स्थिति; स्थान; रुख, द ष्टिकोण; स्तर; प्रतिष्ठा; पद; अवस्था – *vt.* स्थित करना, रख देना
positive (ˈपॉज़िटिव) *a.* निश्चित, स्पष्ट; पक्का; रचनात्मक; असंदिग्ध; धनात्मक (संख्या) – *n.* जो रचनात्मक हो; *Photog.* पाज़िटिव (नैगेटिव के विपरीत) – **positively** *adv.*
possess (पˈज़ैस) *vt.* का स्वामी होना, पर अधिकार होना; नियंत्रण रखना; (दुष्ट आत्मा आदि का किसी को) ग्रस्त करना – **possession** (पˈज़ेंशन) *n.* स्वामित्व, अधिकार; सम्पत्ति; अधिकार में वस्तु – **possessive** (पˈज़ेंसिव) *a.* स्वत्वबोधक, (किसी वस्तु या व्यक्ति पर) बहुत ज्यादा अधिकार या नियंत्रण की भावना रखने वाला – **possessor** *n.* स्वामी, मालिक
possible (ˈपॉसिबल) *a.* संभव; उद्देश्य के लिए उपयुक्त – *n.* संभावित, प्रत्याशी उम्मीदवार – **possibility** (पॉसिˈबिलिटि) *n.* संभावना – **possibly** *adv.* संभवतया, शायद
possum (ˈपॉसम) *n.* दे. OPOSSUM
post[1] (पोस्ट) *n.* खंभा, स्तंभ – *vt.* (सूचना-पट पर) चिपकाना, लगाना – **poster** *n.* पोस्टर, इश्तहार
post[2] (पोस्ट) *n.* डाक; स्थान, कार्य-स्थल; पद; (सैनिक) चौकी; किला – *vt.* डाक में डालना; नवीनतम सूचना देना; स्थान विशेष पर सैनिक आदि तैनात करना; नियुक्त करना; (व्यापार में) खाते में चढ़ाना – *adv.* जल्दी में – **postage** (ˈपोस्टिज) *n.* डाक-शुल्क – **postal** *a.* डाक-, डाक द्वारा – **postal ballot** डाक द्वारा भेजी गयी वोट – **postal order** पोस्टल-ऑर्डर – **postcard** *n.* पोस्ट कार्ड – **postman** (ˈपोस्ट्मन) *n.* पोस्टमैन, डाकिया – **postmark** *n.* डाक-मोहर – **postmaster, postmistress** *n.* पोस्ट आफिस प्रभारी, पोस्टमास्टर – **post office** डाकखाना, पोस्ट ऑफिस
post-(*comb. form*) के पश्चात, के बाद जैसे **postgraduate** *a.*
postdated (पोस्ट्ˈडेटिड) *a.* आगे की तारीख वाला (चैक, पत्र)
posterior (पॉस्ˈटअरिअर) *a.* परवर्ती, पिछला – *n.* नितम्ब, चूतड़
posterity (पॉस्ˈटैरिटि) *n.* भावी पीढ़ियां; वंशज
postgraduate (पोस्ट्ˈग्रैड्युइट) *a.* स्नातकोत्तर (कक्षा, परीक्षा आदि) – *n.* स्नातकोत्तर व्यक्ति
post-haste *adv.* फौरन, तुरंत
posthumous (ˈपॉस्ट्युमस) *a.* मरणोपरांत; पिता की म त्यु के बाद जन्मा
postmortem (पोस्ट्ˈमॉर्टम) *n.* शवपरीक्षा – *a.* म त्यु के बाद
postpone (पोस्टˈपोन) *vt.* स्थगित करना – **postponement** *n.* स्थगन
postscript (ˈपोसस्क्रिप्ट) *n.* पश्चलेख, पुनश्च, पत्र या पुस्तक की समाप्ति के बाद जोड़ी गई सामग्री
postulate (ˈपॉस्ट्युलेट) *vt.* मान लेना, अभिधारणा करना – *n.* अभिधारणा
posture (ˈपॉस्चर) *n.* मुद्रा, भाव, तौर-तरीका; मनःस्थिति, रुख –*v.* रुख अपनाना; विशिष्ट मुद्रा में स्थित होना
posy (ˈपोज़ि) *n.* फूलों का गुच्छा
pot (पॉट) *n.* हंडिया, बरतन – *vt.* पात्र में (सुरक्षित) रखना (**-tt-**); गमले में पौधा लगाना – **potted** *a.* गमले में लगा हुआ – **pot-bellied** *a.* मोटे पेट वाला – **potboiler** *n.* केवल पैसा कमाने के इरादे से लिखी गयी किताब आदि – **pothole** *n.*, सड़क में गड्ढा
potable (ˈपोटबल) *a.* पीने योग्य
potassium (पˈटैसिअम) *n.* पोटैशियम, एक सफेद धातु-पदार्थ

potato (प'टेटो) *n.* आलू (*pl.* **-es.**) – **sweet potato** शकरकंद

potent ('पोटंट) *a.* शक्तिशाली; प्रभावकारी; मैथुन-समर्थ (पुरुष) – **potency** *n.* शक्ति, सामर्थ्य

potential (प'टेंन्शल) *a.* संभावित; अप्रकट – *n.* संभावना – **potentially** *adv.* संभवत – **potentiality** (पटेंन्शि'ऐलिटि) *n.* संभावना; क्षमता

potion ('पोशन) *n.* दवाई की खुराक, ज़हर का घूंट

potter[1] ('पॉटर) *n.* कुम्हार – **pottery** *n.* मिट्टी के बर्तन बनाने का स्थान; मिट्टी के बर्तन बनाने की कला

potter[2] ('पॉटर) *vi.* ढीले-ढाले, अव्यवस्थित ढंग से काम करना; भटकना

potty ('पॉटि) *a. inf.* पागल – *n.* पाखाने के पात्र के लिए बच्चों का शब्द

pouch (पाउच) *n.* थैली; जेब – *vt.* थैली या जेब में रखना

poultice ('पोल्टिस) *n.* पुलटिस (राई, आटे आदि का हलवे जैसा पदार्थ जो फोड़े, चोट आदि पर लगाया जाय)

poultry ('पोल्ट्रि) *n.* पाली गयी मुर्गियां, बत्तख आदि

pounce[1] (पाउन्स) *vi.* – **pounce on** किसी पर टूट पड़ना – *n.* झपट्टा, तेज़ी से नीचे आना

pound[1] (पाउंड) *vt.* कूटना; पीस कर टुकड़े-टुकड़े कर देना या बारीक चूरा बना देना; (फर्श आदि पर) धम-धम करना

pound[2] (पाउंड) *n.* 0.454 किलोग्राम के बराबर भार की एक इकाई; ब्रिटिश मुद्रा (£)

pound[3] (पाउंड) *n.* बाड़ा, कांजी-हाउस; घेरा

pour (पॉर) *vi.* बहना, निकल पड़ना; लोगों की भीड़ का आ जाना; मूसलाधार बरसना – *vt.* उडेलना, बहाना

poverty ('पॉवर्टि) *n.* दरिद्रता, अभाव – **poverty-stricken** गरीब

POW Prisoner of War का संक्षेप

powder ('पाउडर) *n.* चूर्ण, चूरा; (दवाई का) चूर्ण; बारूद – *vt.* पाउडर लगाना; पीस कर चूरा करना – **powdery** *a.* चूरा

power ('पाउअर) *n.* सामर्थ्य, शक्ति, बल; अधिकार; नियंत्रण; प्रभावशाली अथवा अधिकारपूर्ण व्यक्ति या वस्तु; यांत्रिक ऊर्जा; विद्युत-ऊर्जा, बिजली; कार्य करने की इकाई (हार्स पावर आदि); (गणित) घात – **powered** *a.* यंत्र-चलित, विद्युत ऊर्जा-चलित – **powerful** *a.*

pp pages का संक्षेप

PR public relations का संक्षेप

practical (प्रैक्टिकल) *a.* सक्रिय; व्यावहारिक; प्रयोगात्माक; उपयोगी; वास्तविक – **practically** *adv.* – **practicable** *a.* व्यावहारिक, व्यवहार्य, उपयोगी – **practitioner** (प्रैक्'टिशनर) *n.* व्यवसायी (*e.g.* **medical practitioner** चिकित्सक)

practise, US practice (प्रैक्टिस) *vt.* अभ्यास करना, की आदत डालना, कार्यान्वित करना, (के व्यवसाय में) लगा होना – *vi.* अभ्यास करना – **practice** *n.* प्रथा, रिवाज; आदत; अभ्यास; कुशलता; व्यवसाय, पेशा; व्यवहार; आचरण

pragmatic (प्रैग्'मैटिक) *a.* व्यावहारिक – **pragmatism** *n.* व्यावहारिकता

prairie (प्रेअरि) *n.* घास का (व क्ष-रहित) विशाल मैदान – **prairie dog** बिलों में रहने वाला चूहे जैसा एक अमरीकी जानवर

praise (प्रेज़) *n.* प्रशंसा, गुणगान – *vt.* प्रशंसा या सराहना करना; गुणगान करना – **praiseworthy** *a.* प्रशंसनीय

pram (प्रैम) *n.* बच्चा गाड़ी

prance (प्रान्स) *vi.* अकड़ कर चलना; कूदना-फांदना – *n.* कूद-फांद, उछल-कूद

prank (प्रैंक) *n.* नटखटी, शरारत भरा काम; उछल-कूद

prate (प्रेट) *vi.* बकबक करना – *n.* बकबक

prattle (प्रैट्ल) *vi.* बचकानी बातें करना – *n.* बचकानी, मूर्खतापूर्ण बातें

prawn (प्रॉन) *n.* झींगा

pray (प्रे) *vt.* निवेदन करना; विनती करना – *vi.* (प्रभु) प्रार्थना करना – **prayer** (प्रेंअर) *n.* प्रार्थना; विनती, याचना

pre-(*comb. form*) पूर्व-जैसे **prewar** *a.* में

preach (प्रीच) *vi.* प्रवचन करना या उपदेश देना, (धार्मिक या नैतिक) उपदेश देना – *vt.* का प्रचार या समर्थन करना – **preacher** (प्रीचर) *n.* उपदेशक

preamble (प्री ऐंबल) *n.* आमुख, प्रस्तावना

precarious (प्रि कैंअरिअस) *a.* अनिश्चित, अस्थिर, संकटपूर्ण

precaution (प्रि कॉशन) *n.* सावधानी, सतर्कता, एहतियात – **precautionary** *a.* सावधानी के रूप में

precede (प्रि सीड) *vi.* समय, स्थान, क्रम आदि में पहले होना, पूर्ववर्ती होना – **precedence** (प्रेंसिडन्स) *n.* वरीयता – **precedent** (प्रेंसिडंट) *n.* पूर्वोदाहरण, मिसाल

precept (प्रीसेंप्ट) *n.* आचार-नियम, नीति वचन

precinct (प्रीसिंक्ट) *n.* अहाता, दायरा, सीमित क्षेत्र – (~ **s**) *pl.* पड़ोस, परिवेश

precious (प्रेंशस) *a.* बहुत प्रिय, संजोई हुई; बहुमूल्य – **preciousness** *n.*

precipice (प्रेंसिपिस) *n.* खड़ी चट्टान – **precipitous** (प्रि सिपिटस) *a.* सीधी, खड़ी

precipitate (प्रि सिपिटेट) *vt.* जल्दी कराना; ऊंचाई से सीधा नीचे गिराना; *Chem.* ठोस टुकड़े बनकर घोल से प थक हो जाना; (झगड़ा आदि) अचानक पैदा कर देना – *a.* (प्रि सिपिटिट) उतावला, बिना अधिक सोचे किया (कार्य) – *n.* (प्रि सिपिटिट) रासायनिक क्रिया द्वारा घोल से प थक हुआ ठोस पदार्थ – **precipitation** (प्रिसिपि टेशन) *n.* वाष्प के घनीभूत होने से बनी (या गिरने वाली) वर्षा, हिम आदि

précis (प्रेसी) *n.* संक्षेपण, सारांश (*pl.* **précis** (प्रेसीज़))

precise (प्रि साइस) *a.* ठीक-ठाक, सही ढंग से कहा गया; नियमनिष्ठ – **precisely** *adv.* बिल्कुल सही – **precision** (प्रि सिझन) *n.* यथार्थता, बिलकुल स्पष्ट व सही होने का गुण

preclude (प्रि क्लूड) *vt.* घटित होने से रोकना

precocious (प्रि कोशस) *a.* समय से पूर्व विकसित, अकाल प्रौढ़ (बालक) – **precocity,** (प्रि कॉसिटि) *n.*

preconceive (प्रीकन् सीव़) *vt.* पूर्वकल्पना करना – **preco2nception** *n.*

precondition (प्रीकन् डिशन) *n.* आवश्यक शर्त

precursor (प्रि कर्सर) *n.* अग्रदूत

predatory (प्रेंडटरि) *a.* परभक्षी(जानवर, पक्षी); लुटेरा – **predator** (प्रेंडटर) *n.* परभक्षी

predecessor (प्रीडिसेंसर) *n.* पूर्वाधिकारी; पूर्वज

predestine (प्री डेंस्टिन) *vt.* पहले से ही निश्चित अथवा नियत करना – **predestination** *n.* पूर्वनियति, (विधि) विधान, भाग्य

predetermined (प्रिडि टर्मिन्ड) *a.* पूर्वनिश्चित

predicament (प्रि डिकमंट) *n.* उलझन या परेशानी की हालत

predicate *vt.* (प्रेंडिकेट) निश्चयपूर्वक कहना; को आधार बनाना – *n.* (प्रेंडिकिट) गुण, लक्षण; *Grammar* विधेय

predict (प्रि डिक्ट) *vt.* भविष्यवाणी करना – **predictable** *a.* – **prediction** (प्रि डिक्शन) *n.* भविष्यवाणी

predispose (प्रीडिस् पोज़) *vt.* किसी को पहले से तैयार करना, झुकाना; (की ओर) प्रव त करना

predominate (प्रि डॉमिनेट) *vi.* सर्वाधिक महत्वपूर्ण व प्रभावशाली होना – **predominance** *n.* सर्वाधिक महत्व, प्रभाव – **predominant** *a.*

pre-eminent (प्रि´ऍमिनंट) *a.* सर्वश्रेष्ठ, सर्वोत्तम – **pre-eminence** *n.* सर्वोत्तमता – **pre-eminently** *adv.*

pre-emptive (प्रि´ऍम्प्टिव़) *a.* पहले से ही की जाने वाली (कार्यवाही)

preen (´प्रीन) *vt.* चोंच से पंख ठीक-ठाक करना; अपने आप को संवारना

prefabricate (प्री´फ़ैब्रिकेट) *vt.* इमारत के अलग-अलग हिस्सों को बनाना जिन्हें बाद में जोड़ कर इमारत खड़ी की जा सके

preface (´प्रेफ़िस) *n.* भूमिका, प्रस्तावना – *vt.* भूमिका देना

prefect (´प्रीफ़ेक्ट) *n.* प्रशासक, (विभाग) अध्यक्ष; कक्षा में व्यवस्था बनाये रखने का सीमित अधिकार-प्राप्त छात्र

prefer (प्रि´फ़र) *vt.* अधिक चाहना या पसंद करना; किसी को (पद में) आगे बढ़ाना (**-rr-**) – **preferable** (´प्रेफ़रबल) *a.* बेहतर, अधिक वांछनीय – **preferably** *adv.* अच्छा हो कि – **preference** (´प्रेफ़रन्स) *n.* अधिमानता देना – **preferential** (प्रेफ़´रेन्शल) *a.* अधिमान्य; अधिक अच्छा या अधिक लाभकारी

prefix *n.* (´प्रीफ़िक्स) उपसर्ग; नाम से पूर्व जोड़ा गया शब्द (जैसे **Mr.**) – *vt.* (प्री´फ़िक्स) प्रारंभ में जोड़ना; उपसर्ग लगाना

pregnant (´प्रेग्नंट) *a.* गर्भवती, अर्थपूर्ण; मौलिक – **pregnancy** (´प्रेग्नंसि) *n.* गर्भावस्था

prehistoric (प्रीहि´स्टॉरिक) *a.* प्रागैतिहासिक, इतिहासपूर्व समय का

prejudice (´प्रेजुडिस) *n.* , पूर्वाग्रह; पक्षपात; किसी व्यक्ति के हितों की हानि – *vt.* (प्रतिकूल) प्रभाव डालना; हानि पहुंचाना – **prejudicial** (प्रेजु´डिशल) *a.* हानिकर, प्रतिकूल

preliminary (प्रि´लिमिनरि) *a.* प्राथमिक – *n.*

prelude (´प्रेल्यूड) *n. Mus.* मंगलाचरण; पूर्वरंग; प्रस्तावना

premarital (प्री´मैरिट्ल) *a.* विवाहपूर्व

premature (´प्रेम´चर) *a.* उचित समय से पूर्व होने वाली (घटना आदि)

premeditated (प्रि´मेडिटेटिड) *vt.* पूर्वनियोजित – **premeditation** (प्रिमेडि´टेशन) *n.* पूर्व-चिंतन

premier (´प्रेम्यर) *n.* प्रधानमंत्री – *a.* प्रमुख, प्रधान; सर्वप्रथम – **premiership** *n.*

premiere (´प्रेमिएॅअर) *n.* नाटक, फिल्म आदि का प्रथम प्रदर्शन

premise (´प्रेमिस) *n. Logic.* आधार वाक्य, आधारिका –(~ **s**) *pl.* (´प्रेमिसिज़) भवन, अहाता; *Law.* आमुख, आदिखण्ड (किसी दस्तावेज का)

premium (´प्रीमिअम) *n.* बोनस; बीमा किश्त, वास्तविक मूल्य से अधिक राशि, अधिमूल्य; महत्व या सम्मान (*pl.* **-iums**)

premonition (प्रेम´निशन) *n.* (संकट का) पूर्वाभास

prenatal (प्री´नेटल) *a.* जन्मपूर्व

preoccupy (प्री´ऑक्युपाइ) *vt.* किसी एक कार्य में तल्लीन कर देना – **preoccupation** *n.* तल्लीनता – **preoccupied** (प्री´ऑक्युपाइड) *a.* जो किसी काम में तल्लीन हो

prepare (प्रि´पेंअर) *vt.* तैयार करना, बनाना – *vi.* तैयार होना – **preparation** (प्रेप´रेशन) *n.* आयोजन, तैयारी; बनाई गई वस्तु – **preparatory** (प्रि´पैरटरि) *a.* आरंभिक – **preparedness** (प्रि´पेंअरिड्निस) *n.* तैयारी

prepay (प्री´पे) *vt.* पहले से भुगतान करना (**prepaid, prepaying**)

preposition (प्रेप´ज़िशन) *n. Grammar* पूर्वसर्ग जैसे *to, in* आदि

prepossessing (प्रीप´ज़ेसिङ) *a.* प्रभावशाली

preposterous (प्रि´पॉस्टरस) *a.* नितांत हास्यास्पद, मूर्खतापूर्ण

prerequisite (प्री'रेक्विज़िट) *a.* पूर्वापेक्षित, अनिवार्य – *n.* पूर्वापेक्षा, शर्त
prerogative (प्रि'रॉगटिव) *n.* विशेष अधिकार विशे. शासक के परमाधिकार – *a.* विशेषाधिकार प्राप्त
Prez. President का संक्षिप्त
presage *n.* (प्रेंसिज) शकुन, पूर्वाभास – *vt.* (प्रेंसिज, प्रि'सेज) भविष्यवाणी करना, किसी बात का सूचक होना
prescribe (प्रि'स्क्राइब) *v.* नियम निर्धारित करना, आदेश देना; नुस्खा लिखना – **prescription** (प्रि'स्क्रिप्शन) *n.* आदेश; लिखा हुआ नुसखा
present[1] (प्रेंज़ंट) *a.* उपस्थित, विद्यमान; वर्तमान – *n.* वर्तमान काल (**present tense** भी) – **presence** *n.* उपस्थिति; व्यक्तित्व – **presently** *adv.* शीघ्र ही, अभी-अभी
present[2] *vt.* (प्रि'ज़ेण्ट) *vt.* प्रस्तुत करना; परिचय कराना; दिखाना, प्रदर्शित करना; देना– *n.* (प्रेंज़ंट) उपहार, भेंट – **presentable** (प्रि'ज़ेण्टबल) *a.* सामने आने योग्य – **presentation** (प्रिज़ेंन्'टेशन) *n.* प्रस्तुति, पेशकश, प्रदर्शन, अभिनय – **presenter** *n.* कार्यक्रम-प्रस्तुतकर्ता
presentiment (प्रि'ज़ेण्टिमंट) *n.* संकट का पूर्वाभास
preserve (प्रि'ज़र्व) *vt.* सुरक्षित रखना; सड़ने-गलने से बचाना, परिरक्षण करना – *n.* विशेष क्षेत्र; परिरक्षित वस्तु (मुरब्बा आदि) – **preservation** (प्रेंज़र्'वेशन) *n.* – **preservationist** *n.* संरक्षण-समर्थक – **preservative** *n.* खाद्य पदार्थों में मिलाया जाने वाला रासायनिक पदार्थ जिससे वह खराब न हो – *a.* परिरक्षक, परिरक्षी
preside (प्रि'ज़ाइड) *vi.* सभा का अध्यक्ष होना, संचालन करना – **president** (प्रेंज़िडंट) *n.* राष्ट्रपति; प्रधान अथवा मुख्य संचालक – **presidency** *n.* – **presidential** *a.*
press (प्रेंस) *vt.* दबाना; (कपड़े) इस्तरी करना; लगातार अनुरोध करना – *vi.* दबाव डालना; (बहुत) जल्दी करना – *n.* दबाव; दबाने, निचोड़ने आदि का उपकरण; मुद्रणयंत्र, प्रेस; छापाखाना, समाचार-पत्र, (सामूहिक रूप से) पत्रकार, पत्र, पत्रिकाएं आदि – **pressing** *a.* अत्यावश्यक – **press release** प्रेस विज्ञप्ति
pressure (प्रेंशर) *n.* दबाव; प्रभाव; कठिनाइयां; *Physics* दाब, प्रेशर – **pressurize,** US **pressure** *vt.* पर दबाव डालना – **pressure cooker** प्रेशर कुकर
prestige (प्रें'स्टीझ़) *n.* प्रतिष्ठा, इससे उत्पन्न प्रभाव – **prestigious** (प्रें'स्टिजस) *a.* प्रतिष्ठात्मक
prestressed (प्री'स्ट्रेस्ट) *a.* सरिया मिला (कंक्रीट)
presume (प्रि'ज़्यूम) *vt.* मान कर चलना – *vi.* से अनुचित लाभ उठाना – **presumably** *adv.* संभवतया – **presumption** (प्रि'ज़म्प्शन) *n.* ढिठाई, अक्खड़पन; धारणा, परिकल्पना – **presumptive** (प्रि'ज़म्प्टिव) *a.* अनुमानित – **presumptuous** (प्रि'ज़म्प्ट्युअस) *a.* धृष्ट, अक्खड़
presuppose (प्रीस'पोज़) *vt.* (पहले से) मान लेना – **presupposition** (प्रीसप्र'जिशन) *n.* पूर्वधारणा
pretend (प्रि'टेण्ड) *vt.* (झूठा) दावा करना; ढोंग रचना – *vi.* (**pretend to** में) पर दावा जताना – **pretence,** US **pretense** *n.* दावा; छल-कपट; बहाना – **pretender** *n.* (राजगद्दी का) मिथ्या दावेदार – **pretension** (प्रि'टेंन्शन) *n.* दावा, मिथ्याभिमान – **pretentious** *a.* मिथ्याभिमानी, शान दिखाने वाला
preternatural (प्रीटर्'नैचरल) *a.* असाधारण, असामान्य
pretext (प्रीटेंक्सट) *n.* बहाना
pretty (प्रिटि) *a.* मनोहर व आकर्षक – *adv.* बहुत कुछ, पर्याप्त मात्रा में

prevail (प्रि'वेल) *vi.* काबू पाना; प्रचिलित होना – **prevailing** *a.* प्रचिलित, प्रबल – **prevalence** ('प्रेवलंस) *n.* प्रचलन – **prevalent** *a.* बहुप्रचिलित, चालू

prevaricate (प्रि'वैरिकेट) *vi.* गोलमोल बात करना

prevent (प्रि'वेंण्ट) *vt.* रोकना, काम में बाधा डालना – **preventable** *a.* जो रोका जा सके – **prevention** (प्रि'वेंन्शन) *n.* – **preventive** (प्रि'वेंन्टिव) *a./n.* निरोधक, निवारक

preview ('प्रीव्यू) *n.* पूर्व दर्शन

previous ('प्रीविअस) *a.* पूर्ववर्ती, पिछला, पहले का – **previously** *adv.* पहले (से)

prey (प्रे) *n.* शिकार – *vi.* भोजन के लिए शिकार करना; शिकार जैसा बर्ताव करना – **prey on** (को) अत्यधिक चिंतित या परेशान करना

price (प्राइस) *n.* मूल्य, भाव; (*fig.* भी); इनाम; जुए के दाव में संभावना – *vt.* दाम निर्धारित करना, मूल्य लगाना – **priceless** *a.* अमूल्य, बहुमूल्य

prick (प्रिक) *vt.* छेद करना, चुभाना; दुखाना; (कान) खड़े करना – *n.* छेद; छेदन; चुभन; कसक; नुकीला औज़ार या हथियार; नोक – **prickle** *n.* कांटा – *vi.* चुभन महसूस करना *a.* – **prickly heat** पित्ती, घमौरी

pride (प्राइड) *n.* अभिमान, घमंड, गर्व, नाज़; संतोष व गर्व का अनुभव/ विषय; शेरों का झुण्ड – *vt.* गर्व करना

priest (प्रीस्ट) *n.* पुजारी; पुरोहित (**-ess** *fem.*)

prig (प्रिग) *n.* दंभी व्यक्ति

prim (प्रिम) *a.*, उचित अनुचित का अत्यधिक विचार करने वाला

primacy ('प्राइमसि) *n.* कोटि, श्रेणी आदि में प्रमुखता

prima facie ('प्राइम्अ फ़ेशि) *Lat.* प्रथम द ष्टि में, पहली नज़र में

primary ('प्राइमरि) *a.* मुख्य; समय में प्राथमिक; मूल; आरंभिक; मौलिक- **primarily** *adv.*

primate ('प्राइमेट) *n.* स्तनपायी जीवों का एक वर्ग जिसमें बंदर व मनुष्य आते हैं

prime[1] (प्राइम) *a.* प्रथम; मूल, आदि; मुख्य; सर्वोत्तम – *n.* किसी भी वस्तु का प्रथम व सर्वोत्तम अंश; बहार; यौवन; उत्तम स्वास्थ्य– *vt.* (पम्प आदि) इस्तेमाल के लिए तैयार करना – **Prime Minister** (P.M.) प्रधान मंत्री

prime[2] (प्राइम) *vt.* तेल, सरेस आदि का कोट (लेप) लगाकर सतह को रोग़न के लिए तैयार करना, अस्तर चढ़ाना – **primer** *n.* रोगन का अस्तर, रंजकी

primer ('प्राइमर) *n.* प्राथमिक (पाठ्य-) पुस्तक, प्रवेशिका

primitive ('प्रिमिटिव़) *a.* आदिम, प्राचीन; असभ्य

prince ('प्रिन्स) *n.* राजकुमार; छोटे राज्य का शासक; प्रधान, अति उत्तम (**princess** *fem.*) – **princely** *a.* (व्यंगात्मक) मामूली (रकम); शानदार, ठाटबाट वाला

principal ('प्रिन्सिपल) *a.* मुख्य, प्रधान – *n.* प्रधान; नायक; प्राचार्य, प्रिंसिपल; मूलधन – **principality** *n.* राज्य, जागीर

principle ('प्रिन्सिपल) *n.* नैतिक सिद्धांत, नियम; आधारभूत कारण – **principled** *a.* सिद्धांत पर आधारित; सत्यनिष्ठ

print (प्रिंट) *vt.* मुद्रित करना, छापना; छपाई जैसा लिखना; *Photog.* निगेटिव से चित्र बनाना; कपड़े पर रंगीन डिज़ाइन छापना – *n.* छपाई; मुद्रित सामग्री; छपाई जैसा लिखा हुआ; फोटोग्राफ; छापा; ठप्पा; छपा हुआ कपड़ा – **printer** *n.* मुद्रक – **printed circuit** इलेक्ट्रानिकी सरकिट जिसमें विद्युत-रोधी आधार (शीट) पर विभिन्न तारें बनी होती हैं – **print-out** *n.* कम्प्यूटर, टेलीप्रिंटर से निकलने वाली छपी सामग्री

prior (ˈप्राइअर) *a.* पहले का – **priority** (प्राइˈऑरिटि) *n.* प्राथमिकता – **prior to** से पहले- **prioritize** *vt.* महत्व के अनुसार विभिन्न कार्य, समस्याऐं आदि लगाकर क्रम में रखना

prism (ˈप्रिज़्म) *n.* प्रिज़्म, समपार्श्व जो सूर्य किरणों को इसके विभिन्न रंगों में बांट देता है – **prismatic** (प्रिज़्ˈमैटिक) *a.* समपार्श्वीय, इंद्रधनुषी, चमकीला

prison (ˈप्रिज़न) *n.* जेलखाना, कारागार – **prisoner** *n.* कैदी, बंदी

private (ˈप्राइविट) *a.* निजी, व्यक्तिगत; गुप्त; एकांतिक; साधारण; गैर सरकारी – *n.* (सबसे नीचे पद का) सामान्य सैनिक; (लिफाफे पर) निजी – **privacy** (ˈप्राइवसि, ˈप्रिवसि) *n.* एकांत, गोपनीयता – **privately** *adv.* – **private enterprise** निजी उपक्रम/उद्योग – **private parts** गुप्तांग – **privatize** *vt.* (उद्योग आदि) का निजीकरण करना

privation (प्राइˈवेशन) *n.* सुख-साधनों का अभाव, तंगी

privilege (ˈप्रिविलिज) *n.* विशेषाधिकार; अधिकार, वर्ग विशेष को प्राप्त विशेष सुविधाएं – **privileged** *a.* विशेष सुविधाएं प्राप्त (वर्ग अथवा व्यक्ति)

privy (ˈप्रिवि) *a.* जिसे गुप्त जानकारी हो

prize (ˈप्राइज़) *n.* पुरस्कार, इनाम; पुरस्कार में प्राप्त वस्तु (जैसे लाटरी में) – *a.* श्रेष्ठ पुरस्क त अथवा जिसकी पुरस्कार पाने की संभावना हो (जैसे चित्र आदि) – *vt.* महत्व देना; सम्मान देना

pro[1] (ˈप्रो) *a./adv.* के पक्ष में – **the pros and cons** पक्ष और विपक्ष में कही जा सकने वाली बातें

pro[2] *n.* पेशेवर व्यक्ति– *a.* पेशेवर

pro- (*comb. form*) प्रति-, उप-,पूर्व- अग्र- जैसे **proconsul**

proactive (प्रोˈऐक्टिव)*a.*, सक्रिय समर्थक

probable (ˈप्रॉबबल) *a.* संभावित – **probability** (प्रॉबˈबिलिटि) *n.* संभावना – **probably** *adv.* शायद

probation (प्रˈबेशन) *n.* परिवीक्षा, परख-अवधि – **probationer** *n.* परिवीक्षार्थी – **on probation** (कर्मचारी) जिसकी परिवीक्षा चल रही हो

probe (प्रोब) *vt.* ध्यान से खोज-बीन करना; जांच-पड़ताल करना; खोद-खोद कर पूछना – *n.* सलाईनुमा डाक्टरी जांच का औज़ार; पूरी तहकीकात, जांच

probity (ˈप्रोबिटि) *n.* ईमानदारी, सत्यनिष्ठा

problem (ˈप्रॉब्लम) *n.* समस्या, मामला; प्रश्न – **problematic(al)** *a.* संदिग्ध; अनिश्चित; जटिल

proceed (प्रˈसीड) *vi.* आगे बढ़ना, (काम) जारी रखना; (काम) चलते रहना – **proceeds** *pl. n.* विक्रय आदि से प्राप्त आय, लाभ – **procedural** (प्रˈसीजरल) *a.* – **procedure** (प्रˈसीजर) *n.* कार्य प्रणाली, कार्य विधि – **proceeding** *n.* कार्यवाही, कारवाई– *pl.* सभा का कार्य विवरण; मुकदमा, कानूनी कार्रवाई

process (ˈप्रोसेस) *n.* क्रिया या परिवर्तन की श्रंखला; प्रक्रम; प्रक्रिया; विधि; मुकदमा, कार्यवाही – *vt.* उत्पादन आदि की विशेष प्रणाली से (वस्तु) तैयार करना – **processing** *n.* तैयारी की प्रक्रिया (किसी वस्तु की) – **procession** (प्रˈसेशन) *n.* जलूस – **processor** *n.* – *Computers* कम्प्यूटर का वह भाग जो उसकी सारी कार्य प्रणाली को संचालित करता है; तैयार करने वाला (जैसे *food processor*)

proclaim (प्रˈक्लेम) *vt.* सार्वजनिक घोषणा करना – **proclamation** (प्रॉक्लˈमेशन) *n.* घोषणा, एलान

proclivity (प्र´क्लिविटि) *n.* झुकाव, प्रवति

procrastinate (प्रो´क्रैस्टिनेट) *vi.* देर लगाना, टालना – **procrastination** *n.*

procreate (´प्रोक्रिएट) *vi.* (सन्तान) उत्पन्न करना, पैदा करना – **procreation** (प्रोक्रि´एशन) *n.* प्रजनन; उत्पत्ति

proctor (´प्रॉक्अर) *n.* विश्वविद्यालय में कुलानुशासक, प्रॉक्टर

procure (प्र´क्युअर) *vt.* प्राप्त करना, पाना; दिलाना, प्रबंध करना – *vi.* वेश्या की दलाली करना – **procurement** *n.* प्राप्ति; मुख्तारी; प्रबंध

prod (प्रॉड) *vt.* कोंचना, खोदना (**-dd-**) – *n.* अंकुश, खोदनी

prodigal (´प्रॉडिगल) *a.* फिजूल खर्च – *n.* फिजूलखर्च व्यक्ति – **prodigality** *n.* फिजूल खर्ची

prodigy (´प्रॉडिजि) *n.* विलक्षण प्रतिभावान व्यक्ति; अद्‌भुत वस्तु – **prodigious** (प्र´डिजस) *a.* बड़ा, विशाल, असाधारण

produce *vt.* (प्र´ड्यूस) उत्पन्न करना, पैदा करना, बनाना; तैयार करना; पेश करना; नाटक, फिल्म, टेलीविज़न का कार्यक्रम (अभिनय के लिए) प्रस्तुत करना – *n.* (´प्रॉड्यूस) उपज, उत्पादन – **producer** *n.* उत्पादक, (फ़िल्म आदि का), निर्माता – **product** (प्र´डक्ट) *n.* उत्पादन; गुणनफल – **production** (प्र´डक्शन) *n.* उत्पादन क्रिया; उपज, उत्पादन – **productive** *a.* उपजाऊ; सर्जनात्मक – **productivity** *n.* उत्पादकता

Prof. Professor का संक्षेप

profane (प्र´फ़ेन) *a.* ; ईशनिंदात्मक, अधर्मी, अपवित्र – *vt.* दूषित या अपवित्र करना – **profanity** (प्र´फैनिटि) *n.* (ईश) निंदात्मक कथन अथवा आचरण, गाली

profess (प्र´फ़ेस) *vt.* में विश्वास प्रकट करना; खुले आम कहना, घोषित करना; का अभिनय करना – **professedly** (प्र´फ़ेसिड्लि) *adv.* प्रकट रूप से – **profession** (प्र´फ़ेशन) *n.* जीविका व्यवसाय, पेशा विशे. उच्च शिक्षा, विज्ञान, कला संबंधी – **professional** *a.* (डाक्टर, वकील आदि) व्यावसायिक, पेशेवर (खिलाड़ी) – *n.* पेशेवर खिलाड़ी –**professor** (प्र´फ़ेसर) *n.* प्रोफ़ेसर, प्राध्यापक – **professorial** (प्रॉफ़ि´सॉरिअल) *a.* प्रोफेसर, प्राध्यापक, आचार्य

proffer (´प्रॉफ़र) *n./vt.* भेंट (देना)

proficient (प्र´फ़िशंट) *a.* दक्ष, कुशल – **proficiency** (प्र´फ़िशंसि) *n.* दक्षता, कुशलता

profile (´प्रोफ़ाइल) *n.* रूपरेखा, चेहरे का एक ओर का चित्र, पार्श्व चित्र; संक्षिप्त जीवनी

profit (´प्रॉफ़िट) *n.* लाभ – *vi.* (से) लाभ होना या उठाना; हितकर होना – **profitable** *a.* लाभकारी – **profiteer** (प्रॉफ़ि´टीअर) *n.* मुनाफ़ाखोर – *vi.* मुनाफ़ाखोरी करना – **profitless** *a.* लाभहीन, बेकार

profligate (´प्रॉफ़्लिगिट) *a.* चरित्रहीन

profound (प्र´फ़ाउंड) *a.* ज्ञानपूर्ण; गहरा – **profundity** (प्र´फ़न्‌डिटि) *n.* गहराई; गूढ़ता

profuse (प्र´फ़्यूस) *a.* खूब; उदार – **profusion** (प्र´फ़्यूझ़न) *n.* प्रचुरता

progeny (´प्रॉजिनि) *n.* संतान, बच्चे – **progenitor** (प्रो´जेंनिटर) *n.* पूर्वज

programme, US program (´प्रोग्रैम) *n.* योजना; कार्यक्रम, प्रोग्राम – **program** *n.* कम्प्यूटर के लिए विस्त त निर्देश, प्रोग्राम – *vt.* कम्प्यूटर के लिए निर्देश तैयार व नियोजित करना (**-mm-**) – **programmer** *n.* कम्प्यूटर का प्रोग्राम तैयार करने वाला

progress *n.* (´प्रोग्रेस) विकास, उन्नति, प्रगति – *vi.* (प्र´ग्रेस) अग्रसर होना, आगे बढ़ना, उन्नति

करना, सुधरना – **progression** (प्र'ग्रेशन) *n.* सुनिश्चित प्रगति; अग्रगमन – **progressive** *a.* क्रमिक; प्रगतिशील (व्यक्ति)

prohibit (प्र'हिबिट) *vt.* निषेध करना, मना करना – **prohibition** (प्रोइ'बिशन) *n.* मनाही; मद्य-निषेध, शराबबंदी – **prohibitive** (प्र'हिबिटिव़) *a.* निषेधात्मक; बहुत ऊंची (कीमतें) – **prohibitory** *a.* निषेधात्मक

project *n.* ('प्रॉजेक्ट) परियोजना– *vt.* (प्र'जेक्ट) योजना बनाना; दूर फेंकना; दूर प ष्ठभूमि पर दिखाना – *vi.* आगे निकला हुआ होना – **projectile** (प्र'जेक्टाइल) *n.* प्रक्षेपास्त्र – *a.* फेंकने वाली (वस्तु), प्रक्षेपक – **projection** (प्र'जेक्शन) *n.* – **projectionist** *n.* फिल्म प्रोजेक्अर चलाने वाला व्यक्ति – **projector** (प्र'जेक्टर) *n.* पर्दे पर फ़िल्म दिखाने का उपकरण, प्रोजेक्टर

proletariat (प्रोलि'टेंअरिअट) *n.* सर्वहारा; श्रमजीवी वर्ग – **proletarian** *a./n.*

proliferate (प्रो'लिफ़रेट) *v.* तेज़ी से बढ़ना – **proliferation** *n.* फैलाव, बढ़ाव

prolific (प्र'लिफ़िक) *a.* उर्वर, अधिक उत्पन्न करने वाला

prolong (प्र'लॉङ्ग) *vt.* बढ़ाना, लम्बा करना – **prolongation** (प्रोलॉङ्'गेशन) *n.* बढ़ाने/लम्बा करने की क्रिया

promenade (प्रॉम'नाड) *n.* चहलकदमी; (समुद्र तट पर) विचरण स्थल

prominent ('प्रॉमिनंट) *a.* बाहर निकला हुआ; आसानी से नज़र आने वाला; विशिष्ट; विख्यात– **prominence** *n.*

promiscuous (प्र'मिस्क्युअस) *a.* अविवेकी, स्वच्छंद विशे. यौन-संबंधों में

promise ('प्रॉमिस) *v.* वचन देना, वादा करना – *vi.* की संभावना होना – *n.* प्रतिज्ञा, वचन – **promising** *a.* आशाजनक; होनहार

promote (प्र'मोट) *vt.* तरक्की देना; समर्थन देना, बढ़ावा देना; की बिक्री बढ़ाने का प्रयत्न करना – **promoter** *n.* संगठनकर्ता, आयोजक – **promotion** (प्र'मोशन) *n.* पदोन्नति, बढ़ावा

prompt (प्रॉम्प्ट) *a./adv.* तत्काल, ठीक समय पर; तत्पर – *n.* कम्प्यूटर पर संकेत – *v.* प्रोत्साहन देना; सुझाना, जताना; रंगमंच पर पीछे से बोलकर अभिनेता या वक्ता की सहायता करना, अनुबोधन करना – **prompter** *n.* अनुबोधक

promulgate ('प्रॉमल्गेट) *vt.* घोषित करना, जारी करना – **promulgation** *n.* , लागू किया जाना

prone (प्रोन) *a.* अधोमुख, मुंह के बल पड़ा हुआ; (की ओर) प्रव त, झुकाव रखने वाला

pronoun ('प्रोनाउन) *n.* सर्वनाम

pronounce (प्र'नाउन्स) *vt.* (शब्द) उच्चारित करना; सुनाना – *vi.* अपना मत प्रकट करना – **pronounced** *a.* सुस्पष्ट, सुनिश्चित – **pronunciation** (प्रनन्सि'एशन) *n.* उच्चारण

proof ('प्रूफ़) *n.* प्रमाण, सबूत; परीक्षण, जांच; छपाई में प्रूफ़; मादक पेय की तीव्रता का मानक – *a.* अभेध, जो पूरा बचाव, सुरक्षा दे

prop (प्रॉप) *n/vt.* सहारा (देना) **(-pp-)**

propaganda (प्रॉप'गैंड्अ) *n.* राजनीतिक प्रचार, मत-प्रचार – **propagandist** *n.* प्रचारक

propagate ('प्रॉपगेट) *vt.* उपजाना; बढ़ाना, फैलाना, प्रचार करना – *vi.* उत्पन्न करना, पैदा करके संख्या बढ़ाना – **propagation** (प्रॉप'गेशन) *n.*

propel (प्र'पेल) *vt.* आगे धकेलना, ठेलना, नोदन करना **(-ll-)** – **propeller** (प्र'पेलर) *n.* प्रोपेलर, जहाज़ या वायुयान में लगा पंखेनुमा यंत्र – **propulsion** (प्र'पल्शन) *n.* आगे बढ़ाने की क्रिया, नोदन

propensity (प्र'पेंन्सिटि) *n.* झुकाव, प्रवृत्ति, रुचि

proper ('प्रॉपर) *a.* उचित, उपयुक्त; सही; *Grammar* व्यक्तिवाचक (संज्ञा) – **properly** *adv.* उचित ढंग से

property ('प्रॉपर्टि) *n.* सम्पत्ति, स्वामित्व; गुण, विशेषता

prophet ('प्रॉफ़िट) *n.* पैग़म्बर, नबी; भविष्य वक्ता; प्रवर्तक (**-tess** *fem.*) – **prophecy** ('प्रॉफ़िसि) *n.* भविष्यवाणी – **prophesy** ('प्रॉफ़िसाइ) *vi.* भविष्यवाणी करना – **prophetic** (प्र'फेंटिक) *a.* भविष्य सूचक; पैगम्बरी – **prophetically** *adv.*

proportion (प्र'पॉर्शन) *n.* अनुपात, समानुपात; तुलना; अंश – (~**s**) *pl.* आकार मापन – *vt.* के अनुपात में, रखना – **proportional, proportionate** *a.* ठीक अनुपात में – **proportionally** *adv.* अनुपात से

propose (प्र'पोज़) *vt.* प्रस्ताव रखना, सुझाव देना; (चुनाव आदि के लिए) किसी का नाम प्रस्तुत करना; इरादा करना – *vi.* विवाह का प्रस्ताव रखना – **proposal** *n.* प्रस्ताव, विवाह-प्रस्ताव – **proposer** *n.* प्रस्तावक – **proposition** (प्रॉप'ज़िशन) *n.* प्रस्ताव, कथन

propound (प्र'पाउंड) *vt.* विचारार्थ अथवा समाधान रूप में प्रस्तुत करना

proprietor (प्र'प्राइटर) *n.* स्वामी, मालिक (दुकान, होटल आदि का) (**– tress,–trix** *fem.*) – **proprietary** (प्र'प्राइटरि) *a.* मालिकाना, उत्पादन के एक मात्र अधिकार वाली फर्म द्वारा निर्मित (वस्तु)

propriety (प्र'प्राइअटि) *n.* औचित्य, उचित आचरण

propulsion (प्र'पल्शन) दे. PROPEL

pro rata ('प्रो'राट्अ) *Lat.* अनुपात में

prosaic (प्रो'ज़ेइक) *a.* घिसा-पिटा

proscribe (प्रो'स्क्राइब) *vt.* गैरकानूनी करार देना; (पुस्तक आदि) बाधित करना

prose (प्रोज़) *n.* गद्य

prosecute ('प्रॉसिक्यूट) *vt.* चालू रखना; पर मुकदमा चलाना, के विरुद्ध कानूनी कार्रवाई करना – **prosecution** *n.* मुकदमा चलाने या कानूनी कार्रवाई करने का काम; वाद पक्ष, इस्तग़ासा – **prosecutor** *n.* (**public prosecutor** भी) मुक़दमा चलाने वाला अधिकारी (**-trix** *fem.*)

prospect *n.* ('प्रास्पेंक्ट) संभावना; आशा; दृश्य – *v.* (प्र'स्पेंक्ट) खोजना विशे. सोना, पूर्वेक्षण करना – **prospective** (प्रस्'पेंक्टिव़) *a.* प्रत्याशित; भावी – **prospectus** (प्र'स्पेंक्टस) *n.* कम्पनी, स्कूल आदि की विवरण-पत्रिका

prosper ('प्रॉस्पर) *v.* उन्नति करना, फलना- फूलना – **prosperity** (प्रॉ'स्पेंरिटि) *n.* समृद्धि, सम्पन्नता – **prosperous** ('प्रॉस्परस) *a.* समृद्ध

prostitute ('प्रॉस्टिट्यूट) *n.* वेश्या – *vt.* वेश्यावृत्ति करना; दुरुपयोग करना – **prostitution** (प्रॉस्टि'ट्यूशन) *n.* वेश्यावृत्ति

prostrate *a.* ('प्रॉस्ट्रेट) दण्डवत; (ज़मीन पर) पड़ा हुआ; धराशायी – *vt.* (प्रॉस्'ट्रेट) धराशायी कर देना; थका देना – **prostration** (प्रॉस्'ट्रेशन) *n.*

protagonist (प्रो'टैगनिस्ट) *n.* नायक; नेता; समर्थक

protect (प्र'टेंक्ट) *vt.* रक्षा करना, बचाना, संरक्षण प्रदान करना; सुरक्षित रखना – **protection** *n.* रक्षा; संरक्षण – **protective** *a.* संरक्षण देने/बचाव करने वाला – **protector** *n.* संरक्षक, रीजेंट, प्रतिशासक

protégé ('प्रोटिझे) *n.* आश्रित, रक्षित (-ée *fem.*)

protein ('प्रोटीन) *n.* प्रोटीन, भोजन में एक पौष्टिक तत्व

protest *n.* ('प्रोटेंस्ट) विरोध, प्रतिवाद; असहमति – *vi.* (प्र'टेंस्ट) विरोध प्रकट करना – **protester** *n.* विरोधकर्ता – **protestation** (प्रोटेस्'टेशन) *n.* कड़ा विरोध, जोरदार घोषणा/इज़हार

Protestant (´प्रॉटिस्टंट) *n.* ईसाई धर्म में प्रोटेस्टेंट चर्च से संबंधित; प्रोटेस्टेंट चर्च का अनुनायी – **Protestantism** *n.* प्रोटेस्टैंट धर्म

protocol (´प्रोटकॉल) *n.* राजनयिक शिष्टाचार नियम; संधि, समझौते का पूर्वलेख (ड्राफ्ट); कम्प्यूटरों के बीच आकड़ों के आदान-प्रदान के नियम

proton (´प्रोटॉन) *n.* , प्रोटॉन

prototype (´प्रोटटाइप) *n.* आदि प्ररूप, मूल; आदर्श

protract (प्र´ट्रैक्ट) *vt.* लम्बा करना; खींचना; बढ़ाना

protrude (प्र´ट्रूड) *v.* बाहर या आगे निकला हुआ होना, बहिस त

protuberant (प्र´ट्यूबरंट) *a.* उभरा हुआ – **protuberance** *n.* उभार

proud (प्राउड) *a.* अभिमानी, घमंडी, अक्खड़; गर्वीला, स्वाभिमानी; शानदार, वैभवशाली – **proudly** *adv.*

prove (प्रूव़) *vt.* सिद्ध करना, प्रमाणित करना – *vi.* सिद्ध होना, प्रमाणित होना (**proved, proven** *pp.*) – **proven** *a.* सिद्ध, प्रमाणित

provender (´प्राविंडर) *n.* चारा

proverb (´प्रॉव़र्ब) *n.* कहावत, लोकोक्ति – **proverbial** *a.* लोक-प्रसिद्ध

provide (प्र´व़ाइड) *vi.* का प्रबंध करना – *vt.* देना, आवश्यकताओं की पूर्ति करना, मुहैया करना; तैयारी करना – **provider** *n.* प्रबंधक, संभरक – **provided that** बशर्ते कि

provident (´प्रॉव़िडंट) *a.* मितव्ययी, कम खर्च; दूरदर्शी – **providence** *n.* ईश्वर, विधाता; मितव्ययता – **providential** (प्रॉवि´डेंन्शल) *a.* सौभाग्य से

province (´प्रॉव़िन्स) *n.* प्रान्त, क्षेत्र, प्रदेश, कार्यक्षेत्र –*pl.* राजधानी के अतिरिक्त देश का कोई भी भाग – **provincial** (प्र´विन्शल) *a.* प्रान्तीय, प्रादेशिक; संकीर्ण द ष्टिकोण वाला – *n.* देहाती, (राजधानी में) बाहर से आया हुआ

provision (प्र´व़िझन) *n.* व्यवस्था विशे. भविष्य की आवश्यकताओं के लिए; सामग्री, भण्डार – (~ **s**) *pl.* रसद, खाद्य सामग्री; *Law* धारा – *vt.* रसद पहुंचाना या दिलाना – **provisional** *a.* अस्थायी

proviso (प्र´व़ाइज़ो) *n.* शर्त, प्रतिबंध (*pl.* **-os**)

provoke (प्र´व़ोक) *vt.* चिढ़ाना; उत्तेजित करना, उभाड़ना – **provocation** (प्रॉव़´केशन) *n.* उत्तेजना; कारण – **provocative** (प्र´व़ॉकटिव़) *a.* उत्तेजक

prowess (´प्राउइस) *n.* पराक्रम; कौशल

prowl (प्राउल) *vi.* (**prowl about** भी) छिपे-छिपे घूमना विशे. शिकार की खोज में या चोरी के लिए – *n.* खोज – **prowler** *n.*

proximity (प्रॉक्´सिमिटि) *n.* निकटता

proxy (´प्रॉक्सि) *n.* मुख्तार, किसी की ओर से कार्य करने का अधिकार प्राप्त व्यक्ति, परोक्षी; ऐसे अधिकार का पत्र, प्रतिपत्र, मुख्तारी

prude (प्रूड) *n.* व्यक्ति जो यौन सम्बंधी बातों से नाक चिढ़ाये – **prudery** *n.* – **prudish** *a.*

prudent (´प्रूडंट) *a.* सावधान, विवेकपूर्ण, समझदार – **prudence** *n.* समझदारी

prune[1] (प्रून) *n.* सूखा आलू बुखारा

prune[2] *vt.* (सूखी व फालतू टहनियों की) कांट-छांट करना

prurient (´प्रूअरिअंट) *a.* कामुक (विचार आदि)

pry (प्राइ) *vi.* ताक-झांक करना, **US** जबरन खोलना (**pried, prying**)

PS Postscript का संक्षेप

psalm (साम) *n.* भजन, स्तोत्र-**psalmist** *n.* भजनकार

psephology (सें´फ़ॉलजि) *n.* आंकड़ों के आधार पर चुनाव-विश्लेषण – **psephologist** *n.*

pseud(o) (´स्यूडो) *n./a.* छद्म, नकली

pseudonym (´स्यूडनिम) *n.* छद्मनाम; उपनाम

psyche (´साइकि) *n.* मानस, चित्त – **psyched** (साइक्ट) *a.* उत्सुक व उत्तेजित

psychedelic (साइकि'डेलिक) *a.* द ष्टिभ्रम संबंधी

psychic ('साइकिक) *a.* सामान्य अनुभवों से परे अनुभूति संबंधी; आत्मिक; मानसिक, अति भौतिक – **psychiatric** (साइकि'ऐट्रिक) *a.* मनोविक ति संबंधी – **psychiatrist** (साइ'काइअट्रिस्ट) *n.* मनोरोग विशेषज्ञ – **psychiatry** (साइ'काइअट्रि) *n.* मनोरोग विज्ञान, मानसिक रोग चिकित्सा – **psychoanalysis** *n.* मनोविश्लेषण, मानसिक रोगों का अध्ययन व चिकित्सा– **psychoanalyst** *n.* मनोविश्लेषक – **psychological** *a.* मनोवैज्ञानिक, **psychologist** (साइ'कॉलजिस्ट) *n.* मनोवैज्ञानी – **psychology** (साइ'कॉलजि) *n.* मनोविज्ञान – **psychopath** ('साइकोपैथ) *n.* मनोविक त व्यक्ति – **psychopathic** (साइको'पैथिक) *a.* मनोरोगमय –**psychotherapy** (साइको'थैरपि) *n.* (शारीरिक) रोग का मनौवैज्ञानिक ढंग से उपचार, मनश्चिकित्सा

PTO Please Turn Over का संक्षेप (क प्या प ष्ठ उलटिये)

pub (पब) *n.* (**public house** का संक्षेप) स्थान जहां शराब बिकती है व जहां यह पी जा सकती है

puberty ('प्यूबर्टि) *n.* यौवनारंभ

public ('पब्लिक) *a.* सार्वजनिक, आम, लोक- (निजी के विपरीत); जनता की सेवा में – *n.* आम जनता, जन साधारण – **publicly** *adv.* सार्वजनिक रूप से – **public address system** (संक्षेप **PA System**) सार्वजनिक संभाषण व्यवस्था (लाउडस्पीकर आदि) – **public limited company** सार्वजनिक कंपनी – **public convenience** जन सुविध ायें (*Toilet*) – **public holiday** सार्वजनिक छुट्टी

publicist ('पब्लिसिस्ट) *n.* जनहित के विषयों पर (समाचार पत्रों आदि में लेख) लिखने वाला; पत्रकार – **publicity** ('पब्लिसिटि) *n.* प्रचार, प्रसिद्धि – *a.* विज्ञापन संबंधी – **publicize** ('पब्लिसाइज) *vt.* (विज्ञापन द्वारा) प्रचार करना

publish ('पब्लिश) *vt.* प्रकाशित करना – **publication** (पब्लि'केशन) *n.* प्रकाशन – **publisher** *n.* प्रकाशक

pudding ('पुडिङ) *n.* एक मीठा पकवान, पुडिंग; हलवा; एक प्रकार की सासिज

puddle ('पड्ल) *n.* गंदे पानी से भरा गड्ढा

puerile ('प्युअराइल) *a.* बचकाना, मूर्खतापूण

puff (पफ़) *n.* झोंका; कश, फूंक; इसकी आवाज़ (जैसे इंजन से धुंआ निकलते समय); एक प्रकार की पेस्ट्री – *vi.* (सिगरेट आदि) फूंकना; हांफना – *vt.* धुंआ निकालना; फुलाना; विज्ञापन द्वारा प्रशंसा करना; (सिगरेट के) कश लगाना – **puffed** *a.* हांफता हुआ; फूला हुआ

puffin ('पफ़िन) *n.* एक समुद्री पक्षी, पफ़िन

pug (पग) *n.* चिपटी नाक वाला छोटा कुत्ता; *sl.* मुक्केबाज़ – **pug nose** चिपटी नाक

pugilist ('प्यूजिलिस्ट) *n.* मुक्केबाज

pugnacious (पग्'नेशस) *a.* लड़ाका – **pugnacity** *n.* झगड़ालूपन

puke (प्यूक) *vi. sl.* उलटी करना – *n.*

pull ('पुल) *vt.* खींचना; तानना; फाड़ना; (नाव) खेना – *n.* खिंचाई; इसमें लगी शक्ति; शराब की चुस्की या घूंट; *inf.* प्रभाव; ध्यान आकर्षित करने की शक्ति – **pull off** *inf.* (कार्य करने में) सफल हो जाना – **pull out** पीछे हट जाना – **pull sth down** (इमारत) गिरा देना – **pull sth off** कोई कठिन कार्य कर लेना– **pull the strings** घटना/व्यक्तियों पर नियंत्रण रखना

pulley ('पुलि) *n.* सामान उठाने की घिरनी, चरखी, गरारी

pulmonary ('पुल्मनरि) *a.* फेफड़े संबंधी

pulp (पल्प) *n.* (फल का) गूदा; (कागज़ आदि की) लुगदी – *vt.* मसल देना, लुगदी (के समान) बना देना

pulpit (´पुल्पिट) *n.* उपदेशक का प्रवचन-मंच
pulsar (´पल्सार) *n.* छोटा अत्यन्त सघन तारा जो रेडियो तरंगे छोड़ता है
pulse[1] (पल्स) *n.* नाड़ी, नब्ज़; कोई भी नियमित कम्पन या स्पंदन – **pulsate** *vi.* धड़कना, कम्पित होना – **pulsation** *n.*
pulse[2] (पल्स) *n.* दाल
pulverize (´पल्वराइज़) *vt.* चूर-चूर कर देना, पीस देना
puma (´प्यूमअ) *n.* अमरीका का एक बाघ जैसा मांसभक्षी जानवर
pumice (´पमिस) *n.* झाँवे के रूप में प्रयुक्त ज्वालामुखी से प्राप्त एक हल्का पत्थर
pummel (´पमल) *vt.* बार-बार मुक्कों से पिटाई करना
pump[1] (पम्प) *n.* पानी का पंप, हवा या द्रव आदि भरने या निकालने का पंप – *vt.* पंप से भरना या निकालना – *vi.* पंप चलाना, पंप के समान कार्य करना
pump[2] *n.* हल्का जूता
pumpkin (´पम्पकिन) *n.* कद्दू; लौकी
pun (पन) *n.* यमक, श्लेष – *vi.* श्लेष (यमक) का प्रयोग करना (**-nn-**)
punch[1] (पंच) *n.* छेद करने या छापा लगाने की मशीन, घूंसा; *inf.* बल, दम – *vt.* छापा लगाना, छेदना; घूंसा मारना
punch[2] *n.* शराब व फलों का रस, मसाला आदि मिलाकर बना पेय
punctual (´पंक्ट्युल) *a.* ठीक समय पर, यथा समय काम करने वाला – **punctuality** (पंक्ट्यु´ऐलिटि) *n.* समय निष्ठा
punctuate (´पंकट्युएट) *vt.* विराम चिन्ह (पूर्ण विराम, अर्ध विराम आदि) लगाना; बीच-बीच में रोकना – **punctuation** *n.* लेखन में लगाये गये विराम चिन्ह
puncture (´पंक्चर) *n.* छेद, पंक्चर – *vt.* छेद कर देना
pundit (´पंडिट) *n.* स्वयंभू विशेषज्ञ
pungent (´पंजंट) *a.* तीखा, तिक्त; *fig.* तिलमिला देने वाला (कथन आदि) – **pungency** *n.* तीखापन, तिक्तता
punish (´पनिश) *vt.* दण्ड देना, सज़ा देना; (किसी से) बहुत ज्यादा काम लेना – **punishable** *a.* दण्डनीय – **punishment** *n.* – **punitive** (´प्यूनिटिव़) *a.* सज़ा देने के लिए या सज़ा देने के इरादे से (कोई कदम)
punter (´पंटर) *n.* जुआरी, बाज़ी लगाने वाला
puny (´प्यूनि) *a.* छोटा व पतला-दुबला
pup (पप) *n.* पिल्ला; सील मछली का छोटा बच्चा
pupa (´प्यूप्अ) *n.* प्यूपा, कोष (*pl.* **pupae** (-पी)) – **pupal** *a.*
pupil (´प्यूपल) *n.* शिष्य; आंख की पुतली
puppet (´पपिट) *n.* कठपुतली – **puppeteer** (पपि´टिअर) *n.* कठपुतली नचाने वाला – **puppetry** *n.* कठपुतली बनाने व नचाने की कला
puppy (´पपि) *n.* पिल्ला
purchase (´पर्चिस) *vt.* ख़रीदना – *n.* ख़रीद; खरीदी हुई वस्तु; भारी बोझा खींचने का कांटा – **purchaser** *n.*
purdah (´पर्ड्अ) *n.* पर्दा-प्रथा, पर्दा
pure (प्युअर) *a.* शुद्ध, असली; साफ़, निर्मल; मासूम; पवित्र; केवल सिद्धांत से संबंधित – **purely** *adv.* – **purification** *n.* – **purificatory** *a.* – **purify** *vt.* शुद्ध करना (**-ified, -ifying**)– **purity** (´प्युअरिटि) *n.* शुद्धता, पवित्रता
puree (´प्युअरे) *n.* फल, सब्ज़ियों आदि का गूदे सहित निचोड़, - *vt.*
purgatory (´पर्गटरि) *n.* (रोमन कैथलिक चर्च में) अस्थायी नर्क
purge (पर्ज) *vt.* शुद्ध करना, साफ़ करना; हटाना; निकाल फेंकना – *n.* साफ करने, हटाने, निकाल

फेंकने आदि की क्रिया – **purgation** *n.* शुद्धिकरण –**purgative** *a./n.* जुलाब

purloin (पर्'लॉइन) *vt.* चोरी करना, चुपचाप (कुछ) गायब कर देना

purple ('पर्पल) *a./n.* जामुनी (रंग)

purport *vt.* (पर्'पॉर्ट) सत्य होने का दावा करना; संकेत या आभास देना; अर्थ रखना – *n.* ('पर्पॉर्ट) अभिप्राय, तात्पर्य

purpose ('पर्पस) *n.* प्रयोजन, कारण; उद्देश्य, इरादा; लक्ष्य – *vt.* प्रयोजन या उद्देश्य रखना – **purposeful** *a.* सोद्देश्य – **purposely** *adv.* – **on purpose** जानबूझ कर

purr (पर) *n.* बिल्ली की (पुचकारने पर) घुरघुराने की आवाज़ – *vi.* घुरघराना

purse ('पर्स) *n.* बटुआ; (धन) साधन; इनाम स्वरूप राशि – *vt.* (ओंठ) सिकोड़ना – *vi.* सिकुड़ना

pursue (पर्'स्यू) *vt.* पीछा करना; में लगा रहना; जारी रखना – *vi.* (पकड़ने के लिए) के पीछे जाना; जारी रखना – **pursuer** *n.* पीछा करने वाला – **pursuit** *n.* पीछा, खोज; व्यवसाय

purvey (पर्'वे) *vt.* (रसद) पहुंचाना या (उसका) प्रबंध करना

purview ('पर्व्यू) *n.* सीमा, क्षेत्र

pus (पस) *n.* पीप, मवाद

push (पुश) *vt.* ढकेलना, ठेलना, धक्का देना; आगे बढ़ाना, जोर डालना– *vi.* आगे बढ़ना; निरंतर प्रयास से प्रगति करना – *n.* धक्का; उत्साह व आत्मविश्वास; सैनिक अभियान, चढ़ाई – **pusher** *n.* ठेलने वाला; महत्वाकांक्षी व्यक्ति – **pushing** *a.* उत्साही व महत्वाकांक्षी – **push-button** केवल बटन दबा कर चलने वाला(टिलिफोन आदि) – **pushchair** *n.* बच्चा-गाड़ी

puss (पुस) *n.* बिल्ली; **pussy** भी

pustule ('पस्ट्यूल) *n.* पीप भरी फुंसी

put (पुट) *vt.* रखना; लगाना; (दबाव) डालना; (संगीत में) ढालना; व्यक्त करना; फेंकना (विशे. *shot-put* की खेल में गोला) (**put, putting**) – *n.* फेंक – **put across** व्यक्त करना – **put off** स्थगित करना; मायूस करना – **put up** (टैंट आदि) खड़ा करना; ठहराना; (उम्मीदवार) खड़ा करना – **put up with** सहन करना

putrid ('प्यूट्रिड) *a.* सड़ा हुआ – **putrefy** *v.* सड़ाना या सड़ना –**(-efied-efying)**– **putrefaction** (प्यूट्रि'फ़ैक्शन) *n.* सड़ने की क्रिया

puttee ('पटि) *n.* पैर पर लपेटने की पट्टी

putty ('पटि) *n.* शीशा लगाने व लकड़ी की वस्तुओं में सुराख भरने में प्रयुक्त पदार्थ, पुटीन; सुनार का (ज़ेवर) चमकाने का पाउडर

puzzle ('पज़ल) *v.* उलझन में डालना या पड़ना, चकराना, चकरा देना – *n.* पहेली, चकराने वाली समस्या या खिलौना; वर्ग पहेली – **puzzlement** *n.*

PVC polyvinyl chloride का संक्षेप, कत्रिम पदार्थ जो हल्की वस्तुएं (ब्रीफ़केस आदि) बनाने में प्रयुक्त होता है

pygmy, pigmy ('पिग्मि) *n.* बौना; **(-P-)** अफ़्रीका की एक बौना जाति का सदस्य, पिग्मी – *a.* बौना

pyramid ('पिरमिड) *n.* पिरैमिड, सूची-स्तंभ

pyre (पाइअर) *n.* चिता

pyrotechnics (पाइरो'टेक्निक्स) *n.* आतिशबाज़ी; पटाखों आदि का उत्पादन

python ('पाइथन) *n.* अजगर

Q

QED (*Lat.* quod erat demonstrandum का संक्षेप) जो सिद्ध करना था

qr. quarter; quire का संक्षेप

quack (क्वैक) *n.* बत्तख की काँ-काँ की आवाज़; नीम-हकीम, कठवैद्य – *vi.* (बत्तख़ का) काँ-काँ करना – **quackery** *n.* नीम-हकीमी

quad (क्वॉड) quadrangle; quadraphonic; quadruplet का संक्षिप्त रूप

quadr-, quadri- (*comb. form*) चार

quadrangle (ˈक्वॉड्रैंगल) *n.* चतुर्भुज; चुतुर्भुजीय चौक, प्रांगण – **quadrangular** *a.*

quadrant (ˈक्वॉड्रण्ट) *n.* व त्त का चतुर्थ भाग

quadraphonic (क्वाड्र ˈफ़ॉनिक) *a.* (संगीत आदि सुनने के लिए) चार अलग-अलग (लाउड) स्पीकर वाली ध्वनि-व्यवस्था

quadrilateral (क्वॉड्रि ˈलैटरल) *a.* चुतर्भुजी – *n.* चतुर्भुज

quadruped (ˈक्वॉड्रूपेंड) *n.* चौपाया

quadruple (ˈक्वॉड्रुपल) *a.* चौगुना – *v.* चौगुना हो जाना या कर देना

quadruplet (ˈक्वॉड्रुप्लिट) *n.* एक ही मां के चार एक साथ जन्मे बच्चों में से प्रत्येक, चतुष्क

quaff (क्वॉफ़) *v.* एक घूंट में बहुत सारा पी जाना

quag (क्वैग), **quagmire** (ˈक्वैग्माइअर) *n.* दलदल

quail[1] (क्वेल) *n.* बटेर

quail[2] *vi.* डरना, कांपना, घबरा जाना

quaint (क्वेंट) *a.* पुराने ढंग का या अजीब और दिलचस्प, सनकी

quake (क्वेक) *vi.* कांपना, सिहरना

qualify (ˈक्वालिफ़ाइ) *vi.* योग्य होना या बनना – *vt.* कम या हल्का कर देना; सीमित कर देना; योग्य बना देना; चुने जाना (**-fied, -fying**) – **qualification** (क्वॉलिफ़िˈकेशन) *n.* योग्यता; गुण; सीमा, प्रतिबंध

quality (ˈक्वॉलिटि) *n.* गुण, विशेषता, स्वभाव; योग्यता; लक्षण, धर्म – **qualitative** (ˈक्वॉलिटटिव़) *a.* गुणात्मक

qualm (ˈक्वाम) *n.* संदेह, आशंका (विश. किसी कार्य के नैतिक रूप से ठीक न होने की)

quandary (ˈक्वॉण्ड्रि) *n.* – **in a quandary** उलझन, दुविधा में

quantity (ˈक्वॉन्टिटि) *n.* निर्धारित या काफी अधिक राशि या संख्या – **quantify** (ˈक्वॉन्टिफ़ाइ) *vt.* का परिमाण बताना या निर्धारित करना – **quantitative** (ˈक्वॉन्टिटटिव़) *a.*

quarantine (ˈक्वॉरंटीन) *n.* छूत के रोग के रोगी को बिल्कुल अलग रखना ताकि रोग फैल न सके, संगरोधन – *vt.*

quarrel (ˈक्वॉरल) *n.* झगड़ा, गर्मा-गरम बहस, कलह – *vi.* झगड़ा करना, दोष निकालना (**-ll-**) – **quarrelsome** *a.* झगड़ालू

quarry[1] (ˈक्वॉरि) *n.* शिकार का पशु-पक्षी

quarry[2] *n.* खुली खान, खदान – *v.* खदान से (पत्थर) निकालना (**quarried, quarrying**)

quart (क्वॉर्ट) *n.* द्रव माप जो चौथाई गैलन या 1.1 लिटर के बराबर है

quarter (ˈक्वॉर्टर) *n.* चौथाई भाग; **US, C** 25 सैंट का सिक्का; 28 पाउंड के बराबर भार का माप; इलाका, क्षेत्र; दया, क्षमा – *pl.* निवास स्थान – *vt.* चार भागों में बांटना, ठहराना – **quarterly** *a.* त्रैमासिक, तिमाही – *n.* त्रैमासिक पत्रिका – **quarter-final** *n.* खेल प्रतिस्पर्धा का वह चरण जहां आठ खिलाड़ी/टीम रह जांय, क्वार्टर-फाइनल

quartz (क्वॉर्ट्स) *n.* क्वार्टज़, स्फटिक, कांचमणि

quasar (´क्वेज़ार) *n.* प थ्वी से बहुत दूर सितारे जैसा पिण्ड जो शक्तिशाली रेडियो तरंगे छोड़ता है, क्वेज़ार

quash (क्वॉश) *vt.* रद्द कर देना, (फैसला) उलट देना; कुचल देना, दबा देना

quasi- (´क्वेज़ाइ, ´क्वाज़ि) (*comb. form*) प्रतीयमानतः, लगने वाला

quatercentenary (क्वैटरसेंन्´टीनरि) *n.* चार सौंवी वर्षगांठ, चतुश्शती

quaver (´क्वेव़र) *vt.* थरथराते स्वर में बोलना या गाना – *vi.* (आवाज का) कांपना, थरथराना – *n. Music* अर्धपाद स्वर, स्वर कंपन

quay (´की) *n.* (**quay side** भी) जहाज़ी घाट

queasy (´क्वीज़ि) *a.* – **feel queasy** मिचली आना

queen (क्वीन) *n.* रानी; देश की शासिका महारानी; शतरंज में वज़ीर; (*queen bee*) रानी-मधु मक्खी; ताश में बेगम **queenly** *adv.* – **queen mother** सम्राट की माता, राजमाता

queer (क्विअर) *a.* विचित्र, अजीब, विलक्षण

quell (क्वेंल) *vt.* कुचल देना, दबा देना; शांत करना

quench (क्वेंन्च) *vt.* प्यास बुझाना; आग बुझाना

querulous (´क्वेंरूलस) *a.* शिकायती, चिड़चिड़ा (व्यक्ति)

query (´क्विअरि) *n.* प्रश्न, प्रश्न-चिन्ह – *vt.* पूछना (**queried, querying**)

quest (क्वेंस्ट) *n./vt.* खोज, तलाश (करना)

question (´क्वेंस्चन) *n.* प्रश्न, सवाल; समस्या, विवाद का विषय; संदेह का विषय – *vt.* प्रश्न पूछना, से पूछताछ करना; संदेह प्रकट करना, आपत्ति करना – **questionable** *a.* संदेहपूर्ण – **questionnaire** (क्वेंस्च´नेंअर) *n.* विषय-विशेष पर प्रश्नमाला, प्रश्नावली

queue (´क्यू) *n.* पंक्ति, कतार – *vi.* पंक्ति में खड़े होना

quibble (´क्विबल) *n.* निरर्थक बहस या आपत्ति, बहाना, टालमटोल – *v.* बाल की खाल निकालना

quick (क्विक) *a.* तेज, फुर्तीला – *n.* मर्म (स्थान), दर्द फौरन महसूस करने वाला (नाखून के नीचे) मांस – *adv.* जल्दी, तुरन्त – **quicken** *v.* तेज़ करना या होना, चाल बढ़ाना; सजीव या अधिक क्रियाशील होना या करना – **quickly** *adv.* – **quicklime** *n.* अनबुझा चूना – **quicksand** *n.* जान लेवा बलुआ दलदल – **quicksilver** *n.* पारा

quid pro quo (´क्विड प्रो´क्वो) *Lat.* बदले में दी गयी चीज़

quiet (´क्वाइअट) *a.* शांत, चुप, आडम्बरहीन, सादा – *n.* शांति, नीरवता – *v.* शांत करना या हो जाना – **quieten** *v.* शांत करना या हो जाना – **quietly** *adv.* चुपचाप, धीरे से – **quietness, quietude** (´क्वाइअट्यूड) *n.* शांति

quill (क्विल) *n.* बड़ा पंख; पंख-कलम; साही का कांटा

quilt (क्विल्ट) *n.* रज़ाई – *vt.* रजाई, गद्दी आदि बनाना

quinine (क्वि´नीन) *n.* कुनीन (मलेरिया की दवाई)

quintal (´क्विंटल) *n.* 100 किलोग्राम भार

quintuplet (´क्विन्ट्युप्लिट) *n.* एक ही माँ के एक साथ पैदा हुए पांच बच्चों में से एक, पंचज

quip (क्विप) *n./v.* चुटकुला (छोड़ना)

quire (क्वाइअर) *n.* कागज़ों का दस्ता

quirk (क्वर्क) *n.* व्यक्तिगत चारित्रिक विशेषता; (भाग्य का) आकस्मिक मोड़

quit (क्विट) *vi.* कुछ करना बंद कर देना; चले जाना – *vt.* छोड़ देना, से चले जाना; (नौकरी) छोड़ देना (**quitting** *pr. p.*, **quitted** *pt./pp.*)

quite (क्वाइट) *adv.* बिलकुल, पूर्णतया; कुछ सीमा तक – *interj.* बिल्कुल ठीक! ऐसा ही!

quiver¹ (´क्विवर) *vi.* कांपना, थरथराना – *n.* कम्पन

quiver^2 *n.* तरकश

quixotic (क्विक् 'सॉटिक) *a.* अव्यावहारिक

quiz (क्विज़) *n.* किसी विषय में ज्ञान-परीक्षण की प्रश्नोत्तरी; परीक्षा; पूछताछ (**-zz-**) – *vt.* प्रश्न पूछना, पूछताछ करना – **quizzical** *a.* प्रश्नात्मक; उपहासपूर्ण – **quizmaster** *n.* प्रश्नोंत्तरी कार्यक्रम में प्रश्नकर्ता

quorum ('कॉरम) *n.* कोरम, गणपूर्ति, उपस्थिति सदस्यों की न्यूनतम संख्या जो सभा की कार्यवाही की वैधता के लिए आवश्यक है

quota ('क्वोट्अ) *n.* कोटा, नियत अंश, नियत प्रवेश-संख्या (*pl.* **-s**)

quote (क्वोट) *vt.* उद्‌ध त करना; कथन पुष्टि हेतु उद्धरण देना; वस्तुओं का भाव बताना – **quotation** *n.* उद्धरण; भाव

quotient ('क्वोशंट) *n.* भागफल

q.v. *Lat. quod vide* (जिसे देखिए) का संक्षेप

R

rabbi (रैबाइ) *n.* यहूदी विद्वान अथवा धर्मगुरू (*pl.* **rabbis** (इज़))

rabbit (रैबिट) *n.* खरगोश

rabble (रैबल) *n.* शोर मचाते लोगों की भीड़; निम्न वर्ग

rabid (रैबिड) *a.* पागल (कुत्ता, बंदर आदि); प्रचण्ड, उग्र; कट्टर

rabies (रैबीज़) *n.* पागल कुत्ते आदि के काटने से उत्पन्न रोग, जलातंक, रैबीज़

raccoon, racoon (र'कून) *n.* उत्तरी अमरीका का एक छोटा रीछ जैसा प्राणी

race[1] (रेस) *n.* दौड़ प्रतियोगिता; प्रतिद्वंदिता, मुकाबला; तेज़ जल धारा विशे. पनचक्की की ओर जाती हुई – (~ **s**) *pl.* घुड़दौड़ – *vt.* तेजी से चलाना या दौड़ाना – *vi.* तेज़ी से दौड़ना; इंजन आदि का तेज़ी से घूमना – **racecourse** *n.* घुड़दौड़ का मैदान

race[2] (रेस) *n.* जाति, प्रजाति, नस्ल; वंश – **racial** (रेशल) *a.* – **racialism, racism** *n.* प्रजातिवाद, जातिवाद –**racialist** (रेशलिस्ट), **racist** *a./n.* जातिवाद समर्थक

rack[1] (रैक) *n.* (**luggage rack** भी) रखने का लकड़ी का रैक, टांड – *vt.* यातना देना – **racking** *a.* घोर (पीड़ा)

rack[2] (रैक) *n.* नाश, तबाही विशे. **rack and ruin** में

racket[1] (रैकिट) *n.* शोरगुल, हल्ला; धोखाधड़ी का धंधा – **racketeer** (रैकि'टिअर) *n.* ठग-व्यापारी – **racketeering** *n.* धोखाधड़ी

racket[2] *n.* टैनिस आदि खेलने का बल्ला, रैकट

raconteur (रैकॉन्'टर) *n.* कुशल कथा-वाचक, कहानी सुनाने वाला

racy (रेसि) *a.* सजीव, उत्साह भरा

radar (रेडार) *n.* रडार, एक इलेक्ट्रॉनिकी उपकरण जो रेडियो-तरंगों के द्वारा दूर किसी ठोस वस्तु की पहचान व स्थिति बता सकता है

radial (रेडिअल) दे. RADIUS

radiate (रेडिएट) *v.* विकिरण करना या होना (प्रकाश या ताप किरणों का); बिखेरना, केंद्र से चारों ओर फैलना/फैलाना – **radiance** (रेडिअन्स) *n.* कांति, चमक – **radiant** *a.* कांतिमय, चमकदार– **radiation** *n.* विकीरण, प्रसारण; नाभिक (न्यूक्लियर) क्षय में विकीरण होने वाले कण; (**radiation therapy** भी) विकीरण से कैंसर आदि का उपचार – **radiator** (रेडिएटर) *n.* कमरे के लिए हीटर; कार को ठण्डा रखने का उपकरण, रेडियेटर

radical (रैडिकल) *a.* आमूल, बुनियादी, पूर्ण; अतिवादी, उग्र – *n.* उग्र सुधारवादी; मूलांकुर, जड़ – **radicalism** *n.* अतिवाद, आमूल परिवर्तनवाद

radio (रेडिओ) *n.* रेडियो (प्रसारण साधन); रेडियो (यंत्र); रेडियो प्रसारण व कार्यक्रम – *vt.* बेतार द्वारा संदेश भेजना

radioactive (रेडिओ'ऐक्टिव़) *a.* रेडियोधर्मी (किरणें) – **radioactivity** *n.* रेडियोधर्मिता

radiography (रेडि'ऑग्रफ़ि) *n.* एक्स-रे चित्रण, विकिरणी चित्रण

radiology (रेडि'ऑलजि) *n.* विकिरण-चिकित्सा विज्ञान–**radiologist** *n.* विकिरण-चिकित्सा विशेषज्ञ – **radiotherapy** *n.* ऐक्सरे द्वारा रोग-निदान व उपचार, विकिरण-चिकित्सा

radio-telephone *n.* बेतार टेलीफोन

radio telescope सितारों की खोज व अंतरिक्षयान की स्थिति जानने में प्रयुक्त एक उपकरण

radish (रैडिश) *n.* मूली

radium (रेडिअम) *n.* रेडियोधर्मी धातु, रेडियम

radius (रेडिअस) *n.* व त्त में त्रिज्या, अर्धव्यास; बाज़ू

की हड्डी, बहिप्रकोष्ठिका (*pl.* **radii** (´रेडिआइ), **radiuses**) – **radial** *a.* त्रिज्यीय; किरणों का

raffle (´रैफ़ल) *n.* लाटरी जिसमें टिकट पर इनाम के रूप में वस्तुएं दी जाती हैं – *vt.* लाटरी द्वारा बांटना

raft (राफ़्ट) *n.* लकड़ी के लट्ठों का बेड़ा

rafter (´राफ़्टर) *n.* छत की एक मुख्य कड़ी

rag[1] (रैग) *n.* कपड़े का टुकड़ा, चिथड़ा; रैग टाइम संगीत की एक रचना –(~ **s**) *pl.* फटे कपड़े – **ragged** (´रैगिड) *a.* फटा-पुराना, जीर्ण-शीर्ण – **ragtime** *n.* जाज़ पियानो संगीत की शैली

rag[2] (रैग) *vt.* सताना, तंग करना, (विशे. कॉलिज में) मज़ाक करके परेशान करना

ragamuffin (´रैगमफ़िन) *n.* गंदा, फटेहाल व्यक्ति या लड़का

rage (रेज) *n.* रोष, बेहद गुस्सा – *vi.* आगबबूला होकर बोलना या कुछ करना; (तूफ़ान, युद्ध आदि का) प्रचण्ड हो जाना, (महामारी आदि) बुरी तरह फैल जाना – **all the rage** बहुत प्रचिलित, फ़ैशन में (है)

raid (रेड) *n.* छापा; हमला – *vt.* छापा मारना, हमला करना – **raider** *n.* छापामार

rail[1] (रेल) *n.* छड़ विशे. जंगले, घेरे की; रेल की पटरी – **railing** *n.* रेलिंग, घेरा, जंगला, बाड़ा – **railway** (´रेल्वे), US **railroad** *n.* रेलवे, रेल-व्यवस्था (**railways** *pl.* भी)

rail[2] (रेल) *vi.* गाली देना, घोर निंदा करना – **raillery** (´रेलरि) *n.* दिल्लगी

rail[3] (रेल) *n.* जलकुक्कुटी

rain (रेन) *n.* बारिश – *vi.* वर्षा होना – *vt.* की बौछार या भरमार करना या होना – **rainy** *a.* – **rainbow** (´रेन्बो) *n.* इन्द्रधनुष – **raincoat** *n.* बरसाती – **rainfall** *n.* वर्षा, वृष्टि-मात्रा – **rainforest** *n.* उष्ण-कटीबंधीय प्रदेशों का घना जंगल – **rain gauge** वर्षा मापी

raise (रेज़) *vt.* उठाना; खड़ा करना; निर्माण करना (मकान आदि); बढ़ाना, ऊपर उठाना, उन्नत करना; (आवाज़) ऊंची करना; (प्रश्न) उठाना; (मवेशी आदि) पालना; फसल उगाना; वसूल करना – *n.* बढ़ौती, वृद्धि

raisin (´रेज़न) *n.* किशमिश

rake[1] (रेक) *n.* घास आदि समेटने का पाँचा, जेली – *vt.* पाँचे से समेटना; सफाई करना; छानबीन करना; (मशीनगन से) एक सिरे से दूसरे तक गोलीबारी करना

rake[2] *n.* लम्पट, दुश्चरित्र – **rakish** *a.*

rally (´रैलि) *vt.* पुन: एकत्र करना विशे. बिखरे हुओं को – *vi.* एकत्र होना; स्वास्थ्य लाभ करना, संभल जाना; मजबूत स्थिति में आना (शेयर आदि) (**rallied, rallying**) – *n.* रैली, जमघट, कार आदि की रैली; *Tennis* खिलाड़ियों का देर तक लगातार एक दूसरे की ओर गेंद पर स्ट्रोक लगाना

RAM (रैम) *Computers* **Random Access Memory** का संक्षेप

ram (रैम) *n.* मेढ़ा, मेष; टक्कर मारने या कूटने का यंत्र, दुरमूट – *vt.* टक्कर मारना, कूटना, ठूंसना (**-mm-**)

Ramadan (रैम´डान) *n.* रमज़ान

ramble (´रैम्बल) *vi.* भ्रमण, सैर करना, बहकी-बहकी बातें करना; (मकान आदि) बेतरतीबी से फैले या बने होना – *n.* सैर

ramification (रैमिफ़ि´केशन) *n.* शाखा विस्तार, बंट जाने की क्रिया; परिणाम, महत्व

ramp (रैम्प) *n.* ढाल, ढलान (दो तलों या मंज़िलों को जोड़ने वाला)

rampage *vi* (रैम्´पेज) तोड़-फोड़ करना – *n.* (´रैम्पेज) क्रोधोन्माद, तोड़-फोड़

rampant (´रैम्पंट) *a.* उग्र, फैला हुआ

rampart (´रैम्पार्ट) *n.* सुरक्षा के लिए बना परकोटा

ramshackle (´रैम्शैकल) *a.* टूटा-फूटा

ran (रैन) RUN का *pt.*

ranch (रांच) *n.* अमरीका में पशु-पालन के लिए फार्म, पशु फार्म – **rancher** *n.*

rancid (रैन्सिड) *a.* (मक्खन आदि) बासी, खट्टा

rancour (रैंकर) *n.* अत्यधिक घृणा

random (रैंडम) *a.*, बेतरतीब – **random access memory (RAM)** *Computers* कम्प्यूटर की स्मृति (आंकड़े संग्रह-स्थल) जहां आंकड़े/जानकारी बदली, हटायी या किसी भी क्रम में देखी जा सकती है – **at random** यों ही, यादृच्छया

rang **RING** का *pt.*

range (रेंज) *n.* सीमा; पंक्ति; पहुँच; क्षेत्र; दूरी, परास; चांद मारी का मैदान; श्रेणी, वर्ग; एक प्रकार का चूल्हा – *vt.* क्रमबद्ध करना, वर्गीकृत करना; घूमना, विचरना – *vi.* फैल जाना; विचरना; एक छोर से दूसरे तक पहुँचना; (कीमतों में) उतार-चढ़ाव होना – **ranger** *n.* पार्क, वन आदि का रखवाला, रेंजर

rank[1] (रैंक) *n.* पंक्ति; क्रम; सामाजिक वर्ग; पद, दर्जा –(~**s**)*pl.* सामान्य सैनिक; जन साधारण (**rank and file** भी) – *vt.* पंक्तिबद्ध करना, वर्गीकृत करना – *vi.* पद, श्रेणी, स्थान होना; विशेषता होना

rank[2] *a.* बहुत फैलने वाला; गंवारू

rankle (रैंकल) *vi.* कड़ुवाहट का कारण बने रहना, कसकना

ransack (रैन्सैक) *vt.* , छान मारना; लूट लेना

ransom (रैन्सम) *n.* फिरौती, मुक्तिधन – *vt.* की फिरौती देना

rant (रैंट) *vi.* बकना, प्रलाप करना

rap[1] (रैप) *n.* ठक-ठक, खटखट – *v.* ठकठकाना – *vi.* संगीत की लय पर गुनगुनाना **(-pp-)**

rapacious (र'पेशस) *a.* लोभी, लालची – **rapacity** (र'पैसिटि) *n.* लालच; हिंसात्मक प्रवृत्ति

rape[1] (रेप) *vt.* बलात्कार करना – *n.* बलात्कार; – **rapist** *n.* बलात्कारकारी

rape[2] *n.* पौधा जिसके सरसों जैसे दानों **(rapeseed)** का तेल निकलता है, तोरिया

rapid (रैपिड) *a.* तेज़, शीघ्रगामी – **rapidity** (र'पिडिटि) *n.* तेज़ी, शीघ्रता – **rapidly** *adv.* – **rapids** *pl. n.* नदी का तेज धार वाला भाग

rapport (रे'पॉर) *n.* घनिष्ठता, तालमेल

rapprochement (रैप्रॉश्'मॉ) *n.* पुनर्मेल, विशे. राष्ट्रों का

rapt (रैप्ट) *a.* तल्लीन, भावमग्न – **rapture** (रैप्चर) *n.* अत्यधिक प्रसन्नता, हर्षातिरेक – **rapturous** *a.* अति प्रसन्न, हर्षोन्मत्त

rare (रेंअर) *a.* असाधारण, कभी-कभी होने वाली (घटना आदि), दुर्लभ; विरल – **rarely** (रेअर्लि) *adv.* कभी-कभी – **rarity** (रेंअरिटि) *n.* दुर्लभ वस्तु; विरलता; दुष्प्राप्यता

raring (रेंअरिङ) *a.* – **raring to go** किसी काम के लिए तत्पर या तैयार

rascal ('रास्कल) *n.* बदमाश; शरारती (युवा) व्यक्ति

rash[1] (रैश) *a.* जल्दबाज़, लापरवाह – **rashly** *adv.* अंधाधुंध

rash[2] *n.* शरीर पर छोटे-छोटे दाने; एक-सी कई (बुरी) घटनाओं का तांता

rasp (रास्प) *n.* कानों को अखरने वाली किरकिराने की आवाज़; मोटी रेती (औज़ार) – *v.* रेती से रगड़ना; किरकिराना; कर्कश स्वर में बोलना; अखरना

raspberry ('राज़्बरि) *n.* रसभरी (फल)

rat (रैट) *n.* चूहा – *vi.* (*on* के साथ) किसी के बारे में भेद देना, दग़ा देना, साथ छोड़ना **(tt–)** – **rat race** जीवन में सफलता के लिए होड़

rate (रेट) *n.* दर, भाव; गति – **(rates)** *pl.* स्थानीय सम्पत्ति-कर – *vt.* मूल्य निर्धारित करना– **at any rate** फिर भी

rather ('रादर) *adv.* कुछ-कुछ; बल्कि; अधिक पसंद

ratify (रैटिफ़ाइ) *vt.* (समझौता आदि की) संपुष्टि करना, अनुसमर्थन करना (**-ified -ifying**) – **ratification** (रैटिफ़ि´केशन) *n.* सम्पुष्टि, अनुसमर्थन

rating (रैटिंग) *n.* मूल्य निर्धारण, दर निर्धारण; वर्गीकरण विशे. जहाज़ का; नाविक

ratio (रैशिओ) *n.* अनुपात

ration (रैशन) *n.* राशन, रसद – *vt.* रसद वितरित करना; राशन-व्यवस्था (किसी वस्तु पर) लागू करना

rational (रैशनल) *a.* विवेकी, बुद्धि सम्पन्न; तर्कपूर्ण – **rationale** (रैश´नाल) *n.* तर्क का आधार – **rationalism** *n.* तर्क बुद्धिवाद (रैश´नैलिटि) *n.* विवेक, तर्कशीलता – **rationalization** *n.* तर्क के बल पर उचित सिद्ध करने की क्रिया – **rationalize** *vt.* बुद्धिसंगत बना देना, कार्य-कुशलता बढ़ाने के लिए व्यवस्था सुधार करना

rattle (रैट्ल) *vi.* खड़खड़ाना – *vt.* झनझना कर खड़खड़ की आवाज़ करना; *inf.* घबरा देना – *n.* **rattlesnake** *n.* अमरीकी महाद्वीप का ज़हरीला सांप

raucous (´रॉकस) *a.* कर्कश, कर्णकटु

raunchy (´रॉन्चि) *a. sl.* कामुक; गन्दा

ravage (रैविज) *vt.* उजाड़ना, बर्बाद करना

rave (रेव़) *vi.* प्रलाप करना, बेसिरपैर की बातें करना; अत्यधिक प्रशंसा करना – **raving** *a.*

raven (रेव़न) *n.* कौए जैसा बड़ा पक्षी, द्रोण-काक

ravenous (रैव़नस) *a.* बहुत भूखा

ravine (र´वीन) *n.* नदी के बहाव से बनी तंग घाटी, खड्ड

ravish (रैविश) *vt.* सम्मोहित करना; बलात्कार करना – **ravishing** (रैविशिङ) *a.* अत्यंत सुंदर, सम्मोहक

raw (रॉ) *a.* कच्चा (खाद्य पदार्थ, माल आदि); प्राक तिक अवस्था में; अनुभवहीन; संवेदनशील; ठंडा (मौसम); हरा (घाव) – **raw deal** (किसी के साथ) पक्षपात या अन्याय – **rawhide** *n.* कच्ची खाल या चमड़ा, इसकी बनी चाबुक

ray (रे) *n.* किरण, केंद्र बिन्दु से निकलती हुई कोई भी रेखा – *vi* विकीर्ण होना; चारों और फैलना

rayon (´रेऑन) *n.* रेयन (कपड़ा)

raze (रेज़) *vt.* मिटा देना, नष्ट कर देना

razor (´रेज़र) *n.* दाढ़ी बनाने या बाल काटने का उस्तरा, रेज़र – **razor blade** उस्तरे का फल, ब्लेड – **razor-thin** *a.* वोटों के बहुत कम अंतर से (जीत)

re- (*comb. form*) पुनः, दुबारा, फिर के अर्थ में

reach (रीच) *vt.* पहुंचना, बढ़ाना, छू लेना; प्राप्त कर लेना – *vi.* तक हाथ बढ़ाना, फैल जाना – *n.* पहुंच, फैलने या पहुंचने की सीमा, विस्तार; दो मोड़ों के बीच नदी का भाग

react (रि´ऐक्ट) *vi.* प्रतिक्रिया करना या दिखाना – **reaction** *n.* प्रतिक्रिया, रासायनिक अभिक्रिया, रासायनिक या नाभिक परिवर्तन, अनुक्रिया – **reactionary** (रि´ऐक्शनरि) *a./n.* प्रतिक्रियावादी (व्यक्ति)– **reactor** (रि´ऐक्टर) *n.* परमाणु ऊर्जा उत्पन्न करने में प्रयुक्त उपकरण, रिऐक्टर

read (रीड) *vt.* पढ़ना; का अध्ययन करना; समझना; अर्थ लगाना; पढ़कर सुनाना; (मापक यंत्र द्वारा) माप (ताप, दाब आदि) बतलाना – *vi.* पढ़ते होना; (यह) लिखा होना (**read** (रॅड) *pt./pp.*) – **readability** (रीड´बिलिटि) *n.* – **readable** (´रीडबल) *a.* पठनीय; रोचक – **reader** *n.* पाठक; विश्वविद्यालय में लेक्चरार से ऊपर का पद, रीडर; स्कूल की पाठ्य पुस्तक; प्रकाशक को दी गई पाण्डुलिपि को पढ़कर उसके गुण-दोष आंकने वाला व्यक्ति; प्रूफ़-संशोधक, प्रूफ़-वाचक – **reading** *n.* पाठ्य सामग्री, अध्ययन, पठन – **read between the lines** छिपा अर्थ निकालना

ready (ˊरैंडि) *a.* – **readily** *adv.* तुरंत; खुशी से, इच्छा से – **readiness** *n.* तत्परता; इच्छा – **ready-made** *a.* पहले से तैयार (भोज्य पदार्थ, कपड़े)

real (ˊरिअल) *a.* वास्तविक, असली; अचल (सम्पत्ति, जमीन व मकान) – **realism** *n.* यथार्थवाद – **realist** *n.* – **realistic** (रिअˊलिस्टिक) *a.* यथार्थवादी – **reality** (रिˊऐलिटि) *n.* वास्तविकता – **really** *adv.* वास्तव में – **realty** (ˊरिअल्टि) *n.* अचल सम्पत्ति – **real estate** अचल सम्पत्ति

realize (ˊरिअलाइज़) *vt.* समझ जाना; स्पष्ट अनुभव करना; वास्तविकता में लाना; साकार कर देना; धनराशि में परिवर्तित, वसूल करना करना – **realization** *n.* स्पष्ट अनुभव, अनुभूति; साकार होने की स्थिति, वसूली, प्राप्ति

realm (रैल्म) *n.* राज्य; क्षेत्र

ream[1] (रीम) *n.* कागज़ के 480 या 500 पन्ने, रिम

ream[2] (रीम) *vt.* बढ़ाना, धातु में छिद्र चौड़ा करना

reap (रीप) *v.* फसल काटना– **reaper** (ˊरीपर) *n.* फसल काटने वाला व्यक्ति

rear[1] (रिअर) *n.* पिछला भाग – **rear admiral** नौसेना में एक उच्च अधिकारी

rear[2] (रिअर) *vt.* पालन-पोषण करना व पढ़ाना-लिखाना; जानवर, पक्षी आदि पालना; सिर उठाना – *vi.* (**rear up** भी) घोड़े का पिछली टांगो पर खड़ा हो जाना

reason (ˊरीज़न) *n.* कारण, हेतु; विवेक, बुद्धि, सोचने की शक्ति; मति, संतुलन; समझदारी या तर्क-शक्ति – *vi.* तर्क के आधार पर निष्कर्ष निकालना – *vt.* (प्राय: *with* के साथ) तर्क देकर समझाना – **reasonable** *a.* समझदार, पर्याप्त, तर्क संगत

reassure (रीअˊशुअर) *vt.* को आश्वासन देना

rebate *n.* (ˊरीबेट) छूट, वापिस किया गया अंश – *vt.* (रिˊबेट) (भुगतान राशि से) काटना

rebel *vi.* (रिˊबेंल) विद्रोह करना, बग़ावत करना (-ll-) – *n.* (ˊरेंबल) विद्रोही, बाग़ी – *a.* विद्रोही – **rebellion** (रिˊबेंल्यन) *n.* विद्रोह, सशस्त्र विद्रोह – **rebellious** *a.* विद्रोही (प्रव ति वाला)

reboot (रीˊबूट) *vt/vi.* कम्प्यूटर बंद करके फौरन दुबारा चलाना/चलना

rebound *vi.* (रिˊबाउण्ड) टकरा कर लौटना; (षडयंत्र, आदि का) करने वाले को ही हानि पहुंचाना – *n.* (ˊरीबाउण्ड) टकरा कर लौटने की क्रिया

rebuff (रिˊबफ़) *n./vt.* कोरा जवाब (देना)

rebuke (रिˊब्यूक) *vt.* फटकारना, डांटना – *n.* फटकार, डांट-डपट

rebut (रिˊबट) *vt.* खण्डन करना – **rebuttal** *n.*

recalcitrant (रिˊकैल्सिट्रंट) *a./n.* अक्खड़, बिल्कुल आज्ञा न सुनने या मानने वाला – **recalcitrance** *n.* अक्खड़पन, हठ

recall (रिˊकॉल) *vt.* याद करना, (स्वयं को) याद आना, याद होना; वापस बुलाना; वापस लेना; वापस बुला लेना – *n.* वापसी का हुक्म; याद रखने की क्षमता

recant (रिˊकैंट) *vt.* कथन वापिस लेना, मुकर जाना

recap (ˊरीकैप) *v./n.* recapitulate, recapitulation का संक्षेप

recapitulate (रीकˊपिट्युलेट) *vt.* मुख्य बातों को दोहराना – **recapitulation** *n.* सार-कथन

recce (ˊरैकि) *n. inf.* reconnaissance का संक्षेप

recede (रिˊसीड) *vi.* पीछे हटना, दूर हो जाना

receipt (रिˊसीट) *n.* रसीद, पावती; प्राप्ति

receive (रिˊसीव़) *vt.* पाना, लेना; स्वीकार करना; अनुभव करना, (अतिथियों का) स्वागत करना; (टेलीफोन) सुनना – **receiver** *n.* प्राप्त कर्ता, सरकारी खज़ांची, आदाता; चोरी का माल प्राप्त करने वाला (व्यापारी); टेलीफोन का सुनने में काम आने वाला भाग, रिसीवर; रेडियो या टी.वी. सेट

recent ('रीसंट) *a.* हाल का, कुछ समय पहले का, नूतन – **recently** *adv.*

receptacle (रि'सेप्टकल) *n.* कुछ भी रखने का पात्र (थैला, बाक्स आदि) या स्थान

reception (रि'सेप्शन) *n.* प्राप्ति, स्वागत, स्वागत-समारोह, रिसेप्शन; स्वागत-कक्ष; रेडियो प्रसारण में प्राप्त रेडियो-संकेतों का अभिग्रहण गुण (साफ सुनाई देने का गुण) – **receptionist** *n.* स्वागत-अधिकारी

receptive (रि'सेप्टिव़) *a.* ग्रहणशील, नये विचार, सुझाव आदि ग्रहण करने का इच्छुक व करने में समर्थ

recess (रि'सेस) *n.* आला, ताक; मध्यावकाश

recession (रि'सेशन) *n.* व्यापार में मंदी; पीछे हटने की क्रिया

recharge (री'चार्ज) *v.* विद्युत बैटरी को पुन: चार्ज करना; *India* मोबाइल फोन (फीस देकर) पुन: चालू करना

recipe ('रेसिपि) *n.* नुसखा, पकवान बनाने के निर्देश

recipient (रि'सिपिअंट) *a./n.* पाने वाला

reciprocal (रि'सिप्रकल) *a.* पारस्परिक, आपसी; आगे-पीछे घूमने वाला (इंजन का पिस्टन आदि); एकान्तर– **reciprocate** (रि'सिप्रकेट) *vt.* आदान-प्रदान करना, लेना-देना; लौटाना –*vi.* आगे-पीछे घूमना

recite (रि'साइट) *vt.* कविता पाठ करना, पढ़कर सुनाना – **recital** *n.* संगीत कार्यक्रम, गायन विशे. एक व्यक्ति का; कविता पाठ; तथ्यों का विवरण, घटना वर्णन– **recitation** (रेसि'टेशन) *n.*

reckless ('रेक्लिस) *a.* दु:साहसी, असावधान, लापरवाह – **recklessness** *n.* लापरवाही, दुस्साहस

reckon ('रेकन) *v.* गिनना; शामिल करना; मानना; समझना

reclaim (रि'क्लेम) *vt.* (भूमि को) क षि योग्य बनाना; वापस मांगना; सुधारना; किसी से कोई वस्तु वापिस मांगना – **reclamation** (रेक्ल'मेशन) *n.* भूमि-उद्धार

recline (रि'क्लाइन) *vi.* लेट जाना

recluse (रि'क्लूस) *a./n.* एकांतवासी (विशे. सन्यासी)

recognize ('रेकग्नाइज़) *vt.* पहचानना; मान्यता देना; मानना; कद्र करना – **recognition** (रेकग्'निशन) *n.* मान्यता; (दावे आदि की) मंजूरी; पहचान

recoil (रि'कॉइल) *vi.* डर या नफरत से पीछे हटना; बंदूक, तोप आदि का चलाने पर पीछे धक्का देना – *n.* पीछे धक्का, झटका

recollect (रेक'लेक्ट) *vt.* याद करना, स्मरण करना –**recollection** *n.* याद/स्मरण करने की क्रिया

recommend (रेक'मेण्ड) *vt.* सिफ़ारिश करना, उपयुक्त बताना; (विशेषता द्वारा) आकर्षक बनाना – **recommendation** *n.* सिफ़ारिश

recompense ('रेकम्पेन्स) *vt.* पुरस्कार या हरजाना देना, कमी पूरी करना – *n.*

reconcile ('रेकन्साइल) *vt.* मेल-मिलाप करना, झगड़े का निपटारा कराना; तथ्यों का मिलान करना; हालात आदि से समझौता करना – **reconcilable** *a.* समाधान योग्य, संगत – **reconciliation** (रेकन्सिलि'एशन) *n.* मेल-मिलाप, समझौता

recondite (रि'कॉन्डाइट) *a.* गहन, गूढ़, दुर्बोध, बहुत कम ज्ञात

recondition (रीकन्'डिशन) *vt.* मरम्मत करके (मशीन आदि को) चालू हालत में ले आना

reconnaissance (रि'कॉनिसन्स) *n.* शत्रु की टोह लेने की क्रिया; सर्वेक्षण

reconnoitre (रेक'नॉइटर) *vt.* शत्रु की स्थिति, शक्ति आदि की टोह लगाना –*vi.* सर्वेक्षण करना

reconsider (रीकन्'सिडर) *v.* (निर्णय बदलने के इरादे से) पुन: विचार करना – **reconsideration** *n.*

reconstitute (री´कॉन्स्टिट्यूट) *vt.* (खाद्य पदार्थ को) मूल प्राकृतिक अवस्था में लाना विशे. पानी मिलाकर

record *n.* (´रेकॉर्ड) अभिलेख, रिकार्ड; विवरण, लेखा; रजिस्टर, फाइल; ग्रामोफोन रिकार्ड; घटना इतिहास – *vt.* (रि´कॉर्ड) लिपिबद्ध करना, लिखना, दर्ज करना – *v.* ध्वनि, वीडिओ (टेलीविज़न) कार्यक्रम ग्रामोफोन रिकार्ड या (कैसट) टेप पर रिकार्ड करना – **recorder** *n.* कार्यक्रम रिकार्ड करने वाला व्यक्ति या वस्तु; लेखा, वृत्त आदि लिखने वाला व्यक्ति – **recording** *n.* रिकार्ड करने की क्रिया, रिकार्ड किया गया कार्यक्रम – **record player** रिकार्ड बजाने व सुनाने का यंत्र, रिकार्ड प्लेयर

recount[1] (रि´काउंट) *vt.* (घटना का) वर्णन करना

recount[2] *n.* (´रीकाउंट) वोटों की फिर से गिनती – *vt.* (री´काउंट)

recoup (रि´कूप) *vt.* क्षतिपूर्ति कर लेना

recourse (रि´कॉर्स) *n.* शरण, सहारा; अपील का अधिकार

recover (रि´कव़र) *vt.* (पद, खोयी वस्तु) पुन: प्राप्त करना, दुबारा पाना – *vi.* स्वास्थ्य लाभ करना – **recovery** *n.* वसूली; स्वास्थ्य लाभ

recreation (रेक्रि´एशन) *n.* मनोरंजन, मन बहलाव, विश्राम

recrimination (रिक्रिमि´नेशन) *n.* गाली-गलौज व आपस में दोषारोपण, प्रत्यारोप

recruit (रि´क्रूट) *n.* नया भरती हुआ सैनिक, रंगरूट; समाज, सभा आदि का नया सदस्य – *vt.* सैनिक भरती करना – **recruitment** *n.* भरती

rectangle (´रेक्टैंगल) *n.* आयत – **rectangular** (रेक्´टैंग्युलर) *a.* आयताकार

rectify (´रेक्टिफ़ाइ) *vt.* ठीक करना, (भूल) सुधारना (**-fied, -fying**) – **rectification** (रेक्टिफ़ि´केशन) *n.* संशोधन

rectitude (´रेक्टिट्यूड) *n.* ईमानदारी, नैतिक आचरण

rector (´रेक्टर) *n.* चर्च का प्रभारी पुरोहित; कालिज, विश्वविद्यालय आदि का अध्यक्ष, रेक्टर, महाचार्य

rectum (´रेक्टम) *n.* मलाशय (*pl.* **-ta**) – **rectal** *a.* मलाशय संबंधी

recumbent (रि´कम्बंट) *a.* लेटा हुआ

recuperate (रि´कूपरेट) *vi.* बीमारी के बाद स्वास्थ्य लाभ करना – *vt.* (स्वास्थ्य) लाभ करना; (घाटा) पूरा करना – **recuperation** *n.*

recur (रि´कर) *vi.* पुन: घटित होना, मन में दुबारा आना (**-rr-**) – **recurrence** *n.* पुनरावृत्ति– **recurrent** *a.*

recycle (री´साइकल) *vt.* किसी (औद्योगिक) उत्पादन को क्रिया-विशेष द्वारा दुबारा उपयोग के लिए तैयार करना

red (रेंड) *a.* लाल (रंग) – *n.* लाल रंग; साम्यवादी – **redden** *v.* लाल करना या होना, (शर्म आदि से) चेहरा लाल पड़ना – **reddish** *a.* – **red alert** (विस्फोट आदि) बड़े खतरे की चेतावनी – **redbreast** (रेंड्ब्रेस्ट) *n.* रोबिन पक्षी – **red carpet** भव्य, शानदार (स्वागत) – **Red Cross** रेड क्रास संस्था – **red flag** साम्यवादी पार्टी का प्रतीक – **red-handed** *a. inf.* रंगे हाथों (पकड़े जाना) – **red herring** मुख्य विषय से ध्यान हटाने के लिए प्रस्तुत किया गया विषय – **red-hot** *a.* गुस्से में – **Red Indian** उत्तरी अमरीका का मूल निवासी – **red tape** अत्यधिक दफ्तरी कार्यवाही, लालफीता – **red letter day** महत्वपूर्ण, चिरस्मर्णीय दिवस

redeem (रि´डीम) *vt.* ऋण चुकाना; बंधक वस्तु छुड़ा लेना; मोचन करना; पाप मुक्त करना; पूर्ति करना – **redemption** *n.* मुक्ति, उद्धार; पुन: प्राप्ति – **redeeming** *a.* अच्छा (पहलू)

redouble (रि´डबल) *v.* बढ़ना, बढ़ाना; तेज़ करना

redoubtable (रि´डाउटबल) *a.* विकट, जिसके लिए भय मिश्रित सम्मान हो

redress (रि`ड्रैस) *vt.* ठीक कर देना, सुधारना – *n.*
reduce (रि`ड्यूस) *vt.* कम करना; घटाना; निर्बल कर देना, बल पूर्वक किसी स्थिति विशेष में लाना; वज़न घटा लेना – **reducible** *a.* – **reduction** (रि`डक्शन) *n.* कमी, घटाव; छूट, कटौती, लघुकरण; न्यूनीकरण
redundant (रि`डन्डंट) *a.* अनावश्यक, फ़ालतू; अतिरिक्त – **redundancy** *n.*
reed (रीड) *n.* नरकुल, सरकंडा; बांसुरी; रीड, वाद्यों की कम्पिका
reef (रीफ़) *n.* (**coral reef** भी) समुद्री सतह से उभरती हुई चट्टान या प्रवाल, (*coral*) शैलभित्ति, प्रवालभित्ति
reek (रीक) *n.* बदबू, दुर्गन्ध – *vi.* से दुर्गंध निकलना
reel (रील) *n.* चरखी; फ़िल्म की रील; फिरकी, बौबिन; इस पर लिपटा धागा; तेज़ न त्य; इसके साथ संगीत; लड़खड़ाना – *vt.* रील में लपेटना – *vi.* लड़खड़ाना; डगमगाना
refer (रि`फ़र) *vi.* से संबंध रखना, की ओर संकेत करना, जिकर करना – *vt.* सूचनार्थ देखना; (को) सूचना का स्रोत बताना; निर्णय या राय के लिए भेजना; का श्रेय देना (**-rr-**) – **referee** (रैंफ़`री) *n.* खेलकूद में रेफ़री; निर्णायक; किसी के चरित्र आदि का साक्षी – *v.* खेलकूद में रेफरी का कार्य करना – **reference** (`रैंफ़रन्स) *n.* निर्देशन; संदर्भ; हवाला, प्रमाण; प्रमाणपत्र; व्यक्ति जिससे किसी के चरित्र संबंधी पूछताछ की जा सके – **reference book** संदर्भ ग्रंथ – **reference point** मानक – **referendum** (रैंफ़`रैंण्डम) *n.* जनमत-संग्रह (*pl.* **-dums, -da**)
refill *vt.* (सिलिंडर आदि) दुबारा भरना- *n.* दुबारा भरा हुआ; बाल प्वाइंट पेन का सिक्का
refine (रि`फ़ाइन) *vt.* शुद्ध या परिष्क त करना; स्वाद सुधारना – **refined** *a.* सुसंस्क त – **refinement** *n.* परिष्कार, शोधन; स्वभाव, व्यवहार आदि में सुरुचि – **refinery** (रि`फ़ाइनरि) *n.* चीनी, तेल आदि का शोधक कारखाना
reflect (रि`फ़्लैक्ट) *vt.* प्रकाश किरणें आदि परावर्तित करना; (*fig.*) बदनाम करना; (व्यवहार आदि) – *vi.* चिंतन करना – **reflection, reflexion** (रि`फ़्लैक्शन) *n.* परावर्तन (प्रकाश, ताप या ध्वनि का); प्रतिबिम्ब; विचार, अनुचिंतन; विचार-अभिव्यक्ति – **reflective** *a.* चिंतनशील, विचारशील; परावर्तक – **reflector** *n.* परावर्ती सतह जैसे शीशा
reflex (`रीफ़्लेक्स) *n.* अनैच्छिक अथवा सहज क्रिया – *a.* अनैच्छिक (मांस-पेशी की क्रिया) – **reflexive** *a. Grammar* निजवाचक (क्रिया), सर्वनाम – **reflex action** प्रतिवर्ती क्रिया, सहज क्रिया
reform (रि`फ़ॉर्म) *v.* सुधारना; सुधरना – *n.* सुधार – **reformation** (रैंफ़र्`मेशन) *n.* 16 व शताब्दी योरुप में धार्मिक व राजनीतिक सुधारवादी आन्दोलन – **reformer** *n.* सुधारक
refract (रि`फ्रैक्ट) *vi.* प्रकाश किरण आदि का एक माध्यम से दूसरे में जाते समय दिशा बदलना – **refraction** (रि`फ्रैक्शन) *n.* अपवर्तन – **refractive** (रि`फ्रैक्टिव़) *a.* अपवर्तक
refrain[1] (रि`फ़्रेन) *vi.* – **refrain from doing** कोई (कार्य) न करना
refrain[2] *n.* कविता या गीत में टेक
refresh (रि`फ्रैंश) *vt.* ताज़ा करना, नयी शक्ति प्रदान करना, स्फूर्ती देना – **refresher** *n.* ताज़ा करने वाला – **refreshment** *n.* जलपान; स्फूर्तिदायक वस्तु
refrigerate (रि`फ्रिजरेट) *vt.* (पानी आदि) जमाना; ठण्डा करना – **refrigeration** (रिफ्रिजर्`एशन) *n.* ठंडा करने/जमाने की क्रिया,

प्रशीतन – **refrigerator** (रि'फ्रिजरेटर) *n.* रेफ्रिजरेटर

refuge ('रैंफ़्यूज) *n.* शरण, शरण-स्थान – **refugee** (रैंफ्यु'जी) *n.* शरणार्थी

refund *vt.* (रि'फ़ंड) (पैसा) लौटाना – *n.* ('रीफ़ंड) वापस करने की क्रिया; वापस किया धन

refurbish (री'फ़र्बिश) *vt.* चमकाना

refuse[1] (रि'फ़्यूज़) *v.* इनकार करना, 'न' कहना – **refusal** *n.* इनकार, अस्वीक ति

refuse[2] ('रैंफ़्यूस) *n.* कूड़ा-करकट

refute (रि'फ़्यूट) *vt.* (कथन का) खण्डन करना – **refutation** (रिफ़्यू'टेशन) *n.* खण्डन

regain (रि'गेन) *vt.* फिर से पाना, हासिल करना

regal ('रीगल) *a.* राजसी – **regality** (री'गैलिटि) *n.* राजाधिकार

regale (रि'गेल) *vt.* मनोरंजन करना; दावत देना

regard (रि'गार्ड) *vt.* ध्यानपूर्वक देखना; मानना, समझना; सम्मान देना; ध्यान देना; से सम्बंध रखना – *n.* टकटकी, ध्यान; सम्मान; संदर्भ, संबंध – *pl.* शुभकामनाएं – **regarding** *a.* के संदर्भ में – **regardless** *a.* लापरवाह – *adv.* (*of* के साथ) की परवाह न करते हुए

regatta (रि'गैट्अ) *n.* नौका-दौड़

regenerate (रि'जेंनरेट) *v.* नवजीवन प्रदान करना; नैतिक सुधार करना; पुनः रचना या बनना– **regeneration** (रिजेंन'रेशन) *n.* पुनरुज्जीवन

reggae ('रैगे) *n.* वैस्ट इंडीज़ की एक लोकप्रिय संगीत शैली

regime (रे'ज़ीम) *n.* शासन-प्रणाली; शासन

regimen ('रैंजिमेंन) *n.* (चिकित्सक द्वारा) निर्देशित खान-पान आदि; पथ्यापथ्य

regiment ('रैंजिमंट) *n.* सैन्य दल, रेजीमेंट – *vt.* कड़े अनुशासन में रखना – **regimental** *a.* रेजीमेंट का – **regimentation** *n.* कड़ा अनुशासन लागू करने की क्रिया

region ('रीजन) *n.* क्षेत्र, इलाका, प्रदेश; शरीर का कोई भाग– **regional** *a.* क्षेत्रीय, प्रादेशिक

register ('रैंजिस्टर) *n.* रजिस्टर, सूची, पंजिका; लिखित रिकार्ड; स्वर-विस्तार – *v.* सूचक यंत्र, मन, मुख आदि पर अंकित करना या होना – *vt.* पंजीक त करना, दर्ज करना; लिख कर देना; पत्र की रजिस्ट्री कराना – **registrar** *n.* पंजीयक; हस्पताल का एक वरिष्ठ डाक्टर, कालिज, विश्वविद्यालय आदि का रजिस्ट्रार – **registration** *n.* पंजीकरण – **registry** *n.* पंजीक त करना; रजिस्टर रखने का स्थान विशे. जन्म, विवाह आदि सम्बंधित

regress *vi.* (रि'ग्रेस) लौट जाना, पीछे आ जाना (पूर्व स्थान, स्थिति में) – *n.* ('रीग्रेस) – **regression** (रि'ग्रेशन) *n.* प्रतिगमन, अवनति

regret (रि'ग्रेट) *vt.* (के लिए) खेद प्रकट करना – *n.* खेद, अनुताप, दुःख – **regretful** *a.* खेद सूचक; दुःखी, खिन्न – **regretfully** *adv.* खेद से – **regrettable** *a.* खेदजनक

regular ('रैंग्युलर) *a.* सामान्य; नियमित, नियत, समतल; नियमनिष्ठ, सुव्यवस्थित – *n.* नियमित सैनिक– **regularity** (रैंग्यु'लैरिटि) *n.* नियमितता, नियम की पाबंदी, नियम निष्ठा – **regularize** ('रैंग्युलराइज़) – *vt.* नियमित या सुव्यवस्थित करना; (नौकरी में) पक्का करना; (अनियमित कार्य को) वैध घोषित करना

regulate ('रैंग्युलेट) *vt.* (मात्रा) नियंत्रित करना; (यंत्र) ठीक कर देना, समंजित करना; व्यवस्थित व नियमित करना – **regulation** *n.* नियम, विनियम – **regulator** *n.* यंत्र का वह भाग जो गति, बहाव आदि को नियंत्रित करे

regurgitate (रि'गर्जिटेट) *v.* उगलना

rehabilitate (रीअ'बिलिटेट) *vt.* बीमारी, कारावास आदि के बाद समाज में स्थान पाने में सहायता करना; विकलांग को आत्मनिर्भर बनाना; कलंक दूर करना, पुनर्वास करना – **rehabilitation** *n.* पुनर्वास; स्वास्थ्य लाभ

rehash (री हैश) *vt.* बिना अधिक परिवर्तन के लेखन या फिल्म के अंश दुबारा प्रयोग में लाना

rehearse (रि´हर्स) *vt.* नाटक आदि का पूर्वाभ्यास करना – **rehearsal** *n.* रिहर्सल, पूर्वाभ्यास

reign (रेन) *n.* शासनकाल – *vi.* शासन करना; का बोलबाला होना

reimburse (रीइम्´बर्स) *vt.* (कर्मचारी द्वारा खर्च की गई रकम) अदा करना, प्रतिपूर्ति करना – **reimbursement** *n.*

rein (रेन) *n.* लगाम; बागडोर – *vt.* रोकना, लगाम लगाना – **give rein to** खुली छूट देना

reincarnation (रीइन्कार्´नेशन) *n.* पुनर्जन्म, पुनर्वतार

reindeer (´रेन्डिअर) *n.* रेण्डियर (ठण्डे प्रदेश का हिरन)

reinforce (रीइन्´फ़ॉर्स) *vt.* सुद ढ़ या मजबूत करना; कुमुक भेजना – **reinforcement** *n.* कुमुक (मोर्चे पर सेना की सहायता के लिए भेजे सैनिक)

reinstate (रीइन्´स्टेट) *vt.* पुन: नियुक्त करना, पुन: प्रतिष्ठित करना

reiterate (री´इटरेट) *vt.* बार-बार दोहराना

reject *vt.* (रि´जेक्ट) अस्वीकार करना; अलग कर देना; निकाल देना – *n.* (´रीजेक्ट) निकाली या अलग की गई वस्तु या व्यक्ति – **rejection** *n.* अस्वीक ति

rejoice (रि´जॉइस) *v.* किसी बात पर हर्ष मनाना, खुशी मनाना

rejoin (री´जॉइन) *vt.* फिर से जोड़ना, से मिल जाना

rejoinder (रि´जाइंडर *n.* उत्तर, प्रत्युत्तर

rejuvenate (रि´जूविनेट) *vt.* फिर से जवान बना देना– **rejuvenation** *n.* पुनर्यौवन, कायाकल्प

relapse (रि´लैप्स) *vi.* फिर से बीमार पड़ने या बुरी आदतों का शिकार होना – *n.*

relate (रि´लेट) *vt.* वर्णन करना; सम्बंध दिखलाना – *vi.* (*to* के साथ) से सम्बद्ध होना – **relating** to के बारे में

relation (रि´लेशन) *n.* रिश्ता, संबंध; रिश्तेदार; वर्णन – **relationship** *n.* संबंध, नाता – **relative** (´रैंलटिव़) *a.* आपेक्षिक; (से) सम्बद्ध – *n.* सम्बंधी, रिश्तेदार – **relatively** *adv.* अपेक्षाक त

relax (रि´लैक्स) *v.* ढीला या शिथिल करना या होना; (व्यवहार में) नरम पड़ जाना; विश्राम करना – – **relaxing** *a.* आरामदेह – **relaxation** *n.* विश्राम, आराम; ढील

relay (´रीले) *n.* नयी टोली जो पहली का स्थान ले; *Radio, Television* अन्य स्टेशन से रिले द्वारा कार्यक्रम प्राप्त करने वाला स्टेशन – (रि´ले) *vt.* सन्देश पहुंचवाना (**relayed, relaying**) – **relay race** रिले-दौड़

release (रि´लीस) *vt.* छोड़ना, जाने देना; रिहा करना; (फिल्म आदि का) सार्वजनिक प्रदर्शन चालू करना; प्रकाशन की आज्ञा देना; (नियम आदि से) मुक्त करना; (सूचना आदि) जारी करना – *n.* रिहाई, मुक्ति, छुटकारा; फिल्म आदि का प्रदर्शन, बिक्री आदि आरंभ

relegate (´रैंलिगेट) *vt.* निकाल देना; पद कम कर देना – **relegation** *n.* पद-अवनति

relent (रि´लेंण्ट) *vi.* नरम पड़ जाना – **relentless** *a.* निर्दय; कठोर; निरंतर

relevant (´रैंलिव़ण्ट) *a.* प्रस्तुत विषय से सम्बद्ध, प्रासंगिक – **relevance** *n.* प्रासंगिकता

reliable, reliance दे. **RELY**

relic (´रैंलिक) *n.* स्म ति चिन्ह

relief (रि´लीफ़) *n.* राहत, आराम; घोर विपत्ति से पीड़ित लोगों को धन, भोजन आदि की सहायता; ड्यूटी पर दूसरे कर्मचारी का आना, बदल; एवजी; नियमित गाड़ी, वायुयान आदि में जगह न होने पद अतिरिक्त यात्रियों को ले जाने वाली गाड़ी आदि; (नक्काशी आदि में) उभार; सुस्पष्टता – **relieve** *vt.* राहत देना; सहायता करना; (ड्यूटी से) भार मुक्त करना; स्पष्ट दिखाना, उभारना; हलका करना (एकरसता को)

religion (रि'लिजन) *n.* धर्म – **religious** *a.* धार्मिक, कर्तव्यनिष्ठ

relinquish (रि'लिंक्विश) *vt.* त्याग देना

relish ('रैलिश) *v.* स्वाद लेना, पसंद करना – *n.* स्वाद, रस

reluctant (रि'लक्टंट) *a.* अनिच्छुक – **reluctance** *n.* अनिच्छा

rely (रि'लाइ) *vi.* (पर) निर्भर होना, भरोसा रखना (**relied, relying**) – **reliability** *n.* विश्सनीयता, भरोसा – **reliable** *a.* विश्वसनीय, भरोसेमंद – **reliance** *n.* भरोसा, विश्वास – **reliant** *a.* आत्मविश्वासी

remain (रि'मेन) *vi.* रह जाना, शेष या बाकी रहना; बना रहना – **remains** *pl. n.* अवशेष; म त शरीर – **remainder** *n.* शेषफल, बाकी; बचा हुआ – *vt.* कम कीमत पर बचा माल (विशे. पुस्तकें) बेचना

remake (री'मेक) *vt.* पुरानी फिल्म/गाने को नया रूप देना – (रीमेक) *n.*

remand (रि'मांड) *vt.* (हवालात में) वापस भेजना – **remand home** युवा-अपराधियों को रखने का स्थान

remark (रि'मार्क) *vi.* ज(*on* के साथ) के बारे में कहना – *vt.* टिप्पणी करना – *n.* टिप्पणी, कथन – **remarkable** *a.* असाधारण, उल्लेखनीय

remedy ('रैमिडि) *n.* निदान, इलाज, दवा – *vt.* का इलाज करना, सुधारना (**-edied, -edying**) – **remedial** (रि'मीडिअल) *a.* खास कमियाँ दूर करने के लिए बनाया गया (पाठ्यक्रम आदि), उपचारी

remember (रि'मेंम्बर) *vt.* याद करना या रखना– *vi.* (के) मन में रहना – **remembrance** *n.* स्मरण शक्ति; स्म ति चिन्ह

remind (रि'माइंड) *vt.* याद दिलाना – **reminder** *n.* स्मरण-पत्र, अनुस्मारक

reminisce (रैंमि'निस) *vi* अतीत व अतीत के अनुभवों के बारे में बात करना, लिखना – **reminiscence** *n.* स्मरण किये अनुभव, संस्म ति – (~ s) *pl.* संस्मरण – **reminiscent** *a.*

remiss (रि'मिस) *a.* लापरवाह

remit *v.* (रि'मिट) (डाक से) माल मंगाने के लिए रकम भेजना; छूट देना; लौटाना; कम करना – **remission** *n.* कमी; कारावास की अवधि में छूट; क्षमा – **remittance** *n.* रकम भेजना, भेजी गई रकम

remix ('रीमिक्स) *n. India* पुराने गाने नये रूप में

remnant ('रैम्नंट) *n.* टुकड़ा (विशे. कपड़े का)

remonstrate ('रैमन्स्ट्रेट) *vi.* विरोध करना – **remonstrance** *n.*

remorse (रि'मॉर्स) *n.* पश्चाताप – **remorseful** *a.* – **remorseless** *a.* निष्ठुर

remote (रि'मोट) *a.* सुदूर; अलग; (व्यक्ति) जो अलग-अलग रहे; बहुत कम (संभावना आदि) – **remote access** *Computers* दूर से स्थापित सम्बंध – **remote sensing** प थ्वी के बारे में जानकारी खोजने व संग्रह करने में उपग्रह (सैटलाइट) का उपयोग – **remote control** टी.वी. आदि अनेक उपकरणों को दूर से नियंत्रण करने का इलेक्ट्रॉनिक उपकरण

remove (रि'मूव़) *vt.* हटाना, दूर ले जाना; मिटाना (धब्बा आदि); स्थान बदलना; उतारना; बर्खास्त करना – *vi.* रहने का स्थान बदल लेना, चले जाना –**removal** *n.* स्थानांतरण; पदच्युति, दूर करना

remuneration (रिम्यून'रेशन) *n.* पारिश्रमिक – **remunerative** *a.* लाभकारी (कार्य)

renaissance (र'नेसन्स) *n.* पुनर्जागरण

renal ('रीनल) *a.* गुरदे का

rend (रॅण्ड) *v.* फाड़ना, चीरना (**rent, rending**)

render ('रॅन्डर) *vt.* प्रस्तुत करना; बदले में देना; बना देना; चित्रित करना; अनुवाद करना; पलस्तर करना – **rendering** *n.* प्रस्तुति

rendezvous ('रॉन्डिवू) *n.* पूर्व निश्चित मिलने का स्थान; पूर्व निश्चित भेंट; अड्डा

renegade (ˊरॅनिगेड) *n.* विश्वासघाती
renege (रिˊनीग) *vi.* (*on* के साथ) मुकर जाना
renew (रिˊन्यू) *vt.* नया या नवीन करना; दोहराना (प्रतिज्ञा आदि); पुन: आरंभ करना – **renewal** *n.* नवीनीकरण
renounce (रिˊनाउन्स) *vt.* त्याग देना; दावा या पद छोड़ देना; सन्यास लेना – **renunciation** (रिनन्सिˊएशन) *n.* त्याग, सन्यास
renovate (ˊरॅनवेट) *vt.* पुरानी अच्छी स्थिति में ले आना, मरम्मत करना– **renovation** *n.*
renown (रिˊनाउन) *n.* ख्याति, प्रसिद्धि
rent[1] (रॅण्ट) *n.* जमीन, मकान आदि का किराया – *vt.* किराये पर देना
rent[2] (रॅण्ट) *n.* चीर, दरार; REND का *pt./pp.*
renunciation *n.* दे RENOUNCE
repair[1] (रिˊपॅअर) *vt.* मरम्मत करना, ठीक करना – *n.* मरम्मत – **repairable** *a.* – मरम्मत योग्य – **reparation** (रॅपˊरेशन) *n.* भूल सुधार; हरजाना
repartee (रॅपार्ˊटी) *n.* व्यंगपूर्ण उत्तर
repast (रिˊपास्ट) *n. formal* भोजन
repatriate (रीˊपैट्रिएट) *vt.* स्वदेश वापस भेजना – **repatriation** *n.*
repay (रिˊपे) *vt.* (रकम) वापिस लौटना; का बदला चुकाना (**repaid, repaying**)
repeal (रिˊपील) *n./vt.* रद्द करना
repeat (रिˊपीट) *vt.* दोबारा कहना, करना – *vi.* फिर घटित होना – *n.* फिर पेश करने की क्रिया, आवृति विशे. टी.वी. कार्यक्रम की – **repeatedly** *adv.* बार-बार – **repetition** (रॅपिˊटिशन) *n.* दोहराना, पुनरावृत्ति; दुहराई गई वस्तु – **repetitive** (रिˊपॅटिटिव़) *a.* आवृत्तीय
repel (रिˊपॅल) *vt.* मार भगाना, दूर हटाना; को घृणित लगना – **repellent** (रिˊपॅलंट) *a.*– कीड़ों आदि से वस्तुओं की सुरक्षा करने वाला पदार्थ, कीट-निवारक
repent (रिˊपॅण्ट) *vi.* – **repent of** पश्चाताप करना – *vt.* (कार्य, गलती) के लिए पछताना – **repentance** (रिˊपॅन्टन्स) *n.* पश्चताप – **repentant** *n.* पश्चातापी
repercussion (रीपर्ˊकशन) *n.* अप्रत्यक्ष (कु) प्रभाव; उलटा असर; प्रतिध्वनि
repertoire (ˊरॅपट्वार) *n.* नाटक मंडली का अभिनय करने या गाने का नाटकों व गानों का संग्रह, रंग पटल, नाटक चक्र – **repertory (theatre, group)** *n.* लगातार अपने संग्रह से नाटक करने वाली मण्डली (सहित रंगशाला)
repetition, repetitive दे. REPEAT
replace (रिˊप्लेस) *vt.* का स्थान ले लेना, एक के स्थान पर दूसरी वस्तु लेनी या देनी; के स्थान पर दूसरा नियुक्त करना, को बदल देना; वापस रख देना – **replacement** *n.* स्थानापन्न, एक वस्तु के स्थान पर दूसरी वस्तु, प्रतिवस्तु
replay *n.* (ˊरीप्ले) खेल के किसी भाग का टी.वी. पर फौरन ही दुबारा दिखाया जाना, विशे. धीमी गति में (**action replay** भी); मैच का दुबारा खेला जाना – *vt.* (रीˊप्ले) (मैच) का दोबारा खेला जाना; टी.वी. पर धीमी गति से दुबारा दिखाना
replenish (रिˊप्लॅनिश) *vt.* फिर से भरना, परिपूर्ण करना – **replenishment** *n.* भराई, पुन:पूर्ति
replete (रिˊप्लीट) *a.* भरापूरा
replica (ˊरॅप्लिक्अ) *n.* प्रतिकृति, मूल (चित्र आदि) की एकदम नकल
reply (रिˊप्लाइ) *v.* उत्तर देना (**replied, replying**) – *n.* उत्तर
report (रिˊपॉर्ट) *n.* रिपोर्ट, विवरण; समाचार, बच्चे की स्कूल में प्रगति का लिखित विवरण; अफवाह; (कु)ख्याति; (बंदूक चलने का) धड़ाका – *vt.* सूचना देना, रिपोर्ट देना, विवरण देना; शिकायत करना – **reporter** *n.* संवाददाता – **report to** के सम्मुख उपस्थित होना

repose (रि´पोज़) *n.* शांति, धैर्य; निद्रा – *vi.* आराम करना– *vt.* , रखना; (विश्वास, आस्था) रखना – **repository** (रि´पॉज़िटरि) *n.* मूल्यवान वस्तुओं को सुरक्षित रखने का स्थान; भंडार

reprehensible (रिप्रि हि´न्सिबल) *a.* निन्दनीय, खराब

represent (रॅप्रि´ज़ेन्ट) *vt.* का द्योतक होना, का प्रतिनिधित्व करना; का प्रतीक होना या बनना; वर्णन करना – **representation** *n.* प्रतिनिधत्व; अभिनय; चित्रण; प्रतिवेदन; प्रतिरूप – **representative** *n.* प्रतिनिधि; (चल-) बिक्री कर्ता – *a.* प्रतिनिधक, नमूने के तौर पर

repress (रि´प्रॅस) *vt.* दमन करना, दबा कर रखना – **repression** *n.* दमन – **repressive** *a.*

reprieve (रि´प्रीव़) *vt.* फांसी का दिया जाना स्थगित या रद्द करना – *n.* दण्ड स्थगित या रद्द करने की क्रिया; अस्थायी राहत; जानबख्शी

reprimand (रॅप्रिमाण्ड) *n.* फटकार, डांट – *vt.*

reprisal (रि´प्राइज़ल) *n.* प्रतिशोध, बदला

reproach (रि´प्रोच) *vt.* उलाहना देना, धिक्कारना – *n.* फटकार, निन्दा; बदनामी – **reproachful** *a.* उलाहने भरा

reprobate (रॅप्रोबेट) *a.* भ्रष्ट, पापात्मा

reproduce (रीप्र´ड्यूस) *v.* की प्रतिलिपि या प्रतिक ति बनाना, नकल करना; बच्चे पैदा करना – **reproduction** *n.* उत्पत्ति-क्रिया; उत्पादन; जन्म देना; प्रतिक ति – **reproductive** *a.*

reprove (रि´प्रूव़) *vt.* निंदा करना, फटकारना – **reproof** *n.*

reptile (रॅप्टाइल) *n.* रेंगने वाला जीव – **reptilian** (रॅप्´टिलिअन) *a.* सरी-स प-संबंधी

republic (रि´पब्लिक) *n.* गणतंत्र, गणराज्य – **republican** *a./n.* गणतंत्र का (समर्थक)

repudiate (रि´प्यूडिएट) *vt.* के अधिकार या वैधता को अस्वीकार करना – **repudiation** *n.* खण्डन, परित्याग

repugnant (रि´पग्नंट) *a.* घिनावना, अरुचिकर, प्रतिकूल – **repugnance** *n.*

repulse (रि´पल्स) *vt.* पीछे धकेल देना; खदेड़ना; हमला बेकार कर देना, दो टूक जवाब देना – **repulsion** *n.* घ णा, अरुचि – **repulsive** *a.* घ णास्पद, अरुचिकर

repute (रि´प्यूट) *n.* प्रतिष्ठा, नाम – **reputable** (रॅप्युटबल) *a.* माना हुआ, प्रतिष्ठित – **reputation** *n.* प्रतिष्ठा

request (रि´क्वॅस्ट) *n.* अनुरोध, निवेदन – *vt.* मांगना

Requiem (रॅक्विआऍम) *n.* ईसाई धर्म में म त-आत्मा के लिए एक अनुष्ठान; शोक-गीत

require (रि´क्वाइअर) *vt.* मांगना, आवश्यक होना; आदेश देना – **requirement** *n.* शर्त; मांग; ज़रूरत

requisite (रॅक्विज़िट) *a.*– आवश्यक- *n.*

requisition (रॅक्वि´ज़िशन) *n.* (**for** के साथ) माल, सामग्री आदि के लिए औपचारिक रूप से मांग, अभिग्रहण – *vt.* मांग पेश करना; काम में लगाना

requite (रि´क्वाइट) *vt.* बदला चुकाना

rescind (रि´सिंड) *vt.* रद्द करना

rescue (रॅस्क्यू) *vt.* (मुसीबत से) बचाना, छुड़ाना –*n.* बचाव, उद्धार – **rescuing** *n.* बचाव कार्य

research (रि´सर्च) *n.* खोज, अनुसंधान, शोध – *v.* शोध या अनुसंधान करना – **researcher** *n.* अनुसंधानकर्ता, शोधक

resemble (रि´ज़ेम्बल) *vt.* के सद श होना – **resemblance** *n.* साद श्यता

resent (रि´ज़ेण्ट) *vt.* का बुरा मानना; कुढ़ना – **resentful** *a.* – **resentment** *n.* नाराज़गी

reserve (रि´ज़र्व) *vt.* बचा कर रखना; आरक्षित करना; (कुछ करने का) अधिकार रखना – *n.* (~**s**) *pl.* भी) संकट काल में उपयोग के लिए सुरक्षित धन; निधि; रिज़र्व-सेना; आरक्षित क्षेत्र,

संकोच – **reservation** (रेंज़र्'वेशन) *n.* आरक्षण, आरक्षित वस्तु; संदेह; अपवाद – **reserved** *a.* संकोची, अल्पभाषी

reservoir (रेंज़र्व्‌वार) *n.* पानी की टंकी (सार्वजनिक उपयोग के लिए); द्रव, गैस आदि रखने का पात्र

resettle (री'सेंट्‌ल) *vi./vt.* पुनर्वास करना – **resettlement** *n.* पुनर्वास

reside (रि'ज़ाइड) *vi.* निवास करना, रहना – **residence** (रेंज़िडन्स) *n.* घर, निवास – **resident** *a./n.* निवासी, स्थित – **residential** *a.* आवासी, रिहायशी

residue (रेंज़िड्यू) *n.* अवशेष, बचा हुआ – **residual** (रि'ज़िड्युअल) *a.* बचा हुआ

resign (रि'ज़ाइन) *vt.* छोड़ देना – *vi.* त्यागपत्र देना; (अपनी स्थिति को) स्वीकार कर लेना – **resignation** (रेंज़िग्'नेशन) *n.* त्यागपत्र, पदत्याग, इस्तीफा – **resigned** *a.* सहने को तैयार, संतुष्ट

resilient (रि'ज़िलिअंट) *a.* (द ष्टिकोण) लचीला – **resilience** *n.* लचक

resin (रेंज़िन) *n.* राल, धूना (चिपचिपा तरल पदार्थ)

resist (रि'ज़िस्ट) *v.* विरोध करना, प्रभाव न होने देना – **resistance** *n.* विरोध; रोध, मुकाबला – **resistant** *a.* प्रतिरोधी

resolute (रेंज़लूट, रेंज़ल्यूट) *a.* , अटल, पक्का, क त संकल्प – **resolution** *n.* संकल्प, द ढ़ता; प्रस्ताव; फैसला

resolve (रि'ज़ॉल्व) *vt.* निश्चय करना; संकल्प करना; प्रस्ताव पारित करना; (अंशों में) बांटना;ञ(शंका) समाधान करना – *n.* संकल्प, प्रस्ताव

resonance (रेंज़नन्स) *n.* गहरी गूंज; अनुनाद – **resonant** *a.* गुंजायमान

resort (रि'ज़ॉर्ट) *vi.* का सहारा लेना – *n.* मनोरंजन स्थल; आश्रय

resound (रि'ज़ाउंड) *vi.* गूंजना, देर तक बजते रहने – **resounding** *a.* ज़ोरदार

resource (रि'ज़ॉर्स, रि'सॉर्स) *n.* साधन; युक्ति, उपाय – (~ **s**) *pl.* आर्थिक सम्पदा के स्रोत, सम्पदा, धन – **resourceful** *a.* उपाय-कुशल, सूझबूझ वाला–**resourcefulness** *n.*

respect (रि'स्पेंक्ट) *n.* आदर-भावना; पक्ष; संबन्ध – *vt.* आदर करना; ध्यान रखना – **respectability** – *n.* सम्मानीयता – **respectable** (रि'स्पेंक्टबल) *a.* आदरणीय, काफी अच्छा – **respectful** *a.* आदरपूर्ण – **respecting** *prep.* के विषय में – **respective** *a.* अपना-अपना – **respectively** *adv.* क्रमानुसार, क्रमशः

respire (रि'स्पाइअर) *v.* सांस लेना – **respiration** (रेंस्प'रेशन) *n.* श्वास लेने की क्रिया – **respirator** *n.* मुंह पर लगाने का उपकरण जो क त्रिम श्वास-क्रिया में प्रयुक्त होता है – **respiratory** *a.* श्वास-सम्बंधी

respite (रेंस्पिट, रेंस्पाइट) *n.* विश्राम; राहत

resplendent (रि'स्प्लेंन्‌डंट) *a.* चमकता हुआ; भव्य

respond (रि'स्पॉण्ड) *vi.* उत्तर देना; प्रतिक्रिया दिखाना; उत्तर स्वरूप कार्य करना; (**respond to** में) पर (दवा का) असर होना – **respondent** *a.*, प्रतिवादी – **response** *n.* उत्तर, प्रतिक्रिया – **responsive** *a.* सहज में प्रतिक्रिया दिखाने वाला

responsible (रि'स्पॉन्सिबल) *a.* उत्तरदायी; विश्वसनीय; उत्तरदायित्व वाला (कार्य, पद आदि); महत्वपूर्ण– **responsibility** *n.* उत्तरदायित्व; कर्तव्य

rest[1] (रेंस्ट) *n.* आराम, चैन; सहारा; विराम विशे. संगीत में; आश्रय – *vi* आराम करना, सुस्ताना; सहारा लेना, निर्भर होना – *vt.*आराम देना; पर रखना, टिकाना– **restful** *a.* शांत; आरामदेह –

restless *a.* बेचैन, चिंतित – **rest area** *US* विश्रामस्थल – **resting place** कब्र – **restroom** *US* (*toilet*) जन-सुविधा

rest² (रॅस्ट) *n.* शेष, बचा हुआ

restaurant (ˈरॅस्टराँ, ˈरॅस्टरॉन्ट) *n.* रेस्तराँ, भोजनालय – **restaurateur** (रॅस्टरˈटर) *n.* रेस्तराँ-मालिक

restitution (रॅस्टिˈट्यूशन) *n.* (खोयी वस्तु, अधिकार की) वापसी; क्षतिपूर्ति

restive (ˈरॅस्टिव़) *a.* बेचैन, अशांत

restore (रिˈस्टॉर) *vt.* दुबारा बना देना, पुरानी स्थिति में ला देना; वापिस कर देना – **restoration** (रॅस्टˈरेशन) *n.* पुनरुद्धार – **restorative** (रिˈस्टॉरटिव़) *a.* पुष्टिकर – *n.*

restrain (रिˈस्ट्रेन) *vt.* कुछ करने से रोकना – **restraint** *n.* रोक, नियंत्रण; आत्मसंयम

restrict (रिˈस्ट्रिक्ट) *vt.* सीमित करना; सीमा में रखना – **restriction** *n.* नियंत्रण, प्रतिबंध

result (रिˈज़ल्ट) *vi.* परिणाम होना / निकालना; (के रूप में) अंत होना – *n.* परिणाम, फल – **resultant** *a.* परिणामिक

resume (रिˈज़्यूम) *vt.* दुबारा शुरू करना – **résumé** (ˈरॅज़्युमे) *n.* संक्षेप, सारांश; व्यक्तिगत विवरण (विशे० नौकरी के लिए) – **resumption** *n.* पुनरारंभ

resurgence (रिˈसर्जन्स) *n.* पुनरुत्थान, पुनः क्रियाशील होना – **resurgent** *a.* पुनः क्रियाशील

resurrect (रॅज़ˈरॅक्ट) *vt.* पुनर्जीवित करना; दोबारा काम में ले लेना – **resurrection** *n.* पुनरुज्जीवन; नवजागरण

resuscitate (रिˈससिटेट) *vt.* जीवित करना या होश में लाना – **resuscitation** *n.*

retail (ˈरीटेल) *n.* खुदरा, फुटकर, परचून – *adv.* खुदरा (बिक्री) – *v.* खुदरा बेचना या बिकना; (रिˈटेल) विस्तार से सुनाना – **retailer** *n.* खुदरा व्यापारी

retain (रिˈटेन) *vt.* रखना; अधिकार में रखना; नौकर रखना – **retainer** *n.* प्रतिधारण शुल्क, वकील आदि की व्यावसायिक परामर्श देते रहने की फीस – **retention** *n.* धारण; याद रखने की क्षमता – **retentive** *a.* धारण शक्ति-सम्पन्न

retaliate (रिˈटैलिएट) *v.* जवाबी कार्यवाही करना – **retaliation** *n.* बदला, प्रतिशोध – **retaliatory** *a.*

retard (रिˈटार्ड) *vt.* धीमा कर देना; विकास में बाधक होना – **retardation** *n.* – **retarded** (रिˈटार्डिड) *a.* कम विकसित, विशे. मानसिक रूप से

retch (रॅच) *vi.* उबकाई आना

reticent (ˈरॅटिसंट) *a.* मौन – **reticence** *n.*

retina (ˈरॅटिन्अ) *n.* आंख का परदा, दृष्टि पटल

retinue (ˈरॅटिन्यू) *n.* अनुयाइयों या नौकरों का दल

retire (रिˈटाइअर) *vi.* सेवा निवृत होना; चले जाना; पीछे हट जाना; सोने के लिए चले जाना – **retired** *a.* सेवा-निवृत – **retirement** *n.* सेवा निवृत्ति – **retiring** *a.* संकोची

retort (रिˈटॉर्ट) *vt.* प्रत्युत्तर देना; प्रतिकार करना – *vi.* प्रत्युत्तर देना, ईंट का जवाब पत्थर से देना – *n.* प्रत्युत्तर; (कांच का) भभका

retouch (रीˈटच) *vt.* संवारना

retrace (रिˈट्रेस) *vt.* का आरंभ से अवलोकन करना– **retrace one's steps** उसी रास्ते से वापिस लौटना

retract (रिˈट्रैक्ट) *v.* पीछे हट जाना; से मुकर जाना, समेट लेना – **retraction** *n.*

retread *vt.* (रीˈट्रॅड) पुराने रबड़ टायर पर रबड़ की परत चढ़ाना – *n* (रीट्रॅड) रबड़ की परत चढ़ा पुराना टायर

retreat (रिˈट्रीट) *vi.* पीछे हटना – *n.* पीछे हटने की क्रिया; शरण स्थल; एकांतवास

retrench (रिˈट्रॅन्च) *vt.* छटनी करना – **retrenchment** *n.* छटनी

retribution (रॆंट्रि´ब्यूशन) *n.* प्रतिफल, विशे. बुरे कामों का

retrieve (रि´ट्रीव़) *vt.* वापिस लाना; (स्थिति) संभाल लेना; (कम्प्यूटर से जानकारी) पुनः प्राप्त करना – **retrievable** *a.* – **retrieval** *n.* पुनः प्राप्ति – **retriever** *n.* गया कुत्ता मरा शिकार उठाकर लाने के लिए सधाया जाता है

retroactive *a.* पूर्व प्रभावी

retrofit (रॆंट्रोफिट) *vt.* मशीन में कुछ नया उपकरण जोड़ना

retrograde (रॆंट्रोग्रेड) *a.* प्रतिक्रियावादी

retrorocket (रॆंट्रोरॉकिट) *n.* राकेट का इंजन जो अन्तरिक्ष यान की गति धीमी करता है

retrospect (रॆंट्रोस्पॆक्ट) *n.* बीती बातों का सर्वेक्षण – **retrospection** *n.* सिंहावलोकन – **retrospective** *a.* किसी पिछली तारीख से लागू

return (रि´टर्न) *vi.* लौटाना, वापिस आना या जाना – *vt.* लौटाना, वापिस करना; घोषित करना; चुनना – *n.* वापिसी; लाभ; सरकारी रपट, घोषणा – **returning officer** चुनाव अधिकारी

reunion (री´यून्यन) *n.* पुनर्मिलन

rev (रॆव) *inf. n.* इंजन के चक्कर – *v.* (बहुधा *up* के साथ) इंजन की गति बढ़ाना

revalue (री´वैल्यू) *v.* मुद्रा का विनिमय मूल्य बढ़ाना – **revaluation** *n.* पुनर्मूल्यन

revamp (री´वैम्प) *vt.* नया बनाना; सुधारना

reveal (रि´व़ील) *vt.* प्रकट करना, बताना; प्रदर्शित करना – **revelation** (रॆव़´लेशन) *n.* प्रकट होने या रहस्य खुलने की क्रिया

revel (रॆव़ल) *vi.* बहुत पसंद करना, रंगरलियां मनाना (-ll-) – *n.* (प्रायः *pl*) रंगरलियां – **reveller** *n.* रंगरलियां मनाने/मौज उड़ाने वाला – **revelry** *n.* आमोद प्रमोद, रंगरलियां

revenge (रि´व़ेन्ज) *n.* बदला, प्रतिशोध – *vt.* का बदला/प्रतिशोध लेना – *v. refl.* अपना बदला लेना – **revengeful** *a.* प्रतिशोधी

revenue (रॆंव़िन्यू) *n.* आय, राजस्व

reverberate (रि´व़बेरिट) *v.* गूंजना – **reverberation** *n.* गूंज, प्रतिध्वनि

revere (रि´व़िअर) *vt.* आदर करना; श्रद्धा रखना – **reverence** (´रेव़रंस) *n.* आदर, श्रद्धा – **reverend** (´रेव़रंड) *a.* श्रद्धेय (विशे. पादरी के नाम के साथ प्रयुक्त) – **reverent** *a.* श्रद्धालु

reverie (रॆंव़रि) *n.* दिवास्वप्न

reverse (रि´व़र्स) *v.* (कार आदि को) पीछे की ओर चलाना या चलना – *vt.* उलटा या औंधा कर देना; बिल्कुल बदल जाना – *n.* उलटी, विपरीत या दूसरी दिशा; पराजय – *a.* उलटा, विपरीत – **reversal** *n.* विपर्यय – **reversible** *a.* जिसे उलटा जा सके

revert (रि´व़र्ट) *vi.* **revert to** पहली स्थिति/ विषय पर आ जाना – **reversion** *n.*

review (रि´व्यू) *vt.* पुनर्विचार करना; समीक्षा करना – *n.* समीक्षा; समीक्षात्मक लेखों की पत्रिका; सेना का निरीक्षण – **reviewer** *n.* समीक्षक

revile (रि´व़ाइल) *vt.* गाली देना – **reviler** *n.*

revise (रि´व़ाइज़) *vt.* संशोधन करना, सुधारना; परीक्षा के लिए पढ़े हुए पाठ को फिर पढ़ना; (विचारों) में परिवर्तन या रद्दोबदल करना – **revision** (रि´विज़न) *n.*

revive (रि´व़ाइव) *v.* फिर जी उठना या जीवित कर देना; फिर प्रयोग में आ जाना – **revival** *n.* पुनर्जीवन, पुनर्जागरण

revoke (रि´व़ोक) *vt.* वापिस लेना (आदेश आदि); रद्द करना – **revocation** (रॆव़´केशन) *n.* रद्द करने की क्रिया

revolt (रि´व़ोल्ट) *n.* विद्रोह, बगावत – *vi.* विद्रोह करना; से घ णा अनुभव करना – *vt.* वीभत्सा उत्पन्न करना – **revolting** *a.* वीभत्स

revolve (रि´व़ॉल्व) *vi.* के गिर्द घूमना; पर केन्द्रित होना – *vt.* को घुमाना – **revolution** (रॆव़´लूशॅन) *n.* क्रांति; परिक्रमा – **revolutionary** *a./n.*

क्रांतिकारी (व्यक्ति, विचार) – *n.* – **revolutionize** *vt.* क्रांति लाना

revolver (रि´वॉल्वर) *n.* रिवाल्वर

revulsion (रि´वल्शन) *n.* घोर घ णा, जुगप्सा

reward (रि´वॉर्ड) *vt.* पुरस्कार या पारिश्रमिक देना – *n.* पुरस्कार – **rewarding** *a.* सार्थक

rhesus (´रीसस) *n.* दक्षिणी एशिया का छोटी पूंछ का बन्दर – **rhesus factor (Rh Factor** भी) मानव के रक्त की विभिन्न श्रेणियों को एक दूसरी से अलग करने वाली विशेषता

rhetoric (´रेंटरिक) *n.* प्रभावपूर्ण लेखन या भाषण की कला; वाक्यपटुता; शब्दाडम्बर – **rhetorical** *a.* प्रश्न जिसका उत्तर प्रश्न में ही निहित हो

rheumatism (रू´मटिज़म) *n.* गठिया – **rheumatic** *a.* गठिया संबंधी

rhinoceros (राइ´नॉसरस) *n.* गैंडा

rhododendron (रोड´डेंन्ड्रन) *n.* एक सदाबहार फूलों वाली झाड़ी

rhombus, rhomb (´रॉम्बस, रॉम) *n.* समचतुर्भुज; छै कोनों वाली आक ति

rhyme, rime (राइम) *n.* तुक, तुकबंदी (वाला काव्य) – *vt.* तुकबंदी करना

rhythm (´रिदम) *n.* लय, ताल; सामंजस्य – **rhythmic(al)** *a.* तालबद्ध

rib (रिब) *n.* पसली; धारी (स्वेटर आदि की) – *vt.* पट्टी लगाना, बुनाई में धारी डालना (**-bb-**)

ribald (´रिबल्ड) *a.* अश्लील, गंदा – **ribaldry** *n.* घटिया, अश्लील बातें

ribbon (´रिबन) *n.* फीता, पट्टी; किसी वस्तु का पतला, लम्बा टुकड़ा

rice (राइस) *n.* चावल

rich (रिच) *a.* अमीर; उपजाऊ; प्रचुर, (खाद्य पदार्थ) जिसमें चरबी और चीनी बहुत हो; मूल्यवान; विविधतापूर्ण – *n.* धनी वर्ग – **riches** *pl. n.* धन-दौलत, सम द्धि – **richly** *adv.* पूर्ण रूप से

rick[1] (रिक) *n.* पुआल का ढेर

rick[2] *n./vt.* मोच (आ जाना); मांसपेशी खिंच जान

rickets (´रिकिट्स) *n.* बच्चों को विटामिन डी की कमी से होने वाला रोग, सूखा रोग -**rickety** (´रिकिटि) *a.* डावांडोल; खस्ता हाल

rickshaw (´रिक्शॉ) *n.* रिक्शा

ricochet (´रिकशे, ´रिकशेंट) *vi.* (गोली का) ठोस वस्तु या जल से टकरा कर रास्ता बदल लेना

rid (रिड) *vt.* छुड़ाना, दूर करना (**rid, ridding**) – **riddance** *n.* छुटकारा, राहत; आराम

ridden (´रिड्न) RIDE का *pp* – *a.* (*in combination*) पीड़ित, प्रभावित

riddle[1] (´रिडल) *n.* पहेली, रहस्यमयी वस्तु या व्यक्ति

riddle[2] *vt.* (गोलियों से) छलनी कर देना

ride (राइड) *v.* चढ़ना, सवारी करना; (घोड़े आदि पर) चढ़कर पार करना – *vi.* घोड़े या गाड़ी आदि की सवारी करना – *vt.* यात्रा करना (**rode, ridden, riding**) – *n.* घोड़े आदि पर सवारी; घुड़दौड़ का रास्ता – **rider** *n.* सवार; अनुपूरक खण्ड (करार आदि में); दस्तावेज़ में जोड़ा गया अंश; गणित का प्रश्न – **take sb for a ride** को धोखा देना, बेवकूफ बनाना

ridge (रिज) *n.* जमीन का लंबा, संकरा, ढलान वाला भाग, पहाड़ी; मेढ़; दो ढलानों के मिलन की रेखा

ridiculous (रि´डिक्युलस) *a.* हास्यास्पद; बेतुका, मूर्खतापूर्ण – **ridicule** (´रिडिक्यूल) *vt.* खिल्ली उड़ाना, उपहास करना- *n.*

riding (´राइडिङ) *n.* घुड़सवारी

rife (राइफ़) *a.* (भ्रष्टाचार आदि) फैला हुआ

riffraff (´रिफ़्रैफ़) *n.* घटिया, कमीने लोग

rifle (´राइफ़ल) *vt.* छान डालना और उड़ा लेना- *n.* बंदूक, राइफल

rift (रिफ़्ट) *n.* दरार, दरज; *fig.* अनबन

rig (´रिग) *vt.* जहाज़ में मस्तूल आदि लगाना; साज़ सामान से लैस करना; अस्थायी ढांचा खड़ा करना;

बेइमानी से कोई व्यवस्था करना, धांधली (करना जैसे चुनाव में) (**-gg-**) – *n.* (भूमि/समुद्र से) तेल निकालने के लिए भारी मशीन

right (राइट) *a.* उचित, ठीक; न्यायसंगत, सच्चा; उपयुक्त; शुद्ध; दाहिना; *Politics* रूढ़िवादी दक्षिण पंथी; सीधा– *vt.* सीधा करना; खड़ा करना – *vi.* सीधे (खड़े) हो जाना – *n.* अधिकार, हक; रूढ़िवादी राजनीतिक दल– *adv.* सीधे; उचित रूप से; ठीक; दायें या दाईं ओर – **rightful** *a.* – **rightly** *adv.* – **right angle** 90° का कोण – **rightist** *n.* दक्षिणपंथी

righteous (ˊराइचस) *a.* न्यायप्रिय; भला – **righteousness** *n.* न्यायप्रियता; सदाचारिता

rigid (ˊरिजिड) *a.* अनम्य; कठोर; कड़ा – **rigidity** *n.* कठोरता; कड़ापन

rigmarole (ˊरिग्मरोल) *n.* निरर्थक शब्दों का समूह, बकवास

rigour (ˊरिगर) *n.* कठोरता, सख्ती, कड़ाई; कठिनाई, कष्ट – **rigorous** *a.* कठोर, कड़ा, सख्त

rim (रिम) *n.* किनारा; (ऐनक का) घेरा; (पहिए का) बाहरी गोला, हाल – **rimmed** *a.* हाशिएदार, किनारे वाला

rind (राइंड) *n.* (नींबू आदि का) छिलका, छाल

ring[1] (रिंङ) *n.* अंगूठी; छल्ला; चक्र, मंडल, घेरा; (व्यक्तियों का) गिरोह, गुट्ट; अखाड़ा विशे. मुक्केबाजी का; घेरा – *vt.* घेरा डालना– **ringer** *n.* घण्टी बजाने वाला; – **ring finger** सबसे छोटी से बड़ी उंगली, अनामिका – **ringleader** *n.* सरदार, सरग़ना – **ringlet** *n.* घुंघराले बालों का छल्ला – **ring master** (सर्कस में) रिंग-मास्टर – **ring road** चक्राकार मार्ग, मुद्रिका मार्ग – **ringworm** (ˊरिंग्वर्म) *n.* दाद

ring[2] *vi.* (घण्टी का) बजना; गूंजना – *vt.* (घण्टी) बजाना; टेलीफोन करना (**rang** *pt,.* **rung** *pp.*) – *n.* घण्टी की आवाज़; टेलीफोन (कॉल)

rink (रिंक) *n.* (**ice rink** भी) स्केटिंग या कर्लिंग (**curling**) के खेल के लिए जमाई बर्फ की तह

rinse (रिन्स) *vt.* खंगालना, धोना – *n.*

riot (ˊराइअट) *n.* दंगा; गड़बड़, अव्यवस्था; रंगरलियां; हो-हल्ला, बाहुल्य– *vi.* दंगा या बलवा करना – **riotous** *a.* उपद्रवी – **rioter** *n.* दंगाई

RIP requiescat in pace (*Lat.* rest in peace) ईश्वर (उसकी) आत्मा को शांति दे

rip (रिप) *vt.* फाड़ना, चीरना – *vi.* फटना, चिरना (**-pp-**) – **ripcord** *n.* पैराशूट खोलने की रस्सी – **rip-off** *n. sl.* चोरी

rip[2] *n.* – **rip-roaring** *a.* शानदार(*rip-roaring success*)

ripe (राइप) *a.* पका हुआ; युक्ति-युक्त (फैसला, निर्णय) – **ripen** *v.* पकना, विकसित होना

ripple (ˊरिपल) *n.* छोटी लहर; कलकल – *vi.* लहरिया बनना; (आवाज़ का) ऊंची और नीची होना – *vt.* छोटी लहरें उठाना

rise (राइज़) *vi.* उठना; ऊपर को जाना; (सूर्य आदि का) उदित होना; तरक्की करना; मूल्य या कीमत का बढ़ना; विद्रोह करना; (सभा का) विसर्जित या स्थगित होना; उत्पन्न होना, निकलना; (हवा, आवाज़) तेज़ होना (**rose, risen, rising**) – *n.* ऊपर उठने की क्रिया; ऊंचा ढलान, व द्धि, विशे. वेतन की – **rising** *n.* विद्रोह

risk (रिस्क) *n.* जोखिम, खतरा – *vt.* खतरा मोल लेना; दांव पर रखना – **risky** *a.* जोखिम भरा, खतरनाक – **at one's own risk** अपनी जिम्मेवारी पर

rite (राइट) *n.* धार्मिक क त्य, संस्कार या अनुष्ठान – **ritual** (ˊरिचुअल) *n.* धर्म विधि; कर्मकाण्ड; नियमित लेकिन घिसी-पिटी कार्यवाही या व्यवहार – *a.* – **ritualism** *n.* कर्मकाण्ड

rival (ˊराइवल) *n.* प्रतिद्वन्द्वी, प्रतिस्पर्धी – *vt.* प्रतिस्पर्धा करना, होड़ करना (**-ll-**) – *a.* प्रतिद्वंद्वी – **rivalry** *n.* प्रतिस्पर्धा, होड़

riven (ˈरिव़न) *a.* फटा या चिरा हुआ
river (ˈरिव़र) *n.* नदी
rivet (ˈरिव़िट) *n.* धातु के टुकड़ों को जोड़ने की कील, रिवट – *vt.* रिवट लगाना, पक्का जोड़ लगाना
Riviera (रिविˈएँरुअ) *n. US* समुद्र तट पर पर्यटक-स्थल
rivulet (ˈरिव्युलिट) *n.* छोटी सरिता
rly. railway का संक्षेप
road (रोड) *n.* मार्ग; सड़क; गली, बाज़ार; *fig.* दिशा – **roadblock** *n.* नाकाबन्दी – **road rage** एक (कार) चालक का सड़क पर दूसरे से हिंसक व्यवहार – **road sense** सड़क पर गाड़ी आदि चलाने की समझ – **roadshow** *n.* पत्रिका, कंपनी, राजनीतिक दल आदि का चलता फिरता प्रदर्शन
roam (रोम) *vi.* इधर उधर घूमना
roar (रॉर) *v.* दहाड़ना, गरजना – *n.* गरज, दहाड़ – **roaring** *a. inf.* खूब चलता (व्यापार, दुकान)
roast (रोस्ट) *v.* भूनना, सेंकना, बहुत गरम करना या होना – *n.* भुना हुआ मांस का टुकड़ा – *a.* भुना हुआ
rob (रॉब) *vt.* लूटना; धोखा देना; छल से छीनना (**-bb-**) – **robber** *n.* डाकू – **robbery** *n.* डकैती
robe (ˈरोब) *n.* लबादा, चोगा – *vt.* वस्त्र पहनाना – *vi.* वस्त्र पहनना
robin (ˈरॉबिन) *n.* रॉबिन चिड़िया
robot (ˈरोबॉट) *n.* मानव की भांति काम करने वाली मशीन, रोबॉट; यंत्रमानव– **robotic** *a.* रोबॉट सम्बंधी– **robotics** (रोˈबॉटिक्स) *n.* यंत्रमानव विज्ञान
robust (रोˈबस्ट) *a.* हट्टा-कट्टा, हृष्ट-पुष्ट
rock[1] (रॉक) *n.* चट्टान, ऊबड़ खाबड़ पत्थर; एक मिठाई – **rocky** *a.* – **rock bottom** सब से कम
rock[2] (रॉक) *v.* झुलाना, डुलाना – *n.* एक लोकप्रिय संगीत शैली – **rocker** *n.*, झूला कुर्सी, दोलन कुर्सी – **rock-and-roll** *n.* एक लोकप्रिय न त्य
rocket (ˈरॉकिट) *n.* आतिशबाज़ी (जो जलाने पर हवा में उठ जाय); अन्तरिक्ष यान ले जाने वाला उपकरण, राकेट – *vi.* तेज़ी से ऊपर उठना
rod (रॉड) *n.* पतली, सीधी छड़, छड़ी; डंडा, बेंत
rode (रोड) RIDE का *pt.*
rodent (ˈरोडंट) *n.* कुतरने वाला जीव, जैसे चूहा
rodeo (ˈरोडिओ) *n. US, A* बिना काठी के घुड़सवारी और घोड़े पर बैठ कर पशु हांकने की प्रतियोगिता
roe[1] (रो) *n.* (**roe deer** भी) छोटे कद का हिरण
roe[2] (रो) *n.* मत्स्यादंड (खाने में प्रयुक्त मछली का अंडाशय)
rogue (रोग) *n.* बदमाश, दुष्ट, नटखट बच्चा या आदमी; गुस्सैल जंगली पशु जो अपने झुण्ड से अलग रहता हो – **roguish** *a.* बदमाश जैसा व्यवहार; शरारत भरा
role, rôle (रोल) *n.* (अभिनेता की) भूमिका; विशिष्ट क त्य या कर्तव्य
roll (रोल) *v.* लुढ़काना – *vt.* लपेटना; बेलन से समतल करना – *vi.* लहराना; जहाज़ का डोलना; विमान का कलाबाज़ी खाना; गड़गड़ाहट की आवाज़ करना; (मशीन का) चलना – *n.* लुढ़कने, झूलने, डोलने या लहराने की क्रिया; गोल तह किए या लपेटे कागज़ की गड्डी; उस प्रकार गोलाकार कोई पदार्थ, सूची, तालिका; बेलन; के आकार की रोटी; गड़गड़ाहट जैसे ढोल आदि की – **roller** *n.* धातु या लकड़ी का बेलन टिकिया, बत्ती, गोली; लुढ़काव; लम्बी लहर (समुद्र में) – **roll back** कटौती करना; (कर प्रस्ताव आदि) वापिस लेना – **roll call** हाज़िरी लेना (स्कूल/सेना में) – **rolled gold** धातु जिस पर सोने का पानी चढ़ा हो – **roller bearings** इस्पात का पुर्ज़ा जो धुरी में लगता है – **roll-out** *n.* नये उत्पाद का

सार्वजनिक अनावरण – **roller skate** पहिए लगे जूते के नीचे बांधने के स्केट जिन्हें पहन कर तेज़ी से भागा जा सकता है – **rolling pin** बेलन (रोटी बेलने का)

rollicking (ˈरॉलिकिङ) *a.* उछल कूद कर के आनंद मनाता हुआ

roly-poly (ˈरोलिˈपोलि) *n.* एक प्रकार का हलवा – *a.* गोल-मटोल, मुटल्ला

ROM *Computers* Read Only Memory का संक्षेप

Roman (ˈरोमन)– *n.* रोम निवासी – **Roman Catholic** ईसाई चर्च का वह अंग जो पोप की प्रभुता को स्वीकार करता है – **Roman numerals** I, V, X, L, C, D, M रोमन शैली के अंक जिनका क्रमशः 1, 5, 10, 50, 100, 500, 1000 का मूल्य है

romance (रˈमैन्स, ˈरोमैन्स) *n.* उत्कट और सुखद प्यार; प्रेमाख्यान; रहस्यपूर्ण या उत्तेजक गुण; साहस व शौर्य कथा; कहानी जिसकी घटनाएं साधारण से हट कर हों; ऐसा साहित्य – **romantic** (रोˈमैंटिक) *a.* जिसमें प्यार का वर्णन हो; रोमांसवादी (साहित्य); कल्पना व भावुकतापूर्ण, प्रक ति प्रेम-सम्बंधी – *n.* रूमानी – **romanticism** *n.* रोमांसवाद, स्वच्छंदतावाद; भावना, कल्पना व प्रक ति-प्रेम से जुड़ी कला, साहित्य धारा

romp (ˈरॉम्प) *vi.* उछल कूद करना; खुशी से खेलना (बच्चों का) – *n.* उछलकूद

rood (रूड) *n.* क्रास; क्रास की मूर्ति

roof (रूफ़) *n.* छत; ऊपर का भाग; किसी वस्तु का ढक्कन (*pl.* **roofs**) – *vt.* छत डालना, छाजन डालना – **roofing** *n.* छत बनाने का सामान, खपरैल – **the roof of the mouth** तालू

rook[1] (रुक) *n.* कौए की जाति का पक्षी – *vt. sl.* धोखा देना; ठगना

rook[2] (रुक) *n.* शतरंज का एक मोहरा, रुख़, हाथी

rookie (ˈरुकि) *n. inf.* रंगरूट, नया भरती हुआ, विशे. सेना में

room (रूम) *n.* स्थान; पर्याप्त स्थान; कमरा; (**bedroom** भी) शयनकक्ष; गुंजाइश; अवसर – *pl.* निवास स्थान – **roomy** *a.* खुला– **room-mate** *n.* कमरे में साथी

roost (रूस्ट) *n.* पक्षी की छतरी, बसेरा – *vi.* छतरी पर बैठना – **rooster** *n.* **US** पालतू मुर्गा

root (रूट) *n.* (पौधे, पेड़ की) जड़, मूल; मूल, कंद (खाद्य जड़); महत्वपूर्ण अंग; स्रोत; उद्गम; मूल कारण; *Anatomy* दांत, बाल, नाखून आदि की जड –*v.* जड़ पकना; जड़ से उखाड़ना; खोदना; खोखला करना

rope (रोप) *n.* रस्सा – *vt.* रस्से से बांधना या घेरना

rosary (ˈरोज़रि) *n.* प्रार्थनाओं की श्र खला; माला, सूमिरनी

rose[1] (रोज़) *n.* गुलाब; छेद वाली टूंटी; गुलाबी रंग – *a.* गुलाबी रंग का – **rosy** *a.* गुलाबी रंगत वाला चेहरा; आशावान, उजज्वल – **rosewood** *n.* शीशम की लकड़ी; सुगंधित लकड़ी

rose[2] **RISE** का *pt.*

rosin (ˈरॉज़िन) *n.* गंधा-बरोज़ा

roster (ˈरॉस्टर) *n.* (**duty roster** भी) कर्मचारियों की सूची उनके काम के समय सहित, रोस्टर

rostrum (ˈरॉस्ट्रम) *n.* चबूतरा, मंचिका, व्याख्यान-पीठ (*pl.* – **trums**, – **tra**)

rot (रॉट) *vt.* सड़ाना, गलाना – *vi.* सड़ना, गलन; खराब हो जाना (**-tt-**) – *n.* क्षय; सड़न, गलन; रोग जिससे शरीर गलने लगे; *inf.* बकवास, बेकार की बात – **rotten** *a.*

rota (ˈरोट्अ) *n.* कर्मचारियों की सूची

rotary (ˈरोटरि) *a.* चक्रवात (गति); ऐसी गति द्वारा संचालित – **rotate** *v.* गोलाई में घूमना या घुमाना – **rotation** *n.* घूमने की क्रिया; क्रमे, बारी

rote (रोट) *n.* बार बार दोहराने की क्रिया

rotor (ˈरोटर) *n.* मोटर, इंजन आदि का घूमने वाला भाग, घूर्णक

rotten (ˈरॉट्न) देखिए **ROT**

rotund (रोˈटंड) *a.* गोल मटोल; – **rotundity** *n.* गोलाई; आडम्बर

rouble (ˈरूबल) *n.* रूस की मुद्रा, रूबल

rouge (रूझ़) *n.* गालों पर लगाने का लाल रंग, रूज – *v.* (चेहरे पर) रूज लगाना

rough (रफ़) *a.* खुरदरा, ऊबड़-खाबड़; मोटी, कर्कश (आवाज़); प्रचण्ड, तूफानी (मौसम); गुस्ताख; असभ्य; लगभग; अनगढ़; कच्ची (योजना) – *vt.* खुरदरा बनाना; मोटे तौर पर योजना आदि तैयार करना; (**rough it**) बिना सुविधाओं के जीना – *n.* खुरदरी या अनगढ़ अवस्था; स्थूल रेखाचित्र – **roughen** *vt.* खुरदरा करना – **roughly** *adv.* मोटे तौर पर – **roughage** (ˈरफ़िज) *n.* भोजन का वह भाग जो पचता नहीं लेकिन पेट साफ़ करने में सहायक होता है (शाक, भाजी आदि) – **rough and ready** *a.* काम चलाऊ

roulette (रूˈलेंट) *n.* जुए का एक खेल

round (राउंड) *a.* गोल, गोलाकार; मुड़ा हुआ; पूरा, पूर्ण; लगभग ठीक; बड़ा, काफ़ी; गोल मटोल; निश्चित – *adv.* गोलाई में या घुमा फिरा कर (जाने वाला) – *n.* गोल वस्तु; आवर्ती काम; प्रतियोगिता का एक चरण, चक्कर; दौरा; मुक्केबाज़ी आदि जैसे खेलों में खेल का एक दौर; गोली, कारतूस; फेरा; गोलाकार गति – *prep.* आसपास; सभी ओर – *v.* गोल बन जाना या बनाना – *vt.* इर्द-गिर्द घूमना – **roundly** *adv.* पूरी तरह – **roundabout** – *a.* घुमा फिरा कर कही गयी (बात) – **round-the-clock** *a.* चौबीस घंटे (काम आदि)– **round up** पशुओं को इकट्ठे कर के हांकना; अपराधियों को गिरफ्तार करना

rouse (राउज़) *vt.* जगाना, जाग्रत करना; उत्साहित करना; भड़काना – *vi.* नींद से जागना – **rousing** *a.* शानदार (स्वागत)

rout (राउट) *n.* घोर पराजय; भगदड़; हो-हल्ला – *vt.* तितर बितर करना; खदेड़ देना

route (रूट) *n.* मार्ग, नियत या चुना हुआ रास्ता – **route map** मार्ग दर्शक मानचित्र

routine (रूˈटीन) *n.* प्रक्रिया की नियमितता – *a.* साधारण; नियमित

rove (रोव़) *v.* इधर-उधर घूमना; मटरगश्ती करना – **rover** (ˈरोव़र) *n.* घुमक्कड़ व्यक्ति

row¹ (रो) *n.* पंक्ति, कतार; दर्जा

row² (रो) *v.* (नाव) खेना, चप्पू चलाना – *n.* नाव खेने की क्रिया – **rowing boat (rowboat** भी) चप्पू वाली नाव

row³ (राउ) *inf. n.* झगड़ा, उपद्रव – *vi.* लड़ना-झगड़ना, हल्ला मचाना

rowdy (ˈराउडि) *a.* ऊधमी – *n.* ऐसा व्यक्ति

royal (ˈरॉइअल) *a.* शाही, राजसी; वैभवशाली, शानदार – **royalist** *n.* राजतंत्रवादी, राजभक्त – **royalty** (ˈरॉइल्टि) *n.* राजत्व; राजसत्ता; राजा या रानी; स्वत्व शुल्क; रायल्टी (जो पुस्तक की बिक्री पर लेखक को या आविष्कारक को उसके आविष्कार के व्यापारिक उपयोग पर प्रतिवर्ष मिलती है) – **royal blue** गहरा नीला

RP Received Pronunciation का संक्षेप, ब्रिटेन में अंग्रेजी के उच्चारण का मानक रूप

RSVP répondez s'il vous plaît (*Fr.* कृपया उत्तर दें) का संक्षेप

rub (रब) *vt.* मलना, रगड़ना, घिसना; घिस या रगड़ कर सुखाना; मांजना, चमकाना; हाथ फेरना; छीलना; रगड़ कर हटाना या साफ़ करना – *vi.* रगड़ खाना, छिल जाना; घिस जाना (**-bb-**) – *n.* रगड़ने आदि की क्रिया; रुकावट, बाधा

rubber¹ (ˈरबर) *n.* रबर, रबड़; लिखे को मिटाने का रबड़; रगड़ने की वस्तु – *a.* रबड़ का बना

rubber² (ˈरबर) *n.* कई खेलों, प्रतियोगिताओं की अयुग्म संख्या (3, 5 आदि); तीन में से दो जीती गयी प्रतियोगिताएं

rubbish (´रबिश) *n.* कूड़ा करकट, रद्दी माल; बकवास – **rubbish bin** कूड़ेदान – **rubbish dump** कूड़े का ढेर

rubble (´रबल) *n.* ईंट पत्थरों के टुकड़े, रोड़ी

rubella (रू´बॅल्अ) *n.* खसरा

ruby (´रूबि) *n.* माणिक्य, याकूत (लाल रंग का हीरा) रूबी; उस का रंग – *a.* इस रंग का

ruck (रक) *n.* भीड़; जनसाधारण

rucksack (´रक्सैक) *n.* पीठ पर उठाने का थैला, पिट्ठू

ruckus (´रकस) *n. inf.* हो-हल्ला; उपद्रव, हंगामा

rudder (´रडर) *n.* नाव की पतवार; विमान में उस की दिशा बदलने का उपकरण

ruddy (´रडि) *a.* स्वस्थ, लाल या गुलाबी रंग का

rude (रूड) *a.* अशिष्ट, उजड्ड; गुस्ताख़, ढीठ; कच्चा; अनगढ़ – **rudely** *adv.*

rudiments (´रूडिमन्ट्स) *pl. n.* मूल तत्व; प्रारंभिक सिद्धांत – **rudimentary** *a.* प्रारंभिक, प्राथमिक, अल्पविकसित

rue (रू) *v.* शोक मनाना; दुःख होना – **rueful** (´रूफुल) *a.*

ruff[1] (रूफ़) *v.* कलफ़ लगा झालरदार कॉलर; (पक्षियों का) कंठा; समुद्र तट का एक पक्षी, गेहवाला – **ruffle** (´रफ़ल) *vt.* शिकन या सिलवट डालना, बाल खराब या अस्त व्यस्त कर देना; तंग या परेशान करना

ruffian (´रफ़िअन) *n.* गुण्डा, बदमाश

rug (रग) *n.* ग़लीचा, कालीन; मोटा ऊनी शाल या कम्बल

rugby (´रग्बिल) *n.* (**rugby football** भी) फुटबाल खेल का एक प्रकार जिसमें गेंद हाथों में उठाई जाती है

rugged (´रगिड) *a.* ऊबाड़-खाबड़; कठोर, कड़ा

ruin (´रूइन) *n.* विनाश, पतन; खण्डहर; धन सम्पत्ति या पद से वंचित होने की स्थिति; (~ **s**) *pl.* खण्डहर – *vt.* तबाह या नष्ट करना, बरबाद करना – **ruinous** *a.* विनाशकारी

rule (रूल) *n.* नियम, नियमावली; सिद्धांत; विधान; शासन; रिवाज़; नियंत्रण; मापने की चपती – *vt.* पर राज करना, का शासन चलाना; को वश में रखना; निर्णय करना; सीधी रेखाएं डालना – *vi.* शासन करना; निर्णय करना, फ़ैसला देना – **ruler** *n.* शासक; मापने की चपती, रूलर, फुट्टा – **ruling** *n.* निर्णय

rum (रम) *n.* गन्ने से बनी शराब, रम

rumble (´रम्बल) *vi.* (बादलों का) गड़-गड़ाना; (किसी गाड़ी का) चलते हुए गड़गड़ की आवाज़ करना – *n.* गड़गड़ाहट

ruminate (´रूमिनेट) *vi.* (पशु का) जुगाली करना; मनन करना, सोचना

rummage (´रमिज) *v.* छान डालना, तलाशी लेना

rummy (´रमि) *n.* ताश का एक खेल, रमी

rumour (´रूमर) *n.* अफवाह – *vt.* अफ़वाह फैलाना

rump (रम्प) *n.* (पशु का) पुट्ठा

rumple (´रम्पल) *v./n.* शिकन, सिल्वट

run (रन) *vi.* दौड़ना, तेज़ चलना; जल्दी से जाना; बहना (द्रव आदि, का); (नाक) बहना; भाग जाना; दौड़, प्रतियोगिता में भाग लेना; चुनाव में खड़े होना; घूमना; जारी रहना (यंत्र आदि का); फैल जाना; (कार्यक्रम आदि) चलना – *vt.* दौड़ते हुए पार करना; (खतरा आदि) मोल लेना; दौड़ना; समाचार पत्र का छापना, प्रकाशित करना; प्रबन्ध करना; (व्यवसाय) चलाना; (मशीन, गाड़ी आदि) चलाना (**ran** *pt.*, **run** *pp.*; **running** *pr. p.*) – *n.* दौड़, दौड़ने की क्रिया; भीड़; रुख; रास्ता; *Theatre* अवधि; (*series*) क्रम; भारी मांग; क्रिकेट में रन – **runner** *n.* दौड़ने वाला, धावक; सन्देश वाहक, हरकारा; व्यक्ति या जहाज़ जो तस्करी करता हो; कपड़े या कालीन की पट्टी – **running** *a.* लगातार जारी रहने वाला; एक के बाद एक आने वाला; दौड़ में भाग लेने वाला – *n.* प्रबन्ध –

runny *a.* जिससे स्राव निकलता हो, जैसे **runny nose** – **run down** शिथिल होना या करना; बदनाम करना – **run-of-the-mill** *a.* साधारण, सामान्य (नौकरी आदि) – **runway** *n.* हवाई-पट्टी

rung¹ (रंग) *n.* सीढ़ी, जीने का डंडा

rung² (रंग) RING¹ का *pp.*

running देखिए RUN

rupee (रू'पी) *n.* रूपया

rupture ('रप्चर) *n.* फटन, दरार – *v.* फटना, दरार पड़ना; अलग करना

rural ('रुअरल) *a.* ग्रामीण

ruse (रूज़) *n.* चाल, धोखा

rush¹ (रश) *vt.* जल्दी, अचानक या हड़बड़ा कर आगे ले जाना या धकेलना; पिल पड़ना– *vi.* जल्दी करना – *n.* दौड़; झपटने या टूट पड़ने की क्रिया; (भावों का) आवेग; (~ s) – *a.* जल्दी में किया गया (काम आदि)– **rush hour** प्रातः और संध्या का वह समय जब बहुत से लोग काम पर जाते या लौटते हैं

rush² (रश) *n.* एक दलदली पौधा; जलबेंत; बेंत

rusk (रस्क) *n.* एक प्रकार का कड़ा बिस्कुट, रस

russet ('रसिट) *a.* गेरुआ

rust (रस्ट) *n.* जंग, मोरचा– *vi.* ज़ंग या मोरचा लगना – **rusty** *a.* जिसे जंग लगा हो

rustic ('रस्टिक) *a.* देहाती; ग्राम्य, गंवारू, अनगढ़ – *n.* देहाती, ग्रामवासी; किसान – **rusticate** ('रस्टिकेट) *vt.* विश्व विद्यालय से कुछ समय के लिए निकाल देना – **rustication** *n.* विश्व विद्यालय से अस्थायी निर्वासन

rustle¹ ('रसल) *vi.* (सूखे पत्तों का) सरसराना – *n.* सरसराहट

rustle² ('रसल) *vi.* US मवेशी चुराना

rut¹ (रट) *n.* लीक; स्वभाव या जीवन शैली जिसका अभ्यास हो चुका हो; नाली, खांचा

ruthless ('रूथ्लिस) *a.* निर्दयी, निष्ठुर; बेरहम – **ruthlessly** *adv.* बेरहमी से

rye (राइ) *n.* गेहूं जैसा अनाज

S

Sabbath (´सैबथ) *n.* शनिवार जब यहूदी और कुछ ईसाई सम्प्रदाय विश्राम दिवस मनाते हैं; इतवार, जब ईसाई पूजा-अर्चना करते और विश्राम दिवस मनाते हैं – **sabbatical** (स´बैटिकल) *a./n.* विश्व-विद्यालय के कर्मचारियों आदि को अध्ययन करने के लिए दी गयी छुट्टी

sabotage (´सैबटॉझ़) *n.* सड़कों, मशीनों आदि की तोड़-फोड़ या विध्वंस जो जानबूझ कर किया जाय – *v.* तोड़-फोड़ करना – **saboteur** (सैब´टर) *n.* तोड़-फोड़ करने वाला

sabre (´सेबर) *n.* घुड़सवारों की टेढ़ी घुमावदार तलवार

saccharin (´सैकरिन) *n.* बनावटी शक्कर, सैक्रीन – **saccharine** (´सैकरीन) *a. lit./fig.* अत्यधिक मीठा

sachet (´सैशे) *n.* छोटा लिफाफ़ा या थैली

sack (सैक) *n.* बोरा; लूटपाट *inf.* बर्ख़ास्तगी – **sack-cloth** *n.* बोरे बनाने का मोटा कपड़ा

sacrament (´सैक्रमंट) *n.* ईसाई धर्म का संस्कार, विशे. यशु मसीह के अन्तिम भोज से संबंधित – **sacramental** *a.*

sacred (´सेक्रिड) *a.* पवित्र; धार्मिक

sacrifice (´सैक्रिफ़ाइस) *n.* त्याग; त्यक्त वस्तु; बलि, कुर्बानी – *vt.* बलि देना; त्याग करना – **sacrificial** (सैक्रि´फ़िशल) *a.* बलि, बलिदान के लिए

sacrilege (´सैक्रिलिज) *n.* किसी पवित्र वस्तु का दुरुपयोग या अपवित्रीकरण – **sacrilegious** (सैक्रि´लिजस) *a.* धर्म विरोधी, अपवित्रकारी

sacrosanct (´सैक्रोसैङ्क्ट) *a.* परम पावन

sad (सैड) *a.* उदास, दुखी; असन्तोषजनक; बुरी हालत में – **sadden** *vt.* दुखी या उदास कर देना – **sadly** *adv.* से – **sadness** *n.* उदासी

saddle (´सैड्ल) *n.* घोड़े की काठी, ज़ीन; साइकल की गद्दी; मांस का पारचा – *vt.* ज़ीन या काठी डालना – *a.* काठी जैसा

sadism (´सैडिज़्म) *n.* परपीड़न से (काम-) सुख प्राप्त करने की प्रव त्ति – **sadist** *n.* – **sadistic** *a.*

s.a.e. stamped/ self addressed envelope का संक्षेप

safari (स´फ़ारि) *n.* शिकारियों का दल, विशे. अफ्रीका में

safe (सेफ़) *a.* खतरे से बाहर, सुरक्षित; जिसमें खतरा न हो, निरापद; सावधान, सतर्क, विश्वसनीय – *n.* तिजोरी; गोश्त आदि के लिए हवादार आल्मारी – **safely** *adv.* बिना खतरे के, सुरक्षित, बिना दुर्घटना के, सही सलामत – **safety** (´सेफ़्टि) *n.* सुरक्षा, बचाव – **safeguard** *n.* सुरक्षा, बचाव के उपाय – *vt.* सुरक्षा करना – **safety glass** चकनाचूर न होने वाला कांच

safflower (´सैफ़्लाउअर) *n.* कांटेदार पौधा जिसके फूलों से रंग और तेल प्राप्त होता है, कुसुम्य

saffron (´सैफ़्रन) *n.* केसर– *a.* नारंगी

sag (सैग) *vi.* झोल पड़ना, बैठ जाना; एक ओर लटक जाना; धसकना (बोझ से); स्थान से हट जाना; थक जाना; (कपड़ों का) लटकना **(-gg-)**

saga (´साग़ अ) *n.* वीरगाथा (विशे. प्राचीन नॉर्स वीरों की); आख्यान

sagacious (स´गेशस) *a.* विचक्षण, दूरदर्शी – **sagaciously** *adv.* – **sagacity** *n.* विचक्षणता

sage[1] (सेज) *n.* मनीषी, पण्डित – *a.* बुद्धिमान

sage[2] *n.* एक सुगन्धित जड़ी, तानतानी, कसूरी मेथी

Sagittarius (सैजि´टेंअरिअस) *n.* राशि चक्र की नौवीं राशि जिसका काल 21 नवम्बर से 20 दिसम्बर तक होता है, धनुराशि

sago (´सेगो) *n.* साबूदाना

said (सेंड) **SAY** का *pt./pp.*

sail (सेल) *n.* जहाज़ का पाल; नाव चलाने की क्रिया, जहाज़ में यात्रा; जहाजों के लिए सामूहिक शब्द; पवन चक्की का पंखा – *vi.* जहाज़ में यात्रा करना; आराम से चलना (बिना बाधा के); समुद्री यात्रा प्रारंभ करना – *vt.* नाव चलाना – **sailor** *n.* नाविक, जहाज़ी

saint (सेंट) *n.* संत, धर्मात्मा; रोमन कैथलिक सम्प्रदाय में म त्योपरांत दी जाने वाली सम्मान सूचक उपाधि – **saintliness** *n.* पवित्रता – **saintly** *a.* संत जैसा (व्यवहार)

sake (सेक) *n.* कारण; खातिर; प्रयोजन; परिणाम – **for the sake of** की खातिर

salacious (स´लेशस) *a.* कामुकतापूर्ण, अश्लील

salad (´सैलड) *n.* सलाद – *a.*

salami (स´लामि) *n.* एक मसालेदार सासिज

salary (´सैलरि) *n.* वेतन, तनख्वाह – **salaried** *a.* वेतन भोगी

sale (सेल) *n.* बिक्री; कम कीमत पर माल बेचने की क्रिया; नीलामी – **saleable** *a.* बिकने योग्य – **salesman** (´सेल्ज़मन) *n.* दुकानदार का सहायक; कम्पनी की ओर से माल बेचने के लिए घूमने फिरने वाला – **salesmanship** *n.* प्रभावी ढंग से माल बेचने की कला

salient (´सेलिअंट) *a.* प्रमुख; उल्लेखनीय

saline (´सेलाइन) *a.* नमकीन – **salinity** *n.* खारापन

saliva (स´लाइवअ) *n.* लार; थूक

sallow (´सैलो) *a.* पीला, फीका

sally (´सैलि) *n.* धावा, विशे. सैनिकों का; चुटकुला या वैसी कोई बात – *vi.* झपट पड़ना; चल पड़ना (**sallied, sallying**)

salmon (´सैमन) *n.* (*pl.* **salmon**) बड़े आकार की चमकीली मछली, सामन; उसके मांस का गुलाबी रंग – *a.* गुलाबी रंग का

salon (´सैलौं, ´सैलॉन) *n.* (फैशनेबुल घरों में मेहमानों की) बैठक; नाई की दुकान

saloon (स´लून) *n.* यात्री जहाज़ का बड़ा कमरा; विशेष प्रयोजन (बिलियर्ड्स आदि) के लिए सार्वजनिक कक्ष; (*US* **sedan**) कार जिसमें दो या चार दरवाज़े और 4 या 6 यात्रियों के बैठने का स्थान हो – **saloon bar** होटल में मदिरालय, शराबघर

salsa (´सैल्सअ, *US* साल्सअ) *n.* दक्षिण अमरीका का न त्य-संगीत; एक प्रकार की सॉस

salt (सॉल्ट) *n.* नमक, लवण – *vt.* नमक लगाना; नमक में डाल कर सुरक्षित रखना – **salty** *a.* नमकीन, नमक जैसा – **saltcellar** *n.* नमकदानी

salubrious (स´लूब्रिअस) *a.* स्वास्थ्य वर्धक; लाभकारी

salutary (´सैल्युटरि) *a.* हितकर, लाभप्रद

salute (स´लूट) *vt.* नमस्कार करना, अभिवादन करना; प्रशंसा करना – *vi.* सलामी देना, सलूट मारना – *n.* अभिवादन, नमस्कार का शब्द; हाथ उठाकर सलाम करने की क्रिया (जैसे सेना में); (सेना में सम्मान प्रदर्शन के लिए) तोपों की सलामी – **salutation** (सैल्यु´टेशन) *n.* सलूट मारने, सलामी देने की क्रिया

salvage (´सैल्विज) *n.* सम्पत्ति/सम्मान अदि को नष्ट होने से बचाने की क्रिया; इस प्रकार बचाई सम्पत्ति – *vt.*

salvation (सैल्´वेशन) *n.* मुक्ति, मोक्ष; निस्तार

salve (सैल्व, साल्व) *n.* मरहम, मलहम – *vt.* मरहम लगाना; शांत करना

salver (´सैल्वर) *n.* चौकोर थाली (या ट्रे) जिसमें भोजन या चिट्ठी आदि रख कर लाई जाय

salvo (´सैल्वो) *n.* बन्दूकों, तोपों आदि का इकट्ठे छूटना; (गोलों की) बौछार (*pl.* – **vo(e)s**)

same (सेम) *a.* वैसा ही, वही; जो बदला न हो; एक जैसा, एकरूप; जिस की चर्चा अभी हुई हो – **sameness** *n.* साद श्य; एकरूपता, नीरसता

sampan (´सैम्पैन) *n.* एक छोटी नाव, साम्पान

sample (ʹसाम्पल) *n.* नमूना – *vt.* बानगी लेना या देना; परखना– **sampler** *n.* कशीदाकारी में नौसिखिए का अभ्यास; नमूने विशे० संगीत के

sanatorium (सैनʹटॉरिअम) *n.* पुराने रोगियों का अस्पताल; आरोग्य-स्थान; सैनिटोरिअम (*pl.* – **riums – ria**)

sanctify (ʹसैंक्टिफ़ाइ) *vt.* पवित्र या शुद्ध करना; पाप मुक्त करना (**-fied -fying**) – **sanctification** *n.* पवित्रीकरण – **sanctity** (ʹसैंक्टिटि) *n.* पवित्रता, पुनीतता – **sanctuary** (ʹसैंक्ट्युअरि) *n.* पवित्र-स्थान; शरण-स्थल; अभयवन, पशुविहार – **sanctum** *n.* (मंदिर में) पवित्र स्थान; (व्यक्ति का) निजी कमरा

sanctimonious (सैंक्टिʹमोनिअस) *a.* जो पवित्रता का ढोंग करे, पाखण्डी

sanction (ʹसैंक्शन) *n.* मंजूरी, अनुमति; आदेश या अधिकार, संस्वीकृति; कानून के उल्लंघन का दण्ड – (~**s**) *pl.* एक राज्य द्वारा दूसरे के विरुद्ध किसी कानून या अधिकार का उल्लंघन करने पर किया गया बायकाट या अन्य कार्यवाही – *vt.* अनुमति, आदेश या अधिकार देना

sand (सैंड) *n.* रेत, बालु – (~**s**) *pl.* रेत भरा स्थान जैसे मरुस्थल या समुद्र तट – *vt.* रेगमाल से रगड़ना; रेत से ढकना या रेत मिलाना – **sandy** *a.* रेत जैसा, उस के रंग का; जिसमें या जिस पर रेत चढ़ा हो – **sandbag** *n.* रेत का बोरा जो गोलों आदि से बचने के लिए/ मोर्चेबन्दी में, बाढ़ से बचने के लिए या हथियार के रूप में प्रयुक्त होता है – *vt.* ऐसे बोरे से मारना – **sand dune** रेत का टीला – *vt.* – **sandpaper** *n.* रेगमार – **sandpiper** *n.* टिटिहरी की जाति का पक्षी – **sandstone** *n.* बालू-पत्थर

sandal (ʹसैण्ड्ल) *n.* सैंडल

sandalwood (ʹसैंडल्वुड) *n.* चंदन

sandwich (ʹसैंड्विच) *n.* सैन्डविच – *vt.* दो चीजों के बीच रखना

sane (सेन) *a.* स्वस्थ मन वाला; समझदार – **sanity** (ʹसैनिटि) *n.* मानसिक संतुलन/स्वास्थ्य

sang (सैंग) SING का *pt.*

sanguine (ʹसैंग्विन) *a.* हंसमुख, आत्मविश्वास वाला; लाल रक्तिम वर्ण वाला – **sanguinary** *a.*, रक्तपात पूर्ण; खून का प्यासा

sanitary (ʹसैनिटरि) *a.* सफ़ाई, स्वच्छता-सम्बंधी – **sanitation** *n.* , सफ़ाई व्यवस्था; स्वच्छता – **sanitary towel, napkin** रजस्वला स्त्री द्वारा प्रयुक्त कपड़ा

sank (सैंक) SINK का *pt.*

sap[1] (सैप) *n.* पेड़-पौधों का रस (दूध) – **sapling** *n.* पौधा

sap[2] (सैप) *v.* धीरे-धीरे या गुप्त रूप से नष्ट कर देना; दुर्बल या कमज़ोर कर देना

sapphire (ʹसैफ़ाइअर) *n.* नीलम, नीलमणि; गहरा नीला रंग – *a.*

sarcasm (ʹसार्कैज़म) *n.* व्यंग्य, ताना – **sarcastic** (सार्ʹकैस्टिक) *a.* व्यंग्यपूर्ण, कटु – **sarcastically** *adv.*

sardine (सार्ʹडीन) *n.* एक छोटी मछली, सार्डीन

sardonic (सार्ʹडॉनिक) *a.* व्यंग्यात्मक; उपहासपूर्ण

sartorial (सार्ʹटॉरिअल) *a.* दरज़ी का या उससे संबंधित; पुरुषों के पहनावे का

sash (सैश) *n.* कमरबन्द; शरीर के गिर्द लपेटा चौड़ा फ़ीता

sashay (ʹसैशे) *vi.* आकर्षक चाल से चलना

sat (सैट) **SIT** का *pt./pp.*

Satan (ʹसेटन) *n.* शैतान – **satanic(al)** (सʹटैनिकल) *a.* शैतानी

satchel (ʹसैचल) *n.* (विशे. स्कूल का) बस्ता

sated (ʹसेटिड) *a.* छका या अघा हुआ

satellite (ʹसैटलाइट) *n.* उपग्रह (प्राकृतिक या मानव-निर्मित); पिछलग्गू; अधीन राज्य

satiate (ʹसेशिएट) *vt.* पूर्णतया तृप्त करना; छका देना – **satiety** (सʹटाइटि) *n.*

satin (सैटिन) *n.* रेशम, रेयॉन आदि का मुलायम, चमकदार कपड़ा, साटन

satire (ˈसैटाइअर) *n.* व्यंग्य-रचना; भ्रष्टता और मूर्खता का परदा फाश करने के लिए व्यंग्य का प्रयोग – **satirical** (सˈटिरिकल) *a.* व्यंग्यात्मक; कटु – **satirist** (ˈसैटरिस्ट) *n.* व्यंगकार – **satirize** (ˈसैटराइज़) *vt.* व्यंग्य करना

satisfy (ˈसैटिस्फ़ाइ) *vt.* संतुष्ट करना; (की) इच्छा पूरी करना; अदा करना; पूरा करना (शर्तें आदि); पूरी या समुचित मात्रा में देना; विश्वास दिलाना (**-fied, -fying**) – **satisfaction** *n.* सन्तोष, तुष्टि – **satisfactory** *a.* संतोषजनक

saturate (ˈसैचरेट) *vt.* तर-बतर कर देना; सराबोर कर देना – **saturation** *n.* सराबोर करने, भिगोने की क्रिया या उसका परिणाम – **saturation point** , परिपूर्णता

Saturday (ˈसैटर्डे) *n.* शनिवार

Saturn (ˈसैटर्न) *n.* एक ग्रह, शनि – **saturnine** (ˈसैटर्नाइन) *a.* उदास; निस्तेज

satyr (ˈसैटर) *n.* वन देवता; आधा नर आधा बकरा

sauce (सॉस) *n.* सॉस, चटनी – *vt.* सास/चटनी लगाना/डालना – **saucepan** *n.* देगची जिसमें लम्बा दस्ता (हैंडल) लगा हो

saucer (ˈसॉसर) *n.* तश्तरी, प्लेट; हल्का सा गड्ढा

sauna (ˈसौन्अ) *n.* भाप स्नान, भाप-स्नानघर

saunter (ˈसॉन्टर) *vi.* चहलकदमी करना

sausage (ˈसॉसिज) *n.* पशु की अंतड़ी में कीमा भर कर बना व्यंजन; सॉसिज

sauté (ˈसोटे) *a.* थोड़ा-सा तेल डाल कर जल्दी-जल्दी तला हुआ

savage (ˈसैविज) *a.* जंगली; भीषण, खूंखार; असभ्य; वहशी; कड़ी (आलोचना) – *n.* जंगली या वहशी कबीले का सदस्य; बर्बर –*vt.* नशंसता से आक्रमण करना; कटु आलोचना करना – **savagely** *adv.* – **savagery** *n.* नशंसता, क्रूरता; बर्बरता

save (सेव़) *vt.* बचा कर लाना, रक्षा करना; बचा कर रखना (भविष्य के लिए); जमा करना – *vi.* बचत करना; धन बचाना – *prep. obs.* के सिवाए – **saving** *a.* मितव्ययी; उद्धार – *prep.* के सिवाए – *n.* बचत – **savings** *pl.* धन दौलत, बचाकर रखा धन

saviour (ˈसेव्यर) *n.* उद्धारक; (**S-**) यशु मसीह

savour (ˈसेव़र) *n.* विशिष्ट स्वाद; सुगंध – *vi.* विशिष्ट स्वाद या सुगंध होना – *vt.* सुगंध, स्वाद देना; आनंद लेना; अच्छा लगना – **savoury** *a.* स्वादिष्ट, सुगंधित; मसालेदार

savoy (सˈवॉइ) *n.* बन्दगोभी की एक किस्म

savvy (ˈसैवि) *sl. vt.* समझना – *n.* समझ, बुद्धि – *a.* समझ वाला

saw[1] (ˈसॉ) *n.* आरा, आरी – *vt.* आरे से काटना, चीरना – *vi.* आरा चलाना (**sawed, sawn, sawing**) – **sawdust** *n.* लकड़ी का बुरादा

saw[2] (ˈसॉ) SEE का *pt.*

say (से) *vt.* कहना, बोलना; बयान देना; अभिव्यक्त करना; उदाहरण देना; विचार या राय प्रकट करना (**said** *pt./pp.*, **saying** *pr. p.*, **says** *3rd pers. sing. pres. ind.*) – *n.* (अपनी) बात; कहने का अवसर; निर्णय करने में भाग लेने का अधिकार – **saying** *n.* कहावत, लोकोक्ति

scab (स्कैब) *n.* (घाव का) खुरंड; त्वचा की बीमारी, पामा; पौधों की एक बीमारी

scabbard (ˈस्कैबर्ड) *n.* तलवार की म्यान

scabies (ˈस्केबीज़) *n.* त्वचा की एक बीमारी, खुजली, ख़ारिश

scaffold (ˈस्कैफ़ल्ड) *n.* मज़दूरों के लिए अस्थायी चबूतरा, पाड़; फांसी का तख्ता – **scaffolding** *n.* पाड़ बनाने का सामान

scald (ˈस्कॉल्ड) *vt.* गरम द्रव या भाप से झुलस देना; तरल पदार्थ को लगभग उबाल बिन्दु तक गरम करना – *n.* झुलसने से हुआ घाव

scale[1] (स्केल) *n.* (मछलियों, रींगने वाले जीवों की

त्वचा का) शल्क, छिलका; बॉयलरों में जमने वाले पदार्थ की तह; परत, पपड़ी – *vt.* छिलका उतारना; दांतों पर जमा मैल उतारना – *vi.* छिलकों या परतों में उतरना

scale² (स्केल) *n.* (मुख्यतया *pl.* में) तराज़ू, कांटा, तुला

scale³ (स्केल) *n.* माप, मापदण्ड; पैमाना, स्वरग्राम; अनुपात; (सापेक्ष) माप; मापक्रम, श्रेणी; क्रम; सोपान – *vt.* चढ़ना (पर्वत आदि की चोटी पर) – *a.* आनुपातिक – **scale up** *or* **down** आकार के अनुपात में बढ़ाना या घटाना

scallop (ˈस्कॉलप) *n.* घोंघा

scalp (ˈस्कैल्प) *n.* सिर की खाल (बालों समेत) – *vt.* बालों समेत सिर की खाल उतारना

scalpel (ˈस्कैल्पल) *n.* शल्य क्रिया करने वाले (सर्जन) का चाकू

scam (ˈस्कैम) *n. inf.* कांड, घोटाला

scamp (स्कैम्प) *n.* शरारती पुरुष या बच्चा

scamper (ˈस्कैम्पर) *vi.* भागना, चौकड़ी भरना

scan (स्कैन) *vt.* ध्यान से देखना; छानबीन करना; लय के साथ पढ़ना; परीक्षण करना; रेडार (RADAR) से चारों दिशाओं में खोजना; सरसरी निगाह डालना; विशेष मशीन की सहायता से वस्तु, व्यक्ति का कम्प्यूटर पर बिंब बनाना – *vi.* कविता का छन्द के अनुसार होना (**-nn-**) – *n.* छानबीन; परीक्षण – **scanner** *n.* टोह लगाने, पहचान करने या बिंब बनाने वाला इलेक्ट्रॉनिक उपकरण

scandal (ˈस्कैण्ड्ल) *n.* कलंक, बुराई; कांड, बदनामी; चुगली, चुगलखोरी – **scandalize** (ˈस्कैंडलाइज) *vt.* आघात पहुंचना, विक्षुब्ध करना – **scandalous** *a.* लज्जाजनक; अपमानजनक – **scandal monger** चुगलख़ोर, बदनामी करने वाला

scant (स्कैन्ट) *a.* बहुत कम; अपर्याप्त – **scantily** *adv.* – **scanty** *a.* कम

scapegoat (ˈस्केप्गोट) *n.* बलि का बकरा

scar (स्कार) *n.* घाव का निशान, दाग; किसी भावनात्मक कष्ट का परिणाम; दुख की याद – *v.* घाव का भर कर निशान छोड़ जाना (**-rr-**) – **scarred** *a.*

scarce (स्केअर्स) *n.* दुर्लभ; विरल; अपर्याप्त, कम – **scarcely** *adv.* बड़ी मुश्किल से, नहीं के बराबर –**scarcity** *n.* अभाव, कमी

scare (स्कैंअर) *vt.* डराना – **scared** *a.* भयभीत – **scary** *a.* डरावना – **scarecrow** *n.* पक्षियों को डराने के लिए खेत में रखा फूस का आदमी, धूहा, डरावा; गन्दे कपड़े पहने या घटिया दिखने वाला व्यक्ति – **scaremonger** *n.* आतंक या सनसनी फैलाने वाला

scarf (स्कार्फ़) *n.* गुलूबंद, रूमाल (*pl.* **scarfs, scarves**)

scarlet (ˈस्कार्लिट) *n.* चमकीला लाल रंग; इस रंग का कपड़ा; विशे. फौजी वरदी – *a.* इस रंग का; चरित्रहीन, विशे. ऐसी (स्त्री) – **scarlet fever** बुखार जिसमें लाल दाने निकल आते हैं

scathing (ˈस्केदिंग) *a.* अत्यन्त कटु या कठोर; हानिकर

scatter (ˈस्कैटर) *vt.* बिखेरना – *vi.* तितर बितर हो जाना – **scatterbrain** *n.* मूर्ख

scavenge (ˈस्कैविन्ज) *v.* कूड़ कबाड़ में काम की, खाने की चीज़ें खोजना; मरे हुए जानवर खाना (जैसे गिद्ध द्वारा) – **scavenger** *n.* कूड़ कबाड़ इकट्ठा करने वाला; पशु या पक्षी जो गन्दगी या कूड़ कबाड़ आदि पर जीता है (जैसे गिद्ध)

scene (सीन) *n.* घटनास्थल; नाटक का अंश, दृश्य; घटना; तमाशा, प्रदर्शन – **scenery** (ˈसीनरि) *n.* प्राकृतिक दृश्य, परिदृश्य; मंच-सज्जा – **scenic** (ˈसीनिक) *a.* सुरम्य, नाटक मंच का – **scenario** (सिˈनारिओ) *n.* नाटक के कथानक का संक्षेप या उसकी व्यवस्था; दृश्य विधान (*pl.* **-ios**) – **behind the scenes** *fig.* पर्दे के पीछे

scent (सेंन्ट) *n.* कोई गंध, विशे. सुगंध; खोज; सुराग, निशान; इतर, खुशबू – *vt.* सूंघ लेना या सूंघ कर पता लगा लेना; का सन्देह होना, खटका होना; सुगन्धित कर देना

sceptic, US skeptic (ˊस्केप्टिक) *n.* संशयवादी, संशयात्मा; अविश्वासी व्यक्ति – **sceptical** (ˊस्केप्टिकल) *a.* संशयात्मा; अविश्वासी – **scepticism** *n.* सदेहवाद, संशयवाद

sceptre (ˊसेप्टर) *n.* (सम्राट की शक्ति का प्रतीक) राजदण्ड; राजसी वैभव

schedule (ˊशेड्यूल) *n.* किसी परियोजना की प्रक्रिया की योजना; सूची, अनुसूची; कार्यक्रम – *vt.* सूची का कार्यक्रम में लिखना; किसी समय विशेष पर करने की योजना बनाना – **scheduled caste** *India* अनुसूचित जाति – **on schedule** नियत समय पर

scheme (स्कीम) *n.* योजना, स्कीम; रूपरेखा; परियोजना; इरादा; षड़यंत्र – *v.* योजना बनाना, विशे. गुप्तरूप से – **schemer** *n.* षड़यंत्रकारी – **scheming** *a.* मनसूबेबाज़; षड़यंत्रकारी

schism (ˊसिज़म, ˊस्किज़म) *n.* राजनीतिक दल या चर्च में फूट के परिणाम स्वरूप बना दल; पंथ

schizophrenia (स्किट्सो ˊफ्रीनिअ) *n.* मानसिक रोग जिसमें व्यक्तित्व के बारे में भ्रम हो जाता है, खंडित मनस्कता, स्किज़ोफ्रेनिया – **schizophrenic** *a./n.*

scholar (ˊस्कॉलर) *n.* देखिए **SCHOOL**[1]

school[1] (स्कूल) *n.* पाठशाला, स्कूल; स्कूल का भवन; विचार सम्प्रदाय – *vt.* पढ़ाना; नियंत्रण में लाना, सिखाना; प्रशिक्षित करना **schooling** *n.* स्कूल-शिक्षा – **scholar** (ˊस्कॉलर) *n.* विद्वान, पण्डित; छात्र व त्ति प्राप्त छात्र – **scholarly** *a.* विद्वान, पण्डित – **scholarship** *n.* विद्वता, पाण्डित्य; छात्रव त्ति – **scholastic** *a.* विद्यालयी, शैक्षिक; पण्डिताऊ

school[2] (स्कूल) *n.* मछलियों विशे. व्हेल मछलियों का झुण्ड

schooner (ˊस्कूनर) *n.* छोटा जहाज़ ; बड़ा गिलास

sciatica (साइˊऐटिक्अ) *n.* नितम्ब और जांघ की नाड़ी में पीड़ा – **sciatic** *a.* नितम्ब का; इस रोग से संबंधित

science (ˊसाइअन्स) *n.* विज्ञान; शास्त्र – **scientific** *a.* वैज्ञानिक; व्यवस्थाबद्ध – **scientifically** *adv.* – **scientist** *n.* वैज्ञानिक – **science fiction** वैज्ञानिक ज्ञान के आधार पर भावी घटनाओं की कल्पित कहानियां आदि, विज्ञान-गल्प

sci-fi (ˊसाइफ़ाइ) *n.* science fiction का संक्षेप

scimitar (ˊसिमिटर) *n.* खड्ग, शमशीर

scintillating (ˊसिंटिलेटिङ) *a.* रोचक, बढ़िया

scion (ˊसाइअन) *n.* राजवंशज; उत्तराधिकारी

scissors (ˊसिज़र्ज़) *pl. n.* (विशे. **pair of scissors**) कैंची

scoff (स्कॉफ़) *vt.* खिल्ली उड़ाना, उपहास करना

scold (स्कोल्ड) *v.* डांटना, झिड़कना; भर्त्सना करना; गुस्सा/नाराज़ होना – *n.* डांट डपट करने वाला – **scolding** *n.* डांट

scoop (स्कूप) *n.* बेलचे जैसा छोटा उपकरण जो कलछी, डोई या गोलची के रूप में प्रयुक्त होता है; उसमें समाई मात्रा; विशेष समाचार (जो किसी एक ही संवाददाता को प्राप्त हो) – *vt.* कलछी आदि से डालना; समेटना

scooter (ˊस्कूटर) *n.* स्कूटर

scope (स्कोप) *n.* गुंजाइश; विस्तार, प्रसार; विषय-क्षेत्र; परास, मार; मौका, अवसर; (व्यक्ति की) सामर्थ्य

scorch (स्कॉर्च) *v.* ऊपरी तल का झुलस जाना, झुलसा देना; सूख जाना; सिकुड़ जाना; भुन जाना – *n.* झुलसने की क्रिया

score (स्कॉर) *n.* खेल में प्राप्त अंक; बीस का समूह, कोड़ी; बहुत अधिक (विशे. *pl.* में); *Music* स्वर-लिपि, प्रबंध लेख; चिन्ह या खांचा, विशे. हिसाब रखने या गिनती करने के लिए लगाया

गया; कारण; हिसाब; शिकायत, झगड़ा – *vt.* खेल में अंक प्राप्त करना; निशान लगाना; काटना; संगीत-लेखन करना – *vi.* खेल में खिलाड़ियों द्वारा प्राप्त बिन्दुओं का हिसाब रखना; सफल होना – **score board** स्कोर बोर्ड

scorn (स्कॉर्न) *n.* तिरस्कार; उपहास – *vt.* घ णा करना – **scornful** *a.* तिरस्कारपूर्ण – **scornfully** *adv.* तिरस्कार से

Scorpio ('स्कॉर्पिओ) *n.* राशिचक्र की आठवीं राशि व श्चिक जिसका समय 23 अक्तूबर से 21 नवम्बर तक होता है

scorpion ('स्कॉर्पिअन) *n.* बिच्छू

Scot (स्कॉट) *n.* स्काटलैंड का निवासी – **Scottish** *a.* स्कॉटलैंड का – **Scotch** *n.* स्कॉच व्हिस्की

scotch (स्कॉच) *vt.* समाप्त कर देना

scot-free (स्कॉट्'फ्री) *a.* **get off scot-free** सज़ा से बच जाना

scoundrel ('स्काउन्ड्रल) *n.* बदमाश

scour[1] (स्काउअर) *vt.* साफ़ करना; मांजना

scour[2] (स्काउअर) *v.* (किसी चीज़ की खोज में) तेज़ी से किसी क्षेत्र में घूमना, छान डालना

scourge (स्कर्ज) *n.* चाबुक, कोड़ा; बीमारी

scout (स्काउट) *n.* टोह लगाने के लिए भेजा गया व्यक्ति; गुप्तचर; (स्कूल में) स्काउट

scowl (स्काउल) *vi.* त्यौरी चढ़ाना; क्रोध भरी द ष्टि से देखना; बिसूरना – *n.* नाराज़ होने या बिसूरने की क्रिया

scrabble ('स्क्रैबल) *vi.* अव्यवस्थित ढंग से हाथों या पंजों से खरोचना

scrag (स्क्रैग) *n.* दुबला पतला आदमी या जानवर; भेड़ की गरदन के मांस का छोर – **scraggy** ('स्क्रैगि) *a.* दुबला पतला; मरियल

scramble ('स्क्रैम्बल) *vi.* हाथ पांव के बल चलना या चढ़ना; रेंगना; (किसी चीज़ के लिए) संघर्ष करना, छीना झपटी करना; (विमान कर्मचारियों का) जल्दी में विमान को उड़ाकर ले जाना – *vt.* मिलाना; अण्डे फैंट कर दूध के साथ पकाना; इलैक्ट्रॉनिक उपकरण से बातचीत को अबोधगम्य (जो समझ न आये) बना देना – *n.* रेंगने की क्रिया; चढ़ाई; छीना झपटी; ऊबड़ खाबड़ भूमि पर मोटर साइकलों की दौड़

scrap (स्क्रैप) *n.* टुकड़ा; कतरन; (**scrap iron** भी) लोहा-लंगर; हाथापाई, मारपीट (**-pp-**) – (~ **s**) *pl.* टुकड़े – *v.* बेकार समझ कर फैंक देना या बेकार वस्तु के टुकड़े कर देना – *vi. inf.* हाथापाई या मारपीट करना – **scrappy** *a.* जिसकी गुणवत्ता एक सी न हो, जो ठीक से न बना हो – **scrap dealer** कबाड़ी

scrape (स्क्रेप) *vt.* खुरचना; खुरचकर साफ़ करना; खड़खड़ की आवाज़ करना – *n.* खुरचने की क्रिया या उसकी आवाज़; *inf.* उलझन, विशे. किसी शरारत के कारण उत्पन्न अटपटी स्थिति – **scraper** *n.* खुरचनी, रांपी – **get into a scrape** किसी मुसीबत में पड़ जाना – **scrape through** किसी प्रकार सफल हो जाना

scratch (स्क्रैच) *vt.* खरोंचना; खुजलाना; खरोंच के निशान डालना; (घुड़दौड़, प्रतियोगिता आदि से) नाम काट देना या वापिस ले लेना – *vi.* खुजलाने के लिए पंजों या नाखूनों से काम लेना – *n.* खरोंचने का घाव, निशान या आवाज़; दौड़ प्रारंभ करने की रेखा – *a.* काम चलाऊ; जल्दी में तैयार किया गया

scrawl (स्क्रॉल) *vt.* घसीट कर लिखना – *n.* असावधानी पूर्वक लिखी लिखावट

scrawny ('स्क्रॉनि) *a.* दुबला पतला

scream (स्क्रीम) *vi.* चीख़ना, विशे. डर या पीड़ा से – *vt.* चीख मार कर कहना – *n.* चीख़

scree (स्क्री) *n.* कंकड़-पत्थर जो ढुलकते रहें; ऐसे पत्थरों से ढकी ढलान, शैल मलबा

screech (स्क्रीच) *vi.* चीखना – *n.* चीख़; ब्रेक लगने पर टायरों के घिसने की आवाज़

screen (स्क्रीन) *n.* परदा, पट; चिक; सिनेमाघर का परदा; कार आदि के आगे का कांच– *vt.* शरण देना, छिपाना; चलचित्र दिखाना; निरीक्षण या छानबीन करना – **the screen** सिनेमा – **screenplay** *n.* पटकथा – **screen saver** कम्प्यूटर-पटल पर स्थित चित्र आदि को नुकसान से बचाने के लिए कुछ समय बाद उसका स्थान ले लेने वाला अस्थिर

screw (स्क्रू) *n.* पेच, पेंच; पेंच जैसी कोई भी वस्तु; जहाज़ आदि का पंखा; फेर – *vt.* पेंच से कसना; मोड़ना– **screwdriver** *n.* पेचकस

scribble (स्क्रिबल) *v.* घसीटना; लापरवाही से रेखाएं खींचना – *n.* घसीट

scribe (स्क्राइब) *n.* लेखक; लिपिक – *v.* किसी तीखी चीज़ से रेखा कुरेदना

scrip (स्क्रिप) *n.* कम्पनी का प्रतिभूति पत्र, शेयर

script (स्क्रिप्ट) *n.* लिपि; फिल्म, नाटक, रेडियो या टी.वी. कार्यक्रम का आलेख, स्क्रिप्ट; परीक्षा में उत्तर पुस्तिका

scripture (ˊस्क्रिप्चर) *n.* धर्मग्रंथ; बाइबल – **scriptural** (ˊस्क्रिप्चरल) *a.*

scrotum (ˊस्क्रोटम) *n.* अण्डकोषों की थैली, फ़ोता (*pl.* **-ta**)

scrounge (स्क्राउंज) *v. inf.* मांग-तांग कर गुज़ारा करना – **scrounger** *n.*

scrub[1] (स्क्रब) *vt.* पानी और ब्रुश से साफ़ करना; खुरचना (**-bb-**) – *n.* साफ़ करने या रगड़ने की क्रिया

scrub[2] (स्क्रब) *n.* झाड़, झाड़ी – **scrubby** *a.* झाड़-झंखाड़ भरा

scruff (स्क्रफ़) *n.* – **by the scruff of the neck** गुद्दी, गरदन के पिछले भाग से पकड़ कर – **scruffy** *a.* गंदा, मैला-कुचैला

scrum(mage) (स्क्रम, ˊस्क्रमिज) *n.* *Rugby* खेल का फिर से शुरू होना जब अगले खिलाड़ी धक्का पेल कर गेंद को हथियाने की कोशिश करते हैं; भीड़

scruple (ˊस्क्रूपल) *n.* नैतिक द ष्टि से अच्छे बुरे के बारे में संशय, धर्म संकोच; झिझक (पाप पुण्य की) – *vi.* झिझकना – **scrupulous** (ˊस्क्रूप्युलस) *a.* ईमानदारी, छोटी छोटी बातों का ध्यान रखने वाला; धर्मभीरू – **scrupulously** *adv.* – **scrupulousness** *n.* ईमानदारी

scrutiny (ˊस्क्रूटिनि) *n.* सूक्ष्म परीक्षण; छानबीन; वोटों आदि की सरकारी जांच; पैनी द ष्टि – **scrutinize** *vt.* सावधानी पूर्वक जांच करना

scuba (ˊस्क्यूब्अ) *n.* – **scuba-diving** *n.* पानी के नीचे सांस लेने के उपकरण स्क्यूबा की सहायता से समुद्र के अंदर तैरना

scuffle (ˊस्कफ़ल) *vi.* हाथापाई करना – *n.*

scullery (ˊस्कलरि) *n.* बर्तन मांजने का स्थान

sculpture (ˊस्कल्प्चर) *n.* मूर्ति कला; मूर्ति, प्रतिमा – *vt.* मूर्तिकला के माध्यम से अपने को व्यक्त करना – **sculpt** *v.* – **sculptural** *a.* मूर्तिकला संबंधी – **sculptor** (ˊस्कल्प्टर) *n.* मूर्तिकार (**sculptress** *fem.*)

scum (स्कम) *n.* झाग, फेन; कचरा, बेकार का भाग

scurrilous (ˊस्करिलस) *a.* गंवारू, अभद्र (भाषा आदि); गाली गलौज भरी (भाषा)

scurry (ˊस्करि) *vi.* अचानक या तेज़ी से दौड़ पड़ना (**scurried, scurrying**) – *n.* गहमागहमी, भागदौड़; हलचल

scurvy (ˊस्कर्वि) *n.* विटामिन सी की कमी से उत्पन्न रोग, स्कर्वी

scuttle[2] (ˊस्कट्ल) *vi.* तेज़ी से दौड़ जाना

scuttle[3] *vt.* जहाज़ को डुबाने के लिए उसमें छेद कर देना; (योजना, आशा आदि) विफल कर देना

scythe (साइद) *n.* दरांती – *vt.* दरांती से काटना

SE southeast(ern) का संक्षेप

sea (सी) *n.* समुद्र; लहरें; उफान; बहुत बड़ी मात्रा; लम्बा चौड़ा क्षेत्र – **sea change** स्थिति में महत्वपूर्ण परिवर्तन – **seafaring** (ˊसीफ़ेंअरिङ) *a.* समुद्री यात्रा करने वाला – **seafood** *n.* समुद्र

से प्राप्त भोजन (मछली आदि) – **sea horse** मछली जिसका मुंह घोड़े जैसा होता है – **sea lion** बड़े आकार की सील मछली – **seaman** *n.* नाविक – **seasickness** *n.* जहाज़ के चलने से होने वाली मतली – **seasick** *a.* – **seaside** *n.* तट पर स्थित स्थान, विशे. स्वास्थ्यवर्द्धक स्थान – **seaweed** *n.* समुद्री शैवाल – **seaworthy** *a.* समुद्री यात्रा योग्य (जहाज़ आदि)

seal[1] (सील) *n.* मुहर, मोहर, मुद्रा; मुहर का निशान; उपकरण जो पानी, हवा, तेल आदि को निकलने से रोकता है (**sealer** भी) – *vt.* मोहर लगाना; प्रमाणित करना; अनुसमर्थन करना; अधिकार देना; अच्छी किस्म का होने के चिन्ह के रूप में मुहर लगाना; गुप्त रखना; तय करना; पानी, हवा को निकलने से रोकने की व्यवस्था करना – **sealing wax** लाख

seal[2] (सील) *n.* सील मछली – **sealskin** *n.* सील मछली की खाल, चमड़ा

seam (सीम) *n.* सीवन; जोड़; पतली परत या पपड़ी – *vt.* धारी या शिकन डालना – **seamless** *a.* बिना जोड़ का; अबाध – **seamy** *a.* घिनौना; सीवन वाला – **seamstress** *n.* दरज़िन

sear (सिअर) *vt.* झुलसाना; दाग़ना; कठोर बना देना

search (सर्च) *v.* ढूंढना, तलाश करना; तलाशी लेना; छानबीन करना; मुआयना करना – *n.* तलाश, खोज तलाशी – **searching** *a.* पैना; कड़ा; पूरा – **searchlight** *n.* बिजली का तेज़ प्रकाश फेंकने वाला उपकरण, खोज-बत्ती, सर्चलाइट

season (ˈसीज़न) *n.* ऋतु, मौसम, किसी बात, काम, व्यापार के होने की अवधि, काल; उचित समय; मौका – *vt.* खाद्य पदार्थ में नमक-मिर्च लगाना; पूर्णरूप से तैयार करना या अधिक उपयोगी बनाना; (अधिक) अनुभवी बनाना – **seasonable** *a.* मौसम के अनुकूल; उपयुक्त – **seasonal** *a.*, मौसमी – **seasoned** *a.* अनुभवी – **seasoning** *n.* मिर्च-मसाले – **season ticket** निश्चित अवधि के लिए जारी किया गया टिकट

seat (सीट) *n.* (जहाज, गाड़ी, सिनेमा आदि में) बैठने का स्थान, आसन; नितम्ब; आधार; बैठने का अधिकार (संसद आदि में), सीट; स्थान जहां कोई वस्तु स्थित हो; रोग का स्थान; देहात में निवास-स्थान; पायजामा, पतलून आदि का पिछला भाग – *vt.* बिठाना; बैठने के स्थान की व्यवस्था करना; स्थापित करना, बैठाना – **seat belt** विमान या कार की सीट पर लगी पेटी

secede (सिˈसीड) *vi.* (किसी संघ या चर्च से विधिवत) अलग हो जाना – **secession** (सिˈसेशन) *n.* संबंध-विच्छेद – **secessionist** *n.* अलगाववादी

seclude (सिˈक्लूड) *vt.* अलग रखना – **secluded** *a.* दूरस्थ (स्थान), एकांत – **seclusion** (सिˈक्लूझ़न) *n.* एकांत

second (ˈसेंकण्ड) *a.* दूसरा; वैकल्पिक; अतिरिक्त – *n.* दूसरे स्थान पर व्यक्ति या वस्तु; सहायक; सैकिंड; क्षण; विशे. *pl.* में, घटिया माल, दूसरे दर्जे का माल – *vt.* समर्थन करना; प्रस्ताव का समर्थन करना – **secondly** *adv.* – **second-hand** *a.* पुराना (जो एक बार किसी ने प्रयुक्त किया हो)

secondary (ˈसेंकण्डरि) *a.* सहायक, गौण; कम महत्व का; किसी अन्य से विकसित या उस पर आश्रित; *Education* माध्यमिक – **secondarily** *adv.*

secret (ˈसीक्रिट) *a.* गुप्त, गोपनीय – *n.* रहस्य, भेद – **secrecy** *n.* गोपनीयता, छिपाव – **secretive** *a.* जिसे बातें छिपाने की आदत हो, चुप्पा; घुन्ना – **secretiveness** *n.* बातें छिपाने की आदत – **secretly** *adv.*

secretary (ˈसेंक्रट्रि) *n.* सचिव, मंत्री – **secretarial** (सेक्रिˈटेंरिअल) *a.* दफ्तरी (कार्य), लिपिकीय – **secretariat** (सेंक्रिˈटेंअरिअट) *n.* सचिवालय, मंत्रालय – **secretaryship** *n.* सचिव का कार्य या पद

secrete (सि'क्रीट) *vt.* छिपाना, गुप्त रखना; ग्रन्थि का स्राव छोड़ना – **secretion** *n.* छिपाव; स्रवण

sect (सेक्ट) *n.* सम्प्रदाय, पंथ, मत – **sectarian** *a.* साम्प्रदायिक; संकुचित विचारों का

section ('सेक्शन) *n.* काटा हुआ हिस्सा, भाग; विभाग; अनुभाग; खण्ड, टुकड़ा; (दस्तावेज़ का) भाग, अनुच्छेद, वर्ग; काटने की क्रिया, काट; किसी कटी हुई वस्तु का रेखाचित्र; (सेना की) टुकड़ी – **sectional** *a.* अनुभागीय; वर्गीय; प्रांतीय

sector ('सेक्टर) *n.* क्षेत्र, अंचल, खण्ड; व त्त खण्ड

secular ('सेक्युलर) *a.* लौकिक, सांसारिक, दुनियावी; धर्म-निरपेक्ष; चिरकालिक, चिरंतन – **secularism** *n.* धर्म-निरपेक्षता

secure (सि'क्युअर) *a.* सुरक्षित, निरापद; भय, चिंता से मुक्त, निश्चिंत; पक्का, मजबूत, निश्चित; विश्वस्त, विश्वसनीय – *vt.* कब्ज़ा करना; सुरक्षित करना; जमानत देना (कर्ज़ आदि की); पक्का, सुद ढ़ करना; बांधना – **securely** *adv.* – **security** *n.* सुरक्षा; आश्वासन; ज़मानत, प्रत्याभूति; जामिन (जमानत देने वाला) – **security guard** चौकीदार

sedan (सि'डैन) *n.* (**saloon** भी) US चार दरवाज़ों वाली कार

sedate[1] (सि'डेट) *a.* शांत; गंभीर

sedate[2] (सि'डेट) *vt.* शामक (नींद की गोली) देकर शांत करना – **sedation** (सि'डेशन) *n.* इस प्रकार शामक देने की क्रिया – **sedative** ('सेडटिव़) *a.* शामक, शांत करने वाली (औषधि) – *n.* शामक, नींद लाने की दवा

sedentary ('सेडन्टरि) *a.* (काम) जो बैठे बैठे किया जाय; बैठा रहने वाला

sedge (सेंज) *n.* दलदल में उगने वाली बड़ी घास, नरकट

sediment ('सेडिमंट) *n.* तलछट **sedimentary** *a.* तलछटी – **sedimentation** *n.* तलछट का बनना

sedition (सि'डिशन) *n.* राजद्रोह – **seditious** *a.* राजद्रोहात्मक (कार्य)

seduce (सि'ड्यूस) *vt.* किसी गलत काम, विशे. संभोग के लिए राज़ी करना; (स्त्री) का शील भंग करना; बहकाना; प्रलोभन देना; आक ष्ट करना – **seduction** *n.* ऐसा काम – **seductive** *a.* सम्मोहक – **seducer** *n.* (**seductress** (सि'डक्ट्रिस) *fem.*)

see (सी) *vt.* देखना, निहारना; समझना; निरीक्षण, जांच करना; पता लगाना; विचार, चिंतन, मनन करना; अनुभव करना; साक्षात्कार करना, मिलना; ध्यान रखना; साथ जाना –*vi.* देख सकना; विचार करना; समझना (**saw, seen, seeing**) – **seeing** *conj.* यह देखते हुए कि..., को ध्यान में रखते हुए – **see sb off** को स्टेशन आदि पर विदा करना

seed (सीड) *n.* बीज; मूल, उद्‌गम; वीर्य, शुक्र – *vt.* बीज बोना; टैनिस या अन्य खेलों में खिलाड़ियों के मैचों की व्यवस्था इस ढंग से करना कि सब से अच्छे खिलाड़ी एक-दूसरे से बाद में खेलें – *vi.* बीज उगाना – **seedling** *n.* पौध, पौद **seedy** *a.* फटीचर

seek (सीक) *vt.* खोजना, मांगना – *vi.* पता लगाना, छान डालना (**sought** (सॉट), **seeking**)

seem (सीम) *vi.* लगना, प्रतीत होना; दिखना, जान पड़ना – **seeming** *a.* दिखने में, प्रतीयमान – **seemingly** *adv.* देखने में, ऊपर से

seen (सीन) SEE का *pp.*

seep (सीप) *vi.* धीरे-धीरे रिसना

seer (सिअर) *n.* मनीषी; भविष्यवक्ता

seesaw ('सीसॉ) *n.* बच्चों का खेल, झूमा-झूमी, ढेंकी; इस खेल में प्रयुक्त तख्ता – *vi.* ऊपर नीचे होना

seethe (सीद) *vi.* फेन उठना; मन ही मन में बहुत गुस्से, आवेश में होना; लगातार हलचल की स्थिति होना (जैसे अपार भीड़ का-आगे पीछे होना) (**seethed, seething**)

segment (ˈसेगमंट) *n.* किसी वस्तु का कटा हुआ टुकड़ा; खण्ड; फांक – *v.* टुकड़े करना, खण्डों में बांटना – **segmental** *a.* – **segmentation** (सेगमेंन् ˈटेशन) *n.* खण्डीकरण

segregate (ˈसेग्रिगेट) *vt.* अलग करना – **segregation** (सेग्रि ˈगेशन) *n.* अलग करने या रखने की क्रिया/स्थिति, प थक्करण

seismic (ˈसाइज़्मिक) *a.* भूकम्प संबंधी – **seismograph** (ˈसाइज़्मग्राफ़) *n.* भूकम्प मापी (**seismometer** भी)

seize (सीज़्) *vt.* पकड़ लेना; कस कर जकड़ लेना; जीत लेना; (अवसर आदि का) लाभ उठाना – *vi.* मशीन में बेयरिंग या पिस्टन का गरम हो कर बंद हो जाना – **seizable** *a.* – **seizure** (ˈसीझ़र) *n.* जब्ती; रोग का दौरा

seldom (ˈसेल्डम) *adv.* कभी- कभार, यदा-कदा

select (सि ˈलेक्ट) *vt.* छांटना, चुन लेना; पसंद करना – *a.* चुनिंदा; छंटा हुआ; विशिष्ट – **selection** *n.* चयन, चुनाव, पसंद, संकलन – **selective** *a.* चयनात्मक, वरणात्मक; वरणशील

self (सेल्फ़) *pron.* आत्मवाचक या बल देने के लिए प्रयुक्त (*pl.* **selves** (सेल्व्ज़)) – *a.* (रंग) जो सभी जगह एक सा हो; इक रंगा (कपड़ा); एकरूप – *n.* व्यक्तित्व; स्वयं – **selfish** *a.* स्वार्थी; लालची – **selfless** *a.* निःस्वार्थ

self- (*comb. form*) अपना, निज, स्व, आत्म आदि जैसे निम्नलिखित शब्दों में – **self-addressed** स्वनामांकित – **self-centred** स्वकेन्द्रित – **self-confident** आत्मविश्वासी – **self-contained** स्वतःपूर्ण – **self-control** आत्मसंयम – **self-defence** आत्मरक्षा – **self-employed** स्वनियोजित – **self-evident** स्वतःसिद्ध – **self-help** स्वावलंबन, आत्मनिर्भरता – **self-interest** आत्महित, स्वार्थ – **self-pity** आत्मदया – **self-reliant** आत्मनिर्भर – **self-sacrifice** आत्म-बलिदान, आत्म-त्याग – **self-supporting** स्वावलंबी

self-absorbed *a.* स्वयं में खोया हुआ, निमग्न

self-appointed *a.* स्वयं-नियुक्त

self-appraisal *n.* (कार्य का) स्वयं-मूल्यांकन

self-assertive *a.* स्वाग्रही, आत्मविश्वासपूर्ण

self-conscious (सेल्फ़् ˈकॉन्शस) *a.* आत्मचेतन, संकोची; जिसे अपने क त्यों और स्थितियों की गंभीर अनुभूति हो

self determination (सेल्फ़डिटर्मि ˈनेशन) *n.* व्यक्ति या राष्ट्र का अपने भाग्य का स्वयं फैसला करने का अधिकार, आत्म-निर्णय

self-made (सेल्फ़् ˈमेड) *a.* (व्यक्ति) जो बिना किसी की सहायता के उन्नति कर पाया हो, स्वनिर्मित

self-possessed (सेल्फ़् प ˈज़ेस्ट) *a.* शांत, धीर – **self-possession** (सेल्फ़् प ˈज़ेशन) *n.* धीरज, आत्मसंयम

self-respect (सेल्फ़रि ˈस्पेक्ट) *n.* आत्मसम्मान, खुद्दारी

self-righteous (सेल्फ़् ˈराइचस) *a.* जिसे अपने अच्छा होने का घमण्ड हो, दंभी

self-service (सेल्फ़् ˈसर्विस) *a./n.* दुकान या रेस्तोरां जहां लोग अपनी पसन्द की चीज़ें स्वयं ही उठाते, परोसते हैं, स्वयं सेवा

self-sufficient (सेल्फ़् ˈसफ़िशंट) *a.* आत्मनिर्भर

sell (सेल) *vt.* बेचना, बेचने के लिए रखना; बिक्री करना, राज़ी करना; *inf.* धोखा या विश्वासघात करना – *vi.* बिकना (**sold, selling**) – **seller** *n.* – **sellout** *n.* सारे माल, टिकटों आदि का बिक जाना; विश्वासघात

semantic (सि ˈमैन्टिक) *a.* शब्दों के अर्थ से संबंधित – **semantics** *n.* शब्दों के अर्थों का अध्ययन, अर्थ विज्ञान

semblance (ˈसेम्ब्लन्स) *n.* (झूठी) प्रतीति या आभास; आक ति; झलक; साद श्य

semen (ˈसीमेन) *n.* वीर्य, शुक्र

semester (सि ˈमेस्टर) *n.* US कई विश्व-विद्यालयों, कालिजों में छह महीने का सत्र

semi- (*comb. form*) आधा, आंशिक, अपूर्ण, जैसे **semicircle**

semi-automatic *a.* अर्द्ध-स्वचलित (बंदूक)

semibreve (ˈसैमिब्रीव़) *n.* आधा स्वर

semicircle (ˈसैमि सर्कल) *n.* अर्धवृत्त – **semicircular** (सेमिˈसर्क्युलर) *a.* अर्धवृत्ताकार

semicolon (सैमिˈकॉलन) *n.* एक विराम चिन्ह, अर्धविराम (;)

semiconductor (सैमिकन्ˈडक्टर) *n.* ठोस पदार्थ जिसमें से विद्युत प्रवाहित हो सकती है; सेमीकंडक्टर लगा उपकरण

semi-final (सैमिˈफ़ाइनल) *n.* मैच, प्रतियोगिता जो अन्तिम से पहले की हो; सेमीफ़ाइनल

seminal (ˈसैमिनल) *a.* जिसमें विकसित होने की सामर्थ्य हो; प्रभावशाली; वीर्य, बीज संबंधी

seminar (ˈसैमिनार) *n.* (छात्र समूहों की) विचार गोष्ठी; गोष्ठी

semiprecious (सैमिˈप्रैशस) *a.* कीमती पत्थर जो हीरों से कम मूल्य के हों

semi-skilled (सैमिˈस्किल्ड) *a.* अर्ध-प्रशिक्षित; अर्ध-कुशल

semolina (सैमˈलीन्अ) *n.* सूजी

senate (ˈसैनिट) *n.* राज्य, विश्व विद्यालय का ऊपरी सदन, सीनेट, अधिसभा; राज्य परिषद – **senator** (ˈसेनटर) *n.* सीनेट-सदस्य

send (सैण्ड) *vt.* भेजना; पहुंचाना; रवाना करना; रेडियो द्वारा (संदेश) भेजना (**sent, sending**) – **send-off** *n.* विदाई अवसर

senile (ˈसीनाइल) *a.* जो सठिया गया हो, जराग्रस्त – **senility** (सिˈनिलिटि) *n.* जरा, जीर्णता, सठियाने की स्थिति, सठियाना

senior (ˈसीनिअर, ˈसीन्यर) *a.* जो पद या स्थिति में बड़ा हो, प्रवर, वरिष्ठ; ज्येष्ठ; अग्रज, अधिक आयु का – *n.* वरिष्ठ, वय प्राप्त व्यक्ति – **seniority** *n.* वरिष्ठता; प्रवरता – **senior citizen** वयोवृद्ध व्यक्ति

sensation (सैन्ˈसेशन) *n.* अनुभूति, अनुभव; प्रतीति; चेतना; उत्तेजित भावनाएं; उत्तेजना; सनसनी; हलचल, हड़बड़ी – **sensational** *a.* सनसनीखेज़ – **sensationalism** *n.*

sense (सैन्स) *n.* इन्द्रिय, ज्ञानेन्द्रिय; संवेदन, अनुभूति; मानसिक सतर्कता; चेतना, होश; अर्थ; बोधगम्य अर्थ; समझ, समझदारी – *vt.* समझ लेना, बूझ लेना, भाँप लेना – **senseless** *a.* बेहोश; मूर्खतापूर्ण; निरर्थक

sensible (ˈसैन्सिबल) *a.* समझदार, विवेकशील; जिस का ज्ञान इन्द्रियों से सम्भव हो; सचेत; जिसे ध्यान रहता हो– **sensibility** *n.* संवेदनशीलता – (~ **ties**) *pl.* भावनाएं – **sensibly** *adv.*

sensitive (ˈसैन्सिटिव) *a.* संवेदनशील; नाजुक मिजाज; अत्यधिक संवेदी, सूक्ष्मग्राही, अस्थिर – **sensitively** *adv.* – **sensitivity, sensitiveness** *n.* अतिसंवेदनशीलता, भावुकता, चिड़चिड़ापन

sensor (ˈसैन्सर) *n.* उपकरण जो इशारा पाने पर काम करता है

sensory (ˈसैन्सरि) *a.* इन्द्रियों से सम्बन्धित, ज्ञानेद्रियों का

sensual (ˈसैन्स्युअल) *a.* इन्द्रियों का; विषयासक्त – **sensuality** *n.* विषयासक्ति, कामुकता

sensuous (ˈसैन्स्युअस) *a.* इन्द्रियों द्वारा ज्ञेय, विशे. सौन्दर्यबोध के मामले में; इन्द्रियग्राह्य

sent (सैन्ट) **SEND** का *pt./pp.*

sentence (ˈसैन्टन्स) *n.* वाक्य; न्यायालय का फैसला, दण्डादेश, सज़ा – *vt.* सज़ा देना; दोषी ठहराना

sentiment (ˈसैन्टिमंट) *n.* तर्क की बजाय भावना से प्रभावित होने की प्रवृत्ति; भाव; भावना की अभिव्यक्ति; विचार – **sentimental** *a.* भावुक, दुर्बल; बात बात पर रो देने वाला – **sentimentality** *n.* भावुकता, भावप्रवणता

sentinel (ˈसैन्टिनल) *n.* संतरी

sentry ('सेंन्ट्रि) *n.* संतरी

separate *vt.* ('सेंपरेट) अलग करना; बांटना – *vi.* अलग होना; बिछड़ जाना – *a.* ('सेंपरिट) अलग-थलग; कटा हुआ; विशिष्ट, निजी– **separable** *a.* – **separately** *adv.* – **separation** (सेंप'रेशन) *n.* अलग होने की क्रिया, *Law.* पति पत्नी का तलाक लिए बिना अलग अलग रहना – **separator** *n.* दूध से क्रीम निकालने का उपकरण

sepia ('सीपिअ) *n.* एक मछली के स्राव से बना ललाई लिए भूरा रंग – *a.* इस रंग का

Sept. September का संक्षेप

September ('सेंप्टेंम्बर) *n.* सितम्बर

septic ('सेंप्टिक) *a.* (घाव) जिसमें पीव पड़ गयी हो

septuagenarian (सेंप्ट्युअजि- 'नेंअरिअन) *a.* 70 और 80 साल के बीच की आयु का – *n.*

sepulchre ('सेंपल्कर) *n.* समाधि, मकबरा

sequel ('सीक्वल) *n.* परिणाम; (कहानी का) आगे घटनाक्रम, उत्तरकथा

sequence ('सीक्वन्स) *n.* क्रमबद्ध करने की क्रिया; कथाक्रम; फिल्म का भाग या घटना

sequin ('सीक्विन) *n.* सितारा जो स्त्रियों की ओढ़नी आदि पर टांका जाता है

serene (सि'रीन) *a.* शांत, प्रशांत; स्वच्छ; चुपचाप; धीर – **serenely** *adv.* – **serenity** (सि'रेंनिटि) *n.* शांति; स्वच्छता

serf (सर्फ़) *n.* दास, गुलाम – **serfdom, serfhood** *n.* गुलामी

serge (सर्ज) *n.* एक प्रकार का मजबूत ऊनी कपड़ा, सर्ज

sergeant, serjeant ('सार्जन्ट) *n.* सेना, पुलिस में एक अधिकारी, सार्जेन्ट – **sergeant major** *US* रेजिमेंट में गैर.कमीशन प्राप्त अधिकारियों में सबसे बड़ा – **sergeant at arms** संसद, न्यायालय का एक अधिकारी

series ('सिअरीज़) *n.* श्रृंखला; क्रम, सिलसिला; रेडियो, टी.वी. आदि कार्यक्रमों का क्रम, धारावाहिक (जिसमें पात्र वही लेकिन घटनाएं अलग अलग हों) (*pl.* **series**) – **serial** ('सिअरिअल) *n.* धारावाहिक; धारावाहिक प्रकाशन – **serialize** *v.* धारावाहिक के रूप में (किस्तों में) प्रकाशित/प्रस्तुत करना

serious ('सिअरिअस) *a.* गंभीर; संगीन; सच्चा; महत्वपूर्ण; चिंताजनक – **seriously** *adv.* गंभीरता से

sermon ('सर्मन) *n.* प्रवचन; उपदेश; धर्मोपदेश – **sermonize** *vi.* प्रवचन या उपदेश देना

serpent ('सर्पन्ट) *n. literary* सांप, सर्प – **serpentine** ('सर्पंटाइन) *a.* सांप की तरह बल खाता हुआ, लहरिया

serrated (सेंरिटिड) *a.* दंदानेदार, आरी जैसे दांतों वाला

serum ('सिअरम) *n.* शरीर का द्रव, विशे. लहू का द्रव भाग जो टीका बनाने के काम आता है, सीरम

serve (सर्व़) *v.* (मुख्य *vt.*) नौकरी करना; दुकान में ग्राहकों को सामान आदि दिखाना; भोजन परोसना; नियमित रूप से सामान आदि देना; सेना में नौकरी करना; समय बिताना (किसी काम, जेल आदि में); के लिए काम आना, उपयोगी होना; (टेनिस आदि खेलों में) गेंद फैंकना; (अदालत के समन) भेजना – *n.* गेंद फैंकने की क्रिया – **servant** ('सर्वेन्ट) *n.* निजी या घरेलू नौकर – **service** ('सर्विस) *n.* नौकरी, सेवा; सहायता; गाड़ी आदि की मरम्मत, सफाई आदि; प्रयोग के लिए उद्यत होने की स्थिति; सरकारी नौकरी; रकाबियों आदि का समूह (जैसे *dinner service*); सार्वजनिक पूजा, अर्चना की विधि –(~**s** *pl.* सशस्त्र सेनाएं – *vt.* यंत्र आदि की पूरी मरम्मत – **serviceable** *a.* जो चालू हालत में हो; टिकाऊ; इस्तेमाल के योग्य – **serviceman** *n.* सैनिक, नौसैनिक या वायुसैनिक – **service road** संकरी सड़क जो मकानों, दुकानों तक जाती है – **service**

station स्थान जहां कारों आदि के लिए तेल, पेट्रोल और मरम्मत आदि की व्यवस्था हो

serviette (सर्वि'एॅट) *n.* खाने की मेज़ पर रखने का छोटा तौलिया

servile ('सर्वाइल) *a.* दासों जैसा; जिसमें आत्मनिर्भरता न हो; चापलूस – **servility** (सर्'विलिटि) *n.* चापलूसी, जी हज़ूरी

servitude ('सर्विट्यूड) *n.* दासता, गुलामी

sesame ('सेंसमि) *n.* तिल

session ('सेंशन) *n.* न्यायालय आदि की बैठक; सभा; अधिवेशन; किसी कार्यक्रम की अवधि, सत्र; स्कूल या विश्वविद्यालय का वर्ष

set (सेंट) *v.* (मुख्य *vt.*) रखना; बैठाना; बिठाना; जड़ना; (खाने की मेज़) लगाना, तैयार करना; सुद ढ़ या पक्का हो जाना; निश्चित करना, ठहराना; तय करना, देना; संगीत पर बैठाना; (बाल) बनाना; (सूर्य का) अस्त होना; की ओर बढ़ना, चलना (**set, setting**) – *a.* नियत, निश्चित, स्थिर; जानबूझ कर किया गया; औपचारिक; पूर्व निश्चित; अपरिवर्तनीय – *n.* स्थिरीकरण स्थिर, निश्चित होने की क्रिया; भाव-भंगिमा, ठवन, रेडियो या टेलीविज़न का सेट; रंगमंच या सिनेमा में मंच सज्जा; वस्तुओं का समूह; व्यक्तियों का समूह जो एक जैसे समझे जाते हों; *Maths* संख्याओं का समूह, समुच्चय; एक जैसी वस्तुओं का समूह – **set aside** *v.* (कार्य विशेष के लिए धन आदि) अलग रख देना; (निर्णय) रद्द कर देना – **setback** *n.* धक्का – **setup** *n.* स्थिति; संगठन – **set up** स्थापित करना

settee (सें'टी) *n.* कोच, सोफ़ा

setting ('सेंटिङ) *n.* प ष्ठभूमि; परिवेश, अड़ौस-पड़ौस; मंच सज्जा; जमाने या जड़ने का काम; चौखटा; (रत्न आदि जड़ने का) स्थान; मेज़ पर एक व्यक्ति के खाने के बरतन, चम्मच आदि; (सूर्य का) अस्तगमन; गाने के लिए संगीत

settle ('सेंट्ल) *vt.* व्यवस्थित करना; स्थापित, सुरक्षित, पक्का करना; निर्णय करना; झगड़ा आदि निपटाना; भुगतान करना – *vi.* बैठ जाना; तह में बैठ जाना या धंस जाना; स्पष्ट हो जाना; समझौता करना – **settlement** *n.* समझौता, निपटारा; बस्ती; कानून के अनुसार दी गयी राशि – **settler** *n.* अधिवासी; उपनिवेश बनाने वाला

set top box उपकरण जो सेटलाइट आदि से आते संकेतों को साधारण टी.वी. पर देखने युक्त बनता है

seven ('सेंवन) *a./n.* सात – **seventh** *a.* सातवां – **seventeen** (सेंवन्'टीन) *a./n.* सत्रह – **seventy** *a./n.* सत्तर

sever ('सेंवर) *v.* अलग, करना; काट देना – **severance** ('सेंवरन्स) *n.* प थक्करण; (संबंध) विच्छेद

several ('सेंवरल) *a.* कुछ; थोड़े से; व्यक्तिगत; विभिन्न; अलग-अलग – *pron.* (थोड़ी सी) संख्या – **severally** *adv.* अलग-अलग

severe (सि'विअर) *a.* सख्त, कड़ा; श्रम साध्य; जिसे करना कठिन हो; तीखा (स्वर); सादा; प्रचंड – **severely** *adv.* – **severity** (सि'वेंरिटि) *n.* प्रचण्डता; सख्ती

sew (सो) *v.* सिलाई करना (**sewed** *pt.*, **sewn** *pp.*, **sewing** *pr. p.*) – **sewing** *n.* सिलाई

sewage ('सूइज) *n.* नाली में बहता मल व अन्य गंदगी – **sewer** ('सूअर) *n.* भूमिगत नाला – **sewerage** ('सूअरिज) *n.* नालियों की व्यवस्था

sex (सेंक्स) *n.* नर या मादा होने की स्थिति, लिंग; योनि, सैक्स; संभोग – *a.* योनि-, लिंग-, लैंगिक – *vt.* यह पता लगाना कि नर है या मादा – **sexism** *n.* लिंग पर आधारित भेदभाव – **sexist** *n./a.* – **sexual** ('सेंक्स्युल) *a.* यौन- लैंगिक, मैथुन-संबंधी – **sexually** *adv.* – **sexy** ('सेंक्सि) *a.* कामुक, कामोत्तेजक – **sexual harassment** (विशे० स्त्रियों से) दफ्तर आदि में छेड़ छाड़ – **sexual intercourse** संभोग

sextant (सॅक्स्टंट) *n.* ग्रहों की स्थिति मापने का यंत्र, सैक्सटैंट

sf. science fiction का संक्षेप

shabby (ʹशैबि) *a.* बदरंग, फटा पुराना; फटेहाल; कमीना; घटिया– **shabbily** *adv.* – **shabbiness** *n.*

shack (शैक) *n.* झोंपड़ी

shackle (ʹशैकल) *n.* बेड़ी; बन्धन – *vt.* हथकड़ी या बेड़ी पहनाना; बंधन में रखना

shade (शेड) *n.* छाया, साया; स्थान जहां अंधेरा हो; रंग की गहराई, रंगत; भूत, प्रेत; परदा; परदे के रूप में प्रयुक्त कोई वस्तु; **US** खिड़की की झिलमिली – *pl.* **US** *sl.* काला चश्मा, धूप की ऐनक – *vt.* धूप से बचाना; छाया में रखना; (चित्र में) छाया दिखाना – **shady** *a.* छायादार; संदेहजनक

shadow (ʹशैडो) *n.* परछांई; छाया; (हल्का) आभास – *vt.* परछांई डालना; पीछा करना, निगाह रखना – **shadowy** *a.* परछांई जैसा – **shadow boxing** काल्पनिक प्रतिद्वंदी से मुक्केबाज़ी; *fig.* भी

shaft (शाफ्ट) *n.* डंडा, बल्ला; हत्था, दस्ता; तीर; किरण; प्रकाश किरण; इंजन का सीधा डंडा जो उसे चलाता है, शाफ्ट; खान में जाने का रास्ता, कूपक

shaggy (ʹशैगि) *a.* झबरा; उलझे बालों वाला; मैला–कुचैला

shake (शेक) *v.* हिलना; हिलाना; कांपना; (हाथ) मिलाना; घबरा देना या विचलित करना; लहराना; घुमाना (**shook, shaken**) – *n.* हिलाने, कंपाने आदि की क्रिया; स्पंदन; डगमगाहट; झटका; *inf.* क्षण भर – **shakily** *adv.* – **shaky** *a.* अस्थिर, डगमगाता; असुरक्षित; कच्चा, कमज़ोर – **shake sb off** से पीछा छुड़ाना – **shake-up** *n.* कंपनी आदि में आमूल परिवर्तन

shall (शैल) *v. aux.* आभार, आदेश, शर्त या अभिप्राय की अभिव्यक्ति के लिए क्रियाभावों और उसके समासों में प्रयुक्त (**should** *pt.*)

shallow (ʹशैलो) *a.* छिछला, उथला; ओछा (व्यक्ति), कम बुद्धि व ज्ञान वाला – *n.* छिछली जगह – **shallowness** *n.* उथलापन; ओछापन; कम बुद्धि व ज्ञान

sham (शैम) *a./n.* जाली; नकली (वस्तु) – *v.* बनना; स्वांग भरना; का अभिनय करना (**-mm-**)

shamble (ʹशैम्बल) *vi.* पैर घसीट कर चलना

shambles (ʹशैम्बल्ज़) *n.* – **in a shambles** अव्यवस्था की स्थिति या स्थान में

shame (शेम) *n.* शर्म, लज्जा; कलंक, बदनामी; लज्जा की बात; खेद का विषय – *vt.* शर्मिन्दा करना; लाज दिला कर कोई काम करने पर मजबूर करना – **shameful** *a.* लज्जाजनक, शर्मनाक – **shamefully** *adv.* – **shameless** *a.* बेशर्म– **shamefaced** *a.* लज्जित

shampoo (शैम्ʹपू) *n.* शैम्पू; इससे धोने की प्रक्रिया – *vt.* शैम्पू से बाल धोना

shan't (शांट) shall not का संक्षेप

shanty (ʹशैंटि) *n.* झुग्गी

shape (शेप) *n.* शक्ल, आकार, आक ति; सांचा; ढांचा; डील डौल, रूप; *inf.* स्थिति, विशे. शारीरिक स्वास्थ्य की – *vt.* बनाना, गढ़ना, रूप या आकार देना – *vi.* (**shape up** भी) विकसित होना (**shaped, shaping**) – **shapeless** *a.* बेडौल– **shapely** *a.* सुडौल

share (शेंअर) *n.* भाग, हिस्सा, अंश; नियत हिस्सा (कोटा); खेप; कम्पनी का हिस्सा, शेअर – *v.* बाँट लेना, हिस्सा देना, लेना; किसी चीज़ को करने में दूसरों का साथ देना; हाथ बंटाना; सहभागी होना – **shareholder** *n.* कम्पनी आदि का हिस्सेदार – **shareware** (ʹशेंअर्वेंअर) *n.* कम्प्यूटर साफ्टवेयर जो खरीद से पहले परख के लिए मुफ्त मिले

shark (शार्क) *n.* शार्क मछली, हांगर व्यक्ति जो दूसरों को धोखा देकर धन ऐंठता हो

sharp (शार्प) *a.* तीखा, पैना, तीक्ष्ण; नुकीला; तेज़; अचानक (जो धीरे धीरे न आए); फुर्तीला; कठोर; बेइमान, चालाक; तीखा (स्वर); सुस्पष्ट – *adv.* तुरंत, ध्यान से – **sharpen** *vt.* तेज़ करना – **sharper** *n.* धोखेबाज़– **sharply** *adv.* – **sharpness** *n.* तीखापन, चालाकी – **sharpshooter** *n.* पक्का निशानेबाज़

shatter (ˈशैटर) *v.* टुकड़े-टुकड़े या चकनाचूर कर देना; (योजना आदि) विफल बना देना, पर पानी फेर देना; (व्यक्ति को) बुरी तरह ढा देना – *vi.* टूट जाना, टुकड़े टुकड़े हो जाना

shave (शेव़) *v.* हजामत करना; तराशना, छीलना – *vi.* दाढ़ी बनाना (**shaved, shaven, shaving**) – *n.* दाढ़ी या हजामत – **shavings** *pl. n.* छीलन– **close/near shave** बाल-बाल बचने की घटना

shawl (शॉल) *n.* शाल

she (शी) *pron.* त तीय पुरुष, एकवचन स्त्रीलिंग सर्वनाम, वह (स्त्री)

sheaf (शीफ़) *n.* पूला, पूली (फूस की गठड़ी); कागज़ (खुले) (*pl.* **sheaves**)

shear (शिअर) *vt.* बाल, ऊन आदि कतरना; काट कर टुकड़े करना (**sheared** *pt.* **shorn, sheared** *pp.*, **shearing** *pr. p.*) – **shearer** *n.* – **shears** *pl. n.* बड़ी कैंची, कैंचा

sheath (शीथ) *n.* म्यान (तलवार या चाकू की); लिंग पर चढ़ाने का पतला रबड़ का खोल (कंडोम) – **sheathe** (शीद) *vt.* म्यान में रखना; खोल चढ़ाना

shed[1] (शेंड) *n.* सायबान, छप्पर

shed[2] (शेंड) *vt.* (आंसू, लहू) बहाना; (पत्ते) गिराना, झाड़ना; छोड़ देना (**shed, shedding**)

sheen (शीन) *n.* चमक

sheep (शीप) *n.* भेड़ – **sheepish** *a.* संकोची; लज्जित– **sheepdog** *n.* कई नस्लों के कुत्ते जो भेड़ों की रखवाली करते हैं

sheer[1] (शिअर) *a.* सीधी खड़ी (चट्टान आदि); बहुत महीन या झीना (कपड़ा); पारदर्शी; शुद्ध; निरा, मात्र – *adv.* एकदम

sheer[2] *vi.* रास्ते से हट जाना

sheet[1] (शीट) *n.* चादर, खेस; किसी बारीक चीज़ की चौड़ी पट्टी, चादर (लोहे आदि की); विस्तार – *vt.* चादर से ढंकना

sheet[2] *n.* पाल के कोने से बंधा रस्सा – **sheet anchor** आपात स्थिति में काम आने वाला बड़ा लंगर; मुख्य अवलंब, सहारा

sheik(h) (शेक) *n.* अरब सरदार, शेख़

shelf (शेल्फ़) *n.* दीवार में लगा तख्ता, ताक (*pl.* **shelves**) – **shelf life** वस्तु (वि० भोज्य पदार्थ) की अवधि जिसके अंदर उसे बेचा जा सकता है

shell (शेंल) *n.* खोल, आवरण, कोष; छिलका; खोपड़ी (नारियल, कछुए की); (मोती की) सीप, सीपी; (तोप का) गोला; अन्दर की चीज़ें निकाल कर बचा खोल – *vt.* ख़ोल, छिलका, आवरण उतारना; (तोप से) गोले बरसाना – **shellfish** *n.* कई प्रकार की मछलियां जिनका शरीर कवचित होता है, शंख मीन – **shell out** *inf.* अदा करना

shellac (श ˈलैक, ˈशैलक) *n.* लाख (जो पॉलिश के काम आती है)

shelter (ˈशेंल्टर) *n.* आश्रय, शरण; शरणास्थल; सुरक्षित स्थान – *vt.* शरण देना; छिपाना – *vi.* शरण लेना – **sheltered** *a.* सुरक्षित (स्थान); आराम का (जीवन)

shelve (शेंल्व़) *vt.* शेल्फ (खाने) में रखना; स्थगित करना – *vi.* थोड़ा थोड़ा ढलवां होना

shepherd (ˈशेंपर्ड) *n.* गडरिया, चरवाहा (**shepherdess** *fem.*) – *vt.* मार्गदर्शन करना, देखभाल, रखवाली करना

sherbet ('शर्बट) *n.* शरबत

sheriff ('शेरिफ़) *n.* **US** पुलिस अधिकारी; शैरिफ़

sherry ('शेरि) *n.* एक तेज़ शराब

shield (शील्ड) *n.* ढाल; ढाल जैसा कोई अन्य उपकरण; कवच, परित्राण; खेलों में जीत के लिए दी जाने वाली शील्ड – *vt.* (**shield from** में) ओट देना; रक्षा करना

shift (शिफ्ट) *v.* हटाना, खिसकाना; (विचार आदि) बदल देना – *vi.* स्थान परिवर्तित करना; (विचार, नीति आदि) बदल जाना – *n.* (मज़दूरों की) पाली; परिवर्तन; हटाने की क्रिया; स्त्री का लहंगे (स्कर्ट) से नीचे पहनने का वस्त्र – **shiftiness** *n.* टालमटोल करने की प्रक ति – **shiftless** *a.* असमर्थ; जिसमें चरित्र बल न हो – **shifty** *a.* बहानेबाज़; संदिग्ध चरित्र वाला

shilling ('शिलिङ) *n.* ब्रिटेन का पुराना सिक्का

shimmer ('शिमर) *vi.* झिलमिलाना, टिमटिमाना, झिलमिलाहट, टिमटिमाहट – *n.*

shin (शिन) *n.* घुटने के नीचे टांग का अगला भाग, नरहर, नली – *vi.* (**up** के साथ) बाहों और टांगों से ऊपर चढ़ना

shine (शाइन) *vi.* चमकना; औरों से आगे निकल जाना – *vt.* चमकाना (**shone, shining**) – *n.* चमक – **shiny** *a.* चमकदार

shingle[2] ('शिंगल) *n.* कंकड़ों का ढेर

ship (शिप) *n.* जहाज़, जलपोत – *vt.* जहाज़ पर चढ़ाना; (माल आदि) भेजना; खरीदने के लिए उप्लब्ध होना – *vi.* जहाज़ पर चढ़ना; उसमें नौकरी करना (**-pp-**) – **shipment** *n.* जहाज़ द्वारा (माल) भेजने की क्रिया; ऐसा माल – **shipping** *n.* जहाज़; नौवहन – **shipwreck** *n.* जहाज़ का तूफान या टक्कर के कारण टूट जाना – **shipyard** *n.* जहाज़ निर्माण और उनकी मरम्मत का कारखाना – **be shipwrecked** *a.* (नाविक, यात्री आदि का) जहाज़ नष्ट होने के बाद बच जाना

shoot (शर्क) *vt.* (काम से) जी चुराना; अपना कर्तव्य निभाने से भागना

shirt (शर्ट) *n.* कमीज़

shit (शिट) *n.* मल, विष्ठा – *interj. sl.* बकवास! (क्रोध, जुगुप्सा आदि व्यक्त करने के लिए प्रयुक्त शब्द)

shiver ('शिवर) *vi.* कांपना, बहुधा डर या गुस्से से – *n.* सिहरन, कंपकपी

shoal[1] (शोल) *n.* छिछले पानी का क्षेत्र; रेती

shoal[2] (शोल) *n.* मछलियों का गोल, झुण्ड

shock[1] (शॉक) *vt.* धक्का या आघात पहुंचाना; नफ़रत या घ णा पैदा करना – *n.* धक्का, आघात; झटका; संक्षोभ; शारीरिक या मानसिक आघात का नाड़ियों पर प्रभाव; दहशत; बिजली का धक्का

shock[2] (शॉक) *n.* पूलों का ढेर

shock[3] (शॉक) *n.* बालों का गुच्छा

shoddy ('शॉडि) *a.* बेकार; घटिया; घटिया सामान से बना

shoe (शू) *n.* जूता; (घोड़े की) नाल; (बेंत पर लगी) शाम (*pl.* **shoes**) – *vt.* जूते पहनाना; नाल लगाना (**shod** *pt./pp.*, **shoeing** *pr. p.*)– **shoelace** *n.* तस्मा, फीता – **shoestring** *a./n. fig.* – **on a shoestring** बहुत कम साधनों से

shone (शोन) **shine** का *pt./pp.*

shoo (शू) *interj.* भाग जाओ! – *vt.* भगा देना, चलता कर देना

shook (शुक) **SHAKE** का *pt.*

shoot (शूट) *v.* गोली चला कर घायल कर देना या मार देना; गोली दाग़ना; तेज़ी से भेजना, खिसकाना या धकेलना; फोटो या चलचित्र खींचना; तेज निगाह से देखना– *vi.* शिकार करना; (कोंपल का) निकलना (**shot, shooting**) – *n.* टहनी; कोंपल, बन्दूक आदि चलाने की प्रतियोगिता; शिकार के लिए अभियान – **shooter** *n.* – **shooting star** उल्का

shop (शॉप) *n.* दुकान; कारीगर की दुकान; कारखाने का भवन – *vi.* (**go shopping** भी) खरीदारी के लिए जाना – **shop floor** कारखाने का भाग जहां मशीनें लगी हों; कारखाने के मज़दूर – **shopkeeper** *n.* दुकानदार – **shoplifter** *n.* दुकानों से उठाइगीरी करने वाला – **talk shop** (बिमौके) अपने काम, पेशे आदि की बात करना

shore[1] (शॉर) *n.* तट, किनारा

shore[2] (शॉर) *vt.* सहारा देना (**shore up** भी)

short (शॉर्ट) *a.* छोटा; ठिगना, आवश्यकता से कम; अपूर्ण; रूखा– *adv.* अचानक; बिना अंत तक पहुंचे – *n.* तेज़ शराब; छोटा चलचित्र (**short film** भी) – *pl.* घुटनों से ऊपर तक की निकर या जांघिया – **shortage** (´शार्टिज) *n.* कमी – **shorten** *v.* – **shortly** *adv.* शीघ्र ही – **short-change** *vt.*, कुछ भी उचित से कम देना – **short circuit** *Electricity* सर्किट का सम्पूर्ण न होना (जो सांयोगिक होता है) जिससे फ्यूज उड़ जाता है – **shortcoming** *n.* कमज़ोरी, दोष – **shortfall** *n.* कमी – **shorthand** *n.* शार्ट हैंड, आशु लेखन – **short-sighted** *a.* जिसकी दूर की नज़र खराब हो, निकट-द ष्टि – **short-tempered** *a.* गुस्सैल

shot (शॉट) *n.* गोली दागने की क्रिया; गोली या गोला; छर्रों भरा कारतूस; निशानेबाज़, गोली दाग़ने वाला; प्रयत्न, कोशिश; फोटोचित्र; चलचित्र का एक छोटा अंश; खुराक; *inf.* टीका - **shoot** का *pt./pp.*

should (शुड) **SHALL** का *pt.*, चाहिये

shoulder (´शोल्डर) *n.* कंधा, कंधे से मिलती जुलती वस्तु; सड़क का किनारा – *vt.* अपने जिम्मे लेना; बोझ उठाना

shout (शाउट) *n.* चिल्लाहट, चीख – *vi.* ज़ोर से चिल्लाना

shove (शव़) *vt.* धकेलना

shovel (´शव़ल) *n.* बेलचा – *vt.* बेलचे से हटाना या उठाना (**-ll-**)

show (शो) *vt.* दिखाना, प्रदर्शित करना; इशारा करना; व्याख्या करना; सिद्ध करना; रास्ता दिखाना – *vi.* सामने आना, प्रकट होना (**showed, shown, showing**) – *n.* प्रदर्शन; प्रदर्शनी; तमाशा; नाटक या अन्य कलात्मक प्रदर्शन; इशारा; प्रतियोगिता; दिखावा; झलक, आभास – **showy** *a.* तड़क भड़क वाला; आडम्बरपूर्ण – **showdown** *n.* मुठभेड़, बल-परीक्षा – **show off** ऐसी (प्रदर्शित) वस्तु जिसकी सभी प्रशंसा करें; प्रशंसा पाने के लिए कोई काम करना – **show-off** *n.* ऐसा करने वाला व्यक्ति

shower (´शाउअर) *n.* (वर्षा की) बौछार; बौछार जैसी कोई अन्य वस्तु; (स्नानघर में लगा) फुहारा (**shower bath** भी) – *vt.* दिल खोल कर देना – *vi.* फुहारा स्नान करना

shrank (श्रैंक) SHRINK का *pt.*

shrapnel (´श्रैप्नल) *n.* गोले के टुकड़े

shred (´श्रेंड) *n.* धज्जी, छोटा टुकड़ा, थोड़ी सी मात्रा – *vt.* धज्जियां उड़ाना, टुकड़े टुकड़े कर देना (**shred** या **shredded, shredding**)

shrew (श्रू) *n.* चूहे जैसा जीव, छछूंदर; लड़ाका स्त्री

shrewd (श्रूड) *a.* समझदार; चालाक – **shrewdness** *n.*

shriek (श्रीक) *n.* चीख़ – *v.* चीख़ मारना

shrill (श्रिल) *a.* कर्णभेदी, तीखी

shrimp (श्रिम्प) *n.* झींगा मछली; *inf.* छोटे कद-काठ का आदमी

shrine (श्राइन) *n.* समाधि, मकबरा या रौज़ा जो किसी संत, सूफ़ी आदि से सम्बन्धित हो

shrink (श्रिंक) *vi.* सिकुड़ना, संकुचित हो जाना; पीछे हट जाना; झिझकना या डर जाना – *vt.* सिंकोड़ना (**shrank** *pt.*, **shrunken, shrunk** *pp.*, **shrinking** *pr. p.*) – *n. sl.*

मनोरोग चिकित्सक – **shrinkage** (´श्रिंकिज) *n.* ह्रास, कमी; संकुचन

shrivel (´श्रिवल) *vi.* सिकुड़ कर छोटा हो जाना; मुरझा जाना, कुम्हलाना (**-ll-**)

shroud (श्राउड) *n.* कफ़न; कफ़न जैसी कोई वस्तु जो ढक ले – *vt.* कफ़न में लपेटना; परदा डालना

shrub (श्रब) *n.* झाड़ी – **shrubbery** (´श्रबरि) *n.* झाड़ी-झुरमुट

shrug (श्रग) *vi.* (उपेक्षा या अज्ञान जताने के लिए) कंधे उचकाना – *vt.* उचकाना (**-gg-**) – *n.* कंधे उचकाने की क्रिया

shrunk(en) (´श्रंक(न)), **shrink** का *pp.*

shuck (शक) *n.* छिलका; छींबी; फली

shudder (´शडर) *vi.* कांपना या थर्रा जाना (विशे. डर से) – *n.* कंपकपी; थरथराहट

shuffle (´शफ़ल) *vi.* (पैर) हिलाना; टालमटोल करना – *vt.* (ताश के पत्ते) फैंटना – *n.* फैंटने या फिर से तरतीब देने की क्रिया

shun (शन) *vt.* से बचना; से दूर रहना (**-nn-**)

shunt (शंट) *vt.* एक ओर धकेलना, रास्ता बदलना; रेलगाड़ी को एक पटरी से दूसरी पर ले जाना

shut (शट) *v.* बंद करना; न आने देना, प्रवेश निषिद्ध करना (**shut, shutting**) – **shutter** (´शटर) *n.* खिड़की की झिलमिली या जालीदार पट; कैमरे का कपाट, शटर – **shut up** *interj.* खामोश!

shuttle (´शट्ल) *n.* करघे की फिरकी, भरनी, ढरकी; सिलाई मशीन की फिरकी; बस, गाड़ी आदि जो पास-पास के स्थानों के बीच आती जाती हो (**shuttle service** भी) – **shuttlecock** *n.* (बैडमिन्टन के खेल में) चिड़िया

shy[1] (शाइ) *a.* झेंपू, शर्मीला, डरपोक; झिझकने वाला; दूर – *vi.* डर कर पीछे हट जाना; अचानक झिझक दिखाना (**shied, shying**) – *n.* घोड़े का बिदकना – **shyly** *adv.* – **shyness** *n.* संकोच, झिझक, शर्मीलापन

shy[2] (शाइ) *vt.* (से) बचना – *n.* फेंकना

sibling (´सिब्लिंग) *n.* सहोदर भाई या बहिन – *a.* सहोदर

sibyl (´सिबिल) *n.* नबिया, भविष्यवादिनी

sick (सिक) *a.* जिसे मतली या कै आ रही हो; रोगी, *inf.* घिनावना; *inf.* – **sicken** *v.* बीमार पड़ जाना या करना; घ णा जगाना – **sickly** *a.* अस्वस्थ, जो बीमार ही रहता हो, जिससे मतली आये – **sickness** *n.* बीमारी, रोग

sickle (´सिकल) *n.* दरान्ती, हंसिया

side (साइड) *n.* वस्तु की सतह विशे. खड़ी हालत में बाहर या भीतरी सतह; दो सतहों वाली वस्तु की एक सतह; पक्ष, बाजू, तरफ, पार्श्व; शरीर का भाग जो दाईं या बाईं ओर हो; पहलू, अंग; विवाद के पक्षों में से एक; टीम – *a.* पक्ष या बाजू में, गौण, आनुषंगिक, साथ का – *vi.* किसी का पक्ष समर्थन करना (प्राय: *with* के साथ) – **siding** *n.* गौण रेल पटरी जहां गाड़ियां या माल डिब्बे खड़े कर दिए जाते हैं – **sideboard** *n.* खाने के कमरे की अल्मारी जिसमें बरतन रखे जाते हैं – **sideburns** *pl. n.* गलमुच्छे – **side effect** दवाई का उपचार के अलावा अतिरिक्त प्रभाव, गौण प्रभाव – **side issue** गौण विषय – **sidelong** *a.* तिरछा; परोक्ष – *adv.* तिरछे (देखना)– **sidetrack** *v.* मुख्य विषय से परे जाना; विषयान्तर करना – *n.* विषयान्तर – **sidewalk** *n.* **US** पटरी, फुटपाथ – **sideways** *adv.* बाजू से, तिरछे

sidle (´साइडल) *vi.* दबे पांव या चोरी चोरी किसी के पास पहुंचना; तिरछे चलना; खुशामद करना

siege (सीज) *n.* घेराबन्दी, घेरा

siesta (सि´एॅस्ट्अ) *n.* दोपहर के बाद की नींद

sieve (सिव़) *n.* छलनी, चालनी, छालनी – *v.* छानना

sift (सिफ़्ट) *vt.* छानना; ध्यान से निरीक्षण करना; *fig.* झूठ-सच को पहचानना – **sifter** *n.* छलनी

sigh (साइ) *n./v.* ठंडी सांस (खींचना, भरना) – **sigh for** की प्रबल इच्छा होना, ललकना

sight (साइट) *n.* देखने की सामर्थ्य, दृष्टि; देखने की क्रिया; देखी वस्तु; दृश्य; झलक; देखने में सहायक उपकरण, तकनी, दर्शा; नज़ारा, तमाशा- *vt.* देखना, निशाना लगाना – **sight-seeing** *n.* सैर-सपाटा – **sight-seer** *n.* पर्यटक

sign (साइन) *n.* चिन्ह, निशान, संकेत; नाम या सूचना का पट्ट; प्रतीक; लक्षण; शकुन; प्रमाण, साक्ष्य – *vt.* हस्ताक्षर करना; अनुमोदन करना – *vi.* इशारा, संकेत करना; हस्ताक्षर करना – **signboard** *n.* सूचनापट्ट; नामपट्ट – **sign language** संकेत भाषा – **signpost** *n.* दिशा-निर्देश संकेतक

signal ('सिग्नल) *n.* संकेत, विशे. रेलवे सिगनल; किसी कार्यवाही का सूत्रपात करने वाली बात, इशारा; *Radio* प्रसारित या प्राप्त सन्देश – *a.* उल्लेखनीय – *vt.* संकेत देना – *vi.* संकेत के माध्यम से आदेश देना **(-ll-)**

signatory ('सिग्नटरि) *n.* हस्ताक्षरकर्ता

signature (सिग्निचर) *n.* हस्ताक्षर

signet ('सिग्निट) *n.* छोटी मुहर

significant ('सिग्'निफ़िकंट) *a.* सार्थक; अर्थपूर्ण; महत्वपूर्ण – **significance** *n.* महत्व; सार्थकता; अभिप्राय – **significantly** *adv.*

signify ('सिग्निफ़ाइ) *vt.* अर्थ होना; प्रकट, सूचित करना; व्यक्त करना – *vi.* महत्वपूर्ण होना **(signified, signifying)**

silence ('साइलन्स) *n.* मौन, खामोशी – *vt.* चुप करा देना; बन्द करा देना – **silencer** *n.* इंजन या पिस्तौल आदि की आवाज़ कम करने का उपकरण, पुर्ज़ा – **silent** *a.* चुप, मौन– **silently** *adv.*

silhouette (सिलू'ऍट) *n. vt.* छायाकृति बनाना

silica ('सिलिक्अ) *n.* एक प्राकृतिक पदार्थ, सिलिका जिससे कांच बनता है

silicon ('सिलिकन) *n.* रेत, मिट्टी आदि में पाया जाने वाला भुरभुरा धातुज पदार्थ, सिलीकॉन – **silicone** ('सिलिकोन) *n.* सिलीकान जैसे कई संश्लिष्ट पदार्थ जो चिकित्सा उद्योग में काम आते हैं – **silicon chip** देखिए CHIP

silk (सिल्क) *n.* रेशम; रेशमी कपड़ा – **silken** *a.* रेशमी; मुलायम, चिकना – **silky** *a.* रेशमी, रेशम जैसा (नरम) मुलायम – **silkworm** *n.* रेशम का कीड़ा

sill (सिल) *n.* खिड़की के नीचे की कगार (पत्थर की पट्टी); दहलीज़

silly ('सिलि) *a.* मूर्ख; तुच्छ

silo ('साइलो) *n.* अनाज, चारा रखने का गड्ढा या मीनार जैसा गोदाम (*pl.* **-los**)

silt (सिल्ट) *n.* पानी के नीचे जमा कीचड़, गाद – *v.* कीचड़ आदि से भर जाना

silvan *a.* देखिए SYLVAN

silver ('सिल्वर) *n.* चांदी; उससे बनी चीज़ें (**silver ware** भी); चांदी का सिक्का; चाकू छुरियां (खाने की मेज पर) – *a.* चांदी का बना; चांदी जैसा या उस के रंग का – *vt.* चांदी का पानी चढ़ाना – **silvery** *a.* – **silver birch** भोजपत्र का पेड़ – **silver jubilee** रजत-जयंती

simian ('सिमिअन) *a.* बन्दर जैसा या उसका

similar ('सिमिलर) *a.* समान, सदृश, से मिलता-जुलता – **similarity** (सिमिलैरिटि) *n.* सादृश्य – **similarly** *adv.* वैसे ही

simile ('सिमिलि) *n.* उपमा

similitude (सि'मिलिट्यूड) *n.* सादृश्य

simmer ('सिमर) *vi.* बुदबुदाना (उबाल अंक के आसपास गरम हो कर)

simper ('सिम्पर) *vi.* मूर्खता से या बहुत बनते हुए मुस्कराना या कोई बात कहना

simple ('सिम्पल) *a.* साधारण; जो जटिल न हो, सादा; सीधा-सादा, मूर्ख– **simpleton** ('सिम्पल्टन) *n.* बुद्धू – **simplicity** *n.* सादगी; स्पष्टता – **simplification** *n.* सरलीकरण – **simplify** *vt.* सरल, स्पष्ट या

आसान बनाना (**-plified, -plifying**) – **simply** *adv*.

simulate (ंसिम्युलेट) *vt*. स्वांग रचना; नकल करना; किसी स्थिति विशेष की परिस्थितियों को (क त्रिम रूप से) दोबारा उत्पन्न करना – **simulation** *n*. अनुकरण; स्वांग, ढोंग

simultaneous (सिमल्ंटेनिअस) *a*. समकालिक – **simultaneity** (सिमल्टंनीइटि) *n*. **simultaneousness** *n*. समकालिकता – **simultaneously** *adv*. साथ-साथ

sin (सिन) *n*. पाप, गुनाह – *vi*. पाप करना (**-nn-**) – **sinful** *a*. पापमय – **sinner** *n*.

since (सिन्स) *prep*. किसी काल विशेष के बाद की अवधि में या लगातार; से, के बाद से – *conj*. के बाद से; क्योंकि – *adv*. उसी समय से – **since then** तब से

sincere (सिन्ंसिअर) *a*. निष्कपट, सच्चा– **sincerely** *adv*. – **sincerity** (सिन्ंसेरिटि) *n*. शुद्ध हृदयता, निष्कपटता

sinecure (ंसाइनिक्युअर) *n*. नौकरी जिसमें वेतन मिले लेकिन काम न हो, दायित्व हीन पद

sine die (ंसाइनि ंडाइ) *Lat*. अनिश्चितकाल के लिए (स्थगित)

sinew (ंसिन्यू) *n*. मांसपेशी को हड्डी से जोड़ने वाली कड़ी, कंडरा – *pl*. मांसपेशियां; बल, बाहुबल

sing (सिङ) *vi*. गाना; गुनगुनाना; बजना, गूंजना; सनसनाना (कानों का); चहचहाना – *vt*. गीत गाना; प्रशंसा या गुणगान करना; कविता या गीत में किसी के गुण गाना (**sang, sung, singing**) – **singer** *n*. – **singsong** *n*. गाने बजाने की महफ़िल – *a*. एक सुरा

singe (सिन्ज) *vi*. झुलसाना (**singed, singeing**)

single (ंसिंगल) *a*. एक, एक ही, एक मात्र; अविवाहित; एक के लिए; एकांगी; एक ओर की यात्रा का (टिकट) – *n*. (**single ticket** भी) एकतरफा टिकट; अविवाहित व्यक्ति; दो प्रतिद्वंदियों का खेल (जैसे टेनिस); (क्रिकेट) एक रन – *vt*. – **single out** चुन लेना – **singly** *adv*. – **single file** इकहरी पंक्ति में खड़े लोग या सजाई गयी वस्तुएं – **single-handed** *a*. अकेले ही

singular (ंसिंग्युलर) *a*. उल्लेखनीय, असाधारण, विशिष्ट *Grammar* एकवचन – **singularity** *n*. विशेषता

sinister (ंसिनिस्टर) *a*.धमकी भरा; अशुभ, अमंगल

sink (सिंक) *vi*. डूब जाना; गिर जाना; ढह जाना; धंस जाना (न व आदि का)– *vt*. डुबाना; खोदना (कुआं आदि); पूंजी लगाना (**sank** *pt*., **sunk, sunken** *pp*., **sinking** *pr. p.*) – *n*. नाबदान (झूठे बरतन आदि रखने का स्थान) सिंक

Sino (ंसाइनो-) (*comb. form*) चीन का, चीनी

sinuous (ंसिन्युअस) *a*. घुमावदार, टेढ़ा मेढ़ा

sinus (ंसाइनस) *n*. खोपड़ी की हड्डियों में हवा जाने का रास्ता, शिरानाल – **sinusitis** (साइनंसाइटिस) *n*. शिरानाल की सूजन

sip (सिप) *v*. घूंट घूंट पीना, चुस्कियों से पीना (**-pp-**) – *n*.

siphon, syphon (ंसाइफ़न) *n*. हवा के दबाव से तरल पदार्थ को बोतल आदि से निकालने का उपकरण – *v*. इस उपकरण से (द्रव) निकालना; कम मात्रा में निकालना

sir (सर) *n*. पुरुष के लिए आदर सूचक सम्बोधन

sire (साइअर) *n*. पिता, विशे. घोड़े या फालतू पशु का – *v*. पैदा करना, का पिता बनना, होना

siren (ंसाइअरन) *n*. भोंपू, विशे. खतरे की चेतावनी देने वाला

sirloin (ंसर्लॉइन) *n*. गाय के पुट्ठे का मांस

sissy (ंसिसि) *a./n*. कमज़ोर, कायर पुरुष

sister (ंसिस्टर) *n*. बहन, संघिनी, सिस्टर; वरिष्ट नर्स, सिस्टर – *a*. से संबंधित, से जुड़ा हुआ – **sisterly** *a*. बहन जैसा – **sister-in-law** *n*. भाभी; साली; सहलज; देवरानी; जेठानी; ननद

sit (सिट) *v.* (मुख्यतया *intr.*) बैठना; बैठे रहना; तस्वीर बनवाने के लिए बैठना; सरकारी अधिकारी होना, (सभा का) सत्र, अधिवेशन, बैठक होना; बने रहना; परीक्षा देना; बच्चे की देखभाल करना – **sit in** (मज़दूरों का) धरना देना – **sit on the fence** दोनों पक्षों में से किसी को न चुनना – **sitting duck** आसान शिकार

sitar (सि´टार) *n.* सितार

sitcom (´सिट्कॉम) *n. situation comedy* का संक्षेप, मानोरंजनक टी. वी. कार्यक्रम जिसकी हर कड़ी में पात्र वही पर कहानी अलग हो

site (साइट) *n.* स्थल, स्थान; भवन के लिए या उस के साथ का स्थान (**building site** भी); दे० **website**

situate (´सिट्युएट) *v.* रखना; स्थापित करना – **situation** (सिट्युएशन) *n.* स्थल, स्थान, स्थिति; परिस्थिति; रोज़गार, नौकरी; पद

six (सिक्स) *a./n.* छै की संख्या – **sixth** *a.* छटा – *n.* छटा हिस्सा – **sixteen** (सिक्स्टीन) *n./a.* सोलह की संख्या – **sixty** *n./a.* साठ

size[1] (साइज़) *n.* आकार; माप – *vt.* आकार के अनुसार रखना, तरतीब देना – **siz(e)able** *a.* काफ़ी बड़ा

size[2] (साइज़) *n.* एक प्रकार की सरेस (**sizing** भी)

sizzle (´सिज़ल) *v./n.* तले जाने की कड़-कड़ की आवज़ (करना)

skate (स्केट) *n.* जूते के नीचे लगा पतरा जिससे बर्फ पर फिसलते हैं, स्केट – *vi.* इस प्रकार के जूते पहन कर फिसलना – **skateboard** *n.* पहिए वाले स्केटों पर लगा तख्ता – **skating** *n.* जूतों के नीचे पहिए लगे उपकरण से फिसलना

skeleton (´स्केलिटन) *n.* कंकाल, अस्थि पंजर, दुबला-पतला व्यक्ति; रूपरेखा; प्रारूप; ढांचा; केन्द्र – *a.* कम से कम संख्या (कर्मचारियों आदि की); रूपरेखा के रूप में बना; सार रूप में – **skeletal** *a.* कंकाल

sketch (स्केँच) *n.* कच्चा नक्शा, खाका; संक्षिप्त विवरण; निबन्ध; हास्य नाटिका – *v.* रूपरेखा बनाना – **sketchy** *a.* अपूर्ण; अपर्याप्त

skew (स्क्यू) *vi.* तिरछे चलना

skewer (´स्क्युअर) *n.* मांस भूनने की सीख

ski (स्की) *n.* पैर के नीचे बांधी लम्बी पतरी जिसकी सहायता से बर्फ़ पर फिसलते हैं, स्की (*pl.* **skis** (स्कीज़)) – *v.* स्की पहन कर बर्फ़ पर फिसलना (**skied, skiing**) – **skier** *n.*

skid (स्किड) *v.* (एक ओर) फिसल जाना, विशे. मोटरगाड़ी आदि का (**-dd-**) – *n.* इस प्रकार फिसलने की क्रिया- **skid row** बस्ती जाहां गरीब शराबी लोग रहते हो

skiff (स्किफ़) *n.* छोटी नाव, डोंगी

skill (स्किल) *n.* निपुणता; दक्षता, कारीगरी, कौशल – **skilled** *a.* कुशल; प्रशिक्षित (मज़दूर) – **skilful** *a.* विशेषज्ञ, माहिर

skillet (´स्किलिट) *n.* व्यंजन तलने का छोटा बरतन

skim (स्किम) *vt.* मलाई, झाग, फेन, मल आदि उतारना, काछना; हल्के से छूते हुए तेज़ी से निकल जाना; तेज़ी से पढ़ जाना – *vi.* इस प्रकार चलना (**-mm-**) – **skim(med) milk** सपरेटा दूध

skimpy (´स्किम्पि) *a.* अपर्याप्त, कम (तन पर वस्त्र)

skin (स्किन) *n.* चमड़ी, खाल, त्वचा; (फल का) छिलका – **skinny** *a.* दुबला, पतला, मरियल – **skinflint** *n.* कंजूस, – **skin-deep** *a.* ऊपरी, हल्का – **skin-tight** *a.* चुस्त (कपड़े)

skip (स्किप) *vi.* फुदकना; रस्सी फांदना – *vt.* अनदेखी कर देना; छोड़ देना (**-pp-**) – *n.* फांदने की क्रिया

skipper (´स्किपर) *n.* जहाज़, विमान या टीम का कप्तान – *vt.* कप्तान के रूप में काम करना

skirmish (´स्कर्मिश) *n.* छोटे समूहों में भिडंत

skirt (स्कर्ट) *n.* स्त्रियों स्कर्ट; – *vt.* इर्द गिर्द जाना, सीमा के साथ-साथ (दीवार आदि) होना

skit (स्किट) *n.* प्रहसन

skittish ('स्किटिश) *a.* चंचल; उछल-कूद मचाने वाला

skittles ('स्किट्ल्ज़) *n.* नाइन पिन्स (**nine pins**) नाम का खेल

skive (स्काइव़) *v.* काम या जिम्मेदारी से बचना

skulduggery (स्कल्'डगरि) *n. inf.* छलकपट; चालबाजी

skulk (स्कल्क) चुपके से चल देना

skull (स्कल) *n.* खोपड़ी, कपाल – **skullcap** *n.* चुस्त टोपी

skunk (स्कंक) *n.* उत्तरी अमरीका का जीव जो अपनी गुदा से अत्यंत दुर्गन्धयुक्त द्रव छोड़ता है

sky (स्काइ) *n.* आकाश; अन्तरिक्ष (*pl.* **skies**) – **sky-diving** *n.* विमान से कूद कर पैराशूट देर से खोलने का करतब – **skylark** *n.* भरत, चातक पक्षी – **skylight** *n.* छत में बनी खिड़की, वातायन – **skyline** *n.* आकाश की प ष्ठभूमि में इमारतों, पेड़ों और पहाड़ियों की रूपरेखा – **skyscraper** ('स्काइस्क्रेपर) *n.* बहुत ऊंची इमारत

slab (स्लैब) *n.* (पत्थर की) पटिया

slack[1] (स्लैक) *a.* ढीला; धीमा; लापरवाह; मन्दा (जब काम न हो) – *n.* ढीला हिस्सा – *vi.* बेकार बैठे रहना; आलस करना – – **slacken** *v.* (**slacken off** भी) ढीला हो जाना; मंद पड़ जाना

slack[2] (स्लैक) *n.* कोयले का चूरा; कोयले के छोटे छोटे टुकड़े

slacks (स्लैक्स) *pl. n.* सामान्य समय (विशेष अवसर के विपरीत) में पहनी जाने वाली पतलून

slag (स्लैग) *n.* धातु का मल (जो उबलते हुए ऊपर आ जाता हैं)

slain **SLAY** का *pp.*

slake (स्लेक) *vt.* (प्यास) बुझाना; चूना बुझाना

slam (स्लैम) *v.* धम्म से बन्द करना (ढक्कन आदि); जोर से मारना, पटकना; दे मारना; *inf.* कटु, तीव्र आलोचना करना (**-mm-**) – *n.* धमाके से पटकने, दे मारने की आवाज़

slander ('स्लाण्डर) *n.* किसी के बारे में दुर्भावना से कही गयी या झूठी बात का आरोप, बदनामी – *v.* की बदनामी करना **-slanderous** *a.*

slang (स्लैङ) *n.* बोल-चाल की भाषा

slant (स्लांट) *v.* तिरछा करना; मोड़ना; (समाचार आदि पर) अपना रंग चढ़ाना – *n.* ढलान; द ष्टिकोण; विचार – *a.* ढालू; तिरछा – **slanting** *a.* एक ओर झुका हुआ

slap (स्लैप) *n.* थप्पड़ – *vt.* थप्पड़ मारना; पटक देना; (**~ against**) पानी का टकराना (**-pp-**) – **slapstick** *n.* प्रहसन – **slap sth on sb** का हुक्म (विशे० जो अनुचित हो) दे देना

slash (स्लैश) *vt.* काटना; चीरना; कीमतें घटा देना

slat (स्लैट) *n.* लकड़ी या धातु की लम्बी पट्टी

slate (स्लेट) *n.* स्लेट पत्थर; लिखने की स्लेट – *vt.* स्लेटें लगाना; आलोचना करना

slattern ('स्लैटर्न) *n.* फूहड़ और दुष्चरित्र स्त्री

slaughter ('स्लॉटर) *n.* वध, हत्या – *vt.* **slaughterhouse**. *n.* कसाईघर

slave (स्लेव़) *n.* गुलाम, दास (जिसे कोई अधिकार प्राप्त न हों) – *vi.* (**slave away** भी) दासों के समान (कठोर) परिश्रम करना – **slavery** (स्लेव़रि) *n.* गुलामी – **slavish** (स्लेविश) *a.* गुलामों जैसा; नीच – **slave driver** जो नौकरों से बहुत काम कराए

slaver ('स्लैवर) *vi.* मुंह से लार टपकाना

slay (स्ले) *vi.* कत्ल करना, वध करना

sleazy ('स्लीज़ि) *a.* गन्दा, घिनावना

sledge[1], **sled** (स्लेंज, स्लेंड) *n.* बर्फ पर फिसल कर चलने वाली गाड़ी, हिम गाड़ी – *v.*

sledge[2], **sledgehammer** (स्लेंज, 'स्लेंज़हैमर) *n.* भारी हथौड़ा, घन

sleek (स्लीक) *a.* चिकना, चमकदार, नरम

sleep (स्लीप) *n.* न द, निद्रा; आराम – *vi.* सोना

(**slept, sleeping**) – **sleeper** *n.* सोने वाला प्राणी; रेल की पटड़ी के नीचे लगा शहतीर; रेल शायिका – **sleepily** *adv.* – **sleepiness** *n.* – **sleepless** *a.* – **sleepy** *a.* – **sleeping partner** निष्क्रिय हिस्सेदार – **sleep-walk** *vi.* नींद में चलना

sleet (स्लीट) *n.* वर्षा के साथ बर्फ़ या ओलों का गिरना

sleeve (स्लीव़) *n.* आस्तीन, बांह; (इंजन में) शाफ्ट का आवरण; ग्रामोफोन रिकार्ड का आवरण

sleigh (स्ले) *n.* बर्फ़गाड़ी, स्लेज

sleight (स्लाइट) *n.* कौशल; छल कपट, कुटिलता, धूर्तता – **sleight of hand** हाथ की सफाई; जादू के करतब

slender ('स्लेंण्डर) *a.* दुबला-पतला; कम, नगण्य; दुर्बल, कमज़ोर – **slenderness** *n.*

slept (स्लेंप्ट) SLEEP का *pt./pp.*

sleuth (स्लूथ) *n.* जासूस, गुप्तचर

slew (स्लू) **SLAY** का *pt.*

slice (स्लाइस) *n.* कतला, फांक (फल की); हिस्सा, भाग, अंश; चपटी छुरी – *vt.* कतले या फांकें बनाना

slick (स्लिक) *a.* चिकना; चिकनी चुपड़ी बातें करने वाला; खुशामदी; ऊपर से आकर्षक – *vt.* चिकना या चमकदार बनाना – *n.* फिसलन वाला क्षेत्र; पानी पर तेल की परत (**oil slick** भी)

slide (स्लाइड) *v.* फिसलना, सरकना (जैसे बर्फ़ पर); बिना दिखे निकल जाना; (नैतिक) पतन होना (**slid** *pt.*, **slid** *pp.*, **sliding** *pr. p.*) – *n.* फिसलने या सरकने की क्रिया; चट्टान का खिसकना; खुर्दबीन या सूक्ष्म अनुवीक्षण यंत्र के नीचे रखने का कांच का छोटा सा टुकड़ा; फोटो जो फिल्म पर हो कागज़ पर नह , स्लाइड

slight (स्लाइट) *a.* छोटा; तुच्छ; पतला-छरहरा – *vt.* उपेक्षा या तिरस्कार करना – *n.* तिरस्कार; अनादर – **slightly** *adv.* थोड़ा-सा

slim (स्लिम) *a.* दुबला पतला, छरहरा – *v.* व्यायाम और भोजन पर नियंत्रण कर के वजन घटाना (**-mm-**)

slime (स्लाइम) *n.* चिकनी, गाढ़ी गन्दगी या कीचड़ – **slimy** *a.* कीचड़ जैसा, गंदा; चापलूस

sling (स्लिङ) *n.* गलपट्टी (घायल अंग को सहारा देने की पट्टी); भारी वजन उठाने का रस्सा आदि – *vt.* रस्से से उठाना; फेंक देना; लटकाना (**slung, slinging**)

slink (स्लिंक) *vi.* दबे पांव या चोरों की तरह आना जाना; चुपके से आना (**slunk** (स्लंक), **slinking**)

slip (स्लिप) *v.* सरकाना, खिसकाना; सरक या खिसक जाना; भूल जाना – *vi.* फिसल जाना; हाथ से फिसल जाना (किसी वस्तु का); भूल कर बैठना (बहुधा **up** के साथ प्रयुक्त); (स्वास्थ्य या नैतिक स्तर का) गिर जाना – *vt.* आसानी से पहनना या उतारना; बुरी स्थिति में पहुंच जाना (**-pp-**) – *n.* फिसलने या खिसकने की क्रिया; भूल; साया या पेटीकोट; कागज़ का पुर्ज़ा या पर्ची; पौधे की कलम – **slipped disc** रीढ़ की हड्डी में चकत्ती (डिस्क) के खिसकने से उत्पन्न पीड़ा, मेरुदण्ड-पीड़ा – **slipshod** (स्लिप्शॉड) *a.* फूहड़ ढंग से किया गया; लापरवाही से (किया गया)

slipper ('स्लिपर) *n.* घर में पहनने का हल्का जूता, स्लीपर

slippery ('स्लिपरि) *a.* फिसलने वाला; पकड़ में न आने वाला; बदलने वाला; अविश्वसनीय

slit (स्लिट) *vt.* चीरना; टुकड़े करना (**slit, slitting**) – *n.* चीर

slither ('स्लिदर) *vi.* फिसलते हुए जाना

sliver ('स्लिव़र) *n.* किसी चीज़ का छोटा, पतला टुकड़ा, छिपटी

slobber ('स्लॉबर) *v.* लार टपकाना

slog (स्लॉग) *vt.* (बल्लेबाज़ का) ज़ोर से गेंद को मारना – *vi.* बड़ी मेहनत से पढ़ाई या कोई काम करना (**-gg-**) – *n.*

slogan (स्लोगन) *n.* नारा
sloop (स्लूप) *n.* छोटा, एक मस्तूल का जहाज़
slop (स्लॉप) *vi.* (**slop over** भी) (तरल पदार्थ का) छलकना – *vt.* छलकाना, गिराना (**-pp-**) – *n.* छलका हुआ द्रव; पेय (शरबत आदि); गंदा पानी – *pl.* तरल रूप में गन्दगी – **sloppy** *a.* लापरवाह, बेढंगा
slope (स्लोप) *vt.* ढाल, ढलान या चढ़ाई होना – *n.* ढाल, चढ़ाई
slosh (स्लॉश) *n.* पतला कीचड़– *v.* पानी आदि गिराना, बिखेरना या बिखरना; चोट मारना– **sloshed** *a. sl.* शराब के नशे में धुत्त
slot(स्लॉट) *n.* छिद्र, छेद (सिक्कों के लिए); झिर्री – *vt.* छेद में डालना; छांटना; *inf.* श्रंखलाबद्ध करना, किसी संगठन में स्थान देना (**-tt-**)
sloth (स्लोथ) *n.* दक्षिणी अमरीका का एक बहुत धीरे चलने वाला जीव, स्लोथ; आलस्य – **slothful** *a.* आलसी, सुस्त
slouch (स्लाउच) *vi.* आलस्य से या भोंडे ढंग से बैठना या चलना – *n./a.*
slough[1] (स्लाउ) *n.* दलदल
slough[2] (स्लफ़) *n.* सांप की केंचुली – *v.* केंचुली उतारना; उतर जाना
sloven ('स्लव़न) *n.* फूहड़, मैला-कुचैला व्यक्ति – **slovenly** *a./adv.*
slow (स्लो) *a.* धीमा, मंदगति का; मंद-बुद्धि – *v.* की गति कम कर देना, धीमा कर देना या पड़ जाना – **slowly** *adv.* धीरे-धीरे – **slow motion** *a.* मंदगति से दिखाई जाने वाली (फिल्म)
sludge (स्लज) *n.* कीचड़; बर्फ़ पिघलने से बना कीचड़
slug[1] (स्लग) *n.* केंचुआ; गोली – **sluggard** ('स्लगर्ड) *n.* आलसी – **sluggish** ('स्लगिश) *a.* धीमा, सुस्त; आलसी– **sluggishness** *n.*
slug[2] (स्लग) *v.* चोट मारना; कठोर परिश्रम से काम करना – *n.* भारी चोट; शराब का बड़ा घूंट
slugfest ('स्लग्फ़ेंस्ट) *n.***US** गर्मा-गर्मी
sluice (स्लूस) *n.* नहर का पानी नियंत्रित करने का द्वार, जलद्वार – *vt.* पानी डालना, छोड़ना
slum (स्लम) *n.* गंदी बस्ती
slumber ('स्लम्बर) *n./vi.* न द, सोना
slump (स्लम्प) *v.* धम्म से गिरना; भोंडे ढंग से आराम करना; अचानक कीमत, परिमाण या आदर कम हो जाना – *n.*
slung (स्लंग) **SLING** का *pt./pp.*
slunk (स्लंक) **SLINK** का *pt./pp.*
slur (स्लर) *vt.* (पर) ध्यान न देना; अस्पष्ट उच्चारण करना; निन्दा करना; निन्दा करना (**-rr-**) – *n.* तिरस्कार
slurp (स्लर्प) *v. inf.* सड़प-सड़प की आवाज करते हुए पीना या खाना
slurry ('स्लरि) *n.* गारा, घोल
slush (स्लश) *n.* कीचड़; अत्यधिक भावुकता
slut (स्लट) *n.* गन्दी (दुष्चरित्र स्त्री)
sly (स्लाइ) *a.* धूर्त; धोखेबाज – **slyly** *adv.*
smack[1] (स्मैक) *n.* स्वाद, गंध; पुट; – *sl.* हैरोइन (एक नशीला पदार्थ) – *vi.* का स्वाद या गंध होना, का पुट होना, का संकेत या आभास होना
smack[2] (स्मैक) *vt.* थप्पड़ मारना; होंठ खोलते और बंद करते समय "मच-मच" की आवाज़ करना – *n.* ऐसी आवाज; थप्पड़; चटाक (की आवाज़); चुमकार (चूमने की आवाज़) – *adv. inf.* पूरी तरह; प्रत्यक्ष रूप से
small (स्मॉल) *a.* छोटा; महत्वहीन; तुच्छ; नाटा – *n.* पतला अंश, विशे. पीठ का गड्ढा – **small arms** हल्के (पिस्तौल आदि) हथियार – **small change** रेज़मारी, छुट्टा – **small fry** सामान्य छोटे लोग – **small hours** आधी रात के बाद का समय – **smallpox** *n.* चेचक -**small talk** इधर-उधर की रस्मी बातें
smarmy ('स्मार्मि) *a. inf.* चापलूस
smart (स्मार्ट) *a.* चतुर, चालाक; बना ठना; तीक्ष्ण

– *v.* पीड़ा देना; पीड़ा अनुभव करना – *n.* तीव्र पीड़ा – **smarten** (ˈस्मार्टन) *vt.* सजाना, संवारना– **smartly** *adv.* – **smartness** *n.* – **smart card** छोटा प्लास्टिक कार्ड जिसमें इलेक्ट्रानिकी रूप में (व्यक्ति के बारे में) जानकारी भरी हो

smash (स्मैश) *vt.* टुकड़े- टुकड़े/चकना-चूर कर देना; नष्ट कर देना– *n.* करारी चोट– **smashing** *a. inf.* बढ़िया; आकर्षक

smattering (ˈस्मैटरिङ) *n.* थोड़ी सी (ऊपरी) जानकारी

smear (स्मिअर) *vt.* चिकनाई आदि पोतना या लेपना; गंदगी लगाना – *n.* गन्दगी, मैल का धब्बा

smell (स्मेंल) *vt.* सूंघना – *vi.* गन्ध आना; (**smelt** या **smelled, smelling**) – *n.* गंध-शक्ति– **smelly** *a.* जिससे दुर्गन्ध आ रही हो

smelt (स्मेंल्ट) *vt.* कच्ची धातु को पिघलाना

smile (स्माइल) *n.* मुस्काराहट – *v.* मुस्कराना

smelt[2] (स्मेंल्ट) *n.* सामन जाति की मछली

smile (स्माइल) *n.* मुस्काराहट – *v.* मुस्कराना

smirch (स्मर्च) *vt.* मलिन करना; कलंक लगाना – *n.* धब्बा; कलंक

smirk (स्मर्क) *n.* मूर्खता या तिरस्कारपूर्ण मुस्कराहट –*v.* इस प्रकार मुस्कराना

smite (स्माइट) *vt.* मारना, प्रहार करना; आक्रमण करना (**smote, smitten, smiting**)

smith (स्मिथ) *n.* लोहार; सुनार आदि

smithereens (स्मिदˈरीन्ज) *pl. n.* छोटे छोटे टुकड़े

smock (स्मॉक) *n.* ढीला-ढाला कुरता

smog (स्मॉग) *n.* धुएं और कोहरे का सम्मिश्रण

smoke (स्मोक) *n.* धुआं; तम्बाकू पीने की क्रिया – *vi.* धुआं छोड़ना – *vt.* तम्बाकू पीना; धुएं के सामने रखना (विशे. मछली का आग के पास सुखाना) – **smoker** *n.* **smokily** *adv.* – **smoky** *a.* धुएं से भरा – **smokescreen** *n.* छिपाव

smooch (स्मूच) *v. int.* चूमना, गले लगाना

smooth (स्मूद) *a.* मुलायम; चिकना; शान्त; जिस पर शीघ्र विश्वास हो जाय; (सवारी) जिसमें झटके न लगें – *vt.* मुलायम, चिकना बनाना; शांत करना – **smoothly** *adv.*

smote (स्मोट) **SMITE** का *pt.*

smother (ˈस्मदर) *v.* गला घोंटना

smoulder (ˈस्मोल्डर) *vi.* सुलगना; मन ही मन कुढ़ना

smudge (स्मज) *v.* धब्बा या दाग डालना; मैला या गंदा करना – *n.*

smug (स्मग) *a.* आत्मसंतुष्ट व दंभी

smuggle (ˈस्मगल) *vt.* तस्करी करना; छिपा कर ले जाना – **smuggler** *n.* तस्कर

smut (स्मट) *n.* कालिख या उसका कण; अश्लील बातें अथवा साहित्य

snack (स्नैक) *n.* हल्का भोजन; नाश्ता

snag (स्नैग) *n.* कठिनाई, बाहर को निकला भाग; कपड़े में तीखी चीज़ से बड़ी खोंच; बाधा – *vt.* बाधा में फंस जाना

snail (स्नेल) *n.* घोंघा

snake (स्नेक) *n.* सांप – *v.* सांप के समान रेंगना – **snaky** *a.* सांप जैसा

snap (स्नैप) *v.* अचानक टूट जाना, तड़कना; चटपट् या कटकट की आवाज़ करना; काटने को दौड़ना; गुस्से से अचानक कुछ कहना; फोटो लेना – *n.* टूटने, तड़कने आदि की क्रिया; चट की आवाज़ से बंद होने वाला बटन; *inf.* फोटो – *a.* अचानक; बिना तैयारी के – **snappy** *a.* कटखना; *sl.* जल्दी (करने, जाने वाला); *sl.* फैशनेबल – **snapdragon** *n.* पौधा जिसके फूल मुंह की तरह खुल जाते हैं – **snapshot** *n.* फोटो – **snap your fingers** उंगलिया चटकाना

snare (स्नेंअर) *n.* जाल, फंदा – *vt.* फंदे या जाल से पकड़ना (पक्षी आदि)

snarl (स्नार्ल) *n.* (कुत्ते की) गुर्राहट – **snarl-up** *n.* ट्रैफिक जैम, यातायात में रुकावट

snatch (स्नैच) *v.* झपट्टा मार कर छीन लेना; झपटना; पकड़ लेना – *n.* झपट्टा; टुकड़ा

snazzy (ˈस्नैज़ि) *a. inf.* फैशनेबल, तड़क भड़क वाला

sneak (स्नीक) *vi.* दबे पांव आना जाना; चोरी से आना, चुपके-चुपके घूमना – *n.* घटिया या नीच व्यक्ति; मुख़बिर – **sneaking** *a.* अप्रकट/ गुप्त (संदेह); नज़र-चोर (व्यक्ति) – **sneak preview** (फिल्म का) पूर्वप्रदर्शन

sneakers (ˈस्नीकर्ज़) *pl. n. US* खेल कूद के लिए पहनने के लचीले जूते

sneer (स्निअर) *n.* तिरस्कार या उपहास करने वाली बात या भाव भंगिमा – *v.*

sneeze (स्नीज़) *vi.* छ कना – *n.* छ क

snick (स्निक) *n.* खांचा; छोटी सी काट

snicker (ˈस्निकर) *n./v.* SNIGGER

snide (स्नाइड) *a.* दुर्भावपूर्ण; घमण्ड या दंभ युक्त

sniff (स्निफ़) *vi.* (नाक से सांस ख चते समय) सूं-सूं करना; (*at* के साथ) नाक भौं सिकोड़ना – *vt.* (नाक से) सूंघना – *n.* सूंघने की क्रिया – **sniffle** *vi.* सूं सूं करना विशे. जुकाम के कारण

snigger (ˈस्निगर) *n.* दबी दबी तिरस्कार या अवहेलना युक्त हंसी – *v.* इस प्रकार हंसना

snip (स्निप) *vt.* कतरना या टुकड़ा काटना (-**pp**-) – *n.* कतरन; काट; तराश; *inf.* सस्ता सौदा

snipe (स्नाइप) *n.* एक जलपक्षी, चाहा – *v.* शत्रु पर छिप कर गोली चलाना; – **sniper** *n.* छिप कर शत्रु पर गोली चलाने वाला सैनिक – **snipe at** परोक्ष रूप से आलोचना करना

snob (स्नॉब) *n.* व्यक्ति जो ऊंच नीच का बहुत ध्यान रखता हो, घमंडी, दंभी – **snobbery** (स्नॉबरि) *n.* वर्णदंभ, घमंड, अकड़ – **snobbish** (स्नॉबिश) *a.* दंभ-भरा

snooker (ˈस्नूकर) *n.* बिलियर्ड जैसा खेल

snoop (स्नूप) *v.* दूसरों के मामलों में दख़ल देना या टांग अड़ाना; ताक झांक करना – **snooper** *n.*

snooty (ˈस्नूटि) *a. sl.* घमण्डी, दंभी

snooze (स्नूज़) *vi.* झपकी लेना; ऊंघना – *n.* झपकी

snore (स्नॉर) *vi.* खर्राटे लेना – *n.* खर्राटा

snorkel (ˈस्नॉर्कल) *n.* गोता लगाते समय सांस लेने की नली – *vi.* ऐसी नली लगा कर तैरना

snort (स्नार्ट) *vi.* तिरस्कार से फुफकारना

snout (स्नाउट) *n.* (पशु की) थूथनी

snow (स्नो) *n.* (गिरने वाली) बर्फ़ – *v.* बर्फ़ की तरह गिरना या बिखेरना; बर्फ़ से भर देना – **snowy** *a.* बर्फ़ जैसा– **snowball** *n.* बर्फ़ का गोला – *v.* तेज़ी से बढ़ना; बर्फ़ के गोलों से खेलना या उन्हें एक दूसरे पर फैंकना – **snow-blindness** *n.* बर्फ़ के कारण (अस्थायी) अंधापन – **snow-capped** *a.* बर्फ़ीली चोटी वाले (पहाड़) – **snowdrift** *n.* बर्फ़ के गिरने से बना ढेर – **snowdrop** *n.* छोटा घण्टी के आकार का सफेद फूल – **snowfall** *n.* हिमपात – **snowflake** *n.* गिरती बर्फ का हल्का टुकड़ा – **snow line** ऊंचा प्रदेश जहां बर्फ़ कभी नह पिघलती

snub (स्नब) *vt.* (किसी की अवहेलना कर के) अपमान करना (-**bb**-) – *n.* अवहेलना, अपमान – *a.* छोटा और भोथरा – **snub-nosed** *a.* चपटी नाक वाला

snuff[1] (स्नफ़) *n.* नसवार

snuff[2] (स्नफ़) *v.* (मोमबत्ती आदि) बुझा देना

snuffle (ˈस्नफ़ल) *vi.* सूं सूं करते हुए मुश्किल से सांस लेना

snug (स्नग) *a.* आरामदेह, सुखद – **snuggle** (ˈस्नगल) *vi.* प्यार से या गरमी के लिए (किसी से) सट जाना

so (सो) *adv.* इतना, इस हद तक, इतना अधिक; इस प्रकार; बहुत; ऐसी दशा में; इसलिए – *conj.* इस कारण; जिस से कि – *interj.* अच्छा !– **so-called** *a.* तथाकथित

soak (सोक) *v.* भीगना, पानी में डूबा रहना, तरबतर

होना; तरबतर या सराबोर कर देना, भिगो देना; तरल पदार्थ में पड़े होना – *n.* तरबतर होने, भीगने की स्थिति

soap (सोप) *n.* साबुन – *vt.* साबुन लगाना

soar (सॉर) *vi.* ऊंचे उड़ना; कीमतों आदि का बहुत अधिक बढ़ जाना

sob (सॉब) *vi.* सिसकना (-**bb**-) – *n.* सिसकी – **sob story** सहानुभूति पाने के लिए कही गयी दुखों की कहानी

sober ('सोबर) *a.* जिसने शराब न पी रखी हो; संयमी; मद्धिम; गंभीर, सीधा सादा; संयत स्वभाव वाला – *v.* शान्त कर देना (या हो जाना, नशा उतर जाना) – **sobriety** (सो'ब्राइअटि) *n.* संयम; संयत स्वभाव

soccer ('सॉकर) *n.* फुटबाल का खेल

sociable ('सोशबल) *a.* मिलनसार; स्नेही – **sociability** (सोश'बिलिटि) *n.* मिलनसारी

social ('सोशल) *a.* सामाजिक; मिलनसार – *n.* अनौपचारिक सम्मिलन – **socialization** *n.* – **socialize** *v.* व्यवहार में मिलनसार होना; सामाजिक बनाना – **socially** *adv.*

socialism ('सोशलिज़्म) *n.* समाजवाद – **socialist** *a./n.* समाजवादी

society (स'साइअटि) *n.* समाज; साहचर्य; साथ; संघ; क्लब; (**high society** भी) उच्च वर्ग

sociology (सोसि'ऑलजि) *n.* समाज शास्त्र – **sociologist** (सोसि'ऑलजिस्ट) *n.* समाज शास्त्री

sock[1] (सॉक) *n.* जुराब, मोज़ा

sock[2] (सॉक) *sl. vt.* मारना (घूंसा आदि) – *n.* घूंसे आदि की चोट

socket ('सॉकिट) *n.* छेद जिसमें कोई वस्तु समा जाय; (आंख की) कोटर – **wall socket** दीवार में बिजली का साकिट

sod (सॉड) *n.* मिट्टी का ढेला जिस पर घास उगी हो; घास की थिगली

soda ('सोड्अ) *n.* सोडियम का सम्मिश्रण; (**soda water** भी) सोडा वाटर – **soda water** (US **soda pop** भी) सोडा वाटर, सोडा

sodden ('सॉडन) *a.* तरबतर, सराबोर

sodium ('सोडियम) *n.* धातु और क्षार का सम्मिश्रण – **sodium bicarbonate** मीठा सोडा, खाने का सोडा

sodomy ('सॉडमि) *n.* गुदा मैथुन, लौंडिबाजी

sofa ('सोफ़अ) *n.* सोफ़ा

soft (सॉफ्ट) *a.* नरम, मुलायम; म दु; आसान; शांत; भला; बहुत ढीला या नरम– **soften** (सॉफ़न) *v.* नरम या अधिक नरम बनना या बनाना; (क्रोध आदि) शांत करना – **softly** *adv.* धीरे से – **softness** *n.* नरमी – **soft drink** पेय जिसमें अल्कोहल न हो – **soft-spoken** *a.* म दुभाषी – **software** *n.* कम्प्यूटर के प्रोग्राम, टेप आदि

soggy ('सॉगि) *a.*; गीला और भारी

soil[1] (सॉइल) *n.* मिट्टी; भूमि; देश; प्रदेश

soil[2] *v.* मैला, गंदा करना या हो जाना

sojourn ('सॉजर्न, 'सजर्न) *vi.* (कुछ समय) ठहराना या टिकना – *n.* निवास; प्रवास

solace ('सॉलिस) *n.* (मुसीबत में) दिलासा, सांत्वना

solar ('सोलर) *a.* सूर्य का, सौर्य – **solar system** सौर मंडल

sold (सोल्ड) **SELL** का *pt./pp.*

solder ('सॉल्डर) *n.* टांका लगाने की नरम गलनशील धातु (रांगा आदि) – *vt.* टांका लगाना – **soldering iron** टांका लगाने का उपकरण

soldier ('सोल्जर) *n.* सैनिक, फौजी (सिपाही) – *vi.* – **soldiering** *n.* सेना में नौकरी, (**on** के साथ) द ढ़तापूर्वक करते रहना

sole[1] (सोल) *a.* एक मात्र, अकेला; अनुपम; अनन्य – **solely** *adv.* अकेले; के बल, सिर्फ़, मात्र

sole[2] (सोल) *n.* तलवा (पैर का); तला (जूते का) – *vt.* तला लगाना

solemn (´सॉलम) *a.* गंभीर; औपचारिक– **solemnity** (स´लेम्निटि) *n.* गंभीरता; धूमधाम; महत्ता – **solemnization** (सॉलम्नाइ´ज़ेशन) *n.* – **solemnize** *vt.* विधिवत पूर्ण करना, मनाना – **solemnly** *adv.* गंभीरता से

solicit (स´लिसिट) *vt.* प्रार्थना करना; अनुचित प्रस्ताव करना – *vi.* (विश्या का ग्राहक को) लुभाना, फंसाना – **solicitation** *n.* अनुरोध; प्रलोभन – **solicitor** (स´लिसिटर) *n.* वकील जो कानूनी राय देता या दस्तावेज़ तैयार करता है – **solicitude** (स´लिसिट्यूड) *n.* चिंता; उत्सुकता

solid (´सॉलिड) *a.* ठोस, सघन; पक्का; विश्वस्त – *n.* घनाक ति; पिण्ड – **solidarity** (सॉलि´डैरिटि) *n.* एकजुटता; एकात्मकता – **solidification** *n.* – **solidify** *v.* ठोस बनना, बनाना; जम जाना; घनीभूत हो जाना (-**ified, -ifying**)

soliloquy (स´लिलक्वि) *n.* (विशे. नाटक में) अकेले में बोलना; स्वगत भाषण

solitary (´सॉलिटरि) *a.* अकेला, एक भी – *n.* एकांतवासी – **solitaire** (´सॉलिटेयर) *n.* खेल जो एक ही आदमी खेलता है; एक नग जो किसी आभूषण में जड़ा हो – **solitariness** *n.* एकाकीपन, अकेलापन – **solitude** (´सॉलिट्यूड) *n.* अकेलापन; एकांत– **solitary confinement** कालकोठरी की सज़ा

solo (´सोलो) *n.* एक गायक के लिए संगीत रचना; ताश का एक खेल (*pl.* **solos**) – *a.* जिसमें अकेला वादक या गायक हो; अकेला

solstice (´सॉल्स्टिस) *n.* वर्ष में सब से छोटा या सबसे बड़ा दिन

solve (सॉल्व़) *vt.* हल करना; रास्ता निकालना; समाधान करना; उत्तर पाना – **solubility** (सॉल्यु´बिलिटि) *n.* – **soluble** (´सॉल्युबल) *a.* जो तरल पदार्थ में घुल जाय; जिस का हल या समाधान हो – **solution** (स´लूशन) *n.* हल, समाधान; घुलाने या मिलाने की क्रिया; मिश्रण, घोल – **solvable** *a.* – **solvency** (´सॉल्वंसि) *n.* – **solvent** (´सॉल्वंट) *a.* जो अपनी देनदारी चुका सके – *n.* तरल पदार्थ जो अन्य पदार्थों को घुला सके, विलायक द्रव्य

sombre (´सॉम्बर) *a.* अंधकारमय; निरानंद

some (सम) *a.* कुछ ; कोई; लगभग, करीब – *pron.* कुछ; कुछ लोग – **somebody** *n.* कोई व्यक्ति; महत्वपूर्ण (बड़ा) व्यक्ति – **somehow** *adv.* किसी (न किसी) प्रकार – **something** *n.* कुछ (अनिर्दिष्ट वस्तु) – **sometime** *adv.* पहले – *a.* पहला – **sometimes** *adv.* कभी कभार, यदा कदा – **somewhat** *adv.* किसी हद तक – **somewhere** *adv.*

somersault (´समर्सॉल्ट) *n.* कलाबाज़ी

somnambulist (सॉम्´नैम्ब्युलिस्ट) *n.* जिसे न द में चलने की बीमारी हो

son (सन) *n.* बेटा, पुत्र – **son-in-law** *n.* जंवाई

sonar (´सोनार) *n.* पानी में गूंज से जहाज़, पनडुब्बी आदि का पता लगाने का उपकरण

son et lumière (सों ए ´लूमिएँअर) *Fr.*, ध्वनि-प्रकाश प्रदर्शन

song (सॉन्ग) *n.* गाना, गायन

sonic (´सॉनिक) *a.* ध्वनि की लहरों से सम्बन्धित – **sonic boom** ध्वनि की गति से भी तेज़ चलने वाले विमान की कड़ाकेदार ध्वनि

sonnet (´सॉनिट) *n.* चौदह पदों की कविता, चतुर्दश पदी

sonorous (स´नॉरस) *a.* जिससे गंभीर ध्वनि निकले; गुंजायमान; सुरीला

soon (सून) *adv.* जल्दी, शीघ्र ही

soot (सूट) *n.* कालिख; काजल

soothe (सूद) *vt.* शांत करना; पीड़ा आदि कम करना

sop (सॉप) *n.* रोटी आदि का (भिगोया) टुकड़ा; (खुश

करने के लिए) रियायत – *vt.* पानी आदि में भिगोना; (**up** के साथ) सुखा देना (**-pp-**)

sophisticated (स'फ़िस्टिकेटिड) *a.* सुसंस्कृत; दुनियादार – **sophistication** *n.* कृत्रिमता; दुनियादारी; परिष्कृत व्यवहार

soporific (सॉप'रिफ़िक) *a.* (दवा) निद्राजनक

sorcerer ('सार्सरर) *n.* जादूगर; जादू-टोना करने वाला (**sorceress** *fem.*) – **sorcery** *n.* जादू टोना

sordid ('सॉर्डिड) *a.* नीच, गंदा; घिनावना; घटिया

sore (सॉर) *a.* दुखता, पीड़ा भरा; खीज उत्पन्न करने वाला – *n.* फोड़ा आदि; स्थान जहां सूजन आदि हो – **sorely** *adv.* बहुत बुरी तरह – **sore point** क्रोध/खेद का विषय

sorghum ('सॉर्गम) *n.* एक प्रकार की जवार

sorrow ('सॉरो) *n.* मानसिक क्लेश, दुख, व्यथा; शोक; उदासी – *vi.* शोक मनाना – **sorrowful** *a.* शोक भरा – **sorrowfully** *adv.*

sorry ('सॉरि) *a.* दुखी; जिसे किसी पर दया आए; दयनीय; शर्मिंदा – **I'm sorry** क्षमा कीजिए; मुझे खेद है

sort (सार्ट) *n.* किस्म या प्रकार; वर्ग, श्रेणी – *vt.* श्रेणीबद्ध करना, छांटना

sortie ('सॉर्टि) *n.* घिरी हुई सेना का धावा बोलना; एक हवाई जहाज़ की दुश्मन के ठिकाने पर बम गिराने के लिए उड़ान

SOS *n. abbr.* (*save our soul*) संकट का सूचक अन्तर्राष्ट्रीय संकेत; सहायता के लिए पुकार, गुहार

so-so ('सो सो) *a. inf.* मध्यम दर्जे का

sot (सॉट) *n.* शराबी; जो हर समय धुत रहता हो

sought (सॉट) **SEEK** का *pt./pp.*

souk (सूक) *n.* (अरब देशों में) बाज़ार

soul (सोल) *n.* आत्मा, रूह; मूर्त रूप, अवतार; जीव, जीवात्मा; व्यक्ति

sound[1] (साउंड) *n.* ध्वनि; शोर – *vi.* ध्वनि या नाद करना; लगना; आभास देना – *vt.* आवाज़ निकालना; कहना – **soundproof** *a.* ध्वनिरोधक – **sound track** चलचित्र के साथ रिकार्ड की गयी आवाज़

sound[2] (साउंड) *a.* अच्छी हालत में; ठोस, पक्का, मजबूत; विवेकशील; कानून के अनुसार; जो अपनी देनदारी निभा सके; प्रभावोत्पादक; निर्दोष; बेएब; सलामत; गहन, गहरा – **soundly** *adv.* पूरी तरह से

sound[3] (साउंड) *vt.* गहराई नापना (पानी आदि की), जांचना, परखना; (किसी के) विचार मालूम करना; टोह लेना

soup (सूप) *n.* यख़नी, शोरबा; *fig.* कठिन परिस्थिति

sour (साउअर) *a.* खट्टा, अम्ल; जो सड़ या बिगड़ गया हो; फटा (दूध); चिड़चिड़ा; अप्रिय – *v.* बिगाड़ना या बिगड़ जाना

source (सॉर्स) *n.* स्त्रोत; झरना; जड़, आधार; सूत्र

souse (साउस) *v.* में डुबोना, भिगोना; अचार में डालना – *n.* अचार डालने आदि की क्रिया; अचार के लिए नमक मिला तरल पदार्थ

south (साउथ) *n.* दक्षिणी दिशा; देश का दक्षिणी प्रदेश – *a./adv.* दक्षिणी – **southerly** ('सदर्लि) *a.* दक्षिणी – *n.* दक्षिण से आने वाली वायु – **southern** ('सदर्न) *a.* दक्षिणी – **southwards** ('साउथ्वर्ड्ज़) *a.* दक्षिणी – *adv.* दक्षिण की ओर – **South Pole** दक्षिणी ध्रुव

souvenir (सूव'निअर) *n.* निशानी, स्मृति चिन्ह, यादगार

sovereign ('सॉव्रिन) *n.* सम्राट या साम्राज्ञी; बीस शिलिंग मूल्य का पुराना सोने का सिक्का, पौंड – *a.* सर्वोच्च; प्रभावोत्पादक – **sovereignty** ('सॉवरन्टि) *n.* प्रभुसत्ता; स्वतंत्र राज्य

sow[1] (सो) *vi.* बोना, बीज डालना – *vt.* बिखेरना (बीज आदि); फैलाना, छितराना (**sowed** *pt.*, **sown**, **sowed** *pp.*, **sowing** *pr. p*) – **sower** *n.* बीज डालने वाला

sow[2] (साउ) *n.* सूअरी, मादा सूअर
soya (ˈसॉइअ), (US) **soybean** *n.* सोयाबीन
sozzled (ˈसॉज़ल्ड) *a. sl.* शराब में धुत
spa (स्पा) *n.* (गरम) पानी का झरना जिसमें स्वास्थ्यवर्धक तत्व हों; ऐसा स्थान जहां इस प्रकार का झरना हो
space (स्पेस) *n.* स्थान, जगह; गुंजाइश; अन्तराल, काल, अवधि; खाली स्थान; क्षेत्र; विस्तार; दूरी; आकाश; अन्तरिक्ष –*vt.* (**space out** भी) थोड़ी थोड़ी दूरी पर रखना– **spacious** (ˈस्पेशस) *a.* विस्त त, लम्बा-चौड़ा – **space-age** *a. inf.* अत्याधुनिक – **spacecraft, spaceship** *n.* अन्तरिक्ष यान– **space probe** अंतरिक्ष-खोज
spade[1] (स्पेड) *n.* कुदाल, बेलचा – **spade work** प्रारंभिक, श्रमसाध्य काम
spade[2] (स्पेड) *n.* (ताश में) हुकम का पत्ता
spaghetti (स्प ˈगेटि) *n.* सेवियों जैसा खाद्य पदार्थ, नूडल
spam (स्पैम) *n.* बिना मांगे ई-मेल द्वारा भेजी जाने वाली प्रचार-सामग्री
span (स्पैन) *n.* बित्ता, बालिश्त; विस्तार, फैलाव, पाट; चौड़ाई; मेहराब आदि का पाट (**-nn-**)
spangle (ˈस्पैङगल) *n.* सितारा (चुनरी आदि पर टांकने का) – *vt.* सितारे या चमकी टांकना
spaniel (ˈस्पैनिअल) *n.* लम्बे कानों और रेशमी बालों वाले कुत्ते की नस्ल
spank (स्पैंक) *vt.* थप्पड़ या चपत मारना, विशे. चूतड़ों पर – *n.*
spanner (ˈस्पैनर) *n.* काबले या पेच को कस कर पकड़ने का औज़ार, पाना
spar[1] (स्पार) *n.* कड़ी या शहतीर विशे. जहाज़ के मस्तूल की
spar[2] (स्पार) *vi.* मुक्केबाजी का अभ्यास करना
spare (स्पेंअर) *vt.* दया करना; छोड़ देना, इस्तेमाल न करना; के बिना काम चलाना; दे देना – *a.* अतिरिक्त, फालतू; दुबला पतला; अल्प, कम, अपर्याप्त – *n.* मशीन का अतिरिक्त पुर्ज़ा – **sparing** (ˈस्पेंअरिङ) *a.* मितव्ययी, किफ़ायत से काम लेने वाला
spark (स्पार्क) *n.* चिनगारी; बिजली के तारों से निकलता क्षणिक प्रकाश; जीवंतता, ओज, स्फूर्ति; चमक; जिन्दादिली; विनोदप्रियता; आभास, पुट; कार आदि के इंजन में बिजली की चिन्गारी जो ईंधन (तिल) में आग लगाती है – *v.* चिनगारियां छोड़ना; प्रज्वलित करना; उकसाना – **spark(ing) plug** इंजन में चिनगारी उत्पन्न करने वाला पुर्ज़ा
sparkle (ˈस्पार्कल) *vi.* चमकना, दमकना; चिनगारी छोड़ना; टिमटिमाना – *n.* चिनगारी, शोला; चमक, कांति; तड़क भड़क – **sparkler** *n.* फुलझड़ी – **sparkling** *a.* चमकता-दमकता हुआ, प्रकाशमान; जिन्दादिल
sparrow (ˈस्पैरो) *n.* गौरैया, चिड़िया
sparse (स्पार्स) *a.* छितरा या बिखरा हुआ
spartan (ˈस्पार्टन) *a.* उद्यमी, संयमी
spasm (ˈस्पैज़म) *n.* मांसपेशी की अचानक ऐंठन– **spasmodic** (स्पैज़ ˈमॉडिक) *a.* अनियमित
spastic (ˈस्पैस्टिक) *a.* जिसे एंठन के दौरे पड़ते हों; जिसका मस्तिष्क निष्क्रिय हो गया हो – *n.*
spat[1] (स्पैट) **SPIT** का *pt.*
spat[2] (स्पैट) *n.* मामूली झगड़ा
spate (स्पेट) *n.* बाढ़
spatial (स्पेशल) *a.* स्थान का या उस में स्थित
spatter (ˈस्पैटर) *vt.* छिड़कना; छ टें डालना – *vi.* छ टें पड़ना – *n.*
spatula (ˈस्पैट्युलअ) *n.* चपटी कलछी जैसा बरतन
spawn (स्पॉन) *n.* मछली या मेंढक के अंडे; (बहुधा तिरस्कार में) संतान, सन्तति – *vi.* (मछली या मेंढक का) अंडे देना
spay (स्पे) *vt.* पशु का अंडाशय निकाल देना
speak (स्पीक) *vi.* बोलना; बातचीत करना; भाषण देना – *vt.* कहना; घोषणा करना; अभिव्यक्ति

करना (**spoke, spoken, speaking**) – **speakable** *a.* – **speaker** *n.* वक्ता; (बहुधा **S-**) विधान सभा का अध्यक्ष; लाउड स्पीकर का संक्षेप –**speakerphone** *n.* ऊंची ध्वनि वाला टेलीफोन जिसे प्रयोग के लिए हाथ में पकड़ने की आवश्यकता न हो

spear (स्पिअर) *n.* बरछा, भाला– *vt.* भाले या बरछे से बेधना, घायल करना – **spearhead** *n.* हरावल दस्ता, किसी आक्रमण/अभियान का अग्रणी दल – *vt.* का अग्रणी होना

spearmint (ˈस्पिअर्मिंट) *n.* पोदीने की एक किस्म

special (स्पेशल) *a.* विशेष, ख़ास–**specialist** *n.* विशेषज्ञ –**specialization** –*n.* विशेषज्ञता – **specialize** *vi.* विशेषज्ञता प्राप्त करना – **specially** *adv.* विशेष रूप से – **specialty** (ˈस्पेशल्टि), **speciality** (स्पेशिˈऐलिटि) *n.* विशेषता, दक्षता; (होटल आदि का) विशेष पकवान जिसके लिए वह प्रसिद्ध हो

species (ˈस्पीशीज) *n.* जाति, वर्ग, विशे. जीवों का; वर्ग; उपवर्ग (*pl.* **species**)

specific (स्पिˈसिफ़िक) *a.* विशिष्ट, विशेष, किसी वस्तु या जाति की विशेषता अथवा गुण – **specifically** *adv.* विशेष रूप से – **specify** *vt.* निश्चित रूप से या विस्तार से बताना (**ified, -ifying**) – **specification** *n.* वस्तु का विस्त त ब्यौरा (आकार-प्रकार, परिमाण आदि)

specimen (ˈस्पेसिमिन) *n.* नमूना, बानगी

specious (ˈस्पीशस) *a.* जो सत्य लगे लेकिन मिथ्या हो

speck (स्पेक) *n.* कण; धब्बा – *vt.* धब्बा डालना – **speckle** *n./vt.* धब्बा, चित्ती (डालना)

specs (स्पेक्स) *pl.n.* ऐनक

spectacle (ˈस्पेक्टकल) *n.* प्रदर्शन; प्रदर्शित वस्तु; तमाशा – (~ **s**) *pl.* ऐनक, चश्मा – **spectacular** (स्पेक्ˈटैक्युलर) *a.* भव्य, शानदार; तड़क भड़क वाला – *n.* शानदार (नाटक, संगीत आदि का) कार्यक्रम – **spectator** (स्पेक्ˈटेटर) *n.* दर्शक

spectre (ˈस्पेक्टर) *n.* भूत, प्रेत; काली छाया

spectrum (ˈस्पेक्ट्रम) *n.* प्रकाश-किरण के रंगों की पट्टी, वर्णक्रम, स्पैक्ट्रम (*pl.* **spectra**)

speculate (ˈस्पेक्युलेट) *vi.* अटकल लगाना; अनुमान करना; सट्टेबाज़ी करना – **speculation** *n.* अनुमान – **speculative** *a.* सट्टे का; अव्यावहारिक, अनिश्चित – **speculator** *n.* अटकलबाज़, सट्टेबाज़

speech (स्पीच) *n.* वाणी; भाषा, बोली; भाषण – **speechless** *a.* मूक, मौन; हक्का-बक्का

speed (स्पीड) *n.* चाल, रफ्तार; गति; फोटो की फिल्म की संवेदनशीलता – *vi.* तेज़ी से चलना; तीव्र गति से गाड़ी चलाना – *vt.* आगे बढ़ाना; जल्दी कराना (**sped, speeded** *pt./pp.*) – **speeding** *n.* तेज़ गाड़ी चलाना –**speedy** *a.* फुर्तीला; शीघ्र कार्य करने वाला – **speedboat** *n.* हल्की तेज़ चलने वाली नाव (जिसमें इंजन लगा हो) – **speedometer** *n.* गतिमापक यंत्र

spell[1] (स्पेल) *vt.* वर्तनी या हिज्जे करना; का सूचक या परिणाम होना (**spelled** या **spelt** *pt./pp.*, **spelling** *pr. p.*) – **spelling** *n.* – **spell out** स्पष्ट कहना, पूरा ब्यौरा देना

spell[2] (स्पेल) *n.* सम्मोहन; जादू – **spellbound** *a.* मंत्रमुग्ध

spell[3] (स्पेल) *n.* संक्षिप्त अवधि, दौर; काम की अवधि

spend (स्पेण्ड) *vt.* खर्च या व्यय करना; काम में समय लगाना; पूरी तरह व्यय करना, समाप्त कर देना (**spent** *pt./pp.* **spending** *pr. p.*) – **spendthrift** (ˈस्पेण्ड्थ्रिफ्ट) *n.* फिज़ूलखर्च आदमी

sperm (स्पर्म) *n.* (**spermatozoon** (स्पर्मटˈज़ोअन) भी) शुक्र, शुक्राणु

spew (स्प्यू) *v.* उगलना

sphere (स्फ़िअर) *n.* गोला, गोल; परास; कार्यक्षेत्र; दर्जा; स्थिति; क्षेत्र – **spherical** (ˈस्फ़ेरिकल) *a.* गोलाकार

sphinx (स्फ़िंक्स) *n.* मिस्र की एक मूर्ति जिसका धड़ शेर का और मुंह मानव का है; रहस्यमय व्यक्ति

spice (स्पाइस) *n.* मसाला; मसाले – *vt.* में मसाले डालना; रोचक बनाना – **spicy** (ˈस्पाइसि) *a.* मसालेदार; चटपटा; *inf.* तनिक अशिष्ट या अश्लील

spick-and-span (ˈस्पिकन् ˈस्पैन) *a.* साफ़-सुथरा

spider (ˈस्पाइडर) *n.* मकड़ी

spike (स्पाइक) *n.* तीखी नोक; बड़ी सील, कीला; फूलों का लम्बा गुच्छा जिसमें फूल डंठल से लगे हों – *vt.* कील से बेधना या गाड़ना; बेकार या बेअसर कर देना; पेय में शराब मिलाना – **spiky** *a.*

spill (स्पिल) *vt.* छलकाना; गिरा देना; बिगाड़ देना; बहाना – *vi.* छलकना, गिरना, बहना (**spilt** या **spilled** *pt./pp.*) – *n.* छलकने की क्रिया; छलकी हुई मात्रा – **spillage** (ˈस्पिलिज) *n.* – **spillover** *n.* अतिरिक्त मात्रा

spin (स्पिन) *v.* चक्कर खाना या देना; कातना, बटना (धागा)(**spun** *obs.* **span** *pt.*, **spun** *pp.*, **spinning** *pr. p.*) – *n.* कताई; (विमान का) चक्कर खाते हुए नीचे को गिरना; तेज़ दौड़ या सवारी – **spinning** *n.* कताई – **spinner** *Cricket* धीमी गति का गेंदबाज़ – **spinning wheel** चरखा – **spin doctor** राजनीतिक नेता अथवा संगठन की जनता के सम्मुख अच्छी छवि बनाने वाला व्यक्ति – **spin dry** कपड़े धोने की मशीन में कपड़े डाल कर उन्हें निचोड़ने के लिए घुमाना – **spin-dryer** *n.*

spinach (ˈस्पिनिज, ˈस्पिनिच) *n.* पालक

spindle (ˈस्पिन्डल) *n.* तकला, तकली – **spindly** (ˈस्पिंड्लि) *a.* लम्बा और दुबला

spine (स्पाइन) *n.* रीढ़ की हड्डी मेढ़; पुस्तक का पुट्ठा; कांटा – **spinal** (ˈस्पाइनल) *a.* रीढ़ का – **spineless** *a.* कायर, भीरू

spinney (ˈस्पिनि) *n.* पेड़ों का झुरमुट, बनी

spinster (ˈस्पिन्स्टर) *n.* अविवाहिता स्त्री, चिरकुमारी

spiral (ˈस्पाइअरल) *n.* लगातार वक्र जो स्थिर बिन्दु से दूर होती जाय; कुंडली; इस जैसी कोई वस्तु – *a.* कुंडली जैसा – *vi. fig.* तेज़ी से बढ़ना (लागत, कीमत आदि का)

spire (स्पाइअर) *n.* मीनार के ऊपर का तीखा भाग; तीखी डंडी

spirit (ˈस्पिरिट) *n.* आत्मा, स्वभाव; जिन्दादिली; फुर्ती; जीवंतता; साहस; मनोदशा; आवश्यक गुण या अर्थ; अभिप्राय; सार; भूत-प्रेत; शराब – (~ **s**) *pl.* मिज़ाज, मनोदशा; तीखी शराब – *vt.* गायब कर देना – **spirited** *a.* साहसी; जिन्दादिल – **spiritless** *a.* निर्जीव निरुत्साह – **spiritual** (ˈस्पिरिचुअल) *a.* आत्मिक; ईश्वरीय, आध्यात्मिक – *n.* नीग्रो लोगों का भजन – **spiritualism** (ˈस्पिरिचुअलिज़्म) *n.* प्रेतात्मवाद; आध्यात्मवाद – **spiritualist** *n.* – **spirituality** *n.* आध्यात्मिकता; अभौतिकता; साधना – **spiritually** *adv.*

spit[1] (स्पिट) *vi.* थूकना – *vt.* मुंह से बाहर निकालना (**spat, spit** *pt./pp.* **spitting** *pr. p.*) – *n.* थूकने की क्रिया; थूक – **spittle** (ˈस्पिटल) *n.* थूक – **spittoon** (स्पिˈटून) *n.* थूकदान

spit[2] (स्पिट) *n.* सीख जिस पर मांस भूनते हैं; रेतीला कोना जो समुद्र में बढ़ा हुआ हो – *vt.* सीख घुसेड़ना (**-tt-**)

spite (स्पाइट) *n.* द्वेष, दुर्भावना – *vt.* द्वेष की भावना से (किसी को) विफल कर देना – **spiteful** *a.* द्वेषपूर्ण – **spitefully** *adv.* – **in spite of** *prep.* के बावजूद

splash (स्पलैश) *v.* छिड़कना; पानी के छ टे डालना; छपछप करना; (समाचार पत्र में) मोटे अक्षरों

में छापना – *n.* छपछप की आवाज़; रंग का टुकड़ा; प्रदर्शन (का प्रभाव); –**splashdown** *n.* अंतरिक्ष-यान का समुद्र में उतरना

splatter (स्प्लैटर) *v./n.* छिड़कना, छ टे (डालना)

splay (स्प्ले) *a.* फैला हुआ; तिरछा; बाहर की ओर मुड़ा हुआ

spleen (स्प्लीन) *n.* तिल्ली

splendid (स्प्लेंण्डिड) *a.* भव्य, शानदार; उत्क ष्ट – **splendidly** *adv.* – **splendour** (स्प्लेंण्डर) *n.* शान शौकत, भव्यता; गौरव

splice (स्प्लाइस) *vt.* गूंथ कर जोड़ना; लकड़ी के टुकड़े (एक दूसरे पर रख कर) जोड़ना

splint (स्प्लिन्ट) *n.* टूटी हड्डी को सीधा रखने की खपची

splinter (स्प्लिन्टर) *n.* पतला टुकड़ा –*vi.* चूर चूर या टुकड़े-टुकड़े हो जाना

split (स्प्लिट) *v.* चीरना, फाड़ना; अलग करना; (**split, splitting**) – *n.* दरार; फटन– **split second** पलक झपकते

splurge (स्प्लर्ज) *v.* रुपया पानी की तरह बहाना – *n.*

splutter (स्प्लटर) *v.* सीत्कार करना; सीत्कार करते हुए बड़बड़ाना; (पटाखों आदि का) पट-पट की आवाज़ करना – *n.*

spoil (स्पॉइल) *vt.* हानि, क्षति पहुंचाना; बिगाड़ना (विशे. बच्चों को लाड़ प्यार से)–*vi.* खराब होना (**spoiled** या **spoilt** *pt./pp.* **spoiling** *pr. p.*) – (~s) *n.* लूट का माल – **spoilt** *a.* बिगड़ा हुआ (बच्चा) – **spoilsport** *n.* रंग में भंग डालने वाला

spoke[1] (स्पोक) SPEAK का *pt.*, **spoken** *pp.* – **spokesman** (स्पोक्स्मन) *n.* प्रवक्ता (**spokeswoman** *fem.*) – **spokesperson** *n.* प्रवक्ता

spoke[2] (स्पोक) *n.* पहिए की अर

sponge (स्पंज) *n.* तरल पदार्थ सोखने के लिए प्रयुक्त स्पंज या उस जैसा कोई और पदार्थ – *vt.* स्पंज से सोखना – *v.* औरों के टुकड़ों पर पलना; मुफ्तखोरी करना – **sponger** (स्पंजर) *n. sl.* मुफ्तखोर – **spongy** (स्पंजि) *a.* स्पंज जैसा; गीला और नरम

sponsor (स्पॉन्सर) *n.* प्रायोजक; किसी पक्ष (या प्रस्ताव) का समर्थक या उस के लिए धन जुटाने वाला– *vt.* ऐसे समर्थक के रूप में कार्य करना – **sponsorship** *n.* विज्ञापन आदि देने, किसी कार्यक्रम का प्रयोजन करने की क्रिया

spontaneous (स्पॉन् टेंन्यस) *a.* स्वेच्छा से किया गया; स्वत; सहज – **spontaneity** (स्पांट नीइटि) *n.* सहजता; स्वेच्छा – **spontaneously** *adv.* अपने आप से, सहज ही – **spontaneousness** *n.*

spoof (स्पूफ़) *n.* हल्का व्यंग्य या नकल

spool (स्पूल) *n.* चरख़ी, फिरकी

spoon (स्पून) *n.* चम्मच, चमचा – *vt.* चमचे से उठाना – **spoonful** *n.* चम्मच भर

sporadic (स्प रैडिक) *a.* जो रुक रुक कर या कह -कह हो; छिटपुट – **sporadically** *adv.* कभी-कभी; कह -कह

sport (स्पॉर्ट) *n.* खेल; खेल-कूद (प्रतियोगिता); व्यायाम; मनोरंजन; उपहास; हंसमुख व्यक्ति (जो हार कर भी हंसता रहे) – *vt.* धारण करना (विशे. दिखावे के लिए) – *vi.* खेलना – **sporting** *a.* खेल का; न्यायप्रियता या विशाल-हृदयता का व्यवहार करने वाला – **sportsman** *n.* खिलाड़ी; हार कर भी हंसता रहने वाला व्यक्ति – **sportsmanlike** *a.* सच्चे खिलाड़ी जैसा (व्यवहार)

spot (स्पॉट) *n.* चित्ती; धब्बा, दाग़; दोष; फुंसी; स्थान; कठिन स्थिति; स्थान – *vt.* चित्ती या धब्बे डालना; देख लेना; पता लगाना (**-tt-**) – **spotless** *a.* निष्कलंक, बेदाग; शुद्ध – **spotlight** *n.* आकर्षण का केन्द्र; लोक प्रसिद्धि

spouse (स्पाउज़) *n.* पति या पत्नी
spout (स्पाउट) *v.* उगलना – *n.* टोंटी; धारा; फुहारा
sprain (स्प्रेन) *n./vt.* मोच (आना); मुड़कना
sprang (स्प्रैंग) **SPRING** का *pt.*
sprawl (स्प्रॉल) *vi.* पसर कर बैठना या लेटना; अव्यवस्थित ढंग से फैलना या बढ़ना (बस्ती, नगर का) – *n.*
spray (स्प्रे) *n.* तरल पदार्थ को फुहार के रूप में छोड़ने का उपकरण – *vt.* फुहार छोड़ना – **spray gun** रंग करने की पिचकारी
spread (स्प्रेड) *v.* फैलाना; खोलना; बिछाना; छितरा देना; बांट देना; तह खोलना; ढक देना; लगाना (मक्खन आदि) – *vi.* फैलना, बिछना, खुलना (**spread, spreading**) – *n.* फैलाव; विस्तार; दावत; रोटी चुपड़ने का मक्खन आदि – **spread-eagle(d)** *a.* जिसकी बाहें और टांगें फैली हुई हों – **spreadsheet** *Computers* एक प्रकार का कम्प्यूटर कार्यक्रम
spree (स्प्री) *n.* रंगरलियां; आमोद-प्रमोद (का दौरा)
sprig (स्प्रिग) *n.* छोटी टहनी (जैसे पोदीने की); ऐसी बनावट; बिना सिर की छोटी कील
sprightly ('स्प्राइट्लि) *a.* ज़िन्दादिल, प्रसन्नचित्त; फुर्तीला – **sprightliness** *n.* ज़िन्दादिली; फुर्ती
spring (स्प्रिंग) *vi.* उछलना; लपकना; झपटना; उगना, उत्पन्न होना; प्रकट होना; बढ़ना; मुड़ या फट जाना – *vt.* अप्रत्याशित रूप से सामने लाना; आ टपकना; फंदा ख चना (**sprang, sprung, springing**) – *n.* उछलने, लपकने, झपटने की क्रिया; कमानी, स्प्रिंग; झरना; वसन्त ऋतु – **springy** *a.* लचकदार – **spring onion** हरी प्याज़ – **spring roll** एक प्रकार का नमकीन व्यंजन
springbok ('स्प्रिंग्बॉक) *n.* दक्षिणी अफ्रीका का बारहसिंगा
sprinkle (स्प्रिंकल) *vt.* छिड़कना; छितराना; बुरकाना – **sprinkler** *n.* फौहारा – **sprinkling** *n.* छोटी मात्रा या संख्या
sprint (स्प्रिंट) *vt.* थोड़ी दूरी तक तेज़ी से भागना – *n.* ऐसी दौड़ – **sprinter** *n.* धावक
sprout (स्प्राउट) *vi.* अंकुर निकलना, बीज का अंकुरित होना; ऊपर उठना – *n.* अंकुर
spruce[1] (स्प्रूस) *n.* देवदार की एक किस्म
spruce[2] (स्प्रूस) *a.* साफ़-सुथरा; बनाठना
sprung (स्प्रंग) **SPRING** का *pp.*
spry (स्प्राइ) *a.* फुर्तीला; चुस्त
spume (स्प्यूम) *n./vi.* झाग, फेन (निकलना, उठना)
spun (स्पन) **SPIN** का *pt./pp.*
spur (स्पर) *n.* घुड़सवार की महमेज़; प्रेरणा; उत्तेजना– *vt.* तेज़ी से थोड़ा दौड़ाना (**spur on** भी) (**-rr-**) – **on the spur of the moment** तत्काल
spurious ('स्प्युअरिअस) *a.* जाली, नकली, खोटा
spurn (स्पर्न) *vt.* तिरस्कार से ठुकराना
spurt (स्पर्ट) *v.* फूट निकलना, फुहारा छूटना या छोड़ना
sputnik ('स्पुत्निक) *n.* रूस के अन्तरिक्ष यान का नाम
sputter ('स्पटर) *v.* बड़बड़ाना; (आग का) चिटकना
sputum ('स्प्यूटम) *n.* थूक (*pl.* – **ta**)
spy (स्पाइ) *n.* गुप्तचर, जासूस – *vi.* जासूस का काम करना – *vt.* देख लेना (**spied, spying**)- **spyware** *n.* कम्प्यूटर साफ्टवेयर जो इंटरनेट पर या मोबाइल फोन पर आपकी गति विधियां चुपचाप रिकर्ड कर लेता है
sq. square का संक्षेप
squabble ('स्क्वॉबल) *vi.* तू-तू मैं-मैं करना – *n.*
squad (स्क्वॉड) *n.* दस्ता, विशे. सैनिकों का – **squadron** ('स्क्वॉड्रन) *n.* घुड़सवारों, जहाज़ों या विमानों का दस्ता
squalid ('स्क्वॉलिड) *a.* गन्दा; नीच; फटेहाल – **squalor** ('स्क्वॉलर) *n.* गन्दगी; फटेहाली
squall (स्क्वॉल) *n.* चीख़; हवा का तेज़ झोंका; थोड़ी देर का तूफ़ान – *vi.* चीखना

squander (´स्क्वॉण्डर) *vt.* रुपया पानी की तरह बहाना

square (स्क्वेंअर) *n.* वर्ग; वर्गाकार क्षेत्र; (नगर में) वर्गाकार चौक; वर्गफल; गुनिया, कोनिया (औज़ार) –*a.* वर्गाकार; ईमानदार; सच्चा; समतल; बराबर; चौरस; क्षेत्र का नाप (इतने वर्ग फुट आदि)– *vt.* वर्गाकार बनाना; वर्गफल निकालना –*vi.* अनुकूल होना – **squarely** *adv*. पूरी तरह; ठीक से – **square meal** पेट भर खाना – **square metre** वर्ग मीटर – **square root** वर्गमूल

squash (स्क्वॉश) *vt.* कुचलना; समाप्त कर देना; अपमानित करना– *n.* कुचले फलों का रस; स्क्वैश; भीड़-भाड़; टैनिस जैसा खेल

squat (स्क्वॉट) *vi.* पालथी मारकर बैठना; (ज़मीन पर) अनधिक त कब्ज़ा कर लेना (**-tt-**) – *a.* ठिगना और मोटा

squawk (स्क्वॉक) *n.* छोटी कर्कश आवाज़ या चीख़, विशे. पक्षी की – *v.* ऐसी चीख़ निकालना

squeak (स्क्वीक) *n./v.* च -च या चूं-चूं (करना)

squeal (स्क्वील) *n.* लम्बी, तीखी चीख – *vi.* ऐसी चीख़ मारना

squeamish (´स्क्वीमिश) *a.* जिसे जल्दी मतली आ जाय; नाज़ुक-मिज़ाज

squeeze (स्क्वीज़) *vt.* दबाना; भ चना; निचोड़ना; बलपूर्वक प्रवेश करना; गले लगाना– *n.*

squib (स्क्विब) *n.* छोटा-सा पटाख़ा; महत्वहीन व्यक्ति

squid (स्क्विड) *n.* एक प्रकार की मछली, समुद्रफेनी

squint (स्क्विंट) *vi.* भैंगा होना; तिरछी नज़र से देखना – *n.* भैंगापन

squire (स्क्वाइअर) *n.* जम दार

squirm (स्क्वर्म) *vi.* कुलबुलाना; झेंपना – *n.*

squirrel (´स्क्विरल) *n.* गिलहरी

squirt (स्क्वर्ट) *v.* फुहारा या पिचकारी छोड़ना – *n.* फुहारा

St. Saint; Strait; Street का संक्षेप

st. stone (वज़न) का संक्षेप

stab (स्टैब) *v.* (छुरे आदि से) प्रहार करना; छुरा घोंपना (**-bb-**)– *n.* छुरे से प्रहार या उसका घाव; टीस; हूक

stabilize (´स्टैबिलाइज़) *vt.* स्थिर करना, मजबूत या द ढ़ करना; फिर सन्तुलन लाना विशे. कीमतों, मजदूरी आदि में – **stabilizer** *n.* जहाज़, विमान आदि का सन्तुलन बनाए रखने का उपकरण; बिजली की वोल्टता स्थिर रखने का उपकरण

stable[1] (´स्टेबल) *n.* अस्तबल, घुड़साल; किसी मालिक के घोड़ों के लिए प्रयुक्त शब्द – *vt.* अस्तबल में रखना

stable[2] (´स्टेबल) *a.* स्थिर, अचल; द ढ़; द ढ़ निश्चय – **stability** (स्ट´बिलिटि) *n.* स्थिरता, स्थायित्व; द ढ़ता

stack (स्टैक) *n.* वस्तुओं का तरतीब से लगा ढेर; (ईंट का) चट्टा; (ताश की) गड्डी; चिमनी; *Computers* जानकारी संग्रह करने की प्रणाली जिसके अंतर्गत आखिरी जानकारी सबसे पहले ली जा सकती है – *vt.* ढेर लगाना

stadium (´स्टेडिअम) *n.* स्टेडियम (*pl.* **-s, -ia.**)

staff (स्टाफ़) *n.* कर्मचारी-गण; सोटा, लाठी (*pl.* **staffs, staves**) – *vt.* कर्मचारी देना

stag (स्टैग) *n.* नर हिरण – *a.* केवल पुरुषों के लिए, जैसे **stag party**

stage (स्टेज) *n.* (विकास की) अवस्था, चरण; चबूतरा; (**the stage** भी) रंगमंच; कार्यवाही का स्थल; पड़ाव (यात्रा में ठहरने का स्थान); दो पड़ावों के बीच की दूरी; अन्तरिक्ष में जाने वाले राकेट का वह भाग जो उससे अलग हो जाता है – *vt.* नाटक आयोजित करना – **stagy** *a.*नाटकीय – **stage direction** नाट्य निर्देश – **stage-manage** किसी सार्वजनिक घटना (वि० राजनीतिक) को योजनाबद्ध तरीके से स्वाभाविक रूप देकर प्रस्तुत करना

stagger (स्टैगर) *vi.* लड़खड़ाना – *vt.* स्तंभित या आश्चर्यचकित कर देना; टेढ़े-मेढ़े ढंग से रखना; (कार्यक्रमों आदि को) भिन्न-भिन्न समय रखना – *n.* लड़खड़ाहट – **staggered** *a.* स्तंभित; भिन्न-भिन्न समय पर – **staggering** *a.* आश्चर्यचकित करने वाला

stagnate (स्टैग्'नेट) *vi.* बहाव, प्रवाह रुक जाना; विकास या प्रगति रुक जाना – **stagnant** ('स्टैग्नंट) *a.* निश्चल, ठहरा हुआ – **stagnation** *n.* गतिहीनता

staid (स्टेड) *a.* गंभीर, सौम्य; संतुलित, शांत

stain (स्टेन) *v.* धब्बा या निशान लगाना; लकड़ी पर तरल रंग लगाना; कलंक या बदनामी लाना – *n.* कलंक; धब्बा; बदनामी – **stainless** *a.* बेदाग; निष्कलंक – **stainless steel** जंग-रहित इस्पात – **stained glass window** खिड़की जिसमें रंगीन कांच लगे हों

stairs (स्टेंअर्ज़) *pl. n.* सीढ़ी, जीना – **staircase, stairway** *n.* ज़ीना

stake (स्टेक) *n.* खूंटा, खूंटी; बाज़ी की रकम – *vt.* खूंटियां गाड़ना; बाज़ी लगाना; खतरे में डालना – **be at stake** जोखिम में/दांव पर होना – **stakeholder** *n.* भागीदार

stale (स्टेल) *a.* पुराना; बासी; घिसा पिटा; ओजहीन; ऊबाने वाला; जिसमें रुचि न हो – **stalemate** ('स्टेल्मेट) *n.* *Chess* ऐसी स्थिति कि खिलाड़ी अगली चाल न चल सके; ज़िच, गतिरोध

stalk[1] (स्टॉक) *n.* पौधे का डंठल; उस जैसी अन्य वस्तु (वि० कुछ जानवरों में)

stalk[2] (स्टॉक) *v.* दबे पांव पीछा करना; अकड़ कर धीमी चाल चलना – *n.* शिकार का पीछा करने की क्रिया; आतंकित करते हुए आस-पास घूमना; छाया होना

stall (स्टॉल) *n.* अस्तबल में घोड़े का स्थान; प्रदर्शनी आदि में स्टाल; गिरजा घर में बैठने का स्थान – *v.* स्टाल में रखना; घोड़े को थान पर बांधना; (कीचड़, बर्फ में) फंसे रहना; कार के इंजन का अचानक बंद हो जाना, देरी करना; रोकना; टाल मटोल करना – **stalls** *pl. n.* सिनेमा या थियेटर में (आगे के परदे के पास का) स्थान

stallion ('स्टैल्यन, 'स्टैलिअन) *n.* घोड़ा जो नस्ल बढ़ाने के काम आए

stalwart ('स्टॉल्वर्ट) *a.* बलवान; बहादुर; द ढ़निश्चय, पक्का (समर्थक) – *n.*

stamina ('स्टैमिन्अ) *n.* कठोर परिश्रम की शक्ति; ओजस्विता; दम

stammer ('स्टैमर) *v.* हकलाना – *n.* हकलाहट – **stammerer** *n.*

stamp (स्टैम्प) *vi.* (भूमि पर) पैर पटकना – *vt.* छाप या मुहर लगाना; डाक का टिकट चिपकाना; मन में बिठा देना – *n.* पैर पटकने की क्रिया; मुहर, छाप; मुहर (लगाने का उपकरण); डाक टिकट

stampede (स्टैम्'पीड) *n.* भगदड़ – *v.* भगदड़ मचाना

stance (स्टैंस) *n.* मुद्रा; खड़े होने का अंदाज़; रवैया; द ष्टिकोण

stand (स्टैन्ड) *v.* खड़े होना या करना; रहना; स्थित होना; द ढ़ रहना, स्थिर रहना; डटना, न हिलना; सहना, झेलना; सिद्धान्तों पर डटे रहना; चुनाव में खड़े होना; का प्रतीक होना; (*offer, decision*) वैध होना; (**not stand**) पसंद (न) होना; झेलना (*can't stand any more noise*) – *vt. inf.* (किसी को) दावत देना, खिलाना-पिलाना (**stood, standing**) – *n.* स्थिर रहने की स्थिति; द ष्टिकोण, रवैया; (बस का) रुकने का स्थान, अड्डा; (स्टेडियम में) धानी, मंच जहां दर्शक बैठते हैं; लोकप्रिय संगीतकारों, गायकों का कह (कार्यक्रम हेतु) – **standing** *n.* ख्याति; दर्जा; अवधि – *a.* सीधा खड़ा; स्थायी; ठहरा हुआ – **stand by** का साथ देना/की सहायता करना – **stand for** का प्रतीक होना – **stand-off** *n.* समझौता न होने की स्थिति – **stand up for** का समर्थन करना

standard (ˈस्टैन्डर्ड) *n.* मापदंड, मानदंड, कसौटी; स्तर; गुण; झण्डा; मानक वज़न या माप; स्कूल की कक्षा – *a.* सामान्य; नियमित; औसत; माना हुआ, प्रामाणिक – **standardization** *n.* – **standardize** (ˈस्टैंडर्डाइज़) *vt.* किसी मानक के अनुरूप बनाना

standpoint (ˈस्टैन्ड्पॉइंट) *n.* द ष्टिकोण

stank (स्टैंक) **STINK** का *pt.*

stanza (ˈस्टैंज़ुअ) *n.* (कविता का) बंद (*pl.* – **zas**)

staple (ˈस्टेपल) *n.* U अक्षर के आकार का कागज़ नत्थी करने के लिए प्रयुक्त (स्टील का) पिन, स्टेपल; मुख्य उत्पादन – *a.* मुख्य – *vt.* स्टेपल से नत्थी करना – **stapler** (ˈस्टेप्लर) *n.* कागज़ नत्थी करने का छोटा उपकरण

star (स्टार) *n.* तारा; तारे का चिह्न (*); प्रसिद्ध खिलाड़ी, अभिनेता आदि – *vt.* तारों से सजाना; तारे का चिह्न लगाना; मुख्य गायक नर्तक आदि के रूप में आना – *vi.* फिल्म आदि में मुख्य भूमिका निभाना (**-rr-**) – *a.* प्रमुख; सबसे महत्वपूर्ण या प्रसिद्ध – **starry** *a.* तारों भरा – **star-crossed** *a.* किस्मत का मारा – **stardom** *n.* ख्याति-प्राप्त अभिनेता होना – **starfish** *n.* तारे जैसा छोटे आकार का समुद्री जीव – **starlet** *n.* छोटी अभिनेत्री

starch (स्टार्च) *n.* मांड, कलफ़ – *vt.* कलफ़ लगाना – **starchy** *a.* जिसमें कलफ़ लगा हो; औपचारिक; रूखा

stare (स्टेंअर) *n./vi.* टकटकी लगा कर देखना, घूरना

stark (स्टार्क) *a.* कड़ा, कठोर; खाली; एकदम (नंगा); निर्जन – *adv.* पूरी तरह

starling (ˈस्टार्लिंग) *n.* एक पक्षी, तेलियर

start (स्टार्ट) *vt.* शुरू करना; चालू करना – *vi.* शुरू करना; रवाना होना; चौंक उठना – *n.* शुरूआत; चौंकने की क्रिया; किसी दौड़ में आगे होने की स्थिति – **starter** *n.* कार आदि के इंजन का बिजली का उपकरण जो उसे चलाता है; दौड़ में प्रतियोगी या उस का प्रवर्तक – **start-up** *a.* नये व्यवसाय से सम्बंधित

startle (ˈस्टार्टल) *vt.* चौंका देना; डरा देना

starve (स्टार्व़) *v.* भूखों मारना या भूखों मरना – **starvation** *n.* भुखमरी

stash (स्टैश) *vt. inf.* छिपा कर रखना

state (स्टेट) *n.* दशा परिस्थिति; राज्य; सरकार; शान-शौकत – *vt.* कहना; वर्णन करना – **stately** *a.* राजसी – **statement** *n.* कथन – **statesman** *n.* राजमर्मज्ञ, राजनेता – **statesmanship** *n.* राजमर्मज्ञता

static (ˈस्टैटिक) *a.* गतिहीन; स्थायी – *n.* रेडियो में आने वाली कड़कड़ की आवाज़ – *pl.* भौतिकी की शाखा, स्थैतिकी – **statically** *adv.*

station (ˈस्टेशन) *n.* ; रेलवे स्टेशन; पुलिस थाना या दमकल विभाग का दफ्तर; रेडियो या टी.वी. का प्रसारण केन्द्र; बस का अड्डा; चौकी; नौकरी; पद; दर्जा; स्थिति – *vt.* तैनात करना – **stationary** *a.* स्थिर, अचल; जो बदले नह

stationer (ˈस्टेशनर) *n.* लिखने की सामग्री बेचने वाला – **stationery** *n.* लिखने की सामग्री

statistics (स्टˈटिस्टिक्स) *n.* आंकड़े; उनका अध्ययन, सांख्यिकी – **statistical** *a.* – **statistician** (स्टैटिस्ˈटिशन) *n.* सांख्यिकीविद

statue (स्टैट्यू) *n.* मूर्ति, प्रतिमा – **statuary** (ˈस्टैट्युअरि) *n.* मूर्तियों के लिए सामूहिक नाम – **statuesque** (स्टेट्युˈऐस्क) *a.* मूर्ति के सामान; सर्वांग सुन्दर

stature (ˈस्टैचर) *n.* कद, ऊंचाई; महिमा, बड़प्पन

status (ˈस्टेटस) *n.* पद, दर्जा; स्थिति; प्रतिष्ठा; महत्व – **status quo** (ˈस्टेटस ˈक्वो) यथापूर्व स्थिति – **status symbol** कोई बात/वस्तु जो प्रतिष्ठा का प्रतीक हो

statute (ˈस्टैट्यूट) *n.* संविधि – **statutory** (ˈस्टैट्युटरि) *a.* लिखित कानून के अनुसार निर्दिष्ट; संविहित

staunch (´स्टॉन्च) *vt.* (लहू बहने से) रोकना – *a.* विश्वस्त; निष्ठावान; पक्का

stave (स्टेव़) *n.* लकड़ी के पीपे की खपची– *vt.* छेद करना; न होने देना (**stove, staved** *pt./pp.*, **staving** *pr. p.*)

stay¹ (स्टे) *vi.* रुकना; ठहरना; अस्थायी निवास करना, टिकना; प्रतीक्षा करना – *vt.* रोकना; स्थगित करना (**stayed, staying**) – *n.* ठहरने की क्रिया; ठिकाना; प्रवास; रोकथाम; स्थगन – **stay up** देर से सोने जाना

stay² (स्टे) *n.* टेक, सहारा

STD Subscriber Trunk Dialling, sexually transmitted diseases का संक्षेप

stead (स्टॅड) *n.* स्थान – **in stead of** के स्थान में

steady (´स्टॅडि) *a.* स्थिर; नियमित; संयमित; अध्यवसायी; विश्वस्त – *vt.* स्थिर करना – **steadily** *adv.* लगतार, नियमित रूप से – **steadiness** *n.* संतुलन, धैर्य – **steadfast** (´स्टॅड्फ़स्ट; ´स्टॅड्फ़ास्ट) *a.* पक्का, सुस्थिर, अटल

steak (स्टेक) *n.* मांस, विशे. गोमांस का मोटा टुकड़ा

steal (स्टील) *vi.* चोरी करना; दबे पांव या चोरी छिपे जाना – *vt.* चुरा लेना, ले उड़ना (**stole, stolen, stealing**) – **steal the show** सबसे बाज़ी मार जाना

stealth (स्टॅल्थ) *n.* छिपाव; दुराव – **stealthily** *adv.* चोरी-छिपे, गुप्त – **stealthy** *a.* गुप्त, दुराव पूर्ण

steam (स्टीम) *n.* भाप, *inf.* शक्ति; ऊर्जा – *vi.* भाप छोड़ना; भाप उठना; भाप से चलना – *vt.* भाप से पकाना – **steamy** *a.* गरम और आर्द्र – **steamer** *n.* भाप से चलने वाला जहाज़ – **steam-engine** *n.* भाप से चलने वाला इंजन -**steamroller** *vt.* विरोध के बावजूद कुछ करा लेना

steel (स्टील) *n.* इस्पात; इस्पात से बना हथियार – *vt.* कठोर बनाना – **steel-works** *n.* इस्पात का कारखाना

steep¹ (स्टीप) *a.* उठता हुआ; ढालू; प्रवण; *inf.* कठिन; बहुत अधिक (कीमत आदि); *inf.* जो तर्कसंगत न हो, बेतुका

steep² (स्टीप) *v.* भिगोना, डुबोना – *n.*

steeple (´स्टीपल) *n.* गिरजा का मीनार – **steeplechase** (´स्टीपल्चेस) *n.* घुड़दौड़; बाधा दौड़

steer¹ (स्टिअर) *vt.* जहाज़ या कार चलाना – *vi.* अपना रास्ता निर्दिष्ट करना – **steering wheel** वाहन में दिशा मोड़ने का पहियानुमा उपकरण

steer² (स्टिअर) *n.* बधिया बैल

stellar (´स्टॅलर) *a.* सितारों सम्बन्धी

stem¹ (स्टॅम) *n.* डंठल, डंडी; तना; लम्बा पतला भाग जैसे पाइप की डंडी – **stem from** से उत्पन्न होना

stem² (स्टॅम) *vt.* रोकना, रोक या बाधा लगाना (**-mm-**)

stench (स्टॅन्च) *n.* दुर्गन्ध, बदबू

stencil (´स्टॅन्सिल) *n.* स्टेन्सिल; उस पर अंकित शब्द – *vt.* स्टॅसिल काटना (**-ll-**) –**stenciller** *n.*

stenography (स्ट´नॉग्रफ़ि) *n.* आशुलेखन – **stenographer** *n.* आशुलेखक, स्टैनोग्राफ़र – **stenographic** *a.*

step (स्टॅप) *vi.* कदम उठाना और रखना, चलना – *vt.* कदमों में नापना (**-pp-**) – *n.* कदम; कदमों की आवाज़; चाप चिन्ह; चलने का तरीका; (नृत्य में) कदम रखने का तरीका; चाल; गति; माप; प्रक्रिया का चरण या अवस्था; सीढ़ी या ज़ीना; सोपान; पदोन्नति – *pl.* (**pair of steps**) सीढ़ी या जीना जो एक स्थान से उठाकर दूसरे स्थान पर ले जाया जा सके – **step-ladder** *n.* चौड़े तख़्तों वाली सीढ़ी

stepchild (´स्टॅप् चाइल्ड) *n.* सौतेला बच्चा – **stepbrother** *n.* – **stepfather** *n.* – **stepmother** *n.* – **stepsister** *n.*

stereophonic (स्टेंरिअ'फ़ॉनिक) *a.* (आवाज़) जो कई दिशाओं से आती सुनाई पड़े; स्टीरियो – **stereo** ('स्टिअरिओ) *a./n.* इस प्रकार की आवाज़ का बाजा या उसका रिकार्ड

stereotype ('स्टेंरिअटाइप) *n.* मुद्रण फलक (धातु की प्लेट जिस पर उभरे अक्षर होते हैं और जो छपाई में काम आती है); ऊबाने वाली घिसी पिटी बात; परम्परा या रूढ़ि पर आधारित बात – *vt.* एक ही सांचे में ढालना; रूढ़िबद्ध बना देना

sterile ('स्टेंराइल) *a.* बंजर (भूमि); बन्ध्या (स्त्री); फलहीन (पौधा); जीवाणु या रोगाणु हीन – **sterility** (स्टें'रिलिटि) *n.* अनर्वरता; बन्ध्यता – **sterilization** (स्टेंरिलाइ'ज़ेशन) *n.* बन्ध्यीकरण; जीवाणुनाशन – **sterilize** *vt.* बन्ध्य बनाना; जीवाणुहीन बनाना

sterling ('स्टर्लिंग) *a.* खरा; मूल्यवान; ब्रिटिश मुद्रा में – *n.* ब्रिटिश मुद्रा – **a pound sterling** एक ब्रिटिश पाउंड

stern[1] (स्टर्न) *a.* कठोर, सख्त मिज़ाज – **sternness** *n.* कठोरता

stern[2] (स्टर्न) *n.* जहाज़ का पिछला भाग

sternum ('स्टर्नम) *n.* छाती के बीच की हड्डी; उरोस्थि

steroid ('स्टेंरॉइड) *n.* स्टीरॉयड, शरीर में उत्पन्न होने वाला रासायनिक पदार्थ, अनेक रोगों के उपचार में प्रयुक्त क त्रिम स्टीरॉयड

stethoscope ('स्टेंथस्कोप) *n.* डाक्टर का उपकरण – **stethoscopic** (स्टेंथ'स्कॉपिक) *a.*

stevedore ('स्टीविडॉर) *n.* जहाज़ में माल लादने या उतारने वाला मज़दूर

stew (स्ट्यू) *n.* धीमी आग पर बन्द बरतन में पकाया व्यंजन, दमपुख्त– *vt./vi.* दमपुख्त करना

steward ('स्ट्युअर्ड) *n.* सम्पत्ति का प्रबन्धक; घुड़दौड़ का अधिकारी; जहाज़ या विमान में कर्चचारी जो यात्रियों को भोजन आदि देता है – **stewardess** *n.* विमान आदि की परिचारिका – **stewardship** *n.* परिचारक का कार्य

stick (स्टिक) *n.* छड़ी; छड़ी जैसी कोई वस्तु – *vt.* गोंद चिपकाना; चुभाना, भोंकना; छेद करना; का आगे को निकले होना – *vi.* चिपकना; रुक जाना; फंस जाना; रहना; चिपके या बंधे होना; आगे को निकले होना (**stuck** *pt./pp.*) – **sticker** *n.* गोंद लगा लेबल आदि, स्टिकर – **sticky** *a.* जिस पर गोंद या कोई चिपचिपा पदार्थ लगा हो; उमस भरा (मौसम)

stickler ('स्टिक्लर) *n.* – **be a stickler for** किसी बात पर बहुत बल देना या आग्रह करना

stiff (स्टिफ़) *a.* कड़ा; कठिन; गाढ़ा; औपचारिक, प्रचण्ड या ताज़ी जैसे समीर – **stiffen** *vt.* कड़ा करना – *vi.* कड़ा हो जाना – **stiffness** *n.* – **stiff-necked** *a.* हठी, ज़िद्दी, अकड़वाला

stifle ('स्टाइफ़ल) *vt.* दम घोंटना; दबाना

stigma ('स्टिग्मअ) *n.* कलंक का टीका; लांछन, बदनामी (*pl.* **stigmas, stigmata**)

stile (स्टाइल) *n.* किसी बाड़ के साथ बनी सीढ़ियां

still[1] (स्टिल) *a.* निश्चल, अचल; नीरव – *vt.* चुप करा देना – *adv.* अभी तक; अब तक भी; (और) भी – *n.* फोटो, विशे. चलचित्र के किसी द श्य का – **stillness** *n.* नीरवता– **stillborn** *a.* (बच्चा) जो मरा हुआ पैदा हो

still[2] (स्टिल) *n.* अर्क, शराब आदि बनाने की भट्ठी

stilt (स्टिल्ट) *n.* पैर बांसा, गेड़ी; बड़ा शहतीर या टेक (भवन के लिए) – **stilted** *a.* आडम्बरपूर्ण (शैली आदि)

stimulus ('स्टिम्युलस) *n.* प्रेरणा; प्रोत्साहन (*pl.* – **uli** (स्टिम्यूलाइ)) – **stimulant** ('स्टिम्युलंट) *n.* औषधि जो उद्दीपक का काम करे – **stimulate** *vt.* उत्साहित, उत्तेजित या प्रेरित करना – **stimulating** *a.* उत्तेजक; उद्दीपक – **stimulation** *n.* उद्दीपन; प्रोत्साहन

sting (स्टिंग) *vt.* डंक मारना, डसना; अत्यधिक पीड़ा पहुंचाना – *vi.* पीड़ा का अनुभव करना (*pt.* **pp.**

stung, stinging *pr. p.*) – *n.* – **stinging** *a. inf.* करारा (जवाब आदि) – **sting operation** अपराधियों को रंगे हाथों पकड़ने की (पुलिस, पत्रकारों की) गुप्त योजना का कार्यान्वन

stingy ('स्टिन्जि) *a.* कंजूस

stink (स्टिंक) – *vi.* दुर्गन्ध फैलाना; *sl.* जघन्य होना (**stank, stunk, stinking**) – *n.* दुर्गन्ध

stint (स्टिंट) *vt.* कम देना, थोड़ा-थोड़ा देना – *n.* निर्धारित अंश, नियत काम या समय; सीमा

stipend ('स्टाइपेंन्ड) *n.* (छात्र) वृत्ति, वज़ीफ़ा

stipulate ('स्टिप्युलेट) *vi.* (किसी करार में) शर्त लगाना – **stipulation** *n.* शर्त

stir (स्टर) *v.* हिलाना; उकसाना या उत्तेजित करना (**-rr-**) – *n.* गड़बड़; हंगामा – **stir-fry** *vt.* पकवान को तलते समय लगातार चलाते रहना

stirrup ('स्टिरप) *n.* रकाब (जिसमें घुड़सवार अपने पैर रखता है)

stitch (स्टिच) *n.* टांका, तोपा; पसली में अचानक ज़ोर का दर्द; कपड़े का छोटे से छोटा टुकड़ा – *v.* (कपड़ा) सीना, टांका लगाना, तोपा भरना

stoat (स्टोट) *n.* नेवले की जाति का जीव

stock (स्टॉक) *n.* माल (बिक्री का); सामान; भण्डार; संग्रह; निधि; कम्पनी आदि के हिस्से; प्रतिष्ठा, साख; मवेशी; पौधा या टहनी जिस से कलम काटी जाय; बन्दूक का कुन्दा; औजार का दस्ता; मांस का शोरबा; फूलदार पौधा; वंश – *a.* जो भण्डार में पड़ा हो; मानक; घिसा-पिटा (शब्द आदि) – *vt.* (भण्डार में) रखना; के पास होना – **stocky** *a.* भारी भरकम – **stockbroker** *n.* कम्पनियों के शेयर का दलाल – **stock exchange** शेयर बाज़ार – **stockholder** *n.* शेयरधारी – **stock market** शेयर बाजार – **stockpile** *v.* कोई माल बहुत अधिक मात्रा में खरीद कर रखना – **stocktaking** *n.* दुकान मे पड़े माल का लेखा-जोखा

stockade (स्टॉ'केड) *n.* बाड़ा, अहाता

stocking ('स्टॉकिंग) *n.* मोज़ा, जुराब

stodgy ('स्टॉजि) *a.* भारी; नीरस

stoic ('स्टोइक) *a.* निर्लिप्त, विरक्त – *n.* धीर व्यक्ति – **stoicism** ('स्टोइसिज़म) *n.* विरक्ति

stoke (स्टोक) *v.* कोयला झोंकना; भट्ठी को जलाए रखना – **stoker** *n.*

stole (स्टोल) STEAL का *pt., pp.* **stolen**

stomach ('स्टॅमक) *n.* आमाशय, मेदा; भूख; इच्छा – *vt.* सहना, बर्दाश्त करना – **stomach ache** पेट दर्द

stone (स्टोन) *n.* पत्थर, शिलाखंड; फल की गुठली; गुर्दे की पथरी; कीमती पत्थर; 14 पौंड का वज़न – *a.* पत्थर का (बना); सख्त – *vt.* पत्थर फैंकना, मारना – **stonily** *adv.* – **stony** ('स्टोनि) *a.* पत्थर का या उस जैसा; रूखा; कठोर – **stonewall** *vi.* काम में बाधा डालना – **at a stone's throw** थोड़ी दूर पर

Stone Age पाषाण युग

stood STAND का *pt./pp.*

stooge (स्टूज) *n. Theatre* अभिनेता जो दूसरों का उपहास पात्र होता है; *sl.* कठपुतली

stool (स्टूल) *n.* चौकी, स्टूल; पाख़ाना, मल

stoop (स्टूप) *vi.* (आगे या नीचे को) झुकना; झपटना; अपने को गिराना, नीचता करना – *n.* शरीर के आगे को झुके होने की स्थिति; झुकी हुई कमर, झुकाव

stop (स्टॉप) *vt.* रोकना; करने न देना; बाधा डालना; (काम) रोक देना; (से) बाज़ आना – *vi.* रुकना, बन्द कर देना (काम आदि); ठहर जाना (**-pp-**) – *n.* रुकने की क्रिया, ठहराव, विराम; (बस आदि का) रुकने का स्थान; विराम-चिह्न; गति कम या अधिक करने का उपकरण; बाजे का भाग – **stoppage** ('स्टॉपिज) *n.* – **stopper** ('स्टॉपर) *n.* बोतल का काग या ढक्कन – **stopcock** *n.* (पानी आदि के पाइप पर लगा) स्टाप काक – **stopgap** *n.* अस्थायी विकल्प –

stopover *n.* यात्रा के दौरान रुकने की अवधि – **stopwatch** *n.* दौड़ आदि में समय नापने की घड़ी

store (स्टॉर) – *vt.* (गोदाम, भण्डार में) रखना, पास रखना – *n.* दुकान; बाहुल्य; (गोदाम में माल); गोदाम, भण्डार – *pl.* माल का भण्डार; रसद (खाने पीने का सामान) – **storage** *n.*

storey (ˈस्टॉरि) *n.* (मकान की) मंज़िल, तल्ला

stork (स्टॉर्क) *n.* लम्बी टांगों वाला जल पक्षी, चमरधेंघ

storm (स्टॉर्म) *n.* तूफ़ान; किले आदि पर धावा; उपद्रव– *vt.* धावा बोलना, आक्रमण कर के अधिकार कर लेना – *vi.* आगबबूला हो जाना; गरजना – **stormy** (ˈस्टॉर्मि) *a.* तूफानी, प्रचण्ड; उत्तेजनापूर्ण

story (ˈस्टॉरि) *n.* कहानी, किस्सा, कथा; *inf.* झूठ

stout (स्टाउट) *a.* मोटा; बलिष्ठ; द ढ़ (निश्चय) – *n.* एक प्रकार की बीअर

stove (स्टोव़) *n.* चूल्हा, स्टोव

stow (स्टो) *vt.* एक ओर संभाल कर रख देना – **stowage** (ˈस्टोइज) *n.* – **stowaway** (ˈस्टोअवे) *n.* जहाज़ में छिप कर यात्रा करने वाला

straddle (ˈस्ट्रैडल) *vt.* टांगें फैला कर बैठना; के दोनों ओर स्थित होना – *n.*

strafe (स्ट्राफ़) *vt.* विमान से गोली बरसाना या राकेट से आक्रमण करना

straggle (ˈस्ट्रैगल) *vi.* भटक जाना; पीछे रह जाना – **straggler** (ˈस्ट्रैग्लर) *n.*

straight (स्ट्रेट) *a.* सीधा, ईमानदार; नियम के अनुसार; जिसमें पानी न मिला हो (शराब); नीरस, भाव-शून्य – *n.* सीधी स्थिति या भाग – *adv.* प्रत्यक्ष, सीधे – **straighten** (ˈस्ट्रेटन) *v.* सीधा करना – **straightaway** *adv.* तुरन्त, फौरन – **straightforword** *a.* निष्कपट ; स्पष्टवादी

strain[1] (स्ट्रेन) *vt.* कस कर तानना; पूरी शक्ति से या उससे भी अधिक ख चना; निथारना – *vi.* अत्यधिक प्रयास करना – *n.* तनाव; भीषण प्रयत्न; मोच; संगीत या कविता की तान या लय; विशेषता (काम आदि का) दबाव, बोझ; श्रान्ति; लिखने या बोलने की शैली या लहजा; प्रकार – **strained** *a.* तनावपूर्ण (संबंध); अस्वाभाविक – **strainer** *n.* चलनी, छलनी

strain[2] (स्ट्रेन) *n.* नस्ल, जाति; वर्ग (विशे. जीव-विज्ञान में); चिन्ह, निशान

strait (स्ट्रेट) *n.* जलडमरूमध्य – (~ **s**) *pl.* कठिनाई या विपत्ति की स्थिति, तंग, संकीर्ण; कठोर – *a.* तंग, संकरा; सख्त (बर्ताव में) – **straiten** (ˈस्ट्रेटन) *vt.* संकुचित करना – **straitjacket** *n.* हिंसक पागलों की बाहें बांधने का जैकिट – **strait-laced** *a.* संयमी; कठोर – **in straitened circumstances** तंग हाली में

strand[1] (स्ट्रैंड) *v.* जहाज़ का तट पर जा चढ़ना; कठिनाई या असहायावस्था में छोड़ना या पहुंचाया जाना – *n. Poet.* तट, किनारा – **stranded** *a.* बेसहारा

strand[2] (स्ट्रैंड) *n.* रस्से, तार आदि की लड़ी; विचार, कहानी आदि का एक तार

strange (स्ट्रेंज) *a.* अजीब, अजनबी; विलक्षण – **stranger** *n.* अज्ञात व्यक्ति; विदेशी; अजनबी – **strangeness** *n.*

strangle (ˈस्ट्रैङगल) *vt.* गला घोंट कर मार डालना; दमन करना, मुंह बंद करना – **strangulate** (ˈस्ट्रैङग्युलेट) – *vt.* दबाना; गला घोंटना – **strangulation** – *n.* – **stranglehold** *n. fig.* गलघोंटू पकड़; वर्चस्व

strap (स्ट्रैप) *n.* पट्टा, पट्टी तस्मा, विशे. चमड़े का – *vt.* पट्टे से बांधना या पीटना (**-pp-**) – **strapless** *a.* बगैर पट्टी की (चोली) – **strapped** *a.* तंगहाल, खाली जेब – **strapping** *a.* लम्बे कद का और हष्ट-पुष्ट

stratagem (ˈस्ट्रैटिजम) *n.* चाल, युक्ति; दांव-पेच – **strategy** (ˈस्ट्रैटिजि) *n.* रणनीति; युद्ध कला

stratum (ˈस्ट्राटॅम) *n.* तह, विशे. चट्टानों की; समाज का वर्ग (*pl.* – **ta**) – **stratification** *n.* स्तरीकरण

straw (स्ट्रॉ) *n.* पुआल; फूस; तिनका, त ण; पानी आदि पीने की प्लास्टिक की पतली नलकी – **straw in the wind** भविष्यसूचक संकेत – **straw poll** अनोपचारिक जनमत संग्रह

strawberry (स्ट्रॉबरि) *n.* स्ट्रॉबॅरी फल

stray (स्ट्रे) *vi.* इधर-उधर घूमना; भटक जाना – *a.* भटका या रास्ता भूला हुआ; कभी कभार होने वाला, इक्का-दुक्का; छुटपुट – *n.* पशु जो रेवड़ से अलग हो गया हो

streak (स्ट्रीक) *n.* धारी; पुट; तनिक आभास – *vt.* धारियां डालना या बनाना – **streaker** *n.* सार्वजनिक स्थान में नंगा भागने वाला

stream (स्ट्रीम) *n.* धारा, सरिता; प्रवाह; बहाव; स्कूली बच्चों का समूह जो एक जैसी योग्यता के आधार पर एक कक्षा में रखा जाय – *vi.* बहना; हवा में हिलाना – **streamer** *n.* कागज़ की झण्डी या पट्टी

streamlined (ˈस्ट्रीम्लाइन्ड) *a.* (कार, विमान आदि) हवा जिसकी गति में बाधक न हो; *fig.* सरल और कारगर – **streamlining** *n.*

street (स्ट्रीट) *n.* गली, बाज़ार – **street people** बेघर लोग

strength (स्ट्रेंङ्थ) *n.* शक्ति, बल, ताकत; प्रचण्डता, भीषणता; बल; आवश्यक या पूरी संख्या – **strengthen** *v.* शक्तिशाली, मज़बूत बनाना, सुद ढ़ करना

strenuous (ˈस्ट्रेन्युअस) *a.* श्रम साध्य; कठोर; अनवरत (प्रयत्न आदि)

stress (स्ट्रेस) *n.* बल; दबाव; तनाव – *vt.* बल देना; बलाघात करना

stretch (स्ट्रेंच) *vt.* ख चना, लम्बा करना; अत्यधिक प्रयत्न करना; कसना; आगे बढ़ कर पकड़ना – *vi.* पहुंचना; लचक होना; विस्तार होना; (टांगे) फैलाना – *n.* विस्तार; दौर, अवधि – **stretcher** (ˈस्ट्रेंचर) *n.* घायलों को ले जाने की डोली, स्ट्रेचर – **stretch out** लेट जाना

strew (स्ट्रू) *vt.* बिखेरना, छितराना (**strewed** *pt.*, **strewn** या **strewed** *pp.*, **strewing** *pr. p.*)

stricken (ˈस्ट्रिकन) *a.* आक्रांत, पीड़ित; STRIKE का *pp.*

strict (स्ट्रिक्ट) *a.* कड़ा, कठोर, नियमनिष्ठ; सुनिश्चित – **strictness** *n.*

stricture (ˈस्ट्रिक्चर) *n.* आलोचना; संकोचन

stride (स्ट्राइड) *vi.* लम्बे-लम्बे डग या कदम भरना (**strode, stridden, striding**) – *n.* कदम; उसकी दूरी; नियमित चाल

strident (ˈस्ट्राइडंट) *a.* जिसका स्वर कर्कश हो; कर्णभेदी (आवाज़)

strife (स्ट्राइफ़) *n.* संघर्ष; कलह, झगड़ा

strike (स्ट्राइक) *v.* प्रहार करना; चोट मारना; (माचिस) जलाना; (सांप का) डंक मारना; आक्रमण करना; (घड़ी का) घण्टे बजाना – *vt.* प्रभाव डालना; ध्यान में आना; (तिल, सोने आदि के) भंडार, खान का पता लगाना – *vi.* हड़ताल करना (**struck** *pt.*, **stricken** (स्ट्रिकन), **struck** (स्ट्रक) *pp.*, **striking** *pr. p.*) – *n.* हड़ताल; आक्रमण; हमला – **striker** *n.* हड़ताली – **striking** *a.* प्रभावशाली; उल्लेखनीय – **strike off** हटाना, काटना (नाम आदि)

string (स्ट्रिंग) *n.* रस्सी, सुतली, डोरी; लड़, लड़ी; पंक्ति; श्रं खला; (पौधों का) रेशा; वाद्य (सितार आदि) का तार – (~ s) *pl.* शर्तें – *vt.* धागा या डोरी डालना; लड़ी या माला बनाना; पंक्ति या श्रेणीबद्ध करना (**strung, stringing**) – **stringed** *a.* तारों वाला (वाद्य यंत्र) – **stringy** (ˈस्ट्रिंजि) *a.* डोरी जैसा; रेशेदार

stringent ('स्ट्रिन्जन्ट) *a.* कड़ा, अनम्य – **stringency** ('स्ट्रिन्ज़न्सि) *n.* कठोरता – **stringently** *adv.*

strip (स्ट्रिप) *vt.* उघाड़ना, नंगा करना (**strip down** भी); वस्त्र या आवरण उतारना; वंचित करना (**of** के साथ प्रयुक्त) – *vi.* अपने कपड़े उतारना (**-pp-**) – *n.* लम्बा, संकरा टुकड़ा, पट्टी – **strip(tease)** *n.* नृत्यघर या रंग-मंच पर नर्तकी द्वारा एक-एक कर के सब कपड़े उतारने की क्रिया, निर्वस्त्र नृत्य – **strip cartoon** व्यंग्य चित्रों की पट्टी

stripe (स्ट्राइप) *n.* धारी; (सेना में) फीता, फीती – – **striped** (स्ट्राइप्ट) *a.* धारीदार

stripling ('स्ट्रिप्लिंग) *n.* नवयुवक; पट्ठा

strive (स्ट्राइव़) *vi.* घोर प्रयास करना (**strove, striven, striving**)

strode (स्ट्रोड) **STRIDE** का *pt.*

stroke (स्ट्रोक) *n.* सहलाना; आघात, प्रहार; अचानक कार्यवाही या घटना; रक्ताघात का दौरा; कलम या ब्रुश से बनाया निशान; घड़ी के घण्टे की आवाज़; (*complete movement*) चरण; गेन्द आदि को बल्ले से मारने की क्रिया या शैली; तैराकी की विधि; सहलाना – **at a stroke** एक ही वार में

stroll (स्ट्रॉल) *vi.* सैर करना, चहलकदमी करना – *n.* सैर, चहलकदमी – **stroller** *n.* **US** बच्चा गाड़ी

strong (स्ट्रॉङ) *a.* तगड़ा, बलवान; हृष्ट-पुष्ट; स्वस्थ; मज़बूत; ज़ोरदार, शुद्ध (तिज़ाब आदि); विशाल (संख्या में) – **stronghold** *n.* गढ़ – **strongly** ***adv.*** जोरदार शब्दों में, बलपूर्वक – **strong-arm** *a.* ज़ोर-ज़बरदस्ती का – **strong box** तिजोरी, सेफ़ – **strongroom** *n.* अभेद्य कक्ष (जैसा बैंकों में है) – **strong-willed** *a.* मज़बूत इच्छा शक्ति वाला

strove (स्ट्रोव़) **STRIVE** का *pt.*

struck (स्ट्रक) **STRIKE** का *pt./pp.*

structure ('स्ट्रक्चर) *n.* ढांचा; संरचना; रूप; संगठन – **structural** *a.* संरचनात्मक; रूपात्मक, संगठन संबंधी

struggle ('स्ट्रगल) *vi.* संघर्ष करना; सामना करना; कठिनाई से आगे बढ़ना; परिश्रम करना – *n.* संघर्ष

strum (स्ट्रम) *vt.* वीणा आदि के तार छेड़ना; *inf.* झंकारना (**-mm-**)

strung (स्ट्रंग) **STRING** का *pt./pp.*

strut (स्ट्रट) *vi.* अकड़ कर या ऐंठ कर चलना; इठलाना

stub (स्टब) *n.* सिगरेट या पेंसिल का छोटा टुकड़ा; चेक का प्रतिपन्ना – *vt.* (पैर की उंगलियों का) किसी चीज़ से टकराना; सिगरेट आदि दबा कर बुझा देना (**-bb-**)

stubble ('स्टबल) *n.* (कटे घास आदि की) खूंटी; थोड़ी उगी दाढ़ी

stubborn ('स्टबर्न) *a.* ज़िद्दी, अड़ियल – **stubbornness** *n.* हठ, जिद

stucco ('स्टको) *n.* पलस्तर

stuck (स्टक) STICK का *pt./pp.*

stud[1] (स्टड) *n.* गुलमेख, फुलिया (बड़े सिर वाला काबला); दोहरा बटन; सीधी खड़ी टेक (दीवार की) – *vt.* जड़ना (**-dd-**)

stud[2] (स्टड) *n.* नस्ल बढाने के लिए रखा गया जानवर विशे० घोड़ा

student दे० STUDY

studio ('स्ट्यूडिओ) *n.* कलाकार, चित्रकार की कार्यशाला; भवन जहां चलचित्र, टी.वी. और रेडियो कार्यक्रम तैयार किए जाते हैं (*pl.* – **s**)

study ('स्टडि) *vi.* अध्ययन करना, पढ़ना – *vt.* (का) अध्ययन करना; विचार करना; जांच करना (**studied, studying**) – *n.* ज्ञानवर्धन; अध्ययन; अध्ययन-कक्ष; अध्ययन के बाद लिखी पुस्तक या रिपोर्ट; रेखाचित्र – **student** ('स्ट्यूडंट) *n.* छात्र – **studied** *a.* सोच समझ

कर किया गया – **studious** (ˈस्ट्यूडिअस) *a.* अध्ययनशील – **studiously** *adv*.

stuff (स्टफ़) *v.* ठूंस कर भर देना; बहुत अधिक खाना; तैयार सम्मिश्रण से भरना – *n.* सामग्री; कपड़ा; कोई भी पदार्थ – **stuffing** *n.* भरने के लिए प्रयुक्त सामग्री – **stuffy** (ˈस्टफ़ि) *a.* घुटन भरा; *inf.* नीरस, पुराणपंथी

stumble (ˈस्टम्बल) *vi.* लड़खड़ाना – *n.* ठोकर, लड़खड़ाहट, भूल – **stumbling block** रुकावट, बाधा

stump (स्टम्प) *n.* (कटे पेड़, अंग का) ठूंठ; (सिगरेट का) टुकड़ा, टोटा; क्रिकेट की विकेट का डंडा – *vt.* घबरा देना, चक्कर में डाल देना; *Cricket* गेंद को विकेट पर मार खिलाड़ी को आउट कर देना – *vi.* पैर पटकते चलना

stun (स्टन) *vt.* प्रहार कर के अचेत कर देना; आश्चर्यचकित या स्तंभित कर देना (**-nn-**) – **stunner** *n.* अति आकर्षक स्त्री – **stunning** *a.*

stung STING का *pt./pp.*

stunk (स्टंक) **STINK** का *pt./pp.*

stunt[1] (स्टंट) *vt.* विकास रोक देना; बौना बना देना – **stunted** *a.* बौना, छोटे कद का

stunt[2] (स्टंट) *n.* करतब, कलाबाज़ी आदि; साहसिक काम; नाटकबाज़ी – **stuntman** *n.* कलाबाज़

stupefy (ˈस्ट्यूपिफ़ाइ) *vt.* संवेदन शून्य या जड़ कर देना; सुन्न, सतंभित या आश्चर्यचकित कर देना (**-efied, -efying**) – **stupefaction** (स्ट्यूपिˈफ़ैक्शन) *n.* हक्का-बक्का होना

stupendous (स्ट्यूˈपॅण्डस) *a.* आश्चर्यजनक, हैरतअंगेज़, विशाल

stupid (ˈस्ट्यूपिड) *a.* मन्दबुद्धि, जड़मति– **stupidity** (स्ट्यूˈपिडिटि) *n.* मूर्खता – **stupidly** *adv.*

stupor (ˈस्ट्यूपर) *n.* चकराए या किंकर्तव्यविमूढ़ होने की स्थिति; संवेदनशून्यता

sturdy (ˈस्टर्डि) *a.* हट्टा-कट्टा, तगड़ा – **sturdily** *adv.* – **sturdiness** *n.* हृष्ट- पुष्टता, तगड़ापन

sturgeon (ˈस्टर्जन) *n.* मछली जिससे केविआर (कच्चे अंडे) और सरेस निकलती है

stutter (ˈस्टटर) *v.* हकलाना; बोलने में कठिनाई होना – *n.* हकलाहट

sty[1] (स्टाइ) *n.* सूअर-बाड़ा; गन्दी जगह

style (स्टाइल) *n.* शैली; रंग-ढंग; पद्धति; प्रणाली; प्रकार, किस्म; लालित्य, चारुता; डिज़ाइन, फैशन – *vt.* नया आकार, रूप देना, विशेष प्रकार का बनाना; नाम देना – **stylish** (ˈस्टाइलिश) *a.* फैशनेबल – **stylishly** *adv.*

stylus (ˈस्टाइलस) *n.* तेज़ नोक की कलम (स्टैंसिल आदि पर लिखने के लिए); रिकार्ड पर चलने वाली सुई (*pl.* – **li,** – **luses**)

stymie (ˈस्टाइमि) *vt.* बाधा या रुकावट डालना

styrene (ˈस्टाइरीन) *n.* रंगहीन द्रव जो नकली रबड़, प्लास्टिक आदि बनाने में काम आता है

suave (स्वाव़) *a.* चिकना- चुपड़ा; मीठा – **suavity** (ˈस्वाविटि) *n.* सौम्यता, विनम्रता, (बातचीत, व्यवहार में) मधुरता

subaltern (ˈसबल्टर्न) *n.* सेना में कप्तान से निचले पद का अधिकारी

subcommittee (ˈसब्कमिटि) *n.* उपसमिति

subconscious (सब्ˈकॉन्शस) *a.* बिना ज्ञान के होने या रहने वाला – *n. Psychology* चेतना का वह भाग जिसका ज्ञान व्यक्ति को नह होता, अवचेतन

subcontinent (सब्ˈकॉन्टिनंग) *n.* उप- महाद्वीप

subdivide (सब्ˈडिवाइड) *vt.* फिर से विभाजित करना – **subdivision** (ˈसब्डिविझन) *n.* प्रविभाजन; अनुमण्डल या तहसील

subdue (सब्ˈड्यू) *v.* अधीन या वश में करना – **subdued** *a.* डरा हुआ; शांत; मद्धिम (प्रकाश)

subject *n.* (ˈसब्जिक्ट) विषय, मामला; कर्ता; अहम्; प्रजा – *a.* पराधीन; पर निर्भर – *vt.* (सबˈजॆक्ट)

अधीन करना; (*passive* में) (*to* के साथ) का अनुभव कराना –**subjection** (सब् 'जेंक्शन) *n.* अधीन करने या होने की क्रिया; परितंत्रता, अधीनता, दासता – **subjective** (सब् 'जैंक्टिव्) *a.* व्यक्तिनिष्ठ; जो तटस्थ न हो; आत्म-; जो मन में हो; जो कलाकार के व्यक्तित्व की अभिव्यक्ति हो – **subjectivity** (स्ब्जेंक् 'टिविटि) *n.* आत्मापरकता, व्यक्तिपरकता– **be subject to** (कानून के) अधीन होना

sub judice (सब् 'जूडिसि) *Lat.* न्यायालय के विचाराधीन

subjugate ('सब्जुगेट) *vt.* अधीन या वश में करना; परास्त करना – **subjugation** *n.* आधीन बनाने या होने की स्थिति, अधीनता

sublet (सब् 'लेंट) *vt.* (किराएदार द्वारा) मकान किसी और को किराए पर दे देना; शिकमी (पट्टा) देना (**sublet, subletting**)

sublime (स 'ब्लाइम) *a.* उदात्त; उत्क ष्ट; उच्च, महान; भव्य; श्रद्धेय– **sublimely** *adv.* – **sublimity** (स 'ब्लिमिटि), **sublimeness** *n.* उच्चता, भव्यता, उत्क ष्टता

subliminal (स 'ब् 'लिमिनल) *a.* अवचेतनीय

submarine ('सब्मरीन) *n.* पनडुब्बी – *a.* समुद्र के नीचे; समुद्री

submerge (सब् 'मर्ज) *v.* पानी में डूब जाना या डुबो देना – **submersion** (सब् 'मर्शन) *n.*

submit (सब् 'मिट) *vi.* अधीनता स्वीकार करना, झुक जाना; हार मानना – *vt.* विचार के लिए पेश करना, निवेदन करना – **submission** *n.* आत्मसमर्पण, अधीनता; अनुरोध – **submissive** *a.* आज्ञाकारी, विनम्र

subordinate (स 'बॉर्डिनिट) *a.* छोटे दर्जे या कम महत्व का; अधीनस्थ, मातहत – *n.* अधीनस्थ कर्मचारी, मातहत – *vt.* अधीन करना, वश में करना – **subordinately** *adv.* – **subordination** (सबॉर्डि 'नेशन) *n.* अध ीनिता, मातहत होना; गौणता

subscribe (सब् 'स्क्राइब) *v.* चन्दा देना; किसी दस्तावेज़ के नीचे अपना नाम लिखना; (का) समर्थन करना; (पत्रिका का) ग्राहक बनना; कंपनी के शेयर खरीदने के लिए आवेदन करना – **subscriber** *n.* ग्राहक, चंदा देने वाला – **subscription** (सब् 'स्क्रिप्शन) *n.* चंदा; ग्राहकी

subsection ('सब्सेंक्शन) *n.* उपधारा (किसी कानून की)

subsequent ('सब्सिक्वन्ट) *a.* बाद का, अनुवर्ती – **subsequently** *adv.* के बाद

subservient (सब् 'सर्विअंट) *a.* आज्ञाकारी

subside (सब् 'साइड) *vi.* घट जाना, उतर जाना (बाढ़ के पानी का); धंस जाना (भूमि का)– **subsidence** (सब् 'साइडन्स- 'सिडंस) *n.* धंस जाने की क्रिया

subsidiary (सब् 'सिडिअरि) *a.* पूरक, सहायक – *n.*

subsidize ('सब्सिडाइज़) *vt.* आर्थिक सहायता देना; अनुदान देना – **subsidy** ('सब्सिडि) *n.* आर्थिक सहायता

subsist (सब् 'सिस्ट) *vi.* बना रहना, जीवित रहना; गुज़ारा या निर्वाह करना – **subsistence** *n.*, जीवन-निर्वाह

subsonic (सब् 'सॉनिक) *a.* ध्वनि की गति से कम गति वाला (यान आदि)

substance ('सब्स्टन्स) *n.* पदार्थ, सार; सम्पत्ति – **substantial** (सब् 'स्टैन्शल) *a.* पर्याप्त, महत्वपूर्ण; वास्तविक, अस्तित्व वाला – **substantially** *adv.* – **substantiate** *vt.* प्रमाण देना; प्रमाणित करना

substitute ('सब्स्टिट्यूट) *v.* के स्थान पर रखना – *n.* स्थानापन्न वस्तु या व्यक्ति; ऐवजी; सहायक – **substitution** *n.* प्रतिस्थापन

subterfuge ('सब्टर्फ्यूज) *n.* चाल; झूठा बहाना

subterranean, subterraneous (सब्ट 'रेनिअन, सब्ट 'रेनिअस) *a.* भूमि के नीचे; छिपा हुआ

subtitle (ˈसब्टाइटल) *n.* उपशीर्षक; फिल्म के संवाद का दूसरी भाषा में लिखित अनुवाद जो उसके साथ ही पढ़ा जा सकता है

subtle (ˈसटल) *a.* ; प्रखर; सूक्ष्म; चातुर्यपूर्ण; जटिल; कोमल; जिसमें सूक्ष्म विभेद हो – **subtlety** (ˈसटल्टि) *n.* सूक्ष्मता, जटिलता; बारीकी

subtract (सब्ˈट्रैक्ट) *vt.* घटाना – **subtraction** *n.* घटाने की क्रिया

subtropical (सब्ˈट्रॉपिकल) *a.* उष्ण कटिबन्ध के साथ लगते प्रदेश का

suburb (ˈसबर्ब) *n.* नगर के साथ लगती बस्ती – **suburban** (ˈसबर्बन) *a.*

subvert (सब्ˈव़र्ट) *vt.* तख्ता पलटना; बिगाड़ देना – **subversion** (सब्ˈव़र्शन) – **subversive** (सब्ˈव़र्सिव़) *a.* तोड़-फोड़ सम्बन्धी

subway (ˈसब्वे) *n.* भूमि के नीचे बना रास्ता; भूमिगत पथ; US भूमि के नीचे चलने वाली रेल

succeed (सक्ˈसीड) *vi.* सफल होना; उद्देश्य पूर्ति करना; बाद में आना; परवर्ती होना – *vt.* बाद में आना; (का) स्थान लेना; का उत्तराधिकारी होना – **success** (सक्ˈसेंस) *n.* सफलता; उप्लब्धि; सफल प्रयास – **successful** *a.* सफल – **successfully** *adv.* – **succession** (सक्ˈसेंशन) *n.* उत्तराधिकार; अनुक्रमण; सिलसिला – **successive** *a.* निरन्तर – **successively** *adv.* लगातार – **successor** *n.* उत्तराधिकारी

succinct (सक्ˈसिंक्ट) *a.* सारगर्भित; संक्षिप्त

succour (ˈसकर) *n./vt.* मुसीबत में मदद (करना)

succulent (ˈसक्युलंट) *a.* रसीला, मोटे, गूदेदार पत्तों वाला (पौधा) – *n.* ऐसा पौधा

succumb (सˈकम) *vi.* झुक जाना; मर जाना, (का) शिकार बनना

such (सच) *a.* (इस) प्रकार का; इतना (अधिक); ऐसा – **such as** जैसे के, उदाहरणार्थ – **such-and-such** कौन सा/कब/किस (जगह आदि)

suck (सक) *vt.* चूसना; मुंह में लेना; सोख लेना – *n.* चूसने या सोखने की क्रिया – **sucker** *n.* व्यक्ति या वस्तु जो चूस या सोख ले; पौधे की जड़ या तने के निचले भाग से फूटी कोंपल; *inf.* व्यक्ति जो आसानी से धोखे में आ जाय, बुद्धू

suckle (ˈसकल) *v.* बच्चे को स्तनपान कराना; मां का दूध पीना – **suckling** *n.* दूधमुहां बच्चा

suction (ˈसक्शन) *n.* द्रव का चूसा जाना या हवा का ख चा जाना; दबाव में अन्तर के कारण प्रव त्त बल

sudden (ˈसडन) *a.* अचानक, जल्दी से (किया गया) – **suddenly** *adv.* अचानक – **suddenness** *n.* आकस्मिकता, हड़बड़ी

suds (सड्स) *pl. n.* साबुन मिले पानी का झाग, फेन

sue (स्यू) *vt.* (पर) मुकदमा चलाना; न्याय मांगना – *vi.* अनुनय विनय करना, चिरौरी करना, दांत निपोरना

suede (स्वेड) *n.* कमाया हुआ मख़मल जैसा चमड़ा – *a.* ऐसे चमड़े का बना

suffer (ˈसफ़र) *v.* भोगना (कष्ट, पीड़ा, कमी आदि); (नुकसान) उठाना; करने देना – **sufferable** *a.* – **sufferance** (ˈसफ़रन्स) *n.* मौन अनुमति, सहिष्णुता – **sufferer** *n.* बीमार, रोगी – **suffering** *n.* कष्ट, मुसीबत

suffice (सॅˈफ़ाइस) *v.* काफ़ी होना – **sufficiency** (सˈफ़िशन्सि) *n.* पर्याप्ति – **sufficient** *a.* पर्याप्त

suffix (ˈसफ़िक्स) *n.* प्रत्यय; अन्त में जोड़ा भाग – *vt.* प्रत्यय लगाना; अन्त में जोड़ना

suffocate (ˈसफ़केट) *vi.* दम घुट कर मरना – *vt.* दम घोंट कर मार डालना – **suffocation** (सफ़ˈकेशन) *n.* घुटन

suffrage (ˈसफ़्रिज) *n.* वोट या मताधिकार

suffuse (सˈफ़्यूज़) *vt.* से भर देना, पर फैल जाना – **suffusion** (सˈफ़्यूझ़न) *n.*

sugar (ˊशुगर) *n.* चीनी, शक्कर, खांड – *vt.* शक्कर मिलाना; मीठा बनाना (शक्कर से) – **sugary** *a.* मीठा, चीनी जैसा – **sugar beet** *n.* चुकन्दर जिस से चीनी बनती है – **sugarcane** *n.* गन्ना

suggest (ˊसजेस्ट) *vt.* प्रस्ताव रखना; सुझाव देना; की सिफारिश करना; इशारा करना – **suggestibility** (सजेस्टिˊबिलिटि) *n.* – **suggestible** *a.* जो जल्दी किसी की बात मान ले – **suggestion** (सˊजेस्चन) *n.* इशारा; सुझाव; प्रभाव (किसी के मन में कोई बात बैठाने की क्रिया) – **suggestive** (सˊज़ेस्टिव) *a.* जिसमें कोई सुझाव हो; जिसमें अश्लीलता का पुट हो

suicide (ˊसूइसाइड) *n.* आत्महत्या – **suicidal** (सूइˊसाइड्ल) *a.* आत्मघातक

suit (सूट, स्यूट) *n.* कपड़ों का जोड़ा, सूट; (ताश का) रंग; वाद, मुकदमा – *v.* अनुकूल या माफ़िक होना; स्वीकार्य, उचित होना – **suitability** (सूटˊबिलिटि, ˊस्यू–) *n.* – **suitable** (ˊसूटबल, ˊस्यू) *a.* अनुकूल; शोभनीय; उचित – **suitably** *adv.* उचित ढंग से – **suitcase** (ˊसूट्केस, ˊस्यू-) *n.* सूटकेस

suite (स्वीट) *n.* मेज-कुर्सी का सेट जो कमरे के अनुकूल हो; कमरों का सेट; नौकर-चाकर

suitor (ˊसूटर, ˊस्यूटर) *n.* प्रेमी

sulk (सल्क) *vi.* मुंह फुलाए बैठना; रूठना – *n.* ऐसी मनोदशा – **sulky** *a.*

sullen (ˊसलन) *a.* जो किसी से बात न करना चाहे; रूठा हुआ; उदास

sully (ˊसलि) *vt.* पर कलंक (का टीका) लगाना; बदनामी लाना; दूषित करना (**sullied, sullying**)

sulphur (ˊसल्फ़र) *n.* गंधक – **sulphuric** (सल्ˊफ्युअरिक) *a.* गंधक का – **sulphurous** (ˊसल्फ़रस) *a.*

sultan (ˊसल्टन) *n.* मुस्लिम देश का शासक, सुल्तान – **sultana** (सल्ˊटान्अ) *n.* सुल्तान की पत्नी, सुल्ताना; एक प्रकार की किशमिश – **sultanate** (ˊसल्टनेट) *n.* सल्तनत

sultry (ˊसल्ट्रि) *a.* उमस (वाला मौसम); कामोत्तेजक

sum (सम) *n.* जोड़ (राशियों का); राशि; गणित का सवाल; कुल मिलाकर – *v.* जोड़ निकालना; संक्षेप या सार तैयार करना (**-mm-**)

summary (ˊसमरि) *n.* संक्षेप या सार, सारांश – *a.* जल्दी किया गया (न्याय) – **summarily** *adv.* तेज़ी से; अचानक; सरसरी तौर पर – **summarize** (ˊसमराइज़) *vt.* संक्षेप तैयार करना, संक्षिप्त रूप से कहना या सामने रखना

summer (ˊसमर) *n.* ग्रीष्म ऋतु, गरमी का मौसम – *vi.* गरमी का मौसम बिताना

summit (ˊसमिट) *n.* चोटी, शिखर

summon (ˊसमन) *vt.* (किसी सभा आदि की) बैठक के लिए बुलाना; बुला भेजना; साक्षी को न्यायालय में आने का आदेश देना; (**up** के साथ) (साहस, शक्ति) बटोरना – **summons** (ˊसमन्ज़) *n.* (न्यायालय में) उपस्थिति का आदेश

sumo (ˊसूमो) *n.* जापानी शैली की कुश्ती

sumptuous (ˊसम्प्ट्युअस) *a.* शानदार, वैभवशाली

sun (सन) *n.* सूर्य, सूरज; सूरज की किरणें, धूप – *vt.* धूप लगाना (**-nn-**) – **sunless** *a.* – **sunny** (ˊसनि) *a.* सूर्य जैसा; गरम; हंसमुख – **sun-baked** *a.* धूप से तपा व सूखा – **sunbathing** (ˊसन्बेदिंग) *n.* कपड़े उतार कर (या कुछ पहन कर) धूप सेंकना – **sunbeam** *n.* सूरज की किरण – **sunburn** *n.* धूप से त्वचा पर उभरे दाने – **sundown** *n.* सूर्यास्त, संध्या – **sunflower** *n.* सूर्यमुखी (फूल) – **sunglasses** *pl. n.* धूप का चश्मा – **sunspot** *n.* सूर्य पर कभी कभी दिखाई देने वाला धब्बा – **sunstroke** *n.* लू, गरमी

sundae (ˈसन्डि, ˈसन्डे) *n.* आइसक्रीम पर कटे फल डालकर बनाया व्यंजन
Sunday (ˈसन्डे) *n.* इतवार, रविवार
sunder (ˈसन्डर) *vt.* अलग कर देना
sundry (ˈसन्ड्रि) *a.* नाना प्रकार के; कई – **sundries** *pl. n.* फुटकर मदें (वस्तुऐं)
sung (संग) **SING** का *pp.*
sunk (संक), **sunken** (ˈसंकन) **SINK** का *pp.*
sup (सप) *vt.* घूंट-घूंट पीना – *vi.* रात का भोजन करना (**-pp-**) – *n.* किसी तरल पदार्थ का घूंट
super (ˈसूपर) *a. inf.* बहुत बढ़िया
super- (*comb. form*) अधि-, उपरि-, वाह्य, परा, अति, महा, उच्च, परम आदि के अर्थ में प्रयुक्त, जैसे **superhuman** (सूपर्ˈह्यूमन), **superman** (ˈसूपर्मैन)
superannuation (सूपरैन्युˈएशन) *n.* सेवा-निवर्तन; सेवा निव त्ति पेन्शन; कर्मचारी का पेन्शन निधि में योगदान
superb (सूˈपर्ब) *a.* शानदार, भव्य; महान, राजसी; उत्क ष्ट – **superbly** *adv.* शानदार ढंग से
supercilious (सूपर्ˈसिलिअस) *a.* घमण्डी, उपेक्षक – **superciliousness** *n.*
superficial (सूपर्ˈफ़िशल) *a.* ऊपरी, सतही; जिसमें पूरी सावधानी न बरती गयी हो; उथला, छिछला; सरसरी – **superficiality** (सूपरफ़िशिˈऐलिटि) *n.* छिछोरापन; सतहीपन
superfluous (सूˈपर्फ्लुअस) *a.* अतिरिक्त; अनावश्यक– **superfluity** *n.* बाहुल्य, प्राचुर्य; अनावश्यक राशि या मात्रा
superhighway (ˈसूपर्हाइवे) *n.* इंटरनेट द्वारा तीव्र गति से लेख, सामग्री, चित्र, ध्वनि आदि भेजने की प्रणाली, सुपरहाइवे
superimpose (सूपरम्ˈपोज़) *vt.* अध्यारोपित करना
superintend (सूपरिन्ˈटेंण्ड) *v.* अधीक्षक होना; निरीक्षण करना; निगरानी रखना (काम, कर्मचारियों पर) – **superintendence** *n.* अधीक्षण; निरीक्षण; संचालन; देख-रेख – **superintendent** (सूपरिन्ˈटेंन्डंट) *n.* अधीक्षक, विशे. पुलिस का उच्च अधिकारी
superior (सूˈपिअरिअर) *a.* (गुण या मात्रा में) अधिक श्रेष्ठ; उत्क ष्ट; ऊपरी; पद या गुण में अधिक ऊंचा; उत्तम; अभिमानी – **superiority** (सूपिअरिˈऑरिटि) *n.* श्रेष्ठता, उत्तमता; उच्चता
superlative (सूˈपर्लटिव़) *a.* सर्वोच्च, सर्वोत्तम; सर्वश्रेष्ठ; *Grammar* (विश्लेषण अथवा क्रिया विशेषण) उत्तमतासूचक – *n.*
superman (ˈसूपर्मैन) *n.* बहुत अधिक शारीरिक अथवा मानसिक शक्ति वाला मानव, अतिमानव
supermarket (ˈसूपर्मार्किट) *n.* सुपर बाज़ार
supernatural (सूपर्ˈनैचरल) *a.* प्रक ति के नियमों के परे, अलौकिक; लोकोत्तर, चमत्कारपूर्ण
supersede (सूपर्ˈसीड) *vt.* (का) स्थान लेना; हटा देना; किसी दूसरे का स्थान लेना – **supersession** *n.* अधिक्रमण, निवर्तन, एक (नियम आदि) का स्थान दूसरे द्वारा लिया जाना
supersonic (सूपर्ˈसॉनिक) *a.* ध्वनि की गति से अधिक तेज़
superstition (सूपर्ˈस्टिशन) *n.* अंधविश्वास – **superstitious** *a.* अंधविश्वासी
superstructure (ˈसूपर्स्ट्रक्चर) *n.* न व के ऊपर का ढांचा, अधिरचना
supervise (ˈसूपर्वाइज़) *vt.* देखरेख, निगरानी या निरीक्षण करना – **supervision** (सूपर्ˈविझ़न) *n.* अधीक्षण, निगरानी – **supervisor** (ˈसूपर्वाइज़र) *n.* अधीक्षक – **supervisory** *a.* अधीक्षण सम्बन्धी
supine (सूˈपाइन) *a.* चित्त (लेटा हुआ); निष्क्रिय, आलसी
supper (ˈसपर) *n.* रात का (हल्का) भोजन
supplant (सˈप्लांट) *vt.* किसी का स्थान ले लेना

supple (´सपल) *a.* लचीला, नम्य
supplement *n.* (´सप्लिमंट) परिशिष्ट, संपूरक; पत्रिका का (किसी विषय पर) अतिरिक्त या विशेष संस्करण; समाचार पत्रों का (सचित्र) परिशिष्ट; अधिराशि – *vt.* (´सप्लिमेंन्ट) जोड़ना; बढ़ाना; कमी पूरी करना – **supplementary** (–´मेंन्टरि) *a.* अनुपूरक
suppliant (´सप्लिअंट) *a./n.* प्रार्थी
supplicate (´सप्लिकेट) *v.* अनुनय-विनय करना; याचन करना – **supplication** *n.* अनुनय-विनय – **supplicatory** *a.*
supply (स´प्लाइ) *vt.* देना, मुहैया कराना, संभरण या आपूर्ति करना; प्रदान करना (**supplied, supplying**) – *n.* आपूर्ति; संभरण; सामान; भण्डार; रसद; खाद्य सामग्री
support (सॅ´पॉर्ट) *vt.* थामना; संभालना; बनाए रखना; सहारा या समर्थन देना; भरणपोषण करना; सिद्ध करना – *n.* टेक, आधार; सहारा; सहायता, समर्थन; भरणपोषण; प्रमाण – **supporter** *n.* समर्थक, अनुयायी – **supporting** *a.* (फिल्म में भूमिका) गौण; सहायक – **supportive** *a.*
suppose (स´पोज़) *vt.* मान लेना; सही मान लेना; समझना; संभाव्य समझना; (केवल *passive* में) से करने की आशा या अपेक्षा होना; की जिम्मेदारी होना – **supposed** *a.* कल्पित, माना हुआ – **supposedly** (स´पोज़िड्लि) *adv.* माना हुआ – **supposition** (सप´ज़िशन) *n.* कल्पना; अभिधारणा – **supposing** *conj.* यदि
suppress (स´प्रेस) *vt.* दबाना, दमन करना; रोकना, प्रकाशित न होने देना या मुद्रित प्रतियां वापिस ले लेना – **suppression** *n.* दमन; निषेध
suppurate (´सप्युरेट) *vi.* में पीव या मवाद पड़ना
supra- (*comb. form*) ऊपर, अति-, पर- जैसे, **supranational** (सूप्र´नैश्नल) *a.* अधिराष्ट्रीय
supreme (सु´प्रीम) *a.* सर्वोच्च; सर्वोपरि – **supremacy** (सू´प्रेमसि) *n.* सर्वोच्चता; परमाधिकार
surcharge (´सर्चार्ज) *n.* अधिशुल्क / अधिमूल्य – *vt.*
sure (शुअर) *a.* निश्चित; भरोसेमंद; निस्सन्देह – *adv. inf.* निश्चय ही, अवश्य – **surely** *adv.* – **surety** *n.* जमानतदार, जमानती; जमानत, प्रतिभूति
surf (सर्फ़) *n.* (तट से टकराती) लहरें – *v.* लहरों में तैरना या (नाव के पीछे रस्से से बंधे) तख्ते पर खड़े हो कर समुद्र विहार करना; *Computers* इंटरनेट पर उपलब्ध विभिन्न जानकारी-स्थलों (*websites*) का बेतरतीब अवलोकन करना – **surfer** *n.* व्यक्ति जो बहुधा तख्ते पर खड़े होकर समुद्र विहार करता हो; *Computers* इंटरनेट पर बेतरतीब जानकारी का अवलोकन करने वाला – **surfboard** *n.* तख्ता जिस पर समुद्र विहार किया जाता है, तख्ता
surface (´सर्फ़िस) *n.* सतह, बाहरी हिस्सा; प ष्ठ; फलक; तल; ऊपरी रंगरूप; सतही रूप; धारणा – *a.* सतही, ऊपरी का; बाहरी; जो सतह तक ही रहे, छिछला – *vi.* सतह पर आना
surfeit (´सर्फ़िट) *n.* ; अत्याधिकता; अधिकता से उत्पन्न अघाव या अफराक – *v.* बहुत अधिक खाना या खिलाना
surge (सर्ज) *n.* लहर; मात्रा में अचानक व द्धि ; अचानक (भावनाएं) उमड़ने की स्थिति – *vi.* उमड़ना; (मूल्य आदि) तेजी से बढ़ना
surgeon (´सर्जन) *n.* शल्य चिकित्सक, सर्जन – **surgery** (´सर्जरि) *n.* ऑपरेशन की क्रिया; डॉक्टर या दांतों के डॉक्टर का कमरा (जहां मरीज़ देखे जाते है) – **surgical** (´सर्जिकल) *a.* शल्य चिकित्सा संबंधी, शल्य- – **surgically** *adv.*
surly (´सर्लि) *a.* चिड़चिड़ा, बदमिज़ाज
surmise (सर्´माइज़) *n./v.* अनुमान, अटकल (लगाना)

surmount (सर्ˊमाउंट) *vt.* पार कर लेना (बाधा आदि); पर विजयी होना – **surmountable** *a.*
surname (ˊसर्नेम) *n.* कुलनाम
surpass (सर्ˊपास) *vt.* आगे निकल जाना; मात देना; (औरों से) बढ़ कर या श्रेष्ठ होना – **surpassing** *a.* सर्वोत्तम, सर्वश्रेष्ठ
surplus (ˊसर्प्लस) *n.* आधिक्य, बढ़ती, अधिशेष, बचत
surprise (सर्ˊप्राइज़) *vt.* आश्चर्यचकित करना, चौंका देना; अकस्मात टूट पड़ना – *n.* आश्चर्य; अप्रत्याशित बात या घटना; आकस्मिक, अचानक आगमन – **surprising** *a.* आश्चर्यजनक; अनोखा – **surprisingly** *adv.* आश्यर्चजनक रूप से
surrender (सˊरेंण्डर) *vt.* सौंपना; के हवाले करना – *vi.* हथियार डालना, आत्मसमर्पण करना; हार मान लेना – *n.* आत्मसमर्पण
surreptitious (सरप्ˊटिशस) *a.* चोरी छिपे किया गया; गुप्त, प्रछन्न
surround (सˊराउण्ड) *vt.* घेर लेना; घेरा डालना; बाड़ा लगाना; किनारा लगाना – *n.* हाशिया, किनारा – **surrounding** *a.* आस पास का – **surroundings** *pl. n.* वातावरण; परिवेश; अड़ोस-पड़ोस
surveillance (सर्ˊवेलन्स) *n.* निगरानी; निगाह रखने की क्रिया – **surveillant** *a./n.*
survey (ˊसर्वे) *vt.* चारों ओर देखना, पर्यवलोकन करना; सर्वेक्षण करना – *n.* सर्वेक्षण; निरीक्षण; सर्वेक्षण की रिपोर्ट – **surveyor** *n.* सर्वेक्षक, निरीक्षक
survive (सर्ˊवाइव) *vt.* (किसी के बाद) जीते रहना, बने रहना – *vt.* (किसी विपत्ति आदि से) जीवित बच जाना, बच निकलना – **survival** (सर्ˊवाइवल) *n.* (व्यक्तियों, वस्तुओं के) बने, जीवित रहने की स्थिति – **survivor** *n.* व्यक्ति जो दुर्घटना आदि से बच निकला हो, उत्तरजीवित
susceptible (सˊसेंप्टबल) *a.* – **susceptible to** आसानी से प्रभावित हो जाने या झुक जाने वाला; भावप्रवण – **susceptibility** *n.* भावप्रवणता
suspect *vt.* (सˊस्पेंक्ट) किसी के निर्दोष होने पर सन्देह करना – *a.* (ˊससपेंक्ट) संदिग्ध चरित्र वाला – *n.* संदिग्ध व्यक्ति
suspend (सˊस्पेण्ड) *vt.* लटका देना; स्थगित करना; निलम्बित या मुअत्तिल करना; (नियम, कानून आदि पर) अमल स्थगित करना; तरल पदार्थ में रखना – **suspenders** *pl. n.* जुराबों को कसा रखने के फीते, गेटिस
suspense (सˊस्पेंन्स) *n.* चिंता व उत्तेजना की स्थिति, विशे. किसी समाचार की प्रतीक्षा में; चिन्ता; असमंजस – **suspension** (सˊस्पेंन्शन) *n.* लटके होने की स्थिति; गाड़ी की धुरी की कमानियां; निलंबन; स्थगन – **suspension bridge** झूला-पुल
suspicion (सˊसपिशन) *n.* सन्देह करने या सन्देहभाजन होने की स्थिति; हल्का आभास या पुट – **suspicious** *a.*संदिग्ध (व्यक्ति); जिसे संदेह हो, संदेही, शक्की – **suspiciously** *adv.*
sustain (सˊस्टेन) *vt.* उठाए रखना; सहारा देना; बने रहना; जीवित रखना; पुष्टि करना – **sustainable** *a.* – **sustenance** *n.* आहार – **sustained** *a.* निरंतर
suture (ˊसूचर) *n.* सीवन
swab (स्वॉब) *n.* फाहा, फुरेरी; झाड़न
swaddle (ˊस्वॉड्ल) *vt.* कपड़ों में लपेटना (शिशु आदि को)
swag (स्वैग) *n. sl.* चोरी का माल
swagger (ˊस्वैगर) *vi.* अकड़ कर चलना
swallow[1] (ˊस्वॉलो) *vt.* निगलना; (निराशा) छिपाना, दबाना – *n.* निगलने की क्रिया
swallow[2] (ˊस्वॉलो) *n.* एक पक्षी, अबाबील
swam (स्वैम) **SWIM** का *pt.*
swamp (स्वॉम्प) *n.* दलदल – *vt.* जलमग्न कर देना; की भरमार या बौछार कर देना; बाढ़ सी ला देना

swan (स्वॉन) *n.* राजहंस

swap (स्वॉप), **swop** (स्वॉप) *inf. n/v.* अदला-बदली (करना) (**-pp-**)

swarm (स्वॉर्म) *n.* झुंड (वि० मधुमक्खियों का); विशाल भीड़ – *vi.* (मधुमक्खियों का) बड़ी संख्या में इकट्ठे उड़ना; भीड़ करना

swarthy (स्वॉर्दि) *a.* सांवला

swat (स्वॉट) *vt.* (मक्खी, मच्छर आदि) मारना (**-tt-**)

swath (स्वॉथ) *n.* कटी फसल की कतार, हंसिये की कटान (**swathe** (स्वेद) भी)

swathe (स्वेद) *vt.* पट्टियां बांधना; कपड़े में लपेटना

sway (स्वे) *vi.* डोलना, झूलना; (अपने) विचारों में डांवांडोल होना – *vt.* दूसरों के विचारों को प्रभावित करना – *n.* नियंत्रण, अधिकार; शक्ति; झूलने की क्रिया

swear (स्वेंअर) *vt.* कसम खाना, शपथ लेना, कसम दिलाना – *vi.* कसम खा कर कहना; बद्दुआ देना (**swore, sworn, swearing**) – **swearword** *n.* गाली, अपशब्द

sweat (स्वेंट) *n.* पसीना – *v.* पसीना ला देना; पसीना आना; कठोर परिश्रम करना (**sweat** या **sweated** *pt./pp.*, **sweating** *pr. p.*) – **sweat shirt** लम्बी आस्तीन की स्वेटर

sweater (स्वेंटर) *n.* स्वेटर

sweep (स्वीप) *vi.* झाडू लगाना; जल्दी से या अकड़ कर (शान से) चलना; फैलना – *vt.* झाडू से साफ़ करना; जल्दी से या आवेश में उठा ले जाना (**swept, sweeping**) – *n.* साफ़ करने, बुहारने की क्रिया; प्रवाह, बहाव, धारा; चौड़ा घुमाव; परास या पहुंच; (**chimney sweep** भी) चिमनी साफ़ करने वाला – **sweeper** *n.* सफाई करने वाला, जमादार – **sweeping** *a.* विस्त त; आमूल (सुधार आदि) – **sweeping victory** शानदार जीत

sweet (स्वीट) *a.* मीठा, प्रिय, रुचिकर; शुद्ध (वायु); दयाशील; कमनीय; ताज़ा; सुगन्धित, अच्छी हालत में; (*fig.*) सुरीला; आकर्षक – *n.* मिठाई; भोजनोपरांत मिष्ठान्न; प्रिय/प्रिये – **sweeten** (स्वीटन) *v.* मधुर बनाना; मीठा करना – **sweetly** *adv.* प्यार से – **sweetheart** *n.* प्रेमी या प्रेमिका – **sweet pea** मटर का पौधा – **sweet potato** शकरकंदी

swell (स्वेंल) *v.* फैल जाना – *vi.* गर्व से फूले न समाना; भावों का उमड़ना; सूजना (**swelled, swollen, swelling**) – *n.* सूजना, फूलना; समुद्र की लहर

swelter (स्वेंल्टर) *vi.* गरमी से तंग आना – **sweltering** *a.* उमस वाली (गर्मी)

swept (स्वेंप्ट) **SWEEP** का *pt./pp.*

swerve (स्वर्व) *vi.* अचानक मुड़ना या दिशा बदल लेना; पथ से हटना; कर्तव्य से विमुख होना – *n.* मुड़ने या रास्ता बदलने की क्रिया

swift (स्विफ़्ट) *a.* तेज़; फुरतीला – *n.* अबाबील जैसा पक्षी – **swiftly** *adv.* तेज़ी से

swig (स्विग) *n.* लम्बा या बड़ा घूंट

swim (स्विम) *vi.* तैरना; बहना; चक्कर आना – *vt.* तैर कर पार करना; तैराकी प्रतियोगिता में भाग लेना – *n.* तैराकी, तैरना (**swam, swum, swimming**) – **swimmer** *n.* तैराक – **swimming costume** (**swimsuit** भी) (वि० लड़कियों की) तैराकी की पोशाक – **swimming trunks** तैराकी की निकर

swindle (स्विन्डल) *n./v.* धोखा, छल (करना)

swine (स्वाइन) *n.* सूअर; नीच !, कमीना ! (*pl.* **swine**)

swing (स्विंग) *v.* झूलना, झुलाना; डोलना, डुलाना; घूमना; (विचार आदि) बदलना – *vi.* फांसी पर चढ़ना; प्रहार करना (**at** के साथ) (**swung** *pt./pp.*) – *n.* झूलने, डोलने आदि की क्रिया; झूला; उतार चढ़ाव (विशेषकर वोटों में)

swipe (स्वाइप) *v.* लम्बे हाथ से प्रहार करना

swirl (स्वर्ल) *v.* भंवर पड़ना – *n.* भंवर; बहाव

swish (स्विश) *v.* सरसराहट की आवाज़ करना या होना – *n.* सरसराहट

switch (स्विच) *n.* स्विच, बिजली का बटन; अचानक परिवर्तन या कायापलट; लचीली छड़ी या टहनी; पशु की पूंछ के बालों का गुच्छा; स्त्रियों की कृत्रिम चोटी – *vi.* बदलना; स्थान बदलना; झूलना – *vt.* स्विच दबाना; अचानक (पार्टी आदि) बदल लेना; पतली छड़ी से मारना– **switchboard** *n.* स्विचबोर्ड, बिजली के खटकों या टेलीफ़ोन के कनेक्शनों का समूह – **switch on/off** बत्ती जलाना/बुझाना

swivel (ˈस्विव़ल) *n.* घूमने वाली लड़ी; चूल छल्ला – *vi.* चूल/छल्ले पर घूमना (-tt-)

swollen (ˈस्वोलन) **SWELL** का *pp.*

swoon (स्वून) *n./vi.* मूर्च्छा (आना)

swoop (स्वूप) *vi.* झपटना – *n.* झपटने की क्रिया; आकस्मिक आक्रमण

swop (स्वॉप) *vt.* देखिए **SWAP**

swore (स्वॉर) *pt.* **sworn, SWEAR** का *pt.*

swot (स्वॉट) *inf. v.* बहुत मेहनत से पढ़ाई करना (-tt-) – *n.* परिश्रमी विद्यार्थी

swum (स्वम) **SWIM** का *pp.*

swung (स्वङ) **SWING** का *pt./pp.*

sycophant (ˈसिकफ़ंट) *n.* चापलूस – **sycophancy** *n.* चापलूसी – **sycophantic** (सिकˈफ़ैंटिक) *a.*

syllable (ˈसिलबल) *n.* अक्षर, शब्द-उच्चारण इकाई (*button* के दो **syllable** है: **bu-tton** (ब-ट्न))

syllabus (ˈसिलबस) *n.* पाठ्यक्रम, पाठ्य विवरण (*pl.* **-es, bi** (-बाइ))

sylvan (ˈसिल्व़न) *a.* वन्य, वन, वक्ष संबंधी

symbol (ˈसिंबल) *n.* प्रतीक, चिह्न, संकेत – **symbolic** (सिम्ˈबॉलिक) *a.* प्रतीकात्मक – **symbolize** (ˈसिम्बलाइज़) *vt.* प्रतीक रूप में प्रयोग करना

symmetry (ˈसिमिट्रि) *n.* (वस्तु के) भागों के आकार-प्रकार में समता, सुडौलपन – **symmetrical** (सिˈमैट्रिकल) *a.* सममित; संतुलित, सुडौल

sympathy (ˈसिम्पथि) *n.* सहानुभूति, हमदर्दी; दया – **sympathetic** (सिम्पˈथैटिक) *a.* सहानुभूतिशील, हमदर्द; अनुकूल – **sympathize** *vi.* सहानुभूति रखना/प्रकट करना

symphony (ˈसिम्फ़नि) *n.* आरकेस्ट्रा द्वारा बजाई जाने वाली संगीत-रचना, संध्वनिकता, सिम्फ़नि; स्वर संगति

symposium (सिम्ˈपोज़िअम) *n.* परिसंवाद, परिचर्चा, विचार-गोष्ठी

symptom (ˈसिम्प्टम) *n.* रोग लक्षण, लक्षण; आसार – **symptomatic** *a.*

syn- (*comb. form*) साथ, के साथ, समान

synagogue (ˈसिनगॉग) *n.* यहूदी पूजा स्थल या प्रार्थना भवन; यहूदी प्रार्थना-सभा

synchronize (ˈसिंक्रनाइज़) *vt.* एक ही समय में घटित होने देना या करना, समय मिला देना – *vi.* समकालिक करना या होना, एक ही समय पड़ना

syndicate (ˈसिंडिकिट) *n.* सिंडिकेट, अभिषद्, व्यवसाय-संघ; प्रकाशन-संघ – *v.* संघ बनाना – *vt.* कई समाचार-पत्रों, टी.वी. कार्यक्रमों में (लेख आदि) एक साथ प्रकाशित/प्रसारित कराना

syndrome (ˈसिन्ड्रोम) *n.* रोग के विभिन्न लक्षणों का संयोग; लक्षण-समुच्चय

synergism (ˈसिनरजिज़्म), **synergy** (ˈसिनर्जि) *n.* दो दवाइयों, मांस-पेशियों आदि का प्रभावोत्पादन जो उन दोनों के प्रथक-प्रथक प्रभाव के योग से अधिक होता है

synod (ˈसिनड, ˈसिनॉड) *n.* (ईसाई धर्म में) धर्म सभा

synonym (ˈसिनमिम) *n.* पर्याय, समानार्थी शब्द – **synonymous** *a.* समानार्थक, पर्यायवाची **synonymy** (सिˈनॉनिमि) *n.* समानार्थकता

synopsis (सि´नॉप्सिस) *n.* सारांश, रूपरेखा

syntax (´सिंटैक्स) *n.* वाक्य रचना, वाक्य-विन्यास

synthesis (´सिंथिसिस) *n.* संश्लेषण, संयोजन, विभिन्न तत्वों का मेल (*pl.* -**theses** (-सीज़) – **synthesize** (´सिंथिसाइज़) *v.* संश्लेषण करना, मिलाना, (मिलाकर) कत्रिम रीति से बनाना – **synthesizer** *n.* एक इलैक्ट्रॉनिकी वाद्य – **synthetic** (सिन्´थेटिक) *a.* कत्रिम, संश्लेषणात्मक, संश्लेषित

syphilis (´सिफ़िलिस) *n.* उपदंश या आतशक रोग

syphon दे० SIPHON

syringe (´सिरिंज) *n.* पिचकारी; (इंजेक्शन लगाने की) सिरिंज – *vt.* फुहार मारना

syrup (´सिरप) *n.* चाशनी; गाढ़ा शीरा – **syrupy** *a.*

system (´सिस्टम) *n.* व्यवस्था, योजना; तंत्र; पद्धति; शारीरिक तंत्र-व्यवस्था – **systematic** (सिस्टि´मैटिक) *a.* सुव्यवस्थित; आयोजित – **systemic** (सि´स्टेमिक) *a.* सर्वांगी (रोग, विष आदि); (कीटनाशक) जिसे पौधा पूरी तरह सोख ले – *n.* ऐसा कीटनाशक – **system disk** कम्प्यूटर भाषा में विषय विशेष पर कंप्यूटर-डिस्क में भरा प्रोग्राम

T

tab (टैब) *n.* कपड़ों पर लगा लेबिल; पट्टी, टैब; *US* (वस्तु का) मूल्य; बिल; *inf.* गोली (मादक पदार्थ की) – **keep tabs on** पर निगरानी रखना

table (टेबल) *n.* मेज, टेबिल; भोजन; सारणी; खेल प्रतियोगिता-श्रेणी; *Maths* पहाड़ा – *vt.* मेज पर रखना; (विधेयक आदि) विधान सभा के सम्मुख प्रस्तुत करना – **tableland** *n.* पठार – **tablespoon** *n.* भोजन आदि परोसने का चमचा – **table tennis** टेबल टेनिस (खेल) – **turn the tables (on sb)** पांसा पलट देना

tableau (टैब्लो) *n.* झाँकी, नाटकीय द श्य (*pl.* – **leaux** (-लोज़))

tablet (टैब्लिट) *n.* दवाई की गोली; साबुन आदि की टिकिया; (शिला) लेख आदि में प्रयुक्त पत्थर, लकड़ी आदि

tabloid (टैब्लॉइड) *n.* लोकप्रिय छोटे आकार का सनसनीखेज सुर्खियों वाला सचित्र- समाचारपत्र

taboo (टबू) *a.* वर्जित, निषिद्ध

tabular (टैब्युलर) *a.* सारणीबद्ध, तालिकाबद्ध – **tabulate** *vt.* आँकड़ों, तथ्यों आदि को सारणीबद्ध करना – **tabulation** (टैब्युलेशन) *n.* सारणीकरण

tacit (टैसिट) *a.* अनकहा (अर्थ); मौन – **tacitly** *adv.* – **taciturn** *a.* अल्पभाषी, प्राय: मौन

tack[1] (टैक) *n.* चपटी कील, बिरिंजि, कच्चा टाँका; *Naut.* जहाज़ का टेढ़ा-मेढ़ा (पवनाभिमुख) रास्ता; दिशा; *inf.* भोजन – *vt.* बिरिंजी से जड़ना, कच्चा टाँका लगाना, जोड़ना, संलग्न करना – *vi.* जहाज़ का टेढ़े-मेढ़े चलना, दिशा बदलना

tack[2] (टैक) *n.* घुड़सवारी का साज-सामान

tackle (टैकल) *n.* भारी वस्तु उठाने का साज-सामान, टैकल; *Sport* भिड़ंत, जूझ – *vt.* कस कर पकड़ना; सामना करना; से जूझना

tacky (टैकि) *a.* चिपचिपा

tact (टैक्ट) *n.* व्यवहार-कौशल – **tactful** *a.* व्यवहार-कुशल, व्यवहारशील – **tactfully** *adv.* – **tactless** *a.* स्थिति को बिना सोचे-समझे बोलने, कार्य करने वाला (व्यक्ति व्यवहार, बात)

tactics (टैक्टिक्स) *pl. n.* रणकौशल; चालू युक्ति, दाँवपेच – **tactical** (टैक्टिकल) *a.* निपुण, कुशल; सामरिक; स्थिति को देखते हुए (चाल)

tadpole (टैड्पोल) *n.* मेंढक का बच्चा, बेंगची

taffeta (टैफ़िट्अ) *n.* मुलायम रेशमी, रेयन आदि का वस्त्र, टाफ्टा

tag[1] (टैग) *n.* (वस्तु से बंधा) मूल्य का लेबिल; जूते के फीते आदि का नुकीला धातु का अंश; संक्षिप्त घिसा-पिटा उद्धरण; लटकन; जोड़ा गया अंश – *vt.* (से) जोड़ देना; बांध देना; पीछे-पीछे चलना **(-gg-)**

tag[2] (टैग) *n.* बच्चों का एक खेल, छुआछुई – *vt.* छूना

tail (टेल) *n.* पूंछ, दुम; किसी वस्तु का निचला, पिछला या घटिया भाग; *inf.* पीछा करने वाला व्यक्ति (जासूस) – (~ **s**) *pl.* सिक्के का वह भाग जिधर उसका मूल्य लिखा हो, पट; *inf.* एक प्रकार का कोट, टेलकोट – *vt.* पूंछ काटना; *inf.* पीछे लगे रहना, पीछा करना – **tailed** *a* – **tailback** *n.* रुकावट से उत्पन्न सड़क पर वाहनों की लम्बी पंक्ति – **tailboard** *n.* ट्रक आदि का पिछला तख्ता – **tail coat** एक सांयकालीन कोट – **tail end** अंतिम सिरा – **taillight** *n.* वाहन की पिछली बत्ती – **tailpiece** *n.* लेख में जोड़ा गया अंश, पश्चलेख – **tailspin** *n.* वायुयान का गोल घूमते हुए नीचे आना – **turn tail** भाग जाना

tailor (टेलर) *n.* दरज़ी – **tailoring** *n.* सिलाई – **tailor-made** *a.* दरज़ी का सिला (वस्त्र), पहनने में बिलकुल ठीक; *fig.* बिलकुल उपयुक्त

taint (टेंट) *v.* दूषित करना या होना; छूत लगना – *n.* दोष, खराबी

take (टेक) *vt.* पकड़ना, हाथ में लेना, पाना, लेना, ले लेना, ग्रहण करना, (पद) संभालना; मानना, समझना; ले जाना; स्वीकार करना; (स्थान आदि) दिखाना; खाना या पीना; घटाना; (उपाय) करना, (कदम) उठाना आदि; पर कब्ज़ा करना – *vi.* प्रभावकारी होना; जाना (**took, taken, taking**) -*n.* विशे० *Cinema* (लिया गया) दृश्य – **takings** *pl. n.* आय, (व्यापार में) प्राप्ति – **take-off** *n.* हवाई जहाज़ का उड़ान-आरंभ का क्षण – **take in** समझ लेना; (वस्त्र) छोटा करना; धोखा देना – **be taken aback** आश्चर्यचकित होना – **take off** उड़ान भरना; *inf.* चले जाना; *inf.* नकल उतारना; (वस्त्र) उतारना – **take to** पसंद करना

talcum powder (टैलकम-) (चेहरे आदि पर लगाने का) टेल्कम पाउडर

tale (टेल) *n.* कहानी, किस्सा

talent (टैलंट) *n.* प्रतिभा, योग्यता – **talented** *a.* प्रतिभा संपन्न, प्रवीण

talisman (टैलिज़्मन) *n.* ताबीज़

talk (टॉक) *vi.* बोल सकना; बात करना, बातचीत करना – *vt.* के विषय में बात करना; व्यक्त करना, (भाषा) बोल सकना – *n.* वार्ता; बातचीत, विचार-विमर्श; अफ़वाह – **talkative** *a.* बातूनी

tall (टॉल) *a.* लम्बा (व्यक्ति); ऊंचा (भवन); महत्वपूर्ण, महान; अविश्वनीय (कहानी आदि) – **tall order** *inf.* कठिन काम – **tall story** अविश्वसनीय कहानी

tallow (टैलो) *n.* चरबी – *vt.* चरबी लगाना

tally (टैलि) *vi.* (से) मेल खाना, (के) अनुरूप होना; हिसाब में दर्ज़ करना (**tallied, tallying**) – *n.* हिसाब, लेखा; कुल संख्या – **tallier** *n.*

talon (टैलन) *n.* पंजा

tamarind (टैमरिंड) *n.* इमली

tambourine (टैम्ब'रीन) *n.* डफली, खंजरी

tame (टेम) *a.* पालतू, घरेलू; नीरस; शांत, दब्बू – *vt.* पालतू बनाना, वश मे करना

tamper (टैम्पर) *vi.* – **tamper with** हेर-फेर कर देना

tan (टैन) *a./n.* भूरा, कत्थई – *v.* (अधिक धूप से) तांबे जैसा रंग हो जाना या कर देना; पशु की खाल को चमड़े में परिवर्तित करना (**-nn-**) – **tanner** *n.* चर्मशोधक – **tannery** (टैनरि) *n.* चमड़ा बनाने का कारखाना, टैनरी

tang (टैङ) *n.* तीखा स्वाद, तेज़ गंध; संकेत; नोक – **tangy** (टैंजि) *a.* तीखे स्वाद वाला

tangent (टैजंट) *n.* स्पर्श-रेखा – *a.* स्पर्शी – **tangential** (टैन्'जेंन्शल) *a.* स्पर्श-रेखीय; (तर्क आदि) जो किसी विषय से अधिक सम्बद्ध न हो

tangerine (टैंज'रीन) *n.* संतरा

tangible (टैंजबल) *a.* स्पर्शनीय; वास्तविक

tangle (टैंगल) *n.* गुत्थी, उलझन; उलझी हुई शाखाएं आदि – *vt.* उलझाना

tango (टैंगो) *n.* एक दक्षिण अमरीकी न त्य (*pl.* **-gos**)

tank (टैंक) *n.* टंकी, हौज़; सेना का टैंक – **tanker** (टैंकर) *n.* द्रव पदार्थ-वाहक जहाज़, ट्रक आदि

tankard (टैंकर्ड) *n.* (शराब, विशे० बीयर का) पीने का बड़ा प्याला

tannin (टैनिन्) दे. **TAN**

tantalize (टैंटलाइज़) *vt.* तरसाना, ललचाना

tantamount (टैंटमाउंट) *a.* – **tantamount to** (के) समान/बराबर होना

tantrum (टैंट्रम) *n.* बच्चे की तरह मचलने की क्रिया, झल्लाहट

tap[1] (टैप) *v.* धीमे से खटखटाना; थपकी देना; किसी स्त्रोत का अपनी योजना के लिए उपयोग करना (**-pp-**) – *n.* ठक-ठक; थपकी

tap[2] (टैप) *n.* टोंटी, डाट; चूड़ी काटने का औज़ार (सुम्बा) – *vt.* टोंटी लगाना, (टोंटी से) निकालना; दूसरों की बातचीत सुनने के लिए टेलीफोन तार से (गुप्त रूप से) तार जोड़ना (**-pp-**)

tape (टेप) *n.* पट्टी, फ़ीता; (**magnetic tape** भी) टेपरिकार्डर का टेप – *vt.* (संगीत आदि) टेपरिकार्डर में भरना; टेप करना – **tape measure** इंची-टेप – **tape recorder** टेपरिकॉर्डर – **tapeworm** (टेप्वर्म) *n.* पेट का कीड़ा, फीताकमि, टेपवर्म – **have (someone) taped** *inf.* किसी को भाँपना

taper (ˊटेपर) *vi.* एक सिरे पर पतला होते जाना; धीरे-धीरे कम होते जाना – *n.* पतली मोमबत्ती

tapestry (ˊटैपिस्ट्रि) *n.* परदों का विशेष प्रकार का कपड़ा

tapioca (टैपिˊओक्अ) *n.* पकवानों में प्रयुक्त कसावा की जड़ से प्राप्त श्वेतसार (स्टार्च), टैपियोका

tapir (ˊटेपर) *n.* सूअर के समान एक अमरीकी जानवर, टेपर

tar[1] (टार) *n.* डामर, तारकोल – *vt.* तारकोल लगाना, तारकोल डालना (**-rr-**)

tar[2] (टार) *n. inf.* नाविक

tarantula (टˊरैन्ट्युल्अ) *n.* ज़हरीली बड़ी मकड़ी

tardy (ˊटार्डि) *a.* धीमा, सुस्त

target (ˊटार्गिट) *n.* लक्ष्य, निशाना

tariff (ˊटैरिफ़) *n.* आयात-शुल्क, सीमा-शुल्क; दर-सूची

tarnish (ˊटार्निश) *v.* बदरंग हो जाना या कर देना, धब्बे पड़ जाना; (की छवि) खराब कर देना – *n.*

tarpaulin (टार्ˊपॉलिन) *n.* तिरपाल

tarry (ˊटैरि) *vi.* रुकना, ठहरना, पीछे रह जाना (**tarried, tarrying**)

tart[1] (टार्ट) *n.* एक मीठा करारा पकवान; *inf. offens.* वेश्या

tart[2] (टार्ट) *a.* तीखा; तेज़ कड़ुवा

tartan (ˊटार्टन) *n.* चारखाना, ऊनी कपड़ा (विशे. स्कॉटलैंड) के कुछ वर्गों द्वारा पहना जाने वाला

tartar (ˊटार्टर) *n.* दांतों पर जमा मैल

task (टास्क) *n.* कार्य, काम, नियत कार्य – *vt.* काम देना या से काम लेना – **task force** विशेष कार्य पूरा करने के लिए भेजी गई सैनिक नौ-सैनिक, टुकड़ी – **taskmaster** *n.* निरीक्षक – **take to task** डांटना

tassel (ˊटैसल) *n.* धागों का गूंथ कर बना फुंदना, झब्बा

taste (टेस्ट) *n.* स्वाद, ज़ायका; स्वाद शक्ति; (*fig.*) वस्तु का कुछ अनुभव; पुट, अल्प मात्रा; पसंद; सुरुचि – *vt.* चखना; अनुभव करना – *vi.* का विशिष्ट स्वाद होना – **tasteful** *a.* सुरुचिपूर्ण – **tastefully** *adv.* – **tasteless** *a.* स्वादहीन, फीका – **tasty** *a.* चटपटा, स्वादिष्ट – **taste bud** जीभ पर स्वाद कलिका

tattered (ˊटैटर्ड) *a.* फटा हुआ, चिथड़े-चिथड़े - **tatters** *pl.n.* चिथड़े

tattoo[1] (टैˊटू) *n.* रात का बिगुल; सैनिक परेड

tattoo[2] (टैˊटू) *v.* शरीर पर नाम आदि गोदना (**tattooed, tattooing**) – *n.* गोदा गया नाम आदि

tatty (ˊटैटि) *a.* फटा-पुराना; फटेहाल (व्यक्ति) – **tattiness** *n.*

taught (टॉट) **TEACH** का *pt./pp.*

taunt (टॉण्ट) *vt.* ताने मारना – *n.* ताना

Taurus (ˊटॉरस) *n.* वृष राशि (21 अप्रैल से 21 मई के बीच जन्मे व्यक्तियों की राशि)

taut (टॉट) *a.* कसा हुआ, तना हुआ

tavern (ˊटैवर्न) *n.* शराबखाना, सराय

tax (टैक्स) *n.* कर, टैक्स, महसूल; *fig.* भार – *vt.* टैक्स लगाना; भार डालना; का आरोप लगाना, दोष देना; (धैर्य) समाप्त करना – **taxation** (टैक्ˊसेशन) *n.* कराधान, टैक्स-व्यवस्था –

taxpayer *n.* करदाता – **tax evasion** टैक्स की चोरी – **tax return** व्यक्तिगत आय का टैक्स सम्बंधी ब्यौरा, टैक्स-विवरणी

taxi (ˈटैक्सि), **taxicab** *n.* टैक्सी (*pl.* **taxis** (ˈटैक्सीज़)) – *vi.* वायुयान का ज़मीन पर (उतरते या चढ़ते समय) दौड़ना (**taxied** *pt./pp.* **taxiing** *pr. p.*)

taxidermy (ˈटैक्सिडर्मि) *n.* म त जानवर की खाल भरकर उसे जीता-जागता स्वरूप देने की कला

TB tuberculosis का संक्षेप

tea (टी) *n.* चाय – **high tea** तीसरे पहर का चाय सहित भोजन – **teaspoon** *n.* छोटा चम्मच

teach (टीच) *vt.* शिक्षा देना, पढ़ाना – *vi.* अध्यापन कार्य करना (**taught** (टॉट), **teaching**) – **teacher** *n.* शिक्षक – **teaching** *n.* अध्यापन, शिक्षा

teak (टीक) *n.* सागौन, इसकी लकड़ी

team (टीम) *n.* खिलाड़ियों की टीम; दल; (जानवरों की) जोड़ी – **teamster** *n.* US ट्रक चालक– **team spirit** दल के सदस्यों में आपस में सहयोग की भावना – **teamwork** *n.* सामूहिक कार्य

tear[1] (टिअर) *n.* आंसू – **tearful** *a.* आंसू भरा, रोआँसा – **teardrop** *n.* आंसू की बूंद – **tear gas** आंसू-गैस

tear[2] (टॅअर) *vt.* फाड़ना, चीरना – *vi.* फट जाना; तेजी से भागना (**tore, torn, tearing**) – *n.* (कपड़े में) खोंच, चीर

tease (टीज़) *vt.* तंग करना, परेशान करना, चिढ़ाना– *n.* तंग करने वाला

teat (टीट) *n.* (जानवर के) स्तनाग्र, थन; चूची; दूध पिलाने की बोतल का रबड़ निप्पल

tech. (टॅक) **technical, technology** का संक्षिप्त रूप

technical (ˈटॅक्निकल) *a.* तकनीकी, तकनीक से सम्बंधित; तकनीकी कार्य में कुशल; नियमानुसार, पूर्णतया विधिक, कानूनी; **technicality** (–ˈकैलिटि) *n.* कानूनी बारीकी – **technically** *adv.* – **technician** (टॅक्ˈनिशन) *n.* किसी विशेष तकनीक में पारंगत, कुशल, तकनीशियन, यंत्रविद – **technique** (टॅक्ˈनीक) *n.* तकनीक, प्रविधि, विशेष कौशल से सम्पन्न करने की कार्य-प्रणाली

Technicolor (ˈटॅक्निकलर) *n.* **R** फिल्मों में रंगीन फोटोग्राफी, टेक्नीकलर

technology (टॅक्ˈनॉलजि) *n.* प्रौद्योगिकी; तकनीकी विधियां, कौशल, ज्ञान आदि – **technological** (टॅक्नˈलॉजिकल) *a.* प्रौद्योगिकीय – **technologist** (टेक्ˈनॉलजिस्ट) *n.*

teddy bear (ˈटॅडि-) मुलायम रीछ जैसा खिलौना

tedious (ˈटीडिअस) *a.* उबाऊ, नीरस – **tedium** (ˈटीडिअम) *n.* ऊब, नीरसता, उबाऊपन

teem (टीम) *vi.* (से) भरा होना; भरपूर होना

teens (टीन्ज़) *pl. n.* 13 से 19 वर्ष की आयु, किशोरावस्था – **teenage** (ˈटीनेज) *a.* किशोरावस्था का/सम्बंधी – **teenager** *n.* किशोर, किशोरी

teeter (ˈटीटर) *n.* झूमाझूमी – *vi.* ऊपर-नीचे डोलना, लड़खड़ाना

teeth (टीथ) *n.* **TOOTH** का *pl.*

teethe (टीद) *vi.* (बच्चे के) दांत निकलना – **teething troubles** (किसी कार्य में) आरंभिक कठिनाइयां

teetotal (टीˈटोट्ल) *a.* शराब बिलकुल न छूने वाला – **teetotaller** *n.* मद्यत्यागी

tele- (*comb. form*) दूर, दूर से

telecast (ˈटॅलकास्ट) *n./v.* टेलिविज़न कार्यक्रम (प्रसारित करना)

telecommunications (टॅलिकम्यूनि ˈकेशन्ज़) *n.* संचार विज्ञान व प्रौद्योगिकी

teleconference (ˈटॅलिकॉन्फ़रन्स) *n.* टेलीफोन/विडियो पर कई लोगों का विचार-विनिमय

telegram (´टेंलिग्रैम) *n.* तार, टेलीग्राम

telegraph (´टेंलिग्राफ़) *n.* टेलीग्राफ, तार भेजने का उपकरण– *v.* तार भेजना – **telegraphic** *a.* – **telegraphist** (टि´लेंग्रफिस्ट) *n.* – **telegraphy** *n.* टेलीग्राफ़-विज्ञान, तार-संचार

telepathy (टि´लेंपथि) *n.* एक मस्तिष्क का दूसरे मस्तिष्क पर दूर से ही प्रभाव, दूरसंवेदन

telephone (´टेंलिफ़ोन) *n.* टेलीफोन –*v.* टेलीफ़ोन करना – **telephonic** (टेंलि´फ़ॉनिक) *a.*

telephoto (´टेंलिफ़ोटो) *a.* दूर की वस्तु का आवर्धित (बड़ा) बिम्ब बनाने वाला (लैन्स)

teleprinter (´टेंलिप्रिंटर) *n.* दूर मुद्रक, टेलिप्रिंटर

telescope (´टेंलिस्कोप) *n.* दूरबीन, टेलीस्कोप – *v.* एक दूसरे में धंस जाना या दब जाना – **telescopic** *a.*

television (´टेंलिविझ़न) *n.* टेलीविज़न – **televise** (´टेंलिवाइज़) *vt.* टेलीविज़न पर दिखाना, प्रसारित करना

tell (टेंल) *vt.* बताना, कहना; आदेश देना; वर्णन करना, सुनाना; सूचित करना; (दो वस्तुओं का अंतर) पहचानना; गिनना; चेतावनी देना – *vi.* (का) वर्णन करना; प्रभाव डालना (**told, telling**) – **teller** *n.* (कहानी) सुनाने वाला बैंक-खज़ांची – **telling** *a.* प्रभावकारी, ज़ोरदार – **telltale** *n.* चुगलखोर; स्पष्ट संकेत – *a.* सूचक, भेद देने वाला (संकेत)

temerity (टि´मेंरिटि) *n.*, गुस्ताखी

temp (टेंम्प) *n. inf.* अस्थायी कर्मचारी

temper (´टैम्पर) *n.* मनोदशा, मिज़ाज; क्रोध (प्रायः चिल्लाना भी); स्वभाव; स्टील आदि का कड़ापन – *vt.* (कठोरता) मंद करना; नरम करना; (स्टील आदि) कड़ा करना – **bad-tempered** *a.* गुस्सैल

temperament (´टेंम्प्रमंट) *n.* स्वभाव, मिज़ाज – **temperamental** *a.* तुनक मिज़ाज; मनमौजी

temperate (´टेंम्परिट) *a.* संतुलित, संयमी; न अधिक गर्म न अधिक ठण्डी (जलवायु), शीतोष्ण – **temperance** (´टेंम्परन्स) *n.* संयम, शराब से परहेज़, मिताचार

temperature (´टेंम्प्रिचर) *n.* ताप, तापमान, *inf.* बुखार

tempest (´टेंम्पिस्ट) *n.* तूफान – **tempestuous** (टेंम्´पेंसट्युअस) *a.* तेज़, उग्र, तूफानी

template (´टेंम्पलिट) *n.* सांचा, (गत्ते या प्लास्टिक में) काटी गई आकृति जो (कपड़े आदि पर) उतारी जा सके; *Computers* प्रतिमान/नमूना जिससे और अनुकृति तैयार की जा सकें

temple[1] (´टेंम्पल) *n.* मंदिर, पूजास्थल

temple[2] (´टेंम्पल) *n.* कनपटी

tempo (´टेंम्पो) *n.* गति, रफ्तार; ताल

temporal (´टेंम्परल) *a.* काल (समय) सम्बंधी; सांसारिक

temporary (´टेंम्परिर) *a.* अस्थायी, कुछ समय के लिए – **temporarily** *adv.*

tempt (टेंम्प्ट) *vt.* लुभाना, लालच देना, बहकाना (विशे. अनुचित कार्य करने के लिए); की ओर झुकाव करना, आकर्षित करना – **temptation** (टेंम्प्´टेशन) *n.* प्रलोभन, लालच

ten (´टेंन) *n./a.* दस – **tenth** *a./n.* दसवां (भाग)

tenable (´टेंनबल) *a.* तर्कसंगत, समर्थन योग्य (बात, तर्क आदि)

tenacious (टि´नेशस) *a.* दृढ़, पक्का, हठी – **tenaciously** *adv.* – **tenacity** (टि´नैसिटि) *n.* दृढ़ता, हठ

tenant (´टेंनंट) *n.* किरायेदार; पट्टेधारी, काश्तकार आदि – **tenancy** *n.*

tend[1] (टेंण्ड) *vi.* (कुछ) करने की प्रवृत्ति होना; (की ओर) ले जाना; का कारण बनना – **tendency** (´टेंन्डन्सि) *n.* झुकाव, प्रवृति – **tendentious** (टेंन्´डेंन्शस) *a* विवादास्पद

tend[2] (टेंण्ड) *vt.* की देखभाल करना; सेवा या परिचर्या करना, तिमारदारी करना – **tender**

n. जहाज पर छोटी नौका; (**bar tender** भी) परिचारक, क्लब आदि में सदस्यों को शराब आदि देने वाला

tender[1] (टॅण्डर) *a.* कोमल, नरम – **tenderness** *n.* – **tender-hearted** *a.* दयालु

tender[2] (टॅण्डर) *vt.* प्रस्तुत करना – *vi* ठेके की निविदा (अर्ज़ी) देना – *n.* निविदा, टेण्डर; भुगतान के रूप में कानूनन दिया जा सकने वाला धन का रूप (जैसे नोट, सिक्के)

tendon (टॅण्डन) *n.* कंडरा, नस (जो मांसपेशी को हड्डी से जोड़ती है)

tenement (टॅनमंट) *n.* अनेक कमरों या कोठरियों वाली इमारत जिसमें अनेक परिवार रहते हैं, चाल

tenet (टॅनिट) *n.* सिद्धांत, मत

tenner (टॅनर) *n. inf.* दस का नोट

tennis (टॅनिस) *n.* टेनिस का खेल, लान टेनिस

tenor (टॅनर) *n.* जीवन-प्रवाह; भाव, तात्पर्य, कहने का मतलब

tense[1] (टॅन्स) *n. Grammar* क्रिया का काल

tense[2] (टॅन्स) *a.* तना हुआ, खिंचा हुआ; तनावपूर्ण (स्थित), बेचैन – *v.* तन जाना, खिंच जाना; बेचैन कर देना – **tension** (टॅन्शन) *n.* खिंचाव, तनाव, बेचैनी; तनातनी, वैर

tent (टॅण्ट) *n.* तम्बू, खेमा

tentacle (टॅण्टकल) *n.* कुछ प्राणियों के लंबे पतले व लचीले अवयव जो शिकार पकड़ने के काम आते हैं, स्पर्शक

tentative (टॅण्टटिव़) *a.* प्रयोगात्मक; कामचलाऊ; झिझक भरा; सुझाव के रूप में प्रस्तुत

tenterhooks (टॅण्टरहुक्स) *pl. n.* – **on tenterhooks** बेचैन, चिंतित, व्यग्र

tenuous (टॅन्युअस) *a.* कच्चा, थोथा (तर्क आदि); पतला, बारीक

tenure (टॅन्युअर) *n.* , काश्तकारी; कार्यकाल

tepid (टॅपिड) *a.* गुनगुना (पानी); ढीला, उदासीन

tequila (टि'कील्अ) *n.* मेक्सिकन शराब

term (टर्म) *n.* शब्द, पद; अवधि, (स्कूल, न्यायालय आदि का) सत्र; सीमा – (~**s**) *pl.* शर्तें, (आपसी) सम्बंध – *vt.* नाम रखना, नाम देना – **terms of reference** विचारार्थ विषय की सीमाएं

terminal ('टर्मिनल) *a.* आखरी; टर्मिनस सम्बंधी; (बीमारी) जिसमें म त्यु निश्चित हो – *n.* अंतिम छोर, सिरा; (बैटरी आदि) का सिरा; हवाई अड्डे में स्थान जहां से यात्री आते या जाते हैं, अंतिम या आरंभिक बस अड्डा, बस टर्मिनल

terminate ('टर्मिनेट) *vt.* समाप्त करना – *vi.* समाप्त होना, (बस आदि का) अंतिम स्टेशन, अड्डा होना – **terminable** *a.* समापन योग्य – **termination** (टर्मि'नेशन) *n.* समापन, अंत

terminology (टर्मि'नॉलजि) *n.* पारिभाषिक शब्दावली; शब्दावली-अध्ययन – **terminological** *a.* शब्दावली सम्बंधी

terminus ('टर्मिनस) *n.* अंतिम छोर, अंतिम सीमा; अंतिम रेलवे स्टेशन, बस अड्डा आदि, टर्मिनस (*pl.* – **ni** (नाइ))

termite ('टर्माइट) *n.* दीमक (**white ant** भी)

terrace (टॅरस) *n.* ऊंचा समतल स्थान, चबूतरा; पहाड़ी पर काटा गया समतल भाग; (ढाल पर बने) मकानों की श्रं खला; (प्राय: *pl.*) फुटबॉल स्टेडियम में दर्शकों के बैठने की सीढ़ियां; खुली छत; छज्जा – *vt.* (पहाड़ी पर) सीढ़ीनुमा स्थान बनाना – **terraced** *a.* ढालू, ढलान पर; सीढ़ीनुमा (*terraced garden/hillside*)

terra cotta (टॅरअ'कॉट्अ) (गहरी भूरी) पक्की मिट्टी के बर्तन या इसकी मूर्ति

terra firma (टॅर्अ'फर्म्अ) *n.* प थ्वी

terrain (टॅरेन) *n.* भूभाग

terrestrial (ट'रॅस्ट्रिअल) *a.* प थ्वी का, स्थलीय, स्थलचर

terrible (टॅरबल) *a.* डरावना; बहुत अधिक, बहुत गंभीर; बहुत खराब (वस्तु) – **terribly** *adv.* बहुत अधिक (अच्छा, बुरा)

terrier (टेंरिअर) *n.* एक छोटे कुत्ते की नस्ल, टेरियर

terrific (टरिफ़िक) *a.* बहुत अधिक; *inf.* अच्छा, बढ़िया; भय व विस्मय उत्पन्न करने वाला

terrify (टेंरिफ़ाइ) *vt.* भयभीत करना, आतंकित करना

territory (टेंरिटरि) *n.* क्षेत्र, प्रदेश, इलाका, राज्य क्षेत्र; ज्ञान क्षेत्र – **territorial** (टेंरिटॉरिअल) *a.* राज क्षेत्रीय, प्रादेशिक

terror (टेंरर) *n.* आतंक; *inf.* परेशान करने वाला व्यक्ति या वस्तु – **terrorism** *n.* आतंकवाद – **terrorist** (टेंररिस्ट) *n./a.* आतंकवादी – **terrorize** (टेंरराइज़) *vt.* आतंकित करना, आतंक फैलाना – **terror-stricken** *a.* बहुत डरा हुआ, भयभीत

terry (टेंरि) *a./n.* अनकटी बुनाई वाला (तौलिये के प्रकार का मोटा कपड़ा)

terse (टर्स) *a.* अत्यंत संक्षिप्त व रूखा

tertiary (टर्शरि) *a.* तीसरा, ततीय – *n.*

Terylene (टेंरलीन) *n.* **R** टेरिलीन (कपड़ा)

test (टेंस्ट) *vt.* परखना, जांचना, परीक्षण करना, परीक्षा लेना – *n.* (कठिन) परीक्षा; परीक्षण– **testing** *a.* कठिन – **test case** मिसाल कायम करने के लिए अदालत में ले जाया गया कोई मामला – **test match** क्रिकेट में टेस्ट मैच – **test tube** परखनली, टेस्ट-ट्यूब – **test-tube baby** क त्रिम गर्भाशय में पनपा बच्चा

testament (टेंस्टमंट) *n. Law* वसीयत (नामा) – **the Old/New Testament** बाइबल के दो मुख्य भाग

testicle (टेंस्टिकल) *n.* नर की अण्डग्रंथि, अण्ड

testify (टेंस्टिफ़ाइ) *v.* बयान देना; गवाही देना; (का) सबूत होना (**-ified, -ifying**)

testimony (टेंस्टिमनि) *n. Law* प्रमाण; गवाही – **testimonial** (टेंस्टिमोनिअल) *n.* चरित्र, योग्यता आदि का प्रमाण-पत्र; व्यक्ति के सम्मान में उसे दिया गया उपहार, थैली

testy (टेंस्टि) *a.* चिड़चिड़ा, गरममिज़ाज

tetanus (टेंटनस) *n.* टेटनस, एक भयंकर संक्रामक रोग (**lock-jaw** भी)

tête-à-tête (टेट् अटेट) *Fr.* दो व्यक्तियों की एकांत में बातचीत

tether (टेंदर) *n.* जानवार को बांधने का रस्सा या ज़ंजीर – *vt.* खूंटे पर बांधना

text (टेंक्स्ट) *n.* मूल-पाठ; उद्वरण, अवतरण; विषय वाक्य (विशे. धार्मिक-ग्रंथ से) – **textual** (टेंक्स्ट्युअल) *a.* मूलपाठ विषयक – **textbook** *n.* पाठ्य-पुस्तक

textile (टेंक्स्टाइल) *n.* कपड़ा, वस्त्र – *a.*

texture (टेंक्स्चर) *n.* प्रक ति; गठन, बनावट, बुनावट

than (दैन, दन) *conj.* से, अपेक्षाक त, की बनिस्बत, की तुलना में

thank (थैंक) *vt.* आभार प्रकट करना, धन्यवाद देना; को जुम्मेवार ठहराना – **thanks** *pl. n.* धन्यवाद – **thankful** *a.* आभारी, शुक्रगुज़ार – **thankless** *a.* क तघ्न, नाशुक्रा; व्यर्थ (का कार्य) – **thanks to** *prep.* के कारण

that (दैट) *a.* (*pl.* **those**) – *pron.* वह ; जो, जिसे – *adv.* इतना – *conj* कि

thatch (थैच) *n.* छप्पर बनाने का घास-फूस – *vt.* छप्पर बनाना – **thatcher** *n.*

thaw (थॉ) *v.* पिघलना, पिघलाना; (व्यवहार में) अधिक मैत्रीपूर्ण हो जाना, नरम पड़ना, ढीला पड़ना – *n.* पिघलने की क्रिया

the (दी, द) *definite article* ('किसी भी' के विपरीत) विशेष व्यक्ति, वस्तु आदि से पहले प्रयुक्त

the have-nots *pl. n.* गरीब लोग

the haves *pl. n.* अमीर लोग

theatre (थिअटर) *n.* थियेटर, रंगशाला, नाट्य-साहित्य, नाट्य-कला, व्याख्यान आदि का बड़ा कमरा; शल्य कक्ष, आपरेशन का कमरा –

theatrical (थिऐट्रिकल) *a.* रंगशाला संबंधी; अतिनाटकीय– **theatrically** *adv.* – **theatricals** *pl. n.* शौकिया नाटक प्रदर्शन, अव्यवसायी नाट्य-अभिनय – **theatregoer** n. नियमित नाट्य-दर्शक

theft (थेफ्ट) *n.* चोरी

their (दैअर) **them** का *a./pron.;* **they** का *possessive* उनका; इनका; **theirs** *poss. pron.* उनका, इनका

them (दैम, दम) *pron.* उन्हें, उनको, इन्हें, इनको – **themselves** *pron.* वे ही, वे स्वयं, उन्होंने ही

theme (थीम) *n.* विषय (वस्तु); प्रसंग; मूल विषय; (संगीत में) विषय-धुन, टेक की धुन – **thematic** (थि´मैटिक) *a.* विषयक – **theme song** फिल्म आदि में बार-बार आने वाला एक गीत, कथानक

then (दैन) *adv.* तब, उस समय; उसके बाद; और भी, तो – *conj.* अत: – **the-then president** उस समय राष्ट्रपति

thence (दैन्स) *adv. obs.* वहां से; इसलिए

theocracy (थि´ऑक्रिसि) *n.* पुजारियों का शासन, धर्मतंत्र; ईशतंत्र – **theocratic** (थिअ´क्रैटिक) *a.* धर्मतंत्रीय (शासन)

theology (थि´ऑलजि) *n.* धर्मशास्त्र, ईश्वर मीमांसा – **theological** (थिअ´लॉजिकल) *a.* धर्मशास्त्रीय, ईश्वर मीमांसीय

theorem (´थिअरम) *n.* प्रमेय, तर्क द्वारा सिद्ध किया जा सकने वाला साध्य

theory (´थिअरि) *n.* सिद्धांत (व्यवहार के विपरीत); वाद, मत – **theoretical** *a.* सैद्धांतिक (न कि व्यावहारिक), मीमांसात्मक

therapy (´थेरपि) *n.* उपचार, चिकित्सा – **therapeutic** *a.* चिकित्सा-संबंधी; आरोग्यकर, रोगहर –**therapeutics** *pl. n.* चिकित्सा कला –**therapist** *n.* चिकित्सक

there (दैअर) *adv.* वहां, उस स्थान पर; उधर – **thereafter** *adv.* इसके बाद – **thereby** (दैअर्´बाइ) *adv.* उसके द्वारा – **therefore** (´दैअर्फॉर) *adv.* अत:; इसलिए – **therefrom** *adv.* उससे – **therein** *adv.* उसमें – **thereupon** (दैअर्अ´पॉन) *conj.* उस पर, फौरन उसके बाद

therm (थर्म) *n.* थर्म, ऊष्मा (गर्माइश) मापी इकाई – **thermal** (´थर्मल) *a.* गरम; ऊष्म *-pl.* गरम बनियान आदि

thermo- (*comb. form*) ऊष्मा संबंधी

thermodynamics (थर्मोडाइ´नैमिक्स) *n.* ऊर्जा के विभिन्न रूपों में अंतर तथा अंतर्परिवर्तन के अध्ययन सम्बंधी विज्ञान, ऊष्मा-गति की

thermometer (थर्´मॉमिटर) *n.* थर्मामीटर

thermonuclear (थर्मो´न्यूक्लिअर) *a.* ताप-नाभिकीय

Thermos (´थर्मस) **R** थर्मस-बोतल

thermostat (´थर्मस्टैट) *n.* ताप को स्थायी बनाये रखने का उपकरण, तापस्थायी

thesaurus (थि´सॉरस) *n.* पर्याय (व विलोम) शब्दकोश

these (दीज़) *pl. pron.* ये, *pl. a.* ये (*not 'those'*) – **these books** ये किताबें

thesis (´थीसिस) *n.* (विश्वविद्यालय की डिग्री, डिप्लोमा आदि के लिए प्रस्तुत) शोध-प्रबंध; धारणा, अभिधारणा (*pl.* **theses** (-सीज़))

they (दे) *pl. pron.* वे; ये; लोग

they'd (देड) they had; they would का संक्षेप

they'll (देइल) they will का संक्षेप

they've (देव) they have का संक्षेप

thick (थिक) *a.* मोटा; गहरी (धुंध आदि); गाढ़ा; घना (जंगल); *inf.* मंदबुद्धि, मोटी अक्ल वाला; भारी (आवाज़); *inf.* घनिष्ठ (मित्र) – *n.* – **thicken** *vi.* (पदार्थ) गाढ़ा, मोटा या घना होना – *vt.* गाढ़ा आदि करना – **thickly** *adv.* –

thickness *n.* मोटाई; गाढ़ापन; सघनता – **thicket** ('थिकिट) *n.* (पेड़ों का) झुरमुट – **thickset** ('थिक्सेंट) *a.* नाटा व गठीला; घना – **thick-skinned** *a. fig.* मोटी चमड़ी वाला (व्यक्ति) – **through thick and thin** हमेशा

thief (थीफ़) *n.* चोर (*pl.* **thieves** (थीव्ज़)) – **thieve** *v.* चोरी करना

thigh (थाइ) *n.* जांघ, जंघा

thimble ('थिम्बल) *n.* (दरज़ी द्वारा कपड़े सीते वक्त उंगली पर चढ़ने के लिए) अंगुश्ताना

thin (थिन) *a.* पतला, बारीक, महीन; दुबला-पतला; विरल, कम; हल्का (दर्शकगण, बादल आदि); *col.* कम संभावना वाला – *v.* पतला, बारीक या कम होना या करना, घटना; छंटना – **thinner** *n.* गाढ़े द्रव को पतला करने में प्रयुक्त द्रव, थिनर – **thinness** *n.*

thing (थिङ) *n.* वस्तु, पदार्थ, चीज़; कोई भी विचार-वस्तु, बात

think (थिंक) *vi.* सोचना, विचार करना; ध्यान करना; धारणा रखना – *vt.* समझना, मानना; विश्वास रखना (**thought** (थॉट) *pt./pp.*, **thinking** *pr. p*). – **thinkable** *a.* कल्पनीय, संभव – **thinker** *n.* दार्शनिक, विचारक – **thinking** *n.* चिन्तन, सोच-विचार – *a.* मननशील

third (थर्ड) *a.* तृतीय, तीसरा – *n.* तीसरा भाग – **third degree** दे. **degree** – **third party** (*Law, Insurance etc.*) तिसरैत, तृतीय पक्ष, दो पक्षों की कानूनी कार्यवाही आदि में अकस्मात ही फंस जाने वाला तीसरा व्यक्ति – **Third World** अफ्रीका, एशिया व लैटिन अमरीका के विकासशील देश

thirst (थर्स्ट) *n.* प्यास; तीव्र इच्छा – *v.* प्यास लगना, प्यासा होना – **thirstily** *adv.* – **thirsty** ('थर्स्टि) *a.* प्यासा

thirteen ('थर्'टीन) *a./n.* तेरह – **thirty** ('थर्टि) *n./a.* तीस

this (दिस) *a./pron.* यह (*pl.* **these**)

thistle ('थिसल) *n.* कांटेदार पौधा, भटकटैया

thong (थाङ) *n.* चमड़े का पट्टा; कोड़ा

thorax ('थॉरैक्स) *n.* छाती, सीना

thorium ('थॉरिअम) *n.* एक रेडियोधर्मी धातुक तत्व, थोरियम

thorn (थॉर्न) *n.* कांटा, कांटेदार झाड़ी – **thorny** ('थॉर्नि) *a.* कांटेदार

thorough ('थर्अ) *a.* पूर्ण; पक्का, विस्तार के साथ, ध्यानपूर्वक व अच्छी तरह किया गया – **thoroughly** *adv.* – **thoroughfare** ('थर्अफ़ेअर) *n.* आम रास्ता, खुली सड़क

those (दोज़) *pron.* **That** का *pl.*, वे, वो; वो ही

thou (दाउ) *pron. obs.* तू (*pl.* **ye, you**)

though (दो) *conj.* यद्यपि, हालांकि, भले ही – *adv.* पर, फिर भी

thought (थॉट) *n.* सोच-विचार, चिंतन; विचार, धारणा, ख्याल; मत; विचारधारा – THINK का *pt./pp.* – **thoughtful** *a.* लिहाज़ करने वाला; विचारशील; विचारमग्न – **thoughtless** *a.* बेलिहाज़; लापरवाह, बिना सोचे-समझे किया गया (कार्य)

thousand ('थाउजंड) *n./a.* हजार

thrash (थ्रैश) *vt.* पिटाई करना; बुरी तरह हराना – *vi.* हाथ-पैर पटकना, छटपटाना

thread (थ्रेड) *n.* तागा, सूत; पेच पर चूड़ी; (कहानी आदि में) सिलसिला, क्रम; विषय – *vt.* (सुई) पिरोना; फ़िल्म, टेप आदि मशीन में लगाना; (माला) पिरोना, गूंथना – **threadbare** ('थ्रेड्बेअर) *a.* फटा-पुराना, घिसा-पिटा

threat (थ्रेट) *n.* धमकी, आशंका; वस्तु या व्यक्ति जिससे खतरा हो – **threaten** ('थ्रेटन) *vt.* धमकी देना; आशंका उत्पन्न करना

three (थ्री) *n./a.* तीन – **three-dimensional, 3-D** *a.* जिसके तीन आयाम हों – **three-ply** *a.* तीन तारों/धागों वाली

(ऊन, लकड़ी आदि) – **three-R'S-the three R's** पढ़ना, लिखना व गणित

thresh (थ्रेश) *vt.* धान आदि को कूट-पीट कर दाना निकालना

threshold (´थ्रेशोल्ड) *n.* द्वार की देहली, देहलीज; प्रवेश द्वार; आरंभ; संवेदना

threw (थ्रू) **THROW** का *pt.*

thrice (थ्राइस) *adv.* तीन बार; तिगुना

thrift (थ्रिफ्ट) *n.* मितव्ययता, किफ़ायत – **thrifty** *a.*

thrill (थ्रिल) *n.* रोमांच, खुशी व उत्तेजना की लहर, कँपकँपी – *vt.* पुलकित/रोमांचित कर देना, खुशी की लहर दौड़ा देना – *vi.* रोमांचित/पुलकित होना – **thriller** *n.* रोमांचक, रहस्यपूर्ण पुस्तक, फिल्म आदि – **thrilling** *a.* रोमांचक, उत्तेजनापूर्ण

thrive (थ्राइव़) *vi.* फलना-फूलना; उन्नति करना, सफल होना (**throve, thrived** *pt.*, **thriven, thrived** *pp.*, **thriving** *pr. p.*)

throat (थ्रोट) *n.* कंठ, गला; हलक, श्वास नली

throb (थ्रॉब) *vi.* धड़कना, कंपित होना (**-bb-**) – *n.* धड़कन, स्पंदन

throes (थ्रोज़) *pl. n.* अत्यधिक पीड़ा होने की स्थिति; वेदना – **in the throes of** *inf.* उलझा हुआ, जूझता हुआ

thrombosis (थ्रॉम्´बोसिस) *n.* रक्तवाहिका या हृदय में जमे हुए खून का टुकड़ा (थक्का) बन जाना, धनास्रता

throne (थ्रोन) *n.* (राज) सिंहासन, गद्दी; राजा या रानी के अधिकार व कर्तव्य

throng (थ्रॉङ) *n.* भीड़ – *vt.* भीड़ लगाना; भीड़ में आना

throttle (´थ्रॉट्ल) *n.* मोटरकार आदि के इंजन में तेल प्रवाह व गति नियंत्रक वाल्व – *vt.* गला घोंटना; दबाना; (द्रव प्रवाह आदि) नियंत्रित करना

through (थ्रू) *prep.* के आर-पार, के पार; में से; के कारण; के द्वारा, के जरिये – *adv.* आर-पार, अंत तक – *a.* पूर्ण, समाप्त; *inf.* समाप्त सम्बंध; खुला (रास्ता); सीधी (गाड़ी, बस) – **throughout** *adv.* पूर्णतया; शुरू से अंत तक – *prep.* (के) हर भाग में, सारा (दिन, रात आदि) – **throughput** (´थ्रूपुट) *n.* तैयार की गई सामग्री की मात्रा (विशे. कंप्यूटर द्वारा) – **through and through** पूरी तरह से – **carry through** पूरा करना

throve (थ्रोव़) **THRIVE** का *pt.*

throw (थ्रो) *vt.* फेंकना; उतार देना; पटकना, फेंकना; डाल देना; (पार्टी आदि) देना; गिराना (**threw, thrown, throwing**) – *n.* फेंक, फेंकने की दूरी – **throwaway** *a.* सस्ती (वस्तुएं) – **throwback** (´थ्रोबैक) *n.* भूतकाल की वस्तु/उससे मिलती-जुलती वस्तु

thrush (थ्रश) *n.* बाम्कार या कस्तूरी पक्षी

thrust (थ्रस्ट) *v.* धकेलना; घोंपना, भोंकना; (**thrust, thrusting**) – *n.* प्रहार, घोंपना; (इंजन का) धकेलने का बल, प्रणोद

thud (थड) *n.* धम की आवाज़ – *vi* धम-धम करना (**-dd-**)

thug (ठग) *n.* ठग, गुण्डा

thumb (थम) *n.* अंगूठा – *vt.* (पुस्तक के पन्नों को) अंगूठा लगा-लगाकर मैला कर देना; मुफ्त सवारी लेने के लिए वाहनों को संकेत देना - **thumbnail** *a.* वस्तु, व्यक्ति आदि का अति संक्षिप्त (विवरण)

thump (थम्प) *n.* (मुट्ठी से) प्रहार, ऐसे ठोकने की आवाज़ – *vt.* (मुट्ठी से) ठोकना

thunder (´थंडर) *n.* बादलों की गरज, गड़गड़ाहट, कड़क – *vi.* गरजना; (व्यक्ति का) गुस्से में चिल्लाना, गरजना – *vt.* ऊंची आवाज़ में कहना – **thunderous** (´थंडरस) *a.* गरजन भरा, ज़ोरदार (तालियां) – **thunderbolt, thunderclap** *n.* बिजली की कड़क; अप्रत्याशित, अप्रिय घटना – **thunderstorm**

n. गरजन वाला तूफान – **thunderstruck** *a.* भौंचक, स्तंभित

Thursday (´थर्ज़्डे) *n.* बृहस्पतिवार

thus (दस) *adv.* इस प्रकार, इसलिए

thwack (थ्वैक) *vt.* मारना – *n.* प्रहार

thwart (थ्वॉर्ट) *vt.* विफल करना, नाकाम करना

thy (दाइ) *a.* तेरा – **thyself** *pron.* तुम स्वयं

thyme (टाइम) *n.* बनआजवायन, थाइम

thyroid gland (´थाइरॉइड) शारीरिक विकास नियंत्रक ग्रंथि, अवटुग्रंथि

tiara (´टिआर्‌अ) *n.* छोटा मुकुट; त्रिमुकुट

tick[1] (टिक) *n.* घड़ी की टिक-टिक; (सही का) निशान (✓); *inf.* क्षण – *vt.* (सही का) निशान लगाना – *vi.* टिकटिक करना – **tick off** निशान लगाना; डांटना

tick[2] (टिक) *n.* (कुत्तों आदि के लगने वाली) चिचड़ी, किलनी

ticket (´टिकिट) *n.* टिकट, लेबिल; **US** चुनाव में पार्टी के उम्मीदवारों की सूची; यातायात नियम उल्लंघन का चालान – *vt.* लेबिल लगाना; टिकट बांटना – **ticket collector** टिकट कलैक्टर – **ticket office** टिकट घर

tickle (´टिकल) *vt.* गुदगुदाना; खुश करना; *fig.* मनोरंजन करना; का पसंद आना – *vi.* झुनझुनी होना – *n.* गुदगुदी – **ticklish** *a.* नाज़ुक

tide (टाइड) *n.* ज्वार-भाटा; धारा – **tidal** (´टाइडल) *a.* ज्वारीय – **tidal wave** बड़ी समुद्री लहरें – **tide over** सहायता करना विशे. कर्ज़ा आदि देकर

tidings (´टाइडिंग्ज़) *pl. n.* समाचार

tidy (´टाइडि) *a.* ठीक-ठाक; साफ-सुथरा *inf.* काफ़ी बड़ा – *vt.* (**tidy up** भी) ठीक-ठाक करना

tie (टाइ) *v.* (खेल में दो खिलाड़ियों या टीमों का अंक, गोल आदि) बराबर होना; बराबर रहना – *vt.* बांधना, गांठ लगाना; बांध देना, मुक्त न रहने देना (**tied, tying**) – *n.* बंधनी (रस्सी आदि), बंध; बंधन, (मैत्री) संबंध, टाई; (खेल में) बराबरी, बराबरी का खेल – **tied** *a.* बराबरी का (खेल) – **tie-dyeing** *n.* बंधनी रंगाई – **tie-up** *n.* (दो कंपनियों में) गठबंधन

tier (टिअर) *n.* पंक्ति; एक के ऊपर एक बैठने /सोने के स्थान

tiff (टिफ़) *n.* मामूली सा झगड़ा, अनबन

tiger (´टाइगर) *n.* बाघ

tight (टाइट) *a.* (रस्सा) कसा हुआ, तना हुआ; (कपड़े) तंग, चुस्त; मज़बूत; जिसमें पानी आदि न आ सके; ठसाठस; (बजट) जिसमें ज्यादा खर्च की गुंजाइश न हो; बहुत व्यस्त (प्रोग्राम); कड़ा (नियंत्रण); *inf.* नशे में; *inf.* कंजूस – **tights** *pl. n.* एकदम चुस्त पतलून – **tighten** (´टाइटन) *v.* कसना – **tightly** *adv.* – **tightrope** (´टाइट्रोप) *n.* कलाबाज़ों द्वारा तानी गई रस्सी

tile (टाइल) *n.* टाइल; खपरा, खपरैल – *vt.* खपरा बिछाना या लगाना – **tiled** *a.* – **tiling** *n.*

till[1] (टिल) *prep.* (समय) तक – *conj.* जब तक कि ... न

till[2] (टिल) *n.* नकदी रखने की दराज़ या तिजौरी

till[3] (टिल) *vt.* जोतना, हल चलाना – **tillage** (´टिलिज) *n.* – **tiller** *n.* किसान

tilt (टिल्ट) *vt.* झुकाना, तिरछा करना – *vi.* झुकना– *n.* झुकाव; घुड़सवारों की बरछेबाज़ी – **at full tilt** पूरी रफ्तार से

timber (´टिम्बर) *n.* इमारती लकड़ी; कटाई-चिराई योग्य पेड़

timbre (´टिम्बर, ´टैम्बर) *n.* ध्वनिरूप, ध्वनिगुणता

time (टाइम) *n.* समय; काल; युग; अवधि; अवसर, अवकाश; बार (जैसे एक बार); *Music* ताल – *vt.* (उचित) समय चुनना या निश्चित करना; (कुछ करने में लगे रहे) समय का हिसाब रखना – **timely** (´टाइम्लि) *a.* समयोचित, ठीक समय पर – **timer** *n.* समय-मापक (व्यक्ति अथवा

उपकरण) – **time bomb** टाइम-बम – **time-consuming** *a.* जिसमें समय ज़्यादा लगे – **time-lag** *n.* कालान्तर, दो घटनाओं के बीच का अंतर – **timepiece** (ˈटाइम्पीस) *n.* घड़ी – **timetable** *n.* समय-सारणी, टाइम-टेबिल – **Greenwich Mean Time** अंतर्राष्ट्रीय मानक समय – **time and again** बार-बार

timid (ˈटिमिड) *a.* कायर; संकोची – **timidity** *n.* भीरुता; संकोच – **timidly** *adv.* – **timorous** *a.* डरा हुआ, भीरू

tin (टिन) *n.* टिन, टीन (एक धातु), रांगा; टीन, कनस्तर – *vt.* टीन के डब्बे में बंद करना (विशे. खाद्य-पदार्थ) **(-nn-)**– **tinfoil** *n.* (खाना आदि लपेटने के लिए) धातु की पन्नी – **tin-pot** *a. inf* घटिया, बेकार

tincture (ˈटिंक्चर) *n.* टिंचर; झलक, पुट – *vt.* पर हलका सा रंग चढ़ाना; का पुट देना

tinder (ˈटिंडर) *n.* आग जलाने की सूखी लकड़ियां आदि

tinge (टिंज) *n.* झलक, रंगत; पुट, गंध – *vt.* हलका सा रंग चढ़ाना; पुट देना

tingle (ˈटिंगल) *vi.* झुनझुनाहट या सनसनी होना – *n.* झुनझुनाहट

tinker (ˈटिंकर) – *vi.* (मशीन के पुर्ज़ों को) छेड़ना या गड़बड़ करना, बिना जानकारी मरम्मत करने का प्रयत्न करना

tinkle (ˈटिंकल) *v.* (घंटी की) टनटन आवाज़ होना या करना – *n.* टनटन, टनटनाना

tinsel (ˈटिन्सल) *n.* भड़कीली सजावटी वस्तु; सस्ती, दिखावटी वस्तु

tint (टिंट) *n.* रंग; आभा, झलक, रंगत – *vt.* हलका रंग चढ़ाना

tiny (ˈटाइनि) *a.* बहुत छोटा

tip[1] (टिप) *n.* नोक, अग्रभाग, सिरा; नोक पर लगी वस्तु – *vt.* सिरा लगाना **(-pp-)**

tip[2] (टिप) *n.* बख्शीश, इनाम; उपयोगी संकेत, युक्ति, गुप्त सूचना – *vt.* बख्शीश देना; गुप्त सूचना देना **(-pp-)**

tip[3] (टिप) *vt.* उलटना, झुकाना, तिरछा करना; हलका सा स्पर्श करना – *vi.* उलट जाना **(-pp-)** – *n.* कूड़ा इकट्ठा करने का स्थान, घर

tipple (ˈटिपल) *n.* शराब – **tippler** *n.* शराबी

tipsy (ˈटिप्सि) *a.* हलके से नशे में

tiptoe (ˈटिप्टो) *vi.* पंजों के बल चलना; दबे पांव चलना – *n.* – **on tiptoe** दबे पांव

tiptop (टिप्ˈटॉप) *a.* उत्क ष्ट, बहुत बढ़िया

tirade (टाइˈरेड) *n.* लम्बा उत्तेजना व निंदा पूर्ण भाषण

tire (टाइअर) *vt.* थका देना, ऊबा देना; खीज पैदा कर देना – *vi.* थक जाना, ऊब जाना – **tired** *a.* थका हुआ; ऊबा हुआ – **tiring** *a.* थकाने या ऊबाने वाला – **tiresome** (ˈटाइअर्सम) *a.* थकाऊ, उबाऊ, खीज उत्पन्न करने वाला

tissue (ˈटिशू) *n.* शरीर, पौधे आदि का टिशू, ऊतक; पतला मुलायम कागज (विशे. इसका रूमाल); महीन बुना हुआ कपड़ा – **tissue paper** टिशू पेपर, पतला मुलायम कागज़

tit (टिट) *n.* गंगरा चिड़िया; अनेक छोटी चिड़ियाओं की किस्म

titanic (टाइˈटैनिक) *a.* विशालकाय

titbit (ˈटिट्बिट) *n.* चटपटे खाने का ग्रास; मज़ेदार, चटपटी खबर

tit for tat जैसे को तैसा

titillate (ˈटिटिलेट) *vt.* गुदगुदी करना; सहलाना व पुलकित करना; उत्तेजित करना – **titillation** *n.* गुदगुदी; सहलाने या पुलकित करने की क्रिया

title (ˈटाइट्ल) *n.* पुस्तक का नाम; शीर्षक; नाम; उपाधि; अधिकार या अधिकार पत्र; *Sports* खेल-प्रतियोगिता में सर्वविजय सूचक – **titled** *a.* कुलीन वर्ग से, अभिजात – **title deed**

(मकान आदि के) मालिक होने के कानूनी दस्तावेज़, अधिकार-पत्र – **titular** *a.* केवल नाम के लिए

titter ('टिटर) *vi.* दबी हुई हंसी हंसना

tittle-tattle *n./vi.* गपशप (करना)

tizz (टिज़), **tizzy** ('टिज़ि) *n. inf.* घबराहट, चिंता की स्थिति

TNT Trinitro Toluene का संक्षेप; एक विस्फोटक

to (टू) *prep.* की ओर (*to the top*); तक (*from Monday to Friday*); को (*Give it to him*); तुलना में (*3 goals to 2*), अनुपात में; (व्याकरण) अनियत वृति के लिए (*I want to go*) – *adv.* ठीक, ठीक-ठाक; पास, बंद (*The wind blew the door to*)

toad (टोड) *n.* टोड, एक प्रकार का मेंढक – **toady** *n.* चाटुकार, चापलूस – (– **ies** *pl.*) – *vi.* चापलूसी करना (**toadied, toadying**) – **toadstool** ('टोड्स्टूल) *n.* (प्राय: ज़हरीला) कुकुरमुत्ता, खुंभी

toast (टोस्ट) *n.* (डबलरोटी का) टोस्ट; किसी की सफलता पर खुशी प्रकट करने, शुभकामना देने आदि के लिए पिया गया जाम; शुभकामना का पात्र – *vt.* टोस्ट सेंकना; की सलामती आदि का जाम पीना; आग पर सुखाना, तापना – **toaster** *n.* टोस्ट सेंकने का विद्युत-उपकरण, टोस्टर

tobacco (ट'बैको) *n.* तम्बाकू

toboggan (ट'बॉगन) *n.* बर्फगाड़ी – *vi.* बर्फगाड़ी से फिसलते जाना

today (ट'डे) *n.* आज – *adv.* इस समय, आजकल

toddle ('टॉड्ल) *vi.* (बच्चे का) गिरते-पड़ते चलना, ठुमकना; *inf.* टहलना – *n.* ठुमकना – **toddler** *n.* बच्चा जो चलना सीख रहा हो

toddy ('टॉडि) *n.* ताड़ी

to-do *n. inf.* बतंगड़, हंगामा (*pl.* **-dos**).

toe (टो) *n.* पैर की उंगली या अंगूठा; पैर के अंगूठे आकार या स्थान की कोई वस्तु; खुर या सुम – **toe the line** के अनुसार काम करना

toffee ('टॉफ़ि) *n.* टाफी

tofu ('टोफू) *n.* सोयाबीन का पनीर

together (ट'गेंदर) *adv.* साथ में, साथ-साथ, इकट्ठे *inf.* (सु)संगठित

toggle ('टॉगल) *n.* ज़ंजीर या रस्सी पर लगी एक प्रकार की खूंटी या चपटी गिल्ली; कम्प्यूटर की एक कुंजी (बटन) – **toggle switch** बिजली का स्विच जो ऊपर-नीचे व आगे-पीछे किया जा सकता है

togs (टॉग्ज़) *inf. pl. n.* वस्त्र, पहनावा

toil (टॉइल) *n.* कठोर परिश्रम, कठिन काम – *vi.* कठिन परिश्रम करना

toilet ('टॉइलिट) *n.* शौचघर, टट्टी; नहाना-धोना व श्रंगार; प्रसाधन – *a.* प्रसाधन-(सामग्री)

token ('टोकन) *n.* चिह्न, प्रमाण; प्रतीक, टोकन (धन के स्थान पर प्रयुक्त); उपहारकार्ड जिसे देकर विशेष मूल्य तक की वस्तुएं प्राप्त की जा सकती हैं – *a.* नाममात्र का, मामूली सा

told (टोल्ड) **TELL** का *pt./pp.*

tolerate ('टॉलरेट) *vt.* सहना; करने देना – **tolerable** ('टॉलरबल) *a.* सहनीय, पर्याप्त, ठीक-ठीक – **tolerance** *n.* उदारता का दृष्टिकोण, सहिष्णुता, सहनशीलता – **tolerant** *a.* सहिष्णु, सहनशील – **tolerantly** *adv.* – **toleration** *n.* बर्दाश्त, उदारता

toll[1] (टोल) *vt.* घंटा बजाना– *n.*घंटे की ध्वनि

toll[2] (टोल, टॉल) *n.* कर, मार्गकर; दुर्घटना, विपत्ति आदि में क्षति, नुकसान

tomato (ट'माटो) *n.* टमाटर (*pl.* - **toes**)

tomb (टूम) *n.* मकबरा, समाधि – **tombstone** ('टूम्स्टोन) *n.* समाधि-प्रस्तर

tombola (टॉम्बोल्अ) *n.* तम्बोला (एक प्रकार की लाटरी)

tomboy ('टॉम्बॉइ) *n.* लड़कों जैसे वस्त्र पहनने व उनके समान आचरण करने वाली लड़की

tomcat (´टॉम्कैट) बिलाव

tome (टोम) *n.* बड़ी पुस्तक या उसका प थक भाग, ब हद् ग्रंथ

tomorrow (ट´मॉरो) *adv./n.* (*fig.* भी) आने वाला कल – **the day after tomorrow** परसों – **a week tomorrow** कल से पूरे एक सप्ताह बाद

tom-tom *n.* ढोल (बजाना)

ton (टन) *n.* टन (= 1016 किलोग्राम या 2240 पाउंड) (दूसरा नाम **long ton**); **US** टन (= 907 किलोग्राम या 2000 पाउंड) (दूसरा नाम **short ton**) – **tonnage** (´टनिज) *n.* भार ले जाने की क्षमता, (जहाज का) प्रति टन महसूल; ज़हाज़ (सामूहिक रूप से)

tone (टोन) *n.* स्वर, ध्वनि; लहज़ा, स्वर-शैली, स्वर का उतार-चढ़ाव; रंग, रंगत, आभा; सामान्य वातावरण; भाव; स्वास्थ्य, शक्ति – *vt.* सुर मिलाना; उचित रंग भरना, मेल मिलाना – **toner** *n.* रंग गहरा या हल्का करने वाला पदार्थ; फोटोकापी मशीन व कम्प्यूटर में छपाई की स्याही – **tonal** *a.* स्वर सम्बंधी, रंग-सम्बंधी

tongs (टॉङ्ज़) *pl. n.* चिमटा, संडसी; (बालों की) चिमटी

tongue (टङ) *n.* जीभ; जीभ के आकार की वस्तु; भाषा; वाणी; स्वर – **tongue-tied** *a. fig.* जिसकी ज़ुबान एकदम बंद हो, अवाक, मौन

tonic (´टॉनिक) *n.* बलवर्धक, स्फूर्तिदायक दवा; *Mus.* मूल स्वर; प्रथम स्वर – *a.* बलवर्धक, स्फूर्तिदायक; सुर -तान विषयक

tonight (ट´नाइट) *n.* आज की रात – *adv.* आज रात को

tonne (टन) *n.* मीट्रिक टन, 1000 किलोग्राम

tonsil (´टॉन्सल) *n.* टॉन्सिल, गले की ग्रंथि – **tonsillitis** (टॉन्सि´लाइटिस) *n.* टॉन्सिल बढ़ना या उनकी सूजन

tonsure (´टॉन्शर) *n.* मुण्डन, सिर का भाग जिसके बाल बिलकुल साफ कर दिये हों – *vt.* मुण्डन करना

too (टू) *adv.* भी, के अतिरिक्त; आवश्यकता से अधिक – **too much** बहुत अधिक

took (टूक) **TAKE** का *pt.*

tool (टूल) *n.* औजार; (*fig.*) किसी की कठपुतली; साधन– *vt.* औज़ार काम में लाना विशे. पत्थर काटने के – **tooling** *n.* नक्काशी; मशीन चालू करने के लिए औज़ारों की व्यवस्था

toot (टूट) *n.* भोंपू

tooth (टूथ) *n.* दांत; दांते के आकार की वस्तु; दांता (*pl.* **teeth**)

tootle (´टूट्ल) *inf. v.* भोंपू बजाना – *vi.* आराम से जाना, आगे बढ़ना

top[1] (टॉप) *n.* शीर्ष, शिखर, चोटी; सर्वोच्च कोटि; प्रथम स्थान (परीक्षा आदि में); ऊपरी भाग का वस्त्र; ढक्कन; मचान – *vt.* सिरा काटना; चोटी पर पहुंचना, से ऊंचा या बढ़िया होना; सर्वप्रथम आना; ढंकना (**-pp-**) – **topmost** *a.* सर्वोच्च; उच्चतम – **top-dress** *vt.* मिट्टी, खाद आदि फैलाना – **top-dressing** *n.* – **top-heavy** *a.* असंतुलित – **top-notch** *a.* उत्क ष्ट – **top-secret** *a.* अति गोपनीय – **topsoil** (´टॉप्साइल) *n.* ऊपरी उपजाऊ मिट्टी – **top brass** उच्च अधिकारी (-वर्ग)

top[2] (टॉप) *n.* लट्टू

topaz (´टौपैज़) *n.* पुखराज रत्न

topic (´टॉपिक) *n.* व्याख्यान, बातचीत आदि का विषय; प्रसंग – **topical** (टॉपिकल) *a.* प्रासंगिक, सामयिक

topography (ट´पॉग्रफ़ि) *n.* स्थल-आक ति-(विवरण)

topple (´टॉपल) *v.* लुढ़का देना, लुढ़क जाना; *fig.* (सत्ता आदि) उलट देना

topsy-turvy (´टॉप्सि ´टर्वि) *a.* उलटा-पुलटा, अव्यवस्थित

torch (टॉर्च) *n.* बैटरी की टार्च; मशाल; कोई भी तेज गर्म लौ वाला उपकरण – **torch-bearer** *n.* मशालची; पथ-प्रदर्शक

tore (टॉर) **TEAR** का *pt.* (**torn** *pp.*)

torment *v.* (टॉर् 'मेंण्ट) यातना देना; तंग करना – *n.* ('टॉर्मेण्ट) तकलीफ, यातना, परेशानी – **tormentor, -er** *n.*

tornado (टार् 'नेडो) *n.* टॉर्नेडो, बवंडर, तूफान (*pl.* **-does**)

torpedo (टॉर् 'पीडो) *n.* पनडुब्बी से छोड़ा जाने वाला जहाज़ डुबाने का अस्त्र, टॉरपीडो (*pl.* **-does**) – *vt.* टॉरपीडो से या उसके समान वार करना

torpid ('टॉर्पिड) *a.* सुस्त, भावशून्य – **torpor** ('टॉर्पर) *n.* निष्क्रियता, भावशून्यता – **torpidity** *n.*

torrent ('टॉरंट) *n.* बहुत तेज़ धारा, मूसलाधार वर्षा – **torrential** (टॉ 'रेन्शल) *a.* वेगवान, बौछार जैसा

torrid ('टॉरिड) *a.* बहुत गरम व सूखा (मौसम, प्रदेश); अत्यंत भावप्रधान (विशे. काम भावना में); कठिनाईभरी – **Torrid Zone** उष्ण कटिबंध

torsion ('टॉर्शन) *n.* मरोड़, ऐंठन

torso ('टॉर्सो) *n.* धड़, धड़-मूर्ति (*pl.* **-sos, -si** (-सि))

tortoise ('टॉर्टस) *n.* कछुआ – **tortoiseshell** ('टॉर्टस्शेल) *n.* कछुए का कवच – *a.*

tortuous ('टॉर्ट्युस) *a.* टेढ़ा-मेढ़ा, चक्करदार; टेढ़ा; कपटी

torture ('टॉर्चर) *n.* यातना, बहुत अधिक पीड़ा – *vt.* यंत्रणा देना

Tory ('टॉरि) *n.* ब्रिटेन व कनाडा की रूढ़िवादी टोरी राजनीतिक दल का सदस्य; अनुदार दली

toss (टॉस) *vt.* उछालना; (सिर) झटकना – *vi.* उछलना, हचकोले खाना, करवटें बदलना – *n.* उछाल (सिक्के का), टॉस; झटका

tot[1] (टॉट) *n.* नन्हा बालक; छोटी मात्रा

tot[2] (टॉट) *v.* (*up* के साथ) जोड़ना, कुल योग होना (**-tt-**)

total ('टोट्ल) *n.* जोड़, योग, सम्पूर्ण राशि, जमा – *a.* पूरा, सारा – *vi.* कुल योग होना – *vt.* जोड़ना (**-ll-**) – **totality** (टो 'टैलिटि) *n.* सम्पूर्णता

totalitarian (टोटैलि 'टेंअरिअन) *a.* सर्वाधिकारी; तानाशाही

totem ('टोटम) *n.* गणचिह्न, कुलचिह्न, टोटेम

totter ('टॉटर) *vi.* लड़खड़ाना, डगमगाना

touch (टच) *n.* स्पर्श, छूना; स्पर्श-इंद्रिय; (ब्रुश से) घसीट; पुट; हल्की सी चपत या हल्का सा धक्का; अल्पमात्रा, थोड़ा सा – *vt.* स्पर्श करना, छूना; से सटा होना; तक पहुंचना; से सम्बंधित होना; की भावनाओं को प्रभावित करना – *vi.* छूते होना; (**on** के साथ) का जिक्र करना – **touching** *a.* मर्मस्पर्शी, हृदयस्पर्शी – *prep.* से सम्बंधित – **touchy** ('टचि) *n. a.* चिड़चिड़ा, भावुक – **touchstone** ('टच्स्टोन) कसौटी

tough (टफ़) *a.* मज़बूत, जो आसानी से कट या फट न सके; पक्का; कठोर; कठिनाइयां सह सकने वाला; मुश्किल; चबाने में सख्त; दुर्भाग्यपूर्ण – *n. inf.* गुण्डा – **toughen** *v.* – **toughness** *n.*

tour (टुअर) *n.* दौरा, यात्रा, पर्यटन – *vt.* दौरा लगाना, यात्रा करना – **tourism** ('टुअरिज़्म) *n.* पर्यटन; पर्यटन उद्योग – **tourist** ('टुअरिस्ट) *n.* पर्यटक, सैलानी

tour de force (टुर ड 'फ़ॉर्स) *Fr.* शक्ति या कौशल का प्रदर्शन, उत्क ष्ट रचना, अभिनय आदि

tournament ('टुअर्नमंट) *n.* खेल-प्रतियोगिता, टूर्नामेंट

tourniquet ('टुअर्निके) *a.* पट्टी, खून बहने से रोकने के लिए पट्टी, रक्तबंध

tousled ('टाउज़्ल्ड) *a.* उलझे हुए (बाल)

tout (टाउट) *vi.* दलाली करना; का प्रचार करना; (रेल, सिनेमा की टिकट) ब्लैक करना – *n.*

tow (टो) *vt.* रस्सी से ख च कर ले जाना – *n.* खिंचाई; खींचा जाने वाला जहाज, कार आदि

toward(s) (ट´वॉर्ड(ज़)) *prep.* की ओर, के विषय में; के लिए, के हेतु (**toward** भी)

towel (´टाउअल) *n.* तौलिया

tower (´टाउअर) *n.* मीनार, टावर, गढ़ – *vi.* (से) बहुत ऊंचा होना

town (टाउन) *n.* कस्बा – **township** (´टाउन्शिप) *n.* छोटा कस्बा

toxic (´टॉक्सिक) *a.* विषैला, ज़हरीला – **toxicity** *n.* विषाक्तता – **toxin** (´टॉक्सिन) *n.* बैक्टीरिया से उत्पन्न विष, जीव-विष – **toxic waste** उद्योग द्वारा विसर्जित हानिकारक कचरा, द्रव आदि

toy (टॉइ) *n.* खिलौना; छोटी प्रतिक ति – *a.* बहुत छोटा – *vi.* से खेलना, खिलवाड़ करना

trace (ट्रेस) *n.* चिह्न, संकेत, निशान, बहुत थोड़ी मात्रा – *vt.* (के रास्ते) पर चलना; खोज निकालना; रूपरेखा बनाना, खाका बनाना; मान चित्र, नकशे आदि की नकल बनाना – **tracing** *n.* अनुरेखण – **trace element** मिट्टी में बहुत ही अल्प मात्रा में पाये जाने वाले रासायनिक तत्व – **tracing paper** पारदर्शी अनुरेखण- कागज़

trachea (ट्र´कीअ) *n.* श्वासप्रनाल, सांस की नली (*pl.* **tracheae** (ट्र´कीई))

trachoma (ट्र´कोमअ) *n.* कुकरे, रोहे

track (ट्रैक) *n.* किसी वाहन आदि के चलने से बने निशान, लीक, चिन्ह; रास्ता; दौड़ का रास्ता, ट्रैक; रेल की पटरी; टैंक आदि के पहियों पर चढ़ी घूमने वाली लोहे की पट्टी; ग्रामाफ़ोन रिकार्ड आदि में रिकार्ड किए संगीत का एक भाग – *vt.* खोज पर चलना; खोज निकालना – **tracker dog** खोजी कुत्ता – **track events** दौड़ने कूदने आदि की खेल प्रतियोगिताएं – **track record** व्यक्ति, कम्पनी आदि की पिछली सफलताएं व उपलब्धियां – **tracksuit** *n.* दौड़ने कूदने आदि के खिलाड़ियों की गर्म पोशाक, ट्रैक-सूट

tract[1] (ट्रैक्ट) *n.* भूभाग, विस्तार-क्षेत्र

tract[2] (ट्रैक्ट) *n.* पुस्तिका (विशे. धार्मिक)

traction (´ट्रैक्शन) *n.* ख चने की क्रिया

tractor (´ट्रैक्टर) *n.* ट्रैक्टर

trade (ट्रेड) *n.* व्यापार, लेन-देन; कोई भी लाभकारी कार्य; व्यवसाय – *v.* व्यापार करना, लेन/देन करना – **trader** *n.* व्यापारी – **trademark, trade name** *n.* ट्रेडमार्क, मार्का – **tradesman** (´ट्रेड्ज़्मन) *n.* दुकानदार, कुशल कारीगर – **trade union** मज़दूर-संघ – **trade wind** भूमध्य-रेखा की ओर निरंतर चलने वाली पवन, व्यापारिक पवन

tradition (ट्र´डिशन) *n.* परम्परा – **traditional** *a.* परम्परागत

traffic (´ट्रैफ़िक) *n.* सड़क-यातायात; (अवैध) व्यापार – *vi.* अवैध व्यापार करना विशे. नशीली दवाओं का (**trafficked, trafficking**) – **traffic lights** यातायात नियंत्रक रंगीन बत्तियां

tragedy (´ट्रैजिडि) *n.* दुःखद घटना; दुखान्त नाटक अथवा अन्य साहित्यिक रचना, त्रासदी – **tragedian** (ट्र´जीडिअन) *n.*, त्रासदीकार, त्रासदी अभिनेता – **tragic** *a.* दुःखांत; बहुत दुःखद, कारुणिक – **tragically** *adv.* – **tragicomedy** *n.* त्रासिक कामदी

trail (ट्रेल) *vt.* घसीटना, ख चना – *vi.* पीछे घसीटा जाना; (पौधे का) फैल जाना, लटकना – *n.* चिह्न, पदचिह्न; पगडण्डी – **trailer** *n.* एक वाहन से बंधकर चलने वाला दूसरा वाहन, ट्रेलर

train (ट्रेन) *vt.* प्रशिक्षण देना, सिखाना; (बंदूक का) निशाना बांधना – *vi.* (खेलकूद का) अभ्यास करना – *n.* रेलगाड़ी, ट्रेन; विचारों की धारा; सिलसिला, ताँता; कारवां, ताँता; वस्त्र का पीछे ज़मीन पर लटकता भाग; सेवक-दल – **training** *n.* – **trainee** (ट्रे´नी) *n.* प्रशिक्षणार्थी

trait (ट्रेट) *n.* विशेषता

traitor (ट्रेटर) *n.* विश्वासघाती; देशद्रोही, गद्दार – **traitorous** *a.* विश्वासघात करने वाला

trajectory (ट्र'जेक्टरि) *n.* उड़ान-पथ, प्रक्षेप-पथ

tram (ट्रैम) *n.* ट्राम गाड़ी – **tramcar** *n.*

tramp (ट्रैम्प) *vi.* पैदल यात्रा करना विशे. आवारा फिरना; धम-धम पैर पटकते चलना – *n.* आवारागर्द, घुमक्कड़; सैर, पदयात्रा; माल-जहाज़ जो ग्राहकों की इच्छानुसार किसी भी बंदरगाह से माल उठाता है

trample (ट्रैम्पल) *vt.* कुचलना, रौंदना

trampoline (ट्रैम्पलीन) *n.* जिमनास्टिक या कलाबाज़ी के करतब दिखाने के लिए तानी गई मजबूत कैनवस की चादर

trance (ट्रान्स) *n.* बेहोश या चकराये होने की स्थिति; परम आनंद अथवा स्वयं में तल्लीनता की स्थिति, आत्म विस्म ति

tranquil (ट्रैंक्विल) *a.* शांत, शांतिमय – **tranquillity** *n.* – **tranquillize** *vt.* शांत करना – **tranquillizer** *n.* (तनाव दूर करके) शांत करने की औषधि, उपशामक

trans- (*comb. form*) के पार, के परे

transact (ट्रैन्'ज़ैक्ट) *vt.* पूरा करना; सौदा करना – **transaction** *n.* सौदा; कार्यसम्पादन; कारबार संचालन; संस्था की कार्रवाई का ब्यौरा – **transactions** *pl. n.* संस्था की कार्रवाई का ब्यौरा

transcend (ट्रैन्'सेंण्ड) *vt.* से बढ़कर होना, परे होना – **transcendent** *a.*; सामान्य अनुभव से परे; लोकातीत – **transcendence** (ट्रैन्'सेंण्डन्स) *n.* – **transcendental** (ट्रैनसेंन्'डेन्टल) *a.* अनुभवातीत, लोकोत्तर; गूढ़

transcribe (ट्रैन्'स्क्राइब) *vt.* प्रतिलिपि बनाना; बाद में रेडियो-प्रसारण के लिए रिकार्ड करना; भाषा की ध्वनियों को एक विशेष वर्णमाला में लिखना – **transcript** *n.* प्रतिलिपि, प्रतिलेख – **transcription** *n.*

transfer *vt.* (ट्रैन्स्'फ़र, ट्रान्स-) स्थानांतरण करना; एक व्यक्ति से दूसरे को देना (संपत्ति, रोग, अधिकार); (जानकारी, आंकड़े आदि) स्थानंतरित करना (-**rr**-) – *n.* (ट्रैन्सफ़र) स्थानांतरण, बदली, तबादला – **transfer(r)able** *a.* – **transference** *n.* स्थानांतरण

transfigure (ट्रैन्स्'फ़िगर) *vt.* रूपांतरित करना, बदलना – **transfiguration** (ट्रैन्सफ़िग्यु'रेशन) *n.*

transfix (ट्रैन्स्'फ़िक्स) *vt.* जड़वत् कर देना, स्तंभित कर देना; बेधना

transform (ट्रैन्स्'फ़ॉर्म) *vt.* आकार, चरित्र, स्वरूप आदि बदल देना – **transformation** *n.* परिवर्तन, रूपांतर

transfusion (ट्रैन्स्'फ्यूझन) *n.* रुधिर-आदान

transgress (ट्रैन्ज़्'ग्रेस) *vt.* नियम भंग करना; पाप करना, (सीमा) अतिक्रमण करना – **transgression** (ट्रैन्ज़्'ग्रेशन) *n.* अतिक्रमण; नियम भंग की क्रिया – **transgressor** *n.*

trans(s)hip (ट्रैन्'शिप) *vt.* एक जहाज़, गाड़ी आदि से दूसरे पर (माल) पहुंचाना – **transhipment** *n.* वाहनान्तरण

transient (ट्रैन्ज़िअंट) *a.* क्षणिक, क्षणभंगुर

transistor (ट्रैन्'ज़िस्टर) *n.* ट्रांजिस्टर, अनेक उपकरणों में प्रयुक्त एक इलेक्ट्रॉनिकी साधन; ट्रांजिस्टर-रेडियो

transit (ट्रैन्सिट, ट्रैन्ज़िट) *n.* पारगमन, गुज़रना – **transition** *n.* एक स्थिति से दूसरी में परिवर्तन, संक्रमण – **transitional** *a.* – **transitive** (ट्रैन्सिटिव़) *a.* (*active*) सकर्मक (क्रिया) – **transitory** (ट्रैन्सिटरि) *a.* अस्थायी, अल्पकालिक; क्षणिक – **in transit** रास्ते में

translate (ट्रैन्स्'लेट, ट्रान्स्'लेट) *vt.* अनुवाद करना – **translation** *n.* अनुवाद – **translator** *n.*

translucent (ट्रैन्स्'लूसंट, ट्रान्स-) *a.* पारभासक अर्धपारदर्शी – **translucence** *n.*

transmit (ट्रैन्ज़्'मिट, ट्रान्स-) *vt.* पहुंचाना, भेजना, प्रेषित करना; (रेडियो, टेलीविज़न कार्यक्रम) प्रसारित करना – **transmission** (ट्रैंज़् 'मिशन) *n.* प्रसारण; भेजने की क्रिया – **transmitter** *n.* प्रेषक; प्रसारक-यंत्र, ट्रांसमिटर

transmute (ट्रैन्ज़्'म्यूट) *vt.* रूप, स्वभाव, प्रक ति बदल देना – **transmutation** *n.* रूपांतरण

transparent (ट्रैन्स्'पैरंट) *a.* पारदर्शी; स्पष्ट – **transparency** (ट्रैन्स'पैरन्सि) *n.* पारदर्शिता; पीछे से प्रकाश डालने से देखा जाने वाला फ़ोटो-चित्र – **transparently** *adv.*

transpire (ट्रैन्स्'पाइअर) *vi.* पता चलना; *inf.* घटित होना; (पौधों का) पत्तों के द्वारा वाष्प छोड़ना – **transpiration** (ट्रैन्स्प'रेशन) *n.*

transplant *vt.* (ट्रैन्स्'प्लांट) प्रतिरोपित करना; (पौधा) एक स्थान से हटा कर दूसरे स्थान पर लगाना; एक व्यक्ति के शरीर का अंग (हृदय, गुर्दा आदि) दूसरे के शरीर में लगाना – *n.* ('ट्रैन्स्प्लांट) प्रतिरोपण; प्रतिरोपित वस्तु – **transplantation** *n.* प्रतिरोपण

transport *vt.* (ट्रैन्स'पॉर्ट, ट्रान्स-) वहन करना, ढोना; ले जाना – *n.* ('ट्रैन्स्पॉर्ट, ट्रान्स-) परिवहन; सैनिको को ले जाने वाले जहाज, वायुयान आदि – **transportation** *n.* परिवहन, ढोने की क्रिया

transpose (ट्रैन्स्'पोज़, -ट्रान्स-) *vt.* दो वस्तुओं का स्थान (क्रम) बदलना; स्वर-परिवर्तन करना – **transposition** (ट्रैन्स्प'ज़िशन) *n.*

transverse (ट्रैन्ज़्'वर्स, ट्रान्ज़्-) *a.* आड़ा, अनुप्रस्थ

trap (ट्रैप) *n.* फन्दा, जाल; घात; चाल; मुसीबत (जिसमें व्यक्ति फंसा हो); गैस निकलने से रोकने के लिए पाइप-व्यवस्था – *vt.* पकड़ना; फंसाना; चाल में फंसाना (**-pp-**) – **trapdoor** *n.* छत या फर्श में दरवाज़ा

trapeze (ट्र'पीज़) *n.* कलाबाज़ी का झूला (विशे. सरकस में)

trappings ('ट्रैपिंग्ज़) *pl. n.* साज-सामान

trash (ट्रैश) *n.* कूड़ा-करकट, रद्दी; बकवास

trauma ('ट्रॉमअ) *n.* मानसिक आघात, सदमा – **traumatic** *a.* मानसिक आघात पहुंचाने वाला **-traumatize** *vt.* को मानसिक आघात पहुंचाना

travail ('ट्रैवेल) *n./vi.* कठिन परिश्रम (करना)

travel ('ट्रैवल) *v.* (लम्बी) यात्रा करना, चलना (**-ll-**) – *n.* यात्रा, पर्यटन – *pl.* यात्रा (व त्तांत) – **traveller** *n.* – **travelogue** ('ट्रैवलॉग) *n.* यात्रा-फिल्म, यात्रा-विवरण, सफ़रनामा

traverse ('ट्रैवर्स) *vt.* पार करना; (तोप का) घूमना – *n.* आड़ी रखी हुई वस्तु – *a.* आड़ा

travesty ('ट्रैविस्टि) *n.* भोंडी नकल; उपहास, विडम्बना

tray (ट्रे) *n.* ट्रे, तश्तरी

treachery *n.* धोखा, विश्वासघात – **treacherous** ('ट्रेचरस) *a.* विश्वासघाती

tread ('ट्रेड) *vt.* पर पैर रखना; कुचलना; दमन करना – *vi.* चलना (**trod** *pt.*, **trodden** *or* **trod** *pp.*, **treading** *pr. p*) – *n.* चाल, चलने का ढंग, पगध्वनि; सीढ़ी (जिस पर कदम रखा जाता है) का ऊपरी तल, सोपान-पाद; टायर का ज़मीन को छूने वाला भाग

treadle ('ट्रेड्ल) *n.* मशीन का पहिया घुमाने के लिए पाँव से घुमाया जाने वाला भाग

treason ('ट्रीज़न) *n.* राजद्रोह, गद्दारी; विश्वासघात

treasure ('ट्रेझ़र) *n.* खज़ाना, कोष – *vt.* बहुमूल्य मानना, संजोए रखना, (दिल में) बनाए रखना – **treasurer** *n.* खज़ांची – **treasury** ('ट्रेझ़रि) *n.* खज़ाना, राजकोष

treat (ट्रीट) *n.* आनन्द, मनोरंजन – *vt.* बरताव करना, पेश आना; का इलाज करना ; (*of* के साथ) विषय पर बातचीत करना; खिलाना-पिलाना; समझना, मानना; रासायनिक पदार्थ छिड़कना, लगाना – *vi.* मोल-तोल करना – **treatment** *n.* इलाज;

व्यवहार; कला वस्तु, विषय को प्रस्तुत करने का ढंग, प्रतिपादन

treatise (ˈट्रीटिज़) *n.* शोधात्मक पुस्तक, निबंध

treaty (ˈट्रीटि) *n.* संधि, संधिपत्र

treble (ˈट्रेबल) *a./v.* तिगुना (होना, करना)

tree (ट्री) *n.* वृक्ष

trek (ट्रेक) *n./vi.* लम्बी यात्रा (करना); विशे. पैदल यात्रा –**trekker** *n.* – **go trekking** पहाड़ों में लंबी पैदल यात्रा करना

trellis (ˈट्रेलिस) *n.* बेलों को चढ़ाने की जाफ़री, जाली

tremble (ˈट्रेम्बल) *vi.* काँपना, डर से थरथराना – *n.* कँपकँपी

tremendous (ट्रिˈमेंण्डस) *a.* विशाल, बहुत अधिक; *inf.* आश्चर्यजनक, असाधारण; *inf.* बहुत बढ़िया

tremor (ˈट्रेमर) *n.* कँपकँपी; हल्का भूकम्प

tremulous (ˈट्रेम्युलस) *a.* काँपता हुआ

trench (ट्रेन्च) *n.* खाई, खंदक विशे. युद्ध में बचाव-साधन के रूप में –**trench coat** एक प्रकार की बरसाती

trenchant (ˈट्रेन्चंट) *a.* चुभता, कटु

trend (ट्रेण्ड) *n.* प्रवृत्ति, झुकाव; सामान्य दिशा; प्रचलन, फैशन – **trendy** *inf. a.* नये ज़माने का (विचार); नये फैशन के (कपड़े)

trepidation (ट्रेपिˈडेशन) *n.* घबराहट, डर

trespass (ˈट्रेस्पस) *vi.* (किसी स्थान) में अनाधिकार प्रवेश करना – *n.* अनाधिकार प्रवेश

tresses (ˈट्रेसिज़) *pl. n.* लट, जुल्फ़

trestle (ˈट्रेसल) *n.* लकड़ी का ढांचा, घोड़ी, टिकटिकी

tri- (*comb. form*) त्रि–, तीन

triad (ˈट्राइऐड) *n.* त्रय, त्रयी, तीन का वर्ग

trial (ˈट्राइअल) *n.* परीक्षण; प्रयोग; *Law* मुकदमा; संकट

triangle (ˈट्राइऐंगल) *n.* त्रिकोण

tribe (ट्राइब) *n.* जनजाति, कबीला; (व्यवसाय) वर्ग – **tribal** *a.* जनजाति-सम्बंधी

tribulation (ट्रिब्युˈलेशन) *n.* दुःख-तकलीफ, कष्ट, मुसीबत– **tribunal** (ट्राइˈब्यूनल) *n.* न्यायालय; अधिकरण, विशे. मामले की जांच व निर्णय के लिए नियुक्त न्यायाधिकरण; जज का बैठने का स्थान

tributary (ˈट्रिब्युटरि) *n.* सहायक नदी

tribute (ˈट्रिब्यूट) *n.* श्रद्धांजलि, प्रशंसा; एक राज्य द्वारा दूसरे को दिया जाने वाला कर, खिराज – **pay tribute to** को श्रद्धांजलि अर्पित करना

trick (ट्रिक) *n.* दांव-पेच; धोखा, हाथ की सफाई; चाल, ढब (*trick of the trade*); शरारत; ताश में, एक हाथ; पारी – *vt.* धोखा देना, छलना, शरारत करना – **trickery** (ˈट्रिकरि) *n.* – **trickster** *n.* चालबाज – **tricky** *a.* कठिन, जटिल; चालाक, धूर्त

trickle (ˈट्रिकल) *vi.* बूंद-बूंद या पतली धार में टपकना या बहना – *n.* बूंद-बूंद; अल्प मात्रा

tricolour (ˈट्राइकलर) *a.* तिरंगा – *n.* तिरंगा झंडा जैसे भारत का

tricycle (ˈट्राइसिकल) *n.* तिपहिया साइकिल

trident (ˈट्राइडंट) *n.* त्रिशूल

triennial (ट्राइˈऐंनिअल) *a.* त्रैवार्षिक – *n.*

trifle (ˈट्राइफ़ल) *n.* , मामूली चीज़, बहुत थोड़ी राशि – *vi.* खिलवाड़ करना; व्यर्थ बातों या काम में समय गँवाना – **trifler** *n.* – **trifling** *a.* मामूली, महत्वहीन

trigger (ˈट्रिगर) *n.* बंदूक आदि का घोड़ा – *vt.* (प्राय: *off* के साथ) शुरू करना –**trigger-happy** *a.* नासमझी का आचरण करने वाला, विशे. अस्त्रों के उपयोग में

trigonometry (ट्रिगˈनॉमिट्रि) *n.* त्रिकोणमिति (गणित की एक शाखा)

trill (ट्रिल) *vi.* कांपती आवाज़ में गाना; धीमें स्वर में गाना; कूजना – *n.* स्वर कम्पन

trillion (ट्रिल्यन) *n.* एक लाख करोड़, 10^{12}

trilogy (ट्रिलजि) *n.* तीन सम्बंधित (साहित्यिक) रचनाओं की श्रंखला; त्रयी

trim (ट्रिम) *a.* साफ़-सुथरा; चुस्त; छरहरा; ठीक-ठाक, सुव्यवस्थित, देखने में आकर्षक – *vt.* कतरना, छांटना; संवारना; व्यवस्थित करना, (खर्चा) कम करना (-**mm**-) – *n.* सजावट; सुव्यवस्था; ठीक कटे हुए बाल – **trimming** *n.* (प्राय: *pl.*) सजावट; गोटा-पट्टी – **in good trim** अच्छी अवस्था में; स्वस्थ

trinity (ट्रिनिटि) *n.* तीन का समूह, त्रिक; (**T**-) ईश्वर के तीन रूप, त्रिमूर्ति

trinket (ट्रिंकिट) *n.* सस्ता, साधारण गहना

trio (ट्रीओ) *n.* तीन का वर्ग, त्रिक; (*pl.* -s)

triode (ट्राइओड) *n. Electronics* तीन इलैक्ट्रोड का वाल्व

trip (ट्रिप) *n.* छोटी आमोद यात्रा; लड़खड़ाहट; *inf.* नशीली दवा का भ्रांतिजनक प्रभाव – *vi.* लड़खड़ाना, गिर जाना; भूल करना; फुदकना, थिरकना, नाचना – *vt.* गिरा देना – **tripper** *n*, पर्यटक, सैलानी

tripartite (ट्राइ पार्टाइट) *a.* त्रिभागी, त्रिपक्षीय, त्रिदलीय

tripe (ट्राइप) *n.* पकाने के लिए तैयार किया गया गाय-बैल का पेट का भाग; *inf.* बकवास

triple (ट्रिपल) *a.* तिगुना – *v.* तिगुना करना या होना – **triplet** (ट्रिप्लिट) *n.* तीन समान वस्तुएं; एक ही स्त्री के तीन एक साथ जन्मे बच्चों में से कोई – **triple jump** तीन छलांगों वाली कूद प्रतियोगिता

triplicate *a.* (ट्रिप्लिकिट) त्रिविध, तेहरा – *vt.* (ट्रिप्लिकेट), तीन प्रतियां बनाना – *n.* (ट्रिप्लिकिट) तीन गुना या तेहरा होने की स्थिति; तीन प्रतियों में से कोई

tripod (ट्राइपॉड) *n.* तिपाई, तीन टांगों का स्टैंड

trite (ट्राइट) *a.* घिसा-पिटा, मामूली

triumph (ट्राइअम्फ़) *n.* बहुत बड़ी सफलता; विजय; विजयोल्लास – *vi.* अपूर्व सफलता पाना, जीतना – **triumphal** (ट्राइ अम्फ़ल) *a.* – **triumphant** *a.* विजयी; उल्लासभरा

trivia (ट्रिविअ) *pl. n.* मामूली वस्तुएं – **trivial** *a.* महत्वहीन, साधारण – **triviality** (ट्रिवि ऐलिटि) *n.* ओछापन; बहुत मामूली बात – **trivialize** *vt.* गंभीर विषय/बात का महत्व घटा देना, मज़ाक में लेना

trod (ट्रॉड) *pt.* **trodden, trod** TREAD का *pp.*

trolley (ट्रॉलि) *n.* (होटल आदि में) खाने-पीने की सामग्री इधर-उधर ले जाने वाली ट्राली; ठेला; **US** ट्राम – **trolley bus** (ट्राम की तरह) बिजली से चलने वाली बस

trollop (ट्रॉलप) *n.* असंयमी स्त्री, कुलटा

trombone (ट्रॉम् बोन) *n.* तुरही (बाजा)

troop (ट्रूप) *n.* दल, टोली; झुंड; (सेना का) रिसाला, घुड़सवार सेना की टुकड़ी – (~ **s**) *pl.* सैनिक – *vi.* टोली बनाकर चलना; एकत्र हो जाना – **trooper** *n.* घुड़सवार सैनिक

trope (ट्रोप) *n.* अलंकार (जैसे उपमा)

trophy (ट्रोफ़ि) *n.* पुरस्कार, ट्राफी

tropic (ट्रॉपिक) *n.* कर्क-रेखा (**tropic of Cancer**) या मकर-रेखा (**tropic of Capricorn**) – *pl.* उष्णकटिबंध – **tropical** *a.* उष्णकटिबंधीय; बहुत गरम (मौसम)

trot (ट्रॉट) *vi.* (घोड़े का) दुलकी चाल से चलना; (व्यक्ति का) छोटे डग भरते हुए दौड़ना (-**tt**-) – *n.* दुलकी चाल; तेज़ चाल – **trotter** *n.* घुड़दौड़ में दुलकी चाल से दौड़ने वाला घोड़ा

trouble (ट्रबल) *n.* तकलीफ; परेशानी; मुसीबत; असुविधा; ध्यान; मशीन में खराबी – *vt.* कष्ट देना; परेशान करना – *vi.* दुःखी होना, के बारे में चिंतित होना; विशेष ध्यान देना, प्रयत्न करना – **troubled** *a.* परेशान, अशांतिपूर्ण (क्षेत्र) –

troublemaker *n.* झगड़ा कराने वाला व्यक्ति – **troubleshooter** *n.* सुलह-सफाई कराने वाला व्यक्ति – **troublesome** *a.* कष्टकारी, परेशान करने वाला

trough (ट्रॉफ़) *n.* पशुओं के खाने-पीने की नांद; दो लहरों के बीच का स्थान, गर्त; *Meteorology* कम दबाव वाला क्षेत्र

trounce (ट्राउन्स) *vt.* बुरी तरह से पीटना या हरा देना

troupe (ट्रूप) *n.* कलाकार-मण्डली – **trouper** *n.* कलाकार-मण्डली का सदस्य

trousers (ˈट्राउज़र्ज़) *pl. n.* पतलून; पायजामा

trousseau (ˈट्रूसो) *n.* दुल्हन का वस्त्र-संग्रह व साज़-समान

trout (ट्राउट) *n.* मीठे जल की कर्बुरी मछली, ट्राउट

trowel (ˈट्राउअल) *n.* करनी, पाटा, खुरपा

truant (ˈट्रूअंट) *n.* बिना छुट्टी अनुपस्थित रहने वाला व्यक्ति विशे. स्कूल से बच्चा – *a.*

truce (ट्रूस) *n.* युद्ध विराम; अस्थायी शांति

truck[1] (ट्रक) *n.* ट्रक

truck[2] (ट्रक) *n.* लेन-देन विशे. **have no truck with** में

truculent (ˈट्रक्युलंट) *a.* लड़ाका, अवज्ञाकारी

trudge (ट्रज) *vi.* थके-थके चलना

true (ट्रू) *a.* सच, ठीक, सही, खरा; असली – **truism** (ˈट्रूइज़म) *n.* स्वयंसिद्ध तथ्य – **truly** *adv.* सचमुच, वास्तव में – **truth** (ट्रूथ) *n.* सच्चाई; सच बात – **truthful** *a.* सच्चा, सत्यवादी – **truthfully** *adv.* – **true colours** असली रूप/चेहरा (व्यक्ति का)

truffle (ˈट्रफ़ल) *n.* एक प्रकार की खुम्भी; आकार में मिलती-जुलती एक मिठाई

truism *n.* दे. TRUE

trump[1] (ट्रम्प) *n.* तुरुप का पत्ता – **trump card** अचूक युक्ति, ब्रह्मास्त्र – **trump up** गढ़ना

trump[2] (ट्रम्प) *n.* तुरही; तुरही की आवाज़

trumpet (ˈट्रम्पिट) *n.* तुरही (बाजा) – *vi.*

truncate (ट्रंङˈकेट) *vt.* काट कर छोटा कर देना

truncheon (ˈट्रंचन) *n.* गदा, डण्डा

trundle (ˈट्रंड्ल) *vi.* भारी-भरकम वस्तु जैसे बस का बेढंगा चलना, लुढ़कना

trunk (ट्रंक) *n.* पेड़ का तना; धड़; सन्दूक; सूंड – (~ **s**) *pl.* पुरुष की तैरने की पोशाक – **trunk call** ट्रंककाल, लंबी दूरी पर टेलीफोन से बातचीत – **trunk line** रेलवे या टेलीफोन की मुख्य लाइन – **trunk road** मुख्य मार्ग, राजमार्ग

truss (ट्रस) *vt.* कस कर बांध देना – *n.* सहारा; हर्निया रोग में बांधी जाने वाली पेटी

trust (ट्रस्ट) *n.* आस्था, पक्का विश्वास, भरोसा; आपसी होड़ रोकने व कीमतें न गिरने देने के लिए बना (अवैध) व्यापार संघ; संभालने का उत्तरदायित्व; धरोहर – *vt.* भरोसा करना, विश्वास करना, आशा करना, संभालने के लिए सौंपना – **trustee** (ट्रˈस्टी) *n.* न्यासी, ट्रस्टी, जिसे संपत्ति संभालने को दी हो – **trustworthy** (ˈट्रस्ट्वर्दि) *a.* विश्वसनीय, भरोसेमंद; ईमानदार; सुरक्षित

truth (ट्रूथ) दे. TRUE

try (ट्राइ) *vi.* प्रयास करना, कोशिश करना – *vt.* (कुछ करने का) प्रयास करना; प्रयोग करके देखना; परखना; पर अधिक भार डालना, परेशान करना; पर मुकदमा चलाना; (**tried, trying**) – *n.* प्रयत्न, प्रयास – **tried** *a.* सिद्ध, आज़माया हुआ – **trying** *a.* कष्टकर; कठिन

tryst (ट्रिस्ट) *n.* (प्रेमियों की) पूर्व निश्चित भेंट, मिलन स्थल

T-shirt, tee-shirt *n.* टी-शर्ट

tsunami (सुˈनामि) *n.* भूकम्प से उत्पन्न विशाल, विनाशकारी समुद्री लहर

tub (टब) *n.* टब, नांद; स्नान (का टब)

tube (ट्यूब) *n.* नली; टुथपेस्ट, तरल दवाइयों आदि की ट्यूब; **UK** (*underground*) भूमिगत रेलवे – **tubular** *a.*

tuber (´ट्यूबर) *n.* कंद (आलू आदि)
tuberculosis (ट्युबर्क्यु´लोसिस) *n.* तपेदिक
tuck (टक) *vt.* छिपा लेना; ठूंस देना; समेटना; चुन्नट डालना; तह लगाना; लपेटना – *n.* चुनट; *inf.* अल्पाहार
Tuesday (´ट्यूज़्डे) *n.* मंगलवार
tuft (टफ़्ट) *n.* परों, बालों आदि का गुच्छा
tug (टग) *vt.* झटके से ख चना; झटका देना (**-gg-**) – *n.* झटका; नावों, जहाजों आदि को ख चने वाली नाव; झटका – **tug of war** रस्साकशी का खेल
tuition (ट्यू´इशन) *n.* शिक्षण, शिक्षाशुल्क; (*private tuition*) व्यक्तिगत शिक्षण, ट्यूशन
tulip (´ट्यूलिप) *n.* ट्यूलिप फूल (का पौधा)
tumble (´टम्बल) *v.* धड़ाम से गिरना या गिराना, कलाबाज़ी खाना; सिलवटें डालना, गड़बड़ कर देना – *n.* गिरना, कलाबाज़ी – **tumbler** *n.* गिलास; कलाबाज; ताले का खटका – **tumble-down** *a.* टूटा-फूटा
tummy (´टमि) *n. inf.* (बच्चों की ज़बान में) पेट
tumour (´ट्यूमर) *n.* अर्बुद, रसौली
tumult (´ट्यूमल्ट) *n.* कोलाहल, शोरगुल – **tumultuous** (ट्यू´मल्ट्युअस) *a.* उपद्रवी; शोर भरा
tuna (´ट्यून्अ) *n.* दे. TUNNY
tundra (´टण्ड्अ) *n.* विशाल उत्तर ध्रुवीय व क्षरहित प्रदेश, टुण्ड्रा का मैदान
tune (ट्यून) *n.* धुन, लय, राग; वाद्य-यंत्र के स्वर ठीक करना; स्वर-संगति; तालमेल; मानसिक अवस्था – *vt.* सुर मिलाना; सुचारू रूप से चलने के लिए मशीन (का इंजन) ट्यून करना, ठीक करना; रेडियों की ध्वनि ठीक करना – **tuner** *n.* – **tune in** रेडियो या टेलीविज़न पर स्टेशन लगाना
tunnel (´टनल) *n./vi.* सुरंग (बनाना); बिल (बनाना) (**-ll-**) – **tunneller** *n.*
tunny (´टनि) *n.*(*tuna* भी) एक खाई जाने वाली बड़ी समुद्री मछली
tup (टप) *n.* मेढ़ा
turban (´टर्बन) *n.* पगड़ी, साफा
turbid (´टर्बिड) *a.* गँदला (पानी); धुंधला; अव्यवस्थित – **turbidity** *n.*
turbine (´टर्बिन, ´टर्बाइन) *n.* टर्बाइन
turbo- (*comb. form*) टर्बाइन से सम्बंधित या उससे चलने वाला –**turbojet** *n.* जेट विमान
turbulent (´टर्ब्युलंट) *a.* अशांत, अस्त-व्यस्त; उग्र, तूफ़ानी – **turbulence** *n.* विक्षोभ; विप्लव; अशांति, विशे. वायुमण्डल में
turf (टर्फ़) *n.* घास की थिगली; घास का लान (मैदान) (*pl.* **turfs, turves**) – *vt.* (लान पर) घास लगाना– **the turf** घुड़दौड़, घुड़दौड़ का मैदान
turgid (´टर्जिड) *a.* फूला हुआ; बड़े-बड़े शब्दों युक्त, शब्दाडम्बरपूर्ण; उफनती हुई (नदी) – **turgidity** *n.* सूजन; स्फीति; शब्दाडम्बर
turkey (´टर्कि) *n.* खाया जाने वाला एक बड़ा पक्षी, टर्की, पीरू
turmeric (´टर्मरिक) *n.* हल्दी
turmoil (´टर्मॉइल) *n.* शोरगुल, हुल्लड़, खलबली
turn (टर्न) *v.* मोड़ना, मुड़ना, घूमना, घुमाना, (की) स्थिति अथवा दिशा बदलना, मुंह घुमाना; (*into* के साथ) स्वभाव या प्रक ति बदलना – *vt.* गढ़ना, बनाना – *n.* घुमाव, मोड़; झुकाव आदि; परिवर्तन, पलटा; बारी; दौर; फेरा, चक्कर– **turner** *n.*– **turnaround** *n.* आमूल परिवर्तन (बुरी से अच्छी स्थिति में) – **turncoat** *n.* दलबदलू – **turnout** *n.* भीड़, जमाव – **turnover** *n.* अवधिविशेष में कुल बिक्री; उत्पादन– **turnstile** (´टर्न्स्टाइल) *n.* चक्रद्वार, गोल घूमने वाला द्वार – **turntable** (´टर्न्टेबल) *n.* घूम-चक्कर – **turn-up** *n.* पतलून में नीचे मोहरी का मोड़ – **turn down** इनकार कर देना; (ध्वनि आदि)

कम करना) – **turn off** (सुनना, सोचना आदि) बंद कर देना – **turn up** आ जाना, मिल जाना

turnip (ˊटर्निप) *n.* शलजम

turpentine (ˊटर्पन्टाइन) *n.* तारपीन का तेल, गंधाबरोजा

turpitude (ˊटर्पिट्यूड) *n.* भ्रष्टता, चरित्रहीनता

turquoise (ˊटर्क्वॉइज़) *n.* फ़िरोज़ा मणि – *a.* फिरोज़ी रंग

turret (ˊटरिट) *n.* बुर्ज, कंगूरा; युद्धपोत, टैंक आदि पर तोप के घूमने के लिए लगा लोहे का कंगूरा

turtle (ˊटर्ट्ल) *n.* समुद्री कछुआ – **turtleneck (sweater)** *n.* गोल बंद गला (ऐसा स्वेटर)

tusk (टस्क) *n.* हाथी का दांत; जंगली सूअर आदि का बड़ा दांत, खाँग

tussle (ˊटसल) *n./v.* संघर्ष, हाथापाई (करना)

tutelage (ˊट्यूटिलिज) *n.* संरक्षण, अभिभावक का कार्य या पद

tutor (ˊट्यूटर) *n.* ट्यूटर, एक छात्र अथवा छोटे ग्रुप को शिक्षा देने वाला शिक्षक, अनुशिक्षक, निजी शिक्षक – *v.* ट्यूटर के रूप में कार्य करना – **tutorial** (ट्यूˊटॉरिअल) *n.* (कालिज में) अध्यापक द्वारा एक छोटे छात्र समूह को दिया जाने वाला शिक्षण समय

TV television का संक्षेप

twang (ट्वैङ) *n.* (वाद्य में) टन की आवाज़; टंकार, नाक से निकली ध्वनि – *v.*

tweak (ट्वीक) *vt.* चिकोटी काटना, (कान, नाक) मरोड़ना – *n.* चिकोटी

tweed (ट्वीड) *n.* मोटा ऊनी कपड़ा – *pl.* ट्वीड का बना सूट

tweet (ट्वीट) *n. vi* च-च (करना)

tweezers (ˊट्वीज़र्ज़) *pl. n.* चिमटी

twelve (ट्वेल्व़) *n./a.* बारह – **twelfth** (ट्वेल्फ़्थ) *a.* बारवां – *n.* – **twelve o'clock** दोपहर बारह बजे; मध्यरात्रि का समय

twenty (ˊट्वेन्टि) *n./a.* बीस – **twentieth** (ˊट्वेन्टिइथ) *a.* बीसवां – *n.*

twice (ट्वाइस) *adv.* दो बार; दुगना

twiddle (ˊट्विड्ल) *vi.* फ़िराना, मोड़ना

twig (ट्विग) *n.* टहनी

twilight (ˊट्वाइलाइट) *n.* सांध्य प्रकाश, झुटपुटा

twin (ट्विन) *n.* जुड़वा (बच्चों) में से एक – *a.* जुड़वां – *v.* जोड़ा बनाना, जोड़ा बनना

twine (ट्वाइन) *v.* (पौधे का) गुंथना, (के चारों ओर) लिपटना – *n.* सुतली, डोरा

twinge (ट्विंज) *n.* टीस, हूक; पश्चाताप

twinkle (ˊट्विंकल) *vi.* टिमटिमाना, चमकना; (आँखे) झपकना – *n.* टिमटिमाहट, चमक– **twinkling** *n.* पल भर, क्षण भर

twirl (ट्वर्ल) *vt.* घुमाना, मरोड़ना; चक्कर खिलाना – *vi.* घूमना, चक्कर खाना, फिरना

twist (ट्विस्ट) *v.* गूंथना, बटना; तोड़-मरोड़ देना; बदल देना – *n.* मरोड़, घुमाव, मरोड़ी या गूंथी वस्तु (धागा, रस्सी आदि)

twit (ट्विट) *n. inf.* मूर्ख व्यक्ति, बुद्धू – *vt.* चिढ़ाना, ताना मारना (**-tt-**)

twitch (ट्विच) *v.* झटका देना; फड़कना; खिंच जाना – *n.*

twitter (ट्विटर) *vi.* (चिड़ियों का) चहकना – *n.* चहचहाहट

two (टू) *n./a.* दो – **twofold** *a./adv.* दुगना – **two-faced** *a.* कपटी, धोखेबाज़; दो मुंहा – **two fold** *a.* दो भागों में; दुगना – **two-ply** *a.* दो धागे, तारों वाला (ऊन आदि) – **two-way** *a.* दुतरफी (सड़क, व्यापार आदि)

tycoon (टाइˊकून) *n.* (**business tycoon** भी) शक्तिशाली उद्योगपति

type (टाइप) *n.* वर्ग, जाति, प्ररूप; प्रकार; नमूना; प्रतीक, टाइप (छपाई, टाइप के धातु-अक्षर) – *vt.* टंकण (टाइप) करना; का प्रतीक होना, वर्गीकरण करना – **typescript** (ˊटाइप्स्क्रिप्ट)

n. टाइप प्रति – **typewrite** *v.* टंकण (टाइप) करना – **typewriter** (ˊटाइप्राइटर) *n.* टाइपराइटर – **typist** (ˊटाइपिस्ट) *n.* टंकक, टाइपिस्ट

typhoid (ˊटाइफ़ॉइड) *n.* आंत्रज्वर, मोतीझरा, टाइफ़ाइड – *a.* – **typhus** (ˊटाइफ़स) *n.* एक छूत की बीमारी

typhoon (टाइˊफून) *n.* प्रचण्ड तूफ़ान, चक्रवात

typical (ˊटिपिकल) *a.* प्रतिनिधक, नमून के रूप में; विशिष्ट

typify (ˊटिपिफ़ाइ) *vt.* का प्रतीक अथवा नमूना होना **(-ified, -ifying)**

tyrant (ˊटाइरंट) *n.* अत्याचारी, तानाशाह – **tyrannical** (टिˊरैनिकल) *a.* अत्याचारी, निरंकुश – **tyrannize** (ˊटिरनाइज़) *v.* तानाशाही करना, अत्याचार करना – **tyranny** (ˊटिरनि) *a.* तानाशाही, अत्याचार

tyre (टाइअर) *n.* टायर; बैलगाड़ी के पहिये पर लोहे की हाल

tyro (ˊटाइरो) *n.* नौसिखिया

U

ubiquitous (यू´बिक्विटस) *a.* सर्वव्यापक, सब जगह मौजूद
udder (´अडर) *n.* (गाय आदि का) थन
UFO Unidentified Flying Object (उड़न तश्तरी) का संक्षेप
ugly (´अग्लि) *a.* कुरूप, बदसूरत; (*fig.*) घिनौना; अनिष्ट सूचक – **ugliness** *n.* कुरूपता, घिनौनापन
UHF ultra high frequency का संक्षेप
UK United Kingdom का संक्षेप
ulcer (´अल्सर) *n.* फोड़ा, व्रण; (*mouth ulcer* भी) छाला – **ulcerous** *a.* व्रण-संबंधी
ult. ultimate; ultimo का संक्षेप
ulterior (अल्´टिअरिअर) *a.* परवर्ती, छिपा हुआ (इरादा); अप्रत्यक्ष
ultimate (´अल्टिमिट) *a.* अंतिम; सबसे महत्वपूर्ण; उच्चतम – **ultimately** *adv.* अंत में, आखिरकार – **ultimatum** (अल्टि´मेटम) *n.* अंतिम चेतावनी, अंतिम रूप से प्रस्तुत (समझौते की) शर्तें, अल्टीमेटम (*pl.* **-s, -ta**) – **ultimo** (´अल्टिमो) *adv.* गत मास का
ultra- (*comb. form*) परे, से भी अधिक, चरम जैसे **ultramodern** *a.* में
ultra high frequency बहुत कम दैर्घ्य की रेडियो की तरंग-पट्टी
ultramarine (अल्ट्रम´रीन) *n.* नीला रंजक (रंग)
ultrasonic (अल्ट्र´सॉनिक) *a.* पराध्वनि, मनुष्य की श्रवण शक्ति से परे की ध्वनि तरंगों सम्बन्धी – **ultrasound** *n.* पराध्वनि; एक प्रकार का डाक्टरी, परीक्षण
ultraviolet (अल्ट्र´वाइअलिट) *a.* पराबैंगनी (सूर्य की किरणें)
ultra vires (अल्ट्र´वाइरीज़) *Law* अवैध, गैर कानूनी
umbilical (अम्´बिलिकल) *a.* नाभि (के आस पास) का – **umbilical cord** नाल; अंतरिक्ष यात्री को अंतरिक्षयान से जोड़ने वाली डोरी
umbrage (´अम्ब्रिज) *n.* नाराज़गी, असंतोष
umbrella (अम्´ब्रेलअ) *n.* छाता, छतरी
umpire (´अम्पाइअर) *n.* खेल-निर्णायक, अम्पायर; पंच, मध्यस्थ – *v.* किसी खेल में अम्पायर का कार्य करना
umpteen (अम्प्´टीन) *inf. a.* बहुत से – **for the umpteenth time** बहुत बार पहले और एक बार फिर
UN United Nations का संक्षेप
un- (*comb. form*) नकारात्मक (जैसे **unfair, unreal** में), विपरीत आदि
unacceptable *a.* अमान्य
unaccompanied *a.* अकेला
unaccustomed *a.* अनभ्यस्त
unaffected *a.* अप्रभावित; सीधा-साधा
unanimous (यू´नैनिमस) *a.* एकमत, सर्वसम्मत – **unanimously** *adv.* एकमत से – **unanimity** (यून´निमिटि) *n.* सर्वसम्मति
unapproachable *a.* अप्राप्य, जो आसानी से किसी से न मिले
unassuming (अन´स्यूमिङ) *a.* विनीत
unattached *a.* गैर शादीशुदा; असम्बद्ध, असंलग्न
unattractive *a.* अनाकर्षक
unauthorized *a.* अनधिकृत
unavailing (अन´वेलिङ) *a.* व्यर्थ, निष्फल
unaware *a.* अनजान, बेखबर – **unawares** *adv.* अनजाने, अकस्मात
unbearable *a.* असहनीय
unbelievable *a.* अविश्वसनीय; बहुत (अच्छा या बुरा)
unbias(s)ed (अन्´बाइअस्ट) *a.* निष्पक्ष
unbreakable *a.* न टूटने वाला

unbroken *a.* अखण्ड, निरंतर

uncalled-for *a.* अनावश्यक

uncanny (अन्'कैनि) *a.* भयानक, रहस्यमय, अस्वभाविक

unceasing *a.* निरंतर

unceremonious (अन्सेंरि'मोनिअस) *a.* अनौपचारिक, बेतकल्लुफ़

uncertain (अन'सर्टन) *a.* अनिश्चित, अस्थिर; अचानक बदलने वाला (मिज़ाज) ढीला

uncharacteristic *a.* (की) प्रकृति/चरित्र के विपरीत

uncharitable *a.* अनुचित

unchecked *a.* बेरोक, अनियंत्रित

uncle ('अंकल) *n.* चाचा; ताऊ; मामा; मौसा; फूफा

uncomfortable *a.* बेआराम; परेशान, बेचैन

uncommitted *a.* निरपेक्ष, स्वतंत्र

uncommonly *adv.* असामान्य, असाधारण

uncomplimentary (अन्कॉम्पि- लि'मेंण्टरि) *a.* निन्दात्मक, अपमानजनक

unconcerned *a.* उदासीन

unconditional *a.* बिना शर्त (बातचीत आदि)

unconscionable *a.* अनैतिक; बहुत अधिक

unconscious *a.* मूर्छित, बेहोश; (अपने विचारों से) अनजान, अनभिज्ञ, अनजाने में किया (कार्य आदि) – *n.* अचेतन मन (में विचार) – **unconsciously** *adv.* – **unconsciousness** *n.* मूर्छा, बेहोशी

unconstitutional *a.* असंवैधानिक

unconventional *a.* गैर-पारम्परिक

uncoordinated *a.* असम्बद्ध

uncouth (अन्'कूथ) *a.* गंवार, असभ्य

uncritical *a.* जो जांच-परख न करे

unctuous ('अंक्ट्युअस) *a.* चिकना; बातचीत, व्यवहार में चिकना-चुपड़ा

undecided *a.* अनिश्चयी

undemanding *a.* बिना चुनौती (काम); जो अधिक कुछ न चाहे

under ('अंडर) *prep.* के नीचे; के अंदर; के भीतर; से कम; के अनुसार, के अंतर्गत, के नाम से; के राज्यकाल या समय में – *adv.* के नीचे – *a.* निचला

under- (*comb. form*) नीचे (के), अंदर के, कम आदि जैसे **underline, underpass**

underarm *a.* (माप) बगल से कमर तक; *Sport* (गेंदबाज़ी में) कंधे से नीचे हाथ घुमाते हुए

undergo (अंडर्'गो) *vt.* भुगतना, सहना, झेलना (– **went, – gone, – going**)

undergraduate (अंडर्'ग्रैड्युइट) *n.* पूर्वस्नातक

underground *a.* भूमिगत, जमीन के नीचे; गुप्त, छिपा हुआ – *adv.* गुप्त रूप से – *n.* सरकार का गुप्त परंतु संगठित प्रतिरोध; भूमिगत-रेल व्यवस्था

underhand ('अंडर्हैंड) *a.* गुप्त, धोखे या बेइमानी का (तरीका आदि)

underline *vt.* रेखांकित करना; पर बल देना

underling ('अंडर्लिङ) *n.* मातहत; नौकर

undermine *vt.* नीचे से खोखला कर देना; हिला देना (आत्मविश्वास, स्थिति आदि), जड़ें खोदना

underneath *adv.* (के) नीचे, (के तले) –*prep.* के नीचे – *a./n.* निचला भाग

underpass *n.* रेल-मार्ग अथवा सड़क आदि के नीचे से गुजरने वाली सड़क का भाग, अंडरपास

underrate *vt.* को (वास्तविक योग्यता) से कम समझना, कम महत्व देना

undersell *vi.* सामान्य दाम से कम पर बेचना

undersigned ('अंडर्साइन्ड) *n.* व्यक्ति जिसके/जिनके मसविदे, अर्ज़ी आदि के नीचे हस्ताक्षर हों

understand (अंडर्'स्टैंड) *v.* समझना, जान जाना – *vt.* अर्थ या परिणाम निकालना, मान लेना (– **stood, – standing**) – **understanding** *n.* समझ; विचार समझौता; शर्त – *a.* हमदर्द

understudy (´अंडर्स्टडि) *n.* आवश्यकता होने पर नियमित अभिनेता या (अभिनेत्री) का स्थान लेने वाला व्यक्ति
undertake (अंडर्´टेक) *vt.* की जिम्मेवारी अपने ऊपर लेना; हाथ में लेना; वचन देना (– **took,** – **taken,** – **taking**) – **undertaker** *n.* अन्त्येष्टि-प्रबंधक – **undertaking** *n.* कार्य, उद्यम, कारोबार, उपक्रम, जिम्मेवारी; आश्वासन
undertone (´अंडर्टोन) *n.* मंद या हल्का स्वर, दबी आवाज़; अभिप्राय, अंतर्निहित अर्थ
underwear (´अंडर्वेंअर) *n.* (**underclothes** भी) नीचे पहनने के कपड़े
underworld (´अंडर्वर्ल्ड) *n.* अपराधी-समाज; *Myth.* पाताललोक
underwrite (´अंडर्राइट) *vt.* भुगतान का वचन देना – **underwriter** *n.* बीमा-एजेंट
undeserved *a.* अयोग्य, अपात्र
undesirable *a.* अवांछनीय
undeterred *a.* अटल, निर्भीक
undisciplined *a.* अनुशासनहीन, अनियंत्रित
undiscovered *a.* अज्ञात
undies (´अंडिज़) *pl. n. inf.* स्त्रियों के नीचे पहनने के वस्त्र
undo *vt.* (गांठ आदि) खोलना; बिगाड़ देना; उलट देना; रद्द कर देना, तबाह कर देना – **undoing** *n.* सर्वनाश का कारण – **undone** *a.* बर्बाद; अपूर्ण
undoubted *a.* जिस के विषय में कोई संदेह न हो – **undoubtedly** *adv.* निस्संदेह
undress *vi.* कपड़े उतारना
undue *a.* अनुचित, अत्यधिक
undulate (´अनड्युलेट) *v.* लहरों के समान नीचे ऊपर होना, लहराना
unearned *a.* अनअर्जित
unearth *vt.* खोज निकालना
unearthly *a.* अलौकिक, डरावना – **unearthly hour** असमय (बहुत सवेरे या बहुत रात को)
uneasy (अन्´ईज़ि) *a.* अशांत, बेचैन, चिंतित – **uneasiness** *n.*
uneconomic *a.* घाटे वाला (उद्योग)
unemotional *a.* भावुकता से पर
unemployed *a.* बेरोज़गार, बेकार – **unemployment** *n.* बेरोज़गारी
unending (अन्´एन्डिंग) *a.* अनंत, लगातार
unequalled *a.* अद्वितीय, बेजोड़
unequivocal *a.* स्पष्ट (उत्तर)
unerring (अन्´अरिंग) *a.* ठीक, बिलकुल सही, अचूक
unethical *a.* नैतिक स्तर पर अमान्य, अनैतिक
uneven (अन्´ईवन) *a.* ऊंचा-नीचा; असमान
uneventful *a.* सामान्य, घटना रहित
unexpected (अनिक्´स्पैक्टिड) *a.* अप्रत्याशित – **unexpectedly** *adv.* अचानक
unfailing *a.* ; अचूक
unfair *a.* अनुचित
unfaithful *a.* बेवफा, क तघ्न
unfamiliar *a.* अपरिचित; अनभिज्ञ
unfasten (अन्´फ़ासन) *vt.* खोलना; ढीला करना
unfavourable *a.* प्रतिकूल, (के) विरुद्ध
unfeeling *a.* कठोर, हृदयहीन
unfinished *a.* अपूर्ण
unfit *a.* अस्वस्थ; अयोग्य; अनुपयुक्त
unfold (अन्´फ़ोल्ड) *vt.* खोलना; *fig.* प्रकट करना – *vi.* खुलना; *fig.* सामने आना
unforeseen (अन्फ़ॉर्´सीन) *a.* अप्रत्याशित
unforgettable (अन्फ़र्´गैटबल) *a.* अविस्मरणीय
unfortunate (अन्´फ़ॉर्चनिट) *a.* अभागा; दुर्भाग्यपूर्ण; खेदजनक
unfounded *a.* निराधार
unfriendly *a.* शत्रुतापूर्ण, रूखा
ungainly *a.* बेढंगा, भद्दा
ungracious *a.* अक तज्ञ, उपकार न मानने वाला
ungrateful *a.* अक तज्ञ

unguarded *a.* बेखबर; जिसकी रक्षा न की जाय, अरक्षित

unhappy *a.* दुःखी; अभागा – **unhappy with** से अप्रसन्न/नाखुश

unharmed *a.* सकुशल

unhealthy *a.* हानिकर; अस्वस्थ

unheard-of (अन्'हर्‌डॉव़) *a.* अभूतपूर्व, असाधारण

unhelpful *a.* जो मद्द न करना चाहे; बेकार

unhurried *a.* शांत, आराम से किया (काम)

unhurt *a.* अक्षत, ठीक-ठाक

unhygienic *a.* गंदा, अस्वास्थ्यकर

uni- (*comb. form*) एक-, इक- जैसे **uniform**, **unicorn** आदि में

unidentified *a.* अज्ञात

uniform ('यूनिफ़ॉर्म) *n.* वर्दी – *a.* जिसमें परिवर्तन न हो, अपरिवर्ती, एकसमान, एकरूप, एकसार – **uniformity** (यूनि'फ़ॉर्‌मिटि) *n.* एकरूपता – **uniformly** *adv.*

unify ('यूनिफ़ाइ) *v.* एक कर देना या हो जाना (-**ified**, -**ifying**) – **unification** (यूनिफ़ि'केशन) *n.* एकीकरण

unilateral (यूनि'लैटरल) *a.* एकतरफ़ा, एकपक्षीय – **unilaterally** *adv.*

unimaginative *a.* नीरस, कल्पनाशक्तिहीन

unimportant *a.* महत्वहीन, मामूली

uninhabited *a.* सुनसान, निर्जन

uninhibited *a.* बेझिझक

uninspired *a.* नीरस, उबाऊ

unintelligible *a.* जो समझ न आये, दुर्बोध

unintentional *a.* अनजाने में किया/कहा

uninteresting *a.* नीरस

uninterrupted *a.* निरंतर

union ('यूनिअन) *n.* संयोजन, जोड़; एकता, मेल मिलाप; संघ, सभा; श्रमिकसंघ, यूनियन – **unionism** *n.* संघवाद, यूनियनबाज़ी

unique (यू'नीक) *a.* अद्वितीय, बेमिसाल, एकमात्र, बेजोड़

unisex ('यूनिसेक्स) *a.* जो स्त्री व पुरुषों दोनों इस्तेमाल कर सकें (*unisex dresses*)

unison ('यूनिसन) *n. Mus.* स्वरमेल; मैत्री, मेल-मिलाप

unit ('यूनिट) *n.* इकाई; एकक; मात्रक; भाग; (अस्पताल में) चिकित्सा विभाग; दल, टुकड़ी

unite (यू'नाइट) *vt.* एक करना, जोड़ना, संगठित करना, मिलाना – *vi.* एक हो जाना, संगठित हो जाना – **unity** ('यूनिटि) *n.* एकता; मेल-मिलाप; सहयोग; इकाई; *Maths* एक (की संख्या)

universe ('यूनिवर्स) *n.* सृष्टि, ब्रह्माण्ड; विश्व – **universal** (यूनि'वर्सल) *a.* सार्वभौमिक; किसी समाज के सभी सदस्यों पर लागू

university (यूनि'वर्सिटि) *n.* विश्वविद्यालय

unjustified *a.* सरासर गलत

unkempt *a.* अस्त-व्यस्त; मैला-कुचैला

unleash (अन्'लीश) *vt.* खोल देना, छोड़ देना; *fig.* खुला छोड़ देना

unless (अन्'लेस) *conj.* यदि ... नहीं; जब तक .. नहीं

unlike *a.* अलग; असमान – *prep.* से भिन्न, के विपरीत – **unlikely** *a.* लगभग असंभव

unlucky *a.* बदकिस्मत, भाग्यहीन

unmanageable *a.* बेकाबू

unmentionable *a.* अनुल्लेखनीय

unmistakable (अन्‌मिस्'टेकबल) *a.* सुस्पष्ट, साफ़

unmitigated (अन्'मिटिगेटिड) *a.* पूरी तरह (खराब, विनाशकारी), पक्का

unmoved *a.* अविचलित

unnatural *a.* अस्वाभाविक, बनावटी

unnecessary *a.* अनावश्यक

unnoticed *a.* चुपचाप; अलक्षित, जिसपर ध्यान न जाय

UNO United Nations Organization का संक्षेप
unofficial (अन्‌अ´फ़िशल) *a.* गैर सरकारी
unopposed *a.* निर्विरोध
unorthodox *a.* शास्त्र विरुद्ध, परंपरा विरुद्ध
unpack *vt.* (सामान) खोलना
unpalatable (अन्´पैलटबल) *a.* अप्रिय; अस्वादिष्ट, बेस्वाद (भोजन)
unparalleled *a.* अद्वितीय, लाजवाब, बेमिसाल
unpardonable *a.* अक्षम्य (अपराध)
unpleasant *a.* अप्रिय; रूखा; अरुचिकर
unplug *vt.* (बिजली का) प्लग निकालना
unpopular *a.* जो लोक प्रिय न हो
unprecedented *a.* अभूतपूर्व
unpredictable (अनप्रि´डिक्टबल) *a.* जिसके व्यवहार, स्वभाव आदि के बारे में कुछ न कहा जा सके
unquestionably (अन्´क्वेस्चनब्लि) *adv.* निस्सदेह, निर्विवाद
unravel (अन्´रैवल) *vt.* सुलझाना, खोलना
unrealistic *a.* अवास्तविक
unreasonable *a.* तर्क विरुद्ध, असंगत
unrelenting *a.* लगातार; कठोर, नरम न पड़ने वाला
unremitting (अन्‌रि´मिटिङ) *a.* निरंतर
unreservedly (अन्‌रि´ज़र्विड्लि) *adv.* निस्संकोच, पूरी तरह से
unresolved *a.* (समस्या) जो सुलझी न हो
unrest *n.* अशांति, गड़बड़ी
unrestrained *a.* बेलगाम, असंयत
unrivalled *a.* बेजोड़, अद्धितीय
unruffled *a.* शांत
unruly *a.* बेकाबू
unsafe *a.* असुरक्षित
unsavoury (अन्´सेवरि) *a.* अरुचिकर; *fig.* अप्रिय
unscathed (अन्´स्केद्ड) *a.* सही-सलामत
unscheduled *a.* जो पूर्वनियोजित न हो
unscrupulous (अन्´स्क्रूप्युलस) *a.* बेईमान
unshaven (अन्´शेवन) *a.* दाढ़ी बढ़ाए (व्यक्ति)
unsightly *a.* कुरूप, भद्दा
unskilled *a.* बेहुनर (मजदूर)
unsolicited *a.* बिन मांगा, अनचाहा
unspoken *a.* अनकही
unstuck (अन्´स्टक) *a.* – **come unstuck** अलग हो जाना; *fig.* निष्फल होना
unsuitable *a.* अनुपयुक्त
unsweetened *a.* फीका (दूध आदि)
unsympathetic *a.* असहानुभूतिपूर्ण
unsystematic *a.* अव्यवस्थित
untapped (अन्´टैप्ट) *a.* (स्रोत) जिन्हें अभी इस्तेमाल न किया हो, अप्रयुक्त
untenable (अन्´टेनबल) *a.* (सिद्धांत आदि) जिसका समर्थन न किया जा सके
unthinkable *a.* असंभव, कल्पनातीत; अव्यवहारिक
until (अन्´टिल) *conj.* जब तक, जब तक ... न – *prep.* तक
untimely (अन्´टाइम्लि) *a.* असामयिक, बेमौके; अकाल (मत्यु)
unto (´अंटू) *prep. obs.* (**to**) को
untold (अन्´टोल्ड) *a.* अनकही (कहानी)
untouched (अन्´टच्ट) *a.* अछूता; अक्षत – **untouchable** (अन्´टचबल) *a.* जो छुआ न जा सके, अस्पश्य – *n.* अछूत
untoward (अन्ट´वर्ड) *a.* अप्रिय, अनुचित
untrustworthy *a.* अविश्वसनीय
unusable *a.* जो इस्तेमाल न हो सके, घटिया
unused (अन्´यूज्ड) *a.* जो प्रयोग में न लाया गया हो; (अन्´यूस्ट) अनभ्यस्त (जिसे किसी वस्तु कार्य आदि का अभ्यास न हो)
unusual (अन्´यूझुअल) *a.* असाधारण, असामान्य, विरला
unveil (अन्´वेल) *vt.* (मूर्ति आदि का) अनावरण करना

unwanted *a.* अनचाहा, अवांछित
unwarranted *a.* अनावश्यक, अनुचित
unwavering (अन्'वेव़रिंग) *a.* अटल, (इरादे का) पक्का
unwell *a.* अस्वस्थ
unwieldy (अन्'वील्डि) *a.* भारी-भरकम; भद्दा; संभालने में मुश्किल
unwilling *a.* अनिच्छुक
unwise *a.* अविवेकपूर्ण, गलत (फैसला आदि)
unwitting (अन्'विटिङ) *a.* अनजाने में (किया कार्य आदि); अनभिज्ञ
unwrap (अन्'रैप) *vt.* खोलना
up (अप) *prep.* के ऊपर, पर – *adv.* ऊपर, की ओर; सीधा ; सो कर उठा हुआ ; समाप्त, पूरा (*Drink it up!*) (**upper** *comp.*, **uppermost** *sup.*) – **upward** *a./adv.* – **upwards** *adv.* – **up against** का सामना होना
up^2 (अप) (*comb. form*) उच्च-, ऊर्ध्व- जैसे **uproot, upgrade** आदि में
upbraid (अप्'ब्रेड) *vt.* डांटना, झिड़कना
upbringing ('अप्ब्रिंगिंग) *n.* पालन-पोषण व लिखाई-पढ़ाई
upcoming ('अप्कमिंग) *a.* आने वाला (*upcoming film*)
update (अप्'डेट) *vt.* नवीनतम करना (जानकारी, तकनीक आदि)
upfront (अप्'फ्रंट) *a. inf.* (व्यवहार आदि में) स्पष्ट, खुला
upgrade (अप्'ग्रेड) *vt.* पदोन्नति करना; बेहतर बनाना
upheaval (अप्'हीव़ल) *n.* क्रांति; उथल-पुथल
uphill *a.* चढ़ाई वाला; कठिन(काम)
uphold (अप्'होल्ड) *vt.* बनाए रखना, कायम रखना (**upheld, upholding**)
upholstery (अप्होल्स्टरि) *n.* गद्दियां, कवर आदि; कार की गद्दियों पर लगाने का कपड़ा
upkeep ('अप्कीप) *n.* देख-रेख, संभाल
uplift *vt.* (अप्'लिफ्ट) ऊपर उठाना; सुधारना – *n.* ('अप्लिफ्ट) उत्थापन; मानसिक, सामाजिक या भावनात्मक स्तर पर सुधार
upon (अ'पॉन) *prep.* के ऊपर
upper ('अपर) *a.* ऊपरी – **up** का *comp.* उच्चतर, अधिक ऊपर – *n.* जूते का ऊपरी भाग – **uppermost** *a.* – **up** का *sup.* उच्चतम, सर्वोच्च
upright ('अप्राइट) *a.* सीधा; *fig.* सच्चा, ईमानदार – *adv.* खड़ा – *n.* खड़ी वस्तु जैसे खंभा
uprising ('अप्राइज़िङ) *n.* विद्रोह, बग़ावत
uproar ('अप्रॉर) *n.* कोलाहल, शोरगुल – **uproarious** (अप्'रॉरिअस) *a.* शोर भरा
upset *vt.* (अप्'सेट) उलट देना, चिंतित कर देना; (पेट) गड़बड़ कर देना (**upset, upsetting**) – *n.* ('अप्सेट) आशा के विपरीत (खेल में) हार; गड़बड़
upshot ('अप्शॉट) *n.* निष्कर्ष, परिणाम
upstairs ('अप्'स्टेअर्ज़) *adv.* ऊपर
upstart ('अप्स्टार्ट) *n.* व्यक्ति जिसे सहसा धन, शक्ति आदि प्राप्त हुए हों
upstream ('अप्'स्ट्रीम) *a.* जलधारा के प्रतिकूल (दिशा)
up-to-date ('अप् टू 'डेट) *a.* आज तक का आधुनिकतम
upturn ('अप्टर्न) *n.* (किस्मत का) पलटा, सुधार; वद्धि
upward ('अप्वर्ड) *a.* ऊपर की ओर जाने वाला; से ज्यादा – **upward(s)** *adv.* ऊपर की ओर
uranium (यु'रेनिअम) *n.* सफेद रेडियोधर्मी धातु, यूरेनियम
Uranus (यु'रेनस) *n.* ; युरेनस नक्षत्र
urban ('अर्बन) *a.* नगरीय, शहरी – **urbanize** *vt.* शहरीकरण करना
urbane (अर्'बेन) *a.* भद्र, विनम्र, सुसभ्य – **urbanity** (अर्'बैनिटि) *n.*

urchin (´अर्चिन) *n.* नटखट, मैला-कुचैला बालक

urge (अर्ज) *vt.* अनुरोध करना; आग्रह करना; उकसाना, भड़काना – *n.* तीव्र इच्छा – **urgency** (´अर्जन्सि) *n.* तुरंत कार्य करने की आवश्यकता – **urgent** *a.* अत्यावश्यक, बहुत ज़रूरी

urine (´युअरिन) *n.* मूत्र, पेशाब – **urinal** (´युअरिनल) *n.* पुरुषों का मूत्रालय, पेशाबघर – **urinate** (´युअरिनेट) *vi.* पेशाब करना

urn (अर्न) *n.* कलश, घट विशे. भस्म-कलश; अस्थि कलश

US USA United States (of America) का संक्षेप

us (अस) *pron. pl.* हम, हमें

use (यूज़) *vt.* प्रयोग करना, उपयोग करना, व्यवहार में लाना; का फायदा उठाना; की आदत होना; (*up* के साथ) खर्च कर डालना – *n.* (यूस) प्रयोग, उपयोग; प्रयोजन; उपयोगिता– **usable** (´यूज़बल) *a.* प्रयोग करने योग्य, काम लेने लायक – **usage** (´यूसिज,-ज़िज) *n.* प्रयोग, उपयोग; उपयोग या व्यवहार का ढंग; रिवाज़ प्रथा – **used** (यूज्ड) *a.* काम में लाया हुआ, पुराना – **useful** (´यूसफुल) *a.* उपयोगी, लाभदायक – **useless** *a.* – **usefully** *adv.* – **usefulness** *n.* उपयोगिता – **uselessness** *n.* – **used to** (यूस्ट-) *a.* का अभ्यस्त, आदी – *vt.* ... करता था – **used to go** जाया करता था – **user-friendly** *a.* (कम्प्यूटर आदि) आसानी से समझ आने व काम लिए जाने योग्य

usher (´अशर) *n.* प्रवेशक (सिनेमा आदि में), गेटकीपर (**usherette** (अश´रैंट) *fem.*) – *vt.* प्रारंभ करना, घोषित करना; उद्घाटित करना

usual (´यूझुअल) *a.* सामान्य, आम – **usually** *adv.* प्रायः, सामान्यतः, अकसर – **as usual** हमेशा की तरह

usurp (यू´ज़र्प) *vt.* हड़प लेना, हथिया लेना – **usurpation** *n.* अनाधिकार ग्रहण – **usurper** *n.*

usury (´यूझ़रि) *n.* सूदखोरी– **usurer** (´यूझ़रर) *n.* सूदखोर

utensil (यू´टेंन्सल) *n.* बरतन-भाँडे, घर में काम आने वाले औज़ार

uterus (´यूटरस) *n.* गर्भाशय, बच्चेदानी

utility (यू´टिलिटि) *n.* उपयोग; लाभ; उपयोगी वस्तु – *a.* व्यावहारिक या प्रायोगिक – **utilitarian** (यूटिलि´टैंअरिअन) *a.* (वस्तु) जो सुंदर नहीं परंतु उपयोगी हो – **utilization** (यूटिलाइ´ज़ेशन) *n.* उपयोग – **utilize** *vt.* का उपयोग करना

utmost (´अट्मोस्ट) *a.* परम, चरम; अंतिम (स्थान, नगर आदि) भरसक – *n.* अधिकतम मात्रा, सीमा आदि

Utopia (यू´टोपिअ) *n.* काल्पनिक आदर्श राज्य अथवा समाज, राम राज्य – **utopian** *a.* आदर्श परंतु अव्यावहारिक

utter[1] (´अटर) *vt.* कहना, बोलना; आवाज़ निकालना – **utterance** *n.* बोली; अभिव्यक्ति; बोले गये शब्द, कथन, उक्ति

utter[2] (´अटर) *a.* पूरा, निरा – **utterly** *adv.*

U-turn *n.* "U-" आकार का मोड़; किसी की राजनीतिक पालिसी (नीति) में उलटाव

V

vacant (वे़कंट) *a.* खाली; शून्य (भाव) – **vacancy** (वे़कन्सि) *n.* खाली जगह; (होटल में) खाली कमरा; खाली पद, नौकरी की जगह

vacate (व़ 'केट) *vt.* छोड़ना; खाली करना – **vacation** (व़ 'केशन) *n.* अवकाश, विश्वविद्यालयों व न्यायालयों में लम्बी छुट्टी

vaccinate (वै़क्सिनेट) *vt.* किसी रोग-विशेष से बचाव का टीका लगाना – **vaccination** *n.* टीका – **vaccine** *n.* टीके की दवाई

vacillate (वै़सिलेट) *vi.* विचारों में अस्थिर होना, डांवांडोल होना – **vacillation** (वै़सि 'लेशन) *n.* दुविधा; अस्थिरता

vacuum (वै़क्युअम) *n.* शून्य, रिक्त स्थान; निर्वात (*pl.* **-uums, -ua**) – *v.* वैक्युम-क्लीनर से सफ़ाई करना – **vacuum cleaner** धूल-मिट्टी खींच कर सफाई करने का यंत्र, वैक्युम क्लीनर – **vacuum flask** निर्वात फ्लास्क, थर्मस बोतल

vagabond (वै़गबॉण्ड) *n.* आवारागर्द; घुमक्कड़; आवारा (भिखारी या चोर) – *a.* आवारा

vagaries (वे़गरिज़) *n.* वस्तु/व्यक्ति का व्यवहार जिसका अनुमान या नियंत्रण कठिन हो, सनक, तरंग

vagina (व़ 'जाइन्अ) *n.* स्त्री- योनि

vagrant (वे़ग्रंट) *a./n.* आवारा; घुमक्कड़

vague (वे़ग) *a.* अस्पष्ट; धुंधली – **vaguely** *adv.*

vain (वे़न) *a.* दंभी, व्यर्थ, निष्फल

vainglory (वे़न्ग्लॉरि) *n.* आत्म- श्लाघा, शेख़ी– **vainglorious** *a.*

valedictory (वै़लि- 'डिक्टरि) *n.* विदाई का भाषण – *a.*

valentine (वैलन्टाइन) *n.* (**valentine card** भी) सेंट वैलंटाइन- दिवस (14 फरवरी) को भेजा गया प्रेम-पत्र; उपहार (पाने वाला व्यक्ति)

valiant (वै़ल्यंट) *a.* शूरवीर, साहसी

valid (वै़लिड) *a.* ठोस (बहाना); तर्कसंगत; कानूनन सही – **validity** (व़ 'लिडिटि) *n.* मान्यता– **validate** (वै़लिडेट) *vt.* विधिमान्य बनाना

valley (वै़लि) *n.* घाटी

valour (वै़लर) *n.* पराक्रम, बहादुरी

value (वै़ल्यु) *n.* मूल्य; उपयोगिता; महत्व – *pl.* सिद्धांत; मान्यता; नैतिक मूल्य – *vt.* का मूल्य आंकना; कदर करना, को महत्वपूर्ण समझना – **valuable** *a.* बहुमूल्य, मूल्यवान – *n.* (प्राय: *pl.*) बहुमूल्य वस्तुएं – **valuation** (वै़ल्यु 'एशन) *n.* आंका गया मूल्य

valve (वै़ल्व) *n.* (*in machine*) वाल्व, पाइप में प्रवाह-नियंत्रक साधन; *Anat.* शरीर में (विशे. दिल में) वाल्व; रेडियो या टेलिविज़न का वाल्व

vamp[1] (वैम्प) *inf. n.* पुरुषों को लुभाने वाला स्त्री – *v.* लुभाना, मोहित करना

vamp[2] (वैम्प) *n.* पैबंद (**revamp** भी); जूते के ऊपरी भाग का अगला भाग – *vt.* पैबंद लगाना, मरम्मत करना

vampire (वै़म्पायर) *n.* (लोक कथाओं में) रक्त चूसने वाला प्रेत

van[1] (वै़न) *n.* वैन, बंद मोटर गाड़ी, (विशे. मालवाहक); माल ले जाने व गार्ड के उपयोग का रेल डब्बा

vandal (वैंड्ल) *n.* बर्बर, संपत्ति (विशे. कला वस्तुओं) को जानकर नष्ट करने वाला – **vandalism** (वैंडलिज़म) *n.* बर्बरता, कला विध्वंस – **vandalize** *vt.* (कलाक तियां) नष्ट करना

vane (वे़न) *n.* पवनदिशा-सूचक, वातसूचक

vanguard (वै़न्गार्ड) *n.* अग्रणीत, अगुआ; अग्रगामी दल, मोरचा

vanilla (व'निलअ) *n.* वैनिला फूलों की बेल; इसके बीज; इसका सुगंधित अरक
vanish (वैनिश) *vi.* ग़ायब हो जाना
vanity (वैनिटि) *n.* मिथ्याभिमान, घमण्ड
vanquish (वैंक्विश) *vt.* परास्त करना, हरा देना, काबू पा लेना – **vanquished** *n.* पराजित लोग
vantage ('वांटिज) *n.* लाभ, अनुकूल परिस्थिति – **vantage point** स्थान जहां से सामने बहुत कुछ देखा जा सके
vapid (वैपिड) *a.* फीका, नीरस
vapour (वेपर) *n.* भाप, कोहरा – **vaporize** *v.* वाष्प बनना, वाष्प में बदलना – **vaporizer** *n.*
variable (वेंरिअबल) दे. VARY
varicose (वैरिकोस) *a.* सूजी हुई, गुथी हुई (शिराएं)
variety (व'राइटि) *n.* विविधता; विविध वस्तुओं का संग्रह – **variety show** रंगारंग कार्यक्रम
various (वेंअरिअस) *a.* विभिन्न, अनेक; (*several*) तरह-तरह के
varnish ('वार्निश) *n.* वारनिश, रोग़न – *vt.* वारनिश करना
varsity ('वार्सिटि) *n. US* खेल प्रतियोगिता में कालिज की मुख्य टीम; *India* UNIVERSITY का संक्षेप
vary (वेंअरि) *vt.* परिवर्तित करना – *vi.* से भिन्न होना या हो जाना – (**varied, varying**) – **variability** *n.* – **variable** *a.* परिवर्तनीय, परिवर्तनशील, बदल जाने वाला – *n.* परिवर्तनशील वस्तु – **variance** *n.* अनबन, विवाद, झगड़ा, अंतर, फ़र्क – **variant** *a.* भिन्न – *n.* रूपांतर; वैकल्पिक रूप, पाठांतर – **variation** *n.* परिवर्तन, रूपांतरण, विभिन्नता – **varied** *a.* विविध; परिवर्तित; रंग बिरंगा
vase (वाज़) *n.* फूलदान, कलश
Vaseline (वैसिलीन) *n.* R वैसलीन
vast (वास्ट) *a.* विशाल; बहुत बड़ी – **vastly** *adv.* अत्यधिक – **vastness** *n.* विशालता; विस्तार
vat (वैट) *n.* टंकी, बड़ा टब, कुण्ड
vault[1] (वॉल्ट) *n.* मेहराबदार छत; मेहराबदार भवन; तहख़ाना
vault[2] (वॉल्ट) *v.* (को) लांघना, छलांग मारना – *n.* ऐसी छलांग
vaunted ('वॉन्टिड) *a.* – **much vaunted** जिसकी बहुत प्रशंसा व चर्चा हों
VC Vice-Chairman, Vice-Chancellor, का संक्षेप
VCR Video Cassette Recorder का संक्षेप
VD Venereal Disease का संक्षेप
veal (वील) *n.* बछड़े का मांस
veer (विअर) *vi.* दिशा परिवर्तन करना; विचार, रूख बदल लेना
vegan ('वीगन) *n.* शुद्ध शाकाहारी जो दूध-दही आदि का भी प्रयोग न करे
vegetable (वेंजिटेबल) *n.* वनस्पति; शाक; सब्ज़ी– *a.* वनस्पति विषयक – **vegetable marrow** विलायती कद्दू
vegetarian (वेंजि'टेंअरिअन) *n.* (*inf.* **veggie** भी) शाकाहारी – *a.* – **vegetarianism** *n.* शाकाहारवाद
vegetate (वेंजिटेट) *vi.* (पौधों का) उगना, बढ़ना; नीरस, निष्क्रिय जीवन बिताना – **vegetation** *n.* वनस्पति, पेड़-पौधे – **vegetative** (वेंजिटटिव़) *a.*
vehement ('वीइमंट) *a.* तीव्र, उग्र (भावनाएं आदि); ज़ोरदार – **vehemence** *n.* तीव्रता, उग्रता
vehicle ('वीइकल) *n.* वाहन, सवारी; (*fig.*) अभिव्यक्ति का माध्यम या साधन – **vehicular** (वि'हिक्युलर) *a.* वाहन संबंधी
veil (वेल) *n.* पर्दा, घूंघट, बुरका – *vt.* घूंघट, बुरके, आदि से (मुंह) ढंकना; ढंकना – **veiled** *a.* छिपा हुआ (*veiled threat*)

vein (व़िन) *n.* रक्त को दिल की ओर ले जाने वाली शिरा; रग, नस; पत्ते, पतंगे आदि की नसें; खनिज-युक्त चट्टान में रंग जैसे निशान; धारी

velocity (वि़ 'लॉसिट) *n.* वेग

velvet ('वे़ल्विट) *n.* मख़मल – **velveteen** *n.* मख़मल जैसा सूती कपड़ा – **velvety** *a.* मखमली

vend ('वे़ण्ड) *vt.* बेचना – **vendor** *n.* फेरीवाला

vendetta (वे़न् 'डेट्‌अ) *n.* हिंसक प्रतिशोध

veneer (वि़ 'निअर) *n.* मामूली लकड़ी (के फर्नीचर) पर बढ़िया लकड़ी की परत, काष्ठ परत; (*fig.*) दिखावटी व्यवहार

venerable ('वे़नरबल) *a.* पूजनीय, श्रद्धेय – **veneration** (वे़न 'रेशन) *n.*

venereal (वि़ 'निअरिअल) *a.* मैथुन संचारित (रोग), यौन (रोग)

Venetian blind (वि़ 'नीशन-) पतली पट्टियों से बनी खिड़की

vengeance ('वे़न्जन्स) *n.* प्रतिशोध, बदला – **vengeful** *a.* प्रतिशोधी

venison ('वे़निज़न, -सन) *n.* हिरन का मांस

venom ('वे़नम) *n.* विष, ज़हर; द्वेष, वैर की भावना – **venomous** *a.* विषैला

vent (वे़ण्ट) *n.* छेद, निकास – *vt. fig.* (दबी भावनाओं को) व्यक्त करना

ventilate ('वे़ण्टिलेट) *vt.* हवा आने-जाने का प्रबंध करना, हवादार बनाना – **ventilation** *n.* हवा का मुक्त रूप से आने-जाने का प्रबंध, संवातन – **ventilator** *n.* रोशनदान

ventriloquist (वे़न् 'ट्रिलक्विस्ट) *n.* व्यक्ति जो इस प्रकार बोल सके कि आवाज़ कहीं और से अथवा किसी अन्य व्यक्ति से आती जान पड़े, पेटबोला – **ventriloquism** *n.* पेटबोली

venture ('वे़न्चर) *vt.* दांव पर लगाना, खतरे में डालना – *vi.* कुछ करने या कहीं जाने का साहस होना – *n.* जोखिम भरा काम, साहसिक कार्य, सट्टेबाज़ी – **venturesome** ('वे़न्चर्सम) *a.* साहसिक

venue ('वे़न्यू) *n.* मिलन-स्थल, घटनास्थल

Venus ('वीनस) *n.* शुक्र नक्षत्र

veracity (वे़ 'रैसिटि) *n.* सच्चाई

veranda(h) (व 'रैंड़अ) *n.* बरामदा, दालान

verb (वर्ब) *n. Grammar* क्रिया – **verbal** *a.* मौखिक, ज़बानी; शाब्दिक, शब्दश; क्रिया विषयक – **verbatim** (वर् 'बेटिम) *adv./a.* शब्दशः

verbose (वर् 'बोस) *a.* शब्दजाल- पूर्ण – **verbosity** (वर् 'बॉसिटि) *n.* शब्दाडंबर

verdant ('वर्डंट) *a.* हरा-भरा (मैदान)

verdict ('वर्डिक्ट) *n.* ज्यूरी का निर्णय; निर्णय, पंच-फैसला; परीक्षण के बाद दी गयी राय

verge (वर्ज) *n.* किनारा, सिरा, छोर; सड़क के किनारे घास की पट्टी – *vi.* तक पहुंच जाना, के नज़दीक होना

verify ('वे़रिफ़ाइ) *vt.* सत्य सिद्ध करना, कथन आदि को सत्य प्रमाणित करना; की सत्यता जांचना (– **ified**, – **ifying**) – **verification** *n.* सत्यापन, सत्यता की जांच

veritable ('वे़रिटबल) *a.* वास्तविक, खरा

vermicelli (वर्मि 'सेलि) *n.* सेवई

vermilion (वर् 'मिल्यन) *n.* सिंदूर – *a.* सिंदूरी

vermin ('वर्मिन) *pl. n.* हानि पहुंचाने वाले जीव, कीड़े

vernacular (वर् 'नैक्युलर) *n.* देश या स्थान विशेष की जन भाषा – *a.* जनभाषी, देशी

versatile ('वर्सटाइल) *a.* सर्वतोमुखी प्रतिभा वाला (व्यक्ति), हरफ़नमौला – **versatility** (वर्स 'टिलिटि) *n.*

verse (वर्स) *n.* छंद; पद्य; पद्य-पंक्ति; कविता; बाइबल का एक पैरा – **versed in** कुशल

version ('वर्शन) *n.* विशेष द ष्टिकोण से विवरण, बयान; अनुवाद; रूपांतर

versus ('वर्सस) *prep.* प्रति, विरुद्ध, बनाम

vertebra (ˈवर्टिब्रअ) *n.* रीढ़ का छोटा भाग, कशेरुका (*pl.* **-brae** (-ब्री))
vertex (ˈवर्टेक्स) *n.* शीर्ष (*pl.* **vertices** (-सीज़))
vertical (ˈवर्टिकल) *a.* खड़ा, सीधा – **vertically** *adv.* सीधे/खड़े रूप में
vertigo (ˈवर्टिगो) *n.* (सिर में) चक्कर
verve (वर्व) *n.* उत्साह, जोश; ओज, बल
very (ˈवेरि) *a.* बिलकुल, ठीक वही; पक्का; असली – *adv.* बहुत, काफी हद तक
vessel (ˈवेसल) *n.* द्रव-पात्र, बरतन; जहाज़, बड़ी नाव; शरीर में वाहिका, नलिका
vest (वेस्ट) *n.* बनियान, बंडी आदि; जैकिट – *vt.* को देना, प्रदान करना; (से) सम्पन्न करना; पहनाना – **vested interest** निहित स्वार्थ
vestibule (ˈवेस्टिब्यूल) *n.* प्रवेश-कक्ष
vestige (ˈवेस्टिज) *n.* अवशेष, निशानी
vestry (ˈवेस्ट्रि) *n.* चर्च में वस्त्रागार; सभाकक्ष
vet (वेट) *n.* **Veterinary Surgeon** का संक्षेप – *vt.* परीक्षण करना; जांचना (**-tt-**)
veteran (ˈवेटरन) *n.* अनुभवी व्यक्ति; पुराना सैनिक; (**war veteran** भी) सेवानिव त्त सैनिक – *a.* अनुभवी
veterinary (ˈवेटरिनरि) *a.* पशु-रोग संबंधी – **veterinary surgeon** पशु- चिकित्सक
veto (ˈवीटो) *n.* निषेधाधिकार, वीटो; मनाही (*pl.* **-es**) – *vt.* वीटो का प्रयोग करना; निषेध करना
vex (वेक्स) *vt.* नाराज़ करना, खिजाना, परेशान करना – **vexation** *n.* खीज; परेशानी – **vexed** *a.* नाराज़, खिजा हुआ; परेशान; उलझा हुआ (प्रश्न); विवादग्रस्त (मामला)
VHF Very High Frequency का संक्षेप
via (ˈवाइअ) *adv.* के रास्ते, बरास्ता
viable (ˈवाइअबल) *a.* व्यवहार्य, कारगर; जीवनक्षम; स्वतंत्र रूप से जीवित रहने व विकसित होने योग्य – **viability** (वाइअˈबिलिटि) *n.* व्यवहार्यता, कारगर होना; जीवन क्षमता
viaduct (ˈवाइअडक्ट) *n.* घाटी पर बना सड़क या रेल का पुल
vibrate (वाइˈब्रेट) *v.* दोलन करना, दोलायमान होना; दोलन द्वारा (प्रकाश या ध्वनि) उत्पन्न करना; गूंजना – *vi.* काँपना – **vibrant** (ˈवाइब्रंट) *a.* कम्पायमान; गूंजता हुआ; ओजपूर्ण, फुर्तीला लगने वाला – **vibration** *n.* कंपन, दोलन – (~ **s**) *pl. inf.* स्थान, व्यक्ति आदि के बारे में सहज ही कुछ अनुभूति
vicar (ˈविकर) *n.* पल्ली (पैरिश) का पादरी, विकर – **vicarage** (ˈविकरिज) *n.* विकर का घर
vicarious (विˈकेअरिअस, वाइ-) *a.* कल्पना द्वारा स्वयं अनुभव किया गया (दूसरे का सुख, आनंद, दुःख आदि), प्रतिस्थानिक – **vicariousness** *n.*
vice[1] (वाइस) *n.* व्यसन, बुरी लत, बुराई; पापाचार जैसे वेश्याव त्ति; दोष, त्रुटि
vice[2] (वाइस) *n.* बढ़ई आदि का शिकंजा
vice- (*comb. form*) के स्थान पर, उप- जैसे *vice-chairman, vice-chancellor* आदि में
vice-chancellor *n.* (विश्वविद्यालय का) उप-कुलपति
vice-president *n.* उप-राष्ट्रपति
viceroy (ˈवाइसरॉइ) *n.* वाइसराय, बड़े लाट – **viceregal** (वाइस्ˈरीगल) *a.* वाइसराय का
vice versa (ˈवाइसिˈवर्सअ) *Lat.* इसके विपरीत
vicinity (विˈसिनिटि) *n.* पास-पड़ोस, आस-पास, समीपता
vicious (ˈविशस) *a.* दुष्ट, क्रूर, खूंखार; ख़तरनाक; भ्रष्ट, पापमय; अनैतिक – **viciously** *adv.* – **vicious circle** दुष्चक्र
vicissitude (विˈसिसिट्यूड) *n.* किस्मत का फेर – *pl.* भाग्य का उतार-चढ़ाव
victim (ˈविक्टिम) *n.* शिकार, पीड़ित या सताया हुआ व्यक्ति, वर्ग आदि – **victimization** (विक्टिमाइˈज़ेशन) *n.* – **victimize** (ˈविक्टिमाइज़) *vt.* अनुचित दण्ड देना; सताना

victor (ˈविक्टर) *n.* विजेता – **victorious** (विकिˈटॉरिअस) *a.* विजयी – **victory** (ˈविक्टरि) *n.* विजय, जीत, फ़तह

vide (ˈवाइडि) *Lat.* देखिए

videlicet (विˈडीलिसेंट) *Lat.* अर्थात, यानि (प्रायः *namely* पढ़ा जाता है); संक्षेप में *viz.*

video (ˈविडिओ) *a.* टेलिविज़न-चित्र प्रसारण संबंधी अथवा प्रसारण में प्रयुक्त (उपकरण आदि) – *n.* टेलिविज़न कार्यक्रम रिकार्ड करने का यंत्र, उपस्कर – **video camera** वीडियो फिल्म बनाने का कैमरा – **video cassette** कैसट जिसमें फ़िल्म आदि रिकार्ड की गई हो – **video cassette recorder** टी. वी. कार्यक्रम, फिल्म रिकार्ड करने व बाद में दिखाने का उपकरण, विडियो कैसट रिकार्डर, वीडियो – **video compact disc (VCD)** प्लास्टिक डिस्क जिसपर फिल्म आदि रिकार्ड करके वी.सी.डी. प्लेयर पर देखी जा सके – **video conferencing** व्यवस्था जिसमें विभिन्न स्थानों में बैठे लोग वीडियो के पर्दे पर एक-दूसरे को देख-सुनकर वार्तालाप कर सकें – **video game** वीडियो-पट पर इलैक्ट्रानिकी नियंत्रण द्वारा संचालित खेल

vie (वाइ) *vi.* (**vie with/for** में) से या के लिए होड़ लगाना, मुकाबला करना, प्रतिस्पर्धा करना **(vied, vying)**

view (व्यू) *n.* दृष्टि, निगाह, नज़र; चित्र; दृश्य; मत; दृष्टिकोण; उद्देश्य – *vt.* देखना, निहारना; सर्वेक्षण करना; विचार करना – **viewer** *n.* दर्शक; (फिल्म) अन्वीक्षक; टेलिविज़न दर्शक; फोटो स्लाइड देखने का उपकरण – **viewpoint** *n.* दृष्टिकोण; दूर तक भू-दृश्य देख सकने का स्थान, प्रेक्षण स्थान

vigil (ˈविजिल) *n.* जागरण; निगरानी, सतर्कता – **vigilance** *n.* सतर्कता, चौकसी – **vigilant** *a.* सतर्क, चौकस

vignette (विˈन्येंट) *n.* साहित्यक लघु-लेख; शब्द चित्र; फोटो, चित्र जिसकी पृष्ठभूमि छायित की हुई हो

vigour (ˈविगर) *n.* बल, शक्ति, ओज, उत्साह – **vigorous** *a.* ज़ोरदार; उत्साही; बलवान

vile (वाइल) *a.* दुष्ट, भ्रष्ट; शर्मनाक; घटिया – **vileness** *n.* दुष्टता; घिनौनापन

villa (ˈविल्अ) *n.* गांव में आलीशान मकान, ग्राम-निवास; उपनगरीय-निवास

village (ˈविलिज) *n.* गांव – **villager** *n.* ग्राम निवासी

villain (ˈविलन) *n.* बदमाश; खलनायक; *inf.* शरारती व्यक्ति – **villainous** *a.* दुष्ट; नीच – **villainy** *n.* दुष्टता

vim (विम) *n. inf.* उत्साह, जोश

vindicate (ˈविंडिकेट) *vt.* निर्दोष ठहराना; सच या उचित सिद्ध करना – **vindication** *n.* दोष निवारण, सच सिद्ध होना; समर्थन

vindictive (विन्ˈडिक्टिव) *a.* प्रतिशोधी, बदले की भावना या इच्छा रखने वाला; नाराज़गी से प्रेरित

vine (वाइन) *n.* अंगूर की बेल – **vineyard** (ˈविन्यर्ड) *n.* अंगूर का बाग – **vintage** (ˈविंटिज) *n.* एकत्र अंगूर; अंगूर की फसल; वर्ष-विशेष की (अंगूरी) शराब; (शराब के बनने का) वर्ष, समय – *a.* पुरानी बढ़िया (शराब); किसी कलाकार की कृति – **vintner** (ˈविंट्नर) *n.* अंगूरी-शराब का व्यापारी

vinegar (ˈविनिगर) *n.* सिरका

vinyl (ˈवाइनिल) *n.* एक प्लास्टिक पदार्थ

violate (ˈवाइअलेट) *vt.* (कानून, समझौते आदि का) उल्लंघन करना, भंग करना, अतिक्रमण करना; बलात्कार करना; अपवित्र अथवा दूषित करना – **violable** *a.* – **violation** *n.* उल्लंघन, अतिक्रमण; दूषण, अपवित्र किया जाना – **violator** *n.*

violent (ˈवाइअलंट) *a.* उग्र; हिंसात्मक; ज़ोरदार – **violence** (ˈवाइअलंस) *n.* हिंसा; तीव्रता, उग्रता– **violently** *adv.*

violet ('व़ाइअलिट) *n.* बैंगनी रंग; नील पुष्प, बनफ़्शा – *a.* बैंगनी

violin (व़ाइअ'लिन) *n.* वायलिन, बेला – **violinist** *n.* वायलिन-वादक

VIP Very Important Person का संक्षेप

viper ('व़ाइपर) *n.* विषैला सांप, वाइपर

virago (वि'रागो) *n.* झगड़ालू स्त्री, कर्कशा (*pl.* -**go(e)s**)

virgin ('व़र्जिन) *n.* कुमारी, कुँआरी – *a.* कुमारी; शुद्ध, अछूती (वस्तु); कभी न जोती गई (भूमि) – **virginity** (व़र्'जिनिटि) *n.* कौमार्य; शुद्धता; अछूतापन

Virgo ('व़र्गो) *n.* कन्या राशि (23 अगस्त से 23 सितंबर की अवधि के बीच जन्मे व्यक्तियों की)

virile ('विराइल) *a.* मैथुन समर्थ; पुरुषोचित, बलशाली, तेजस्वी – **virility** (वि'रिलिटि) *n.* पौरुष, मरदानगी

virtual ('व़र्चुअल) *a.* वास्तविक (यद्यपि औपचारिक या प्रत्यक्ष रूप में नहीं), असली – **virtually** *adv.* वस्तुतः, असल में

virtue ('व़र्चू) *n.* गुण, सद्‌गुण; विशेषता – **virtuous** ('वर्चुअस) *a.* सच्चरित्र; नेक; गुणवान – **virtuously** *adv.*

virtuoso (व़र्चु'ओज़ो) *n.* प्रवीण, पारंगत विशे. किसी ललित कला में (*pl.* **-sos, -si** (-सी)) – **virtuosity** (व़र्चु'ऑसिटि) *n.*

virulent ('विरुलंट) *a.* तेजी से असर करने वाली (बीमारी); विषाक्त, ज़हरीला, अति हानिकारक, सांघातिक; कटु, कड़ुवा, तीव्र (आलोचना आदि)

virus ('व़ाइरस) *n.* सूक्ष्म जीवाणु जिनमें से कुछ छूत के रोग फैलाते हैं, वाइरस; *Computers* किसी कम्प्यूटर प्रोग्राम में छिपे निर्देश जो अंकित/संग्रहीत जानकारी को खराब या नष्ट कर सकते है

visa ('व़ीज़अ) *n.* किसी देश में प्रवेश की अनुमति, वीज़ा, प्रवेशपत्र

visage ('विज़ज) *n.* चेहरा, मुख

vis-a-vis (वीज़ा'वी) *Fr.* की तुलना में; के संबंध में; के विपरीत

viscera ('विसर्‌अ) *pl. n.* अंतड़ियां

viscous ('विस्कस) *a.* गाढ़ा व चिप- चिपा – **viscosity** (विस्'कॉसिटि) *n.*

visible ('विज़िबल) *a.* दृष्टिगोचर, स्पष्ट – **visibility** *n.* दृष्टि सीमा, दृष्टि क्षेत्र; हवा में स्पष्ट दिखाई देने की सीमा – **visibly** *adv.* स्पष्टतया

vision ('विझ़न) *n.* दृष्टि; अंतर्दृष्टि; स्वप्न– **visionary** *a.* काल्पनिक, अव्यावहारिक – *n.* स्वप्नद्रष्टा; अव्यावहारिक व्यक्ति

visit ('विज़िट) *v.* मिलने जाना या आना, भेंट करना; कुछ समय के लिए (किसी के यहां) ठहरना; *Computers* इंटरनैट पर वेबसाइटों का अवलोकन करना – *n.* भेंट, मुलाकात – **visitation** (विज़ि'टेशन) *n.* औपचारिक निरीक्षण; विपत्ति, महामारी ; किसी अलौकिक जीव का आगमन – **visitor** *n.* आगंतुक; पर्यटक

visor, vizor ('व़ाइज़र) *n.* हेलमेट का (प्रायः शीशे का) ऊपर-नीचे किया जा सकने वाला अग्र भाग; (कार में) सूर्य किरणें रोकने वाला शेड, टोपी पर शेड, वाइज़र

vista ('विस्ट्‌अ) *n.* दृश्य विशे. दूर तक का

visual ('विझ़ुअल) *a.* दृष्टि संबंधी – **visualization** (विझ़ुअलाइ'ज़ेशन) *n.* कल्पना – **visualize** *vt.* (सजीव) कल्पना करना – **visual aid** दृश्य उपकरण जो प्रशिक्षण में काम आये

vital ('व़ाइट्‌ल) *a.* जीवन के लिए अत्यावश्यक; सजीव, आवश्यक– **vitals** *pl. n.* शरीर के प्रमुख अंग – **vitality** *n.* जीवन शक्ति, तेजस्विता – **vitalize** *vt.* में जान डालना, सजीव या क्रियाशील बनाना – **vitally** *adv.* आवश्यक रूप से – **vital statistics** छाती, कमर, नितम्बों का माप; जीवन-संबंधी आंकड़े

vitamin (ˈविटमिन, ˈवाइ-) *n.* विटामिन
vitiate (ˈविशिएट) *vt.* खराब करना, दूषित करना; बेअसर कर देना
vivacious (विˈवेशस) *a.* सजीव, हंसमुख, ज़िंदादिल, फुर्तीला – **vivacity** (विˈवैसिटि) *n.* सजीवपन, ज़िंदादिली
viva voce (ˈवाइव्अ ˈवोचि) *Lat. adv.* मौखिक रूप में – *n.* मौखिक परीक्षा (प्रायः **viva**)
vivid (ˈविविड) *a.* चमकीला, तेज़; स्पष्ट; सजीव – **vividly** *adv.* स्पष्ट रूप से (वर्णन, चित्रण आदि करना) – **vividness** *n.* जीवंतता, स्पष्टता
vivisection (विविˈसेक्शन) *a.* जीवित प्राणी की चीर-फाड़ करना, उस पर प्रयोग करना
vixen (ˈविक्सन) *n.* लोमड़ी (मादा); झगड़ालू, मदमिज़ाज औरत
viz. (**namely** भी) VIDELICET का संक्षेप
vizier (विˈज़िअर) *n.* वज़ीर
vizor (ˈवाइज़र) दे. VISOR
vocabulary (वˈकैब्युलरि) *n.* शब्दावली, शब्द संग्रह
vocal (ˈवोकल) *a.* उच्चरित, बोला गया; मौखिक; स्पष्ट बात कहने वाला, खूब बोलने वाला – *n.* गायन, कंठ संगीत – **vocalist** *n.* गायक – **vocalize** *vt.* उच्चारण करना
vocation (वोˈकेशन) *n.* व्यवसाय (-विशेष की ओर प्रव त्ति), पेशा – **vocational** *a.* व्यवसाय संबंधी
vociferous (वोˈसिफ़रस) *a.* शोर भरा, ज़ोरदार; चिल्लाने वाला
vodka (ˈवॉड्क्अ) *n.* वोदका, एक रूसी शराब
vogue (ˈवोग) *n.* प्रचलन, फैशन
voice (ˈवॉइस) *n.* वाणी, ध्वनि, आवाज़, राय; (किसी विषय पर) बोलने का अधिकार – *vt.* व्यक्त करना, कहना – **voiceless** *a.*
void (ˈवॉइड) *a.* रिक्त, अभावग्रस्त; अमान्य – *n.* रिक्ति, शून्य – *vt.* अमान्य या रद्द करना, खाली करना – **void of** से खाली
voile (ˈवॉइल) *n.* महीन कपड़ा, वायल
vol. volume का संक्षेप
volatile (ˈवॉलटाइल) *a.* वाष्पशील (जैसे spirit); (स्थिति) जिसका अचानक बदलने या बिगड़ने की संभावना हो; चंचल – **volatility** (वॉलˈटिलिटि) *n.*
volcano (वॉल्ˈकेनो) *n.* ज्वालामुखी (*pl.* -**no(e)s**) – **volcanic** *a.*
vole (ˈवोल) *n.* मूस (चूहे जैसा जन्तु)
volition (वˈलिशन) *n.* इच्छा शक्ति, संकल्प शक्ति
volley (ˈवॉलि) *n.* (गोलियों, गोलों की) बौछार; (प्रश्नों, गालियों आदि की) झड़ी, बौछार; *Sports* जमीन पर टप्पा खाने से पहले गेंद पर वार – *v.* (गोलियों की) बौछार होना; (प्रश्नों आदि की) झड़ी लगना; टप्पे से पहले गेंद मारना – **volleyball** *n.* वॉलीबॉल
volt (ˈवोल्ट) *n.* विद्युत बल की इकाई, वोल्ट – **voltage** (ˈवोल्टिज) *n.* वोल्टता, वोल्टेज
volte-face (ˈवॉल्ट्ˈफ़ास) *Fr. n.* विचारों आदि में एकदम पलटा; काया पलट
voluble (ˈवॉल्युबल) *a.* धारा प्रवाह बोलने वाला, बातूनी
volume (ˈवॉल्यूम) *n.* आयतन; मात्रा, राशि, ढेर; आवाज़ की ऊंचाई; रेडियो, टी.वी. पर ध्वनि-नियंत्रक; पुस्तक; पुस्तक का एक खंड, जिल्द – **volumetric** (वॉल्युˈमैट्रिक) *a.* आयतन माप संबंधी – **voluminous** *a.* भारी भरकम, बहुत अधिक विस्त त
voluntary (ˈवॉलंटरि) *a.* स्वैच्छिक, मर्जी का; बिना पारिश्रामिक लिए किया गया; स्वयंसेवी; दान-आश्रित (संस्था आदि); अनायास, सहज भाव से – **voluntarily** *adv.* – **volunteer** (वॉलन्ˈटिअर) *n.* वालंटियर, स्वयंसेवक – *v.* वालंटियर के रूप में (सेवा) अर्पित करना
voluptuous (वˈलप्चुअस) *a.* विलासमय; ऐन्द्रिय सुख संबंधी; कामोत्तेजक (स्त्री) **voluptuousness** *n.*

vomit (ˈव़ॉमिट) *v.* उलटी करना, वमन करना – *n.* वमन, उलटी, कै

voodoo (ˈवूडू) *n.* जादू-टोना विशे. वेस्ट इंडीज में

voracious (व़ॉˈरेशस) *a.* लालची, पेटू, जिसकी तप्ति न हो – **voraciously** *adv.* – **voracity** (व़ॉˈरैसिटि) *n.* लालच, पेटूपन

vote (व़ोट) *n.* मत; मतदान; मताधिकार; मतदान का परिणाम; वोट – *v.* वोट देना, मत देना; चुनना; स्वीक ति देना; (विधेयक) पास करना – **voter** *n.* मतदाता

vouch (व़ाउच) *vi.* (प्राय: *for* के साथ) का जिम्मा लेना, की सच्चाई आदि की गवाही देना – **voucher** *n.* वाउचर, खर्च का पुरज़ा; नगदी के स्थान पर उसी राशि का पुर्ज़ा – **vouchsafe** (व़ाउच्ˈसेफ़) *vt.* कुछ देने अथवा करने की क पा करना, का वायदा करना

vow (व़ाउ) *n.* प्रतिज्ञा, वचन, व्रत – *vt.* प्रतिज्ञा करना; प्रतिज्ञा द्वारा (बदले आदि की) धमकी देना

vowel (ˈव़ाउअल) *n.* स्वर; स्वर अंकित करने वाला अक्षर (*a, e, i, o, u*)

voyage (ˈव़ॉइइज) *n.* यात्रा विशे. समुद्री या हवाई यात्रा; *fig.* – *vi.* यात्रा करना – **voyager** (ˈवॉइअजर) *n.* (समुद्री) यात्री

VCD video compact disc का संक्षेप

vs. versus का संक्षेप

vulcanize (ˈव़ल्कनाइज़) *vt.* विशेष क्रिया द्वारा (रबड़ का) टिकाऊपन बढ़ाना, वल्कनित करना – **vulcanization** *n.*

vulgar (ˈव़ल्गर) *a.* असभ्य, अशिष्ट; अश्लील; भद्दा– **vulgarism** (ˈव़ल्गरिज़म) *n.* भाषा में ग्राम्य, अभद्र भाषा का प्रयोग – **vulgarity** (वल्ˈगैरिटि) *n.* अभद्रता, कुरूचि

vulnerable (ˈव़ल्नरबल) *a.* अतिसंवेदनशील, नाज़ुक; असुरक्षित; आसानी से मान जाने वाला – **vulnerability** *n.*

vulture (ˈव़ल्चर) *n.* गिद्ध

vying VIE का *pr. p.*

W

wacky (वैकि) *a. inf.* बेवकूफी व शरारत भरा (सुझाव आदि)

wad (वॉड) *n.* गद्दी; नोटों की गड्डी; राशि – *vt.* मोटा अस्तर लगाना; रूई आदि भर कर गद्दी बनाना (**-dd-**) – **wadding** *n.* भराई का पदार्थ

waddle (ˈवॉड्ल) *vi.* बतख की तरह चलना – *n.* बतख की चाल

wade (विड) *vi.* पैदल पार करना विशे. पानी – **wader** *n.* पैदल (पानी) पार करने वाला व्यक्ति अथवा पक्षी

wafer (ˈवेफ़र) *n.* पतला कुरमुरा बिस्कुट – **wafer thin** बहुत पतला

waffle (ˈवॉफ़ल) *n.* पतली मीठी रोटी

waft (वाफ्ट) *vt.* उड़ा ले जाना – *vi.* बह जाना – *n.* हवा का झोंका; महक

wag (वैग) *vt.* (पूंछ) हिलाना– *vi.* (पूंछ) हिलना (**-gg-**) – *n.* हिलाना; – *inf.* मसखरा, दिल्लगीबाज़ – **waggish** *a.* – **wagtail** (वैग्टेल) *n.* एक छोटी चिड़िया

wage (विज) *n.* वेतन, मजदूरी (प्राय: *pl.* में) – *vt.* जारी रखना – **wage war** युद्ध करना

wager (ˈवेजर) *vt.* शर्त लगाना, दांव पर लगाना – *n.* शर्त, दांव

wag(g)on (ˈवैगन) *n.* भारी माल वाहक चौपहिया गाड़ी; मालगाड़ी का डिब्बा, वैगन – **wag(g)oner** *n.* गाड़ीवान

waif (वफ़) *n.* बेघर व्यक्ति, विशे. बच्चा

wail (वल) *v.* रोना, बिलखना – *n.* विलाप, रुदन

waist (विस्ट) *n.* कमर – **waistcoat** *n.* वास्कट

wait (विट) *v.* प्रतीक्षा करना, इंतज़ार करना, राह देखना; तैयार रहना; कार्य, प्रस्थान आदि, ठहरना, रुकना – *vi.* होटल आदि में बैरे का काम करना – *n.* प्रतीक्षा, प्रतीक्षाकाल – **waiter** *n.* वेटर, बैरा (**waitress** *fem.*)

waive (विव़) *vt.* (अधिकार आदि) छोड़ देना; पर आग्रह न करना – **waiver** *n.* छोड़ देने का लिखित बयान, अभित्याग

wake[1] (विक) *v.* जगाना, जागना; जाग त या सचेत होना होश में आना या लाना (**woke, woken, waking**) – *n.* शव के पास रात भर जागना; (प्राय: *pl.*) – **waken** *v.* **wake** के अर्थ में

wake[2] (विक) *n.* जहाज़ आदि के पानी में चलने से उत्पन्न लहरें, अनुजल; पीछे बने रास्ते के निशान

walk (वॉक) *v.* चलना, चलाना, टहलना – *vt.* पैदल पार करना, पैदल पार करवाना, चलवाना – *n.* चाल, भ्रमण, सैर; पगडंडी; व्यवसाय, धन्धा – **walker** *n.* – **walking stick** छड़ी – **walkout** *n.* वाक आउट, सदन त्याग; हड़ताल – **walkover** *n.* निर्विरोध विजय

Walkman (ˈवॉक्मन) **R** हाथ में लेकर घूमने वाला (स्टीरियो की सुविधा सहित) छोटा कैसट रिकार्डर

wall (वॉल) *n.* दीवार – *vt.* दीवार से घेरना या बंद करना – **wallpaper** *n.* दीवारें ढंकने का सजावटी कागज़, वाल पेपर, भित्तिपत्र – **wall-to-wall (carpet)** *a.* जो कमरे के सारे फर्श को ढंके (जैसे गलीचा)

wallaby (ˈवॉलबि) *n.* कंगारू जैसा छोटा जीव

wallet (ˈवॉलिट) *n.* बटुआ, मनी बैग

wallop (ˈवॉलप) *inf. vt.* खूब मारना, जोर से वार करना – *n.* पिटाई, वार

wallow (ˈवॉलो) *vi.* लोटना; (में) लिप्त हो जाना, डूब जाना – *n.*

walnut (ˈवॉल्नट) *n.* अखरोट

walrus (ˈवॉल्रस) *n.* वालरस (समुद्री जीव) (*pl.* **walruses** *or* **walrus**)

waltz (वॉल्स) *n.* वाल्स, बालरूम-न त्य; इसके साथ संगीत – *v.*

WAN (वैन) *n.* wide area network का संक्षेप, एक बड़े क्षेत्र में आपस में जुड़े कम्प्यूटरों की व्यवस्था

wan (वॉन) *a.* पीला (चेहरे का रंग), फीका, निस्तेज

wand (वॉण्ड) *n.* (**magic wand** भी) (जादूगर की) छड़ी

wander (ˈवॉण्डर) *v.* निरर्थक इधर-उधर घूमना, भ्रमण करना – *vi.* भटक जाना, विषय से भटक जाना – *n.* – **wanderer** *n.* घुमक्कड़

wane (विन) *vi.* (चांद का) घटना, कम हो जाना; ख्याति कम हो जाना – *n.* चांद के घटने की क्रिया; ख्याति कम होने की क्रिया

wangle (ˈवैंगल) *inf. vt.* जोड़-तोड़ लगाकर काम निकालना – *n.* जोड़-तोड़, चालबाज़ी

wannabe (ˈवानबी) *n. US* किसी बड़े अभिनेता आदि जैसा लगने के लिए उनके तौर-तरीके, पहनावे की नकल करने वाला व्यक्ति, नकलची

want (वॉन्ट) *v.* चाहना; की आवश्यकता होना, अभाव होना – *n.* इच्छा; आवश्यकता; अभाव, कमी – **wanted** *a.* जिसकी तलाश हो (विशे. अपराधी की) – **wanting** *a.* आवश्यक; नियत स्तर से नीचे

wanton (ˈवॉन्टन) *a.* व्यभिचारी, लम्पट; चंचल, निरर्थके; अनियंत्रित, मनमाना – *n.* व्यभिचारी, कुलटा स्त्री

war (वॉर) *n.* युद्ध, लड़ाई; संघर्ष; शत्रुता – *vi.* युद्ध करना (**-rr-**) – **warlike** *a.* सामरिक; युद्धप्रिय – **warrior** (वॉरिअर) *n.* योद्धा, लड़ाकू – **warfare** *n.* युद्ध; युद्ध स्थिति – **warhead** *n.* प्रक्षेपास्त्र आदि में स्फोटक सामग्री – **warmonger** (ˈवॉर्मंगर) *n.* युद्ध भड़काने वाला – **warship** *n.* युद्धपोत

warble (ˈवॉर्बल) *vi.* (पक्षियों का) कूजना, चहचहाना; गाना – **warbler** *n.* एक कूजने वाला पक्षी

ward (वॉर्ड) *n.* नगर का प्रशासनिक भाग, हल्का, वार्ड; हस्पताल, जेल आदि में वार्ड; अभिभावक के संरक्षण में नाबालिग; अभिभावकता, अभिरक्षा – **warder** *n.* जेलर (**wardress** *fem.*) – **ward off** बचाव करना

warden (ˈवॉर्डन) *n.* होस्टल, पार्क, अभ्यारण्य का कार्यभारी, वार्डन, छात्रपाल – **wardenship** *n.* वार्डन का पद व कार्य

wardrobe (ˈवॉर्ड्रोब) *n.* कपड़े रखने या टांगने की आलमारी; व्यक्ति का वस्त्रसंग्रह

ware (वेंअर) *n.* सामान; वस्तु-समूह – *pl.* सौदा, माल – **warehouse** (ˈवेंअर्हाउस) *n.* माल-गोदाम, भंडार

warm (वॉर्म) *a.* सुहाने योग्य गरम; गरम (कपड़े); प्रेमपूर्ण, स्नेही, हार्दिक; उत्साही, जोशीला; चटकीला (रंग) – *v.* गरमाना, गरम करना; उत्साहित होना, जोश में आना; जोश दिलाना – **warmly** *adv.* – **warmth** (वॉर्म्थ) *n.* सुहानी गर्माहट; स्नेह; उत्तेजना; क्रोध

warn (वॉर्न) *vt.* सतर्क या सावधान करना, सचेत करना; चेतावनी देना; पूर्व सूचना देना – **warning** *n.* चेतावनी; पूर्व सूचना

warp (वॉर्प) *v.* संवलित होना, की आक ति बिगड़ जाना; (मानसिक अथवा नैतिक स्तर पर) विक त हो जाना; *fig.* बिगाड़ देना – *n.* संवलन, विक ति, विकार

warrant (ˈवॉरंट) *n.* जमानत या गारंटी; तलाशी या गिरफ्तारी वारंट, अधिपत्र – *vt.* सच्चाई आदि का आश्वासन देना; अधिकार देना; उचित सिद्ध करना – **warrantee** (वॉरन्ˈटी) *n.* व्यक्ति जिसे आश्वासन दिया गया हो, समाश्वासित – **warrantor** (ˈवॉरंटर) *n.* आश्वसन देने वाला व्यक्ति, कंपनी – **warranty** (ˈवॉरंटि) *n.* माल की गुणवत्ता के बारे में आश्वासन

warren (ˈवॉरन) *n.* (अनेक बिलों से बनी) खरगोशों की आबादी

warrior (ˈवॉरिअर) *n.* दे. **WAR**

wart (वॉर्ट) *n.* मस्सा, चर्मकील – **warthog** अफ्रीका का खांगदार जंगली सूअर

wary (वॅंअरि) *a.* सतर्क, सावधान – **warily** *adv.* फूंक-फूंक कर, झिझकते-झिझकते

was (वाज़, वज़) **be** का *pt.* था, थी

wash (वॉश) *v.* धोना, नहा लेना – *vi.* धोने योग्य होना– *vt.* बहाना, बहा ले जाना; (लहरों का) टकराना, के ऊपर से बहना – *n.* धुलाई; स्नान; एक समय धुले कपड़े; जहाज़ के चलने से उठी तरंग; रंग का पतला लेप – **washable** *a.* धोया जा सकने वाला – **washer** *n.* वाशर, छल्ला – **washing** *n.* धुलाई वाले कपड़े – **washout** *n. inf.* घोर असफलता – **washroom** *n.* (*toilet*) जन-सुविधा – **washing-up** *n.* बर्तन धोने का काम

wasp (वॉस्प) *n.* भिड़, ततैया

waste (वेस्ट) *vt.* गंवाना; फ़ज़ूलखर्ची करना; (मौके का) फायदा न उठा सकना – *vi.* घटना; (व्यक्ति का) घुलना – *n.* कूड़ा-करकट, रद्दी; उजाड़, ऊसर – *a.* बेकार, रद्दी; उजाड़; बंजर – **wastage** (ˈवेस्टिज) *n.* अपव्यय, बर्बादी; हानि – **wasteful** *a.* खर्चीला – **wastefully** *adv.* – **wastrel** (ˈवेस्ट्रल) *n.* फजूलखर्च; निकम्मा व्यक्ति

watch (वॉच) *vt.* ध्यान से देखना, पर निगरानी रखना, चौकसी करना – *vi.* उत्सुकता से प्रतीक्षा करना, की राह देखना; की ताक में रहना – *n.* घड़ी; चौकसी, निगरानी, पहरा – **watchful** *a.* – **watchmaker** *n.* घड़ीसाज – **watchman** *n.* पहरेदार – **watchword** *n.* संकेत-शब्द; नारा

water (ˈवॉटर) *n.* पानी; आंसू; मूत्र – *vt.* पानी देना या डालना, सिंचाई करना – *vi.* मुंह में पानी आना, आंखों में आंसू आना; पानी भरना – **watery** *a.* जलीय; पानी जैसा – **water buffalo** भैंस – **water closet** शौचघर – **watercolour** *n.* जलरंग – **waterfall** *n.* जलप्रपात– **water lily** पानी पर तैरने वाला पौधा, जल-कुमुद – **waterlogged** *a.* पानी से भरा हुआ (क्षेत्र) – **watermark** *n.* कागज़ पर लगा जल-चिन्ह, जलांक – **watermelon** *n.* तरबूज़ – **waterproof** *a.* जिस पर पानी का असर न हो, वॉटर प्रूफ़ – *v.* वाटरप्रूफ़ बनाना – *n.* वाटर प्रूफ़ वस्त्र – **watershed** *n.* दो नदी-क्षेत्रों की विभाजक रेखा (ऊंची भूमि), महत्वपूर्ण परिवर्तन लाने वाली घटना – **watertight** *a.* जलरोधी, इस प्रकार बंद कि पानी भीतर न जा सके; पक्का, ठोस (तर्क आदि)

watt (वॉट) *n.* विद्युत ऊर्जा की इकाई, वाट – **wattage** (वॉटिज) *n.* वाट-संख्या, वाट में विद्युत ऊर्जा की मात्रा

wattle (ˈवॉट्ल) *n.* टहनियों के ताने-बाने से बना बाड़ा, टट्टर

wave (विव़) *v.* लहराना; हाथ हिलाना (स्वागत या विदाई के संकेत रूप में); हाथ हिलाकर संकेत करना – *n.* लहर; तरंग; हिलोर; *Physics* (रेडियो) तरंग, विद्युत या चुंबकीय तरंग; (लोकप्रियता की) लहर; आवेग– **wavy** *a.* लहरिया

waver (वेव़र) *vi.* हिचकिचाना, आगा-पीछा करना; डाँवाँडोल होना, डगमगाना

wax[1] (वैक्स) *n.* मोम; कान का मैल – *vt.* मोम लगाना – **waxy** *a.* मोम जैसा

wax[2] (वैक्स) *vi.* (चन्द्रमा की कलाओं का) बढ़ना; चमकना

way (वे) *n.* ढंग; तरीका; साधन; रास्ता; दिशा; प्रगति; दशा, हालत, आदत; स्वभाव – **wayfarer** *n.* पथिक, राही – **waylay** *vt.* घात में बैठना; हमला करना (**-laid, -laying**)– **wayside** *n.* सड़क का किनारा – *a.* किनारे का – **wayward** *a.* सनकी; मौजी; अड़ियल – **under way** शुरू हो चुका (काम)

W.C. Water Closet का संक्षेप, शौचालय

we (वी) *pron.* हम

weak (वीक) *a.* कमज़ोर, नाज़ुक; आसानी से प्रभाव में आ जाने वाला; हल्का – **weaken** *vt.* कमजोर कर देना – *vi.* कमज़ोर हो जाना – **weakling** *n.* कमज़ोर व्यक्ति – **weakly** *a.* कमज़ोर; रोगी – *adv.* – **weakness** *n.* कमज़ोरी

weal (वील) *n.* छड़ी या कोड़े की मार का निशान

wealth (वॅल्थ) *n.* धन-दौलत; बहुतायत – **wealthy** *a.* धनी, सम द्ध

wean (वीन) *vt.* (बच्चे का) मां का दूध छुड़ाना; मना लेना; (से) अलग कराने में सफल होना

weapon (वॅपन) *n.* शस्त्र, हथियार

wear (वॅअर) *vt.* पहनना; (ऐनक, पेटी आदि) लगाना; (भाव आदि) प्रदर्शित करना; घिसकर (छेद आदि) बना देना; निर्बल कर देना; *inf.* करने देना; सहना – *vi.* (वस्तु का देर तक) चलना; घिस जाना; (समय) धीरे-धीरे बीतना (**wore, worn, wearing**) – *n.* पहनावा, कपड़े; घिसावट; टिकाऊपन – **wearer** *n.*

weary (विअरि) *a.* थका-मांदा; निढाल; थकाने वाला, उबाऊ – *v.* थक जाना या थका देना (**wearied, wearying**) – **wearily** *adv.* – **wearisome** *a.* उबाऊ

weasel (वीज़ल) *n.* एक छोटा शिकारी जानवर, कथियान्याल

weather (वॅदर) *n.* किसी दिन का मौसम – *a.* हवा की दिशा में – *vt.* मौसम से प्रभावित होना; सह लेना, झेलना; से बचकर निकल आना – **weathercock** *n.* पवन दिशासूचक, वातसूचक, बादनुमा

weave (वीव़) *vt.* बुनना; (कहानी की) रचना करना; टेढ़े-मेढ़े चल कर रास्ता निकालना (**weaved** *pt.*) – *vi.* बुनाई का काम करना (**wove, woven, weaving**) – **weaver** *n.* जुलाहा, बुनकर

web (वॅब) *n.* बुना हुआ कपड़ा, मकड़ी का जाला; जलमुर्गी, मेंढक आदि के पैरों की उंगलियों के बीच झिल्ली; ताना-बाना (*fig.* भी) – **webbing** *n.* निवार – **website** *n.* इंटरनेट पर जानकारी स्थल – **world wide web** (संक्षेप **w.w.w.**) विश्वव्यापी कम्प्यूटर संचार व्यवस्था (दि. **internet**)

wed (वॅड) *vt.* से विवाह करना; जोड़ना (**-dd-**) – **wedding** *n.* विवाह, विवाह संस्कार, विवाह समारोह – **wedlock** *n.* विवाह, बंधन, विवाहित अवस्था

we'd (वीड, विड) we had; we would का संक्षेप

wedge (वॅज) *n.* लकड़ी या धातु की फ़न्नी, पच्चर; (केक आदि का) टुकड़ा – *vt.* पच्चर लगाना; फन्नी से दो भाग कर देना; तंग जगह भीड़ आदि में फंस जाना या घुसा देना

Wednesday (वॅन्ज़्डे) *n.* बुधवार

weed (वीड) *n.* जंगली पौधा, खर-पतवार – *vt.* खरपतवार साफ करना – **weedy** *a.* घासपात से भरा; *inf.* पतला, कमज़ोर – **weed killer** खरपतवार नाशक दवाई – **weed out** छांटना, निकालना

week (वीक) *n.* सप्ताह; सप्ताह में काम के कुल घण्टे या दिन – **weekly** *a.* साप्ताहिक – *n.* साप्ताहिक पत्रिका – **weekday** *n.* शनिवार व रविवार के अतिरिक्त सप्ताह का अन्य कोई भी दिन – **weekend** *n.* शनिवार व रविवार

weep (वीप) *v.* रोना; के लिए अफसोस करना, शोक मनाना (**wept, weeping**) – **weeping willow** बैंस जाति का व क्ष, नम्रा

weevil (वीविल) *n.* घुन

weft (वॅफ्ट) *n.* (बुनाई में) बना, भरनी

weigh (वे) *vt.*, वज़न करना; पर विचार करना– *vi.* भारी या वज़नी होना; परेशान करना – **weight** (वेट) *n.* वज़न; बाट; भार तोलने की इकाई; महत्व; प्रभाव – *vt.* भारी करना –

weightily *adv.* – **weighty** *a.* भारी; महत्वपूर्ण – **weighbridge** (वेब्रिज) *n.* ट्रक आदि जैसे वाहन तौलने की मशीन, तुला-चौकी

weir (विअर) *n.* नदी पर छोटा बांध, वीयर

weird (विअर्ड) *a.* अलौकिक, भयानक; अजीबो-ग़रीब

welcome (वैल्कम) *a.* अभिनंदन योग्य; सुखदायी; जिसे छूट/इजाज़त हो, जिसकी छूट/इजाज़त हो – *n.* स्वागत – *vt.* स्वागत करना, अभिनन्दन करना (**-comed, -coming**)

weld (वैल्ड) *vt.* , झलाई करना, वेल्ड करना; एक करना – *n.* वेल्ड किया गया जोड़ – **welder** *n.* वेल्ड करने वाला व्यक्ति, वेल्डिंग करने की मशीन

welfare (वैल्फ़ेअर) *n.* कल्याण, भलाई

well[1] (वैल) *adv.* अच्छा, अच्छी तरह, ठीक ठीक तरह; काफ़ी, बहुत, बिल्कुल – *a.* अच्छा, स्वस्थ; उचित, ठीक (**better** *comp.*, **best** *sup.*) – *interj.* अच्छा !; ओह !; क्या !, हां! तो संतुलित *n.* – **wellbeing** *n.* कल्याण, स्वास्थ्य – **well-disposed** *a.* अनुकूल, (की ओर) मित्रतापूर्ण, कपालु – **well-mannered** *a.* शिष्ट, सभ्य – **well-off** *a.* खुशहाल, धनी

well[2] (वैल) *n.* कुआँ; झरना – *vi.* उमड़ आना, तेजी से बाहर आना

welter (वैल्टर) *n.* बड़ी मात्रा/संख्या

welterweight (वैल्टर्वेट) *n. Boxing* 63.5 से 66.5 किलोग्राम का भार; इस भार का मुक्केबाज

wend (वैण्ड) *v. lit.* धीरे-धीरे दूर तक जाना, यात्रा करना

went (वैण्ट) GO का *pt.*

wept (वैप्ट) WEEP का *pt./pp.*

were (वर) BE का *pt.*, WAS का *pl.* थे; होता, होते (*If I were there*)

west (वैस्ट) *n.* पश्चिम; पाश्चत्य देश (यूरोप) – *a.* पश्चिमी – *adv.* पश्चिम की ओर – **westerly** *a.* – **westward** *a./adv.* – **westwards** *adv.* पश्चिम की ओर – **western** *a.* पश्चिमी, पाश्चत्य – *n.* पश्चिमी संयुक्त राज्य अमरीका के चरवाहों अथवा सीमांतवासियों पर फिल्म, कहानी आदि – **westerner** *n.* पश्चिमवासी विशे० यूरोप व अमरीका का – **westernization** *n.* पाश्चात्यीकरण

wet (वैट) *a.* गीला; तर; बरसाती (मौसम); (क्षेत्र) जहां शराबबंदी न हो (**wetter** *comp.*, **wettest** *sup.*) – *vt.* गीला करना, भिगोना; पेशाब करना (बच्चे द्वारा) (**wetted, wetting**) – *n.* आर्द्रता, नमी

we've (वीव़, 'विव़) we have का संक्षेप

whack (वैक) *vt.* ज़ोर से सटाक की आवाज़ के साथ मारना – *n.* जोरदार मार; सटाक की आवाज़

whale (विल) *n.* व्हेल मछली – **whaler** *n.* व्हेल-शिकारी (व्यक्ति, जहाज़) – **whale of a** *inf.* बहुत बड़े, बहुत बढ़िया की मिसाल

wharf (वॉर्फ़) *n.* बंदरगाह, नदी आदि पर माल चढ़ाने उतारने का प्लेटफार्म, जहाज़ घाट (*pl.* **wharves** (वार्व्ज़))

what (वॉट, वट) *pron.* क्या – *a.* कौन; कौन-सा; जो कुछ; कितना; कितना बड़ा, कितना अजीब – *interj.* विस्मय, क्रोध आदि का सूचक – **whatever** (वॉट् 'ऍव़र) *pron.* जो कुछ, जो भी – **whatsoever** (वॉट्सो 'ऍव़र) *a.* कोई भी/कुछ भी (नह)

wheat (वीट) *n.* गेहूँ

wheedle ('वीड्ल) *v.* फुसलाना, मनाना

wheel (वील) *n.* चक्र, पहिया; पहिये के आकार वाली वस्तु; घूमने की क्रिया; (कार आदि का) स्टीयरिंग-व्हील, चालन-चक्का – *vt.* (गाड़ी आदि) घुमाना; (उलटा) मोड़ देना – *vi.* घूमना, मुड़ना – **wheeler** *n.* पहियों वाला वाहन – **wheelbarrow** *n.* एक पहिये व दो हैंडल वाला ठेला (प्राय: कूड़ा ले जाने का) – **wheelchair** *n.* पहियों वाली कुर्सी (रोगियों के लिए)

wheeze (वीज़) *vi.* घरघर करते हुए कठिनाई से सांस लेना – *n.* घरघराहट
whelp (व्ह्लेप) *n.* पिल्ला, शेर का बच्चा – *v.* (कुतिया का) बच्चे देना
when (वेन) *adv.* कब – *conj.* जबकि; यद्यपि; तब से – *pron.* जब; तब – **whenever** *adv./conj.* कभी भी, जब भी
whence (वेन्स) *adv/conj. obs.* कहां से; जहां से; कैसे
where (वेंअर) *adv./conj.* कहां, जहां – **whereabouts** (वेंअरबाउट्स) *adv./conj.* कहां – *n.* पता-ठिकाना – **whereas** *conj.* क्योंकि; जबकि – **whereby** *conj.* जिससे – **whereupon** *conj* किस पर; जिस पर; तत्पश्चात – **wherever** *adv.* कह भी, जहां कह – **wherewithal** (वेंअर्विदॉल) *n.* आवश्यक (आर्थिक) साधन
whet (वेट) *vt.* धार लगाना, पैनी करना; तीव्र करना, बढ़ाना (**-tt-**) – **whetstone** *n.* (औजार तेज करने का पत्थर) सान
whether (वेंदर) *conj.* कि (*I don't know whether she is here or abroad*); चाहे (*I would say it whether he likes it or not*)
whey (वे) *n.* छाछ, तोड़, दही का पानी
which (विच) *a.* कौन, कौन-सा – *pron.* जो, कौन – **whichever** *pron.* जो भी, जो कोई
whiff (विफ़) *n.* हवा, गंध का झोंका
while (वाइल) *conj.* जबकि, जब तक, हालांकि – *vt.* (समय) व्यतीत करना, गुज़ारना – *n.* (कुछ) समय, देर – **whilst** *conj.* जबकि
whim (विम) *n.* सनक, झक, तरंग – **whimsical** *a.* सनकी
whimper (विम्पर) *vi.* ठिनकना, रोते हुए शिकायत करना – *n.* ठिनकना, शिकायत
whine (वाइन) *n.* चिल्लाहट; झीखना – *vi.* रिरियाना, चिल्लाना
whip (विप) *vt.* चाबुक मारना, कोड़े लगाना; फेंटना; तेजी से निकालना – *vi.* तेज़ी से अन्दर आना या बाहर जाना (**-pp-**) – *n* . कोड़ा, चाबुक; संसद में किसी पार्टी का सचेतक, व्हिप – **whipping boy** बलि का बकरा
whir (वर) *v.* (**whirr** भी) घूं-घूं की आवाज़ के साथ घूमना या घुमाना; इधर-उधर भागदौड़ करना (**-rr-**) – *n.* घूं-घूं का शोर; भाग-दौड़
whirl (वर्ल) *vt.* तेजी से घुमाना, तेजी से चक्कर देना; (कार आदि) बहुत तेज चलाना – *vi.* तेजी से घूमना, चक्कर खाना या चलना – *n.* घुमाव, चक्कर; घबराहट, चकराने की स्थिति, चक्कर; भागदौड़ – **whirligig** *n.* लट्टू – **whirlpool** *n.* भंवर – **whirlwind** *n.* बवण्डर – *a.*
whisk (विस्क) *v.* हल्का सा झाड़ना, साफ करना; तुरंत ले जाना; फेंटना – *n.* हल्की झाड़ू; (अंडा फेंटने की) फेंटनी, रई
whisker (विस्कर) *n.* बिल्ली आदि की मूंछ; (प्रायः *pl.*) दाढ़ी (प्रायः कनपटी वाली), गलमुच्छा
whisky (विस्कि) *n.* एक तेज़ शराब, व्हिस्की (**US whiskey**)
whisper (विस्पर) *v.* फुसफुसाना, कान में कहना; सरसराहट होना – *n.* फुसफुसाहट, कानाफूसी, सरसराहट खुसुर-पुसुर
whistle (विसल) *vi.* सीटी बजाना, सीटी की आवाज करना – *vt.* सीटी बजाकर बुलाना, रोकना आदि – *n.* सीटी; सीटी की आवाज़ – **whistleblower** *n. inf.* भांडाफोड़ करने वाला
whit (विट) *n.* लेशमात्र
white (वाइट) *a.* सफेद, गौरवर्ण, गोरा; (डर से) हल्का पीला, रंग में हल्का – *n.* सफेद रंग; सफेद भाग; (अंडे की) सफेदी; गोरी जाति का व्यक्ति – **whiten** *v.* सफेद करना – **whiteness** *n.* सफेदी – **whitish** *a.* सफेद – **white ant** दीमक – **white-collar** *a.* सफेदपोश (कर्मचारी) – **white flag** शांति अथवा आत्मसपर्मण का प्रतीक

– **white goods** घरेलू सुख-सुविधा का बिजली का भारी सामान जैसे रेफ्रिजरेटर, धुलाई-मशीन आदि – **white lie** झूठ जिससे किसी की हानि न हो, निष्पाप झूठ – **whitewash** *n.* पुताई, सफेदी –*vt.* सफेदी करना; छिपाना, लीपा-पोती करना

whither (ʹविदर) *adv. obs.* कहां, किधर; जहां, जिधर

whittle (ʹविट्ल) *vt.* काटना, (चाकू से) छीलना

whiz(z) (विज़्) *n.* सनसनाहट की आवाज – *v.* सनसनाहट करते हुए जाना; *inf.* तेज़ी से निकल जाना (**-zz-**) – **whiz(z) kid** आयु को देखते हुए अत्यंत कुशल, बुद्धिमान या सफल व्यक्ति

WHO World Health Organization का संक्षेप

who (हू) *pron.* कौन; जो – **whodunit** (ʹहूडनिट) *n. inf.* जासूसी कहानी – **whoever** *pron.* जो कोई; जो भी

who'd (हूड) who had, who would का संक्षेप

whole (होल) *a.* सम्पूर्ण, पूरा-पूरा, अखंड, समूचा; स्वस्थ – *n.* सम्पूर्ण इकाई अथवा व्यवस्था, समष्टि – **wholly** *adv.* – **wholegrain** *a.* बिना छिलका उतारे अनाज, दाल आदि से बना – **whole-hearted** *a.* हार्दिक; उत्साहपूर्ण – **wholemeal** *a.* आटा (बगैर सूजी आदि निकाले) – **wholesale** *n.* थोक बिक्री – *a.* थोक; बड़े पैमाने पर – **wholesaler** *n.* थोक-व्यापारी – **wholesome** *a.* पुष्टिकर; लाभकारी

whom (हूम) *pron.* किसे, किससे; जिसे, जिससे

whoop (वूपʹहूप) *n.* खुशी, उत्तेजना आदि से भरी ऊंची आवाज़

whooping cough (ʹहूपिंग-) काली खांसी

whore (हॉर) *n.* वेश्या

whose (हूज़) *pron.* किसका, जिसका

why (वाइ) *adv.* क्यों – **whys** *pl.n.* कारण

wick (विक) *n.* (मोमबत्ती लैंप की) बत्ती

wicked (ʹविकिड) *a.* दुष्ट, पापी, बहुत बुरा ; शरारती – **wickedness** *n.* दुष्टता; बुराई; शरारत

wicker (ʹविकर) *n.* टोकरी आदि बुनने की खपची – **wickerwork** *n.* टोकरा, टोकरी

wicket (ʹविकिट) *n.* छोटा फाटक; *Cricket* विकेट, क्रिकेट पिच

wide (वाइड) *a.* विशाल, विस्तीर्ण; चौड़ा; खुला; उदार; बड़ा; निशाने से बहुत दूर; – *adv.* पूरी तरह से; बिल्कुल गलत, लक्ष्य से दूर – *n.* *Cricket* बल्लेबाज़ की पहुंच से बाहर फेंकी गयी गेंद – **widen** *v.* – **widely** *adv.* – **width** (विड्थ) *n.* चौड़ाई – **widespread** *a.* दूर-दूर तक फैला हुआ, व्यापक

widow (ʹविडो) *n.* विधवा – *vt.* विधवा बना देना – **widower** *n.* विधुर – **widowhood** *n.* वैधव्य

wield (वील्ड) *vt.* (लाठी आदि) पकड़ कर इस्तेमाल करना, घुमाना, चलाना; नियंत्रित करना

wife (वाइफ़) *n.* पत्नी (*pl.* **wives** (वाइव्ज़))

wig (विग) *n.* विग, नकली बालों की टोपी

wiggle (ʹविगल) *v.* (पैर की उंगलियाँ) हिलाना-डुलाना, झटके देना

wild (वाइल्ड) *a.* जंगली (पशु, पौधा); बंजर, उजाड़ (भूमि); जंगली, असभ्य; तूफानी; बेलगाम, चंचल; अटकल-पच्चू; उत्तेजित; ऊधमी; *inf.* हुल्लड़ व हो-हल्ला भरी (पार्टी आदि) – **wildly** *adv.* – **wildness** *n.* – **wildcat** *n.* बनबिलाव – **wild goose chase** निरर्थक परिश्रम – **wildlife** *n.* वन्य-जीवन (वन्यप्राणी व पेड़-पौधे)

wilderness (ʹविल्डर्निस) *n.* उजाड़ भूमि, बीहड़

wildfire (ʹवाइल्ड्फ़ाइअर) *n.* भयानक काबू न पाई जा सकने वाली आग, दावानल; तेज़ी से फैलने वाली वस्तु (जैसे अफवाह)

wile (वाइल) *n.* चाल– **wily** *a.* चालाक, चालबाज

wilful (ˈविल्फ़ुल) *a.* हठीला, जिद्दी; जानबूझकर किया गया (कार्य) – **wilfully** *adv.* – **wilfulness** *n.*

will (विल) *v. aux.* भविष्यकाल सूचक सहायक क्रिया (**would** *pt.*) – *vi.* इच्छा होना – *vt.* चाहना; इरादा रखना; वसीयत करना – *n.* इच्छाशक्ति, संकल्पशक्ति, द ढ़संकल्प; इच्छा; वसीयत – **willing** *a.* इच्छुक; तैयार; मन से दिया गया, किया गया आदि – **willingly** *adv.* – **willingness** *n.* – **willpower** *n.* आत्मसंयम

will-o'-the-wisp (विल्अदˈविस्प) *n.* हाथ न आ सकने वाली वस्तु या व्यक्ति; छलाव

willow (ˈविलो) *n.* (**weeping willow** भी) बैंस जाति के अनेक व क्ष, इनकी लकड़ी

willy-nilly (ˈविलिˈनिलि) *adv./a.* चाहे-अनचाहे (होने वाला कार्य)

wilt (विल्ट) *v.* मुरझा जाना; मुरझा देना

win (विन) *vi.* सफल होना, जीतना – *vt.* मेहनत व प्रयत्न से प्राप्त करना, हासिल करना; तक पहुंचना; मोह लेना; में सफल होना; का समर्थन पा लेना, को राजी कर लेना; मना लेना (**won, winning**) – *n.* विजय, जीत – **winner** *n.* – **winning** *a.* मोहक – **winnings** *pl. n.* दांव आदि पर जीती गई रकम

wince (विन्स) *vi.* चौंकना, पीछे हटना (दर्द आदि से) – *n.*

winch (विंच) *n.* मोटे तार से ख च कर भार उठाने की मशीन, विंच – *vt.* विंच से (वस्तु को) उठाना

wind[1] (विण्ड) *n.* हवा; सांस; अफारा; निरर्थक बातें; संकेत, भनक – *vt.* दम फुलाना; गंध पा लेना – **windward** *n.* हवा के सामने की दिशा – **windy** *a.* तूफानी; बादी या वातग्रस्त; लम्बा-चौड़ा (भाषण) – **wind-bag** *n.* बातूनी – **windbreak** तूफान से बचाव के लिए व क्ष-पंक्ति – **windcheater** *n.* गर्म जाकिट जिसमें बुना हुआ गला, कलाईबंद व कमरबंद होते हैं – **windfall** *n.* अप्रत्याशित या अचानक लाभ – **wind instrument** सुषिर-वाद्य जैसे शहनाई – **windmill** *n.* पवनचक्की – **windpipe** *n.* श्वास नली – **windscreen** *n.* कार आदि में सामने लगा शीशा, विंड-स्क्रीन

wind[2] (वाइंड) *vi.* लिपटना; घूमते, मोड़ खाते जाना (जैसे नदी) – *vt.* लपेटना; कुण्डली मारना; (घड़ी को) चाबी देना (**wound** (वाउंड), **winding**) – *n.* घुमाव, मोड़; एक फेर

window (ˈविंडो) *n.* खिड़की, आक ति या प्रकार्य में इसके समान वस्तु; दुकान के शीशे के पीछे प्रदर्शन हेतु रखे सामान का स्थान – **window-dressing** *n.* , ऊपरी दिखावा, टीमटाम – **windowpane** *n.* खिड़की का कांच – **window shopping** बिना खरीदने के इरादे दुकानों के चक्कर मारना, विंडोशापिंग – **windowsill** खिड़की के नीचे लगा पत्थर

wine (वाइन) *n.* (अंगूर से बनी) शराब

wing (विंङ) *n.* पक्षी का पंख, पर; हवाई जहाज़ का पंख; भवन का पक्ष, खंड; रंगमंच का पर्श्वभाग; राजनीतिक दल का धड़ा, पक्ष – *vi.* उड़ जाना; बहुत तेज चलना, जाना – **winged** *a.* पंखों या परों वाला – **winger** *n. Sport* मैदान के दायें या बायें भाग का खिलाड़ी

wink (विंक) *v.* झपकाना, पलक मारना, आंख मारना; टिमटिमाना – *n.* झपक, कनखी, झपकी

winnow (ˈविनो) *vt.* अनाज फटकना

winsome (ˈविन्सम) *a.* आकर्षक, मोहक

winter (ˈविंटर) *n.* शीतकाल, जाड़ा – **wintry** *a.* ठण्डा, शीतकालीन, सर्दियों जैसा

wipe (वाइप) *vt.* पोंछना – *n.* पोंछन – **wiper** *n.* पोंछने का कपड़ा; स्वचलित पोंछने का उपकरण (जैसे कार में), वाइपर – **wipe out** मिटा देना, सत्यानाश कर देना; *sl.* मार देना

wire (वाइअर) *n.* धातु की तार; तार का बना बाड़ा, तार, टेलिग्राम – *vt.* तार लगाना; तार भेजना – **wired** *a.* कम्प्यूटर व्यवस्था से जुड़ा हुआ; उत्तेजित, उद्‌दिग्न – **wiring** *n.* बिजली के (घर, फैक्ट्री आदि में) लगे तार – **wiry** *a.* तार जैसा; पतला परंतु तगड़ा **-go down to the wire** खेल, वार्ता आदि अंत में जाकर सफल होना

wireless (ˊवाइअर्‌लिस) *n.* बेतार; रेडियो का पुराना नाम – *a.*

wise[1] (वाइज़्) *a.* बुद्धिमान, अक्लमंद – **wisdom** (ˊविज़्डम) *n.* बुद्धिमानी, विवेक, अक्लमंदी; (संचित) ज्ञान; समझदारी – **wisely** *adv.* – **wiseacre** (ˊवाइज़ेकर) *n.* व्यक्ति जो बुद्धिमान दिखाई देना चाहता हो – **wisdom tooth** अकलदाढ़

wish (विश) *vi.* (की) इच्छा होना – *vt.* चाहना, इच्छा करना – *n.* इच्छा, चाह; अभिलाषा; इच्छित वस्तु – **wishful** *a.* इच्छुक, आकांक्षी; बहुत अधिक आशावान

wisp (विस्प) *n.* हल्का, पतला लच्छा (बालों, धुँए आदि का); धुएँ की हल्की लकीर; फूस की छोटी सी पूली, आँटी – **wispy** *a.*

wistful (ˊविस्ट्‌फुल) *a.* उत्कंठित; विचारमग्न, उदास – **wistfully** *adv.* ललचाया-सा (दिखना)

wit (विट) *n.* बिलकुल असंगत बातों को जोड़ने की सूझ; जिसे दूर की सूझे; समझ, बुद्धि; हाज़िरजवाबी – **witticism** (ˊविटिसिज़्म) *n.* चटकीला मज़ाक – **wittingly** *adv.* जानबूझ कर – **witless** *a.* मूर्ख – **witty** *a.* विनोदपूर्ण, हाज़िरजवाब – **slow-witted** *a.* मंदबुद्धि

witch (विच) *n.* डायन; जादूगरनी; भद्दी, दुष्ट स्त्री – **witchcraft** (ˊविच्क्राफ़्ट) *n.* जादू-टोना

with (विद) *prep.* के साथ ; सहित , (व्यक्ति आदि) से (*be patient with her*); से, के द्वारा ; के कारण, से (*shaking with anger*); अपेक्षा-सूचक, से (*can't compare me with him*) – **within** *prep./adv.* में, अंदर – **without** *prep.* के बिना

withdraw (विद्‌ˊड्रॉ) *v.* हटाना, निकाल लेना; (पैसे) निकालना वापस लेना; पीछे ख च लेना; (शब्द) वापिस लेना (**-drew, -drawn, -drawing**) – **withdrawal** (विद्‌ˊड्रॉअल) *n.* पीछे हटना; नशीली दवा लेना बंद कर देना; बैंक से पैसा निकालने की क्रिया – **withdrawn** *a.* चुप-चुप, गैर मिलनसार, खिंचा-खिंचा

wither (ˊविदर) *v.* सूख जाना, मुरझा जाना, धीरे-धीरे खत्म हो जाना – **withering** *a.* तिरस्कार भरी (निगाह)

withhold (विद्‌ˊहोल्ड) *vt.* रोकना; रोक रखना; (भुगतान, मंजूरी आदि) न देना, रोक लेना (**-held, holding**) – **withholder** *n.*

withstand (विद्‌ˊस्टैंड) *vt.* विरोध करना; का सामना करना; झेलना, सहन करना (**-stood, -standing**)

witness (ˊविट्‌निस) *n.* (*eye witness* भी) दर्शक; साक्षी, गवाह; प्रत्यक्षदर्शी – *vi.* गवाही देना – *vt.* देखना, प्रमाणित या सिद्ध करना; (समझौते आदि के) साक्षी के रूप में हस्ताक्षर करना

wizard (ˊविज़र्ड) *n.* ओझा, जादूगर; (किसी कार्य क्षेत्र में) सिद्धहस्त या अत्यंत कुशल व्यक्ति, उस्ताद – **wizardry** *n.* जादूगरी; कौशल, कमाल

wizened (ˊविज़न्ड) *a.* मुर्झाया हुआ; झुर्रीदार

wobble (ˊवॉबल) *vi.* लड़खड़ाना, डगमगाना – *n.* डगमगाहट – **wobbly** *a.* लड़खड़ाता, डगमगाता

woe (वो) *n.* शोक; व्यथा, दुर्भाग्य – **woebegone** (ˊवोबिगॉन) *a.* दुःखी या उदास (चेहरा) – **woeful** *a.* शोकमय, दयनीय; बहुत ख़राब – **woefully** *adv.*

wolf (वुल्फ़) *n.* भेड़िया (*pl.* **wolves** (वुल्व्ज़)) – *vt.* निगलना, भकोसना – **cry wolf** झूठमूठ ही किसी खतरे का शोर मचाना

woman (ˈवुमन) *n.* स्त्री, नारी; स्त्री जाति (*pl.* **women** (ˈविमिन)) – **womanhood** *n.* नारीत्व – **womanish** *a.* स्त्री-जैसा (पुरुष) – **womanize** (ˈवुमनाइज़) *vi. inf.* अनके स्त्रियों से सम्बंध रखना, व्यभिचार करना – **womankind** (ˈवुमन्काइंड) *n.* स्त्री-जाति – **womanly** *a.* नारी सुलभ

womb (वूम) *n.* गर्भाशय, बच्चेदानी, कोख

won (वन) **WIN** का *pt./pp.*

wonder (ˈवंडर) *n.* आश्चर्य, विस्मय; आश्चर्यजनक या अदभुत वस्तु, चमत्कार – *vi.* जानने के लिए उत्सुक होना, चकित होना, विस्मित होना, हैरान होना – **wonderful** *a.* प्रशंसनीय, अदभुत, बढ़िया, कमाल का – **wondrous** (ˈवंड्रस) *a.* विस्मयकारी, आश्चर्यजनक; अजीब

wont (वोंट) *n. formal* रीति, प्रथा – *a. formal* आदी – **wonted** *a.* स्वाभाविक, प्रचिलित

won't (वोन्ट) will not का संक्षेप

woo (वू) *vt.* का समर्थन पाने का प्रयत्न करना; प्रेम जताना, प्रणय निवेदन करना – **wooer** *n.* प्रणय-निवेदक, प्रेमी

wood (वुड) *n.* लकड़ी; वन, जंगल – **wooded** *a.* व क्षों से भरा – **wooden** *a* लकड़ी का बना; भावशून्य (चेहरा) – **woody** *a.* – **woodcarving** *n.* लकड़ी पर नक्काशी – **woodland** *n.* जंगल, वनस्थली – **woodpecker** *n.* कठफोड़ा – **woodwork** *n.* (घर, दफ्तर आदि में) लकड़ी का काम – **woodworm** *n.* घुन

woof (वूफ़) *interj.* (कुत्ते की) भौं भौं – *vi.* (कुत्ते का) भौंकना

wool (वुल) *n.* ऊन – **woollen** *a.* ऊनी, गरम – **woolly** *a.* ऊनी; अस्पष्ट, उलझे विचारों वाला – *n.*

word (वर्ड) *n.* शब्द; कथन; बातचीत; संदेश; सूचना, वचन, वायदा; आदेश – *vt.* (किसी विशेष ढंग से) शब्दों में व्यक्त करना – **wording** *n.* शब्दचयन, वाक्य रचना – **wordy** *a.* शब्दाडम्बरपूर्ण – **word processor** एक कम्प्यूटर-व्यवस्था जो लिखित सामग्री को भविष्य में प्रयोग के लिए बनाए रखती है, शब्द-संसाधक

wore (वॉर) **WEAR** का *pt./pp.*

work (वर्क) *n.* कार्य, काम, क्रिया; परिश्रम; व्यवसाय, नौकरी; क ति, रचना; पुस्तक; सुई का काम, सुईकारी – (~ **s**) *pl.* कारखाना; (अच्छे या बुरे) कर्म; व्यक्ति द्वारा किया गया कुल कार्य, रचनाऐं आदि; घड़ी आदि के कल-पुर्ज़े – *vt.* (मशीन आदि) चलाना; बनाना – *vi.* परिश्रम करना; चालू होना; व्यवसाय आदि में लगे होना; सफल होना; (दवाई का) असर करना – **workable** *a.* – **worker** *n.* – **workaholic** (वर्कˈहॉलिक) *n.* जिसे खूब काम करने का नशा-सा हो – **working class** श्रमिक वर्ग, वेतनभोगी वर्ग – **workman** *n.* श्रमिक, कारीगर, कर्मकार – **workload** *n.* काम (दफ्तर आदि में) – **workmanship** *n.* शिल्पी, कारीगरी– **workshop** *n.* कारखाना, वर्कशाप – **work-to-rule** केवल-नियमानुसार -कार्य-हड़ताल

world (वर्ल्ड) *n.* विश्व, संसार; मानवजाति, लोग; समाज – *a.* विश्व- – **worldly** *a.* सांसारिक;

worm (वर्म) *n.* कीड़ा; इससे मिलती वस्तु – (~ **s**) *pl.* क मि रोग विशे. आंतों का – *vi.* रेंगना – *vt.* धीरे-धीरे अपना स्थान बना लेना या किसी का क पा पात्र बन जाना; चालाकी से (भेद) निकाल लेना; दवाई देकर कीड़ों से छुटकारा दिलाना

worn (वॉर्न) **WEAR** का *pp.* – *a.* घिसा हुआ – **worn-out** *a.* फटी पुरानी (वस्तु); थका मंदा (व्यक्ति)

worry (ˈवरि) *vi.* (बहुत अधिक) चिंतित होना– *vt.* परेशान करना, तंग करना, सताना; (कुत्ते का शिकार को) पकड़ कर झंझोड़ना, फाड़ खाना (**worried, worrying**) – *n.* चिंता

worse (वर्स) *a./adv.* **BAD** या **BADLY** का *comp.*, (से) अधिक खराब – *n.* –**worst** *a./adv.* **BAD** या **BADLY** का *sup.*, सबसे बुरा – *n.* – **worsen** *v.* (हालत आदि) बिगड़ना, बिगाड़ना

worship (ˈवर्शिप) *vt.* पूजा करना, पर श्रद्धा रखना, का भक्त होना (**-pp-**) – *n.* पूजा, पूजन; भक्ति, आराधना – **worshipful** *a.* – **worshipper** *n.* उपासक

worsted (ˈवुस्टिड) *n.* ऊनी धागा – *a.* विशेष प्रकार का ऊनी (वस्त्र)

worth (वर्थ) *a.* के योग्य; के मूल्य का – *n.* महत्व; योग्यता; मूल्य; गुण, उपयोगिता; किसी राशि के बदले में मिलने वाली मात्रा – **worthy** *a.* आदरणीय, प्रशंसनीय; सुयोग्य – *n.* प्रतिष्ठित व्यक्ति – **worthily** (ˈवर्दिलि) *adv.* – **worthiness** (ˈवर्दिनिस) *n.* – **worthless** (ˈवर्थलिस) *a.* बेकार, निकम्मा – **worthwhile** (ˈवर्थ्वाइल) *a.* लाभकर, सार्थक

would (वुड) *v. aux.* इच्छा सूचक; संभावना सूचक; **WILL** का *pt.* – **would-be** *a.* होने वाला, बनने का इच्छुक (*would-be bride*)

wound[1] (वूंड) *n.* घाव, जख्म, चोट; ठेस – *vt.* घायल करना, चोट पहुंचाना; ठेस पहुंचाना

wound[2] (वाउंड) **WIND**[2] का *pt./pp.*

wove (वोव़) WEAVE का *pt.* – **woven** (ˈवोव़न) WEAVE का *pp.*

wow (वाउ) *interj.* वाह!

wrangle (ˈरैंगल) *vi.* झगड़ा करना, बहस करना – *n.* झगड़ा, तू-तू मैं-मैं – **wrangler** *n.* US, C चरवाहा, काउबॉय

wrap (रैप) *v.* ढकना, लपेटना (कागज आदि में); ओढ़ना (**-pp-**) – **wrap, wrapper** *n.* ढीला वस्त्र, गाउन; रैपर, कवर (किताब आदि का) – **wrapping** *n.* लपेटने का पदार्थ (कागज़ आदि)

wrath (रॉथ) *n.* रोष, क्रोध – **wrathful** *a.*

wreak (रीक) *vt.* बदला लेना; का कारण बनना – **wreak vengeance on** से बदला लेना – **wreak havoc on** के विनाश का कारण बनना

wreath (रीथ) *n.* समाधि, कब्र आदि पर चढ़ाने की चक्राकार तार में पिरोई फूलमाला – **wreathe** (रीद) *vt.* इस प्रकार की फूलमाला बनाना; लपेटना, लिपटना; (धुएं का) छल्ले बनाते हुए ऊपर उठना

wreck (रेंक) *n.* जहाज़ का नष्ट होना; क्षतिग्रस्त अथवा बरबाद जहाज़, भग्नपोत; विध्वंस, बरबादी; विध्वंसित वस्तु – *vt.* विध्वंस करना – **wreckage** (ˈरेंकिज) *n.* मलबा (नष्ट जहाज़ आदि का) – **wrecker** *n.* विध्वंसक; US दुर्घटनास्थल से क्षतिग्रस्त गाड़ी हटाने वाला वाहन

wren (रेंन) *n.* एक कूजने वाली चिड़िया

wrench (रेंन्च) *vt.* मरोड़ना; बिगाड़ना; छीन लेना; मोच खाना – *n.* मरोड़; रेन्च (औज़ार); पाना (औज़ार)

wrest (ˈरेंस्ट) *vt.* छीन लेना; ज़ोर से मरोड़ना

wrestle (ˈरेंस्ल) *vi.* कुश्ती लड़ना; का सामना करना, संघर्ष करना, जूझना – *n.* – **wrestler** *n.* पहलवान – **wrestling** *n.* पहलवानी

wretch (रेंच) *n.* कमीना आदमी; अभागा दुःखी व्यक्ति – **wretched** (ˈरेंचिड) *a.* अभागा, दुःखी; बदकिस्मत; घटिया, बेकार – **wretchedness** *n.* दुःख; गरीबी; अभागापन

wriggle (ˈरिगल) *v.* रेंगना; तड़पना, छटपटाना, कुलबुलाना – *n.*

wring (रिङ) *vt.* कपड़े मरोड़ना; (पैसा) ऐंठना; पीड़ा देना, कपड़े निचोड़ना (**wrung, wringing**)

wrinkle (रिंकल) *n.* झुर्री, शिकन; (कपड़े पर) शिकन, सिलवट – *v.* झुर्रियां या शिकन पड़ना; नाक चढ़ाना – *vt.* शिकन डालना

wrist (रिस्ट) *n.* कलाई, पहुंचा – **wrist watch** हाथ की घड़ी

writ (रिट) *n.* न्यायालय अथवा अन्य किसी अधिकारी का लिखित आदेश

write (राइट) *vi.* लिख सकना, पत्र लिखना; रचना करना – *vt.* लिखना; रचना करना; (पत्र) लिखना (**wrote, written, writing**) – **writer** *n.* लेखक, लिखने वाला – **write-off** *n. inf.* क्षतिग्रस्त वस्तु जिसे बिलकुल न सुधारा जा सके, बेकार – **write-up** *n.* लिखित (प्रकाशित) विवरण, लेख

writhe (राइद) *v.* (जैसे) दर्द में छटपटाना, तड़पना – *vi.* परेशानी व शर्मिंदगी महसूस करना (**writhed** *pt./pp.*, **writhing** *pr. p.*)

wrong (रॉङ) *a.* गलत, अशुद्ध; अनुचित; अनैतिक, बुरा; असत्य; (मशीन का) खराब (होना); अन्यायपूर्ण; गैर कानूनी – *adv.* गलती से – *n.* अन्याय; हानि; पाप, बुराई – *vt.* के साथ अन्याय करना; के बारे में गलत सोचना – **wrongdoer** *n.* अधर्मी; पापी – **wrongful** *a.* – **wrongfully** *adv.* – **wrongly** *adv.*

wrote (रोट) **WRITE** का *pt.*

wrought (रॉट) *a.* गढ़ा हुआ (धातु) – **wrought iron** लोहे का शुद्ध रूप

wrung (रङ) **WRING** का *pt./pp.*

wry (राइ) *a.* मरोड़ा हुआ; तिरछा, टेढ़ा; व्यंगपूर्ण, व्यंगात्मक, कटु

WTO World Trade Organization का संक्षेप

X

X Christ, Christian, Cross, Roman numeral 10 (दस का अंक) का चिह्न; अशुद्धि, गलती, पसन्द, चुम्बन, हस्ताक्षर, वयस्क फिल्म का सूचक-चिह्न – *n.* अज्ञात, रहस्यमय व्यक्ति या कारण

x *Maths.* अज्ञात संख्या, राशि

xenophobia (ज़ेंन'फ़ोबिअ) *n.* विदेशियों व अज्ञातजनों से घृणा या भय, अज्ञातजनभीति

xerography (ज़ि'रॉग्रफ़ि) *n.* फोटोस्टेट प्रतिलिपि बनाने की प्रक्रिया, ज़ीरोग्राफ़ी – **Xerox** ('ज़िअरॉक्स) *n.* **R** ज़ीरोग्राफ़ी प्रक्रिया, ज़ीरोग्राफ़ी यंत्र

Xmas ('ऍक्स्मस) *n.* Christmas का संक्षेप

X-rated *a.* फिल्म जो अत्यधिक सेक्स व हिंसापूर्ण होने के कारण नाबालिग़ नहीं देख सकते

x-rays *pl. n.* एक्स-रे, एक्स-रे फ़ोटो – **x-ray** *v.* एक्स-रे फोटो लेना

Y

yacht (यॉट) *n.* नौका-दौड़, नौका-विहार आदि में प्रयुक्त पाल अथवा इंजन युक्त नाव, याट – **yachting** *n.* नौका-विहार – **yachtsman** (ˈयॉट्स्मन) *n.*
yak (यैक) *n.* तिब्बत की सुरागाय, याक
yam (यैम) *n.* जिमीकंद
yank (यैंक) *v.* झटके से खींचना – *n.* झटका
Yank, Yankee (यैंक, ˈयैंकि) *a./n. sl.* अमरीकावासी
yap (यैप) *vi.* (छोटे कुत्ते का) भूंकना; बकना; निरर्थक बोलना (**-pp-**) – *n.* भौंक; बकबक
yard[1] (यार्ड) *n.* गज़ (= 0.915 मीटर); – **yardstick** *n.* मानदण्ड; *fig.* कसौटी
yard[2] (यार्ड) *n.* बाड़ा, अहाता, यार्ड (जैसे रेलवे यार्ड)
yarn (यार्न) *n.* धागा, सूत; *fig.* किस्सा – *vi.* किस्सा सुनाना
yawn (यॉन) *vi.* जम्हाई लेना; रिक्त स्थान या बड़ी खाई होना; *fig.* बहुत अंतर होना – *n.* जंभाई
yd. yard(s) का संक्षेप
ye (यी, यि) *pron. obs.* तुम
yea (ये) *interj. obs.* हां
yeah (यॅअ) *interj.* हां
year (यिअर) *n.* वर्ष, साल – **yearly** *a./adv.* वार्षिक, सालाना
yearn (यर्न) *vi.* (किसी चीज़ के लिए) ललकना, लालायित होना, तरसना; (पर) तरस आना – **yearning** *n.* लालसा; तरस
yeast (यीस्ट) *n.* खमीर, यीस्ट
yell (यॅल) *v.* ज़ोर से चिल्लाना; चीखना – *n.* चिल्लाहट
yellow (ˈयॅलो) *a.* पीला; *inf.* कायर, डरपोक – *n.* पीलापन, पीतवर्ण – **yellow fever** पीत ज्वर (एक संक्रामक रोग) – **yellow card** (फुटबाल में) अनुचित व्यवहार के लिए रेफरी द्वारा खिलाड़ी को चेतावनीस्वरूप दिखाया जाने वाला कार्ड, यलो कार्ड
yelp (यॅल्प) *vi.* (कुत्ते का) चीखना, कराहना – *n.*
yen[1] (यॅन) *n.* जापानी मुद्रा
yen[2] (यॅन) *n. inf.* लालसा, उत्कंठा, चाह
yeoman (ˈयोमन) *n. Hist.* भूमिधर (किसान); सहायक, मातहत
yes (यॅस) *interj.* सहमति-सूचक शब्द, हाँ – **yes-man** *n.* जी हजूरी करने वाला
yesterday (ˈयॅस्टर्डे) *n.* बीता हुआ कल, अभी बीता समय – *adv.*
yet (यॅट) *adv.* अभी, अभी तक, यद्यपि, इसके अतिरिक्त फिर भी – *conj.* परंतु, फिर भी
yeti (ˈयॅटि) *n.* येति, हिममानव
yew (यू) *n.* एक सदाबहार व क्ष, यू
Yiddish (ˈयिडिश) *a./n.* जर्मन व हीब्रू से बनी मिश्रित बोली
yield (यील्ड) *vt.* पैदा करना, उत्पन्न करना, लाभ देना; सौंपना; आत्मसमर्पण करना – *vi.* पैदा करना; झुक जाना; (रास्ता) दे देना – *n.* पैदावार; लाभ; प्राप्ति
YMCA Young Men's Christian Association का संक्षेप
yog(h)urt (ˈयॉगर्ट) *n.* एक प्रकार का दही
yoke (योक) *n.* बैलों आदि का जूआ; बहंगी; जोड़ा; गर्दन, कंधे आदि पर वस्त्र का भाग; बंधन; अधिकार, हुकूमत – *vt.* जूआ लगाना, जोतना; जोड़ना
yokel (ˈयोकल) *n.* (तिरस्कारपूर्ण शब्द) देहाती, गंवार
yolk (योक) *n.* अण्डे की ज़र्दी
yon (यॉन) *a. obs.* वहां का, उधर का – **yonder** *a.* वहां का, उधर का – *adv.* वहां, उधर, उस ओर

yore (यॉर) *n. Poet.* प्राचीन काल

yorker (ˈयॉर्कर) *n. Cricket* गेंद जो सीधा बल्ले के नीचे टप्पा खाये

you (यू) *pron.* तू, तुम, आप

young (यङ) *a.* (आयु में) छोटा, किशोर, जवान; अनाड़ी, कच्चा, अनुभवहीन; आरंभिक स्थिति में; चुस्त, फुरतीला – *n.* (पशु का) बच्चा, बच्चे – **youngster** *n.* बच्चा

your (यॉर) *a.* तुम्हारा, आपका – **yours** (यॉर्ज़) *pron.* तुम्हारा – **yourself** (यॉर्ˈसैल्फ़) *pron.* आप (तुम) स्वयं (*pl.* **yourselves**) (यॉर्ˈसैल्व्ज़)

youth (यूथ) *n.* यौवन, किशोरावस्था; (नव)युवक; नौजवान लड़के-लड़कियां – **youthful** *a.* जवान, युवा (*pl.* **youths**)

you've (यूव़) you have का संक्षेप

yowl (याउल) *v.* रोने के स्वर में चिल्लाना – *n.*

Yuletide (ˈयूल्टाइड) *n.* क्रिसमस-पर्व

yummy (ˈयमि) *a. inf.* स्वादिष्ट

yuppie (ˈयपि) *n.* तरुण शहरी डॉक्टर, वकील, मैनेजर आदि – *a.*

YWCA Young Women's Christian Association का संक्षेप

Z

zany (´ज़ेनि) *a.* हास्यजनक, अजीब (विशे. व्यवहार में)

zap (ज़ैप) *vt. sl.* नष्ट करना, हमला करना, मौत के घाट उतारना; *Computers* स्क्रीन (पर अंकित सामग्री) को साफ़ कर देना – *vi.* दूर-नियंत्रण से टेलिविज़न के चैनल तेज़ी से बदलना (**-pp-**) – **zapper** *n.* दूर-नियंत्रण, रिमोटकंट्रोल; विध्वंसक हथियार या उपकरण

zeal (ज़ील) *n.* उत्साह, जोश – **zealot** (´ज़ेलट) *n.* कट्टरपंथी, अत्यधिक उत्साही व्यक्ति – **zealous** (´ज़ेलस) *a.* उत्साही, जोशीला – **zealously** *adv.*

zebra (´ज़ेब्रअ ´ज़ीब्रअ,) *n.* ज़ेबरा (जंगली जानवर) – **zebra crossing** सड़क पर सफेद धारियों से बना पैदल-पारपथ

zeitgeist (´ज़ाइट्गाइस्ट) *n.* लोगों के विचारों में अभिव्यक्त किसी काल-विशेष की भावना

zenith (´ज़ेनिथ) *n.* ठीक सिर के ऊपर आकाश का बिंदु, शिरोबिंदु; चरम बिंदु, चोटी, पराकाष्ठा

zephyr (´ज़ेफ़र) *n.* मंद समीर, हलकी हवा

zero (´ज़िअरो) *n.* शून्य, सिफर, **0** का अंक; कुछ नहीं; शून्यांक; अधोबिंदु (*pl.* **zero(e)s**)

zest (ज़ेस्ट) *n.* मज़ा, रस; जोश; रुचि; नारंगी या नींबू का छिलका – **zestful** *a.*

zigzag (´ज़िग्ज़ैग) *n.* टेढ़ी-मेढ़ी रेखा या टेढ़ा-मेढ़ा रास्ता – *vi.* टेढ़े-मेढ़े चलना (**-zagged** *pt./pp.*, **-zagging** *pr. p.*)

zinc (ज़िंक) *n.* जस्ता, ज़िंक (धातु)

zip (ज़िप) *n.* धातु की दो हिस्सों में बंटी खुलने व बंद होने वाली ज़ंजीर (बटनों के स्थान पर प्रयुक्त), ज़िप (**zipper, zip fastener** भी); सनसनाहट; उत्साह, जोश, फुर्ती – *vt.* ज़िप से बंद करना (**zip up** भी) – *v.* तेज़ी से आना, जाना

zodiac (´ज़ोडिऐक) *n.* राशिचक्र – **signs of the zodiac** राशि – **zodiacal** (ज़ो´डाइअकल) *a.* राशिचक्रीय

zone (ज़ोन) *n.* क्षेत्र, मण्डल; कटिबंध (जैसे – **Temperate Zone**) – **zonal** *a.* मण्डलीय

zoo (ज़ू) *n.* चिड़ियाघर (**zoological gardens** का संक्षिप्त)

zoology (ज़ो´ऑलजि, ज़ू´ऑलजि) *n.* प्राणि-विज्ञान – **zoological** (ज़ोअ´लॉजिकल, ´ज़ूअ) *a.* – **zoologist** (ज़ो´ऑलजिस्ट, ज़ू´ऑलजिस्ट) *n.* प्राणि-विज्ञानी

zoom (ज़ूम) *v.* ज़ोर-ज़ोर से शूँ की आवाज़ करना, गुंजारना; (जहाज़) तेज़ी से ऊपर उड़ना या उड़ाना; (कीमतें) तेज़ी से बढ़ना – *vi.* (कैमरे का) लेन्स इस प्रकार प्रयोग करना कि वस्तु बिलकुल पास आती या दूर जाती प्रतीत हो – **zoom lens** इस उपयोग में आने वाला लेन्स

zucchini (ज़ु´कीनि) *n.* U.S. कद्दू की एक किस्म